thomson.com

changing the way the world learns

To get extra value from this book for no additional cost, go to:

http://www.thomson.com/wadsworth.html

thomson.com is the World Wide Web site for Wadsworth/ITP and is your direct source to dozens of on-line resources. *thomson.com* helps you find out about supplements, experiment with demonstration software, search for a job, and send e-mail to many of our authors. You can even preview new publications and exciting new technologies.

thomson.com: *It's where you'll find us in the future.*

American Government and Politics Today

1997–1998 EDITION

STEFFEN W. SCHMIDT
Iowa State University

MACK C. SHELLEY II
Iowa State University

BARBARA A. BARDES
University of Cincinnati

West / Wadsworth
I(T)P® An International Thomson Publishing Company

Belmont, CA • Albany, NY • Bonn • Boston • Cincinnati • Detroit • Johannesburg
London • Los Angeles • Madrid • Melbourne • Mexico City • Minneapolis / St. Paul
New York • Paris • Singapore • Tokyo • Toronto • Washington

Editor: Clyde H. Perlee, Jr.
Development Editor: Jan Lamar
Production, Art, and Design: Bill Stryker
Promotion Managers: John Tuvey and Ellen Stanton
Copy Editor: Pat Lewis
Cover Photographs: Background © Carr Clifton; upper left © Ira Wyman, Sygma; upper right © PhotoDisc;
lower left © PhotoDisc; lower right © Rick Friedman, Black Star
Compositor: Parkwood Composition Service
Printer: West Publishing Company

Printed in the United States of America
   3 4 5 6 7 8 9 10

For more information, contact Wadsworth Publishing Company, 10 Davis Drive, Belmont, CA 94002, or electronically at
http://www.thomson.com/wadsworth.html

International Thomson Publishing Europe
Berkshire House 168-173
High Holborn
London, WC1V 7AA, England

Thomas Nelson Australia
102 Dodds Street
South Melbourne 3205
Victoria, Australia

Nelson Canada
1120 Birchmount Road
Scarborough, Ontario
Canada M1K 5G4

International Thomson Publishing GmbH
Königswinterer Strasse 418
53227 Bonn, Germany

International Thomson Editores
Campos Eliseos 385, Piso 7
Col. Polanco
11560 México D.F. México

International Thomson Publishing Asia
221 Henderson Road
#05-10 Henderson Building
Singapore 0315

International Thomson Publishing Japan
Hirakawacho Kyowa Building, 3F
2-2-1 Hirakawacho
Chiyoda-ku, Tokyo 102, Japan

International Thomson Publishing Southern Africa
Building 18, Constantia Park
240 Old Pretoria Road
Halfway House, 1685 South Africa

Library of Congress Cataloging-in-Publication Data

Schmidt, Steffen W.
   American government and politics today / Steffen W. Schmidt,
   Mack C. Shelley II, Barbara A. Bardes. 1997–1998 ed.
   Includes index.
ISBN: 0–314–20495–4 (Hard)
ISBN: 0–314–21952–8 (Loose-Leaf Edition)
ISSN: 1079–0071
1997–1998 EDITION
   1. United States—Politics and government. I. Shelley, Mack C. 1950–   II. Bardes, Barbara A.   III. Title
JK274.S428 1997
320.973–dc20

Contents in Brief

Contents

CHAPTER 3
Federalism 67

PART TWO
Civil Rights and Liberties   101

CHAPTER 4
Civil Liberties 103

PART THREE
People and Politics   209

CHAPTER 7
Public Opinion 211

CHAPTER 8
Interest Groups 246

CHAPTER 9
Political Parties 279

CHAPTER 10
Campaigns, Candidates, and Elections 313

CHAPTER 13

The Presidency 433

CHAPTER 14
The Bureaucracy 471

PART FIVE
Public Policy 535

CHAPTER 17
Economic Policy 571

Features of Special Interest

Preface

As the twentieth century draws to a close, American voters and political leaders face a host of challenging questions: How can the high cost of government be reduced? What programs will have to be sacrificed in the process? Is turning responsibility over to the states for certain programs, such as welfare, really a solution? Other questions are equally pressing: What can or should be done to halt the continued unequal treatment of women and various minority groups in our society, given the growing perception that affirmative action is not the solution? How can soaring campaign costs be contained so that we can avoid the prospect of a government by the wealthy few? How can the government control crime and terrorism without restraining our civil rights and liberties to an unacceptable degree? What laws should be devised to regulate electronic communications in the age of the Internet?

There are no easy answers to these and other questions facing American society today. But then, there were no easy answers to questions that were equally challenging for Americans in the past. How major political issues in the past were resolved has had a lasting impact on American society. So will the ways in which some of today's important issues are resolved.

Readers of this text will learn about these issues and the government institutions and processes that have framed—and continue to frame—their outcomes. Students will come to understand that politics is not an abstract process but a very human enterprise, one involving interaction among individuals from all walks of life. They will be encouraged to think critically about issues facing American government and society today and consider how alternative outcomes of these issues will affect their lives—including their civil rights and liberties, their employment opportunities, their economic welfare, and their ability to participate in the American political system. Finally, they will learn how they themselves can become active, informed participants in the political process—which is the ultimate aim of this book. As you will see, many of the special features and pedagogical elements described in the remaining pages of this Preface were designed with this ultimate goal in mind.

1996 ELECTION RESULTS INCLUDED AND ANALYZED

Because we believe that students respond positively to up-to-date information about political events, we have included the latest presidential, congressional, and state election results from November 1996. These results are discussed throughout the book but particularly in those chapters that most directly relate to campaigns and elections or their outcomes. For example, in Chapter 10 ("Campaigns, Candidates, and Elections"), we look closely at the 1996 elections with respect to campaign expenses, the candidates who ran, and voting behavior. In Chapter 12 ("The Congress"), we examine how the elections affected Congress, including the changes in committee chairs that resulted from the elections.

New to this edition are special features highlighting the 1996 elections. These features, which are entitled *Elections '96*, relate to topics covered in the chapters. For example, in Chapter 3 ("Federalism"), the feature discusses the implications of the 1996 elections for the new federalism; in Chapter 6 ("Striving for Equality"), the feature deals with the topic of political leadership by women with reference to the 1996 elections; in Chapter 7 ("Public Opinion"), the feature looks at the gender gap in the 1996 elections; and so on. These features offer students the latest, most up-to-date information in those areas that are most strongly affected by the outcomes of the elections.

A SPECIAL LOOSE-LEAF VERSION

New to the 1997–1998 Edition is a special loose-leaf version of the text. The loose-leaf edition offers the complete text of *American Government and Politics Today*, 1997–1998 Edition, in shrinkwrapped and three-hole-punched pages. The loose-leaf format allows instructors to present topics covered in the text in any order that is right for their courses at a substantially reduced price to their students.

SPECIAL PEDAGOGICAL AIDS AND HIGH-INTEREST FEATURES

The 1997–1998 Edition of *American Government and Politics Today* contains numerous pedagogical aids and high-interest features to assist both students and instructors in the learning/teaching process. The following list summarizes these special elements.

1. *A Preview of Contents to Each Chapter.* To give the student an understanding of what is to come, each chapter starts out with a topical outline of its contents.

2. *What If . . .* To stimulate student interest in the chapter topics, each chapter begins with a hypothetical situation that we call *What If . . .* Some important *What If . . .* examples follow:

- "What If . . . Citizens' Militias Were Banned?" (Chapter 4).
- "What If . . . There Were No More Newspapers?" (Chapter 11).
- "What If . . . We Switched to a Flat Tax?" (Chapter 17).

3. *Margin Definitions.* Because terminology is often a stumbling block to understanding, each important term is printed in boldface, and a definition of the term appears in the margin adjacent to the boldfaced term. To help students locate these important terms quickly when reviewing the chapter materials, we list each boldfaced term and the page number on which it can be found in the *Key Terms* list at the end of the chapter. Additionally, all of the boldfaced terms and their definitions are contained in the *Glossary* at the end of the text, in which the terms are listed alphabetically.

4. *Did You Know . . . ?* Throughout the text, in the margins, are various facts and figures that we call *Did You Know . . . ?* They add relevance, humor, and a certain amount of fun to the student's task of learning about American government and politics. The following are examples of the *Did You Know . . . ?* feature:

- Did You Know . . . That the Pledge of Allegiance was written by two journalists as a promotional stunt for a children's magazine, *Youth's Companion*, to be recited by children on Columbus Day in 1892? (Chapter 1).

- Did You Know . . . That 64 percent of Americans believe that the Constitution declared English as the national language of the United States? (Chapter 2).
- Did You Know . . . That because Texas was the only state to enter the Union after having sovereign status, it is the only state that can fly its state flag at the same height as the U.S. flag? (Chapter 19).

5. *Thinking Politically about . . .* Most chapters in this edition contain a special new feature entitled *Thinking Politically about . . .* This feature is designed to help the student think critically (and politically) about contemporary political issues or events. Each of these features concludes with a *For Critical Analysis* question. The following examples indicate the kinds of issues and topics treated in these features:

- "Thinking Politically about the Right to Bear Arms" (Chapter 2).
- "Thinking Politically about School Vouchers" (Chapter 4).
- "Thinking Politically about Foreign Aid" (Chapter 18).

6. *Politics and . . .* Every chapter is further enlivened with special features entitled *Politics and . . . ,* in which we take a closer look at some of the interesting aspects of topics discussed in the chapter. The following list shows the titles to some of these features:

- *Politics and Information:* The Internet and Views on Civil Liberties (Chapter 4).
- *Politics and the Constitution:* The Changing Meaning of Equal Protection (Chapter 15).
- *Politics and Diversity:* Immigrants and High Technology (Chapter 16).

7. *Politics and the Fifty States.* Any text on American government and politics necessarily must focus on laws and developments affecting all of the states. To offset somewhat this broad emphasis on national events, in addition to the extensive coverage of state and local law in Chapter 19, we have included in this edition a new feature, called *Politics and the Fifty States,* that focuses solely on state issues. Listed here are some examples of the topics covered in this feature.

- "The Impact of Immigration" (Chapter 1).
- "The Death Penalty" (Chapter 4).
- "Which States Get Media Coverage?" (Chapter 11).

8. *Getting Involved.* Because we believe that the best way for students to get a firmer understanding of the American political system is by direct participation, we offer suggestions on ways for them to get involved in the system. At the end of each chapter, there are suggestions on where to write, whom to call, and what to do. When available, Internet addresses and locators have been included. Some examples of this feature follow:

- Your Civil Liberties: Searches and Seizures (Chapter 4).
- Be a Critical Consumer of Opinion Polls (Chapter 7).
- Communicating with the White House (Chapter 13).

9. *Critical Perspectives.* A continuing feature of this text is the *Critical Perspective.* There is one *Critical Perspective* in every chapter of this book. They are only part of the expanded political analysis in this edition. Each *Critical Perspective* is a short essay in which we examine newer theories about what has happened in American political history, what is happening now, or what might happen in the future. The student is asked to examine a particular theory more critically than he or she might normally do within the text itself. The *Critical Perspectives* that have been chosen for this edition follow:

- Chapter 1: "The Election of 1996: Change in American Politics."
- Chapter 2: "Was Madison Really a Nationalist?"
- Chapter 3: "Competitive Federalism."
- Chapter 4: "Free Speech versus the Regulation of Cyberspace."
- Chapter 5: "Does Racism Still Matter?"
- Chapter 6: "Should More Juvenile Criminals Be Tried as Adults?"
- Chapter 7: "Can War Make the President More Popular?"
- Chapter 8: "The Logic of Collective Action."
- Chapter 9: "What Is the Future of the Political Parties?"
- Chapter 10: "Controlling the Campaign Money Machine."
- Chapter 11: "Media Agendas and Political Agendas."
- Chapter 12: "Gridlock or Constitutional Balance?"
- Chapter 13: "Which Presidential Style Is Best?"
- Chapter 14: "Can Common Sense Be Put Back into Government?"
- Chapter 15: "Do Personal Policy Preferences Shape Supreme Court Decisions?"
- Chapter 16: "Drugs and a Constitutional Alternative."
- Chapter 17: "Has the American Economy Been Globalized?"
- Chapter 18: "Can the United Nations Keep the Peace?"
- Chapter 19: "Should Cities Be Able to Stop Sports Franchises from Moving Away?"

10. *Concept Overviews.* New to this edition are *Concept Overviews*, which summarize some of the key changes that have occurred over time with respect to the law or political practices discussed within the chapters. For example, in Chapter 3 ("Federalism"), a *Concept Overview* lists some of the ways in which the relationship between the states and the national government has changed during the course of the twentieth century.

11. *Point-by-Point Chapter Summaries.* At the end of each chapter, the essential points in the chapter are presented in a point-by-point format for ease of review and understanding.

12. *Questions for Review and Discussion.* To elicit student interest and discussion in and out of class, there are two to five questions for review and discussion at the end of each chapter.

13. *Logging On.* In keeping with the electronic age, we provide students with suggestions on how to access information on the Internet that relates to topics covered in the chapters. For this edition, students can access the home page for one of the text's authors, Steffen W. Schmidt. The Uniform Resource Locator (URL) for this home page is given at the top of each *Logging On* feature.

14. *Selected References.* Important and understandable references are given at the end of each chapter. Each reference is annotated to indicate its usefulness and the area that it covers.

15. *Tables, Charts, and Photographs.* As you can readily see, the text uses tables and charts, as well as photographs, to summarize and illustrate important institutional, historical, and economic facts.

EMPHASIS ON CRITICAL THINKING

Whenever feasible, we have gone beyond mere factual narrative to discuss the rationale underlying specific political decisions and the likely consequences of those decisions in the future. For example, in our discussion of interest groups in Chapter 8, we not only describe how interest groups function in the American political system but also examine the potential consequences of interest-group politics for a representative democracy. As another example, in Chapter 16, when discussing welfare reform, we look at the controversy surrounding the welfare reform bill of 1996 and at some of its potential consequences for state governments.

Special features in the 1997–1998 Edition also emphasize critical thinking. In addition to the *Critical Perspectives,* the features entitled *Thinking Politically about . . .* mentioned earlier in this Preface were designed specifically to engage the student in critical thought concerning contemporary political issues. Furthermore, we have expanded the number of questions *For Critical Analysis* for this edition. *Every feature in the text now concludes with one or more of these questions.* Finally, if the student uses our accompanying booklet, *Handbook on Critical Thinking and Writing in American Politics,* with the exercises in critical thinking, he or she will have a strong basis for analyzing not only American politics but all other college subjects as well.

INTERNATIONAL COVERAGE INTEGRATED THROUGHOUT

In addition to the chapter covering foreign policy, numerous features throughout the text focus on global issues or on political developments, events, or structures in other nations of the world. Some examples of some of the features discussing international affairs or political issues or institutions in other countries are the following:

• Chapter 2 ("The Constitution") includes a special feature, in the section discussing the Bill of Rights, that examines the controversy over whether Britain needs a bill of rights.
• Chapter 6 ("Striving for Equality") contains a feature exploring some of the possible reasons for the worldwide decline in political leadership by women.
• Chapter 15 ("The Judiciary") has a feature introducing the student to the civil law system characteristic of many nations and comparing the civil law system to the common law system.

THE ANNOTATED U.S. CONSTITUTION AND OTHER APPENDICES

So that this book can serve as a reference, we have included important documents for the student of American government to have close at hand. Of course, every college American government text includes the U.S. Constitution. We believe that this document—and students' understanding of it—is so important that we have included a fully annotated U.S. Constitution as Appendix B. Although our brief summaries of constitutional provisions should not be thought of as a substitute for a word-for-word analysis, they will help the student understand the finer points within each part of our Constitution.

In addition to the U.S. Constitution and a special appendix on survival skills (see the next section), we have also included the following appendices:

• *The Declaration of Independence.*
• *The Presidents of the United States.*
• *Federalist Papers Nos. 10, 51, and 78.*
• *How to Do Research in Political Science.*
• *Justices of the U.S. Supreme Court in the Twentieth Century.*
• *Party Control of Congress in the Twentieth Century.*
• *Spanish Equivalents for Important Terms in American Government and Political Science.*

A SPECIAL APPENDIX ON SURVIVAL SKILLS

Students, as citizens, need certain survival skills. We include in this edition a special appendix called *A Citizen's Survival Guide*. It includes the following sections:

- You and the Political System.
- You and the Justice System.
- You and Your Personal Protection.
- You and Your Employer.

A FULL SUPPLEMENTS PACKAGE

In conjunction with a number of our colleagues, we have developed numerous supplementary teaching materials to accompany *American Government and Politics Today*, 1997–1998 Edition. The text, along with the supplements listed below, constitutes a total learning/teaching package that we believe is the best available today. For further information on these supplements, contact your West/ITP sales representative.

Printed Supplements

- *Study Guide.*
- *Instructor's Manual* (also available in computerized form).
- *Test Bank* (also available in computerized form).
- *Logging On: Internet Exercises.*
- *Handbook of Selected Legislation and Other Documents.*
- *Readings in American Government and Politics Today,* 1977–1998 Edition.
- *A Handbook on Critical Thinking and Writing.*
- *The Rise and Fall of the Soviet Union, 1917–1991.*
- *Handbook of Selected Court Cases.*
- *College Survival Guide.*
- *Transparency Acetates.*
- *The 1996 Elections: In Divided Government We Trust.*

Multimedia Resources

- CD-ROM Resources to Accompany *American Government and Politics Today,* 1997–1998 Edition.
- A computerized version of the *Instructor's Manual;* available in ASCII format.
- WESTEST—A computerized version of the *Test Bank;* available for IBM PCs and compatible computers or for the Apple Macintosh family of microcomputers.
- Videos of the Dallas County Community College District telecourse "Government by Consent."
- *West's American Government Videodisc.*
- The Lecture Builder™—Software to accompany *West's American Government Videodisc.*
- An interactive videodisc covering two lessons—interest groups and political action committees (PACs).
- Interactive software that allows students to interact with the interactive videodisc.
- Your Research Data Analysis for *American Government and Politics Today.*

FOR USERS OF PREVIOUS EDITIONS

As always, we want to thank you for your past support. Here we wish to let you know what changes have been made in the 1997–1998 Edition. Of course, all textual materials—text, figures, tables, features, and so on—have been revised as necessary to reflect the political developments that have occurred since the last edition. In addition, we have rewritten many sections in the text, added numerous new features, and updated the text extensively to reflect the results of the November 1996 elections. We summarize here the features and other elements that we have added to the 1997–1998 Edition, as well as the most significant changes in chapter coverage.

1. Generally, we have employed a more analytical approach to political issues and events.

2. New special features added to this edition include the following, each of which has already been described in this Preface:

- *Thinking Politically about . . .*
- *Elections '96.*
- *Concept Overviews.*
- *Politics and the Fifty States.*

3. *For Critical Analysis* questions now conclude each feature in the text.

4. The following *What If . . .* features are new:

- "What If . . . Every Citizen Used the Internet?" (Chapter 1).
- "What If . . . Federally Owned Lands Were Given to the States?" (Chapter 3).
- "What If . . . Citizens' Militias Were Banned?" (Chapter 4).
- "What If . . . A Moratorium Were Placed on All Immigration?" (Chapter 5).
- "What If . . . There Were Forced Retirement at Age Sixty-Five?" (Chapter 6).
- "What If . . . The Government Regulated the Polling Industry?" (Chapter 7).
- "What If . . . There Were No More PACs?" (Chapter 8).
- "What If . . . There Were Three Parties?" (Chapter 9).
- "What If . . . There Were No Newspapers?" (Chapter 11).
- "What If . . . Members of Congress Were Required to Spend Six Months Each Year in Their Districts?"
- "What If . . . The First Lady Were a Paid Government Employee?" (Chapter 13).
- "What If . . . Some Agencies Were Privatized?" (Chapter 14).
- "What If . . . Supreme Court Justices Were Elected?" (Chapter 15).
- "What If . . . Welfare Programs Were *Completely* Controlled by the States?" (Chapter 16).
- "What If . . . We Switched to a Flat Tax?" (Chapter 17).
- "What If . . . All States Allowed Gambling?" (Chapter 19).

5. We have included many new *Critical Perspectives* in this edition. They are as follows:

- Chapter 1: "The Election of 1996: Change in American Politics."
- Chapter 2: "Was Madison Really a Nationalist?"
- Chapter 4: "Free Speech versus the Regulation of Cyberspace."
- Chapter 5: "Does Racism Still Matter?"
- Chapter 6: "Should More Juvenile Criminals Be Tried as Adults?"
- Chapter 10: "Controlling the Campaign Money Machine."
- Chapter 14: "Can Common Sense Be Put Back into Government?"
- Chapter 15: "Do Personal Policy Preferences Shape Supreme Court Decisions?"

- Chapter 17: "Has the American Economy Been Globalized?"
- Chapter 19: "Should Cities Be Able to Stop Sports Franchises from Moving Away?"

6. We have made hundreds of changes and updates to the chapters of this book for the 1997–1998 Edition. Here we list just a few of these revisions:

- Chapter 1 ("Politics and American Government: Stability and Change") has been revised to emphasize not only the continuity of American political institutions but also some new elements in the contemporary political landscape that pose challenges for our society and political leaders. These elements include a growing underclass of Americans who are alienated from the political process, a decline in the influence of the two major political parties, ethnic divisiveness, and terrorism at home and abroad.
- Chapter 3 ("Federalism") has been significantly revised, and many sections have been completely rewritten. The chapter now presents a more streamlined and up-to-date presentation of the evolution—and recent "devolution"—of national government powers.
- Chapter 4 ("Civil Liberties") includes substantially revised sections on the incorporation issue, commercial advertising, school prayer and aid to public schools, and privacy issues (including the courts' current positions on abortion and assisted suicide).
- Chapter 6 ("Striving for Equality") now offers a thoroughly revised and expanded discussion of gender discrimination and other topics relating to the status of women in American society. The sections on the rights of older Americans, persons with disabilities, and gays and lesbians have been virtually rewritten and discuss the latest developments in these areas. The problem of juvenile crime is emphasized by the inclusion of a *Critical Perspective* on this topic.
- Chapter 7 ("Public Opinion") contains new textual discussions and features on developments in polling techniques, including "push polls" and "deliberative polls." The discussion of the media's influence on the formation of public opinion has been rewritten to reflect the growing influence of the media, particularly TV, on younger Americans.
- Chapter 8 ("Interest Groups") opens with a discussion of the 1996 farm bill and the role interest groups played in the process of passing that legislation. A new section and a special feature analyze the question of whether civic participation is declining in America. Additionally, a new section examines the issue of pluralism in the context of a representative democracy.
- Chapter 10 ("Campaigns, Candidates, and Elections") includes coverage of the 1996 campaign as well as the latest developments in campaign financing, including the extensive use of "soft money" and "bundling" to raise funds.
- Chapter 12 ("The Congress") has been updated to include a discussion of term limits and the Supreme Court's position on this issue. The chapter also describes recent developments with respect to race-based congressional redistricting.
- Chapter 15 ("The Judiciary") has been significantly revised and rewritten. The chapter now includes a restructured discussion of the sources of American law and expanded coverage of jurisdictional requirements. A new section on the role of the judiciary in American government incorporates the topic of judicial review and includes a new subsection on judicial interpretation of the laws. Generally, more emphasis is placed on the policymaking role of the judiciary, particularly the Supreme Court, and the impact of Supreme Court decisions on American society.
- Chapter 16 ("Domestic Policy") now contains a substantially revised discussion of the policymaking process and new sections dealing with the wel-

fare reform bill of 1996 and immigration. The section on crime has been updated to include the latest data on this issue.

7. The following appendices are new to this edition:

• Appendix D—*Federalist Papers* Nos. 10, 51, and 78 (*Federalist Paper* No. 78 was added for this edition).
• Appendix G—Party Control of Congress in the Twentieth Century.

8. New supplements for the 1997–1998 Edition include the following:

• *Logging On: Internet Activities.*
• *Handbook of Selected Legislation and Other Documents.*
• *The 1996 Elections: In Divided Government We Trust.*

ACKNOWLEDGMENTS

Since we started this project a number of years ago, a sizable cadre of individuals has helped us in various phases of the undertaking. The following academic reviewers offered numerous constructive criticisms, comments, and suggestions during the preparation of all previous editions:

Danny M. Adkison
Oklahoma State University

Sharon Z. Alter
William Rainey Harper College, Illinois

William Arp III
Louisiana State University

Kevin Bailey
North Harris Community College, Texas

Dr. Charles T. Barber
University of Southern Indiana, Evansville, Indiana

Clyde W. Barrow
Texas A&M University

Lynn R. Brink
North Lake College, Irving, Texas

Barbara L. Brown
Southern Illinois University at Carbondale

Kenyon D. Bunch
Fort Lewis College, Durango, Colorado

Ralph Bunch
Portland State University, Oregon

Carol Cassell
University of Alabama

Frank J. Coppa
Union County College, Cranford, New Jersey

Robert E. Craig
University of New Hampshire

Doris Daniels
Nassau Community College, New York

Carolyn Grafton Davis
North Harris County College, Texas

Marshall L. DeRosa
Louisiana State University, Baton Rouge, Louisiana

Michael Dinneen
Tulsa Junior College, Oklahoma

Gavan Duffy
University of Texas at Austin

George C. Edwards III
Texas A&M University

Mark C. Ellickson
Southwestern Missouri State University, Springfield, Missouri

John W. Epperson
Simpson College, Indianola, Indiana

Daniel W. Fleitas
University of North Carolina at Charlotte

Elizabeth N. Flores
Del Mar College, Texas

Joel L. Franke
Blinn College, Brenham, Texas

Barry D. Friedman
North Georgia College

Robert S. Getz
SUNY–Brockport, New York

Kristina Gilbert
Riverside City College

William A. Giles
Mississippi State University

Donald Gregory
Stephen F. Austin State University, Nacogdoches, Texas

Forest Grieves
University of Montana

Dale Grimnitz
Normandale Community College, Bloomington, Minnesota

Stefan D. Haag
Austin Community College, Texas

Jean Wahl Harris
University of Scranton, Scranton, Pennsylvania

David N. Hartman
Rancho Santiago College, Santa Ana, California

Robert M. Herman
Moorpark College, California

Richard J. Herzog
Stephen F. Austin State University, Nacogdoches, Texas

Paul Holder
McClennan Community College, Waco, Texas

Michael Hoover
Seminole Community College, Sanford, Florida

J. C. Horton
San Antonio College, Texas

Willoughby Jarrell
Kennesaw College, Georgia

Loch K. Johnson
University of Georgia

Donald L. Jordan
United States Air Force Academy, Colorado

John D. Kay
Santa Barbara City College, California

Charles W. Kegley
University of South Carolina

Bruce L. Kessler
Shippensburg University, Pennsylvania

Nancy B. Kral
Tomball College

Dale Krane
Mississippi State University

Samuel Krislov
University of Minnesota

Harry D. Lawrence
Southwest Texas Junior College,
Uvaide, Texas

Ray Leal
Southwest Texas State University,
San Marcos, Texas

Sue Lee
Center for Telecommunications, Dallas
County Community College District

Carl Lieberman
University of Akron, Ohio

Orma Linford
Kansas State University

Eileen Lynch
Brookhaven College

James D. McElyea
Tulsa Junior College, Oklahoma

William P. McLauchlan
Purdue University, Indiana

William W. Maddox
University of Florida

S. J. Makielski, Jr.
Loyola University, New Orleans

Jarol B. Manheim
George Washington University

J. David Martin
Midwestern State University, Texas

Bruce B. Mason
Arizona State University

Steve J. Mazurana
University of Northern Colorado

Thomas J. McGaghie
Kellogg Community College, Michigan

Stanley Melnick
Valencia Community College, Florida

Robert Mittrick
Luzurne County Community College,
Pennsylvania

Helen Molanphy
Richland College, Texas

Keith Nicholls
University of Alabama

Stephen Osofsky
Nassau Community College, New York

John P. Pelissero
Loyola University of Chicago

Neil A. Pinney
Western Michigan University

Michael A. Preda
Midwestern State University, Texas

Charles Prysby
University of North Carolina

Donald R. Ranish
Antelope Valley College, California

Curt Reichel
University of Wisconsin

Russell D. Renka
Southeast Missouri State University

Paul Rozycki
Charles Stewart Mott Community
College, Flint, Michigan

Eleanor A. Schwab
South Dakota State University

Len Shipman
Mount San Antonio College, California

Scott Shrewsbury
Mankato State University, Minnesota

Gilbert K. St. Clair
University of New Mexico

Carol Stix
Pace University, Pleasantville,
New York

Gerald S. Strom
University of Illinois at Chicago

John R. Todd
North Texas State University

Benjamin Walter
Vanderbilt University, Tennessee

B. Oliver Walter
University of Wyoming

Thomas L. Wells
Old Dominion University, Virginia

Jean B. White
Weber State College, Utah

Allan Wiese
Mankato State University, Minnesota

Robert D. Wrinkle
Pan American University, Texas

The 1997–1998 Edition of this text is the result of our working closely with reviewers who each offered us penetrating criticisms, comments, and suggestions for how to improve the text. Although we haven't been able to take account of all requests, each of the reviewers listed below will see many of his or her suggestions taken to heart.

David C. Benford, Jr.
Tarrant County Junior College

John A. Braithwaite
Coastline College

Frank J. Coppa
Union County College

Larry Elowitz
Georgia College

Donald Gregory
Stephen F. Austin State University

Robert Jackson
Washington State University

William W. Lamkin
Glendale Community College

Stanley Melnick
Valencia Community College

George E. Pippin
Jones County Community College

Walter V. Powell
Slippery Rock University

John D. Rausch
Fairmont State University

Michael W. Sonnlietner
Portland Community College

Ron Velton
Grayson County College

Mark J. Wattier
Murray State University

Lance Widman
El Camino College

J. David Woodard
Clemson University

Many individuals helped during the research and editorial stages of this edition. We wish to thank William Eric Hollowell, Sherry Downing-Alfonso, Cara Bardes, Lavina Miller, Suzanne Jasin, and Roxie Lee. Clyde Perlee, Jr., our untiring editor at West/ITP continued to offer strong support and guidance at every phase of this edition. Our project editor, Bill Stryker, helped us in this new design and photo research program. He remains the object of our sincere appreciation, as does Jan Lamar for her extensive developmental guidance and her ability to get all the teaching supplements out on time.

Any errors that remain are our own. We welcome any and all comments from instructors and students alike. Comments that we have received on previous editions have helped us improve this text. Nonetheless, we know that we need to continue to make changes as the needs of instructors and students change.

Steffen Schmidt
Mack Shelley
Barbara Bardes

PART ONE
The American System

1
American Government and Politics: Stability and Change

CHAPTER OUTLINE

- ☆ Political Change in the United States
- ☆ What Is Politics?
- ☆ The Need for Government and Power
- ☆ Who Governs?
- ☆ Do We Have a Democracy?
- ☆ Ideas and Politics: Political Culture
- ☆ The Changing Face of America
- ☆ Ideas and Politics: Ideology

Every Citizen Used the Internet?

BACKGROUND

A FEW YEARS AGO, ONLY COMPUTER FANATICS EVEN KNEW ABOUT THE INTERNET. TODAY, AT LEAST 60 MILLION PEOPLE USE IT, AND BY THE END OF THIS CENTURY, IT IS PROJECTED THAT OVER 120 MILLION PEOPLE WILL BE USING IT WORLDWIDE. SOME 70,000 NETWORKS ARE CONNECTED TO THE INTERNET, WHICH PROVIDES ACCESS TO THOUSANDS OF SOURCES OF INFORMATION ABOUT GOVERNMENT AND POLITICS—AS WELL AS ABOUT SCIENCE, BUSINESS, AND HEALTH. IN A SHORT TIME, THE INTERNET HAS BECOME A VITAL FORCE IN EDUCATION, BUSINESS, COMMUNICATION, AND ECONOMICS. IT IS ON THE WAY TO BECOMING A FORCE IN POLITICS AS WELL. WHAT WOULD RESULT IF EVERY CITIZEN COULD AND DID USE THE INTERNET?

WHAT IF EVERY CITIZEN USED THE INTERNET?

If every citizen used the Internet routinely, the results in terms of an informed citizenry could be amazing. Citizens easily could access information placed on the Web by government agencies, including government regulations, explanations of tax forms, and court decisions. They also could access quickly the enormous number of materials—ranging from presidential speeches to committee hearings—that Congress and the White House place on the electronic network for individuals to read and copy for their own use. Newspapers and magazines put their stories on the Web, as do serious journals of opinion and science. A citizen who wanted to study, for example, the debate over affirmative action could have access to thousands of documents from hundreds of sources and then make up his or her own mind about this important issue.

DRAWBACKS TO INTERNET USE

The drawbacks to this situation are several. First, sources on the Internet are only as good as the organization that sponsors them. The Internet is completely unedited, meaning that a fraudulent or unethical organization can originate material as easily as a reputable company or government agency. Nor does the organization need to explain whether there is any political slant to the material.

Second, the multiplicity of information sources will overwhelm some individuals in the same way that six hundred channels of cable TV can. Others will find electronic connections much less satisfying than person-to-person talk.

POLITICAL PARTICIPATION VIA THE INTERNET

Widespread use of the Internet could have important effects with respect to political participation. All citizens could read messages from their elected representatives and government officials and "talk back" to them.

Another possibility for the use of the Internet might be electronic voting from one's home. All that is necessary is a system, such as one involving voter passwords, that protects the election from vote fraud. The ease of voting and the ability to have complete privacy and freedom from the pressure of going to the polls might increase voter turnout greatly.

One of the most unpredictable elements of having everyone "online" is the possible creation of new political organizations, publications, and interest groups as a result of electronic conversations. In 1835, the French observer Alexis de Tocqueville wrote about the great American habit of joining together in groups to pursue common objectives. It is likely that the Internet will make this even more possible for more citizens.

FOR CRITICAL ANALYSIS

1. *How much time do you think most people would spend connecting to government officials if they were able to do so? What questions would they be most likely to ask these officials?*

2. *With universal connection, do you think the government should or would try to "edit" electronic messages to assure truth and protect safety and security?*

Politics is about change—change in the laws and policies that guide a nation, change in the desires of the people, change in the ranks of government officials, and change in the very structures of government. Some of this dynamism is inherent in the nature of politics as a struggle for a better society. Sometimes, external forces—such as the Internet (as discussed in the opening *What If . . .*), the aftermath of war, and economic depression—force political change on a society.

In recent years, the world has witnessed tremendous changes in the way that many nations are governed. The once monolithic Soviet Union dissolved into a federation of separate states. The most important of the successor states, Russia, has approved a constitution and has held parliamentary and presidential elections. The same kinds of institutional change have taken place in all of the Eastern European nations that used to be part of the Soviet bloc, as well as in a number of Caribbean and Central American states. At the same time, several other nations, including Liberia and Yugoslavia, literally have come apart through ethnic struggles and civil war.

Political change also means the creation of new political groups and parties that contend for places in the government. Not only did Russia reemerge as a separate nation, but dozens of political parties, ranging from the Women's party to the revived and revised Communist party, were created. In Russia's first parliamentary elections, the Communists won a large number of seats, probably in response to the lack of economic progress for most people. In the presidential elections, however, Boris Yeltsin won the presidency after a runoff. His election portends even further changes for this large and powerful nation, although the direction and durability of those changes are uncertain.

POLITICAL CHANGE IN THE UNITED STATES

As the United States approaches the end of the twentieth century, the electorate seems more restless than it has been for many decades. In the period following World War II, the Democratic party was able to control both the House of Representatives and the Senate for long periods of time, while the party controlling the presidency changed more frequently. The timetable for political change seems to have speeded up in the 1990s. In 1988, the voters elected a Republican president, George Bush, who faced a Democratic Congress. In 1992, the voters turned Bush out of office, electing Bill Clinton, a Democrat, to the presidency and keeping both chambers of Congress under Democratic control. In the 1994 midterm elections, only two years after Clinton's election, the Republicans won control of both the House and the Senate, and Newt Gingrich launched his drive to fulfill the Contract with America. As discussed in this chapter's *Critical Perspective,* in 1996 the voters sent a decidedly mixed message to the government about their desire for change. Bill Clinton was reelected to the presidency, but the voters returned the Republican majorities in both the House and the Senate. Both the president and the Republicans interpreted the voters' message as supporting cooperation between the presidency and Congress and moderate policy changes.

The electorate has shown a real desire for new political processes. Many voters have switched to voting by mail. In 1996, the state of Washington held a primary election by mail. Voters in many states have approved term limits for their legislatures. At the national level, Congress finally passed a line-item veto, which allows the president to veto selected portions of spending legislation, although the law did not take effect until after the 1996 election. Whether or not the electorate desired it, the presidential primary system was revamped completely in 1996 due to changes in the dates for presidential primaries and caucuses set by the various states.

The willingness of Americans to debate new initiatives and to demand changes in the way the government works is at the core of our democratic nation. Change—even revolutionary change—is a tribute to the success of a political system. As Abraham Lincoln put it, "This country with all its institutions, belongs to the people who inhabit it. Whenever they shall grow weary of the existing government, they can exercise their Constitutional right of amending it, or the revolutionary right to dismember or overthrow it."[1]

In the chapters that follow, we will look more closely at the **institutions** of our government and how they have changed over the decades. We will examine how the political processes of the nation work to accomplish those changes. To begin, we will look at why political institutions and processes are necessary in any society and what purposes they serve.

INSTITUTION

A long-standing, identifiable structure or association that performs functions for society.

WHAT IS POLITICS?

Why do nations and people struggle so hard to establish a form of government and continue to expend so much effort in *politics* to keep that government functioning? Politics and forms of government are probably as old as human society. There are many definitions of politics, but all try to explain how human beings regulate conflict within their society. As soon as humans began to live in groups, particularly groups that were larger than their immediate families, there arose the need to establish rules about behavior, property, the privileges of individuals and groups, and how people would survive together. **Politics** can be best understood as the process of, as Harold Lasswell put it, "who gets what, when, and how."[2] To another social scientist, David Easton, politics should be defined as the "authoritative allocation of values."[3] Politics, then, is the struggle or process engaged in by human beings to decide which members of society get benefits or privileges and which are excluded from certain benefits or privileges.

In the early versions of human society, the tribe or village, politics was relatively informal. Tribal elders or hereditary chiefs were probably vested with the power to decide who married whom, who was able to build a hut on the best piece of land, and which young people succeeded them into the positions of leadership. Other societies were "democratic" from the very beginning, giving their members some form of choice of leadership and rules. Early human societies rarely had the concept of property, so few rules were needed to decide who owned which piece of property or who inherited that piece. The concepts of property and inheritance are much more modern. As society became more complex and humans became settled farmers rather than hunters and gatherers, the problems associated with property, inheritance, sales and exchanges, kinship, and rules of behavior became important to resolve. Politics developed into the process by which some of these questions were answered.

Inevitably, conflicts arise in society, because members of a group are distinct individuals with unique needs, values, and perspectives. At least three

POLITICS

According to David Easton, the "authoritative allocation of values" for a society; according to Harold Lasswell, "who gets what, when, and how" in a society.

[1]*Oxford Dictionary of Quotations*, 3d ed. (Oxford, England: Oxford University Press, 1980), p. 314.
[2]Harold Lasswell, *Politics: Who Gets What, When and How* (New York: McGraw-Hill, 1936).
[3]David Easton, *The Political System* (New York: Knopf, 1953).

different kinds of conflicts that may require the need for political processes arise in a society:

1. People may differ over their beliefs, either religious or personal, or over basic issues of right and wrong. The kind of debate that has arisen in recent years on abortion is an example of this kind of conflict.

2. People within a society may differ greatly in their perception of what the society's goals should be. In early society, that debate may have been over whether the group should move to a new territory or stay settled in its current situation. Today, Americans differ over whether balancing the federal budget should be the most important item on the public agenda, or whether finding a way to reduce crime and violence in our cities is the most important issue.

3. People compete for scarce resources; jobs, income, and property are examples. The question of who will pay for Medicare benefits, for example, is really a discussion of whether younger people will pay for the health care of the older persons in the society or whether retirees must pay more for this health insurance.

THE NEED FOR GOVERNMENT AND POWER

If *politics* refers to conflict and conflict resolution, **government** refers to the structures by which the decisions are made that resolve conflicts or allocate values. In early human societies, such as families and small tribes, there was no need for formal structures of government. Decisions were made by acknowledged leaders in those societies. In families, all members may meet together to decide values and priorities. Where there is a community that makes decisions and allocates values through informal rules, politics exists—but not government. Within most contemporary societies, these activities continue in many forms. For example, when a church decides to build a new building or hire a new minister, that decision may be made politically, but there is in fact no government. Politics can be found in schools, social groups, and any other organized group. When a society, however, reaches a certain level of complexity, it becomes necessary to establish a permanent or semipermanent group of individuals to act for the whole, to become the government.

Governments range in size from the volunteer city council and one or two employees of a small town to the massive and complex structures of the U.S. government or those of any other large, modern nation. Generally, governments not only make the rules but also implement them through the use of police, judges, and other government officials. Some governments may be relatively limited in their power to make rules about the conduct of the individuals in the society. Other governments may have the power not only to decide public laws but also, as in the former Soviet Union, to control all enterprises within the society.

Authority and Legitimacy

In addition to instituting and carrying out laws regulating individual behavior, such as traffic laws and criminal laws, most modern governments also attempt to carry out public policies that are intended to fulfill specific national or state goals. For example, a state may decide that its goal is to reduce teenage consumption of alcohol and the driving accidents caused by such behavior. To do that, the state may institute extremely strong penalties for drinking, along with a statewide education program for teenagers and younger children about the dangers of drinking and driving. The U.S. gov-

DID YOU KNOW...
That the word *politkos* (pertaining to citizen or civic affairs) was used by the Greeks thousands of years ago and that the English word *politics* entered the language around 1529?

GOVERNMENT

A permanent structure (institution) composed of decision makers who make society's rules about conflict resolution and the allocation of resources and who possess the power to enforce them.

AUTHORITY

The features of a leader or an institution that compel obedience, usually because of ascribed legitimacy. For most societies, government is the ultimate authority in the allocation of values.

LEGITIMACY

A status conferred by the people on the government's officials, acts, and institutions through their belief that the government's actions are an appropriate use of power by a legally constituted governmental authority following correct decision-making policies. These actions are regarded as rightful and entitled to compliance and obedience on the part of citizens.

POWER

The ability to cause others to modify their behavior and to conform to what the power holder wants.

COMPLIANCE

Accepting and carrying out authorities' decisions.

TOTALITARIAN REGIME

A form of government that controls all aspects of the political and social life of a nation. All power resides with the government. The citizens have no power to choose the leadership or policies of the country.

ernment has instituted and attempted to implement a series of environmental laws meant to improve air and water quality. Environmental laws have required citizens to follow certain rules, such as to use unleaded gasoline. Such laws also have forced citizens to buy only certain types of automobiles and to pay higher costs for those vehicles in order to reimburse automobile manufacturers for the equipment they have installed to control emissions.

Why do citizens obey these laws and subject themselves to these regulations? One reason citizens obey government is because it has the **authority** to make such laws. By authority, we mean the ultimate right to enforce compliance with decisions. Americans also believe the laws should be obeyed because they possess **legitimacy**—that is, they are appropriate and rightful. The laws have been made according to the correct and accepted political process by representatives of the people. Therefore, they are accepted by the people as legitimate and having political authority.

The Question of Power

Another and perhaps more basic answer as to why we comply with the laws and rules of the government is because we understand that government has the **power** to enforce the law. We obey environmental laws and pay taxes in part because we acknowledge the legitimacy of the law. We also know that the government has the power to coerce our compliance with the law. Governments differ in the degree to which they must rely on coercion to gain **compliance** from their citizens. In authoritarian nations, the use of force is far more common than in democratic nations, in which most citizens comply with the law because they accept the authority of the government and its officials. In authoritarian or **totalitarian regimes,** the will of the government is imposed frequently and is upheld by the use of force.

The concept of power also involves the ability of one individual or a group to influence the actions of another individual or group of individuals. We frequently speak of the power of the president to convince Congress to pass laws, or the power of the American Association of Retired Persons to influence legislation. We also speak frequently of the power of money to influence political decisions. These uses of power are informal, including the use of rewards for compliance rather than the threat of coercion. More often than not, political power in the government is a matter of influence and persuasion rather than coercion.

WHO GOVERNS?

One of the most fundamental questions of politics has to do with which person or groups of people control society through the government. Who possesses the power to make decisions about who gets what and how the benefits of the society are distributed among the people?

Sources of Political Power

At one extreme is a society governed by a totalitarian regime. In such political systems, a relatively small group of leaders or perhaps a single individual—a dictator—makes all political decisions for the society. Every aspect of political, social, and economic life is controlled by the government. The power of the ruler is total (thus, the term *totalitarianism*).

Many of our terms for describing the distribution of political power are derived from the ancient Greeks, who were the first Western people to study politics systematically. A society in which political decisions were controlled by a small group was called an **oligarchy,** meaning rule by a few members of the **elite,** who generally benefited themselves. Another form of rule by the few was known as **aristocracy,** meaning rule by the most virtuous, most talented, or the best suited to the position. Later, in European history, *aristocracy* meant rule by the titled or the upper classes. In contrast to such a top-down form of control was the form known as **anarchy,** or the condition of no government. Anarchy exists when each individual makes his or her own rules for behavior, and there are no laws and no government.

The Greek term for rule by the people was **democracy.** Although most Greek philosophers were not convinced that democracy was the best form of government, they understood and debated the possibility of such a political system. Within the limits of their culture, some of the Greek city-states operated as democracies.

The Athenian Model of Direct Democracy

The government of the ancient Greek city-state of Athens is often considered to be the historical model for a **direct democracy.** In fact, the system was not a pure system of direct democracy, because the average Athenian was not a participant in every political decision. Nonetheless, all major issues, even if decided by the committees of the ruling council, were put before the assembly of all citizens for a vote. The most important feature of Athenian democracy was that the **legislature** was composed of all of the citizens. Women, foreigners, and slaves were excluded, because they were not citizens. Direct democracy in Athens is considered to have been an ideal form of democracy, because it demanded a high level of participation from every citizen.

Direct democracy also has been practiced in some Swiss cantons and, in the United States, in New England town meetings and in some midwestern township meetings. New England town meetings, which can include all of the voters who live in the town, continue to make important decisions for the community—such as levying taxes, hiring city officials, and deciding local

OLIGARCHY

Rule by a few members of the elite, who generally make decisions to benefit their own group.

ELITE

An upper socioeconomic class that controls political and economic affairs.

ARISTOCRACY

Rule by the best suited, through virtue, talent, or education; in later usage, rule by the upper class.

ANARCHY

The condition of having no government and no laws. Each member of the society governs himself or herself.

DEMOCRACY

A system of government in which ultimate political authority is vested in the people. Derived from the Greek words *demos* ("the people") and *kratos* ("authority").

DIRECT DEMOCRACY

A system of government in which political decisions are made by the people directly, rather than by their elected representatives; probably possible only in small political communities.

LEGISLATURE

A government body primarily responsible for the making of laws.

This town meeting in New Hampshire allows every citizen of the town to vote directly and in person for elected officials, for proposed policies, and, in some cases, for the town budget. To be effective, such a form of direct democracy requires that the citizens stay informed about local politics and devote time to discussion and decision making.

INITIATIVE

A procedure by which voters can propose a law or a constitutional amendment.

REFERENDUM

An act of referring legislative (statutory) or constitutional measures to the voters for approval or disapproval.

RECALL

A procedure allowing the people to vote to dismiss an elected official from state office before his or her term has expired.

CONSENT OF THE PEOPLE

The idea that governments and laws derive their legitimacy from the consent of the governed.

ordinances—by majority vote. Some states provide a modern adaptation of direct democracy for their citizens: in most states, representative democracy is supplemented by the **initiative** or the **referendum**—a process by which the people may vote directly on laws or constitutional amendments. The **recall** process, which is available in over one-third of the states, allows the people to vote to remove an incumbent from state office.

The Dangers of Direct Democracy

Although they were aware of the Athenian model, the framers of the U.S. Constitution—for the most part—were opposed to such a system. For many centuries preceding this country's establishment, any form of democracy was considered to be dangerous and to lead to instability. But in the eighteenth and nineteenth centuries, the idea of government based on the **consent of the people** gained increasing popularity. Such a government was the main aspiration of the American and French revolutions, as well as of many subsequent ones. The masses, however, were considered to be too uneducated to govern themselves, too prone to the influence of demagogues (political leaders who manipulate popular prejudices), and too likely to abrogate minority rights.

James Madison defended the new scheme of government set forth in the U.S. Constitution, while warning of the problems inherent in a "pure democracy":

> A common passion or interest will, in almost every case, be felt by a majority of the whole . . . and there is nothing to check the inducements to sacrifice the weaker party or an obnoxious individual. Hence it is that such democracies have ever been spectacles of turbulence and contention, and have ever been found incompatible with personal security or the rights of property; and have in general been as short in their lives as they have been violent in their deaths.[4]

Like many other politicians of his time, Madison feared that pure, or direct, democracy would deteriorate into mob rule. What would keep the majority of the people, if given direct decision-making power, from abusing the rights of minority groups?

Representative Democracy

REPUBLIC

The form of government in which sovereignty rests with the people, who elect agents to represent them in lawmaking and other decisions.

REPRESENTATIVE DEMOCRACY

A form of government in which representatives elected by the people make and enforce laws and policies.

The framers of the U.S. Constitution attempted to craft a system of government that would ensure the continuation of a **republic,** meaning a government in which the power rests with the people, who elect representatives to govern them and to make the laws and policies. To eighteenth-century Americans, the idea of a republic also meant a government based on common beliefs and virtues that would be fostered within small communities. The rulers were to be amateurs—good citizens—who would take turns representing their fellow citizens, in a way similar to the Greek model.[5]

The U.S. Constitution creates a form of republican government known as a **representative democracy.** The people hold the ultimate power over the government through the election process, but policy decisions are all made by elected officials. Even this distance between the people and the government was not sufficient. Other provisions in the Constitution made sure that the Senate and the president would be selected by political elites rather than by the people, although later changes to the Constitution allowed the voters

---

[4]James Madison, in Alexander Hamilton, James Madison, and John Jay, *The Federalist Papers,* No. 10 (New York: Mentor Books, 1964), p. 81. See Appendix D.
[5]See Chapter 2 for a discussion of the founders' ideas.

to elect directly members of the Senate. This modified form of democratic government came to be widely accepted throughout the Western world as a compromise between the desire for democratic control and the needs of the modern state.

Principles of Democratic Government.   All representative democracies rest on the rule of the people as expressed through the election of government officials. In the 1790s, only free white males were able to vote, and in some states, they had to be property owners as well. Women did not receive the right to vote in national elections in the United States until 1920, and the right to vote was not really secured by African Americans until the 1960s. Today, **universal suffrage** is the rule.

Granting every person the right to participate in the election of officials recognizes the equal voting power of each citizen. This emphasis on the equality of every individual before the law is central to the American system. Because everyone's vote counts equally, the only way to make fair decisions is by some form of **majority** will. But to ensure that **majority rule** does not become oppressive, modern democracies also provide guarantees of minority rights. If certain democratic principles did not protect minorities, the majority might violate the fundamental rights of members of certain groups, especially groups that are unpopular or dissimilar to the majority population. In the past, the majority has imposed such limitations on African Americans, Native Americans, and Japanese Americans, to name only a few.

One way to guarantee the continued existence of a representative democracy is to hold free, competitive elections. Thus, the minority always has the opportunity to win elective office. For such elections to be totally open, freedom of the press and speech must be preserved so that opposition candidates may present their criticisms of the government.

Constitutional Democracy.   Another key feature of Western representative democracy is that it is based on the principle of **limited government.** Not only is the government dependent on popular sovereignty, but the powers of the government are also clearly limited, either through a written document or

DID YOU KNOW . . .
That in 1996, there were over 500,000 elected officials in the United States, which was more than all the bank tellers in the country?

UNIVERSAL SUFFRAGE

The right of all adults to vote for their representatives.

MAJORITY

More than 50 percent.

MAJORITY RULE

A basic principle of democracy asserting that the greatest number of citizens in any political unit should select officials and determine policies.

LIMITED GOVERNMENT

A form of government based on the principle that the powers of government should be clearly limited either through a written document or through wide public understanding; characterized by institutional checks to ensure that government serves the public rather than private interests.

Volunteers register voters in the Spanish Harlem section of New York City. By setting up a table in the neighborhood, the election officials make registration more convenient for voters as well as less threatening. Both political parties often conduct voter registration drives in the months before general elections.

through widely shared beliefs. The U.S. Constitution sets down the fundamental structure of the government and the limits to its activities. Such limits are intended to prevent political decisions based on the whims or ambitions of individuals in government rather than on constitutional principles.

DO WE HAVE A DEMOCRACY?

The sheer size and complexity of American society seem to make it unsuitable for direct democracy on a national scale. Some scholars suggest that even representative democracy is difficult to achieve in any modern state. They point to the low level of turnout for presidential elections and the even lower turnout for local ones. Polling data have shown that many Americans are neither particularly interested in politics nor well informed. Few are able to name the persons running for Congress in their district, and even fewer can discuss the candidates' positions. Members of Congress claim to represent their constituents, but few constituents follow the issues, much less communicate their views to their representatives. For the average citizen, the national government is too remote, too powerful, and too bureaucratic to be influenced by one vote.

Democracy for the Few

If ordinary citizens are not really making policy decisions with their votes, who is? One answer suggests that elites really govern the United States. Proponents of **elite theory** see society much as Alexander Hamilton did, who said,

> All communities divide themselves into the few and the many. The first are the rich and the wellborn, the other the mass of the people. . . . The people are turbulent and changing; they seldom judge or determine right. Give therefore to the first class a distinct, permanent share in the government. They will check the unsteadiness of the second, and as they cannot receive any advantage by a change, they therefore will ever maintain good government.

Elite theory describes an American mass population that is uninterested in politics and willing to let leaders make the decisions. Some versions of elite theory posit a small, cohesive elite class that makes almost all the important

ELITE THEORY

A perspective holding that society is ruled by a small number of people who exercise power in their self-interest.

Elites may have far more power and influence on the political system than do voters from the lower and middle classes. Because they share an educational background from selective schools, a higher income level, and common lifestyles, they are more likely to see government policy makers on a social basis and to form friendships with elected officials.

decisions regarding the nation,[6] whereas others suggest that voters choose among competing elites. New members of the elite are recruited through the educational system so that the brightest children of the masses allegedly have the opportunity to join the elite stratum.

In such a political system, the primary goal of the government is stability, because elites do not want any change in their status. Major social and economic change only takes place if elites see their resources threatened. This selfish interest of the elites does not mean, however, that they are necessarily undemocratic or always antiprogressive. Whereas some policies, such as favorable tax-avoidance laws, may be perceived as elitist in nature, other policies benefit many members of the public. Political scientists Thomas Dye and Harmon Ziegler propose that American elites are more devoted to democratic principles and rights than are most members of the mass public.[7]

Many observers contend that economic and social developments in the last several years have strengthened the perception that America is governed by an elite, privileged group. These observers believe that "the rich get richer and the poor get poorer" in this country and that, as a consequence, more and more Americans are becoming alienated from the political process. Already, there is a growing underclass of Americans that has little say in government and has little hope of being able to in the future—because the possibility of joining the elite stratum is so remote. Wealthier citizens have educational opportunities that poorer individuals simply cannot afford. Moreover, as you will read in Chapter 10, political campaigns are expensive, and campaign costs have increased steadily each year. Today, candidates for political office, unless they can afford the "price" of winning, have to drop out of the race— or not enter it in the first place. Many predict that if present trends continue, we will indeed have a "democracy for the few."

Democracy for Groups

A different school of thought looks at the characteristics of the American electorate and finds that our form of democracy is based on group interests. Even if the average citizen cannot keep up with political issues or cast a deciding vote in any election, the individual's interests will be protected by groups that represent him or her.

Theorists who subscribe to **pluralism** as a way of understanding American politics believe that people are naturally social and inclined to form associations. In the pluralists' view, politics is the struggle among groups to gain benefits for their members. Given the structures of the American political system, group conflicts tend to be settled by compromise and accommodation so that each interest is satisfied to some extent.[8]

Pluralists see public policy as resulting from group interactions carried out within Congress and the executive branch. Because there are a multitude of interests, no one group can dominate the political process. Furthermore, because most individuals have more than one interest, conflict among groups does not divide the nation into hostile camps.

There are a number of flaws in some of the basic assumptions of this theory. Among these are the relatively low number of people who formally join interest groups, the real disadvantages of pluralism for the poorer citizens,

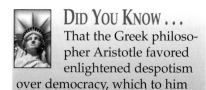

DID YOU KNOW ...
That the Greek philosopher Aristotle favored enlightened despotism over democracy, which to him meant mob rule?

PLURALISM

A theory that views politics as a conflict among interest groups. Political decision making is characterized by bargaining and compromise.

---

[6]Michael Parenti, *Democracy for the Few,* 7th ed. (New York: St. Martin's Press, 1995).

[7]Thomas Dye and Harmon Ziegler, *The Irony of Democracy,* 10th ed. (Duxbury, Mass.: Wadsworth, 1996).

[8]David Truman, *The Governmental Process* (New York: Knopf, 1951); and Robert Dahl, *Who Governs?* (New Haven, Conn.: Yale University Press, 1961).

HYPERPLURALISM

A situation that arises when interest groups become so powerful that they dominate the political decision-making structures, rendering any consideration of the greater public interest impossible.

and pluralism's belief that group decision making always reflects the best interests of the nation.

With these flaws in mind, critics see a danger that groups may become so powerful that all policies become compromises crafted to satisfy the interests of the largest groups. The interests of the public as a whole, then, cannot be considered. Critics of pluralism have suggested that a democratic system can be virtually paralyzed by the struggle between interest groups. This struggle results in a condition sometimes called **hyperpluralism,** meaning that groups and their needs control the government and decision making rather than the government's acting for the good of the nation.

Both pluralism and elite theory attempt to explain the real workings of American democracy. Neither approach is complete, nor can either be proved. Viewing the United States as run by elites reminds us that the founders themselves were not great defenders of the mass public. In contrast, the pluralist view underscores both the advantages and the disadvantages of Americans' inclination to join, to organize, and to pursue benefits for themselves. It points out all of the places within the American political system in which interest groups find it comfortable to work. With this knowledge, the system can be adjusted to keep interest groups within the limits of the public good.

IDEAS AND POLITICS: POLITICAL CULTURE

In spite of its flaws and weaknesses, most Americans are proud of their political system and support it with their obedience to the laws, their patriotism, or their votes. Given the diverse nature of American society and the wide range of ethnic groups, economic classes, and other interests, what gives Americans a common political heritage? One of the forces that unites Americans is the **political culture,** which can be defined as a patterned set of ideas, values, and ways of thinking about government and politics. For Americans, the political culture includes such symbolic elements as the flag, the Statue of Liberty, and the Lincoln Memorial. It includes ideas such as the belief that one is innocent until proven guilty. Political culture also encompasses deeply held values, including equality, liberty, and the right to hold property.

POLITICAL CULTURE

The collection of beliefs and attitudes toward government and the political process held by a community or nation.

The degree to which Americans subscribe to a single set of values is surprising if you consider that virtually all U.S. citizens are descended from immigrants. The process by which such beliefs and values are transmitted to individuals is known as **political socialization.** Historically, the political parties played an important role in teaching new residents how to participate in the system in return for their votes. Frequently, the parties also provided the first economic opportunities, in the form of jobs, to immigrants and their families.

POLITICAL SOCIALIZATION

The process through which individuals learn a set of political attitudes and form opinions about social issues. The family and the educational system are two of the most important forces in the political socialization process.

A fundamental source of political socialization is, of course, the family. The beliefs and attitudes transmitted to children by their parents play a large role in the formation of political views and values. Yet another major force for the socialization of Americans—past and present—has been the school system. The educational process continues to socialize the children of both immigrants and native-born Americans by explicitly teaching such basic political values as equality and liberty and by emphasizing patriotism.

A Political Consensus

Usually, the more homogeneous a population, the easier it is to have a political culture that is based on consensus. One of the reasons that Great Britain can maintain a limited government without a written constitution is that

Certain groups within the United States insist on maintaining their own cultural beliefs and practices. The Amish, pictured here, are descended from German religious sects and live in close communities in Pennsylvania, Ohio, Indiana, and Illinois, as well as in other states. The more conservative Amish groups do not use modern conveniences, such as automobiles or electricity, and have resisted immunizations and mandatory schooling for their children.

there exists substantial agreement within the population with respect to the political decision-making process of government. Even in a nation that is heterogeneous in geography and ethnic background, such as the United States, it is possible for shared cultural ideas to develop. We have already discussed one of the most fundamental ideas in American political culture—democracy. There are other concepts related to the notion of democracy that are also fundamental to American political culture, although individual Americans may interpret their meaning quite differently. Among these are liberty, equality, and property.

Liberty. The term **liberty** can be defined as the greatest freedom of individuals that is consistent with the freedom of other individuals in the society. In the United States, our civil liberties include religious freedom—both the right to practice whatever religion one chooses and freedom from any state-imposed religion. Our civil liberties also include freedom of speech—the right to express our opinions freely on matters, including government actions. Freedom of speech is perhaps one of our most prized liberties, because a democracy could not endure without it. These and other basic guarantees of liberty are not found in the body of the U.S. Constitution but in the Bill of Rights, the first ten amendments to the Constitution.

The process of ensuring liberty for all Americans did not end with the adoption of the Bill of Rights but has continued throughout our history. Political issues often turn on how a particular liberty should be interpreted or the extent to which it should be limited in the interests of society as a whole. Some of the most emotionally charged issues today, for example, have to do with whether our civil liberties include the liberty to have an abortion or (for terminally ill persons) to commit assisted suicide.

Equality. The Declaration of Independence states, "All men are created equal." Today, that statement has been amended by the political culture to include groups other than white males—women, African Americans, Native Americans, Asian Americans, and others. The definition of **equality,** however, has been disputed by Americans since the Revolution.[9] Does equality

LIBERTY

The greatest freedom of individuals that is consistent with the freedom of other individuals in the society.

EQUALITY

A concept that all people are of equal worth.

---

[9]Richard J. Ellis, "Rival Visions of Equality in American Political Culture," *Review of Politics,* Vol. 54 (Spring 1992), p. 254.

INALIENABLE RIGHTS

Rights held to be inherent in natural law and not dependent on government; as asserted in the Declaration of Independence, the rights to "life, liberty, and the pursuit of happiness."

PROPERTY

Anything that is or may be subject to ownership. As conceived by the political philosopher John Locke, the right to property is a natural right superior to human law (laws made by government).

POPULAR SOVEREIGNTY

The concept that ultimate political authority rests with the people.

FRATERNITY

From the Latin *fraternus* (brother), a term that came to mean, in the political philosophy of the eighteenth century, the condition in which each individual considers the needs of all others; a brotherhood. In the French Revolution of 1789, the popular cry was "liberty, equality, and fraternity."

mean simply political equality—the right to register to vote, to cast a ballot, and to run for political office? Does equality mean equal opportunity for individuals to develop their talents and skills? If the latter is the meaning of equality, what should the United States do to ensure equal opportunities for those who are born poor, disabled, or female? As you will read in later chapters of this book, much of America's politics has concerned just such questions. Although most Americans believe strongly that all persons should have the opportunity to fulfill their potential, many disagree about whether it is the government's responsibility to eliminate economic and social differences.

Property.   Many Americans probably remember that the **inalienable rights** asserted in the Declaration of Independence are the rights to "life, liberty, and the pursuit of happiness." The inspiration for that phrase, however, came from the writings of an English philosopher, John Locke (1632–1704), who clearly stated that people's rights were to life, liberty, and **property.** In American political culture, the pursuit of happiness and property are considered to be closely related. Americans place great value on owning land, on acquiring material possessions, and on the monetary value of jobs. Property can be seen as giving its owner political power and the liberty to do whatever he or she wants. At the same time, the ownership of property immediately creates inequality in society. The desire to own property, however, is so widespread among all classes of Americans that socialist movements, which advocate the redistribution of wealth and property, have had a difficult time securing a wide following here.

Democracy, liberty, equality, and property—these concepts lie at the core of American political culture. Other issues—such as majority rule, **popular sovereignty,** and **fraternity**—are closely related to them. These fundamental principles are so deeply ingrained in U.S. culture that most Americans rarely question them.

The Stability of the Culture

Political culture plays an important role in holding society together, because the system of ideas at the core of that culture must persuade people to support the existing political process through their attitudes and participation. If people begin to doubt the ideas underlying the culture, they will not transmit those beliefs to their children or support the existing political processes. As the number of immigrants to the United States continues to rise, especially on the East and West Coasts, and as society gives more recognition to the cultures of the groups within it, we might expect that the old cultural beliefs, especially beliefs in the importance of individualism and self-determination, might be eroded.

Consider that some subgroups, such as Native Americans and the Amish, have made concerted efforts to preserve their language and cultural practices. Many immigrant groups, including Hispanics, Asian Americans, and Caribbean Americans, maintain their language and cultural values within American cities and states. The question is whether these subgroups also subscribe to the values of the American political culture.

Everett C. Ladd believes that polling data provide strong evidence that these subgroups do subscribe to such values. Ladd asserts that "the populace at large [is] distinguished by strong attachments to individualism, but these attachments are remarkably uniform across social lines."[10] Ladd's data show

---

[10]Everett C. Ladd, "E Pluribus Unum Still: The Uniting of America," *Public Perspective,* May/June 1992, pp. 3–5.

Hispanic Americans join together to support a political candidate. Like other ethnic groups, these Hispanic voters seek to have their concerns heard by the candidates. In return, political candidates try to show their appreciation for the culture of the ethnic voters by delivering a speech in their language or promising more benefits for the group.

that 66 percent of the people believe that one gets ahead by personal hard work rather than lucky breaks or help from others. Different ethnic groups within the society almost all have the same view: 69 percent of Hispanics, 71 percent of Native Americans, and 60 percent of African Americans say that hard work makes the difference. When asked whether they were very proud to be an American, 96 percent of all respondents answered in the affirmative. Again, there were virtually no differences between ethnic groups, age groups, or income groups. As Figure 1–1 shows, pride in living in the United States is high for almost all Americans regardless of ethnic identity. Ladd concludes that such evidence suggests that the basic beliefs and symbols of the political culture still command loyalty from Americans regardless of their other conflicts. (For a discussion of Americans' religious beliefs and their effects on the political scene, see this chapter's *Politics and Values*.)

THE CHANGING FACE OF AMERICA

The face of America is changing as its citizens age, become more diverse, and generate new needs for laws and policies. Long a nation of growth, the United States has become a middle-aged nation with a low birthrate and an increasing number of older citizens who want services from the government. The 1990 census showed that between 1980 and 1990, the U.S. population grew only 9.8 percent, the second lowest rate of growth in the history of taking such measurements.

Several aspects of this population trend have significant political consequences. As Figure 1–2 shows, the population is aging quickly; the median

Figure 1–1

How Different Groups Feel about Living in the United States

Question: Do you agree or disagree that..."I'd rather live in the U.S. than anywhere else?"
Percent Agreeing

White	95%
African American	87%
Hispanic	92%

SOURCE: Survey by ABC News, April 8–9, 1992, as reprinted in *Public Perspective*, March/April 1992.

POLITICS AND VALUES
Americans and Religion

Given the strongly religious origins of the original colonies in the seventeenth and eighteenth centuries, it may not seem surprising that U.S. culture today is replete with religious symbols and practices. These practices spill over into the political arena in many ways. Our coins and paper currency bear the motto "In God We Trust," daily sessions of Congress begin with a prayer, and presidents take the oath of office resting one hand on the Bible.

In fact, Americans continue to express a high degree of association with religion and religious groups—more than that expressed by any other Western nation. A recent *U.S. News* poll found that 62 percent of Americans believed that religion is an increasing influence on their lives while only 16 percent felt that religion's influence on their personal lives was decreasing. Although more than 60 percent of Americans claimed to be formally affiliated with a religious group, only 40 percent actually attended any religious service during a week.

According to one survey, almost one in three white Americans is affiliated with an evangelical church, believes that the Bible contains no errors, or reports being born again. Many scholars define as truly fundamentalist or evangelical those who report both being born again and believing in the Bible as being without error. That group would include about 20 percent of white American adults.

Given such widespread avowals of religious belief, it is not surprising that religion has influenced American culture and politics. Many Americans believe that prayer should be allowed in schools, but the Supreme Court has ruled that such practices violate the Constitution. Cities and school districts struggle to find appropriate ways to celebrate religious holidays, but pressure to celebrate the holidays

of the majority group—Christians—leads to protests both from other religious bodies and from those who feel that no public entity should recognize religion in any way.

Religious views and leaders have also played a direct role in the American political arena. In recent decades, the strongest force for the insertion of religion into American politics has come from the political right. President Jimmy Carter himself sought support as a born-again, or evangelical, Christian. Pat Robertson, a fundamentalist minister with a wide following from his television show "The 700 Club," campaigned for the Republican presidential nomination in 1988 but met with limited success.

For many decades, Americans seemed to feel that churches should be relatively apolitical. As recently as 1965, the Gallup Poll found that 55 percent of Americans believed that churches should keep out of political matters while 40 percent felt that churches should get involved. A recent survey released by the Pew Research Center for the People and the Press shows that those proportions have been reversed: in 1996, 54 percent of Americans said that churches should express their views on political issues.* Additionally, almost 30 percent favored having their religious leaders promote political stands from the pulpit.

The growing support for the discussion of political issues in churches is contradicted, however, by a continuing fear that particular denominations may become too powerful. The Pew study also reports that 44 percent of Americans believe that Protestants should have less power rather than more while 53 percent say that Catholics should have less power. Fifty-one percent say that evangelicals should have less power, and 49 percent would like to reduce the power of Jews.

All of this suggests that religion will continue to be involved in American politics and that the relationship between religious affiliation and the political beliefs of individuals may also strengthen and have an increasing effect at the pools.

For Critical Analysis
Do you believe that religious leaders ought to try to convince their followers to take specific political positions or to vote for specific candidates?

*Reported by the Pew Research Center for the People and the Press, 1996.

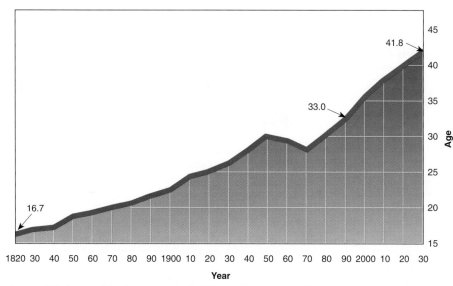

Figure 1–2
● ● ● ● ● ● ● ● ● ● ● ● ● ● ● ● ● ● ●
The Median Age of the U.S.
Population: 1820 to 2030

SOURCE: U.S. Bureau of the Census, as cited in *Universal Almanac, 1996* (Kansas City, Mo.: Andrews and McMeel, 1996).

age (the age at which half the people are older and half are younger) will reach thirty-five by the year 2000. Even more startling is the fact that almost 13 percent of the population is now sixty-five years old or older. By the year 2030, more than 21 percent of the population will be retired or approaching retirement. If the current retirement and pension systems remain in place, including Social Security, a very large proportion of each worker's wages will have to be deducted to support benefits for the retired.

Ethnic Change

The ethnic character of the United States is also changing. (See this chapter's *Politics and the Fifty States*.) Whites have a very low birthrate, whereas African Americans and Hispanics have more children per family. As displayed in Table 1–1, including the effects of immigration, the proportion of whites has decreased, and the proportions of Hispanics, African Americans, and Asian Americans have increased.

Although studies—such as that of Everett Ladd discussed earlier—show that the various groups in this country share many common values, conflicts between ethnic and racial groups also exist. These conflicts all too often erupt into "hate speech" or "hate crimes," which pose an increasing threat to polit-

Table 1–1

Resident Population Distribution by Race and Hispanic Origin, 1980 to 1990

RACE/HISPANIC ORIGIN*	1980 NUMBER	1980 PERCENTAGE	1990 NUMBER	1990 PERCENTAGE	CHANGE NUMBER	CHANGE PERCENTAGE
Total population	226,545,805	100.0%	248,709,873	100.0%	22,164,068	9.8
White	188,371,622	83.1	199,686,070	80.3	11,314,448	6.0
Black	26,495,025	11.7	29,986,060	12.1	3,491,035	13.2
American Indian, Eskimo, or Aleut	1,420,400	0.6	1,959,234	0.8	538,834	37.9
Asian or Pacific Islander	3,500,439	1.5	7,273,662	2.9	3,773,223	107.8
Other race	6,758,319	3.0	9,804,847	3.9	3,046,528	45.1
Hispanic origin	14,608,673	6.4	22,354,059	9.0	7,745,386	53.0

*Persons of Hispanic origin may be of any race.

SOURCE: U.S. Bureau of the Census release, as cited in *Universal Almanac, 1996* (Kansas City, Mo.: Andrews and McMeel, 1996).

POLITICS AND THE FIFTY STATES
The Impact of Immigration

Although Americans rarely think of immigration as a force for change, the number of individuals who have immigrated to the United States has grown rapidly in the last decade. Immigration now makes up more than 30 percent of the population growth in the United States. The impact of immigration on states and local communities, however, varies greatly. The top five states in terms of the percentage of their residents who are foreign born are California, 21.7 percent; New York, 15.8 percent; Hawaii, 14.7 percent;

Florida, 12.8 percent; and New Jersey, 12.5 percent.

Clearly, issues that arise from the influx of many people from other nations and cultures are more likely to be hotly debated in those states that receive many immigrants. In those states, the need to educate children who speak another language, the provision of welfare benefits to immigrants, and the impact of affirmative action admissions to universities all have become matters of political debate and often are subject to

statewide referenda. States that receive few new residents from other nations are far less likely to consider such issues to be important topics for debate and action.

For Critical Analysis
How does the number of immigrants in a state affect state policies and state spending?

SOURCE: Data reported by the U.S. Bureau of the Census, and published in *The Universal Almanac, 1996* (Kansas City, Mo.: Andrews and McMeel, 1996), p. 314.

ical stability. There is no reason to assume that these and other divisive forces at work in our society cannot be overcome, but there is also no reason to ignore them. Consider, for example, the results of a recent *Newsweek* poll, in which respondents were asked the following question: "One hundred years from today, will the United States still exist as one nation?" Forty-eight percent of the African American respondents answered "No" to this question, as did 26 percent of white respondents and 38 percent of Hispanic respondents.

Immigrants are also likely to shape American politics in the future. Few Americans think of the current period in our history as being as volatile as the early years of the twentieth century, when millions of Europeans immigrated to the United States. Yet, as Figure 1–3 shows, the percentage of population growth attributed to immigration was almost as high in the past decade as it was before World War I. In 1994, more than 1.7 million persons immigrated

Figure 1–3
• • • • • • • • • • • • • • • • • • • •
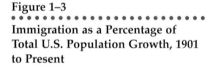
Immigration as a Percentage of Total U.S. Population Growth, 1901 to Present

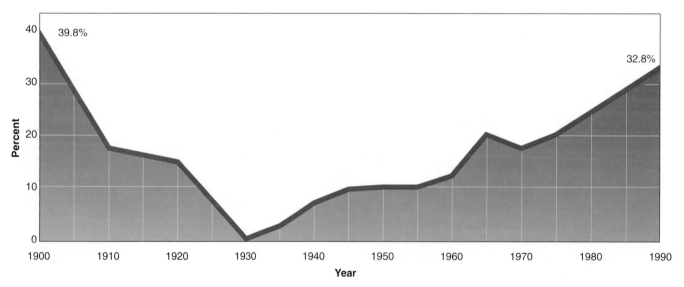

SOURCE: U.S. Immigration and Naturalization Service, Population Reference Bureau, *Population Bureau (1986)*, and U.S. Bureau of the Census, *1990 Census Profile (1991)*, as cited in *Universal Almanac 1996* (Kansas City, Mo.: Andrews and McMeel, 1996).

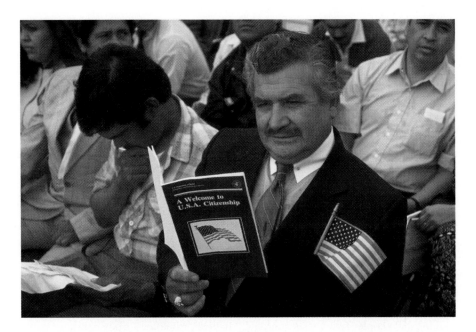

Each year thousands of immigrants are sworn in as new U.S. citizens. The U.S. Constitution in Article VI, Section 8, declares that Congress shall have the power to "establish a uniform Rule of Naturalization." Naturalization is the process by which individuals who are not yet citizens become United States citizens. Such individuals are called naturalized citizens as opposed to native-born citizens. There are myriad requirements to become a naturalized citizen. Because it is often difficult to do so, many immigrants remain in this country without proper documentation.

to the United States legally, with the greatest number coming from Mexico, but sizable numbers from Asian nations as well. These changes are placing strain on the cohesiveness of U.S. political culture and on the willingness of citizens to support the political structures of the nation.

Other Trends

Other changes in the face of America have more to do with our changing society. More Americans continue to fill the urban places of the nation in comparison with rural areas. By 1997, more than 75 percent of the population lived in an urban environment. Women continued to increase their participation in the educational system. By the beginning of this decade, as many women as men had completed their high school educations, and the percentage of women who had completed college continued to grow.

Change also continues in the structure of American families, although the traditional two-parent family is still very strong. Just twenty years ago, more than 85 percent of children lived in a two-parent family. Today, 71 percent of children under age eighteen live in two-parent families, and 25 percent live with only one parent. About one-fourth of the children of one-parent families live in poverty.

Other changes also have consequences for social policies. Although the national government has been committed to ending poverty since the mid-1960s, 13.5 percent of all Americans still live in households that have incomes below the official poverty line. Although this number is large, it is below the 22 percent figure recorded in 1960. Far more alarming is the trend in prison populations. Since 1980, the number of persons incarcerated in state and federal prisons has increased from about 329,000 to more than 1,000,000, an increase of over 200 percent.

Also emerging as a part of the American landscape are citizens' militias or "patriot" groups. While members of these groups might say that they are proud to be Americans, many in these groups view the national government as the enemy—not the protector—of civil rights and liberties. Animosity toward the national goverment, for whatever reason, is thought to have motivated the 1995 bombing of the Oklahoma City Federal Building and some other terrorist acts against government bureaucrats, particularly in the West.

For Americans, terrorism always seemed to be a problem for other countries. Recently, though, terrorism on American soil has occurred, such as the bombing of the Murrah Federal Building in Oklahoma City. In 1995, a crude, but effective, home-made bomb was detonated at the base of this building, killing 168 persons and injuring hundreds of others. It is thought that members of a local militia group were responsible.

POLITICS AND IDEOLOGY
Beyond Ideology: Terrorism

One of the most troubling aspects of certain political ideology is that, if carried to an extreme, it can lead to violent acts that destroy the life, liberty, and property of others. Terrorism, at least to a significant extent, is linked to extremist political views. Sometimes, these views are held by a group. For example, if a bomb explodes in London, people assume that it is probably the work of the Irish Republican Army. The numerous bombings in Paris in 1995 were almost all tied to Algerian extremists. The killing of Israeli athletes during the 1972 Olympics in Munich, Germany, was connected to long-standing Palestine-Israel hostilities. Terrorist acts also have been sponsored by national governments, particularly by the Middle Eastern nations of Libya, Iraq, Iran, and the Sudan. Still other terrorist acts have been the work of a single individual, such as the Unabomber, a loner who conducted an almost two-decade reign of terror in the United States.

Traditionally, the United States has been a relatively safe haven from terrorism, with fewer terrorist incidents than any nation in the world. Since 1993, however, when a powerful terrorist bomb exploded in New York's World Trade Center, a rash of terrorist acts has occurred in this country. The bombing of the Oklahoma City Federal Building in 1995 killed 168 persons and injured hundreds of others. In July 1996, TWA flight 800 exploded shortly after it left New York for Paris, killing 230 people. Two weeks later, pipe bomb hidden in a knapsack exploded at a public concert held to celebrate the Olympics in Atlanta, Georgia, killing two persons and injuring more than one hundred others. These and other terrorist acts have caused U.S. political leaders to look with some urgency for solutions to the problem of terrorism.

In April 1996, Congress took action by providing $1 billion over four years to combat terrorism. Congress also modified immigration and political-asylum rules in an attempt to make it more difficult for potential terrorists to enter this country. Congress has considered an antiterrorism bill that would tighten airport security and allow suspected terrorists to be prosecuted under federal racketeering laws. On the international level, the United States joined six other nations at a summit meeting in June 1996 to launch a joint international effort to contain terrorism. The meeting was held shortly after a truck bomb exploded in a military complex in Saudi Arabia, killing nineteen Americans.

The battle against terrorism will be difficult, because the "enemy" often is invisible, and terrorist acts, by their very nature, are random, diverse, and unpredictable. Furthermore, Americans have not yet decided on just how far they want the government to go in its efforts to protect them from terrorist attacks. President Clinton has proposed that the government should be given more extensive wiretapping authority, so that law-enforcement personnel could monitor more closely the activities of suspected terrorists or potential terrorists. The question before Congress is whether such authority would be too invasive of the liberties and privacy rights of U.S. citizens. There are no easy answers to this question. As President Clinton said in a July 1996 speech, terrorism "may well be the most significant security challenge of the twenty-first century for the people of the United States and to civilized people everywhere."

For Critical Analysis
What liberties and privacy rights would you be willing to sacrifice in order to achieve protection against terrorist acts?

An Atlanta Police bomb squad truck arrives at Centenial Olympic Park after an explosion rocked the park in the morning hours of July 27, 1996. Over 200 people were injured in the blast. As of 1997, no suspect had been apprehended.

Finally, recent national surveys have found that about one-fifth of all Americans are barely literate and have difficulty dealing with simple documents. Each of these statistics raises political questions for the society as a whole. These facts challenge voters and their representatives to change policies in order to reduce poverty, crime, and illiteracy—if society can agree on how to accomplish these tasks. Another challenging problem of our time is terrorism, as discussed in the *Politics and Ideology* on the facing page.

DID YOU KNOW . . .
That about 14 percent of all legal immigrants to the United States plan to live in the Los Angeles/Long Beach, California, area?

IDEAS AND POLITICS: IDEOLOGY

An **ideology** is a closely linked set of beliefs about the goal of politics and the most desirable political order. True ideologies are well-organized theories that can guide virtually every decision that an individual or society can make. As discussed in this chapter's *Politics and Comparative Systems: Competing Visions of Power*, the major ideologies of our time are usually represented as a continuum from far left to far right according to their views of the power of government. Few Americans, however, derive their views on politics from the more extreme ideologies. In fact, the U.S. political spectrum has been dominated for decades by two relatively moderate ideological positions: **liberalism** and **conservatism.**

American liberals believe that government should take strong positive action to solve the nation's economic and social problems. They believe that it is the obligation of the government to enhance opportunities for the economic and social equality of all individuals. Liberals tend to support programs to reduce poverty, endorse progressive taxation to redistribute income from wealthier classes to the poorer, and rely on government regulation to guide the activities of business and the economy.

Conservatives take a quite different approach to the role of government in the economy, believing that the private sector probably can outperform the government in almost any activity. Believing that the individual is primarily responsible for his or her own well-being, conservatives are less supportive of government initiatives to redistribute income or to craft programs that will change the status of individuals.

In the moral sphere, conservatives tend to support more government regulation of social values and moral decisions than do liberals. Thus, conservatives tend to oppose gay rights legislation and propose stronger curbs on pornography. Liberals usually support wider tolerance of different life choices and oppose government attempts to regulate personal behavior and morals.

Individuals in the society may not accept the full range of either liberal or conservative views. It is not unusual for Americans to be quite liberal on economic issues and supportive of considerable government intervention in the economy while holding conservative views on moral and social issues. Such a mixture of views makes it difficult for American political parties to identify themselves solely with either a conservative or liberal viewpoint, because such a position may cost them votes on specific issues.

There are also smaller groups of Americans who consider themselves to be communists, socialists, or libertarians, but these groups play a minor role in the national political arena. The limited role played by these and other alternative political perspectives is reinforced by the fact that they receive little positive exposure in classrooms, the media, or public discourse.

IDEOLOGY

A comprehensive and logically ordered set of beliefs about the nature of people and about the institutions and role of government.

LIBERALISM

A set of beliefs that includes the advocacy of positive government action to improve the welfare of individuals, support for civil rights, and tolerance for political and social change.

CONSERVATISM

A set of beliefs that includes a limited role for the national government in helping individuals, support for traditional values and lifestyles, and a cautious response to change.

POLITICS AND COMPARATIVE SYSTEMS
Competing Visions of Power

Political ideologies offer their adherents well-organized theories. These theories propose goals for the society and the political means by which those goals can be achieved. At the core of every political ideology is a set of values that guides its theory of governmental power. If we compare political ideologies on the basis of how much power the government should have within a society, we can array them on a continuum from left to right, as shown in the first box below.

For each of these ideological positions, the amount of power granted to the government is intended to achieve a certain set of goals within the society, and the perfect society would completely achieve these values. The values are arrayed in the second box below.

In the United States, there are adherents of each of these ideological positions. Given widely shared cultural values, however, only two of these belief systems consistently have played a central part in American political debates: liberalism and conservatism.

For Critical Analysis

What kinds of activities do you believe the government should control? When is government action most effective? Does answering those questions help you identify with one of the ideological positions described below?

How Much Power Should the Government Have?

MARXISM-LENINISM	SOCIALISM	LIBERALISM	CONSERVATISM	LIBERTARIANISM
Central control of economy and political system.	Active government control of major economic sectors	Positive government action in economy and to achieve social goals.	Positive government action to support capitalism; action to uphold certain values.	Government action only for defense; almost no regulation of economy or individual behavior.

What Values Should the Government Pursue?

MARXISM-LENINISM	SOCIALISM	LIBERALISM	CONSERVATISM	LIBERTARIANISM
Total equality and security; unity and solidarity.	Economic equality; community.	Political liberty; economic security; equal opportunity.	Political liberty; economic liberty; order.	Total political and economic liberty for individuals.

AMERICA'S POLITICS: UNFINISHED WORK

Although the U.S. government is one of the oldest democratic regimes in the world and its Constitution remains relatively unchanged more than two hundred years after it was written, the U.S. political system has been dynamic since its founding. As you will read in the chapters that follow, Americans have changed their ideas about who votes and who controls the government, constantly expanded their list of rights and liberties, originated and then revised a number of political parties, and significantly altered their view of the role of the national government in their lives and businesses.

Like the people of the nations of Eastern Europe and the former Soviet republics, the citizens of the United States have often pressed to make their government more responsive to the needs of the society and more effective in its functioning. What makes Americans different from the people of those other nations is a long and stable history that encourages them to try to modify the political structures and processes rather than invent totally new ones. Changing the political machinery has brought changes in the past—witness the social legislation of the New Deal in the 1930s and the Great Society in the 1960s—and Americans generally believe that change can occur again.

CRITICAL PERSPECTIVE

The Elections of 1996: Change in American Politics

From a purely historical perspective, the elections of 1996 constituted a watershed event. Bill Clinton became the first Democrat to be reelected to a second term as president since Franklin Roosevelt's reelection to a second term in 1936. The Republicans retained control of both houses of Congress in two successive elections for the first time since 1928. While these electoral outcomes were historic, what did they say about change in American politics? Some commentors have suggested that the real message conveyed by the voters in the 1996 elections was that the voters wanted very little change from either party.

Divided Government

After the 1994 Republican "revolution," the president and the Republican leaders of Congress struggled to define a working relationship. In the first year following the 1994 elections, the young Republican majority in the House rushed to pass the legislation on their agenda, including the line-item veto and many changes within Congress, while the president seemed to sit back and wait for their bills. By late 1995, the Clinton administration took another approach to the Republican majority, with the president using the veto to establish his position in opposition to Republican budgets and other legislation. Using such phrases as "gridlock" and "train wreck," both parties tried to use partial government shutdowns to force their way. Not only did the public disapprove of this tactic, but polls showed that the Republicans were viewed as the cause of the shutdowns. With both the president and the Republican legislators looking toward the elections of 1996, Congress and the president began working together and produced some major legislation, including the Telecommunications Act, the new farm law, the welfare reform, and the budget.

Voting for a "divided government" is not new for Americans. Having the presidency and Congress in different political hands has occurred often in the twentieth century. Divided government takes advantage of the checks and balances built into the Constitution to keep either branch from assuming too much power. In 1996, the voters seemed to say, "Change stalemate to productive work."

"Grass Roots" Politics and Political Change

What other changes were produced by the 1996 elections? As is often the case in the United States, political change comes from the grass roots. Several states had election results that reaffirmed broad changes in the electorate. In the South, Republicans continued to increase their lead in House and Senate seats, confirming the conversion of the southern states to that party. In contrast, President Clinton won formerly Republican strongholds in New England, and voters swept Democrats into governorships in New Hampshire and Indiana.

Perhaps the most attention was given to the numerous initiatives and referenda on state ballots. In California, voters picked their way through a number of issues, voting to end affirmative action in state hiring and in admissions to state universities. Californians also approved the medicinal use of marijuana, defeated propositions aimed at easing the way for shareholder suits against corporations, and restricted managed-care plans. More states rejected gambling initiatives than passed them. What can one make of this mix of liberal and conservative decisions? At least one conclusion is clear: the voters are willing and able to make decisions on policy issues at the local level.

Campaign Financing

Perhaps the most startline change in the 1996 elections was the brazen fund-raising activities undertaken by both the Republican and Democratic parties, by business groups and many corporate political committees, and by organized labor. More than $2 billion may have been raised and spent on the 1996 elections. By the end of the campaign, concerns were raised about foreign contributions and about the ability of corporations and labor unions to find legal ways to skirt the laws governing campaign financing. If nothing else, the potential for corruption and the saturation of campaign advertising raised a cry for campaign finance reform.

For Critical Analysis

1. What message to you think voters are sending by voting for divided government?

2. To what extent do you think voter decisions on state initiatives or referenda are influenced by campaign advertising rather than by the policy choices involved in the issues?

CONCEPT OVERVIEW
Changes in the Understanding of Democracy

The concept of democracy and the types of society to which it was suited have changed significantly over time. We look here at some of the changes that have occurred in the understanding and practice of democracy since its origins in ancient Greece.

THEN	NOW
• Democracy limited to small cities.	• Democracy practiced in large nations.
• Voting was in a public forum.	• Voting is by ballot.
• Citizens voted directly on policy ("direct democracy").	• Citizens vote for representatives, who vote for policies ("representative democracy").
• Voting limited to citizens— usually defined as free males born in the city.	• Universal suffrage for all citizens, including males, females, and members of all races.
• Officeholders were amateurs; citizens took turns holding office.	• Officeholders tend to be career politicians.
• High citizen involvement and participation were essential to democracy.	• Relatively low levels of interest and knowledge characterize citizens, particularly younger ones.
• Political involvement was regarded as part of good character.	• Political involvement often is viewed as corrupting and undesirable.

What are some of the American political tasks that remain unfinished? Clearly, Americans struggle to keep a cohesive society as people become more diverse in terms of ethnic and racial backgrounds, generational expectations, and economic level. How can a wider range of Americans participate in the political process and make the process work for them? What kinds of institutions and policies can meet the demands of world markets, the needs of an aging population, the expectations of a society with instant media access, and the hopes of the youngest generations for jobs and opportunities similar to those given to their parents and grandparents? Many alternatives are up for debate: decentralization to the states, new approaches to welfare and education reform, universal access to the Internet to connect all Americans, and hundreds more.

The remainder of this book will examine the roots and structures of contemporary American government and politics, with particular attention to the ways in which they have changed over time. At the end of each chapter, we will consider the unfinished business of the subject at hand—whether it is the expansion of civil liberties or the attempts to curb the power of interest groups. Without a doubt, there is enough unfinished business to last many decades. Also without a doubt, Americans will make political changes as they see fit.

GETTING INVOLVED
Seeing Democracy in Action

One way to begin understanding the American political system is to observe a legislative body in action. There are thousands of elected legislatures in the United States at all levels of government. You might choose to visit the city council, a school board, the township board of trustees, the state legislature, or the U.S. Congress. Before attending a business session of the legislature, try to find out how the members are elected. Are they chosen by the "at-large" method of election so that each member represents the whole community, or are they chosen by specific geographic districts or wards? Some other questions you might want to ask are these: Is there a chairperson or official leader of the body who controls the meetings and who may have more power than the other leaders? What are the responsibilities of this legislature? Are the members paid political officials, or do they volunteer their services? Do the officials serve as full-time or part-time employees?

When you visit the legislature, keep in mind the theory of representative democracy. The legislators or council members are elected to represent their constituents. Observe how often the members refer to the voters, to their constituents, or to the special needs of their community or electoral district. Listen carefully for the sources of conflict within a community. If there is a debate, for example, over a zoning decision that involves the issue of land use, try to figure out why some members oppose the decision. Perhaps the greatest sources of conflict in local government are questions of taxation and expenditure. It is important to remember that the council or board is also supposed to be working toward the good of the whole; listen for discussions of the community's priorities.

If you want to follow up on your visit and learn more about representative government in action, try to get a brief interview with one of the members of the council or board. In general, legislators are very willing to talk to students, particularly students who also are voters. Ask the member how he or she sees the job of representative. How can the wishes of the constituents be identified? How does the representative balance the needs of the ward or district with the good of the whole community? You also might ask the member how he or she keeps in touch with constituents and informs them of the activities of the council or board.

For a different view of democracy in action, watch the activities of the House of Representatives or Senate on one of the C-SPAN channels on cable television. These public television channels show speeches and actions on the floor of both chambers, broadcast committee hearings when possible, and televise interviews with government officials and the journalists who cover government and politics. If you watch the action on the floor of the House, for example, notice how few members actually are present. Is the member addressing his or her colleagues, or the voters back home? Why do you think members use large charts and graphs? Most observers of Congress believe that members dress differently and use a different speaking style since the proceedings have been televised.

Think about the advantages and disadvantages of representative democracy. Do you think the average citizen would take the time to consider all of the issues that representatives must debate? Do you think that, on the whole, the elected representatives act responsibly for their constituents?

To find out when and where the local legislative bodies meet, look up the number of the city hall or county building in the telephone directory, and call the clerk of council. You might also check cable television listings. In many communities, city council meetings and county board meetings can be seen on public access channels. For information on the structure of your local government, contact the local chapter of the League of Women Voters.

KEY TERMS

anarchy 9	hyperpluralism 14	pluralism 13
aristocracy 9	ideology 23	political culture 14
authority 8	inalienable rights 16	political socialization 14
compliance 8	initiative 10	politics 6
consent of the people 10	institution 6	popular sovereignty 16
conservatism 23	legislature 9	power 8
democracy 9	legitimacy 8	property 16
direct democracy 9	liberalism 23	recall 10
elite 9	liberty 15	referendum 10
elite theory 12	limited government 11	representative democracy 10
equality 15	majority 11	republic 10
fraternity 16	majority rule 11	totalitarian regime 8
government 7	oligarchy 9	universal suffrage 11

CHAPTER SUMMARY

❶ The willingness of Americans to debate new initiatives and to demand changes in the way the government works is at the core of our democratic nation. Americans worked hard to establish this form of government and continue to expend effort in politics to keep it functioning. *Politics* was defined by Harold Lasswell as the process of "who gets what, when, and how" in a society. David Easton defined it as the "authoritative allocation of values" in a society. The prerogative of government to make allocative decisions is based on authority, legitimacy, and power. Sources of power include direct democracy, a system of government in which political decisions are made by the people directly.

❷ Fearing the problems of a direct democracy, the framers of the Constitution set up a representative, or indirect, democracy. The people control the government through the election of representatives. Decisions are made by majority rule, although the rights of minorities are protected.

❸ Some scholars believe that most of the power in our society is held by elite leaders who actively influence political decisions, while the masses are apathetic. The pluralist viewpoint, in contrast, suggests that groups that represent the different interests of the people struggle for political power. In pluralist theory, the political process is characterized by bargaining and compromise between groups.

❹ The American political system is characterized by a set of cultural beliefs that includes liberty, equality, and property. These beliefs are passed on to each generation of Americans by the process of political socialization. Additionally, the demographic make-up of the population is changing—it is growing older and more diverse, and includes more immigrants.

❺ Americans' ideas about how government should act in their lives vary widely. These views may be included in liberal, conservative, or other ideological positions. Certain ideology, when carried to an extreme, can lead to terrorist acts.

QUESTIONS FOR REVIEW AND DISCUSSION

❶ How do the groups that you belong to govern themselves? How does your church, fraternity, sorority, or club choose officers and make decisions? To what extent are the principles of democracy accepted by that group?

If your group is not democratically organized, how is its decision-making power organized?

❷ Given the great diversity of the population of the United States in terms of ethnic origin, religion, age, native country, and region, how are common beliefs created and shared with new generations? What institutions—school, church, the family, or the community—shaped your own beliefs about politics and government?

❸ How is your personal life shaped by government? How do the policies decided and implemented by the national and state governments place limits on your personal liberty? To what extent do those policies improve the quality of your life and its opportunities? Do you feel that you or your family had a part in deciding those policies?

LOGGING ON: WELCOME TO THE INTERNET

Back Forward Home Reload Images Open Print Find Stop

Go To: http://www.public.iastate.edu/~sws/homepage.html

What's New? What's Cool? Handbook Net Search Net Directory Software

As mentioned in this chapter's opening *What If . . .* , increasingly people are using the Internet, and particularly the World Wide Web, to do research, participate in online discussion groups, send and receive e-mail, and the like. Your college or university probably is connected directly to the Internet and pays thousands of dollars a year for this hookup—so that its faculty, administrators, and students can use the Internet. Each chapter in this book ends with Internet uniform resource locators, or URLs, that you can use to access sources containing information on topics covered within the chapters—or on related topics that you might find interesting. If you want to view the home page of Steffen W. Schmidt, one of the authors of this text, go to the URL given at the top of this "screen."

A great guide to political science home pages on the Web can be found at

http://www.trincoll.edu/pols/home.html#main

You can access all kinds of materials on such topics as federalism, state issues, people, and so on at this site. Start here. You can't go wrong!

Another interesting Web resource is found at

http://www.lib.lsu.edu/socsci/american.html

You can follow the major topics found in this textbook through the many excellent links provided by this site. The home page lists the following contents: Associations, Federal Government, U.S. Agencies, Discussion Groups, and Indexes to Other Resources. These are hot links. There is a Congressional Quarterly gopher and a Congressional Quarterly on the Web. The section on the Federal Government includes such topics as the 1996 Elections, the Clinton Administration, the U.S. Budget, the WhiteHouse Web Server, the House of Representatives Home Page, and the U.S. Senate Home Page. The section on U.S. Agencies has links such as the Central Intelligence Agency, the Environmental Protection Agency, the Science and Technology Information Service, the Social Security Administration, and many others. There are also several discussion groups, including the following:

alt.politics.clinton

alt.politics.democrats.d

alt.politics.elections

A textbook Web site that is interesting can be found at

http://moby.ucdavis.edu/Approaching Democracy

Another resource on the Web is PoliticsUSA, which is a joint venture undertaken by the American Political Network and the National Journal, Inc., two publishers with strong reputations for editorial quality. Go to

http://www.politicsusa.com/

SELECTED REFERENCES

Brimelow, Peter. *Alien Nation.* New York: Random House, 1995. The author of this study examines the data on both legal and illegal immigration and presents a detailed case for restricting immigration into the United States. He analyzes the social, economic, and cultural costs to society of relatively unrestricted immigration.

Chiswick, Barry R., ed. *Immigration, Language, and Ethnicity: Canada and the United States.* Lanham, Md.: AEI Press, 1992. This collection of essays reviews the history of immigration policies in Canada and the United States, and it also gives an excellent portrait of the demographic and social characteristics of recent immigrants. Additionally, it discusses some of the issues raised by immigration with regard to language and wage policies.

Dahl, Robert A. *Modern Political Analysis,* 4th ed. Englewood Cliffs, N.J.: Prentice-Hall, 1991. Dahl's book contains definitions and explanations of politics and political analysis, political influence, political systems, and political socialization.

Elazar, Daniel J. *The American Mosaic: The Impact of Space, Time, and Culture on American Politics.* Boulder, Colo.: Westview Press, 1994. Continuing his work on the development of regional cultures in the United States, Elazar investigates the influence of place and time on the political culture of specific regions. He proposes that an individual's specific location in the nation at a particular time will shape his or her political culture, as well as define an outlook on national politics.

Fishkin, James S. *The Voice of the People.* New Haven: Yale University Press, 1995. In this controversial book, Fishkin argues that the many voices that politicians hear today—polls, call-in radio shows, talk shows, network news reports—do not represent the will of the people. He proposes instituting the "deliberative poll" to instruct holders of political office. This poll would be taken of a select group of people who have met with the candidates and have carefully debated the issues presented to them.

Lapham, Lewis H. *The Wish for Kings.* New York: Grove Press, 1993. In a very controversial essay, Lapham criticizes the U.S. political system for having lapsed into an oligarchy ruled by elected officials who behave arrogantly and are supported by the ruling class. The public is apathetic and generally fearful about its own interests and admiring of media stars. Lapham suggests that a monarchy might be a more honest route to the goals of government than are elected politicians.

Lasch, Christopher. *The Revolt of the Elites and the Betrayal of Democracy.* New York: W. W. Norton, 1995. Although democracy appears to be in ascendance throughout the world, Lasch sees it as threatened by the rise of a new elite. This elite group, international in character, consists of privileged individuals who have access to power and who are disengaged from their respective nations. They are linked electronically and through economic ties, and they are much more concerned for their own welfare than for that of the other members of their societies.

Lasswell, Harold. *Politics: Who Gets What, When and How.* New York: McGraw-Hill, 1936. This classic work defines the nature of politics.

Reed, Ralph. *Politically Incorrect: The Emerging Faith Factor in American Politics.* Washington, D.C.: Word Publications, 1994. The leader of the Christian Coalition, the most influential evangelical interest group, presents his view of how religion should play a role in American politics.

Stanley, Harold W., and Richard G. Niemi. *Vital Statistics on American Politics,* 5th ed. Washington, D.C.: Congressional Quarterly Press, 1995. This valuable reference work contains over two hundred tables and figures on a wide range of topics covering almost all aspects of American politics.

Tocqueville, Alexis de. *Democracy in America.* Edited by Phillips Bradley. New York: Vintage Books, 1945. Life in the United States was described by a French writer who traveled through the nation in the 1820s.

Wilcox, Clyde. *God's Warriors: The Christian Right in Twentieth-Century America.* Baltimore: Johns Hopkins University Press, 1992. Wilcox examines the history of the Christian Right movement in the United States and its recent rise to political prominence on national issues. He provides an extensive analysis of the types of individuals who share the beliefs of the Christian Right and suggests the potential for more political activity by that movement.

2
The Constitution

CHAPTER OUTLINE

The Constitution Were Easier to Amend?

BACKGROUND

ONE OF THE REASONS FOR THE BREVITY OF THE CONSTITUTION IS THE DIFFICULTY INVOLVED IN CHANGING IT. TO CHANGE A CONSTITUTION, WHETHER IT BE A STATE CONSTITUTION OR THE U.S. CONSTITUTION, A CONSTITUTIONAL AMENDMENT MUST BE PASSED. AN AMENDMENT MAY SPECIFY A CIVIL LIBERTY OR RIGHT OF CITIZENS THAT WAS NOT INCLUDED IN THE ORIGINAL CONSTITUTION, OR IT MAY MAKE A CHANGE IN A PROVISION THAT ORIGINALLY WAS INCLUDED IN THE CONSTITUTION.

AS YOU WILL READ IN THIS CHAPTER, PASSING AN AMENDMENT TO THE U.S. CONSTITUTION REQUIRES GREAT EFFORT ON THE PART OF THOSE WHO WISH TO DO SO. INDEED, IN THE OVER TWO HUNDRED YEARS SINCE THE CONSTITUTION WAS WRITTEN, ONLY TWENTY-SEVEN AMENDMENTS HAVE BEEN PASSED—ALTHOUGH CONGRESS HAS CONSIDERED OVER ELEVEN THOUSAND.

WHAT IF THE CONSTITUTION WERE EASIER TO AMEND?

What if it were easier to amend the Constitution? One thing is certain: there would be more amendments. How many and what kind are unknown, of course. At a minimum, we can look at what has happened in states that have relatively easy constitutional amendment procedures.

The U.S. Constitution is about 7,000 words long. The average state constitution is more than three times as long as the federal Constitution. For example, the Louisiana Constitution of 1921 (which was replaced by a new constitution in 1974) contained over 250,000 words. Nineteen states have constitutions that have been amended 100 times or more. Consider that the citizens of Alabama by 1997 had been asked to approve over 650 amendments, of which they adopted over 450! If the U.S. Constitution could be amended more easily, it possibly would become more similar to state constitutions and would become quite long.

CONSTITUTIONAL AMENDMENT VERSUS LEGISLATION

Additionally, state legislators seem to have a difficult time distinguishing between constitutional law and statutory law. (Normally, constitutions provide only general principles.) The Louisiana Constitution has an amendment declaring Huey Long's birthday a legal holiday. The South Dakota Constitution has an amendment authorizing a cordage and twine plant at the state penitentiary. The Alabama Constitution has an amendment establishing the Alabama Heritage Trust Fund.

Clearly, the easier it is for a constitution to be amended, the more this process will be used. When a constitution can be amended easily, we get constitutional amendments. Furthermore, in states that allow their constitutions to be amended easily, constitutional amendments often are proposed in an attempt to override unfavorable state court decisions.

Thus, if the U.S. Constitution could be amended more easily, organized special interest groups possibly would lobby Congress to amend the Constitution rather than simply to pass new laws. The basic and relatively limited powers and rights outlined in the U.S. Constitution perhaps would lose some of their importance if they became part of a lengthier and more complicated document.

FOR CRITICAL ANALYSIS

1. *What is the distinction between constitutional law and the statutes that Congress normally passes?*
2. *Who has benefited from the difficulty of amending the U.S. Constitution?*
3. *What would be the benefit of making the amending process for the U.S. Constitution less difficult?*

We the People of the United States, in Order to form a more perfect Union, establish Justice, insure domestic Tranquillity, provide for the common defence, promote the general Welfare, and secure the Blessings of Liberty to ourselves and our Posterity, do ordain and establish this Constitution for the United States of America.

Every schoolchild in America has at one time or another been exposed to these famous words from the Preamble to the U.S. Constitution. The document itself is remarkable. As this chapter's *What If . . .* just pointed out, the U.S. Constitution, compared with others in the states and in the world, is relatively short. Because amending it is difficult (as you will see later in this chapter), it also has relatively few amendments. Perhaps even more remarkable is the fact that it has remained largely intact for over two hundred years.

How and why this Constitution was created is a story that has been told and retold. It is worth repeating, because the historical and political context in which this country's governmental machinery was formed is essential to understanding American government and politics today. The Constitution was not the result of completely creative thinking. Many of its provisions were grounded in contemporary political philosophy. The delegates to the Constitutional Convention in 1787 brought with them two important sets of influences: their political culture and their political experience. In the years between the first settlements in the New World and the writing of the Constitution, Americans had developed a political philosophy about how people should be governed and had tried out numerous forms of government. These experiences gave the founders the tools with which they constructed the Constitution.

DID YOU KNOW . . .
That the first English claim to territory in North America was made by John Cabot, on behalf of King Henry VII, on June 24, 1497?

INITIAL COLONIZING EFFORTS

The first British outpost in North America was set up by Sir Walter Raleigh in the 1580s for the purpose of harassing the Spanish treasure fleets. The group, known as the Roanoke Island Colony, stands as one of history's great mysteries: After a three-year absence to resupply the colony, Raleigh's captain, John White, returned in 1590 to find signs that the colony's residents apparently had moved north to Chesapeake Bay. White was unable to search further, and no verifiable evidence of the fate of the "lost colony" has ever been

The first British settlers who landed on the North American continent faced severe tests of endurance. This woodcut depicts a cold existence for the settlers in the late 1500s and early 1600s.

REPRESENTATIVE ASSEMBLY

A legislature composed of individuals who represent the population.

recorded. Local legends in North Carolina maintain that the lost colonists survived and intermarried with the Native Americans, and that their descendants live in the region today.

In 1607, the British government sent over a group of farmers to establish a trading post, Jamestown, in what is now Virginia. The Virginia Company of London was the first to establish successfully a permanent British colony in the Americas. The king of England gave the backers of this colony a charter granting them "full power and authority" to make laws "for the good and welfare" of the settlement. The colonists at Jamestown, Virginia, instituted a **representative assembly,** setting a precedent in government that was to be observed in later colonial adventures.

Jamestown was not a commercial success. Of the 105 men who landed, 67 died within the first year. But 800 new arrivals in 1609 added to their numbers. By the spring of the next year, frontier hazards had cut their numbers to 60. Of the 6,000 people who left England for Virginia between 1607 and 1623, 4,000 of them perished. The historian Charles Andrews has called this the "starving time for Virginia."[1]

Separatists, the *Mayflower,* and the Compact

The first New England colony was established in 1620. A group of mostly extreme Separatists, who wished to break with the Church of England, came over on the ship *Mayflower* to the New World, landing at Plymouth (Massachusetts). Before going on shore, the adult males—women were not considered to have any political status—drew up the Mayflower Compact, which was signed by forty-one of the forty-four men aboard the ship on November 21, 1620. The reason for the compact was obvious. This group was outside the jurisdiction of the Virginia Company of London, which had chartered their settlement in Virginia, not Massachusetts. The Separatist leaders feared that some of the *Mayflower* passengers might conclude that they were no longer under any obligations of civil obedience. Therefore, some form of public authority was imperative. As William Bradford (a printer and editor in Philadelphia) recalled in his accounts, there were "discontented and muti-

[1]Charles M. Andrews, *The Colonial Period of American History,* Vol. 1 (New Haven, Conn.: Yale University Press, 1934), p. 110.

The signing of the compact aboard the *Mayflower.* In 1620, the Mayflower Compact was signed by almost all of the men aboard the ship *Mayflower,* just before disembarking at Plymouth, Massachusetts. It stated, "We . . . covenant and combine ourselves togeather into a civil body politick . . .; and by vertue hearof to enacte, constitute, and frame such just and equal laws . . . as shall be thought [necessary] for the generall good of the Colonie."

nous speeches that some of the strangers amongst them had let fall from them in the ship; That when they came a shore they would use their owne libertie; for none had power to command them."[2]

The compact was not a constitution. It was a political agreement in which the signers agreed to submit to majority-rule government, pending the receipt of a royal charter. The Mayflower Compact's historical and political significance is twofold: it depended on the consent of the affected individuals, and it served as a prototype for similar compacts in American history. According to Samuel Eliot Morison, the compact proved the determination of the English immigrants to live under the rule of law, based on the *consent of the people*.[3]

More Colonies, More Government

Another outpost in New England was set up by the Massachusetts Bay Colony in 1630. Then followed Rhode Island, Connecticut, New Hampshire, and others. By 1732, the last of the thirteen colonies, Georgia, was established. During the colonial period, Americans developed a concept of limited government, which followed from the establishment of the first colonies under Crown charters. Theoretically, London governed the colonies. In practice, owing partly to the colonies' distance from London, the colonists exercised a large measure of self-government. The colonists were able to make their own laws, as in the Fundamental Orders of Connecticut in 1639. The Massachusetts Body of Liberties in 1641 supported the protection of individual rights and was made a part of colonial law. In 1682, the Pennsylvania Frame of Government was passed. Along with the Pennsylvania Charter of Privileges of 1701, it established the rationale for our modern Constitution and Bill of Rights. All of this legislation enabled the colonists to acquire crucial political experience. After independence was declared in 1776, the states quickly set up their own constitutions.

BRITISH RESTRICTIONS AND COLONIAL GRIEVANCES

The Navigation Acts of 1651 were the earliest general restrictions on colonial activity. These acts imposed the condition that only English ships (including ships of its colonies) could be used for trade within the British Empire. The Proclamation of 1763 declared that no colonial settlement could be established west of the Appalachians. In 1764, the Sugar Act was passed, in part to pay for the French and Indian War. Many colonists were unwilling to pay the required tax.

Further regulatory legislation was to come. In 1765, the British Parliament passed the Stamp Act, providing for internal taxation, or, as the colonists' Stamp Act Congress assembled in 1765 called it, "taxation without representation." The colonists boycotted the Stamp Act. The success of the boycott (the Stamp Act was repealed a year later) generated a feeling of unity within the colonies. The British, however, continued to try to raise revenues in the colonies. When duties on glass, lead, paint, and other items were passed in 1767, the colonists boycotted the purchase of English commodities in return.

---

[2]John Camp, *Out of the Wilderness: The Emergence of an American Identity in Colonial New England* (Middleton, Conn.: Wesleyan University Press, 1990).
[3]See Morison's "The Mayflower Compact" in Daniel J. Boorstin, ed., *An American Primer* (Chicago: University of Chicago Press, 1966), p. 18.

Milestones in Early U.S. Political History

1585	British outpost set up in Roanoke.
1607	Jamestown established; Virginia Company lands settlers.
1620	Mayflower Compact signed.
1630	Massachusetts Bay Colony set up.
1639	Fundamental Orders of Connecticut adopted.
1641	Massachusetts Body of Liberties adopted.
1682	Pennsylvania Frame of Government passed.
1701	Pennsylvania Charter of Privileges written.
1732	Last of thirteen colonies established.
1756	French and Indian War declared.
1765	Stamp Act; Stamp Act Congress meets.
1770	Boston Massacre.
1774	First Continental Congress.
1775	Second Continental Congress; Revolutionary War begins.
1776	Declaration of Independence signed.
1777	Articles of Confederation drafted.
1781	Last state signs Articles of Confederation.
1783–1789	"Critical period" in U.S. history; weak national government.
1786	Shays' Rebellion.
1787	Constitutional Convention.
1788	Ratification of Constitution.
1791	Ratification of Bill of Rights.

King George III (1738–1820) was king of Great Britain and Ireland from 1760 until his death on January 29, 1820. Under George III, the first attempt to tax the American colonies was made. Ultimately, the American colonies, exasperated at renewed attempts at taxation, proclaimed their independence on July 4, 1776.

FIRST CONTINENTAL CONGRESS

The first gathering of delegates from twelve of the thirteen colonies, held in 1774.

SECOND CONTINENTAL CONGRESS

The 1775 congress of the colonies that established an army.

The colonists' fury over taxation climaxed in the Boston Tea Party: colonists dressed as Mohawk Indians dumped almost 350 chests of British tea into the Boston Harbor as a gesture of tax protest. In retaliation, the British Parliament passed the Coercive Acts (the "Intolerable Acts") in 1774, which closed Boston Harbor and placed the government of Boston under direct British control. The colonists were outraged—and they responded.

THE COLONIAL RESPONSE: THE CONTINENTAL CONGRESSES

New York, Pennsylvania, and Rhode Island proposed the convening of a colonial congress. The Massachusetts House of Representatives requested that all colonies hold conventions to select delegates to be sent to Philadelphia for such a congress. The **First Continental Congress** was held at Carpenter's Hall on September 5, 1774. It was a gathering of delegates from twelve of the thirteen colonies (Georgia did not attend until 1775). At that meeting, there was little talk of independence. The Congress passed a resolution requesting that the colonies send a petition to King George III expressing their grievances. Resolutions were also passed requiring that the colonies raise their own troops and boycott British trade. The British government condemned the Congress's actions, treating them as open acts of rebellion.

The delegates to the First Continental Congress declared that in every county and city, a committee was to be formed whose mission was to spy on the conduct of friends and neighbors and to report to the press any violators of the trade ban. The formation of these committees was an act of cooperation among the colonies, which represented a step toward the creation of a national government.

By the time the **Second Continental Congress** met in May 1775 (this time all of the colonies were represented), fighting already had broken out between the British and the colonists. One of the main actions of the Second Congress was to establish an army. It did this by declaring the militia that had gathered around Boston an army and naming George Washington as commander in chief. The participants in that Congress still attempted to reach a peaceful settlement with the British Parliament. One declaration of the Congress stated explicitly that "we have not raised armies with ambitious designs of separating from Great Britain, and establishing independent states." But by the beginning of 1776, military encounters had become increasingly frequent.

Public debate was acrimonious. Then Thomas Paine's *Common Sense* appeared in Philadelphia bookstores. The pamphlet was a colonial best seller.[4] Many agreed that Paine did make common sense when he argued that

> a government of our own is our natural right: and when a man seriously reflects on the precariousness of human affairs, he will become convinced, that it is infinitely wiser and safer, to form a constitution of our own in a cool and deliberate manner, while we have it in our power, than to trust such an interesting event to time and chance.[5]

Students of Paine's pamphlet point out that his arguments were not new—they were common in tavern debates throughout the land. Rather, it was the near poetry of his words—which were at the same time as plain as the alphabet—that struck his readers.

---

[4]To do relatively as well today, a book would have to sell between eight and ten million copies in its first year of publication.

[5]*The Political Writings of Thomas Paine,* Vol. 1 (Boston: J. P. Mendum Investigator Office, 1870), p. 46.

DECLARING INDEPENDENCE

The Resolution of Independence

On April 6, 1776, the Second Continental Congress voted for free trade at all American ports for all countries except Great Britain. This act could be interpreted as an implicit declaration of independence. The next month, the Congress suggested that each of the colonies establish state governments unconnected to Britain. Finally, on July 2, the Resolution of Independence was adopted by the Second Continental Congress:

> RESOLVED, That these United Colonies are, and of right ought to be free and independent States, that they are absolved from allegiance to the British Crown, and that all political connection between them and the state of Great Britain is, and ought to be, totally dissolved.

The actual Resolution of Independence was not legally significant. On the one hand, it was not judicially enforceable, for it established no legal rights or duties. On the other hand, the colonies were already, in their own judgment, self-governing and independent of Britain. Rather, the Resolution of Independence and the subsequent Declaration of Independence were necessary to establish the legitimacy of the new nation in the eyes of foreign governments, as well as in the eyes of the colonists themselves. What the new nation needed most was supplies for its armies and a commitment of foreign military aid. Unless it appeared in the eyes of the world as a political entity separate and independent from Britain, no foreign government would enter into a contract with its leaders. (Many historians believe that Paine, in a series of articles written in 1778 and collectively called *The Crisis*, was the first to use the term *United States*.)[6]

July 4, 1776—The Declaration of Independence

By June 1776, Thomas Jefferson already was writing drafts of the Declaration of Independence in the second-floor parlor of a bricklayer's house in Philadelphia. On adoption of the Resolution of Independence, Jefferson had argued that a declaration putting forth clearly the causes that compelled the colonies to separate from England was necessary. The Second Congress assigned the task to him, and he set to work, enumerating the major grievances. Some of his work was amended to gain unanimous acceptance (for example, his condemnation of the slave trade was eliminated to satisfy Georgia and North Carolina), but the bulk of it was passed intact on July 4, 1776. On July 19, the modified draft became "the unanimous declaration of the thirteen United States of America." On August 2, it was signed by the members of the Second Continental Congress.

A revolutionary concept of the Declaration was the assumption, inspired by the ideas of John Locke, that people have **natural rights** ("unalienable Rights"), including the rights to "life, liberty, and the pursuit of happiness." Governments are established to secure these rights, and governments derive their power "from the consent of the governed."[7] The Declaration claimed

"You know, the idea of taxation with representation doesn't appeal to me very much either."

Drawing by Handelsman; © 1970 The New Yorker Magazine, Inc.

NATURAL RIGHTS

Rights held to be inherent in natural law, not dependent on governments. John Locke stated that natural law, being superior to human law, specifies certain rights of "life, liberty, and property." These rights, altered to become "life, liberty, and the pursuit of happiness," are asserted in the Declaration of Independence.

---

[6]A. J. Ayer, *Thomas Paine* (New York: Atheneum, 1988), p. 42.

[7]Not all scholars were truly influenced by Locke. For example, Jay Fliegelman states that "Jefferson's fascination with Homer, Ossian, Patrick Henry, and the violin is of greater significance than his indebtedness to Locke." Jay Fliegelman, *Declaring Independence: Jefferson, Natural Language, and the Culture of Performance* (Stanford, Calif.: Stanford University Press, 1993).

UNICAMERAL LEGISLATURE

A legislature with only one legislative body, as compared with a bicameral (two-house) legislature, such as the U.S. Congress. Nebraska is the only state in the union with a unicameral legislature.

CONFEDERATION

A political system in which states or regional governments retain ultimate authority except for those powers they expressly delegate to a central government. A voluntary association of independent states, in which the member states agree to limited restraints on their freedom of action.

STATE

A group of people occupying a specific area and organized under one government; may be either a nation or a subunit of a nation.

Members of the Second Continental Congress signed the Declaration of Independence on July 4, 1776. Minor changes were made in the document in the following two weeks. On July 19, the modified draft became the "unanimous declaration of the thirteen United States of America." On August 2, the members of the Second Continental Congress signed it. The first official printed version carried only the signatures of the Congress's president, John Hancock, and its secretary, Charles Thompson.

that whenever government "becomes destructive to these ends, it is the Right of the People to alter or to abolish it, and to institute a new government."

Although the colonists had formally declared independence from Britain, the fight to gain actual independence continued for five more years—until the British General Cornwallis surrendered at Yorktown in 1781. In 1783, after Britain formally recognized the independent status of the United States in the Treaty of Paris, Washington disbanded the army. During these years of military struggles, the states faced the additional challenge of creating a system of self-government for an independent United States.

THE RISE OF REPUBLICANISM

Not everyone had agreed with the notion of independence. There were recalcitrant colonists in the middle and lower southern colonies who demanded that independence be preceded by the formation of a strong central government. But the anti-Royalists in New England and Virginia, who called themselves Republicans, were against a strong central government. They opposed monarchy, executive authority, and virtually any form of restraint on the power of local groups. These so-called Republicans were a major political force from 1776 to 1780. Indeed, they almost prevented victory over the British by their unwillingness to cooperate with any central authority.

During this time, all the states adopted written constitutions. Eleven of the constitutions were completely new. Two of them—those of Connecticut and Rhode Island—were old royal charters with minor modifications. Republican sentiment led to increased power for the legislatures. In Pennsylvania and Georgia, **unicameral** (one-body) **legislatures** were unchecked by executive or judicial authority. Basically, the Republicans attempted to maintain the politics of 1776. In almost all states, the legislature was predominant.

THE ARTICLES OF CONFEDERATION: OUR FIRST FORM OF GOVERNMENT

The fear of a powerful central government led to the passage of the Articles of Confederation. The term **confederation** is important; it means a voluntary association of *independent* **states,** in which the member states agree to only

limited restraints on their freedom of action. As a result, confederations seldom have an effective executive authority.

On June 6, 1776, Richard Henry Lee proposed that a confederation be established. So the Second Continental Congress appointed thirteen men to a drafting committee. Satisfied that progress was occurring, on August 20, 1776, the Second Continental Congress agreed to proceed with the second draft of what would become the Articles of Confederation. Four issues remained for settlement: (1) the equal representation of all states in the Congress, (2) the basis for the apportionment of common expenses, (3) the grant of powers to the central government over western lands, and (4) the distribution of power between the states and the central legislative body to define the precise location of sovereignty.

The final form of the Articles of Confederation was achieved by November 15, 1777. It was not until March 1, 1781, however, that the last state, Maryland, agreed to ratify what was called the Articles of Confederation and Perpetual Union. Well before the final ratification of the Articles, however, many of them were implemented: the Continental Congress and the thirteen states conducted American military, economic, and political affairs according to the standards and the form specified by the Articles.[8]

Under the Articles, the thirteen original colonies, now states, established on March 1, 1781, a government of the states—the Congress of the Confederation. The Congress was a unicameral assembly of so-called ambassadors from each state, with each state possessing a single vote. Each year, the Congress would choose one of its members as its president, but the Articles did not provide for a president of the United States. The Congress was authorized in Article X to appoint an executive committee of the states "to execute in the recess of Congress, such of the powers of Congress as the United States, in Congress assembled, by the consent of nine [of the thirteen] states, shall from time to time think expedient to vest with them." The Congress was also allowed to appoint other committees and civil officers necessary for managing the general affairs of the United States. The Articles did not establish a separate judicial institution, although Congress had certain judicial functions. In addition, the Congress could regulate foreign affairs and establish coinage and weights and measures. But it lacked an independent source of revenue and the necessary executive machinery to enforce its decisions throughout the land. Figure 2–1 illustrates the structure of the government under the Articles of Confederation; Table 2–1 summarizes the powers—and the lack of powers—of Congress under that system.

Article II of the Articles of Confederation guaranteed that each state retains its sovereignty:

> Each state retains its sovereignty, freedom and independence, and every power, jurisdiction, and right, which is not by this Confederation expressly delegated to the United States in Congress assembled.

Accomplishments under the Articles

Although the Articles of Confederation had many defects, there were also some accomplishments during the eight years of their existence. Certain states' claims to western lands were settled. Maryland had objected to the claims of Massachusetts, New York, Connecticut, Virginia, the Carolinas, and Georgia. It was only after these states consented to give up their land claims

---

[8]Robert W. Hoffert, *A Politics of Tensions: The Articles of Confederation and American Political Ideas* (Niwot, Colo.: University Press of Colorado, 1992).

DID YOU KNOW...
That on July 4, 1776, on the day the Declaration of Independence was signed, King George III of England wrote in his diary, "Nothing of importance happened today"?

Figure 2–1
● ●
The Structure of the Confederal Government under the Articles of Confederation

Congress
Congress had one house. Each state had two to seven members, but only one vote. The exercise of most powers required approval of at least nine states. Amendments to the Articles required the consent of all the states.

⬇

Committee of the States
A committee of representatives from all the states was empowered to act in the name of Congress between sessions.

⬇

Officers
Congress appointed officers to do some of the executive work.

⬇

The States

Table 2–1

Powers of the Congress of the Confederation

CONGRESS HAD POWER TO	CONGRESS LACKED POWER TO
• Declare war and make peace.	• Provide for effective treaty-making power and control foreign relations; it could not compel states to respect treaties.
• Enter into treaties and alliances.	
• Establish and control armed forces.	
• Requisition men and money from states.	• Compel states to meet military quotas; it could not draft soldiers.
• Regulate coinage.	• Regulate interstate and foreign commerce; it left each state free to set up its own tariff system.
• Borrow money and issue bills of credit.	
• Fix uniform standards of weight and measurement.	• Collect taxes directly from the people; it had to rely on states to collect and forward taxes.
• Create admiralty courts.	
• Create a postal system.	• Compel states to pay their share of government costs.
• Regulate Indian affairs.	
• Guarantee citizens of each state the rights and privileges of citizens in the several states when in another state.	• Provide and maintain a sound monetary system or issue paper money; this was left up to the states, and monies in circulation differed tremendously in value.
• Adjudicate disputes between states upon state petition.	

to the United States as a whole that Maryland signed the Articles of Confederation. Another accomplishment under the Articles was the passage of the Northwest Ordinance of 1787, which established a basic pattern of government for new territories north of the Ohio River.

Finally, the Articles created a sort of "first draft" for the Constitution of the United States that was to follow. In a sense, it was an unplanned experiment applying some of the principles of government set forth in the Declaration of Independence.

Weaknesses of the Articles

Although Congress had the legal right to declare war and to conduct foreign policy, it did not have the right to demand revenues from the states. It could only *ask* for them. Additionally, the actions of Congress required the consent of nine states. Any amendments to the Articles required the unanimous consent of the Congress and confirmation by every state legislature. Furthermore, the Articles did not create a national system of courts.

Basically, the functioning of the government under the Articles depended on the goodwill of the states. Article III of the Articles simply established a "league of friendship" among the states—no national government was intended.

Probably the most fundamental weakness of the Articles, and the most basic cause of their eventual replacement by the Constitution, concerned the lack of power to raise money for the militia. The Articles lacked any language giving Congress coercive power to raise money (by levying taxes) to provide adequate support for the military forces controlled by Congress. When states refused to send money to support the government (not one state met the financial requests made by Congress under the Articles), Congress resorted to selling off western lands to speculators or issuing bonds that sold for less than their face value. Due to a lack of resources, the Continental Congress was forced to disband the army, even in the face of serious Spanish and British military threats.

Shays' Rebellion and the Need for Revision of the Articles

By 1786, in Concord, Massachusetts, the scene of one of the first battles of the Revolution, there were three times as many people in prison for debt as there were for all other crimes combined. In Worcester County, Massachusetts, the ratio was even higher—twenty to one. Most of the prisoners were small farmers who could not pay their debts owing to the disorganized state of the economy.

In August 1786, mobs of musket-bearing farmers led by former revolutionary captain Daniel Shays seized county courthouses and disrupted the trials of the debtors in Springfield, Massachusetts. Shays and his men then launched an attack on the federal arsenal at Springfield, but they were repulsed. Shays' Rebellion demonstrated that the central government could not protect the citizenry from armed rebellion or provide adequately for the public welfare.

DRAFTING THE CONSTITUTION

The Annapolis Convention

The Virginia legislature called for a meeting of all the states to be held at Annapolis, Maryland, on September 11, 1786—ostensibly to discuss commercial problems only. It was evident to those in attendance (including Alexander Hamilton and James Madison) that the national government had serious weaknesses that had to be addressed if it were to survive. Among the important problems to be solved were the relationship between the states and the central government, the powers of the national legislature, the need for executive leadership, and the establishment of policies for economic stability.

At this Annapolis meeting, a call was issued to all of the states for a general convention to meet in Philadelphia in May 1787 "to consider the exigencies of the union." When the Republicans, who favored a weak central government, realized that the Philadelphia meeting would in fact take place, they approved the convention in February 1787. They made it explicit, however, that the convention was "for the sole and express purpose of revising the Articles of Confederation." Those in favor of a stronger national government—the Federalists, as they were to be called—had different ideas.

The Philadelphia Convention

The designated date for the opening of the convention was May 14, 1787. Because few of the delegates had actually arrived in Philadelphia by that time, however, it was not formally opened in the East Room of the Pennsylvania State House until May 25.[9] By then, fifty-five of the seventy-four delegates chosen for the convention had arrived. (Of those fifty-five, only about forty played active roles at the convention.) Rhode Island was the only state that refused to send delegates.

---

[9]The State House was later named Independence Hall. This was the same room in which the Declaration of Independence had been signed eleven years earlier.

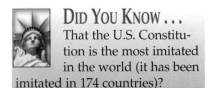

DID YOU KNOW . . .
That the U.S. Constitution is the most imitated in the world (it has been imitated in 174 countries)?

The Working Environment

The conditions under which the delegates worked for 115 days were far from ideal and were made even worse by the necessity of maintaining total secrecy. The framers of the Constitution felt that if public debate were started on particular positions, delegates would have a more difficult time compromising or backing down to reach agreement. Consequently, the windows were usually shut in the East Room of the State House. Summer quickly arrived, and the air became heavy, humid, and hot by noon of each day. Also, when the windows were open, flies swarmed into the room. The delegates did, however, have a nearby tavern and inn to which they retired each evening. The Indian Queen became the informal headquarters of the delegates.

Factions among the Delegates

We know much about the proceedings at the convention because James Madison kept a daily, detailed personal journal. A majority of the delegates were strong nationalists—they wanted a central government with real power, unlike that of the central government under the Articles of Confederation. George Washington and Benjamin Franklin preferred limited national authority based on a separation of powers. They were apparently willing to accept any type of national government, however, as long as the other delegates approved it. A few advocates of a strong central government, led by Gouverneur Morris of Pennsylvania and John Rutledge of South Carolina, distrusted the ability of the common people to engage in self-government.

Among the nationalists were several monarchists, including Alexander Hamilton, who was chiefly responsible for the Annapolis Convention's call for the Constitutional Convention. In a long speech on June 18, he presented his views: "I have no scruple in declaring . . . that the British government is the best in the world and that I doubt much whether anything short of it will do in America."

Another important group of nationalists were of a more democratic stripe. Led by James Madison (see this chapter's *Critical Perspective*) of Virginia and James Wilson of Pennsylvania, these democratic nationalists wanted a central government founded on popular support.

George Washington presided over the Constitutional Convention of 1787. Although the convention was supposed to have started on May 14, 1787, few of the delegates had actually arrived in Philadelphia by that date. It formally opened in the East Room of the Pennsylvania State House (later named Independence Hall) on May 25. Only Rhode Island did not send any delegates.

CRITICAL PERSPECTIVE

Was Madison Really a Nationalist?

Modern scholars point to all of the hard work that James Madison devoted to making sure that the republic envisioned by the delegates to the Constitutional Convention in the summer of 1787 became a reality. At age thirty-six, he became perhaps the leading figure in shaping the Constitution that summer. Perhaps even more important, he joined forces with Alexander Hamilton to provide what clearly were the arguments in favor of the ratification of the Constitution by state conventions. Specifically, he authored or coauthored many convincing articles of *The Federalist Papers.* As you will learn in this chapter, he sponsored the Bill of Rights at the first Congress. Finally, President Washington used Madison as a key adviser.

Did Madison Change His Mind?

Because Madison had a celebrated alliance with Alexander Hamilton at the time our republic was made, Hamilton believed that Madison was an advocate of strong central government. Quite naturally, Hamilton considered Madison a turncoat who "deserted" him when Madison opposed Hamilton's idea that the national government should take over the debts of the states and form a national bank.

Later, Madison joined forces with Thomas Jefferson to draft the Kentucky and Virginia Resolutions of 1798. These resolutions, which were passed by the Kentucky and Virginia legislatures, declared the Alien and Sedition Acts of 1798 unconstitutional. In essence, these resolutions reflected a more or less Anti-Federalist (state-centered) position, because they implied that the national government's powers were constitutionally limited and that certain powers reserved to the states could be protected by the states. Some scholars argue that those resolutions started the movement for states' rights that eventually resulted in the Civil War.

A New Interpretation

Professor Lance Banning of the University of Kentucky has developed an alternative view of Madison. In Banning's view, Madison acted consistently throughout his life.* In the first place, Banning shows that Madison's own native state of Virginia was desperately in need of the protection of a union, which it was not getting under the Articles of Confederation. Virginia was prey to naval attack and was experiencing numerous slave uprisings. Madison thought that if the states, under the Articles, started fighting each other, Virginia and the South in general would lose their liberties. So, he felt compelled to seek a national government.

Madison, even though he was in alliance with Hamilton, did not share Hamilton's view that the new central government should resemble the great empires of the Old World in form and power. Rather, Madison simply wanted to protect the existing revolutionary gains—no more "swollen taxes" or "powerful executives." Once the Constitution was ratified, Madison was determined that it should be strictly interpreted. Unlike Hamilton, he had no desire to give the central government more powers. He felt that if the national government had more powers, the United States would soon have "a government without any limits at all."

At the heart of understanding Madison, according to Banning, is the realization that Madison simply wanted to secure religious liberties and prevent the states from turning America into armed and hostile nations.

Federalist Paper No. 10 Means Something, Though

Not everyone agrees with this relatively new interpretation of Madison's intellectual career. Some critics of Banning's work note that in *Federalist Paper* No. 10, Madison specifically pointed out the superiority of a large republic. If one takes to heart the logic of *Federalist Paper* No. 10, it leads to the conclusion that the nation should allow for the concentration of the majority of power in a national government.

For Critical Analysis

1. Is Madison's insistence on the passage of the Bill of Rights consistent with Banning's view of Madison's intellectual consistency? Explain.

2. The political philosopher Montesquieu believed that only small republics could succeed. Madison, in contrast, argued that individual liberties would be safer in a large republic. What are the arguments in favor of each of these opposing views?

The Sacred Fire of Liberty: James Madison and the Founding of the Federal Republic (Ithaca, N.Y.: Cornell University Press, 1995).

Elbridge Gerry (1744–1814), from Massachusetts, was a patriot during the Revolution. He was a signatory of the Declaration of Independence and later became governor of Massachusetts (1810–1812). He became James Madison's new vice president when Madison was reelected in December 1812.

BICAMERAL LEGISLATURE

A legislature made up of two chambers, or parts. The U.S. Congress, composed of the House of Representatives and the Senate, is a bicameral legislature.

Still another faction consisted of nationalists who were less democratic in nature and who would support a central government only if it were founded on very narrowly defined republican principles. This group was made up of a relatively small number of delegates, including Edmund Randolph and George Mason of Virginia, Elbridge Gerry of Massachusetts, and Luther Martin and John Francis Mercer of Maryland.

Most of the other delegates from Maryland, New Hampshire, Connecticut, New Jersey, and Delaware were concerned about only one thing—claims to western lands. As long as those lands became the common property of all states, they were willing to support a central government.

Finally, there was a group of delegates who were totally against a national authority. Two of the three delegates from New York quit the convention when they saw the nationalist direction of its proceedings.

Politicking and Compromises

The debates at the convention started on the first day. James Madison had spent months reviewing European political theory. When his Virginia delegation arrived ahead of most of the others, it got to work immediately. By the time George Washington opened the convention, Governor Edmund Randolph of Virginia was immediately able to present fifteen resolutions. In retrospect, this was a masterful stroke on the part of the Virginia delegation. It set the agenda for the remainder of the convention—even though, in principle, the delegates had been sent to Philadelphia for the sole purpose of amending the Articles of Confederation. They had *not* been sent to write a new constitution.

The Virginia Plan.   Randolph's fifteen resolutions proposed an entirely new national government under a constitution. It was, however, a plan that favored the large states, including Virginia. Basically, it called for the following:

1. A **bicameral** (two-house) **legislature,** with the lower house chosen by the people and the smaller upper house chosen by the lower house from nominees selected by state legislatures. The number of representatives would be proportional to a state's population, thus favoring the large states. The legislature could void any state laws.
2. The creation of an unspecified national executive, elected by the legislature.
3. The creation of a national judiciary appointed by the legislature.

It did not take long for the smaller states to realize they would fare poorly under the Virginia plan, according to which Virginia, Massachusetts, and Pennsylvania would form a majority in the national legislature. The debate on the plan dragged on for a number of weeks. It was time for the small states to come up with their own plan.

The New Jersey Plan.   On June 15, lawyer William Paterson of New Jersey offered an alternative plan. After all, argued Paterson, under the Articles of Confederation all states had equality; therefore, the convention had no power to change this arrangement. He proposed the following:

1. The fundamental principle of the Articles of Confederation—one state, one vote—would be retained.
2. Congress would be able to regulate trade and impose taxes.
3. All acts of Congress would be the supreme law of the land.
4. Several people would be elected by Congress to form an executive office.
5. The executive office would appoint a Supreme Court.

Basically, the New Jersey plan was simply an amendment of the Articles of Confederation. Its only notable feature was its reference to the **supremacy doctrine,** which was later included in the Constitution.

The "Great Compromise."   The delegates were at an impasse. Most wanted a strong national government and were unwilling even to consider the New Jersey plan. But when the Virginia plan was brought up again, the small states threatened to leave. It was not until July 16 that the **Great Compromise** was achieved. Roger Sherman of Connecticut proposed the following:

1. A bicameral legislature in which the House of Representatives would be apportioned according to the number of free inhabitants in each state, plus three-fifths of the slaves.
2. An upper house, the Senate, which would have two members from each state elected by the state legislatures.

This plan, also called the Connecticut Compromise because of the role of the Connecticut delegates in the proposal, broke the deadlock. It did exact a political price, however, because it permitted each state to have equal representation in the Senate. Having two senators represent each state in effect diluted the voting power of citizens living in more heavily populated states and gave smaller states disproportionate political powers. But the Connecticut Compromise resolved the large-state/small-state controversy. In addition, the Senate acted as part of a checks-and-balance system against the House, which many feared would be dominated by, and responsive to, the masses.

The Great Compromise also settled another major issue—how to deal with slaves in the representational scheme. Slavery was legal everywhere except in Massachusetts, but it was concentrated in the South. The South wanted slaves to be counted equally in determining representation in Congress. Equal representation, however, meant equal taxation, and the South wanted to avoid equal taxation. Sherman's three-fifths compromise solved the issue, satisfying those northerners who felt that slaves should not be counted at all and those southerners who wanted them to be counted as free whites. Actually, Sherman's Connecticut plan spoke of three-fifths of "all other persons" (and that is the language in the Constitution itself). It is not hard to figure out, though, who those other persons were.

Slavery and Other Issues.   The slavery issue was not completely eliminated by the three-fifths compromise. Many delegates were opposed to slavery and wanted it banned entirely in the United States. Charles Pinckney of South Carolina led strong southern opposition to the idea of a ban on slavery. Finally, the delegates agreed that Congress could limit the importation of slaves after 1808. The compromise meant that the issue of slavery itself was never addressed. The South won twenty years of unrestricted slave trade and a requirement that escaped slaves in free states be returned to their owners in slave states.

The agrarian South and the mercantile North were in conflict. The South was worried that the northern majority in Congress would pass legislation unfavorable to its economic interests. Because the South depended on exports of its agricultural products, it feared the imposition of export taxes. In return for acceding to the northern demand that Congress be given the power to regulate commerce among the states and with other nations, the South obtained a promise that export taxes would not be imposed. Even today, such taxes are prohibited. The United States is one of the few countries that does not tax its exports.

DID YOU KNOW . . .
That Alexander Hamilton wanted the American president to hold office for life and to have absolute veto power over the legislature?

SUPREMACY DOCTRINE

A doctrine that asserts the superiority of national law over state or regional laws. This principle is rooted in Article VI of the Constitution, which provides that the Constitution, the laws passed by the national government under its constitutional powers, and all treaties constitute the supreme law of the land.

GREAT COMPROMISE

The compromise between the New Jersey and the Virginia plans that created one chamber of the Congress based on population and one chamber that represented each state equally; also called the Connecticut Compromise.

An American slave market from a painting by Taylor. The writers of the Constitution did not ban slavery in the United States but did agree to limit the importing of new slaves after 1808. Nowhere are the words *slavery* or *slaves* used in the Constitution. Instead, the Constitution uses such language as "no person held in service" and "all other persons."

SEPARATION OF POWERS

The principle of dividing governmental powers among the executive, the legislative, and the judicial branches of government.

MADISONIAN MODEL

The model of government devised by James Madison in which the powers of the government are separated into three branches: executive, legislative, and judicial.

James Madison (1751–1836) contributed to the colonial cause by bringing to it a deep understanding of government and political philosophy. These resources first proved valuable in 1776, when he helped to draft the constitution for the new state of Virginia. Madison was prominent in disestablishing the Anglican Church when he was a representative of his county in the Virginia legislature from 1784 to 1786. At the Annapolis Convention, he supported New Jersey's motion to hold a federal constitutional convention the following year. Madison earned the title "master builder of the Constitution" because of his persuasive logic during the Constitutional Convention. His contributions to *The Federalist Papers* showed him to be a brilliant polemicist.

There were other disagreements. The delegates could not decide whether to establish only a Supreme Court or to create lower courts as well. They deferred the issue by mandating a Supreme Court and allowing Congress to establish lower courts. They also disagreed over whether the president or the Senate would choose the Supreme Court justices. A compromise was reached, with the agreement that the president would nominate the justices and the Senate would confirm the nomination.

These compromises, as well as others, resulted from the recognition that if one group of states refused to ratify the Constitution, it was doomed.

Working toward Final Agreement

The Connecticut Compromise was reached by mid-July. The makeup of the executive branch and the judiciary, however, was left unsettled. The remaining work of the convention was turned over to a five-man Committee of Detail, which presented a rough draft of the Constitution on August 6. It made the executive and judicial branches subordinate to the legislative branch.

The Madisonian Model. The major issue of **separation of powers** had not yet been resolved. The delegates were concerned with structuring the government to prevent the imposition of tyranny—either by the majority or by a minority. It was Madison who devised a governmental scheme—sometimes called the **Madisonian model**—to achieve this: the executive, legislative, and judicial powers of government were to be separated so that no one branch had enough power to dominate the others. The separation of powers was by function, as well as by personnel, with Congress passing laws, the president enforcing and administering laws, and the courts interpreting laws in individual circumstances.

Each of the three branches of government would be independent of the others, but they would have to cooperate to govern. According to Madison, in *Federalist Paper* No. 51 (see Appendix D), "the great security against a gradual concentration of the several powers in the same department consists in giving to those who administer each department the necessary constitutional means and personal motives to resist encroachments of the others."

The "constitutional means" Madison referred to is a system of **checks and balances** through which each branch of the government can check the actions of the other branches. For example, Congress can enact laws, but the president has veto power over congressional acts. The Supreme Court has the power to declare acts of Congress and of the executive branch unconstitutional, but the president appoints the justices of the Supreme Court, with the advice and consent of the Senate. (The Supreme Court's power to declare acts unconstitutional was not mentioned in the Constitution, although arguably the framers assumed that the Court would have this power—see the discussion of judicial review later in this chapter.) Figure 2–2 outlines these checks and balances.

The Executive. Some delegates favored a plural executive made up of representatives from the various regions. This was abandoned in favor of a single chief executive. Some argued that Congress should choose the executive. To make the presidency completely independent of the proposed Congress, however, an **electoral college** was adopted, probably at James Wilson's suggestion. To be sure, the electoral college created a cumbersome presidential election process. It could even result in a candidate who came in second in the popular vote becoming president by being the top vote getter in the electoral college. The electoral college insulated the president, however, from direct popular control. The seven-year single term that some of the delegates had proposed was replaced by a four-year term and the possibility of reelection.

THE FINAL DOCUMENT

On September 17, 1787, the Constitution was approved by thirty-nine delegates. Of the fifty-five who had attended originally, only forty-two remained.

CHECKS AND BALANCES

A major principle of the American governmental system whereby each branch of the government exercises a check on the actions of the others.

ELECTORAL COLLEGE

A group of persons called electors selected by the voters in each state and Washington, D.C.; this group officially elects the president and vice president of the United States. The number of electors in each state is equal to the number of each state's representatives in both houses of Congress. The Twenty-third Amendment to the Constitution permits Washington, D.C., to have as many electors as a state of comparable population.

Figure 2–2
• •
Checks and Balances

The major checks and balances among the three branches are illustrated here. Some of these checks are not mentioned in the Constitution, such as judicial review—the power of the courts to declare federal or state acts unconstitutional—or the president's ability to refuse to enforce judicial decisions or congressional legislation. Checks and balances can be thought of as a confrontation of powers or responsibilities. Each branch checks the action of another; two branches in conflict have powers that can result in balances or stalemates, requiring one branch to give in or both to reach a compromise.

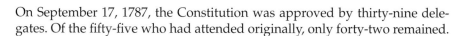

The Supreme Court can declare presidential actions unconstitutional.

The president nominates federal judges; the president can refuse to enforce the Court's decisions; the president grants pardons.

THE JUDICIARY

The Supreme Court can declare congressional laws unconstitutional.

Congress can rewrite legislation to circumvent the Court's decisions; the Senate confirms federal judges; Congress determines the number of judges.

The president proposes laws and can veto congressional legislation; the president makes treaties, executive agreements, and executive orders; the president can refuse, and has refused, to enforce congressional legislation; the president can call special sessions of Congress.

THE PRESIDENCY

The Congress makes legislation and can override a presidential veto of its legislation; the Congress can impeach and remove a president; the Senate must confirm presidential appointments and consent to the president's treaties based on a two-third's concurrence; the Congress has the power of the purse and provides funds for the president's programs.

THE CONGRESS

DID YOU KNOW . . .
That of the fifty-five delegates who attended the Constitutional Convention, sixteen failed to sign the final document, and some of the thirty-nine signatories approved only with reservations?

Only three delegates refused to sign the Constitution. Others disapproved of at least parts of it but signed anyway to begin the ratification debate.

The Constitution that was to be ratified established the following fundamental principles:

1. Popular sovereignty, or control by the people.
2. A republican government in which the people choose representatives to make decisions for them.
3. Limited government with written laws, in contrast to the powerful monarchical English government against which the colonists had rebelled.
4. Separation of powers, with checks and balances among branches to prevent any one branch from gaining too much power.
5. A federal system that allowed for states' rights, because the states feared too much centralized control (the federal system of government created by the Constitution is discussed in detail in Chapter 3).

As mentioned earlier, the Constitution is remarkably brief. The language of the Constitution is also remarkable (see this chapter's *Politics and Language* for details).

THE DIFFICULT ROAD TO RATIFICATION

RATIFICATION
Formal approval.

The founders knew that **ratification** of the Constitution was far from certain. Indeed, because it was almost guaranteed that many state legislatures would not ratify it, the delegates agreed that each state should hold a special convention. Elected delegates to these conventions would discuss and vote on the Constitution. Further departing from the Articles of Confederation, the delegates agreed that as soon as nine states (rather than all thirteen) approved the Constitution, it would take effect, and Congress could begin to organize the new government.

The Federalists Push for Ratification

FEDERALIST
The name given to one who was in favor of the adoption of the U.S. Constitution and the creation of a federal union. The Federalists favored a strong central government.

ANTI-FEDERALIST
An individual who opposed the ratification of the new Constitution in 1787.

The two opposing forces in the battle over ratification were the Federalists and the Anti-Federalists. The **Federalists**—those in favor of a strong central government and the new Constitution—had an advantage over their opponents, the **Anti-Federalists,** who wanted to prevent the Constitution as drafted from being ratified. In the first place, the Federalists had assumed a positive name, leaving their opposition the negative label of *Anti*-Federalist. More important, the Federalists had attended the Constitutional Convention and knew of all the deliberations that had taken place. Their opponents had no such knowledge, because those deliberations had not been open to the public. Thus, the Anti-Federalists were at a disadvantage in terms of information about the document. The Federalists also had time, power, and money on their side. Communications were slow. Those who had access to the best communications were Federalists—mostly wealthy bankers, lawyers, plantation owners, and merchants living in urban areas, where communication was better. The Federalist campaign was organized relatively quickly and effectively to elect Federalists as delegates to the state ratifying conventions.

The Anti-Federalists, however, had at least one strong point in their favor: they stood for the status quo. In general, the greater burden is placed on those advocating change.

The Federalist Papers. In New York, opponents of the Constitution were quick to attack it. Alexander Hamilton answered their attacks in newspaper

POLITICS AND LANGUAGE
The Art of Constitutional Writing

One of the explanations offered as to why the U.S. Constitution is the oldest living written constitution in the world is that it is vague and ambiguous. The Constitution either does not address many important issues (such as slavery) or addresses certain issues in an extremely loose manner (such as by stating that Congress shall have the power to "make all laws which shall be necessary and proper" to the exercise of its expressed powers—see Chapter 3).

One of the reasons for this vagueness, of course, is that it was impossible to achieve consensus on certain issues, such as whether slavery should be banned. Another reason is that a constitution, if it is to endure, must be worded sufficiently loosely that its basic principles can be adapted to changing conditions. If a constitution formalizes in writing the particular political views of its time, it will not serve a future age when those views give way to others.

Consider the gender issue. At the time the Constitution was written, no state permitted women to vote. Nowhere in the Constitution, however, were women specifically excluded from voting or otherwise participating in the political process—the Constitution was silent on the issue. The framers of the Constitution did not use the terms *male* and *female*. Rather, they used neutral terms, such as *citizens*, *persons*, or *people*. (When a masculine pronoun such as *he* or *him* was used, it was also used in reference to a previously stated person, citizen, or official—a common practice in formal legal documents until relatively recently.) Therefore, when women were given the right to vote (in 1920, with the Nineteenth Amendment), the provisions of the original Constitution remained applicable without changing the initial language used. Similarly, when women began to be elected to Congress, there was no need to change the language of the Constitution.

For Critical Analysis
When the Constitution is silent on an issue, how can a court decide whether a law concerning that issue is constitutionally valid?

columns over the signature "Caesar." When the Caesar letters had little effect, Hamilton switched to the pseudonym Publius and secured two collaborators—John Jay and James Madison. In a very short time, those three political figures wrote a series of eighty-five essays in defense of the Constitution and of a republican form of government. These widely read essays appeared in New York newspapers from October 1787 to August 1788 and were reprinted in the newspapers of other states. Although we do not know for certain who wrote every one, it is apparent that Hamilton was responsible for about two-thirds of the essays. These included the most important ones interpreting the Constitution, explaining the various powers of the three branches, and presenting a theory of judicial review. Madison's *Federalist Paper* No. 10 (see Appendix D), however, is considered a classic in political theory; it deals with the nature of groups—or factions, as he called them. In spite of the rapidity with which *The Federalist Papers* were written, they are considered by many to be perhaps the best example of political theorizing ever produced in the United States.[10]

The Anti-Federalist Response.   The Anti-Federalists used such pseudonyms as Montezuma and Philadelphiensis in their replies. Many of their attacks against the constitution were also brilliant. They claimed that it was a document written by aristocrats and would lead to aristocratic tyranny. More important, the Anti-Federalists believed that the Constitution would create an overbearing and overburdening central government inimical to personal liberty. (The Constitution said nothing about liberty of the press, freedom of

---

[10]Some scholars believe that *The Federalist Papers* played only a minor role in securing ratification of the Constitution. Even if this is true, they still have lasting value as an authoritative explanation of the Constitution.

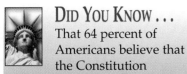

religion, or any other individual liberty.) They wanted to include a list of guaranteed liberties, or a bill of rights. Finally, the Anti-Federalists decried the weakened power of the states.

The Anti-Federalists cannot be dismissed as a bunch of unpatriotic extremists. They included such patriots as Patrick Henry and Samuel Adams. They were arguing what had been the most prevalent view of the time. This view derived from the French political philosopher Montesquieu (1689–1755), who believed that liberty was only safe in relatively small societies governed by direct democracy or by a large legislature with small districts. The Madisonian view favoring a large republic, particularly expressed in *Federalist Papers* No. 10 and No. 51 (see Appendix D), was actually the more *un*popular view of the time. Madison was probably convincing because citizens were already persuaded that a strong national government was necessary to combat foreign enemies and to prevent domestic insurrections. Still, some researchers believe it was mainly the bitter experiences with the Articles of Confederation, rather than Madison's arguments, that created the setting for the ratification of the Constitution.[11]

The March to the Finish

The struggle for ratification continued. Strong majorities were procured in Delaware, Pennsylvania, New Jersey, Georgia, and Connecticut. After a bitter struggle in Massachusetts, ratification passed by a narrow margin on February 6, 1788. By the spring, Maryland and South Carolina had ratified by sizable majorities. Then on June 21 of that year, New Hampshire became the ninth state to ratify the Constitution. Although the Constitution was formally in effect, this meant little without Virginia and New York, the latter not ratifying for yet another month. (See Table 2–2.)

THE BILL OF RIGHTS

Bills of rights had been included in state constitutions at least as early as 1776, when George Mason of Virginia wrote the Virginia Declaration of Rights. That document was modeled on the traditional rights established in England and present in the British Bill of Rights of 1689. (Note that Britain's Bill of Rights enumerates the rights of Parliament. Britain does not have a bill of rights for its citizens, or even a written constitution. See this chapter's *Politics and Comparative Systems* for a discussion of the current debate over whether Britain should have a bill of rights.)

Ratification of the U.S. Constitution in several important states could not have proceeded if the Federalists had not assured the states that amendments to the Constitution would be passed to protect individual liberties against incursions by the national government. Many of the recommendations of the state ratifying conventions included specific rights that were considered later by James Madison as he labored to draft what became the Bill of Rights. (Although called the Bill of Rights, essentially the first ten amendments to the Constitution were a "bill of limits," because the amendments limited the

LET'S SEE NOW ...WE'LL GIVE THEM FREEDOM, BUT NOT TOO MUCH FREEDOM; LIBERTY BUT NOT TOO MUCH LIBERTY; DEMOCRACY, BUT NOT TOO MUCH DEMOCRACY...

---

[11]Of particular interest is the view of the Anti-Federalist position contained in Herbert J. Storing, *What the Anti-Federalists Were For* (Chicago: University of Chicago Press, 1981). Storing also edited seven volumes of the Anti-Federalist writings, *The Complete Anti-Federalist* (Chicago: University of Chicago Press, 1981). See also Josephine F. Pacheco, *Antifederalism: The Legacy of George Mason* (Fairfax, Va.: George Mason University Press, 1992).

POLITICS AND COMPARATIVE SYSTEMS
Does Britain Need a Bill of Rights?

Great Britain has no single written document that serves as its constitution. Therefore, it is difficult to obtain a clear outline that indicates how the rights of British citizens are protected. In place of one document, Britain has a collection of customs and practices, as well as judicial decisions handed down in numerous court cases. In fact, what is regarded as the British constitution today consists of various statutes, judicial decisions, conventions, constitutional commentaries, authoritative opinions, letters, and works of scholarship. These include the Magna Carta (1215), the 1689 Bill of Rights, the Reform Act of 1832, laws passed by Parliament, and various charters.

Ironically Britain—a country that traditionally has been regarded as a "beacon of liberty" in the world—is now the only country in Western Europe that has no written bill of rights for its citizens. Should it?

According to the majority of respondents to recent opinion polls,* Britain should have a bill of rights.

The British Labour party and the Liberal Democrats also support the idea. Those in favor of a bill of rights point out that although Britain was once regarded as a beacon of liberty, its beacon now has become a fading light. In the nineteenth century, when government was relatively small, British citizens had substantial freedoms—essentially, they were free to do anything not specifically prohibited by law. Today, numerous laws and administrative regulations constrain the liberties of British citizens—and individuals have little recourse against the official power of the government bureaucrats who implement these laws and regulations.

Furthermore, although Parliament may protect citizens' rights, it also may eliminate a right previously granted by a single parliamentary vote. For example, a criminal suspect's right to remain silent has long been a legal hallmark in Great Britain, as in the United States. In 1994, however, the British Parliament passed an act that substantially modified this right

by providing that a criminal defendant's silence may be interpreted as evidence of the defendant's guilt.

Traditionalists argue that there is no need for a bill of rights. They contend that British liberties are better protected by Parliament than they would be by a bill of rights. After all, a bill of rights would effectively remove the power to protect citizens' rights and liberties from Parliament and place that power in the hands of unelected court judges—who would have to interpret and apply the bill of rights to specific cases. This would allow conservative judges to restrict British freedoms, rather than protect those freedoms.

For Critical Analysis—
If Britain were to pass a bill of rights, who should decide which rights are sufficiently fundamental to be included in the bill of rights?

*"Britain's Constitution: Why Britain Needs a Bill of Rights," *The Economist*, October 21, 1995, pp. 64–66.

Table 2–2

Ratification of the Constitution

STATE	DATE	VOTE FOR–AGAINST
Delaware	Dec. 7, 1787	30–0
Pennsylvania	Dec. 12, 1787	46–23
New Jersey	Dec. 19, 1787	38–0
Georgia	Jan. 2, 1788	26–0
Connecticut	Jan. 9, 1788	128–40
Massachusetts	Feb. 6, 1788	187–168
Maryland	Apr. 28, 1788	63–11
South Carolina	May 23, 1788	149–73
New Hampshire	June 21, 1788	57–46
Virginia	June 25, 1788	89–79
New York	July 26, 1788	30–27
North Carolina	Nov. 21, 1789*	187–77
Rhode Island	May 29, 1790	34–32

*Ratification was originally defeated on August 4, 1788, by a vote of 184–84.

DID YOU KNOW ...
That the delegates to the Constitutional Convention signed the document by geographic order, starting with New Hampshire (the northernmost state) and finishing with Georgia (the southernmost state)?

powers of the national government in regard to the rights and liberties of individuals.)

Ironically, a year earlier Madison had told Jefferson, "I have never thought the omission [of the Bill of Rights] a material defect" of the Constitution. But Jefferson's enthusiasm for a bill of rights apparently influenced Madison, as did his desire to gain popular support for his election to Congress. He promised in his campaign letter to voters that, once elected, he would force Congress to "prepare and recommend to the states for ratification, the most satisfactory provisions for all essential rights."

Madison had to cull through more than two hundred state recommendations. It was no small task, and in retrospect he chose remarkably well. (One of the rights appropriate for constitutional protection that he left out was equal protection under the laws—but that was not commonly regarded as a basic right at that time. It wasn't until 1868 that an amendment guaranteeing that no state shall deny equal protection to any person was ratified. The Supreme Court has applied this guarantee to certain actions of the federal government as well.)

The final number of amendments that Madison and a specially appointed committee came up with was seventeen. Congress tightened the language somewhat and eliminated five of the amendments. Of the remaining twelve, two—dealing with the apportionment of representatives and the compensation of the members of Congress—were not ratified immediately by the states. Eventually, Supreme Court decisions led to legislative reforms relating to apportionment. The amendment relating to compensation of members of Congress was ratified 203 years later—in 1992!

On December 15, 1791, the national Bill of Rights was adopted when Virginia agreed to ratify the ten amendments. The basic structure of American government had already been established. Now the fundamental rights and liberties of individuals were protected, at least in theory, at the national level. The proposed amendment that Madison characterized as "the most valuable amendment in the whole lot"—which would have prohibited the *states* from infringing on the freedoms of conscience, press, and jury trial—had been eliminated by the Senate. Thus, the Bill of Rights as adopted did not limit state power, and individual citizens had to rely on the guarantees contained in the particular state constitution or state bill of rights. The country had to wait until the violence of the Civil War before significant limitations on state power in the form of the Fourteenth Amendment became part of the national Constitution.

In interpreting and applying provisions in the Constitution and the Bill of Rights, the courts frequently look to the intentions of the framers. In deciding why the framers included a certain provision, the historical context naturally becomes important. For example, what did the framers mean by the "right of the people to keep and bear Arms" in the Second Amendment? This question is explored in this chapter's *Thinking Politically about the Right to Bear Arms.*

THE MOTIVES OF THE FRAMERS

In 1913, historian Charles Beard published *An Economic Interpretation of the Constitution of the United States,* charging that the Constitution had been produced primarily by wealthy property owners who desired a stronger government able to protect their property rights.[12] Beard also claimed that the

---

[12]Charles A. Beard, *An Economic Interpretation of the Constitution of the United States* (New York: Macmillan, 1913; New York: Free Press, 1986).

Thinking Politically about the Right to Bear Arms

"A well regulated Militia, being necessary to the security of a free State, the right of the people to keep and bear Arms shall not be infringed." So reads the Second Amendment to the U.S. Constitution. Does this amendment protect the right of *individuals* to bear arms or the right of *state governments* to maintain a "well regulated Militia"? How this question is answered has significant political implications. In an era of widespread crime and violence caused by individuals wielding guns, Congress has imposed certain restrictions on the sale or resale of handguns and has banned outright the sale of assault weapons. Many wish Congress would go further and ban the sale of handguns entirely. Others think Congress already has gone too far.

Do individuals have a constitutionally protected right to bear arms? According to many legal scholars, if they do have a right, it is not found in the Constitution. Generally, legal scholars and jurists consistently have interpreted the Second Amendment to mean that only states, not individuals, have such a constitutional right. This conclusion is based on an analysis of the intention of the framers. This intention, in turn, is determined by the historical context of those times. When the Constitution and Bill of Rights were written, one of the major concerns of the states was the need to protect their sovereignty against possible encroachment by the new national government. The right to maintain volunteer armed forces (state militias) was seen as essential.

In contrast, many Americans, particularly members of arms-bearing "citizens' militias" and other "patriot" groups, interpret this amendment to mean that *individuals* have a constitutional right to bear arms. A common theme among the citizens' militias that have sprung up around the country in the last decade or so (see the *What If . . .* that opens Chapter 4 for details on these groups) is that individuals need to have some means of defending themselves against the federal government. According to many members of these groups, the federal government has become too large, too impersonal, and too indifferent to human rights. Some militia members believe that the U.S. government is conspiring with other nations to destroy democracy in this country and the sovereignty of our nation. Many other Americans also believe that individuals have a constitutional right to bear arms—as anyone who has listened to radio talk shows realizes.

Public opinion polls have shown that most Americans support the idea of some form of gun control, such as licensing requirements for handguns. Why, then, has Congress found it difficult to gain consensus on any significant handgun-control legislation? The answer, in part, is that opponents of such legislation have a powerful interest group lobbying for their interests: the National Rifle Association (NRA). This organization, which was founded over a century ago, has lobbied for over three decades against any federal or state restrictions on the ownership or use of handguns. The NRA has over two million members and millions of dollars to spend on lobbying efforts, to contribute to the campaigns of those candidates who endorse the NRA's views, and to pay for advertising.

For Critical Analysis
How do powerful interest groups, such as the NRA, affect our "representative" democracy?

Constitution had been imposed by undemocratic methods to prevent democratic majorities from exercising real power. He pointed out that there was never any popular vote on whether to hold a constitutional convention in the first place. Furthermore, most people in the country (white males without property, as well as women and slaves) were not even eligible to vote on the Constitution, and only about one-sixth of adult white males actually voted for ratification.

Beard's thesis gave rise to a long-standing debate over the purpose of the Constitution. Was it designed to protect all of the people against the power of government and their own excesses? Or was it written to serve the interests of the people and groups that wielded economic power in the United States after the Revolution? Recall from Chapter 1 that the *elite theory* of American government assumes that our democracy is in essence an oligarchy in which decisions are made by an elite group—or competing elite groups—of wealthy and powerful individuals. Beard's thesis accords with this view.

DID YOU KNOW . . .

That term limits were included among the fifteen resolutions of the Virginia plan submitted to the Constitutional Convention in Philadelphia, but they were put aside "as entering too much into detail for general propositions"?

Were the delegates to the Constitutional Convention an elite group? Was the Constitution truly favored by a majority of Americans? We look at these questions here. A further issue is whether the motives of the framers even matter to today's world.

Who Were the Delegates?

Who were the fifty-five delegates to the Constitutional Convention? They certainly did not represent a cross section of eighteenth-century American society. Indeed, most were members of the upper class. Consider the following facts:

1. Thirty-three were members of the legal profession.
2. Three were physicians.
3. Almost 50 percent were college graduates.
4. Seven were former chief executives of their respective states.
5. Six were large plantation owners.
6. Eight were important businesspersons.

They were also relatively young by today's standards: James Madison was thirty-six, Alexander Hamilton was only thirty-two, and Jonathan Dyton of New Jersey was twenty-six. The venerable Benjamin Franklin, however, was eighty-one and had to be carried in on a portable chair borne by four prisoners from a local jail. Not counting Franklin, the average age was just over forty-two.

Additionally, all of the delegates were white and male. In contrast, some of the demographics of the 535 members of the 105th Congress, which took office in January 1997, are as follows: 38 are African Americans, 18 are Hispanics, and 57 are women.

Was the Constitution Truly Favored by the Majority?

Political scientists and historians still debate whether the Constitution actually was favored by a popular majority. The delegates at the various state ratifying conventions had been selected by only 150,000 of the approximately 4 million citizens of that time. That does not seem very democratic—at least not by today's standards. (On election day in 1996, for example, 91.4 million persons—of 185 million people of voting age—voted in the presidential election.) Even Federalist John Marshall believed that in some of the adopting states a majority of the people opposed the Constitution.[13] Indeed, some historians have suggested that if a Gallup poll could have been taken at that time, the Anti-Federalists would probably have outnumbered the Federalists.[14]

We have to realize, however, that the adoption of the Constitution was probably as open a process as was reasonable at that time. Transportation and communication were rudimentary and slow. It would have been difficult to discover the true state of popular opinion, even if the leaders of the new nation had been concerned enough to do so.

Do the Motives of the Framers Really Matter?

Many today contend that the motives of the framers do not really matter. What matters, they assert, is that the framers created a constitutional edifice that has endured for over two hundred years. The principles of government

---

[13]Beard, *An Economic Interpretation of the Constitution*, p. 299.
[14]Jim Powell, "James Madison—Checks and Balances to Limit Government Power," *The Freeman*, March 1996, p. 178.

set forth in the Constitution were sufficiently broad to enable succeeding generations of Americans to adapt those principles to a changing society. The *Concept Overview: Changes in the Constitution* near the end of this chapter indicates some of the significant ways in which we have departed from the framers' vision of American society and politics.

Others argue that the motives of the framers are indeed important. As you will read in Chapter 15, the judiciary itself is divided on the issue. Generally, conservative jurists take the position that the Constitution should be interpreted in accordance with the intention of the framers who drafted it. Liberal justices, in contrast, tend to stress that interpretations of the Constitution must take into account the changes in social values and mores that have taken place over the last two centuries.

DID YOU KNOW...
That the total cost to the federal taxpayer for getting the Constitution written was $1,586?

ALTERING THE CONSTITUTION: THE FORMAL AMENDMENT PROCESS

The U.S. Constitution consists of 7,000 words. It is shorter than every state constitution except that of Vermont, which has 6,880 words (see this chapter's *Politics and the Fifty States*). One of the reasons the federal Constitution is short is that the framers intended it to be only a framework for governing, to be interpreted by succeeding generations. One of the reasons it has remained short is because the formal amending procedure does not allow for changes to be made easily. Article V of the Constitution outlines the way in which amendments may be proposed and ratified (see Figure 2–3).

Two formal methods of proposing an amendment to the Constitution are available: (1) a two-thirds vote in each house of Congress or (2) a national convention that is called by Congress at the request of two-thirds of the state legislatures.

Ratification can occur by one of two methods: (1) by a positive vote in three-fourths of the legislatures of the various states or (2) by special conventions called in the states for the specific purpose of ratifying the proposed amendment and a positive vote in three-fourths of them. The second method has been used only once, to repeal Prohibition. That situation was exceptional

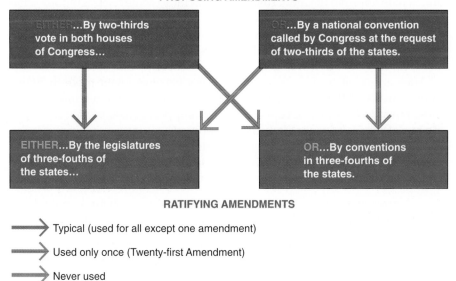

PROPOSING AMENDMENTS

EITHER...By two-thirds vote in both houses of Congress...

OR...By a national convention called by Congress at the request of two-thirds of the states.

EITHER...By the legislatures of three-fouths of the states...

OR...By conventions in three-fourths of the states.

RATIFYING AMENDMENTS

→ Typical (used for all except one amendment)

→ Used only once (Twenty-first Amendment)

→ Never used

Figure 2–3
● ● ● ● ● ● ● ● ● ● ● ● ● ● ● ● ● ● ●
The Formal Constitutional Amending Procedure

There are two ways of proposing amendments to the U.S. Constitution and two ways of ratifying proposed amendments. Among the four possibilities, the usual route has been proposal by Congress and ratification by state legislatures. Only in the case of the ratification of the Twenty-first Amendment in 1933, which repealed the Eighteenth Amendment (Prohibition), was ratification by state conventions used. The Constitution has never been amended by two-thirds of the states requesting a national convention to be called by Congress and then having the proposed amendment ratified by the legislatures of three-fourths of the states or by state conventions in three-fourths of the states.

POLITICS AND THE FIFTY STATES
Length of State Constitutions

The length of state constitutions varies considerably from state to state. Here we list the number of words contained in the ten longest and the ten shortest state constitutions.

TEN LONGEST CONSTITUTIONS		TEN SHORTEST CONSTITUTIONS	
State	**Word Length**	**State**	**Word Length**
Alabama	220,000	Vermont	6,880
Texas	80,806	New Hampshire	9,200
California	54,645	Connecticut	9,564
Louisiana	54,112	Indiana	10,230
New York	51,700	North Carolina	11,000
Colorado	45,679	Utah	11,000
Missouri	42,000	Montana	11,866
Maryland	41,349	Kansas	11,900
Arkansas	40,720	Iowa	13,430
Ohio	36,900	Maine	13,500

For Critical Analysis
What factors might explain the greater length of state constitutions relative to the U.S. Constitution?

because it involved an amendment (the Twenty-first) to repeal an amendment (the Eighteenth, which had created Prohibition). State conventions were necessary for repeal of the Eighteenth Amendment because the "pro-dry" legislatures in the more conservative states would never have passed the repeal. (Note that Congress determines the method of ratification to be used by all states for each proposed constitutional amendment.)

Many Amendments Proposed, Few Accepted

Congress has considered more than eleven thousand amendments to the Constitution. Only thirty-three have been submitted to the states after having been passed by Congress, and only twenty-seven have been ratified (see Table 2–3). It should be clear that the process is much more difficult than a graphic depiction like Figure 2–3 can indicate. Because of competing social and economic interests, the requirement that two-thirds of both the House and Senate approve the amendments is difficult to achieve. Thirty-four senators, representing only seventeen sparsely populated states, could block any amendment. For example, the Republican-controlled House passed the Balanced Budget Amendment within the first one hundred days of the 104th Congress in 1995, but it was defeated in the Senate by one vote.

After approval by Congress, the process becomes even more arduous. Three-fourths of the state legislatures must approve the amendment. Only those amendments that have wide popular support across parties and in all regions of the country are likely to be approved.

Why was the amendment process made so difficult? The framers feared that a simple amendment process could lead to a tyranny of the majority, which could pass amendments to oppress disfavored individuals and groups.

Limits on Ratification

A reading of Article V of the Constitution reveals that the framers of the Constitution specified no time limit on the ratification process. The Supreme Court has held that Congress can specify a time for ratification as long as it is "reasonable." Since 1919, most proposed amendments have included a requirement that ratification be obtained within seven years. This was the case with the proposed Equal Rights Amendment. When three-fourths of the states had not ratified in time, Congress extended the limit for an additional three years and three months. That extension expired on June 30, 1982, and the amendment had still not been ratified. Another proposed amendment, which would have guaranteed congressional representation to the District of Columbia, fell far short of the thirty-eight state ratifications needed before its August 22, 1985, deadline.

On May 7, 1992, the Michigan state legislature became the thirty-eighth state to ratify the Twenty-seventh Amendment (on congressional compensation)—one of the two "lost" amendments of the twelve that originally were sent to the states in 1789. Because most of the amendments proposed in recent years have been given a time limit of only seven years by Congress, it was questionable for a while whether the amendment would become effective even if the necessary number of states ratified it. Is 203 years too long a lapse of time between the proposal and the final ratification of an amendment? It apparently was not, because the amendment was certified as legitimate by archivist Don Wilson of the National Archives on May 18, 1992.

DID YOU KNOW...
That 52 percent of Americans do not know what the Bill of Rights is?

Table 2–3

Amendments to the Constitution

AMENDMENTS	SUBJECT	YEAR ADOPTED	TIME REQUIRED FOR RATIFICATION
1st–10th	The Bill of Rights	1791	2 years, 2 months, 20 days
11th	Immunity of states from certain suits	1795	11 months, 3 days
12th	Changes in electoral college procedure	1804	6 months, 3 days
13th	Prohibition of slavery	1865	10 months, 3 days
14th	Citizenship, due process, and equal protection	1868	2 years, 26 days
15th	No denial of vote because of race, color, or previous condition of servitude	1870	11 months, 8 days
16th	Power of Congress to tax income	1913	3 years, 6 months, 22 days
17th	Direct election of U.S. senators	1913	10 months, 26 days
18th	National (liquor) prohibition	1919	1 year, 29 days
19th	Women's suffrage	1920	1 year, 2 months, 14 days
20th	Change of dates for congressional and presidential terms	1933	10 months, 21 days
21st	Repeal of the Eighteenth Amendment	1933	9 months, 15 days
22d	Limit on presidential tenure	1951	3 years, 11 months, 3 days
23d	District of Columbia electoral vote	1961	9 months, 13 days
24th	Prohibition of tax payment as a qualification to vote in federal elections	1964	1 year, 4 months, 9 days
25th	Procedures for determining presidential disability, presidential succession, and filling a vice presidential vacancy	1967	1 year, 7 months, 4 days
26th	Prohibition of setting minimum voting age above eighteen in any election	1971	3 months, 7 days
27th	Prohibition of Congress's voting itself a raise that takes effect before the next election	1992	203 years

The National Convention Provision

The Constitution provides that a national convention requested by the legislatures of two-thirds of the states can propose a constitutional amendment. Congress has received approximately 400 convention applications since the Constitution was ratified; every state has applied at least once. Less than 20 applications were submitted during the Constitution's first 100 years, but more than 150 have been filed in the last two decades. No national convention has been held since 1787, and many national political and judicial leaders are uneasy about the prospect of convening a body that conceivably could do as the Constitutional Convention did—create a new form of government. The state legislative bodies that originate national convention applications, however, appear not to be uncomfortable with such a constitutional modification process; more than 230 state constitutional conventions have been held. The major national convention campaigns have reflected dissatisfaction, as one scholar has noted, "of a conservative and rural hue, with the social and economic policies associated with the federal government."[15]

The Constitution is silent about many of the procedures that would be required at a national convention, and significant questions abound about the nature and process of such a convention: Does Congress have wide or narrow discretion in determining the acceptability and/or validity of applications? If sufficient numbers of applications are submitted, but Congress refuses to call a convention, do the states have any other recourse? Is a vote of Congress necessary to authorize the issuance of a call for a national convention? Can the president veto such an action? When and where would the convention meet? How would the delegates be elected? Would they represent the states or the people as an aggregate? Can the convention be limited to one specific issue? Does Congress have any legal authority to set convention ground rules? Members of Congress have proposed legislation that would provide constitutional convention procedural controls, but no such act has been passed.

INFORMAL METHODS OF CONSTITUTIONAL CHANGE

Formal amendments are one way of changing our Constitution, and, as is obvious by their small number, they have not been resorted to very frequently. If we discount the first ten amendments (the Bill of Rights), which passed soon after the ratification of the Constitution, there have been only seventeen formal alterations of the Constitution in the more than two hundred years of its existence.

But looking at the sparse number of formal constitutional changes gives us an incomplete view. The brevity and ambiguity of the original document has permitted great changes in the Constitution by way of changing interpretations over time. As the United States grew, both in population and territory, new social and political realities emerged. Congress, presidents, and the courts found it necessary to interpret the Constitution's provisions in light of these new realities. The Constitution has proved to be a remarkably flexible document, adapting itself time and again to new events and concerns.

---

[15]Russell L. Caplan, *Amending the Constitution by National Convention* (New York: Oxford University Press, 1988).

Congressional Legislation

The Constitution gives the Congress broad powers to carry out its duties as the nation's legislative body. For example, Article I, Section 8, of the Constitution gives Congress the power to regulate foreign and interstate commerce. Although there is no clear definition of foreign commerce or interstate commerce in the Constitution, Congress has cited the *commerce clause* as the basis for passing thousands of laws that have defined the meaning of foreign and interstate commerce. Similarly, Article III, Section 1, states that the national judiciary shall consist of one supreme court and "such inferior courts, as Congress may from time to time ordain and establish." Through a series of acts, Congress has used this broad sanction to establish the federal court system of today.

Presidential Actions

Even though the Constitution does not expressly authorize the president to propose bills or even budgets to Congress, presidents since the time of Woodrow Wilson (who served as president from 1913 to 1921) have proposed hundreds of bills to Congress each year. Presidents have also relied on their Article II authority as commander in chief of the nation's armed forces to send American troops abroad into combat, although the Constitution provides that Congress has the power to declare war. Presidents have also conducted foreign affairs by the use of **executive agreements,** which are legally binding documents made between the president and a foreign head of state. The Constitution does not mention such agreements.

EXECUTIVE AGREEMENT

A binding international agreement made between chiefs of state that does not require legislative sanction.

Judicial Review

Another way of changing the Constitution—or of making it more flexible—is through the power of judicial review. **Judicial review** refers to the power of U.S. courts to invalidate actions undertaken by the legislative and executive branches of government. A state court, for example, may rule that a statute enacted by the state legislature is unconstitutional. Federal courts (and ultimately, the United States Supreme Court) may rule unconstitutional not only acts of Congress and decisions of the national executive branch but also state statutes, state executive actions, and even provisions of state constitutions.

JUDICIAL REVIEW

The power of the Supreme Court or any court to declare unconstitutional federal or state laws and other acts of government.

The Constitution does not specifically mention the power of judicial review. Those in attendance at the Constitutional Convention, however, probably expected that the courts would have some authority to review the legality of acts by the executive and legislative branches. Indeed, Alexander Hamilton, in *Federalist Paper* No. 78 (see Appendix D), explicitly outlined the concept of judicial review. Whether the power of judicial review can be justified constitutionally is a question we explore in Chapter 15, in the context of the role of the judiciary. For now, suffice it to say that in 1803, the Supreme Court claimed this power for itself in *Marbury v. Madison*,[16] in which the Supreme Court ruled that a particular provision of an act of Congress was unconstitutional.

Through the process of judicial review, the Supreme Court adapts the Constitution to modern situations. Electronic technology, for example, did not exist when the Constitution was ratified. Nonetheless, in this century the Supreme Court used the Fourth Amendment guarantees against unreason-

---

[16] 1 Cranch 137 (1803). (See the appendix to Chapter 2 for information on how court decisions are referenced.) See the *Politics and the Law* in Chapter 15 for a discussion of the *Marbury v. Madison* case and its significance.

able searches and seizures to place limits on wiretapping and other electronic eavesdropping methods by government officials. Additionally, the Supreme Court has changed its interpretation of the Constitution in accordance with changing times. It ruled in 1896 that "separate-but-equal" public facilities for African Americans were constitutional; but by 1954 the times had changed, and the Supreme Court reversed that decision.[17]

Woodrow Wilson summarized the Supreme Court's work when he described it as "a constitutional convention in continuous session." Basically, the law is what the Supreme Court says it is at any point in time. Consider just one example. By 1995, twenty-four states had enacted laws or amended their constitutions to limit the terms of congresspersons. The U.S. Constitution, however, does not mention term limits. Thus, it fell to the Supreme Court to decide whether state laws requiring term limits passed constitutional muster. In *Terms Limits v. Arkansas*,[18] the Court held that they did not—an Arkansas state constitutional amendment limiting the terms of members of Congress was declared unconstitutional. As a result, the term-limits laws in all twenty-four states were invalidated. The Court stated that only an amendment to the U.S. Constitution could limit the terms served by members of Congress.

Interpretation, Custom, and Usage

The Constitution has also been changed through its interpretation by both Congress and the president. Originally, the president had a staff consisting of personal secretaries and a few others. Today, because Congress delegates specific tasks to the president and the chief executive assumes political leadership, the executive office staff alone has increased to several thousand persons. The executive branch provides legislative leadership far beyond the intentions of the Constitution.

Changes in the ways of doing political business have also altered the Constitution. The Constitution does not mention political parties, yet these informal, "extraconstitutional" organizations make the nominations for offices, run the campaigns, organize the members of Congress, and in fact change the election system from time to time. The emergence and evolution of the party system, for example, has changed the way of electing the president. The Constitution calls for the electoral college to choose the president. Today, the people vote for electors who are pledged to the candidate of their party, effectively choosing the president themselves. Perhaps most strikingly, the Constitution has been adapted from serving the needs of a small, rural republic with no international prestige to providing a framework of government for an industrial giant with vast geographic, natural, and human resources.

THE CONSTITUTION: UNFINISHED WORK

The U.S. Constitution has been called a "living" constitution because the framers embodied it with sufficient flexibility so that its meaning and application could change as the nation and its people changed. As we fully develop the age of technology, information, and communication, this inherent flexibility undoubtedly will be pushed to its limits at times. For example, how can our constitutional right to free speech be applied to electronic communications via the Internet? How can privacy rights be protected in an electronic age? Furthermore, how can any state or national law protect rights in an electronic jurisdiction that is essentially international in scope?

---

[17]*Brown v. Board of Education of Topeka,* 347 U.S. 483 (1954).
[18]115 S.Ct. 1842 (1995).

CONCEPT OVERVIEW
Changes in the Constitution

There have been many changes in the Constitution in the more than two hundred years since its ratification. We list here just a few of the more significant changes.

THEN	NOW
• No mention of judicial review.	• The doctrine of judicial review is well established (first affirmed by the Supreme Court in *Marbury v. Madison* in 1803).
• Slavery not prohibited.	• Slavery abolished (by the Thirteenth Amendment of 1865 and subsequent laws).
• No provision for equal protection of the laws.	• A right to equal protection of the laws (granted by the Fourteenth Amendment in 1868—see Chapter 4).
• Voting rights severely restricted (to property-owning white males).	• Minimal restrictions, such as age and residency requirements, on voting rights (see Chapters 5 and 6).
• No provision for a national income tax.	• National income tax (provided for by the Sixteenth Amendment in 1913).
• No limit on presidential terms.	• Presidential terms limited to two elected terms (by the Twenty-second Amendment in 1951).
• Senators elected by state legislatures.	• Senators elected directly by the people (provided for by the Seventeenth Amendment in 1913).
• No privacy rights.	• Privacy rights (inferred from the First, Third, Fourth, Fifth, and Ninth Amendments).

A further issue involves striking a balance between the rights of the fifty sovereign states and the powers of the national government. This has never been easy, and during the 1860s, the nation resorted to civil war to resolve the issue. As the end of the twentieth century draws near, there again seems to be a growing movement toward states' rights and away from national government involvement. We examine the challenges posed by a federal form of government—and how those challenges have been dealt with in the past—in Chapter 3. We return to this theme again in later chapters of this text, particularly in Chapters 16 and 17.

These are just a few examples of unfinished work in the area of constitutional law. In a sense, the Constitution itself is "unfinished"—at least to the extent that is must be adapted continuously to the ever-changing needs of the nation.

GETTING INVOLVED
How Can You Affect the U.S. Constitution?

The Constitution is an enduring document that has survived more than two hundred years of turbulent history. It is also a changing document, however. Twenty-seven amendments have been added to the original Constitution. How can you, as an individual, actively help to rewrite the Constitution?

One of the best ways is to work for (or against) a constitutional amendment. At the time of this writing, national coalitions of interest groups are supporting or opposing proposed amendments concerning a balanced federal budget and antiabortion laws. If you want an opportunity to change the Constitution—or to assure that it is not changed—you could work for or with one of the alliances of groups interested in the fate of these amendments.

The following contacts should help you get started on efforts to affect the U.S. Constitution directly.

BALANCED BUDGET AMENDMENT

Critics of a balanced budget amendment often stress that the focus on balancing the federal budget obscures other, more important national priorities. They fear that a balanced budget amendment, while it would help to reduce the federal budget deficit, would do so at the expense of other national goals, such as those relating to education, the environment, employment, and health care. To learn more about the arguments against the passage of a balanced budget amendment, you can contact Americans for Democratic Action, 1625 K St. N.W., Washington, D.C. 20006 (202-785-5980).

Other groups argue to the contrary. They believe that forcing Congress to "live within its means" is essential if the government is to endure and that passing a balanced budget amendment is one way to obtain this goal. For information on this perspective on the issue, you can contact The Heritage Foundation, 214 Massachusetts Ave. N.E., Washington, D.C. 20002 (202-546-4400).

ABORTION

One of the organizations whose primary goal is to secure the passage of the Human Life Amendment is the American Life League, P.O. Box 1350, Stafford, VA 22555 (703-690-2049) [it can be reached online at http://www.ahoynet.com/~all/index.html]. The Human Life Amendment would recognize in law the "personhood" of the unborn, secure human rights protections for the fetus from the time of fertilization, and prohibit abortion under any circumstances.

The National Abortion and Reproductive Rights Action League, 1156 15th St. N.W., Suite 700, Washington, DC 20005 (202-973-3000) [its URL is http://www.naral/org], is a political action and information organization working on behalf of "pro-choice" issues—that is, the right of women to have control over reproduction. The organization has roughly 500,000 members.

KEY TERMS

Anti-Federalist 48

bicameral legislature 44

checks and balances 47

confederation 38

electoral college 47

executive agreement 59

Federalist 48

First Continental Congress 36

Great Compromise 45

judicial review 59

Madisonian model 46

natural rights 37

ratification 48

representative assembly 34

Second Continental Congress 36

separation of powers 46

state 38

supremacy doctrine 45

unicameral legislature 38

CHAPTER SUMMARY

❶ An early effort by Great Britain to establish North American colonies was unsuccessful. The first English colonies were established at Jamestown in 1607 and Plymouth in 1620. The Mayflower Compact created the first formal government. By the mid-1700s, other British colonies had been established along the Atlantic seaboard from Georgia to Maine.

❷ In 1763, the British tried to reassert control over their increasingly independent-minded colonies through a series of taxes and legislative acts. The colonists responded with boycotts of British products and protests. Representatives of the colonies formed the First Continental Congress in 1774. The delegates sent a petition to the king of England expressing their grievances. The Second Continental Congress established an army in 1775 to defend colonists against any attacks by British soldiers.

❸ On July 4, 1776, the Second Continental Congress approved the Declaration of Independence. Perhaps the most revolutionary aspects of the Declaration were its assumptions that people have natural rights to life, liberty, and the pursuit of happiness; that governments derive their power from the consent of the governed; and that people have a right to overthrow oppressive governments. During the Revolutionary War, however, all of the colonies adopted written constitutions that severely curtailed the power of executives, thus giving their legislatures predominant powers. By the end of the Revolutionary War, the states had signed the Articles of Confederation, creating a weak government with few powers. The Articles proved to be unworkable because the national government had no way to assure compliance by the states with such measures as securing tax revenues.

❹ General dissatisfaction with the Articles of Confederation prompted delegates to call the Philadelphia Convention in 1787. Although the delegates originally convened with the idea of amending the Articles, the discussions soon focused on creating a constitution for a new form of government. The Virginia plan and the New Jersey plan were offered but did not garner widespread support. A compromise offered by the state of Connecticut helped to break the large-state/small-state disputes dividing the delegates. The final version of the Constitution provided for the separation of powers and for checks and balances.

❺ Fears of a strong central government prompted the addition of the Bill of Rights to the Constitution. The Bill of Rights secured a wide variety of freedoms for Americans, including the freedoms of religion, speech, and assembly. It was initially applied only to the federal government, but amendments to the Constitution following the Civil War made it clear that the Bill of Rights also applied to the states.

❻ An amendment to the Constitution may be proposed by either a two-thirds vote in each house of Congress or by a national convention called by Congress at the request of two-thirds of the state legislatures. Ratification can occur by either a positive vote in three-fourths of the legislatures of the various states or by special conventions called in the states for the specific purpose of ratifying the proposed amendment and a positive vote in three-fourths of these state conventions. Informal methods of constitutional change include congressional legislation, presidential actions, judicial review, and changing interpretations of the Constitution.

QUESTIONS FOR REVIEW AND DISCUSSION

❶ Under the Articles of Confederation, Congress had no power to regulate interstate commerce. The absence of this power encouraged the states to engage in a certain type of legislation. What type of legislation was this, and what effect do you think it had on economic growth?

❷ The writing of the Constitution can be seen as the first real working of group interest, or pluralism, in the United States. What kinds of bargains or compromises were struck in the writing of this document? How were the various interests in the thirteen colonies protected by the provisions of the Constitution?

❸ Although the Constitution calls for separation of powers, a more accurate description of the system might be one of "separate branches sharing powers." What provisions of the Constitution require that the branches cooperate, or "share," power in order for the government to function?

❹ In this chapter, there are four subsections under the heading "Informal Methods of Constitutional Change."

Of the four methods, which do you think is most important, and why? Give examples to back up your argument.

⑤ The Anti-Federalists expressed many fears in their writings. Two of the most important involved taxation and the centralization of government. With respect to taxation, they feared that the central government would expand its taxing power slowly and would end up restricting how much the states and cities could tax because the federal government would be taking so much. Do you think this prediction was accurate? Why or why not? The second major fear of the Anti-Federalists was that the capital city would cause the central government to lose touch with its constituents. Have members of Congress lost touch with their home states by living in Washington, D.C.? Why or why not?

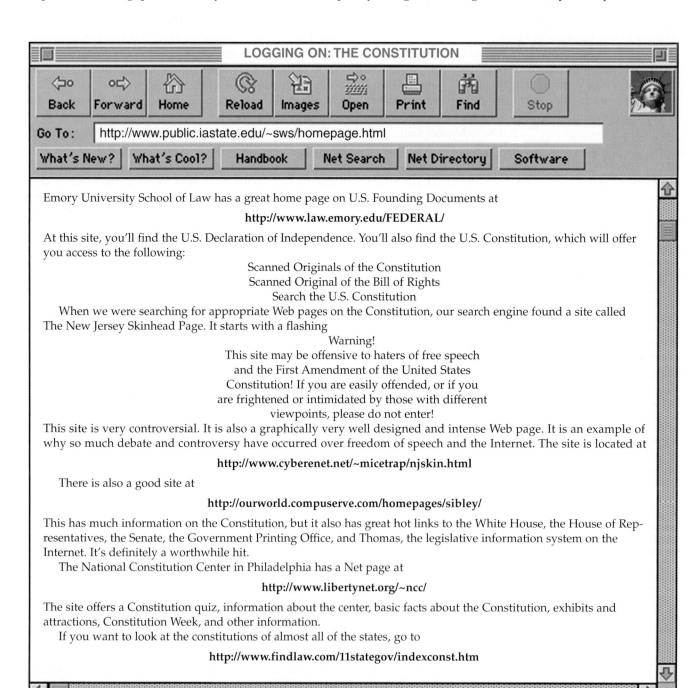

LOGGING ON: THE CONSTITUTION

Back | Forward | Home | Reload | Images | Open | Print | Find | Stop

Go To: http://www.public.iastate.edu/~sws/homepage.html

What's New? | What's Cool? | Handbook | Net Search | Net Directory | Software

Emory University School of Law has a great home page on U.S. Founding Documents at

http://www.law.emory.edu/FEDERAL/

At this site, you'll find the U.S. Declaration of Independence. You'll also find the U.S. Constitution, which will offer you access to the following:

Scanned Originals of the Constitution
Scanned Original of the Bill of Rights
Search the U.S. Constitution

When we were searching for appropriate Web pages on the Constitution, our search engine found a site called The New Jersey Skinhead Page. It starts with a flashing

Warning!
This site may be offensive to haters of free speech
and the First Amendment of the United States
Constitution! If you are easily offended, or if you
are frightened or intimidated by those with different
viewpoints, please do not enter!

This site is very controversial. It is also a graphically very well designed and intense Web page. It is an example of why so much debate and controversy have occurred over freedom of speech and the Internet. The site is located at

http://www.cyberenet.net/~micetrap/njskin.html

There is also a good site at

http://ourworld.compuserve.com/homepages/sibley/

This has much information on the Constitution, but it also has great hot links to the White House, the House of Representatives, the Senate, the Government Printing Office, and Thomas, the legislative information system on the Internet. It's definitely a worthwhile hit.

The National Constitution Center in Philadelphia has a Net page at

http://www.libertynet.org/~ncc/

The site offers a Constitution quiz, information about the center, basic facts about the Constitution, exhibits and attractions, Constitution Week, and other information.

If you want to look at the constitutions of almost all of the states, go to

http://www.findlaw.com/11stategov/indexconst.htm

SELECTED REFERENCES

Beard, Charles A. *An Economic Interpretation of the Constitution of the United States.* New York: Macmillan, 1913; New York: Free Press, 1986. This classic interpretation of the motives of the founders of the republic emphasizes the founders' economic interests in the success of the nation.

Biskupic, Joan, and Elder Witt. *The Supreme Court and Individual Rights.* Washington, D.C.: Congressional Quarterly Books, 1996. This study of Supreme Court cases focuses on the freedoms guaranteed in the Bill of Rights and subsequent laws and how those rights have been defined and applied in the twentieth century.

Epstein, Lee, and Thomas G. Walker. *Constitutional Law for a Changing America: A Short Course.* Washington, D.C.: Congressional Quarterly Books, 1996. An examination of the constitutional powers of the three branches of government, important cases in the development of constitutional law, and the political context in which judicial decisions are made—including behind-the-scenes stories and photographs.

Gerber, Scott Douglas. *To Secure These Rights: The Declaration of Independence and Constitutional Interpretation.* New York: New York University Press, 1995. A very readable account of the judicial function in regard to constitutional interpretation and the role of the Supreme Court in protecting the rights of individuals.

Hamilton, Alexander, James Madison, and John Jay. *The Federalist Papers.* Cambridge, Mass.: Harvard University Press, 1961. The complete set of columns from the *New York Packet* defending the new Constitution is presented.

Huyler, Jerome. *Locke in America: The Moral Philosophy of the Founding Era.* Lawrence, Kans.: University Press of Kansas, 1995. A penetrating analysis of the role played by John Locke's political philosophy in the founding of American government.

Pacheco, Josephine F., ed. *Antifederalism: The Legacy of George Mason.* Fairfax, Va.: George Mason University Press, 1992. A collection of essays that examines the concept of antifederalism and how the persistence of this political idea has been instrumental in shaping our nation.

Rakove, Jack N. *Original Meanings: Politics and Ideas in the Making of the Constitution.* New York: Knopf, 1996. The author, a professor at Stanford University, places the drafting of the Constitution in its historical and political context, and offers insights into the difficulty of interpreting that document. He contends that although in some ways the issues facing the framers of the Constitution were similar to those of today, in other ways, they were vastly different.

Redish, Martin H. *The Constitution as Political Structure.* New York: Oxford University Press, 1995. The author contends that the Supreme Court, by using the commerce clause of the Constitution to strike down state legislation impeding the free flow of interstate commerce, has acted contrary to the separation of powers and limited national government powers envisioned by the framers of the Constitution.

Storing, Herbert J. *The Complete Anti-Federalist.* 7 vols. Chicago: University of Chicago Press, 1981. The views of those opposed to the Constitution are examined.

Tully, James. *Strange Multiplicity: Constitutionalism in an Age of Diversity.* New York: Cambridge University Press, 1995. The author explores what the concepts of constitutionalism and sovereignty mean in an age of cultural diversity.

Wood, Gordon S. *The Radicalism of the American Revolution.* New York: Knopf, 1992. This study of the American revolution puts it in the perspective of other revolutions. The author examines the meaning of the American Revolution in a modern context.

APPENDIX TO CHAPTER TWO
How to Read Case Citations and Find Court Decisions

Many important court cases are discussed in references in footnotes throughout this book. Court decisions are recorded and published. When a court case is mentioned, the notation that is used to refer to, or to cite, the case denotes where the published decision can be found.

State courts of appeals decisions are usually published in two places, the state reports of that particular state and the more widely used *National Reporter System* published by West Publishing Company. Some states no longer publish their own reports. The *National Reporter System* divides the states into the following geographic areas: Atlantic (A. or A.2d, where *2d* refers to *Second Series*), South Eastern (S.E. or S.E.2d), South Western (S.W. or S.W.2d), North Western (N.W. or N.W.2d), North Eastern (N.E. or N.E.2d), Southern (So. or So.2d), and Pacific (P. or P.2d).

Federal trial court decisions are published unofficially in West's *Federal Supplement* (F.Supp.), and opinions from the circuit courts of appeals are reported unofficially in West's *Federal Reporter* (F., F.2d, or F.3d). Opinions from the United States Supreme Court are reported in the *United States Reports* (U.S.), the *Lawyers' Edition of the Supreme Court Reports* (L.Ed.), West's *Supreme Court Reporter* (S.Ct.), and other publications. The *United States Reports* is the official publication of United States Supreme Court decisions. It is published by the federal government. Many early decisions are missing

from these volumes. The citations of the early volumes of the *U.S. Reports* include the names of the actual reporters, such as Dallas, Cranch, or Wheaton. *McCulloch v. Maryland,* for example, is cited as 17 U.S. (4 Wheat.) 316. Only after 1874 did the present citation system, in which cases are cited based solely on their volume and page numbers in the *United States Reports,* come into being. The *Lawyers' Edition of the Supreme Court Reports* is an unofficial and more complete edition of Supreme Court decisions. West's *Supreme Court Reporter* is an unofficial edition of decisions dating from October 1882. These volumes contain headnotes and numerous brief editorial statements of the law involved in the case.

State courts of appeals decisions are cited by giving the name of the case; the volume, name, and page number of the state's official report (if the state publishes its own reports); the volume, unit, and page number of the *National Reporter;* and the volume, name, and page number of any other selected reporter. Federal court citations are also listed by giving the name of the case and the volume, name, and page number of the reports. In addition to the citation, this textbook lists the year of the decision in parentheses. Considere, for example, the case *United States v. Curtiss-Wright Export Co.,* 299 U.S. 304 (1936). The Supreme Court's decision of this case may be found in volume 299 of the *United States Reports* on page 304. The case was decided in 1936.

3
Federalism

CHAPTER OUTLINE

Federally Owned Lands Were Given to the States?

BACKGROUND

THE FEDERAL GOVERNMENT OWNS NEARLY 30 PERCENT OF THE LANDS IN THE UNITED STATES. IN THE TWELVE WESTERN MOST STATES, THIS FIGURE IS NEARLY 50 PERCENT. TRADITIONALLY, THE U.S. GOVERNMENT HAS ALLOWED STATE RESIDENTS TO USE FEDERAL LANDS FOR CATTLE GRAZING AND OTHER PURPOSES. RECENTLY, HOWEVER, IN THE INTERESTS OF ENVIRONMENTAL PROTECTION, THE FEDERAL GOVERNMENT HAS TIGHTENED THE REINS ON LOCAL USE OF FEDERAL LAND AND WATER RESOURCES. IN MANY AREAS OF THE WEST, THIS HAS LED TO A GROWING HOSTILITY TOWARD THE FEDERAL GOVERNMENT—AND PARTICULARLY TO THE BUREAUCRATS WHO ENFORCE FEDERAL LAND-USE POLICIES. SOME SUGGEST THAT THE ONLY SOLUTION TO THIS PROBLEM IS TO GIVE FEDERALLY OWNED LANDS BACK TO THE STATES.

WHAT IF FEDERALLY OWNED LANDS WERE GIVEN TO THE STATES?

Certainly, the return of federal lands to the states would reduce the threat of armed confrontations between local and national officials. Currently, a number of rebels in the increasingly "Wild West" are defying federal government orders and using federal lands without permits. Others have resorted to violent acts, such as shooting at a Forest Service biologist in California or bombing the van of a Nevada forest ranger while it was parked in his driveway. The Forest Service has advised forest rangers to travel in pairs, as a safety precaution, and to maintain frequent radio contact with district offices.

It is equally certain that federal lands would be used much differently than they are now. Each state could decide how the land would be used. It could retain ownership of these lands and either manage the lands itself or contract out management responsibilities to public (or private) corporations. Income generated by the lands would then go into state coffers instead of to the federal government. Currently, the federal government receives over $1.1 billion a year in fees from these lands. Of course, the states would have to pay for the costs involved in land management, and some estimates show that these costs may exceed the revenues received—at least in the short run. Alternatively, a state could give tracts of land to local governments, auction off long-term leases, or even sell these lands to private parties. The long-run financial benefits realized by the states from ownership of federal lands would depend, in large part, on how efficiently the lands were managed or the uses to which the lands are put.

WHAT ABOUT THE ENVIRONMENT?

Some of the biggest supporters of the movement for state ownership of federal lands are groups, such as the mining and timber industries, that would like to put the lands to commercial use. These interest groups could pressure state legislatures to privatize the lands so that they could purchase them for increased logging, mining, and other commercial activities. At the same time, in many respects state and local governments may be in a better position to regulate environmental decisions. Federal regulatory schemes must be applied uniformly across the nation regardless of regional and local differences, whereas state and local governments can tailor policies to fit the needs of citizens in a particular area. Whether the public interest would be served better by state and local regulation of the environment than by national regulation is not all that clear, however.

FOR CRITICAL ANALYSIS

1. *What might be some other ramifications of turning over federal lands to the states?*
2. *What compromise solution might be reached between the federal government and state and local governments over the ownership or use of public lands?*

There are many separate governments in this country. One national government and fifty state governments, plus local governments, create a grand total of more than 85,000 governments in all! The breakdown can be seen in Table 3–1. Those 85,000 governments contain about 500,000 elected office-holders.

Visitors from France or Spain are often awestruck by the complexity of our system of government. Consider that a criminal action can be defined by state law, by national law, or by both. Thus, the alleged criminal can be prosecuted in the state court system or in the federal court system (or both). Often, economic regulation over exactly the same matter exists at the local level, the state level, and the national level—generating multiple forms to be completed, multiple procedures to be followed, and multiple laws to be obeyed. Numerous programs are funded by the national government but administered by state and local governments.

There are various ways of ordering relations between central governments and local units. *Federalism* is one of these ways. Understanding federalism and how it differs from other forms of government is important in understanding the American political system. Indeed, some of the most pressing political issues today, including the one discussed in this chapter's opening *What If . . .* , would not arise if we did not have a federal form of government in which governmental authority is divided between the central government and various subunits.

THREE SYSTEMS OF GOVERNMENT

There are basically three ways of ordering relations between central governments and local units: (1) a unitary system, (2) a confederal system, and (3) a federal system. The most popular, both historically and today, is the unitary system.

Table 3–1

The Number of Governments in the United States Today

With more than 85,000 separate governmental units in the United States today, it is no wonder that intergovernmental relations in the United States are so complicated. Actually, the number of school districts has decreased over time, but the number of special districts created for single purposes, such as flood control, has increased from only about 8,000 during World War II to over 30,000 today.

Federal government		1
State governments		50
Local governments		86,692
Counties	3,043	
Municipalities	19,296	
(mainly cities or towns)		
Townships	16,666	
(less extensive powers)		
Special districts	33,131	
(water, sewer, etc.)		
School districts	14,556	
	86,692	
TOTAL		86,743

SOURCE: U.S. Department of Commerce, *Statistical Abstract of the United States* (Washington, D.C.: U.S. Government Printing Office, 1996).

A Unitary System

UNITARY SYSTEM

A centralized governmental system in which local or subdivisional governments exercise only those powers given to them by the central government.

A **unitary system** of government is the easiest to define. Unitary systems allow ultimate governmental authority to rest in the hands of the national, or central, government. Consider a typical unitary system—France. There are departments and municipalities in France. Within the departments and the municipalities are separate government entities with elected and appointed officials. So far, the French system appears to be very similar to the United States system, but the similarity is only superficial. Under the unitary French system, the decisions of the governments of the departments and municipalities can be overruled by the national government. The national government also can cut off the funding of many departmental and municipal government activities. Moreover, in a unitary system such as that in France, all questions related to education, police, the use of land, and welfare are handled by the national government.[1] Great Britain, Sweden, Israel, Egypt, Ghana, and the Philippines also have unitary systems of government, as do most countries today.

A Confederal System

CONFEDERAL SYSTEM

A system of government consisting of a league of independent states, each having essentially sovereign powers. The central government created by such a league has only limited powers over the states.

You were introduced to the elements of a **confederal system** of government in Chapter 2, when we examined the Articles of Confederation. A confederation is the opposite of a unitary governing system. It is a league of independent states in which a central government or administration handles only those matters of common concern expressly delegated to it by the member states. The central governmental unit has no ability to make laws directly applicable to individuals unless the member states explicitly support such laws. The United States under the Articles of Confederation and the Confederate States during the American Civil War were confederations.

There are few, if any, confederations in the world today that resemble those that existed in the United States. Switzerland is a confederation of twenty-three sovereign cantons, and several republics of the former Soviet Union formed the Commonwealth of Independent States. Countries have formed organizations with one another for limited purposes: military/peacekeeping, as in the case of the North Atlantic Treaty Organization or the United Nations; or economic, as in the case of the European Union (formerly the European Community) or the economic unit created by the North American Free Trade Agreement. These organizations, however, are not true confederations.

A Federal System

FEDERAL SYSTEM

A system of government in which power is divided by a written constitution between a central government and regional, or subdivisional, governments. Each level must have some domain in which its policies are dominant and some genuine political or constitutional guarantee of its authority.

The **federal system** lies between the unitary and confederal forms of government. In a federal system, authority is divided, usually by a written constitution, between a central government and regional, or subdivisional, governments (often called constituent governments). The central government and the constituent governments both act directly on the people through laws and through the actions of elected and appointed governmental officials. Within each government's sphere of authority, each is supreme, in theory. Contrast a federal system to a unitary one in which the central government is supreme and the constituent governments derive their authority from it. Australia, Canada, Mexico, India, Brazil, and Germany are examples of nations with federal systems. See Figure 3–1 for a comparison of the three systems.

---

[1]In the past decade, legislation has altered somewhat the unitary character of the French political system.

WHY FEDERALISM?

Why did the United States develop in a federal direction? We look here at that question as well as at some of the arguments for and against a federal form of government.

A Practical Solution

As you saw in Chapter 2, the historical basis of the federal system was laid down in Philadelphia at the Constitutional Convention, where strong national government advocates opposed equally strong states' rights advocates. This dichotomy continued through to the ratifying conventions in the several states. The resulting federal system was a compromise. The supporters of the new constitution were political pragmatists—they realized that without a federal arrangement, there would be no ratification of the new constitution. The appeal of federalism was that it retained state traditions and local power while establishing a strong national government capable of handling common problems.

Even if the colonial leaders had agreed on the desirability of a unitary system, the problems of size and regional isolation would have made such a system difficult operationally. At the time of the Philadelphia Convention, the thirteen colonies taken together were larger geographically than England or France. Slow travel and communication, combined with geographic spread, contributed to the isolation of many regions within the colonies. For example, it could take up to several weeks for all of the colonies to be informed about one particular political decision.

Other Arguments for Federalism

The arguments for federalism in the United States and elsewhere involve a complex set of factors, some of which we already have noted. First, for big countries, such as the United States, India, and Canada, federalism allows many functions to be "farmed out" by the central government to the states or provinces. The lower levels of government, accepting these responsibilities, thereby can become the focus of political dissatisfaction rather than the national authorities. Second, even with modern transportation and commu-

Figure 3–1
● ● ● ● ● ● ● ● ● ● ● ● ● ● ● ● ● ●

The Flow of Power in Three Systems of Government

In a unitary system, the flow of power is from the central government to the local and state governments. In a confederal system, the flow of power is in the opposite direction—from the state and local governments to the central government. In a federal system, the flow of power is, in principle, both ways.

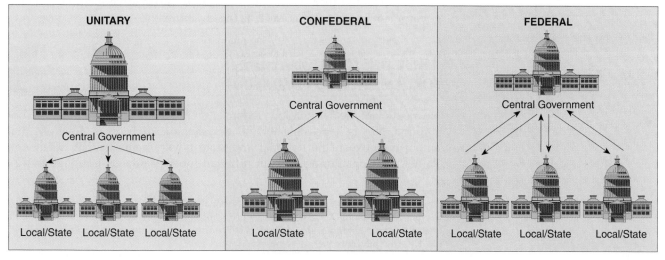

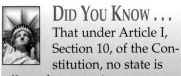

DID YOU KNOW ...
That under Article I, Section 10, of the Constitution, no state is allowed to enter into any treaty, alliance, or confederation?

nications systems, the sheer geographic or population size of some nations makes it impractical to locate all political authority in one place. Finally, federalism brings government closer to the people. It allows more direct access to, and influence on, government agencies and policies, rather than leaving the population restive and dissatisfied with a remote, faceless, all-powerful central authority.

In the United States, federalism historically has yielded many benefits. State governments long have been a training ground for future national leaders. Presidents Ronald Reagan and Bill Clinton made their political mark as state governors. The states themselves have been testing grounds for new government initiatives, such as unemployment compensation, which began in Wisconsin, and air-pollution control, which was initiated in California. Of course, some actions pioneered at the state level, such as Prohibition, were disastrous.

Additionally, the American way of life always has been characterized by a number of political subcultures, which divide along the lines of race and ethnic origin, wealth, education, and, more recently, age, degree of religious fundamentalism, and sexual preference. The existence of diverse political subcultures would appear to be at odds with a political authority concentrated solely in a central government. Had the United States developed into a unitary system, the various political subcultures certainly would have been less able to influence government behavior (relative to their own regions and interests) than they have been, and continue to be, in our federal system.

Arguments against Federalism

Not everyone thinks federalism is such a good idea. Some see it as a way for powerful state and local interests to block progress and impede national plans. Others see dangers in the expansion of national powers at the expense of the states. President Ronald Reagan said, "The Founding Fathers saw the federalist system as constructed something like a masonry wall. The States are the bricks, the national government is the mortar. . . . Unfortunately, over the years, many people have increasingly come to believe that Washington is the whole wall."[2]

Smaller political units are more likely to be dominated by a single political group, and the dominant groups in some cities and states have resisted implementing equal rights for all minority groups. (This was essentially the argument that James Madison put forth in *Federalist Paper* No. 10, which you can read in Appendix D to this text.) Others point out, however, that the dominant factions in other states have been more progressive than the national government in many areas, such as the environment.

THE CONSTITUTIONAL BASIS FOR AMERICAN FEDERALISM

No mention of the designation "federal system" can be found in the U.S. Constitution. Nor is it possible to find a systematic division of governmental authority between the national and state governments in that document. Rather, the Constitution sets out different types of powers (see Figure 3–2).

---

[2]Text of the address by the president to the National Conference of State Legislatures, Atlanta, Georgia (Washington, D.C.: The White House, Office of the Press Secretary, July 30, 1981), as quoted in Edward Millican, *One United People, The Federalist Papers and the National Idea* (Lexington, Ky.: The University Press of Kentucky, 1990).

These powers can be classified as (1) the powers of the national government, (2) the powers of the states, and (3) prohibited powers. The Constitution also makes it clear that if a state or local law conflicts with a national law, the national law will prevail.

Powers of the National Government

The powers delegated to the national government include both expressed and implied powers, as well as the special category of inherent powers. Most

Figure 3–2

• •

The American Federal System—The Division of Powers between the National Government and the State Governments

Here we look at the constitutional powers of both the national government and the state governments together. Then we look at the powers denied by the Constitution to each level of government.

SELECTED CONSTITUTIONAL POWERS

National Government	National and State Governments	State Governments
IMPLIED "To make all Laws which shall be necessary and proper for carrying into Execution the foregoing Powers, and all other Powers vested by this Constitution in the Government of the United States, or in any Department or Officer thereof." (Article 1, Section 8, Clause 18)	**CONCURRENT** ■ To levy and collect taxes ■ To borrow money ■ To make and enforce laws ■ To establish courts ■ To provide for the general welfare ■ To charter banks and corporations	**RESERVED TO THE STATES** ■ To regulate intrastate commerce ■ To conduct elections ■ To provide for public health, safety, and morals ■ To establish local governments ■ To ratify amendments to the federal constitution ■ To establish a state militia
EXPRESSED ■ To coin money ■ To conduct foreign relations ■ To regulate interstate commerce ■ To levy and collect taxes ■ To declare war ■ To raise and support the military ■ To establish post offices ■ To establish courts inferior to the Supreme Court ■ To admit new states		

SELECTED POWERS DENIED BY THE CONSTITUTION

National Government	National and State Governments	State Governments
■ To tax articles exported from any state ■ To violate the Bill of Rights ■ To change state boundaries ■ To suspend the right of *habeas corpus* ■ To make *ex post facto* laws ■ To subject officeholders to a religious test	■ To grant titles of nobility ■ To permit slavery ■ To deny citizens the right to vote because of race, color, or previous servitude ■ To deny citizens the right to vote because of sex	■ To tax imports or exports ■ To coin money ■ To enter into treaties ■ To impair obligations of contracts ■ To abridge the privileges or immunities of citizens or deny due process and equal protection of the laws

ENUMERATED POWERS

Powers specifically granted to the national government by the Constitution. The first seventeen clauses of Article I, Section 8, specify most of the enumerated powers of Congress.

of the powers expressly delegated to the national government are found in Article I, Section 8, of the Constitution. These **enumerated powers** include setting standards for weights and measures, making uniform naturalization laws, admitting new states, establishing post offices, and declaring war. Another important enumerated power is the power to regulate commerce among the states—a topic we deal with later in this chapter.

The implied powers of the national government are also based on Article I, Section 8, which states that the Congress shall have the power

> To make all laws which shall be necessary and proper for carrying into Execution the foregoing Powers, and all other Powers vested by this Constitution in the Government of the United States, or in any Department or Officer thereof.

ELASTIC CLAUSE, OR NECESSARY AND PROPER CLAUSE

The clause in Article I, Section 8, that grants Congress the power to do whatever is necessary to execute its specifically delegated powers.

This clause is sometimes called the **elastic clause,** or the **necessary and proper clause,** because it provides flexibility to our constitutional system. It gives Congress all those powers that can be reasonably inferred but that are not expressly stated in the brief wording of the Constitution. The clause was first used in the Supreme Court decision of *McCulloch v. Maryland*[3] (discussed later in this chapter) to develop the concept of implied powers. Through this concept, the national government has succeeded in strengthening the scope of its authority to meet the numerous problems that the framers of the Constitution did not, and could not, anticipate.

A special category of national powers that is not implied by the necessary and proper clause consists of what have been labeled the inherent powers of the national government. These powers derive from the fact that the United States is a sovereign power among nations, and as such, its national government must be the only government that deals with other nations. Under international law, it is assumed that all nation-states, regardless of their size or power, have an *inherent* right to ensure their own survival. To do this, each nation must have the ability to act in its own interest among and with the community of nations—by, for instance, making treaties, waging war, seek-

---

[3]4 Wheaton 316 (1819). See the appendix to Chapter 2 for more information about how court decisions are referenced.

When the Los Angeles earthquake destroyed billions of dollars of property, the state government looked to the federal government for financial aid for the quake's victims. Proponents of a strong central government argued that the states alone cannot handle significant local emergencies and that is why the federal government must step in.

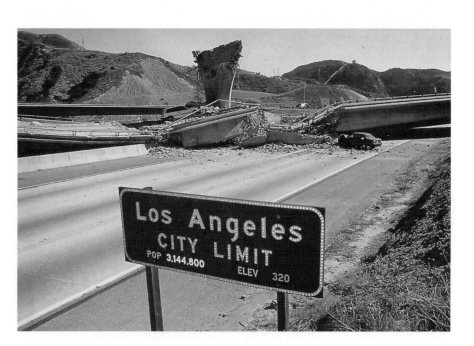

ing trade, and acquiring territory.[4] The national government has these powers whether or not they have been enumerated in the Constitution. Some constitutional scholars categorize inherent powers as a third type of power, completely distinct from the delegated powers (both expressed and implied) of the national government.

Powers of the State Governments

The Tenth Amendment states that the powers not delegated to the United States by the Constitution, nor prohibited by it to the states, are reserved to the states, or to the people. These are the reserved powers that the national government cannot deny to the states. Because these powers are not expressly listed—and because they are not limited to powers that are expressly listed—there is sometimes a question as to whether a certain power is delegated to the national government or reserved to the states. State powers have been held to include each state's right to regulate commerce within its borders and to provide for a state militia. States also have the reserved power to make laws on all matters not prohibited to the states by the national or state constitutions and not expressly, or by implication, delegated to the national government. The states also have **police power**—the authority to legislate for the protection of the health, morals, safety, and welfare of the people.

The ambiguity of the Tenth Amendment has allowed the reserved powers of the states to be defined differently at different times in our history. When there is widespread support for increased regulation by the national government, the Tenth Amendment tends to recede into the background. When the tide turns the other way, as it has in recent years (see the discussion of the new federalism later in this chapter), the Tenth Amendment is resurrected to justify arguments supporting increased states' rights.

In certain areas, the states share **concurrent powers** with the national government. Most concurrent powers are not specifically stated in the Constitution; they are only implied. An example of a concurrent power is the power to tax. The types of taxation are divided between the levels of government. States may not levy a tariff (a set of taxes on imported goods); the federal government may not tax real estate; and neither may tax the facilities of the other. If the state governments did not have the power to tax, they would not be able to function other than on a ceremonial basis. Other concurrent powers include the power to borrow money, to establish courts, and to charter banks and corporations. Concurrent powers are normally limited to the geographic area of the state and to those functions not delegated by the Constitution exclusively to the national government—such as the coinage of money and the negotiation of treaties.

Prohibited Powers

The Constitution prohibits or denies a number of powers to the national government. For example, the national government has expressly been denied the power to impose taxes on goods sold to other countries (exports). Moreover, any power not delegated expressly or implicitly to the federal government by the Constitution is prohibited to it. For example, the national government cannot create a national public school system.

POLICE POWER

The authority to legislate for the protection of the health, morals, safety, and welfare of the people. In the United States, most police power is a reserved power of the states.

CONCURRENT POWERS

Powers held jointly by the national and state governments.

---

[4]See especially *United States v. Curtiss-Wright Export Co.*, 299 U.S. 304 (1936), which upheld the validity of a joint resolution of Congress delegating the power to the president to prohibit arms shipments to foreign belligerents.

DID YOU KNOW...
That Abraham Lincoln, the "Great Emancipator," claimed on taking office that he would not attack slavery as an institution and that he even wanted a constitutional amendment to make the right to own slaves irrevocable?

SUPREMACY CLAUSE
The constitutional provision that makes the Constitution and federal laws superior to all conflicting state and local laws.

The states are also denied certain powers. These are found in Article I, Section 10, as well as in the Thirteenth, Fourteenth, Fifteenth, Nineteenth, Twenty-fourth, and Twenty-sixth Amendments. For example, no state is allowed to enter into a treaty on its own with another country.

The Supremacy Clause

The supremacy of the national constitution over subnational laws and actions can be found in the **supremacy clause** of the Constitution. The supremacy clause (Article VI, Paragraph 2) states the following:

> This Constitution and the Laws of the United States which shall be made in Pursuance thereof; and all Treaties made . . . under the Authority of the United States, shall be the supreme Law of the Land; and the Judges in every State shall be bound thereby, any Thing in the Constitution or Laws of any State to the Contrary notwithstanding.

In other words, states cannot use their reserved or concurrent powers to thwart national policies. All national and state officers, as well as judges, must be bound by oath to support the Constitution. Hence, any legitimate exercise of national governmental power supersedes any conflicting state action.[5] Of course, deciding whether a conflict actually exists is a judicial matter, as you will soon read about in the case of *McCulloch v. Maryland.*

Some political scientists believe that national supremacy is critical for the longevity and smooth functioning of a federal system. Nonetheless, the application of this principle has been a continuous source of conflict. Indeed, as you will see, the most extreme result of this conflict was the Civil War.

HORIZONTAL FEDERALISM

So far we have examined only the relationship between central and state governmental units. The states, however, have numerous commercial, social, and other dealings among themselves. These interstate activities, problems, and

---

[5]An excellent example of this is President Dwight Eisenhower's disciplining of Arkansas governor Orval Faubus by federalizing the National Guard to enforce the court-ordered desegregation of Little Rock High School.

The only indication that a motorist has crossed state boundary on Interstate 95 is the "Welcome to Maine" sign posted there. There are no border posts, and no visa, passport, or special permission is needed to change states. Different traffic laws may apply, however.

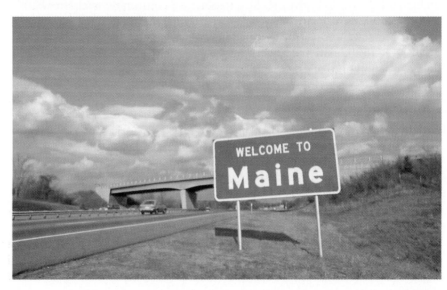

policies make up what can be called **horizontal federalism.** The national Constitution imposes certain "rules of the road" on horizontal federalism, which have had the effect of preventing any one state from setting itself apart from the other states. The three most important clauses in the Constitution relating to horizontal federalism, all taken from the Articles of Confederation, require that

1. Each state give full faith and credit to every other state's public acts, records, and judicial proceedings.
2. Each state extend to every other state's citizens the privileges and immunities of its own citizens.
3. Each state agree to render persons who are fleeing from justice in another state back to their home state when requested to do so.

The Full Faith and Credit Clause

Article IV, Section 1, of the Constitution provides that "Full Faith and Credit shall be given in each State to the public Acts, Records, and judicial Proceedings of every other State." This clause applies only to civil matters. It ensures that rights established under deeds, wills, contracts, and the like in one state will be honored by other states. It also ensures that any judicial decision with respect to such property rights will be honored, as well as enforced, in all states. The **full faith and credit clause** originally was put in the Articles of Confederation to promote mutual friendship among the people of the different states. In fact, it has contributed to the unity of American citizens, because it protects their legal rights as they move about from state to state. This is extremely important for the conduct of business in a country with a very mobile citizenry.

Privileges and Immunities

Privileges and immunities are defined as special rights and exemptions provided by law. Article IV, Section 2, indicates that "The Citizens of each State shall be entitled to all Privileges and Immunities of Citizens in the several States." This clause indicates that states are obligated to extend to citizens of other states protection of the laws, the right to work, access to courts, and other privileges they grant their own citizens. It means, quite simply, that a resident of Alabama cannot be treated as an alien (noncitizen) when that person is in California or New York. He or she must have access to the courts of each state, to travel rights, and to property rights.[6]

Interstate Extradition

Article IV, Section 2, states that "[a] person charged in any State with Treason, Felony, or another Crime who shall flee from Justice and be found in another State, shall on Demand of the executive Authority of the State from which he fled, be delivered up, to be removed to the State having jurisdiction of the Crime." The language here appears clear, yet governors of one state were not legally required to **extradite** (render to another state) a fugitive from justice until 1987. Furthermore, the federal courts will not order such an action; it is rather the moral duty of the governor to extradite. In 1993, David Walters, the

---

[6]Out-of-state residents have been denied lower tuition rates at state universities, voting rights, and immediate claims to welfare benefits.

HORIZONTAL FEDERALISM

Activities, problems, and policies that require state governments to interact with one another.

FULL FAITH AND CREDIT CLAUSE

A section of the Constitution that requires states to recognize one another's laws and court decisions. It ensures that rights established under deeds, wills, contracts, and other civil matters in one state will be honored by other states.

PRIVILEGES AND IMMUNITIES

Special rights and exceptions provided by law. Article IV, Section 2, of the Constitution requires states not to discriminate against one another's citizens. A resident of one state cannot be treated as an alien when in another state; he or she may not be denied such privileges and immunities as legal protection, access to courts, travel rights, or property rights.

EXTRADITE

To surrender an accused or convicted criminal to the authorities of the state from which he or she has fled; to return a fugitive criminal to the jurisdiction of the accusing state.

governor of Oklahoma, claimed that New York governor Mario Cuomo had disregarded this moral duty when Cuomo refused to extradite convicted murderer Thomas Grasso from New York to Oklahoma. Walters claimed that Cuomo, an outspoken opponent of the death penalty, was trying to keep "Oklahoma from exercising its right to capital punishment." It was only after George Pataki, a death-penalty supporter, took office as New York's governor in January 1995 that Grasso was sent to Oklahoma and later executed.

The Peaceful Settlement of Differences between States

INTERSTATE COMPACT

An agreement between two or more states. Agreements on minor matters are made without congressional consent, but any compact that tends to increase the power of the contracting states relative to other states or relative to the national government generally requires the consent of Congress. Such compacts serve as a means by which states can solve regional problems.

States are supposed to settle their differences peacefully. In so doing, they may enter into agreements called **interstate compacts**—if consented to by Congress. In reality, congressional consent is necessary only if such a compact increases the power of the contracting states relative to other states (or to the national government). Typical examples of interstate compacts are the establishment of the Port of New York Authority by the states of New York and New Jersey and the regulation of the production of crude oil and natural gas by the Interstate Oil and Gas Compact of 1935.

DEFINING CONSTITUTIONAL POWERS—THE EARLY YEARS

Recall from Chapter 2 that constitutional language, to be effective and to endure, must have some degree of ambiguity. Certainly, the powers delegated to the national government and the powers reserved to the states contain elements of ambiguity, thus leaving the door open for different interpretations of federalism. Disputes over the boundaries of national versus state powers have characterized this nation from the beginning. In the early 1800s, the most significant disputes arose over differing interpretations of the implied powers of the national government under the necessary and proper clause and the respective powers of the national government and the states in regard to commerce.

Although political bodies at all levels of government play important roles in the process of settling such disputes, ultimately it is the Supreme Court that casts the final vote. As might be expected, the character of the referee will have an impact on the ultimate outcome of any boundary dispute. From 1801 to 1835, the Supreme Court was headed by Chief Justice John Marshall, a Federalist who advocated a strong central government. We look here at two cases decided by the Marshall Court: *McCulloch v. Maryland*[7] and *Gibbons v. Ogden*.[8] Both cases are considered milestones in the movement toward national government supremacy.

McCulloch v. Maryland (1819)

The U.S. Constitution says nothing about establishing a national bank. Article I, Section 8, gives Congress the power "[t]o coin Money, regulate the Value thereof, and of foreign Coin, and fix the Standard of Weights and Measures." Nonetheless, at different times Congress chartered two banks—the First and Second Banks of the United States—and provided part of their initial capital; they were thus national banks.

---

[7]4 Wheaton 316 (1819).
[8]9 Wheaton 1 (1824).

The government of Maryland imposed a tax on the Second Bank's Baltimore branch. It was an attempt to put that branch out of business. The branch's cashier, James William McCulloch, refused to pay the Maryland tax. Maryland took McCulloch to its state court. In that court, the state of Maryland won. Because similar taxes were being levied in other states, the national government appealed the case to the Supreme Court, then headed by Chief Justice John Marshall.

The Constitutional Questions.   Congress has the authority to make all laws that are "necessary and proper" for the execution of Congress's expressed powers. One of the issues before the Court was whether the national government had the implied power, under the necessary and proper clause, to charter a bank and contribute capital to it.

Some looked at the word *necessary* and contended that the national government had only those powers *indispensable* to the exercise of its designated powers. To them, chartering a bank and contributing capital to it were not necessary, for example, to coin money and regulate its value. Nothing was specifically stated in the Constitution about the creation by the national government of a national bank.

Others disagreed. They believed that the word *necessary* could not be looked at in its strictest sense. If one were to interpret the necessary and proper clause literally, it would have no practical effect.

The other important question before the Court was the following: If the bank was constitutional, could a state tax it? In other words, was a state action that conflicted with a national government action invalid under the supremacy clause?

Marshall's Decision.   Three days after hearing the arguments in the case, Chief Justice John Marshall announced the decision of the Court. (It is said that Marshall made his decision in this case even before he heard the opposing arguments.) It is true, Marshall said, that Congress's power to establish a national bank was not expressed in the Constitution. He went on to say, however, that if establishing such a national bank aided the national government in the exercise of its designated powers, then the authority to set up such a bank could be implied. To Marshall, the necessary and proper clause embraced "all means which are appropriate" to carry out "the legitimate ends" of the Constitution. Only when such actions are forbidden by the letter and spirit of the Constitution are they thereby unconstitutional. There was nothing in the Constitution, according to Marshall, "which excludes incidental or implied powers; and which requires that everything granted shall be expressly and minutely described." It would be impossible to spell out every action that Congress might legitimately take—the Constitution "would be enormously long and could scarcely be embraced by the human mind."

In perhaps the single most famous sentence ever uttered by a Supreme Court justice, Marshall said, "[W]e must never forget it is a constitution we are expounding." In other words, the Constitution is a living instrument that has to be interpreted to meet the "practical" needs of government.

Having established this doctrine of implied powers, Marshall then answered the other important question before the Court and established the doctrine of national supremacy. Marshall stated that no state could use its taxing power to tax an arm of the national government. If it could, "the declaration that the Constitution . . . shall be the supreme law of the land, is empty and unmeaning declamation."

John Marshall (1755–1835) was the fourth chief justice of the Supreme court. When Marshall took over, the court had little power and almost no influence over the two other branches of government. Some scholars have declared that Marshall is the true architect of the American constitutional system, because he single-handedly gave new power to the Constitution. Early in his career, he was an attorney and was elected to the first of four terms in the Virginia Assembly. He was instrumental in the fight to ratify the Constitution in Virginia. Prior to being named to the Supreme Court, he won a seat in Congress in 1799 and in 1800 became secretary of state to John Adams.

Marshall's decision became the basis for strengthening the national government's power from that day on. The Marshall Court enabled the national government to grow and to meet problems that the Constitution's framers were unable to foresee. Today, practically every expressed power of the national government has been expanded in one way or another by use of the necessary and proper clause.

Gibbons v. Ogden (1824)

COMMERCE CLAUSE

The section of the Constitution in which Congress is given the power to regulate trade among the states and with foreign countries.

One of the more important parts of the Constitution included in Article I, Section 8, is the so-called **commerce clause,** in which Congress is given the power "[t]o regulate Commerce with foreign Nations, and among the several States, and with the Indian Tribes." What exactly does "to regulate commerce" mean? What does "commerce" entail? The issue here is essentially the same as that raised by *McCulloch v. Maryland:* How strict an interpretation should be given to a constitutional phrase?

The background to the case was as follows. Robert Fulton, inventor of the steamboat, and Robert Livingston, American minister to France, secured a monopoly of steam navigation on the waters in New York State from the New York legislature in 1803. They licensed Aaron Ogden to operate steam-powered ferryboats between New York and New Jersey. Thomas Gibbons, who had obtained a license from the U.S. government to operate boats in interstate waters, decided to compete with Ogden, but he did so without New York's permission. Ogden sued Gibbons. The New York state courts granted Ogden an **injunction,** prohibiting Gibbons from operating in New York waters. Gibbons appealed to the Supreme Court.

INJUNCTION

An order issued by a court to compel or restrain the performance of an act by an individual or government official.

The Issue before the Court.   There were actually several issues before the Court in this case. The first issue had to do with how the term *commerce* should be defined. New York's highest court had defined the term narrowly to mean only the shipment of goods, or the interchange of commodities, *not* navigation or the transport of people. The second issue was whether the national government's power to regulate interstate commerce extended to commerce within a state (*intra*state commerce) or was limited strictly to commerce among the states (*inter*state commerce). The third issue was whether the power to regulate interstate commerce was a concurrent power (as the New York court had concluded) or an exclusive national power.

Marshall's Decision.   As might be expected, because Marshall had interpreted the necessary and proper clause liberally in *McCulloch v. Maryland,* he used the same approach, five years later, in interpreting the commerce clause. Marshall defined *commerce* as *all* commercial intercourse—all business dealings—including navigation and the transport of people. He stated that to hold otherwise, as the New York court had by defining the term narrowly, would eventually "explain away the Constitution." Marshall also held that the commerce power of the national government could be exercised in state jurisdictions, even though it cannot reach *solely* intrastate commerce.

Finally, Marshall emphasized that the power to regulate interstate commerce was an *exclusive* national power. If the states were to regulate commerce with foreign nations or among the several states, they would exercise the very power granted to Congress. Furthermore, said Marshall, "This power, like all other vested in Congress, is complete in itself." In other words, the power of the national government to regulate commerce has no limitations, other than those specifically found in the Constitution. Based on this reasoning, Marshall held that because Gibbons was duly authorized by the national government to navigate in interstate waters, he could not be prohibited from doing so by a state court.

Marshall's expansive interpretation of the commerce clause in *Gibbons v. Ogden* allowed the national government to exercise increasing authority over all areas of economic affairs throughout the land. Congress did not immediately exploit this broad grant of power. In the 1930s and subsequent decades, however, the commerce clause became the primary constitutional basis for national government regulation—as you will read later in this chapter.

STATES' RIGHTS AND THE RESORT TO CIVIL WAR

We usually think of the Civil War simply as the fight to free the slaves. The facts are quite different. Freedom for the slaves was an important aspect of the Civil War, but not the only one—and certainly not the most important one, say many scholars. At the heart of the controversy that led to the Civil War was the issue of national government supremacy versus the rights of the separate states. Essentially, the Civil War brought to an ultimate and violent climax the ideological debate that had been outlined by the Federalist and Anti-Federalist parties even before the Constitution was ratified.

The Shift Back to States' Rights

As we have seen, while John Marshall was chief justice of the Supreme Court, he did much to increase the power of the national government and to reduce that of the states. During the Jacksonian era (1829–1837), however, a shift back to states' rights began. The question of the regulation of commerce became one of the major issues in federal-state relations. The business community preferred state regulation (or, better yet, no regulation) of commerce.

When Congress passed a tariff in 1828, the state of South Carolina attempted to nullify the tariff (render it void), claiming that in cases of con-

The Civil War was not fought over just the question of slavery. Rather, the supremacy of the national government was at issue. Had the South won, presumably any state or states would have the right to secede from the Union.

flict between a state and the national government, the state should have the ultimate authority over its citizens. The concept of **nullification** eventually was used by others to justify the **secession** of the southern states from the Union. (See this chapter's *Politics and Comparative Systems* for a discussion of separatist tendencies in Canada and Europe.)

NULLIFICATION

The act of nullifying, or rendering void. Prior to the Civil War, southern supporters of states' rights claimed that a state had the right to declare a national law to be null and void and therefore not binding on its citizens, on the assumption that ultimate sovereign authority rested with the several states.

SECESSION

The act of formally withdrawing from membership in an alliance; the withdrawal of a state from the federal union.

War and the Growth of the National Government

The ultimate defeat of the South permanently ended any idea that a state within the Union can successfully claim the right to secede. Ironically, the Civil War—brought about in large part because of the South's desire for increased states' rights—resulted in the opposite: an increase in the political power of the national government.

Thousands of new employees were hired to run the Union war effort and to deal with the social and economic problems that had to be handled in the aftermath of war. A billion-dollar ($1.3 billion, which is over $11 billion in today's dollars) national government budget was passed for the first time in 1865 to cover the increased government expenditures. The first (temporary) income tax was imposed on citizens to help pay for the war. Both the increased national government spending and the nationally imposed income tax were precursors to the expanded role of the national government in the American federal system.[9] Civil liberties were curtailed in the Union and in the Confederacy in the name of the wartime emergency. The distribution of pensions and widow's benefits also boosted the national government's social role. The North's victory set the nation on the path to a modern industrial economy and society.

THE CONTINUING DISPUTE OVER THE DIVISION OF POWER

Although the outcome of the Civil War firmly established the supremacy of the national government and put to rest the idea that a state could secede from the Union, the war by no means ended the debate over the division of powers between the national government and the states. The debate can be viewed as progressing through at least three stages since the Civil War: dual federalism, cooperative federalism, and the new federalism.

Dual Federalism

DUAL FEDERALISM

A system of government in which the states and the national government each remain supreme within their own spheres. The doctrine looks on nation and state as coequal sovereign powers. It holds that acts of states within their reserved powers could be legitimate limitations on the powers of the national government.

During the decades following the Civil War, the prevailing doctrine was that of **dual federalism**—a doctrine that emphasizes a distinction between federal and state spheres of government authority. Generally, the states exercised their police powers to regulate affairs within their borders, such as intrastate commerce, and the national government stayed out of purely local affairs. The courts tended to support the states' rights to exercise their police powers and concurrent powers in regard to the regulation of intrastate activities. For example, in 1918, the Supreme Court ruled that a 1916 federal law banning child labor was unconstitutional because it attempted to regulate a local prob-

---

[9]The future of the national government's powerful role was cemented with the passage of the Sixteenth Amendment (ratified in 1913), which authorized the federal income tax. Annual federal government outlays now exceed one-fifth of annual total national income.

POLITICS AND COMPARATIVE SYSTEMS
Separatist Movements in Canada and Europe

Residents of the Canadian province of Quebec, for the most part, share a common language (French) and culture. For years, they have sought greater autonomy from the central Canadian government. Time and again, however, the Quebec separatists have failed to garner the necessary votes in support of separating from Canada and dealing with other countries of the world as a sovereign nation. In a 1995 referendum, though, they almost succeeded—coming within only a few thousand votes of achieving their goal of independence.

Canada is not the only country currently facing a separatist surge. Many European countries have also been contending with nationalist groups that desire to achieve sovereign status. For example, the Sardinian Action party of Italy seeks to establish an independent Sardinia. Because they share similar aims, the Sardinian nationalists as well as other European separatist groups, such as the Basque National party in Spain and the Scottish Nationalist party, have been watching developments in Quebec closely. Generally, these and other European nationalist groups have been encouraged by the near success of the Quebec movement, concluding that it will force the Canadian government to undertake meaningful negotiations with Quebec over the issue. According to Mario Carboni, a leader of the Sardinian Action party, "Quebec's success shows that a pacifist, democratic movement for greater autonomy can work. We, too, are working for a referendum that would lead to a fundamental re-evaluation of the Italian state's relationship with Sardinia."*

For Critical Analysis
If Quebec eventually succeeds in achieving independence, will the federal system in Canada be strengthened or weakened?

*As quoted in Ian Mather and Alex Standish, "Europe Braced for Separatist Surge," *The European*, November 2–8, 1995, p. 1.

Two Canadian citizens display their loyalties in the separatist movement.

lem.[10] In the 1930s, however, the doctrine of dual federalism receded into the background as the nation attempted to deal with the Great Depression.

Cooperative Federalism

Franklin D. Roosevelt was inaugurated on March 4, 1933, as the thirty-second president of the United States. In the previous year, nearly 1,500 banks had failed (and 4,000 more would fail in 1933). Thirty-two thousand businesses closed down, and one-fourth of the labor force was unemployed. The national government had been expected to do something about the disastrous state of the economy. But for the first three years of the Great Depres-

---

[10]*Hammer v. Dagenhart,* 247 U.S. 251 (1918). This decision was overruled in *United States v. Darby,* 312 U.S. 100 (1940).

In the 1800s, very young children worked in coal mines. Today, child labor laws prohibit employers from hiring such young Americans. Some argue that even in the absence of child-labor laws, few, if any, children would still be working in the mines, because the United States is a much richer country that it was a hundred years ago. Presumably, today's parents, no longer at subsistence income levels, would opt to have their children go to school.

sion, the national government did very little. That changed with the new Democratic administration's energetic intervention in the economy. FDR's "New Deal" included numerous government spending and welfare programs, in addition to voluminous regulations relating to economic activity. The U.S. Supreme Court, still abiding by the legal doctrine of dual federalism, rejected as an unconstitutional interference in state powers virtually all of Roosevelt's attempt at national regulation of business. It was not until 1937 that the Court, responding to Roosevelt's Court-packing threat and worsening economic conditions (including the outbreak of violent labor disputes), ruled that manufacturing could be regulated as interstate commerce by the national government.[11]

Some political scientists have labeled the era since 1937 as an era characterized by **cooperative federalism,** in which the states and the national gov-

COOPERATIVE FEDERALISM

The theory that the states and the national government should cooperate in solving problems.

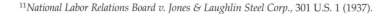

[11]*National Labor Relations Board v. Jones & Laughlin Steel Corp.,* 301 U.S. 1 (1937).

This housing development in Minnesota was one of the many projects sponsored by the New Deal's Works Progress Administration (WPA) in the 1930s. The federal government's efforts to alleviate unemployment (in this case, among construction workers) during the Great Depression signaled a shift from dual federalism to cooperative federalism.

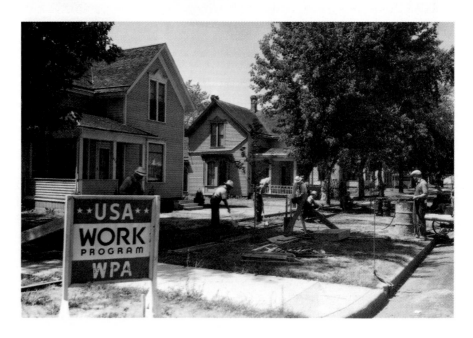

ernment cooperate in solving complex common problems. The New Deal programs of Franklin Roosevelt, for example, often involved joint action between the national government and the states. Federal grants (discussed later) were given to the states to help pay for public works projects, housing assistance, Aid to Families with Dependent Children, unemployment compensation, and other programs. The states, in turn, were required to implement the programs and pay for at least some of the costs involved. Others see the 1930s as the beginning of an era of national supremacy, in which the power of the states has been consistently diminished.

The Growth of National-Level Powers

Even if the Great Depression had not occurred, we probably still would have witnessed a growth of national-level powers as the country became increasingly populated, industrial, interdependent with other countries, and a world power. This meant that problems and situations that once were treated locally would begin to have a profound impact on Americans hundreds or even thousands of miles away.

For example, if one state is unable to maintain an adequate highway system, the economy of the entire region may suffer. If another state maintains a substandard educational system, the quality of the work force, the welfare rolls, and the criminal justice agencies in other states may be affected. Environmental pollution does not respect state borders, nor do poverty, crime, and violence. National defense, space exploration, and an increasingly global economy also call for national—not state—action. So the ascendancy of national supremacy had a very logical and very real set of causes. Our more mobile, industrial, and increasingly interdependent nation demanded more uniform and consistent sets of rules, regulations, and governmental programs.

Certainly, the 1960s and 1970s saw an even greater expansion of the national government's role in domestic policy. The "Great Society" program of Lyndon Johnson's administration (1963–1969) created the Job Corps, Operation Head Start, Volunteers in Service to America (VISTA), Medicaid, and Medicare. The Civil Rights Act of 1964 prohibited discrimination in public accommodations, employment, and other areas on the basis of race, color, national origin, religion, or gender. The economy was regulated further in the 1970s by national laws protecting consumers, employees, and the environment. Today, few activities are beyond the reach of the regulatory arm of the national government.

Federal Grants-in-Aid. As part of the system of cooperative federalism, the national government gives back to the states (and local governments) a significant amount of the tax dollars it collects—an estimated $255 billion a year in fiscal year 1997. Federal grants typically have taken the form of **categorical grants-in-aid,** which are grants to state and local governments designed for very specific programs or projects. For some of the categorical grant programs, the state and local governments must put up a share of the money, usually called **matching funds.** For other types of programs, the funds are awarded according to a formula that takes into account the relative wealth of the state, a process known as **equalization.**

Grants-in-aid in the form of land grants were given to the states even before the ratification of the Constitution. Cash grants-in-aid started in 1808, when Congress gave money to the states to pay for the state militias. It was not until the twentieth century, however, that the federal grants-in-aid program became significant. Grants-in-aid and the restrictions and regulations

President Johnson displays his signature on The War on Poverty Bill after he signed it into law in a ceremony in the rose garden at the White House August 20, 1964.

CATEGORICAL GRANTS-IN-AID

Federal grants-in-aid to states or local governments that are for very specific programs or projects.

MATCHING FUNDS

For many categorical grant programs, money with which the state must "match" the federal funds. Some programs only require the state to raise 10 percent of the funds, whereas others approach an even share.

EQUALIZATION

A method for adjusting the amount of money that a state must put up to receive federal funds. The formula used takes into account the wealth of the state or its ability to tax its citizens.

DID YOU KNOW...
That local governments, which can be created as well as abolished by their state, have no independent existence according to the Constitution, unlike the state and national governments?

that accompany them started to mushroom during Roosevelt's administration. The major growth began in the 1960s, however, when the dollar amount of grants-in-aid quadrupled to help pay for the Great Society programs of the Johnson administration. Grants became available in numerous areas, including the fields of education, pollution control, conservation, recreation, and highway construction and maintenance.

Nowhere can the shift toward a greater role for the central government in the United States be seen better than in the shift toward increased central government spending as a percentage of total government spending. Figure 3–3 shows that in 1929, on the eve of the Great Depression, local governments accounted for 60 percent of all government outlays, whereas the federal government accounted for only 17 percent. After Roosevelt's New Deal had been in place for several years during the Great Depression, local governments gave up half their share of the government spending pie, dropping to 30 percent, and the federal government increased its share to 47 percent. Estimates are that in 1997, the federal government accounts for about 66 percent of all government spending.

Expanding the Commerce Power of the National Government. The full effect of Chief Justice John Marshall's broad interpretation of the commerce clause has only been realized in the twentieth century. In particular, the commerce clause has been used to justify national regulation of virtually any activity, even what would appear to be a purely local activity. For example, in 1942, the Supreme Court held that wheat production by an individual farmer intended wholly for consumption on his own farm was subject to federal regulation—because the home consumption of wheat reduced the demand for wheat and thus could have a substantial effect on interstate commerce.[12]

The commerce clause has also been used to validate congressional legislation even in what would seem to be social and moral matters—concerns traditionally regulated by the states. For example, in 1964 a small hotel in Georgia challenged the constitutionality of the Civil Rights Act of that year, claiming that Congress has exceeded its authority under the commerce clause

---

[12]*Wickard v. Filburn,* 317 U.S. 111 (1942).

Figure 3–3
• •
The Shift toward Central Government Spending

Before the Great Depression, local governments accounted for 60 percent of all government spending, with the federal government accounting for only 17 percent. By 1960, federal government spending was up to 64 percent, local governments accounted for only 19 percent, and the remainder was spent by state governments. The estimate for 1997 is that the federal government accounts for 66 percent and local governments for 15.5 percent.

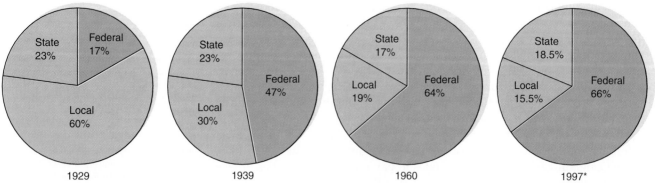

*Estimated
SOURCE: U.S. Department of Commerce, Bureau of the Census, *Government Finances* (Washington, D.C.: U.S. Government Printing Office, 1996).

by regulating local, intrastate affairs. The Supreme Court held that the 1964 act was constitutional, concluding that "[i]f it is interstate commerce that feels the pinch, it does not matter how local the operation that applies the squeeze."[13] By 1980, the Supreme Court acknowledged that the commerce clause had "long been interpreted to extend beyond activities actually in interstate commerce to reach other activities, while wholly local in nature, which nevertheless substantially affect interstate commerce."[14] (See this chapter's *Politics and the Environment* for a discussion of how the commerce power of the national government affects states' attempt to regulate the disposal of hazardous waste.)

The Supremacy Clause and Federal Preemption. The supremacy clause also plays a significant role in respect to constitutional justification for the growth of national-level powers. Recall from earlier in this chapter that the states and the national government share certain regulatory powers, called concurrent powers. Under the supremacy clause, however, national government legislation in a concurrent area *preempts* (takes precedence over) any conflicting state and local law or rule in that area. Figure 3–4 presents in graphic form the growth in the number of federal laws that have preempted state laws since 1900. As you can see, this number grew dramatically during the Johnson administration in the 1960s—and has not declined significantly since then.

---

[13]*Heart of Atlanta Motel v. United States,* 379 U.S. 241 (1964).
[14]*McLain v. Real Estate Board of New Orleans, Inc.,* 444 U.S. 232 (1980).

Figure 3–4

● ●

Federal Laws That Preempt State Laws

This graph shows the number of federal laws that preempt state authority. As you can see, the greatest growth in federal preemption is in laws regulating the environmental, health, or safety areas. Laws affecting commerce, energy, labor, and transportation run a close second.

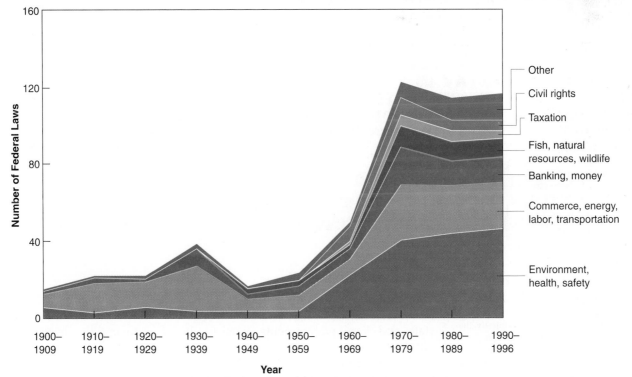

SOURCE: U.S. Advisory Commission on Intergovernmental Relations, plus authors' estimates.

POLITICS AND THE ENVIRONMENT
The Commerce Clause and Hazardous Waste Disposal

In the United States, more than 240 million tons of hazardous waste are generated annually by nearly 80,000 different sources. Under federal law, the waste can be disposed of only at licensed facilities. Nearly 4,700 facilities are licensed, but these facilities are located in only sixteen states. Thus, large quantities of hazardous waste move in interstate commerce every day. States, however, have found it difficult to control the amount of hazardous waste being transported into their states for disposal at intrastate waste disposal sites. Why? The answer is that states, although they can regulate commerce within their borders, do not have the power to regulate interstate commerce.*

Consider just one example. One of this country's largest licensed facilities for hazardous waste disposal is located in Emelle, Alabama. The site receives waste from sources in Alabama and from sources outside the state. The state of Alabama became concerned about the volume of waste entering the facility and its effect on the environment and on the public's health and safety. In an attempt to curb the amount of waste disposed of at the site, Alabama imposed a fee on all waste received at the facility. To discourage sources outside the state from using the facility, Alabama imposed a higher fee on waste that was generated outside the state.

The firm operating the waste disposal facility sued the state, seeking an injunction against enforcement of the higher fee. At issue was whether Alabama's different treatment of out-of-state waste violated the commerce clause. Ultimately, the United States Supreme Court held that it did—Alabama had discriminated against interstate commerce in violation of the commerce clause.[†] The court based its ruling on the well-established principle that no state should be allowed to isolate itself from a problem common to all of the states. There are those who believe, however, that environmental concerns are sufficiently pressing that the Court should allow the states (Alabama, in this case) to exercise control over hazardous waste disposal.

For Critical Analysis
How else, other than by imposing higher fees on out-of-state waste, can states regulate the disposal of out-of-state waste within their borders?

*This principle was set forth in *Gibbons v. Ogden*, as discussed earlier in this chapter.

†*Chemical Waste Management, Inc. v. Hunt*, 504 U.S. 334 (1992). For a similar ruling on this issue, see *Oregon Waste Systems, Inc. v. Department of Environmental Quality of the State of Oregon*, 114 S.Ct. 1345 (1994).

A sign cautions people at a hazardous waste area in Times Beach, Missouri.

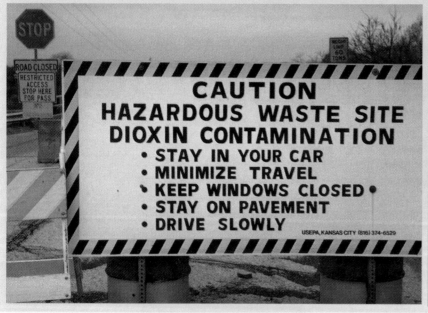

NEW FEDERALISM

A plan to limit the national government's power to regulate, as well as to restore power to state governments. Essentially, the new federalism is designed to give the states greater ability to decide for themselves how government revenues should be spent.

The New Federalism

The third phase of federalism was labeled by President Richard Nixon (1969–1974) as the **new federalism.** Its goal is to restore more power to the state and local governments, particularly by reducing the restrictions attached to federal grants.

No state or local official likes all of the strings attached to myriad grants-in-aid because these strings essentially allow the national government to legislate state behavior. If a state does not comply with a particular requirement, the national government may withhold federal funds for other programs. A classic example of the power of the federal government to sanction the states for lack of compliance occurred during the administration of Ronald Reagan (1981–1989). Reagan threatened to withhold federal highway funds unless the states raised the minimum drinking age to twenty-one years. As part of the new federalism, governors and mayors succeeded in convincing Washington that fewer restrictions should be placed on federal grants to the states.

Under Nixon's program of *revenue sharing,* money was given directly to states and localities without any strings attached—that is, the national government returned to state and local governments a certain portion of federal taxes. This program, which lasted through 1986, allowed local officials to make the decisions about how the money was to be spent. The problem with the revenue-sharing process was that it generated specific constituencies among governments, but not among voters. Consequently, there were no well-organized groups of people lobbying Congress to increase revenue sharing. So, when the federal government budget continued to be in the red during the 1980s, it was relatively easy for the members of Congress to let the program die.

President Ronald Reagan went further in the direction begun by Nixon. Reagan's administration even took steps to privatize various federal programs, including some programs relating to low-cost housing, prisons, and hospitals. Analysis shows, however, that the new federalism was—and perhaps continues to be—more talk than action. Although many agree with the underlying goal of the new federalism, in reality, there are a number of political obstacles to making the new federalism a reality. (See this chapter's *Critical Perspective* for a proposed alternative to the new federalism.)

The Politics of Block Grants.   The difficulties of building a new federalism are apparent in the politics of the block grant, one of the major tools of the new federalism. **Block grants** place fewer restrictions on grants-in-aid given to state and local governments by grouping a number of categorical grants

BLOCK GRANTS

Federal programs that provide funding to the state and local governments for general functional areas, such as criminal justice or mental-health programs.

CRITICAL PERSPECTIVE
Competitive Federalism

The most common view of federalism focuses on nation-state relationships—that is, the allocation of power between our federal government based in Washington, D.C., and the fifty state governments. In this sense, most discussions of federalism center around intergovernmental relations. Are the state governments cooperating with the national government in order to carry out our national policies? Under this common notion of federalism, state and local governments become viewed as administrative units of the national government, put there to carry out more efficiently the management of federal programs.

Political scientist Thomas R. Dye, of Florida State University, argues that federalism should be viewed *not* as how the national and state governments cooperate but as how competition—the creation of "opposite and rival" interests among governments—benefits the nation. He refers specifically to competition among the states and, in this sense, wants us to think of competitive federalism rather than any other type.*

Competition among the States and Its Benefits

Dye argues that constitutional limits on governmental power do not enforce themselves. Rather, it is only through the encouragement of competition within and among governments that those who work in government will be provided with personal motives to enforce the constitutional limitations on governmental power. Dye sees competitive federalism as a marketplace across states, with state governments vying for more "customers." He sees the same competition across municipalities, each attempting to attract more citizens. When viewed in this light, Dye argues that federalism does the following:

● Facilitates party competition, because state and local governments provide a political base of offices for the opposition party when it has lost national elections.

● Stimulates political participation because of the over eight-five thousand separate governments in the United States that must be staffed. The existence of so many opportunities for direct citizen involvement in government contributes to a sense of political effectiveness.

● Assists in managing conflict, because federalism allows for diverse peoples to be brought together in a single nation.

● Guards against an oversupply of government-provided goods and services, because competing jurisdictions will attempt to eliminate undesired government goods and services to reduce taxes. All voters don't necessarily have to be able to "vote with their feet" (move to another state) to create this incentive. Comparative information about tax rates and levels of government services is all that is necessary.

● Inspires policy responsiveness as different jurisdictions test different levels of public spending per capita.

● Places revenue constraints on policymakers, because citizen-voters can "vote with their feet" if their tax burdens become too high.

under one broad purpose. Governors and mayors generally prefer block grants because they give the states more flexibility in how the money is spent.

Out of the numerous block grants that were proposed from 1966 until the election of Ronald Reagan in 1980, only five were actually legislated. At the Reagan administration's urging, Congress increased the number to nine. By the beginning of the 1990s, such block grants accounted for slightly over 10 percent of all federal aid programs. With the Republican sweep of Congress in the 1994 elections, block grants again became the focus of attention. Republicans proposed reforming welfare and a number of other federal programs by transforming the categorical grants-in-aid to block grants and transferring more of the policymaking authority to the states. Congress succeeded, in part, in achieving these goals when it enacted the welfare reform bill of 1996 (discussed in Chapter 16).

The problem with block grants is that they are based on problematic assumptions. One such assumption is that state governments will not respond to pressure by interest groups to use federal funds in a way that is

POLITICS AND THE FIFTY STATES
Medicaid Expenditures

Medicaid, the federally mandated program to pay health-care costs for the poor, varies across the nation, depending on the number of poor people in each state's population and the health-care legislation and overall level of health care in each state. The table below shows the ten states having the highest and lowest Medicaid expenditures. As you can see, New York's expenditures far exceed those of the other states.

For Critical Analysis

Should the federal government provide national health coverage for the poor when it does not do so for other income groups?

TEN STATES WITH THE HIGHEST MEDICAID EXPENDITURES		TEN STATES WITH THE LOWEST MEDICAID EXPENDITURES	
New York	$15,281	Wyoming	$114
California	$ 8,692	Alaska	$187
Texas	$ 4,407	Arizona	$209
Pennsylvania	$ 4,213	Montana	$217
Illinois	$ 4,070	Delaware	$219
Ohio	$ 3,653	Vermont	$222
Florida	$ 3,518	South Dakota	$231
Massachusetts	$ 3,248	North Dakota	$253
New Jersey	$ 2,802	Hawaii	$270
Michigan	$ 2,802	Idaho	$275

SOURCE: U.S. Health Care Financing Administration. Data are in millions of dollars.

physical disabilities to public buildings, sidewalks, and other areas. As mentioned earlier, under the supremacy clause of the Constitution, federal laws preempt conflicting state and local laws.

No accurate analysis exists of the overall costs state and local governments have incurred as a result of federal mandates. Certain mandates, however, clearly are very costly. For example, one mandate involves eligibility for Medicaid. Medicaid is the federally subsidized, state-run health-care program for low-income Americans. The estimated cost of the programs for the states is over $70 billion in 1997. The cost of the Medicaid program for each of the selected states is detailed in this chapter's *Politics and the Fifty States.*

Table 3–2 shows the projected cost to the states of other federal mandates through 1998. Although Congress passed legislation in 1996 to curb

Table 3–2

The Projected Cost of Federal Mandates to the States through 1998

MANDATE	FISCAL YEARS 1994–1998 PROJECTED TOTAL COSTS (IN BILLIONS OF DOLLARS)
Underground storage tank regulations	1.041
Clean Water Act/wetlands	29.303
Clean Air Act	3.652
Solid waste disposal	5.476
Safe Drinking Water Act	8.644
Asbestos removal	.747
Lead-based paint	1.628
Endangered species	.189
Americans with Disabilities Act	2.196
Fair Labor Standards Act*	1.122
TOTAL	53.998

*Exempt employee & other costs.
SOURCE: National Association of Towns and Townships.

Thinking Politically about Federal Mandates

A central question in the political debate over federalism today concerns unfunded federal mandates—mandates in federal legislation calling for actions that the states must pay for. One of the major "planks" in the Republican platform of 1994 was a promise to end unfunded mandates to state and local governments. By March 1995, the Republican-controlled 104th Congress had indeed succeeded in passing a bill to regulate the use of such federal mandates. On close analysis, however, the 1995 legislation was mostly symbolic; it accomplished little actual change in the use of unfunded federal mandates. Why is this? A closer look at the politics of unfunded federal mandates provides the answer.

Imagine for a moment that you are a member of Congress from, say, Oregon. Your constituents have made it clear that they expect you to vote for a bill protecting endangered species,

such as the spotted owl, in the Oregon forests. If you fail to follow your constituents' wishes in this respect, your "job" as their representative may end. The result is that even if you support the idea of eliminating unfunded federal mandates in theory, the reality you face may force you to reach a compromise: on the one hand, you vote for a bill ending unfunded federal mandates; on the other, you agree to include in the bill certain conditions that render the bill largely ineffective.

The 1995 bill passed by Congress did just this. The bill requires the Congressional Budget Office (CBO) to prepare cost estimates for any new mandate that will impose more than $50 million in costs on state and local governments or more than $100 million on the private sector. On the basis of CBO estimates, a member of Congress may make a point of order challenging the mandate. The bill also provides, however, that a congressional point of

order can be overridden by a simple majority vote—rather than the larger majority (such as three-fifths) proposed by several legislators.

Furthermore, although the Republicans had sought to repeal previously legislated mandates dealing with such matters as civil rights and discrimination, the compromise bill that President Clinton signed exempts these matters. The act also exempts legislation concerning such issues as constitutional rights, voting rights, and national security. In short, the act exempts the matters that account for many of the most costly unfunded mandates imposed on state and local governments during the last decade.

For Critical Analysis

How can members of Congress surmount the political obstacles they face in trying to end unfunded federal mandates?

unfunded federal mandates, the legislation was essentially more rhetoric than reality (see the feature entitled *Thinking Politically about Federal Mandates* for a further discussion of this issue).

The Federal Courts and the New Federalism. Many supporters of the new federalism argue that the national government has exceeded the regulatory powers granted to it by the Constitution. In fact, one of the rallying cries of the new federalism has been that the national government has gone too far in the direction of exercising powers reserved to the states under the Tenth Amendment to the Constitution. To a limited extent, the federal courts have agreed with this contention.

In 1992, for example, the United States Supreme Court held that requirements imposed on the state of New York under federal law regulating low-level radioactive waste were inconsistent with the Tenth Amendment and thus unconstitutional. According to the Court, the act's "take title" provision, which required states to accept ownership of waste or regulate waste according to Congress's instructions, exceeded the enumerated powers of Congress. Although Congress can regulate the handling of such waste, "it may not conscript state governments as its agents" in an attempt to enforce a program of federal regulation.[15]

---

[15]*New York v. United States,* 505 U.S. 144 (1992).

Changes in Federalism

One way to understand how our perception of federalism has changed over time is to compare today's federalism with the "New Deal" federalism initiated by Franklin Roosevelt in the 1930s. We list here a few of the significant conditions and attitudes of each era.

THEN	NOW
• The states were unable to meet needs.	• The national government is unable to meet needs.
• National government growing.	• State and local governments growing.
• Introduction of grants-in-aid.	• Move to block grants.
• Government has the solutions.	• Solutions may be impossible.
• Positive attitude toward national government regulation.	• National government regulation viewed by many as a problem.
• Sharp partisan differences.	• Partisan differences blurred.
• Economic centralization.	• Economic decentralization.
• States varied in regulation of business.	• Most regulation of business is by the national government.

In a widely publicized 1995 case, *United States v. Lopez*,[16] the Supreme Court held that Congress had exceeded its constitutional authority under the commerce clause when it passed the Gun-Free School Zones Act in 1990. The Court stated that the act, which banned the possession of guns within one thousand feet of any school, was unconstitutional because it attempted to regulate an area that had "nothing to do with commerce, or any sort of economic enterprise." This marked the first time in sixty years that the Supreme Court had placed a limit on the national government's authority under the commerce clause.

Some argue that these and a few other cases curbing national government authority[17] indicate that the federal courts are reversing their position in regard to the constitutional powers of the national government. Others contend that it would be foolish to draw such a conclusion. It is notable that, just a few days after the *Lopez* case was decided, the Supreme Court again declared that what appeared (to many) to be fundamentally local activities sufficiently affected interstate commerce to be subject to federal legislation.[18]

FEDERALISM: UNFINISHED WORK

According to some political observers, the remainder of the 1990s will see an increasing conflict between Washington, D.C., and state and local govern-

---

[16]115 S.Ct. 1624 (1995).

[17]See, for example, *Seminole Tribe of Florida v. Florida,* 116 S.Ct. 1114 (1996).

[18]*United States v. Robertson,* 115 S.Ct. 1732 (1995).

DID YOU KNOW . . .
That the city of Columbus, Ohio, estimates that its cost of meeting federal environmental mandates will increase to 23 percent of the city's budget by the year 2000 and that part of this cost goes for testing city drinking water for 52 different pesticides—including those used only on pineapples and rice, neither of which is grown in Ohio?

ments. Relations between the national government and the states are often acrimonious, and there is even a growing acrimony between local governments and their state capitals. The issue concerns state mandates that require local governments to undertake certain actions, such as spending a specified amount on certain types of welfare recipients.

There is no question that the relations between the various governments in the United States—federal, state, and local—have become strained. The new federalism envisioned by Nixon and developed by subsequent political administrations—the shift of power back to the states—is considered by many to be at least a partial solution to federal-state disputes. The new federalism, however, has yet to become a reality. Its future success depends on whether certain political obstacles can be overcome. Cooperative federalism resulted in the growth of a national bureaucracy that became firmly entrenched and that seeks to perpetuate itself (see Chapter 14). The senators and representatives in Congress must heed the wishes of their constituents if they are to retain their positions. They must also heed the wishes of various interest groups (see Chapter 8). Even those groups who vote Republican may pressure Congress to pass national regulatory legislation if such regulation is in the groups' political interest.

The success of the new federalism also depends on the voting public. Essentially, the question before the voters has to do with which government—federal, state, or local—can best be entrusted with control over certain areas, such as environmental pollution, aid for the poor and disadvantaged, and other areas that have been regulated for decades by the national government. There are no easy answers to this question.

GETTING INVOLVED
Writing Letters to the Editor

Just about every day an issue concerning federalism is discussed in the media. Advocates of decentralization—a shift of power from federal to state or local governments—argue that we must recognize the rights of states to design their own destinies and master their own fates. Advocates of centralization—more power to the national government—see the shift in power under decentralization as undermining the national purpose, common interests, and responsibilities that bind us together in pursuit of national goals.

The big question is how much the national government should do for the people. Is it within the power of the national government to decide what the law should be on abortion? Before 1973, each state set its own laws without interference from the national government. Who should be responsible for the homeless? Should the national government subsidize state and local efforts to help them?

You may have valid, important points to make on these or other issues. One of the best ways to make your point is by writing an effective letter to the editor of your local newspaper (or even to a national newspaper such as the *New York Times*). First, you should familiarize yourself with the kinds of letters that are accepted by the newspapers to which you want to write. Then, follow these rules for writing an effective letter:

1. Use a computer, and double-space the lines. If possible, use a spelling checker and grammar checker.

2. Your lead topic sentence should be short, to the point, and powerful.

3. Keep your thoughts on target—choose only one topic to discuss in your letter. Make sure it is newsworthy and timely.

4. Make sure your letters are concise; never let your letter exceed a page and a half in length (double-spaced).

5. If you know that facts were misstated or left out in current news stories about your topic, supply the facts. The public wants to know.

6. Don't be afraid to express moral judgments. You can go a long way by appealing to the readers' sense of justice.

7. Personalize the letter by bringing in your own experiences.

8. Sign your letter, and give your address (including your e-mail address, if you have one) and your telephone number.

9. Send your letter to the editorial office of the newspaper or magazine of your choice. Many publications now have e-mail addresses and home pages on the World Wide Web. The Web sites often give information on where you can send mail. Use these addresses, because more and more editors are "wired."

10. With appropriate changes, you can send your letter to other newspapers and magazines as well. Make sure, however, that the letters are not exactly the same. If your letter is not published, try again. Eventually, one will be.

KEY TERMS

block grant 89

categorical grant-in-aid 85

commerce clause 80

concurrent powers 75

confederal system 70

cooperative federalism 84

dual federalism 82

elastic clause 74

enumerated powers 74

equalization 85

extradite 77

federal mandate 92

federal system 70

full faith and credit clause 77

horizontal federalism 77

injunction 80

interstate compact 78

matching funds 85

necessary and proper clause 74

new federalism 88

nullification 82

police power 75

privileges and immunities 77

secession 82

supremacy clause 76

unitary system 70

CHAPTER SUMMARY

1 There are three basic models for ordering relations between central governments and local units: (a) a unitary system (in which ultimate power is held by national government), (b) a confederal system (in which ultimate power is retained by the states), and (c) a federal system (in which governmental powers are divided between the national government and the states). A major reason for the creation of a federal system in the United States is that it reflected a compromise between the views of the Federalists (who wanted a strong national government) and those of the Anti-Federalists (who wanted the states to retain their sovereignty), thus making ratification of the Constitution possible.

2 The Constitution expressly delegated certain powers to the national government in Article I, Section 8. In addition to these expressed powers, the national government has implied and inherent powers. Implied powers are those that are reasonably necessary to carry out the powers expressly delegated to the national government. Inherent powers are those held by the national government by virtue of its being a sovereign state with the right to preserve itself.

3 The Tenth Amendment to the Constitution states that powers not delegated to the United States by the Constitution, nor prohibited by it to the states, are reserved to the states, or to the people. In certain areas, the Constitution provides for concurrent powers, which are powers that are held jointly by the national and state governments. The classic example of a concurrent power is the power to tax.

4 The supremacy clause of the Constitution states that the Constitution, congressional laws, and national treaties are the supreme law of the land. States cannot use their reserved or concurrent powers to override national policies.

5 The three most important clauses in the Constitution relating to horizontal federalism require that (a) each state give full faith and credit to every other state's public acts, records, and judicial proceedings; (b) each state extend to every other state's citizens the privileges and immunities of its own citizens; and (c) each state agree to return persons who are fleeing from justice to another state back to their home state when requested to do so.

6 Two landmark Supreme Court cases expanded the constitutional powers of the national government. Chief Justice John Marshall's expansive interpretation of the "necessary and proper" clause of the Constitution in *McCulloch v. Maryland* (1819) enhanced the implied power of the national government. Marshall's broad interpretation of the commerce clause in *Gibbons v. Ogden* (1824) further extended the constitutional regulatory powers of the national government.

7 At the heart of the controversy that led to the Civil War was the issue of national government supremacy versus the rights of the separate states. The notion of nullification eventually led to the secession of the Confederate states from the Union. But the effect of the South's desire for increased states' rights and the subsequent Civil War was an increase in the political power of the national government.

8 Since the Civil War, federalism has evolved through at least three phases: dual federalism, cooperative federalism, and the new federalism. In dual federalism, each of the states and the federal government remain supreme within their own spheres. The era since the Great Depression has sometimes been labeled as one of cooperative federalism, in which states and the national government cooperate in solving complex common problems. Others view it as the beginning of an era of national supremacy, because from the era of Franklin Roosevelt to the present, the national government continually has expanded its regulatory powers and activities.

9 The goal of the *new federalism,* so labeled by President Nixon, is to decentralize federal programs and return more decision-making authority to the states. Revenue sharing—giving money to the states with no strings attached—was one solution to the states' dissatisfaction with the many strings attached to federal grants-in-aid. The block grant, which groups various categorical grants together, has been utilized as another way to give more authority to the states in respect to the use of federal funds. Curbing unfunded federal mandates is seen as yet another step on the road to a new federalism. The new federalism may take some time to build because of the numerous political obstacles to its implementation.

QUESTIONS FOR REVIEW AND DISCUSSION

1 The Advisory Commission on Inter-governmental Relations (ACIR) has, among other things, recommended that Congress and the states consider a constitutional amendment that would give two-thirds of the states the power to declare null and void an act of Congress. If such an amendment were passed, what might be some of the results?

2 At the time of the framing of the Constitution, state

governments existed as sovereign political units. All but Rhode Island sent delegates to the Constitutional Convention. Does this mean that the state governments formally helped to create the Constitution? The Constitution was ratified through ratification conventions composed of citizens of each state. Does this therefore mean that the approval of the Constitution was made by, and rests with, the people?

3 "The federal government, because it is more efficient, can collect taxes more easily than can the combination of all fifty state governments. Therefore, the federal government should do so and remit taxes to the states in the form of revenue sharing." Do you agree with this statement? Why or why not?

4 How would our system of government differ if there were no division of powers between the national government and the states?

5 As the western states joined the Union, they agreed that they would give up forever any claims to unappropriated public lands within their borders. Now, however, many westerners claim that having to forfeit these public lands on entry into the Union was an invalid action. In part, they base their argument on the fact that the thirteen original states did not have to forfeit control over public lands as a condition of joining the Union. Do you agree with the westerners' argument? Why has control over public lands become such a burning issue in the West only recently?

LOGGING ON: FEDERALISM

Go To: http://www.public.iastate.edu/~sws/homepage.html

The Web has many and varied sites related to federalism. The following are excellent places to start your search.
Use the **Alta Vista** search engine at

http://altavista.digital.com

Type *federalism* in the Web search, and you will get over five thousand hits with many interesting sites on the topic.
One of the most interesting we found is the States' Federalism Summit site at

http://www.csg.org/federalism.html

The States' Federalism Summit—composed of the executive committees of the Council of State Governments, the National Conference of State Legislatures, the National Governors' Association, the American Legislative Exchange Council, and the State Legislative Leaders Foundation—believes that further action is necessary to restore a proper and healthy balance to the nation's federal system.
Another good location is the Brookings Institution at

http://www.brook.edu/

The Brookings Institution is the nation's oldest think tank. A private, independent, nonprofit research organization, the institution seeks to improve the performance of American institutions, the effectiveness of government programs, and the quality of U.S. public policies. It addresses current and emerging policy challenges and offers practical recommendations for dealing with them, expressed in language that is accessible to policymakers and the general public alike.
If you prefer a more libertarian approach to government and issues such as federalism, the Cato Institute—which says that it is "promoting public policy based on limited government, free markets, individual liberty, and peace"—has a Web page at

http://www.cato.org/

Do you want to read the original *Federalist Papers?* Go to

gopher://spinaltap.micro.umn.edu:70/11/Ebooks/By%20Title/Fedpap

The ELECTRONIC POLICY NETWORK—"providing you with timely information and leading ideas about national policy and politics"—has an interesting Web site with links to dozens of hot links on public policy and federalism at

http://epn.org/

SELECTED REFERENCES

Beer, Samuel H. *To Make a Nation: The Rediscovery of American Federalism.* Cambridge, Mass.: Harvard University Press, 1993. This study of the purpose of American federalism begins with European political thought. The author discusses the originality of American federalism in both theory and practice. He contrasts the nation-centered federalism of the Constitution's framers and the state-centered federalism of their opponents.

Bensel, Richard F. *Yankee Leviathan: The Origins of Central State Authority.* New York: Cambridge University Press, 1990. In this analysis of state formation, Bensel looks closely at the changes in political structure caused by the Civil War.

Fix, Michael, and Daphne A. Kenyon, eds. *Coping with Mandates: What Are the Alternatives?* Lanham, Md.: University Press of America, 1990. This excellent examination of the mandates issue focuses on the history of mandates and their relationship to policy goals, the burden that mandates place on state and local governments, and the potential of alternative approaches to the mandates issue.

Hamilton, Alexander, John Jay, and James Madison. *The Federalist: A Collection of Essays Written in Favor of the New Constitution.* Edited by George W. Carey and James McClellan. Dubuque, Ia.: Kendall/Hunt, 1990. This student-oriented edition makes these classic essays accessible to this generation and includes an introduction, analytical notes, a glossary, and an index.

Lehmann, Scott. *Privatizing Public Lands.* New York: Oxford University Press, 1995. The author reviews the history of publicly owned lands in the United States and argues for the continued federal ownership of all lands that are currently owned by the federal government.

Ottosen, Garry K. *Making American Government Work: A Proposal to Reinvigorate Federalism.* Lanham, Md.: University Press of America, 1992. The author contends that the divided responsibilities and fragmented power between the states and the national government have made American government unworkable. He believes that the solution to this problem is to reinvigorate federalism. He examines the critical issue of competition between and among the states.

Peterson, Paul E. *The Price of Federalism.* Washington, D.C.: Brookings Institution, 1995. The author looks at theories of federalism, arguing that how we divide power among governments is a central question in self-government. He states that the United States seems to have arrived at a rational division of labor among the various levels of government and suggests that certain functions (such as building roadways) are best performed at the state and local level whereas other functions (such as Social Security) are best handled at the federal level.

Pickvance, C. G., and E. Preteceille. *State and Locality: A Comparative Perspective on State Restructuring.* Irvington, N.Y.: Columbia University Press, 1991. The authors offer an insightful comparative study of the relationship between central and local governments in several nations, including the United States.

Rich, Michael J. *Federal Policymaking and the Poor: National Goods, Local Choices, and Distributional Outcomes.* Princeton, N.J.: Princeton University Press, 1993. This is a study of the impact of federal programs designed to help needy people. There is an extensive analysis of the Community Development Block Grant Program, the principal federal program for aiding cities. The author points out that the redistributive power of federal programs depends on choices made by local government officials.

Riker, William H. *Federalism.* Boston: Little, Brown, 1964. This classic discussion of federalism offers a highly critical account of the American version of this form of government.

Walker, David B. *The Rebirth of Federalism: Slouching toward Washington.* Chatham, N.J.: Chatham House, 1995. This history of American federalism offers an excellent analysis of federalism's current "feeble" condition. The book links the failure of true federalism to the decline of trust in the national government during the 1990s.

Zimmerman, Joseph F. *State-Local Relations: A Partnership Approach.* 2d ed. Westport, Conn.: Praeger, 1995. The author has revised and updated his classic study of state-local relations. Zimmerman examines numerous aspects of the relations between state and local governments, including the legal and constitutional basis for state government authority, the control by state governments over local governing units and how that control has changed over time, and the state-local partnership in terms of fiscal relations.

PART TWO
Civil Rights
and Liberties

4
Civil Liberties

CHAPTER OUTLINE

Citizens' Militias Were Banned?

BACKGROUND

CITIZENS' MILITIAS ARE PRIVATE, LOOSELY ORGANIZED PARAMILITARY GROUPS. THEY ARE THE MILITANT, EXTREMIST EDGE OF A LARGER GROUP OF AMERICANS WHO CALL THEMSELVES "PATRIOTS." MILITIA MEMBERS AND OTHER PATRIOTS ARE DRAWN TOGETHER BY A COMMON FEAR OF BIG GOVERNMENT, WHICH THEY BELIEVE, HAS SIMPLY GOTTEN TOO BIG AND TOO POWERFUL—AND TOO INDIFFERENT TO INDIVIDUALS' (AND STATES') RIGHTS. THEY WANT LESS FEDERAL GOVERNMENT REGULATION AND MORE LOCAL CONTROL OVER THEIR LIVES. ALTHOUGH IT IS ESTIMATED THAT ONLY ABOUT TEN THOUSAND AMERICANS ARE ACTIVELY INVOLVED IN MILITIAS, THOSE WHO IDENTIFY WITH THE BROADER PATRIOT MOVEMENT MAY NUMBER IN THE HUNDREDS OF THOUSANDS.

THOSE JOINING MILITIAS ARE PREDOMINANTLY WHITE MEN AND WOMEN WHO ENJOY USING HIGH-POWERED WEAPONS AND PARTICIPATING IN SEMIMILITARY MANEUVERS. THEY MAY BE FUNDAMENTALIST CHRISTIANS OR NEO-NAZIS, OR THEY MAY FAVOR LOCAL CONTROL OF PUBLIC LANDS. THEIR PRIMARY ALLEGIANCE IS TO THE CONSTITUTION, AS THEY INTERPRET THAT DOCUMENT, AND THEY ARE PARTICULARLY DEDICATED TO THE RIGHT TO BEAR ARMS. A MAJOR CATALYST OF THE MILITIA MOVEMENT HAS BEEN FEDERAL GUN-CONTROL LEGISLATION. SOME AMERICANS FEEL THAT THESE MILITIAS REPRESENT A SERIOUS THREAT TO CIVIL ORDER AND SHOULD BE BANNED.

WHAT IF CITIZENS' MILITIAS WERE BANNED?

Clearly, a ban on citizens' militias would divide Americans into two camps. Supporters of the ban would argue that no government should permit armed individuals to join together in subversive groups. They also would stress the violent potential of these extremist factions and the threat they pose to society. As examples of this threat, they would point to such terrorist acts as the 1995 bombing of the Federal Building in Oklahoma City, which killed 160 persons, and various incidents of violence in the West over land-control issues.

Militia members would, of course, oppose the ban. Militia leaders and their followers would claim that the government's ban is proof in itself that their fears of the national government are well founded. Extremists might use the ban as part of a propaganda campaign to recruit more moderate militia members and other patriots into an underground, armed movement against the federal government. The end result might be that Americans would witness even more terrorism and more violence. Opponents of the ban would include not only militia members and patriots but, very likely, also a large number of Americans who would be concerned about the implications of the ban for our constitutional rights.

CONSTITUTIONAL ISSUES

A major constitutional issue would be the militia members' rights under the First Amendment to the Constitution—their freedoms of speech, expression, and assembly. Another issue would center on the right to bear arms, which is guaranteed by the Second Amendment. How should this amendment be interpreted? Do all individuals have a right to bear arms, or can this right be exercised only by persons authorized by a state to do so? Inevitably, civil libertarian groups, such as the American Civil Liberties Union (ACLU), would become involved in the dispute. The ACLU, for example, probably would bring lawsuits against the federal government challenging the constitutionality of the ban.

FOR CRITICAL ANALYSIS

1. *If the decision were yours to make, would you ban citizens' militias? Why or why not?*
2. *If a state government—and not the national Congress—were to ban militias within state borders, would the issues be different? Explain.*

Most Americans believe that they have more individual freedom than virtually any other people on earth. For the most part, this opinion is accurate. The freedoms that we take for granted—religion, speech, press, and assembly—are relatively unknown in some parts of the world. In some nations today, citizens have little chance of living without government harassment if they choose to criticize openly, through speech or print, the government or its actions. Indeed, if the United States suddenly had the same rules, laws, and procedures about verbal and printed expression that exist in certain other countries, American jails would be filled overnight with transgressors. Certainly, citizens' militias such as those discussed in this chapter's opening *What If . . .* would not be tolerated in some nations.

CIVIL LIBERTIES AND THE FEAR OF GOVERNMENT

Without government, people live in a state of anarchy. With unbridled government, men and women may end up living in a state of tyranny. The framers of the Constitution wanted neither extreme. As was pointed out in Chapter 2, the Declaration of Independence was based on the idea of natural rights. These are rights discoverable in nature and history, according to such philosophers as John Locke (1632–1704) and John Dickinson (1732–1808), and cannot be taken away by any human power.

Linked directly to the strong prerevolutionary sentiment for natural rights was the notion that a right was first and foremost a *limitation* on any government's ruling power. To obtain ratification of the Constitution by the necessary nine states, the Federalists had to deal with the colonists' fears of a too-powerful national government. The **Bill of Rights** was the result. These first ten amendments to the U.S. Constitution were passed by Congress on September 25, 1789, and ratified by three-fourths of the states by December 15, 1791. When we speak of civil liberties in the United States, we are referring mostly to the specific limitations on government outlined in the Bill of Rights (although there are such limitations in the Constitution's main text itself, including the prohibition against *ex post facto* laws and others found in Section 9 of Article I).

Here we must make a distinction between the technical definitions of *civil liberties* and *civil rights*. **Civil liberties** represent something that the government *cannot do*, such as abridge a freedom by, for example, taking away someone's freedom of speech. In contrast, **civil rights** represent something that the government *must do*, such as guaranteeing to individuals a power or privilege. The right to vote is one such civil right. In this chapter we will examine civil liberties, and in the following chapter, civil rights.

As you read through these chapters, bear in mind that the Bill of Rights, like the rest of the Constitution, is relatively brief. The framers set forth broad guidelines, leaving it up to the courts to interpret these constitutional mandates and apply them to specific situations. Thus, judicial interpretations shape the true nature of the civil liberties and rights that we possess. Because judicial interpretations change over time, so do our liberties and rights. As you will read in the following pages, there have been numerous conflicts over the meaning of such simple phrases as *freedom of religion* and *freedom of the press*. To understand what freedoms we actually have, we need to examine some of those conflicts. One important conflict has to do with whether the national Bill of Rights limited state governments as well as the national government.

BILL OF RIGHTS

The first ten amendments to the U.S. Constitution. They contain a listing of the freedoms that a person enjoys and that cannot be infringed upon by the government, such as the freedoms of speech, press, and religion.

CIVIL LIBERTIES

Those personal freedoms that are protected for all individuals and generally that deal with individual freedom. Civil liberties typically involve restraining the government's actions against individuals.

CIVIL RIGHTS

Those powers or privileges that are guaranteed to individuals or protected groups and that are protected from arbitrary removal by government or by individuals.

THE NATIONALIZATION OF THE BILL OF RIGHTS

Most citizens do not realize that, as originally intended, the Bill of Rights limited only the powers of the national government. At the time the Bill of Rights was ratified, there was little concern over the potential of state governments to curb civil liberties. For one thing, state governments were closer to home and easier to control. For another, most state constitutions already had bills of rights. Rather, the fear was of the potential tyranny of the national government. The Bill of Rights begins with the words, "Congress shall make no law . . . ." It says nothing about *states* making laws that might abridge citizens' civil liberties. Chief Justice John Marshall's decision in *Barron v. Mayor of Baltimore*,[1] a case decided in 1833, confirmed this interpretation: the Bill of Rights limited only the national government and not the state governments.

State bills of rights were similar to the national one, but there were some differences. Furthermore, each state's judicial system interpreted the rights differently. A citizen in one state, therefore, effectively had a different set of civil rights from a citizen in another state. In other words, a citizen in the state of Virginia could not sue successfully in a federal court if the state of Virginia passed a law that curbed a liberty guaranteed by the national Bill of Rights. It was not until the Fourteenth Amendment was ratified in 1868 that civil liberties guaranteed by the national Constitution began to be applied to the states.

The Fourteenth Amendment

The Fourteenth Amendment was passed as a standard that would guarantee both due process and equal protection under the laws for all persons. Section 1 of that amendment provides as follows:

> No State shall make or enforce any law which shall abridge the privileges or immunities of citizens of the United States; nor shall any State deprive any person of life, liberty, or property, without due process of law; nor deny any person within its jurisdiction the equal protection of the laws.

Section 5 of the amendment explicitly gives Congress the power to enforce the provisions of the amendment by appropriate legislation. Note the use of the terms *citizen* and *person*. *Citizens* have political rights, such as the right to vote and run for political office. The Fourteenth Amendment makes it clear that citizens have certain privileges and immunities (see Chapter 3). All *persons*, however, including legal *and* illegal immigrants, have a right to due process of law and equal protection under the laws.

The Incorporation Issue

There was no question that the Fourteenth Amendment applied to state governments. For decades, however, the courts were reluctant to hold that the liberties spelled out in the national Bill of Rights were protected under the Fourteenth Amendment. It was not until 1925, in *Gitlow v. New York*,[2] that the United States Supreme Court held that the Fourteenth Amendment protected the freedom of speech guaranteed by the First Amendment to the Constitution.

---

[1] 7 Peters 243 (1833).
[2] 268 U.S. 652 (1925).

The *Gitlow* decision was a landmark case in respect to the limitations on the powers of state governments. This is because, for many Americans, the First Amendment is the most significant part of the Bill of Rights. The First Amendment sets forth our basic freedoms of religion, speech, the press, assembly, and the right of petition. It is thus the mainstay of the statement in the Declaration of Independence that all people should be able to enjoy life, liberty, and the pursuit of happiness.

Only gradually, and never completely, did the Supreme Court accept the **incorporation theory**—the view that most of the protections of the Bill of Rights are incorporated into the Fourteenth Amendment's protection against state government. Table 4–1 shows the rights that the Court has incorporated into the Fourteenth Amendment and the case in which it first applied each protection. As you can see in that table, in the fifteen years following the *Gitlow* decision, the Supreme Court incorporated into the Fourteenth Amendment the other basic freedoms (of the press, assembly, the right to petition, and religion) guaranteed by the First Amendment.

These and the later Supreme Court decisions listed in Table 4–1 have bound the fifty states to accept for their respective citizens most of the guarantees that are contained in the U.S. Bill of Rights. Today, for all intents and purposes, the national Bill of Rights must be applied uniformly by individual state governments to their laws and practices. The exceptions usually involve the right to bear arms, the right to refuse to quarter soldiers, and the right to a grand jury hearing.

DID YOU KNOW ...
That Samuel Argall, governor of Virginia from 1616 to 1618, punished those who failed to attend church with prison terms and forced labor, and that he banned all forms of amusement on Sunday?

INCORPORATION THEORY
The view that most of the protections of the Bill of Rights are incorporated into the Fourteenth Amendment's protection against state governments.

FREEDOM OF RELIGION

In the United States, freedom of religion consists of two principal precepts as they are presented in the First Amendment. The first has to do with the separation of church and state, and the second guarantees the free exercise of religion.

The Separation of Church and State

The First Amendment to the Constitution states, in part, that "Congress shall make no law respecting an establishment of religion." In the words of Presi-

Table 4–1

Incorporating the Bill of Rights into the Fourteenth Amendment

YEAR	ISSUE	AMENDMENT INVOLVED	COURT CASE
1925	Freedom of speech	I	*Gitlow v. New York*, 268 U.S. 652.
1931	Freedom of the press	I	*Near v. Minnesota*, 283 U.S. 697.
1932	Right to a lawyer in capital punishment cases	VI	*Powell v. Alabama*, 287 U.S. 45.
1937	Freedom of assembly and right to petition	I	*De Jonge v. Oregon*, 299 U.S. 353.
1940	Freedom of religion	I	*Cantwell v. Connecticut*, 310 U.S. 296.
1947	Separation of state and church	I	*Everson v. Board of Education*, 330 U.S. 1.
1948	Right to a public trial	VI	*In re Oliver*, 333 U.S. 257.
1949	No unreasonable searches and seizures	IV	*Wolf v. Colorado*, 338 U.S. 25.
1961	Exclusionary rule	IV	*Mapp v. Ohio*, 367 U.S. 643.
1962	No cruel and unusual punishment	VIII	*Robinson v. California*, 370 U.S. 660.
1963	Right to a lawyer in all criminal felony cases	VI	*Gideon v. Wainwright*, 372 U.S. 335.
1964	No compulsory self-incrimination	V	*Malloy v. Hogan*, 378 U.S. 1.
1965	Right to privacy	I	*Griswold v. Connecticut*, 381 U.S. 479.
1966	Right to an impartial jury	VI	*Parker v. Gladden*, 385 U.S. 363.
1967	Right to a speedy trial	VI	*Klopfer v. North Carolina*, 386 U.S. 213.
1969	No double jeopardy	V	*Benton v. Maryland*, 395 U.S. 784.

ESTABLISHMENT CLAUSE

The part of the First Amendment prohibiting the establishment of a church officially supported by the national government. It is applied to questions of state and local government aid to religious organizations and schools, questions of the legality of allowing or requiring school prayers, and questions of the teaching of evolution versus fundamentalist theories of creation.

dent Jefferson, the **establishment clause** was designed to create a "wall of separation of Church and State."[3] Perhaps Jefferson was thinking about the religious intolerance that characterized the first colonies. Although many of the American colonies were founded by groups in pursuit of religious freedom, they were quite intolerant nonetheless of religious nonconformity within their own communities. Jefferson undoubtedly was also aware that state religions were the rule; among the original thirteen American colonies, nine of them had official religions.

As interpreted by the Supreme Court, the establishment clause in the First Amendment means at least the following:

> Neither a state nor the federal government can set up a church. Neither can pass laws which aid one religion, aid all religions, or prefer one religion over another. Neither can force nor influence a person to go to or to remain away from church against his will or force him to profess a belief or disbelief in any religion. No person can be punished for entertaining or professing religious beliefs or disbeliefs, for church attendance or nonattendance. No tax in any amount, large or small, can be levied to support any religious activities or institutions, whatever they may be called, or whatever form they may adopt to teach or practice religion. Neither a state nor the federal government can, openly or secretly, participate in the affairs of any religious organizations or groups and vice versa.[4]

The establishment clause covers all conflicts about such matters as the legality of allowing or requiring school prayers, the teaching of evolution versus fundamental theories of creation, and state and local government aid to religious organizations and schools.

The Issue of School Prayer. Do the states have the right to promote religion in general, without making any attempt to establish a particular religion? That is the question in the issue of school prayer and was the precise question

---

[3]The impenetrability of this wall has been called into question by a book that got a warm endorsement from President Bill Clinton. In *The Culture of Disbelief* (New York: Basic Books, 1993), Yale professor Stephen Carter argues that American law and politics have suffered by excluding religion from public discourse.
[4]*Everson v. Board of Education*, 330 U.S. 1 (1947).

Fundamentalists Vicki Frost and her husband challenged certain textbooks as being too secular and violating their freedom of religion. Other people have argued that public schools cannot teach about religion because that would be a violation of the establishment clause.

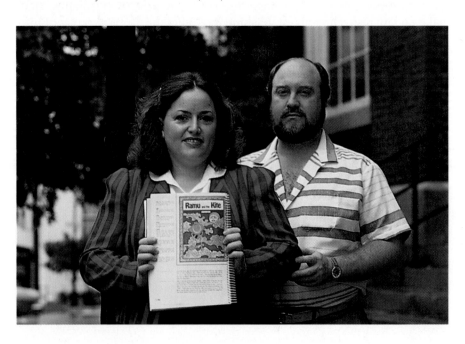

presented in 1962 in *Engel v. Vitale*,[5] the so-called Regents' Prayer Case in New York. The State Board of Regents of New York had suggested that a prayer be spoken aloud in the public schools at the beginning of each day. The recommended prayer was as follows:

> Almighty God, we acknowledge our dependence upon Thee,
> And we beg Thy blessings upon us, our parents, our teachers, and our Country.

Such a prayer was implemented in many New York public schools.

The parents of a number of students challenged the action of the regents, maintaining that it violated the establishment clause of the First Amendment. At trial, the parents lost. The Supreme Court, however, ruled that the regents' action was unconstitutional because "the constitutional prohibition against laws respecting an establishment of a religion must mean at least that in this country it is no part of the business of government to compose official prayers for any group of the American people to recite as part of a religious program carried on by any government." The Court's conclusion was based in part on the "historical fact that governmentally established religions and religious persecutions go hand in hand."[6] In 1963, the Supreme Court outlawed daily readings of the Bible and recitation of the Lord's Prayer in public schools.[7]

Although the Supreme Court has ruled repeatedly against officially sponsored prayer and Bible-reading sessions in public schools, other means for bringing some form of religious expression into public education have been attempted. In 1983, the Tennessee legislature passed a bill requiring public school classes to begin each day with a minute of silence. Alabama also had a similar law. In 1985, the Supreme Court struck down as unconstitutional the Alabama law authorizing one minute of silence in all public schools for prayer or meditation. The majority of the Court concluded that because the law specifically endorsed prayer, it appeared to support religion.[8]

More recently, the courts have dealt with cases involving prayer in public schools outside the classroom, particularly prayer during graduation ceremonies. In 1992, in *Lee v. Weisman*,[9] the Supreme Court held that it was unconstitutional for a school to invite a rabbi to deliver a nonsectarian prayer at graduation. The Court said nothing about *students* organizing and leading prayers at graduation ceremonies, however, and since then the lower courts have disagreed on this issue. For example, in *Jones v. Clear Creek Independent School District*,[10] a federal appellate court concluded that a graduation prayer was allowable when requested by a majority of the seniors. Another federal appellate court held to the contrary—that prayers, even if approved by student vote, cannot be said at graduation ceremonies.[11] It is certainly possible that by the time you read this book, another school-prayer case will have reached the Supreme Court.

Religious Student Publications. A related issue concerns whether public university funds can be used to subsidize publications by religious student organizations. For example, in *Rosenberger v. University of Virginia*,[12] the Uni-

Children pray in school. Such in-school prayer is in violation of Supreme Court rulings based on the First Amendment. A Supreme Court ruling does not necessarily carry with it a mechanism for enforcement everywhere in the United States, however.

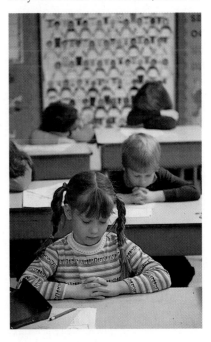

[5]370 U.S. 421 (1962).
[6]*Engel v. Vitale*, 421.
[7]*Abington School District v. Schempp*, 374 U.S. 203 (1963).
[8]*Wallace v. Jafree*, 472 U.S. 38 (1985).
[9]505 U.S. 577 (1992).
[10]977 F.2d 963 (1992).
[11]*American Civil Liberties Union of New Jersey v. Blackhorse Pike Regional Board of Education*, 84 F.3d 1471 (3d Cir. 1993).
[12]115 S.Ct. 2510 (1995).

versity of Virginia collected mandatory fees each semester from all students and placed them in a special fund. Grants were given from the fund to various student organizations. The university refused to grant money to a Christian group to pay for the printing of a newsletter, arguing that to give such financial assistance would violate the establishment clause. When the case reached the Supreme Court in 1995, the Court held that the university's policy unconstitutionally discriminated against religious speech. The Court pointed out that the money came from student fees, not general taxes, and was used for a specific purpose—the neutral payment of bills for student groups.

Forbidding the Teaching of Evolution.   For a good part of this century, certain religious groups, particularly in the southern states, have opposed the teaching of evolution in the schools. To these groups, evolutionary theory directly counters their religious belief that human beings did not evolve but were created fully formed, as described in the biblical story of the creation. State and local attempts to forbid the teaching of evolution, however, have not passed constitutional muster in the eyes of the United States Supreme Court. For example, in 1968, the Supreme Court held, in *Epperson v. Arkansas,*[13] that an Arkansas law prohibiting the teaching of evolution violated the establishment clause, because it imposed religious beliefs on students. The Louisiana legislature passed a law requiring the teaching of the biblical story of the Creation alongside the teaching of evolution. In 1987, the Supreme Court declared that this law was unconstitutional, in part because it had as its primary purpose the promotion of a particular religious belief.[14]

State and local groups in the so-called Bible Belt continue their efforts against the teaching of evolution. In 1996, the Tennessee legislature was considering a bill that would allow a school to fire any teacher who presents evolution as fact. A proposed amendment to the bill would also protect teachers who want to teach the biblical theories of the Creation along with evolution. Alabama has approved a disclaimer to be inserted in biology textbooks, indicating that evolution is "a controversial theory some scientists present as a scientific explanation for the origin of living things." A school district in Georgia adopted a policy that creationism could be taught along with evolution. No doubt, these laws and policies will be challenged on constitutional grounds.

Aid to Church-Related Schools.   Throughout the United States, all property owners except religious, educational, fraternal, literary, scientific, and similar nonprofit institutions must pay property taxes. A large part of the proceeds of such taxes goes to support public schools. But not all school-age children attend public schools. Fully 12 percent attend private schools, of which 85 percent have religious affiliations. Numerous cases have reached the Supreme Court in which the Court has tried to draw a fine line between permissible public aid to students in church-related schools and impermissible public aid to religion.

It is at the elementary and secondary levels that these issues have arisen most often. In a series of cases, the Supreme Court has allowed states to use tax funds for lunches, textbooks, diagnostic services for speech and hearing problems, standardized tests, and transportation for students attending

---

[13]393 U.S. 97 (1968).
[14]*Edwards v. Aguillard,* 482 U.S. 578 (1987).

church-operated elementary and secondary schools.[15] In a number of cases, however, the Supreme Court has held state programs helping church-related schools to be unconstitutional. In *Lemon v. Kurtzman*,[16] the Court ruled that direct state aid could not be used to subsidize religious instruction. The Court in the *Lemon* case gave its most general statement on the constitutionality of government aid to religious schools, stating that the aid had to be secular in aim, that it could not have the primary effect of advancing or inhibiting religion, and that the government must avoid "an excessive entanglement with religion." All laws under the establishment clause are now subject to the three-part *Lemon* test. In other cases, the Court has denied state reimbursements to religious schools for field trips and for developing achievement tests.

Issues concerning the use of public funds for church-related schools are likely to continue as state legislators search for new ways to improve the educational system in this country. One alternative to the current public educational system would allow students to use public funds for private schools, including church-operated schools. (See this chapter's feature entitled *Thinking Politically about School Vouchers* for a discussion of the arguments for and against this alternative.)

The Free Exercise of Religious Beliefs

The First Amendment constrains Congress from prohibiting the free exercise of religion. Does this **free exercise clause** mean that no type of religious practice can be prohibited or restricted by government? Certainly, a person can hold any religious belief that he or she wants; or a person can have no religious belief. When, however, religious *practices* work against public policy and the public welfare, the government can act. For example, regardless of a child's or parent's religious beliefs, the government can require certain types of vaccinations. Similarly, public school students can be required to study from textbooks chosen by school authorities. The sale and use of marijuana for religious purposes has been held illegal, because a religion cannot make legal what would otherwise be illegal. Conducting religious rites that result in beheaded and gutted animals being left in public streets normally is not allowed.

The courts and lawmakers are constantly faced with a dilemma. On the one hand, no law may be made that requires someone to do something contrary to his or her religious beliefs or teachings, because this would interfere with the free exercise of religion. On the other hand, if certain individuals, because of their religious beliefs, are exempted from specific laws, then such exemptions might tend to favor religion and be contrary to the establishment clause. The original view of the Court was that although religious beliefs are protected by the law, acting on those beliefs may not be. For instance, children of Jehovah's Witnesses are not required to say the Pledge of Allegiance at school,[17] but their parents cannot prevent them from accepting medical treatment (such as blood transfusions) if in fact their lives are in danger. Generally, any laws that infringe in any way on the free exercise of religion in public places must be justified by a *compelling state interest*, however. In 1993, to provide clear guidelines to the courts on this issue, Congress affirmed the compelling-interest standard legislatively with the passage of the Religious

FREE EXERCISE CLAUSE

The provision of the First Amendment guaranteeing the free exercise of religion.

---

[15]See *Everson v. Board of Education*, 330 U.S. 1 (1947); *Meek v. Pittenger*, 421 U.S. 349 (1975); and *Committee for Public Education v. Regan*, 444 U.S. 646 (1980).
[16]403 U.S. 602 (1971).
[17]*West Virginia State Board of Education v. Barnette*, 319 U.S. 624 (1943).

Thinking Politically about School Vouchers

Many parents are dismayed at what they perceive as the declining quality of their children's education in the public school system. Of course, there are alternatives—private schools or home-schooling—but these alternatives are costly. Furthermore, parents who send their children to private schools have to pay, in addition to private-school tuition, the taxes that support the public school system.

One of the proposed methods for making private schools affordable for more Americans is the voucher system. Under a voucher system, parents could use educational vouchers (state-issued credits) to "purchase" education at any school, private or public. Proponents of school vouchers argue that the use of vouchers would enhance the quality of education by, among other things, introducing more accountability into education. Those schools that perform well would attract more students; those that do

not simply would have to close their doors. Furthermore, the use of vouchers would allow parents to exercise more control over the education of their children. Religious groups and other groups and individuals would be in a better position to ensure that their children's education is consistent with their religious or cultural beliefs.

Opponents of school vouchers argue that a voucher system would be questionable constitutionally because state funds could be used to pay for church-operated schools. Another argument raised by opponents is that the use of vouchers eventually would destroy educational standards. This is because the state exercises greater control over the standards and policies of the public school system than it does over private schools. Furthermore, the use of vouchers could result in an educational flexibility that could have serious repercussions for society. Fundamentalist Christians, black Muslims,

and other groups could establish private schools in which children are taught to condemn those who do not share their views. Opponents argue that such schools would breed hatred, intolerance, and, ultimately, social anarchy.

If one thinks politically about school vouchers, though, what really is at issue in this debate? Some argue that it is the welfare of public school teachers, who stand to lose the most if state funds were channeled to private schools. Consider, for example, the following fact: leading the opposition to school vouchers is the most powerful teachers' union in the United States, the National Education Association (NEA), and its state affiliates. Public schools are unionized, and public school teachers depend on NEA lobbying efforts in state legislatures for their employment benefits and income, and job security generally. If these teachers were forced to find jobs in private schools, they would not have the powerful NEA to defend their interests. They might have less job security, lower salaries, and fewer benefits.

Clearly, the NEA has a vested interest in continuing the public school system. To expect it to support reforms that reduce the income going to public schools (and thus the influence of the NEA over education) would be, in effect, to assume that it will act against its interests.

For Critical Analysis
Which students would benefit most from a voucher system? Which students would benefit least?

Fully 85 percent of all private schools have some religious affiliation, as does this private, all-female Catholic school. A true school voucher system would allow parents to use state funds to send their children to such schools.

Freedom Restoration Act. The Supreme Court has held that even animal sacrifices cannot be banned by a municipality if those sacrifices are part of established religious practices.[18]

FREEDOM OF EXPRESSION

Perhaps the most frequently invoked freedom that Americans have is the right to free speech and a free press without government interference. These rights guarantee each person a right of free expression by all means of communication and ensure all persons a full discussion of public affairs. Each of us has the right to have our say, and all of us have the right to hear what others say. For the most part, Americans can criticize public officials and their actions without fear of reprisal or imprisonment by any branch of our government.

Permitted Restrictions on Expression

At various times, restrictions on expression have been permitted. A description of several such restrictions follows.

Clear and Present Danger. When a person's remarks present a clear and present danger to the peace or public order, they can be curtailed constitutionally. Justice Oliver Wendell Holmes used this reasoning in 1919 when examining the case of a socialist who had been convicted for violating the Espionage Act. Holmes stated:

> The question in every case is whether the words are used in such circumstances and are of such a nature as to create a *clear and present danger* that they will bring about the substantive evils that Congress has a right to prevent. It is a question of proximity and degree. [Emphasis added.][19]

Thus, according to the **clear and present danger test,** expression may be restricted if evidence exists that such expression would cause a condition, actual or imminent, that Congress has the power to prevent. Commenting on this test, Justice Louis D. Brandeis in 1920 said, "Correctly applied, it will reserve the right of free speech . . . from suppression by tyrannists, well-meaning majorities, and from abuse by irresponsible, fanatical minorities."[20] A related concept is the **preferred-position doctrine.** Only if the government is able to show that limitations on speech are absolutely necessary to avoid imminent, serious, and important evils are such limitations allowed.

The Supreme Court modified the clear and present danger test in the early 1950s. At the time, there was considerable tension between the United States and the Soviet Union. The Soviet Union's government was run by the Communist party. Twelve members of the American Communist party were convicted of violating a statute that made it a crime to conspire to teach, advocate, or organize the violent overthrow of any government in the United States. The Supreme Court affirmed the convictions, significantly modifying the clear and present danger test in the process. The Court applied a "grave and probable danger rule." Under this rule, "the gravity of the `evil' discounted by its improbability justifies such invasion of free speech as is neces-

CLEAR AND PRESENT DANGER TEST

The test proposed by Justice Holmes for determining when government may restrict free speech. Restrictions are permissible, he argued, only when speech provokes a "clear and present danger" to the public order.

PREFERRED-POSITION DOCTRINE

A judicial doctrine under which limitations on speech are permissible only if they are necessary to avoid imminent, serious, and important evils.

[18]*Church of Lukumi Babalu Aye v. Hialeah,* 508 U.S. 520 (1993).
[19]*Schenck v. United States,* 249 U.S. 47 (1919).
[20]*Schaefer v. United States,* 251 U.S. 466 (1920).

sary to avoid the danger." This rule gave much less protection to free speech than did the clear and present danger test.[21]

BAD-TENDENCY RULE

A rule stating that speech or other First Amendment freedoms may be curtailed if there is a possibility that such expression might lead to some "evil."

The Bad-Tendency Rule.   According to the **bad-tendency rule,** speech or other First Amendment freedoms may be curtailed if there is a possibility that such expression might lead to some "evil." In *Gitlow v. New York,*[22] a member of a left-wing group was convicted of violating New York state's criminal anarchy statute when he published and distributed a pamphlet urging the violent overthrow of the U.S. government. In its majority opinion, the Supreme Court held that although the First Amendment afforded protection against state incursions on freedom of expression, Gitlow could be punished legally in this particular instance because his expression would tend to bring about evils that the state had a right to prevent.

PRIOR RESTRAINT

Restraining an action before the activity has actually occurred. It involves censorship, as opposed to subsequent punishment.

No Prior Restraint.   Restraining an activity before that activity has actually occurred is referred to as **prior restraint.** It involves censorship, as opposed to subsequent punishment. Prior restraint of expression would require, for example, a permit before a speech could be made, a newspaper published, or a movie or TV show exhibited. Most, if not all, Supreme Court justices have been especially critical of any governmental action that imposes prior restraint on expression:

> A prior restraint on expression comes to this Court with a "heavy presumption" against its constitutionality. . . . The government thus carries a heavy burden of showing justification for the enforcement of such a restraint.[23]

One of the most famous cases concerning prior restraint involved the so-called Pentagon Papers. On June 13, 1971, the *New York Times* carried its first article about the forty-seven-volume, classified *U.S. Government History of American Policy in Vietnam from 1945 to 1967.* The *Washington Post* also began a similar series on the secret study, based on documents it had secured. The U.S. attorney general obtained a court order suspending the publication of these materials by both the *Times* and the *Post.* Both cases reached the Supreme Court within days, and the justices were deeply divided on the constitutional issues. Did Americans have the right to know (and the press the right to inform them) of information that the government claimed might endanger national security? Would such publication jeopardize U.S. national security in the long run? The Court ruled six to three in favor of the newspapers' right to publish the information.[24] This case affirmed the no prior restraint doctrine.

The Protection of Symbolic Speech

SYMBOLIC SPEECH

Nonverbal expression of beliefs, which is given substantial protection by the courts.

Not all expression is in words or in writing. Gestures, movements, articles of clothing, and other forms of expressive conduct are considered **symbolic speech.** Such speech is given substantial protection today by our courts. For example, in 1989, in *Texas v. Johnson,*[25] the Supreme Court ruled that state laws that prohibited the burning of the American flag as part of a peaceful protest also violated the freedom of expression protected by the First Amendment. Congress responded by passing the Flag Protection Act of 1989, which

---

[21]*Dennis v. United States,* 341 U.S. 494 (1951).

[22]268 U.S. 652 (1925).

[23]*Nebraska Press Association v. Stuart,* 427 U.S. 539 (1976). See also *Near v. Minnesota,* 283 U.S. 697 (1931).

[24]*New York Times Co. v. United States* and *United States v. The Washington Post,* 403 U.S. 713 (1971).

[25]488 U.S. 884 (1989).

was ruled unconstitutional by the Supreme Court in June 1990.[26] Congress and President Bush immediately pledged to work for a constitutional amendment to "protect our flag"—an effort that has yet to be successful.

More recently, the Supreme Court ruled that a city statute banning bias-motivated disorderly conduct (including, in this case, the placing of a burning cross in another's front yard as a gesture of hate) was an unconstitutional restriction of speech.[27] Freedom of speech can also apply to group-sponsored events. In 1995, the Supreme Court held that forcing the organizers of Boston's St. Patrick's Day parade to include gays and lesbians violated the organizers' freedom of speech.[28]

Symbolic speech is an area in which the First Amendment freedoms of speech and religion may overlap considerably. For example, the placement of religious symbols in public forums, such as a crucifix in a public school classroom or a cross in a public square, involves not only freedom of (symbolic) speech but also freedom of religion. (See this chapter's *Politics and Diversity* for a further discussion of this topic.)

The Protection of Commercial Speech

Commercial speech is usually defined as advertising statements. Can advertisers use their First Amendment rights to prevent restrictions on the content of commercial advertising? Until the 1970s, the Supreme Court held that such speech was not protected by the First Amendment. By the mid-1970s, however, more and more commercial speech was brought under First Amendment protection. According to Justice Harry A. Blackmun, "Advertising, however tasteless and excessive it sometimes may seem, is nonetheless dissemination of information as to who is producing and selling what product for what reason and at what price."[29] If consumers are to make more intelligent marketplace decisions, there must be a "free flow of commercial information," according to Blackmun and the Court. Thus, for example, the federal government cannot prohibit the mailing of unsolicited advertisements (although unsolicited advertisements by fax have been prohibited because they impose costs on recipients), a state cannot prohibit the advertising of drug prices by pharmacies, and a town cannot prohibit the use of "for sale" signs by sellers of homes. Generally, the Court has considered a restriction on commercial speech valid as long as it (1) seeks to implement a substantial government interest, (2) directly advances that interest, and (3) goes no further than necessary to accomplish its objective.

Certain types of commercial advertising may implement one substantial government interest but be contrary to another government interest. In such cases, the courts have to decide which interest takes priority. Liquor advertising is a good example of this kind of conflict. In *Liquormart v. Rhode Island*,[30] the issue concerned a Rhode Island law that banned the advertising of liquor prices. Rhode Island argued that the ban served the state's goal of discouraging liquor consumption (because the ban discouraged bargain hunting and thus kept liquor prices high). The United States Supreme Court, however, held that the ban was an unconstitutional infringement of commercial speech. The Court stated that "[t]he First Amendment directs us to be espe-

COMMERCIAL SPEECH

Advertising statements, which have increasingly been given First Amendment protection.

---

[26]*United States v. Eichman*, 496 U.S. 310 (1990).

[27]*R.A.V. v. City of St. Paul, Minnesota*, 505 U.S. 377 (1992).

[28]*Hurley v. Irish-American Gay, Lesbian and Bisexual Group of Boston*, 115 S.Ct. 2338 (1995).

[29]*Virginia State Board of Pharmacy v. Virginia Citizens Consumer Council, Inc.*, 425 U.S. 748 (1976).

[30]116 S.Ct. 1495 (1996).

POLITICS AND DIVERSITY
Religious Symbols Go to Court

Municipalities often spend tax dollars to decorate streets and government offices during the holiday season. Most of these decorations are not religious and apparently offend few individuals. What about blatantly religious scenes, however? Does any government in the United States have the legal right to use public monies for the display of religious scenes or to permit the display of religious symbols on government (public) property? Do such actions violate the establishment clause of the First Amendment?

A major test of a municipality's ability to spend public funds on religious scenes during the Christmas season occurred in 1984. The city of Pawtucket, Rhode Island, included a crèche—a model depicting Mary, Joseph, and others around the crib of Jesus in the stable at Bethlehem—in a larger, nonreligious Christmas display, which included reindeer, candy-striped poles, and a Christmas tree. The entire display, although it was located in a private park, was the city's official display and had been both erected and maintained by city employees. This case, known as *Lynch v. Donnelly,** was decided in favor of the municipal government. The crèche

could be included as long as it was just one part of a holiday display.

What about the simultaneous display by a local government of symbols from different religions? In *County of Allegheny v. American Civil Liberties Union,*† the American Civil Liberties Union (ACLU) sued Allegheny County, where Pittsburgh, Pennsylvania, is located, because of what the ACLU claimed were "frankly religious displays." These displays included a crèche in the county courthouse and a menorah (a nine-branched candelabrum used in celebrating Chanukah) near the annual Christmas tree on the steps of its city-county building. Although the county displays nonreligious holiday symbols in the courthouse, they are not displayed alongside the crèche, as they were in the *Lynch* case. Therefore, the Supreme Court held that the presence of the crèche was unconstitutional. Displaying the menorah, however, did not violate the First Amendment, because the menorah was situated in close proximity to the Christmas tree.

In 1995, the Court had to decide whether the Ku Klux Klan (KKK) should be allowed to place an unattended cross in the statehouse plaza in

Columbus, Ohio, during the Christmas season. The Court ruled in favor of the KKK. Because the square was a forum for the discussion of public questions and for public activities, the presence of the cross did not indicate the government's endorsement of a religious belief. Neither *Allegheny* nor *Lynch,* stated the Court, "even remotely assumes that the government's neutral treatment of private religious expression can be unconstitutional."‡

Clearly, court judges and justices do not have an easy job. In addition to their other duties, they periodically have to function as, in Justice Kennedy's words, a kind of "theology board."

For Critical Analysis

Would a local government ordinance prohibiting the placement of any religious symbol on public property violate the establishment clause? Why or why not?

*465 U.S. 668 (1984).

†492 U.S. 573 (1989).

‡*Capitol Square Review and Advisory Board v. Pinette,* 115 S.Ct. 2440 (1995).

cially skeptical of regulations that seek to keep people in the dark for what the Government perceives to be their own good."

Unprotected Speech: Obscenity

Numerous state and federal statutes make it a crime to disseminate obscene materials. All such state and federal statutes prohibiting obscenity have been deemed constitutional if the definition of obscenity conforms with that of the then-current U.S. Supreme Court. Basically, the courts have not been willing to extend constitutional protections of free speech to what they consider obscene materials. For example, in *Roth v. United States,*[31] the Supreme Court stated, "Obscenity is not within the area of constitutionally protected speech or press."

---

[31]354 U.S. 476 (1957).

But what is obscenity? Justice Potter Stewart once said that even though he could not define obscenity, "I know it when I see it."[32] The problem, of course, is that even if it were agreed on, the definition of obscenity changes with the times. Victorians deeply disapproved of the "loose" morals of the Elizabethan Age. The works of Mark Twain and Edgar Rice Burroughs have at times been considered obscene (after all, Tarzan and Jane were not legally wedded).

The Supreme Court has grappled from time to time with the problem of specifying an operationally effective definition of obscenity. In the *Roth* case in 1957, the Court coined the phrase "utterly without redeeming social importance." Since then, Supreme Court justices have viewed numerous films to determine if they met this criterion. By the 1970s, the justices had recognized the failure of the *Roth* definition. In *Miller v. California*,[33] Chief Justice Warren Burger created a formal list of requirements, known as the *Roth-Miller* test of obscenity, that currently must be met for material to be legally obscene. Under this test, material is obscene if (1) the average person finds that it violates contemporary community standards; (2) the work taken as a whole appeals to a prurient interest in sex; (3) the work shows patently offensive sexual conduct; and (4) the work lacks serious redeeming literary, artistic, political, or scientific merit.

The problem, of course, is that one person's prurient interest is another person's artistic pleasure. The Court went on to state that the definition of prurient interest would be determined by the community's standards. The Court avoided presenting a definition of obscenity, leaving this determination to local and state authorities. Consequently, the *Miller* case has had widely inconsistent applications. Obscenity remains a constitutionally unsettled area. Many women's rights activists, often in alliance with religious fundamentalists, have pushed for antipornography laws on the basis that pornography violates women's rights. In regard to child pornography, the Supreme Court has upheld state laws making it illegal to sell materials showing sexual performances by minors. In 1990, the Court ruled that states can outlaw the possession of child pornography in the home. The Court reasoned that the ban on private possession is justified because owning the material perpetuates commercial demand for it and for the exploitation of the children involved.[34]

Public concern over access to pornographic materials via the Internet led Congress to enact the Communications Decency Act of 1996. The act would impose criminal penalties on those who make "indecent" materials available online to persons under the age of eighteen. The controversy and constitutional questions surrounding this act are explored in this chapter's *Critical Perspective*.

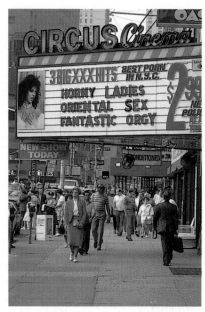

The Constitution does not specifically protect pornography, but rather guarantees freedom of speech in general. Local laws differ considerably concerning what is and is not pornographic and therefore in what is and is not legal.

Unprotected Speech: Slander

Can you say anything you want about someone else? Not really. Individuals are protected from **defamation of character,** which is defined as wrongfully hurting a person's good reputation. The law has imposed a general duty on all persons to refrain from making false, defamatory statements about others. Breaching this duty orally involves the wrongdoing called **slander.**[35]

DEFAMATION OF CHARACTER

Wrongfully hurting a person's good reputation. The law has imposed a general duty on all persons to refrain from making false, defamatory statements about others.

SLANDER

The public uttering of a false statement that harms the good reputation of another. The statement must be made to, or within the hearing of, persons other than the defamed party.

---

[32]*Jacobellis v. Ohio,* 378 U.S. 184 (1964).
[33]413 U.S. 5 (1973).
[34]*Osborne v. Ohio,* 495 U.S. 103 (1990).
[35]Breaching it in writing involves the wrongdoing called *libel,* which is discussed in the next major section.

CRITICAL PERSPECTIVE
Free Speech versus the Regulation of Cyberspace

On February 8, 1996, President Clinton signed into law the Communications Decency Act (CDA), which makes it a criminal offense to transmit "indecent" speech or images to minors (persons under the age of eighteen) or to make such speech or images available online to minors. Penalties for violations include fines up to $250,000 and imprisonment for up to two years. On the same day, former Grateful Dead lyricist John Perry Barlow placed on the Internet a message entitled "A Declaration of the Independence of Cyberspace." The message was addressed to the "Governments of the Industrial World" and stated, in part, "On Behalf of the future, I ask you of the past to leave us alone. You are not welcome among us. You have no sovereignty where we gather." Barlow is one of many critics who resent the government's intrusion into the cyberspace speech forum. Although the debate over whether cyberspace should be regulated is still in its beginning stages, the battlelines have been drawn.

Arguments for and against Regulation

Groups such as the Christian Coalition, the Family Research Council, and the National Coalition for the Protection of Children and Families support government censorship of the Internet and the provisions of the CDA. These groups stress the fact that dozens of "adult" computer bulletin board systems (BBSs), with hundreds of thousands of pornographic images, are available to everyone, including children, who have access to the Internet.

Opponents of the legislation include cyberenthusiasts such as Barlow, the American Civil Liberties Union (ACLU), the Electronic Frontier Foundation, Planned Parenthood, and others. One of the major opposing arguments is that, unlike other media, particularly radio and television, Internet users *choose* where to go and what to read or see. It is not as if someone is forcing children to view pornographic or sexually explicit materials. Opponents point out that parents—through "parental control" software and services created by online service providers—can choose the areas of cyberspace that they want their children to access. Thus, parents, and not the government, should be the ones to regulate what materials their children do or do not access via the Internet. Government regulation through the CDA, argues the ACLU, effectively restricts expression on the Net to that appropriate only for children.

Legal Issues

For the most part, the battle over free speech in cyberspace will be decided in legislatures and courtrooms across the country. Legislators and jurists will have to find ways to overcome the difficul-

---

Legally, slander is the public uttering of a false statement that harms the good reputation of another. Slanderous public uttering means that the defamatory statements are made to, or within the hearing of, persons other than the defamed party. If one person calls another dishonest, manipulative, and incompetent when no one else is around, that does not constitute slander. The message is not communicated to a third party. If, however, a third party accidentally overhears defamatory statements, the courts have generally held that this constitutes a public uttering and therefore slander, which is prohibited.

Fighting Words and Hecklers' Veto

FIGHTING WORDS

Words that, when uttered by a public speaker, are so inflammatory that they could provoke the average listener to violence; the words are usually of a racial, religious, or ethnic type.

The Supreme Court has prohibited types of speech "which by their very utterance inflict injury or intend to incite an immediate breach of peace that governments may constitutionally punish."[36] The reference here is to a prohibition on public speakers from using **fighting words.** These may include

---

[36]*Cohen v. California,* 403 U.S. 15 (1971).

CRITICAL PERSPECTIVE
Free Speech versus the Regulation of Cyberspace, Continued

ties of adapting traditional laws and legal concepts to the new frontier of the cyberworld. A major difficulty is jurisdictional in nature. Barlow's comment that the U.S. government has "no sovereignty" over the Internet is well founded—no one government, state or national, can exercise sovereignty over a realm that has no physical borders. Speech that is legal in one country may not be so in another, and vice versa. Similarly, what is deemed pornographic in one community of the United States may not be so in another.

In fact, one of the problems with the CDA is that it defines indecency in terms of community standards—but what physical community's standards can or should apply to Internet communications? The ACLU and other organizations have challenged the constitutionality of the CDA on just this ground—that it subjects persons to criminal penalties without specifically identifying the crimes to which these penalties attach. In the first ruling on the issue, in February 1996, a federal district court in Pennsylvania agreed that the lack of a specific definition of what actions were prohibited by the act may render it unconstitutional and unenforceable. On the basis of this conclusion, the court ordered a temporary restraining order prohibiting the government from enforcing the section of the CDA pertaining to indecent materials.* Five

months later, another federal district court held that the act was unconstitutional because it was overbroad—it also impermissibly regulated the protected speech of adults.† The issue will surely come before the Supreme Court at some point in the future. In the meantime, several state legislatures are considering legislation, such as California's proposed Online Parental Control Act that would narrow the scope of the indecency ban.

For Critical Analysis

1. Many argue that Internet users themselves should be the ones to determine how cyberspeech should be regulated. How would you argue in favor of such "self-rule"? How would you argue against it?

2. Is it technologically possible for the government to regulate the Internet?

*American Civil Liberties Union v. Reno, 929 F. Supp. 824 (E.D.Pa. 1996). This case is not published in West's *Federal Supplement* (see the appendix to Chapter 2).

†Shea v. Reno, 930 F.Supp. 916 (S.D.N.Y. 1996)

racial, religious, or ethnic slurs that are so inflammatory that they will provoke the "average" listener to fight.

Under the Supreme Court leadership of Chief Justice Warren Burger, fighting words were more and more narrowly construed. For example, a four-letter word used in reference to the draft and emblazoned on a sweater is not considered a fighting word unless it is directed at a specific person. As discussed earlier in this chapter, the Supreme Court has held that municipalities cannot ban cross burnings and other expressions of racial bias because such activities are protected speech.

Members of a crowd listening to a speech are prohibited from exercising a **hecklers' veto.** The boisterous and disruptive behavior of hecklers poses the threat of disruption or violence, so hecklers are vetoing the essential rights of the speaker.

HECKLERS' VETO

Boisterous and generally disruptive behavior by listeners of public speakers that, in effect, vetoes the public speakers' right to speak.

Free Speech and Violence

Some state universities have challenged the boundaries of the protection of free speech provided by the First Amendment with the issuance of campus speech and behavior codes. Such codes are designed to prohibit so-called "hate speech"—abusive speech attacking persons on the basis of their ethnicity, race, or other criteria. For example, a University of Michigan code banned "any behavior, verbal or physical, that stigmatizes or victimizes an individual on the basis of race, ethnicity, religion, sex, sexual orientation, creed, national origin, ancestry, age, marital status, handicap or Vietnam-era veterans status." A federal court found that the code violated students' First Amendment rights.[37] Although many people assert that such codes are necessary to stem violence on American campuses, the courts generally have held, as in the University of Michigan case, that they are unconstitutional restrictions on the right to free speech.

In a June 1995 speech, Senate Majority Leader and future presidential nominee Bob Dole focused public attention on another free-speech issue when he delivered a stinging critique of the film and music industry. Dole maintained that the entertainment industry stretched the limits of free speech too far by permitting the American public, and particularly American youth, to be exposed to extremely violent films and song lyrics. He claimed that the leaders of the industry should not be allowed to "hide behind the lofty language of free speech in order to profit from the debasing of America." Following this speech, Dole was chided by some for being so tardy in jumping on the moral bandwagon and criticized by others for advocating censorship.

Both campus speech and behavior codes and recent criticisms of the film and music industry raise a controversial issue: whether rights to free speech can (or should) be traded off to reduce violence in America. This issue extends to hate speech transmitted on the Internet as well, which is a growing concern for many Americans. Even though the percentage of Americans using the Internet is now relatively small, that percentage is growing and will continue to do so. Those who know how to navigate the online world can find information on virtually any topic, from how to build bombs to how to wage war against the government. Here again, the issue is whether free speech on the Internet should be restrained in the interests of protecting against violence. (See this chapter's *Politics and Information* for a discussion of the potential influence of certain types of Internet communications on people's political views.)

FREEDOM OF THE PRESS

Freedom of the press can be regarded as a special instance of freedom of speech. Of course, at the time of the framing of the Constitution, the press meant only newspapers, magazines, and perhaps pamphlets. As technology has modified the ways in which we disseminate information, so too have the laws touching on freedom of the press been modified. What can and cannot be printed still occupies an important place in constitutional law, however.

Defamation in Writing

Libel is defamation in writing (or in pictures, signs, and films, or any other communication that has the potentially harmful qualities of written or printed words). As with slander, libel is an **actionable** wrong only if the defamatory statements are observed by a third party. If one person writes another a private letter wrongfully accusing him or her of embezzling funds,

LIBEL
A written defamation of a person's character, reputation, business, or property rights. To a limited degree, the First Amendment protects the press from libel actions.

ACTIONABLE
Furnishing grounds for a lawsuit. Actionable words, for example, in the law of libel are such words that naturally imply damage to the individual in question.

---

[37]*Doe v. University of Michigan,* 721 F.Supp. 852 (1989).

POLITICS AND INFORMATION
The Internet and Views on Civil Liberties

Until recently, one would have said that television and talk radio have had the most influence on shaping political opinion. Some argue that today and in the future, the expansion of "anything goes" on the Internet will have an even deeper influence, not only in promoting freedom of speech but also in influencing our political views on just about everything. But not all of this proliferation of sometimes "offensive" views is considered beneficial to society. Specifically, many are worried that militia groups have been able to use the Internet to increase their numbers. For example, the militia have transmitted over the Internet a political satire published in 1967 called *Report from*

Iron Mountain. That publication presents purported evidence of a government conspiracy against the American public. It is a classic work for militia members, some of whom believe that it is a real government report that concludes that war is necessary for society to flourish. In actuality, the book was written during the Vietnam War to mock government politics.

We should not exaggerate the potential influence of the new "medium" of the Internet. Currently, to gain access to information on the Internet, you must do more than simply turn on your radio or TV. Additionally, all current studies seem to show that most people visit Internet

sites that are already of interest to them. This means that they are predisposed to hold certain views or opinions and that an Internet site will not necessarily cause them to change their opinions.

In any event, Congress's recent attempts to regulate certain speech on the Internet has made millions of Americans aware of today's free speech issues.

For Critical Analysis
If speech is not regulated at all on the Internet, why are there still regulations governing speech on radio and television?

that does not constitute libel. It is interesting that the courts have generally held that dictating a letter to a secretary constitutes communication of the letter's contents to a third party, and therefore, if defamation has occurred, the wrongdoing of libel is actionable.

Newspapers are often involved in libel suits. *New York Times Co. v. Sullivan*[38] explored an important question about libelous statements made about **public figures**—public officials and employees who exercise substantial governmental power, as well as any persons who are generally in the public limelight. Sullivan, a commissioner of the city of Montgomery, Alabama, sued the *New York Times* for libel because it had printed an advertisement critical of the actions of the Montgomery police during the civil rights movement. Under Alabama law, the jury found that the statements were in fact libelous on their face, so that damages could be awarded to Sullivan without proof of the extent of any injury to him. The jury awarded him a half-million dollars, and the Alabama Supreme Court upheld the judgment.

The United States Supreme Court, however, unanimously reversed the judgment. It found that Alabama's libel laws as applied to public officials in the performance of their duty deprived critics of their rights of free speech under the First and Fourteenth Amendments.[39] Speaking for the Court, Justice William J. Brennan, Jr., stated that libel laws such as those in Alabama would inhibit the unfettered discussion of public issues. The Court indicated that only when a statement was made with **actual malice**—that is, with either knowledge of its falsity or a reckless disregard of the truth—against a public official could damages be obtained. If the Court had upheld the Alabama judgment, virtually any criticism of public officials could be suppressed.

PUBLIC FIGURES

Public officials, movie stars, and generally all persons who become known to the public because of their positions or activities.

ACTUAL MALICE

Actual desire and intent to see another suffer by one's actions. Actual malice in libel cases generally consists of intentionally publishing any written or printed statement that is injurious to the character of another with either knowledge of the statement's falsity or a reckless disregard of the truth.

---

[38]376 U.S. 254 (1964).
[39]Remember that the Supreme Court has held that the Fourteenth Amendment "nationalizes" most of the liberties listed in the Bill of Rights.

In the *New York Times* case, the Supreme Court set a standard that has since been applied to public figures generally. Statements made about public figures, especially when they are made via a public medium, are usually related to matters of general public interest; they are made about people who substantially affect all of us. Furthermore, public figures generally have some access to a public medium for answering disparaging falsehoods about themselves, whereas private individuals do not. For these reasons, public figures have a greater burden of proof (they must prove that the statements were made in actual malice) in defamation cases than do private individuals.

A Free Press versus a Fair Trial: Gag Orders

Another major issue relating to freedom of the press concerns newspaper reports of criminal trials. Amendment VI of the Bill of Rights guarantees a fair trial. In other words, the accused have rights. The Bill of Rights also guarantees freedom of the press. What if the two appear to be in conflict? Which one prevails?

Jurors certainly may be influenced by reading news stories about the trial in which they are participating. In the 1970s, judges increasingly issued **gag orders,** which restricted the publication of news about a trial in progress or even a pretrial hearing. A landmark case, *Nebraska Press Association v. Stuart,*[40] was decided by the Supreme Court in 1976, based on the trial of E. C. Simants, who was charged with the murder of a neighboring family. Because the murder occurred in the course of a sexual assault, details of the crime were lurid. A local Nebraska judge issued an order prohibiting the press from reporting information gleaned in a pretrial hearing. Because there were only 860 people in the town, the judge believed that such publicity would prejudice potential jurors. The Supreme Court unanimously ruled that the Nebraska judge's gag order had violated the First Amendment's freedom of the press clause. Chief Justice Warren Burger indicated that even pervasive adverse pretrial publicity did not necessarily lead to an unfair trial and that prior restraints on publication were not justified. Some justices even went so far as to indicate that gag orders are never justified.

In spite of that *Nebraska Press Association* ruling, the Court has upheld certain types of gag orders. In *Gannett Company v. De Pasquale,*[41] the highest court held that if a judge found a reasonable probability that news publicity would harm a defendant's right to a fair trial, the court could impose a gag rule: "Members of the public have no constitutional right under the Sixth and Fourteenth Amendments to *attend* criminal trials."

The *Nebraska* and *Gannett* cases, however, involved pretrial hearings. Could a judge impose a gag order on an entire trial, including pretrial hearings? In *Richmond Newspapers, Inc. v. Virginia,*[42] the Court ruled that actual trials must be open to the public except under unusual circumstances.

Confidentiality and Reporters' Work Papers

Does freedom of the press mean that news reporters have a right to keep their sources and working papers confidential? To an extent, yes. Courts, however, have often claimed that this right must take second place to the needs of criminal prosecutors to obtain information. In several cases, for example, police

GAG ORDER

An order issued by a judge restricting the publication of news about a trial in progress or a pretrial hearing in order to protect the accused's right to a fair trial.

---

[40]*Nebraska Press Association v. Stuart,* 427 U.S. 539 (1976).
[41]443 U.S. 368 (1979).
[42]448 U.S. 555 (1980).

officers have been permitted to search newspaper offices for documents related to cases under investigation.

One important case concerned the *Stanford Daily*. The campus newspaper of Stanford University had its offices searched by police officers with a search warrant. They were looking for photographs that would identify demonstrators who may have been responsible for injuries to the police. In this particular case, in 1978, the Supreme Court ruled that the protection of confidentiality, and therefore the protection of the First Amendment's guarantee of a free press, was less important under the specific circumstances than the needs of law-enforcement agencies to secure information necessary for prosecution.[43]

Congress responded to the *Stanford Daily* case by enacting the Privacy Protection Act of 1980. This law applies to state as well as federal law-enforcement personnel. It limits their power to obtain evidence from the news media by means of a search warrant and in many instances requires that they use a subpoena. Additionally, more than half of the states have enacted so-called shield laws. These laws protect reporters against having to reveal their sources and other confidential information. Nonetheless, some courts continue to give more weight to law-enforcement needs than to news reporters' needs to keep their sources and notes confidential. For example, in 1993 a federal appeals court ruled that a reporter's material only had to be "relevant" to a case to have to be relinquished to parties in a federal criminal trial.[44]

Other Information Channels: Motion Pictures, Radio, and TV

The framers of our Constitution could not have imagined the ways in which information is disseminated today. Nonetheless, they fashioned the Constitution into a flexible instrument that could respond to social and technological changes. First Amendment freedoms have been applied differently to newer forms of information dissemination.

Motion Pictures: Some Prior Restraint.   The most onerous of all forms of government interference with expression is prior restraint. As was noted, the Supreme Court has not declared all forms of censorship unconstitutional, but it does require an exceptional justification for such restraint. Only in a few cases has the Supreme Court upheld prior restraint of published materials.

The Court's reluctance to accept prior restraint is less evident in the case of motion pictures. In the first half of the twentieth century, films were routinely submitted to local censorship boards. In 1968, the Supreme Court ruled that a film can be banned only under a law that provides for a prompt hearing at which the film is shown to be obscene. Today, few local censorship boards exist. Instead, the film industry regulates itself primarily through the industry's rating system.

Radio and TV: Limited Protection.   Of all forms of communication, television is perhaps the most influential, and radio runs a close second. Radio and television broadcasting has the most limited First Amendment protection. The reason that broadcasting initially acquired more limited protection than the printed media is that the number of airwave frequencies were at the time limited. In 1934, the national government established the Federal Communications Commission (FCC) to regulate electromagnetic wave frequencies. No one has a right to use the airwaves without a license granted by the FCC. The

---

[43]*Zurcher v. Stanford Daily*, 436 U.S. 547 (1978).
[44]*United States v. Cutler*, 6 F.3d 67 (2d Cir. 1993).

Radio "shock jock" Howard Stern apparently offended the sensitivities of the Federal Communications Commission (FCC). That regulatory body fined Stern's radio station owner hundreds of thousands of dollars for Stern's purportedly obscene outbursts on radio. The extent to which the FCC can regulate speech over the air involves the First Amendment. Today, both on the radio and on TV, what is considered permissive and acceptable would probably have been considered "obscene" three decades ago.

FAIRNESS DOCTRINE

An FCC regulation affecting broadcasting media, which required that fair or equal opportunity be given to legitimate opposing political groups or individuals to broadcast their views.

FCC grants licenses for limited periods and imposes numerous regulations on broadcasting.

Although Congress has denied the FCC the authority to censor what is transmitted, the FCC can impose sanctions on those radio or TV stations broadcasting "filthy words," even if the words are not legally obscene.[45] From 1993 through 1995, the FCC fined some radio stations that broadcast the talk show hosted by Howard Stern a total of over $1.5 million for what the agency considered to be indecent radio programs. Also, the FCC has occasionally refused to renew licenses of broadcasters who presumably have not "served the public interest." Perhaps one of the more controversial of the FCC's rulings was its **fairness doctrine,** which was in effect from 1949 to 1987. The doctrine imposed on owners of broadcast licenses an obligation to present "both" sides of significant public issues.

THE RIGHT TO ASSEMBLE AND TO PETITION THE GOVERNMENT

The First Amendment prohibits Congress from making any law that abridges "the right of the people peaceably to assemble and to petition the Government for a redress of grievances." Inherent in such a right is the ability of private citizens to communicate their ideas on public issues to government officials, as well as to other individuals. The Supreme Court has often put this freedom on a par with the freedom of speech and the freedom of the press. Nonetheless, it has allowed municipalities to require permits for parades, sound trucks, and demonstrations, so that public officials may control traffic or prevent demonstrations from turning into riots.[46] This became a major issue in 1977 when the American Nazi party wanted to march through the largely Jewish suburb of Skokie, Illinois. The American Civil Liberties Union defended the Nazis' right to march (in spite of its opposition to the Nazi philosophy). The Supreme Court let stand a lower court's ruling that the city of

---

[45]*Federal Communications Commission v. Pacifica Foundation,* 438 U.S. 726 (1978).
[46]*Davis v. Massachusetts,* 167 U.S. 43 (1897).

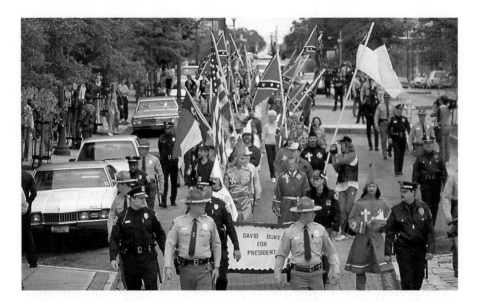

With their right to assemble and demonstrate protected by the Constitution, members of the modern Ku Klux Klan march in Wilmington, North Carolina. The police escort is charged with making sure that neither the marchers nor the observers provoke any violence.

Skokie had violated the Nazis' First Amendment guarantees by denying them a permit to march.[47]

The right to assemble has been defined broadly. For example, municipal and state governments do not have the right to require any organization to publish its membership list. This was decided in *NAACP v. Alabama*.[48] The state of Alabama had required the National Association for the Advancement of Colored People (NAACP) to publish a list of its members. The Supreme Court held that the requirement was unconstitutional because it violated the NAACP's right of assembly, which the Court addressed in terms of freedom of association.

The courts generally have interpreted the right to parade and protest more narrowly than pure forms of speech or assembly. The Supreme Court has generally upheld the right of individuals to parade and protest in public places, but it has ruled against parades and protests when matters of public safety were at issue. In *Cox v. New Hampshire*, for example, the Court ruled that sixty-eight Jehovah's Witnesses had violated a statute prohibiting parading without a permit and upheld the right of a municipality to control its public streets.[49]

MORE LIBERTIES UNDER SCRUTINY: MATTERS OF PRIVACY

During the past several years, a number of civil liberties that relate to the right to privacy have become important social issues. Among the most important issues are those concerning sexual freedom, abortion, and the "right to die."

The Right to Privacy

No explicit reference is made anywhere in the Constitution to a person's right to privacy. The courts did not take a very positive approach toward the right

---

[47]Smith v. Collin, 439 U.S. 916 (1978).
[48]357 U.S. 499 (1958).
[49]312 U.S. 569 (1941).

to privacy until relatively recently. For example, during Prohibition, suspected bootleggers' telephones were routinely tapped, and the information obtained was used as a legal basis for prosecution. In *Olmstead v. United States*,[50] the Supreme Court upheld such an invasion of privacy. Justice Louis Brandeis, a champion of personal freedoms, strongly dissented to the majority decision in this case. He argued that the framers of the Constitution gave every citizen the right to be left alone. He called such a right "the most comprehensive of rights and the right most valued by civilized men."

In the 1960s, the highest court began to modify the majority view. In 1965, in *Griswold v. Connecticut*, the Supreme Court overthrew a Connecticut law that effectively prohibited the use of contraceptives, holding that the law violated the right to privacy.[51] Justice William O. Douglas formulated a unique way of reading this right into the Bill of Rights. He claimed that the First, Third, Fourth, Fifth, and Ninth Amendments created "penumbras, formed by emanations from those guarantees that help give them life and substance," and he went on to talk about zones of privacy that are guaranteed by these rights. When we read the Ninth Amendment, we can see the foundation for his reasoning: "The enumeration in the Constitution of certain rights, shall not be construed to deny or disparage others retained by the people." In other words, just because the Constitution, including its amendments, does not specifically talk about the right to privacy does not mean that this right is denied to the people.

In a reversal of this trend, the Supreme Court ruled in 1986 (by a vote of five to four) that the right to privacy does not protect homosexual acts between consenting adults. It ruled that a Georgia law prohibiting sodomy—oral or anal sex—was constitutional.[52] About half the states have sodomy laws, which are generally intended to restrict homosexual activities.

An important privacy issue, created in part by new technology, is the amassing of information on individuals by government. The average American citizen has personal information filed away in dozens of agencies—such as the Social Security Administration and the Internal Revenue Service. Because of the threat of indiscriminate use of private information by nonauthorized individuals, Congress passed the Privacy Act in 1974. This was the first law regulating the use of federal government information about private individuals. Under the Privacy Act, every citizen has the right to obtain copies of personal records collected by federal agencies and to correct inaccuracies in such records.

Privacy Rights and Abortion

Historically, abortion was not a criminal offense before the "quickening" of the fetus (the first movement of the fetus in the uterus, usually between the sixteenth and eighteenth weeks of pregnancy). During the last half of the nineteenth century, however, state laws became more severe. By 1973, performance of an abortion was a criminal offense in most states.

Roe v. Wade. In *Roe v. Wade*,[53] the United States Supreme Court accepted the argument that the laws against abortion violated "Jane Roe's" right to pri-

---

[50]277 U.S. 438 (1928). This decision was overruled later in *Katz v. United States*, 389 U.S. 347 (1967).
[51]381 U.S. 479 (1965).
[52]*Bowers v. Hardwick*, 478 U.S. 186 (1986).
[53]410 U.S. 113 (1973). Jane Roe was not the real name of the woman in this case. It is a common legal pseudonym used to protect a person's privacy.

vacy under the Constitution. The Court did not answer the question about when life begins. It simply said that "the right to privacy is broad enough to encompass a woman's decision whether or not to terminate her pregnancy." The Court did not say that such a right was absolute, although it implied an absolute right by asserting that any state could impose certain regulations that would safeguard the health of the mother and protect potential life *after* the first three months of pregnancy.

Thus, the Court balanced different interests when it decided that during the first trimester (three months) of pregnancy, abortion was an issue solely between a woman and her doctor. The state could not limit abortions except to require that they be performed by licensed physicians. During the second trimester, to protect the health of the mother, the state was allowed to specify the conditions under which an abortion could be performed. During the final trimester, the state could regulate or even outlaw abortions except when necessary to preserve the life or health of the mother.

After *Roe*, the Supreme Court issued decisions in a number of cases defining and redefining the boundaries of state regulation of abortion. Twice the Court has struck down laws that required a woman who wished to have an abortion to undergo counseling designed to discourage abortions.[54] The Court has held, however, that the government can prohibit doctors in medical clinics that receive federal funding from discussing abortion with their patients.[55]

The *Webster* and *Casey* Decisions. In 1989, the Supreme Court announced its decision in *Webster v. Reproductive Health Services*,[56] a case that challenged very restrictive state laws on abortion. In a narrow five-to-four majority, the Court upheld the restrictions that Missouri placed on the performing of abortions, opening the way for many other states to enact similar or more restrictive laws. Specifically, the ruling allowed states to pass laws that, like the Missouri statute, ban the use of public hospitals or other taxpayer-supported facilities from performing abortions; bar public employees, including doctors and nurses, from assisting in abortions; and require the performance of viability tests on any fetus thought to be at least twenty weeks old. Although the *Webster* decision did not overturn the right to have an abortion, the Court's ruling was a major victory for antiabortion forces. The ultimate effect of the *Webster* decision was to make obtaining an abortion more difficult in some states than in others.

In a 1992 decision, *Planned Parenthood v. Casey*,[57] the Supreme Court upheld a Pennsylvania statute, portions of which were similar to the Missouri law upheld in *Webster*. The Pennsylvania law required that a woman who wished to have an abortion receive specific counseling and wait twenty-four hours. A married woman was required to notify her husband. Unmarried girls under the age of eighteen and not self-supporting were required by the act to obtain the consent of one of their parents or the permission of a state judge. In a five-to-four vote, the Supreme Court upheld all of the law's provisions except the husband-notification requirement.

The Controversy Continues. Although the Supreme Court has never overruled the *Roe v. Wade* decision, some argue that the *Webster* and *Casey* deci-

[54]*Thornburgh v. American College of Obstetricians and Gynecologists,* 476 U.S. 747 (1986); *City of Akron v. Akron Center for Reproductive Health, Inc.,* 462 U.S. 416 (1983).
[55]*Rust v. Sullivan,* 500 U.S. 173 (1991).
[56]492 U.S. 490 (1989).
[57]505 U.S. 833 (1992).

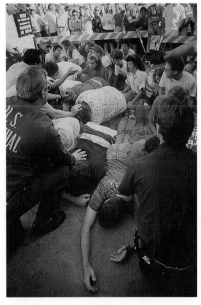

Antiabortion forces increased their demonstration throughout the 1990s. The clash between the pro-choice and the antiabortion forces have resulted in several individuals being killed. The courts imposed restrictions on what antiabortion forces could do in their demonstrations around abortion clinics.

sions have effectively nullified the holding in *Roe.* Certainly, state laws and court decisions have directly challenged the *Roe* decision.

In 1990, for example, the territory of Guam banned all abortions except those necessary to save a woman's life or to preserve her health. Similar laws making abortion illegal have been passed in Louisiana and Utah, and nearly half of the states have laws restricting teenagers' access to abortion. California joined these states in 1996, when the California Supreme Court held that a 1987 state law requiring parent notification or judicial intervention for minors seeking an abortion does not infringe on privacy rights provided by the state constitution.[58]

Antiabortion forces continue to push for laws banning abortion, to endorse political candidates who support their views, and to organize protests. Because of several episodes of violence attending protests at abortion clinics, in 1994 Congress passed the Freedom of Access to Clinic Entrances Act. The act prohibits protesters from blocking entrances to such clinics. The Supreme Court has also ruled that abortion protesters can be prosecuted under laws governing racketeering.[59]

Antiabortion forces have as yet met with little success by arguing that these actions unconstitutionally restrain their right to free speech. In 1995, a federal appeals court upheld the constitutionality of prohibiting protesters from entering a fifteen-foot "buffer zone" around abortion clinics and from giving unwanted counseling to those entering the clinics.[60]

Privacy Rights and the "Right to Die"

The question of whether the right to privacy includes the right to die is now a major point of controversy. Suicide and **euthanasia,** or mercy killing, are both illegal; but many extremely ill people do not want their lives prolonged through expensive artificial measures. These situations often end up in court, because hospitals and doctors sympathetic to the patient's wishes do not want to be legally or morally responsible for giving the order to stop treatment, even with the patient's and family's consent.

The 1976 case involving Karen Ann Quinlan was one of the first publicized right-to-die cases.[61] The parents of Quinlan, a young woman who had been in a coma since age twenty-one and kept alive by a respirator, wanted her respirator removed. The New Jersey Supreme Court ruled that the right to privacy includes the right of a patient to refuse treatment and that patients unable to speak can exercise that right through a family member or guardian. In its ruling on a 1985 case, the New Jersey Supreme Court set some clear guidelines for when care could be withheld for patients who cannot express their own wishes.[62] Care can be withheld if (1) the patient definitely would have refused treatment, (2) evidence suggests that treatment would have been refused, and (3) the burdens of continuing care are greater than the benefits.

In the 1990s, the most controversial aspect of right-to-die issues has to do with whether terminally ill persons have the right to end their lives through physician-assisted suicide. In particular, the activities of Dr. Jack Kevorkian of Michigan—who has yet to be convicted under Michigan law for assisting people who want to "die with dignity"—have focused public attention on this issue. Currently, over half of the states have laws specifically banning assisted suicide, and most of the other states prohibit the practice under their general homicide statutes.

EUTHANASIA

Killing incurably ill people for reasons of mercy.

---

[58]*American Academy of Pediatrics v. Lungren,* 12 Cal.4th 1007 (1996).
[59]*National Organization of Women v. Joseph Scheidler,* 509 U.S. 951 (1993).
[60]*ProChoice Network v. Schenck,* 67 F.3d 377 (2d Cir. 1995).
[61]*In re Quinlan,* 70 N.J. 10 (1976).
[62]*In re Conroy,* 98 N.J. 321 (1985).

In a historic shift in the attitude of the courts toward assisted suicide, in March 1996 a federal appeals court held that Washington state's ban on physician-assisted suicide violated the U.S. Constitution, which, according to the court, protects the right to die. The court could see little difference between assisting a terminally ill person in ending his or her life and withdrawing life-sustaining treatment from terminally ill patients. Furthermore, said the court, "What interest can the state possibly have in requiring the prolongation of a life that is all but ended?"[63] Two months later, another federal appeals court held that a similar New York law banning assisted suicide was unconstitutional.[64]

The implications of these decisions have alarmed many Americans, including several state attorneys general. Certainly, the decisions have intensified the controversy over this issue, which no doubt will come before the Supreme Court in the near future.

THE GREAT BALANCING ACT: THE RIGHTS OF THE ACCUSED VERSUS THE RIGHTS OF SOCIETY

The United States has one of the highest violent crime rates in the world. It is not surprising, therefore, that many citizens have extremely strong opinions about the rights of those accused of criminal offenses. When an accused person, especially one who has confessed to some criminal act, is set free because of an apparent legal "technicality," many people may feel that the rights of the accused are being given more weight than the rights of society and of potential or actual victims. Why, then, give criminal suspects rights? The answer is partly to avoid convicting innocent people, but mostly because all citizens have rights, and criminal suspects are citizens.

The courts and the police must constantly engage in a balancing act of competing rights. At the basis of all discussions about the appropriate balance is, of course, the U.S. Bill of Rights. The Fourth, Fifth, Sixth, and Eighth Amendments deal specifically with the rights of criminal defendants.

Rights of the Accused

The basic rights of criminal defendants are outlined below. When appropriate, the specific amendment on which a right is based also is given.

Limits on the Conduct of Police Officers and Prosecutors
- No unreasonable or unwarranted searches and seizures (Amend. IV).
- No arrest except on probable cause (Amend. IV).
- No coerced confessions or illegal interrogation (Amend. V).
- No entrapment.
- Upon questioning, a suspect must be informed of his or her rights.

Defendant's Pretrial Rights
- **Writ of *habeas corpus*** (Article I, Section 9).
- Prompt arraignment (Amend. VI).
- Legal counsel (Amend. VI).
- Reasonable bail (Amend. VIII).
- To be informed of charges (Amend. VI).
- To remain silent (Amend. V).

WRIT OF *HABEAS CORPUS*

Habeas corpus means, literally, "you have the body." A writ of *habeas corpus* is an order that requires jailers to bring a person before a court or judge and explain why the person is being held in prison.

---

[63]*Compassion in Dying v. Washington*, 85 F.3d 1440 (9th Cir. 1996).
[64]*Quill v. Vacco*, 80 F.3d 716 (2d Cir. 1996).

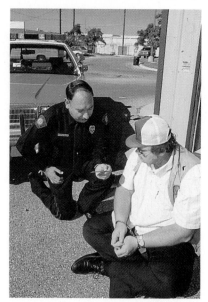

This individual is being read his *Miranda* rights by the arresting officer. These rights were established in the 1966 case *Miranda v. Arizona*. The rights concern minimum procedural safeguards. They are also known as the *Miranda* warnings and include informing arrested persons prior to questioning (1) that they have the right to remain silent, (2) that anything they say may be used as evidence against them, and (3) that they have the right to the presence of an attorney.

Trial Rights

- Speedy and public trial before a jury (Amend. VI).
- Impartial jury selected from a cross section of the community (Amend. VI).
- Trial atmosphere free of prejudice, fear, and outside interference.
- No compulsory self-incrimination (Amend. V).
- Adequate counsel (Amend. VI).
- No cruel and unusual punishment (Amend. VIII).
- Appeal of convictions.
- No double jeopardy (Amend. V).

Extending the Rights of the Accused

During the 1960s, the Supreme Court, under Chief Justice Earl Warren, expanded significantly the rights of accused persons. In a case decided in 1963, *Gideon v. Wainwright*,[65] the Court held that if a person is accused of a felony and cannot afford an attorney, an attorney must be made available to the accused person at the government's expense. Although the Sixth Amendment to the Constitution provides for the right to counsel, the Supreme Court had established a precedent twenty-one years earlier in *Betts v. Brady*,[66] when it held that only criminal defendents in capital cases automatically had a right to legal counsel.

Three years later, the Court issued its decision in *Miranda v. Arizona*.[67] The case involved Ernesto Miranda, who was arrested and charged with the kidnapping and rape of a young woman. After two hours of questioning, Miranda confessed and was later convicted. Miranda's lawyer appealed his conviction, arguing that the police had never informed Miranda that he had a right to remain silent and a right to be represented by counsel. The Court, in ruling in Miranda's favor, enunciated the *Miranda* rights that are now familiar to virtually all Americans:

> Prior to any questioning, the person must be warned that he has a right to remain silent, that any statement he does make may be used against him, and that he has a right to the presence of an attorney, either retained or appointed.

Many people, particularly police officials, complained that the *Miranda* ruling distorted the Constitution by placing the rights of criminal suspects above the rights of society as a whole. Others, however, agreed with the Court that criminal law enforcement would be more reliable if it were based on independently secured evidence rather than on confessions obtained under coercive interrogation conditions in the absence of counsel.

As part of a continuing attempt to balance the rights of criminal defendants against the rights of society, Congress and the courts subsequently have created several exceptions to the *Miranda* ruling. For example, the Omnibus Crime Control and Safe Streets Act of 1968 provided that in federal cases, a voluntary confession could be used as evidence even if the accused person was not informed of his or her rights. Even in cases that are not tried in federal courts, confessions have been allowed into evidence in certain circumstances. For example, in 1984 the Supreme Court held that when "public safety" required action (in this case, to find a loaded gun), police could interrogate the suspect before advising him of his right to remain silent.[68]

---

[65]372 U.S. 335 (1963).
[66]316 U.S. 455 (1942).
[67]384 U.S. 436 (1966).
[68]*New York v. Quarles*, 467 U.S. 649 (1984).

The Exclusionary Rule

At least since 1914, judicial policy has prohibited the admission of illegally seized evidence at trials in federal courts. This is the so-called **exclusionary rule.** Improperly obtained evidence, no matter how telling, could not be used by prosecutors. This includes evidence obtained by police in violation of a suspect's *Miranda* rights or of the Fourth Amendment. The Fourth Amendment protects against unreasonable searches and seizures and requires that a search warrant may be issued by a judge to a police officer only on probable cause (a demonstration of facts that permit a reasonable belief that a crime has been committed). The question that must be determined by the courts is what constitutes an "unreasonable" search and seizure.

The reasoning behind the exclusionary rule is that it forces police officers to gather evidence properly, in which case their due diligence will be rewarded by a conviction. There have always been critics of the exclusionary rule who argue that it permits guilty persons to be freed because of innocent errors.

This rule was first extended to state court proceedings in the 1961 Supreme Court decision *Mapp v. Ohio.*[69] In this case, the Court overturned the conviction of Dollree Mapp for the possession of obscene materials. Police found pornographic books in her apartment after searching it without a search warrant despite her refusal to let them in.

In 1984, the Supreme Court held that illegally obtained evidence could be admitted at trial if law-enforcement personnel could prove that they would have obtained the evidence legally anyway.[70] In another case decided in the same year, the Court held that a police officer who used a technically incorrect search warrant form to obtain evidence had acted in good faith and therefore the evidence was admissible at trial. The Court thus created the "good faith" exception to the exclusionary rule.[71]

Other exceptions to the rule made by the courts during the 1980s and 1990s have tended to further weaken criminal defendants' rights and, according to many critics, have allowed law-enforcement personnel to exercise power a little too arbitrarily. Who is to say, for example, whether a police officer was acting in "good faith" when obtaining evidence against a criminal suspect? Others argue that these exceptions have not altered the basic fact that the numerous rights of criminal defendants' make justice difficult—if not impossible—to obtain (see the feature entitled *Politics and Criminal Justice* for a further discussion of this view).

The Death Penalty

Capital punishment remains one of the most debated aspects of our criminal justice system. Those in favor of it maintain that it serves as a deterrent to serious crime and satisfies society's need for justice and fair play. Those opposed to the death penalty to not believe it has any deterrent value and hold that it constitutes a barbaric act in an otherwise civilized society. Recent public opinion polls have demonstrated that a large majority of Americans favor using the death penalty more frequently, and most states currently provide for the death penalty. (See this chapter's *Politics and the Fifty States* for a list indicating which states have the death penalty and which do not.)

---

[69]367 U.S. 643 (1961).
[70]*Nix v. Williams*, 467 U.S. 431 (1984).
[71]*Massachusetts v. Sheppard*, 468 U.S. 981 (1984).

DID YOU KNOW...
That the state of North Carolina commissioned a $27,000 study to determine why inmates want to escape from prison?

EXCLUSIONARY RULE

A policy forbidding the admission at trial of illegally seized evidence.

Capital punishment became a viable alternative after a 1972 Supreme Court ruling. In 1992, Arizona executed its first inmate in twenty-nine years, Delaware its first in forty-six years, and California its first in twenty-five years. By 1996, about one prisoner a week was being executed.

POLITICS AND THE FIFTY STATES
The Death Penalty

At the time the Constitution and Bill of Rights were written and ratified, the death penalty was widely accepted, and many offenses were punishable by death. Today, all but thirteen states impose the death penalty, and virtually all death sentences are for murder. The following list indicates the states that have the death penalty and the method of execution that is used in each state.

STATES IMPOSING THE DEATH PENALTY	METHOD OF EXECUTION	STATES IMPOSING THE DEATH PENALTY	METHOD OF EXECUTION
Alabama	Electrocution	Nebraska	Electrocution
Arizona	Lethal injection or lethal gas	Nevada	Lethal injection
Arkansas	Lethal injection or electrocution	New Hampshire	Lethal injection or hanging
California	Lethal injection or lethal gas	New Jersey	Lethal injeciton
Colorado	Lethal injection or lethal gas	New Mexico	Lethal injection
Connecticut	Electrocution	North Carolina	Lethal injection or lethal gas
Delaware	Lethal injection or hanging	Ohio	Lethal injection or electrocution
Florida	Electrocution	Oklahoma	Lethal injection
Georgia	Electrocution	Oregon	Lethal injection
Idaho	Lethal injection	Pennsylvania	Lethal injection
Illinois	Lethal injection	South Carolina	Electrocution
Indiana	Electrocution	South Dakota	Lethal injection
Kansas	Lethal injection	Tennessee	Electrocution
Kentucky	Electrocution	Texas	Lethal injection
Louisiana	Lethal injection	Utah	Lethal injection or firing squad
Maryland	Lethal injection or lethal gas	Virginia	Electrocution
Mississippi	Lethal injection or lethal gas	Washington	Lethal injection or hanging
Missouri	Lethal injection or lethal gas	Wyoming	Lethal injection or lethal gas
Montana	Lethal injection or hanging		

SOURCE: *The Book of the States, 1996–1997 Edition.* Lexington, Ky.: The Council of State Governments, 1996.

For Critical Analysis
What factors do you think influence a state's choice to impose (or not to impose) the death penalty?

murderers were being executed at a rate of about one a week. There also may be federal executions soon. Although the federal government has not executed in over thirty-six years, as of September 1996, eleven individuals had been sentenced to death for federal crimes; their cases are now pending on appeal.

Sanity Issues.   Issues surrounding the sanity of death-row inmates have come up in the last decade. In 1986, the Supreme Court ruled that the U.S. Constitution bars states from executing convicted killers who have become insane while waiting on death row *(Ford v. Wainwright).*[73] Despite this ruling, in 1989 the Supreme Court held that mentally retarded persons may be executed for murder *(Penry v. Lynaugh).*[74] In the same year, the Court found that defendants who were as young as sixteen could be executed if they had com-

---

[73]477 U.S. 399 (1986).
[74]492 U.S. 302 (1989).

mitted a murder (*Stanford v. Kentucky*).[75] Finally, in *Murray v. Giarratano*,[76] the Court held that indigent death-row inmates have no constitutional right to a lawyer for a second round of state court appeals.

Racial Bias.   The Supreme Court also must wrestle with issues involving racial discrimination and the death penalty. When the Court considered statistical evidence regarding one state's death-sentencing process, which the defendant claimed was racially discriminatory, the Court held that some disparities are an inevitable part of the criminal justice system and do not necessarily violate the Constitution.[77] In Georgia, in 1978, the defendant, a black man, was convicted of armed robbery and murder—shooting a white police officer in the face during the robbery of a store. The jury recommended the death penalty, and the trial court followed the recommendation. On appeal, the defendant presented a statistical study based on more than two thousand murder cases that occurred in Georgia during the 1970s. The study purported to show that the death sentence was imposed more often on black defendants convicted of killing whites than on white defendants convicted of killing blacks. The Supreme Court decided that the statistics did not prove that race enters into capital sentencing decisions or that it was a factor in the defendant's case. The Court stated that the unpredictability of jury decisions does not justify their condemnation, because it is the jury's function to make difficult judgments. The Court explained that any method for determining guilt or punishment has its weaknesses and the potential for misuse. Despite such imperfections, the Court concluded, constitutional guarantees are met when the method has been made as fair as possible.

CIVIL LIBERTIES: UNFINISHED WORK

During the 1950s, 1960s, and 1970s, the United States Supreme Court made numerous landmark decisions establishing new liberties for all Americans. During the 1980s and early 1990s, federal judges issued fewer important decisions regarding civil liberties. At the state level, though, the state supreme courts continued to expand civil liberties beyond what the federal courts were willing to do. We can expect this trend toward increased state authority and expanded civil liberties to continue and to serve as an example of the flexibility of the American system of government.

In the future, the courts certainly will have to grapple with several significant issues concerning First Amendment freedoms. One issue concerns the emerging use of the Internet for personal communications and business transactions. Adapting traditional legal concepts and doctrines to the realm of cyberspace—and establishing new laws and guidelines—will take time and will certainly elicit controversy. So will decisions as to whether the Internet should be regulated and who the regulators should be. "Hate speech" and disorderly protests will also force difficult trade-offs to be made between the constitutional guarantee of free speech and society's need to reduce violence.

There is also much unfinished work with respect to religious freedom. The desire of many Americans to express publicly their religious beliefs presents an ongoing challenge to courts and legislators, who at some point will need to issue more definitive guidelines on such issues as school prayer, the teach-

---

[75]*Stanford v. Kentucky*, 492 U.S. 361 (1989).
[76]492 U.S. 1 (1989).
[77]*McCleskey v. Kemp*, 481 U.S. 279 (1987).

CONCEPT OVERVIEW

CONCEPT OVERVIEW
Changes in Civil Liberties

Our civil liberties are in a constant state of evolution. Here are just a few of the changes in civil liberties that have occurred since the Constitution and the Bill of Rights were adopted (by 1791).

THEN	NOW
• Bill of Rights applied only to the national government, not state governments.	• Bill of Rights applies to actions by both the national government and state governments.
• No restrictions on free speech by federal courts.	• Numerous restrictions on free speech by federal courts.
• No *Miranda* rights.	• *Miranda* rights.
• No exclusionary rule.	• Exclusionary rule.
• No significant privacy rights.	• Significant privacy rights in many circumstances and jurisdictions.
• Assisted suicide generally illegal.	• Assisted suicide legal in some states.
• Religion and values taught in schools.	• Laws prohibit religious teaching in public schools.
• Religious displays and public prayer were common.	• Few publicly supported religious displays; public prayer is rare.
• Death penalty for many offenses.	• Death penalty primarily for murder.

ing of evolution, and the use of public funds for education in church-related schools.

The growing hostility toward the national government and the emergence of citizens' militias, particularly in the western states, no doubt will engender even more debate over the Second Amendment's provision concerning the right to bear arms. Part of the unfinished work of the government in regard to constitutional liberties is whether these militias should—and legally can—be banned in the interests of civil order.

The abortion issue as it relates to privacy and other constitutional matters has yet to be resolved and constitutes some of the major unfinished work in the area of civil liberties. Whether our civil liberties include a right to "assisted suicide" is another pressing question that will not be easy to decide.

Finally, because crime continues to be a major problem in this country, the rights of accused persons probably will continue to be challenged. As American society looks for new ways to halt crime, it also must attempt to maintain some kind of balance between the rights of accused persons and the rights of those who suffer from criminal wrongdoing. If past experience is any indication, this work will remain unfinished for generations to come.

GETTING INVOLVED
Your Civil Liberties: Searches and Seizures

What happens if you are stopped by members of the police force? Your civil liberties protect you from having to provide any other information than your name and address. Indeed, you are not really required to produce identification, although it is a good idea to show this to the officers. Normally, even if you have not been placed under arrest, the officers have the right to frisk you for weapons, and you must let them proceed. The officers cannot, however, check your person or your clothing further if, in their judgment, no weaponlike object is produced. The officers may search you only if they have a search warrant or probable cause that they will likely find incriminating evidence if the search is conducted. Normally, it is unwise to resist physically the officers' attempt to search you if they do not have probable cause or a warrant; it is usually best simply to refuse orally to give permission for the search, preferably in the presence of a witness. Also, it is usually advisable to tell the officer as little as possible about yourself and the situation that is under investigation. Being polite and courteous, though firm, is better than acting out of anger or frustration and making the officers irritable. If you are arrested, it is best to keep quiet until you can speak with a lawyer.

If you are in your car and are stopped by the police, the same fundamental rules apply. Always be ready to show your driver's license and car registration quickly. You may be asked to get out of the car. The officers may use a flashlight to peer inside if it is too dark to see otherwise. None of this constitutes a search. A true search requires either a warrant or probable cause. No officer has the legal right to search your car simply to find out if you may have committed a crime. Police officers can conduct searches that are incident to lawful arrests, however.

If you are in your residence and a police officer with a search warrant appears, you should examine the warrant before granting entry. A warrant that is correctly made out will state the exact place or persons to be searched, a description of the object sought, and the date of the warrant (which should be no more than ten days old), and it will bear the signature of a judge or magistrate. If the search warrant is in order, you should not make any statement. If you believe the warrant to be invalid, you should make it clear orally that you have not consented to the search, preferably in the presence of a witness. If the warrant later is proved to be invalid, normally any evidence obtained will be considered illegal.

Officers who attempt to enter your home without a search warrant can do so only if they are pursuing a suspected felon into the house. Rarely is it advisable to give permission for a warrantless search. You, as the resident, must be the one to give permission if any evidence obtained will be considered to be legal. The landlord, manager, or head of a college dormitory cannot give legal permission. A roommate, however, can give permission for a search of his or her room, which may allow the police to search those areas in which you have personal belongings.

If you find yourself a guest in a location that is being legally searched, you may be legally searched also. But unless you have been placed under arrest, you cannot be compelled to go to the police station or into a squad car.

If you would like to find out more about your rights and obligations under the laws of searches and seizures, you might wish to contact the following organizations:

THE AMERICAN CIVIL LIBERTIES UNION
132 West 43d St.
New York, NY 10036
1-800-775-ACLU
http://www.aclu.org/

LEGAL DEFENSE FUND
755 Riverpoint Dr.
West Sacramento, CA 95605
1-800-882-9906

KEY TERMS

actionable 120	establishment clause 108	libel 120
actual malice 121	euthanasia 128	preferred-position doctrine 113
bad-tendency rule 114	exclusionary rule 131	prior restraint 114
Bill of Rights 105	fairness doctrine 124	public figures 121
civil liberties 105	fighting words 118	slander 117
civil rights 105	free exercise clause 111	symbolic speech 114
clear and present danger test 113	gag order 122	writ of *habeas corpus* 129
commercial speech 115	hecklers' veto 119	
defamation of character 117	incorporation theory 107	

CHAPTER SUMMARY

❶ To deal with American colonists' fears of a too-powerful national government, after the adoption of the U.S. Constitution, Congress proposed a Bill of Rights. These ten amendments to the Constitution were ratified by the states by the end of 1791. The amendments represent civil liberties—that is, they are limitations on the government.

❷ Originally, the Bill of Rights limited only the power of the national government, not that of the states. Gradually, however, the Supreme Court accepted the incorporation theory under which no state can violate the Bill of Rights.

❸ The First Amendment protects against government interference with the freedom of religion by requiring a separation of church and state and by guaranteeing the free exercise of religion. The separation of church and state is mandated in the establishment clause. Under this clause, the Supreme Court has ruled against officially sponsored prayer, Bible-reading sessions, and "meditation, prayer, or silent reflection" in public schools. The Court has also struck down laws forbidding the teaching of evolution or requiring the teaching of the biblical story of the Creation. The government can provide financial aid to religious schools if the aid is secular in aim, the aid does not have the primary effect of advancing or inhibiting religion, and the government avoids "an excessive entanglement with religion."

❹ The First Amendment protects against government interference with the freedom of speech, which includes symbolic speech (expressive conduct). Restrictions are permitted when expression presents a clear and present danger to the peace or public order, or when expression has a bad tendency (that is, when it might lead to some "evil"). Expression may be restrained before it occurs, but such prior restraint has a "heavy presumption" against its constitutionality. Commercial speech (advertising) by businesses has received First Amendment protection. Speech that has not received First Amendment protection includes expression judged to be obscene, utterances considered to be slanderous, and speech constituting fighting words or a hecklers' veto.

❺ The First Amendment protects against government interference with the freedom of the press, which can be regarded as a special instance of freedom of speech. Speech by the press that does not receive protection includes libelous statements made with actual malice. Publication of news about a criminal trial may be restricted by a gag order under unusual circumstances. The press may be asked to cooperate in criminal investigations by revealing its sources or providing other evidence in response to subpoenas or search warrants. In many states, shield laws protect reporters from having to reveal their sources and confidential information.

❻ The First Amendment protects the right to assemble peaceably and to petition the government. Permits may be required for parades, sound trucks, and demonstrations to maintain the public order, and a permit may be denied to protect the public safety. To avoid government interference with freedom of association, an organization cannot be required to publish a list of its members.

❼ Under the Ninth Amendment, rights not specifically mentioned in the Constitution are not denied to the people. Among these unspecified rights is a right to privacy, which has been implied through the First, Third, Fourth,

Fifth, and Ninth Amendments. Questions concerning whether an individual's privacy rights include a right to have an abortion or a "right to die" continue to elicit controversy. Another issue with serious implications is whether a terminally ill person has the right to commit physician-assisted suicide. The Supreme Court has yet to rule on the latter issue.

⑧ The Constitution includes protections for the rights of persons accused of crimes. Under the Fourth Amendment, no one may be subject to an unreasonable search or seizure or arrested except on probable cause. Under the Fifth Amendment, an accused person has the right to remain silent. Under the Sixth Amendment, an accused

person must be informed of the reason for his or her arrest. The accused also has the right to adequate counsel, even if he or she cannot afford an attorney, and the right to a prompt arraignment and a speedy and public trial before an impartial jury selected from a cross section of the community. Under the Eighth Amendment, cruel and unusual punishment is prohibited. The exclusionary rule forbids the admission in court of illegally seized evidence. There is a "good faith exception" to the exclusionary rule: illegally seized evidence need not be thrown out owing to, for example, a technical defect in a search warrant. Whether the death penalty is cruel and unusual punishment continues to be debated.

QUESTIONS FOR REVIEW AND DISCUSSION

❶ The Bill of Rights initially applied only to the federal government. Does this mean that the states' governments had an unlimited ability to bridle their citizens' basic civil liberties? Why or why not?

❷ "If parents had the ability to choose freely which schools their children attended, the school prayer issue would be much less important." Do you agree or disagree with this statement? Explain your answer.

❸ The Supreme Court has often made the distinction between free speech and less-protected commercial speech. Why do you think a distinction has been made between "regular" speech and commercial speech?

❹ What is the trade-off between judges' issuing gag orders and the public's "right to know"? In other words, whose freedoms and liberties are at issue when a gag order is instituted by a judge?

❺ As the use of the Internet becomes more widespread, Americans will have access to information on virtually every possible topic, including a wide range of political views on civil liberties. How will this information affect political debate on the issues discussed in this chapter?

❻ Today there are numerous "drug exceptions" to the Fourth Amendment's prohibition against unreasonable searches and seizures. What are the advantages and drawbacks involved in allowing such drug exceptions, which are typically used when the possibility of illegal drug manufacture, sale, or use is involved?

❼ "As long as there is the possibility of one innocent person's being put to death under capital punishment laws, such laws should be deemed unconstitutional." Do you agree or disagree with this statement? Why?

LOGGING ON: CIVIL LIBERTIES

Go To: http://www.public.iastate.edu/~sws/homepage.html

The leading civil liberties organization, the American Civil Liberties Union (ACLU), can be found at

http://www.aclu.org/

Here are some of the current choices on its home page: Church and State; Criminal Justice; Cyber-Liberties; Death Penalty; Free Speech; Lesbian and Gay Rights; Reproductive Rights; Students' Rights. As you can see, the ACLU offers a wide array of information. It's also interesting to see how the ACLU defines civil liberties for its own work.

A group called the Liberty Counsel can be found at

http://www.lc.org/

The Liberty Counsel, according to its Web page description,

is a nonprofit religious civil liberties education and legal defense organization established to preserve religious freedom. Established in 1989, Liberty Counsel provides information on First Amendment religious rights, and *pro bono* [free or at a reduced price] legal defense to defend those rights. Educational materials available through Liberty Counsel include a variety of information brochures on subjects such as students' and teachers' rights on public school campuses, prayers in public schools, political activity of nonprofit organizations, equal access, and more. Liberty Counsel also publishes a monthly newsletter, *The Liberator*. Additionally, Liberty Counsel produces a two-minute radio program, "Freedom's Call," dealing with First Amendment civil liberties.

The home page of Human & Civil Rights Organizations of America Members is found at

http://www.charitiesusa.com/charitiesusa/fedmain/hcroamain.html

Its teaser reads, "Help stop racial discrimination, fight religious bigotry, prosecute hate crimes, end unfair sex bias, defend democratic principles, and promote equality, freedom and justice for all. (800) 626-6347." The last time we hit the site, the list of members included AARP's Legal Counsel for the Elderly, Advocates for Fair Family Support, AIDS National Interfaith Network, Alternative Gifts International, American Civil Liberties Union Foundation, American Council of the Blind, American Youth Hostels, Catholic Legal Immigration Services, Democracy for China Fund, Blind Children and Adults Action Fund of America, Disability Rights Education and Defense Fund, Medicare Beneficiaries Defense Fund, National Victim Center, Special Olympics International, and dozens of others.

SELECTED REFERENCES

Brownlie, Ian. *Basic Documents on Human Rights*. 3d ed. New York: Oxford University Press, 1993. This compact handbook gives a useful collection of sources on human rights throughout the world. It includes recent U.N. declarations; European conventions; and Latin American, African, and Asian human rights developments.

Calvi, James V., and Susan Coleman. *Cases in Constitutional Law: Summaries and Critiques*. Englewood Cliffs, N.J.:

Prentice-Hall, 1994. Of the 122 significant Supreme Court cases involving the Constitution included in this book, dozens apply to civil liberties, including freedom of religion (Chapter 6); freedom of speech, press, and association (Chapter 7); and the rights of accused persons (Chapter 8).

Cushman, Robert. *Cases in Civil Liberties*. 6th ed. Englewood Cliffs, N.J.: Prentice-Hall, 1994. This collection of Supreme Court cases includes introductory notes that place each opinion in its social, economic, and political context. The book includes cases involving the nationalization of the Bill of Rights, all First Amendment rights, and the power to protect individuals.

Dworkin, R.M. *Freedom's Law: The Moral Reading of the American Constitution.* Cambridge, Mass.: Harvard University Press, 1996. The author passionately defends freedom of speech and freedom of conscience. He urges a broad reading of the First Amendment in the interests of promoting an open and tolerant society.

Fish, Stanley. *There's No Such Thing as Free Speech and It's a Good Thing, Too.* New York: Oxford University Press. 1995. The author, a noted professor of law, takes a different approach to writing about the First Amendment. Using literary allusions and wit, he presents a set of essays that lays out his view that the powers must always define what free speech is. He believes that speech (by Nazi groups, for example) can be dangerous and provides a rationale for necessary limits on free speech.

Fiss, Owen M. *The Irony of Free Speech.* Cambridge, Mass.: Harvard University Press, 1996. The author, a professor at Yale Law School, argues that the state "might become the friend, rather than the enemy, of freedom" by suppressing certain types of speech, such as hate speech and pornography.

Greenawalt, Kent. *Fighting Words: Individuals, Communities and Liberties of Speech.* Princeton, N.J.: Princeton University Press, 1995. The author compares the treatment of free speech questions in the United States and Canada, examining such issues as hate speech, obscenity, and workplace harassment.

Lewis, Anthony. *Gideon's Trumpet.* New York: Vintage, 1964. This classic work discusses the background and facts of *Gideon v. Wainwright*, the 1963 Supreme Court case in which the Court held that the state must make an attorney available for any person accused of a felony who cannot afford a lawyer.

Moe, Terry M., ed. *Private Vouchers.* Stanford, Calif.: The Hoover Institution, 1995. This collection of essays focuses on the school voucher movement, one of today's most controversial forces for change in American education.

Pacheco, Josephine S., ed. *To Secure the Blessings of Liberty: Rights in American History.* Lanham, Md.: University Press of America and Center for the Study of Constitutional Rights, 1993. The essays in this book examine the expanding concepts of liberty by demonstrating the relevance of the Bill of Rights in today's world.

Rauch, Jonathan. *Kindly Inquisitors: The New Attacks on Free Thought.* Chicago: University of Chicago Press, 1993. The author attempts to move beyond the First Amendment in defending morality. He examines fundamentalists' beliefs, intellectual egalitarian beliefs, and humanitarian beliefs, the latter involving the "political correctness" movement.

Shriffin, Steven H. *The First Amendment, Democracy, and Romance.* Cambridge, Mass.: Harvard University Press, 1990. In this highly readable and well-researched work, Shriffin argues that the First Amendment should be interpreted more broadly and that emotion, as well as logic, has its place in the law.

Stone, Geoffrey R., Richard A. Epstein, and Cass R. Sunstein, *The Bill of Rights in the Modern State.* Chicago: University of Chicago Press, 1992. This collection of essays written by prominent constitutional scholars explores some of today's most controversial constitutional issues. Such issues as freedom of religion, freedom of speech, and constitutional interpretation are discussed from a variety of perspectives.

Waldron, Jeremy. *Liberal Rights: Collected Papers 1981–1991.* New York: Cambridge University Press, 1993. The author deals with freedom, toleration, and neutrality in arguing for a robust conception of liberty. He defends the right of people to act in ways that others might not approve of. He also argues that the state should be neutral with respect to religious and ethical systems.

5
Civil Rights

CHAPTER OUTLINE

A Moratorium Were Placed on All Immigration?

BACKGROUND

AMERICA HAS ALWAYS BEEN A LAND OF IMMIGRANTS—AND IT CONTINUES TO BE. TODAY, NEARLY 9 PERCENT (ABOUT 23 MILLION) OF THE PEOPLE LIVING IN THIS COUNTRY WERE BORN ELSEWHERE, AND THE NUMBER OF IMMIGRANTS IS RISING AT A RAPID PACE. IN FACT, THE RATE OF IMMIGRATION IS NOW HIGHER THAN IT HAS BEEN AT ANY TIME SINCE 1940. RISING IMMIGRATION RATES WORRY SOME AMERICANS, WHO FEAR THAT RECENT IMMIGRANTS ARE GETTING JOBS THAT SHOULD GO TO NATIVE-BORN AMERICANS OR THAT STATE BUDGETS CAN NO LONGER ENDURE THE STRAIN OF PROVIDING PUBLIC BENEFITS FOR IMMIGRANTS. ONE WAY TO ADDRESS THESE PROBLEMS, ACCORDING TO SOME, WOULD BE TO PLACE A MORATORIUM ON ALL IMMIGRATION.

WHAT IF THE GOVERNMENT PLACED A MORATORIUM ON ALL IMMIGRATION?

Certainly, a moratorium on immigration would reduce the economic costs (for medical care, public schooling, and other services) faced by some states, such as California, due to large numbers of new immigrants. Additionally, more jobs would be available to native-born American workers (at least, in the short run). Instead of hiring cheaper new immigrant labor, U.S. employers would hire American workers, who would then receive the wages and employment benefits that currently go to new immigrants. Of course, a moratorium on immigration would not solve the problem of illegal immigration, which troubles many Americans.

ECONOMIC EFFECTS

Many contend that a moratorium on immigration would have a negative impact on the U.S. economy. Historically, immigrants have contributed significantly to U.S. economic growth. Today, a large percentage of the "best and brightest" individuals hired by American corporations are scientists from other countries. Over one-fourth of those with doctoral degrees who are engaged in research and development for American companies are foreign-born individuals. A moratorium on immigration would prevent U.S. firms from recruiting highly skilled computer scientists, civil engineers, and others who help to make U.S. companies competitive on a global level.

Entrepreneurship rates also are high among immigrants. In fact, some of today's leading high-tech companies have been founded or led by immigrants (see Chapter 16 for a further discussion of immigration and the contributions of immigrants to the American economy).

FOR CRITICAL ANALYSIS

1. *What might be some of the reasons for the growing anti-immigration sentiment in this country?*

2. *How can you explain the fact that a significant percentage of the "best and brightest" in American corporations are foreign born?*

We hold these Truths to be self-evident, that all Men are created equal . . .

These words from the Declaration of Independence are beautiful, to be sure. When they were written in 1776, however, the term *men* had a somewhat different meaning than it has today. It did not include slaves, women, or Native Americans. So individuals in these groups were not considered equal. It has taken this nation over two hundred years to approach even a semblance of equality among all Americans. The struggle for equality has not been easy, and, as you will read in the following pages, the struggle continues. The struggle perhaps is best described as an effort to strengthen and to expand constitutional guarantees to *all* persons in our society.

Minority rights have often been called civil rights. As with our civil liberties, our civil rights are not written in stone—they change over time. In fact, the tremendous expansion of the civil rights of minority groups during the past several decades has caused some Americans to believe that these groups may have too many rights. Similarly, as you read in this chapter's opening *What If . . . ,* the rights of immigrants to receive certain public benefits and services are now being called into question by some Americans. In a word, our civil rights are dependent on society's perception of fairness and justice—and this perception changes over time.

In this chapter and in the one that follows, we examine the rights of various minorities and groups: African Americans, Mexican Americans and other Hispanics, Native Americans, Asian Americans, women, gays and lesbians, the elderly, and juveniles—to name just some of them. As you read these chapters, bear in mind that there are many minority groups that we do not discuss here. Arab Americans from Middle Eastern countries also struggle for equal treatment in the United States, as do persons from India, various island nations, and other countries. The fact that these groups are not singled out for special attention in the following pages should not be construed to mean that their struggle for equality is any less significant than the struggle of the larger groups that we do discuss.

The quest for the expansion of minority rights has been called the civil rights movement. Because the modern civil rights movement started with the struggle for African American equality, that story is told first.

AFRICAN AMERICANS AND THE CONSEQUENCES OF SLAVERY IN THE UNITED STATES

Article I, Section 2, of the U.S. Constitution states that congressional representatives and direct taxes are to be apportioned among the states according to their respective numbers. These numbers were to be obtained by adding to the total number of free persons "three fifths of all other Persons." The "other persons" were, of course, slaves. A slave was thus equal to three-fifths of a white person. As Abraham Lincoln stated sarcastically, "All men are created equal, except Negroes." Before 1863, the Constitution thus protected slavery and made equality impossible in the sense we use the word today. African American leader Frederick Douglass pointed out that "Liberty and Slavery—opposite as Heaven and Hell—are both in the Constitution."

The constitutionality of slavery was confirmed just a few years before the outbreak of the Civil War in the famous *Dred Scott v. Sanford*[1] case of 1857. The Supreme Court held that slaves were not citizens of the United States, nor

[1]19 Howard 393 (1857).

DID YOU KNOW...
That the original Constitution failed to describe the status of a citizen or how this status could be acquired?

This portrait is of Dred Scott (1795–1858), an American slave who was born in South Hampton County, Virginia. He was the nominal plaintiff in a test case that sought to obtain his freedom on the ground that he lived in the free state of Illinois. Although the Supreme Court ruled against him, he was soon emancipated and became a hotel porter in St. Louis.

DID YOU KNOW . . .

That slaves in several states, including Texas, Oklahoma, Arkansas, and Louisiana, did not learn about the Emancipation Proclamation until more than two years after it was issued in 1863?

were they entitled to the rights and privileges of citizenship. The Court also ruled that the Missouri Compromise, which banned slavery in the territories north of 36° 30′ latitude (the southern border of Missouri), was unconstitutional. The *Dred Scott* decision had grave consequences. Most observers contend that the ruling contributed to making the Civil War inevitable.

With the emancipation of the slaves by President Lincoln's Emancipation Proclamation in 1863 and the passage of the Thirteenth, Fourteenth, and Fifteenth Amendments during the Reconstruction period following the Civil War, constitutional inequality was ended. The Thirteenth Amendment (1865) states that neither slavery nor involuntary servitude shall exist within the United States. The Fourteenth Amendment (ratified on July 9, 1868) tells us that *all* persons born or naturalized in the United States are citizens of the United States. It states, furthermore, "No State shall make or enforce any law which shall abridge the privileges or immunities of the citizens of the United States; nor shall any State deprive any person of life, liberty or property, without due process of law; nor deny to any person within its jurisdiction the equal protection of the laws." The Fifteenth Amendment seems equally impressive: "The right of citizens of the United States to vote shall not be denied or abridged by the United States or by any State on account of race, color, or previous condition of servitude." Pressure was brought to bear on Congress to include in the Fourteenth and Fifteenth Amendments a prohibition against discrimination based on sex, but with no success.

As we shall see, the words of these amendments had little immediate effect. Although slavery was legally and constitutionally ended, African American political and social inequality has continued to the present time. In the following sections, we discuss several landmarks in the struggle of African Americans to overcome this inequality.

The Civil Rights Acts of 1865 to 1875

At the end of the Civil War, President Lincoln's Republican party controlled the national government and most state governments, and the so-called Radical Republicans, with their strong antislavery stance, controlled that party.

Abraham Lincoln reads the Emancipation Proclamation on July 22, 1862. The Emancipation Proclamation did not abolish slavery (that was done by the Thirteenth Amendment, in 1865), but it ensured that slavery would be abolished if and when the North won the Civil War. After the Battle of Antietam on September 17, 1862, Lincoln publicly announced the Emancipation Proclamation and declared that all slaves residing in states that were still in rebellion against the United States on January 1, 1863, would be freed once those states came under the military control of the Union Army.

The Radical Republicans pushed through the Thirteenth, Fourteenth, and Fifteenth Amendments to the Constitution (the "Civil War amendments"). From 1865 to 1875, they succeeded in getting Congress to pass a series of civil rights acts that were aimed at enforcing these amendments. Even Republicans who were not necessarily sympathetic to a strong antislavery position wanted to undercut Democratic domination of the South. What better way to do so than to guarantee African American suffrage?

The first Civil Rights Act in the Reconstruction period that followed the Civil War was passed in 1866 over the veto of President Andrew Johnson. That act extended citizenship to anyone born in the United States and gave African Americans full equality before the law. The act further authorized the president to enforce the law with national armed forces. Many considered the law to be unconstitutional, but such problems disappeared in 1868 with the adoption of the Fourteenth Amendment.

Among the six other civil rights acts in the nineteenth century, one of the more important ones was the Enforcement Act of May 31, 1870, which set out specific criminal sanctions for interfering with the right to vote as protected by the Fifteenth Amendment and by the Civil Rights Act of 1866. Equally important was the Civil Rights Act of April 20, 1872, known as the Anti–Ku Klux Klan Act. This act made it a federal crime for anyone to use law or custom to deprive an individual of his or her rights, privileges, and immunities secured by the Constitution or by any federal law. Section 2 of that act imposed detailed penalties or damages for violation of the act.

The last of these early civil rights acts, known as the Second Civil Rights Act, was passed on March 1, 1875. It declared that everyone is entitled to full and equal enjoyment of public accommodations, theaters, and other places of public amusement, and it imposed penalties for violators. This act, however, was virtually nullified by the *Civil Rights Cases* of 1883 discussed below.

The civil rights acts of the 1870s are of special interest, because they were an indication that congressional power or authority applied both to official, or government, action and to private action. The theory behind the acts was that if a state government failed to act, Congress could act in its absence. Thus, Congress could legislate directly against private individuals who were violating the constitutional rights of other individuals when state officials failed to protect those rights. At the time, this was a novel theory, and it was not implemented in practice until the 1960s.

DID YOU KNOW...
That by the time of the American Revolution, African Americans made up nearly 25 percent of the American population of about three million?

The Ineffectiveness of the Civil Rights Acts

The Reconstruction statutes, or civil rights acts, ultimately did little to secure equality for African Americans in their civil rights. Both the *Civil Rights Cases* and the case of *Plessy v. Ferguson* effectively nullified these acts.

The *Civil Rights Cases.* The Supreme Court invalidated the 1875 Civil Rights Act when it held, in the *Civil Rights Cases*[2] of 1883, that the enforcement clause of the Fourteenth Amendment (which states that "[n]o State shall make or enforce any law which shall abridge the privileges or immunities of citizens") was limited to correcting actions by states in their official acts; thus, the discriminatory acts of private citizens were not illegal. ("Individual invasion of individual rights is not the subject matter of the Amendment.") The 1883 Supreme Court decision met with widespread approval throughout most of the United States.

---

[2]109 U.S. 3 (1883).

of classrooms, libraries, and cafeterias. In 1951, Oliver Brown decided that his eight-year-old daughter, Linda Carol Brown, should not have to go to an all-nonwhite elementary school twenty-one blocks from her home, when there was a white school only seven blocks away. The National Association for the Advancement of Colored People (NAACP), formed in 1909, decided to help Oliver Brown. The results were monumental in their impact on American society. Actually, a series of cases, first argued in 1952, contested state laws permitting or requiring the establishment of separate school facilities based on race. Following the death of Chief Justice Frederick M. Vinson and his replacement by Earl Warren, the Supreme Court asked for rearguments.

Brown v. Board of Education of Topeka. The 1954 unanimous decision in *Brown v. Board of Education of Topeka*[4] established that public school segregation of races violates the equal protection clause of the Fourteenth Amendment. Concluding that separate schools are inherently unequal, Chief Justice Warren stated that "to separate [African Americans] from others of similar age and qualifications solely because of their race generates a feeling of inferiority as to their status in the community that may affect their hearts and minds in a way unlikely ever to be undone." Warren said that separation implied inferiority, whereas the majority opinion in *Plessy v. Ferguson* had said the opposite.

"With All Deliberate Speed." The following year, in *Brown v. Board of Education*[5] (sometimes called the second *Brown* decision), the Court asked for rearguments concerning the way in which compliance with the 1954 decision should be undertaken. The Supreme Court declared that the lower courts must ensure that African Americans would be admitted to schools on a nondiscriminatory basis "with all deliberate speed." The high court told lower federal courts that they had to take an activist role in society. The district courts were to consider devices in their desegregation orders that might include "the school transportation system, personnel, [and] revision of school districts and attendance areas into compact units to achieve a system of determining admission to the public schools on a nonracial basis."

Jim Crow laws required the segregation of the races, particularly in public facilities such as this theater. The name "Jim Crow" originates from a nineteenth-century vaudeville character who was called Jim (which was a common name) Crow (for a black-colored bird). Thus, the name "Jim Crow" was applied to laws and practices affecting African Americans.

Reactions to School Integration

One unlooked-for effect of the "all deliberate speed" decision was that the term *deliberate* was used as a loophole by some officials, who were able to delay desegregation by showing that they were indeed acting with all deliberate speed but still were unable to desegregate. Another reaction to court-ordered desegregation was "white flight." In some school districts, the public school population became 100 percent nonwhite when white parents sent their children to newly established private schools, sometimes known as "segregation academies."

The white South did not let the Supreme Court ruling go unchallenged. Arkansas's Governor Orval Faubus used the state's National Guard to block the integration of Central High School in Little Rock in September 1957. The federal court demanded that the troops be withdrawn. Finally, President Dwight Eisenhower had to federalize the Arkansas National Guard and send it to quell the violence. Central High became integrated.

The universities in the South, however, remained segregated. When James Meredith, an African American student, attempted to enroll at the University

---

[4]347 U.S. 483 (1954).
[5]349 U.S. 294 (1955).

After the *Brown* decision, aggressive white reaction followed for a number of years, particularly with respect to the attempt to desegregate the school system in Little Rock, Arkansas. After the local school board secured approval of the federal courts for desegregation, Governor Orval Faubus sent in the state's National Guard to preserve order when a handful of African American students entered Little Rock Central High School on September 2, 1957. The National Guard was withdrawn after a few weeks and replaced by a white mob. President Dwight Eisenhower sent in five hundred soldiers on September 24, many of whom remained there for the rest of the school year. (The high school was closed in 1958).

of Mississippi in Oxford in 1962, violence flared there, as it had in Little Rock. Two men were killed, and a number of people were injured in campus rioting. President John Kennedy sent federal marshals and ordered federal troops to maintain peace and protect Meredith. One year later, George Wallace, governor of Alabama, promised "to stand in the schoolhouse door" to prevent two African American students from enrolling at the University of Alabama in Tuscaloosa. Wallace was forced to back down when Kennedy federalized the Alabama National Guard.

An Integrationist Attempt at a Cure: Busing

In most parts of the United States, the process of achieving racial balance in schools has been made difficult because of residential concentration by race. Although it is true that a number of school boards in northern districts created segregated schools by drawing school district lines arbitrarily, the residential concentration of African Americans and other minorities in well-defined geographic locations has contributed to the difficulty of achieving racial balance. This concentration results in *de facto* segregation.

Court-Ordered Busing.   The obvious solution to both *de facto* and *de jure* segregation seemed to be transporting some African American schoolchildren to white schools and some white schoolchildren to African American schools. Increasingly, the courts ordered school districts to engage in such **busing** across neighborhoods. Busing led to violence in some northern cities such as in south Boston, where African American students were bused into blue-collar Irish Catholic neighborhoods. Indeed, busing was unpopular with many groups. In the mid-1970s, almost 50 percent of African Americans interviewed were opposed to busing, and approximately three-fourths of the whites interviewed held the same opinion.[6] Nonetheless, through the next decade, the Supreme Court fairly consistently came down on the side of upholding busing plans in the cases it decided.

DE FACTO SEGREGATION

Racial segregation that occurs not as a result of deliberate intentions but because of past social and economic conditions and residential patterns.

DE JURE SEGREGATION

Racial segregation that occurs because of laws or administrative decisions by public agencies.

BUSING

The transportation of public school students from areas where they live to schools in other areas to eliminate school segregation based on residential patterns.

---

[6]Diane Ravitch, "Busing: The Solution That Has Failed to Solve," *New York Times,* December 21, 1975, section 4, p. 3.

To remedy *de facto* segregation, the courts often imposed busing requirements on school districts. Busing meant transporting children of white neighborhoods to nonwhite schools, and vice versa. Busing has been one of the most controversial domestic policies in the history of this country. Initially, bused students had to be escorted by police because of potential violence. This scene was photographed in Boston in the 1970s.

Changing Directions. In an apparent reversal of previous decisions, the Supreme Court in June 1986 allowed the Norfolk, Virginia, public school system to end fifteen years of court-ordered busing of elementary schoolchildren.[7] The Norfolk school board supported the decision because of a drop in enrollment from 32,500 whites attending public schools in 1970, when busing was ordered, to fewer than 14,000 in 1985.

In 1991, the Supreme Court held, in *Board of Education v. Dowell*,[8] that a school board only needs to show that it has complied in "good faith" with a desegregation decree. In *Dowell*, the Supreme Court instructed a lower court administering the decree that if school racial concentration was a product of residential segregation that resulted from "private decision making and economics," its effects may be ignored entirely.

In *Freeman v. Pitts*,[9] decided in 1992, the Supreme Court also stressed the importance of "local control over the education of children." In *Freeman*, a Georgia school district, which had once been segregated by law and was operating under a federal district court–administered desegregation decree, was allowed to regain partial control over its schools, although it was judged to have not complied with certain aspects of the decree. In 1995, the Supreme Court ruled in *Missouri v. Jenkins*[10] that the state of Missouri could stop spending money to attract a multiracial student body through major educational improvements. This decision dealt a potentially fatal blow to the use of magnet schools for racial integration. (See this chapter's *Politics and Race* for a discussion of the resegregation of schools and the search for alternatives to integration in the ongoing quest for equal educational opportunities.)

---

[7]*Riddick v. School Board of City of Norfolk*, 627 F.Supp. 814 (E.D.Va. 1984); *certiorari* denied, 479 U.S. 938 (1986)—see Chapter 15 for a discussion of the meaning of the term *certiorari*.
[8]498 U.S. 237 (1991).
[9]503 U.S. 467 (1992).
[10]115 S.Ct. 2038 (1995).

POLITICS AND RACE
From Integration Back to Segregation

There have been many changes in the U.S. educational system since *Brown v. Board of Education* in 1954. Instead of the school system becoming increasingly integrated, however, evidence shows that there has been a renewed growth of segregation in American schools during the 1990s. According to the National School Boards Association's report, "The Growth of Segregation in American Schools," the Northeast has the most segregated schools in the country and the South, the most integrated. But even in the South, the trend is toward more segregation. By the mid-1990s, less than 40 percent of African American students attended predominantly white schools, compared with 44 percent in 1987.

Nationwide, one out of every three African American and Hispanic stu-

dents goes to a school with more than 90 percent minority enrollment. In the largest U.S. cities, fifteen out of sixteen African American and Hispanic students go to schools with almost no whites.

Has the cause been renewed racism? Not according to many observers. The major cause is the rapid decline in the relative proportion of whites who live in big cities. Whites have left big cities, whereas immigration and high minority birth rates have increased the minority presence in those urban areas.

In the face of continuing *de facto* segregation based on social and economic circumstances and the courts' recent opinions on busing, the integrationist approach to solving the problem of inequality in schools has gradu-

ally lost favor. Increasingly, the emphasis has been on improving poor conditions in urban schools through school-funding equalization. By the mid-1990s, for example, several school-financing cases had been filed across the country, all basically alleging that poor conditions in urban schools violate state constitutional guarantees of equal educational opportunity. The goal of a racially balanced school, envisioned in the *Brown* decision, has given way to the goal of better educated children, however that goal is attained.

For Critical Analysis
Can the government do anything further to prevent **de facto segregation**? *If so, what? If not, why not?*

Rosa Parks was born on February 4, 1913, in Tuskegee, Alabama. She was active in the Montgomery Voters' League and the NAACP League Council. After she instigated the successful boycott of the Montgomery bus system, she was fired from her job and moved to Detroit. In 1987, she founded the Rosa Raymond Parks Institute for Self-Development, offering guidance to disadvantaged African Americans.

THE CIVIL RIGHTS MOVEMENT

The *Brown* decision applied only to public schools. Not much else in the structure of existing segregation was affected. In December 1955, a forty-three-year-old African American woman, Rosa Parks boarded a public bus in Montgomery, Alabama. When the bus became crowded and several white people stepped aboard, Parks was asked to move to the rear of the bus, the "colored" section. She refused, was arrested, and was fined $10; but that was not the end of the matter. For an entire year, African Americans boycotted the Montgomery bus line. The protest was headed by a twenty-seven-year-old Baptist minister, Dr. Martin Luther King, Jr. During the protest period, he went to jail, and his house was bombed.[11] In the face of overwhelming odds, however, King won. In 1956, the federal district court issued an injunction prohibiting the segregation of buses in Montgomery. The era of civil rights protests had begun.

King's Philosophy of Nonviolence

The following year, in 1957, King formed the Southern Christian Leadership Conference (SCLC). King's philosophy of nonviolent civil disobedience was influenced, in part, by Mahatma Gandhi's (1869–1948) life and teachings. Gandhi had led Indian resistance to the British colonial system from 1919 to 1947. He used tactics such as demonstrations and marches, as well as pur-

---

[11]Read King's "Letter from the Birmingham Jail" for a better understanding of this period.

Dr. Martin Luther King, Jr. at the August 1963 March on Washington for Jobs and Freedom.

poseful, public disobedience to unjust laws, while remaining nonviolent. King's followers successfully used these methods to widen public acceptance of their case.

For the next decade, African Americans and sympathetic whites engaged in sit-ins, freedom rides, and freedom marches. In the beginning, such demonstrations were often met with violence, but the contrasting image of nonviolent African Americans and violent, hostile whites created strong public support for the civil rights movement. When African Americans in Greensboro, North Carolina, were refused service at a Woolworth's lunch counter, they organized a sit-in that was aided day after day by sympathetic whites and other African Americans. Enraged customers threw ketchup on the protestors. Some spat in their faces. The sit-in movement continued to grow, however. Within six months of the first sit-in the Greensboro Woolworth's, hundreds of lunch counters throughout the South were serving African Americans.

The sit-in technique was also successfully used to integrate interstate buses and their terminals, as well as railroads engaged in interstate transportation. Although buses and railroads that were engaged in interstate transportation were prohibited by law from segregating African Americans from whites, they stopped doing so only after the sit-in protests.[12]

The civil rights movement gathered momentum in the 1960s. One of the most famous of the violence-plagued protests occurred in Birmingham, Alabama, in the spring of 1963, when Police Commissioner Eugene "Bull" Connor unleashed police dogs and used electric cattle prods against the protestors. The object of the protest had been to provoke a reaction by local officials so that the federal government would act. People throughout the country viewed the event on national television with indignation and horror, and such media coverage played a key role in the process of ending Jim Crow conditions in the United States. The ultimate result was the most important civil rights act in the nation's history, the Civil Rights Act of 1964 (to be discussed shortly).

In August 1963, King organized the massive March on Washington for Jobs and Freedom. Before nearly a quarter-million white and African American spectators and millions watching on television, King told the world his dream:

---

[12]See *Morgan v. Commonwealth of Virginia*, 328 U.S. 373 (1946); and *Henderson v. United States*, 339 U.S. 819 (1950).

DID YOU KNOW...
That by September 1961, more than 3,600 students had been arrested for participating in civil rights demonstrations and that 141 students and 58 faculty members had been expelled by colleges and universities for their part in civil rights protests?

I have a dream that my four little children will one day live in a nation where they will not be judged by the color of their skin but by the content of their character.... When we let freedom ring, when we let it ring from every village and every hamlet, from every state and every city, we will be able to speed up that day when all God's children, black men and white men, Jews and Gentiles, Protestants and Catholics, will be able to join hands and sing in the words of that old Negro Spiritual, "Free at last! Free at last! Thank God almighty, we are free at last!"

King's dream was not to be realized immediately, however. Eighteen days after his famous speech, four African American girls attending Bible class in the basement room of the Sixteenth Street Baptist Church in Birmingham, Alabama, were killed by a bomb explosion.

Police-dog attacks, cattle prods, high-pressure water hoses, beatings, bombings, and the March on Washington—all of these events led to an environment in which Congress felt compelled to act on behalf of African Americans. The second era of civil rights acts, sometimes referred to as the second Reconstruction period, was under way.

Another Approach—Black Power

Not all African Americans agreed with King's philosophy of nonviolence or with the idea that King's strong Christian church background should represent the core spirituality of African Americans. Indeed, Black Muslims and other African American separatists felt that there should be a more militant voice against the politics of cultural assimilation. During the 1950s and 1960s, when King was spearheading nonviolent protests and demonstrations to achieve civil rights for African Americans, black power leaders insisted that African Americans should "fight back" instead of turning the other cheek.

Malcolm Little (who became Malcolm X when he joined the Black Muslims in 1952) and other leaders in the black power movement believed that African Americans fell into two groups: the "Uncle Toms," who accommodated peaceably the white establishment, and the "New Negroes," who took pride in their color and culture and who preferred and demanded racial separation as well as power. Malcolm X was assassinated in 1965, but his teachings continue to influence African Americans. In the early 1990s, he again became an important reference point for a new generation of African Americans and a symbol of African American identity.

Malcolm X strongly opposed the philosophy of nonviolence espoused by Martin Luther King, Jr., and urged African Americans to "fight back" against white supremacy. In the 1990s, several books and a movie by Spike Lee have added to the revival of Malcolm X as a symbol of African American identity.

Another influential African American of the 1990s is the Reverend Louis Farrakhan, whose efforts to help troubled African American youths are not as well publicized as his sometimes controversial rhetoric. In 1993 and 1994, Farrakhan attracted harsh criticism for his public statements about whites, Jews, and others. Among his critics were other African American leaders. In 1996, Farrakhan elicited the ire of U.S. foreign-policy officials during his "friendship tour" of Libya, Iraq, Iran, and the Sudan—which are all considered by the U.S. government to be sponsors of terrorism. Foreign news reporters quoted Farrakhan as condemning the United States during his trip, and Farrakhan acknowledged that he had received a $1 billion pledge to the Nation of Islam from Libya's Muammar Gaddafi. The U.S. government refused to allow Farrakhan to accept the money.

MODERN CIVIL RIGHTS LEGISLATION AND ITS IMPLEMENTATION

In the wake of the Montgomery bus boycott, public sentiment for stronger civil rights legislation put pressure on Congress and President Dwight Eisenhower to act. The action taken was relatively symbolic. The Civil Rights Act of 1957 established a Civil Rights Commission and a new Civil Rights Division within the Justice Department. (President Ronald Reagan tried to abolish the commission in 1983; Congress extended its life for another twenty years, after working out a compromise in which the president and congressional leaders would select its members.) The Civil Rights Act of 1960 provided that whenever a pattern or practice of discrimination was documented, the Justice Department could bring suit, even against a state. The act also set penalties for obstructing a federal court order by threat of force and for illegally using and transporting explosives. But the 1960 Civil Rights Act, as well as that of 1957, had little substantive impact.

The same cannot be said about the Civil Rights Acts of 1964 and 1968 or the Voting Rights Act of 1965 (discussed in the next sections). Those acts marked the assumption by Congress of a leading role in the enforcement of the constitutional notion of equality for *all* Americans, as provided by the Fourteenth and Fifteenth Amendments.

The Civil Rights Act of 1964

As the civil rights movement mounted in intensity, equality before the law came to be "an idea whose time has come," in the words of conservative Senate Minority Leader Everett Dirksen. The Civil Rights Act of 1964, the most far-reaching bill on civil rights in modern times, forbade discrimination on the basis of race, color, religion, gender, and national origin. The major provisions of the act were as follows:

1. It outlawed arbitrary discrimination in voter registration.
2. It barred discrimination in public accommodations, such as hotels and restaurants, whose operations affect interstate commerce.
3. It authorized the federal government to sue to desegregate public schools and facilities.
4. It expanded the power of the Civil Rights Commission and extended its life.
5. It provided for the withholding of federal funds from programs administered in a discriminatory manner.
6. It established the right to equality of opportunity in employment.

In 1963, a historic civil rights bill was before Congress. Many opposed the bill as too radical. To galvanize senators and representatives to pass the bill, Martin Luther King, Jr., organized the March on Washington for Jobs and Freedom. On August 28, 1963, nearly a quarter-million Americans appeared in Washington to call for its passage. At the time, it was the largest demonstration in the capital's history.

DID YOU KNOW ...

That during the Mississippi Summer Project in 1964, organized by students to register African American voters, there were 1,000 arrests, 35 shooting incidents, 30 buildings bombed, 25 churches burned, 80 people beaten, and at least 6 murders?

FILIBUSTER

In the Senate, unlimited debate to halt action on a particular bill.

CLOTURE

A method invoked to close off debate and to bring the matter under consideration to a vote in the Senate.

EQUAL EMPLOYMENT OPPORTUNITY COMMISSION (EEOC)

A commission established by the 1964 Civil Rights Act to (1) end discrimination based on race, color, religion, gender, or national origin in conditions of employment and (2) promote voluntary action programs by employers, unions, and community organizations to foster equal job opportunities.

Several factors led to the passage of the 1964 act. As noted earlier, there had been a dramatic change in the climate of public opinion owing to violence perpetrated against protesting African Americans and whites in the South. Second, the assassination of President John F. Kennedy in 1963 had, according to some, a significant effect on the national conscience. Many believed the civil rights program to be the legislative tribute that Congress paid to the martyred Kennedy. Finally, the 1964 act could be seen partly as the result of President Lyndon B. Johnson's vigorous espousal of the legislation after his gradual conversion to the civil rights cause. The act was passed in Congress only after the longest **filibuster** in the history of the Senate (eighty-three days) and only after **cloture** was imposed for the first time to cut off a civil rights filibuster.

The Civil Rights Act of 1968 and Other Housing-Reform Legislation

Martin Luther King, Jr., was assassinated on April 4, 1968. Nine days after King's death, President Johnson signed the Civil Rights Act of 1968, which forbade discrimination in most housing and provided penalties for those attempting to interfere with individual civil rights (giving protection to civil rights workers, among others). In the same year, the Supreme Court prohibited discrimination in the sale and rental of all housing, using as a precedent the Civil Rights Act of April 9, 1866.[13] The Court held that Section 1 of the earlier act contains a broad prohibition against any racial discrimination in the sale or rental of property. It therefore forbids private development companies from refusing to rent to an individual simply because he or she is African American. The Court noted that racial discrimination "herds men into ghettos and makes their ability to buy property turn on the color of their skin."

Additional legislation continued where the Fair Housing Act (Title VIII of the Civil Rights Act of 1968) left off. The Home Mortgage Disclosure Act of 1975 and the Community Reinvestment Act of 1977 added enforcement provisions to the federal government's rules pertaining to discriminatory mortgage-lending practices. In 1990, the Financial Institution Reform, Recovery, and Enforcement Act required lenders to report to the federal government the race, gender, and income of all mortgage-loan seekers, along with the final decision on their loan applications.

In a sense, housing-reform advocates have refocused their objectives. The Civil Rights Act of 1968 was thought to be a step in the direction of creating an environment that would promote integrated neighborhoods. Subsequent legislation has evolved that aims more to create leverage for minorities to obtain a fair share of housing resources.

Employment and Affirmative Action

Title VII of the Civil Rights Act of 1964 is the cornerstone of employment-discrimination law. It prohibits discrimination in employment based on race, color, religion, gender, or national origin. Under Title VII, executive orders were issued that banned employment discrimination by firms that received any federal funding. The 1964 Civil Rights Act created a five-member commission, the **Equal Employment Opportunity Commission (EEOC),** to administer Title VII.

The EEOC can issue interpretive guidelines and regulations, but these do not have the force of law. Rather, they give notice of the commission's

---

[13]*Jones v. Mayer,* 329 U.S. 409 (1968).

enforcement policy. The EEOC also has investigatory powers. It has broad authority to require the production of documentary evidence, to hold hearings, and to **subpoena** and examine witnesses under oath.

To put teeth in the 1964 law, President Johnson applied the concept of affirmative action in 1965. **Affirmative action** can be defined as remedial steps taken to improve work opportunities for women, racial and ethnic minorities, and other persons considered to have been deprived of job opportunities in the past on the basis of their race, color, religion, gender, or national origin.

Backlash against Affirmative Action

By the early 1970s, U.S. Labor Department regulations imposing numerous employment goals and timetables had been applied to every company that did more than $10,000 worth of business of any sort with the national government. Affirmative action plans were also required whenever an employer had been ordered to develop such a plan by a court or by the EEOC because of past discrimination. Finally, labor unions that had been found to discriminate against women or minorities were required to follow affirmative action plans.

Affirmative action programs have been controversial because they sometimes result in discrimination against majority groups, such as white males (or discrimination against other minority groups that may not be given preferential treatment under a particular affirmative action program). At issue in the current debate over affirmative action programs is whether such programs, because of their inherently discriminatory nature, violate the equal protection clause of the Fourteenth Amendment to the Constitution.

The *Bakke* Case.   An early case addressing this issue involved an affirmative action program implemented by the University of California at Davis. Alan Bakke, a Vietnam War veteran and engineer who had been turned down for medical school at the Davis campus of the University of California, discovered that his academic record was better than those of some of the minority applicants who had been admitted to the program. He sued the University of California regents, alleging **reverse discrimination.** The UC–Davis Medical School had held sixteen places out of one hundred for educationally "disadvantaged students" each year, and the administrators at that campus admitted to using race as a criterion for admission for these particular minority slots. At trial in 1974, Bakke said that his exclusion from medical school violated his rights under the Fourteenth Amendment's provision for equal protection of the laws. The trial court agreed. On appeal, the California Supreme Court agreed also. Finally, the regents of the university appealed to the United States Supreme Court.

On June 28, 1978, the Supreme Court handed down its decision in *Regents of the University of California v. Bakke.*[14] The Court did not actually rule against affirmative action programs but did hold that Bakke must be admitted to the UC–Davis Medical School because its admission policy had used race as the *sole* criterion for the sixteen "minority" positions. But Justice Lewis Powell, speaking for the Court, indicated that race can be considered "as a factor" among others in admissions (and presumably hiring) decisions. In other words, it is legal to give special consideration to "afflicted minority groups" in an effort to remedy past discrimination. Race can be one of many criteria for admission, but not the only one. So affirmative action programs, but not specific quota systems, were upheld as constitutional.

---

[14]438 U.S. 265 (1978).

SUBPOENA

To serve with a legal writ requiring a person's appearance in court to give testimony.

AFFIRMATIVE ACTION

A policy in job hiring that gives special consideration or compensatory treatment to traditionally disadvantaged groups in an effort to overcome present effects of past discrimination.

REVERSE DISCRIMINATION

The charge that affirmative action programs requiring preferential treatment or quotas discriminate against those who do not have minority status.

Further Limitations on Affirmative Action.   A number of cases subsequently placed even further limits on affirmative action programs. In 1984, for example, in *Firefighters Local Union No. 1784 v. Stotts*,[15] the Supreme Court said that the layoffs of Memphis firefighters had to be done on the basis of seniority unless there were African American employees who could prove they were victims of racial bias. In 1986, however, in *Wygant v. Jackson Board of Education*,[16] the Court sent the signal that affirmative action could apply to hiring but not to layoffs. This mixed message came from a case brought by a group of white teachers in Jackson, Michigan. The case challenged a labor contract that called for laying off three white teachers for every faculty member belonging to a minority group in order to preserve the school system's racial and ethnic ratios. In a five-to-four vote, the Court's majority said that the Jackson plan violated the Fourteenth Amendment's guarantee of equal protection of the laws.

In 1989, the Supreme Court considered whether whites could challenge employment decisions made on the basis of an earlier judgment that included goals for hiring African Americans as firefighters in the city of Birmingham, Alabama. White firefighters who had not been parties in the earlier proceedings alleged that because of their race, they were being denied promotions in favor of less-qualified African Americans. The Supreme Court held that the white firefighters could challenge those employment decisions.[17] In another 1989 decision, the Court overturned a local government minority-preference program, signaling to dozens of cities and states that hundreds of affirmative action programs might also be invalid.[18]

In regard to racial discrimination, the Court made it harder for minority workers to sue employers.[19] In another ruling, racial harassment was exempted from a widely used antibias law.[20] In 1993, the Court used *Bakke* as a precedent for deciding that a policy of the city of Jacksonville, Florida, requiring that 10 percent of funds spent on city contracts be set aside annually for minority business enterprises, improperly discriminated against white contractors.[21]

By 1990, civil rights activists were arguing that the conservative rulings of the Supreme Court made it difficult for victims of employment discrimination to prove their cases. Believing that the courts could not be counted on to expand civil rights protections, some activists turned to Congress. Congress responded with the Civil Rights Act of 1991, which effectively overturned some of the conservative rulings and made it easier for workers to sue employers. Another section of the act includes racial harassment under the widely used antibias law from which the Supreme Court had exempted it. The act also bars challenges to earlier judgments that include goals for hiring minorities by persons in the same circumstances as the firefighters in the Birmingham case—thus overruling the Supreme Court's 1989 decision on this issue.

The End of Affirmative Action?

The Civil Rights Act of 1991 consisted of amendments to Title VII of the Civil Rights Act of 1964 and other laws prohibiting discrimination. More than anything, the act clarified for the courts some of the ambiguities in the provisions

---

[15]467 U.S. 561 (1984).

[16]476 U.S. 267 (1986).

[17]*Martin v. Wilks*, 490 U.S. 755 (1989).

[18]*Richmond v. J. A. Croson Co.*, 488 U.S. 469 (1989).

[19]*Wards Cove Packing Co. v. Atonio*, 490 U.S. 642 (1989).

[20]*Patterson v. McLean Credit Union*, 491 U.S. 164 (1989).

[21]*Northwestern Florida Chapter of the Association of General Contractors of America v. Jacksonville, Florida*, 508 U.S. 656 (1993).

of those earlier laws. The act did not, and could not, make any pronouncements on the *constitutionality* of affirmative action programs. That is the Supreme Court's job; and as the century draws to a close, the Court is going even further than *Bakke* and subsequent cases in questioning the constitutional validity of affirmative action programs.

For example, in *Adarand Constructors, Inc. v. Peña*,[22] the Supreme Court held that any federal, state, or local affirmative action program that uses racial or ethnic classifications as the basis for making decisions is subject to "strict scrutiny" by the courts. Under a strict-scrutiny analysis, to be constitutional, a discriminatory law or action must be narrowly tailored to meet a *compelling* government interest. In effect, the Court's opinion in *Adarand* means that an affirmative action program cannot make use of quotas or preferences for unqualified persons, and once the program has succeeded, it must be changed or dropped.

In 1996, a federal appellate court issued a decision that also has far-reaching implications. In *Hopwood v. State of Texas*,[23] two white law school applicants sued the University of Texas School of Law in Austin, alleging that they were denied admission because of the school's affirmative action program. The program allowed admitting officials to take race and other factors into consideration when determining which students would be admitted. The federal appellate court held that the program violated the equal protection clause because it discriminated in favor of minority applicants. Significantly, the court directly challenged the *Bakke* decision by stating that the use of race even as a means of achieving diversity on college campuses "undercuts the Fourteenth Amendment." The Supreme Court declined to hear the case, thus letting the lower court's decision stand.

The fact that the Supreme Court did not overrule the *Hopwood* decision has led many observers to conclude that it may be difficult for any affirmative action program to survive a constitutional challenge and that the era of affirmative action may be drawing to a close. Essentially, what seems to be occurring today is the realization by many Americans that the policy of affirmative action has not, in fact, resulted in equal protection of the laws for *most* Americans, including various minority groups that do not qualify for specific affirmative action preferences. Although some groups continue to argue that affirmative action programs are essential in the struggle for equality, other groups contend that the time has come for a "colorblind" society in which racial and ethnic differences should not mandate decisions made by business firms and others in our society. (See this chapter's *Critical Perspective* for a further discussion of this issue.)

THE VOTING RIGHTS ACT OF 1965

The Fourteenth Amendment, ratified on July 9, 1868, provided for equal protection of the laws. The Fifteenth Amendment, ratified on February 3, 1870, stated that "[t]he right of citizens of the United States to vote shall not be denied or abridged by the United States or by any State on account of race, color, or previous condition of servitude." Immediately after the adoption of those amendments, African Americans in the South began to participate in political life—but only because of the presence of federal government troops and northern Radical Republicans who controlled the state legislatures.

---

[22]115 S.Ct. 2097 (1995).
[23]84 F.3d 720 (5th Cir. 1996).

CRITICAL PERSPECTIVE
Does Racism Still Matter?

During the civil rights movement of the 1960s, our nation focused on racism and its effects on the welfare of minority groups, particularly African Americans. Subsequently, affirmative action programs were implemented in an attempt to make up for past discrimination against African Americans, other minorities, and women. Now, thirty years later, the debate over racism has been refueled by critics of affirmative action who argue that affirmative action policies have largely failed as a solution to the problem of racial inequality.

One of the most controversial of these critics is Dinesh D'Souza, an immigrant from India who became a U.S. citizen in 1990. In his book, *The End of Racism: Principles for a Multiracial Society,** D'Souza calls for an end to affirmative action programs and racial preferences because they are based on an erroneous assumption. They assume that race, not culture, is the primary cause of racial inequality. This erroneous assumption, he argues, arose in the 1500s when Europeans, in their explorations of the world, encountered Asians, Africans, and Latin Americans whose societies seemed to be less developed. Race, D'Souza asserts, was a logical way for European explorers to explain the "backwardness" of these other peoples. For five hundred years, says D'Souza, whites believed themselves superior to others and used their power to dominate other races. Today, of course, no one believes this explanation; he argues that we are at the "end of racism" and at the beginning of the era of "cultural responsibility."

D'Souza's Key Contentions

D'Souza stresses that many of the problems attributed to racism are, in fact, moral and cultural in nature. One of D'Souza's main points is that African American culture is perhaps just dysfunctional and that many of the problems (concerning educational attainment, high crime rates, and illegitimacy) experienced by African Americans result from this dysfunctional culture—not from racism. These cultural problems have no political or legal solutions, and race-based government policies therefore should be abolished. Instead of government activism on behalf of African Americans, African Americans should confront the major problems and "reform" their communities on their own.

D'Souza also argues that some discrimination against African Americans is rational rather than racially motivated. He gives as an example the reluctance of taxicab drivers (of all races) to pick up young African American men in certain areas of some cities because of the disproportionately high crime rate among this group. Although the refusal to pick up young African American men is discriminatory and results in some injustice, it may be more unjust to force taxi drivers to take the very real risk of being harmed when they pick up such persons.

The Critics Respond

The End of Racism has been denounced by critics from both sides of the political spectrum. Many believe that D'Souza is completely wrong in his assertion that "the end of racism" has arrived. This may be true for many whites, critics maintain, but not for African Americans who have a different historical experience. D'Souza is also criticized for making race relations a minor issue. In the wake of attacks on affirmative action, including D'Souza's, and general and apparently growing public sentiment toward less government, many Americans worry that this country will return to what they perceive to be a more racist era. This group of critics argues that affirmative action and racial preferences may be imperfect, but they are far better than no programs at all. Some critics have pointed out that D'Souza, himself an immigrant, has benefited from the very programs he would abolish.

For Critical Analysis

1. Can race-based discrimination for any reason ever be justified? Explain.

2. Who would be the primary beneficiaries of a government policy of "hands off" with respect to discrimination in the marketplace? Why?

*New York: The Free Press, 1995.

Historical Barriers to African American Political Participation

The brief enfranchisement of African Americans ended after 1877, when southern Democrats regained control of state governments after the federal troops that occupied the South during the Reconstruction era were withdrawn. Social pressure, threats of violence, and the terrorist tactics of the Ku Klux Klan combined to dissuade African Americans from voting. Southern politicians, using everything except race as a formal criterion, passed laws that effectively deprived African Americans of the right to vote.

White Primaries and Grandfather Clauses. By using the ruse that political party primaries were private, southern whites were allowed to exclude African Americans. The Supreme Court, in *Grovey v. Townsend*,[24] upheld such exclusion. Indeed, it was not until 1944, in *Smith v. Allwright*,[25] that the highest court finally found the **white primary** to be a violation of the Fifteenth Amendment. The Court reasoned that the political party was actually performing a state function in holding a primary election, not acting as a private group. By being denied a vote in the primary, African Americans had been prevented from participating in the selection of public officials from the end of Reconstruction until World War II. The **grandfather clause** restricted the voting franchise to those who could prove that their grandfathers had voted before 1867. Most African Americans were automatically disenfranchised by this provision. In *Guinn v. United States*,[26] in 1915, the Supreme Court held that grandfather clauses were unconstitutional.

Poll Taxes and Literacy Tests. Another device to prevent African Americans from voting was the **poll tax,** requiring the payment of a fee to vote. This practice ensured the exclusion of poor African Americans from the political process. It wasn't until the passage of the Twenty-fourth Amendment, in 1964, that the poll tax as a precondition to voting was eliminated. That amendment, however, applied only to national elections. In *Harper v. Virginia State Board of Elections*,[27] in 1966, the Supreme Court declared that the payment of any poll tax as a condition for voting in any state or national election is unconstitutional.

Actually, the poll tax had reduced the voting participation of both whites and nonwhites in five southern states, but it worked a greater hardship on African Americans, because a higher proportion of them were poor. Also, the poll tax was unequally enforced among whites and nonwhites. The result was that poll-tax states had turnouts in national elections equal to about 50 percent of those in states not having poll taxes.

Literacy tests also were used to deny the vote to African Americans. Such tests asked potential voters to read, recite, or interpret complicated texts, such as a section of a state constitution, to the satisfaction of local registrars.

By the 1960s, the distribution of seats in state legislatures among state voting districts had become another obstacle to African Americans' political participation. The frequent use of area instead of population as a basis for voting districts led to the domination of state legislatures by (white) rural representatives. In 1962, the Supreme Court decided that federal courts could hear

[24]295 U.S. 45 (1935).
[25]321 U.S. 649 (1944).
[26]238 U.S. 347 (1915).
[27]383 U.S. 663 (1966).

The Ku Klux Klan, or KKK, is well known for its burning-cross symbol. The KKK, which first met in Nashville's Maxwell House in April 1867, was organized during the Reconstruction period after the Civil War for the purpose of preventing former slaves from benefiting from the civil rights guaranteed by postwar federal legislation and constitutional amendments. After World War I, the KKK also became anti-Catholic and anti-Semitic.

WHITE PRIMARY

A state primary election that restricts voting to whites only; outlawed by the Supreme Court in 1944.

GRANDFATHER CLAUSE

A device used by southern states to exempt whites from state taxes and literacy laws originally intended to disenfranchise African-American voters. It restricted the voting franchise to those who could prove that their grandfathers had voted before 1867.

POLL TAX

A special tax that must be paid as a qualification for voting. The Twenty-fourth Amendment to the Constitution outlawed the poll tax in national elections, and in 1966 the Supreme Court declared it unconstitutional in all elections.

LITERACY TEST

A test administered as a precondition for voting, often used to prevent African Americans from exercising their right to vote.

cases involving state districting, and in 1964, the Court ruled that population is the only acceptable basis for the distribution of seats in a legislative body.[28]

The Struggle for Voting Rights. As late as 1960, only 29.1 percent of African Americans of voting age were registered in the southern states, in stark contrast to 61.1 percent of whites. In 1965, Martin Luther King, Jr., took action to change all that. Selma, the seat of Dallas County, Alabama, was chosen as the site to dramatize the voting-rights problem. In Dallas County, only 2 percent of eligible African Americans had registered to vote by the beginning of 1965. King organized a fifty-mile march from Selma to the state capital in Montgomery. He didn't get very far. Acting on orders of Governor George Wallace to disband the marchers, state troopers did so with a vengeance—with tear gas, night sticks, and whips.

Once again the national government was required to intervene to force compliance with the law. President Lyndon Johnson federalized the National Guard, and the march continued. During the march, the president went on television to address a special joint session of Congress urging passage of new legislation to ensure African Americans the right to vote. The events during the Selma march and Johnson's dramatic speech, in which he invoked the slogan of the civil rights movement ("We shall overcome"), were credited for the swift passage of the Voting Rights Act of 1965.

Provisions of the Voting Rights Act of 1965

The Voting Rights Act of 1965 had two major provisions. The first one outlawed discriminatory voter-registration tests. The second major section authorized federal registration of persons and federally administered voting procedures in any political subdivision or state that discriminated electorally against a particular group.[29] In part, the act provided that certain political subdivisions could not change their voting procedures without federal approval. The act targeted counties, mostly in the South, in which less than 50 percent of the eligible population was registered to vote. Federal voter registrars were sent to these areas to register African Americans who had been restricted by local registrars. Within one week after the act was passed, forty-five federal examiners were sent to the South. A massive voter-registration drive covered the country.

In 1970, the Voting Rights Act was extended to August 1975. In 1975, Congress extended the act to August 1982, and it was again extended in 1983. The act originally brought federal supervision to areas of the country known for discriminating against African Americans in the voter-registration process. But in 1970 and in 1975, the law was extended to other states and to other groups, including Spanish-speaking Americans, Asian Americans, and Native Americans, including Alaskan natives. As a result of this act, its extensions, and the large-scale voter-registration drives in the South, the number of African Americans registered to vote climbed dramatically. By 1980, 55.8 percent of African Americans of voting age in the South were registered.

By 1986, the number of registered African American voters nationally was more than 11 million. By 1996, there were more than 7,500 African American elected officials in the United States, including the mayors of Atlanta, Detroit, and the District of Columbia. In 1984, the Reverend Jesse Jackson became the first African American candidate to compete seriously for the Democratic

---

[28]*Baker v. Carr,* 369 U.S. 186 (1962); and *Reynolds v. Sim,* 377 U.S. 533 (1964).
[29]In addition, the act indicated that in Congress's opinion, the state poll tax was unconstitutional.

presidential nomination. In 1988, a renewed effort to register thousands more African Americans and other minority voters helped Jackson achieve an impressive total primary and caucus vote. In 1989, Virginia became the first state to elect an African American governor. In 1991, Clarence Thomas, an African American generally considered to be politically conservative, became a justice of the Supreme Court, replacing Thurgood Marshall, the first African American justice.

HISPANICS IN AMERICAN SOCIETY

The second largest minority group in America can be classified loosely as Hispanics—or individuals from Spanish-speaking backgrounds. As you can see in this chapter's *Politics and the Fifty States,* the southwestern states have the largest Hispanic populations. In fact, Hispanics constitute the largest minority group in Arizona, California, New Mexico, and Texas.

Even though this minority group represents 10 percent of the American population, its diversity and geographic dispersion have hindered its ability to achieve political power, particularly at the national level. Mexican Americans constitute the majority of the Hispanic population. The next largest group is Puerto Ricans, followed by Cubans, and finally Hispanics from Central and South America.

Economically, Hispanics in the United States are less well off than non-Hispanic whites but a little better off than African Americans. About 30 percent of Hispanics live in poverty. Unlike the economic situation of African Americans, that of Hispanics is worsening. The percentage of their population below the poverty level rose over 5 percentage points between 1980 and 1996. The unemployment rate for Hispanics decreased less than the rate for any other group, and their real median income actually dropped during that period. Hispanic leaders have attributed these declines to language barriers and lack of training (which lead to low-paying jobs), as well as to continuing immigration (which deflates statistical progress).

Politically, Hispanics are gaining power in some states. By the mid-1990s, over 5 percent of the members of the state legislatures of Arizona, California, Colorado, Florida, New Mexico, and Texas were of Hispanic ancestry.

Mexican Americans

During the early 1800s, Mexico owned California, as well as Arizona, New Mexico, Texas, Utah, Nevada, parts of Wyoming and Oklahoma, and most of Colorado. By 1853, these territories had all been acquired by the United States (by purchase or by war) and were settled mainly by Anglos. It is interesting to note that the treaty ending the Mexican War in 1848 explicitly guaranteed for all former citizens of Mexico then living in U.S. territory the same liberties, protections, and rights as any other American citizens. They did not receive this treatment, though. These Mexicans' rights were frequently violated as Anglos appropriated their land and denigrated their culture.

Mexicans have continued to settle in the United States, immigrating to this country primarily for economic reasons. Some Mexicans look to the United States for employment and a chance to better their lives. Since 1820, slightly more than 8 percent of all immigrants into the United States have been of Mexican origin. Most Mexican Americans still live in the southwestern United States, but many have moved to Indiana, Illinois, Pennsylvania, and Ohio.

POLITICS AND THE FIFTY STATES
Ethnic Groups

As the following table indicates, the ethnic composition of state populations varies from state to state.

STATE	TOTAL POPULATION	% (NON-HISPANIC) WHITE	% BLACK	% AMERICAN INDIAN	% ASIAN	% HISPANIC
Alabama	4,137,511	73	25	0	1	1
Alaska	587,766	74	4	15	4	3
Arizona	3,832,368	71	3	5	2	20
Arkansas	2,394,253	82	16	1	1	1
California	30,895,356	55	7	1	10	27
Colorado	3,464,675	80	4	1	2	13
Connecticut	3,279,116	83	8	0	2	7
Delaware	690,884	78	17	0	2	3
District of Columbia	585,221	27	65	0	2	6
Florida	13,482,716	72	13	0	1	13
Georgia	6,773,364	69	27	0	1	2
Hawaii	1,155,726	30	2	0	59	8
Idaho	1,065,885	92	0	1	1	6
Illinois	11,612,906	74	15	0	3	8
Indiana	5,658,323	89	8	0	1	2
Iowa	2,802,944	96	2	0	1	1
Kansas	2,515,320	88	6	1	1	4
Kentucky	3,753,836	92	7	0	1	1
Louisiana	4,278,889	65	31	0	1	2
Maine	1,236,348	98	0	0	1	1
Maryland	4,917,269	68	25	0	3	3
Massachusetts	5,992,712	87	5	0	3	5
Michigan	9,433,665	82	14	1	1	2
Minnesota	4,468,165	93	2	1	2	1
Mississippi	2,615,208	63	36	0	1	1
Missouri	5,190,719	87	11	0	1	1
Montana	822,347	92	0	6	1	2
Nebraska	1,600,524	92	4	1	1	3
Nevada	1,336,419	78	7	1	3	11
New Hampshire	1,115,087	97	1	0	1	1
New Jersey	7,820,260	73	13	0	4	10
New Mexico	1,581,830	50	2	8	1	39
New York	18,109,491	68	14	0	4	13
North Carolina	6,836,333	75	22	1	1	1
North Dakota	634,031	94	1	4	1	1
Ohio	11,021,419	87	11	0	1	1
Oklahoma	3,205,234	81	8	8	1	3
Oregon	2,971,567	90	2	1	3	4
Pennsylvania	11,995,405	87	9	0	1	2
Rhode Island	1,001,344	89	4	0	2	5
South Carolina	3,602,854	68	30	0	1	1
South Dakota	708,411	91	1	7	1	1
Tennessee	5,025,261	82	16	0	1	1
Texas	17,682,538	60	12	0	2	27
Utah	1,811,215	91	1	1	2	5
Vermont	571,334	98	0	0	1	1
Virginia	6,394,481	75	19	0	3	3
Washington	5,142,746	86	3	2	5	5
West Virginia	1,808,860	96	3	0	0	1
Wisconsin	4,992,664	91	5	1	1	2
Wyoming	464,736	91	1	2	1	6

SOURCE: Bureau of the Census, 1996.

For Critical Analysis
How does the ethnic composition of your state's population affect state and local politics?

Political Participation. Mexican Americans have faced numerous barriers to voting. Not the least of these is the language barrier for those unable to read English. The Voting Rights Act extension of 1970 alleviated this problem somewhat by requiring ballots to be printed in both English and Spanish in districts where at least 5 percent of the registered voters are Spanish speaking.

Mexican Americans, as well as other Hispanics in the United States, have a comparatively low level of political participation in elections. The lower overall participation rate is related to the overall lower socioeconomic status among Hispanics. The gap among ethnic groups has narrowed in recent years, however. Currently, the voting participation rate of Hispanic citizens is only about 10 percentage points less than the national average. Further, when citizens of equal incomes and educational backgrounds are compared, the Hispanic citizens' participation rate is higher than average. Even poor Hispanics are more likely to vote than poor whites.

Mexican Americans have also had some success in sending their own representatives to Congress. In 1976, the Hispanic caucus in the House of Representatives consisted of five people—a California Mexican American, two Texas Mexican Americans, the resident commissioner from Puerto Rico, and a Puerto Rican from New York City. In the 105th Congress, in 1997, the number of Hispanics had risen to 18. Also, the members of President Bill Clinton's first cabinet included two Hispanic Americans—Henry Cisneros, who serves as the secretary of housing and urban development, and Federico Peña, the secretary of transportation. Mexican Americans have also gained political clout in local politics.

Political Organizations. As far back as 1921, the *Hijos de America* (Sons of America) was formed in San Antonio, Texas. Eight years later, in Corpus Christi, the League of the United Latin American Citizens (LULAC) was established. Its goal, then and now, is to facilitate Hispanics' integration into American culture, using English as the primary language tool. Through numerous court battles, LULAC succeeded in removing many discriminatory barriers in public facilities, education, and employment in the Southwest for Hispanics.

DID YOU KNOW . . .
That by the year 2020, Hispanics are expected to become the largest minority in the United States? It is expected that they will constitute 15.7 percent of the U.S. population (up from 9.7 percent in 1997).

Spanish-language billboards in Miami, Florida, demonstrate the pervasiveness of Spanish-speaking cultures in some sections of the United States. Indeed, southern Florida leads the nation in the number of Americans who speak a language other than English at home. In Dade County, 57 percent of the residents do not speak English at home. In the adjacent city of Hialeah, the figure is 90 percent.

Puerto Ricans

Because Puerto Rico is a U.S. commonwealth, its inhabitants are American citizens. As such, they may freely move between Puerto Rico and the United States. In recent years, more Puerto Ricans have emigrated from the United States to Puerto Rico than from the island to the mainland. Currently, Puerto Ricans constitute about 12 percent of the Hispanic population in the United States. Most of them who come to the continental United States reside in the New York–New Jersey area.

In Puerto Rico, Puerto Ricans use U.S. currency, U.S. mails, and U.S. courts. They are also eligible for U.S. welfare benefits and food stamps, but they pay no federal taxes unless they move to the continental United States. By the mid-1990s, almost three-fourths of Puerto Ricans living in Puerto Rico were eligible for food stamps. Those who come to the mainland do not fare much better, owing to economic and language barriers and racial discrimination.

Puerto Ricans have had few political successes on the mainland. There are more than a million Puerto Ricans living in New York City, constituting at least 10 percent of the city's population, but only about 30 percent of them are registered to vote. Other statistics show that currently there are only a few Puerto Rican city council members and only two Puerto Rican members of Congress. In New York City's massive bureaucracy, only a small percentage of the administrators are Puerto Rican.

Cuban Americans

About 5 percent of the Hispanics in the United States are Cubans or Cuban Americans. Unlike their Hispanic brothers and sisters from Mexico and Puerto Rico, Cuban Americans chose to come to the United States for political, as well as economic, reasons. They left Cuba because they opposed the communist government of Fidel Castro. Many of the émigrés came from the educated middle class, and although they had to leave most of their financial assets behind, their education and training helped them to become established economically with relative ease. In Miami, for example, one can find numerous examples of former Cuban professionals who started out as taxi drivers and today own banks, retail stores, and law practices.

A majority of Cuban Americans reside in southern Florida, although some live in New York City and elsewhere. Economically, they constitute a major force in the southern Florida region. Politically, they have been very successful in gaining power within city and county governments. Cuban American members of Congress include Ileana Ros-Lehtinen and Lincoln Diaz-Balart, both elected as Republicans to the House of Representatives from districts in southern Florida. The political influence of Cuban Americans will certainly rise as their percentage of the population increases. In Dade County, Hispanics, particularly Cubans, now constitute the majority of the county's population.

As a group, Cuban Americans are known for being staunchly anticommunist, and they strongly oppose any attempts of the American government to improve relations with communist Cuba. Militant Cuban American organizations have denounced, threatened, or even bombed individuals and institutions in southern Florida that they feel are pro-Castro or procommunist.

Bilingualism

About 85 percent of Hispanic citizens speak English, but all Hispanic groups are concerned about the preservation of their language and heritage. Bilingual education programs are supported by many Hispanic groups as a civil

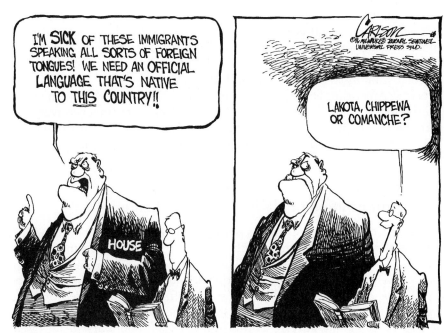

right. This claim was established by the Supreme Court in 1974, when it required a school district in California to provide special programs for Chinese students with language difficulties if there were a substantial number of these children.[30]

There is disagreement over the purpose of bilingual education. Some people feel such programs should be temporary, helping students only until they master English. Others want them to be permanent programs to help immigrant students preserve their cultural heritage. Still others think that bilingual programs simply are not feasible, given the variety of languages spoken by immigrants to this country. For example, the population in the Los Angeles area includes people who speak over one hundred different languages. How can bilingual education programs accommodate all of these people?

In response to public pressure from "America first" groups, as well as for other reasons, nearly half of the states have passed "English-only" laws that require all official speech to be in English. Congress is also considering a bill that would make English the official language of the U.S. government. Employers' policies that require only English to be spoken in the workplace have survived, at least to date, challenges from plaintiffs who allege that such policies violate Title VII of the Civil Rights Act of 1964, which prohibits discrimination based on ethnic origin. For example, in *Long v. First Union Corp. of Virginia*,[31] in which several Hispanic employees objected to an "English-only" policy imposed by their employer, a federal district court held that "[t]here is nothing in Title VII which . . . provides that an employee has a right to speak his or her native tongue while on the job."

NATIVE AMERICANS

When the New World was "discovered," there were about ten million Native Americans, or "Indians," living there. It is estimated that they had inhabited

---

[30]*Lau v. Nichols,* 414 U.S. 563 (1974).
[31]894 F.Supp. 933 (E.D.Va. 1995).

areas from the north slope of Alaska to the southern tip of South America for at least thirty thousand years before Europeans arrived. In the latest census, about two million individuals identified themselves as Native Americans. The five states with the largest Native American populations are Oklahoma, Arizona, California, New Mexico, and Alaska.

Native Americans have not fared well economically, as is evident in Figure 5–1. From the point of view of health, Native Americans are even worse off than their economic status shows. Table 5–1 shows that the death rates per 100,000 of the population are two and sometimes three or more times the national average.

The Appropriation of Native American Lands

When the Confederation Congress passed the Northwest Ordinance in 1787, it stated that "the utmost good faith shall always be observed towards the Indians; their lands and property shall never be taken from them without their consent; and in their property, rights, and liberty, they shall never be invaded or disturbed, unless in just and lawful wars authorized by Congress." In 1789, Congress designated the Native American tribes as foreign nations to enable the government to sign land and boundary treaties with them.

During the next hundred years, many agreements were made with the Native American tribes; however, many were broken by Congress, as well as by individuals who wanted Native American lands for settlement or exploration. In 1830, Congress instructed the Bureau of Indian Affairs to remove all Native American tribes to lands west of the Mississippi River to free land east of the Mississippi for white settlement. From that time on, Native Americans who refused to be "removed" to whatever lands were designated for them were moved forcibly. During the resettlement of the Cherokee tribe in 1838 and 1839, on a forced march known as the "Trail of Tears," nearly four thousand out of fifteen thousand Cherokees died.

With the passage of the Dawes Act (General Allotment Act) of 1887, the goal of Congress became the "assimilation" of Native Americans into American society. Each family was allotted acreage within the reservation to farm, and the rest was sold to whites. The number of acres in reservation status was reduced from 140 million to about 47 million acres. Tribes that refused to cooperate with this plan lost their reservations altogether.

Native American Political Response

Native Americans have been relatively unsuccessful in garnering political power. This is partly because the tribes themselves have no official representation in government and partly because the tribes are small and scattered. In the 1960s, the National Indian Youth Council (NIYC) was the first group to become identified with Indian militancy. At the end of the 1960s, a small group of persons identifying themselves as Indians occupied Alcatraz Island, claiming that the island was part of their ancestral lands. In 1972, several hundred Native Americans marched to Washington and occupied the Bureau of Indian Affairs (BIA). (Founded in 1824 as part of the War Department, today the BIA runs the Indian reservation system with the tribes.) They arrived in a caravan labeled "The Trail of Broken Treaties." In 1973, supporters of the American Indian Movement (AIM) took over Wounded Knee, South Dakota, which had been the site of the massacre of at least 150 Sioux Indians by the

Figure 5–1

• •

Native American and White Family Earnings Compared

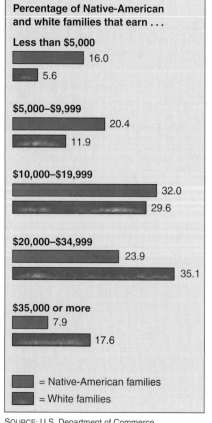

Percentage of Native-American and white families that earn . . .

Less than $5,000
16.0
5.6

$5,000–$9,999
20.4
11.9

$10,000–$19,999
32.0
29.6

$20,000–$34,999
23.9
35.1

$35,000 or more
7.9
17.6

■ = Native-American families
■ = White families

SOURCE: U.S. Department of Commerce.

Table 5–1

Native Americans: Death Rates per 100,000 Population

	NATIVE AMERICANS (INCLUDING ALASKANS)	ALL RACES
Motor-vehicle accidents	43.1	17.0
All other accidents	36.7	16.2
Alcoholism	30.0	9.0
Diabetes	29.1	10.0
Homicide	15.4	9.0
Pneumonia, influenza	13.1	10.1
Suicide	17.5	11.4
Tuberculosis	3.7	0.7

SOURCE: Indian Health Service, Centers for Disease Control, 1996.

U.S. Army in 1890.[32] The goal of these demonstrations was to protest federal policy and to dramatize injustices toward Native Americans.

Native Americans today face the continuing problem of dealing with a divided BIA. Some BIA bureaucrats want to maintain the dependency of the Native Americans on the reservation system run by the agency. Recently, however, the BIA has let more and more tribes control the police, job-training, educational, and social programs that the BIA used to manage. Nonetheless, there are still numerous conflicts between Indian tribes and the BIA, as well as between them and state governments. Native Americans face the additional problem of being a fragmented political group now that large numbers of their population do not live on reservations.

---

[32]This famous incident was the subject of Dee Brown's best-selling book, *Bury My Heart at Wounded Knee* (New York: Holt, Rinehart, and Winston, 1971), published two years before the modern siege.

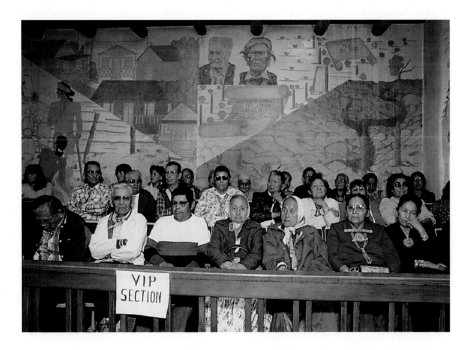

The Navajo Council in Window Rock, Arizona, governs tribal affairs and consists of representatives elected from local areas.

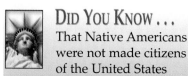

Compensation for Past Injustices

As more Americans became aware of the concerns of Native Americans, Congress started to compensate them for past injustices. In the Native American Languages Act of 1990, for example, Congress declared that Native American languages are unique and serve an important role in maintaining Indian culture and continuity. Under the act, the government shares responsibility with the Indian community for the survival of native languages and native cultures. Courts, too, have shown a greater willingness to recognize Native American treaty rights. For example, in 1985, the Supreme Court ruled that three tribes of Oneida Indians could claim damages for the use of tribal land that had been unlawfully transferred in 1795.[33]

In 1988, Congress passed the Indian Gaming Regulatory Act, allowing Native Americans to have profit-making gambling operations on their land. This has had a rapid and profound effect on economic and social aspects of reservation life and has affected non–Native American public authorities significantly as well. For example, Connecticut Governor Lowell Weicker allowed slot machines at a Mashantucket Pequot casino in his state in exchange for a pledge by the tribe to contribute $100 million a year in gambling profits to a state fund that aids troubled cities and towns.[34] Gambling on Native American property has, in the words of the *New York Times*, "become a multibillion-dollar industry that fuels a renaissance of American Indian tribal fortunes and culture; the trend is reversing a population exodus from reservations."[35]

The rapid expansion of reservation gambling has concerned authorities in some states. Generally, the states have sought tighter regulation of Native American casinos. One of the problems is that state governments cannot simply say "no" to casino gambling on reservations within their borders. Rather, under the 1988 act, states are obligated to negotiate "in good faith" with Indian tribes that wish to operate gambling casinos on tribal lands. The act further provides that if a state refuses to negotiate in good faith, a tribe may sue the state to compel good faith negotiations. In 1996, however, the United States Supreme Court held that the provision of the act permitting suits against states to compel negotiations was an unconstitutional incursion on state sovereignty.[36] Some see this decision as bolstering states' powers with respect to reservation casinos. Others contend that the case marks a step in the direction of allowing Native Americans to operate reservation casinos without dealing with the states—that is, simply by obtaining authorization from the federal government to do so.

ASIAN AMERICANS

Because Asian Americans have a relatively high median income, they are typically not thought of as being victims of discrimination. This certainly was not always the case. The Chinese Exclusion Act of 1882 prevented persons from China and Japan from coming to the United States to prospect for gold or to work on the railroads or in factories in the West. Japanese American students were segregated into special schools after the 1906 San Francisco earthquake so that white children could use their buildings.

---

[33]*County of Oneida v. Oneida Indian Nation,* 470 U.S. 226 (1985).
[34]*New York Times,* April 17, 1993, p. I1.
[35]*New York Times,* January 31, 1993, p. I1.
[36]*Seminole Tribe of Florida v. Florida,* 116 S.Ct. 1114 (1996).

The 1941 Japanese bombing of Pearl Harbor intensified the fear of the Japanese. Executive Order 9066, signed by President Franklin D. Roosevelt on February 19, 1942, set up "relocation" camps for virtually all Japanese Americans living in the United States. The Japanese were required to dispose of their property, usually at below-market prices. The Japanese Americans were subjected to a curfew, excluded from certain "military areas," and finally ordered to report to "assembly" centers, from which they were evacuated to the relocation camps. The Supreme Court upheld the curfew, the exclusion order, and the order to report to assembly centers.[37] It wasn't until 1944 and 1945 that the relocation camps were closed and the prisoners freed, after a December 18, 1944, Supreme Court ruling deemed such activity illegal. Three Japanese Americans who had been jailed for resisting relocation during World War II successfully sued the United States in 1983. They won damages, and their 1942 convictions were overturned because of their claim that the army lied about the possibility of security threats. In 1988, Congress provided funds to compensate former camp inhabitants or their survivors—$1.25 billion for 65,000 people.

Both Japanese Americans and Chinese Americans have overcome initial prejudice to lead America's ethnic groups in median income and median education. Asians who moved to the United States after 1965 represent the most highly skilled immigrant group in American history. Of all Asian Americans in the United States, about 40 percent of those over the age of twenty-five have college degrees, and their median family income is higher than that of non-Hispanic whites.

Recently, however, a new group of Asians has had to fight discrimination—those from Southeast Asia. More than a million Indochinese war refugees, most of them from Vietnam, have come into the United States in the last twenty-five years. Like their predecessors, the newer immigrants have quickly increased their median income; only about one-third of all such households receive welfare of any sort. Most have come with families and have been sponsored by American families or organizations, so they have had good support systems to help them get started. As with Chinese Americans and Japanese Americans, however, once they become established, they are seen as economic threats by those who believe they are being displaced by the new immigrants.

THE MELTING POT

No one really knows when the term *melting pot* was first applied to American society, although the phrase is derived from a play of that name by Israel Zangwill. Perhaps the last lines of Emma Lazarus's sonnet, "The New Colossus," engraved on a tablet inside the base of the Statue of Liberty, best express the melting-pot idea:

> Give me your tired, your poor,
> Your huddled masses yearning to breathe free,
> The wretched refuse of your teeming shore.
> Send these, the homeless, tempest-tossed to me,
> I lift my lamp beside the golden door!

The ethnic groups that came to the United States in the great waves of immigration that began after the Civil War were first northern Europeans and later

---

[37]*Hirabayashi v. United States,* 320 U.S. 81 (1943); and *Korematsu v. United States,* 323 U.S. 214 (1944).

eastern and southern Europeans. Then, as now, they were lured by the American Dream—the promise of economic security and freedom. Assimilation was the way by which the American Dream could be achieved.

Immigration Laws

As mentioned earlier, until the late nineteenth century, the United States imposed few limitations on immigration. Immigration laws then became increasingly restrictive, although one of the largest waves of immigration occurred between 1901 and 1910 and included almost nine million people. After 1965, the government began to ease the restrictions. Between 1981 and 1990, there were an estimated eight to twelve million immigrants, including three to seven million illegal aliens. To deal with illegal immigration, Congress passed the Immigration Reform and Control Act of 1986. The new law authorized more border guards and provided penalties for employers who were caught hiring illegal aliens. The act also granted amnesty to illegal aliens who could prove they had been in the United States since 1981. In 1993, the Supreme Court, in the widely publicized "Haitian boat people" case, ruled eight to one that the Coast Guard's interception of aliens and their forcible return to Haiti violated neither immigration law nor international conventions on refugees.[38]

As discussed in this chapter's opening *What If . . .* , anti-immigration sentiment is rising in America. Complaints that immigrants receive jobs and public benefits that should go to native-born Americans have led to proposals to curb immigration or to limit immigrants' rights. Currently, Congress is considering a bill aimed directly at the problem of illegal immigrant workers (see the feature entitled *Thinking Politically about a National Worker ID Card* for further details on this proposed bill).

Toward a "Universal Nation"

Since 1977, four out of five immigrants have come from Latin America or Asia. If current rates continue, Hispanics will overtake African Americans as the

---

[38]*Sale v. Haitian Centers Council Inc.,* 509 U.S. 155 (1993).

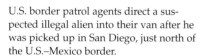

U.S. border patrol agents direct a suspected illegal alien into their van after he was picked up in San Diego, just north of the U.S.–Mexico border.

Thinking Politically about a National Worker ID Card

Hundreds of thousands of persons enter this country illegally every year, generally to find work. These illegal immigrants, or "undocumented workers," may impose costs on state governments and, according to many, take jobs that should go to American workers.

One proposed solution to the problem is a national worker identification (ID) card of some kind. A bill currently before Congress, for example, includes a provision that would create a national computer database containing the "birth certificate of every person born in the United States [to be] verified as pertaining to a particular person at an age no older than sixteen . . . and [that] would be personalized by the addition of a fingerprint or other biometric data." Employers would be required to verify the status of any person who applied for a job by consulting this database.

Proponents of this type of worker ID system, who include not only several Republicans in Congress but also Democratic senator Dianne Feinstein of California, argue that such a program would make it difficult, if not impossible, for illegal immigrants to obtain jobs. Traditional techniques used by illegal immigrants, such as using fake Social Security numbers and fraudulent documents, would no longer be effective under the new system. This is because the identification certificate would also include a digitalized fingerprint or "other biometric data," such as a voice print or a retina scan, which could not be faked. The government easily could monitor employers' hiring practices and weed out any illegal aliens.

Many disagree that a national ID card system for all 130 million American workers would be a feasible solution to the problem of illegal immigration. First of all, argue these opponents, a national computerized worker registry would cost the federal government between $3 billion and $6 billion per year to administer. Some estimate that computer errors alone would result in hundreds of thousands of Americans being denied legal access to the workforce. Second, such a system would represent a giant step in terms of the government's intrusion into the daily lives and activities of Americans. Third, some critics of a national ID card system have already voiced doubts about Congress's constitutional authority to create and implement such a system. Finally, opponents argue that a national worker registry simply would be unworkable. They point out that employers already hire illegal immigrants, even though they know that they are breaking the law, and there is no reason to believe that these employers will comply with the requirements of a national ID card system.

Democrats traditionally have favored government activism to cure economic and social problems. From a political perspective, then, it is perhaps not surprising that the Clinton administration would endorse such a bill or that it might be supported by Democratic senators such as Dianne Feinstein. Why, however, would key Republicans in Congress, such as (former) Senator Alan Simpson of Wyoming and Representative Lamar Smith of Texas, support such a system, given the Republican goal of having less government rather than more? One of the reasons for this seeming paradox might have to do with the growing public mood against immigrants—particularly illegal immigrants. Supporting a proposal to create a national worker ID system is one way to win votes.

For Critical Analysis

Some Americans contend that the United States simply should open its doors to all immigrants. What would be the result of such a policy?

nation's largest minority by the year 2010. By the year 2030, African Americans and Hispanics together will constitute 30 percent of the population.

Ben Wattenberg of the American Enterprise Institute in Washington, D.C., says the United States is becoming the world's first "universal nation." We have always claimed to be one, but this really was not true until relatively recently. The "old guard" Anglo-Saxon Protestants will no longer dominate American political life. We may see intense periods of conflict among African Americans and newly arrived Hispanics and Asians as they vie for jobs and political influence. But if Hispanics and African Americans can form coalitions, perhaps with Asian Americans, their political strength can be increased dramatically, for they will have the numerical strength to make significant changes. African American leader Jesse Jackson has attempted to form such a coalition. His 1984 and 1988 campaigns for the presidency were focused on, and supported by, a "Rainbow Coalition" of African Americans, Hispanics, Native Americans, women, and other underrepresented groups.

America has been challenged and changed—and culturally enriched—time and again by immigrant peoples speaking other languages and observing different customs. In this century, and particularly since the 1950s, this nation has attempted to counter prejudice against immigrant groups by ensuring that they obtain equal rights under the law. Civil rights legislation, particularly during the 1960s, resulted in significant changes in the civil rights of minorities. Some of the most significant of these changes are listed in this chapter's *Concept Overview.* The minority groups discussed in this chapter eventually will come to participate fully in the American system, and someday those thought of as "traditional Americans" may be of Hispanic or Asian origin, as well as Anglo-Saxon.

CONCEPT OVERVIEW
Changes in Civil Rights

There have been many changes in the civil rights of many Americans in the past fifty years, particularly as a result of the civil rights legislation of the 1960s. Here are just a few ways in which our civil rights have expanded in the last five decades.

THEN	NOW
• Numerous legal and other barriers to African American political participation.	• No legal barriers to African American political participation.
• No significant protection of minority groups.	• Significant protection of minority groups.
• No equal employment opportunity.	• Equal employment opportunity (by law).
• No affirmative action.	• Affirmative action (but under attack).
• Bilingual education not required.	• Bilingual education required in some areas.
• Discrimination in housing.	• Discrimination in housing now illegal.
• Few members of minority groups elected to political office.	• Members of minority groups elected to political office as all levels of government.
• Little or no voting participation by minority groups.	• Voter turnout among minority groups equal to that of whites.

CIVIL RIGHTS: UNFINISHED WORK

The future of civil rights in the United States seems clouded in the late 1990s. The nation could better be described as a "salad bowl" than as a "melting pot." As the immigrant population grows, America will become more a nation of minorities, each demanding what it believes to be fair treatment under the law. Some commentators argue that racism will always be a problem in America, because so many groups believe that their own racial or ethnic background is superior to that of others. The resurgence of ethnic pride, in contrast to the concept of the "melting pot," probably means that at least subtle forms of conflict will continue among the various racial and ethnic groups in our society.

Although no nation is capable of legislating morality, our government does have a responsibility to create an environment that does not allow state-sanctioned discrimination against any race, creed, or ethnic group. To be sure, since the 1950s, the gains of African Americans, Hispanics, Native Americans, and Asian Americans have been impressive. The civil rights movement and the legislation and affirmative action programs it prompted have made giant strides toward the goal of equality for all Americans. Nonetheless, discrimination still does exist in America; and for all of the gains accomplished by African Americans, there remains more of an African American underclass than a white underclass. Moreover, many fear that the gains made in civil rights for minorities since the 1960s are now being threatened by a growing backlash against affirmative action programs. Certainly, the most important unfinished work in the area of civil rights will continue to be finding a solution to the problem of how to protect the civil rights of minorities without abridging the rights of other groups in society.

GETTING INVOLVED
Citizenship and Immigrant Rights

A great debate has taken place in recent years over the issue of immigrant rights. The questions have included whether illegal immigrants can become citizens, whether employers are liable for hiring illegal immigrants, and whether the economy can absorb so many new workers. Legislation passed in 1986 created a new process by which illegal aliens who have resided in the United States since 1982 can apply to become legal residents and, after five more years, become citizens. Employers are required to certify the legal status of alien workers or face fines.

Although the law forbids discrimination against anyone on the basis of national origin, the latest rules may, in fact, reinforce prejudices against minorities. Many organizations are concerned with the way in which illegal immigrants are treated by federal and state police and immigration officials. Such groups want to maintain the nation's commitment to relatively free entry to people of all racial, ethnic, religious, political, and economic backgrounds. Their goals are fair immigration rules, greater protection for resident illegal aliens, and a more pluralistic and tolerant culture.

You can become involved in this national controversy over immigration and citizenship policy in a number of ways. You can pay attention to the often contradictory policies that are proposed in Congress to deal with the problem. If you feel deeply enough about this issue, you might wish to join action organizations that lobby through influencing public opinion or by exerting direct pressure on Congress and the executive branch. You can also lobby your local government to enact laws allowing aliens fleeing persecution to live in your community. The following organizations have been involved in the controversy over immigration and citizenship policies. The following groups are generally in favor of the right to immigrate:

CENTER FOR IMMIGRANTS' RIGHTS
48 St. Marks Pl.
New York, NY 10003
212-353-9690
http://tripod.com/work/goodworks/jobs/161.html

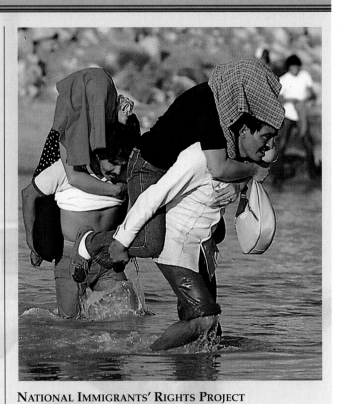

NATIONAL IMMIGRANTS' RIGHTS PROJECT
AMERICAN CIVIL LIBERTIES UNION
132 West 43d St.
New York, NY 10036
212-944-9800
http://www.aclu.org/issues/immigrant/hmir.html

Groups that usually support stricter enforcement of existing immigration laws or a more homogeneous culture include the following:

FEDERATION FOR AMERICAN IMMIGRATION REFORM
1666 Connecticut Ave. N.W.
Washington, DC 20036
202-328-7004
http://www.fairus.org/

U.S. ENGLISH
818 Connecticut Ave. N.W.
Washington, DC 20036
202-833-0100
http://www.us-english.org/

KEY TERMS

affirmative action 155

busing 148

cloture 154

de facto segregation 148

de jure segregation 148

Equal Employment
Opportunity Commission
(EEOC) 154

filibuster 154

grandfather clause 159

literacy test 159

poll tax 159

reverse discrimination 155

separate-but-equal doctrine 146

subpoena 155

white primary 159

CHAPTER SUMMARY

1 The civil rights movement started with the struggle by African Americans for equality. Before the Civil War, African Americans were slaves, and slavery was protected by the Constitution and the Supreme Court. African Americans were not considered citizens or entitled to the rights and privileges of citizenship. In 1863 and during the years after the Civil War, the Emancipation Proclamation and the Thirteenth, Fourteenth, and Fifteenth Amendments (the "Civil War amendments") legally and constitutionally ended slavery. From 1865 to 1875, to enforce the Civil War amendments, Congress passed a number of laws (civil rights acts). African Americans gained citizenship, the right to vote, equality before the law, and protection from deprivation of these rights.

2 Politically and socially, African American inequality continued. The *Civil Rights Cases* (1883) and *Plessy v. Ferguson* (1896) effectively nullified the civil rights acts of 1865 to 1875. In the *Civil Rights Cases,* the Supreme Court held that the Fourteenth Amendment did not apply to private invasions of individual rights. In *Plessy,* the Court upheld the separate-but-equal doctrine, declaring that segregation did not violate the Constitution.

3 African Americans fought unceasingly for equality. Legal segregation was declared unconstitutional by the Supreme Court in *Brown v. Board of Education of Topeka* (1954), in which the Court stated that separation implied inferiority. In *Brown v. Board of Education* (1955), the Supreme Court ordered federal courts to ensure that public schools were desegregated "with all deliberate speed." Segregationists resisted with legal tactics, violence, and "white flight." Integrationists responded with court orders, federal marshals, and busing. Also in 1955, the modern civil rights movement began with a boycott of segregated public transportation in Montgomery, Alabama. Of particular impact was the Civil Rights Act of 1964. The act bans discrimination on the basis of race, color, religion, gender, or national origin in employment and public accommodations. The act created the Equal Employment Opportunity Commission and led to a presidential order for affirmative action to improve opportunities for those who had been deprived of them due to discrimination.

4 Affirmative action programs have been controversial because they can lead to reverse discrimination against majority groups or even other minority groups. In an early case on the issue, *Regents of the University of California v. Bakke* (1978), the Supreme Court held that using race as the sole criterion for admission to a university is improper. Since *Bakke* a number of Supreme Court decisions have further limited affirmative action programs. Recent Supreme Court decisions, particularly *Adarand Constructors, Inc. v. Peña,* and decisions by the lower courts that the Supreme Court has let stand, such as *Hopwood v. State of Texas,* have led some observers to conclude that it will be difficult in the future for any affirmative action program to pass constitutional muster. Some fear that the current backlash against affirmative action threatens the gains made in civil rights since the 1960s.

5 Historically, African Americans had been excluded from the voting process through poll taxes, grandfather clauses, white primaries, and literacy tests. The Twenty-fourth Amendment (ratified in 1964) and a 1966 Supreme Court decision outlawed poll taxes. The Voting Rights Act of 1965 outlawed discriminatory voter-registration tests and authorized federal registration of persons and federally administered procedures in any state or political subdivision evidencing electoral discrimination or low registration rates.

6 Today, Hispanics make up the second largest minority group in the United States. Their diversity and geographic dispersion, however, hinder their ability to exercise unified political power, particularly at the national level. Hispanics have faced discriminatory barriers to political participation. Several Hispanic political organizations have succeeded in removing barriers in public facilities, education, and employment, including the language barrier for those not fluent in English. The Voting Rights Act was amended in 1970 to require that ballots be printed in English and Spanish in districts in which at least 5 percent of registered voters are Spanish speaking. In 1974, the Supreme Court recognized bilingual education as a right.

⑦ In 1787, Congress declared Native American tribes to be foreign nations to enable the government to sign land and boundary treaties with them. Over the next century, many treaties were made, and most were broken. Native Americans were forced westward as white settlement expanded. Congress passed the Dawes Act (General Allotment Act) in 1887 to assimilate Native Americans. Partly because their numbers were so diminished and the tribes so scattered, Native Americans have been unsuccessful in attaining political power.

⑧ The Chinese Exclusion Act of 1882 prevented Chinese persons from coming to work in the western United States in certain occupations. After the San Francisco earthquake of 1906, Japanese American children were segregated so that white children could use their schools. In 1942, at a time of intensified fear of the Japanese because of the bombing of Pearl Harbor, the president ordered the relocation of West Coast residents of Japanese descent to internment camps. In 1988, Congress provided funds to compensate those Americans and their survivors.

QUESTIONS FOR REVIEW AND DISCUSSION

❶ Even though the North fought the Civil War in part to liberate the slaves, the southern states were able to reestablish white domination within a generation after the war. Why did the North allow the disenfranchisement of African Americans in the South, even though it violated the Constitution? How did the Supreme Court's views of the proper powers of government work to support segregation in the South and industrialization in the North?

❷ Why was the Supreme Court, during the first half of this century, able to conclude that the separate-but-equal doctrine was constitutionally acceptable, whereas during the second half it concluded that the doctrine was unconstitutional?

❸ In spite of the *Brown* rulings in 1954 and 1955, most African American and Hispanic students attend classrooms with few or no whites, according to the National School Boards Association. Current figures show that less than 40 percent of African American students attend predominantly white schools in the South, compared with almost 45 percent at the beginning of this decade. What are the factors that create predominantly white or predominantly African American schools? How have those factors changed, if at all, through the years?

❹ What were some of the ways in which African Americans were effectively excluded from the political process during the Reconstruction era?

❺ Different minority groups in the United States have different socioeconomic situations. What are some of the possible explanations for such differences?

❻ To what extent do you believe that legalized gambling on Native American property has altered the culture of Native Americans?

❼ To what extent can the "American" culture absorb other, non–Anglo-Saxon cultures, such as those of Native Americans, Hispanics, or Asians? How would "American culture" be changed if we came to have a multilingual, multiethnic society?

❽ If we are truly a nation of immigrants, how can we justify any restrictions on immigration?

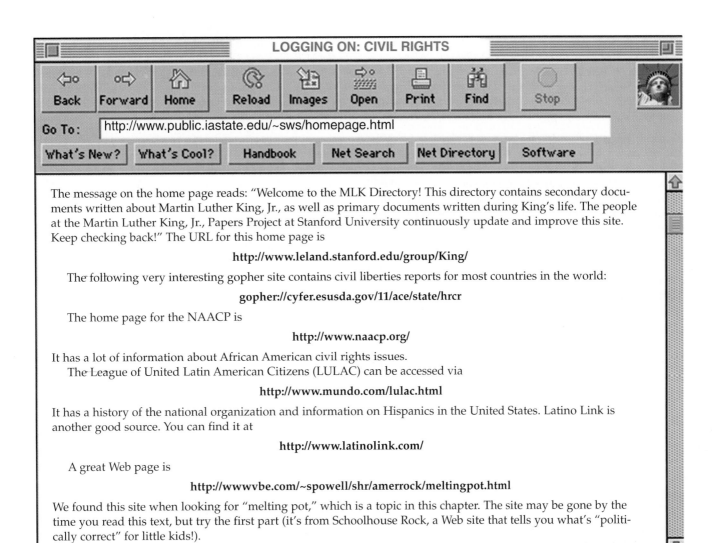

The message on the home page reads: "Welcome to the MLK Directory! This directory contains secondary documents written about Martin Luther King, Jr., as well as primary documents written during King's life. The people at the Martin Luther King, Jr., Papers Project at Stanford University continuously update and improve this site. Keep checking back!" The URL for this home page is

http://www.leland.stanford.edu/group/King/

The following very interesting gopher site contains civil liberties reports for most countries in the world:

gopher://cyfer.esusda.gov/11/ace/state/hrcr

The home page for the NAACP is

http://www.naacp.org/

It has a lot of information about African American civil rights issues.
The League of United Latin American Citizens (LULAC) can be accessed via

http://www.mundo.com/lulac.html

It has a history of the national organization and information on Hispanics in the United States. Latino Link is another good source. You can find it at

http://www.latinolink.com/

A great Web page is

http://wwwvbe.com/~spowell/shr/amerrock/meltingpot.html

We found this site when looking for "melting pot," which is a topic in this chapter. The site may be gone by the time you read this text, but try the first part (it's from Schoolhouse Rock, a Web site that tells you what's "politically correct" for little kids!).

SELECTED REFERENCES

Armor, David. *Forced Justice: School Desegregation and the Law.* New York: Oxford University Press, 1995. The author, based on an examination of the sociological evidence relating to court decisions concerning school integration, argues that neither African Americans nor whites have benefited from integrationist attempts.

Bolick, Clint. *The Affirmative Action Fraud: Can We Restore the American Civil Rights Vision?* Washington, D.C.: The Cato Institute, 1996. Bolick contends that the American civil rights vision has been shattered by proponents of affirmative action in the form of racial preferences. He argues that race-based preferences have dramatically widened the racial divide in the United States.

Brown, Dee. *Bury My Heart at Wounded Knee.* New York: Holt, Rinehart & Winston, 1971. This book is an important examination of the treatment of Native Americans as the frontier pushed westward.

Carmichael, Stokely, and Charles V. Hamilton. *Black Power: The Politics of Liberation in America* (New York: Vintage Books, 1967). This is a classic expression of the politics of racism in the United States and of the struggle to overcome white domination.

Cornell, Stephen. *The Return of the Native: American Indian Political Resurgence.* New York: Oxford University Press, 1988. Cornell's work is considered to be the best study of Native Americans as an important and politicized ethnic minority.

Delgado, Richard. *The Coming Race War?: And Other Apocalyptic Tales of America after Affirmative Action and Welfare.* New York: New York University Press, 1996. The author, a University of Colorado law professor, believes that affirmative action programs should be maintained because American culture is inherently racist.

Eastland, Terry. *Ending Affirmative Action: The Case for Color-blind Justice.* New York: Basic Books, 1996. The author, an editor at *Forbes* magazine, takes issue with affirmative action policies. He argues for a race-neutral, "color-blind" policy in the United States, contending that affirmative action results in unfair treatment and only serves to foster racial resentment.

Fullinwider, Robert K., ed. *Public Education in a Multicultural Society: Policy, Theory, Critique.* New York: Cambridge University Press, 1995. This collection of essays deals with some of the major questions raised by multicultural education in American public schools.

Hollinger, David A. *Postethnic America: Beyond Multiculturalism.* New York: Basic Books, 1995. The author suggests that it is time to move beyond multiculturalism to a "postethnic America" in which the bonds uniting American citizens are emphasized, rather than ethnic differences.

Kinder, Donald R., and Lynn M. Sanders. *Divided by Color: Racial Politics and Democratic Ideals.* Chicago: University of Chicago Press, 1996. The authors, based on an examination of polling data, conclude that the majority of white respondents oppose affirmative action programs.

Kluger, Richard. *Simple Justice.* New York: Knopf, 1975. The history of the 1954 Supreme Court ruling on *Brown v. Board of Education of Topeka* and African Americans' struggle for equality are investigated.

Schwartz, Warren A. *Justice in Immigration.* New York: Cambridge University Press, 1995. A group of leading economists looks at the issue of immigration from various perspectives.

Tatalovich, Raymond. *Nativism Reborn? The Official English Language Movement and the American States.* Lexington, Ky.: University Press of Kentucky, 1995. The author examines the history of the official English movement as well as the possible motives underlying it.

Woodward, C. Vann. *The Strange Career of Jim Crow.* New York: Oxford University Press, 1957. This is the classic study of segregation in the southern United States.

6
Striving for Equality

CHAPTER OUTLINE

There Were Forced Retirement at Age Sixty-five?

BACKGROUND

TRADITIONALLY, MANDATORY RETIRE-MENT POLICIES REQUIRED EMPLOY-EES TO RETIRE AT A CERTAIN AGE, SUCH AS FIFTY-FIVE, SIXTY, OR SIXTY-FIVE. TODAY, IN AN ERA OF IMPROVED HEALTH CARE AND INCREASING LONGEVITY, MANDATORY RETIREMENT AT, SAY, THE AGE OF SIXTY-FIVE NO LONGER MAKES SENSE. TO PROTECT THE INTERESTS OF OLDER WORKERS AGAINST FORCED RETIREMENT, IN 1986 THE FEDERAL GOVERNMENT PROHIBITED MANDATORY RETIREMENT IN ALL BUT A FEW SELECTED OCCUPATIONS, SUCH AS FIREFIGHTING.

WHAT IF EMPLOYEES HAD TO RETIRE AT AGE SIXTY-FIVE?

Imagine for a moment that all employees in the United States were forced to retire from their jobs when they reached the age of sixty-five. What effect would this have on older people, the economy, and American society generally? One thing is certain—the problem of providing Social Security benefits to older people would become even more severe than it now is. The Social Security system is already in trouble (as you will read in Chapter 16), and as the population ages, there will be proportionately fewer younger workers to contribute to Social Security funds through payroll deductions. If, combined with this problem, all workers had to retire at the age of sixty-five, more workers would receive Social Security—which would exacerbate the problem. Forced retirement also would mean that older workers would have less income to provide for

their needs and their future, which would contribute to the problem of poverty among older Americans.

Mandatory retirement at the age of sixty-five would have an obvious disadvantage for employers: they would be deprived of the skills and talents of older workers who would prefer to continue working rather than retire. At the same time, businesses and institutions could save expenses on wages and benefits by hiring younger persons (for less pay than the older workers receive), as those over the age of sixty-five retired from their positions.

SELF-EMPLOYMENT

People who are self-employed would not be affected by a mandatory retirement law—because they are not classified as employees. Rather, such persons, when they agree to do work for others, do so on a contractual basis and are classified as independent contractors. Very likely, many employees over the age of sixty-five who would like to continue working would become self-employed and hire out their services as consultants. Self-employed persons must pay

Social Security taxes, just as employees do, so the mandatory retirement law would have little or no effect with respect to such workers.

FOR CRITICAL ANALYSIS

1. *Who would benefit most from a law mandating retirement at age sixty-five? Who would benefit least?*

2. *How have changes in technology, such as the computerization of the workplace, affected the status of older workers?*

3. *How do you explain the bias against older workers that continues to exist in many workplaces?*

"The paramount destiny and mission of women are to fulfill the noble and benign offices of wife and mother. This is the law of the Creator." Words of centuries ago? Not quite. These words were part of a Supreme Court opinion rendered in the first case tried under the Fourteenth Amendment in 1873. The Court at that time upheld the denial of the right of women to practice law.[1] The sentiment that it is somehow more "natural" for women (than for men) to tend the household and the children is still very much alive. Old ways of thinking die hard, and those who favor complete equality among men and women—socially, politically, and economically—must still struggle with this age-old cultural tradition regarding the proper status of women in society.

In addition to women, other groups in American society have had to deal with the effects of traditional cultural beliefs and social perceptions in their struggle for equality. As indicated in this chapter's opening *What If . . .* , older Americans also have been victims of discrimination. So have persons with disabilities, juveniles, and gays and lesbians. In this chapter, we look closely at these groups and examine some of the problems they have faced—and continue to face—in their ongoing attempt to obtain equality in the eyes of the law.

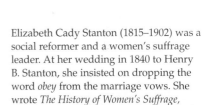

DID YOU KNOW . . .
That in 1916, Jeannette Rankin became the first woman to be elected to the U.S. House of Representatives, four years before the Nineteenth Amendment gave women the right to vote?

WOMEN'S POSITION IN SOCIETY: EARLY POLITICAL MOVEMENTS

In 1776, Abigail Adams wrote to her husband, John Adams, the following words in reference to new laws that would be necessary if a Declaration of Independence was issued:

> I desire you would remember the ladies. . . . If particular care and attention is not paid to the ladies, we are determined to foment a rebellion and will not hold ourselves bound by any laws in which we have no voice or representation.[2]

Despite this request, women, although considered citizens in the early years of the nation, had no political rights.

The first political cause in which women became actively engaged was the slavery abolition movement. Even male abolitionists felt that women should not take an active role on the subject in public, however. When the World Antislavery Convention was held in London in 1840, women delegates were barred from active participation. Responding partly to this rebuff, two American delegates, Lucretia Mott and Elizabeth Cady Stanton, returned from that meeting with plans to work for women's rights in the United States.

In 1848, Mott and Stanton organized the first women's rights convention in Seneca Falls, New York. The three hundred people who attended approved a Declaration of Sentiments: "We hold these truths to be self-evident: that all men *and women* are created equal." In the following twelve years, groups of feminists held seven conventions in different cities in the Midwest and East. With the outbreak of the Civil War, however, advocates of women's rights were urged to put their support behind the war effort, and most agreed.

The Suffrage Issue and the Fifteenth Amendment

"The right of citizens of the United States to vote shall not be denied or abridged by the United States or by any State on account of race, color, or previous condition of servitude." So reads Section 1 of Amendment XV to the

Elizabeth Cady Stanton (1815–1902) was a social reformer and a women's suffrage leader. At her wedding in 1840 to Henry B. Stanton, she insisted on dropping the word *obey* from the marriage vows. She wrote *The History of Women's Suffrage*, which was published in 1886.

---

[1]*Bradwell v. Illinois*, 16 Wall. 130 (1873).
[2]As quoted in Lewis D. Eigen and Jonathan P. Siegel, *The Macmillan Dictionary of Political Quotations* (New York: Macmillan, 1993), p. 324.

SUFFRAGE

The right to vote; the franchise.

Constitution, which was ratified in 1870. The campaign for the passage of this amendment split the women's **suffrage** movement. Militant feminists wanted to add "sex" to "race, color, or previous condition of servitude." Other feminists, along with many men, opposed this view; they wanted to separate African American suffrage and women's suffrage to ensure the passage of the amendment. So, although the African American press supported the women's suffrage movement, it became separate from the racial equality movement. Still, some women attempted to vote in the years following the Civil War. One, Virginia Louisa Minor, was arrested and convicted in 1872. She appealed to the Supreme Court, but the Court upheld her conviction.[3]

Women's Suffrage Associations

Susan B. Anthony and Elizabeth Cady Stanton formed the National Suffrage Association in 1869. According to their view, women's suffrage was a means to achieve major improvements in the economic and social situation of women in the United States. In other words, the vote was to be used to obtain a larger goal. Lucy Stone, however, felt that the vote was the only major issue. Members of the American Women's Suffrage Association, founded by Stone and others, traveled to each state, addressed state legislatures, wrote, published, and argued their convictions. They achieved only limited success. In 1890, the two organizations quit battling and joined forces. The National American Women's Suffrage Association had only one goal—the enfranchisement of women—but it made little progress.

By the early 1900s, small radical splinter groups were formed, such as the Congressional Union, headed by Alice Paul. This organization worked solely for the passage of an amendment to the U.S. Constitution. Willing to use "unorthodox" means to achieve its goal, this group and others took to the streets. There were parades, hunger strikes, arrests, and jailings. Finally, in 1920, seventy-two years after the Seneca Falls convention, the Nineteenth Amendment was passed: "The right of citizens of the United States to vote shall not be denied or abridged by the United States or by any State on account of sex." Women were thus enfranchised. Although today it may seem that the United States was slow to give women the vote, it was really not too far behind the rest of the world (see Table 6–1).

[3]*Minor v. Happersett,* 21 Wall. 162 (1874). The Supreme Court reasoned that the right to vote was a privilege of state, not federal, citizenship. The Court did not consider privileges of state citizenship to be protected by the Fourteenth Amendment.

The words of Susan B. Anthony are still used today by those who work for women's political equality.

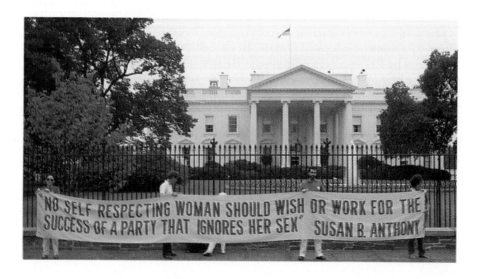

Table 6–1

Years, by Country, in Which Women Gained the Right to Vote

1893: New Zealand	**1919:** Germany	**1945:** Italy	**1953:** Mexico
1902: Australia	**1920:** United States	**1945:** Japan	**1956:** Egypt
1913: Norway	**1930:** South Africa	**1947:** Argentina	**1963:** Kenya
1918: Britain	**1932:** Brazil	**1950:** India	**1971:** Switzerland
1918: Canada	**1944:** France	**1952:** Greece	**1984:** Yemen

SOURCE: Center for the American Woman and Politics, 1995.

WOMEN'S CONTINUED STRUGGLE FOR EQUAL STATUS

Obviously, the right to vote does not guarantee political power. It has been nearly eighty years since women obtained the right to vote in the United States, yet relatively few high political positions have been held by women. In the latter half of the twentieth century, proponents of equal rights for women continue to struggle with traditional cultural beliefs concerning the proper role of women in society, as well as with court decisions upholding laws and policies based on gender classifications.

Women and Political Leadership

Of the more than ten thousand members who have served in the U.S. House of Representatives, only 1 percent have been women. No woman has yet held one of the major leadership positions in the House or Senate. In Congress, the men's club atmosphere prevails, although elections during the 1990s brought substantially more women to Congress than either the Senate or the House had seen before. After the 1994 elections, there were forty-nine women in the House and eight in the Senate. (See this chapter's feature entitled *Elections '96: Political Leadership by Women* for further detail on women in today's Congress.)

Susan B. Anthony (1820–1906) was a leader of the women's suffrage movement who was also active in the antialcohol and antislavery movements. In 1869, with Elizabeth Cady Stanton, she founded the National Suffrage Association. In 1888, she organized the International Council of Women and, in 1904, the International Women's Suffrage Alliance, in Berlin.

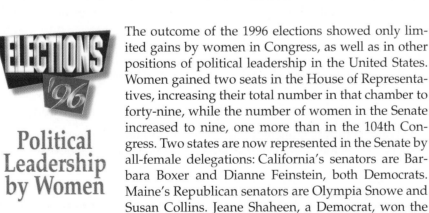

ELECTIONS '96

Political Leadership by Women

The outcome of the 1996 elections showed only limited gains by women in Congress, as well as in other positions of political leadership in the United States. Women gained two seats in the House of Representatives, increasing their total number in that chamber to forty-nine, while the number of women in the Senate increased to nine, one more than in the 104th Congress. Two states are now represented in the Senate by all-female delegations: California's senators are Barbara Boxer and Dianne Feinstein, both Democrats. Maine's Republican senators are Olympia Snowe and Susan Collins. Jeane Shaheen, a Democrat, won the governorship of New Hampshire, becoming the first female chief executive of that state.

Of much more significance than the limited gains in Congress by women was the importance of women's votes in reelecting Bill Clinton to the presidency. The "gender gap," which will be explained in more detail in Chapter 7, appeared in force in 1996. Exit polls showed that women gave 54 percent of their votes to President Clinton and only 37 percent to Bob Dole, while men cast 44 percent of their votes for Clinton and 44 percent for Dole. Democrats had campaigned hard for women's votes and, in this election, succeeded in getting them.

No woman has yet been nominated for president by a major political party—although public opinion polls suggest ever-increasing support for the idea of a female president. (In 1984, Democrats nominated Geraldine Ferraro to be Walter Mondale's vice presidential running mate.)

Women have also been meagerly represented in federal political appointments, although this situation is changing. President Franklin Roosevelt appointed the first woman to a cabinet post—Frances Perkins, who was secretary of labor from 1933 to 1945. In 1969, President Richard Nixon declared that "a woman can and should be able to do any political job that a man can do." But by the time of his resignation in 1974, he had not appointed a woman to either the cabinet or the Supreme Court. His successor, Gerald Ford, appointed a woman as secretary of housing and urban development. President Jimmy Carter (1977–1981) had three women in his cabinet and appointed many female judges. President Ronald Reagan (1981–1989) appointed women to two major cabinet posts and to head the U.S. delegation to the United Nations. He is also credited with a historical first in his appointment of Sandra Day O'Connor to the Supreme Court in 1981. President George Bush (1989–1993) appointed two women to cabinet posts, and a woman served as his international trade negotiator. President Bill Clinton named three women to cabinet posts in his first term and appointed Ruth Bader Ginsburg to the Supreme Court. Despite these changes, however, women have yet to be appointed to any of the "inner" cabinet posts—secretary of state, secretary of the treasury, and secretary of defense.

Women have had more success at attaining elective office in state legislatures and local governments. Several women have been elected to governorships. At the beginning of 1997, of 7,366 state legislators in the United States, over 20 percent were women. Chicago, Houston, and San Francisco have had women mayors, as have 17 percent of U.S. cities with populations of more than thirty thousand.

The representation of women in political office does not reflect their participation as voters. As Table 6–2 indicates, the absolute turnout of female voters nationally is higher than that of male voters.

The United States is not the only country in which women are underrepresented. Indeed, in no country does the percentage of women in political office correspond to the percentage of women in the national population. Furthermore, on a worldwide level, political leadership by women seems to be declining (see this chapter's *Politics and Comparative Systems*).

Gender Discrimination and the Fourteenth Amendment

The Fourteenth Amendment to the U.S. Constitution provides that no *person* shall be denied the *equal protection* of the laws. Nonetheless, laws that include

Table 6–2

Voting and Registration

Voting participation by females has recently been equal to, or greater than, voting participation by males. In both percentage and absolute terms, more females than males voted and registered in 1992.

	PERSONS OF VOTING AGE (MILLIONS)	PERSONS REPORTING THEY REGISTERED (MILLIONS)	PERSONS REPORTING THEY VOTED (PERCENTAGE)
Male	88.6	66.9	60.2
Female	97.1	69.3	62.3

SOURCE: U.S. Department of Commerce, *Statistical Abstract of the United States* (Washington, D.C.: U.S. Government Printing Office, 1996).

POLITICS AND COMPARATIVE SYSTEMS
The Worldwide Decline in Political Leadership by Women

A recent study conducted by the Inter-Parliamentary Union (IPU) indicated that the number of women elected to national legislatures in other countries is declining. Why is this? According to Pierre Cornillion, secretary general of the IPU, the decline can be attributed in part to the collapse of communism in Europe and the consequent resurgence of older forms of government there as well as in Africa. Cornillion pointed out that governments in socialist systems tend to give priority to representation (or apparent representation) of all components of soci-

ety—workers, farmers, intellectuals, and women. He concluded that what we now know is that "representation did not lead to a real sharing of power by women. When free and fair elections came, the parties did not put up women as candidates."*

The study also showed that of the 106 nations that have freely elected legislatures, the United States ranks forty-third with respect to women in positions of political leadership, lower than Russia and many Eastern European and Latin American countries. Worldwide, between 1988 and 1995,

the percentage of seats in national legislatures held by women dropped from nearly 15 percent to 11.3 percent.

For Critical Analysis
How can you explain the fact that although female voter turnout in the United States is as high or higher than that of men, women continue to be underrepresented in Congress?

*As quoted in Barbara Crossette, "Worldwide Study Finds Decline in Election of Women to Offices," *The New York Times*, August 27, 1995.

different provisions for men and women are not always struck down by the Supreme Court. The Court has established standards for determining whether gender classifications are acceptable. Laws with racial classifications are always "suspect" and are invalidated unless the government can prove that the classifications are "necessary to a compelling objective" (in fact, laws with racial classifications have been invalidated in almost every case). Laws that classify by gender are permissible if they "substantially relate to important governmental interests." For example, a law punishing males but not females for statutory rape is valid because of the important governmental interest in preventing teenage pregnancy in those circumstances.[4] A law granting a husband, as "head and master" of the house, the right to unilaterally sell or give away property owned jointly with his wife is not valid.[5] This standard for evaluating the acceptability of gender classifications was established by the Court in 1971 in *Reed v. Reed*,[6] a case involving an Idaho law that gave men preference over women in administering estates of dead relatives.

In determining the validity of a law based on gender classification, the courts thus must weigh the government's interest in passing the law against the equal protection clause of the Fourteenth Amendment. Consequently, it is difficult to predict the outcome of any particular case. Generally, though, since the 1970s, the Court has scrutinized gender classifications closely, and many gender-based laws have failed to pass muster in the Court's eyes. For example, in 1976 the Court held that states cannot set different ages for men and women with respect to when they reach the age of majority (become adults legally).[7] In 1977, the Court ruled that police departments and firefighting units cannot establish arbitrary rules, such as height and weight requirements, that tend to preclude women from joining those occupations.[8]

[4]*Michael M. v. Superior Court*, 450 U.S. 464 (1981).
[5]*Kirchberg v. Feenstra*, 450 U.S. 455 (1981).
[6]404 U.S. 71 (1971).
[7]*Craig v. Borden*, 429 U.S. 190 (1976).
[8]*Dothard v. Rawlinson*, 433 U.S. 321 (1977).

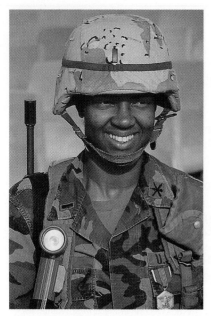

Women took part in Operation Desert Storm in 1991 as officers and enlisted personnel. Although women have been restricted from holding combat positions, they have been allowed to perform their jobs in combat zones.

In 1983, the Court ruled that insurance companies cannot charge different rates for women than for men.[9]

A question that has elicited substantial controversy in recent years has to do with whether women should be allowed to participate in military combat. Generally, the Supreme Court has left this decision up to Congress and the Department of Defense. Although recently women have been allowed to serve as combat pilots and on naval warships, to date they have not been allowed to join infantry combat units. In regard to military training institutes, however, the Supreme Court has made it clear that any state seeking to defend a classification based solely on gender must provide an exceedingly persuasive justification for the state's position. In a 1996 case, *United States v. Virginia*,[10] the Court held that the state-financed Virginia Military Institute's policy of accepting only males violated the equal protection clause. The Court stated that the state of Virginia had failed to provide a sufficient justification for its gender-based classification. The Court did not hold, however, that gender-based classifications are always unconstitutional. In other words, the question remains as to whether other single-sex educational programs around the country would survive the Court's scrutiny.

The Equal Rights Amendment

To obtain truly equal rights for women, proponents of women's rights have tried to garner support for an amendment to the Constitution. The proposed Equal Rights Amendment (ERA), which was first introduced in Congress in 1923 by leaders of the National Women's Party, states as follows: "Equality of rights under the law shall not be denied or abridged by the United States or by any state on account of sex." After years during which the amendment was not even given a hearing in Congress, it was finally approved by both chambers and was sent to the state legislatures for ratification on March 22, 1972.

As was noted in Chapter 2, any constitutional amendment must be ratified by the legislatures (or conventions) in three-fourths of the states before it can become law. Since the early 1900s, most proposed amendments have required that ratification occur within seven years of passage of the amendment by Congress. The states at first responded enthusiastically to the ERA and ratified with little deliberation. Most of the twenty-two states that ratified the ERA in 1972 did so without holding the customary hearings. Hawaii ratified the same day Congress passed the amendment. The Nebraska legislature, anxious to appear promptly responsive, ratified quickly but discovered it had done so improperly and had to do it again.[11] At the same time, opposing forces were becoming organized and militant. In 1972, the platform of the American party (which had nominated former segregationist Alabama governor George Wallace for president in 1968) denounced the ERA as a "socialistic plan to destroy the home." The necessary thirty-eight states failed to ratify the amendment within the seven-year period specified by Congress, in spite of the support given to the ERA in numerous national party platforms, by six presidents, and by both houses of Congress.

In the forefront of the organizations pushing for the adoption of the ERA—and for women's rights in general—has been the National Organization for Women (NOW). NOW was formed in 1966 by writer Betty Friedan and others who were dissatisfied with the lack of aggressive action against sex discrimination by the then-largest women's organizations—the National Feder-

---

[9]*Arizona v. Norris*, 463 U.S. 1073 (1983).
[10]116 S.Ct. 2263 (1996).
[11]The following year, Nebraska rescinded its ratification.

ation of Business and Professional Women's Clubs and the League of Women Voters. NOW immediately adopted a blanket resolution designed "to bring women into full participation in the mainstream of American society *now*, exercising all the privileges and responsibilities thereof in truly equal partnership with men." NOW, whose membership grew from 300 members in 1966 to over 250,000 members in 1997, continues to be one of the leading pressure groups in the struggle for women's rights.

GENDER-BASED DISCRIMINATION IN THE WORKPLACE

Although the ERA did not pass, several efforts were made by the federal government to eliminate sex discrimination in the labor market both before and after the introduction of the amendment in 1972.

Title VII of the Civil Rights Act of 1964

Title VII of the Civil Rights Act of 1964 prohibits **gender discrimination** in the employment context and has been used to strike down employment policies that discriminate against employees on the basis of gender. For example, in 1978, the Supreme Court ruled that an employer (the city of Los Angeles) could not require female employees to make higher pension-fund contributions than male employees earning the same salaries.[12]

Even so-called protective policies have been held to violate Title VII if they have a discriminatory effect. In 1991, for example, the Court held that a fetal protection policy established by Johnson Controls, Inc., the country's largest producer of automobile batteries, violated Title VII. The policy required all women of childbearing age working in jobs that entailed periodic exposure to lead or other hazardous materials to prove that they were infertile or to transfer to other positions. Women who agreed to transfer often had to accept cuts in pay and reduced job responsibilities. The Court concluded that women who are "as capable of doing their jobs as their male counterparts may not be forced to choose between having a child and having a job."[13]

Pregnancy Discrimination.   In 1978, Congress amended Title VII to expand the definition of gender discrimination to include discrimination based on pregnancy. Women affected by pregnancy, childbirth, or related medical conditions must be treated—for all employment-related purposes, including the receipt of benefits under employee-benefit programs—the same as other persons not so affected but similar in ability to work. An employer is required to treat an employee temporarily unable to perform her job owing to a pregnancy-related condition in the same manner as the employer would treat other temporarily disabled employees. The employer must change work assignments, grant paid disability leaves, or grant leaves without pay if that is how it would treat other temporarily disabled employees. Policies concerning an employee's return to work, accrual of seniority, pay increases, and so on also must result in equal treatment.

Sexual Harassment.   Title VII also prohibits **sexual harassment** in the workplace. Sexual harassment occurs when job opportunities, promotions, salary

---

[12]*Los Angeles v. Meinhart,* 435 U.S. 702 (1978).
[13]*United Automobile Workers v. Johnson Controls, Inc.,* 499 U.S. 187 (1991).

GENDER DISCRIMINATION

Any practice, policy, or procedure that denies equality of treatment to an individual or to a group because of gender.

SEXUAL HARASSMENT

Unwanted physical or verbal conduct or abuse of a sexual nature that interferes with a recipient's job performance, creates a hostile environment, or carries with it an implicit or explicit threat of adverse employment consequences.

Paula Jones brought a lawsuit against President Clinton in 1994. Jones was unable to bring a suit for sexual harassment, because the statute of limitations had run out. Nonetheless, she accused Clinton of violating her civil rights when she was an employee of the state of Arkansas and he was the governor. She claimed that he made unwanted sexual advances and acted in an obscene manner. Her lawsuit was stayed during Clinton's first term as president.

increases, and so on are given in return for sexual favors. A special form of sexual harassment, called hostile-environment harassment, occurs when an employee is subjected to sexual conduct or comments that interfere with the employee's job performance or create an intimidating, hostile, or offensive environment.

The problem of sexual harassment received widespread attention in the national media in 1991, when law professor Anita Hill charged that Supreme Court nominee Clarence Thomas had sexually harassed her when they both had worked at the Equal Employment Opportunity Commission (EEOC). Although Thomas was appointed to the Court, Hill's allegations caused a national furor and resulted in a dramatic increase in sexual-harassment claims. In the following five years, the number of sexual-harassment complaints submitted to the EEOC increased dramatically, as you can see in this chapter's *Politics and Discrimination*.

The Supreme Court has upheld the right of women to be free from sexual harassment on the job. In 1986, the Court indicated that creating a hostile environment by sexual harassment violates Title VII, even if job status is not affected.[14] In 1993, the Court said that a victim need not prove psychological harm from sexual harassment to win damages. Justice Sandra Day O'Connor explained that the law protects victims of sexual harassment "before the harassing conduct leads to a nervous breakdown."[15] Additionally, the Civil Rights Act of 1991 greatly expanded the remedies available for victims in cases of sexual harassment. The act specifically states that victims can seek damages in addition to back pay, job reinstatement, and the other remedies previously available.

Wage Discrimination

By 1997, women constituted 46 percent of the U.S. labor force, and that number continues to grow. By the year 2010, women will approach a majority of U.S. workers. Although Title VII and other legislation since the 1960s have mandated employment opportunities for men and women, women continue to earn less, on average, than men do. Currently, for every dollar earned by men, women earn about seventy-six cents.

The Equal Pay Act of 1963.   The issue of wage discrimination was first addressed during World War II (1941–1945), when the War Labor Board issued an "equal pay for women" policy. In implementing the policy, the board often evaluated jobs for their comparability and required equal pay for comparable jobs. The board's authority ended with the war. Supported by the next three presidential administrations, the Equal Pay Act was finally enacted in 1963 as an amendment to the Fair Labor Standards Act of 1938.

Basically, the Equal Pay Act requires employers to pay equal pay for substantially equal work. In other words, males cannot be paid more than females who perform essentially the same job. The Equal Pay Act did not address the fact that certain types of jobs traditionally held by women pay lower wages than the jobs usually held by men. For example, more women than men are secretaries, sales clerks, and nurses, whereas more men than women are construction workers, truck drivers, and plumbers. Even if all secretaries performing substantially similar jobs for a company earned the same salaries, they would still be earning less than the company's truck drivers.

---

[14]*Meritor Savings Bank, FSB v. Vinson*, 477 U.S. 77 (1986).
[15]*Harris v. Forklift Systems, Inc.*, 510 U.S. 17 (1993).

POLITICS AND DISCRIMINATION
The Overburdened EEOC

Compliance with most of the federal laws prohibiting discrimination is monitored by the Equal Employment Opportunity Commission (EEOC). EEOC procedures have been criticized because the process involves so many delays—and any delay in a legal proceeding can be critical because fresh evidence can make or break a case.

Under EEOC procedural rules, a victim of alleged discrimination, before bringing a suit against the employer, must first file a claim with the EEOC within 180 days of the alleged discriminatory act. The EEOC then has 180 days to investigate the dispute and decide whether to bring a suit against the employer on the employee's behalf. If the EEOC decides not to investigate the claim, the victim may bring his or her own lawsuit against the employer—but not before receiving a right-to-sue letter from the EEOC. Although the EEOC has 180 days to take action on the employee's complaint, in reality, the process averages eight months. Why does it take the EEOC so long to process complaints? One reason for

the delay is that the EEOC is simply overburdened. Workers who take their claims to the EEOC face a backlog of over 95,000 cases.

Two events in the early 1990s caused the number of claims filed with the EEOC to skyrocket. First, Anita Hill's sexual harassment charges against Supreme Court nominee Clarence Thomas, during Thomas's 1991 confirmation hearings, opened a Pandora's box of sexual-harassment complaints from other women around the nation. Sexual-harassment claims filed with the EEOC rose by nearly 150 percent in the five years following the confirmation hearings, and today about 16 percent of all claims filed with the EEOC are for sexual harassment. Second, the Americans with Disabilities Act (ADA), which was passed in 1990 and became effective in 1992, significantly increased the EEOC's caseload. Over 17 percent of the almost 90,000 discrimination cases filed with the EEOC during the first full year of the ADA's implementation were for disability-based discrimination, and this percentage has increased

slightly since then. In other words, the number of claims handled by the EEOC has increased dramatically in the 1990s. Its budget, however, has not kept pace—it rose by only 26 percent between 1991 and 1995.

One solution to the problem is to limit the number of cases the EEOC investigates, which is what the commission did in 1996. In its "National Enforcement Plan," the EEOC stated that it will investigate only "priority cases," not all cases, as it did in the past. The plan lists the types of cases that the EEOC wants to investigate and take to litigation and those that it does not. Generally, priority cases are cases that affect many workers, cases involving retaliatory discharge (firing an employee in retaliation for filing a claim with the EEOC), and cases involving types of discrimination that are of particular concern to the EEOC.

For Critical Analysis
Why doesn't Congress simply increase the amount of funds allocated for the EEOC?

Comparable Worth, or Pay Equity.   The concept of **comparable worth,** or pay equity, is that women should receive equal pay not just for equal (that is, the same) work but also for work requiring comparable skill, effort, and responsibility. The comparable worth doctrine attempts to redress the effects of traditional "women's work" being undervalued and underpaid.

The issue of equal pay for comparable work obtained national attention during a strike of female municipal workers in San Jose, California, in 1981. At that time, a study comparing the skill, effort, and responsibility of all city jobs showed that jobs traditionally held by women had pay rates less than those of comparable jobs held by men. The mayor's secretary, for example, was paid $18,000 for work found to be qualitatively equivalent to that of a senior air-conditioning mechanic earning $31,000. The strike was ended by an agreement to raise the women's pay to the level of male workers doing comparable work.

In 1981, the Supreme Court ruled that female workers could sue under Title VII even if they were not performing the same jobs as men.[16] By the

COMPARABLE WORTH

The idea that compensation should be based on the worth of the job to an employer and that factors unrelated to the worth of a job, such as the sex of the employee, should not affect compensation.

---

[16]*Washington County, Oregon v. Gunther,* 452 U.S. 161 (1981).

The "Willmar 8"—female bank employees picket for equal pay. The question of equal pay for equal work has not been fully resolved with the passage of federal legislation. Women still earn, on average, 25 percent less than their male counterparts.

1990's, more than twenty states had adjusted the pay of state government employees. The state of Washington closed the pay gap most successfully, reducing the difference in average pay between men and women to 5 percent.

Defendants in equal-pay cases have successfully relied upon a stipulation that they were only following market wages in their failure to pay women's jobs the same amount as men's jobs. In both *American Federation of State, County, and Municipal Employees v. State of Washington*[17] and *American Nurses Association et al. v. State of Illinois*,[18] the courts allowed the market wage defense to defeat the plaintiffs' claims of intentional discrimination.

The problem with comparable worth is that wages in the United States traditionally have been determined by the forces of supply and demand in the labor market. If pay scales based on comparable worth were implemented, what criteria would be used to determine the value of particular jobs? To date, this question has not been resolved satisfactorily—although, as mentioned, several state governments have modified their pay scales to reduce the "gender gap" with respect to wages.

The Glass Ceiling.   Although increased numbers of women are holding jobs in professions or business enterprises that were once dominated by men, few women hold top positions in their firms. Less than 3 percent of the Fortune 500 companies in America—America's leading corporations—have a woman as one of their five highest-paid executives. Because the barriers faced by women in the corporate world are subtle and not easily pinpointed, they have been referred to as "the glass ceiling."

As mentioned earlier in this chapter, age-old cultural traditions regarding the proper role of women in society die hard. Nowhere is this fact more evident than in the business context. In a Gallup poll released in 1996, for example, 49 percent of the Americans surveyed thought that an arrangement in which the husband works and the wife stays home was ideal. Furthermore, the poll detected a preference among Americans for male supervisors. Even 54 percent of women said they would prefer to work for men. The United States is not alone in these sentiments. The majority of women in most of the twenty-two other nations surveyed in the poll said that they would prefer working for men. Only women in El Salvador and Honduras expressed no obvious preference for male or female bosses.

THE STATUS OF OLDER AMERICANS

Americans are getting older. In colonial times, about half the population was under the age of sixteen. In 1990, the number of people under the age of sixteen was fewer than one in four, and half were thirty-three or older. By the year 2050, at least half could be thirty-nine or older.

Today, 32 million Americans (13 percent of the population) are sixty-five or over. As can be seen in Figure 6–1, it is estimated that by the year 2020, this figure will have reached 53.6 million. From 2010 to 2030, the Bureau of the Census predicts that the portion of the population over age sixty-five will grow 76 percent, while the population under age sixty-five will increase only 6.5 percent (see Figure 6–1).

Thus, the problems of aging and retirement are going to become increasingly important national issues. Because many older people rely on income

[17]770 F.2d 1401 (1985).
[18]783 F.2d 716 (1986).

from Social Security to maintain themselves, the funding of Social Security benefits continues to be a major issue on the national political agenda, as you will read in Chapter 16.

Age Discrimination in Employment

Age discrimination is potentially the most widespread form of discrimination, because anyone—regardless of race, color, national origin, or gender—could be a victim at some point in life. The unstated policies of some companies not to hire or to demote or dismiss people they feel are "too old" have made it difficult for some older workers to succeed in their jobs or continue with their careers. Additionally, older workers have fallen victim at times to cost-cutting efforts by employers. To reduce operational costs, companies may replace older, higher-salaried workers with younger, lower-salaried workers. In spite of their proven productivity, some older workers have suffered from age discrimination in employment.

The Age Discrimination in Employment Act of 1967.   In an attempt to protect older employees from discriminatory practices, Congress passed the Age Discrimination in Employment Act (ADEA) in 1967. The act, which applies to employers, employment agencies, and labor organizations and covers individuals over the age of forty, prohibits discrimination against individuals on the basis of age unless age is shown to be a bona fide occupational qualification reasonably necessary to the normal operation of the particular business.

Specifically, it is against the law to discriminate by age in wages, benefits, hours worked, or availability of overtime. Employers and unions may not discriminate in providing fringe benefits, such as education or training programs, career development, sick leave, and vacations. It is a violation of the act to publish notices or advertisements indicating an age-preference limitation or discrimination based on age. Even advertisements that imply a preference for youthful workers over older workers are in violation of the law.

DID YOU KNOW...
That those eighty-five years of age or older constitute the most rapidly growing segment of the U.S. population, and that by the year 2040, this group will constitute 8 percent of the total population?

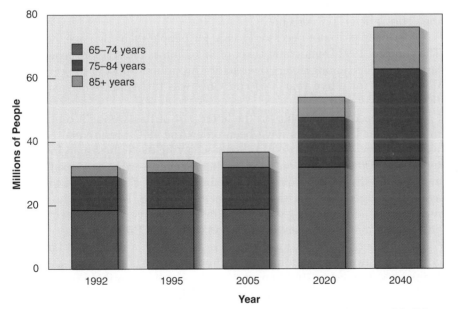

Figure 6–1
• •
Population Projections: Persons Age 65 and Older (in Millions)

SOURCE: U.S. Department of Commerce, *Statistical Abstract of the United States* (Washington, D.C.: U.S. Government Printing Office, 1994).

DID YOU KNOW . . .
That in 1922, at age eighty-seven, Rebecca Latimer Felton was the first and oldest woman to serve in the U.S. Senate—although she was appointed as a token gesture and was allowed to serve only one day?

MANDATORY RETIREMENT

Forced retirement when a person reaches a certain age.

Figure 6–2
● ●

Federal Age Discrimination Complaints and Damages Awarded in Age Discrimination Cases (Fiscal Years Ending September 30)

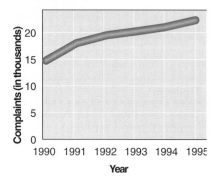

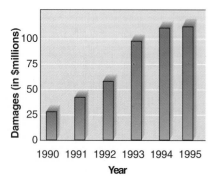

SOURCE: Federal Equal Employment Opportunity Commission and authors' update.

Requesting age on an application is not illegal but may be closely scrutinized in light of the employer's hiring practices.

To succeed in a suit for age discrimination, an employee must prove that the employer's action, such as a decision to fire the employee, was motivated, at least in part, by age bias. Proof that qualified older employees are generally discharged before younger employees or that co-workers continually made unflattering age-related comments about the discharged worker may be enough. In 1996, the Supreme Court held that even if an older worker is replaced by a younger worker falling under the protection of the ADEA—that is, by a younger worker who is also over the age of forty—the older worker is entitled to bring a suit under the ADEA. The Court stated that the issue in all ADEA cases is whether age discrimination has in fact occurred, regardless of the age of the replacement worker.[19]

Figure 6–2 shows the increase in the number of complaints for age discrimination as well as the total size of damage awards.

Mandatory Retirement.   The ADEA, as initially passed, did not address one of the major problems facing older workers—**mandatory retirement** rules, which required employees to retire when they reached a certain age. As discussed in this chapter's opening *What If . . . ,* mandatory retirement rules often meant that competent, well-trained employees who wanted to continue working were unable to do so. In 1978, in an amendment to the ADEA, Congress prohibited mandatory retirement rules with respect to most employees under the age of seventy. Many states had already passed similar statutes. In 1986, Congress outlawed mandatory retirement rules entirely for all but a few selected occupations, such as firefighting.

Age and Political Participation and Leadership

If we use voter participation as a measure of political involvement, it is clear that voter participation increases with age. Table 6–3 shows that, of the six age categories listed, the over-sixty-five age group ranks first in voter registration and in actual turnout on election day. Whereas approximately 61.3 percent of all persons of voting age claim to have voted, in the over-sixty-five category, the voting rate is 70.1 percent.

Older people do not necessarily vote for people their own age, however. The youthful 1992 Democratic ticket of Bill Clinton and Al Gore achieved its largest margins among voters over sixty. Throughout most of the campaign, Clinton was forty-five years old and Gore was forty-four, whereas George Bush was sixty-four.

With respect to leadership, in the latter part of the twentieth century, the most popular U.S. leaders have been older (the 1992 presidential elections were an exception). The three presidents achieving the highest margins of victory since 1950—Eisenhower, Johnson, and Reagan—were sixty-six, fifty-six, and seventy-three, respectively, at the time of their elections. All three ran against younger men. Of the thirty incumbent U.S. senators who sought reelection to additional six-year terms in 1994, twelve were in their sixties, and five were in their seventies; only one was under fifty.

Older Americans work for their interests through a number of large and effective political associations. The National Association of Retired Federal Employees, formed in 1921, currently has about half a million members. In 1947, the National Retired Teachers' Association was established, and today

---

[19]*O'Connor v. Consolidated Coil Caterers Corp.,* 116 S.Ct. 1307 (1996).

Table 6–3

Voter Participation by Age Group

Voter participation seems to be positively correlated with age. The lowest participation is by persons eighteen to twenty years old, and the highest is by those sixty-five and over.

AGE GROUP	PERSONS VOTING AGE (MILLIONS)	PERCENTAGE REPORTING THEY REGISTERED	PERCENTAGE REPORTING THEY VOTED
18–20	9.7	48.3	38.5
21–24	14.6	55.3	45.7
25–34	41.6	60.6	53.2
35–44	39.7	69.2	63.6
45–64	49.1	75.3	70.0
65 and over	30.8	78.0	70.1

SOURCE: U.S. Department of Commerce, *Statistical Abstract of the United States* (Washington, D.C.: U.S. Government Printing Office, 1994), p. 283. Data are for 1992.

it has more than half a million members. The largest group is the American Association of Retired Persons, for those aged fifty and older. Founded in 1958, it has a current membership of more than thirty-three million. The latter two groups have united in a powerful joint effort to ensure beneficial treatment for older Americans by lobbying for legislation at the federal and state levels. They use the same staff in Washington and provide almost the same services to their members, including low-priced group insurance and travel programs.

Age and Government Benefits

Americans over the age of sixty-five receive a disproportionate share of government spending. Almost half the entire federal budget is spent on Medicare and Social Security. Medicare costs recently have risen at about twice the rate of inflation for the economy as a whole. Many entitlement programs, like Medicare and Social Security, have been tied legislatively to external factors so that spending on them has become, to a large degree, uncontrollable and automatic.

Given the higher levels of political participation by older Americans, the number of political leaders that are or will soon be over sixty-five, and the population "bulge" of baby boomers who are approaching retirement age, it seems very likely that the administration of entitlement programs increasingly could become the predominant responsibility of the U.S. government. This likelihood, coupled with the prospect of a constitutional amendment forcing a balanced budget, has prompted one writer to forecast that "the government will, over time, become merely a giant transfer payment pump, a gray source of stipends from familiar entitlement programs for an aging population, and especially for the population that includes Bill Clinton, who was born in 1946, Year One of the baby boom."[20]

THE RIGHTS OF PERSONS WITH DISABILITIES

By the 1970s, persons with disabilities were becoming a political force. Congress passed the Rehabilitation Act in 1973, which prohibited discrimination against persons with disabilities in programs receiving federal aid. A 1978

[20]George Will, *Washington Post*, February 10, 1994.

Lovola West Burgess, former president of the American Association of Retired Persons (AARP). This powerful lobbying group started small but has become perhaps the largest such group in the nation. Anyone over 50 is eligible. All that is required is a small payment for dues (currently $8 a year). In exchange, AARP members obtain relatively lower priced insurance, special air fares and vacation deals, etc. The AARP can effectively counter proposed legislation that will affect its membership. It does so with letter writing campaigns and personal calls by its members to members of Congress. The AARP was instrumental, for example, in causing Congress to rescind an extra tax on senior citizens to pay for catastrophic health insurance.

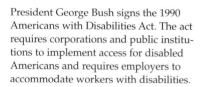

Christopher Reeves speaks to the opening night session of the Democratic National Convention in Chicago. Reeves celebrity status has made him a powerful advocate for disabled Americans.

amendment to the act established the Architectural and Transportation Barriers Compliance Board. Regulations for ramps, elevators, and the like in all federal buildings were implemented. Congress passed the Education for All Handicapped Children Act in 1975. It guarantees that all children with disabilities will receive an "appropriate" education.

The most significant federal legislation with respect to the rights of persons with disabilities, however, is the Americans with Disabilities Act (ADA), which Congress passed in 1990. The ADA requires that all public buildings and public services be accessible to persons with disabilities. The act also mandates that employers must reasonably accommodate the needs of workers or potential workers with disabilities.

Physical Access to Public Buildings and Services.   Physical access means ramps; handrails; wheelchair-accessible restrooms, counters, drinking fountains, telephones, and doorways; and more accessible mass transit. In addition, other steps must be taken to comply: Car-rental companies must provide cars with hand controls for disabled drivers. Telephone companies are required to have operators to pass on messages from the speech-impaired who use telephones with keyboards.

The Right to Reasonable Job Accommodations.   The ADA requires employers to "reasonably accommodate" the needs of persons with disabilities unless to do so would cause the employer to suffer an "undue hardship." The ADA defines persons with disabilities as persons who have physical or mental impairments that "substantially limit" their everyday activities. Health conditions that have been considered disabilities under federal law include blindness, alcoholism, heart disease, cancer, muscular dystrophy, cerebral palsy, paraplegia, diabetes, and acquired immune deficiency syndrome (AIDS).

The ADA does not require that *unqualified* applicants with disabilities be hired or retained. If a job applicant or an employee with a disability, with reasonable accommodation, can perform essential job functions, however, then the employer must make the accommodation. Required accommodations may include installing ramps for a wheelchair, establishing more flexible working hours, creating or modifying job assignments, and creating or improving training materials and procedures. (See this chapter's feature entitled *Thinking Politically about the Americans with Disabilities Act* for some of the issues involved in implementing the ADA.)

President George Bush signs the 1990 Americans with Disabilities Act. The act requires corporations and public institutions to implement access for disabled Americans and requires employers to accommodate workers with disabilities.

Thinking Politically about the Americans with Disabilities Act

In 1990, a Democratic Congress overwhelmingly supported the passage of the Americans with Disabilities Act (ADA). Five years later, House Republican leader Dick Armey of Texas—one of the few House members who voted against the ADA in 1990—called for a rewriting of the act to define the term *disability* more narrowly. The act broadly defines a disability as "a physical or mental impairment that substantially limits one or more of the major life activities" of an individual. The act also mandates that persons with disabilities be "reasonably accommodated." Federal agencies, such as the Equal Employment Opportunity Commission (EEOC), and the courts have been left to fill in the blanks left by Congress. What constitutes a physical or mental impairment? At what point does such an impairment "substantially limit" a "major life activity," and what constitutes a major life activity? Finally, what exactly is required to reasonably accommodate persons with disabilities?

Many commentators have agreed with Armey that the ADA has some serious shortcomings. Because of the broadly drafted provisions of the act, it has been implemented in ways that at times defy common sense. Consider, for example, the situation in which Blair Taylor, who owns a restaurant, found himself. To accommodate persons with disabilities, Taylor was required to install a ramp inside the restaurant, so that all tables would be accessible to those in wheelchairs. To make room for the ramp, he had to give up four tables. Before the modifications were made, sixteen of the twenty-eight tables in the restaurant were accessible to persons using wheelchairs. After the modifications, all twenty-four tables were accessible. To date, the ramp has never been used. "It will never be used," says Blair. "There will never be a time when seventeen wheelchairs are ever going to be in the Barolo Grill at the same time."

In accommodating the needs of employees with disabilities, employers have faced situations that appear equally bizarre. In one case, an employer fired an employee who came to work toting a loaded gun. The jury concluded that the employer had violated the ADA because the employee's behavior was the result of a mental impairment. Therefore, the employer should have accommodated the employee in some way, such as by giving him a leave of absence.*

On the other side of the picture, of course, are the many persons with disabilities who have benefited from the ADA. The ADA clearly highlights the problem of the political and economic trade-offs that have to be made when resources are allocated to benefit specially selected groups in society. It is not enough to state simply that persons with disabilities (or older citizens or any other disadvantaged group) should be given better treatment in the United States. We also must ask who will bear the costs of this improved treatment. This is both an economic and a political question.

For Critical Analysis
In your opinion, should the ADA be rewritten (amended) to define the term disability more narrowly? Why or why not?

*Hindman v. GTE Data Services, Inc. (M.D.Fla. 1994). This case is not published in West's *Federal Supplement* reporter.

THE RIGHTS AND STATUS OF JUVENILES

Approximately seventy-six million Americans—almost 30 percent of the total population—are under twenty-one years of age. The definition of *children* ranges from persons under age sixteen to persons under age twenty-one. However defined, children form a large group of individuals in the United States and have the fewest rights and protections.

The reason for this lack is the common presumption of society and its lawmakers that children are basically protected by their parents. This is not to say that children are the exclusive property of the parents. Rather, an overwhelming case in favor of *not* allowing parents to control the actions of their children must be presented before children can be given authorization to act without parental consent (or before the state can act be given authorization to act on children's behalf without regard to their parents' wishes).

Supreme Court decisions affecting children's rights of today began a process of slow evolution with *Brown v. Board of Education of Topeka*,[21] the landmark civil rights case of 1954. In *Brown*, the Court granted children the status of rights-bearing persons. In 1967, the court expressly held that children have a constitutional right to be represented by counsel at the government's expense in a criminal action.[22] Five years later, the Court acknowledged that "children are 'persons' within the meaning of the Bill of Rights. We have held so over and over again."[23]

Supreme Court decisions affecting the rights of children have also touched upon another very controversial issue: abortion. In 1976, the Court recognized a girl's right to have an abortion without consulting her parents.[24] More recently, however, the Court has allowed state laws to dictate whether consent must be obtained by the child. In 1993, the Court refused to review a case involving a state law that required girls under the age of eighteen to obtain the consent of both parents or a judge prior to an abortion.[25] In effect, then, the state law was upheld.

Voting Rights and the Young

The Twenty-sixth Amendment to the Constitution, ratified on July 1, 1971, reads as follows:

> The right of citizens of the United States, who are eighteen years of age or older, to vote shall not be denied or abridged by the United States or by any State on account of age.

Before this amendment was ratified, the age at which citizens could vote was twenty-one. Why did the Twenty-sixth Amendment specify age eighteen? Why not seventeen or sixteen? And why did it take until 1971 to allow those between the ages of eighteen and twenty-one to vote?

There are no easy answers to such questions. One cannot argue simply that those under twenty-one, or those under eighteen, are "incompetent." Incompetent at what? Certainly, one could find a significant number of seventeen-year-olds who can understand the political issues presented to them as well as can many adults eligible to vote. One of the arguments used for granting suffrage to eighteen-year-olds was that, because they could be drafted to fight in the country's wars, they had a stake in public policy. At the time, the example of the Vietnam War was paramount.

Have eighteen- to twenty-year-olds used their right to vote? Yes and no. Immediately after the passage of the Twenty-sixth Amendment, the percentage of eighteen- to twenty-year-olds registering to vote was 58 percent (in 1972), and 48.4 percent reported that they had voted. But by the 1992 presidential election, of the 9.7 million Americans in the eighteen-to-twenty voting age bracket, 48.2 percent were registered, and 38.5 percent reported that they had voted.

The Rights of Children in Civil and Criminal Proceedings

Children today have limited rights in civil and criminal proceedings in our judicial system. Different procedural rules and judicial safeguards apply in

---

[21]347 U.S. 483 (1954).
[22]*In re Gault*, 387 U.S. 1 (1967).
[23]*Wisconsin v. Yoder*, 406 U.S. 205 (1972).
[24]*Planned Parenthood of Central Missouri v. Danforth*, 428 U.S. 52 (1976).
[25]*Barnes v. Mississippi*, 510 U.S. 976 (1993).

civil and criminal laws. **Civil law** relates in part to contracts among private individuals or companies. **Criminal law** relates to crimes against society that are defined by society acting through its legislatures.

Civil Rights of Juveniles.   Children are defined exclusively by state law with respect to private contract negotiations, rights, and remedies. The legal definition of **majority** varies from eighteen to twenty-one years of age, depending on the state. If an individual is legally a minor, as a rule, he or she cannot be held responsible for contracts that he or she forms with others. In most states, only contracts entered into for so-called **necessaries** (things necessary for subsistence, as determined by the courts) can be enforced against minors. Also, when minors engage in negligent behavior, typically their parents are liable. If, for example, a minor destroys a neighbor's fence, the neighbor may bring suit against the child's parent but not against the child.

Civil law encompasses an area that has recently broken new ground in children's rights: child custody. Child-custody rulings have traditionally given little weight to the wishes of the child. Courts have maintained their right to act on behalf of the child's "best interests"[26] but have sometimes been constrained from doing so by the "greater" rights possessed by adults. For instance, a widely publicized Michigan Supreme Court ruling awarded legal custody of a two-and-a-half-year-old Michigan resident to an Iowa couple, the child's biological parents. A Michigan couple, who had cared for the child since shortly after its birth and who had petitioned to adopt the child, lost out in the custody battle. The court clearly and somewhat regretfully said that the law had allowed it to consider only parents' rights and not the child's best interests.[27]

Children's rights and their ability to articulate their rights for themselves in custody matters were strengthened, however, by several well-publicized rulings in which older children were involved. In 1992, an eleven-year-old Florida boy filed suit in his own name, assisted by his own privately retained legal counsel, to terminate his relationship with his biological parents and to have the court affirm his right to be adopted by foster parents.[28] The court granted his request, although it did not agree procedurally with the method by which the boy initiated the suit. The news media characterized the case as the first instance in which a minor child had "divorced" himself from his parents. In 1992, a New York court recognized the rights of an eleven-year-old boy to dismiss a court-appointed attorney and retain a lawyer of his own choosing to represent his interests in a court battle his parents were waging over his custody.[29] In 1993, a court ruled in favor of a fourteen-year-old Florida girl, who had been mistakenly switched at birth and given to the wrong couple. She sued to have a court declare her legally to be the child of her nonbiological parents.[30]

Criminal Rights of Juveniles.   One of the main requirements for an act to be criminal is intent. The law has given children certain defenses against criminal prosecution because of their presumed inability to have criminal intent. Under the **common law,** children up to seven years of age were considered incapable of committing a crime, because they did not have the moral sense

CIVIL LAW

The law regulating conduct between private persons over noncriminal matters. Under civil law, the government provides the forum for the settlement of disputes between private parties in such matters as contracts, domestic relations, and business relations.

CRIMINAL LAW

The law that defines crimes and provides punishment for violations. In criminal cases, the government is the prosecutor, because crimes are against the public order.

MAJORITY

Full age; the age at which a person is entitled by law to the right to manage his or her own affairs and to the full enjoyment of civil rights.

NECESSARIES

In contract law, necessaries include whatever is reasonably necessary for suitable subsistence as measured by age, state, condition in life, and so on.

COMMON LAW

Judge-made law that originated in England from decisions shaped according to prevailing customs. Decisions were applied to similar situations and thus gradually became common to the nation.

---

[26]*Kingsbury v. Buckner,* 134 U.S. 650 (1980).
[27]*In re Clausen,* 442 Mich. 648 (1993).
[28]*Kingsley v. Kingsley,* 623 So.2d 780 (Fla.App. 1993).
[29]*New York Times,* November 10, 1992, p. 6.
[30]*New York Times,* August 19, 1993, p. 16.

This juvenile is being arrested in the same way as an adult would be, but he does not have the rights under criminal law of an adult. Juveniles normally receive less severe punishment than adults do for similar crimes, however.

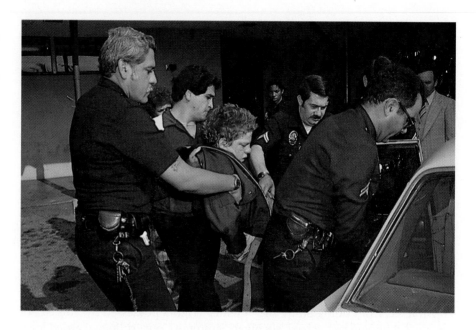

to understand that they were doing wrong. Children between the ages of seven and fourteen were also presumed to be incapable of committing a crime, but this presumption could be challenged by showing that the child understood the wrongful nature of the act. Today, states vary in their approaches. Most states retain the common law approach, although age limits vary from state to state. Other states have simply set a minimum age for criminal responsibility.

All states have juvenile court systems that handle children below the age of criminal responsibility who commit delinquent acts. The aim of juvenile courts is allegedly to reform rather than to punish. In states that retain the common law approach, children who are above the minimum age but are still juveniles can be turned over to the criminal courts if the juvenile court determines that they should be treated as adults. Children still do not have the right to trial by jury or to post bail. Also, in most states parents can still commit their minor children to state mental institutions without allowing the child a hearing.

Although minors still do not usually have the full rights of adults in criminal proceedings, they have certain advantages. In felony, manslaughter, murder, armed robbery, and assault cases, juveniles are usually not tried as adults. They may be sentenced to probation or "reform" school for a relatively few years regardless of the seriousness of their crimes. Most states, however, allow juveniles to be tried as adults (often at the discretion of the judge) for certain crimes, such as murder. When they are tried as adults, they are treated to due process of law and tried for the crime, rather than being given the paternalistic treatment reserved for the juvenile delinquent.

What to do about crime committed by juveniles is a pressing problem for today's political leaders. One approach to the problem is to treat juveniles as adults, which more and more judges seem to be doing. (See this chapter's *Critical Perspective* for a discussion of arguments in favor of and against treating juvenile criminal offenders as adults.) Another is to hold parents responsible for the crimes of their minor children (a minority of the states do so under so-called parental-responsibility laws). These are contradictory approaches, to be sure. Yet they perhaps reflect the divided opinion in our society concerning the rights of children versus the rights of parents.

THE RIGHTS AND STATUS OF GAY MALES AND LESBIANS

Studies indicate that between 3 and 15 percent of the American population may have some varying degree of homosexual orientation. Gay men and lesbians therefore represent one of the most important minorities in the United States. Nonetheless, their rights did not surface as a major issue on the American political and legal scene until the late 1960s.

On June 27, 1969, patrons of the Stonewall Inn, a New York City bar popular with gays and lesbians, responded to a police raid by throwing beer cans and bottles because they were angry at what they felt was unrelenting police harassment. In the ensuing riot, which lasted two nights, hundreds of gays and lesbians fought with police. Before Stonewall, the stigma attached to homosexuality and the resulting fear of exposure had tended to keep most gays and lesbians acquiescent. In the months immediately after Stonewall, however, "gay power" graffiti began to appear in New York City. The Gay Liberation Front and the Gay Activist Alliance were formed, and similar groups sprang up in other parts of the country. Thus Stonewall has been called "the shot heard round the homosexual world."

The status of gays and lesbians again came to national attention in 1977, when Anita Bryant, of Florida orange juice and television commercial fame, organized a "Save Our Children" campaign. Its purpose was to rescind the law protecting the legal rights of gays and lesbians in Dade County, Florida. The Dade County law protected them from discrimination in public accommodations, housing, and employment. Bryant's campaign against the gay community's effort to keep the law on the books was successful. In June 1977, Miami citizens voted 2 to 1 to repeal the law protecting gays and lesbians.

Similar laws were repealed in Eugene, Oregon; Wichita, Kansas; and St. Paul, Minnesota. In the 1990 primary, Broward County, Florida, voters defeated a proposal designed to give gay men and lesbians greater protection against discrimination (the so-called "human rights referendum") by a margin of 3 to 2. A major effort by the gay community in California to get a gay rights bill enacted into law was foiled when Governor Pete Wilson vetoed the bill in October 1991. Today, at least nineteen states still have antihomosexual laws on the books. In the summer of 1986, the Supreme Court upheld by a five-to-four decision an antigay law in the state of Georgia that made homosexual conduct between two adults a crime. Justice Byron White stated that "we are quite unwilling" to "announce . . . a fundamental right to engage in homosexual sodomy."[31]

Changing Public Attitudes

Attitudes toward gays and lesbians are changing, however. Almost one hundred cities throughout the United States currently have laws prohibiting discrimination against homosexuals in the areas of housing, education, banking, labor union employment, and public accommodations. Since 1982, Wisconsin has had on its books a general law prohibiting all discrimination against gays and lesbians. In 1989, Massachusetts passed a law specifically stating that the state does not endorse homosexuality nor recognize homosexual partnerships but that no discrimination against gays or lesbians shall exist. In 1990, St. Paul, Minnesota, passed a new ordinance prohibiting discrimination on

---

[31]*Bowers v. Hardwick*, 478 U.S. 186 (1986).

CRITICAL PERSPECTIVE

Should More Juvenile Criminals Be Tried as Adults?

In 1996, almost three million juveniles were arrested, and about 40 percent of them were under the age of fifteen. Juvenile criminals are responsible for 15 percent of all violent crimes and for over 25 percent of all property crimes. Although males from fourteen to twenty-four years of age constitute only 8 percent of the population, they account for nearly half of all murders. Violence by teenagers will probably only get worse, given the projection that the number of juveniles under seventeen will grow to about 75 million in the next decade and a half.

The Juvenile Justice System

For the most part, juvenile criminal offenders today enter the juvenile justice system, which is completely separate from the adult criminal justice system. The juvenile justice system is based on the legal doctrine of *parens patriae.* These Latin words mean that the state has the power to stand in the place of the parent. All states have juvenile court systems that handle those below the age of criminal responsibility who commit crimes. The aim of these court systems is to reform, rather than to punish.

Therefore, technically, juvenile criminals are not punished; instead, arrangements are made to influence the behavior of juveniles in positive ways. The determination of how to treat a juvenile offender is made by a juvenile judge. When an accused juvenile is found guilty of having committed the offense with which he or she has been charged, the court will declare the juvenile a ward of the court. The options available to juvenile court judges include (a) suspending the judgment, (b) putting the juvenile on probation, (c) sending the juvenile to a training program, (d) fining the juvenile, and (e) committing the juvenile to a juvenile home or camp, or to a special jail for juvenile offenders. When juveniles are institutionalized, they are given sentences in which the length of time is not specified. Release is based, at least in part, on an evaluation of a juvenile's rehabilitation.

Under specified conditions, usually after the passage of several years, many juvenile courts will officially seal all records related to a minor's case. The juvenile then officially has no criminal record.

The Arguments in Favor of Treating Juveniles as Adults

Some concerned politicians, scholars, and certainly many victims of juvenile criminal behavior argue in favor of trying juveniles as adults. They point out that the juvenile justice system has failed to rehabilitate many juvenile offenders. They offer as proof the number of times that juvenile offenders are guilty of repeated acts of serious violence. Not surprisingly, some politicians have jumped on the bandwagon and demanded that juvenile offenders be treated more harshly. In 1996, for example, House Republicans proposed legislation designed to end federal mandates that require states to segregate adults from juveniles in jails and prisons.

The argument is that at a minimum, juveniles automatically should be tried as adults for certain types of criminal acts, such as armed robbery, violent rape, and murder. Additionally, any juvenile

the basis of sexual orientation in housing, education, employment, and public accommodations. In a number of states and localities, laws against "hate crimes" include actions taken against homosexuals, even though the genesis of those laws was crimes against African Americans and Hispanics.

A 1952 law prohibiting gays and lesbians from immigrating to the United States was voided by Congress in October 1990. The Hate Crimes Statistics Act became law on April 23, 1990. It required the Justice Department to collect and publish data for five years on hate-motivated crimes based on religion, race, ethnicity, or sexual orientation.

Recent polls also indicate increasing support for the rights of gays and lesbians. In a survey conducted in 1996, for example, 73 percent of the respondents acknowledged that gays were victims of at least some discrimination, and 84 percent said gays should have equal job opportunities. Only 27 per-

CRITICAL PERSPECTIVE

Should More Juvenile Criminals Be Tried as Adults? Continued

delinquent who has a prior record of violent or serious crimes automatically should be tried as an adult.

In essence, those who argue in favor of trying more juvenile criminals as adults seem to have abandoned the hope that teenage criminal offenders can be rehabilitated. The goal is simply to keep violent criminals of all ages off the streets.

The Arguments against Treating Juveniles as Adults

Many sociologists, criminologists, and others are against the idea of increasing the number of juvenile offenders who are tried as adults and ultimately sent to adult prisons. Among them are William Bennett, John J. DiIulio, Jr., and John Walters. In *Body Count: Moral Poverty and How to Win America's War against Crime and Drugs,** these authors point out that most juvenile criminal offenders are not guilty of repeated acts of serious violence. They argue that juveniles who engage in criminal behavior need useful adult guidance, which they certainly will not find in adult prisons. Statistically, most teenage violent criminals began life as at-risk children. Generally, children are less likely to commit violent crimes when they are around responsible adults during their daily lives. The authors of *Body Count* suggest that the way to "save" such children is through programs that put them in contact with role-model adults. They cite a study showing that low-income, at-risk juveniles who meet with a big sister or a big brother on a regular basis are much less likely than their peers to assault someone.

Others who don't necessarily support these ideas are still against the concept of trying juveniles as adults. They point out that our adult prisons are already overcrowded in virtually every state. Forcing more inmates into these prisons will only worsen the situation for all prisoners.

An Alternative Solution

Many believe that an alternate solution to the problem of juvenile crime lies in reforming the juvenile justice system. They argue that criminal records of juveniles should not be sealed when violent crimes have been involved, especially murder. They contend that more resources should go toward the rehabilitation of at least those young criminal offenders who show the most hope of being reformed.

For Critical Analysis

1. Most juvenile crimes take place in major cities. Why?
2. Why do you think proportionally more violent crime is committed by juveniles today than, say, one hundred years ago?

*New York: Simon & Schuster, 1996.

cent believed that greater efforts are needed to protect homosexual rights, however, and 52 percent thought that there should not be special laws guaranteeing equal rights for homosexuals.[32]

In 1996, in *Romer v. Evans*,[33] the Supreme Court issued a decision that will have a significant impact on the rights of gays and lesbians. The case involved a Colorado state constitutional amendment that invalidated all existing state and local laws protecting homosexuals from discrimination. The Supreme Court held that the amendment violated the equal protection clause of the Constitution because it denied to homosexuals in Colorado—but to no other Colorado residents—"the right to seek specific protection of the law." The Court stated that the equal protection clause simply does not permit Col-

---

[32]As reported in *Newsweek,* June 3, 1996, p. 29.
[33]116 S.Ct. 1620 (1996).

DID YOU KNOW ...
That Albert Einstein was among six thousand signers in Germany in 1903 of a petition to repeal a portion of the German penal code that made homosexuality illegal?

Gays and lesbians have become an important political force in American politics today. These demonstrators believe that constitutional civil rights and liberties, including equal protection of the laws, should extend to gays and lesbians and that laws permitting discrimination against these groups should be repealed.

orado to make homosexuals "unequal to everyone else." The Court's decision may halt efforts in several other states to adopt constitutional amendments of a similar nature.

Gay Men and Lesbians in the Military

The U.S. Department of Defense traditionally has viewed homosexuality as incompatible with military service. Supporters of gay and lesbian rights have attacked this policy in recent years, and in 1993 the policy was modified. In that year, President Bill Clinton announced that a new policy, generally characterized as "don't ask, don't tell," would be in effect. Enlistees would not be asked about their sexual orientation, and gays and lesbians would be allowed to serve in the military as long as they did not declare that they were gay or lesbian, or commit homosexual acts. Military officials endorsed the new policy, after opposing it initially, but supporters of gay rights were not enthusiastic. Clinton had promised during his presidential campaign to repeal outright the long-standing ban.

Several gays and lesbians who have been discharged from military service have protested their discharges by bringing suit against the Defense Department. In one case, a former Navy lieutenant, Paul Thomasson, was dismissed from the service in 1995 after stating "I am gay" in a letter to his commanding admiral. In 1996, a federal appellate court reviewed the case and concluded that the courts should defer, as they traditionally have, to the other branches of government, especially in military policy. A dissenting judge wrote that Thomasson was being punished for "nothing more than an expression of his state of mind."[34] Two other federal appellate courts, however, had ruled earlier that the policy was unconstitutional.[35]

At issue in these cases are the constitutional rights to free speech and the equal protection of the laws. Because the lower courts are in disagreement, it is likely that the Supreme Court will rule on the matter in the future.

Same-Sex Marriages and Child-Custody Issues

Perhaps one of the most sensitive political issues with respect to the rights of gay and lesbian couples is whether they should be allowed to marry, just as heterosexual couples are. The controversy over this issue was fueled recently by a Hawaii Supreme Court ruling that denying marriage licenses to gay couples violates the equal protection clause of the Hawaii constitution. Additionally, the Hawaiian legislature may pass a law recognizing gay marriages. In the wake of these developments, bills that would prohibit such marriages also were introduced in at least thirty-two state legislatures (by 1997, fifteen of these bills had been enacted into law). In September 1996, President Clinton signed into law a congressional bill that allows states to refuse to recognize same-sex marriages.

Another legal challenge faced by gay couples is the difficulty they have obtaining child-custody rights. Courts around the country are wrestling with how much weight, if any, should be given to a parent's sexual orientation when deciding which of two parents should have custody. The courts are split on the issue. In about half the states, courts have held that a parent's sexual orientation should not be a significant factor in determining child custody. Courts in other states, however, tend to give more weight to sexual ori-

[34]*Thomasson v. Perry,* 80 F.3d 915 (4th Cir. 1996).
[35]*Meinhold v. United States Department of Defense,* 34 F.3d 1469 (9th Cir. 1994); *Able v. United States,* 44 F.3d 128 (2d Cir. 1995).

entation. In one case, a court even went so far as to award custody to a father because the child's mother was a lesbian, even though the father had served eight years in prison for killing his first wife. The judge stated that the child should be "given the opportunity and the option to live in a non-lesbian world." The judge's ruling was not disturbed on appeal.[36]

The Gay Community and Politics

The number of gay and lesbian organizations has grown from fifty in 1969 to several thousand by the 1990s. These groups have been active in exerting political pressure on legislatures, the media, schools, and churches. In 1973, some of these organizations succeeded in having the American Psychiatric Association remove homosexuality from its list of disorders. During the 1970s and 1980s, more than half the states repealed sodomy laws. The Civil Service Commission eliminated its ban on the employment of gays and lesbians. In 1980, the Democratic party platform included a gay rights plank. The largest gay rights groups today are the Human Rights Campaign Fund, which hopes to see federal gay rights laws passed, and the National Gay and Lesbian Task Force, which works toward the repeal of state antisodomy laws and the passage of state and local gay rights legislation.

Politicians have not overlooked the potential significance of homosexual issues in American politics. Conservative politicians have been generally critical of gays and lesbians. Liberals, however, have by and large begun to speak out for gay rights. Walter Mondale, former vice president of the United States and the winning contender for the Democratic party nomination for president in 1984, addressed a gay convention and openly bid for the political support of gays and lesbians, as did Bill Clinton in 1992. The gay community also supported Jesse Jackson's 1988 bid for the presidency and Jackson's Rainbow Coalition.

Gays and lesbians have been elected to public offices in increasing numbers. Public awareness of elected officials who were gay or lesbian was significantly heightened when, on November 27, 1978, San Francisco supervisor Harvey Milk—thought to be the first openly gay person elected to office in a major city—was assassinated, along with the city's mayor, George Moscone. The killer, a former supervisor, was angry at the mayor for refusing to reinstate him after he resigned and was unhappy with Milk for supporting the mayor. Many gays and lesbians across the country, however, tended to view the highly publicized event as a "hate crime."

Two members of the 104th Congress, which took office in January 1995, were openly gay—Barney Frank and Gerry Studds, both of Massachusetts. Other liberal members of Congress have vigorously supported gay rights issues.

Gays and lesbians—as well as the other groups of Americans discussed in this chapter—still have many obstacles to overcome in their struggle for equality. Nonetheless, compared to fifty years ago, they have made great strides toward equal treatment, as can be seen in this chapter's *Concept Overview.*

STRIVING FOR EQUALITY: UNFINISHED WORK

To be sure, since the 1950s, the gains of women, children, gays and lesbians, persons with disabilities, and older Americans have been impressive. Nonetheless, fear of people who are different, as well as a general fear of

[36] __ S.2d__ (Fla.App.—1st Dist. 1996). This decision is not yet published.

CONCEPT OVERVIEW

Changes in the Struggle for Equality

In the past fifty years, women and the other groups discussed in this chapter have made great strides in their struggle for equality. Here we summarize briefly their most significant accomplishments in terms of gaining equal treatment under the law.

THEN	NOW
• Women had little legislative protection against employment discrimination, they were underrepresented in legislatures to a far greater extent than they are today, and they had no organizations (such as NOW) to lead the fight for equal treatment in all walks of life.	• Women are protected against employment discrimination by federal (and state) laws, they hold more political offices in national and state governments than ever before, and their interests are championed by many groups (including NOW).
• Older Americans had no legislative protection against age discrimination in employment, often had to comply with mandatory retirement policies and laws regardless of their health or productivity, and had little influence politically.	• Older Americans are protected from age discrimination by federal (and state) laws, normally are not subject to mandatory retirement rules, and wield substantial influence in Congress through organized interest groups.
• Persons with disabilities were not legislatively protected against discrimination, and laws mandating that they have access to public buildings and services were nonexistent.	• Persons with disabilities are protected by laws prohibiting discrimination and mandating access to public buildings and services. Employers must accommodate the needs of persons with disabilities unless to do so constitutes an "undue hardship."
• Juveniles had no status as rights-bearing persons, were not considered to have the right to be represented by counsel, could not vote until they were twenty-one years of age, had little—if any—influence in child-custody determinations, and were generally treated as children rather than as adults in criminal proceedings.	• Juveniles are considered to be rights-bearing persons, have the right to be represented by counsel, can vote at the age of eighteen years, increasingly have more say in child-custody arrangements, and are treated as adults in criminal proceedings more often than previously.
• Gays and lesbians rarely declared their sexual preferences because they feared being ostracized by society if they did so, were not a political force, and had no specific laws protecting their interests.	• Gays and lesbians face less ostracism today and frequently declare their sexual preferences, they are a significant political force, and increasingly state and local laws protecting their interests are being enacted (and upheld by the courts).

change, continues to exist. Consequently, we can be certain that controversy over the role that these groups play, or should play, in our society will continue to foster both private and public debate. What special benefits should be given to older citizens and persons with disabilities, for example? Have affirmative action programs for women and minorities gone too far? How much should society be worried about the rights of children when there is evidence that so much crime is committed by juveniles?

Certainly the expanding proportion of the American population that is over age sixty-five will lead to political and economic conflicts in the future. As senior citizens become a larger percentage of the population, their political power will continue to grow. They will undoubtedly clash repeatedly with those who propose cutting or modifying benefits for older Americans or changing the way in which current programs, such as Social Security and Medicare, are administered.

Women and minorities certainly will continue to push for more political power by being elected to more federal, state, and local offices. Gay and lesbian groups will certainly fight for an increase in the number of statutes that protect their rights.

Positive attitudes toward equality and protective legislation do not always translate into economically feasible programs. What resources are allocated to pay for new benefits will continue to occupy public debate.

GETTING INVOLVED
Dealing with Discrimination

When you apply for a job, you may be subjected to a variety of possibly discriminatory practices—based on your race, color, gender, religion, age, national origin, sexual preference, or disability. You may also be subjected to a battery of tests, some of which you may feel are discriminatory. At both state and federal levels, the government has continued to examine the fairness and validity of criteria used in job-applicant screening. If you believe that you have been discriminated against by a potential employer, you may wish to consider the following steps:

1. Evaluate your own capabilities, and determine if you are truly qualified for the position.
2. Analyze the reasons that you were turned down (or dismissed). Do you feel that others would agree with you that you have been the object of discrimination, or would they uphold your employer's claim?
3. If you still believe that you have been unfairly treated, you have recourse to several agencies and services.

You should first speak to the personnel director of the company and politely explain that you feel you have not been adequately evaluated. If asked, explain your concerns clearly. If necessary, go into explicit detail, and indicate that you feel that you may have been discriminated against. If a second evaluation is not forthcoming, contact the local branch of your state employment agency. If you still do not obtain adequate help, contact one or more of the following agencies, usually found by looking in your telephone directory under "State Government" listings.

1. If a government entity is involved, a state ombudsman or citizen aide who will mediate may be available.
2. You may wish to contact the state civil rights commission, which will at least give you advice even if it does not wish to take up your case.
3. The state attorney general's office will normally have a division dealing with discrimination and civil rights.
4. There may be a special commission or department specifically set up to help you, such as a women's status commission or a commission on Hispanics or Asian Americans. If you are a woman or a member of such a minority, contact these commissions.
5. Finally, at the national level, you can contact the American Civil Liberties Union, 132 West 43d St., New York, N.Y. 10036, 1-800-775-ACLU, or check http://www.aclu.org. You can also contact the most appropriate federal agency: the Equal Employment Opportunity Commission, 1801 L St. N.W., Washington, DC 20507, 1-202-663-4900.

KEY TERMS

civil law 197	gender discrimination 187	sexual harassment 187
common law 197	majority 197	suffrage 182
comparable worth 189	mandatory retirement 192	
criminal law 197	necessaries 197	

CHAPTER SUMMARY

1 In the early years of the United States, women were considered citizens, but they were citizens without political rights. After the first women's rights convention in 1848, the women's movement gained momentum. Women's organizations held seven conventions in the next twelve years and lobbied for the enfranchisement of women. Progress was slow, however, and it was not until 1920, when the Nineteenth Amendment was passed, that women gained the universal right to vote.

2 The right to vote has not guaranteed political power to women. Women have been and continue to be greatly underrepresented in Congress, as well as in the other branches of the federal government. Women have had more success at state and local levels. Nowhere does the representation of women in political office reflect their participation as voters—their national turnout has been higher than that of men.

3 Although the Fourteenth Amendment mandates equal protection under the law for all persons, laws that include different provisions for men and women are not always struck down by the Supreme Court. The Court holds that laws involving classifications on the basis of sex are permissible if they "substantially relate to important governmental interests." The National Organization for Women (NOW) and other women's rights groups worked for the passage of the Equal Rights Amendment (ERA) to the Constitution. The ERA is seen as a way to invalidate state laws that maintain the inferior status of women by discriminating against them.

4 Federal government efforts to eliminate gender discrimination in the labor market include Title VII of the Civil Rights Act of 1964. Title VII has been used to invalidate "protective" laws or policies, such as fetal protection policies, that kept women out of jobs deemed dangerous or onerous. The Supreme Court has upheld the right of women to be free from sexual harassment on the job. Wage discrimination continues to be a problem for women, as does the "glass ceiling" that prevents them from rising to the top of their business or professional firms.

5 Problems associated with aging and retirement are becoming increasingly important as the number of older persons in the United States increases. Many older Americans have lost their jobs due to age bias and cost-cutting efforts by business firms. The Age Discrimination in Employment Act of 1967 prohibits job-related discrimination against individuals over the age of forty on the basis of age, unless age is shown to be a bona fide occupational qualification reasonably necessary to the normal operation of the business. Amendments to the act prohibit mandatory retirement except in a few selected professions. As a group, older people contribute significantly to American political life, ranking first in voter registration and turnout and being well represented in Congress. Through a variety of organizations, older Americans lobby effectively at both the federal and state levels.

6 Persons with disabilities, too, have become an effective political force. In 1973, Congress passed the Rehabilitation Act, which prohibits discrimination against persons with disabilities in programs receiving federal aid. Regulations implementing the act provide for ramps, elevators, and the like in all federal buildings. The Education for All Handicapped Children Act (1975) provides that all children with disabilities receive an "appropriate" education. The Americans with Disabilities Act of 1990 prohibits job discrimination against persons with physical and mental disabilities, requiring that positive steps be taken to comply with the act's requirements. The act also requires expanded access to public facilities, including transportation, and to services offered by such private concerns as car-rental and telephone companies.

7 Although children form a large group of Americans, they have the fewest rights and protections, in part because it is commonly presumed that parents protect their children. The Twenty-sixth Amendment grants the right to vote to those age eighteen or older. In most states, only contracts entered into for necessaries can be enforced against minors. When minors engage in negligent acts, their parents may be held liable. Minors have some defense against criminal prosecution because of their presumed inability at certain ages to have criminal intent. For those below the age of criminal responsibility, there are state juvenile courts. When minors are tried as adults, they receive all of the rights accorded to adults.

❽ Gay rights surfaced as a major issue on the American political and legal scene during the 1970s. At least nineteen states still have antihomosexual laws, and a state law that made homosexual conduct between consenting adults a crime was upheld by the Supreme Court. Public attitudes toward gays and lesbians are changing, however, and today many local governments and some state governments prohibit discrimination against gays and lesbians in education, housing, banking, employment, and public accommodations. In a number of states and localities, laws against "hate crimes" include crimes against gays. In 1996, the Supreme Court held that a state could not ban, by a state constitutional amendment, state and local laws protecting the rights of gays and lesbians. In the same year, however, Congress enacted a bill allowing states not recognize same-sex marriages.

QUESTIONS FOR REVIEW AND DISCUSSION

❶ In your opinion, should women be allowed to participate in military combat in infantry units? Why or why not?

❷ What, if anything, can the government do to overcome the effect of the "glass ceiling" on women in the workplace?

❸ How would the economy be affected if the wages for many "women's jobs" were greatly increased?

❹ Why did it take until modern times for persons with disabilities to receive special treatment through federal legislation?

❺ How does our society balance a concern for the rights of children with an increased fear of crime, a large percentage of which is committed by juveniles?

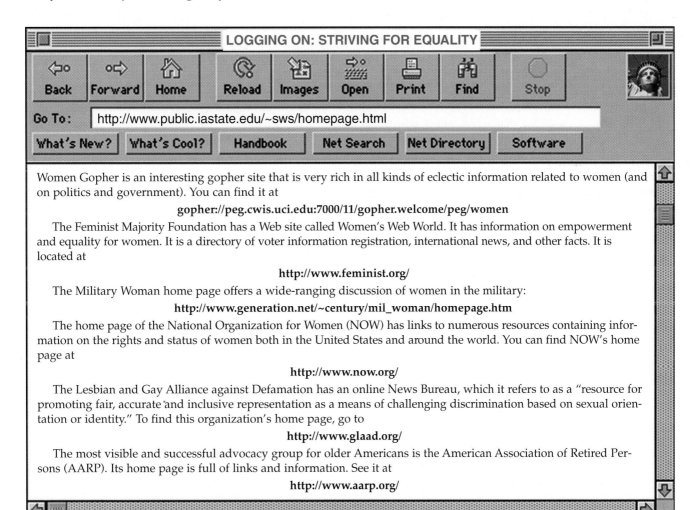

LOGGING ON: STRIVING FOR EQUALITY

Back | Forward | Home | Reload | Images | Open | Print | Find | Stop

Go To: http://www.public.iastate.edu/~sws/homepage.html

What's New? | What's Cool? | Handbook | Net Search | Net Directory | Software

Women Gopher is an interesting gopher site that is very rich in all kinds of eclectic information related to women (and on politics and government). You can find it at

gopher://peg.cwis.uci.edu:7000/11/gopher.welcome/peg/women

The Feminist Majority Foundation has a Web site called Women's Web World. It has information on empowerment and equality for women. It is a directory of voter information registration, international news, and other facts. It is located at

http://www.feminist.org/

The Military Woman home page offers a wide-ranging discussion of women in the military:

http://www.generation.net/~century/mil_woman/homepage.htm

The home page of the National Organization for Women (NOW) has links to numerous resources containing information on the rights and status of women both in the United States and around the world. You can find NOW's home page at

http://www.now.org/

The Lesbian and Gay Alliance against Defamation has an online News Bureau, which it refers to as a "resource for promoting fair, accurate and inclusive representation as a means of challenging discrimination based on sexual orientation or identity." To find this organization's home page, go to

http://www.glaad.org/

The most visible and successful advocacy group for older Americans is the American Association of Retired Persons (AARP). Its home page is full of links and information. See it at

http://www.aarp.org/

SELECTED REFERENCES

Bergman, Barbara R. *In Defense of Affirmative Action.* New York: Basic Books, 1996. Bergman analyzes the progress women and minority groups have made with respect to employment, concentrating especially on how affirmative action programs have assisted women.

Blasius, Mark. *Gay and Lesbian Politics: Sexuality and the Emergence of a New Ethic.* Philadelphia: Temple University Press, 1994. This is an insightful book into the politics of gay and lesbian rights. The author discusses what it means to be gay or lesbian in American culture today and suggests that traditional definitions of gays and lesbians are inadequate.

Duke, Louis Lovelace. *Women in Politics: Outsiders or Insiders?* Englewood Cliffs, N.J: Prentice-Hall, 1993. In this volume, you will read about contemporary women's issues that have been addressed in the political process, as well as about how government institutions and processes influence the lives of American women.

French, Marilyn. *The War against Women.* New York: Summit Books. 1992. This book catalogs what the author views as the losing battle of the sexes that is being waged by women. French discusses the subjugation of women by tradition, religion, and the state; institutional discrimination that prevents women from attaining economic independence, political power, and control over their own bodies; cultural hatred of women; and physical assaults against women.

Held, Virginia. *Feminist Morality: Transforming Culture, Society, and Politics.* Chicago: University of Chicago Press, 1993. The author examines feminine ethics. She shows how social, political, and cultural institutions have been founded upon masculine ideals of morality.

Kaptur, Marcy. *Women of Congress: A Twentieth-Century Odyssey.* Washington, D.C.: Congressional Quarterly Books, 1996.

The author recounts the increasing involvement of American women in politics and their gradual progress toward more influential committee appointments. The author also discusses how men and women in Congress differ with respect to legislative style, ethics, and other factors.

Oliver, Michael. *Understanding Disability: From Theory to Practice.* New York: St. Martin's Press, 1995. This book compares U.S. disability policy and movements for rights for persons with disabilities with those in the United Kingdom. The author places disability in the context of broader societal discrimination.

Paglia, Camille. *Sexual Personae: Art and Decadence from Nefertiti to Emily Dickinson.* New Haven, Conn.: Yale University Press, 1991. This is one of the most controversial books on gender to be published in years. Paglia, a feminist, stands on end most of the principles of politically correct feminism.

Sorensen, Elaine. *Comparable Worth: Is It a Worthy Policy?* Princeton, N.J.: Princeton University Press, 1994. The author examines the current notions of comparable worth and how they have been applied. She assesses the most·and least successful among the definitions. She argues that some of the gender pay gap is due to economic discrimination.

Witt, Linda *et al. Running as a Woman: Gender and Power in American Politics.* New York: Free Press/MacMillan, 1993. The authors of this analysis of the past, present, and future of women in American politics examine the dilemmas facing women as candidates and office holders. They look at the ambivalence that the United States has about the place of women in politics.

PART THREE

People and Politics

7
Public Opinion

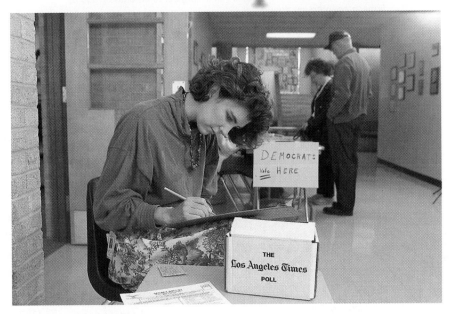

CHAPTER OUTLINE

- ☆ How Powerful Is Public Opinion?
- ☆ Defining and Measuring Public Opinion
- ☆ The Qualities of Public Opinion
- ☆ Measuring Public Opinion: Polling Techniques
- ☆ How Public Opinion Is Formed
- ☆ Political Culture and Public Opinion
- ☆ Public Opinion about Government
- ☆ The Spectrum of Political Beliefs
- ☆ Public Opinion and the Political Process

The Government Regulated the Polling Industry?

BACKGROUND

PUBLIC OPINION POLLS HAVE BECOME DEEPLY INGRAINED IN AMERICAN POLITICAL LIFE—SO MUCH SO THAT SOME POLITICIANS SEEM TO FEAR MAKING A DECISION WITHOUT SEEING SOME POLL DATA FIRST. WHILE THE NUMBER OF OPINION POLLS CONTINUES TO GROW, PUBLIC CONFIDENCE AND INTEREST IN THEM MAY BE SHRINKING DUE TO CERTAIN POLLING PRACTICES, SUCH AS QUESTIONNAIRES THAT ARE CLEARLY BIASED, AND THE MEDIA'S EMPHASIS ON WHO'S AHEAD IN EVERY CAMPAIGN.

WHAT IF THE GOVERNMENT REGULATED THE POLLING INDUSTRY?

Probably the first step that the government would take in regulating the polling industry would be to establish some sort of national board or commission to issue licenses to polling firms that conduct their own polls. Such licensing might require that individuals who conduct polls have certain types of training.

Besides licensing polling firms, a government agency surely would require public disclosure of all of the polling that is done by a company and the sponsorship of such polls. Pollsters might have to report annually on all of the polls they completed, who paid for the polls, how the samples were chosen, who actually conducted the polls, and whether the results were public or private. They also might be required to disclose to respondents the name of the party sponsoring or conducting the poll.

Such regulations would wreak havoc with political polling because the vast majority of polls conducted for candidates are commissioned by a campaign for the private use of the candidate and are never made public. Furthermore, most pollsters believe that if you identify a poll's sponsor as, for example, the Clinton reelection committee, you are less likely to get honest responses from either Republicans or Democrats.

RESTRICTIONS ON POLLS

Government regulators could institute restrictions on polling with respect to time and place of polling or choice of respondents. Opinion polls of voters might be ended some days before the election, as is done in some European nations. Of course, the media that rely on these opinion polls for their news stories would oppose any such restrictions.

A restriction on the respondents to be contacted would greatly undermine the reliability of opinion polls. For example, government regulations might allow individuals to notify all pollsters through a central registry that they did not wish to be called. This would end the possibility of a truly random telephone sample and would diminish greatly the accuracy of poll data.

Government regulations might exclude from surveys certain questions, such as those about sexual orientation. Other kinds of regulations might prohibit certain polling practices, such as the misleading wording or ordering of questions and the influence of interviewers.

ENFORCEMENT PROBLEMS

It is highly unlikely that the new government regulatory body would be successful in implementing policies on these issues or in punishing firms that did not meet the standards. Certainly, political candidates, political parties, and interest groups would defend every question in their respective polls as appropriate and truthful while their opponents cried foul. It seems unlikely that any standard could be set that would not violate free speech principles and eliminate the political uses of polls.

FOR CRITICAL ANALYSIS

1. *What information about public opinion polls and their sponsors ought to be made available to the individuals who are polled?*
2. *Do you think that polling may become so intrusive in our lives that the majority of people will wish to regulate it more closely?*

Public opinion polls have the potential to give voice to the preferences of the people between elections. These preferences may relate to the distribution of power between the national government and the states, and the future role of the nation in the world. Furthermore, public opinion, whether expressed through scientifically conducted opinion polls or directly over the Internet, can express the public's views on specific policy actions in a way that elections cannot. What role, then, does public opinion play in the changing American political system? Is it truly the voice of the people, or is it an instrument to be manipulated by politicians and interest groups? Can political leaders count on public opinion to provide guidance on their actions, or are the results of most opinion polls too ephemeral to be useful.

The very character of public opinion polls may limit their usefulness. After all, the pollster wrote the question, called the respondents, and perhaps forwarded the results to the politicians. Public opinion, as gathered by polls, is not equivalent to constituents' letters to their representatives or to ballots cast in an election. In fact, polls usually include individuals who do not vote and may be flawed in a number of ways. As the chapter-opening *What If . . .* suggests, the polling industry may have created some issues for itself that will lead to more government regulation of these instruments for public expression.

HOW POWERFUL IS PUBLIC OPINION?

At various times in the recent history of the United States, public opinion has played a powerful role in presidential politics. Beginning in 1965, public opinion became more divided over the Vietnam War (1964–1975). Numerous public expressions of opposition to the war took place, as measured by the polls and demonstrations in many cities. By 1968, when Lyndon Johnson was preparing to run for another term, public opinion against the war was expressed through a surge of support for antiwar candidate Senator Eugene McCarthy in the New Hampshire primary. Faced with public disapproval, Johnson dropped out of the race.

As the scandal surrounding the 1972 **Watergate Break-in** unfolded, revealing the role of President Richard Nixon through congressional hearings and tape recordings from his office, a similar groundswell of opinion against the president occurred. In this case, the disastrous fall in the president's approval ratings to less than 25 percent coincided with the decision by the House Judiciary Committee to initiate impeachment proceedings against the president. Nixon, facing an impeachment trial, resigned from office.

Both of these cases illustrate the power of public opinion when there is great public dissatisfaction with the government or with an official. Rarely, however, is public opinion expressed so strongly over a long period of time.

In most situations, public opinion is used by legislators, politicians, and presidents to shore up their own arguments. It provides a kind of evidence for their own point of view. If the results of polls do not support their position, they can either commission their own poll or ignore the polls. The stalemate over the budget between President Bill Clinton and the Republicans in Congress illustrated how difficult it is to learn what the public prefers when the issue is as complex and detailed as the various budget proposals were. Each side claimed public support for its own point of view. Public opinion is more likely to be limiting when it comes to the use of troops overseas, but, as we will see in the *Critical Perspective* on page 234 in this chapter, presidents who are able to limit the casualties among American troops sent on a military

WATERGATE BREAK-IN

The 1972 illegal entry into the Democratic Campaign offices by participants in Richard Nixon's reelection campaign.

Those who wish to have legislation passed often muster the forces of public opinion to help convince Congress to pass it. Here you see citizens voicing their opinions on health-care reform.

DID YOU KNOW ...
That James Madison and others argued in *The Federalist Papers* that because public opinion is potentially dangerous, it should be diffused through a large republic with separation of government powers?

PUBLIC OPINION

The aggregate of individual attitudes or beliefs shared by some portion of adults. There is no one public opinion, because there are many different "publics."

mission have much more freedom from the constraints of public opinion. President Clinton was able to secure such freedom with the almost casualty-free missions of American troops in both Haiti and Bosnia. Public opinion, then, is neither all powerful nor powerless.

DEFINING AND MEASURING PUBLIC OPINION

There is no one public opinion, because there are many different "publics." In a nation of more than 265 million people, there may be innumerable gradations of opinion on an issue. What we do is describe the distribution of opinions among the public about a particular question. Thus, we define **public opinion** as the aggregate of individual attitudes or beliefs shared by some portion of adults.

As the American involvement in keeping the peace in Bosnia increased, the Clinton administration made the case that the fate of that nation was of vital importance to the United States. Poll results from December 1995 clearly showed that the public was of several minds about Bosnia. The *New York Times*/CBS News Survey reported that 26 percent of those polled believed that what happened in Bosnia was very important to the United States, 43 percent felt it was somewhat important, 26 percent felt it was not very important, and 1 percent said it was not important at all. Politicians opposed to increasing American involvement in Bosnia cited the fact that only one-fourth of those polled felt it was very important to our interests. The president cited the 69 percent who believed it was somewhat or very important to U.S. interests. In fact, multiple opinions were reported, and no majority view could be identified.

How is public opinion made known in a democracy? In the case of the Vietnam War, it was made known by numerous antiwar protests, countless articles in magazines and newspapers, and continuing electronic media coverage of antiwar demonstrations. Normally, however, public opinion becomes known in a democracy through elections and, in some states, initiatives or referenda (see Chapter 19). Other ways are through lobbying and interest group activities, which are also used to influence public opinion (see Chapter 8). In the age of the Internet, citizens increasingly are able to send their opinions to government officials electronically.

Union members protest a cut in benefits. A strike can be seen as an expression of public opinion, but if the union does not get support from others, politicians will feel little effect.

Public opinion can be defined most clearly by its effect. As political scientist V. O. Key, Jr., said, public opinion is what governments "find it prudent to heed."[1] This means that for public opinion to be effective, enough people have to hold a particular view with such strong conviction that a government feels its actions should be influenced by that view.

An interesting question arises as to when *private* opinion becomes *public* opinion. Everyone probably has a private opinion about the competence of the president, as well as private opinions about more personal concerns, such as the state of a neighbor's lawn. We say that private opinion becomes public opinion when the opinion is publicly expressed and if the opinion concerns public issues. When someone's private opinion becomes so strong that the individual is willing to go to the polls to vote for or against a candidate or an issue—or is willing to participate in a demonstration, to discuss the issue at work, to speak out on local television or a radio talk show, or to participate in the political process in any one of a dozen other ways—then that opinion becomes public opinion.

THE QUALITIES OF PUBLIC OPINION

At the beginning of the Vietnam War in the 1960s, public opinion about its conduct was not very clear, like a camera that is not focused. As the war progressed and U.S. involvement deepened, public opinion became increasingly clarified. In that case, as in most cases, public opinion has identifiable qualities that change over time. Political scientists have identified at least five specific qualities relating to public opinion: (1) intensity, (2) fluidity, (3) stability, (4) latency, and (5) relevance. In addition, political knowledge affects opinion, and the distribution of opinion on an issue indicates the possibilities for conflict or compromise.

Intensity

How strongly people are willing to express their private opinions determines the **intensity** of public opinion. Consider an example that is in the news regularly—the state of democracy in Haiti. Most Americans do not have strong opinions about the future of democracy in this island nation. They do, however, have more intense opinions about whether American troops should remain in Haiti to keep the peace. Opinions are even more intense about whether Haitians should be allowed to immigrate to the United States in large numbers. Intense opinions held by such groups as the voters of Florida can have a much greater impact on national politics than their numbers would suggest.

INTENSITY

The strength of a position for or against a public policy or an issue. Intensity is often critical in generating public action; an intense minority can often win on an issue of public policy over a less intense majority.

Fluidity

Public opinion can change drastically in a very short period of time. When this occurs, we say that public opinion is fluid. At the end of World War II, for example, the American people were about evenly divided in their opinions of the U.S. wartime ally, the Soviet Union. A 1945 Roper poll showed that about 39 percent of Americans saw the Soviets as peace loving, whereas 38 percent felt they were aggressive. During the years of the Cold War (1947 to, roughly, 1985), American opinion about the aims of the Soviet Union was

---

[1] V. O. Key, Jr., *Public Opinion and American Democracy* (New York: Knopf, 1961), p. 10.

DID YOU KNOW ...
That public opinion pollsters typically measure national sentiment among the nearly 200 million adult Americans by interviewing only about 1,500 people?

FLUIDITY

The extent to which public opinion changes over time.

SOLID SOUTH

A term describing the tendency of the post–Civil War southern states to vote for the Democratic party. (Voting patterns in the South have changed, though.)

STABILITY

The extent to which public opinion remains constant over a period of time.

LATENT PUBLIC OPINION

Unexpressed political opinions that have the potential to become manifest attitudes or beliefs.

RELEVANCE

The extent to which an issue is of concern at a particular time. Issues become relevant when the public views them as pressing or of direct concern to daily life.

very consistent. Between 13 and 17 percent of the American people believed that the Soviet Union was peace loving, and more than 60 percent saw it as aggressive.

Mikhail Gorbachev's leadership of the Soviet Union and his policy of openness toward the West, however, created an extremely fluid state of opinion among Americans. As Americans watched his attempts at internal reform and his willingness to allow the Eastern European nations to pull away from the Russian orbit, American opinion about the Soviet Union changed quickly. Between 1985 and 1990, the number of Americans who saw the Soviet Union as peace loving increased from 17 to 43 percent.[2] The **fluidity** of American opinion was a response to the rapidly changing conditions in the Soviet Union and world politics. Such fluidity in public opinion reflects public awareness of government policy and in turn influences government decision making.

Stability

Many individual opinions remain constant over a lifetime. Taken together, individual opinions that constitute public opinion may also be extremely stable, persisting for many years. Consider the effect of the Civil War on political attitudes in the South. It was the Republicans under Abraham Lincoln who, in the eyes of southerners, were responsible for the Civil War and the ensuing humiliations experienced by a defeated South. Consequently, the South became strongly Democratic. Until the post–World War II period, it was called the **Solid South,** because Democratic candidates nearly always won. We can say that public opinion in the South in favor of Democrats and against Republicans had great **stability.**

Latency

Not all political opinions are expressed by the holders of opinions. There may be potential political opinions—those not yet realized. Political scientists call these **latent,** or quiescent, **public opinions.** Some say, for example, that Adolf Hitler exploited the latent public opinion of post–World War I Germany by forming the National Socialist party. The public was ripe for a leader who would militarize Germany and put Germany back on its feet. Latent public opinion offers golden opportunities for political leaders astute enough to perceive it and act on it politically.

When average citizens are asked to respond to highly complex issues about which they have imperfect knowledge, their opinions may remain latent. Because of the complexity of the issues involved, many Americans cannot realistically predict the future impact of the outcome of the issues on their own lives, much less on public policy.

Relevance

Relevant public opinion for most people is simply public opinion that deals with issues concerning them. If a person has a sick parent who is having trouble meeting medical bills, then public opinion that is focused on the issues of Medicare or Medicaid will be relevant for that person. If another person likes to go hunting with his or her children, gun control becomes a relevant political issue. Of course, **relevance** changes according to events. Public concern

---

[2]Alvin Richman, "The Polls: Changing American Attitudes toward the Soviet Union," *Public Opinion Quarterly,* Vol. 55 (1991), p. 144.

Reprinted with special permission of King Features Syndicate.

about inflation, for example, was at an all-time low during the late 1980s and most of the 1990s. Why? Because the United States had relatively little inflation during that period. Public opinion about the issue of unemployment certainly was relevant during the Great Depression during the 1930s, but not during the 1960s, when the nation experienced 102-months of almost uninterrupted economic growth from 1961 to 1969.

Certain popular books or spectacular events can make a particular issue relevant. The succession of violent acts—ranging from the bombing of the Federal Building in Oklahoma City in 1995 to the bombing of TWA flight 800 in 1996—made violence and terrorism increasingly relevant for many citizens by 1997.

Political Knowledge

People are more likely to base their opinions on knowledge about an issue if they have strong feelings about the topic. Just as relevance and intensity are closely related to having an opinion, individuals who are strongly interested in a question will probably take the time to read about it.

Looking at the population as a whole, the level of political information is modest. Survey research tells us that slightly less than 29 percent of adult Americans can give the name of their congressperson, and just 25 percent can name both U.S. senators from their state. Only 34 percent of adults know that Congress declares war,[3] though almost 70 percent know the majority party in Congress. What these data tell us is that Americans do not expend much effort remembering political facts that may not be important to their daily lives.

Americans are also likely to forget political information quite quickly. Facts that are of vital interest to citizens in a time of crisis lose their significance after the crisis has passed. In the 1985 *New York Times*/CBS News Survey on

---

[3]Michael X. Della Carpini and Scott Keeter, "The Public's Knowledge of Politics," in J. David Dennamar, ed., *Public Opinion, the Press, and Public Policy* (Westport, Conn.: Praeger, 1992), p. 29.

CONSENSUS

General agreement among the citizenry on an issue.

DIVISIVE OPINION

Public opinion that is polarized between two quite different positions.

OPINION POLL

A method of systematically questioning a small, selected sample of respondents who are deemed representative of the total population. These polls are widely used by government, business, university scholars, political candidates, and voluntary groups to provide reasonably accurate data on public attitudes, beliefs, expectations, and behavior.

Vietnam, marking the tenth anniversary of the end of that conflict, 63 percent of those questioned knew that the United States sided with the South Vietnamese in that conflict. Only 27 percent remembered, however, which side in that conflict launched the Tet offensive, which was a major political defeat for American and South Vietnamese forces.[4]

If political information is perceived to be of no use to an individual or is painful to recall, it is not surprising that facts are forgotten. What is more disturbing than forgetting the past is the inability of many citizens to give basic information about current issues. Polls on the U.S. military action in the Persian Gulf in 1991, for example, showed that most Americans tend to learn some basic facts about critical events, but only a few have detailed information. Studies showed that more than half of all Americans knew that the United States provided most of the troops in the Persian Gulf conflict and knew that Iraq's army outnumbered the U.S. forces there. Only 10 percent, however, knew what percentage of U.S. imports come from the Middle East.[5]

Consensus and Division

There are very few issues on which most Americans agree. The more normal situation is for opinion to be distributed among several different positions. Looking at the distribution of opinion can tell us how divided the public is on a question and give us some indication of whether compromise is possible. The distribution of opinion can also tell us how many individuals have not thought about an issue enough to hold an opinion.

When a large proportion of the American public appears to express the same view on an issue, we say that a **consensus** exists, at least at the moment the poll was taken. Figure 7–1 shows the pattern of opinion that might be called consensual. Issues on which the public holds widely differing attitudes result in **divisive opinion** (Figure 7–2). If there is no possible middle position on such issues, we expect that the division will continue to generate political conflict.

Figure 7–3 shows a distribution of opinion indicating that most Americans either have no information about the issue or are not interested enough in the issue to formulate a position. This figure illustrates latent, or quiescent, opinion. Politicians may feel that the lack of knowledge gives them more room to maneuver, or they may be wary of taking any action for fear that the opinion will crystallize after a crisis. It is possible that we would see the latent pattern most often if survey respondents were totally honest. Research has shown that some individuals will express fabricated opinions to an interviewer on certain topics rather than admit their ignorance.

MEASURING PUBLIC OPINION: POLLING TECHNIQUES

The History of Opinion Polls

Although some idea of public opinion can be discovered by asking persons we know for their opinions or by reading the "Letters to the Editor" sections in newspapers, most descriptions of the distribution of opinions are based on **opinion polls.** During the 1800s, certain American newspapers and maga-

[4]*New York Times*/CBS News Survey, February 23–27, 1985.
[5]Della Carpini and Keeter, "Public's Knowledge of Politics," p. 29.

Figure 7–1
• • • • • • • • • • • • • • • • • •
Consensus Opinion

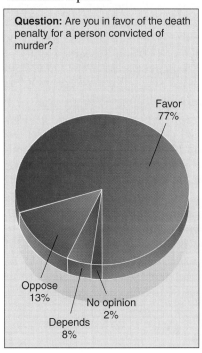

Question: Are you in favor of the death penalty for a person convicted of murder?

Favor
77%

Oppose
13%

Depends
8%

No opinion
2%

SOURCE: *The Gallup Poll,* May 1995.

Figure 7–2
• • • • • • • • • • • • • • • • • •
Divisive Opinion

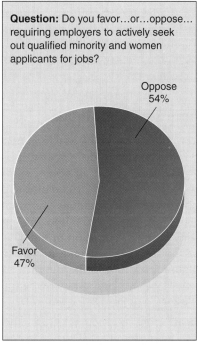

Question: Do you favor...or...oppose... requiring employers to actively seek out qualified minority and women applicants for jobs?

Oppose
54%

Favor
47%

SOURCE: NBC/*Wall Street Journal* Poll, March 1995.

Figure 7–3
• • • • • • • • • • • • • • • • • • • •
Latent Opinion

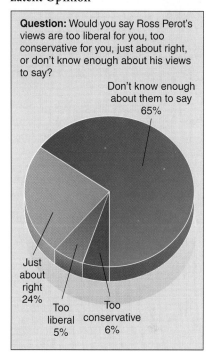

Question: Would you say Ross Perot's views are too liberal for you, too conservative for you, just about right, or don't know enough about his views to say?

Don't know enough about them to say
65%

Just about right
24%

Too liberal
5%

Too conservative
6%

SOURCE: Survey by ABC News/*Washington Post,* June 3–7, 1992, as cited in *Public Perspective,* July/August 1993, p. 86.

zines spiced up their political coverage by doing face-to-face straw polls (unofficial polls indicating the trend of political opinion) or mail surveys of their readers' opinions. In this century, the magazine *Literary Digest* further developed the technique of opinion polls by mailing large numbers of questionnaires to individuals, many of whom were its own subscribers. From 1916 to 1936, more than 70 percent of the magazine's election predictions were accurate.

Literary Digest, however, suffered a major setback in its polling activities when it predicted that Republican candidate Alfred Landon would win over Democratic candidate Franklin D. Roosevelt in 1936, based on more than two million returned questionnaires. Landon won in only two states. A major problem with the *Digest*'s polling technique was its continuing use of nonrepresentative respondents. In 1936, at the bottom of the Great Depression, those people who were the magazine's subscribers were, for one thing, considerably more affluent than the average American.

Several newcomers to the public opinion poll industry accurately predicted Roosevelt's landslide victory. The organizations of these newcomers are still active in the poll-taking industry today: the Gallup poll of George Gallup, and Roper and Associates founded by Elmo Roper. Gallup and Roper, along with Archibald Crossley, developed the modern polling techniques of market research. Using personal interviews with small samples of selected voters (less than a few thousand), they showed that they could predict with accuracy the behavior of the total voting population. We shall see how this is possible.

Government officials during World War II were keenly interested in public opinion about the war effort and about the increasing number of restrictions placed on civilian activities. Improved methods of sampling were used, and by the 1950s, a whole new science of survey research was developed, which soon spread to Western Europe, Israel, and other countries. Survey research centers sprang up throughout the United States, particularly at universities. Some of these survey groups are the American Institute of Public Opinion at Princeton, New Jersey; the National Opinion Research Center at the University of Chicago; and the Survey Research Center at the University of Michigan.

Sampling Techniques

How can interviewing less than two thousand voters tell us what tens of millions of voters will do? Clearly, it is necessary that the sample of individuals be representative of all voters in the population. Consider an analogy. Let's say we have a large jar containing pennies of various dates, and we want to know how many pennies were minted within certain decades (1950–1959, 1960–1969, and so on). There are ten thousand pennies in the jar. One way to estimate the distribution of the dates on the pennies—without examining all ten thousand—is to take a representative sample. This sample would be obtained by mixing the pennies up well and then removing a handful of them—perhaps one hundred pennies. The distribution of dates might be as follows:

- *1950–1959: 5 percent.*
- *1960–1969: 5 percent.*
- *1970–1979: 20 percent.*
- *1980–1989: 30 percent.*
- *1990–present: 40 percent.*

If the pennies are very well mixed within the jar, and if you take a large enough sample, the resulting distribution would probably approach the actual distribution of the dates of all ten thousand coins. (A new type of opinion poll, called the deliberative poll, has been criticized as not being based on a truly random sample—see the feature entitled *Thinking Politically about the Deliberative Poll.*)

The most important principle in sampling, or poll taking, is randomness. Every penny or every person should have a known chance, and especially an *equal chance*, of being sampled. If this happens, then a small sample

This NBC news pollster conducts an interview with a "representative" American. Changes in public opinion are often measured on a regular basis by numerous polling organizations, such as this television network. Indeed, polling results have become ubiquitous. They are reported in newspapers and news magazines virtually every day of the year. TV commentators refer to them in the morning and evening news reports. Some contend that we have become a nation of percentages–*X* percent of Americans believe this and *Y* percent of Americans believe that.

POLITICS AND THE FIFTY STATES
Thinking Politically about the Deliberative Poll

Survey researchers and scholars long have been disappointed by the relative lack of attention and information that members of the public bring to the political sphere. Studies of polling have shown clearly that people will answer questions about issues when they have no knowledge about the subject, answer questions differently depending on the wording and placement of the question, and give different answers depending on the interviewer's race and gender. Professor James Fishkin of the University of Texas proposed a new kind of poll—the deliberative poll—to provide a way to make public opinion more informed and, perhaps, more useful in the political process.

Fishkin proposed that a carefully selected national sample of individuals be invited to participate in the deliberative poll. They would be surveyed about their opinions and then invited to come to a particular place, receive information about the issues, discuss that information in small groups, and hear from politicians directly about the issues. Then they would be surveyed again. It is Fishkin's contention that such a poll would be "a recommending force: these are the conclusions that people

would come to, were they better informed on the issues and had the opportunity and motivation to examine those issues seriously."* Further, he believes that if such a convention were broadcast on television and its results made known to politicians and the public, it could affect election outcomes.

In early 1996, the first American version of such a poll was conducted. Several hundred citizens were selected and then, after being polled, were given expense-paid trips to Austin, Texas, for the discussion of the issues at a National Issues Convention (NIC). The proceedings were televised on public television. The results of the before-and-after polls were publicized and discussed. Generally, people were more likely to change their minds on issues for which they received new facts than they were on issues for which they received no new facts. Changes in opinions were not as drastic on most items as the sponsors expected they would be, however.

The NIC was applauded by many of the politicians who attended the convention for the high level of participation by the voters who chose to come to Austin. The poll was criticized by many others for not being a truly

random sample, for being a very unrealistic way to deal with issues during an election, and for ignoring the ordinary voter, who does not have the time to spend at such a meeting.

Some critics were quick to point out the elitist bias of the method, noting that one of the strengths of regular polling is that everyone in the sample is treated the same—that polls "take Americans as they find them." The NIC, in contrast, reflected the views of the better-educated and higher-income groups that could give time to such deliberation. Moreover, why should the rest of the electorate accept the deliberations of a small group as representative of their own? Of course, most of the people who do polling were among those who criticized the NIC, perhaps because they feared a loss of business in the future.

For Critical Analysis
Should the opinions of voters who have taken the time to become informed and discuss the issues be given more weight by politicians and the media?

*James Fishkin, "Bringing Deliberation to Democracy," *The Public Perspective*, December/January 1996, p. 1.

should be representative of the whole group, both in demographic characteristics (age, religion, race, living area, and the like) and in opinions. The ideal way to sample the voting population of the United States would be to put all voter names into a jar—or a computer—and randomly sample, say, two thousand of them. Because this is too costly and inefficient, pollsters have developed other ways to obtain good samples. One of the most interesting techniques is simply to choose a random selection of telephone numbers and interview the respective households. This technique produces a relatively accurate sample at a low cost.

To ensure that the random samples include respondents from relevant segments of the population—rural, urban, Northeast, South, and so on—most survey organizations randomly choose, say, urban areas that they will consider as representative of all urban areas. Then they randomly select their respondents within that area. A generally less accurate technique is known as *quota sampling*. For this type of poll, survey researchers decide how many persons of certain types they need in the survey—such as minorities, women, or farmers—and then send out interviewers to find the necessary number of these types. This method is often not only less accurate, but it also may be biased if, say, the interviewer refuses to go into certain neighborhoods or will not interview after dark.

Generally, the national survey organizations take great care to select their samples randomly, because their reputations rest on the accuracy of their results. Usually, the Gallup or Roper polls interview about 1,500 individuals, and their results have a very high probability of being correct—within a margin of 3 percent. The accuracy with which the Gallup poll has predicted national election results is reflected in Table 7–1.

Table 7–1

Gallup Poll Accuracy Record

Year	Gallup Final Survey		Election Results		Deviation*
1996	52.0%	CLINTON	49.0%	CLINTON	−3.0
1994	58.0	Republican	51.0	Republican	+7.0
1992†	49.0	CLINTON	43.2	CLINTON	+5.8
1990	54.0	Democratic	54.1	Democratic	−0.1
1988	56.0	BUSH	53.9	BUSH	−2.1
1984	59.0	REAGAN	59.1	REAGAN	−0.1
1982	55.0	Democratic	56.1	Democratic	−1.1
1980	47.0	REAGAN	50.8	REAGAN	−3.8
1978	55.0	Democratic	54.6	Democratic	+0.4
1976	48.0	CARTER	50.0	CARTER	−2.0
1974	60.0	Democratic	58.9	Democratic	+1.1
1972	62.0	NIXON	61.8	NIXON	+0.2
1970	53.0	Democratic	54.3	Democratic	−1.3
1968	43.0	NIXON	43.5	NIXON	−0.5
1966	52.5	Democratic	51.9	Democratic	+0.6
1964	64.0	JOHNSON	61.3	JOHNSON	+2.7
1962	55.5	Democratic	52.7	Democratic	+2.8
1960	51.0	KENNEDY	50.1	KENNEDY	+0.9
1958	57.0	Democratic	56.5	Democratic	+0.5
1956	59.5	EISENHOWER	57.8	EISENHOWER	+1.7
1954	51.5	Democratic	52.7	Democratic	−1.2
1952	51.0	EISENHOWER	55.4	EISENHOWER	−4.4
1950	51.0	Democratic	50.3	Democratic	+0.7
1948	44.5	TRUMAN	49.9	TRUMAN	−5.4
1946	58.0	Republican	54.3	Republican	+3.7
1944	51.5	ROOSEVELT	53.3	ROOSEVELT	−1.8
1942	52.0	Democratic	48.0	Democratic	+4.0
1940	52.0	ROOSEVELT	55.0	ROOSEVELT	−3.0
1938	54.0	Democratic	50.8	Democratic	+3.2
1936	55.7	ROOSEVELT	62.5	ROOSEVELT	−6.8

Note: No Congressional poll done in 1986.
*Average deviation for 30 national elections: 2.4 percent.

TREND IN DEVIATION:

Elections	Average Error
1936–1950	3.6
1952–1996	2.0

†The Ross Perot candidacy created an additional source of error in estimating the 1992 presidential vote. There was no historical precedent for Perot, an independent candidate who was accorded equal status to the major party nominees in the presidential debates and had a record advertising budget. Gallup's decision to allocate none of the undecided vote to Perot, based on past performance of third party and independent candidates, resulted in the overestimation of Clinton's vote.

SOURCE: *The Gallup Poll Monthly,* November 1992; *Time,* November 21, 1994; *Wall Street Journal,* November 6, 1996.

Similar sampling techniques are used in many other, nonpolitical situations. For the Nielsen ratings of television programs, for example, representative households are selected by the A. C. Nielsen Company, and a machine is attached to each household's television set. The machine monitors viewing choices twenty-four hours a day and transmits this information to the company's central offices. A one-point drop in a Nielsen rating can mean a loss of revenue of millions of dollars to a television network. A one-point drop indicates that about 800,000 fewer viewers are watching a particular show. This means that advertisers are unwilling to pay as much for viewing time. Indeed, advertising rates are based in many cases solely on Nielsen ratings. When you consider that only about three thousand families have that little machine attached to their television sets, it is apparent that the science of selecting representative samples has come a long way—at least far enough to convince major advertisers to accept advertising fees based on the results of those samples.

Problems with Polls

Public opinion polls are, as noted above, snapshots of the opinions and preferences of the people at a specific moment in time and as expressed in response to a specific question. Given that definition, it is fairly easy to understand situations in which the polls are wrong. For example, opinion polls leading up to the 1980 presidential election showed President Jimmy Carter defeating challenger Ronald Reagan. Only a few analysts noted the large number of "undecided" respondents to poll questions a week before the election. Those voters shifted massively to Reagan at the last minute, and Reagan won the election.

The famous photo of Harry Truman showing the front page that declared his defeat is another tribute to the weakness of polling. Again, the poll that predicted his defeat was taken more than a week before election day.

Polls may also report erroneous results because the pool of respondents was not chosen in a scientific manner. That is, the form of sampling and the number of people sampled may be too small to overcome **sampling error,** which is the difference between the sample results and the true result if the entire population had been interviewed. The sample would be biased, for example, if the poll interviewed people by telephone and did not correct for the fact that more women than men answer the telephone and that some populations (college students and very poor individuals, for example) cannot be

Interviewers working for the Harris poll call survey respondents. Such telephone surveys have considerable accuracy, because the telephone numbers are selected at random.

SAMPLING ERROR

The difference between a sample's results and the true result if the entire population had been interviewed.

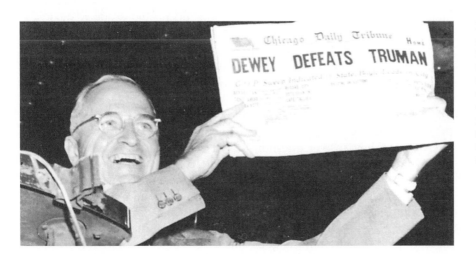

President Harry S Truman holds up the front page of the *Chicago Daily Tribune* issue that predicted his defeat on the basis of a Gallup poll. The poll had indicated that Truman would lose the 1948 contest for his reelection by a margin of 55.5 to 44.5 percent. Gallup's poll was completed more than two weeks before the election, so it missed the undecided voters. Truman won the election with 49.9 percent of the vote.

POLITICS AND TECHNOLOGY
The Interviewer Becomes a Machine

As you have read in this chapter, public opinion pollsters began to develop a scientific bias for sampling the population and asking questions in the late 1930s and during World War II (1941–1945). For several decades after the war, good polls were conducted only by sending out individual interviewers to people's homes. The homes were chosen by complicated national sampling techniques, and numerous methodologies were developed to assure a good sample from within each household.

In the 1960s, the methods for conducting a telephone sample were perfected. Not only could the pollsters use a random sample of telephone numbers to locate their households, but they also could conduct the interviews by telephone, thus cutting costs and assuring their physical security.

The next step in polling technology was computer-assisted telephone interviewing, or CATI. After a computer dials a respondent's telephone number, the interviewer reads the questions from the computer screen and enters the respondent's answers directly into the computer, where they can be analyzed almost instantly. This development cut costs further and made possible "overnight" polls—polls conducted immediately after debates and during crises.

Technology is now close to eliminating the interviewer altogether. With CATS—completely automated telephone surveying—computers and a type of voicemail system are used to complete the entire interview. The computer makes the call, a recording asks the questions, and the respondent is asked to use his or her touch-tone phone to give responses. Again, the data can be analyzed instantly because they are entered directly into the computer. The pollster who developed

CATS, Jay Leve, believes that the system is just as reliable as human interviewers in getting a sample and actually improves on human techniques by eliminating certain interview effects. For example, respondents will not answer the way that they think the interviewer expects or desires them to. The technology bears the commercial name, Bullet Poll. So far, it has been used to conduct more than two thousand surveys in major market areas.

Obviously, this type of technology makes it possible for a company, candidate, or television station to take virtually instant polls and then use them to advantage—on the evening news, for example.

For Critical Analysis
Do you think that people respond as thoughtfully to a recorded poll as to a live interviewer?

found so easily by telephone. Unscientific mail-in polls, telephone call-in polls, and polls completed by the workers in a campaign office are usually very biased and do not give an accurate picture of the public's views.

As poll takers get close to election day, they become even more concerned about their sample of respondents. Some pollsters continue to interview eligible voters, meaning those over eighteen and registered to vote. Many others use a series of questions in the poll and other weighting methods to try to identify "likely voters" so that they can be more accurate in their election-eve predictions. When a poll changes its method from reporting the views of eligible voters to reporting those of likely voters, the results are likely to change dramatically.

Finally, it makes sense to expect that the results of a poll will depend on the questions that are asked. Depending on what question is asked, voters could be said either to support a particular proposal or to oppose it. Furthermore, respondents' answers are also influenced by the order in which questions are asked, the types of answers they are allowed to choose, and in some cases, by their interaction with the interviewer. To some extent, people try to please the interviewer. They answer questions about which they have no information and avoid some answers to try to measure up to the interviewer's expectations. (See the feature entitled *Politics and Technology: The Interviewer Becomes a Machine* for a discussion of a new polling technique that eliminates the effects of the interviewer's expectations in polling.) Most recently, some campaigns have been using "push polls," in which the respondents are given misleading information in the questions asked to get them to vote against a

POLITICS AND ETHICS
Polls That Mislead

Pollsters long have known that the wording of questions can influence the response that a person gives. Different question wordings can provoke extensive political debate about the actual preferences of the public. When President Clinton and the congressional Republicans were unable to resolve their differences over the budget for more than six months, Democrats were cheered by poll results that showed that the majority of Americans opposed "cutting funding for Medicare." Republicans countered by showing poll results that indicated that many Americans supported "decreasing the growth in funding for Medicare." Both parties were depending on question wording for building a case for their own positions.

A far more deliberate use of question wording has surfaced recently in election campaigns. In the weeks before a primary or general election, voters are interviewed in what seems to be a legitimate poll. One or more of the questions in the poll, however, gives the respondent false or misleading information about the opposing candidate in an effort to influence the respondent's vote. Such surveys have become known as "push polls," because they are intended to push the voter to the candidate whose campaign sponsored the poll. Sometimes the information given in the question is simply misleading, while on other occasions it has been closer to scandal or gossip. In another variation, push polls can be used to start rumors about a candidate at a time very close to the election when rebuttal of the information is almost impossible.

The prevalence of push polling in early 1996 led to a statement by the American Association for Public Opinion Research condemning such polls and labeling them marketing ploys. It also led to the introduction of legislation in Virginia to regulate polls by requiring the disclosure of the candidate sponsoring the polls. By the middle of 1996, both major political parties had issued a statement saying that they would not engage in such polls. Similar tactics also may be used by polls about commercial products or any other topic, however. The ultimate result will be a further weakening of public confidence in any poll.

For Critical Analysis
How can you tell whether a survey question is worded "neutrally" or whether it might be biased toward a particular response?

candidate. Obviously, the answers given are likely to be influenced by such techniques. For a further discussion of push polls, see the feature above entitled *Politics and Ethics: Polls That Mislead.*

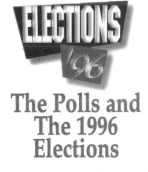

The Polls and The 1996 Elections

The performance of the polls during the presidential campaign of 1996 was exceptional. From the beginning of the campaign, polls showed that President Clinton was the choice of a plurality of voters and that Bob Dole had the support of between 30 and 40 percent of the voters. As shown in Figure 7–4, both candidates had slight "upticks" following their respective party conventions. At the end of the campaign, most of the major polls overestimated President Clinton's percentage of the vote by 3 to 8 percent.

The 1996 polls were also very accurate in measuring the level of the voting public's interest in the campaign. When survey data showed that only 39 percent of the voters were interested in the campaign, as compared to more than 70 percent in 1992, most commentators began to expect a low turnout on election day. Indeed, voter turnout was only 48 percent of eligible voters, the lowest in many decades.

One of the most interesting aspects of public opinion in 1996 was the relative lack of confidence in the president's character. The exit polls on election day found that at least 52 percent of the voters surveyed believed that President Clinton was not honest and could not be trusted. Nonetheless, many of the voters who believed this voted for the president.

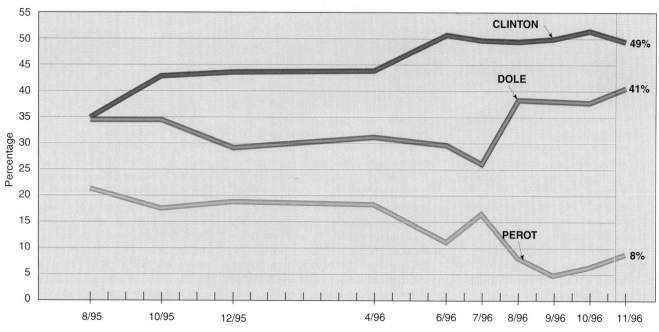

SOURCE: *New York Times*, November 4, 1996, p. A12; and *New York Times*, November 11, 1996.

Figure 7–4
• • • • • • • • • • • • • • • •
Tracking the New York Times/CBS News Poll—Voters' Approval of 1996 Presidential Candidates

POLITICAL SOCIALIZATION

The process by which individuals acquire political beliefs and attitudes.

HOW PUBLIC OPINION IS FORMED

Most Americans are willing to express opinions on political issues when asked. How do individuals acquire these opinions and attitudes? Most views that are expressed as political opinions are acquired through a process known as **political socialization.** By this we mean that individuals acquire their political attitudes, often including their party identification, through relationships with their families, friends, and co-workers. The most important influences in this process are the following: (1) the family, (2) the educational environment and achievement of the individual, (3) peers, (4) religion, (5) economic status and occupation, (6) political events, (7) opinion leaders, (8) the media, and (9) race and other demographic traits. We discuss each of these influences below, as well as the relatively recent phenomenon of the gender gap.

The Importance of the Family

The family is the most important force in political socialization. Not only do our parents' political attitudes and actions affect our adult opinions, but the family also links us to other socialization forces. We acquire our ethnic identity, our notion of social class, our educational opportunities, and our early religious beliefs from our families. Each of these factors can also influence our political attitudes.

How do parents transmit these attachments? Studies suggest that the influence of parents is due to two factors: communication and receptivity. Parents communicate their feelings and preferences to children constantly. Because children have such a strong need for parental approval, they are very receptive to their parents' views.[6]

---

[6]Robert S. Erikson, Norman R. Luttbeg, and Kent L. Tedin, *American Public Opinion: Its Origins, Content and Impact,* 5th ed. (New York: Macmillan, 1994), pp. 141–142.

The clearest legacy of the family is partisan identification. If both parents identify with one party, there is a strong likelihood that the children will begin political life with the same party preference. In their classic study of political attitudes among adolescents, M. Kent Jennings and Richard G. Niemi probed the partisan attachments of high school seniors and their parents during the mid-1960s.[7] They found that Democratic parents tend to produce Democratic children about two-thirds of the time, and Independent and Republican parents both transmit their beliefs about parties only slightly less well. There is still a sizable amount of cross-generational slippage, however. In all, Jennings and Niemi found that 59 percent of the children agreed with their parents' party ties.

In a 1973 reinterview of the same children and their parents, Jennings and Niemi found that the younger people had become notably more independent of partisan ties, whereas their parents went through very little change.[8] By 1973, a majority of the children had deviated from their parents' partisanship.

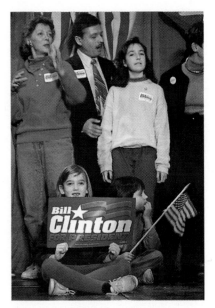

Patriotism is instilled in children through the process of political socialization. The children in this picture know that their parents approve of this display of support for the flag, thus enhancing their patriotic feelings.

Educational Influence on Political Opinion

From the early days of the republic, schools were perceived to be important transmitters of political information and attitudes. Children in the primary grades learn about their country mostly in patriotic ways. They learn to salute the flag, to say the Pledge of Allegiance, and to celebrate national holidays. Later, in the middle grades, children learn more historical facts and come to understand the structure of government and the functions of the president, judges, and Congress. By high school, students have a more complex understanding of the political system, may identify with a political party, and may take positions on issues.

Generally, education is closely linked to political participation. The more education a person receives, the more likely it is that the person will be interested in politics, be confident in his or her ability to understand political issues, and be an active participant in the political process.

Peers and Peer Group Influence

Once a child enters school, the child's friends become an important influence on behavior and attitudes. As young children, and later as adults, friendships and associations in **peer groups** are influential on political attitudes. We must, however, separate the effects of peer group pressure on opinions and attitudes in general from peer group pressure on political opinions. For the most part, associations among peers are nonpolitical. Political attitudes are more likely to be shaped by peer groups when the peer groups are involved directly in political activities.

Individuals who join interest groups based on ethnic identity may find, for example, a common political bond through working for the group's civil liberties and rights. African American activist groups may consist of individuals who join together to support government programs that will aid the African American population. Members of a labor union may feel strong political pressure to support certain pro-labor candidates.

PEER GROUP

A group consisting of members sharing common relevant social characteristics. These groups play an important part in the socialization process, helping to shape attitudes and beliefs.

[7]M. Kent Jennings and Richard G. Niemi, *The Political Character of Adolescence: The Influence of Families and Schools* (Princeton, N.J.: Princeton University Press, 1974).

[8]M. Kent Jennings and Richard G. Niemi, *Generations and Politics* (Princeton, N.J.: Princeton University Press, 1981).

Religious Influence

Religious associations tend to create definite political attitudes, although why this occurs is not clearly understood. Surveys show that Roman Catholic respondents tend to be more liberal on economic issues than are Protestants. Apparently, Jewish respondents are more liberal on all fronts than either Catholics or Protestants. In terms of voting behavior, it has been observed that northern white Protestants are more likely to vote Republican, whereas northern white Roman Catholics more often vote Democratic; everywhere in the United States, Jews mostly vote Democratic. As noted in Chapter 1, in the feature entitled *Politics and Values: Americans and Religion,* the increase in fundamentalist or evangelical Protestants has had a political impact. A recent study by the Pew Center for People and the Press found that 42 percent of white evangelical Protestants are Republican. Less than ten years ago, this figure was 35 percent.

These associations between religious background and political attitudes are partly derived from the ethnic background of certain religious groups and the conditions at the time their forebears immigrated to the United States. Germans who immigrated before the Civil War tend to be Republican regardless of their religious background, whereas Eastern European Catholics, who arrived in the late nineteenth century, adopted the Democratic identity of the cities in which they made their homes. The relationship between religion and party affiliation is shown in Figure 7–5.

Sometimes a candidate's religion enters the political picture, as it did in the 1960 presidential election contest between Democrat John Kennedy and Republican Richard Nixon. The fact that Kennedy was a Catholic—the second Catholic to be nominated by a major party—polarized many voters. Among northern whites, Kennedy was supported by 83 percent of voting Catholics and by 93 percent of Jewish voters but by only 28 percent of the Protestants who voted.

The Influence of Economic Status and Occupation

How wealthy you are and the kind of job you hold are also associated with your political views. Social-class differences emerge on a wide range of issues. Poorer people are more inclined to favor government social-welfare

Figure 7–5
• •
Religion and Party Affiliation

Percentage identifying with each party ...

	Democrat	Republican
Jewish	43%	22%
Baptist	43%	27%
Pentecostal	38%	27%
Catholic	38%	27%
Methodist	35%	36%
Presbyterian	28%	44%
Lutheran	26%	37%
Episcopalian	25%	41%
Mormon	23%	51%

SOURCE: *New York Times,* April 10, 1991.

programs but are likely to be conservative on social issues such as abortion. The upper middle class is more likely to hold conservative economic views but to be tolerant of social change. People in lower economic strata also tend to be more isolationist on foreign-policy issues and are more likely to identify with the Democratic party and vote for Democratic candidates. Support for civil liberties and tolerance of different points of view tend to be greater among those with higher social status and lower among those with lower social status. Probably, it is educational differences more than the pattern of life at home or work that account for this.

The Influence of Political Events

People's political attitudes may be shaped by political events and the nation's reactions to them. In the 1960s and 1970s, the war in Vietnam—including revelations about the secret bombing in Cambodia—and the Watergate break-in and subsequent cover-up fostered widespread cynicism toward government. In one study of the impact of the Watergate scandal of 1972, Christopher Atherton found that schoolchildren changed their image of President Nixon from a "benevolent" to a "malevolent" leader as the scandal unfolded. Negative views also increased about other aspects of politics and politicians. Members of that age group moderated their views, however, as they matured.[9]

When events produce a long-lasting political impact, **generational effects** result. Voters who grew up in the 1930s during the Great Depression were likely to form life-long attachments to the Democratic party, the party of Franklin D. Roosevelt. There was some evidence that the years of economic prosperity under Ronald Reagan during the 1980s may have influenced young adults to identify with the Republican party. A 1990 poll showed that 52 percent of thirteen- to seventeen-year-olds thought of themselves as Republicans, whereas 32 percent of this age group thought of themselves as Democrats. Although the number of younger voters identifying themselves as Republicans declined in 1992, the youngest voters still were more likely to be Republican than Democratic.[10]

GENERATIONAL EFFECT

A long-lasting effect of events of a particular time period on the political opinions or preferences of those who came of political age at that time.

Opinion Leaders' Influence

We are all influenced by those with whom we are closely associated or whom we hold in great respect—friends at school, family members and other relatives, teachers, and so on. In a sense, these people are **opinion leaders,** but on an informal level; that is, their influence over us is not necessarily intentional or deliberate. We are also influenced by formal opinion leaders, such as a president, a lobbyist, a congressperson, or a news commentator, who have as part of their jobs the task of swaying people's views. Their interest lies in defining the political agenda in such a way that discussions about policy options will take place on their terms.

OPINION LEADER

One who is able to influence the opinions of others because of position, expertise, or personality. Such leaders help to shape public opinion.

Media Influence

Clearly, the **media**—newspapers, television, radio broadcasts, and Internet sources—strongly influence public opinion. This is because the media inform the public about the issues and events of our times and thus have an agenda-

MEDIA

The technical means of communication with mass audiences.

---

[9]Erikson, Luttbeg, and Tedin, *American Public Opinion,* p. 153.
[10]"Age, Generation, and Party ID," *Public Perspective,* July/August 1992, p. 16.

DID YOU KNOW...
That the number of radio and television stations with a dominant talk-show format grew from 308 in 1989 to 1,028 in 1996?

setting effect. In other words, to borrow from Bernard Cohen's classic statement on the media and public opinion, the media may not be successful in telling people what to think, but they are "stunningly successful in telling their audience what to think about."[11]

Today, many contend that the media's influence on public opinion is increasing to the point where the media are as influential as the family in regard to public opinion. For example, in her analysis of the role played by the media in American politics,[12] media scholar Doris A. Graber points out that high school students, when asked where they obtain the information on which they base their attitudes, mention the mass media far more than their families, friends, and teachers. This trend, combined with the increasing popularity of more populist and interactive news sources, such as talk shows and the Internet, may alter the nature of the media's influence on public debate significantly in the future. (See Chapter 11 for a more detailed analysis of the role of the media in American political life.)

The Influence of Demographic Traits

African Americans show a much stronger commitment than do whites to steady or more rapid racial desegregation. African Americans tend to be more liberal than whites on social-welfare issues, civil liberties, and even foreign policy. Party preference and voting among African Americans since the 1930s have supported very heavily the Democrats, and wealth has little impact on African American attitudes.

It is somewhat surprising that a person's chronological age has comparatively little impact on political preferences. Still, young adults are somewhat more liberal than older people on most issues, and they are considerably more progressive on such issues as marijuana legalization, pornography, civil disobedience, and racial and sexual equality.

Finally, attitudes vary from region to region, although such patterns probably are accounted for mostly by social class and other differences. Regional differences are relatively unimportant today. There is still a tendency for the South and the East to be more Democratic than the West and the Midwest. More important than region is a person's residence—urban, suburban, or rural. Big cities tend to be more liberal and Democratic because of their greater concentration of minorities and newer ethnic groups. Smaller communities are more conservative and, outside the South, more Republican.

The Gender Gap

GENDER GAP

A term most often used to describe the difference between the percentage of votes a candidate receives from women and the percentage the candidate receives from men. The term was widely used after the 1980 presidential election.

Until the 1980s, there was little evidence that men's and women's political attitudes were very different. The election of Ronald Reagan in 1980, however, soon came to be associated with a **gender gap.** In a May 1983 Gallup poll, 43 percent of the women polled approved of Reagan's performance in office and 44 percent disapproved, versus 49 percent of men who approved and 41 percent who disapproved.

In the 1988 election, the gender gap reappeared, but in a modified form. Although the Democrats hoped that women's votes would add significantly to their totals, a deep split between men and women did not occur. The final polls showed that 54 percent of the men voted for George Bush, as did 50 per-

---

[11]*The Press and Foreign Policy* (Princeton, N.J.: Princeton University Press, 1963), p. 81.
[12]See Doris A. Graber, *Mass Media and American Politics,* 5th ed. (Washington, D.C.: Congressional Quarterly Books, 1996).

cent of the women. The 1992 presidential election again found women more likely than men to vote for the Democrats: 46 percent of women voted for Bill Clinton, compared with 41 percent of the men. Additionally, women were less likely to vote for H. Ross Perot than were men. Throughout his first term, Clinton continued to get higher approval marks from women than from men. For a discussion of the gender gap in the 1996 elections, see the feature entitled *Elections '96: The Gender Gap.*

The Gender Gap

The gender gap reappeared in force in 1996. President Clinton received 54 percent of women's votes and only 44 percent of men's votes. In contrast, only 37 percent of women voters voted for Bob Dole, the Republican candidate, while the same percentage of men voted for Dole (44 percent) as for Clinton. The gender gap was most evident among working women, with 57 percent of that group voting for Clinton and 34 percent voting for Dole.

Republican campaign strategists admitted after the elections that the Clinton campaign did a much better job of relating to women voters. Polling data collected by the *New York Times* also indicated that women were more likely than men to support spending on education and affirmative action programs (which the Republicans opposed) and were more likely than men to oppose the welfare bill passed by Congress and signed by Clinton in 1996. Neither presidential candidate spoke to the issue of abortion, although it was clear that the president supported pro-abortion forces on the issue.

Women also appear to hold different attitudes from their male counterparts on a range of issues other than presidential preferences. They are much more likely to oppose capital punishment, as well as the use of force abroad. Studies have also shown that women are more concerned about risks to the environment, more supportive of social welfare, and more supportive of extending civil rights to gay men and lesbians than are men.[13] These differences of opinion appear to be growing and may become an important factor in future elections at national and local levels.

POLITICAL CULTURE AND PUBLIC OPINION

Americans are divided into a multitude of ethnic, religious, regional, and political subgroups. In many cases, members of these groups hold a particular set of opinions about government policies, about the goals of the society, and about the rights of their group and the rights of others. Given the diversity of American society and the wide range of opinions contained within it, how is it that the political process continues to function without being stalemated by conflict and dissension?

One explanation is rooted in the concept of the American political culture, which can be described as a set of attitudes and ideas about the nation and the government. As discussed in Chapter 1, our political culture is widely shared by Americans of many different backgrounds. To some extent, it consists of symbols, such as the American flag, the Liberty Bell, and the Statue of Liberty. The elements of our political culture also include certain shared

---

[13]*Gallup Poll Monthly,* April 1993, p. 33.

The Million Man March in Washington
D.C., October 16,1995. This march was
organized by the often controversial
Nation of Islam leader, Louis Farrakhan,
and his supporters. One of the major goals
of the march was to inspire black males to
take responsibility for themselves, to
achieve higher levels of personal achievement, and to involve themselves in the
renewal of their communities—values
shared by many Americans. Some criticized Farrakhan and the march because
women were not allowed to participate.

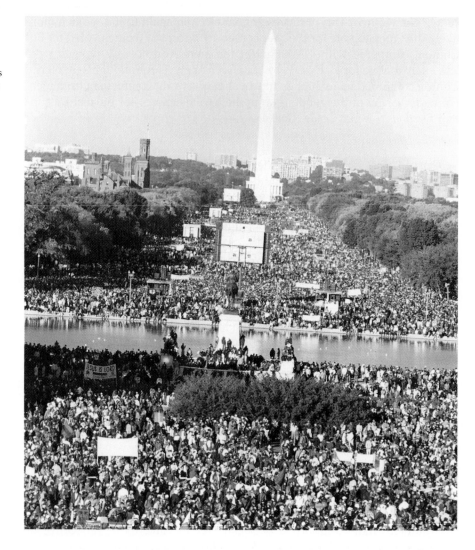

beliefs about the most important values in the American political system
including (1) liberty, equality, and property; (2) support for religion; and
(3) community service and personal achievement. The structure of the government—particularly federalism, the political parties, the powers of Congress, and popular rule—were also found to be important values.[14]

The political culture provides a general environment of support for the
political system. If the people share certain beliefs about the system and a
reservoir of good feeling exists toward the institutions of government, the
nation will be better able to weather periods of crisis, such as Watergate. This
foundation of goodwill may combat cynicism and increase the level of participation in elections as well. During the 1960s and 1970s, survey research
showed that the overall level of **political trust** declined steeply. A considerable proportion of Americans seemed to feel that they could not trust government officials and that they could not count on officials to care about the
ordinary person. This index of political trust reached an all-time low in 1992,
reflecting Americans' cynicism about the government and the presidential
election campaign (see Table 7–2).

POLITICAL TRUST

The degree to which individuals express
trust in the government and political institutions, usually measured through a specific series of survey questions.

---

[14]Donald Devine, *Political Culture of the United States* (Boston: Little, Brown, 1972).

Table 7–2

Trends in Political Trust

QUESTION: How much of the time do you think you can trust the government in Washington to do what is right—just about always, most of the time, or only some of the time?

	1964	1968	1972	1974	1976	1978	1980	1982	1984	1986	1988	1990	1992	1994	1996
Percentage saying:															
Always/Most of the time	76	61	53	36	33	29	25	32	46	42	44	27	23	20	25
Some of the time	22	36	45	61	63	67	73	64	51	55	54	73	75	79	71

SOURCE: *New York Times*/CBS News Surveys; the University of Michigan Survey Research Center, National Election Studies; and *The Washington Post*/Kaiser Family Foundation.

PUBLIC OPINION ABOUT GOVERNMENT

A vital component of public opinion in the United States is the considerable ambivalence with which the public regards many major national institutions. Table 7–3 shows trends from 1973 to 1995 in Gallup public opinion polls asking respondents, at regularly spaced intervals, how much confidence they had in the institutions listed. Over the years, military and religious organizations have ranked highest, but note the decline in confidence in churches following the numerous scandals concerning television evangelists in the late 1980s. Note also the heightened regard for the military after the war in the Persian Gulf in 1991. (The effect of a successful war on public opinion is explored in this chapter's *Critical Perspective.*) The United States Supreme

Table 7–3

Confidence in Institutions Trend

QUESTION: I am going to read a list of institutions in American society. Would you please tell me how much confidence you, yourself, have in each one—a great deal, quite a lot, some, or very little?

	Percentage Saying "Great Deal" or "Quite a Lot"											
	1973	1975	1977	1979	1981	1983	1985	1987	1989	1991	1993	1995
Church or organized religion	66%	68%	65%	65%	64%	62%	66%	61%	52%	56%	53%	57%
Military	NA	58	57	54	50	53	61	61	63	69	67	64
U.S. Supreme Court	44	49	46	45	46	42	56	52	46	39	43	44
Banks and banking	NA	NA	NA	60	46	51	51	51	42	30	38	43
Public schools	58	NA	54	53	42	39	48	50	43	35	39	40
Congress	42	40	40	34	29	28	39	NA	32	18	19	21
Newspapers	39	NA	NA	51	35	38	35	31	NA	32	31	30
Big business	26	34	33	32	20	28	31	NA	NA	22	23	21
Television	37	NA	NA	38	25	25	29	28	NA	24	21	33
Organized labor	30	38	39	36	28	26	28	26	NA	22	26	26
NA = Not asked.												

SOURCE: *The Gallup Report,* May, 1995.

CRITICAL PERSPECTIVE
Can War Make the President More Popular?

The American public has been reluctant to use military force overseas since the end of the Vietnam War. Political leaders have been warned that this antimilitary feeling could translate into a political liability for an interventionist administration. It is worth noting that Americans were also reluctant to engage in World War I, entering it three years after it began in Europe, and that isolationist sentiment kept the nation out of World War II until the Japanese attack on Pearl Harbor in 1941. The "Vietnam syndrome" has not, however, kept presidents from using force. Military incidents since Vietnam include Gerald Ford's rescue of the *Mayaguez* seamen, Jimmy Carter's foray into Iran in an attempt to rescue the hostages, Ronald Reagan's sending of troops to Lebanon and Grenada, George Bush's incursions into Panama to capture Manuel Noriega and into Kuwait and Iraq to expel Iraqi troops from Kuwait, and Bill Clinton's sending of troops to Haiti.

If Americans are so unwilling to risk military involvement, why are presidents so willing to risk the displeasure of the voters? One reason may be the belief that a successful military engagement can enhance the president's popularity, increase patriotic feeling, and even improve the electoral fortunes of the president's party. In a highly regarded study, John Mueller examined the levels of public support for the presidential use of force in Korea and Vietnam.

He finds that the use of American forces initially spurs a "rally round the flag" effect that lifts the president's popularity and builds support for the troops.* The positive effect lasts until the number of casualties and the length of the engagement begin to wear on the public. Continued military action will then have a deleterious effect on the president's approval ratings as the war becomes unpopular.

Mueller's thesis seems to be supported by the relatively weak public opposition to Reagan's use of troops in Grenada and to Bush's military engagement in Panama. The Persian Gulf War, however, provided an excellent test of the degree to which military action, particularly successful military action, could raise a president's popularity. In the spring and summer of 1989, Bush's presidential approval ratings hovered around 55 percent. After Iraq's invasion of Kuwait and Bush's decision to send standby troops to Saudi Arabia, his ratings climbed to the 70 to 75 percent range. The weekly Gallup ratings dipped again from October through December 1990 as the troop buildup increased and the threat of war became clear. In the period between January 11, 1991 (before the air war) and January 17 (the day after the air attacks began), however, his ratings rose from 64 to 82 percent. By mid-March, when it seemed likely that the war would be over soon, 89 percent of those polled approved of the way that Bush was handling his job.†

Court, which many people do not see as a particularly political institution, although it is clearly involved in decisions with vitally important consequences for the nation, also scored well, as did banks and banking until recently. A series of unpopular Supreme Court decisions from 1989 to 1991 and the savings and loan scandals of about the same time caused the public's confidence in both of those institutions to drop significantly by 1991. Even less confidence is expressed in newspapers, big business, television, and organized labor, all of which certainly are involved directly or indirectly in the political process. In 1991, following the check-kiting scandal and other embarrassments, confidence in Congress fell to a record low of 18 percent. (Note that the decreasing confidence in Congress has been paralleled by an increasing confidence in the ability of state and local institutions. See this chapter's *Politics and the Fifty States* on page 236.

Although people may not have much confidence in government institutions, they nonetheless turn to government to solve what they perceive to be the major problems facing the country. Table 7–4, which is based on Gallup polls conducted over the years 1975 to 1996, shows that the leading problems clearly have changed over time. The public tends to emphasize problems that are immediate. It is not at all unusual to see fairly sudden, and even appar-

CRITICAL PERSPECTIVE
Can War Make the President More Popular? Continued

Given the popularity of Bush's actions in the Middle East, political strategists expected that he would be an invincible candidate in 1992. The war was too short and too successful for the rally effect to last, however. By December 1991, his ratings were back at the 50 percent level and continued to decline as the economy limped along.

Not only did the Gulf War give a temporary boost to the president's popularity; it also seemed to inspire patriotism and support for the military throughout the nation. Table 7–3 on page 233 shows that in 1991, the public had more confidence in the military than it did in the church or organized religion, in newspapers, or in any institution of government.

In another study of the Gulf War, Suzanne Parker looked at the question of the breadth of the rally effect on other institutions and public attitudes.[‡] She found that the rally effect carried over to the public's views on the country's financial outlook, to expressed trust in government, to the public's views on Bush's handling of the wider issues of the Middle East, and to the evaluation of Congress. For each of these issues, the rally effect increased public support during the war. Parker drew the same conclusion as Mueller, however: The effect was so short lived that public support

returned almost exactly to prewar levels within eight months after the conflict ended. Thus, the answer to the question of whether war can help a president's popularity is complex: the Persian Gulf War suggests that a successful, short war can raise approval to unprecedented levels but that the effect is brief and may not carry over to the next election campaign.

For Critical Analysis

1. How can you explain the linkage between the use of military force and presidential popularity?

2. Do you think that the desire to gain voter approval has ever been a significant factor in a U.S. president's decision to use military force?

3. Why is the effect of a military venture—even a highly successful one, such as the Persian Gulf War—on presidential popularity so short lived?

[*]John Mueller, *War, Presidents and Public Opinion* (New York: Wiley, 1973).
[†]Gallup poll data reported in John Mueller, *Policy and Opinion in the Gulf War* (Chicago: University of Chicago Press, 1994).
[‡]Suzanne Parker, "Toward an Understanding of 'Rally' Effects: Public Opinion in the Persian Gulf War," *Public Opinion Quarterly*, Vol. 59 (1995), pp. 526–546.

ently contradictory, shifts in public perceptions of what government should do. In recent years, crime and the budget deficit have reached the top of the problems list.

Table 7–4

Most Important Problem Trend, 1975–1996

Year	Problem	Year	Problem
1996	Budget deficit	1985	Fear of war, unemployment
1995	Crime, violence	1984	Unemployment, fear of war
1994	Crime, violence, health care	1983	Unemployment, high cost of living
1993	Health care, budget deficit	1982	Unemployment, high cost of living
1992	Unemployment, budget deficit	1981	High cost of living, unemployment
1991	Economy	1980	High cost of living, unemployment
1990	War in Middle East	1979	High cost of living, energy problems
1989	War on drugs	1978	High cost of living, energy problems
1988	Economy, budget deficit	1977	High cost of living, unemployment
1987	Unemployment, economy	1976	High cost of living, unemployment
1986	Unemployment, budget deficit	1975	High cost of living, unemployment

SOURCE: *Gallup Report*, 1994.; *New York Times*/CBS News Poll, January 1996.

POLITICS AND THE FIFTY STATES
Increasing the Responsibility of State and Local Governments

One of the key points of the Republican revolution of 1994 was the drive to return power over federal programs to the states and local communities. As was described in Chapter 3, the twentieth century has seen a rapid increase in national government authority and revenue collection. Following the Great Depression of the 1930s, the American people seemed to want the national government to take responsibility for their welfare and economic security by regulating business and finance. Looking at some of the earliest public policy polls, we find the results as shown in Graphs 1 and 2.

By 1964, a Gallup poll found that 35 percent of the respondents believed that the federal government has the right amount of power, while 31 percent felt it should use its powers more. Only 28 percent felt it had too much power. By the mid-1970s, however, polls began to show a shift toward believing more in the efficiency of the states—a shift that has been pronounced in recent years. In 1995, the

Los Angeles Times reported poll results as shown in Graph 3.

Another recent survey, by Yankelovich Partners in September 1994, produced the responses depicted in Graph 4.

Clearly, the public has shifted its opinion toward more appreciation for state and local governments and has improved its opinion of what those governments can accomplish. Other polls have shown that the kinds of activities that the people would favor returning to the states include improving public education, reducing crime, providing job training, building housing, and constructing highways.

For Critical Analysis

What were some of the major fears that made people turn to the national government during the 1930s? Are those fears still prevalent today? How do those fears affect opinions on returning government activities to the states?

GRAPH 3

Question: In general, who do you think does the best job of spending tax dollars in an efficient and constructive way: the federal government, your state government, or your local government?

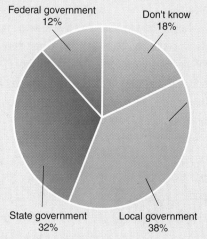

Federal government 12% — Don't know 18% — State government 32% — Local government 38%

SOURCE: *Los Angeles Times* poll, 1995.

GRAPH 1

Question: Which...do you favor..., concentration of power in the federal government or...in the state government?

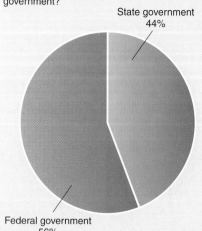

State government 44% — Federal government 56%

SOURCE: Gallup Organization, January 1936.

GRAPH 2

Question: Which do you think is the most honest and efficient in performing its own special duties?

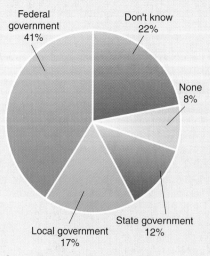

Federal government 41% — Don't know 22% — None 8% — State government 12% — Local government 17%

SOURCE: Roper Organization, July 1939.

GRAPH 4

Question: Would you favor or oppose having your state government assume the governmental powers and functions now exercised by the federal government in Washington?

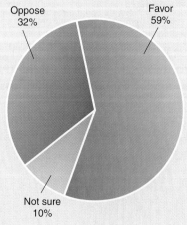

Oppose 32% — Favor 59% — Not sure 10%

SOURCE: Yankelovich Partners, September 1994.

This gives rise to a critically important question: Is government really responsive to public opinion? A study by political scientists Benjamin I. Page and Robert Y. Shapiro suggests that in fact the national government is very responsive to the public's demands for action.[15] In looking at changes in public opinion poll results over time, Page and Shapiro show that when the public supports a policy change, policy changes in a direction congruent with the change in public opinion 43 percent of the time, policy changes in a direction opposite to the change in opinion 22 percent of the time, and policy does not change at all 33 percent of the time. So, overall, the national government could be said to respond to changes in public opinion about two-thirds of the time. Page and Shapiro also show, as should be no surprise, that when public opinion changes more dramatically—say, by 20 percentage points rather than by just 6 or 7 percentage points—government policy is much more likely to follow changing public attitudes.

THE SPECTRUM OF POLITICAL BELIEFS

Political candidates and officeholders in the United States frequently are identified as liberals or conservatives. These terms refer loosely to a spectrum of political beliefs that commonly are arrayed on a continuum from left to right. Each of the terms has changed its meaning from its origins and continues to change as the issues of political debate change. In the United States, however, the terms most frequently refer to sets of political positions that date from the Great Depression.

Liberals are most commonly understood to embrace national government solutions to public problems, to believe that the national government should intervene in the economy to ensure its health, to support social welfare programs to assist the disadvantaged, and to be tolerant of social change. Today, liberals are often identified with pro–women's rights positions, pro–civil rights policies, and opposition to increased defense spending.

In contrast, conservatives usually feel that the national government has grown too large, that the private sector needs less interference from the government, that social-welfare programs should be limited, that state and local governments should be able to make their own decisions, and that the nation's defense should be strengthened. Some conservatives express grave concerns about the decline of family life and traditional values in this country; they would not be tolerant of gay rights laws, for example. Senator Edward Kennedy and 1992 and 1996 presidential candidate Pat Buchanan are examples of today's variety of liberalism and conservatism, respectively.

When asked, Americans usually are willing to identify themselves on the liberal-conservative spectrum. More individuals are likely to consider themselves moderates than as liberals or conservatives. As Table 7–5 shows, although the number of moderates and conservatives has increased and the number of liberals has declined in the past two decades, there has not been a dramatic change in ideological self-identification since 1976.

Most Americans, however, do not fit into the categories as nicely as do Edward Kennedy or Pat Buchanan. Such political leaders, who are quite conscious of their philosophical views and who hold a carefully thought out and a more or less consistent set of political beliefs, can be described as **ideo-**

---

[15]See the extensive work of Page and Shapiro in Benjamin I. Page and Robert Y. Shapiro, *The Rational Public: Fifty Years of Trends in Americans' Policy Preferences* (Chicago: University of Chicago Press, 1992).

Table 7–5

Ideological Self-identification, 1976 to 1996

There has been relatively little change in the distribution of liberals and conservatives, even after the elections of self-described liberal or conservative presidents.

YEAR	LIBERAL	MODERATE	CONSERVATIVE	NO OPINION
1976	21%	41%	26%	12%
1977	21	38	29	12
1978	21	35	27	17
1979	21	42	26	12
1980	19	40	31	11
1981	18	43	30	9
1982	17	40	33	11
1984	17	41	31	11
1986	20	45	28	7
1988	18	45	33	4
1990	20	45	28	6
1992	19	41	34	6
1993	18	45	32	5
1994	18	48	34	0
1995	19	39	37	4
1996	17	45	34	4

SOURCE: *Gallup Reports;* and *New York Times*/CBS News Surveys.

IDEOLOGUE

An individual whose political opinions are carefully thought out and relatively consistent with one another. Ideologues are often described as having a comprehensive world view.

logues. Partly because most citizens are not highly interested in all political issues and partly because Americans have different stakes in politics, most people have mixed sets of opinions that do not fit into one ideological framework. Election research suggests that only a small percentage of all Americans, perhaps less than 10 percent, could be identified as ideologues. The rest of the public conceives of politics more in terms of the parties or of economic well-being.

Some critics of the American political system have felt that elections would be more meaningful and that the nation could face important policy problems more effectively if Americans were more ideological in their thinking. Public opinion research suggests that for most Americans, political issues are

Senator Edward Kennedy (left) of Massachusetts has been a liberal voice throughout his tenure in Congress. Patrick Buchanan (right), who opposed President George Bush during the Republican presidential primaries in 1992 and Robert Dole in 1996, is an outspoken conservative. Buchanan has built a career in television as a political commentator.

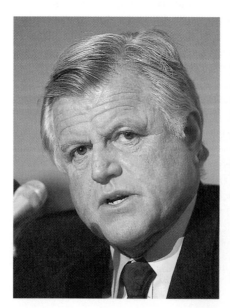
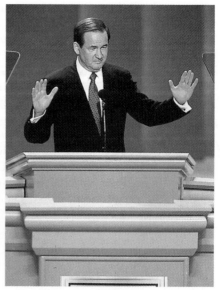

not usually as important as events in their daily lives are. There is no evidence to suggest that forces are in place to turn Americans into highly motivated ideological voters.

PUBLIC OPINION AND THE POLITICAL PROCESS

Surveys of public opinion, no matter what fascinating questions they ask or how quickly they get the answers, are not equivalent to elections in the United States. Because not all Americans are equally interested in politics or equally informed, public opinion polls can suggest only the general distribution of opinion on issues. Many times, only a few citizens have formulated preferences, and these preferences will be changed by events.

Politicians, whether in office or in the midst of a campaign, see public opinion as important to their careers. The president, members of Congress, governors, and other elected officials realize that strong support by the public as expressed in opinion polls is a source of power in dealing with other politicians. It is far more difficult for a senator to say no to the president if the president is immensely popular and if polls show approval of the president's policies. Public opinion also helps political candidates identify the most important concerns among the public and may help them shape their campaigns successfully.

Although opinion polls cannot give exact guidance on what the government should do in a specific instance, the opinions measured in polls do set an informal limit on government action. For example, consider the highly controversial issue of abortion. Most Americans are moderates on this issue; they do not approve of abortion as a means of birth control, but they do feel that it should be available under certain circumstances. Yet sizable groups of people express very intense feelings both for and against abortion. Given this distribution of opinion, most elected officials would rather not try to change policy to favor either of the extreme positions. To do so would clearly violate the opinion of the majority of Americans. In this case, as in many others, public opinion does not make public policy; rather, it restrains officials from taking truly unpopular actions. If officials do act in the face of public opposition, the consequences of such actions will be determined at the ballot box.

PUBLIC OPINION: UNFINISHED WORK

Public opinion is a vital part of the political process—it identifies issues for resolution, provides for a public debate on the issues, gives policymakers some idea of what the voters prefer, and sets boundaries on those same policymakers. The polling industry, however, may be close to putting itself out of business either through public distrust or government regulation.

The science of polling provides powerful information to private and governmental bodies to manipulate the public, to influence markets and the economy, and to shape the public agenda. Yet there is no mechanism to sort out "accurate" and "scientific" polls from marketing devices. The explosion of polls and poll results has also alienated the public. Refusal rates for polls have soared to above 40 percent in some instances. This means that certain groups within the public are no longer willing to cooperate with the pollsters, thus weakening the samples.

At the same time that the public is wearying of the polls and paying less attention to them, the media are increasing their expenditures on them,

DID YOU KNOW...
That when Americans were asked if they think race relations are good or bad in the United States, 68 percent said that they were "bad," but when asked about race relations in their own communities, 75 percent said that they were "good"?

Changes in Public Opinion Polling

As long as there has been an American republic, politicians have tried to ground their decisions in an understanding of what the voters desire. As the chart below indicates, before the invention of random-sample polling in the 1930s, many other sources were used for judging public opinion.

THEN	NOW
• Straw or street-corner polls.	• Random-sample polls.
• Personal interviews.	• Telephone polls; computer-assisted polls; automated polls; talk shows; call-in surveys.
• Polling on public issues.	• Polling on public issues, candidates, and products.
• Polls sponsored by the media.	• Polls sponsored by the media, political parties, interest groups, and candidates.
• Polling was an American phenomenon.	• Polling is a worldwide phenomenon.
• Poor prediction of election results.	• Successful prediction of election results.

polling on almost every conceivable issue. The real danger is that deliberation on the real effects of policies and their impact on society will be drowned out by poll results that substitute for public debate. Whether the answer is to regulate polls, to outlaw polls before elections or at some other point in time, or just to allow the polls to exhaust themselves, any change undoubtedly will provoke strong opposition from the media, as well as from those who see a challenge to First Amendment freedoms.

GETTING INVOLVED
Be a Critical Consumer of Opinion Polls

Americans are inundated with the results of public opinion polls. The polls, often reported to us through television news, the newspaper, *Time*, *Newsweek*, or radio, purport to tell us a variety of things: whether the president's popularity is up or down, whether gun control is more popular now than previously, or who is leading the pack for the next presidential nomination.

What must be kept in mind with this blizzard of information is that not all the poll results are equally good or equally believable. As a critical consumer, you need to be aware of what makes one set of public opinion poll results valid and other results useless or even dangerously misleading.

SELECTION OF THE SAMPLE

How were the people who were interviewed selected? Pay attention only to opinion polls that are based on scientific, or random, samples, in which a known probability was used to select every person who was interviewed. These *probability samples*, as they are also called, can take a number of different forms. The simplest to understand is known as a *random sample*, in which everybody had a known, and possibly an equal, chance of being chosen to be interviewed. As a rule, do not give credence to the results of opinion polls that consist of shopping-mall interviews. The main problem with this kind of opinion taking, which is a special version of a so-called *accidental sample*, is that not everyone had an equal chance of being in the mall when the interview took place. Also, it is almost certain that the people in the mall are not a reasonable cross section of a community's entire population (shopping malls would tend to attract people who are disproportionately younger, female, mobile, and middle class).

Probability samples are useful (and nonprobability samples are not) for the following reason: when you know the odds that the particular sample would have been chosen randomly from a larger population, you can calculate the range within which the real results for the whole population would fall if everybody had been interviewed. Well-designed probability samples will allow the pollster to say, for example, that he or she is 95 percent sure that 61 percent of the public, plus or minus 4 percentage points, supports national

health insurance. It turns out that if you want to become twice as precise about a poll result, you would need to collect a sample four times as large. This tends to make accurate polls quite expensive and difficult to collect. Typically, the Gallup organization seldom interviews more than about 1,500 respondents.

INTERVIEW METHOD

There are other important points to keep in mind when you see opinion poll results. How were people contacted for the poll—by mail, by telephone, in person in their homes, or in some other way? By and large, because of its lower cost, polling firms have turned more and more to telephone interviewing. This method usually can produce highly accurate results. Its disadvantage is that telephone interviews typically need to be short and to deal with questions that are fairly easy to answer. Interviews in person are better for getting useful information about why a particular response was given to a question. They take much longer to complete, however, and are not as useful if results must be generated quickly. Results from mailed questionnaires should be taken with a grain of salt. Usually, only a small percentage of people complete them and send them back.

NONPOLLS

Be particularly critical of telephone "call-in" polls. When viewers or listeners of television or radio shows are encouraged to call in their opinions to an 800 telephone number, the call is free, but the polling results are useless. Only viewers who are interested in the topic will take advantage of calling in, and that group, of course, is not representative of the general public. Polls that use 900 numbers are perhaps even more misleading. The only respondents to those polls are those who care enough about the topic to pay for a call. Both types of polls are likely to be manipulated by interest groups or supporters of a political candidate, who will organize their supporters to make calls and reinforce their own point of view. Remember, when seeing the results of any poll, take a moment and try to find out how the poll was conducted.

KEY TERMS

consensus 218	latent public opinion 216	public opinion 214
divisive opinion 218	media 229	relevance 216
fluidity 216	opinion leader 229	sampling error 223
gender gap 230	opinion poll 218	Solid South 216
generational effect 229	peer group 227	stability 216
ideologue 238	political socialization 226	Watergate break-in 213
intensity 215	political trust 232	

CHAPTER SUMMARY

❶ Public opinion is the aggregate of individual attitudes or beliefs shared by some portion of adults. It has at least five special qualities: (a) intensity—the strength of an opinion; (b) fluidity—the extent to which opinion changes; (c) stability—the extent to which opinion remains constant; (d) latency—quiescent opinions; and (e) relevance—the extent to which an issue is of concern at a particular time. Opinions are also affected by political knowledge and distributed among the public in different ways. Consensus issues are those on which most people agree, whereas divisive issues are those about which people strongly disagree.

❷ Most descriptions of public opinion are based on the results of opinion polls. The accuracy of polls is based on sampling techniques that ensure randomness in the selection of respondents. Polls only measure opinions held on the day they are taken and will not reflect rapidly changing opinions. Certain methodological problems may reduce the accuracy of polls.

❸ Opinions and attitudes are produced by a combination of socialization, information, and experience. Young people, for example, are likely to be influenced by their parents' political party identification. Education has an effect on opinions and attitudes, as do peer groups, religious affiliation, and economic status. Political events may have generational effects, shaping the opinions of a particular age group. Opinion leaders, the media, ethnicity, and gender also affect political views.

❹ A political culture exists in the United States because so many Americans hold similar attitudes and beliefs about how the government and the political system should work. In addition, most Americans are able to identify themselves as liberals, moderates, or conservatives, even though they may not articulate a consistent philosophy of politics, or ideology.

❺ Public opinion can play an important part in the political system by providing information to candidates, by indicating support or opposition to the president and Congress, and by setting limits on government action through public pressure.

QUESTIONS FOR REVIEW AND DISCUSSION

❶ Should public opinion polls be regulated so that consumers can be assured that these polls are accurate and complete? How much harm is done by the overuse of polls and the reporting of inaccurate poll data?

❷ Should public opinion have more influence over public policy than do elections? To what extent should the president and the members of Congress consider public opinion when deciding on policies? What are some of the limits on the value of public opinion as a way to decide public policy?

❸ How are opinions formed on issues or on politicians? Think about your own opinions on health-care policy, for example. What factors—demographic, political, social, or informational—are influencing your thinking?

LOGGING ON: PUBLIC OPINION

Back | Forward | Home | Reload | Images | Open | Print | Find | Stop

Go To: http://www.public.iastate.edu/~sws/homepage.html

What's New? | What's Cool? | Handbook | Net Search | Net Directory | Software

The Center for Public Opinion is a nonpartisan organization that provides polling and survey services. Its services include Issue Identification, Candidate Awareness, Tracking Studies, and New Product Market Analysis. To access this information, go to

http://www.iquest.net/CFPO/cfpo2.htm

The Public Opinion Store allows you to participate in online polls. "The Public Opinion Store will collect the opinions of thousands and then share them with (of all people) our elected representatives. We believe that these are the statistics those elected officials will not want to receive but should!!!!"—says the promo. Explore this interesting site at

http://www.ssquare.com/opinopen.htm

If you do a search on Yahoo using "Public and Opinion", you'll get, among other things, some lists under "Government: Politics: Political Opinion: . . ." After the colon, they list different options: Conservative, Liberal/Progressive, or Libertarian. These contain numerous links to other sources.

Yale University Library, one of the great research institutions, has a Social Science Library and Information Services. If you want to roam around some library sources of public opinion data, this is an interesting site to visit. Their URL for "Resources for Public Opinion Research at Yale" is

http://www.library.yale.edu/socsci/printfor.html

According to its home page, the mission of National Election Studies (NES) "is to produce high quality data on voting, public opinion, and political participation that serves the research needs of social scientists, teachers, students, and policymakers concerned with understanding the theoretical and empirical foundations of mass politics in a democratic society." This is a good place to obtain information related to public opinion. Find it at

http://www.umich.edu/~nes/

SELECTED REFERENCES

Asher, Herbert. *Polling and the Public: What Every Citizen Should Know.* 3d ed. Washington, D.C.: Congressional Quarterly Press, 1995. This brief introduction to the science of polling for the citizen as consumer pays special attention to the use of polls by the media and by political candidates.

Brehm, John. *The Phantom Respondents: Opinion Surveys and Political Representation.* Ann Arbor, Mich.: University of Michigan Press, 1993. This study examines who does not participate in polls and what difference it makes to the outcomes of polls.

Donovan, Robert, and Ray Scherer. *Unsilent Revolution: Television News and American Public Life, 1948–1991.* New York: Cambridge University Press, 1992. The authors explore the effect that television has had on such institutions as politics, current events, and public opinion over the last half-century.

Erikson, Robert S., Norman R. Luttbeg, and Kent L. Tedin. *American Public Opinion: Its Origins, Content, and Impact.* 5th ed. New York: Macmillan, 1994. This book gives an overview of public opinion, its formation, and its distribution within the public. It also explores how public opinion influences public policy.

Fishkin, James S. *The Voice of the People: Public Opinion and Democracy.* New Haven, Conn.: Yale University Press, 1995. In this provocative work, Fishkin lays out his proposal for a deliberative poll and discusses the theoretical framework for using such a gathering for understanding public opinion on major issues.

Herbst, Susan. *Numbered Voices: How Opinion Polling Has Shaped American Politics.* Chicago: University of Chicago Press, 1993. In this study, Herbst inquires into the American fascination with counting opinions and how opinion polls and their results have come to play such an important role in American politics.

Langston, Thomas S. *With Reverence and Contempt: How Americans Think about Their President.* Baltimore, Md.: Johns Hopkins University Press, 1995. This is a qualitative study of how Americans regard the president and the presidency. The author looks at the topic both historically and in terms of reforms that might improve the relationship between the people and the president.

Lavrakas, Paul J., Michael W. Traugott, and Peter V. Miller, eds. *Presidential Polls and the News Media.* Boulder, Colo.: Westview, 1995. The editors, who are preeminent scholars of public opinion, present a set of original essays that include works on exit polling, newspaper coverage of polls, and the character issue in the 1992 election.

McCombs, Maxwell, Edna Einsiedel, and David Weaver. *Contemporary Public Opinions: Issues and the News.* Hilldale, N.J.: Lawrence Erlbaum, 1991. The authors look at how the news media and other forms of information transmission influence the formation of public opinion.

Page, Benjamin I., and Robert Y. Shapiro. *The Rational Public: Fifty Years of Trends in Americans' Policy Preferences.* Chicago: University of Chicago Press, 1992. An examination of public opinion data over more than five decades leads to the conclusion that public opinions are fairly stable and rational and that opinions do have an influence on public policy over time.

Zaller, John R. *The Nature and Origins of Mass Opinion.* New York: Cambridge University Press, 1992. Zaller focuses on the role of the mass media in generating public opinion on public policy, civil rights issues, trust in government, presidential actions, and other matters.

8
Interest Groups

CHAPTER OUTLINE

★ The Role of Interest Groups

★ Major Interest Groups

★ Interest Group Strategies

★ Regulating Lobbyists

★ Interest Groups and Representative Democracy

There Were No More PACs?

BACKGROUND

IN THE EARLY 1970S, CONGRESS BEGAN TO REFORM THE FINANCING OF POLITICAL CAMPAIGNS DUE TO THE INCREASING INFLUENCE OF INDIVIDUAL CITIZENS WHO GAVE ENORMOUS SUMS OF MONEY TO THEIR FAVORITE CANDIDATES. ONE RESULT OF THE REFORMS WAS TO PERMIT THE FORMATION OF POLITICAL ACTION COMMITTEES (PACS) BY CORPORATIONS, GROUPS OF PRIVATE CITIZENS, OR OTHER ASSOCIATIONS. LABOR UNIONS HAD BEEN ABLE TO FORM PACS FOR MANY YEARS. SINCE THE EARLY 1970S, MORE THAN 4,500 PACS HAVE BEEN FORMED, MOST OF THEM BY CORPORATIONS OR OTHER INDEPENDENT GROUPS. CRITICS CHARGE THAT CANDIDATES HAVE BECOME TOO DEPENDENT ON PAC CONTRIBUTIONS AND TOO BEHOLDEN TO PAC DEMANDS.

WHAT IF THERE WERE NO MORE PACS?

If there were no more PACs, the basic structure of campaign financing would be altered totally. Because PACs now provide the bulk of contributions for political campaigns, especially for members of Congress, new rules would be necessary for regulating campaign contributions.

One solution would be to return to the earlier rules, which allowed individuals to give very large contributions to candidates or political parties. This would permit very wealthy individuals or families to support their candidate and, perhaps, to maintain considerable influence over that candidate after he or she is elected. At the same time, without PACs the influence of interest groups and their individual members would be reduced greatly.

Another way to pay for campaign expenses would be to encourage individual contributions but severely limit the amount. The total amount of campaign funds would drop precipitously, and candidates would need to spend almost all of their time raising small amounts of money. Given the high cost of television campaign ads, the need to spend a majority of time on fund-raising activities might discourage many excellent candidates from running for office. At the same time, wealthy candidates could spend their own funds to pay for the campaign.

PUBLIC FINANCING

Yet another solution would be to provide public financing for campaigns. Congress has considered such funding on a number of occasions. Although public financing seems to be the "fair" way to provide support for campaigns, it is always favored more by new candidates than by incumbent representatives and senators. Incumbents fear that their seats will be much less secure because equal funding will give more help to challengers. In addition, with the increased concern for eliminating the federal budget deficit, it is difficult to sell the idea of spending large amounts of public funds on the kinds of campaign advertising that have been utilized in recent years.

Additionally, public funding takes all of the voters' voices out of campaigns. No individual or group could express its preferences or views through campaign contributions if all campaign financing were provided by the government. Civil liberties groups are concerned that public financing would reduce the freedom of speech of individual Americans and, because there would be no involvement by groups, would lead to a further emphasis on media campaigning and image policies.

It seems clear to many that PAC spending has gotten out of control and that reform of campaign financing lies ahead. It is equally clear that the outcomes of any reform of campaign financing will be controversial.

FOR CRITICAL ANALYSIS

1. *How would voters react to learning that a candidate had been funded by a single wealthy family or corporate CEO?*
2. *How important are the voices of interest groups and corporations to the election process? Could we have real choices between candidates without their voices?*

Faced by the imminent expiration of current farm legislation and the beginning of the planting season, Congress passed the first major overhaul of farming law in more than fifty years in March 1996. Despite some misgivings about the new Freedom to Farm Act, President Clinton signed the bill into law. (More details on the act are given in Chapter 16.) American agriculture has been governed by federal policies and controlled by a system of price supports and subsidies since the Great Depression. That system created a series of artificial prices for many crops, including sugar, peanuts, dairy products, and tobacco. The new law phases out many of the **subsidies,** allows farmers to decide what to plant, and moves much of the farming industry into an environment of free-market competition.

The debate over the new legislation involved the members of Congress, the farmers from their respective states and districts, **interest groups** representing growers of specific crops, farmers in general, consumer groups, and the giant corporations that buy the crops. Each of these groups had access to legislators through the **political action committees (PACs)** that had contributed to their election campaigns. Such a debate might be quite different, as the *What If . . .* that opens the chapter suggests, if PACs no longer existed.

During the struggle to write the new legislation, the farm lobbies split into different factions, due, for the most part, to the new realities of foreign trade. Those farmers, such as corn and wheat producers, who see expanding markets for their crops overseas and the companies who trade in those crops favored a free-market system that allows farmers to decide how much to plant and what crops to plant. Farmers who saw only domestic markets for their crops and who were threatened by foreign imports wanted to continue receiving price supports and crop controls from the government. Consumer groups opposed much of the new law because, although free-market farming might lower prices for some crops, in other years prices might rise, thus increasing food prices for ordinary families. Regional debates also broke out. The New England dairy farmers, for example, sought higher prices and protection through a regional pricing agreement, while other regions were willing to phase out dairy supports.

At the end of the debate, Republicans generally were pleased that the new farm legislation would reduce the regulation of farmers, although Democrats feared that the government safety net that protects farmers might have been destroyed.

SUBSIDY

Financial assistance given by the government to business firms or individuals.

INTEREST GROUP

An organized group of individuals sharing common objectives who actively attempt to influence policymakers in all three branches of the government and at all levels. Also called *pressure group* or *lobby*.

POLITICAL ACTION COMMITTEE (PAC)

A committee set up by and representing a corporation, labor union, or special interest group. PACs raise and give campaign donations on behalf of the organizations or groups they represent.

Lobbying activity becomes most intensive the day a vote is being taken on an important issue. Here lobbyists are working frantically on the day that the North American Free Trade Agreement vote was taken in 1993. Not surprisingly, lobbyists are often found in the lobbies of Congress.

THE ROLE OF INTEREST GROUPS

The passage of the Freedom to Farm Act signaled a change in direction in the farming sector of the United States. It involved serious battles between interest groups representing different crops and regions of the nation, consumer groups, corporations who manufacture food products, and multinational corporate interests.

Interests, however, are also likely to be represented by more ordinary people who make their points in Congress and the statehouses of America. When a businesswoman contacts her state representative about a proposed change in the law, she is lobbying the government. When farmers descend on Washington, D.C., in tractors or Americans with disabilities gather in the corridors of city hall, they are also interest groups lobbying their representatives. Protected by the First Amendment's guarantee of the right to assemble and petition the government for the redress of grievances, individuals have joined together in voluntary associations to try to influence the government since the Boston Tea Party (see Chapter 2), which involved, after all, an eighteenth-century trade issue.

As pluralist theories suggest, the structure of American government invites the participation of interest groups. The governmental system has many points of access or places in the decision-making process where interest groups may focus an attack. If a bill opposed by a group passes the Senate, the lobbying efforts shift to the House of Representatives or to the president to seek a veto. If, in spite of all efforts, the legislation passes, the group may even lobby the executive agency or bureau that is supposed to implement the law and hope to influence the way in which the legislation is applied. In some cases, interest groups carry their efforts into the court system, either by filing lawsuits or filing briefs as "friends of the court." The constitutional features of separation of powers and checks and balances encourage interest groups in their efforts.

A Nation of Joiners?

Alexis de Tocqueville (1805–1859), a French social historian and traveler, first commented on Americans' predilection for group action.

Alexis de Tocqueville observed in 1834 that "in no country of the world has the principle of association been more successfully used or applied to a greater multitude of objectives than in America."[1] The French traveler was amazed at the degree to which Americans formed groups to solve civic problems, establish social relationships, and speak for their economic or political interests. Perhaps James Madison, when he wrote *Federalist Paper* No. 10 (see Appendix D), had already judged the character of his country's citizens similarly. He supported the creation of a large republic with several states to encourage the formation of many interests. The multitude of interests, in Madison's view, would work to discourage the formation of an oppressive larger minority or majority interest.

Surely, neither Madison nor de Tocqueville foresaw the formation of more than a hundred thousand associations in the United States. Poll data show that more than two-thirds of all Americans belong to at least one group or association. While the majority of these affiliations could not be classified as "interest groups" in the political sense, Americans do understand the principles of working in groups. As noted in Chapter 1, some scholars maintain that this penchant for group action supports a pluralist interpretation of American politics, in which most government policies become the work of group con-

---

[1]Alexis de Tocqueville, *Democracy in America*, Vol. 1, edited by Phillips Bradley (New York: Knopf, 1980), p. 191.

POLITICS AND CIVIC PARTICIPATION
Are Americans Really "Bowling Alone"?

In a series of recent articles, Robert Putnam, a professor at Harvard University, has commented on the decline of civic participation in the United States.* He calls the phenomenon "Bowling Alone" and sees it as a symbol of the state of democracy in America. Putnam claims not only that voter turnout is declining but that participation in such organizations as the PTA, the Red Cross, the Girl Scouts, and even bowling leagues is also on the decline. He notes that only gardening and other such "hobby" clubs seem to be holding onto their members.

Why is this a serious problem? Putnam proposes that every society is held together and functions because it has accumulated a certain amount of *social capital* or interrelationships of trust that allow people to work and live together. The declining membership in civic organizations may signal a decline in our ability to maintain the stability of American society.

What are the causes of this decline in civic participation? After looking at a number of potential causes, including the increased number of women in the work force, the decline of stable marriages, the pressures of modern jobs, and the suburbanization of our cities, Putnam suggests that the decline has a generational cause. Americans born between 1910 and 1940 seem to be the age group that is most civic minded and most inclined to express social trust. Those born since 1940 demonstrate the declining levels of participation that he fears. One change in society that might account for this is the advent of television as a primary source of entertainment, replacing social interaction.

Some scholars have criticized Putnam and have produced data that indicate that the decline does not exist. Everett Carl Ladd examined poll and membership data and found opposite results.† For example, while PTA membership declined 56 percent between 1962 and 1982, it has increased 28 percent since then. The accompanying graph shows that the percentage of people who are not members of organizations is about where it was twenty years ago, as is the percentage of those who have three or more memberships. Ladd also notes that in the sphere of political activities, although participation in direct campaign work is down, contact with public officials, contributions to campaigns, and work on local political issues have increased over the last two decades.

For Critical Analysis

What motivates people to join groups? Are those motivational forces getting stronger or weaker?

*See the following articles by Robert Putnam: "Tuning In, Tuning Out: The Strange Disappearance of Social Capital in America," *PS: Political Science and Politics*, December 1995, pp. 664–683; and "Bowling Alone, Revisited," *The Responsive Community*, Vol. 18 (Spring 1995), p. 33.

†Everett Carl Ladd, "The Data Just Don't Show Erosion of America's 'Social Capital,'" *The Public Perspective*, June/July 1996, pp. 1–6.

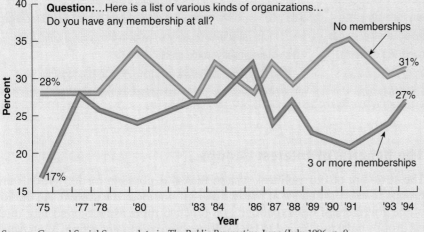

Question: ...Here is a list of various kinds of organizations... Do you have any membership at all?

No memberships — 31%

3 or more memberships — 27%

28%

17%

(X-axis: Year — '75 '77 '78 '80 '83 '84 '86 '87 '88 '89 '90 '91 '93 '94)
(Y-axis: Percent — 15 20 25 30 35 40)

SOURCE: General Social Survey data in *The Public Perspective*, June/July 1996, p. 9.

flict and compromise. (The Freedom to Farm Act, discussed earlier, resulted from such a process.) Some critics might say that the drive to organize interests can go too far, resulting in "hyperpluralism," meaning that so many powerful interests are competing that no real policy change can take place. Furthermore, it is possible that interest groups can become so powerful that the needs and demands of ordinary citizens can be ignored (see the discussion of interest groups and representative democracy later in this chapter).

Recently, American society has been faulted for a perceived decline in participation in group activities, a decline that may threaten society's ability to maintain itself. The debate over this issue is discussed in this chapter's feature entitled *Politics and Civic Participation: Are Americans Really "Bowling Alone"?*

CRITICAL PERSPECTIVE
The Logic of Collective Action

One puzzle that has fascinated political scientists is the question of why some individuals join interest groups, whereas a great many more Americans do not. Everyone has some interest that could benefit from government action. For many groups, however, those remain unorganized interests, or latent interests. Consider the women's movement. Until the 1960s, the interests of women in equal employment or equal educational opportunities had no representation. Even today, the membership of women's groups such as the National Organization for Women (NOW) or Women Employed is but a fraction of the women who share their goals.

It may be, according to the theory of Mancur Olson, that it simply is not rational for individuals to join most groups. His theory of collective action, first published in 1965, is controversial, but it offers an intriguing explanation for interest group membership and strength.

Olson introduces the idea of the "collective good." This concept refers to any public benefit that, if available to any member of the community, cannot be denied to any other member, whether or not he or she participated in the effort to gain the good. For example, women who regard themselves as antifeminists, or at least who would never join such an organization as NOW, still may avail themselves of equal employment opportunities although they never participated in the effort to change the laws. So equal employment is seen as a collective good.

Although collective benefits are usually thought of as coming from such public goods as clean air or national defense, benefits are also bestowed by the government on subsets of the public. The price subsidies to dairy farmers or loans to college students are examples. Olson uses economic theory to propose that it is not rational for interested individuals to join groups that work for group benefits. In fact, it is often more rational for the individual to wait for others to procure the benefits and then share them.

Using agriculture as an example, Olson suggests that the solution to overproduction is for all farmers to cut production. The rational farmer, however, seeing that a small cutback will not really change the overall output, would be smarter to grow as much as possible so that if others cut production, prices would rise, and he or she would profit from their actions. In the same fashion, individuals who would like to obtain a government benefit would probably find it more rational to let others invest in the political effort from which they similarly would profit.

If so little incentive exists for individuals to join together, why are there thousands of interest groups lobbying in Washington?

The Benefits of Interest Groups

The structure of our political system makes it possible for individuals and groups to exert influence at many different points in the system. As the role of the government has expanded and touched more aspects of society, interest groups have multiplied to try to influence government action. Most American governments have legislative, executive, and judicial branches. If, for example, the state legislature passes a law that may hurt a local industry, then the representatives of that industry, the employees whose jobs may be affected, and the citizens of the town in which the industry is located may well feel that they should express their dissatisfaction and try to have the law changed. They may attempt to influence the governor, who could veto the legislation, or they may concentrate on the bureaucracy to forestall the law's implementation. The newly formed interest group may try to block the legislation in the courts. At the next election, the group may try to defeat those representatives who voted for the bill. If it receives no satisfaction at the state level, the group may try to move the debate to the federal level. All of the institutions of government offer it similar access under the First Amendment

CRITICAL PERSPECTIVE
The Logic of Collective Action, Continued

Olson's theory holds that if the contribution of an individual *will* make a difference to the effort, then it is worth it to the individual to join. Thus, smaller groups, which seek benefits only for a small proportion of the population, are more likely to enroll members who will give time and money to the cause. Larger groups, which represent general public interests (the women's movement or Common Cause, for example), will have a difficult time getting individuals to join.

Olson's theory seems to have considerable validity. Certainly, the smaller, more cohesive groups have a larger presence in Washington than their sizes would warrant. Furthermore, these groups seem to have highly motivated members who will pressure their representatives to achieve their goals. If this aspect of Olson's theory is true, then smaller interests will always be overrepresented compared with the public interest.

Some larger interest groups, however, such as the National Education Association (NEA) or the AFL-CIO, are also successful. Olson says that groups can increase their memberships by offering incentives to members. The NEA, for example, provides information, publications, insurance plans, and educational assistance to teachers. Furthermore, many organizations offer such benefits as free travel services (the American Automobile Association), free

admissions to zoos (the Audubon Society), or free admissions to conventions (the American Legion). It is also true that if the cost of membership is low and the group provides other benefits, such as social opportunities, individuals may join, regardless of economic calculations. For the poorer members of the community, however, any cost of group membership is probably too high. Thus, interest groups tend to be middle- and upper-class organizations.

Olson's theory presents complications for a democratic society. If groups that are smallest are likely to be the most cohesive and determined to get benefits, the public interest may be injured. Similarly, if individuals who need the most assistance from the government—the least advantaged—are least likely to organize, policies that extend benefits to them are less likely to be promoted.*

For Critical Analysis

1. What benefits have you gained from groups that you have joined?

2. Why have farmers remained such a potent political group?

*For further reading on this complex and interesting theory, see Mancur Olson, *The Logic of Collective Action* (Cambridge, Mass.: Harvard University Press, 1965).

---

to the Constitution, which guarantees citizens the right to assemble and petition the government for the redress of grievances.

Individuals join interest groups for a variety of reasons. Obviously, the proliferation of interest groups and the growth in their membership require a reciprocity of interests. An interest group must give individuals an incentive to become members of the group, and members of the group must have their needs satisfied through the group's activities, or they will no longer participate. (See this chapter's *Critical Perspective* for a broader look at the reasons for interest group activity.)

Solidary Incentives. Interest groups offer **solidary incentives** for their members. Solidary incentives include companionship, a sense of belonging, and the pleasure of associating with others. Although the National Audubon Society was founded originally to save the snowy egret from extinction, most members join today to learn more about birds and to meet and share their pleasure with other individuals who enjoy bird watching as a hobby. Even though the incentive might be solidary for many members, the society nonetheless also pursues an active political agenda, working to preserve the

SOLIDARY INCENTIVE

A reason or motive having to do with the desire to associate with others and to share with others a particular interest or hobby.

environment and to protect endangered species. Most members may not play any part in working toward larger, more national goals unless the organization can convince them to take political action or unless some local environmental issue arises.

Material Incentives.   For other individuals, interest groups offer direct **material incentives.** A case in point is the American Association of Retired Persons (AARP), which provides discounts, insurance plans, and organized travel opportunities for its members. Because of its exceptionally low dues ($8 annually) and the benefits gained through membership in AARP, it has become the largest—and a very powerful—interest group in the United States. AARP can claim to represent the interests of millions of senior citizens and can show that they actually have joined the group. For most seniors, the material incentives outweigh the membership costs.

Many other interest groups offer indirect material incentives for their members. Such groups as the American Dairy Association or the National Association of Automobile Dealers do not give discounts or freebies to their members, but they do offer indirect benefits and rewards by, for example, protecting the material interests of their members from government policymaking that is injurious to their industry or business.

Purposive Incentives.   Interest groups also offer the opportunity for individuals to pursue political, economic, or social goals through joint action. Such **purposive incentives** offer individuals the satisfaction of taking action for the sake of their beliefs or principles. The individuals who belong to groups focusing on the abortion issue have joined those groups because they are concerned about the issue of whether abortions should be made available to the public. People join such groups because they feel strongly enough about the issues to support the groups' work with money and time.

Interest Groups and Social Movements

Interest groups are often spawned by mass **social movements.** Such movements represent demands by a large segment of the population for change in

MATERIAL INCENTIVE

A reason or motive having to do with economic benefits or opportunities.

PURPOSIVE INCENTIVE

A reason or motive having to do with ethical beliefs or ideological principles.

SOCIAL MOVEMENT

A movement that represents the demands of a large segment of the public for political, economic, or social change.

President Clinton is shown here addressing the American Association of Retired Persons (AARP), which has become one of the most powerful lobbying groups in America. As the population ages, a larger percentage of Americans are over 50. Any president knows the importance of keeping such an important interest group happy. Through its lobbying efforts, the AARP has been effective in preventing any significant reductions in the growth of Social Security benefits.

the political, economic, or social system. Social movements are often the first expression of latent discontent with the contemporary system. They may be the authentic voice of weaker or oppressed groups in society that do not have the means or standing to organize as interest groups. For example, the women's movement of the mid-nineteenth century suffered social disapproval from most mainstream political and social leaders. Because women were unable to vote or take an active part in the political system, it was difficult for women who desired greater freedoms to organize formal groups. After the Civil War, when more women became active in professional life, the first real women's rights group, the National Suffrage Association, came into being.

African Americans found themselves in an even more disadvantaged situation after the end of the Reconstruction period. Not only were they unable to exercise political rights in many southern and border states, but also participation in any form of organization could lead to economic ruin, physical harassment, or even death. The civil rights movement of the 1950s and 1960s was clearly a social movement. Although there were several formal organizations that worked to support the movement—including the Southern Christian Leadership Conference, the National Association for the Advancement of Colored People, and the Urban League—only a social movement could generate the kinds of civil disobedience that took place in hundreds of towns and cities across the country.

Social movements are often precursors of interest groups. They may generate interest groups with specific goals that successfully recruit members through the incentives the group offers. In the case of the women's movement of the 1960s, the National Organization for Women was formed out of a demand to end gender-segregated job advertising in newspapers.

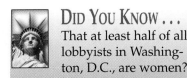

MAJOR INTEREST GROUPS

Thousands of groups exist to influence government. Among the major types of interest groups are those that represent the main sectors of the economy—business, agricultural, and labor groups. In addition, there are many groups whose purpose is to protect the interests of public employees and professionals. In more recent years, a number of "public interest" organizations have been formed to represent the needs of the general citizenry, including some "single-issue" groups. The interests of foreign governments and foreign businesses are also represented in the American political arena. The staff size, membership, and PAC affiliation of some major interest groups are shown in Table 8–1.

Business Interest Groups

Thousands of trade and business organizations attempt to influence government policies. Some groups target a single regulatory unit, whereas others try to effect major policy changes. Three big business pressure groups are consistently effective: (1) the National Association of Manufacturers (NAM), (2) the U.S. Chamber of Commerce, and (3) the Business Roundtable. The annual budget of the NAM is more than $15 million, which it collects in dues from about 12,500 relatively large corporations. Sometimes called the National Chamber, the U.S. Chamber of Commerce represents more than 180,000 businesses. Dues from its members, which include upward of 3,500 local chambers of commerce, approach $30 million a year. Two hundred of

Table 8–1

Characteristics of Selected Interest Groups

Name (Founded)	Staff Size	Members (individuals or as noted)	PAC
Business/Economic			
Business Roundtable (1972)	16	200 corporations	No
The Conference Board, Inc. (1916)	310	3,000 labor unions, colleges & universities, etc.	No
National Association of Manufacturers (1895)	185	12,500 companies	No
U.S. Chamber of Commerce (1912)	1,700	180,000 companies, state & local chambers of commerce, etc.	National Chamber Alliance for Politics
Civil/Constitutional Rights			
AIDS Coalition to Unleash Power (ACT UP–New York) (1987)	volunteer	4,000 (NYC) + national branches	No
American Association of Retired Persons (1958)	1,585	33,000,000	No
American Civil Liberties Union (1920)	162	280,000	No
Amnesty International USA (1961)	91	386,000	No
Handgun Control, Inc. (1974)	28	360,000	Handgun Control Voter Education Fund
Leadership Conference on Civil Rights, Inc. (1950)	8	80 national organizations	No
League of United Latin American Citizens (LULAC) (1929)	5	110,000	No
Mexican-American Legal Defense and Educational Fund (1968)	63	—	No
NAACP Legal Defense and Educational Fund, Inc. (1940)	79	—	No
National Abortion Rights Action League (1969)	45	450,000	NARAL PAC
National Association for the Advancement of Colored People (1909)	100	345,000	No
National Gay and Lesbian Task Force (1973)	15	17,000	No
National Organization for Women, Inc. (1966)	32	250,000	National NOW PAC & National Equality PAC
National Rifle Association of America (1871)	550	2,650,000	Political Victory Fund
National Right to Life Committee, Inc. (1973)	55	—	National Right to Life PAC

the largest corporations in the United States send their chief executive officers to the Business Roundtable. This organization is based in New York, but it does its lobbying in Washington, D.C. Established in 1972, the Roundtable was designed to promote a more aggressive view of business interests in general, cutting across specific industries. Dues paid by the member corporations are determined by the companies' wealth.

Agricultural Interest Groups

American farmers and their workers represent about 2 percent of the U.S. population. In spite of this, farmers' influence on legislation beneficial to their interests has been enormous. As discussed in this chapter's introduction, farmers have succeeded in their aims because they have very strong interest groups. They are geographically dispersed and therefore have many repre-

Table 8–1, *Continued*

Characteristics of Selected Interest Groups

NAME (FOUNDED)	STAFF SIZE	MEMBERS (INDIVIDUALS OR AS NOTED)	PAC
Civil/Constitutional Rights—*continued*			
National Urban League (1910)	185	1,600,000	No
Planned Parenthood Federation of America, Inc. (1916)	253	—	No
Women's Legal Defense Fund (1971)	24	1,500	No
Community/Grassroots			
The American Society for the Prevention of Cruelty to Animals (1866)	203	400,000	No
Association of Community Organizations for Reform Now (ACORN) (1970)	200	80,000	No
Mothers Against Drunk Driving (1980)	260	2,950,000	No
National Anti-Vivisection Society (1929)	15	—	No
Environmental			
Environmental Defense Fund (1967)	110	150,000	No
Greenpeace USA (1971)	250	2,100,000	No
Izaak Walton League of America (1922)	23	52,700	No
League of Conservation Voters (1970)	67	60,000	LCV is a political committee
National Audubon Society (1905)	315	600,000	No
National Wildlife Federation (1936)	608	5,600,000	No
The Nature Conservancy (1951)	1,150	580,000	No
Sierra Club (1892)	325	650,000	Sierra Club Political Committee
The Wilderness Society (1935)	136	383,000	No
World Wildlife Fund (1948)	244	1,000,000	No
International Affairs			
American Israel Public Affairs Committee (1954)	100+	55,000	No
Human Rights Watch (1978)	60	—	No
Accuracy in Media (1969)	15	25,000	No

SOURCE: Foundation for Public Affairs, *Public Interest Profiles 1995–1996* (Washington, D.C.: Congressional Quarterly Press, 1995.)

sentatives and senators to speak for them. The American Farm Bureau Federation, established in 1919, has 3 million members. It was instrumental in getting government guarantees of "fair" prices during the Great Depression in the 1930s.[2] Another important agricultural special interest organization is the National Farmers' Union (NFU).

Labor Interest Groups

Interest groups representing the **labor movement** date back to at least 1886 with the formation of the American Federation of Labor (AFL). In 1955, the AFL joined forces with the Congress of Industrial Organizations (CIO).

LABOR MOVEMENT

Generally, the full range of economic and political expression of working-class interests; politically, the organization of working-class interests.

---

[2]The Agricultural Adjustment Act of 1933 (declared unconstitutional) was replaced by the 1937 Agricultural Adjustment Act and later changed and amended several times.

Union strikers line the streets outside the Caterpillar factory protesting the use of nonunion workers, or "scabs," to replace them on the assembly line.

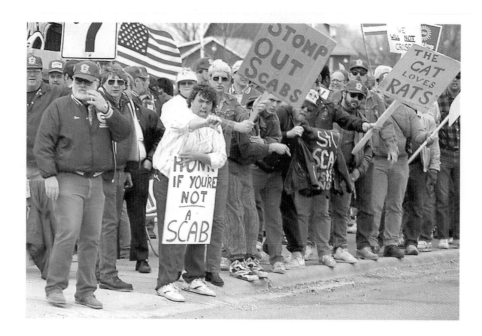

Today, the combined AFL-CIO is an enormous union with a membership exceeding 13 million workers. In a sense, the AFL-CIO is a union of unions.

The political arm of the AFL-CIO is the Committee on Political Education (COPE). COPE's activities are funded by voluntary contributions from union members. COPE has been active in state and national campaigns since 1956.

Other unions are also active politically. One of the most widely known is the International Brotherhood of Teamsters, which was led by Jimmy Hoffa until his expulsion in 1967 because of alleged ties with organized crime. The Teamsters Union was established initially in 1903 and today has a membership of 1.4 million and an annual budget of $73 million.

Another independent union is the United Auto Workers, founded in 1935. It now has a membership of 840,000 with an annual budget of $230 million. Also very active in labor lobbying is the United Mine Workers union, representing about 200,000 members.

Labor group pressure on Congress has been only partly successful. Although unions successfully allied themselves with civil rights groups in the 1960s, they lost on such issues as the Taft-Hartley Act of 1948, which put some limits on the right to strike and the right to organize workers. They were also frustrated in their efforts in 1975 and 1977 to enact a bill designed to facilitate the picketing of construction sites. In 1994, Congress failed to adopt proposed legislation that would have made it more difficult for companies to hire replacements for striking workers.

The role of unions in American society has weakened in recent years, as witnessed by a decline in union membership from over 30 percent of American workers in 1954 to 15.1 percent in 1996 (Figure 8–1). The strength of union membership traditionally lay with blue-collar workers. But in the age of automation and with the rise of the **service sector,** blue-collar workers in basic industries (autos, steel, and the like) represent a smaller and smaller percentage of the total working population. Because of this decline in the industrial sector of the economy, national unions are looking to nontraditional areas for their membership, including migrant farm workers, service workers, and most recently, public employees—such as police officers; firefighting personnel; and teachers, including college professors.

SERVICE SECTOR

The sector of the economy that provides services—such as food services, insurance, and education—in contrast to the sector of the economy that produces goods.

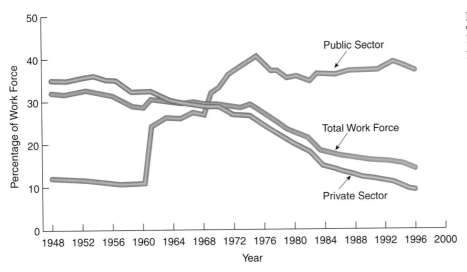

Figure 8–1
● ●
**Decline in Union Membership,
1948 to 1996**

Public Employee Interest Groups

The degree of unionization in the private sector has declined since 1965, but this has been offset by growth in the unionization of public employees. Figure 8–1 shows the growth in the public sector work force. With a total work force of more than 6.6 million, these unions are likely to continue expanding.

Both the American Federation of State, County, and Municipal Employees and the American Federation of Teachers are members of the AFL-CIO's Public Employee Department. Originally, the public employee unions started out as social and professional organizations. Over the years, they have become quite militant and are often involved in strikes. Many of these strikes are illegal, because certain public employees do not have the right to strike and essentially sign a contract so stating. In August 1981, the Professional Air Traffic Controllers Organization (PATCO), in defiance of a court order, went on strike. The issues included wage levels, long hours, excessive stress, insensitive Federal Aviation Administration management, and other problems. President Ronald Reagan, convinced that public opinion was on his side, fired the strikers. Supervisors, nonstrikers, military personnel, and new trainees were rounded up to handle the jobs vacated by the 16,000 terminated air traffic controllers. On July 27, 1982, the union folded as a trustee padlocked the PATCO headquarters office. (It is ironic that PATCO was one of only a few unions to endorse Ronald Reagan's candidacy in 1980.)

A powerful interest group lobbying on behalf of public employees is the National Education Association (NEA), a nationwide organization of about 1.8 million administrators, teachers, and others connected with education. The NEA lobbies intensively for increased public funding of education. The NEA sponsors regional and national conventions each year and has an extensive program of electronic media broadcasts, surveys, and the like.

Interest Groups of Professionals

Numerous professional organizations exist, including the American Bar Association, the Association of General Contractors of America, the Institute of Electrical and Electronic Engineers, the Screen Actors Guild, and others. Some professional groups, such as lawyers and doctors, are more influential than others due to their social status. Lawyers have a unique advantage—a large number of members of Congress share their profession. In terms of money spent on lobbying, however, one professional organization stands out head and shoulders above the rest—the American Medical Association (AMA). Founded in 1947, it is now affiliated with more than 2,000 local and state medical societies and has a total membership of 237,000 and an administrative staff of 1,000. Together with the American Dental Association, the AMA spent an estimated $3.6 million in 1994 congressional campaign contributions in its efforts to influence legislation.

Environmental Groups

Environmental interest groups are not new. The National Audubon Society was founded in 1905 to protect the snowy egret from the commercial demand for hat decorations. The patron of the Sierra Club, John Muir, worked for the creation of national parks more than ninety years ago. But the blossoming of national environmental groups with mass memberships is a relatively recent phenomenon. Since the first Earth Day, organized in 1972, many interest groups have sprung up to protect the environment in general or unique ecological niches. The groups range from the National Wildlife Federation, with a membership of more than 5.6 million and an emphasis on education, to the fairly elite Environmental Defense Fund, with a membership of 150,000 and a focus on influencing federal policy. Other groups include the Nature Conservancy, which seeks members' contributions so the organization can buy up threatened natural areas and either give them to state or local governments or manage them itself, and the more radical Greenpeace Society and Earth First.

Public Interest Groups

PUBLIC INTEREST

The best interests of the collective, overall community; the national good, rather than the narrow interests of a self-serving group.

Public interest is a difficult term to define because, as we noted earlier, there are many publics in our nation of more than 265 million. It is nearly impossible for one particular public policy to benefit everybody, which makes it practically impossible to define the public interest. Nonetheless, over the past few decades, a variety of law and lobbying organizations have been formed "in the public interest."

Nader Organizations. The most well known and perhaps the most effective public interest groups are those organized under the leadership of consumer activist Ralph Nader. The story of Ralph Nader's rise to the top began after

The *Rainbow Warrior*, the flagship of Greenpeace, is both a symbol for the environmental interest group and a resource that can be used for actions at sea to protect the environment. The *Rainbow Warrior* has acted to save dolphins, to protest oil spills, and to stop Japanese and Russian whaling.

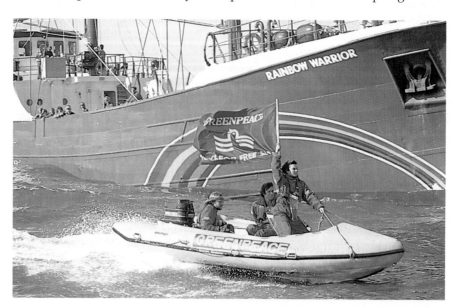

the publication, in 1965, of his book *Unsafe at Any Speed,* a lambasting critique of the purported attempt by General Motors (GM) to keep from the public detrimental information about GM's rear-engine Corvair. Partly as a result of Nader's book, Congress began to consider testimony in favor of an automobile safety bill. GM made a clumsy attempt to discredit Nader's background. Nader sued, the media exploited the story, and when GM settled out of court for $425,000, Nader became the recognized champion of consumer interests. Since then, Nader has turned over much of his income to the more than sixty public interest groups that he has formed or sponsored. In recent years, Nader has opposed tort reform legislation, among other things.

Other Public Interest Groups. Partly in response to the Nader organizations, numerous conservative public interest law firms have sprung up that are often pitted against the consumer groups in court. Some of these are the Mountain States Legal Defense Foundation, the Pacific Legal Foundation, the National Right-to-Work Legal Defense Foundation, the Washington Legal Foundation, and the Mid-Atlantic Legal Foundation.

One of the largest public interest pressure groups is Common Cause, founded in 1968, whose goal is to reorder national priorities toward "the public" and to make governmental institutions more responsive to the needs of the public. Anyone willing to pay dues of $15 a year can become a member. Members are polled regularly to obtain information about local and national issues requiring reassessment. Some of the activities of Common Cause have been (1) helping to ensure the passage of the Twenty-sixth Amendment (giving eighteen-year-olds the right to vote), (2) achieving greater voter registration in all states, (3) supporting the complete withdrawal of all U.S. forces from South Vietnam in the 1970s, and (4) promoting legislation that would limit campaign spending.

Other public interest pressure groups are active on a wide range of issues. The goal of the League of Women Voters, founded in 1920, is to educate the public on political matters. Although generally nonpartisan, it has lobbied for the Equal Rights Amendment and for government reform. The Consumer Federation of America is an alliance of about two hundred local and national organizations interested in consumer protection. The American Civil Liberties Union dates back to World War I, when, under a different name, it defended draft resisters. It generally enters into legal disputes related to Bill of Rights issues.

Ralph Nader began the movement to create public interest groups through the publication, in 1965, of his book *Unsafe at Any Speed,* which criticized General Motors for underplaying the dangers of its Corvair automobile. Since that time, he has founded a number of not-for-profit public interest groups that track business and governmental actions in specific policy arenas.

Single-Issue Groups

A number of interest groups have formed that focus on one issue. The abortion debate has created various groups opposed to abortion (such as Right to Life) and groups in favor of abortion (such as the National Abortion Rights Action League). Other single-issue groups are the National Rifle Association, the Right to Work Committee (an anti-union group), and the Hudson Valley PAC (a pro-Israel group).

Narrowly focused groups such as these may be able to call more attention to their respective causes because they have simple and straightforward goals and because their members tend to care intensely about the issues. Thus, they can easily motivate their members to contact legislators or to organize demonstrations in support of their policy goals.

Foreign Governments

Home-grown interests are not the only players in the game. Washington, D.C., is also the center for lobbying by foreign governments as well as private foreign interests. Large research and lobbying staffs are maintained by governments of the largest U.S. trading partners, such as Japan, South Korea, Canada, and the European Union (EU) countries (see this chapter's *Politics and Economics*). Even smaller nations, such as those in the Caribbean, engage lobbyists when vital legislation affecting their trade interests is considered. Frequently, these foreign interests hire former representatives or former senators to promote their positions on Capitol Hill.

INTEREST GROUP STRATEGIES

Interest groups employ a wide range of techniques and strategies to promote their policy goals. Although few groups are successful at persuading Congress and the president to endorse their programs completely, many are able to prevent legislation injurious to their members from being considered or at least to weaken such legislation. The key to success for interest groups is the ability to have access to government officials. To achieve this, interest groups and their representatives try to cultivate long-term relationships with legislators and government officials. The best of such relationships are based on mutual respect and cooperation. The interest group provides the official with excellent sources of information and assistance, and the official in turn gives the group opportunities to express its views.

The techniques used by interest groups may be divided into those that are direct and indirect. **Direct techniques** include all those ways in which the interest group and its lobbyists approach the officials personally to press their case. **Indirect techniques,** in contrast, include strategies that use the general public or individuals to influence the government for the interest group.

Direct Techniques

Lobbying, publicizing ratings of legislative behavior, and providing campaign assistance are the three main direct techniques used by interest groups.

Lobbying Techniques.   As might be guessed, the term **lobbying** comes from the activities of private citizens regularly congregating in the lobbies of legislative chambers before a session to petition legislators. In the latter part of the nineteenth century, railroad and industrial groups openly bribed state legislators to pass legislation beneficial to their interests, giving lobbying a well-deserved bad name. Today, standard lobbying techniques still include button-holing (detaining and engaging in conversation) senators and representatives in state capitols and in Washington, D.C., while they are moving from their offices to the voting chambers. Lobbyists, however, do much more than that.

Lobbyists engage in an array of activities to influence legislation and government policy. These include, at a minimum, the following:

1. Engaging in private meetings with public officials, including the president's advisers, to make known the lobbyist's clients' interests. Although acting on behalf of a client, often lobbyists furnish needed information to senators and representatives (and government agency appointees) that they could not hope to obtain on their own. It is to the lobbyist's advantage to provide accurate information so that the policymaker will rely on this source in the future.

2. Testifying before congressional committees for or against proposed legislation being considered by Congress.

3. Testifying before executive rulemaking agencies—such as the Federal

---

DIRECT TECHNIQUE

An interest group activity that involves interaction with government officials to further the group's goals.

INDIRECT TECHNIQUE

A strategy employed by interest groups that uses third parties to influence government officials.

LOBBYING

The attempt by organizations or by individuals to influence the passage, defeat, or contents of legislation and the administrative decisions of government.

POLITICS AND ECONOMICS
American and Foreign Interests: A New Alliance

Foreign nations and corporations have employed lobbyists in the United States for many years, usually working for trade preferences and other economic benefits. Some former members of Congress have become lobbyists for these nations, working for Middle Eastern or Asian states. In recent years, the amount of money spent by foreign nations and corporations has continued to grow. The accompanying figure shows that Japan spends far more than any other nation in this effort, with Canada ranking second and Germany third.

With the increase in international trade and the growth of multinational corporations, lobbyists for U.S. corporations are now likely to be working in alliances with those representing foreign nations. Boeing Corporation, the manufacturer of aircraft, frequently works with representatives of the People's Republic of China for improvement of that nation's trade status, because China is such a strong customer for its products. Canadian timber interests found an ally in the U.S. home-building industry, and IBM often works with its Japanese business partners. Sometimes a U.S. firm will take a position against another U.S. firm in trade negotiations or in lobby-

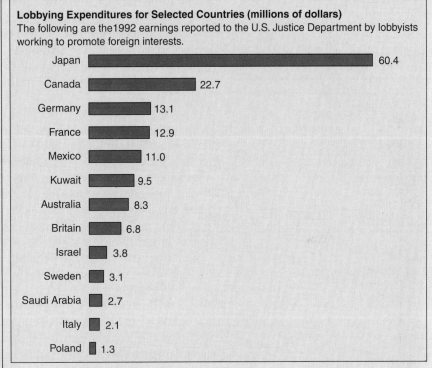

Lobbying Expenditures for Selected Countries (millions of dollars)
The following are the 1992 earnings reported to the U.S. Justice Department by lobbyists working to promote foreign interests.

Japan	60.4
Canada	22.7
Germany	13.1
France	12.9
Mexico	11.0
Kuwait	9.5
Australia	8.3
Britain	6.8
Israel	3.8
Sweden	3.1
Saudi Arabia	2.7
Italy	2.1
Poland	1.3

SOURCE: U.S. Justice Department

ing for legislation that will help it. The question arises as to whether U.S. firms might have a negative effect on the U.S. economy with these political partners.

For Critical Analysis
Should foreign corporations have the same rights to lobby Congress that domestic interest groups have?

Trade Commission or the Consumer Product Safety Commission—for or against proposed rules.

4. Assisting legislators or bureaucrats in drafting legislation or prospective regulations. Often, lobbyists can furnish legal advice on the specific details of legislation.

5. Inviting legislators to social occasions, such as cocktail parties, boating expeditions, and other events. Most lobbyists feel that contacting legislators in a more relaxed social setting is effective. The extent to which legislators feel obligated to lobbyists for entertaining them is hard to gauge.

6. Providing political information to legislators and other government officials. Often the lobbyists will have better information than the party leadership about how other legislators are going to vote. In this case, the political information they furnish may be a key to legislative success.

7. Supplying nominations for federal appointments to the executive branch.

Table 8–2

ADA Ratings for 1995

Americans for Democratic Action (ADA), a liberal political organization, tracks the votes of all senators and representatives on the set of issues that ADA thinks is most important. The "score" for each legislator is the percentage of "correct" votes from the ADA's point of view. Many other interest groups also engage in the ratings game.

SENATOR	HIGHEST RATING
Feingold, D., Wisconsin	100%
Harkin, D., Iowa	100
Wellstone, D., Minnesota	100
Kennedy, D., Massachusetts	100
Kerry, D., Massachusetts	100
Lautenberg, D., New Jersey	100
Leahy, D., Vermont	100
Levin, D., Michigan	100
Moseley-Braun, D., Illinois	100
Sarbanes, D., Maryland	100
Simon, D., Illinois	100

	LOWEST RATING
Burns, R., Montana	0%
Craig, R., Idaho	0
Helms, R., North Carolina	0
Kempthorne, R., Idaho	0
Pressler, R., South Dakota	0
Coats, R., Indiana	0
Coverdell, R., Georgia	0
Faircloth, R., North Carolina	0
Lott, R., Mississippi	0
McConnell, R., Kentucky	0
Nickles, R., Oklahoma	0
Smith, R., New Hampshire	0

SOURCE: *ADA Today,* March 1996, pp. 2–4.

The Ratings Game. Many interest groups attempt to influence the overall behavior of legislators through their rating systems. Each year, the interest group selects those votes on legislation that it feels are most important to the organization's goals. Each legislator is given a score based on the percentage of times that he or she voted in favor of the group's position. The usual scheme ranges from 0 to 100 percent. If a legislator has a score of, for example, 90 percent on the Americans for Democratic Action (ADA) rating, it means that he or she supported that group's position to a high degree (see Table 8–2). A legislator with such a high ADA score is usually considered to be very liberal. The groups that use rating systems range from the American Conservative Union to the League of Conservation Voters (an environmental group). Each year, the league identifies the twelve legislators having what it sees as the worst records on environmental issues and advertises them as the "Dirty Dozen."

Campaign Assistance. Interest groups have additional strategies to use in their attempts to influence government policies. Groups recognize that the greatest concern of legislators is to be reelected, so they focus on their campaign needs. Associations with large memberships, such as labor unions or the National Education Association, are able to provide workers for political campaigns, including precinct workers to get out the vote, volunteers to put up posters and pass out literature, and people to staff telephone banks for campaign headquarters.

In many states where membership in certain interest groups is large, candidates vie for the groups' endorsements in the campaign. Gaining those endorsements may be automatic, or it may require that the candidates participate in a debate or interview with the interest groups. Endorsements are important because an interest group usually publicizes its choices in its membership publication and because the candidate can use the endorsement in his or her campaign literature. Traditionally, labor unions such as the AFL-CIO and the UAW have endorsed Democratic party candidates. Republican candidates, however, often try to persuade union locals at least to refrain from any endorsement. Making no endorsement can then be perceived as disapproval of the Democratic party candidate.

The job of a lobbyist never stops. This Washington lobbyist is trying to convince a member of a congressperson's staff to get the congressperson to vote a particular way. While many critics of lobbyists and interest groups argue that they distort the actions of our government, the First Amendment prohibits the government from regulating their speech.

Reprinted courtesy of Larry Wright and the Detroit News.

Stung by the Republican sweep of Congress in 1994 and the decline in union membership, the AFL-CIO saw 1996 as the year in which labor could influence the outcome of the national elections. The leadership of the largest union voted to raise a war chest of $35 million to support campaign activities in 1996 and to increase membership. Most of the money would be raised through a 15-cent per member monthly assessment on each of its seventy-eight member unions. Led by their new president, John J. Sweeney, the confederated unions pledged to change the balance of power in the elections. Since the unions' contributions to individual candidates are regulated by campaign finance laws, the money, according to the leadership, would be spent for voter education and registration drives. Republicans reacted with shock at this first major effort by organized labor in many years, claiming that the fund raising was simply a campaign tactic to support the Clinton administration and to defeat Republican freshman legislators. Big business and the U.S. Chamber of Commerce voted to raise money in opposition to the labor campaign. See the feature entitled *Elections '96: Interest Groups* for a discussion of how the various groups tried to influence election outcomes.

Interest groups spent far more on electing or defeating candidates in 1996 than in any previous national election. The increase in interest group spending on the campaign was fueled by the demand for "soft money" contributions to the parties and candidates, in addition to the usual PAC spending. Interest groups and their individual members contributed large sums of money to political parties, to independent party committees, and to other "independent" committees that were spending money for educational purposes or to get out the vote, all legal activities.

Organized labor's decision to raise an additional $35 million, targeting Republican seats in the House, presented an open challenge to many business interests. In response, business groups and specific corporations raised even more money than in 1994. Perhaps because labor was openly supporting Democrats, business PAC contributions to Democratic congressional candidates dropped 20 percent in 1996.

Did the groups gain any influence with these campaign contributions? As the election results became known, Republicans believed that they had turned back the challenge from organized labor. The AFL-CIO had targeted up to thirty-two House races and won only twelve. The Christian Coalition—which, prior to the election, had distributed millions of voters' guides supporting Republican candidates—also claimed credit for keeping Republicans in control of the House. The Sierra Club, an environmental group, believed that its dollars were well spent: it claimed credit for Senator Larry Pressler's defeat in South Dakota as well as for victories in seven other Senate seats. The National Rifle Association, which spent nearly $4.5 million on races at all levels, believed that their candidates had won in 80 percent of the races. In contrast, Democrat Carolyn McCarthy, whose husband had been killed on a train, was elected to Congress on the strength of her beliefs in gun control. The question facing the 105th Congress is whether it is possible truly to curb the lavish spending by interest groups in the future.

PACs and Political Campaigns. In the last two decades, the most important form of campaign help from interest groups has become the political contribution from a group's political action committee (PAC). The 1974 Federal Election Campaign Act and its 1976 amendments allow corporations, labor unions, and special interest groups to set up PACs to raise money for candidates. For a PAC to be legitimate, the money must be raised from at least fifty volunteer donors and must be given to at least five candidates in the federal election. PACs can contribute up to $5,000 to each candidate in each election. Each corporation or each union is limited to one PAC. As you might imagine, corporate PACs obtain funds from executives in their firms, and unions obtain PAC funds from their members.

The number of PACs has grown astronomically, as has the amount they spend on elections. There were about 1,000 political action committees in 1976; by the mid-1990s, there were more than 4,600 (see Figure 8–2). The total amount of spending by PACs grew from $19 million in 1973 to an estimated $450 million in 1995–1996. Of all of the campaign money spent by House candidates in 1994, about 32 percent came from PACs.[3]

Interest groups funnel PAC money to candidates who they think can do the most good for them. Frequently, they make the maximum contribution of $5,000 per election to candidates who face little or no opposition. The summary of PAC contributions given in Figure 8–3 shows that the great bulk of campaign contributions goes to incumbent candidates rather than to challengers. Table 8–3 shows the amounts contributed by the top twenty PACs. It is clear that some PACs balance their contributions between Democratic and Republican candidates. Corporations are particularly likely to give money to Democrats in Congress as well as to Republicans, because Democratic incumbents may again chair important committees or subcommittees. Why, might you ask, would business leaders give to Democrats who may be more liberal than themselves? Interest groups see PAC contributions as a way to ensure access to powerful legislators, even if they may disagree with them some of the time. PAC contributions are, in a way, an investment in a relationship.

---

[3]Norman Ornstein, Thomas E. Mann, and Michael J. Malbin, *Vital Statistics on Congress, 1995–1996* (Washington, D.C.: Congressional Quarterly Press, 1996), p. 95.

Figure 8–2

PAC Growth, 1977 to 1995

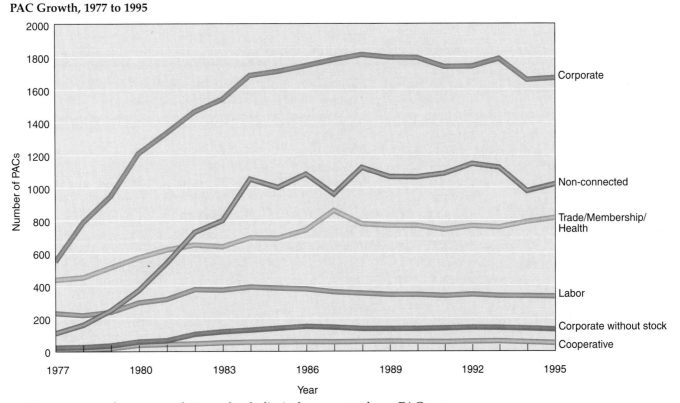

The campaign finance regulations clearly limit the amount that a PAC can give to any one candidate, but there is no limit on the amount that a PAC can spend on an independent campaign, either on behalf of a candidate or party or in opposition to one. As noted in this chapter's feature entitled *Politics in the Fifty States* on page 267, PACs set up in states may circumvent federal limits.

Figure 8–3

PAC Contributions to Congressional Candidates, 1974 to 1994

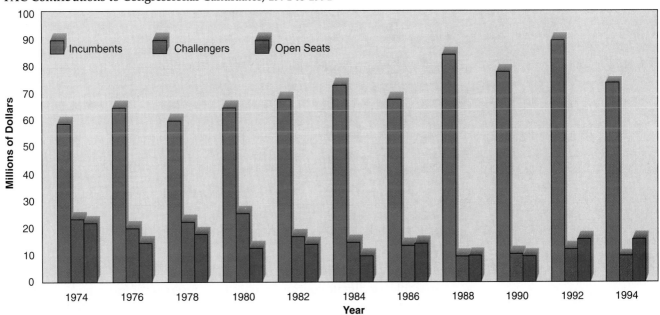

SOURCE: *Congressional Quarterly Weekly Report,* March 22, 1986, p. 657; *Federal Election Commission Report,* 1987, 1989, 1991; and *Vital Statistics on Congress, 1995–1996.*

Table 8–3

The Top Twenty PAC Contributors

Rank	Contributor	Total	PAC %	Dem %	Rep %	Principal Category
1	National Association of Realtors	$3,094,228	100%	55%	44%	Real estate
2	American Medical Association	$2,647,981	100	49	51	Doctors
3	Teamsters Union	$2,438,184	99+	92	8	Teamsters
4	National Education Association	$2,334,715	99+	93	7	Teachers unions
5	United Auto Workers	$1,801,772	99+	99	1	Manufacturing unions
6	Letter Carriers Union	$1,755,478	99+	86	14	Postal unions
7	American Federation of State/County/Municipal Employees	$1,549,720	99+	98	2	Local government unions
8	National Association of Retired Federal Employees	$1,545,122	100	76	24	Federal worker unions
9	Association of Trial Lawyers of America	$1,539,550	100	87	13	Lawyers
10	Carpenters Union	$1,526,534	99+	96	4	Contruction unions
11	National Association of Life Underwriters	$1,487,800	100	51	49	Life insurance
12	Machinists/Aerospace Workers Union	$1,487,495	99+	98	1	Manufacturing unions
13	AT&T	$1,477,200	98	57	43	Long distance
14	American Bankers Association	$1,473,061	100	55	45	Commercial banks
15	National Association of Home Builders	$1,362,550	99+	48	52	Residential construction
16	Laborers Union	$1,359,119	99+	92	8	Construction unions
17	National Auto Dealers Association	$1,313,900	100	38	62	Auto dealers
18	International Brotherhood of Electrical Workers	$1,257,920	99+	97	2	Communication unions
19	Air Line Pilots Association	$1,167,797	100	81	19	Air transport unions
20	American Institute of CPAs	$1,089,294	99+	56	44	Accountants

SOURCE: Adapted from Larry Makinson, *Open Secrets: The Cash Constituents of Congress* (Washington, D.C.: Congressional Quarterly Press, 1992).

Indirect Techniques

Interest groups can try to influence government policy by working through third parties—which may be constituents, the general public, or other groups. Indirect techniques mask the interest group's own activities and make the effort appear to be spontaneous. Furthermore, legislators and government officials are often more impressed by contacts from constituents than from an interest group's lobbyist.

Generating Public Pressure. In some instances, interest groups try to produce a "groundswell" of public pressure to influence the government. Such efforts may include advertisements in national magazines and newspapers, mass mailings, television publicity, and demonstrations. Computers and satellite links make communication efforts even more effective (see this chapter's *Politics and Technology* on page 268). Interest groups may commission polls to find out what the public's sentiments are and then publicize the results. The intent of this activity is to convince policymakers that public opinion overwhelmingly supports the group's position.

Some corporations and interest groups also engage in a practice that might be called **climate control.** This strategy calls for public relations efforts that are aimed at improving the public image of the industry or group and not necessarily related to any specific political issue. Contributions by corporations and groups in support of public television programs, sponsorship of special events, and commercials extolling the virtues of corporate research are examples of climate control. By building a reservoir of favorable public opinion, groups believe it less likely that their legislative goals will be met with opposition by the public.

CLIMATE CONTROL

The use of public relations techniques to create favorable public opinion toward an interest group, industry, or corporation

POLITICS AND THE FIFTY STATES
State PACs for Federal Candidates

Although candidates for the House, the Senate, and the White House can raise money from PACs (political action committees) in a number of ways, all PACs registered with the Federal Election Commission must abide by the limits on expenditures established in 1974. Such PACs can contribute only $5,000 per candidate per election, although there is no limit on their total amount of contributions in an election cycle. Candidates themselves can accept only $1,000 in contributions from individual donors and $5,000 from each PAC for their reelection campaign.

Many candidates and members of Congress have found a way to evade these federal regulations by establishing "state PACs," or political action committees chartered in the states and thus subject only to state regulation. Although some states do have limits on contributions from state PACs to state election campaigns, few states have limits on what a state PAC can spend on the campaign of a federal candidate for the House or the Senate. Nor are state limits on what individuals can contribute to a state PAC as stringent.

Funds that are given to a state PAC are not supposed to go to a federal candidate's campaign funds, so these funding mechanisms are often borderline with respect to their legality. The funds can, however, be spent to assist other candidates at the state level, provide prizes and contributions for local charitable or community events, and pay for local appearances that are not related directly to the campaign.

One example of such a state PAC is the Torricelli PAC, which was established in New Jersey to support the efforts of Robert Torricelli, a Democratic representative who ran for the Senate in 1996. Torricelli's state PAC has raised more than $600,000 since 1984 and has received contributions from corporations far in excess of what they could give to a federal PAC. Torricelli says that the money is spent mostly for other candidates in New Jersey because, as he puts it, "the collapse of local party organizations has put a good deal of the burden on Members of Congress to help other candidates."* Other state PACs that have amassed considerable funds include those of Senator Alfonse D'Amato of New York (a Republican) and Representative William Lipinski of Illinois (a Democrat). As candidates face increasing campaign costs, it is likely that more and more will use state PACs and other types of fund raising to meet their expenses.

For Critical Analysis
Why would a state such as New Jersey or Illinois have fewer rules governing campaign finance than does the federal government? Why would states provide such loopholes in the campaign financing system?

*As quoted by Eliza Newlin Carney in "Backdoor PACs," *The National Journal*, March 2, 1996, p. 470.

Using Constituents as Lobbyists. One of the most effective interest group activities is the use of constituents to lobby for the group's goals. In the "shotgun" approach, the interest group tries to mobilize large numbers of constituents to write, phone or send electronic mail to their legislators or the president. Often, the group provides postcards or form letters for constituents to fill out and mail. These efforts are only effective on Capitol Hill when there is an extraordinary number of responses, because legislators know that the voters did not initiate the communication on their own.

A more influential variation of this technique uses only important constituents. Known as the "rifle" technique, or the "Utah plant manager's theory," the interest group contacts an influential constituent, such as the manager of a local plant in Utah, to contact the senator from Utah.[4] Because the constituent is seen as being responsible for many jobs or other resources, the legislator is more likely to listen carefully to the constituent's concerns about legislation than to a paid lobbyist.

Building Alliances. Another indirect technique used by interest groups is to form an alliance with other groups concerned about the same legislation.

---

[4]Kay Lehman Schlozman and John T. Tierney, *Organized Interests and American Democracy* (New York: Harper & Row, 1986), p. 293.

POLITICS AND TECHNOLOGY
High-tech Lobbying

Interest group activity has exploded in recent years. One particularly important aspect of lobbying in this new era is the use of modern technology to enhance the role of pressure groups.

Lobbying organizations have for many years employed "grass-roots" tactics for influencing the outcomes of government decisions. These tactics have included soliciting citizens to send letters to members of Congress, mobilizing protest movements, and endorsing or attacking candidates during election campaigns.

What is new, exciting, and potentially crucial is the availability of computer-based technology and expanded telecommunications facilities for communicating more effectively and more quickly to targeted segments of the population. For example, consider computerized letter-generating programs. After dialing an 800 telephone number, the caller leaves his or her name and address on a recording, which then generates letters to members of Congress over that person's name. Computerized letter-generating programs also target individuals who are likely to have an interest in legislation.

Television technology has allowed pressure groups to increase their role in American politics. Such use is particularly striking in the case of the New Right groups on the conservative side of the political spectrum. Conservative activist Paul Weyrich has created National Empowerment Television (NET). NET is a satellite network that allows local groups to see public officials debate the issues and to ask questions through an interactive connection. Weyrich believes that the impact on elected officials of his viewing groups and concerns is much stronger than the usual letters and telegrams.

Business pressure groups have adopted the tactics that have been so successful for the New Right. Apart from the more traditional efforts of soliciting letters, telegrams, and phone calls to elected officials, the National Chamber of Commerce has a major high-technology communications system available to send its interpretations of pending legislation and other matters to members; a monthly magazine (*Nation's Business*) with a circulation of 1.25 million; a weekly newsletter (*Washington Report*) that is sent to

nearly a million members and friends of the group; a weekly television program ("It's Your Business") that is carried on more than one hundred stations; a radio show ("What's the Issue?") that discusses major national topics on more than four hundred stations; and Biznet, a highly ambitious closed-circuit, tax-exempt television network.

Of course, the Internet can be used most effectively for lobbying Congress. Whether the computer user calls up an interest group's home page or receives lobbying information from an automatic list, it is extremely easy to "forward" messages to any official of the government. With the new leap into technology for most members of Congress and most government offices, interest groups will quickly disseminate the electronic mail addresses of their favorite targets.

For Critical Analysis
How can elected officials distinguish between computer-generated mail or messages and individualized mail or messages from concerned constituents?

Often, these groups will set up a paper organization with an innocuous name, such as the Citizens Trade Campaign, to represent their joint concerns. In this case, the alliance, comprising environmental, labor, and consumer groups, opposed the passage of North American Free Trade Agreement in 1993. Members of such an alliance share expenses and multiply the influence of their individual groups by combining their efforts.[5] Other advantages of such an alliance are that it looks as if larger public interests are at stake, and it blurs the specific interests of the individual groups involved. These alliances also are efficient devices for keeping like-minded groups from duplicating one another's lobbying efforts.

REGULATING LOBBYISTS

Congress made its first attempt to control lobbyists and lobbying activities through Title III of the Legislative Reorganization Act of 1946, otherwise

---

[5]*San Diego Union-Tribune*, December 4, 1993, p. C1.

"A very special interest to see you, Senator."

Drawing by Steiner © 1994 The New Yorker Magazine, Inc.

known as the Federal Regulation of Lobbying Act. The act actually provided for public disclosure more than for regulation, and it neglected to specify which agency would enforce its provisions. The 1946 legislation defined a lobbyist as any person or organization that received money to be used principally to influence legislation before Congress. Such persons and individuals were supposed to "register" their clients and the purposes of their efforts, and report quarterly on their activities.

The legislation was tested in a 1954 Supreme Court case, *United States v. Harriss*,[6] and was found to be constitutional. The Court agreed that the lobbying law did not violate due process, freedom of speech or of the press, or the freedom to petition. The Court narrowly construed the act, however, holding that it applied only to lobbyists who were influencing federal legislation *directly*.

The result of the act was that a minimal number of individuals registered as lobbyists. National interest groups like the National Rifle Association and the American Petroleum Institute could employ hundreds of staff members who were, of course, working on legislation but only register one or two lobbyists who were engaged *principally* in influencing Congress. There were no reporting requirements for lobbying the executive branch, federal agencies, the courts, or congressional staff. Approximately seven thousand individuals and organizations registered annually as lobbyists, although most experts

---

[6]347 U.S. 612 (1954).

estimated that ten times that number were actually employed in Washington to exert influence on the government.

The reform-minded Congress of 1995–1996 overhauled the lobbying legislation, fundamentally changing the ground rules for those who seek to influence the federal government. The new legislation, approved in late 1995, includes the following provisions:

1. A lobbyist is defined as anyone who spends at least 20 percent of his or her time lobbying members of Congress, their staffs, or executive branch officials.
2. Lobbyists must register with the clerk of the House and the secretary of the Senate within forty-five days of being hired or of making their first contact. The registration requirement applies to organizations that spend more than $20,000 in one year or to individuals who are paid more than $5,000 annually for their work.
3. Semiannual reports must disclose the general nature of the lobbying effort, specific issues and bill numbers, the estimated cost of the campaign, and a list of the branches of government contacted. The names of the individuals contacted need not be reported.
4. Representatives of U.S.-owned subsidiaries of foreign-owned companies and lawyers who represent foreign entities also would be required to register for the first time.
5. The requirements exempt "grass-roots" lobbying efforts and those of tax-exempt organizations, such as religious groups.

The new law is expected to increase the number of registered lobbyists by three to ten times what it currently is. It will make the connections between organizations and specific issues much clearer in the reporting process. The major exemption for grass-roots campaigns, however, might cause interest groups to divert major resources to organizing the folks back home so that they can exert pressure on Congress.

Concurrently with the debate on the new law, both the House and the Senate adopted new rules on gifts and travel expenses: the House adopted a flat ban on gifts, and the Senate limited gifts to $50 in value and to no more than $100 in gifts from a single source in a year. There are exceptions for gifts from family members and for home-state products and souvenirs like T-shirts and coffee-mugs. Both houses ban all-expenses-paid trips, golf outings, and other such junkets. There is an exception for "widely attended" events, however that is defined, or if the member is a primary speaker at an event. The new gift rules stop the broad practice of taking members of Congress to lunch or dinner, but the various exemptions and exceptions undoubtedly will cause much controversy as individual cases are decided by the Senate and House Ethics Committees in future years.

INTEREST GROUPS AND REPRESENTATIVE DEMOCRACY

The significant role played by interest groups in shaping national policy has caused many to question whether we really have a democracy at all. To be sure, most interest groups have a middle-class or upper-class bias. Members of interest groups can afford to pay the membership fees, are generally fairly well educated, and normally participate in the political process to a greater extent than the "average" American. Furthermore, leaders of interest groups tend to constitute an "elite within an elite" in the sense that they usually are from a higher social class than their members. The most powerful interest

Thinking Politically about AARP

The American Association of Retired Persons (AARP) is one of the most powerful interest groups in Washington, D.C., and, according to some, the strongest lobbying group in the United States. It is certainly the nation's largest interest group, with a membership of over thirty-three million. The small membership fee ($8 annually) allows its members to reap the many benefits of belonging to the organization. These benefits include discount rates for various services, mail-order prescriptions, automobile insurance, and credit cards. Most of all, members have a strong voice in Congress representing their interests.

AARP has accomplished much for its members over the years. It played a significant role in the creation of Medicare and Medicaid, as well as in obtaining cost-of-living increases in Social Security payments. Today, though, AARP is under attack. In part, this is because of the changed circumstances of today's older Americans. Whereas they were once among the poorer groups of our society, today they are, on average, the country's wealthiest citizens. In other words, they no longer need special legislation to protect their welfare to the extent

that they once did. Nonetheless, AARP continues to pressure Congress for legislation that benefits this group of Americans.

AARP's actions drew national attention, and sharp criticism, in 1988 because of the role it played in the life and death of the Medicare Catastrophic Care Act of that year. The act was passed in response to concern over the high costs of medical care for catastrophic illnesses, such as strokes and cancer. Because the costs of such care could rob older Americans of their savings, the act guaranteed that the government would pay the bills for catastrophic illnesses. To pay for the program, Congress increased Medicare fees and imposed a surtax on the income of wealthier senior citizens. In other words, the goal was to make the group that would benefit under the new law pay for the benefits. AARP, however, did not believe that the law provided sufficient benefits to justify the price. Thus, AARP representatives lobbied hard, and within eighteen months, Congress repealed the act.

AARP continues to be criticized on various fronts. The National Taxpayers Union, a lobby for fiscal conservatism,

called AARP the champion of an "age-based welfare state." Some people, including a few members of Congress, think that AARP may not be truly accountable to its members and may be abusing its "nonprofit" status. They point to the fact that nearly 60 percent of AARP's annual revenues (which total about $80 million annually) comes not from its membership fees but from its extensive business operations. Others suspect that it is time for the nation to be less concerned about the welfare of older Americans and more concerned about the needs of younger Americans—who, after all, will have to pay the bill for benefits for older Americans. Given our aging population, there will be more and more older Americans—and more members in AARP or other organizations representing the interests of older Americans.

For Critical Analysis

Which members of Congress— Republicans or Democrats— would be more likely to support national legislation benefiting older Americans?

groups—those with the most resources and political influence—are primarily business, trade, or professional groups. In contrast, public interest groups or civil rights groups make up only a small percentage of the interest groups lobbying Congress.

Remember from Chapter 1 that the elite theory of politics presumes that most Americans are uninterested in politics and are willing to let a small, elite group of citizens make decisions for them. Pluralist theory, in contrast, views politics as a struggle among various interest groups to gain benefits for their members. The pluralist approach views compromise among various competing interests as the essence of political decision making. In reality, neither theory describes American politics very accurately. If interest groups led by elite, upper-class individuals are the dominant voices in Congress, then what we see is a conflict among elite groups—which would support the elitist theory, not a pluralist approach.

The results of lobbying efforts—congressional legislation—do not always favor the interests of the most powerful groups, however. In part, this is because not all interest groups have an equal influence on government. Each group has a different combination of resources to use in the policymaking process. While some groups are composed of members who have high social status and enormous economic resources, such as the National Association of Manufacturers, other groups derive influence from their large memberships. The American Association of Retired Persons (AARP), for example, has more members than any other interest group. Its large membership allows it to wield significant power over legislators (see the feature entitled *Thinking Politically about AARP* on page 271). Still other groups, such as environmentalists, have causes that can claim strong public support even from those people who have no direct stake in the issue. Groups such as the National Rifle Association are well organized and have highly motivated members. This enables them to channel a stream of mail toward Congress with a few days' effort.

Even the most powerful interest groups do not always succeed in their demands. Whereas the National Chamber of Commerce may be accepted as having a justified interest in the question of business taxes, many legislators might feel that the group should not engage in the debate over the size of the federal budget deficit. In other words, groups are seen as having a legitimate concern in the issues closest to their interests but not necessarily in broader issues. This may explain why some of the most successful groups are those that focus on very specific issues—such as tobacco farming, funding of abortions, or handgun control—and do not get involved in larger conflicts.

CONCEPT OVERVIEW
Changes in Lobbying

With the growth of the federal government in the twentieth century and the advent of the age of electronic media, interest groups have expanded their activities dramatically since the turn of the century.

THEN	NOW
• Lobbying took place in the halls and offices of legislatures.	• Lobbying takes place in halls and offices of legislatures, executive offices, and regulatory agencies.
• Lobbying took place in person.	• Lobbyists use personal visits, mail, telephone, and electronic connections.
• Lobbying was confined to leaders.	• Lobbying includes leaders, grass-roots groups, and ordinary citizens.
• Lobbying included campaign help through volunteers and in-kind assistance.	• Lobbying uses PACs for primary campaign help.
• Lobbying was not regulated.	• Lobbying is regulated through registration requirements and campaign finance limits.

INTEREST GROUPS: UNFINISHED WORK

The role of interest groups in American politics has been in question since the writing of the Constitution. James Madison, among many others, worried about how to control the "mischiefs of faction" while recognizing that the very business of a democracy is to resolve the conflicts between interests. Today, the power of interest groups is probably greater than ever before: PACs sponsored by interest groups are able to raise and spend huge amounts of money to support candidates and parties; politicians admit that such support buys access, if not influence; groups use modern technology to rally their members; and Congress seems unable to get beyond the adjudication of interests to write policy for the good of all.

In the future, Americans will consider whether to limit the role that interest groups can play in campaigns and elections either by reducing the financial support these groups can give or by eliminating that influence altogether through some public financing scheme. Then, all taxpayers would support campaigns rather than special groups. It is unlikely that there will be any attempt to limit severely the contact that groups have with political decision makers, because their right to access is protected by the First Amendment to the Constitution. Lobbyists could, however, be required to report every contact publicly; interest groups could be required to make public the amount that they spend on attempts to influence government; or the use of the media by specialized groups for their own interest could be regulated.

The existence of interest groups, nonetheless, has great advantages for a democracy. By participating in such groups, individual citizens are empowered to influence government in ways far beyond the ballot. Groups do increase the interest and participation of voters in the system. And, without a doubt, these groups can protect the rights of minorities through their access to all branches of the government. Thus, the future could see a continued expansion of interest groups, particularly among segments of society that have been left out of the debate. The political system might be reformed to encourage such participation, making the struggle among groups more inclusive rather than less. In any case, given the structure of the government with its pluralist enticements for group struggle, it is unlikely that these political associations will disappear soon.

GETTING INVOLVED
The Gun Control Issue

Is the easy availability of handguns a major cause of crime? Do people have a right to possess firearms to defend home and hearth? These questions are part of a long-term and heated battle between organized pro-firearm and anti-firearm camps. The disagreements run deeply and reflect strong sentiments on both sides. The fight is fueled by the one million gun incidents occurring in the United States each year—the murders, suicides, assaults, accidents, robberies, and injuries in which guns are involved. Proponents of gun control seek new restrictions on gun purchases—if not a ban on them entirely—while decreasing existing arsenals of privately owned weapons. Proponents of firearms are fighting back. They claim that firearms are a cherished tradition, a constitutional right, a vital defense need for individuals. They contend that the problem lies not in the sale and ownership of the weapons themselves but in the criminal use of firearms.

The National Coalition to Ban Handguns favors a total ban, taking the position that handguns "serve no valid purpose, except to kill people." The National Rifle Association of America (NRA) opposes a ban. The NRA claims, among other things, that a gun law won't reduce the number of crimes. It is illogical to assume, according to the NRA, that persons who refuse to obey laws prohibiting rape, murder, and other crimes will obey a gun law.

The debate is intense and bitter. Gun control proponents accuse their adversaries of being "frightened little men living in the pseudomacho myth." Gun control opponents brand the other side as "new totalitarians" intent on curbing individual freedom. The NRA, founded in 1871, is currently one of the most powerful single-issue groups on the American political scene, representing the seventy million gun owners in the United States.

In 1993, Congress passed a law instituting a five-day waiting period for all handgun purchases. Most observers saw this as a defeat for the NRA. That group, however, asserted that the law would have no effect on crime. If you agree with the NRA's position and want to get involved in its efforts in opposition to further gun control legislation, contact the NRA at the following address:

THE NATIONAL RIFLE ASSOCIATION
11250 Waples Mill Rd.
Fairfax, VA 22030
703-267-1000
http://www.nra.org

If, however, you are concerned with the increase in gun-related crimes and feel that stricter gun laws are necessary, you can get involved through the following organizations:

THE NATIONAL COALITION TO BAN HANDGUNS
100 Maryland Ave. N.E.
Washington, DC 20002
202-530-0340

HANDGUN CONTROL, INC.
1225 I St. N.W.
Suite 1100
Washington, DC 20006
202-898-0792

KEY TERMS

climate control 260	lobbying 260	purposive incentive 252
direct technique 260	material incentive 252	service sector 256
indirect technique 260	political action committee (PAC) 247	social movement 252
interest group 247		solidary incentive 251
labor movement 255	public interest 258	subsidy 247

CHAPTER SUMMARY

❶ An interest group is an organization whose members share common objectives and who actively attempt to influence government policy. Interest groups proliferate in the United States because they can influence government at many points in the political structure and because they offer solidary, material, and purposive incentives to their members. Interest groups are often created out of social movements.

❷ Major types of interest groups include business, agricultural, labor, public employee, professional, and environmental groups. Other important groups may be considered public interest groups. In addition, single-issue groups and foreign governments lobby the government.

❸ Interest groups use direct and indirect techniques to influence government. Direct techniques include testifying before committees and rulemaking agencies, providing information to legislators, rating legislators' voting records, and making campaign contributions. Contributions are often made through political action committees, or PACs. Most PAC money is given to incumbents

to ensure access for the group. Indirect techniques to influence government include campaigns to rally public sentiment, letter-writing campaigns, influencing the climate of opinion, and using constituents to lobby for the group's interest.

❹ The 1946 Legislative Reorganization Act was the first attempt to control lobbyists and their activities through registration requirements. The Supreme Court narrowly construed the act as applying only to lobbyists who directly seek to influence federal legislation.

❺ In 1995, Congress approved new legislation requiring anyone who spends 20 percent of his or her time influencing legislation to register. Also, any organization spending $20,000 or more and any individual who is paid more than $5,000 annually for his or her work must register. Semiannual reports will include the name of clients, the bills in which they are interested, and the branches of government contacted. Grass-roots lobbying and the lobbying efforts of tax-exempt organizations are exempt from the new rules.

QUESTIONS FOR REVIEW AND DISCUSSION

❶ Which interest groups seem to be among the most powerful in the United States? What characteristics—size, prestige, resources, geographic location, political position—seem to make them more influential than others?

❷ Consider the possibility of removing all interest group influence from campaigns and elections—no contributions of money, assistance, workers, or other material help. How would candidates appeal to the voters' interests? How would the interactions between politi-

cians and groups change after the election? Would the influence of interest groups in Washington, D.C., be lessened significantly?

❸ Imagine that you are a member of Congress considering an important legislative proposal, such as health-care reform. To which interest groups would you be likely to listen? Which of the techniques used by such groups would be likely to influence your attitudes and your decisions? Could you make up your mind without considering the voices of interest groups?

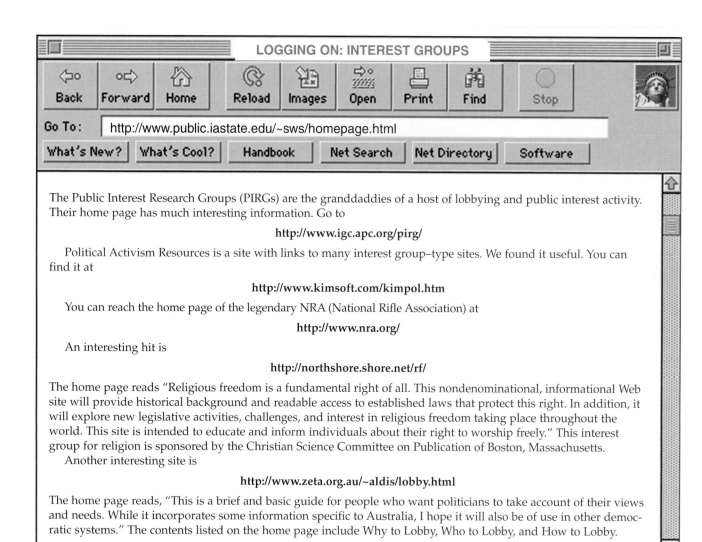

LOGGING ON: INTEREST GROUPS

Go To: http://www.public.iastate.edu/~sws/homepage.html

The Public Interest Research Groups (PIRGs) are the granddaddies of a host of lobbying and public interest activity. Their home page has much interesting information. Go to

http://www.igc.apc.org/pirg/

Political Activism Resources is a site with links to many interest group–type sites. We found it useful. You can find it at

http://www.kimsoft.com/kimpol.htm

You can reach the home page of the legendary NRA (National Rifle Association) at

http://www.nra.org/

An interesting hit is

http://northshore.shore.net/rf/

The home page reads "Religious freedom is a fundamental right of all. This nondenominational, informational Web site will provide historical background and readable access to established laws that protect this right. In addition, it will explore new legislative activities, challenges, and interest in religious freedom taking place throughout the world. This site is intended to educate and inform individuals about their right to worship freely." This interest group for religion is sponsored by the Christian Science Committee on Publication of Boston, Massachusetts.

Another interesting site is

http://www.zeta.org.au/~aldis/lobby.html

The home page reads, "This is a brief and basic guide for people who want politicians to take account of their views and needs. While it incorporates some information specific to Australia, I hope it will also be of use in other democratic systems." The contents listed on the home page include Why to Lobby, Who to Lobby, and How to Lobby.

SELECTED REFERENCES

Birnbaum, Jeffrey. *The Lobbyists*. New York: Times Books/Random House, 1993. This is an excellent account of the work of lobbyists in the halls of Congress as reported by a journalist. Birnbaum reports on some of the conflicts between interest groups and industries, as well as on the exchange of staff between Congress and the associations.

Cammisa, Anne Marie. *Governments as Interest Groups: Intergovernmental Lobbying and the Federal System*. Westport, Conn.: Praeger Publishers, 1995. This book looks closely at the way state and local governments lobby Congress and the executive branch in regard to the writing of national policy that affects local governments. Housing policy, welfare policy and child-care policy are examined with respect to the impact of state and local lobbying.

Cigler, Allan J., and Burdette A. Loomis. *Interest Group Politics*. 4th ed. Washington, D.C.: Congressional Quarterly Press, 1994. This collection of essays deals with interest groups in general and with the politics of specific groups such as the environmental movement, religious groups, abortion groups, and agricultural groups.

Clawson, Dan, Alan Neutstadtl, and Denise Scott. *Money Talks: Corporate PACs and Political Influence*. New York: Basic Books, 1992. How corporations set up PACs, how they decide which candidates to support, and the goals of that support are covered in this excellent investigation.

Greider, William. *Who Will Tell the People? The Betrayal of American Democracy.* New York: Simon & Schuster, 1992. Greider argues that the American political process has degenerated into a "grand bazaar" in which interest groups' money is exchanged for political power and influence.

Makinson, Larry, and Joshua Goldstein. *Open Secrets: The Cash Constituents of Congress.* 3d ed. Washington, D.C.: Congressional Quarterly Press, 1994. This extensive reference book on PACs and Congress includes the actual contributions of the major PACs to the members of congressional committees and to the members of Congress.

Richan, Willard C. *Lobbying for Social Change.* 2d ed. New York: The Haworth Press, 1995. This is a handy guide book for individuals and groups that want to begin successful lobbying efforts. It includes directions on identifying the correct political target, testifying at hearings, and using the media for the group's cause.

Rosenthal, Alan. *The Third House: Lobbyists and Lobbying in the States.* Washington, D.C.: Congressional Quarterly Press, 1993. Interest groups and lobbyists have proliferated not only at the national level but also within states and cities. This study examines the growth of lobbying efforts and interest groups at the state level using comparative data and interviews with lobbyists and state government officials.

Rothenberg, Lawrence S. *Linking Citizens to Government: Interest Group Politics at Common Cause.* New York: Cambridge University Press, 1992. This in-depth exploration and analysis of one of the largest public interest groups in the United States, Common Cause, focuses on the demographics, organization, and policies of the group.

Wilson, James Q. *Political Organizations* (with a new introduction to the 1974 edition). Princeton, N.J.: Princeton University Press, 1995. This is one of the classic works on the formation and membership of interest groups in American society. Wilson looks closely at the motivations of a group's members and the relationship of the members to the leaders of a group.

9
Political Parties

CHAPTER OUTLINE

There Were Three Parties?

BACKGROUND

AMERICAN POLITICS HAS BEEN DOMINATED BY TWO POLITICAL PARTIES—ALTHOUGH NOT ALWAYS TODAY'S REPUBLICANS AND DEMOCRATS—SINCE THE EARLIEST DAYS OF THE FEDERAL REPUBLIC. THE TWO MAJOR PARTIES USUALLY HAVE REPRESENTED DIFFERENT ECONOMIC STRATA IN THE NATION, DIFFERENT REGIONAL STRENGTHS, AND DIFFERENT POSITIONS ON SOCIAL ISSUES. THE LAST TWENTY YEARS HAVE WITNESSED A SEVERE DECLINE IN THE STRENGTH OF PARTY ATTACHMENT AMONG THE ELECTORATE. APPROXIMATELY ONE-THIRD OF THE VOTERS DECLARE THEMSELVES "INDEPENDENTS," AND MORE THAN HALF BELIEVE THAT HAVING A THIRD PARTY IS A GOOD IDEA.

WHAT IF THERE WERE THREE PARTIES?

To be viable, a third party would have to attract a substantial proportion (between 10 and 30 percent) of the electorate, field slates of candidates in most, if not all states, and be able to nominate a viable candidate for the presidency. Presumably, the third party would have a platform or set of principles that would be different enough from those of the Republicans and Democrats to attract adherents and potential candidates for office.

THIRD-PARTY PLATFORMS

What might be some of the issues around which a third party might form? At the present time, some Americans believe that the Republican party is becoming too conservative and the Democratic party is too controlled by its liberal wing. The successful third party might be based on a moderate approach to social issues such as abortion, affirmative action, and gay and lesbian issues. The question of what position it might take on economic issues is less obvious. Would a third party be successful by advocating an entirely new tax system, either more or less federal control of programs, or a new approach to the budget? Americans are quite divided on these issues and seem to prefer slow change to more radical policy decisions.

COMPETING AS A THIRD PARTY

To have real influence on the American political system, a third party must have enough supporters to sign the petitions to get their candidates on the ballot and then to vote the candidates into office. To do this, the party must be able to raise funds to support district and statewide campaigns and television advertising to reach voters.

On the national level, it is difficult, but not impossible, for a third party to get its presidential nominee on the ballot in every state. The two major parties would need to agree to include the third party's candidate in campaign debates. Based on past history, the Federal Election Commission is likely to provide public funding for a third-party candidate who appears to represent a fairly well-organized party. The real difficulty comes in getting a third-party candidate elected to the presidency. The candidate must win a plurality (the most popular votes of any candidate) in enough states to amass a majority of electoral votes in the nation. Given the right candidate—one who generates enormous public excitement—this is a possibility in today's media age.

Remember, though, that the two existing major parties will do everything in their power to prevent a third party from rising to compete with them. Both parties would be likely to change their platforms to try to win over the third-party voters and to try to persuade third-party candidates to join one of the existing major-party tickets in the effort to eliminate the new competitor.

FOR CRITICAL ANALYSIS

1. On which issues do you think the public is most unhappy with the Democrats and Republicans? Could those issues provide a viable platform for a third party?

2. How do you think the dynamics of the presidential campaign would be changed by the addition of a third-party candidate who truly was competitive?

WHAT IS A POLITICAL PARTY?

Almost every political survey completed in the United States includes the question, "Do you consider yourself to be a Democrat, a Republican, or an independent?" The question refers to the respondent's self-identification with a particular political party. Although a majority of Americans are willing to identify themselves with one of the two major parties, more than 30 percent of voters consciously identify themselves as **independents.** As proposed in the *What If . . .* that opens this chapter, independent voters could be attracted to a third party at some point in the future.

In the United States, being a member of a political party does not require paying dues, passing an examination, or swearing an oath of allegiance. If nothing is really required to be a member of a political party, what, then, is a political party?

A **political party** might be formally defined as a group of political activists who organize to win elections, to operate the government, and to determine public policy. This definition explains the difference between an interest group and a political party. Interest groups do not want to operate government, and they do not put forth political candidates—even though they support candidates who will promote their interests if elected or reelected. Another important distinction is that interest groups tend to sharpen issues, whereas American political parties tend to blur their issue positions to attract voters.

A political party is not a **faction** (see Chapter 2). Factions, which historically preceded political parties, were simply groups of individuals who joined together to win a benefit for themselves, like the interest groups of today. They were limited to the period in our political history when there were relatively few elective offices and when only a small percentage of the population could meet the requirements for voting. Today, we still use the term *faction,* but only for a particular group within a political party. For example, we speak of the conservative faction within the Democratic party or the liberal faction within the Republican party. A faction is founded on a particular philosophy, personality, or even geographic region. Sometimes a faction can be based on a political issue. The main feature differentiating a faction from a political party is that the faction generally does not have a permanently organized structure.

FUNCTIONS OF POLITICAL PARTIES IN THE UNITED STATES

Political parties in the United States engage in a wide variety of activities, many of which are discussed in this chapter. Through these activities, parties perform a number of functions for the political system. These functions include the following:

1. *Recruiting candidates for public office.* Because it is the goal of parties to gain control of government, they must work to recruit candidates for all elective offices. Often this means recruiting candidates to run against powerful incumbents or for unpopular jobs. Yet if parties did not search out and encourage political hopefuls, far more offices would be uncontested, and voters would have limited choices.

2. *Organizing and running elections.* Although elections are a government activity, political parties actually organize the voter-registration drives, recruit the

INDEPENDENT

A voter or candidate who does not identify with a political party.

POLITICAL PARTY

A group of political activists who organize to win elections, to operate the government, and to determine public policy.

FACTION

A group or bloc in a legislature or political party acting together in pursuit of some special interest or position.

Supporters of Bob Dole and Jack Kemp lead the cheers for the candidate during the 1996 Republican convention.

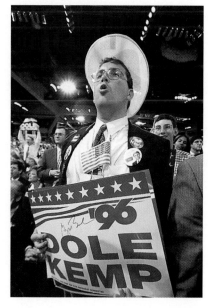

1996 Democratic convention delegates show their support for the Clinton and Gore ticket.

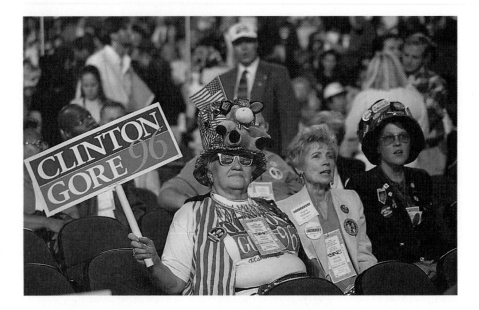

volunteers to work at the polls, provide most of the campaign activity to stimulate interest in the election, and work to increase participation.

3. *Presenting alternative policies to the electorate.* The difference between political parties and factions is that factions are often centered on individual politicians, whereas parties are focused on a set of political positions. The Democrats or Republicans in Congress who vote together do so because they represent constituencies that have similar expectations and demands.

4. *Accepting responsibility for operating the government.* When the party elects the president or governor and members of the legislature, it accepts the responsibility for running the government. This includes staffing the executive branch with managers from the party and developing linkages among the elected officials to gain support for policies and their implementation.

5. *Acting as the organized opposition to the party in power.* The "out" party, or the one that does not control the executive branch, is expected to articulate its own policies and oppose the winning party when appropriate. By organizing the opposition to the "in" party, the opposition party forces debate on the policy alternatives.

Students of political parties, such as Leon D. Epstein, point out that the major functions of American political parties are carried out by a small, relatively loose-knit **cadre,** or nucleus, of party activists.[1] This is quite a different arrangement from the more highly structured, mass-membership party organization typical of certain European working-class parties. American parties concentrate on winning elections rather than on signing up large numbers of deeply committed, dues-paying members who believe passionately in the party's program.

CADRE

The nucleus of political party activists carrying out the major functions of American political parties.

A SHORT HISTORY OF POLITICAL PARTIES IN THE UNITED STATES

Political parties in the United States have a long tradition dating back to the 1790s (see Figure 9–1). The function and character of these political parties, as well as the emergence of the two-party system itself, have much to do with

---

[1]*Political Parties in Western Democracies* (New Brunswick, N.J.: Transaction, 1980).

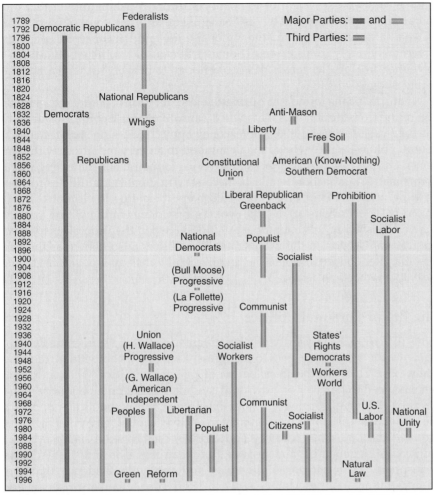

Figure 9–1

American Political Parties Since 1789

The chart indicates the years that parties either ran presidential candidates or held national conventions. The life span for many political parties can only be approximated, because parties existed at the state or local level before they ran candidates in presidential elections, and parties continued to exist at local levels long after they ceased running presidential candidates. Not every party fielding a presidential candidate is represented in the chart. For instance, in 1988, at least nine other parties fielded a presidential candidate in at least one state.

SOURCE: Congressional Quarterly, *Congressional Quarterly's Guide to U.S. Elections,* 2d ed. (Washington, D.C.: Congressional Quarterly, 1985), p. 224; *Congressional Quarterly Weekly Report* (1988), p. 3184; and J. David Gillespie, *Politics at the Periphery* (Columbia, S.C.: University of South Carolina Press, 1993), updated by authors

the unique historical forces operating from this country's beginning as an independent nation.

Generally, we can divide the evolution of our nation's political parties into six periods:

1. The creation of parties, from 1789 to 1812.
2. The era of one-party rule, or personal politics, from 1816 to 1824.
3. The period from Andrew Jackson's presidency to the Civil War, from 1828 to 1860.
4. The post–Civil War period, from 1864 to 1892.
5. The progressive period, from 1896 to 1928.
6. The modern period, from 1932 to the present.

The Formative Years: Federalists and Anti-Federalists

The first partisan political division in the United States occurred prior to the adoption of the Constitution. The **Federalists** proposed adoption of the Constitution, whereas the **Anti-Federalists** were against ratification.

In September 1796, George Washington, who had served as president for almost two full terms, decided not to run again. In his farewell address, he

FEDERALISTS

The first American political party, led by Alexander Hamilton and John Adams. Many of its members had strongly supported the adoption of the new Constitution and the creation of the federal union.

ANTI-FEDERALISTS

Those who opposed the adoption of the Constitution because of its centralist tendencies and attacked the failure of the Constitution's framers to include a bill of rights.

Thomas Jefferson, founder of the Democratic Republicans. His election to the presidency in 1800 was decided in the House of Representatives, because the Democratic Republican party did not carry enough electoral votes.

ERA OF PERSONAL POLITICS

An era when attention centers on the character of individual candidates rather than on party identification.

ERA OF GOOD FEELING

The years from 1817 to 1825, when James Monroe was president and there was, in effect, no political opposition.

DEMOCRATIC PARTY

One of the two major American political parties evolving out of the Democratic (Jeffersonian) Republican group supporting Thomas Jefferson.

WHIG PARTY

One of the foremost political organizations in the United States during the first half of the nineteenth century, formally established in 1836. The Whig party was dominated by the same anti-Jackson elements that organized the National Republican faction within the Democratic (Jeffersonian) Republicans and represented a variety of regional interests. It fell apart as a national party in the early 1850s.

made a somber assessment of the nation's future. Washington felt that the country might be destroyed by the "baneful effects of the spirit of party." He viewed parties as a threat to both national unity and the concept of popular government. Early in his career, Thomas Jefferson did not like political parties either. In 1789, he stated, "If I could not go to heaven but with a party, I would not go there at all."[2]

What Americans found out during the first decade or so after the ratification of the Constitution was that even a patriot-king (as George Washington has been called) could not keep everyone happy. There is no such thing as a neutral political figure who is so fair minded that everyone agrees with him or her. During this period, it became obvious to many that something more permanent than a faction would be necessary to identify candidates for the growing number of citizens who would be participating in elections. Thus, according to many historians, the world's first democratic political parties were established in this country. Also, in 1800, when the Federalists lost the presidential election to the Democratic Republicans (also known as the Jeffersonian Republicans), one of the first peaceful transfers of power from one party to another was achieved.

The Era of Personal Politics

From 1816 to 1828, a majority of voters regularly elected Democratic Republicans to the presidency and to Congress. Two-party competition did not really exist. This was the so-called **era of personal politics,** when attention centered on the character of individual candidates rather than on party identification. Although during elections the Democratic Republicans opposed the Federalist call for a stronger, more active central government, they acquired the Louisiana Territory and Florida, established a national bank, enforced a higher tariff, and resisted European intrusion into the Western hemisphere. Domestic tranquility was sufficiently in evidence that the administration of James Monroe (1817 to 1825) came to be known as the **era of good feeling.**

National Two-Party Rule: Democrats and Whigs

During the era of personal politics, one-party rule did not prevent the Democratic Republican factions from competing against each other. Indeed, there was quite a bit of intraparty rivalry. Finally, in 1824 and 1828, Democratic Republicans who belonged to the factions of Henry Clay and John Quincy Adams split with the rest of the party to oppose Andrew Jackson in those elections. Jackson's supporters and the Clay-Adams bloc formed separate parties, the **Democratic party** and the **Whig party,** respectively. That same Democratic party is now the oldest continuing political party in the Western world.

The Whigs were those Democratic Republicans who were often called the "National Republicans." At the national level, the Whigs were able to elect two presidents—William Henry Harrison in 1840 and Zachary Taylor in 1848. The Whigs, however, were unable to maintain a common ideological base when the party became increasingly divided over the issue of slavery in the late 1840s. During the 1850s, the Whigs fell apart as a national party.

---

[2]Letter to Francis Hopkinson written from Paris while Jefferson was minister to France. In John P. Foley, ed., *The Jeffersonian Cyclopedia* (New York: Russell & Russell, 1967), p. 677.

The Post–Civil War Period

The existing two-party system was disrupted by the election of 1860, in which there were four major candidates. Abraham Lincoln, the candidate of the newly formed **Republican party,** was the victor with a majority of the electoral vote, although with only 39.9 percent of the popular vote. This newly formed Republican party—not to be confused with the Democratic Republicans—was created in the mid-1850s from the various groups that sought to fill the vacuum left by the disintegration of the Whigs. It took the label of Grand Old Party, or GOP. Its first national convention was held in 1856, but its presidential candidate, John C. Frémont, lost.

After the end of the Civil War, the South became heavily Democratic (the Solid South), and the North became heavily Republican. This era of Republican dominance was highlighted by the election of 1896, when the Republicans, emphasizing economic development and modernization under William McKinley, resoundingly defeated the Democratic and Populist candidate, William Jennings Bryan. The Republicans' control was solidified by winning over the urban working-class vote in northern cities. From the election of Abraham Lincoln until the election of Franklin D. Roosevelt in 1932, the Republicans won all but four presidential elections.

The Progressive Movement

In 1912, a major schism occurred in the Republican party when former Republican president Theodore Roosevelt ran for the presidency as a Progressive. Consequently, there were three significant contenders in that presidential contest. Woodrow Wilson was the Democratic candidate, William Howard Taft was the regular Republican candidate, and Roosevelt was the Progressive candidate. The Republican split allowed Wilson to be elected. The Wilson administration, although Democratic, ended up enacting much of

Andrew Jackson earned the name "Old Hickory" for his exploits during the War of 1812. In 1828, Jackson was elected president as the candidate of the new Democratic party.

REPUBLICAN PARTY

One of the two major American political parties, which emerged in the 1850s as an antislavery party. It was created to fill the vacuum caused by the disintegration of the Whig party.

William McKinley campaigns in 1896 on a platform draped with the flag. The decorations are no different from those that candidates used a century later.

FIRESIDE CHAT

One of the warm, informal talks by Franklin D. Roosevelt to a few million of his intimate friends—via the radio. Roosevelt's fireside chats were so effective that succeeding presidents have been urged by their advisers to emulate him by giving more radio and television reports to the nation.

the Progressive party's platform. Left without any reason for opposition, the Progressive party collapsed in 1921.

Republican Warren Harding's victory in 1920 reasserted Republican domination of national politics until the Republicans' defeat by Franklin D. Roosevelt in 1932 in the depths of the Great Depression.

The Modern Era: From the New Deal to the Present

Franklin D. Roosevelt was elected in 1932 and reelected in 1936, 1940, and 1944. The impact of his successive Democratic administrations and the New Deal that he crafted is still with us today. Roosevelt used his enormous personal appeal to unify Democrats under his leadership, and he established direct communication between the president and the public through his radio **"fireside chats."** It wasn't until 1940 that the Republicans made even a small dent in the Democratic hegemony, when Wendell Willkie reduced Roosevelt's popular vote to 54.8 percent from the 60.5 percent and the 57.4 percent of the two previous elections.

In April 1945, Roosevelt died; Vice President Harry Truman became president through succession and, in 1948, through election. The New Deal coalition, under Truman's revised theme of the Fair Deal, continued. It was not until Republican Dwight Eisenhower won the 1952 election that the Democrats lost their control of the presidency. Eisenhower was reelected in 1956.

From 1960 through 1968, the Democrats, led first by John F. Kennedy and then by Lyndon B. Johnson, held national power. Republicans again came to power with Richard Nixon's victory in 1968 and retained it in 1972, but they lost prestige after the Watergate scandal forced Nixon's resignation on August 8, 1974. For this and other reasons, the Democrats were back in power after the presidential elections in 1976. But Democratic president Jimmy Carter was unable to win reelection against Ronald Reagan in 1980. The Republicans also gained control of the Senate in 1980 and retained it in the elections of 1982 and 1984. The 1984 reelection of Ronald Reagan appeared to some pollsters to signal the resurgence of the Republican party as a competitive force in American politics as more people declared themselves to be Republicans than they had in the previous several decades.

In 1988, George Bush won the White House for the Republicans without converting many voters to the party. Democrats gained seats in the House of Representatives and one seat in the Senate. The same phenomenon occurred, in reverse, in 1992. Bill Clinton won the presidency, but the Democrats lost nine seats in the House. The midterm election of 1994 was a stunning reversal for the Democrats. Republicans won majorities in both the House and the Senate, as well as gaining a majority of governorships. In 1996, the voters reelected President Clinton with just under 50 percent of the votes, while returning the Republicans to power in both the House and the Senate. Although Clinton's coattails managed to increase the number of Democrats in the House by eight, the Senate was immune to this effect. Republicans gained two seats in the Senate to hold a majority of fifty-five to forty-five over the Democrats.

THE THREE FACES OF A PARTY

PARTY-IN-ELECTORATE

Those members of the general public who identify with a political party or who express a preference for one party over the other.

Although American parties are known by a single name and, in the public mind, have a common historical identity, each party is really composed of three major subunits. The first subunit is the **party-in-electorate.** This phrase refers to all those individuals who claim an attachment to the political party. They need not be members in the sense that they pay dues or even participate in election campaigns. Rather, the party-in-electorate is the large number of

Americans who feel some loyalty to the party or who use partisanship as a cue to decide who will earn their vote. This is a rather fluid and unstable group, one that can become disenchanted with the candidates and policies offered by the Democrats or Republicans and that can freely switch parties or be drawn to independent or third-party candidates. Needless to say, the party leaders pay close attention to the affiliation of their members in the electorate.

The second subunit, the **party organization,** provides the structural framework for the political party by recruiting volunteers to become party leaders; identifying potential candidates; and organizing caucuses, conventions, and election campaigns for its candidates. It is the party organization and its active workers that keep the party functioning between elections, as well as make sure that the party puts forth electable candidates and clear positions in the elections. When individuals accept paid employment for a political party, they are considered party professionals. Among that group are found campaign consultants; fund raisers; local, state, and national executives; and national staff members. If the party-in-electorate declines in numbers and loyalty, the party organization must try to find a strategy to rebuild the grassroots following.

The **party-in-government** is the third subunit of American political parties. The party-in-government consists of those elected and appointed officials who identify with a political party. Generally, elected officials cannot also hold official party positions within the formal organization. Executives such as the president, governors, and mayors often have the informal power to appoint party executives, but their duties in office preclude them from active involvement in the party organization most of the time.

Ties to a political party are essential to the functioning of government and the operation of the political process in the United States. Republican representatives, senators, and governors expect to receive a hearing at a Republican-controlled White House if they request it. In return, Republican presidents call on party loyalty when they ask the legislators to support their programs. Finally, the electorate at the polls is asked to judge the party-in-government by its policies and candidates. American political parties, although not nearly as ideological as many European parties, do claim to present alternative positions to the voters. If the party organization and the party-in-government are in conflict, the party-in-electorate is likely to look for other party leadership to articulate its preferences.

DID YOU KNOW...
That the political party with the most seats in the House of Representatives chooses the speaker of the House, makes any new rules it wants, gets a majority of the seats on each important committee and chooses their chairs, and hires most of the congressional staff?

PARTY ORGANIZATION

The formal structure and leadership of a political party, including election committees; local, state, and national executives; and paid professional staff.

PARTY-IN-GOVERNMENT

All of the elected and appointed officials who identify with a political party.

PARTY ORGANIZATION

In theory, each of the American political parties has a standard, pyramid-shaped organization (see Figure 9–2). The pyramid, however, does not reflect accurately the relative power and strengths of the individual parts of the party organization. If it did, the national chairperson of the Democratic or Republican party, along with the national committee, could simply dictate how the organization was to be run, just as if it were Exxon Corporation or Ford Motor Company.

In reality, the formal structure of political parties resembles a layer cake with autonomous strata more than it does a pyramid. Malcolm E. Jewell and David M. Olson point out that "there is no command structure within political parties. Rather, each geographic unit of the party tends to be autonomous from the other units at its same geographic level."[3]

---

[3]Malcolm E. Jewell and David M. Olson, *American State Political Parties and Elections,* rev. ed. (Homewood, Ill.: Dorsey Press, 1982), p. 73.

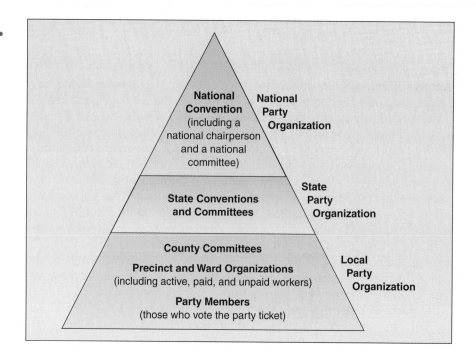

The National Party Organization

Each party has a national organization, the most clearly institutional part of which is the **national convention,** held every four years. The convention is used to nominate the presidential and vice presidential candidates. In addition, the **party platform** is written, ratified, and revised at the national convention. The platform sets forth the party's position on the issues and makes promises to initiate certain policies if the party wins the presidency. Often, platforms represent compromises among the various factions of a party, in an attempt to make peace before the campaign begins.

After the convention, the platform frequently is neglected or ignored by party candidates who disagree with it. Because candidates are trying to win votes from a wide spectrum of voters, it is counterproductive to emphasize the fairly narrow and sometimes controversial goals set forth in the platform. The work of Gerald M. Pomper has shown, however, that once elected, the parties do try to carry out platform promises and that roughly three-fourths of the promises eventually become law.[4] Of course, some general goals, such as economic prosperity, are included in the platforms of both parties.

Choosing the National Committee. At the national convention, each of the parties formally chooses a national standing committee, elected by the individual state parties. This **national committee** is established to direct and coordinate party activities during the following four years. The Democrats include at least two members, a man and a woman, from each state, from the District of Columbia, and from the several territories. Governors, members of Congress, mayors, and other officials may be included as at-large members of the national committee. The Republicans, in addition, add state chairpersons from every state carried by the Republican party in the preceding presidential, gubernatorial, or congressional elections. The selections of national committee members are ratified by the delegations to the national convention.

NATIONAL CONVENTION

The meeting held every four years by each major party to select presidential and vice presidential candidates, to write a platform, to choose a national committee, and to conduct party business. In theory, the national convention is at the top of a hierarchy of party conventions (the local and state conventions are below it) that consider candidates and issues.

PARTY PLATFORM

A document drawn up by the platform committee at each national convention, outlining the policies, positions, and principles of the party; it is then submitted to the entire convention for approval.

NATIONAL COMMITTEE

A standing committee of a national political party established to direct and coordinate party activities during the four-year period between national party conventions.

---

[4]Gerald M. Pomper and Susan S. Lederman, *Elections in America: Control and Influence in Democratic Politics,* 2d ed. (New York: Longman, 1980).

One of the jobs of the national committee is to ratify the presidential nominee's choice of a national chairperson, who in principle acts as the spokesperson for the party. Even though we have placed the national committee at the top of the hierarchy of party organization (see Figure 9–2), it has very little direct influence. Basically, the national chairperson and the national committee simply plan the next campaign and the next convention, obtain financial contributions, and publicize the national party.

Picking a National Chairperson. In general, the party's presidential candidate chooses the national chairperson.[5] The major responsibility of that person is the management of the national election campaign. In some cases, a strong national chairperson has considerable power over state and local party organizations. There is no formal mechanism with which to exercise direct control over subnational party structures, however. The national chairperson does such jobs as establish a national party headquarters, raise and distribute campaign funds, and appear in the media as a party spokesperson.

The national chairperson, along with the national committee, attempts basically to maintain some sort of liaison among the different levels of the party organization. The fact is that the real strength and power of a national party is at the state level.

The State Party Organization

There are fifty states in the Union, plus the territories and the District of Columbia, and an equal number of party organizations for each major party. Therefore, there are more than a hundred state parties (and even more, if we include local parties and minor parties). Because every state party is unique, it is impossible to describe what an "average" state political party is like. Nonetheless, state parties have several organizational features in common.

This commonality can be described in one sentence: each state party has a chairperson, a committee, and a number of local organizations. In principle,

---

[5]If that candidate loses, however, the chairperson is often changed.

Bob Dole addresses the delegates at the 1996 Republican convention in San Diego.

STATE CENTRAL COMMITTEE

The principal organized structure of each political party within each state. This committee is responsible for carrying out policy decisions of the party's state convention.

UNIT RULE

All of a state's electoral votes are cast for the presidential candidate receiving a plurality of the popular vote.

PATRONAGE

Rewarding faithful party workers and followers with government employment and contracts.

each **state central committee**—the principal organized structure of each political party within each state—has a similar role in the various states. The committee, usually composed of those members who represent congressional districts, state legislative districts, or counties, has responsibility for carrying out the policy decisions of the party's state convention, and in some states the state committee will direct the state chairperson with respect to policymaking.

Also, like the national committee, the state central committee has control over the use of party campaign funds during political campaigns. Usually, the state central committee has little, if any, influence on party candidates once they are elected. In fact, state parties are fundamentally loose alliances of local interests and coalitions of often bitterly opposed factions.

State parties are also important in national politics because of the **unit rule**, which awards electoral votes in presidential elections as an indivisible bloc (except in Maine and Nebraska). Presidential candidates concentrate their efforts in states in which voter preferences seem to be evenly divided or in which large numbers of electoral votes are at stake.

Local Party Machinery: The Grass Roots

The lowest layer of party machinery is the local organization, supported by district leaders, precinct or ward captains, and party workers. Much of the work is coordinated by county committees and their chairpersons. In the past, the institution of **patronage**—rewarding the party faithful with government jobs or contracts—held the local organization together. For immigrants and the poor, the political machine often furnished important services and protections. The big-city machine was the archetypal example, and Tammany Hall, or the Tammany Society, which dominated New York City government for nearly two centuries, was perhaps the highest refinement of this political form. (See this chapter's *Politics and Ethics.*)

The last big-city local political machine to exercise a great deal of power was run by Chicago's Mayor Richard J. Daley, who was also an important figure in national Democratic politics. Daley, as mayor, ran the Chicago Democratic machine from 1955 until his death in 1976. The Daley organization, largely Irish in candidate origin and voter support, was split by the successful candidacy of African American Democrat Harold Washington in the racially divisive 1983 mayoral election.

City machines are now dead, mostly because their function of providing social services (and reaping the reward of votes) has been taken over by state and national agencies. This trend began in the 1930s, when the social legislation of the New Deal established Social Security and unemployment insurance. The local party machine has little, if anything, to do with deciding who is eligible to receive these benefits.

Local political organizations, whether located in cities, townships, or at the county level, still can contribute a great deal to local election campaigns. These organizations are able to provide the foot soldiers of politics—individuals who pass out literature and get out the vote on election day, which can be crucial in local elections. In many regions, local Democratic and Republican organizations still exercise some patronage, such as awarding courthouse jobs, contracts for street repair, and other lucrative construction contracts. (The constitutionality of awarding—or not awarding—contracts on the basis of political affiliation increasingly is subject to challenge, however. For the Supreme Court's opinion on the matter, see this chapter's *Politics and the Constitution.*) Local party organizations are also the most important vehicles for recruiting young adults into political work, because political involvement at the local level offers activists many opportunities to gain experience.

POLITICS AND ETHICS
Tammany Hall: The Quintessential Local Political Machine

The Tammany Society dominated New York City politics for nearly two centuries. Founded in 1786 with the express purpose of engaging in cultural, social, and patriotic activities, the society evolved into a major political force and became known as Tammany Hall. In the beginning, it organized and provided social services for the foreign born, who made up the bulk of the Democratic party in New York City.

One of its more notorious leaders was William Tweed, head of the so-called Tweed ring, whose scandals were unearthed by the *New York Times* in 1871. Readers were entertained and horrified by stories of millions of dollars in kickbacks received from giving out government contracts, of how civil and criminal violations were being overlooked, and of phony leases and padded bills that were paid to members of the Tweed ring. As a result of the exposé, Tweed was imprisoned; but the other members of the ring managed to flee the country (as very wealthy men and women). Richard Crocker took over the leadership of Tammany Hall in 1886 and kept it until 1901.

Tammany Hall's influence declined when its slate of candidates was defeated in a reform movement in 1901. It was not until Franklin D. Roosevelt's victory in 1932, however, that Tammany lost its political clout almost completely—but only for a

TWEEDLEDEE AND SWEEDLEDUM.
(A New Christmas Pantomime at the Tammany Hall.)
Clown (to Pantaloon). "Let's Blind them with *this*, and then take *some more*."

couple of decades. In the 1950s, there was a short-lived resurgence in the influence of the Tammany Society. It has enjoyed no political influence in New York City politics since then.

For Critical Analysis
What kinds of organizations provide the services today that political machines did in the past?

THE PARTY AND ITS MEMBERS

The two major American political parties are often characterized as being too much like Tweedledee and Tweedledum, the twins in Lewis Carroll's *Through the Looking Glass.* When both parties nominate moderates for the presidency, the similarities between the parties seem to outweigh their differences. Yet the political parties do generate strong conflict for political offices throughout the United States, and there are significant differences between the parties, both in the characteristics of their members and in their platforms.

POLITICS AND THE CONSTITUTION
Political Patronage and the First Amendment

Traditionally, political patronage has entailed rewarding the party faithful with government jobs and contracts. It has also involved firing (or refusing to hire or award contracts to) those employees or contractors who do not support the views of a newly elected official. How, though, can firing an employee because of his or her political views be squared with the First Amendment's guarantee of free speech and expression?

In a series of decisions over the past three decades, the Supreme Court has had to grapple with the problem of how to balance these First Amendment freedoms with the tradition of political patronage. In a landmark decision in 1976, *Elrod v. Burns,** the Court held that government officials cannot discharge public employees for refusing to support a political party or its candidates unless political affiliation is an appropriate requirement for the job in question. In 1990, in *Rutan v. Republican Party of Illinois,*† the Court went even further: it ruled that not only was firing a public employee for political affiliation an impermissible infringement on the employee's First Amendment rights but so was hiring, promoting, or transferring a public employee on such a basis.

In 1996, the issue of political patronage and First Amendment rights again came before the Supreme

Court. The specific issue was whether a local government could refuse to hire or to continue using the services of *independent contractors* (workers who are not classified as employees) because of their political views. The Court held that the First Amendment protections afforded to public employees against being discharged for refusing to support a political party or its candidates also extend to independent contractors.‡

Clearly, though, political patronage itself is far from dead; and it certainly has its defenders on the Supreme Court. In the 1976 *Elrod* decision, for example, Justice William Rehnquist (now chief justice), joined by Justices Lewis Powell and Warren Burger, dissented from the majority's view and defended the patronage system. These justices could see nothing unconstitutional in conditioning public employment on political affiliation. In the 1990 *Rutan* case, Justice Antonin Scalia—joined by Chief Justice Rehnquist and Justices Anthony Kennedy and Sandra Day O'Connor—wrote a stinging dissent in which he predicted "disastrous consequences for our political system" if the view of the majority on the Court prevailed.

Again in 1996, Justice Scalia dissented from the majority's decision, this time joined by Justice Clarence Thomas. Scalia stated, "There can be

no dispute that, like rewarding one's allies, the . . . act of refusing to reward one's opponents—and at bottom both of today's cases involve exactly that—is an American political tradition as old as the Republic. This is true not only with regard to employment matters . . . but also in the area of government contracts." Scalia concluded that it was inconceivable that the protections given to public employees should extend to the "massive field" of all government contracting. "Yet amazingly, that is what the Court does. . . . It is profoundly disturbing that the varying political practices across this vast country, from coast to coast, can be transformed overnight by an institution whose conviction of what the Constitution means is so fickle."

For Critical Analysis
Justice Scalia, in his dissent from the **Rutan** *decision, stated that the Supreme Court justices themselves owe their appointments to political patronage. What did he mean by this?*

*427 U.S. 347 (1976).
†497 U.S. 62 (1990).
‡*Board of County Commissioners v. Umbehr*, 116 S.Ct. 2342 (1996); *O'Hare Truck Service, Inc. v. City of Northlake*, 116 S.Ct. 2361 (1996).

Differences between the Parties

Although Democrats and Republicans are not divided along religious or class lines to the extent that some European parties are, certain social groups are more likely to identify with each party. Since the New Deal of Franklin D. Roosevelt, the Democratic party has appealed to the more disadvantaged groups in society. African American voters are far more likely to identify with the Democrats, as are members of union households, Jewish voters, and individuals who have less than a high school education. Republicans draw more of their support from college graduates, upper-income families, and professionals or businesspersons. In recent years, more women than men have tended to identify themselves as Democrats than as Republicans.

Hillary Clinton (left) speaking at the 1996 Democratic convention, Elizabeth Dole (right) interacting with 1996 Republican delegates during her "Oprah Winfrey-style" presentation.

The coalition of minorities, the working class, and various ethnic groups has been the core of Democratic party support since the presidency of Franklin D. Roosevelt. The social programs and increased government intervention in the economy that were the heart of Roosevelt's New Deal were intended to ease the strain of economic hard times on these groups. This goal remains important for many Democrats today. In general, Democratic identifiers are more likely to approve of social-welfare spending, to support government regulation of business, to approve of measures to improve the situation of minorities, and to support assistance to the elderly with their medical expenses. Republicans are more supportive of the private marketplace, and many Republicans feel that the federal government should be involved in fewer social programs.

Table 9–1 shows that the general public shares these views on which groups are served by each party. It would seem that a larger proportion of the population falls into those groups that most people think are better served by the Democratic party than by the Republican party, yet the Republican party has captured the presidency in five of the last eight elections. Turning from the interests of specific groups to the interest of the nation as a whole, Table 9–2 shows the percentage of Americans who think that the Republican or Democratic party is better for preserving peace and promoting prosperity. Since 1984, a greater proportion of the public has felt that the Republican party was better able than the Democratic party to keep peace and to keep the

BETTER A THIRD TERMER THAN A THIRD RATER

Table 9–1

Which Party Is Better?

QUESTION: IN THE VIEW OF THE PUBLIC, WHICH PARTY SERVES THE INTERESTS OF GROUPS IN SOCIETY BETTER?

BETTER FOR	REPUBLICAN	DEMOCRAT	SAME/ DON'T KNOW
Business and professional people	65%	19%	16%
White-collar workers	56	25	19
Skilled workers	58	40	22
Small business people	36	45	19
Farmers	27	49	24
Retired people	28	51	21
Unemployed people	20	59	21
Women	26	45	29
Labor union members	22	55	23
African Americans	17	59	24

SOURCE: *Gallup Report*, 1992.

Table 9–2

Public Perceptions of the Parties on Peace and Prosperity

QUESTION: WHICH PARTY IS BETTER FOR KEEPING PEACE?			QUESTION: WHICH PARTY IS BETTER FOR PROSPERITY?		
YEAR	REPUBLICAN	DEMOCRATIC	YEAR	REPUBLICAN	DEMOCRATIC
1980	25%	42%	1980	35%	36%
1982	29	38	1982	34	43
1984	38	38	1984	49	33
1986	34	29	1986	41	30
1988	43	33	1988	52	34
1991	42	33	1991	49	32
1993	36	40	1993	30	31
1994	42	38	1994	48	38
1996	31	44	1996	41	42

SOURCE: *Gallup Report*, 1996.

country prosperous. If it is true, as some researchers suggest, that voters are more likely to consider the good of the whole nation than their individual interests in choosing a presidential candidate, then the somewhat greater success of the Republican party at the presidential level may be due to public perceptions of its effectiveness on the issues of peace and the economy.

Ideology and Party Leadership

The differences separating those who identify with the Democrats and those who identify with the Republicans are magnified greatly among the leadership of the Democrats and the Republicans. Generally, a much greater percentage of Democratic leaders consider themselves to be liberals than do their followers, and Republican elites are far more likely to identify their philosophy as conservative than are their followers. Polls of the national convention delegates demonstrate the wide gap in policy preferences between elites and general party identifiers. Such differences are reflected in the party platforms that are adopted at each party's convention. Democratic platforms recently have stressed equality of opportunity, the government's responsibility to help citizens, and ending tax loopholes for business. Recent Republican platforms seek to ban abortions, oppose programs to remedy discrimination, and support prayer in public schools. It is worth noting, however, that the differences between the attitudes of party elites and party platforms tend to disappear during the election campaign as candidates try to win votes from partisans of all ideological persuasions and from independent voters as well. See this chapter's feature entitled *Thinking Politically about Independent Voters* for a discussion of the character of these "independents."

THE PARTY-IN-GOVERNMENT

After the election is over and the winners are announced, the focus of party activity shifts from getting out the vote to organizing and controlling the government. As you will see in Chapter 12, party membership plays an important role in the day-to-day operations of Congress, with partisanship determining everything from office space to committee assignments and power on Capitol Hill. For the president, the political party furnishes the pool of qualified applicants for political appointments to run the government. Although it is uncommon to do so, presidents can and occasionally do appoint executive

Thinking Politically about Independent Voters

Since the 1970s, many surveys have reported that there are more independent voters than there are either Democrats or Republicans in the electorate. As the graph below shows, the number of Americans who call themselves "independents" has doubled since 1940, increasing from the 16 percent of voters who used that identification in 1940 to somewhere around 39 percent today. Depending on which polling firm is reporting, the number of Americans who continue to call themselves either Democrats or Republicans ranges between 59 and 65 percent.

Are these voters truly "independent," or are they more likely to vote for one party or the other? Since 1948, with the exception of the election of Lyndon Johnson in 1964 and Bill Clin-

ton in 1992, a majority of independent voters have reported that they voted for Republican presidential candidates. Thus, the independent voter has been the "swing" vote that propels Republicans to the White House.

In terms of congressional voting, the pattern has been quite different. Since 1958, a majority of independent voters have reported that they voted for Democratic candidates for Congress in every election except 1994 and 1996. Given this trend of independent voters voting for Republicans for the White House and Democrats for Congress, how likely is it that they could become the basis for a new party?

Polling data on the preferences and characteristics of independent voters and of those with very weak partisan preferences indicate that they are more

likely to be moderates on social issues; in other words, they hold positions in between Republicans and Democrats. They are in the middle-income range ($22,500 to $40,000), have not completed a degree beyond high school, and disapprove of the job that Congress is doing. In 1995, however, 50 percent felt that President Clinton should not be renominated. Organizers of a new party probably would be most discouraged by the fact that these voters are also the least interested in politics and our system of government.

For Critical Analysis
How might the Republicans or Democrats reach out to gain the allegiance and the votes of independent voters?

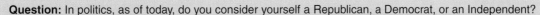
Question: In politics, as of today, do you consider yourself a Republican, a Democrat, or an Independent?

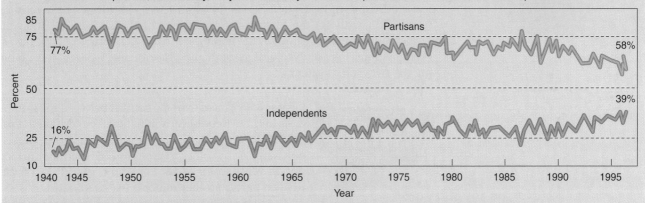

Note: From 1940–1985 data are from personal interviews, from 1986–1995 the results are from telephone surveys. From 1940–1953 the exact question text varies slightly.

Source: Surveys by the Gallup Organization, latest that of August 4–7, 1995.

personnel, such as cabinet secretaries, from the opposition party. As we note in Chapter 13, there are not as many of these appointed positions as presidents might like, and presidential power is limited by the permanent bureaucracy. Judicial appointments, however, offer a great opportunity to the winning party. For the most part, presidents are likely to appoint federal judges from their own party.

All of these party appointments suggest that the winning political party, whether at the national, state, or local level, has a great deal of control in the American system. Because of the checks and balances and the relative lack of cohesion in American parties, however, such control is an illusion. In fact, many Americans, at least implicitly, prefer a "divided government," with the

TICKET SPLITTING

Voting for candidates of two or more parties for different offices. For example, a voter splits her ticket if she votes for a Republican presidential candidate and for a Democratic congressional candidate.

TWO-PARTY SYSTEM

A political system in which only two parties have a reasonable chance of winning.

executive and legislative branches controlled by different parties. The trend toward **ticket splitting**—splitting votes between president and House members—has increased sharply since 1944. Voters seem comfortable with a president affiliated with one party and a Congress controlled by the other. This practice may indicate a lack of trust in government or the relative weakness of party identification among many voters. (See this chapter's *Critical Perspective: What Is the Future of Political Parties?*)

WHY DO WE HAVE A TWO-PARTY SYSTEM?

It would be difficult to imagine a political system in the United States in which there were four, five, six, or seven major political parties. (See this chapter's feature on *Politics and Comparative Systems.*) The United States has a **two-party system,** and that system has been around from about 1800 to the present. Considering the range of political ideology among voters and the variety of local and state party machines, the fact that we still have just two major political parties is somewhat unusual.

Strong competition between the parties at the national level in general has not filtered down to the state level. From 1900 to 1996, the Republicans won thirteen presidential elections and the Democrats, eleven. In state and local elections, however, one-party dominance is the rule in many regions of the United States. The Solid South was almost totally Democratic at all levels of government from 1880 to 1944. The northeastern states and much of the Midwest were solidly Republican from approximately 1860 to 1930. Almost 60 percent of the states today are dominated by either the Republican or the Democratic party.

There are several reasons why two major parties have dominated the political landscape in the United States for almost two centuries. These reasons have to do with (1) the historical foundations of the system, (2) the self-perpetuation of the parties, (3) the commonality of views among Americans, (4) the winner-take-all electoral system, and (5) state and federal laws favoring the two-party system.

The Political Parties

Given two years of extreme conflict between the Democrats and the Republicans in national government, voters had the opportunity in the 1996 elections to choose one party or the other to govern. They had the further option of choosing Ross Perot, the candidate of the Reform party, or other minor party candidates.

The two major parties raised more money than ever before to compete for the presidency and for both houses of Congress. By the end of the campaign, Republican ads began to hint that a Republican Congress was necessary to prevent too much Democratic power. President Clinton, in contrast, aired virtually no ads asking for the election of a Democratic Congress. The outcome of the elections affirmed current partisan trends: 39 percent of the voters declared themselves to be Democrats; 35 percent, Republicans; and 26 percent, Independents. As in 1994, a majority of Independents voted for Republicans for Congress, thus assuring continued Republican control of the House and the Senate. As in past years, only 10 percent of Democrats voted for the Republican presidential candidate (Bob Dole), and only 13 percent of Republicans voted for the Democratic candidate (Bill Clinton). Ross Perot's totals were reduced because most party identifiers were faithful to their candidates. Perot garnered only 17 percent of the votes cast by Independents.

CRITICAL PERSPECTIVE
What Is the Future of the Political Parties?

In 1992, H. Ross Perot's very successful independent campaign for the presidency shocked political party leaders, the media, political pundits, and officeholders alike. How could a candidate who attacked the political party system itself, and who ran solely on his experience as a successful businessman and on his ideas about government, garner 19 percent of the national vote? Not only did Perot win more votes than anyone expected; he also changed the actual methods of campaigning. He forced the other candidates to meet him in three-way, town meeting–style debates. He made campaign announcements on "Larry King Live" on the Cable News Network (CNN), and he made his campaign accessible to everyone through his toll-free 800 number.

Perot's success underlined some of the crises facing the political parties. First, American political parties traditionally have relied on recruiting young Americans into the parties at about the time that they cast their first presidential vote. During the 1980s, Republicans seemed to be gaining ground among younger voters, partly because of the popularity of Ronald Reagan during their formative years. The Clinton campaign in 1992, however, attracted a greater proportion of eighteen- to twenty-nine-year-olds to the Democratic party than the Republicans attracted. Furthermore, an even greater number of younger voters prefer to call themselves independent voters. Perot garnered 22 percent of the votes of this age group and 23 percent of the votes of independents.

Not only do Americans find the message of an independent like Perot attractive, but many also are very intrigued by the formation of a third party. In their book *Mad As Hell: Revolt at the Ballot Box, 1992,* writers Jack W. Germond and Jules Witcover explained the 1992 election as a victory for Bill Clinton that can be attributed to his capitalizing on the alienation and anger of many Americans.

From data collected by the *Time*/CNN poll, it is clear that Americans are willing to consider alternatives to the current two-party system. When asked whether they favored a third party that would run candidates for president, Congress, and state offices against Republicans and Democrats, 54 percent of those questioned answered that they would support such a party.

Washington Post journalist E. J. Dionne, Jr., also finds potential for either a new party or a rebirth of one of the major parties in his discussion of the "Anxious Middle" of America. He analyzes four crises that he believes the United States will face in the future: crises in politics, in economics, in morality, and in the U.S. role in the international order. Dionne suggests that a new reform movement will find supporters and believes that the seeds for a new political movement are planted in the voters' tremendous discontent with the current two major political parties.*

In contrast to these indicators of weaker political parties are signs of strong and vital state and national party organizations. Parties are both raising and spending more money at all levels of party organization. Parties continue to nominate candidates, win office, control governments, and distribute jobs and benefits to their constituents, particularly at the state and local levels.

What may be happening is a change in the meaning of political party for the voter. Voters may be willing to say that they favor one party or another, finding one closer to their personal preferences than another, but such partisan identification does not mean loyalty in the voting booth.

For Critical Analysis

1. Think about how younger Americans find their political identity. How might the current state of politics influence future party identification?

2. What are some of the reasons for voters' discontent with the major political parties?

*E. J. Dionne, Jr., *They Only Look Dead: Why Progressives Will Dominate the Next Political Era* (New York: Simon & Schuster, 1995).

POLITICS AND COMPARATIVE SYSTEMS
One Party, Two Parties, Ten Parties?

Political parties are a phenomenon found in almost all political systems. The number of parties that a nation has, however, may vary from one to dozens. What factors influence the number of parties that a nation has?

As discussed later in the chapter, the United States has only two major political parties and a dozen or so very minor parties. The two-party system is partly the result of historical development and of the kinds of economic and social issues that have divided Americans for two centuries. The system is also influenced strongly by the constitutional structures of the nation. Congressional single-member districts reward only the winner. Losing parties, especially minor parties that have no hope of winning any seats, have little incentive to stay in existence.

Other democratic systems have three-party, four-party, or even ten-party systems. In some European nations, parties are clearly tied to ideological positions, with parties that represent Marxist, socialist, liberal, conservative, and ultraconservative positions on the political continuum. Some nations have political parties that represent regions of the nation that have separate cultural identities, such as the French-speaking and German-speaking regions of Switzerland. Some parties are rooted in religious differences. In some Muslim nations, political parties are based on differences between factions of Islam. Parties also exist that represent specific economic interests—agricultural, maritime, or industrial—and some, such as monarchist parties, speak for alternative political systems.

Like the United States, many other nations have constitutional requirements and legal regulations that either encourage or discourage the formation and growth of new political parties. In general, nations that have single-member, "winner-takes-all" districts have fewer parties than those states that have multiple-member districts or other forms of voting.

Of course, some nations have only one party. The Communist party of the People's Republic of China is the only party allowed to nominate candidates. Some other nations, including Mexico, have one dominant party that always controls the government, even though the system has democratic elections. Whatever the number, however, parties in each nation do represent stated goals and sets of interests.

For Critical Analysis
Are there enough differences between urban and rural voters to support parties for each of these groups? Are there enough differences between Catholics and Protestants in the United States to support political parties for each of these groups?

This handbill was used in the election campaign of 1860. Handbills served the same purpose as today's direct-mail advertisements, appealing directly to the voters with the candidate's message.

The Historical Foundations of the Two-Party System

As we have seen, the first two opposing groups in U.S. politics were the Federalists and the Anti-Federalists. The Federalists, who remained in power and solidified their identity as a political party, represented those with commercial interests, including merchants, shipowners, and manufacturers. The Federalists supported the principle of a strong national government. The Anti-Federalists, who gradually became known as the Democratic Republicans, represented artisans and farmers. They strongly supported states' rights. These interests were also fairly well split along geographic lines, with the Federalists dominant in the North and the Democratic Republicans dominant in the South.

Two relatively distinct sets of interests continued to characterize the two different parties. During Andrew Jackson's time in power, eastern commercial interests were pitted against western and southern agricultural and frontier interests. Before the Civil War, the major split again became North versus South. The split was ideological (over the issue of slavery), as well as economic (the Northeast's industrial interests versus the agricultural interests of the South). After the Civil War and until the 1920s, the Republicans found most of their strength in the Northeast and the Democrats, in the Solid South.

"The euonymus likes partial shade and does equally well under Republican and Democratic Administrations."

Drawing by Farris © 1994 The New Yorker Magazine, Inc.

The West and the Midwest held the balance of power at that time. The period from the Civil War to the 1920s has been called one of **sectional politics.**

Sectional politics gave way to **national politics** as the cities became more dominant and as industry flowed to the South and to the West. Some political scientists classify the period from 1920 to today as one of **class politics,** with the Republicans generally finding support among groups of higher economic status and the Democrats appealing more to working-class constituencies. The modern parties also have reversed their traditional views on the issue of states' rights versus a strong central government. Now, it is the Democrats who advocate a stronger role for the national government, whereas the Republicans want the central government to play less of a role in the political and economic life of the nation.

Self-perpetuation of the Two-Party System

As we saw in Chapter 7, most children identify with the political party of their parents. Children learn at a young age to think of themselves as either Democrats or Republicans. Relatively few are taught to think of themselves as Libertarians or Socialists or even independents. This generates a built-in

SECTIONAL POLITICS

The pursuit of interests that are of special concern to a region or section of the country.

NATIONAL POLITICS

The pursuit of interests that are of concern to the nation as a whole.

CLASS POLITICS

Political preferences based on income level, social status, or both.

DID YOU KNOW ...
That it takes about 700,000 signatures to qualify to be on the ballot as a presidential candidate in all fifty states?

mechanism to perpetuate a two-party system. According to most studies of the process of political socialization, psychological attachment to party identity intensifies during adulthood.[6]

Also, many politically oriented people who aspire to work for social change consider that the only realistic way to capture political power in this country is to be either a Republican or a Democrat. Of course, the same argument holds for those who involve themselves in politics largely for personal gain. Thus, political parties offer avenues for the expression of the personal ambitions of politicians and supply government with men and women anxious to serve the public by satisfying their own goals.[7]

The Political Culture of the United States

Another determining factor in the perpetuation of our two-party system is the commonality of goals among Americans. Most Americans want continuing material prosperity. They also believe that this goal should be achieved through individual, rather than collective, initiative. There has never been much support for establishing the government as the owner of the major means of production. Left-wing political movements wish to limit the ownership of private property. Most Americans take a dim view of such an attitude. Private property is considered a basic American value, and the ability to acquire and use it the way one wishes commonly is regarded as a basic American right.

Another reason we have had a basic consensus about our political system and the two major parties is that we have managed largely to separate religion from politics. Religion was an issue in 1928, when Governor Alfred Smith of New York became the first Roman Catholic to be nominated for the presidency (he was defeated by Republican Herbert Hoover), and again in 1960, when John F. Kennedy was running for president. But religion has never been a dividing force triggering splinter parties. There has never been a major Catholic party or a Protestant party or a Jewish party or a Muslim party.

The major division in American politics has been economic. As we mentioned earlier, the Democrats have been known—at least since the 1920s—as the party of the working class. They have been in favor of government intervention in the economy and more government redistribution of income from the wealthy to those with lower incomes. The Republican party has been known in modern times as the party of the middle and upper classes and commercial interests, in favor of fewer constraints on the market system and less redistribution of income.

Not only does the political culture support the two-party system, but also the parties themselves are adept at making the necessary shifts in their platforms or electoral appeal to gain new members. Because the general ideological structure of the parties is so broad, it has been relatively easy for them to change their respective platforms or to borrow popular policies from the opposing party or from minor parties to attract voter support. Both parties perceive themselves as being broad enough to accommodate every group in society. The Republicans try to gain support from the African American community, and the Democrats strive to make inroads among professional and business groups.

---

[6]See, for example, Lester W. Milbrath, *Political Participation: How and Why Do People Get Involved in Politics?* (Chicago: Rand McNally, 1965), pp. 134–135.
[7]This is the view of, among others, Joseph Schlesinger. See his *Ambition and Politics: Political Careers in the United States* (Chicago: Rand McNally, 1966).

The Winner-Take-All Electoral System

At virtually every level of government in the United States, the outcome of elections is based on the plurality, winner-take-all principle. A plurality system is one in which the winner is the person who obtains the most votes, even if a majority is not obtained. Whoever gets the most votes gets everything. Because most legislators in the United States are elected from single-member districts in which only one person represents the constituency, the candidate who finishes second in such an election receives nothing for the effort.

The winner-take-all system also operates in the **electoral college** (see Chapter 10). In virtually all of the states, the electors are pledged to presidential candidates chosen by their respective national party conventions. During the popular vote in November, in each of the fifty states and in the District of Columbia, the voters choose one slate of electors from those on the state ballot. If the slate of electors wins a plurality in a state, then usually *all* the electors so chosen cast their ballots for the presidential and vice presidential candidates of the winning party. This means that if a particular candidate's slate of electors receives a plurality of 40 percent of the votes in a state, that candidate will receive all the state's electoral votes. Minor parties have a difficult time competing under such a system, even though they may influence the final outcome of the election. Because voters know that minor parties cannot succeed, they often will not vote for minor-party candidates, even if the voters are ideologically in tune with them.

Not all countries, or even all states in the United States, use the plurality, winner-take-all electoral system. Some hold run-off elections until a candidate obtains at least one vote over 50 percent of the votes. Such a system also may be used in countries with multiple parties. Small parties hope to be able to obtain a sufficient number of votes at least to get into a run-off election. Then the small-party candidate can form an alliance with one or more of those parties that did not make the run-off. Such alliances also occur in the United States, but with the winner-take-all system these coalitions normally must be made before the first election, because usually there is no run-off.

Now consider another alternative political system in which there is proportional representation with multimember districts. In Germany, each party submits its preferred list of candidates in order of preference. If, during the national election, party X obtains 12 percent of the vote, party Y gets 43 percent of the vote, and party Z gets the remaining 45 percent of the vote, then in Parliament, party X gets 12 percent of the seats, party Y gets 43 percent of the seats, and party Z gets 45 percent of the seats. Because even a minor party may still obtain at least a few seats in Parliament, the smaller parties have a greater incentive to organize under such electoral systems than they do in the United States.

State and Federal Laws Favoring the Two Parties

Many state and federal election laws offer a clear advantage to the two major parties. In some states, the established major parties need to gather only a few signatures to place their candidates on the ballot, whereas a minor party or an independent candidate must get many more signatures. See this chapter's *Politics and the Fifty States* for a discussion of the widely varying signature requirements. The criterion for making such a distinction is often based on the total party vote in the last general election, penalizing a new political party that did not compete in the election.

At the national level, minor parties face different obstacles. All of the rules and procedures of both houses of Congress divide committee seats, staff

DID YOU KNOW...
That the new Reform party, formed in 1996, used a vote-by-mail process for the first step of its nominating convention and also accepted votes cast by electronic mail?

ELECTORAL COLLEGE

A group of persons called electors who are selected by the voters in each state. This group officially elects the president and the vice president of the United States. The number of electors in each state is equal to the number of each state's representatives in both houses of Congress.

THIRD PARTY

A political party other than the two major political parties (Republican and Democratic). Usually, third parties are composed of dissatisfied groups that have split from the major parties. They act as indicators of political trends and as safety valves for dissident groups.

Eugene V. Debs was the founder of the Socialist party and a candidate for president on that ticket five times. Despite its longevity, the party has had little impact on the American political system.

members, and other privileges on the basis of party membership. A legislator who is elected on a minor-party ticket, such as the Liberal party of New York, must choose to be counted with one of the major parties to get a committee assignment. The Federal Election Commission (FEC) rules for campaign financing also place restrictions on minor-party candidates. Such candidates are not eligible for federal matching funds in either the primary or the general election. In the 1980 election, John Anderson, running for president as an independent, sued the FEC for campaign funds. The commission finally agreed to repay part of his campaign costs after the election in proportion to the votes he received.

THE ROLE OF MINOR PARTIES IN U.S. POLITICAL HISTORY

Minor parties have a difficult, if not impossible, time competing within the American two-party political system. Nonetheless, minor parties have played an important role in our political life. Frequently, dissatisfied groups have split from major parties and formed so-called **third parties,** which have acted as barometers of changes in the political mood.[8] Such barometric indicators have forced the major parties to recognize new issues or trends in the thinking of Americans. Political scientists also believe that third parties have acted as a safety valve for dissident political groups, perhaps preventing major confrontations and political unrest.

Historically Important Minor Parties

Most minor parties that have endured have had a strong ideological foundation that is typically at odds with the majority mindset. Ideology has at least two functions. First, the members of the minor party regard themselves as outsiders and look to one another for support; ideology provides tremendous psychological cohesiveness. Second, because the rewards of ideological commitment are partly psychological, these minor parties do not think in terms of immediate electoral success. A poor showing at the polls therefore does not dissuade either the leadership or the grass-roots participants from continuing their quest for change in American society. Some of the notable third parties include the following:

1. The Socialist Labor party, started in 1877.
2. The Socialist party, founded in 1901.
3. The Communist party, started in 1919 as the radical left wing that split from the Socialist party.
4. The Socialist Workers' party, formerly a Trotskyite group, started in 1938.
5. The Libertarian party, formed in 1972 and still an important minor party.
6. The Reform party, founded in 1996.

As we can see from their labels, several of these minor parties have been Marxist oriented. The most successful was Eugene Debs's Socialist party, which captured 6 percent of the popular vote for president in 1912 and elected more than a thousand candidates at the local level. About eighty mayors were affiliated with the Socialist party at one time or another. It owed much of its success to the corruption of big-city machines and to antiwar sentiment.

---

[8]The term *third party* is erroneous, because sometimes there have been third, fourth, fifth, and even sixth parties. Because it has endured, however, we will use it here.

POLITICS AND THE FIFTY STATES
Getting on the Ballot

Although many Americans (more than half, as of 1996) believe that it would be valuable to have a third major party contend in national elections, state laws make the task of getting a new party on the ballot very complicated. The state laws tend to make it easier to get a new party's presidential candidate on the ballot than to put a full slate of candidates for the House of Representatives on the ballot. If you examine the ballot requirements listed below, you will note that in Louisiana, for example, no signatures are needed to put a presidential candidate on the ballot, but 125,000 signatures of registered party voters are needed to field an entire House slate.

For Critical Analysis

Should the federal government create regulations or enact legislation that would make it easier for third parties to get on the ballot?

Number of Signatures Required for a New Political Party to Get on the November 1996 Ballot

STATE	PRESIDENTIAL CANDIDATE ONLY	FULL SLATE FOR U.S. HOUSE OF REPRESENTATIVES	STATE	PRESIDENTIAL CANDIDATE ONLY	FULL SLATE FOR U.S. HOUSE OF REPRESENTATIVES
Alabama	11,991	35,973	New Mexico	2,339	7,017
Alaska	2,586	4,753	New York	15,000	123,500
Arizona	15,062	15,062	North Carolina	51,904	51,904
Arkansas	0	21,506	North Dakota	7,000	7,000
California	89,006*	89,006*	Ohio	33,463	33,463
Colorado	0	4,800	Oklahoma	41,711	49,751
Connecticut	7,500	18,195	Oregon	18,316	18,316
Delaware	180*†	180*†	Pennsylvania	30,000†	46,351
Dist. of Columbia	3,200†	6,200†	Rhode Island	1,000	2,000
Florida	65,596	196,788	South Carolina	10,000	10,000
Georgia	30,036	180,216	South Dakota	7,792	7,792
Hawaii	3,829	4,889	Tennessee	37,179	37,179
Idaho	9,644	9,644	Texas	43,963	43,963
Illinois	25,000	177,198	Utah	300	500
Indiana	29,822	59,644	Vermont	20	20
Iowa	1,500	3,000	Virginia	16,000†	32,000†
Kansas	16,418	16,418	Washington	200	225
Kentucky	5,000	7,400	West Virginia	6,837	10,904
Louisiana	0	125,000*†	Wisconsin	2,000	10,000
Maine	4,000	8,000	Wyoming	8,000	8,000
Maryland	10,000	85,000†			
Massachusetts	10,000	30,000			
Michigan	30,891	30,891			
Minnesota	2,000	10,000			
Mississippi	0**	0			
Missouri	10,000	10,000			
Montana	10,471	10,471			
Nebraska	5,741	5,741			
Nevada	3,761	3,761			
New Hampshire	3,000	3,000			
New Jersey	800	2,100			

*State requires voter signatories to register as members of that particular party.

**State subjectively decides whether a party is sufficiently "organized" to merit ballot access.

†Estimates.

Notes: Some signature totals are estimates because the formula for calculating the number depends on an event that hasn't happened yet (e.g., the results of a November 1996 election, or the number of registered voters as of January 1, 1997). In Texas and West Virginia, primary voters cannot sign petitions for new party candidates.

SOURCE: *Ballot Access News*, as quoted by John F. Persinos, "Voter Discontent Is Opening an Opportunity for a New Political Force," *Campaigns and Elections*, September 1995.

SPIN-OFF PARTY

A new party formed by a dissident faction within a major political party. Usually, spin-off parties have emerged when a particular personality was at odds with the major party.

Theodore Roosevelt, president of the United States from 1901 to 1909, became president after William McKinley was assassinated. Roosevelt was reelected in 1904. In 1912, unable to gain the nomination of the Republican party, Roosevelt formed a splinter group named the Bull Moose Progressive party but was unsuccessful in his efforts to win the presidency.

Debs's Socialist party was vociferously opposed to American entry into World War I, a view shared by many Americans. The other, more militant parties of the left (the Socialist Labor, Socialist Workers', and Communist parties) have never enjoyed wide electoral success. At the other end of the ideological spectrum, the Libertarian party supports a *laissez-faire* capitalist economic program combined with a hands-off policy on regulating matters of moral conduct.

Spin-off Minor Parties

The most successful minor parties have been those that split from major parties. The impetus for these **spin-off parties,** or factions, has usually been a situation in which a particular personality was at odds with the major party. The most famous spin-off was the Bull Moose Progressive party, which split from the Republican party in 1912 over the candidate chosen to run for president. Theodore Roosevelt rallied his forces and announced the formation of the Bull Moose Progressive party, leaving the regular Republicans to support William Howard Taft. Although the party was not successful in winning the election for Roosevelt, it did succeed in splitting the Republican vote so that Democrat Woodrow Wilson won.

Among the Democrats, there have been three splinter third parties since the late 1940s: (1) the Dixiecrat (States Rights) party of 1948, (2) Henry Wallace's Progressive party of 1948, and (3) the American Independent party supporting George Wallace in 1968. The strategy employed by Wallace in the 1968 election was to deny Richard Nixon or Hubert Humphrey the necessary

majority in the electoral college. Many political scientists believe that Humphrey still would have lost to Nixon in 1968 even if Wallace had not run, because most Wallace voters would probably have given their votes to Nixon. The American Independent party emphasized mostly racial issues, and to a lesser extent, foreign policy. Wallace received 9.9 million popular votes and 46 electoral votes.

Other Minor Parties

Numerous minor parties have coalesced around specific issues or aims. The goal of the Prohibition party, started in 1869, was to ban the sale of liquor. The Free Soil party, active from 1848 to 1852, was dedicated to preventing the spread of slavery.

Some minor parties have had specific economic interests as their reason for being. When those interests are either met or made irrelevant by changing economic conditions, these minor parties disappear. Such was the case with the Greenback party, which lasted from 1876 to 1884. It was one of the most prominent farmer-labor parties that favored government intervention in the economy. Similar to the Greenbacks, but with broader support, was the Populist party, which lasted from about 1892 to 1908. Farmers were the backbone of this party, and agrarian reform was its goal. In 1892, it ran a presidential candidate, James Weaver, who received one million popular votes and twenty-two electoral votes. The Populists, for the most part, joined with the Democrats in 1896, when both parties endorsed the Democratic presidential candidate, William Jennings Bryan.

The Impact of Minor Parties

Minor parties clearly have had an impact on American politics. What is more difficult to ascertain is how great that impact has been. Simply by showing that third-party issues were taken over some years later by a major party really does not prove that the third party instigated the major party's change. The case for the importance of minor parties may be strongest for the spin-off parties. These parties do indeed force a major party to reassess its ideology and organization. There is general agreement that Teddy Roosevelt's Progressive party in 1912 and Robert La Follette's Progressive party in 1924 caused the major parties to take up business regulation as one of their major issues.

Minor parties also can have a serious impact on the outcomes of an election. Although Bill Clinton may well have won the 1992 election in any case, the campaign of H. Ross Perot left its imprint on American politics. Perot was not the candidate of a third party; rather, he was antiparty, attacking both major political parties for being ineffective and beholden to special interests. Perot had a very strong appeal to young voters, to independent voters, and to disaffected party identifiers. In 1996, Perot started the Reform party.

Perot's share of the votes in 1992 could have been divided unevenly between Bush and Clinton, thereby changing the outcome of the election. His success followed the pattern of other third parties that have polled enough votes to affect an election. As Figure 9–3 shows, when a third or minor party makes a strong showing, the incumbent party is likely to lose the White House. Counting 1992, this has happened in six out of the eight elections in which third parties were important.

In 1996 Reform party candidate Perot only received 8 percent of the national vote. This total was enough to affect the margins of both Dole and Clinton, but because Perot drew votes from Republicans, Democrats, and Independents, his campaign did not keep Clinton from being reelected.

Reform Party presidential nominee Ross Perot speaks at the party's national convention in Valley Forge, Pennsylvania.

In eight presidential elections a non–major party's candidate received more than 10 percent of the popular vote—in six of those elections the incumbent party lost. As shown here, only in 1856 and 1924 did the incumbent party manage to hold onto the White House in the face of a significant third-party showing.

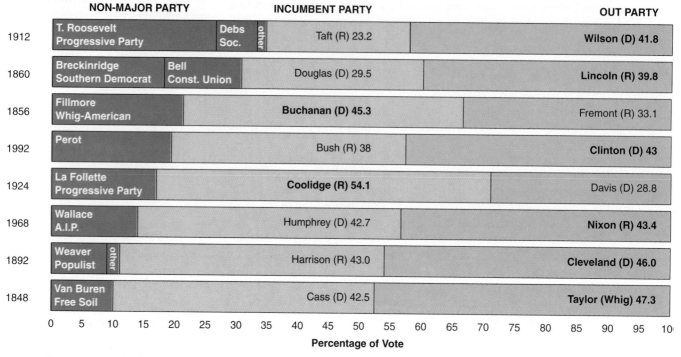

	NON-MAJOR PARTY	INCUMBENT PARTY	OUT PARTY
1912	T. Roosevelt Progressive Party / Debs Soc. / other	Taft (R) 23.2	Wilson (D) 41.8
1860	Breckinridge Southern Democrat / Bell Const. Union	Douglas (D) 29.5	Lincoln (R) 39.8
1856	Fillmore Whig-American	Buchanan (D) 45.3	Fremont (R) 33.1
1992	Perot	Bush (R) 38	Clinton (D) 43
1924	La Follette Progressive Party	Coolidge (R) 54.1	Davis (D) 28.8
1968	Wallace A.I.P.	Humphrey (D) 42.7	Nixon (R) 43.4
1892	Weaver Populist / other	Harrison (R) 43.0	Cleveland (D) 46.0
1848	Van Buren Free Soil	Cass (D) 42.5	Taylor (Whig) 47.3

0 5 10 15 20 25 30 35 40 45 50 55 60 65 70 75 80 85 90 95 100

Percentage of Vote

SOURCE: *Congressional Quarterly Weekly Report*, June 13, 1992, p. 1729.

Figure 9–3
• •
Third-Party Impact on Elections

Calling the U.S. system a two-party system is an oversimplification. The nature and names of the major parties have changed over time, and smaller parties almost always have enjoyed a moderate degree of success. Whether they are splinters from the major parties or expressions of social and economic issues not addressed adequately by factions within the major parties, the minor parties attest to the vitality and fluid nature of American politics.

Courtesy of the Chattanooga Times.

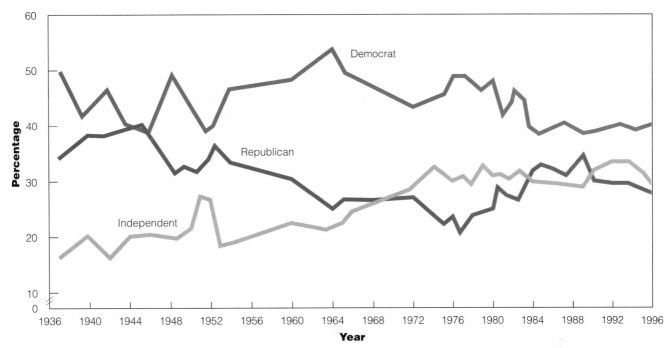

SOURCE: *Gallup Report*, August 1995; *New York Times*/CBS poll, June, 1996.

Figure 9–4
● ●
Party Identification from 1937 to 1996

CONCEPT OVERVIEW
Changes in Political Parties

Since the origin of the American political party system, some features, such as the existence of two major parties, have remained quite stable. Since World War II, however, many of the other features of the political parties have changed significantly—due, perhaps, to changes in the ways that political campaigns are conducted and changes in society.

THEN	NOW
• Presidential nominees were chosen by elites.	• Presidential nominees are chosen by the primary system.
• Parties organized campaigns.	• Candidates organize campaigns.
• Parties raised campaign funds.	• Candidates, PACs, and parties raise funds.
• Door-to-door campaigning.	• Media campaigning, mostly on TV.
• Strong local machines.	• No local machines.
• Patronage politics earned members benefits.	• Little patronage for members.
• Straight-ticket voting frequent.	• Ticket splitting predominates.
• Less than 20 percent independents.	• More than 30 percent independents.

POLITICAL PARTIES: UNFINISHED WORK

PARTY IDENTIFICATION

Linking oneself to a particular political party.

Figure 9–4 on the previous page shows trends in **party identification,** as measured by standard polling techniques from 1937 to 1996. What is evident is the rise of the independent voter combined with a relative strengthening of support for the Republican party, so that the traditional Democratic advantage in party identification is relatively small today.

In the 1940s, only about 20 percent of voters classified themselves as independents. By 1975, this percentage had increased to about 33 percent, and more recent polls show it holding steady at about that level. At times, the Democrats have captured the loyalty of about half the electorate, and the Republicans, until 1960, had more than 30 percent support. By the 1990s, the Democrats could count on less than 40 percent of the electorate and the Republicans, on about 30 percent.

Not only have ties to the two major parties weakened in the last three decades, but also voters are less willing to vote a straight ticket—that is, to vote for all the candidates of one party. The percentage of voters who engage in ticket splitting has increased from 12 percent in 1952 to more than 38 percent in the presidential election of 1996. This trend, along with the increase in the number of voters who call themselves independents, suggests that parties have lost much of their hold on the loyalty of the voters.

There is considerable debate over the reasons for the upsurge in independent voters and split tickets. The increased importance of the media in American politics, the higher educational levels of Americans, and the mobility of American voters may all work to weaken party ties. The work of the political parties in the years to come is to reaffirm their importance to the nation and to the voters. To do this, they will need to move beyond slick media campaigns and money raising to answer the voters' true concerns.

GETTING INVOLVED
Electing Convention Delegates

The most exciting political party event, staged every four years, is the national convention. Surprising as it might seem, there are opportunities for the individual voter to become involved in nominating delegates to the national convention or to become such a delegate. For both the Republican and Democratic parties, most delegates must be elected at the local level—either the congressional district or the state legislative district. These elections take place at the party primary election or at a neighborhood or precinct caucus level. If the delegates are elected in a primary, persons who want to run for these positions must file petitions with the board of elections in advance of the election. If you are interested in committing yourself to a particular presidential candidate and running for the delegate position, check with the local county committee or with the party's national committee about the rules you must follow.

It is even easier to get involved in the grass-roots politics of presidential caucuses. In some states—Iowa being the earliest and most famous one—delegates are first nominated at the local precinct caucus. According to the rules of the Iowa caucuses, anyone can participate in a caucus if he or she is eighteen years old, a resident of the precinct, and registered as a party member. These caucuses, in addition to being the focus of national media attention in January or February, select delegates to the county conventions who are pledged to specific presidential candidates. This is the first step toward the national convention.

At both the county caucus and the convention levels, both parties try to find younger members to fill some of the seats. Contact the state or county political party to find out when the caucuses or primaries will be held. Then gather local supporters and friends, and prepare to join in an occasion during which political persuasion and debate are practiced at their best.

For further information about these opportunities (some states hold caucuses and state conventions in every election year), contact the state party office or your local state legislator for specific dates and regulations. Or write to the national committee for their informational brochures on how to become a delegate.

REPUBLICAN NATIONAL COMMITTEE
Republican National Headquarters
310 1st St. S.E.
Washington, DC 20003
202-863-8500
Fax: 202-863-8820
http://www.mc.org

DEMOCRATIC NATIONAL COMMITTEE
Democratic National Headquarters
430 S.E. Capital St.
Washington, DC 20003
202-863-8000
Fax: 202-863-8081
dnc@democrats.org
http://www.democrats.org

KEY TERMS

CHAPTER SUMMARY

❶ A political party is a group of political activists who organize to win elections, operate the government, and determine public policy. Political parties perform a number of functions for the political system. These functions include recruiting candidates for public office, organizing and running elections, presenting alternative policies to the voters, assuming responsibility for operating the government, and acting as the opposition to the party in power.

❷ The evolution of our nation's political parties can be divided into six periods: (1) the creation and formation of political parties from 1789 to 1812; (2) the era of one-party rule, or personal politics, from 1816 to 1824; (3) the period from Andrew Jackson's presidency to the Civil War, from 1828 to 1860; (4) the post–Civil War period, from 1864 to 1892, ending with solid control by the modern Republican party; (5) the progressive period, from 1896 to 1928; and (6) the modern period, from 1932 to the present.

❸ A political party is composed of three elements: the party-in-electorate, the party organization, and the party-in-government. Each party element maintains linkages to the others to keep the party strong. In theory, each of the political parties has a pyramid-shaped organization with a hierarchical command structure. In reality, each level of the party—local, state, and national—has considerable autonomy. The national party organization is responsible for holding the national convention in presidential election years, writing the party platform, choosing the national committee, and conducting party business.

❹ The party-in-government comprises all of the elected and appointed officeholders of a party. The linkage of party is crucial to building support for programs among the branches and levels of government.

❺ Although it may seem that the two major American political parties do not differ substantially on the issues, each has a different core group of supporters. The general shape of the parties' coalitions reflects the party divisions of Franklin Roosevelt's New Deal. It is clear, however, that party leaders are much further apart in their views than are the party followers.

❻ Two major parties have dominated the political landscape in the United States for almost two centuries. The reasons for this include (1) the historical foundations of the system, (2) the self-perpetuation of the parties, (3) the commonality of views among Americans, (4) the winner-take-all electoral system, and (5) state and federal laws favoring the two-party system. Minor parties have emerged from time to time, often as dissatisfied splinter groups from within major parties, and have acted as barometers of changes in political moods. Spin-off parties, or factions, usually have emerged when a particular personality was at odds with the major party, as when Teddy Roosevelt's differences with the Republican party resulted in formation of the Bull Moose Progressive party. Numerous other minor parties, such as the Prohibition party, have formed around single issues.

❼ From 1937 to the present, independent voters have formed an increasing proportion of the electorate, with a consequent decline of strongly Democratic or strongly Republican voters. Minor parties have also had a serious impact on the outcome of elections. In 1992, for example, the candidacy of H. Ross Perot drew enough support to change the outcome of the presidential election.

QUESTIONS FOR REVIEW AND DISCUSSION

❶ What are the major incentives that keep the political parties alive? To what extent are these incentives shared by party officials and ordinary citizens who think of themselves as Democrats or Republicans?

❷ Why would a third party appeal to today's voters? What would cause party identifiers to turn away from the traditional parties?

❸ What are the major issues and concerns that divide voters today? To what extent are these similar to, or different from, the issues that divided parties in the Great Depression or after the Civil War? How should parties change to respond to the issues that face today's voters?

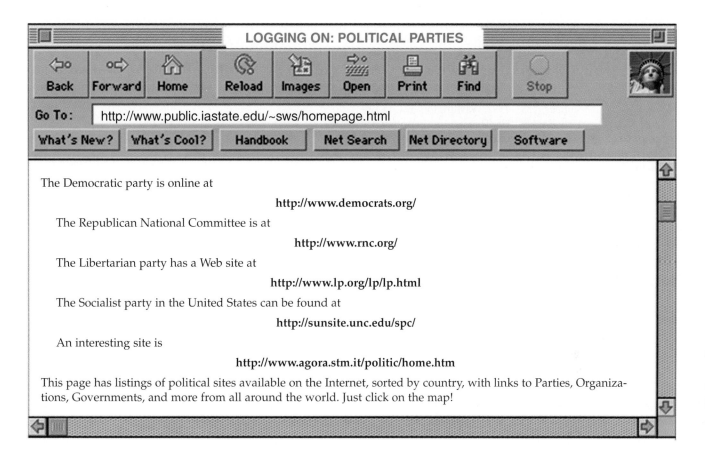

LOGGING ON: POLITICAL PARTIES

Go To: http://www.public.iastate.edu/~sws/homepage.html

The Democratic party is online at

http://www.democrats.org/

The Republican National Committee is at

http://www.rnc.org/

The Libertarian party has a Web site at

http://www.lp.org/lp/lp.html

The Socialist party in the United States can be found at

http://sunsite.unc.edu/spc/

An interesting site is

http://www.agora.stm.it/politic/home.htm

This page has listings of political sites available on the Internet, sorted by country, with links to Parties, Organizations, Governments, and more from all around the world. Just click on the map!

SELECTED REFERENCES

Dionne, E. J., Jr. *They Only Look Dead: Why Progressives Will Dominate the Next Political Era.* New York: Simon & Schuster, 1995. Another commentary on the state of American politics by a noted *Washington Post* journalist. This time, Dionne predicts the possible creation of a third party out of the middle class that is dissatisfied with both parties.

Gillespie, J. David. *Politics at the Periphery.* Columbia, S.C.: University of South Carolina Press, 1993. This work provides both a historical review of the roles played by third parties and minor parties in American politics and a look at the impact of H. Ross Perot on party voting in the 1992 election. The volume is a valuable source of data on third-party voting.

Green, Donald P., and Erick Schickler. *The Grim Reaper, the Stork, and Partisan Change in the North and South, 1952–1992.* New Haven, Conn.: Yale University Press, 1995. The authors discuss party identification and change in the context of generational replacement and regional factors.

Hadley, Charles D., and Lewis Bowman, eds. *Southern State Party Organizations and Activists.* Westport, Conn.: Praeger Publishers, 1995. This collection of original essays examines politics in eleven southern states using data gathered from county party chairpersons.

Keith, Bruce E., *et al. The Myth of the Independent Voter.* Berkeley, Calif.: University of California Press, 1992. The result of extensive survey research, this study examines the implication of the growth of nonpartisanship. The authors contend that most self-declared independents exhibit some degree of partisanship—in fact, often more than do self-declared partisans.

McSweeney, Dean, and John Zvesper. *American Political Parties: The Formation, Decline, and Reform of the American Party System.* New York: Routledge, 1991. This work discusses in detail the evolution of, and influences on, today's American political party system.

Menendez, Albert J. *The Perot Voters and the Future of American Politics.* New York: Prometheus Books, 1995. The author analyzes state-by-state election returns to identify those groups of voters who supported Perot in 1992.

Milkis, Sidney M. *The President and the Parties: The Transformation of the American Party System since the New Deal.* New

York: Oxford University Press, 1993. Milkis argues that the original party system worked against the creation of a modern state and that Franklin D. Roosevelt's shift from party to administrative politics displaced parties and precipitated their decline.

National Party Conventions, 1831–1992. Washington, D.C.: Congressional Quarterly Books, 1995. This volume is a reference guide to all the political party conventions since their origin and includes information about rules, leaders of the parties, platform issues, and candidates.

Schramm, Peter W., and Bradford P. Wilson, eds. *American Political Parties and Constitutional Politics.* Lanham, Md.: Rowman and Littlefield, 1993. This collection of essays explores the role of political parties in American constitutional government and how the parties' movement away from a focus on the Constitution is contributing to party decline.

10
Campaigns, Candidates, and Elections

CHAPTER OUTLINE

Voting Were Compulsory?

BACKGROUND

AMONG THE DEMOCRACIES OF THE WORLD, THE UNITED STATES RANKS FAIRLY LOW IN THE PERCENTAGE OF ELIGIBLE CITIZENS WHO TURN OUT TO VOTE IN LOCAL OR NATIONAL ELECTIONS. MOST HISTORICAL ANALYSES SUGGEST THAT LEVELS OF PARTICIPATION WERE HIGHER IN THE LATE NINETEENTH CENTURY THAN THEY HAVE BEEN IN THE TWENTIETH CENTURY.

WHAT IF VOTING WERE COMPULSORY?

One way to ensure that a much higher percentage of eligible voters would take part in elections would be to make voting compulsory. In theory, the mechanics of such an approach are simple. Every citizen could be required to register to vote at the age of eighteen. At the time of each election, the list of voters would be published for each precinct or township for public inspection. Any registered citizen who did not vote might be sent a ticket, similar to a parking violation, and be required to pay a fine.

In fact, voting is compulsory in Australia, and registration is compulsory in New Zealand. In New Zealand, eligible citizens have an obligation to register at the age of eighteen and are fined if they do not do so. Both nations spend considerable effort and money to make registration easy and convenient for their citizens, however. As a result of this policy, voter turnout rates are higher than 94 percent.

WHAT WOULD BE THE CONSEQUENCES OF UNIVERSAL VOTING?

The immediate effects of compulsory voting might not be that significant. Most studies indicate that the attitudes of nonvoters are quite similar to those of voters, so the results of elections should be much the same as they are today. Surveys suggest that there would be about the same number of voters identifying with the Democrats and about 4 percent fewer identifying with the Republicans. Because nonvoters are less likely to be interested in politics and tend to have less information about the political system, expanding the pool of voters should not change issue preferences of the public. In fact, nonvoters are not perceptibly more conservative or liberal than voters.

The longer-term impact of compulsory voting might be more significant. Those who stay away from the polls today tend to be the poor, the young, minorities, southerners, and the unemployed. Parties and candidates sometimes ignore these groups because they are rarely likely to change the outcome of an election. If these constituent groups were compelled to vote, however, candidates might work much harder to gain their approval and suggest policies that appeal to their respective interests. Younger candidates might win favor among younger voters. Expanded welfare policies or policies to make home ownership easier might be attractive to some of today's nonvoters.

WHAT ARE THE ADVANTAGES AND DISADVANTAGES OF COMPULSORY VOTING?

It does seem that the quality of political debate and interest in government policies would be heightened if a far greater proportion of the electorate went to the polls. Some would argue, however, that the country would be worse off if its least educated, least informed, and least interested citizens voted. Such individuals are likely to make poor choices or to be swayed unduly by campaign rhetoric because they have few facts on which to base their vote.

In addition, the idea of compulsory voting suggests a more authoritarian and controlling regime than most Americans support. Most people would say that if individuals cannot support any of the candidates or disapprove strongly of what the government is doing, it is their right to decide whether to vote and express their views or not to vote.

FOR CRITICAL ANALYSIS

1. *How would compulsory voting change the outcomes of national and state elections, especially in your state?*

2. *Which groups in the population might receive more attention from candidates and political parties if voting were compulsory?*

THE PEOPLE WHO RUN FOR POLITICAL OFFICE

The presidential campaign of 1996 began with the possibility that a political outsider might become the Republican nominee for president instead of the obvious frontrunner—Senate Majority Leader Bob Dole. Given the upsurge in President Bill Clinton's popularity at the end of 1995 and his determined opposition to the proposals of the Republican-controlled Congress, the renomination of the incumbent president was a sure thing. As in other years, the final outcome of the Republican primaries and the general election for president and Congress might have been different if voter turnout had been higher. The *What If . . .* that opens this chapter discusses the possible impact on elections of compulsory voting.

The Republican challengers in the early primaries were an unusual assortment of candidates: Bob Dole, on his third try for the presidential nomination; Patrick Buchanan, articulate conservative commentator; Lamar Alexander, former governor of Tennessee; Senator Richard Lugar of Indiana; Senator Phil Gramm of Texas; Senator Arlen Specter of Pennsylvania; Representative Bob Dornan of California; Alan Keyes, an African American conservative; and a nonpolitician, Steve Forbes, the multimillionaire publisher of *Forbes* magazine. Buchanan challenged Dole from the political right, and the race was close in several states because Buchanan's supporters turned out in large numbers. Gramm, despite his high rate of spending, was rejected by the voters. Steve Forbes mounted the most distinctive challenge to all of the other candidates, spending his own fortune to advertise his "flat tax" proposal. The well-organized Dole campaign, however, quickly eliminated the other candidates and captured the nomination, in terms of delegate votes, by late March.

Due to the **front-loading** of the presidential primaries, which moved most of the big-state primary elections to early in the year, the contest for delegate votes was completed in both parties by late spring. While President Clinton increased his support by using the advantages of the Oval Office, Bob Dole tried to generate enthusiasm among voters before the Republican convention. Both party conventions were held in August and provided virtually no surprises to either the media or the voters. Bob Dole provided some energy for his campaign by choosing Jack Kemp, former member of Congress and cabinet secretary, to be the vice presidential candidate. As the general election

FRONT-LOADING

The practice of moving presidential primary elections to the early part of the campaign, to maximize the impact of certain states or regions on the nomination.

Bob Dole and Jack Kemp at a campaign stop in Media, Pennsylvania, make the most of a photo opportunity posing with an Abraham Lincoln look alike.

campaign opened on Labor Day, however, the 1996 election was much more about whether the Republicans could maintain control of the House and the Senate than whether Bill Clinton would be reelected.

The presidential campaign of 1996 was relatively uneventful. Republican candidate Bob Dole struggled to gain attention for his promise of a 15 percent tax cut for all Americans, while polls showed that most voters were more interested in reducing the budget deficit. President Clinton campaigned across the nation, seeking votes not only in Democratic strongholds like the northeastern states but venturing into the South and continuing to shore up his lead in California. The Clinton campaign, mindful of the potential for a gender gap, emphasized issues such as education, crime reduction, and health care in hopes of winning women's votes.

In the last two weeks of the campaign, Dole began to attack Clinton's character but avoided any outright charges against the administration. After a gallant ninety-six-hour marathon at the end of the campaign, Dole succeeded in gaining 41 percent of the vote. President Clinton was elected with 49 percent of the vote, and Ross Perot garnered 8 percent of the votes cast. Voter turnout, however, was only 48.8 percent, as low as it had been in many decades.

Why They Run

People who choose to run for office can be divided into two groups—those who are "self-starters" and those who are recruited. The volunteers, or self-starters, get involved in political activities to further their careers, to carry out specific political programs, or in response to certain issues or events. The campaign of Senator Eugene McCarthy in 1968 to deny Lyndon Johnson's renomination was rooted in McCarthy's opposition to the Vietnam War. H. Ross Perot's run for the presidency in 1992 was a response to public alienation and discontent with the major parties' candidates.

Issues are important, but self-interest and personal goals—status, career objectives, prestige, and income—are central in motivating some candidates to enter political life. Political office is often seen as the stepping stone to achieving certain career goals. A lawyer or an insurance agent may run for office only once or twice and then return to private life with enhanced status. Other politicians may aspire to long-term political office—for example, county offices such as commissioner or sheriff sometimes offer attractive opportunities for power, status, and income and are in themselves career goals. Finally, we think of ambition as the desire for ever-more-important offices and higher status. Politicians who run for lower office and then set their sights on Congress or a governorship may be said to have "progressive" ambitions.[1]

We tend to pay far more attention to the flamboyant politician or to the personal characteristics of those with presidential ambitions than to their "lesser" colleagues. But it is important to note that there are far more opportunities to run for office than there are citizens eager to take advantage of them. To fill the slate of candidates for election to such jobs as mosquito-abatement district commissioner, the political party must recruit individuals to run. The problem of finding candidates is compounded in states or cities where the majority party is so dominant that the minority candidates have virtually no chance of winning. In these situations, candidates are recruited by party leaders on the basis of loyalty to the organization and civic duty.

---

[1]See the discussion in Linda Fowler, *Candidates, Congress, and the American Democracy* (Ann Arbor, Mich.: University of Michigan Press, 1993), pp. 56–59.

Dwight D. Eisenhower campaigns for president in 1952. Few presidential candidates would take the time to ride in a parade today.

Who Runs?

There are few constitutional restrictions on who can become a candidate in the United States. As detailed in the Constitution, the formal requirements for a national office are as follows:

1. *President.* Must be a natural-born citizen, have attained the age of thirty-five years, and be a resident of the country for fourteen years by the time of inauguration.

2. *Vice president.* Must be a natural-born citizen, have attained the age of thirty-five years, and not be a resident of the same state as the candidate for president.

3. *Senator.* Must be a citizen for at least nine years, have attained the age of thirty by the time of taking office, and be a resident of the state from which elected.

4. *Representative.* Must be a citizen for at least seven years, have attained the age of twenty-five by the time of taking office, and be a resident of the state from which elected.

The qualifications for state legislators are set by the state constitutions and likewise relate to age, place of residence, and citizenship. (Usually, the requirements for the upper house are somewhat higher than those for the lower house.) The legal qualifications for running for governor or other state office are similar.

Race, Gender, and Religion.   In spite of these minimal legal qualifications for office at both the national and state levels, a quick look at the slate of candidates in any election—or at the U.S. House of Representatives—will reveal that not all segments of the population take advantage of these opportunities. Holders of political office in the United States are overwhelmingly white and male. Until this century, politicians were also predominantly of northern European origin and predominantly Protestant. Laws enforcing segregation in the South and many border states, as well as laws that effectively denied voting rights, made it impossible to elect African American public officials in many areas in which African Americans constituted a significant portion of the population. As a result of the passage of major civil rights legislation in the last several decades, the number of African American public officials has increased throughout the United States.

In 1984, Geraldine Ferraro became the first woman to be nominated for vice president by a major party.

Until recently, women generally were considered to be appropriate candidates only for lower-level offices, such as state legislator or school board member. The last ten years have seen a tremendous increase in the number of women who run for office, not only at the state level but for the U.S. Congress as well. Figure 10–1 shows the increase in female candidates. (In 1996, 135 women ran for Congress, and 52 were elected.) Whereas African Americans were restricted from running for office by both law and custom, women generally were excluded by the agencies of recruitment—parties and interest groups—because they were thought to have no chance of winning or because they had not worked their way up through the party organization. Women also had a more difficult time raising campaign funds. Today, it is clear that women are just as likely as men to participate in many political activities, and a majority of Americans say they would vote for a qualified woman or for an African American for president of the United States.

Professional Status.   Not only are candidates for office more likely to be male and white than female or African American, but they are also likely to be professionals, particularly lawyers. Political campaigning and officeholding are simply easier for some occupational and economic groups than for others, and political involvement can make a valuable contribution to certain careers. Lawyers, for example, have more flexible schedules than do other professionals, can take time off for campaigning, and can leave their jobs to hold public office full time. Furthermore, holding political office is good publicity for their professional practice, and they usually have partners or associates to keep the firm going while they are in office. Perhaps most important, many jobs that lawyers aspire to—federal or state judgeships, state attorney offices, or work in a federal agency—can be attained by political appointment. Such appointments most likely come to loyal partisans who have

Figure 10–1
• •
Women Running for Congress

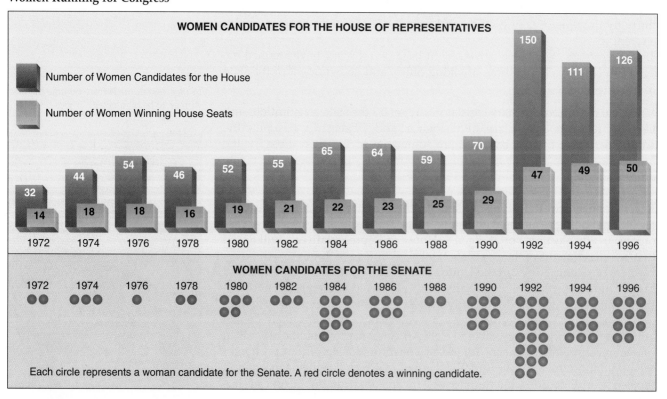

served their party by running for and holding office. Personal ambitions, then, are well served for certain groups by entering the political arena, whereas it could be a sacrifice for others whose careers demand full-time attention for many years.

THE MODERN CAMPAIGN MACHINE

American political campaigns are extravagant, year-long events that produce campaign buttons and posters for collectors, hours of film and sound to be relayed by the media, and eventually winning candidates who become the public officials of the nation. Campaigns are also enormously expensive; the total expenditures for 1996 were estimated at well over $2 billion for all congressional and local races in that year. Political campaigns exhaust candidates, their staff members, and the journalists covering the campaign—to say nothing of the public's patience.

The Changing Campaign

Campaigns seem to be getting longer and more excessive each year. The goal of all the frantic activity of campaigns is the same for all of them—to convince voters to choose a candidate or a slate of candidates for office. Part of the reason for the increased intensity of campaigns in the last decade is that they have changed from being party centered to being candidate centered. The candidate-centered campaign emerged in response to changes in the electoral system, to the importance of television in campaigns, and to technological innovations such as computers.

To run a successful and persuasive campaign, the candidate's organization must be able to raise funds for the effort, get coverage from the media, produce and pay for political commercials and advertising, schedule the candidate's time effectively with constituent groups and prospective supporters, convey the candidate's position on the issues, conduct research on the opposing candidate, and get the voters to go to the polls. When party identification was stronger among voters and before the advent of television campaigning,

DID YOU KNOW...
That the average cost for a U.S. House of Representatives campaign is $525,000 and for a U.S. Senate campaign, $4.5 million?

These campaign workers have volunteered their time to support the candidate or the party of their choice. Political parties and candidates at all levels would have a difficult time conducting their campaigns without such volunteers. Volunteering for a campaign is one way to participate actively in the political process, to learn more about it, and to take advantage of one's rights as a citizen.

a strong party organization on the local, state, or national level could furnish most of the services and expertise that the candidate needed. Political parties provided the funds for campaigning until the 1970s. Parties used their precinct organizations to distribute literature, register voters, and get out the vote on election day. Less effort was spent on advertising for a single candidate's positions and character, because the party label communicated that information to many of the voters.

One of the reasons that campaigns no longer depend on parties is that fewer people identify with them (see Chapter 9), as is evident from the increased number of independent voters. In 1952, about 22 percent of the voters were independent voters, whereas in 1996, between 26 and 33 percent classified themselves as independents, depending on the survey. Independent voters include not only those voters who are well educated and issue oriented but also many voters who are not very interested in politics or well informed about candidates or issues. One campaign goal is to give such voters the most information about the political stance of each candidate.

The Professional Campaign

Whether the candidate is running for the state legislature, for the governor's office, for the U.S. Congress, or for the presidency, every campaign has some fundamental tasks to accomplish. What is most striking about today's campaigns is that most of these tasks are now put into the hands of paid professionals rather than volunteers or amateur politicians.

The most sought-after and possibly the most criticized campaign expert is the **political consultant,** who, for a large fee, devises a campaign strategy, thinks up a campaign theme, and possibly chooses the campaign colors and candidate's portrait for all literature to be distributed. The paid consultant monitors the campaign's progress, plans all media appearances, and coaches the candidate for debates. The consultants and the firms they represent are not politically neutral; most will work only for candidates from one party or only for candidates of a particular ideological persuasion.

Political consultants began to displace volunteer campaign managers in the 1960s, about the same time that television became a force in campaigns.

POLITICAL CONSULTANT

A paid professional hired to devise a campaign strategy and manage a campaign. Image building is the crucial task of the political consultant.

Dick Morris, President Clinton's former top campaign aide, speaks during a brief meeting with the press outside his home in Connecticut. Morris, shown here with his wife Linda McGann, was forced to resign his post as an advisor to the Clinton campaign following news reports that he had a relationship with a prostitute. Morris, however, represents a new breed of political consultant—a professional who will craft a campaign strategy regardless of the candidate's political ideology. Morris, a Republican, has worked successfully with conservative Republicans as well as with Democrats.

Some of the first "superfirms" of consultants operated in California; Ronald Reagan engaged one of these pioneer firms, Spencer-Roberts, to organize his first campaign for governor of California. Several new generations of political consultants have succeeded these early firms. Today's most sought-after firms include those of Roger Ailes (works for Republicans), Bob Squier (Democrats), Carville and Begala (Democrats), and Bob Teeter (Republicans). Following the 1992 campaign, a documentary film about the Clinton campaign, which featured the president's consultants (James Carville and Paul Begala) and campaign staff, was released under the title *The War Room*, a reference to the center of campaign planning.

As more and more political campaigns are run exclusively by professional campaign managers, critics of the campaign system are becoming increasingly vociferous. Their worry is that political consultants are more concerned with plotting campaign strategy and developing the candidate's image than with developing positions on issues. Thomas Edmonds, a conservative consultant, believes that candidates are changing too. He notes that "most modern candidates are more interested in sound bites [brief, memorable comments by news broadcasters] than they are in position papers. They are more interested in how to manipulate the message than what the message really is."[2] A professional campaign manager is a public relations person. He or she looks at an upcoming election as a contest of personalities rather than as a contest between two opposing parties or opposing principles. According to critics, professional campaign managers are willing to do anything to get their candidate to win, even if this means reshaping the public image of the candidate so that it bears little relation to reality.

THE STRATEGY OF WINNING

The goal of every political campaign is the same: to win the election. In the United States, unlike some European countries, there are no rewards for a candidate who comes in second; the winner takes all. The campaign organization must plan a strategy to maximize the candidate's chances of winning. In making these strategic choices, a number of factors are considered.

Candidate Visibility and Appeal

One of the most important concerns is how well known the candidate is. If he or she is a highly visible incumbent, there may be little need for campaigning except to remind the voters of the officeholder's good deeds. If, however, the candidate is an unknown challenger or a largely unfamiliar character attacking a well-known public figure, the campaign must devise a strategy to get the candidate before the public.

In the case of the **independent candidate** or the candidate representing a minor party, the problem of name recognition is serious. There are usually a number of **third-party candidates** in each presidential election. (See Chapter 9 for a figure showing the most successful third parties in American history.) Such candidates must present an overwhelming case for the voter to reject the major-party candidate. Both the Democratic and the Republican candidates use the strategic ploy of labeling third-party candidates as "not serious" and therefore not worth the voter's time.

> **DID YOU KNOW...**
> That Russian president Boris Yeltsin's campaign managers, during his 1996 campaign for the presidency, hired a team of six American political consultants?

INDEPENDENT CANDIDATE

A political candidate who is not affiliated with a political party.

THIRD-PARTY CANDIDATE

A political candidate running under the banner of a party other than the two major political parties.

---

[2]"The Political Campaign Industry," *Campaigns and Elections*, December/January 1994, p. 46.

The First Family aboard "The 21st Century Express" as they kick off their 1996 campaign in Huntington, West Virginia.

Because neither of the major parties can claim a majority of voters in its camp, the task that faces them is threefold. Each party and its presidential candidate must reinforce the party loyalty of its followers, motivate the undecided or independents to vote for their candidate, and—the most difficult task—try to convince some followers of the other major party to cross party lines. The Republicans, having fewer adherents than the Democrats, spend more time and money trying to attract independents and Democrats, whereas the Democrats know that they can win normally if they can secure all of the votes of their party plus a significant share of the independents. To accomplish these tasks, the campaign organization, whether at the presidential level or otherwise, plans a mix of strategies—including televised campaign appearances, debates, and position papers—to sway the voters.

The Use of Opinion Polls and Focus Groups

Because the decision-making power for presidential nominations has shifted from the elites to the masses, one of the major sources of information for both the media and the candidates is polls. Poll taking is widespread during the primaries. Presidential hopefuls will have private polls taken to make sure that there is at least some chance they could be nominated and, if nominated, elected. Also, because the party nominees depend on polls to fine-tune their campaigns, during the presidential campaign itself continual polls are taken. Polls are taken not only by the regular pollsters—Roper, Harris, Gallup, and others—but also privately by each candidate's campaign organization. These private polls, as opposed to the independent public polls conducted by Gallup and others, are for the exclusive and secret use of the candidate and his or her campaign organization.

As the election approaches, many candidates use **tracking polls,** which are polls taken almost every day, to find out how well they are competing for

TRACKING POLL

A poll taken for the candidate on a nearly daily basis as election day approaches.

Bob Dole, former Chairman of the Joint Chiefs of Staff Colin Powell, and Jack Kemp wave to the crowd at Washington International Airport as they prepare to leave for Louisville, Kentucky, where Dole addressed the 97th Veterans of Foreign Wars National Convention.

votes. Tracking polls, by indicating how well the campaign is going, enable consultants to fine-tune the advertising and the candidate's speeches in the last days of the campaign.

Another tactic is the use of the **focus group** to gain insights into public perceptions of the candidate. Professional consultants organize a discussion of the candidate or of certain political issues among ten to fifteen ordinary citizens. The citizens are selected from certain target groups in the population—for example, working men, blue-collar men, senior citizens, or young voters. The group discusses personality traits of the candidate, political advertising, and other candidate-related issues. The conversation is videotaped (and often observed from behind a mirrored wall). Focus groups are expected to reveal more emotional responses to candidates or the deeper anxieties of voters—expressions that consultants believe often are not tapped by more impersonal telephone surveys. The campaign then can shape its messages to respond to these feelings and perceptions.

FOCUS GROUP

A small group of individuals who are led in discussion by a professional consultant to gather opinions and responses to candidates and issues.

WHERE DOES THE MONEY COME FROM?

In a book published in 1932 entitled *Money in Elections,* Louise Overacker had the following to say about campaign financing:

> The financing of elections in a democracy is a problem which is arousing increasing concern. Many are beginning to wonder if present-day methods of raising and spending campaign funds do not clog the wheels of our elaborately constructed mechanism of popular control, and if democracies do not inevitably become plutocracies.[3]

---

[3]Louise Overacker, *Money in Elections* (New York: Macmillan, 1932), p. vii.

CORRUPT PRACTICES ACTS

A series of acts passed by Congress in an attempt to limit and regulate the size and sources of contributions and expenditures in political campaigns.

HATCH ACT

An act passed in 1939 that prohibited a political committee from spending more than $3 million in any campaign and limited individual contributions to a committee to $5,000. The act was designed to control political influence buying.

The purpose of signs like these is to increase name recognition, yet it is doubtful that any one name will be recognized when signs proliferate in number and crowd together as they do here.

Although writing more than sixty years ago, Overacker touched on a sensitive issue in American political campaigns: the connection between money and elections. It is estimated that over $2 billion was spent at all levels of campaigning in 1996. At the federal level alone, a total of more than $416 million is estimated to have been spent in races for the House of Representatives, $200 million in senatorial races, and $600 million in the presidential campaign. Except for the presidential campaign in the general election, all of the other money had to be provided by the candidates and their families, borrowed, or raised by contributions from individuals or PACs (as discussed in Chapter 8). For the general presidential campaign, most of the money comes from the federal government.

Regulating Campaign Financing

The way in which campaigns are financed has changed dramatically in the last two and a half decades, and today candidates and political parties, when trying to increase their funding sources, must operate within the constraints imposed by complicated laws regulating campaign financing.

There have been a variety of federal **corrupt practices acts** designed to regulate campaign financing. The first, passed in 1925, limited primary and general election expenses for congressional candidates. In addition, it required disclosure of election expenses and, in principle, put controls on contributions by corporations. Numerous loopholes were found in the restrictions on contributions, and the acts proved to be ineffective.

The **Hatch Act** (Political Activities Act) of 1939 was passed in another attempt to control political influence buying. That act forbade a political committee to spend more than $3 million in any campaign and limited individual contributions to a committee to $5,000. Of course, such restrictions were easily circumvented by creating additional committees.

In the wake of the scandals uncovered after the 1972 Watergate break-in, Congress and the Supreme Court reshaped the nature of campaign financing. It was discovered during the Watergate investigations that large amounts of money had been illegally funneled to Nixon's Committee to Reelect the President (CREEP). Congress acted quickly to prevent the recurrence of such a situation.

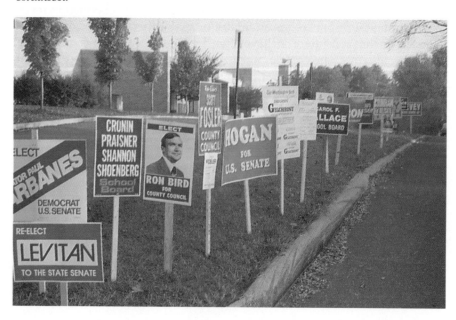

The Federal Election Campaign Acts of 1972 and 1974

The Federal Election Campaign Act of 1972 essentially replaced all past laws and instituted a major reform. The act placed no limit on overall spending but restricted the amount that could be spent on mass-media advertising, including television. It limited the amount that candidates and their families could contribute to their own campaigns and required disclosure of all contributions and expenditures in excess of $100. In principle, the 1972 act limited the role of labor unions and corporations in political campaigns. It also provided for a voluntary $1 check-off on federal income tax returns for general campaign funds to be used by major-party presidential candidates (first applied in the 1976 campaign).

But the act still did not go far enough. In 1974, Congress passed another Federal Election Campaign Act. It did the following:

1. *Created the Federal Election Commission.* This commission consists of six nonpartisan administrators whose duties are to enforce compliance with the requirements of the act.

2. *Provided public financing for presidential primaries and general elections.* Any candidate running for president who is able to obtain sufficient contributions in at least twenty states can obtain a subsidy from the U.S. Treasury to help pay for primary campaigns. Each major party was given $12.4 million for its national convention in 1996. The major party candidates have federal support for almost all of their expenses, provided they are willing to accept campaign-spending limits.

3. *Limited presidential campaign spending.* Any candidate accepting federal support has to agree to limit campaign expenditures to the amount prescribed by federal law.

4. *Limited contributions.* Citizens can contribute up to $1,000 to each candidate in each federal election or primary; the total limit of all contributions from an individual for a set of specific candidates is $25,000 per year. Groups can contribute up to a maximum of $5,000 to a candidate in any election.

5. *Required disclosure.* Periodic reports must be filed by each candidate with the Federal Election Commission, listing who contributed, how much was spent, and for what the money was spent.

The 1972 act also limited the amount that each individual could spend on his or her own behalf. The Supreme Court declared the provision unconstitutional in 1976, stating that it was unconstitutional to restrict in any way the amount congressional candidates or their immediate families could spend on their own behalf: "The candidate, no less than any other person, has a First Amendment right to engage in the discussion of public issues and vigorously and tirelessly to advocate his own election."

The 1974 act, as modified by certain amendments in 1976, allows corporations, labor unions, and special interest groups to set up PACs to raise money for candidates. For a PAC to be legitimate, the money must be raised from at least fifty volunteer donors and must be given to at least five candidates in the federal election. Each corporation or each union is limited to one PAC. As you might imagine, corporate PACs obtain funds from executives, employees, and stockholders in their firms, and unions obtain PAC funds from their members.[4]

---

[4] See Anthony Corrado, *Creative Campaigning: PACs and the Presidential Selection Process* (Boulder Colo.: Westview Press, 1992) for a discussion of how PACs influence early efforts in presidential campaigns.

SOFT MONEY

Campaign contributions that evade contribution limits by being given to parties and party committees to help fund general party activities.

BUNDLING

The practice of adding together maximum individual campaign contributions to increase their impact on the candidate.

Campaign Financing beyond the Limits

Within a few years after the establishment of the tight limits on contributions, new ways to finance campaigns were developed that skirt the reforms and make it possible for huge sums of money to be raised, especially by the major political parties.

Independent Expenditures.   Business corporations, labor unions, and other interest groups discovered that it was legal to make "independent" expenditures in an election campaign so long as the expenditures were not coordinated with those of the candidate or political party. Hundreds of unique committees and organizations blossomed to take advantage of this campaign tactic. Although a 1990 United States Supreme Court decision, *Austin v. Michigan State Chamber of Commerce,*[5] upheld the right of the states and the federal government to limit independent, direct corporate expenditures (such as for advertisements) on behalf of *candidates,* the decision did not stop business and other types of groups from making independent expenditures on *issues.*

In 1996, the Federal Election Commission sued the Christian Coalition, headed by former presidential candidate and television personality Pat Robertson, charging that the coalition illegally promoted Republican candidates through its independent expenditures. The Christian Coalition, which is incorporated, annually raises millions of dollars to produce and distribute voter guidelines and other direct-mail literature to describe candidates' positions on various issues and to promote its agenda. If the suit is successful, it would curtail sharply such independent-expenditure efforts, not only by the Christian right but also by other groups. Other similar suits have not been successful—the courts generally have upheld the right of free speech for organizations.

Soft Money.   Candidates, PACs, and political parties have found other ways to generate **soft money,** that is, campaign contributions that escape the rigid limits of federal election law. Although federal law limits contributions that are spent on elections, there are no limits on contributions to political parties for party activities such as voter education or voter registration drives. This loophole has enabled the parties to raise millions of dollars from corporations and individuals. It has not been unusual for such corporations as Time Warner to give more than half a million dollars to the Democratic National Committee and for the tobacco companies to send more than a million dollars to the Republican party.[6] The parties then spend this money for the convention, for registering voters, and for advertising to promote the general party position. The parties also send a great deal of the money to state and local party organizations, which use it to support their own tickets. (For a discussion of the use of soft money in the 1996 presidential campaign, see this chapter's feature entitled *Politics and Economics: Financing the Presidential Campaign.*

Bundling.   Yet another way to maximize contributions to a candidate or a party is through the practice of **bundling**—collecting $1,000 contributions from a number of individuals in the same firm or family and then sending the quite large check to the candidate of choice. While this practice is in complete compliance with the law, it makes the candidate or party more aware of the source of the funding.

---

[5]494 U.S. 652 (1990).
[6]Paul Allen Beck, *Party Politics in America,* 8th ed. (New York: Longman Publishers, 1996), pp. 293–294.

POLITICS AND ECONOMICS
Financing the Presidential Campaign

In 1992, about $550 million was spent on the presidential campaigns. In 1996, presidential campaign expenditures rose even higher, to an estimated $600 million, making the 1996 presidential campaign the most expensive in history. Where did the money come from? Some of it—$86 million—came from the federal government. That amount, though, constitutes only about 14 percent of $600 million. What about the remaining $514 million? Given the restrictions on campaign contributions, how is it possible to raise funds of this magnitude?

The answer is that individuals and corporations have found *loopholes* (legal ways of evading certain legal requirements) in the federal laws limiting campaign contributions. As discussed elsewhere in this chapter, under laws enacted in 1974, individual campaign contributions to candidates are limited to $1,000, and corporate PAC contributions are limited to $5,000 per PAC. The loophole in the law is that it did not prohibit individu-

als or corporations from contributing to political *parties.* Today, many contributors make donations to the national parties for such activities as voter registration, advertising in the media, campaigns to "get out the vote," and fund-raising events—such as the Democratic party's $10,000-a-ticket fiftieth-birthday dinner for President Bill Clinton in August 1996.

Contributions to political parties, instead of to particular candidates, are referred to as "soft money," because, as one observer said, it is "so squishy." Although clearly it goes to support the candidates, it is difficult to track exactly where the money goes. Although this loophole has existed since the 1970s, there was little widespread awareness or use of it until the 1990s. Today, soft money constitutes an increasing percentage of campaign funds. In the 1996 presidential election, for example, soft money accounted for between $120 and $150 million of each party's campaign funds.

Contributors to the 1996 presidential campaign found other loopholes as well. Corporations donated approximately $25 million to each of the national parties to help defray the costs of the national conventions. This amount was in addition to the portion of the federal funds ($12.4 million to each party) that were given for the same purpose—to pay for the conventions. Other loopholes include in-kind contributions (allowing the party to have the free use of office equipment, for example, instead of making cash contributions) and independent expenditures by interest groups (such as labor unions) to pay for grass-roots campaigns in favor of certain candidates (such as those supporting organized labor).

For Critical Analysis
Should the federal government limit soft-money campaign contributions? What would be the pros and cons of such an action?

The effect of all of these strategies is to increase greatly the amount of money spent for campaigns and party activities. Critics of the system continue to wonder whether the voice of the individual voter or the small contributor is drowned in the flood of big contributions. This chapter's *Critical Perspective* discusses some of the issues that make campaign finance reform so difficult.

RUNNING FOR PRESIDENT: THE LONGEST CAMPAIGN

The American presidential election is the culmination of two different campaigns linked by the parties' national conventions. The **presidential primary** campaign lasts officially from January until June of the election year, and the final presidential campaign heats up around Labor Day.

Primary elections were first mandated in 1903 in Wisconsin. The purpose of the primary was to open the nomination process to ordinary party members and to weaken the influence of party bosses in the nomination process. Until 1968, however, there were fewer than twenty primary elections for the

PRESIDENTIAL PRIMARY

A statewide primary election of delegates to a political party's national convention to help a party determine its presidential nominee. Such delegates are either pledged to a particular candidate or unpledged.

CRITICAL PERSPECTIVE
Controlling the Campaign Money Machine

Since the beginning of the political party system and national presidential campaigns, campaign finance has concerned candidates and parties, as well as the American electorate. Political campaigns are expensive, and with the advent of electronic media and television advertising, the costs continue to escalate. Political candidates and parties always have needed sources of funding for their activities. Citizens also benefit from campaign expenditures. Without advertising, debates, mailings, and personal appearances, the voters would have no information on which to base their votes. Americans, however, traditionally have been suspicious that large campaign contributors might be corrupting the system through their relationships with the president or members of Congress.

Campaign Contributions and the Political Process

As discussed in this chapter, the reform of campaign finance laws in 1972 greatly limited the influence of solitary individuals on campaigns for individual candidates. With the $1,000 limit for contributions per election, wealthy persons must find other avenues for supporting candidates, most likely through PACs and other soft-money practices. Public financing of presidential campaigns also has succeeded to some extent in limiting individual influences on the political process. For every limit or regulation created, however, new methods are devised for funneling money into politics.

Why is it so vital for individuals, corporations, and groups to invest in political campaigns and candidates? For every contribution, there is an interest at stake. Rarely are American individuals or interest groups looking for illegal assistance from officeholders: they want access to make their case; they want small loopholes in tax legislation; they want bureaucratic decisions that will help their interests. So, for instance, when the Clinton administration attacked the tobacco industry, the tobacco companies increased their contributions to the Republican party and to every congressional candidate—incumbent or challenger—who might assist them in their fight to stay in the marketplace. By the summer of 1996, tobacco companies already had become the biggest campaign contributors of the election cycle.

The Difficulty of Reforming Campaign Financing

Is it possible to reform campaign financing to reduce the influence of wealthy individuals and large interest groups? The most strin-

gent reform would include public financing of all presidential and congressional campaign costs. Such a reform probably would outlaw all other contributions to candidates and campaigns. While the idea is appealing, it has proved very difficult for members of Congress, the sitting president, or the political parties to relinquish voluntarily the sources of income that make their success possible. Furthermore, many taxpayers view the idea of paying for all those campaign advertisements as an inappropriate way to spend public money. One state, Maine, will be implementing a public finance system in the near future.

The most recent attempt to control campaign financing involved a bipartisan effort in Congress to limit spending on House and Senate seats and to eliminate contributions from PACs to candidates for Congress. The result was a complete stalemate in Congress and, ultimately, a defense of PACs by many liberals who believed that their limited contributions, publicly recorded, were not the problem. Furthermore, some legislators, such as those who represent very poor districts, claim that without PACs, they would have no chance to raise enough money to stay in office.

The most radical approach, which has been supported by both conservatives and liberals, would impose no limits on contributions but would require complete, early disclosure of every penny given and spent. While this would open the door to huge contributions by corporations or individuals, it also might provide a way for the public to limit influence through the vote. Corruption or perceived influence could be voted out. Although such a free-market approach certainly would support the right of free speech in elections, it depends very heavily on the willingness of the American voter to become informed about candidates, their campaign contributors, and their stands on particular issues.

For Critical Analysis

1. What kind of public information source could track the contributions to hundreds of candidates and make that information available to the public? Would people read this information?

2. What impact would campaign spending limits have on the length and pervasiveness of campaigns? Would shorter, less heavily financed campaigns be as effective as longer, more expensive campaigns in helping voters choose their candidates?

presidency. They were generally **"beauty contests"** in which the contending candidates for the nomination competed for popular votes, but the results had little or no impact on the selection of delegates to the national convention. National conventions were meetings of the party elite—legislators, mayors, county chairpersons, and loyal party workers—who were mostly appointed to their delegations. National conventions saw numerous trades and bargains among competing candidates, and the leaders of large blocs of delegate votes could direct their delegates to support a favorite candidate.

Reforming the Primaries

In recent decades, the character of the primary process and the make-up of the national convention have changed dramatically. The mass public, rather than party elites, now controls the nomination process, owing to extraordinary changes in the party rules. After the massive riots outside the doors of the 1968 Democratic convention in Chicago, many party leaders pushed for serious reforms of the convention process. They saw the general dissatisfaction with the convention, and the riots in particular, as stemming from the inability of the average party member to influence the nomination system.

The Democratic National Committee appointed a special commission to study the problems of the primary system. Known as the McGovern-Fraser Commission, the group over the next several years formulated new rules for delegate selection that had to be followed by state Democratic parties.

The reforms instituted by the Democratic party, which were imitated in most states by the Republicans, revolutionized the nomination process for the presidency. The most important changes require that convention delegates not be nominated by the elites in either party; they must be elected by the voters in primary elections, in caucuses held by local parties, or at state conventions. (See the feature entitled *Politics and Elections: Primaries and Parties* for a description of different types of primaries.) Delegates are mostly pledged to a particular candidate, although the pledge is not formally binding at the convention. The delegation from each state must also include a proportion of women, younger party members, and representatives of the minority groups within the party. At first, virtually no special privileges were given to elected

DID YOU KNOW...
That Philip Morris is the largest "soft money" contributor to the Republican party, having donated at least $1.6 million for the 1996 presidential campaign?

"BEAUTY CONTEST"
A presidential primary in which contending candidates compete for popular votes but the results have little or no impact on the selection of delegates to the national convention, which is made by the party elite.

Riots outside the 1968 Democratic convention in Chicago. The riots influenced the party to reform its delegate selection rules.

POLITICS AND ELECTIONS
Primaries and Parties

Although most Americans assume that the presidential and congressional elections are controlled by the federal government, the only national regulations are those that affect campaign financing and set the day for the national election. States control the system of primaries and caucuses that nominate not only presidents but all candidates at the state level. In the presidential nominating process, some states use a primary election for both parties and some prescribe a caucus system for one or both parties. The same variation exists for other types of nominations at the state level. Some state parties use the primary election, some use caucuses, and some use state-level conventions to nominate candidates for the ticket.

Not only do the states and state parties vary in the devices they use for nominations, but they also may hold different types of primary elections. Among the most likely to be seen are the following:

• **Closed Primary.** In a *closed primary*, the selection of a party's candidates in an election is limited to avowed or declared party members. In other words, voters must declare their party affiliation, either when they register or at the primary election. A closed-primary system tries to make sure that registered voters cannot cross over into the other party's primary in order to nominate the weakest candidate of the opposing party or to affect the ideological direction of that party.
• **Open Primary.** An *open primary* is a primary in which voters can vote in either party primary without disclosing their party affiliation. Basically, the voter makes the choice in the privacy of the voting booth. The voter must,

however, choose one party's list from which to select candidates. Open primaries place no restrictions on independent voters.
• **Blanket Primary.** A *blanket primary* is one in which the voter may vote for candidates of more than one party. Alaska, Louisiana, and Washington all have blanket primaries.
• **Run-off Primary.** Some states have a two-primary system. If no candidate receives a majority of the votes in the first primary, the top two candidates must compete in another primary, called a *run-off primary*.

For Critical Analysis

If you are a candidate who has never run for office before and has not been active in the party, which type of primary election would be to your advantage?

SUPERDELEGATE

A party leader or elected official who is given the right to vote at the party's national convention. Superdelegates are not elected at the state level.

CAUCUS

A closed meeting of party leaders to select party candidates or to decide on policy; also, a meeting of party members designed to select candidates and propose policies.

FRONT-RUNNER

The presidential candidate who appears to have the most momentum at a given time in the primary season.

SUPER TUESDAY

The date on which a number of presidential primaries are held, including those of most of the southern states.

party officials, such as senators or governors. In 1984, however, many of these officials returned to the Democratic convention as **superdelegates.**

The Primary as a Springboard to the White House

As soon as politicians and potential presidential candidates realized that winning as many primary elections as possible guaranteed the party's nomination for president, their tactics changed dramatically. Candidates such as Jimmy Carter concentrated on building organizations in states that held early, important primary elections. Candidates realized that winning early primaries, such as the New Hampshire election in February, or finishing first in the Iowa **caucus** meant that the media instantly would label the winner as the **front-runner,** thus increasing the candidate's media exposure and increasing the pace of contributions to his or her campaign fund.

The states and state political parties began to see that early primaries had a much greater effect on the outcome of the presidential election and, accordingly, began to hold their primaries earlier in the season to secure that advantage. While New Hampshire held on to its claim as the "first" primary, other states moved to the next week. The southern states decided to hold their primaries on the same date, known as **Super Tuesday,** in the hopes of nominating a moderate southerner at the Democratic convention. When California, which had held the last primary (in June), moved its election to March, the primary season was curtailed drastically. In 1996, the presidential nominating process was over in late March, with both Bob Dole and Bill Clinton having enough delegate votes to win their respective nominations. This meant that the campaign was essentially without news until the conventions in August, a gap that did not appeal to the politicians or the media. Both parties began to discuss whether more changes in the primary process were necessary.

On to the National Convention

Presidential candidates have been nominated by the convention method in every election since 1832. The delegates are sent from each state and are apportioned on the basis of state representation. Extra delegates are allowed to attend from states that had voting majorities for the party in the preceding elections. Parties also accept delegates from the District of Columbia, the territories, and certain overseas groups.

At the convention, each political party uses a **credentials committee** to determine which delegates may participate. The credentials committee usually prepares a roll of all delegates entitled to be seated. Controversy may arise when rival groups claim to be the official party organization for a county, district, or state. The Mississippi Democratic party split along racial lines in 1964 at the height of the civil rights movement in the Deep South. Separate all-white and mixed white and African American sets of delegates were selected, and both factions showed up at the national convention. After much debate on party rules, the committee decided to seat the pro–civil rights forces and exclude those who opposed racial equality.

DID YOU KNOW ...
That Abraham LIncoln sold pieces of fence rail that he had split as political souvenirs to finance his campaign?

CREDENTIALS COMMITTEE

A committee used by political parties at their national conventions to determine which delegates may participate. The committee inspects the claim of each prospective delegate to be seated as a legitimate representative of his or her state.

The 1996 Republican National Convention in San Diego, California.

ELECTOR

A person on the partisan slate that is selected early in the presidential election year according to state laws and the applicable political party apparatus. Electors cast ballots for president and vice president. The number of electors in each state is equal to that state's number of representatives in both houses of Congress.

ELECTORAL COLLEGE

The constitutionally required method for the selection of the president and the vice president. To be elected president or vice president, a candidate must have a majority of the electoral votes (currently, 270 out of 538).

Because delegates generally arrive at the convention committed to presidential candidates, no convention since 1952 has required more than one ballot to choose a nominee. Since 1972, candidates have usually come into the convention with enough committed delegates to win.

The typical convention lasts only a few days. The first day consists of speech making, usually against the opposing party. During the second day, there are committee reports, and during the third day, there is presidential balloting. On the fourth day, a vice presidential candidate is usually nominated, and the presidential nominee gives the acceptance speech.

By 1996, the outcome of the two conventions was so predictable that the national networks televised the convention proceedings for no more than two hours each evening. The convention planners concentrated on showing off the most important speeches during that prime-time period.

THE ELECTORAL COLLEGE

Most voters who vote for the president and vice president think that they are voting directly for a candidate. In actuality, they are voting for **electors** who will cast their ballots in the **electoral college.** Article II, Section 1, of the Constitution outlines in detail the number and choice of electors for president and vice president. The framers of the Constitution wanted to avoid the selection of president and vice president by the excitable masses. Rather, they wished the choice to be made by a few supposedly dispassionate, reasonable men (but not women).

 **The Race That Never Was**

Except for a few polls taken near the end of the campaign and the polls taken in the days following the Republican convention, there was little doubt that President Bill Clinton would be reelected to a second term. At one point, the question seemed to become whether it would be a "landslide" or not. The presidential campaign was, in fact, fairly cleanly fought, with relatively few personal attacks made by either party. H. Ross Perot, the nominee of the new Reform party, claimed that he was going to be able to win the election, but he only received 8 percent of the votes, mostly from independent voters.

Presidential debates seemed to have less impact in 1996. The bipartisan, nongovernmental debate commission ruled that Ross Perot had no chance of winning and thus should be excluded from the debates. Clinton and Dole faced off twice, and the vice presidential candidates—Vice President Al Gore and Jack Kemp—met once on national television. The debates were issue oriented and not very memorable.

The *real* race in 1996 was for the control of the House and the Senate. Hundreds of interest groups and corporations got involved in the campaign through "soft money" contributions and spending for educational purposes. All in all, campaign expenditures in 1996 may have exceeded $2 billion.

Both parties and both presidential candidates ended the campaign of 1996 with calls for campaign finance reform. Given the effect of any such reform on the political fortunes of incumbent legislators, it is clear that reform must be undertaken early in the 105th Congress if it is to happen before the next campaign.

The Choice of Electors

Each state's electors are selected during each presidential election year. The selection is governed by state laws and by the applicable party apparatus (see Table 10–1). After the national party convention, the electors are pledged to the candidates chosen. The total number of electors today is 538, equal to 100 senators, 435 members of the House, plus 3 electors for the District of Columbia (subsequent to the Twenty-third Amendment, ratified in 1961). Each state's number of electors equals that state's number of senators (two) plus its number of representatives.

The Electors' Commitment

If a **plurality** of voters in a state chooses one slate of electors, then those electors are pledged to cast their ballots on the first Monday after the second Wednesday in December in the state capital for the presidential and vice pres-

PLURALITY

The total votes cast for a candidate who receives more votes than any other candidate but not necessarily a majority. Most national, state, and local electoral laws provide for winning elections by a plurality vote.

Table 10–1

How Electors Are Selected

By State Political Party Convention	By Political Party's Central Committee	By Political Party
Alabama	California	Arizona
Alaska	District of Columbia	Maryland
Arkansas	Florida	
Colorado	Louisiana	
Connecticut	Massachusetts	
Delaware	Missouri	
Georgia	Montana	
Hawaii	New Jersey	
Idaho	New York	
Illinois	Pennsylvania	
Indiana	South Carolina	
Iowa	Tennessee	
Kansas		
Kentucky		
Maine		
Michigan		
Minnesota		
Mississippi		
Nebraska		
Nevada		
New Hampshire		
New Mexico		
North Carolina		
North Dakota		
Ohio		
Oklahoma		
Oregon		
Rhode Island		
South Dakota		
Texas		
Utah		
Vermont		
Virginia		
Washington		
West Virginia		
Wisconsin		
Wyoming		

SOURCE: Michael J. Glennon, *When No Majority Rules: The Electoral College and Presidential Succession* (Washington, D.C.: Congressional Quarterly, 1993), p. 24.

idential candidates for the winning party.[7] The Constitution does not, however, require the electors to cast their ballots for the candidate of their party.

The ballots are counted and certified before a joint session of Congress early in January. The candidates who receive a majority of the electoral votes (270) are certified as president-elect and vice president–elect. According to the Constitution, in cases in which no candidate receives a majority of the electoral votes, the election of the president is decided in the House from among the candidates with the three highest number of votes (decided by a plurality of each state delegation), each state having one vote. The selection of the vice president is determined by the Senate in a choice between the two highest candidates, each senator having one vote. Congress was required to choose the president and vice president in 1801 (Thomas Jefferson and Aaron Burr), and the House chose the president in 1825 (John Quincy Adams). The entire process is outlined in Figure 10–2.

It is possible for a candidate to become president without obtaining a majority of the popular vote. There have been numerous minority presidents in our history, including Abraham Lincoln, Woodrow Wilson, Harry S Truman, John F. Kennedy, Richard Nixon (in 1968), and Bill Clinton. Such an event can always occur when there are third-party candidates.

---

[7]In Maine and Nebraska, electoral votes are based on congressional districts. Each district chooses one elector. The remaining two electors are chosen statewide.

Figure 10–2
• •
How Presidents and Vice Presidents Are Chosen

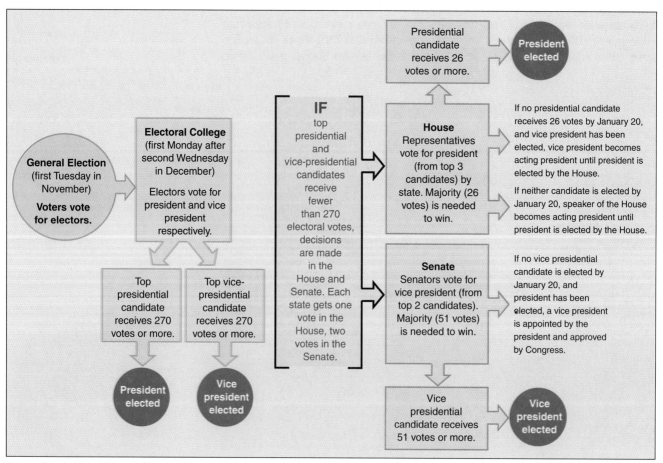

SOURCE: Adapted from Michael J. Glennon, *When No Majority Rules: The Electoral College and Presidential Succession* (Washington, D.C.: Congressional Quarterly, 1993), p. 20.

Perhaps more distressing is the possibility of a candidate's being elected when the candidate's major opposition receives a larger popular vote. This occurred on three occasions—in the elections of John Quincy Adams in 1824, Rutherford B. Hayes in 1876, and Benjamin Harrison in 1888, all of whom won elections without obtaining a plurality of the popular vote.

Criticisms of the Electoral College

Besides the possibility of a candidate's becoming president even though his or her major opponent obtains more popular votes, there are other complaints about the electoral college. The idea of the Constitution's framers was to have electors use their own discretion to decide who would make the best president. But electors no longer perform the selecting function envisioned by the founders, because they are committed to the candidate who has a plurality of popular votes in their state in the general election.[8]

One can also argue that the current system, which gives all of the electoral votes to the candidate who has a statewide plurality, is unfair to other candidates and their supporters. The unit system of voting also means that presidential campaigning will be concentrated in those states that have the largest number of electoral votes and in those states in which the outcome is likely to be close. All of the other states generally get second-class treatment during the presidential campaign.

It can also be argued that there is something of a less-populous-state bias in the electoral college, because including Senate seats in the electoral vote total partly offsets the edge of the more populous states in the House. A state such as Alaska (with two senators and one representative) gets an electoral vote for roughly each 183,000 people (based on the 1990 census), whereas Iowa gets one vote for each 397,000 people, and New York has a vote for every 545,000 inhabitants.

---

[8]Note, however, that there have been revolts by so-called *faithless electors*—in 1796, 1820, 1948, 1956, 1960, 1968, 1972, 1976, and 1988.

DID YOU KNOW ...
That forty-two states do not indicate on the ballot that the voter is casting a ballot for the electors rather than for the president and vice president directly?

Proposed Reforms

Many proposals for reform of the electoral college system have been advanced. The most obvious is to get rid of it completely and simply allow candidates to be elected on a popular-vote basis; in other words, have a direct election, by the people, for president and vice president. This was proposed as a constitutional amendment by President Jimmy Carter in 1977, but it failed to achieve the required two-thirds majority in the Senate in a 1979 vote. An earlier effort in 1969 passed the House, but a Senate vote defeated the proposed amendment due to the efforts of senators from less populous states and the South.

A less radical reform is a federal law that would require each elector to vote for the candidate who has a plurality in the state. Another system would eliminate the electors but retain the electoral vote, which would be given on a proportional basis rather than on a unit (winner-take-all) basis. This method was endorsed by President Richard Nixon in 1969.

The major parties are not in favor of eliminating the electoral college, fearing that it would give minor parties a more influential role. Also, less populous states are not in favor of direct election of the president, because they feel they would be overwhelmed by the large urban vote.

AUSTRALIAN BALLOT

A secret ballot prepared, distributed, and tabulated by government officials at public expense. Since 1888, all states have used the Australian ballot rather than an open, public ballot.

HOW ARE ELECTIONS CONDUCTED?

The United States uses the **Australian ballot**—a secret ballot that is prepared, distributed, and counted by government officials at public expense. Since 1888, all states have used the Australian ballot. Before that, many states used the alternatives of oral voting and differently colored ballots prepared by the

In the voting booth, an official demonstrates how a voter indicates his or her choice in an election.

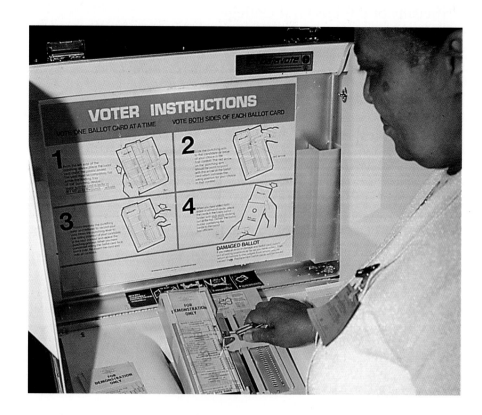

parties. Obviously, knowing which way a person was voting made it easy to apply pressure to change his or her vote, and vote buying was common.

Office-Block and Party-Column Ballots

There are two types of ballots in use in the United States in general elections. The first, called an **office-block ballot,** or sometimes called a **Massachusetts ballot,** groups all the candidates for each elective office under the title of each office. Politicians dislike the office-block ballot, because it places more emphasis on the office than on the party; it discourages straight-ticket voting and encourages split-ticket voting.

A **party-column ballot** is a form of general election ballot in which the candidates are arranged in one column under their respective party labels and symbols. It is also called the **Indiana ballot.** In some states, it allows voters to vote for all of a party's candidates for local, state, and national offices by simply marking a single "X" or by pulling a single lever. Most states use this type of ballot. As it encourages straight-ticket voting, majority parties favor this form. When a party has an exceptionally strong presidential or gubernatorial candidate to head the ticket, the **coattail effect** is increased by the use of the party-column ballot.

Counting the Votes and Avoiding Fraud

State and local election officials tabulate the results of each election after the polls are closed. Although most votes are tallied electronically, there is still the possibility of voting fraud. To minimize this possibility, the use of canvassing boards is common. A **canvassing board** is an official body that tabulates and consolidates the returns and forwards them to the state canvassing authority. It is only in very close elections that the final outcome turns on the official tabulation and certification.

To avoid fraud at the polling places themselves, each party may appoint **poll watchers** to monitor elections. In virtually all polling places throughout the country during partisan elections, major parties have their own poll watchers. Poll watching is particularly important when there is a challenge to

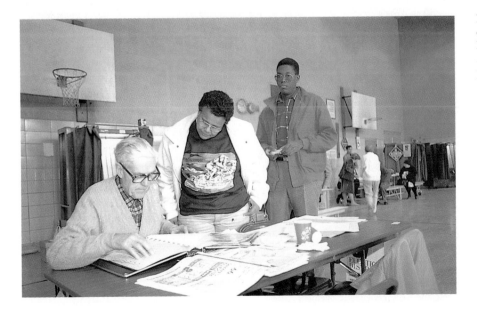

Election judges check the registration of each voter before giving out the ballot. Most local election boards require judges from both political parties at each precinct.

CHALLENGE

An allegation by a poll watcher that a potential voter is unqualified to vote or that a vote is invalid; designed to prevent fraud in elections.

an entrenched, local political machine. At any time, a poll watcher may make a **challenge,** which is an allegation either that a potential voter is unqualified or that his or her vote is invalid. Once a challenge is made, a bipartisan group of election judges in each precinct will decide on the merits of the challenge.

Vote fraud is something regularly suspected but seldom proved. Voting in the nineteenth century, when secret ballots were rare and people had a cavalier attitude toward the open buying of votes, was probably much more conducive to fraud than modern elections are. A recent investigation by Larry J. Sabato and Glenn R. Simpson, however, revealed that the potential for vote fraud is high in many states, particularly through the use of phony voter registrations and absentee ballots.[9]

VOTING IN NATIONAL, STATE, AND LOCAL ELECTIONS

In 1996, there were 196.5 million eligible voters. Of that number, 151.7 million, or 77 percent, actually registered to vote in the general presidential election. Of those who registered, 95.8 million actually went to the polls. The participation rate during the 1996 presidential election was only 63 percent of registered voters, down from 76 percent in 1992, and 48.8 percent of eligible voters (see Table 10–2).

VOTER TURNOUT

The percentage of citizens taking part in the election process; the number of eligible voters that actually "turn out" on election day to cast their ballots.

Figure 10–3 shows that the **voter turnout** in the United States compared with that of selected countries places Americans at the bottom. Figure 10–4 shows voter turnout for presidential and congressional elections from 1896 to

[9]Larry J. Sabato and Glenn R. Simpson, *Dirty Little Secrets: The Persistence of Corruption in American Politics* (New York: Random House, 1996).

Table 10–2

Elected by a Majority?

Most presidents have won a majority of the votes cast in the election. We generally judge the extent of their victory by whether they have won more than 51 percent of the votes. Some presidential elections have been proclaimed *landslides,* meaning that the candidates won by an extraordinary majority of votes cast. As indicated below, however, no modern president has been elected by more than 38 percent of the total voting-age electorate.

YEAR—WINNER (PARTY)	PERCENTAGE OF TOTAL POPULAR VOTE	PERCENTAGE OF VOTING-AGE POPULATION
1932—Roosevelt (D)	57.4	30.1
1936—Roosevelt (D)	60.8	34.6
1940—Roosevelt (D)	54.7	32.2
1944—Roosevelt (D)	53.4	29.9
1948—Truman (D)	49.6	25.3
1952—Eisenhower (R)	55.1	34.0
1956—Eisenhower (R)	57.4	34.1
1960—Kennedy (D)	49.7	31.2
1964—Johnson (D)	61.1	37.8
1968—Nixon (R)	43.4	26.4
1972—Nixon (R)	60.7	33.5
1976—Carter (D)	50.1	26.8
1980—Reagan (R)	50.7	26.7
1984—Reagan (R)	58.8	31.2
1988—Bush (R)	53.4	26.8
1992—Clinton (D)	43.3	23.1
1996—Clinton (D)	49.2	23.2

SOURCE: *Congressional Quarterly Weekly Report,* January 31, 1989, p. 137; *New York Times,* November 5, 1992; and *New York Times,* November 7, 1996.

1996. The last "good" year of turnout for the presidential elections was 1960, when almost 65 percent of the eligible voters actually voted. Each of the peaks in the figure represents voter turnout in a presidential election. Thus, we can also see that voting for U.S. representatives is greatly influenced by whether there is a presidential election in the same year.

The same is true at the state level. When there is a race for governor, more voters participate both in the general election for governor and in the election for state representatives. Voter participation rates in gubernatorial elections are also greater in presidential election years. The average turnout in state elections is about 14 percentage points higher when a presidential election is held. This chapter's *Politics and the Fifty States* shows the voter turnout in each state for the 1994 congressional elections.

Now consider local elections. In races for mayor, city council, county auditor, and the like, it is fairly common for only 25 percent or less of the electorate to vote. Is something amiss here? It would seem obvious that people would be more likely to vote in elections that directly affect them. At the local level, each person's vote counts more (because there are fewer voters). Furthermore, the issues—crime control, school bonds, sewer bonds, and so on—touch the immediate interests of the voters. The facts, however, do not fit the theory. Potential voters are most interested in national elections, when a presidential choice is involved. Otherwise, voter participation in our representative government is very low (and, as we have seen, it is not overwhelmingly great even at the presidential level).

The Effect of Low Voter Turnout

There are two schools of thought concerning low voter turnout. Some view the decline in voter participation as a clear threat to our representative democratic government. Fewer and fewer individuals are deciding who wields political power in our society. Also, low voter participation presumably signals apathy about our political system in general. It also may signal that potential voters simply do not want to take the time to learn about the issues.

Figure 10–3
Voter Turnout in the United States Compared with Other Countries

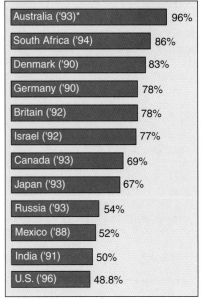

Australia ('93)*	96%
South Africa ('94)	86%
Denmark ('90)	83%
Germany ('90)	78%
Britain ('92)	78%
Israel ('92)	77%
Canada ('93)	69%
Japan ('93)	67%
Russia ('93)	54%
Mexico ('88)	52%
India ('91)	50%
U.S. ('96)	48.8%

*Year of the most recent national election.
SOURCE: *Time* Magazine, May 23, 1994, and authors' update.

Figure 10–4
Voter Turnout for Presidential and Congressional Elections, 1896 to Present

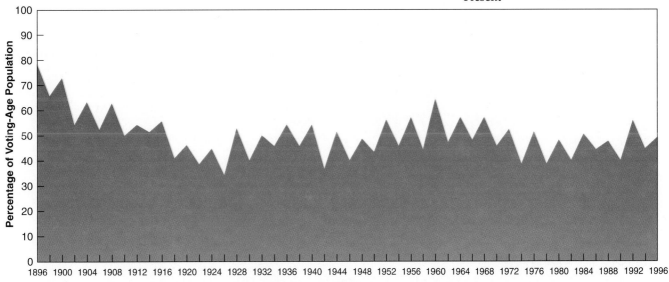

SOURCE: Historical Data Archive, Inter-university Consortium for political and social research: U.S. Department of Commerce, *Statistical Abstract of the United States: 1980*, 101st ed. (Washington, D.C.: U.S. Government Printing Office, 1980), p. 515; William H. Flanigan and Nancy H. Zingale, *Political Behavior of the American Electorate*, 5th ed. (Boston: Allyn and Bacon, 1983), p. 20; *Congressional Quarterly*, various issues; and authors' update.

POLITICS AND THE FIFTY STATES
Voter Turnout

The table below shows the percentage of the persons who registered and the voting turnout in the latest nonpresidential-year congressional elections by state and region of the country. The overall turnout rate for the election was 44.5 percent, which is relatively high for a congressional election. Note that different regions of the country tend to have quite different registration and turnout rates, and that individual states within those regions recorded higher turnout rates. Those state variations may indicate a particularly competitive race in that year. The West North Central (W.N.C.). region, which includes Minnesota, Wisconsin, and the Great Plains states, had the highest registration rate as well as the highest voter turnout rate.

For Critical Analysis
What are some of the political, legal, or cultural factors that might explain differences among the states in registration and voter turnout?

Number of Persons Who Registered and Voted, by State: 1994

State	Voting-Age Population (1000)	Percentage of Voting-Age Population		State	Voting-Age Population (1000)	Percentage of Voting-Age Population	
		Registered	Voted			Registered	Voted
U.S.	190,267	62.0	44.6	DC	440	66.9	55.6
				VA	4,760	60.0	45.7
Northeast	38,386	60.9	45.2	WV	1,396	60.8	33.9
N.E.	9,865	67.8	51.0	NC	5,211	60.8	35.7
ME	909	81.6	58.2	SC	2,681	60.8	45.2
NH	832	64.3	41.2	GA	5,105	54.9	35.4
VT	432	70.7	48.8	FL	10,582	55.5	42.3
MA	4,532	65.6	51.6	E.S.C.	11,662	66.7	41.9
RI	729	64.2	50.6	KY	2,807	62.5	34.5
CT	2,431	68.4	51.3	TN	3,856	63.7	43.0
M.A.	28,521	58.5	43.1	AL	3,136	70.6	45.8
NY	13,599	56.8	44.6	MS	1,863	72.6	44.3
NJ	5,918	61.6	40.3	W.S.C.	20,273	61.0	38.5
PA	9,004	58.9	42.7	AR	1,801	60.0	41.6
Midwest	44,505	68.7	48.7	LA	3,013	70.6	34.2
E.N.C.	31,463	66.4	46.1	OK	2,325	65.8	46.8
OH	8,152	64.6	46.6	TX	13,134	58.2	37.6
IN	4,191	55.6	38.7	West	51,009	58.1	46.4
IL	8,561	63.0	42.8	Mountain	10,911	60.0	45.9
MI	6,921	73.7	52.2	MT	619	73.2	60.7
WI	3,638	77.2	49.6	ID	798	63.0	50.7
W.N.C.	13,042	74.3	55.2	WY	333	69.0	63.5
MN	3,296	80.9	58.4	CO	2,703	64.3	46.4
IA	2,059	71.7	52.5	NM	1,175	58.8	46.8
MO	3,797	72.3	54.5	AZ	2,971	56.0	41.6
ND	441	93.3	61.1	UT	1,231	59.4	44.1
SD	495	75.4	63.9	NV	1,081	49.5	40.1
NE	1,156	72.6	54.3	Pacific	30,098	57.4	46.6
KS	1,798	65.3	50.5	WA	3,924	66.8	46.3
South	66,364	60.7	40.5	OR	2,309	72.7	60.9
S.A.	34,429	58.4	41.2	CA	22,639	54.2	45.0
DE	528	58.7	41.2	AK	393	71.7	59.1
MD	3,726	62.6	46.2	HI	833	51.5	46.0

SOURCE: U.S. Bureau of the Census.

When only a handful of people do take the time, it will be easier, say the alarmists, for an authoritarian figure to take over our government.

Others are less concerned about low voter participation. They believe that a decline in voter participation simply indicates more satisfaction with the status quo. Also, they believe that representative democracy is a reality even if a very small percentage of eligible voters vote. If everyone who does not vote believes that the outcome of the election will accord with his or her own desires, then representative democracy is working. The nonvoters are obtaining the type of government—with the type of people running it—that they want to have anyway.

Factors Influencing Who Votes

A clear association exists between voter participation and the following characteristics: age, educational attainment, minority status, income level, and the existence of two-party competition.

1. *Age.* Look at Table 10–3, which shows the breakdown of voter participation by age group for the 1992 presidential election. It would appear from these figures that age is a strong factor in determining voter turnout on election day. The reported turnout increases with older age groups. Greater participation with age is very likely due to the fact that older voters are more settled in their lives, are already registered, and have had more time to experience voting as an expected activity.

2. *Educational attainment.* Education also influences voter turnout. In general, the more education you have, the more likely you are to vote. This pattern is clearly evident in the 1992 election results, as we can see in Table 10–4. Reported turnout was over 30 percentage points higher for those who had some college education than it was for people who had never been to high school.

3. *Minority status.* Race is important, too, in determining the level of voter turnout. Whites in 1992 voted at a 59 percent rate, whereas the African American turnout rate was 51.5 percent.

4. *Income levels.* Differences in income can also lead to differences in voter turnout. Wealthier people tend to be overrepresented in the electorate. In 1992, turnout among whites varied from less than 40 percent of those with annual family incomes under $15,000 to about 70 percent for people with annual family incomes of $50,000 or more.

5. *Two-party competition.* Another factor in voter turnout is the extent to which elections are competitive within a state. More competitive states generally have higher turnout rates, although the highest average percentage turnout for the past two decades has been in states in which Republicans were elected to most state offices.

The foregoing statistics reinforce one another. White voters are likely to be wealthier than African American voters, who are also less likely to have obtained a college education.

Why People Do Not Vote

For many years, political scientists believed that one reason why voter turnout in the United States was so much lower than in other Western nations was that it was so difficult to register and vote. In most states, registration required a special trip to a public office far in advance of elections. Many experts are now advancing other explanations for low U.S. voter turnout, however.

Table 10–3

Voting in the 1992 Presidential Election by Age Group (in Percentage)

AGE	REPORTED TURNOUT
18–20	38.5
21–24	45.7
25–34	53.2
35–44	63.6
45–64	70.0
65 and over	70.1

SOURCE: U.S. Department of Commerce, *Statistical Abstract of the United States: 1993* (Washington, D.C.: U.S. Government Printing Office, 1993), p. 283.

Table 10–4

Voting in the 1992 Presidential Election by Education Level (in Percentage)

YEARS OF SCHOOL COMPLETED	REPORTED TURNOUT
8 years or less	35.1
9–11 years	42.2
12 years	57.5
1–3 years of college	68.7
4+ years of college	81.0

SOURCE: U.S. Department of Commerce, *Statistical Abstract of the United States: 1993* (Washington, D.C.: U.S. Government Printing Office, 1993), p. 283.

These residents of New York are voting in the 1992 presidential elections. The long lines seemed to indicate a high turnout. Indeed, voter turnout rates during presidential election years are consistently much higher than voter turnout rates during off years.

Political Withdrawal.   Ruy A. Teixeira believes that the factor that has contributed most significantly to the decline in voting turnout since 1960 is not the "cost" of voting but the increasing social and political disconnectedness of American society. Teixeira's study shows that the barriers to voting have been reduced considerably since 1960, whereas turnout continues to decrease. It is true that as the population has become more educated and wealthier, turnout has increased among some groups. But with the decline of church membership, social memberships, and community identity, along with the extraordinary increase in political cynicism and distrust, fewer and fewer citizens feel close enough to government to be interested in voting.[10]

RATIONAL IGNORANCE EFFECT

When people purposely and rationally decide not to become informed on an issue because they believe that their vote on the issue is not likely to be a deciding one; a lack of incentive to seek the necessary information to cast an intelligent vote.

The Rational Ignorance Effect.   Another explanation of why voter turnout is low suggests that citizens are making a logical choice in not voting. If citizens believe that their votes will not affect the outcome of an election, then they have little incentive to seek the information they need to cast intelligent votes. The lack of incentive to obtain costly (in terms of time, attention, and so on) information about politicians and political issues has been called the **rational ignorance effect.** That term may seem contradictory, but it is not. Rational ignorance is a condition in which people purposely and rationally decide *not* to obtain information—to remain ignorant.

If average voters choose to remain rationally ignorant, what determines how they vote when they do vote? According to the rational ignorance theory, voters will simply rely on information that is supplied by candidates and by the mass media. Bits of information picked up from TV news and political advertising, as well as information gleaned from casual conversations with co-workers and friends, will be used as a basis for making a choice among candidates.

Why, then, do even one-third to one-half of U.S. citizens bother to show up at the polls? One explanation is that most citizens receive personal satisfaction from the act of voting. It makes them feel that they are good citizens and

[10]Ruy A. Teixeira, *The Disappearing American Voter* (Washington, D.C.: Brookings Institution, 1992), p. 57.

that they are doing something patriotic. But that feeling is not overriding. Even among voters who are registered and who plan to vote, if the cost of voting goes up (in terms of time and inconvenience), the number of eligible voters who actually vote will fall. In particular, bad weather on election day means that, on average, a smaller percentage of eligible voters will go to the polls.

LEGAL RESTRICTIONS ON VOTING

Legal restrictions on voter registration have existed since the founding of the nation. Most groups in the United States have been concerned with the suffrage issue at one time or another.

Historical Restrictions

In colonial times, only white males who owned property with a certain minimum value were eligible to vote, leaving a far greater number of Americans ineligible than eligible to take part in the democratic process. Because many government functions are in the economic sphere and concern property rights and the distribution of income and wealth, some of the founders of our nation felt it was appropriate that only people who had an interest in property should vote on these issues. The idea of extending the vote to all citizens was, according to South Carolina delegate Charles Pinckney, merely "theoretical nonsense." Of paramount concern to the backers of the Constitution was that the government should be as insulated as possible from the shifting electoral will of the population. A restricted vote meant a more stable government. An unrestricted vote would result, as Elbridge Gerry of Massachusetts declared at the Constitutional Convention, in "the evils . . . [which] flow from the excess of democracy."

The logic behind this restriction of voting rights to property owners was questioned seriously by Thomas Paine in his pamphlet *Common Sense:*

> Here is a man who today owns a jackass, and the jackass is worth $60. Today the man is a voter and goes to the polls and deposits his vote. Tomorrow the jackass

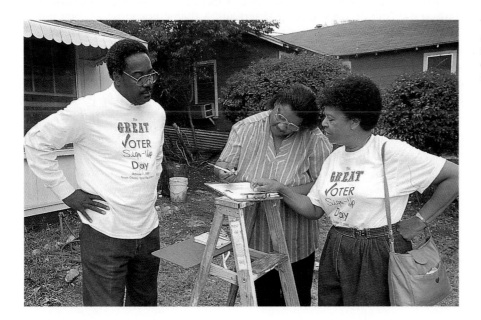

Voter registration is an important part of our political process. This worker is helping a citizen register to vote in the next elections. The requirements for voter registration vary across states.

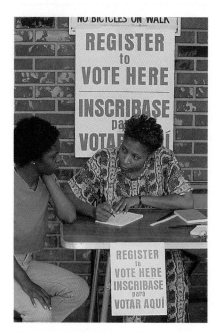

Signs in English and Spanish encourage voters to register for the next election. The Supreme Court has ruled that registration and ballots must be available in other languages if a specified proportion of the citizens speak a language other than English.

REGISTRATION

The entry of a person's name onto the list of eligible voters for elections. Registration requires meeting certain legal requirements relating to age, citizenship, and residency.

dies. The next day the man comes to vote without his jackass and cannot vote at all. Now tell me, which was the voter, the man or the jackass?[11]

The writers of the Constitution allowed the states to decide who should vote. Thus, women were allowed to vote in Wyoming in 1870 but not in the entire nation until the Nineteenth Amendment was ratified in 1920.

It was not until the Jacksonian era of the 1830s that the common man (but not woman) began to be heralded as the backbone of democracy. Men without property were first given the right to vote in the western states. By about 1850, most white adult males in virtually all the states could vote without any property qualification. North Carolina was the last state to eliminate its property test for voting—in 1856.

Extension of the franchise to black males occurred with the passage of the Fifteenth Amendment in 1870. This enfranchisement was short-lived, however, as the "redemption" of the South by white racists rolled back these gains by the end of the century. As discussed in Chapter 5, it was not until the 1960s that African Americans, both male and female, were able to participate in large numbers in the electoral process. Women received full national voting rights with the Nineteenth Amendment in 1920. The most recent extension of the franchise occurred when the voting age was reduced to eighteen by the Twenty-sixth Amendment in 1971.

Current Eligibility and Registration Requirements

Voting requires **registration,** and registration requires satisfying voter qualifications, or legal requirements. These requirements are the following: (1) citizenship, (2) age (eighteen or older), and (3) residency—the duration varying widely from state to state and with types of elections. Since 1972, states cannot impose residency requirements of more than thirty days. Twenty-five states require that length of time, while the other twenty-five states require fewer or no days. In addition, most states disqualify people who are mentally incompetent, prison inmates, convicted felons, and election-law violators.

Each state has different qualifications for voting and registration. In every state except North Dakota, registration must take place before voting. Traditionally, many states expected a personal appearance at an official building during normal working hours in order to register. In 1993, however, Congress passed the "motor voter" bill, which requires that states provide voter registration materials when people receive or renew driver's licenses, that all states allow voters to register by mail, and that voter registration forms be made available at a wider variety of public places and agencies. In general, a person must register well in advance of an election, although voters in Maine, Minnesota, Oregon, and Wisconsin are allowed to register up to, and on, election day.

Some argue that registration requirements are responsible for much of the nonparticipation in our political process. Certainly, since their introduction in the late nineteenth century, registration laws have had the effect of reducing the voting participation of African Americans and immigrants. There also is a partisan dimension to the debate over registration and nonvoting. Republicans generally fear that an expanded electorate would help to elect more Democrats.

The question arises as to whether registration is really necessary. If it decreases participation in the political process, perhaps it should be dropped

[11]Thomas Paine, *Common Sense* (London: H. D. Symonds, 1792), p. 28.

altogether. Still, as those in favor of registration requirements argue, such requirements may prevent fraudulent voting practices, such as multiple voting or voting by noncitizens.

HOW DO VOTERS DECIDE?

Political scientists and survey researchers have collected much information about voting behavior. This information sheds some light on which people vote and why people decide to vote for particular candidates. We have already discussed factors influencing voter turnout. Generally, the factors that influence voting decisions can be divided into two groups: (1) socioeconomic and demographic factors and (2) psychological factors.

Socioeconomic and Demographic Factors

As Table 10–5 indicates, a number of socioeconomic and demographic factors appear to influence voting behavior, including (1) education, (2) income and **socioeconomic status,** (3) religion, (4) ethnic background, (5) gender, (6) age, and (7) geographic region. These influences all reflect the voter's personal background and place in society. Some factors have to do with the family into which a person is born: race, religion (for most people), and ethnic background. Others may be the result of choices made throughout an individual's life: place of residence, educational achievement, or profession. It is also clear that many of these factors are related. People who have more education are likely to have higher incomes and to hold professional jobs. Similarly, children born into wealthier families are far more likely to complete college than children from poorer families. Furthermore, some of these demographic factors relate to psychological factors—as we shall see.

Education.   More education seems to be correlated with voting Republican. As can be seen in Table 10–5, 46 percent of college graduates voted for Bob Dole in the 1996 election, whereas 44 percent voted for Bill Clinton. An exception to the rule that more educated voters vote Republican occurred in

SOCIOECONOMIC STATUS

A category of people within a society who have similar levels of income and similar types of occupations.

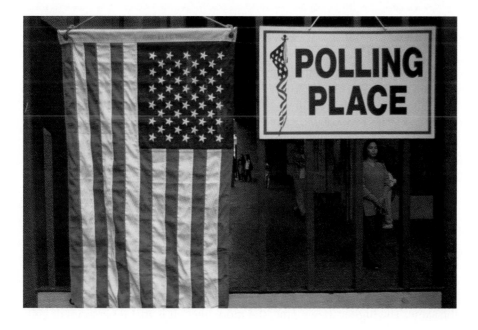

There are a number of factors that determine how voters make decisions at the polling place. Aside from many demographic influences that come into play, there are also psychological factors that help shape the way voters make decisions when they enter the voting booth.

Table 10–5

Vote by Groups in Presidential Elections since 1964 (in Percentages)

	1964		1968			1972		1976			1980		
	LBJ (DEM.)	GOLDWATER (REP.)	HUMPHREY (DEM.)	NIXON (REP.)	WALLACE (IND.)	McGOVERN (DEM.)	NIXON (REP.)	CARTER (DEM.)	FORD (REP.)	McCARTHY (IND.)	CARTER (DEM.)	REAGAN (REP.)	ANDERSON (IND.)
NATIONAL	61.3	38.7	43.0	43.4	13.6	38	62	50	48	1	41	51	7
SEX													
Male	60	40	41	43	16	37	63	53	45	1	38	53	7
Female	62	38	45	43	12	38	62	48	51	*	44	49	6
RACE													
White	59	41	38	47	15	32	68	46	52	1	36	56	7
Nonwhite	94	6	85	12	3	87	13	85	15	*	86	10	2
EDUCATION													
College	52	48	37	54	9	37	63	42	55	2	35	53	10
High school	62	38	42	43	15	34	66	54	46	*	43	51	5
Grade school	66	34	52	33	15	49	51	58	41	1	54	42	3
OCCUPATION													
Professional	54	46	34	56	10	31	69	42	56	1	33	55	10
White collar	57	43	41	47	12	36	64	50	48	2	40	51	9
Manual	71	29	50	35	15	43	57	58	41	1	48	46	5
AGE (Years)													
Under 30	64	36	47	38	15	48	52	53	45	1	47	41	11
30–49	63	37	44	41	15	33	67	48	49	2	38	52	8
50 and older	59	41	41	47	12	36	64	52	48	*	41	54	4
RELIGION													
Protestants	55	45	35	49	16	30	70	46	53	*	39	54	6
Catholics	76	24	59	33	8	48	52	57	42	1	46	47	6
POLITICS													
Republicans	20	80	9	86	5	5	95	9	91	*	8	86	5
Democrats	87	13	74	12	14	67	33	82	18	*	69	26	4
Independents	56	44	31	44	25	31	69	38	57	4	29	55	14
REGION													
East	68	32	50	43	7	42	58	51	47	1	43	47	9
Midwest	61	39	44	47	9	40	60	48	50	1	41	51	7
South	52	48	31	36	33	29	71	54	45	*	44	52	3
West	60	40	44	49	7	41	59	46	51	1	35	54	9
MEMBERS OF LABOR UNION FAMILIES	73	27	56	29	15	46	54	63	36	1	50	43	5

*Less than 1 percent.

Note: 1976 and 1980 results do not include votes for minor-party candidates.

1964, when college graduates voted 52 percent for Democrat Lyndon Johnson and 48 percent for Republican Barry Goldwater. Typically, those with less education are more inclined to vote for the Democratic nominee. In 1984, Democrat Walter Mondale received 43 percent and Republican Ronald Reagan, 57 percent of the vote from high school graduates, whereas those with only a grade school education voted 51 percent for Mondale and 49 percent for Reagan. The same pattern held in 1996, when 46 percent of the college graduates voted for Republican Bob Dole, compared with 28 percent of those who had not completed high school.

Income and Socioeconomic Status. If we measure socioeconomic status by profession, then those of higher socioeconomic status—professionals and businesspersons, as well as white-collar workers—tend to vote Republican. Manual laborers, factory workers, and especially union members are more likely to vote Democratic (but see Table 10–6). The effects of income are much the same. The higher the income, the more likely it is that a person will vote

Table 10–5 (Continued)

Vote by Groups in Presidential Elections since 1964 (in Percentages)

	1984		1988		1992			1996		
	MONDALE (DEM.)	REAGAN (REP.)	DUKAKIS (DEM.)	BUSH (REP.)	CLINTON (DEM.)	BUSH (REP.)	PEROT (IND.)	CLINTON (DEM.)	DOLE (REP.)	PEROT (REF.)
NATIONAL	41	59	45	53	43	38	19	49	41	8
SEX										
Male	36	64	41	57	41	38	21	43	44	10
Female	45	55	49	50	46	37	17	54	38	7
RACE										
White	34	66	40	59	39	41	20	43	46	9
Nonwhite	87	13	86	12	NA	NA	NA	NA	NA	NA
EDUCATION										
College	39	61	43	56	44	39	18	44	46	8
High school	43	57	49	50	43	36	20	51	35	13
Grade school	51	49	56	43	56	28	NA	59	28	11
OCCUPATION										
Professional	34	66	40	59	NA	NA	NA	NA	NA	NA
White collar	47	53	42	57	NA	NA	NA	NA	NA	NA
Manual	46	54	50	49	NA	NA	NA	NA	NA	NA
AGE (Years)										
Under 30	40	60	47	52	44	34	22	54	34	10
30–49	40	60	45	54	42	38	20	48	41	9
50 and older	41	59	49	50	50	38	12	48	44	7
RELIGION										
Protestants	39	61	33	66	33	46	21	36	53	10
Catholics	39	61	47	52	44	36	20	53	37	9
POLITICS										
Republicans	4	96	8	91	10	73	17	13	80	6
Democrats	79	21	82	17	77	10	13	84	10	5
Independents	33	67	43	55	38	32	30	43	35	17
REGION										
East	46	54	49	50	47	35	NA	55	34	9
Midwest	42	58	47	52	42	37	NA	48	41	10
South	37	63	41	58	42	43	NA	46	46	7
West	40	60	46	52	44	34	NA	48	40	8
MEMBERS OF LABOR UNION FAMILIES	52	48	57	42	55	24	NA	59	30	9

*Less than 1 percent.

Note: 1976 and 1980 results do not include votes for minor-party candidates.

SOURCE: *Gallup Report,* November 1984, p. 32; *New York Times,* November 10, 1988, p. 18; *New York Times,* November 15, 1992, p. B9; *New York Times,* November 10, 1996, p. 16.

Republican. Conversely, a much larger percentage of low-income individuals vote Democratic. But there are no hard and fast rules. There are some very poor individuals who are devoted Republicans, just as there are some extremely wealthy supporters of the Democratic party. In some recent elections, the traditional pattern did not hold. In 1980, for example, many blue-collar Democrats voted for Ronald Reagan, although the 1996 election showed those votes going to Bill Clinton.

Religion. In the United States, Protestants have traditionally voted Republican, and Catholics and Jews have voted Democratic. As with the other patterns discussed, however, this one is somewhat fluid. Republican Richard Nixon obtained 52 percent of the Catholic vote in 1972, and Democrat Lyndon Johnson won 55 percent of the Protestant vote in 1964. The Catholic vote was evenly split between Democrat Jimmy Carter and Republican Ronald

Table 10–6

How Democratic Are Labor Voters?

Although union members are more likely to identify themselves as Democrats than Republicans and labor organizations are far more likely to support Democratic candidates, the data below show that in seven of twelve presidential elections, Republicans have captured at least 40 percent of the votes from union households.

| | UNION HOUSEHOLDS VOTING REPUBLICAN FOR PRESIDENT | |
YEAR	CANDIDATES	PERCENTAGE
1952	Eisenhower vs. Stevenson	44%
1956	Eisenhower vs. Stevenson	57%
1960	Kennedy vs. Nixon	36%
1964	Johnson vs. Goldwater	17%
1968	Nixon vs. Humphrey	44%
1972	Nixon vs. McGovern	57%
1976	Carter vs. Ford	36%
1980	Reagan vs. Carter	45%
1984	Reagan vs. Mondale	43%
1988	Bush vs. Dukakis	41%
1992	Clinton vs. Bush	32%
1996	Clinton vs. Dole	30%

SOURCE: *CQ Researcher,* June 28, 1996, p. 560; *New York Times,* November 10, 1996, p. 16.

Reagan in 1980 but went heavily for Reagan in 1984. In 1996, Republican candidate Bob Dole obtained fewer votes from Catholics than did Democratic candidate Bill Clinton.

Ethnic Background.   Traditionally, the Irish have voted for Democrats. So, too, have voters of Slavic, Polish, and Italian heritages. But Anglo-Saxon and northern European ethnic groups have voted for Republican presidential candidates. These patterns were disrupted in 1980, when Ronald Reagan obtained much of his support from several of the traditionally Democratic ethnic groups, with the help of fundamentalist religious groups.

African Americans voted principally for Republicans until Democrat Franklin D. Roosevelt's New Deal. Since then, they have largely identified with the Democratic party. Indeed, Democratic presidential candidates have received, on average, more than 80 percent of the African American vote since 1956.

Gender.   Until recently, there seemed to have been no fixed pattern of voter preference by gender in presidential elections. One year, more women than men would vote for the Democratic candidate; another year, more men than women would do so. Some political analysts believe that a "gender gap" became a major determinant of voter decision making in the 1980 presidential election. Ronald Reagan obtained 15 percentage points more than Jimmy Carter among male voters, whereas women gave about an equal number of votes to each candidate. In 1984, the gender gap amounted to 9 percent nationally, with 64 percent of male voters casting their ballots for Ronald Reagan and 55 percent of female voters doing the same. While the size of the gap has varied over the years, by 1996, women cast 54 percent of their votes for Bill Clinton, the Democrat. The gender gap rarely appears in congressional elections.

Age.   Age clearly seems to relate to an individual's voting behavior. Younger voters have tended to vote Democratic; older voters have tended to vote Republican. It was only the voters under thirty who clearly favored Jimmy

Carter during the Carter-Reagan election in 1980. This trend was reversed in 1984, when voters under thirty voted heavily for Ronald Reagan and again voted Republican in 1988. In 1992, Bill Clinton won back the young voters by 10 percentage points, a margin that expanded to 20 percentage points in 1996.

Geographic Region.   As we noted earlier, the former Solid (Democratic) South has crumbled. In 1972, Republican Richard Nixon obtained 71 percent of the southern vote, whereas Democrat George McGovern only obtained 29 percent. Ronald Reagan drew 52 percent of the southern vote in 1980, however, and 63 percent in 1984.

Democrats still draw much of their strength from large northern and eastern cities. Rural areas tend to be Republican (and conservative) throughout the country except in the South, where the rural vote still tends to be heavily Democratic. On average, the West has voted Republican in presidential elections. Except for the 1964 election between Barry Goldwater and Lyndon Johnson, and again in the 1992 and 1996 elections, the Republicans have held the edge in western states in every presidential election since 1956.

Psychological Factors

In addition to socioeconomic and demographic explanations for the way people vote, at least three important psychological factors play a role in voter decision making. These factors, which are rooted in attitudes and beliefs held by voters, are (1) party identification, (2) perception of the candidates, and (3) issue preferences.

Party Identification.   With the possible exception of race, party identification has been the most important determinant of voting behavior in national elections. As we pointed out in Chapter 7, party affiliation is influenced by family and peer groups, by age, by the media, and by psychological attachment. During the 1950s, independent voters were a little more than 20 percent of the eligible electorate. In the middle to late 1960s, however, party identification began to weaken, and by the mid-1990s, independent voters constituted over 30 percent of all voters. In 1996, the estimated proportion of independent voters was between 26 and 33 percent. Independent voting seems to be concentrated among new voters, particularly among new young voters. Thus, we can still say that party identification for established voters is an important determinant in voter choice.

Perception of the Candidates.   The image of the candidate also seems to be important in a voter's choice for president. To some extent, voter attitudes toward candidates are based on emotions (such as trust) rather than on any judgment about experience or policy. In 1996, voters' decisions were largely guided by their perceptions of who they could trust to run the economy. Bob Dole tried to reduce the voters' trust in Bill Clinton but failed to make an impact.

Issue Preferences.   Issues make a difference in presidential and congressional elections. Although personality or image factors may be very persuasive, most voters have some notion of how the candidates differ on basic issues or at least know that the candidates want a change in the direction of government policy.

Historically, economic issues have the strongest influence on voters' choices. When the economy is doing well, it is very difficult for a challenger,

DID YOU KNOW ...
That noncitizens were allowed to vote in some states until the early 1920s?

particularly at the presidential level, to defeat the incumbent. In contrast, increasing inflation, a rising rate of unemployment, or a high interest rate is likely to work to the disadvantage of the incumbent. Studies of how economic conditions affect the vote differ in their conclusions. Some indicate that people vote on the basis of their personal economic well-being, whereas other studies seem to show that people vote on the basis of the nation's overall economic health.

Foreign policy issues become more prominent in a time of crisis. Although the parties and candidates have differed greatly over policy toward trade with China, for example, foreign policy issues are truly influential only when armed conflict is a possibility. Clearly, public dissension over the war in Vietnam had an effect on elections in 1968 and 1972.

Some of the most heated debates in American political campaigns take place over the social issues of abortion, the role of women, the rights of lesbians and gay males, and prayer in the public schools. In general, presidential candidates would prefer to avoid such issues, because voters who care about these questions are likely to be offended if a candidate does not share their views.

CONCEPT OVERVIEW
The Changing Nature of Campaigns

American political campaigns always have been exciting and innovative. The advent of television, the rise of candidate-centered campaigns, and the revolution in the primary system have produced great shifts in the system since the early years of the twentieth century.

THEN	NOW
• Political parties ran campaigns.	• Candidates and strategists run campaigns with little party input.
• Party elites controlled conventions and nominations.	• Candidates compete for nominations through primaries; delegates are selected by the voters.
• Elections were based on the party ticket.	• The party ticket means little; ticket splitting is prevalent.
• Campaign money was donated by the elites; no reporting requirements.	• Federal campaign law limits individual contributions; PACs make contributions; soft money evades limits.
• Party identification was the major voting determinant.	• Voters are swayed primarily by candidate image, then issues, and then party.
• Voting was restricted to white, male citizens.	• Voting is open to minorities, eighteen-year-old persons, and women.
• Candidates were almost all white males.	• The candidate pool includes women and minorities.

From time to time, drugs, crime, and corruption become important campaign issues. The Watergate affair cost the Republicans a number of congressional seats in 1974, and its aftereffects probably defeated Gerald Ford in 1976. If the president or high officials are involved in truly criminal or outrageous conduct, the issue will undoubtedly influence voters.

All candidates try to set themselves apart from their opposition on crucial issues in order to attract voters. What is difficult to ascertain is the extent to which issues overshadow partisan loyalty or personality factors in the voters' minds. It appears that some campaigns are much more issue oriented than others. Some research has shown that **issue voting** was most important in the presidential elections of 1964, 1968, and 1972, was moderately important in 1980, and was less important in the 1990s.

ISSUE VOTING

Voting for a candidate based on how he or she stands on a particular issue.

CAMPAIGNS, CANDIDATES, AND ELECTIONS: UNFINISHED WORK

Few areas in American politics seem to be in such need of change and reform as campaigns, voting, and elections. Every four years, polls show that the majority of Americans are dissatisfied with the length of campaigns, with vicious campaign strategies, with the caliber of candidates, and with the influence of campaign contributions on the system. Yet very few serious reforms result, and after the campaign fury subsides, most citizens are willing to get on with their personal business and allow the officials elected in that campaign to take office and hold political authority.

As the cost of campaigns rises, though, more and more Americans are becoming concerned about reforming the way in which campaigns are financed. If only the rich can afford to enter the race, what does this mean for the future of our democratic form of government? It seems clear to many that alternate means of financing political campaigns must be found, but what those means might be is a question that is yet to be resolved. In the meantime, both Republicans and Democrats probably will continue to take advantage of loopholes, such as contributions in soft money, to obtain campaign funds. Certainly, they did in 1996, in spite of the fact that both parties argued strongly for campaign finance reform.

Other important issues are those raised by commentators and scholars who indict the whole electoral system for creating cynicism among the electorate and for making real debate and discussion of the most important issues almost impossible to imagine. As you will see in Chapter 11, many of the problems that afflict campaigns and elections in the United States involve the role of the media in the political system.

GETTING INVOLVED
Registering and Voting

In nearly every state, before you are allowed to cast a vote in an election, you must first register. Registration laws vary considerably from state to state, and, depending on how difficult a state's laws make it to register, some states have much higher rates of registration and voting participation than do others.

What do you have to do to register and cast a vote? Most states require that you meet minimum residence requirements. In other words, you must have lived in the state in which you plan to be registered for a specified period of time. You may retain your previous registration, if any, in another state, and you can cast an absentee vote if your previous state permits that. The minimum-residency requirement is very short in some states, such as one day in Alabama or ten days in New Hampshire and Wisconsin. No state requires more than thirty days. Other states with voter residency requirements have minimum-day requirements in between these extremes. Twenty states do not have any minimum-residency requirement at all.

Nearly every state also specifies a closing date by which you must be registered before an election. In other words, even if you have met a residency requirement, you still may not be able to vote if you register too close to the day of the election. The closing date is different in certain states (Connecticut, Delaware, and Louisiana) for primary elections than for other elections. The closing date for registration varies from election day itself (Maine, Minnesota, Oregon, and Wisconsin) to thirty days (Arizona). Delaware specifies the third Saturday in October as the closing date. In North Dakota, no registration is necessary.

In most states, your registration can be revoked if you do not vote within a certain number of years.

This process of automatically "purging" the voter registration lists of nonactive voters happens every two years in about a dozen states, every three years in Georgia, every four years in more than twenty other states, every five years in Maryland and Rhode Island, every eight years in North Carolina, and every ten years in Michigan. Ten states do not require this purging at all.

What you must do to register and remain registered to vote varies from state to state and even from county to county within a state. In general, you must be a citizen of the United States, at least eighteen years old on or before election day, and a resident of the state in which you intend to register.

Using Iowa as an example, you normally would register through the local county auditor or when you obtain your driver's license (under the "motor voter" law of 1993). If you moved to a new address within the state, you would also have to change your registration to vote by contacting the auditor. Postcard registrations must be postmarked or delivered to the county auditor no later than the twenty-fifth day before an election. Party affiliation may be changed or declared when you register or reregister, or you may change or declare a party at the polls on election day. Postcard registration forms in Iowa are available at many public buildings, from labor unions, at political party headquarters, at the county auditors' offices, or from campus groups. Registrars who will accept registrations at other locations may be located by calling your party headquarters or your county auditor.

For more information on voting registration, contact your county or state officials, party headquarters, labor union, or local chapter of the League of Women Voters.

KEY TERMS

Australian ballot 336

"beauty contest" 329

bundling 326

canvassing board 337

caucus 330

challenge 338

coattail effect 337

corrupt practices acts 324

credentials committee 331

elector 332

electoral college 332

focus group 323

front-loading 315

front-runner 330

Hatch Act 324

CHAPTER SUMMARY

1 People may choose to run for political office to further their careers, to carry out specific political programs, or in response to certain issues or events. The legal qualifications for holding political office are minimal at both the state and local levels, but holders of political office still are predominantly white and male and are likely to be from the professional class.

2 American political campaigns are lengthy and extremely expensive. In the last decade, they have become more candidate centered rather than party centered in response to technological innovations and decreasing party identification. Candidates have begun to rely less on the party and more on paid professional consultants to perform the various tasks necessary to wage a political campaign. The crucial task of professional political consultants is image building. The campaign organization devises a campaign strategy to maximize the candidate's chances of winning. Candidates use public opinion polls to gauge their popularity and to test the mood of the country.

3 The amount of money spent in financing campaigns is steadily increasing. A variety of corrupt practices acts have been passed to regulate campaign finance. The Federal Election Campaign Acts of 1972 and 1974 instituted major reforms by limiting spending and contributions; the acts allowed corporations, labor unions, and interest groups to set up political action committees (PACs) to raise money for candidates. New techniques, including bundling and soft money, have been created to raise money.

4 Following the Democratic convention of 1968, the McGovern-Fraser Commission was appointed to study the problems of the primary system. It formulated new rules, which were adopted by all Democrats and by Republicans in many states. These reforms opened up the nomination process for the presidency to all voters.

5 A presidential primary is a statewide election to help a political party determine its presidential nominee at the national convention. Some states use the caucus method of choosing convention delegates. The primary campaign recently has been shortened to the first few months of the election year.

6 In making a presidential choice on election day, the voter technically does not vote directly for a candidate but chooses between slates of presidential electors. The slate that wins the most popular votes throughout the state gets to cast all the electoral votes for the state. The candidate receiving a majority (270) of the electoral votes wins. Both the mechanics and the politics of the electoral college have been sharply criticized. There have been many proposed reforms, including a proposal that direct elections be held in which candidates would be elected on a popular-vote basis.

7 The United States uses the Australian ballot, a secret ballot that is prepared, distributed, and counted by government officials. The office-block ballot groups candidates according to office. The party-column ballot groups candidates according to their party labels and symbols.

8 Voter participation in the United States is low (and generally declining) compared with that of other countries. Some view the decline in voter turnout as a threat to representative democracy, whereas others believe it simply indicates greater satisfaction with the status quo. There is an association between voting and a person's age, education, minority status, and income level. Another factor affecting voter turnout is the extent to which elections are competitive within a state.

9 In colonial times, only white males with a certain minimum amount of property were eligible to vote. The suffrage issue has concerned, at one time or another, most groups in the United States. Current voter eligibility requires registration, citizenship, and specified age and residency requirements. Each state has different qualifications. It is argued that these requirements are responsible for much of the nonparticipation in the political process in the United States.

10 Socioeconomic or demographic factors that influence voting decisions include (a) education, (b) income and socioeconomic status, (c) religion, (d) ethnic background, (e) gender, (f) age, and (g) geographic region. Psychological factors that influence voting decisions include (a) party identification, (b) perception of candidates, and (c) issue preferences.

QUESTIONS FOR REVIEW AND DISCUSSION

❶ Should we change the system of nomination for political office in order to encourage more control by political parties or interest groups? How would the behavior of members of Congress change, for example, if most members were nominated by their respective parties rather than being self-nominated?

❷ How should the presidential campaign be reformed? Consider the advantages and disadvantages of a very short primary season—perhaps with one national primary election—or of simply shortening the entire campaign to three or four months. How would such changes benefit the voters?

❸ How should political campaigns be financed? Should all campaigns be financed by the general public, with strict limits on expenditures? How would such regulations change the nature of campaign advertising and other strategies?

❹ What information does the voter need about a prospective member of Congress or a senator in order to cast an informed ballot? How can campaigns be reformed to provide that information to the electorate?

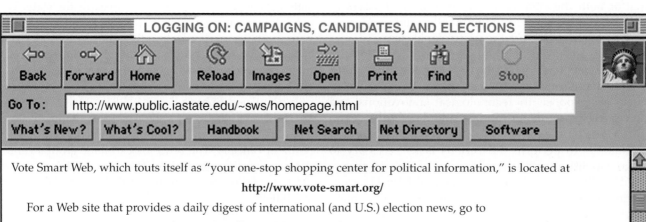

LOGGING ON: CAMPAIGNS, CANDIDATES, AND ELECTIONS

| Back | Forward | Home | Reload | Images | Open | Print | Find | Stop |

Go To: http://www.public.iastate.edu/~sws/homepage.html

| What's New? | What's Cool? | Handbook | Net Search | Net Directory | Software |

Vote Smart Web, which touts itself as "your one-stop shopping center for political information," is located at

http://www.vote-smart.org/

For a Web site that provides a daily digest of international (and U.S.) election news, go to

http://www.klipsan.com/elecnews.htm

The Federal Election Commission's site is worth exploring. It is located at

http://www.fec.gov/

It offers access to a variety of topics, including the Citizen's Guide to Contributions and the Law; Using FEC Services; Financial Information about Candidates, Parties, and PACs; Help for Candidates, Parties, and PACs; About Elections and Election Administration; News Releases; and Media Advisories.

An excellent Web site for political information on the Internet is PoliticsNow, a resource offered jointly by ABC News, the *Washington Post, Newsweek,* the *Los Angeles Times,* and the *National Journal.* This site offers constantly updated news, the latest polling data on public opinion and politics, excerpts from various newspapers, and information on a variety of other political topics. You can locate this site at

http://www.politicsnow.com/

Another good site is AllPolitics, which is a joint project by Cable News Network (CNN) and *Time* magazine. Prior to the 1996 elections, it offered daily tracking polls by CNN, *USA Today,* and Gallup. One feature, "Rate-O-Matic," allowed users to answer a series of questions about campaign issues, after which the users could request Rate-O-Matic to "Find My President." To access AllPolitics, go to

http://www.allpolitics.com

SELECTED REFERENCES

Brown, Clifford W., Lynda W. Powell, and Clyde Wilcox. *Serious Money: Fundraising and Contributions in Presidential Nomination Campaigns.* New York: Cambridge University Press, 1995. The authors present the results of an analysis of individuals who contributed large amounts of money to presidential candidates. They look at the networks that reach these contributors and convince them to give.

Corrado, Anthony. *Creative Campaigning: PACs and the Presidential Selection Process.* Boulder, Colo.: Westview Press, 1992. This book investigates and explains the use of political action committees for presidential campaigns. It shows how a candidate can raise early money to enter the campaign through what the author calls "shadow campaigns."

Euchner, Charles C., and John Anthony Maltese. *Selecting the President: From Washington to Bush.* Washington, D.C.: Congressional Quarterly, 1992. This readable history of presidential elections covers the process of nomination and election, campaign tactics, and the major issues in each campaign.

Glennon, Michael J. *When No Majority Rules: The Electoral College and Presidential Succession.* Washington, D.C.: Congressional Quarterly, 1992. This clear explanation of how the electoral college functions discusses the possible options for the political system if no candidate obtains a majority of electoral votes.

Jackson, John S., III, and William Crotty. *The Politics of Presidential Selection.* New York: Longman Publishers, 1996. This account of how we elect the president and the members of Congress is based on theories of rational decision making by voters and discusses the limits to such decision making for those voters without information.

Mayer, William G., Ed. *In Pursuit of the White House: How We Choose Our Presidential Nominees.* Chatham, N.J.: Chatham House Publishers, 1995. This book contains an excellent collection of articles examining the primary system, campaign financing, and independent and third-party candidates.

Nelson, Michael, ed. *The Elections of 1992.* Washington, D.C.: Congressional Quarterly, 1993. This collection of essays by prominent scholars discusses the issues and events of the 1992 presidential and congressional campaigns.

Sabato, Larry J., and Glenn R. Simpson. *Dirty Little Secrets: The Persistence of Corruption in American Politics.* New York: Random House, 1996. Through an intensive investigation of election practices, the authors document areas of the system where fraud is still possible and, in some states, prevalent.

Simpson, Dick. *Winning Elections: A Handbook in Modern Participatory Politics.* New York: Longman Publishers, 1996. Former alderman and mayoral candidate Simpson gives advice to citizens who would like to get involved in politics at the grass roots.

Sorauf, Frank J. *Inside Campaign Finance: Myths and Realties.* New Haven, Conn.: Yale University Press, 1992. This leading scholar of political parties and elections provides an extensive and balanced treatment of current issues in campaign finance, including the power of political action committees, the ways in which candidates and parties avoid finance regulations, possible reforms of the system, and obstacles to reform.

Teixeira, Ruy A. *The Disappearing American Voter.* Washington, D.C.: Brookings Institution, 1992. This thoughtful study examines the historical causes for the decline in voter turnout in the United States and suggests that the reasons for this decline include the relatively high costs of registration and voting for the citizen and the perceived low benefits of voting to the average person.

11
The Media

CHAPTER OUTLINE

There Were No Newspapers?

BACKGROUND

CURRENTLY, THERE ARE ABOUT 12,000 NEWSPAPERS IN THE UNITED STATES. WHILE THE NUMBER OF DAILY PAPERS IS DECLINING, THE NUMBER OF WEEKLY NEWSPAPERS IS INCREASING, PROBABLY DUE TO THE GROWTH OF THE SUBURBS AND THE NEED FOR LOCAL NEWS OUTLETS THERE. THE NEWSPAPER INDUSTRY AS A WHOLE, HOWEVER, IS "FLAT" IN TERMS OF GROWTH, WHILE THE USE OF TELEVISION—NETWORK AND CABLE—CONTINUES TO SOAR. THE USE OF THE INTERNET, WITH ITS ENORMOUS CAPACITY TO DELIVER INFORMATION TO THE HOME, IS ALSO INCREASING. THESE DEVELOPMENTS HAVE LED SOME OBSERVERS TO SPECULATE THAT NEWSPAPERS MAY NOT HAVE A FUNCTION IN OUR FUTURE SOCIETY.

WHAT IF THERE WERE NO NEWSPAPERS?

What would U.S. citizens lose without newspapers? First, there would be no shortage of news about major events and crises—most people get that kind of news from television. With a number of round-the-clock news channels available on cable television and, of course, radio broadcasts, most major news would be available to citizens.

What about access to the texts of speeches or detailed analyses of policy issues, the kind that is available through major national newspapers? For those individuals who have access to computers, such texts are available online through either free or relatively inexpensive services. For those citizens who are not "online," many library systems also subscribe to the Internet and online services for the public.

Clearly, though, individuals who do not have access to the Internet would be disadvantaged if newspapers disappeared. Additionally, retail establishments and other participants in the marketplace that advertise their products or services also would be disadvantaged by the loss of newspapers. They would need to find another way to reach the public. Advertising on television is much more expensive than in newspapers. Rates for advertising through online service providers, are also high.

News about social events, charities, public institutions, and events that are important to only a relatively small number of people—for example, planning and zoning hearings—would also be hard to obtain in a world without newspapers.

WHO WOULD EDIT AND VERIFY THE NEWS?

Newspapers are organizations that, through the work of journalists and editors gather and present the news. Normally, publishers verify the parts of the news stories that appear in their news pages. The opinion of the newspaper's publisher is marked out clearly on the editorial page. If you don't like the editorial stance of one newspaper, you are free to buy another. In contrast, the line between editorial comment and news coverage is blurred completely on television. Officially, there is no "editorial page" on NBC. There are paid commentators and panel shows of journalists, but they represent themselves, not the owner of the network. Without newspapers, there would be no voice in the media that clearly differentiates opinion from the facts of the news.

The same problem arises with information available via the Internet. It is impossible in some cases to know whether information on the Internet is true or not.

Without newspapers, there could be as much information for people to absorb, but what organizations would sort the news, identify the most important stories, and try to check sources? Without some means of verifying the accuracy of information reported online, that information would not be very useful.

FOR CRITICAL ANALYSIS

1. *Why is it important in a democracy for newspaper publishers to check the sources of their stories and make them known?*

2. *Could the Internet be made available to every citizen? How?*

THE MEDIA'S FUNCTIONS

The study of people and politics—of how people gain the information that they need to be able to choose between political candidates, to organize for their own interests, and to formulate opinions on the policies and decisions of the government—needs to take into account the role played by the media in the United States. Historically, the printed media played the most important role in informing public debate. The printed media developed, for the most part, our understanding of how news is to be reported. Today, however, more than 90 percent of all Americans use television news as their primary source of information. In the future, the Internet may become the most important source of information and political debate for Americans. If that happens, control over the gathering and sharing of news and information will be greatly changed from a system in which the media have a primary role to one in which the individual citizen may play a greater role. The chapter-opening *What If . . .* explores some of the possible consequences of such a change for the future. With that future in mind, it is important to analyze the current relationship between the media and politics.

The mass media perform a number of different functions in any country. In the United States, we can list at least six. Almost all of them can have political implications, and some are essential to the democratic process. These functions are as follows: (1) entertainment, (2) reporting the news, (3) identifying public problems, (4) socializing new generations, (5) providing a political forum, and (6) making profits.

Entertainment

By far the greatest number of radio and television hours are dedicated to entertaining the public. The battle for prime-time ratings indicates how important successful entertainment is to the survival of networks and individual stations.

There is no direct linkage between entertainment and politics; however, network dramas often introduce material that may be politically controversial and that may stimulate public discussion. Made-for-TV movies have focused on many controversial topics, including AIDS, incest, and wife battering.

A television camera records the action on the floor of the 1996 Republican National Convention in San Diego. Because the television networks decided to limit their coverage of each of the party conventions to only two hours, party leaders tried to place their most important speakers in "prime time." Many speeches and discussions during the conventions received little or no media coverage.

PUBLIC AGENDA

Issues that commonly are perceived by members of the political community as meriting public attention and governmental action. The media play an important role in setting the public agenda by focusing attention on certain topics.

Reporting the News

A primary function of the mass media in all their forms—newspapers, radio, television, cable, magazines—is the reporting of news. The media convey words and pictures about events, facts, personalities, and ideas. The protections of the First Amendment are intended to keep the flow of news as free as possible, because it is an essential part of the democratic process. If citizens cannot get unbiased information about the state of their community and their leaders' actions, how can they make voting decisions? Perhaps the most incisive comment about the importance of the media was made by James Madison, who said, "A people who mean to be their own governors must arm themselves with the power knowledge gives. A popular government without popular information or the means of acquiring it, is but a prologue to a farce or a tragedy or perhaps both."[1]

Identifying Public Problems

The power of information is important, not only in revealing what the government is doing but also in determining what the government ought to do—in other words, in setting the **public agenda.** The mass media identify public issues, such as the placement of convicted sex offenders in new homes and neighborhoods. The media then influence the passage of legislation, such as "Megan's Law," which requires police to notify neighbors about the release and/or resettlement of certain offenders. American journalists also work in a long tradition of uncovering public wrongdoing, corruption, and bribery and of bringing such wrongdoing to the public's attention. Closely related to this investigative function is that of presenting policy alternatives. Public policy is often complex and difficult to make entertaining, but programs devoted to public policy increasingly are being scheduled for prime-time television. Most networks produce "news magazine" format shows that sometimes include segments on foreign policy and other issues.

Socializing New Generations

As mentioned in Chapter 7, the media, and particularly television, strongly influence the beliefs and opinions of all Americans. Because of this influence, the media play a significant role in the political socialization of the younger generation, as well as immigrants to this country. Through the transmission of historical information (sometimes fictionalized), the presentation of American culture, and the portrayal of the diverse regions and groups in the United States, the media teach young people and immigrants about what it means to be an American. For example, TV dramas often involve a contest between "good guys" and "bad guys," thereby conveying value judgments as to types of social conduct that are "right" or "wrong." TV talk shows, such as *Oprah*, sometimes focus on controversial issues (such as abortion or assisted suicide) that relate to basic American values (such as liberty). Many children's shows are designed not only to entertain young viewers but also to instruct them in the traditional moral values of American society.

Providing a Political Forum

As part of their news function, the media also provide a political forum for leaders and the public. Candidates for office use news reporting to sustain

---

[1]As quoted in "Castro vs. (Some) Censorship," editorial in the *New York Times,* November 22, 1983, p. 24.

The town meeting of yesterday gave way to the electronic town meeting of today. Here Bill Clinton answers a question asked by a citizen in another location but whose image and voice were transmitted through video conferencing telecommunications equipment. As telecommunications that include video and voice become better and cheaper, politicians will be able to use Clinton's electronic town-meeting concept more and more.

interest in their campaigns, whereas officeholders use the media to gain support for their policies or to present an image of leadership. Presidential trips abroad are an outstanding way for the chief executive to get colorful, positive, and exciting news coverage that makes the president look "presidential." The media also offer a way for citizens to participate in public debate, through letters to the editor, televised editorials, or electronic mail. The question of whether more public access should be provided is discussed later in this chapter.

Making Profits

Most of the news media in the United States are private, for-profit corporate enterprises. One of their goals is to make profits—for employee salaries, for expansion, and for dividends to the stockholders who own the companies. Profits are made, in general, by charging for advertising. Advertising revenues usually are related directly to circulation or to listener/viewer ratings. (Recent developments in the area of media ownership are discussed later in this chapter.)

Several well-known outlets are publicly owned—public television stations in many communities and National Public Radio. These operate without extensive commercials and are locally supported and often subsidized by the government and corporations.

Added up, these factors form the basis for a complex relationship among the media, the government, and the public. Throughout the rest of this chapter, we examine some of the many facets of this relationship. Our purpose is to set a foundation for understanding how the media influence the political process.

HISTORY OF THE MEDIA IN THE UNITED STATES

Many years ago Thomas Jefferson wrote, "Were it left to me to decide whether we should have a government without newspapers, or newspapers

MANAGED NEWS

Information generated and distributed by the government in such a way as to give government interests priority over candor.

High-speed presses made newspapers cheap and easily available. Since this development, the media have played an increasingly important role in American political life.

without a government, I should not hesitate a moment to prefer the latter."[2] Although the media have played a significant role in politics since the founding of this nation, they were not as overwhelmingly important in the past as they are today. For one thing, politics was controlled by a small elite who communicated personally. For another, during the early 1800s and before, news traveled slowly. If an important political event occurred in New York, it was not known until five days later in Philadelphia; ten days later in the capital cities of Connecticut, Maryland, and Virginia; and fifteen days later in Boston. Of course, there were one or more newspapers in each major city, and they served some of the functions that newspapers do today. Most of these early newspapers were weeklies, but a few daily publications existed also.

Roughly three thousand newspapers were being published by 1860. Some of these, such as the *New York Tribune,* were mainly sensation mongers that concentrated on crimes, scandals, and the like. The *New York Herald* specialized in self-improvement and what today would be called practical news. Although sensational and biased reporting often created political divisiveness (this was true particularly during the Civil War), many historians believe that the growth of the printed media played an important role in unifying the country. A few printed publications stand out as being instrumental in changing the fate of the nation. As we pointed out in Chapter 2, Thomas Paine's *Common Sense* was not only a best-seller (selling half a million copies) but also a catalyst for the revolt against the mother country. Later, *The Federalist Papers* were instrumental in creating the atmosphere necessary for the ratification of the Constitution.

The Rise of the Political Press

Americans may cherish the idea of a nonpartisan press, but in the early years of the nation's history, the number of politically sponsored newspapers was significant. The sole reason for the existence of such periodicals was to further the interests of the politicians who paid for their publication. Printing newspapers was relatively expensive in the 1700s and 1800s, and poor transportation facilities meant that they could not be widely distributed. As a consequence, political newspapers had a small clientele who paid a relatively high subscription price.

As chief executive of our government during this period, George Washington has been called a "firm believer" in **managed news.** Although acknowledging that the public had a right to be informed, he felt that some matters should be kept secret and that news that might damage the image of the United States should not be published. Washington, however, made no attempt to control the press.

Several political periodicals were partially subsidized by the government. No one seemed to think it was improper for government-paid employees to work on partisan newspapers. Indeed, the development of the objective news reporting that we value so much today was not due to any increase in idealism. Rather, it was the result of a reduction in the cost of printing newspapers and the consequent rise of the self-supported mass-readership daily.

The Development of Mass-Readership Newspapers

Two inventions in the nineteenth century led to the development of mass-readership newspapers. The first was the high-speed rotary press; the second

[2]As quoted in Richard M. Clurman, "The Media Learn a Lesson," *New York Times,* December 2, 1983, p. A2.

was the telegraph. Faster presses meant lower per-unit costs and lower subscription prices. The telegraph meant instant access to news between major cities at a low cost. By 1848, the Associated Press had developed the telegraph into a nationwide apparatus for the dissemination of all types of information on a systematic basis.

Along with these technological changes came a growing population and increasing urbanization. Daily newspapers could be supported by a larger, more urbanized populace, even if the price per paper was only a penny. Finally, the burgeoning, diversified economy encouraged the growth of advertising, which meant that newspapers could obtain additional revenues from merchants who seized the opportunity to promote their wares to a larger public. The days of dependence on political interests for newspapers were coming to an end.

The Popular Press and Yellow Journalism

Students of the history of journalism have ascertained a change, in the last half of the 1800s, not in the level of biased news reporting but in its origin. Whereas earlier politically sponsored newspapers expounded a particular

In a cartoon attacking yellow journalism, William Randolph Hearst (left) and Joseph Pulitzer (right) are lampooned for emphasizing scandal and gossip in news coverage.

DID YOU KNOW . . .

That the first successful daily newspaper in the United States was the *Pennsylvania Packet & General Advertiser*, which was initially published on September 21, 1784?

YELLOW JOURNALISM

A term for sensationalistic, irresponsible journalism. Reputedly, the term is short for "Yellow Kid Journalism," an allusion to the cartoon "The Yellow Kid" in the old *New York World*, a newspaper especially noted for its sensationalism.

political party's point of view, most mass-based newspapers expounded whatever political philosophy the owner of the newspaper happened to have.

William Randolph Hearst thought the United States should go to war against Spain. He was also interested in selling newspapers. Tensions between the United States and Spain grew over a bloody colonial war that the Spanish were fighting in Cuba. Hearst used this episode to launch his anti-Spanish campaign with screaming headlines. When the U.S. battleship *Maine* exploded in Havana Harbor at 9:40 P.M. on February 15, 1898, killing 260 officers and soldiers, Hearst and others wrote such inflammatory articles that President William McKinley had little choice but to go to war. Spain was blamed for the explosion, even though later investigations could not fix responsibility on anyone.[3]

Even if newspaper heads did not have a particular political axe to grind, they often allowed their editors to engage in sensationalism and what is known as **yellow journalism.** The questionable or simply personal activities of a prominent businessperson, politician, or socialite were front-page material. Newspapers, then as now, made their economic way by maximizing readership. As the *National Enquirer* demonstrates with its current circulation of more than five million, sensationalism is still rewarded by high levels of readership.

The Age of the Electromagnetic Signal

The first scheduled radio program in the United States featured politicians. On the night of November 2, 1920, KDKA-Pittsburgh transmitted the returns of the presidential election race between Warren G. Harding and James M. Cox. The listeners were a few thousand people tuning in on very primitive, homemade sets.

By 1924, there were nearly 1,400 radio stations. But it wasn't until 8 P.M. on November 15, 1926, that the electronic media came into its own in the United States. On that night, the National Broadcasting Company (NBC) made its debut with a four-hour program broadcast by twenty-five stations in twenty-one cities. Network broadcasting had become a reality.

[3]Richard Davis, *The Press and American Politics: The New Mediator,* 2d ed. (Upper Saddle River, N.J.: Prentice-Hall, 1996), p. 52.

KDKA-Pittsburgh broadcast the 1920 presidential election returns.

Australian ballot 336	**challenge** 338	**electoral college** 332
"beauty contest" 329	**coattail effect** 337	**focus group** 323
bundling 326	**corrupt practices acts** 324	**front-loading** 315
canvassing board 337	**credentials committee** 331	**front-runner** 330
caucus 330	**elector** 332	**Hatch Act** 324

DID YOU KNOW...
That the first "wire" story transmitted by telegraph was sent in 1846?

Even with the advent of national radio in the 1920s and television in the late 1940s, many politicians were slow to understand the significance of the **electronic media.** The 1952 presidential campaign was the first to involve a real role for television. Television coverage of the Republican convention helped Dwight Eisenhower win over delegates and the nomination. Even though Eisenhower had problems reading a teleprompter that did not work, his vice presidential running mate, Richard Nixon, put the TV time to good use. Accused of hiding a secret slush fund, Nixon replied to his critics with his famous "Checkers" speech. He denied the attacks, cried real tears, and said that the only thing he ever received from a contributor for his personal use was his dog, Checkers. It was a highly effective performance.

Today, television dominates the campaign strategy of every would-be national politician, as well as that of every elected official. Smart politicians figure out ways to continue to be newsworthy, thereby gaining access to the electronic media. Attacking the president's programs is one way of becoming newsworthy; other ways include holding highly visible hearings on controversial subjects, going on "fact-finding" trips, and gimmicks (such as a walking tour of a state).

The Revolution in the Electronic Media

Just as technological change was responsible for the end of politically sponsored periodicals, technology is increasing the number of alternative news sources today. The advent of pay TV, cable TV, subscription TV, satellite TV, and the like have completely changed the electronic media landscape. When there were basically only three TV networks, it was indeed a "wasteland," as federal communications commissioner Newton Minnow once claimed. But now, with dozens of potential outlets for specialized programs, the electronic media are becoming more and more like the printed media, catering to specialized tastes. This is sometimes referred to as **narrowcasting.** If, for example, you wish to appeal only to health-conscious individuals, you might be able to offer a cable TV station with in-depth programs on nutrition, diet, exercise, sports, and the like. You would not have to appeal to the general advertiser; rather, you could find advertising dollars from vitamin manufacturers, health-food manufacturers, and gymnasium-equipment manufacturers who will pay for less expensive advertising campaigns targeted at their customers.

With the advent of cable and satellite television, which now reaches over sixty-five million homes in the United States, the potential for offering diverse sources of news, entertainment, and information to citizens became a reality. To date, Americans have not responded to the offerings on cable and satellite networks by becoming greater consumers of news or of self-education material. For the most part, the multiple channels available carry more sports, entertainment, movie, shopping, religion, and music video programming. Most viewers are able to choose among several sources for their favorite type of programming. Serious political discussions remain the territory of CNN, C-SPAN, PBS, and the major networks.

Narrow casting has become a reality. Consumers only watch those shows and channels that they like, and the major networks have declining audiences. In the realm of politics, the multiple channels have given more access to political commentators and talk shows, phenomena of the 1990s. By 1997, there were over two dozen talk shows on major channels daily, with many more at the local level. Rush Limbaugh and Larry King have become so well known that politicians believe they must make an appearance on their programs. The appeal of talk shows is primarily emotional rather than informational, with

ELECTRONIC MEDIA

Broadcasting media (radio and television). The term derives from their method of transmission, in contrast to printed media.

NARROWCASTING

Broadcasting that is targeted to one small sector of the population.

the likely result of producing an electorate that may become even more cynical and alienated from the process of politics and government.

THE PRIMACY OF TELEVISION

Television is the most influential medium. As you can see in Figure 11–1, it is the medium of choice for most consumers. It also is big business. National news TV personalities like Dan Rather may earn in excess of several million dollars per year from their TV news–reporting contracts alone. They are paid so much because they command large audiences, and large audiences command high prices for advertising on national news shows. Indeed, news *per se* has become a major factor in the profitability of TV stations. In 1963, the major networks—ABC, CBS, and NBC—devoted only eleven minutes daily to national news. By 1997, the amount of time on the networks devoted to news-type programming had increased to three hours. In addition, a twenty-four-hour-a-day news cable channel—CNN—started operating in 1980. With the addition of CNN–Headline News, CNBC, and other news-format cable channels and shows in the 1980s and 1990s, the amount of news-type programming continues to increase. News is obviously good business.

Television's influence on the political process today is recognized by all who engage in it. Its special characteristics are worthy of attention. Television news is often criticized for being superficial, particularly compared with the detailed coverage available in the *New York Times*, for example. In fact, television news is constrained by its peculiar technical characteristics, the most important being the limitations of time; stories must be reported in only a few minutes. As pointed out in this chapter's *Politics and the Fifty States*, news coverage of the states is very uneven, in part because of these limits.

The most interesting aspect of television is, of course, the fact that it relies on pictures rather than words to attract the viewer's attention. Therefore, the videotapes or slides that are chosen for a particular political story have exaggerated importance. Viewers do not know what other photos may have been

Figure 11–1
● ●
Media Usage by Consumers: 1984 to Present

SOURCE: U.S. Department of Commerce, *Statistical Abstract of the United States, 1996* (Washington, D.C.: U.S. Government Printing Office, 1996), p. 568, plus authors' projections.

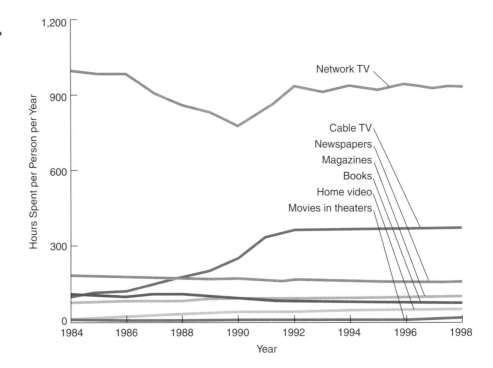

POLITICS AND THE FIFTY STATES
Which States Get Media Coverage?

National news media tend to focus on national events and issues, especially in a presidential campaign. What about in other years? Does news in the states get any national coverage? Doris Graber's analysis of the news coverage from August 1994 through July 1995 shows that the national networks focused predominantly on New York and California (in which their production facilities are located) and on two other states—Texas and Florida—to which the president traveled a great deal in search of support. As the accompanying table shows, the states that have more than 60 percent of the electoral votes received less than 40 percent of all national coverage. Graber notes that media coverage of a particular state depends on whether the president or another prominent politician is visiting that state, the availability of video crews, the ease of access to the area, and the degree to which the networks can plan ahead for the coverage.*

For Critical Analysis
What determines which news is covered?

*Doris A. Graber, *Mass Media and American Politics*, 5th ed. (Washington, D.C.: Congressional Quarterly Press, 1996), p. 112.

Network Coverage of State News: August 1994 to July 1995

ANNUAL NUMBER OF STORIES	STATES		PERCENTAGE OF MENTIONS	PERCENTAGE OF ELECTORAL VOTE
1–24	Alaska Arizona Connecticut Delaware Hawaii Iowa Kentucky Maine Missouri Montana Nebraska Nevada	New Hampshire North Dakota New Mexico North Carolina Ohio South Dakota Utah Vermont West Virginia Wisconsin Wyoming	11.4	27.1
25–50	Alabama Arkansas Georgia Idaho Indiana Illinois Kansas Louisiana Maryland	Massachusetts Minnesota Mississippi New Jersey Oregon Rhode Island South Carolina Tennessee Washington	27.6	32.9
51–100	Colorado Michigan Pennsylvania	Virginia Washington, D.C.	14.7	11.6
101–200	Florida Oklahoma	Texas	17.5	12.1
201–341	California	New York	28.9	16.3

SOURCE: Data compiled from the Vanderbilt Television News Archives.
Note: The sample size was 2,325.

taken or events recorded—they note only those appearing on their screens. Television news can also be exploited for its drama by well-constructed stories. Some critics suggest that there is pressure to produce television news that has a "story line," like a novel or movie. The story should be short, with exciting pictures and a clear plot. In the extreme case, the news media is satisfied with a **sound bite,** a several-second comment selected or crafted for its immediate impact on the viewer.

It has been suggested that these formatting characteristics—or necessities—of television increase its influence on political events. (Newspapers and news magazines are also limited by their formats, but to a lesser extent.) As you are aware, real life is usually not dramatic, nor do all events have a neat or an easily understood plot. Political campaigns are continuing events, lasting perhaps two years or more. The significance of their daily turns and twists are only apparent later. The "drama" of Congress, with its 535 players and

SOUND BITE

A brief, memorable comment that easily can be fit into news broadcasts.

dozens of important committees and meetings, is also difficult for the media to present. What television needs is dozens of daily three-minute stories.

News coverage of a single event, such as the results of the Iowa caucuses or the New Hampshire primary, may be the most important factor in having a candidate being referred to in the media as the "front-runner" in presidential campaigns. (See this chapter's *Critical Perspective* for a discussion of how the media's own needs have negatively affected political campaigns.)

THE MEDIA AND POLITICAL CAMPAIGNS

All forms of the media—television, newspapers, radio, and magazines—have an enormous political impact on American society. Media influence is most obvious during political campaigns. Because television is the primary news source for the majority of Americans, candidates and their consultants spend much of their time devising strategies to use television to their benefit. Three types of TV coverage are generally used in campaigns for the presidency and other offices: advertising, management of news coverage, and campaign debates.

Advertising

President Lyndon Johnson's "Daisy Girl" ad contrasted the innocence of childhood with the horror of an atomic attack.

Perhaps one of the most effective political ads of all time was a short, thirty-second spot created by President Lyndon Johnson's media adviser. In this ad, a little girl stood in a field of daisies. As she held a daisy, she pulled the petals off and quietly counted to herself. Suddenly, when she reached number ten, a deep bass voice cut in and began a countdown: 10, 9, 8, 7, 6 . . . When the voice intoned "zero," the unmistakable mushroom cloud of an

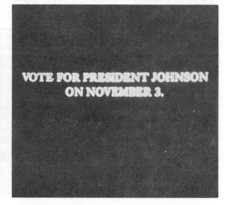

VOTE FOR PRESIDENT JOHNSON ON NOVEMBER 3.

CRITICAL PERSPECTIVE
Media Agendas and Political Agendas

The 1992 presidential election evoked considerable enthusiasm from political scientists and other watchers of the political system because, for the first time in more than twenty years, the percentage of eligible voters who cast ballots increased. The increase was only a few percentage points, but it suggested the reversal of a trend. Some commentators suggested that the increase was due to the increased excitement caused by the three-way contest and the extraordinary campaign waged by independent candidate H. Ross Perot. Others believed that the campaign tactics were not as offensive, particularly in regard to advertising, as they had been in 1988. The news media could also claim some credit: publishers and editors had declared that they would spend less effort on stories concerned with which candidate was running ahead of other candidates and more on issues.

Not all commentators agreed. Thomas E. Patterson, a political scientist, charged the media with continuing to cover the campaign in a way that increased voter cynicism and reduced the ability of the voter to make an educated choice. In his book, *Out of Order,* Patterson examines a great deal of data gathered from the news coverage of the 1992 campaign and concludes that "the United States cannot have a sensible campaign as long as it is built around the news media."* Patterson believes that one of the reasons voters seem to feel that they do not have legitimate choices among the candidates and that they would rather vote for "none of the above" is that the media spend most of their efforts dwelling on bad news and casting doubt on the candidates and the whole notion of the campaign itself. By the end of the campaign, the public—which has few, if any, sources of information besides the media—comes to believe that the candidates are manipulative, untrustworthy, and not well qualified to hold office. Patterson's examination of the data shows that the 1992 presidential debates, held in new formats and including Perot, improved the voters' opinions of the candidates because they were able to see the candidates as "real," without seeing them through the interpretation of the news media. In fact, a study of the campaign found that the public gave the media campaign coverage a grade of C, whereas the debates were assigned an A.

*Thomas E. Patterson, *Out of Order* (New York: Knopf, 1993), p. 25.

Setting the Agenda

After the 1988 campaign, the news media were criticized roundly for their emphasis on the horse race and their acceptance of "dirty campaigning." As a result of this criticism, the major news media, including television networks and national newspapers, decided to improve their coverage of campaigns. They resolved to focus less on the horse race, to be critical of dirty campaign tactics, to correct errors of facts put forward by candidates, and to focus on issues. In their study of the results of this resolution, S. Robert Lichter and Richard E. Noyes found that although the news media *did* increase their coverage of substantive issues, they investigated and commented on the issues that they—the media—had determined were important. Additionally, the media doubled their non-substantive coverage of campaign events and the horse race. Furthermore, the agenda set by the media was not the agenda set by any of the candidates. So, these scholars point out, the voter was unable to connect the candidates to their policy positions and thus could not cast a meaningful vote because the media did not provide sufficient information.†

The Need to Tell a Story Every Day

Although journalists try to report the news without bias, they do need to tell a story every day. Thus, Thomas Patterson says, journalists must create a plot for the campaign story every day. Usually, it involves the campaign itself—who is winning and who is losing. If someone is losing or declining in the polls, it must be the fault of the candidate and his or her staff. Such stories become the news, thus reinforcing the focus on the "game" of the campaign. Patterson finds that the news media do not show any bias related to partisanship; rather, the bias is toward bad news.

Interpreting the campaign for the voters should be done by party leaders and coalition builders. The current state of presidential campaigning, with its long season, multiple competing candidates during the primary season, and relatively weak party influence, by default gives the responsibility of explaining the election

†S. Robert Lichter and Richard E. Noyes, *Good Intentions Make Bad News: Why Americans Hate Campaign Journalism* (Lanham, Md.: Rowman and Littlefield, 1995).

CRITICAL PERSPECTIVE

Media Agendas and Political Agendas, Continued

to the news media. The media, however, focus on bad news and on the campaign game—or worse, decide which issues are most important.

The critiques by Patterson, Lichter and Noyes, and other commentors raise the following question: Whose election is it anyhow? Is it the media's election to sell according to their own agenda and commercial needs, or does it belong to the candidates and the voters? Without a better connection between what the candidates

are saying and what the voters are reading and hearing, campaign coverage will continue to earn poor marks from the public.

For Critical Analysis

1. Why do so many candidates seem to choose negative advertising as a strategy?

2. Why do reporters tend to focus on the "horse race" aspect of any important campaign?

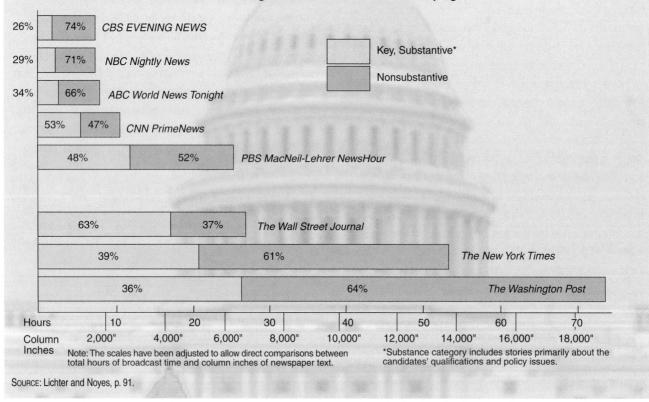

Substantive and Nonsubstantive Coverage of the 1992 Presidential Campaign

	Substantive*	Nonsubstantive	
CBS EVENING NEWS	26%	74%	
NBC Nightly News	29%	71%	
ABC World News Tonight	34%	66%	
CNN PrimeNews	53%	47%	
PBS MacNeil-Lehrer NewsHour	48%	52%	
The Wall Street Journal	63%	37%	
The New York Times	39%	61%	
The Washington Post	36%	64%	

Key: ☐ Substantive*   ▨ Nonsubstantive

Hours: 10   20   30   40   50   60   70

Column Inches: 2,000"   4,000"   6,000"   8,000"   10,000"   12,000"   14,000"   16,000"   18,000"

Note: The scales have been adjusted to allow direct comparisons between total hours of broadcast time and column inches of newspaper text.

*Substance category includes stories primarily about the candidates' qualifications and policy issues.

SOURCE: Lichter and Noyes, p. 91.

atom bomb began to fill the screen. Then President Johnson's voice was heard: "These are the stakes. To make a world in which all of God's children can live, or to go into the dark. We must either love each other or we must die." At the end of the commercial, the message read, "Vote for President Johnson on November 3."

To understand how effective this daisy girl commercial was, you must know that Johnson's opponent was Barry Goldwater, a Republican conservative candidate known for his expansive views on the role of the U.S. military.

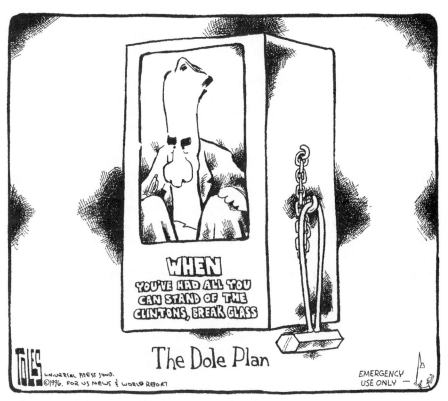

WHEN YOU'VE HAD ALL YOU CAN STAND OF THE CLINTONS, BREAK GLASS

The Dole Plan

EMERGENCY USE ONLY —

The ad's implication was that Goldwater would lead the United States into nuclear war. Although the ad was withdrawn within a few days, it has a place in political campaign history as the classic negative campaign announcement.

Since the daisy girl advertisement, negative advertising has come into its own. Candidates vie with one another to produce "attack" ads and then to counterattack when the opponent responds. The public claims not to like negative advertising, but as one consultant put it, "Negative advertising works." Any advertising "works" when viewers or listeners remember an ad. It is clear that negative ads are more memorable than ones that praise the candidate's virtues. The purpose of campaigns is to confirm the votes of the supporters and attract the votes of independents. Negative advertising, which supporters and independents remember longer than positive advertising, works well. For those members of the other party or supporters of the candidate under attack, no vote gain is expected anyway.

Too many blatantly negative ads by the candidates, of course, can alienate viewers and subject the candidates to criticism by the press and other media. Nonetheless, at least at the national level, negative ads continue to be used extensively. In fact, one study showed that 88 percent of President Clinton's ads from April to September in 1996 essentially consisted of negative messages about Bob Dole and the Republican party.

Management of News Coverage

Using political advertising to get a message across to the public is a very expensive tactic. Coverage by the news media is, however, free; it simply demands that the campaign ensure that coverage takes place. In recent years, campaign managers have shown increasing sophistication in creating newsworthy

SPIN

An interpretation of campaign events or election results that is most favorable to the candidate's campaign strategy.

SPIN DOCTOR

A political campaign adviser who tries to convince journalists of the truth of a particular interpretation of events.

events for journalists to cover. As Doris Graber points out, "To keep a favorable image of their candidates in front of the public, campaign managers arrange newsworthy events to familiarize potential voters with their candidates' best aspects."[4]

To take advantage of the media's interest in campaign politics, whether at the presidential level or perhaps in a Senate race, the campaign staff tries to influence the quantity and type of coverage the campaign receives. (See this chapter's *Politics and the Media* for a discussion of the role books may play in a campaign.) First, it is important for the campaign staff to understand the technical aspects of media coverage—camera angles, necessary equipment, timing, and deadlines—and to plan their political events to accommodate the press. Second, the campaign organization learns that political reporters and their sponsors—networks or newspapers—are in competition for the best stories and can be manipulated through the granting of favors, such as a personal interview with the candidate. Third, an important task for the scheduler in the campaign is the planning of events that will be photogenic and interesting enough for the evening news. A related goal, although one that is more difficult to attain, is to convince reporters that a particular interpretation of an event is correct.

Today the art of putting the appropriate **spin** on a story or event is highly developed. Each presidential candidate's press advisers, often referred to as **spin doctors,** try to convince the journalists that their interpretations of the political events are correct. For example, in 1992 Bill Clinton's people tried to convince the press that he didn't really expect to win the New Hampshire primary anyway, while the Paul Tsongas camp insisted that winning the New England state was a great and unexpected victory. Journalists began to report on the different spins and how the candidates tried to manipulate campaign news coverage.

Going for the Knockout Punch—Presidential Debates

Perhaps of equal importance to political advertisements is the performance of the candidate in a televised presidential debate. After the first such debate in 1960, in which John Kennedy, the young senator from Massachusetts, took on the vice president of the United States, Richard Nixon, candidates became aware of the great potential of television for changing the momentum of a campaign. In general, challengers have much more to gain from debating than do incumbents. Challengers hope that the incumbent may make a mistake in the debate and undermine the "presidential" image. Incumbent presidents are loath to debate the challenger, because it puts their opponent on an equal footing with them.

The presidential debates of 1992 were distinguished by the addition of the independent candidate, H. Ross Perot, and by the use of two different formats. The first and third debates were more formal, with a panel of journalists asking questions of the three candidates. In the second debate, audience members asked the candidates questions directly. Most observers of the three debates noted that the questions posed by the audience were as complex and probing as any raised by the media during the campaign.

Three debates were held in 1996. The first was a formally staged and not very memorable exchange between Bill Clinton and the Republican challenger, Bob Dole. The second, also rather formal, featured the vice presiden-

[4]Doris Graber, *Mass Media and American Policies,* 5th ed. (Washington, D.C.: Congressional Quarterly Press, 1996), p. 59.

POLITICS AND THE MEDIA
Book Wars

Although some voters get their news from the Internet and it sometimes seems that all political campaigning takes place on television, the lowly book continues to play an important role.

Books as Income

Many politicians write books to build public support for their ideas and future campaigns, but the conditions under which they agree to write a book may cast a shadow on their careers. One speaker of the House, Jim Wright of Texas, left Congress after a book scandal. It was found that he had published his biography himself and was reaping the benefits. In his first days as speaker of the House in 1995, Newt Gingrich came under intense fire for signing a book contract with a publishing house owned by Rupert Murdoch, the conservative Australian media giant. Gingrich first accepted a million-dollar advance on the book, but then he returned it and accepted only one dollar instead. He was heavily criticized for taking such a large sum, especially from an outspoken conservative, to boost his political funds.

Books as Policy Platforms

Many other books are written by political figures and elected leaders to put their views in front of the public. For such celebrities as Al Gore, who wrote a best seller about the environment, and Hillary Rodham Clinton, who wrote a book about families and child-

rearing that generated much Republican reaction, publishing a book was a way to gain an audience and enhance their credentials. The royalties went to charities.

Books as Campaign Advertisements

Most candidates have biographies published about them at the beginning of a campaign. Written by a journalist or a professional writer, a campaign biography is an uncritical recounting of the candidate's life that is intended to increase the candidate's likability. In recent years, most candidates also have published autobiographies that were written with the help of "ghost writers."

Books and Journalists

Many journalists have improved their reputations and competed for Pulitzer Prizes by writing books about politics. Bob Woodward and Carl Bernstein wrote a best-selling book (*All the President's Men*) about the Watergate break-in. Woodward has written several other books about presidential administrations and campaigns. Theodore White's series about the campaigns from 1960 to 1988 were exceptional accounts of American politics. The Clinton campaign and his subsequent administration seem to spawn more books than most, perhaps because the president was young and energetic and presented journalists with a complex personality. One of the books about Whitewater, *Bloodsport*, made

the best-seller list. Perhaps the most controversial book was *Primary Colors*, a novel published anonymously about a presidential candidate, his wife, and his entourage. The book was modeled directly on the Clintons. So realistic were the characters and conversations in the book that all of Washington buzzed with discussion about which Clinton staff member had written the book or provided the information. Finally, after an exhaustive investigation, a scholar matched the handwriting on the manuscript with that of Joe Klein, a writer for *Newsweek*. Klein confessed, after which his editor admitted that he had known about the project all along.

The world of journalism exploded with contempt: How could an editor have lied? How could Klein claim to be a journalist when he had lied and written this book and made millions? Didn't the magazine bear responsibility for the book? What is the line between reporting, writing nonfiction, and writing fiction based on reporting? It is unlikely that the exposure of Klein will end the writing of books about politics—whether they be fictional or true stories.

For Critical Analysis

How can you tell if a book about a candidate is meant to be a campaign piece or is a critical or scholarly investigation? Why does it matter?

tial candidates, Al Gore and Dole's Republican running mate, Jack Kemp. The two candidates engaged in relatively mild attacks on the respective presidential candidates. In the final debate, on October 16, Dole and Clinton faced off in a less formal format. They appeared together on a stage surrounded by galleries of people selected by the Gallup organization to represent a cross section of the nation. Ross Perot and Pat Choate, his running mate, were denied access to the dabates by the federal courts.

A family watches the 1960 Kennedy-Nixon debates on television. After the debate, TV viewers thought Kennedy had won, whereas radio listeners thought Nixon had won.

The crucial fact about the practice of televising debates is that, although debates are justified publicly as an opportunity for the voters to find out how candidates differ on the issues, what the candidates want is to capitalize on the power of television to project an image. They view the debate as a strate-

In 1996, President Clinton and Bob Dole faced off in two debates. They were generally civil and respectful toward each other. Neither debate seemed to have much impact on the outcome of the 1996 elections.

gic opportunity to improve their own images or to point out the failures of their opponent. Candidates are very aware not only that the actual performance is important but also that the morning-after interpretation of the debate by the news media may play a crucial role in what the public thinks. Regardless of the risks of debating, the potential for gaining votes is so great that candidates undoubtedly will continue to seek televised debates.

The Media and the 1996 Elections

The media were sharply criticized in 1988 and 1992 for concentrating on the "horse race" in their coverage of the presidential elections of those years. Still smarting from this criticism, in 1996 the major network news operations and many of the major national newspapers tried to include more coverage of substantive issues and candidates' positions on those issues. Some of the newspapers printed whole texts from the presidential candidates' speeches to help inform their readers. National Public Radio aired brief speeches by Bob Dole and Bill Clinton through the last few weeks of the campaign.

The Media's Impact on the Voters

The question of how much influence the media have on voting behavior is difficult to answer. Generally, individuals watch television or read newspapers with certain preconceived ideas about political issues and candidates. These attitudes and opinions act as a kind of perceptual screen that filters out information that makes people feel uncomfortable or that does not fit with their own ideas.

Voters watch campaign commercials and news about political campaigns with "selective attentiveness." That is, they tend to watch those commercials that support the candidate they favor and tend to pay attention to news stories about their own candidates. This selectivity also affects their perceptions of the content of the news story or commercial and whether it is remembered. Apparently, the media are most influential with those persons who have not formed an opinion about political candidates or issues. Studies have shown that the flurry of television commercials and debates immediately before election day has the most impact on those voters who are truly undecided. Few voters who have already formed their opinions change their minds under the influence of the media.

As mentioned earlier in this chapter, the media—particularly TV—have a significant impact on the views of young Americans. Yet a survey conducted in 1996 by the Pew Research Center in Washington, D.C., found that only 22 percent of Americans under the age of thirty said that they regularly watched a network news broadcast. In the last few years, several TV networks have initiated programs or changes to appeal to the younger generation. For example, in the 1992 presidential campaign, both Bill Clinton and Ross Perot appeared on MTV as part of MTV's "Rock the Vote" campaign, which was intended to raise political participation and awareness among young voters. In 1996, C-SPAN introduced a "first time voter" feature and also sent two buses around the nation to conduct taped interviews with young persons (outdoing MTV's one bus). CNN recently hired several younger political

DID YOU KNOW...
That the first radio commercial was a ten-minute spot that sold for $50?

reporters to change its image, and MSNBC was launched in 1996 as a twenty-four-hour cable news channel for young adults.

THE MEDIA AND THE GOVERNMENT

The mass media not only wield considerable power when it comes to political campaigns, but they also, in one way or another, can wield power over the affairs of government and over government officials. Perhaps the most notable example in modern times concerns the activities of *Washington Post* reporters Bob Woodward and Carl Bernstein. These two reporters were assigned to cover the Watergate break-in, and they undertook an investigation that eventually led to the resignation of President Richard Nixon. Other investigations have included the Iran-*contra* scandal, the savings and loan debacle, and, more recently, the Whitewater deals.

The Media and the Presidency

A love-hate relationship clearly exists between the president and the media. During the administration of John F. Kennedy, the president was seen in numerous photos scanning the *New York Times,* the *Washington Post,* and other newspapers each morning to see how the press tallied his successes and failures. This led to frequent jocular comments about his speed-reading ability.

In the United States, the prominence of the president is cultivated by a **White House press corps** that is assigned full time to cover the presidency. These reporters even have a lounge in the White House where they spend their days, waiting for a story to break. Most of the time, they simply wait for the daily or twice-daily briefing by the president's **press secretary.** Because of the press corps's physical proximity to the president, the chief executive cannot even take a brief stroll around the presidential swimming pool without its becoming news. Perhaps no other nation allows the press such access to its highest government official. Consequently, no other nation has its airwaves and print media so filled with absolute trivia regarding the personal lives of the chief executive and his family.

President Franklin D. Roosevelt brought new spirit to a demoralized country and led it through the Great Depression through his effective use of the media, particularly radio broadcasts. His radio "fireside chats" brought hope to millions. Roosevelt's speeches were masterly in their ability to forge a common emotional bond among his listeners. His decisive announcement in 1933 on the reorganization of the banks, for example, calmed a jittery nation and prevented the collapse of the banking industry, which was threatened by a run on banks, from which nervous depositors were withdrawing their assets. His famous Pearl Harbor speech, following the Japanese attack on the U.S. Pacific fleet on December 7, 1941 ("a day that will live in infamy"), mobilized the nation for the sacrifices and effort necessary to win World War II.

Perhaps no president exploited the electronic media more effectively than did Ronald Reagan. The "great communicator," as he was called, was never more dramatic than in his speech to the nation following the October 1983 U.S. invasion of the Caribbean island of Grenada. In this address, the president, in an almost flawless performance, appeared to many to have decisively laid to rest the uncertainty and confusion surrounding the event.

The relationship between the media and the president has thus been reciprocal. Both institutions have used each other, sometimes positively, sometimes negatively. The presidency and the news media are mutually dependent.

WHITE HOUSE PRESS CORPS

A group of reporters assigned full time to cover the presidency.

PRESS SECRETARY

The individual responsible for representing the White House before the media. The press secretary writes news releases, provides background information, sets up press conferences, and so on.

President Franklin D. Roosevelt, the first president to fully exploit the airwaves for his benefit, reported to the nation through radio "fireside chats."

Setting the Public Agenda

Given that government officials have in front of them an array of problems with which they must deal, the process of setting the public agenda is constant. To be sure, what goes on the public agenda for discussion, debate, and, ultimately, policy action depends on many factors—not the least being each official's personal philosophy.

According to a number of studies, the media play an important part in setting the public agenda. Evidence is strong that whatever public problems receive the most media treatment will be cited by the public in contemporary surveys as the most important problems. In recent years, television coverage has brought a number of issues to public attention and, consequently, to the attention of policymakers. For example, videotaped footage of the horrors in Bosnia aroused public concern, and eventually President Bill Clinton sent U.S. troops to Bosnia to enforce the 1995 Dayton peace accords.

A relatively recent use of the media by presidents has been regularly scheduled press conferences. Here President Clinton addresses questions from the Washington press corps. Clinton has proven himself to be quick on his feet when asked even embarrassing questions. He and others before him have learned to memorize the names of virtually all of the members of the Washington press corps.

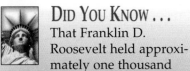

DID YOU KNOW ...
That Franklin D. Roosevelt held approximately one thousand press conferences during his terms as president?

Although the media do not make policy decisions, they do determine to a significant extent the policy issues that need to be decided—and this is an important part of the political process. Because those who control the media are not elected representatives of the people, the agenda-setting role of the media necessarily is a controversial one. The relationship of the media to agenda setting remains complex, though, because politicians are able to manipulate media coverage to control some of its effects, as well as to exploit the media to further their agendas with the public.

GOVERNMENT REGULATION OF THE MEDIA

The United States has perhaps the freest press in the world. Nonetheless, regulation of the media does exist, particularly of the electronic media. Many aspects of this regulation were discussed in Chapter 4, when we examined First Amendment rights and the press.

Controlling Ownership of the Media

The First Amendment does not mention electronic media, which did not exist when the Bill of Rights was written. For many reasons, the government has much greater control over the electronic media than it does over printed media. Through the Federal Communications Commission (FCC), which regulates communications by radio, television, wire, and cable, the number of radio stations has been controlled for many years, in spite of the fact that technologically we could have many more radio stations than now exist. Also, the FCC created a situation in which the three major TV networks have dominated the airwaves.

Most FCC rules have dealt with ownership of news media, such as how many stations a network can own. Recently, the FCC has decided to auction off hundreds of radio frequencies, allowing the expansion of cellular telephone applications.

In 1996, Congress passed, and the president signed, an act that has far-reaching implications for the communications industry—the Telecommunications Act of 1996. The act ended the rule that kept telephone companies from entering the cable business and other communications markets. What this means is that a single corporation—whether AT&T or Disney—can offer long distance and local telephone services, cable television, satellite television, Internet services, and, of course, libraries of films and entertainment. The race is on for companies to control media ownership and to develop all the needed technology. Already, the Disney Company has purchased ABC/Capital Cities Company, and Time Warner has acquired Turner Broadcasting. In the near future, consumers can choose among multiple competitors for all these services delivered to the home. It also will be possible for a single entity to own a television network; the studios that produce shows, news, and movies; and the means to deliver that content to the home via cable, satellite, or the Internet. The question to be faced in the future is how to assure competition in the delivery of the news so that citizens have access to multiple points of view from the media.

Government Control of Content

In general, the broadcasting industry has avoided government regulation of content by establishing its own code. This code consists of a set of rules developed by the National Association of Broadcasters (the lobby for the TV and radio industry) that regulate the amount of sex, violence, nudity, profanity, and so forth that is allowed on the air. (High rates of violent crime among teens has again brought the attention of Congress to media programming.) It should be noted that abiding by the code is voluntary on the part of networks and stations.

Since 1980, there has been continued public debate over whether the government should attempt to control polling and the "early calling" of presidential elections by the television networks. On election night in 1980, before numerous states had closed their polls, the networks predicted, based on exit polls, that Ronald Reagan had been elected. The concern expressed by many was that voters on their way to vote might not bother because the victor had already been declared. It was feared that the resulting drop in turnout would particularly affect state and local races. Because some types of voters, such as factory workers, are more likely to vote late in the day, the outcomes of elections and referenda might be seriously affected.

In 1984, the networks were careful to say that they would not project winners in any state until the polling places *in that state* were closed. With the different time zones and with a concentration of population (and electoral college votes) in the Northeast and Midwest, however, the networks were able to project a winner by 8 p.m. eastern time, which was 5 p.m. on the West Coast.

Some legislators and citizens have called for a ban on exit polls or on releasing them before *all* polling places in the continental United States are closed. Others have called for a federal law establishing a uniform closing time for voting so that voting would end at the same time all over the country, and thus exit polls could not be a factor. In any event, although turnout has been lower than expected in many western states, studies suggest that the early announcement of election results based on exit polls has little effect on election outcomes.

The Telecommunications Act of 1996 included two provisions that allows for some government control of the content of the media. One provision required that television manufacturers include a "V-chip" in each set. The V-chip will allow parents to block programs that include violence or sexual conduct from being viewed on their televisions. The other provision prohibited the transmission of indecent or patently offensive materials on the Internet in such a way that minors could access those materials. Responding to immediate legal challenges to this portion of the new law, two federal district courts held in 1996 that the provision blocking certain content from the Internet was unconstitutional. One court stated that this section was "profoundly repugnant" to the First Amendment's guarantee of free speech. Further regulation of the Internet is obviously a matter of constitutional debate (see Chapter 4).

THE PUBLIC'S RIGHT TO MEDIA ACCESS

Does the public have a right to **media access?** Both the FCC and the courts gradually have taken the stance that citizens do have a right of access to the media, particularly the electronic media. The argument is that the airwaves are public, but because they are used for private profit, the government has the right to dictate how they are used. It does so in many ways. In addition to the equal-time rule for candidates—under which broadcasters who sell airtime to political candidates must make equal time available to opposing candidates

MEDIA ACCESS

The public's right of access to the media. The Federal Communications Commission and the courts gradually have taken the stance that citizens do have a right to media access.

on equal terms—the FCC has also promulgated the **personal attack rule.** This rule allows individuals (or groups) airtime to reply to attacks that have previously been aired.

Technology is giving more citizens access to the electronic media and, in particular, to television. As more cable operators have more airtime to sell, some of that time will remain unused and will be available for public access. At the same time, such developments as the Internet, video magazines for the millions of videocassette recorder owners, and other technological changes are making the issue of media access by the public less important. The public increasingly has relatively cheap access to the electronic media, although not in the traditional forms.

BIAS IN THE MEDIA

Many studies have been undertaken to try to identify the sources and direction of bias in the media, and these studies have reached different conclusions. For example, in a classic study conducted in the 1980s, the researchers found that the media producers, editors, and reporters (the "media elite") had a notably liberal and "left-leaning" bias in their news coverage.[5] Other studies, however, have concluded that there is a pro-Republican and pro-conservative bias in the overall stance of newspapers and major networks. Still other studies assert that the press is "apolitical." For example, Calvin F. Exoo, in his study of politics in the media, suggests that journalists are neither liberal nor conservative. Rather, they are constrained by both the pro-America bias of the media ownership and the journalists' own code of objectivity. Most are more interested in improving their career prospects by covering the winning candidate and pleasing their editors to get better assignments than they are in discussing public policies.[6] Thus, the bias in the media is toward not criticizing the American system and on producing "news" that will attract viewers and readers without threatening the American way of life. This analysis would support Thomas E. Patterson's view that the real bias of the news media is to emphasize bad news and cynicism rather than any partisan position.[7]

Increasingly, the media are being criticized for their failure to provide any context—biased or not—for news events. According to one critic, the focus on the "brief now" of events tends to magnify the trivial and trivialize the important. The media convey the sense that life is just a sequence of random events in a world that "cannot be understood, shaped or controlled."[8]

THE MEDIA AND POLITICS: UNFINISHED WORK

The power of the media and their impact on American society clearly is a controversial and important subject. To what extent the mass media help to clarify issues and to contribute to a more enlightened public, as opposed to distorting and oversimplifying reality, is a topic hotly debated in the United States. The increasing dependence of campaigns and candidates on the media

---

[5]S. Robert Lichter, Stanley Rothman, and Linda S. Lichter, *The Media Elite* (New York: Adler and Adler, 1986).
[6]Calvin F. Exoo, *The Politics of the Mass Media* (St. Paul: West, 1994), pp. 49–50.
[7]Thomas E. Patterson, *Out of Order* (New York: Knopf, 1993).
[8]James Fallows, *Breaking the News: How the Media Undermine American Democracy* (New York: Pantheon Books, 1996).

CONCEPT OVERVIEW
The Changing Media Landscape

Within the last forty years, the range and variety of media available to the general public have expanded to a startling degree. Accompanying this expansion in information services has been a change in the role played by the media: electronic media interpret the news in ways that newspapers and other printed media cannot.

THEN	NOW
• Newspapers and radio were the primary news sources.	• Television is the primary news source.
• Newspaper publishers competed in local markets.	• There is little competition among newspaper publishers in local markets.
• Presidential actions were mostly reported in the printed media; there were no live news conferences on TV.	• Presidential actions are covered live on TV.
• Political campaigns depended on parties and volunteers.	• Political campaigns primarily depend on television advertising and news coverage of the candidates.
• Campaign advertising meant buttons and bumper stickers.	• Campaign advertising means television ads and debates.
• The telephone system was run by a monopoly.	• Telephone, cable, and Internet services are competitive.
• No cable TV existed.	• The majority (64 percent) of Americans have cable TV.

makes this an era of symbolic politics and weakened political attachments. At the same time, the greatly expanded number of media outlets, including cable television and online computer services, has offered Americans more freedom to choose what they watch and read.

By 1996, the Internet had made available literally hundreds of sites allowing voters to read about candidates and "chat" with politicians, journalists, and other voters. Voters could view home pages that were advertisements for candidates and seek information about almost any topic from the great libraries of the nation. Although this interactive political forum was beyond the reach of those Americans who are not connected to the Internet, the vigor and intensity of these Internet exchanges suggest that Americans are willing and eager to express themselves in the arena of national politics. The same lesson was demonstrated in debates in which ordinary citizens, rather than journalists, were allowed to ask the questions. At the same time, the number of partisan talk shows and cable TV channels is increasing, so Americans can choose to listen only to media outlets that support their own positions. Obviously, how to harness the potential of the mass media to allow for national debate about the good of the nation is an issue yet to be resolved.

GETTING INVOLVED
Being a Critical Consumer of the News

Television and newspapers provide an enormous range of choice for Americans who want to stay informed. Still, critics of the media argue that a substantial amount of programming and print is colored either by the subjectivity of editors and producers or by the demands of profit making. Few Americans take the time to become critical consumers of the news, either in print or on the TV screen.

To become a critical news consumer, you must practice reading a newspaper with a critical eye toward editorial decisions. For example, ask yourself what stories are given prominence on the front page of the paper, and which ones merit a photograph? What is the editorial stance of the newspaper? Most American papers tend to have moderate to conservative editorial pages. Who are the columnists given space on the "op-ed" page, the page opposite the paper's own editorial page? For a contrast to most daily papers, occasionally pick up an outright political publication such as the *National Review* or the *New Republic* and take note of the editorial positions.

Watching the evening news can be far more rewarding if you look at how much the news depends on video effects. You will note that stories on the evening news tend to be no more than three minutes long, that stories with excellent videotape get more attention, and that considerable time is taken up with "happy talk" or human interest stories that tap the emotions of the audience.

Another interesting study you might make is to compare the evening news with the daily paper on a given date. You will see that the paper is perhaps half a day behind the news but that the print story contains far more information. Headlines must take the place of videotape in grabbing your attention.

You can also be a more active consumer by voicing your views and suggestions to the producers of television news or to the editors of newspapers and magazines through letters, by telephone, and by electronic mail. These persons are often responsive to criticism and open to constructive suggestions; you might be surprised to find them so accessible.

If you wish to obtain more information on the media and take an active role as a consumer of the news, you can contact one of the following organizations:

NATIONAL ASSOCIATION OF BROADCASTERS
1771 N St. N.W.
Washington, DC 20036
202-429-5300
http://www.nab.org

NATIONAL NEWSPAPER ASSOCIATION
1525 Wilson Blvd.
Arlington, VA 22209
1-800-829-4NNA
nna@as/.com
http://www.oweb.com/nna/nnahome.html

ACCURACY IN MEDIA (A CONSERVATIVE GROUP)
4455 Connecticut Ave. N.W., Suite 330
Washington, DC 20008
202-364-4401
http://www.aim.org

PEOPLE FOR THE AMERICAN WAY (A LIBERAL GROUP)
200 M St. N.W. Suite 400
Washington, DC 20036
202-467-4999
http://www.pfaw.org

KEY TERMS

electronic media 365

managed news 362

media access 379

narrowcasting 365

personal attack rule 380

press secretary 376

public agenda 360

sound bite 367

spin 372

spin doctor 372

White House press corps 376

yellow journalism 364

CHAPTER SUMMARY

1 The media are enormously important in American politics today. They perform a number of functions, including (a) entertainment, (b) news reporting, (c) identifying public problems, (d) socializing new generations, (e) providing a political forum, and (f) making profits.

2 The media have always played a significant role in American politics. In the 1800s and earlier, however, news traveled slowly, and politics was controlled by a small group whose members communicated personally. The high-speed rotary press and the telegraph led to self-supported newspapers and mass readership.

3 The electronic media (television and radio) are growing in significance in the area of communications. New technologies, such as cable television, are giving broadcasters the opportunity to air a greater number of specialized programs.

4 The media wield enormous political power during political campaigns and over the affairs of government and government officials by focusing attention on their actions. Today's political campaigns use political advertising and expert management of news coverage. Of equal importance for presidential candidates is how they appear in presidential debates.

5 The relationship between the media and the president is close; each has used the other—sometimes positively, sometimes negatively. The media play an important role in investigating the government, in getting government officials to understand better the needs and desires of American society, and in setting the public agenda.

6 The media in the United States, particularly the electronic media, are subject to government regulation, although the United States has possibly the freest press in the world. Most Federal Communications Commission rules have dealt with ownership of TV and radio stations. Recent legislation has removed many rules about co-ownership of several forms of media.

7 Studies of bias in the media have reached different conclusions. Some detect a conservative bias, while others find a more liberal stance. Still other studies conclude that the media are apolitical. Recently, the media have been criticized for being biased in favor of cynicism and "bad news," as well as for not providing any context—biased or unbiased—for the events they report.

QUESTIONS FOR REVIEW AND DISCUSSION

1 Why are Americans so fascinated with talk shows? What are the advantages and disadvantages of candidates and politicians presenting their views on these shows?

2 Compare the coverage of a major political event by the printed media, the network news, CNN, and talk shows. What can you learn from each type of presentation? In which format is the most information available? Are different aspects of the event emphasized by different presentations? How does editing change the theme of the story in each case?

3 Discuss the relationships among the media, political candidates, and officeholders. How do the demands on journalists for "news" and "stories" affect their relationship to a candidate? Is it possible for journalists to main-

tain a positive relationship with the president over the long term?

4 What should be the role of mass media in a presidential campaign? How could the media become a vehicle for improving debate over the major issues of a campaign? To what extent should the media focus on the personality and character of the candidates? What impact does the focus on the "horse race" aspect of a campaign have on the voters?

5 Consider the evidence of bias in the media when you watch prime-time network news. Do the media seem to favor the Democrats or the Republicans? Do the stories ever criticize the American political system? Are the video images positive or negative, compared with the words used by the anchors?

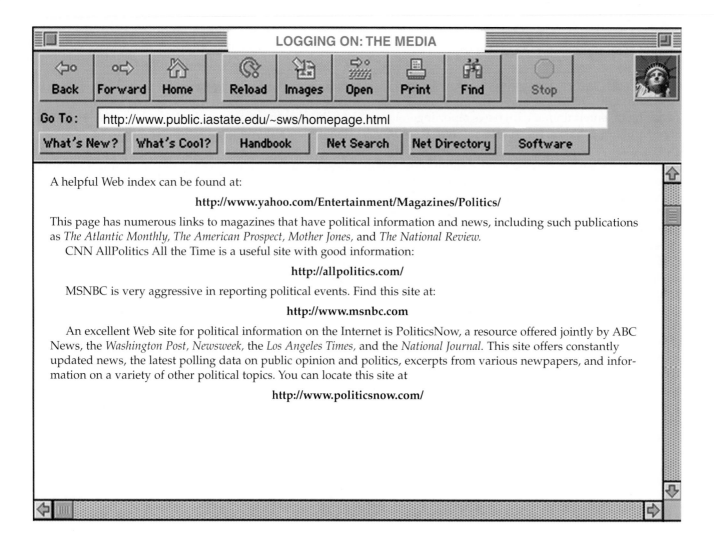

LOGGING ON: THE MEDIA

A helpful Web index can be found at:

http://www.yahoo.com/Entertainment/Magazines/Politics/

This page has numerous links to magazines that have political information and news, including such publications as *The Atlantic Monthly, The American Prospect, Mother Jones,* and *The National Review.*

CNN AllPolitics All the Time is a useful site with good information:

http://allpolitics.com/

MSNBC is very aggressive in reporting political events. Find this site at:

http://www.msnbc.com

An excellent Web site for political information on the Internet is PoliticsNow, a resource offered jointly by ABC News, the *Washington Post, Newsweek,* the *Los Angeles Times,* and the *National Journal.* This site offers constantly updated news, the latest polling data on public opinion and politics, excerpts from various newpapers, and information on a variety of other political topics. You can locate this site at

http://www.politicsnow.com/

SELECTED REFERENCES

Davis, Richard. *The Press and American Politics: The New Mediator.* 2d ed. Upper Saddle River, N.J.: Prentice-Hall, 1996. Davis provides a historical perspective on the development of the media in the United States and their current role as the interpreter of the political scene for most citizens.

Exoo, Calvin F. *The Politics of the Mass Media.* St. Paul: West, 1994. The author presents an extended critique of the hegemony of the media, discussing not only what the mass media are presenting to the public but why they support the system and present the views of the dominant culture.

Gilder, George. *Life after Television: The Coming Transformation of Media and American Life.* New York: Norton, 1993. The author predicts a future when the communications networks that we currently have—telephones and televisions—are made obsolete by fiber-optic computer networks that link everyone in the United States. Gilder believes that such direct connections will enable people to take control of their own democracy and free themselves from the influence of the mass media.

Graber, Doris A. *Mass Media and American Politics.* 5th ed. Washington, D.C.: Congressional Quarterly Press, 1996. In this new edition of a classic work, Graber gives an overview of many aspects of the mass media, including how government regulates the media, how the media decide to cover news, and how the media affect citizens' views of the world.

Grossman, Lawrence K. *The Electronic Republic: Reshaping Democracy in the Information Age.* New York: Viking Press, 1995. The author, a former president of the Public Broadcasting Service and NBC News and now president of Horizons Cable Network, looks at some of the implications of the electronic media and communications technology for our democratic political system.

Jamieson, Kathleen Hall. *Packaging the Presidency: A History and Criticism of Presidential Campaign Advertising.* 3d ed. New York: Oxford University Press, 1996. This is an insightful discussion of presidential campaign advertising as it has evolved over time from printed handbills to television coverage of carefully orchestrated events.

Just, Marion H., *et al. Crosstalk: Citizens, Candidates and the Media in a Presidential Campaign.* Chicago: University of Chicago Press, 1996. The result of a lengthy study, this book analyzes how citizens respond to both the candidates' messages and the interpretations given to those messages by the media in order to form an opinion of the candidates.

Lichter, S. Robert, and Richard E. Noyes. *Good Intentions Make Bad News: Why Americans Hate Campaign Journalism.* Lanham, Md.: Rowman and Littlefield, 1995. The authors examine a large body of data about newspaper and television coverage of the 1992 election to critique the media's performance and suggest reforms for improving campaign coverage.

Mitchell, Greg. *The Campaign of the Century: Upton Sinclair's Race for Governor of California and the Birth of Media Politics.* New York: Random House, 1992. The subject of this book is the 1934 campaign of muckraking novelist Upton Sinclair, who ran for governor of California on an antipoverty platform. Frightened by his "radical" politics, the Hollywood studios and the business community hired consultants and mounted against Sinclair the first major media campaign ever, inventing the idea of political consulting.

Rosenstiel, Tom. *Strange Bedfellows: How Television and the Presidential Candidates Changed American Politics, 1992.* New York: Hyperion, 1993. The author, who is a correspondent for the *Los Angeles Times,* criticizes the press for its treatment of the campaign as a horse race, for searching for gossip rather than news, and for wanting to become pundits rather than journalists. This is an interesting account of the 1992 campaign.

Wriston, Walter. *The Twilight of Sovereignty: How the Information Revolution Is Transforming Our World.* New York: Scribner's, 1993. The author argues that the microchip and satellite technologies have created a world community, with political and economic ramifications far beyond our imagination. He believes that the new technology fosters democracy and can be used to improve economic conditions throughout the world.

PART FOUR
Political Institutions

12
The Congress

Members of Congress Were Required to Spend Six Months Each Year in Their Districts?

BACKGROUND

MEMBERS OF CONGRESS SPEND FAR MORE TIME IN WASHINGTON TALKING TO LOBBYISTS AND OTHER MEMBERS THAN THEY DO AT HOME. IN FACT, ALTHOUGH INCUMBENT MEMBERS OF CONGRESS ARE VERY DIFFICULT TO DEFEAT, A FEW OF THEM ARE CHALLENGED SUCCESSFULLY EACH ELECTION BY NEWCOMERS WHO POINT TO THE MEMBERS' WASHINGTON TOWNHOUSES AND HEAVY INVOLVEMENT WITH POLITICS "INSIDE THE BELTWAY."

WHAT IF MEMBERS WERE REQUIRED TO SPEND SIX MONTHS EACH YEAR IN THEIR DISTRICTS?

Requiring members of Congress to be in their districts for six months each year certainly would strengthen their relationship with the voters. The voters would have far more opportunities to meet with the members in order to express their views. It is likely that members would be even more immersed in problem solving for ordinary citizens than they are now. It is very likely that local interests might be perceived as more powerful than they are now, and national lobbyists would have to compete with local demands. With so much time spent listening to the concerns of local workers, for example, a member of Congress might be more aware of the impact of international trade on his or her constituents.

Spending more time in the district could have the effect of reducing the legislator's tie to the political party. Strong state and regional interests would be likely to force the legislator to vote against the party's position if that position was contrary to constituent interests. If the legislator cultivated good constituency relations, the time spent at home probably would strengthen the power of incumbency. Voters find it much harder to reject someone whom they have met and who may have helped their family or town on an issue than to vote against someone who is always in Washington, D.C. A new person might get to Congress only by running for an open seat.

GETTING THE LEGISLATIVE WORK DONE

If members of Congress had to complete the budget and all legislation in six months so they could go home, could those tasks be completed? To be sure, most legislation could move faster than it does, particularly if members would be willing to delegate more power to committees or to the leadership. One of the problems of a speedier legislative process in Washington, D.C., however, is that not all issues might be raised or all interests considered in the process of writing legislation. Part of a representative democracy involves allowing all who have opinions to contribute to the legislative process. Shortening the time spent in Washington might reduce the amount of influence that the public has on the process. Furthermore, speeding up legislation could, in the long run, produce laws that soon would need to be reconsidered or amended. Time does allow difficult issues to be worked out.

Finally, sending Congress home for six months each year would transfer a great deal of power to the president and to the members of the executive branch to act without a counterbalance. While Americans might like to see more of their representatives at home, they also are unlikely to place their trust in the executive branch for six months each year.

FOR CRITICAL ANALYSIS

1. *Which local interests might receive stronger representation if members spent more time at home? Which interests would be unaffected?*
2. *Do you think that members of Congress could transact some of their business via electronic communications systems? Is face-to-face deliberation necessary?*

Most Americans spend little time thinking about the Congress of the United States, and when they do, their opinions are frequently unflattering. After the Republican victory of 1994 and the budget gridlock of 1995–1996, polls taken in late 1996 showed that less than 30 percent of Americans approved of the job Congress was doing. Nonetheless, 64 percent believed that their own representative deserved to be reelected. This is one of the paradoxes of the relationship between the people and Congress. Members of the public hold the institution in low regard while expressing satisfaction with their individual representatives.

Part of the explanation for these seemingly contradictory appraisals is that members of Congress spend considerable time and effort serving their constituents. If the federal bureaucracy makes a mistake, the senator's or representative's office tries to resolve the issue. What most Americans see of Congress, therefore, is the work of their own representatives in their home states. As suggested in this chapter's opening *What If . . .* , the tie between members of Congress and the voters might be even further strengthened if the members were at home more of the time.

Congress, however, was created to work not just for local constituents but also for the nation as a whole. Understanding the nature of the institution and the process of lawmaking is an important part of understanding how the policies that shape our lives are made.

WHY WAS CONGRESS CREATED?

The founders of the American republic believed that the bulk of the power that would be exercised by a national government should be in the hands of the legislature. As you will recall from Chapter 2, the authors of the Constitution were strongly influenced by their fear of tyrannical kings and powerful, unchecked rulers. They were also aware of how ineffective the confederal Congress had been during its brief existence under the Articles of Confederation.

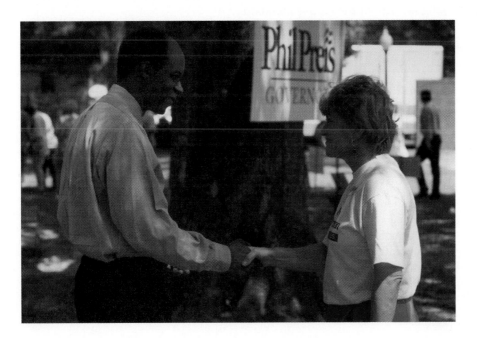

Representative William Jefferson (D.) of Louisiana shakes hands with a constituent during a visit to his home district. In 1996, Jefferson won in an uncontested race for reelection after winning his party's primary election.

The leading role envisioned for Congress in the new government is apparent from its primacy in the Constitution. Article I deals with the structure, the powers, and the operation of Congress, beginning in Section 1 with an application of the basic principle of separation of powers: "All legislative Powers herein granted shall be vested in a Congress of the United States, which shall consist of a Senate and House of Representatives." These legislative powers are spelled out in detail in Article I and elsewhere.

The **bicameralism** of Congress—its division into two legislative houses—was in part an outgrowth of the Connecticut Compromise, which tried to balance the big-state population advantage, reflected in the House, and the small-state demand for equality in policymaking, which was satisfied in the Senate. Beyond that, the two chambers of Congress also reflected the social class biases of the founders. They wished to balance the interests and the numerical superiority of the common citizen with the property interests of the less numerous landowners, bankers, and merchants. This goal was achieved by providing in Sections 2 and 3 of Article I that members of the House of Representatives should be elected directly by "the People," whereas members of the Senate were to be chosen by the elected representatives sitting in state legislatures, who were more likely to be members of the elite. (The latter provision was changed in 1913 by the passage of the Seventeenth Amendment, which provides that senators also be elected directly by the people.)

The elected House, then, was to be the common person's chamber, and the nonelected Senate was to be the chamber of the elite, similar to the division between the House of Commons and the House of Lords in England. Also, the House was meant to represent the people, whereas the Senate was meant to represent the states, in accordance with the intent of the Connecticut Compromise. The issue of who counted as part of "the People" for electing members of the House was left up to the states. The logic of separate constituencies and separate interests underlying the bicameral Congress was reinforced by differences in length of tenure. Members of the House were required to face the electorate every two years, whereas senators could serve for a much more secure term of six years—even longer than the four-year term provided for the president. Furthermore, the senators' terms were staggered so that only one-third of the senators would face the electorate every two years, along with all of the House members.

THE POWERS OF CONGRESS

The Constitution is both highly specific and extremely vague about the powers that Congress may exercise. The first seventeen clauses of Article I, Section 8, specify most of the **enumerated powers** of Congress—that is, powers expressly given to that body.

Enumerated Powers

The enumerated, or expressed, powers of Congress include the right to impose taxes and import tariffs; borrow money; regulate interstate commerce and international trade; establish procedures for naturalizing citizens; make laws regulating bankruptcies; coin (and print) money and regulate its value; establish standards of weights and measures; punish counterfeiters; establish post offices and postal routes; regulate copyrights and patents; establish lower federal courts; punish pirates and others committing illegal acts on the high seas; declare war; raise and regulate an army and a navy; call up and regulate the state militias to enforce laws, to suppress insurrections, and to repel invasions; and govern the District of Columbia.

The most important of the domestic powers of Congress, listed in Article I, Section 8, are the rights to collect taxes, to spend money, and to regulate commerce, whereas the most important foreign policy power is the power to declare war. Other sections of the Constitution give Congress a wide range of further powers. Generally, Congress is also able to establish rules for its own members, to regulate the electoral college, and to override a presidential veto.

Some functions are restricted to only one house. Under Article II, Section 2, the Senate must advise on, and consent to, the ratification of treaties and must accept or reject presidential nominations of ambassadors, Supreme Court justices, and "all other Officers of the United States." But the Senate may delegate to the president, the courts, or department heads the power to make lesser appointments. Congress may regulate the appellate jurisdiction of the Supreme Court, regulate relations between states, and propose amendments to the Constitution.

The amendments to the Constitution provide for other congressional powers. Congress must certify the election of a president and a vice president or itself choose these officers if no candidate has a majority of the electoral vote (Twelfth Amendment). It may levy an income tax (Sixteenth Amendment) and determine who will be acting president in case of the death or incapacity of the president or vice president (Twentieth Amendment, Sections 3 and 4, and Twenty-fifth Amendment, Sections 2, 3, and 4). In addition, Congress explicitly is given the power to enforce, by appropriate legislation, the provisions of several other amendments.

The Necessary and Proper Clause

Beyond these numerous specific powers, Congress enjoys the right under Article I, Section 8 (the "elastic," or "necessary and proper," clause), "[t]o make all Laws which shall be necessary and proper for carrying into Execution the foregoing Powers [of Article I], and all other Powers vested by this Constitution in the Government of the United States, or in any Department or Officer thereof." As discussed in Chapter 3, this vague statement of con-

The president appoints Supreme Court justices only with the advice and consent of the Senate. On occasion, presidents have nominated individuals who were not confirmed by the Senate. Here, in contrast, President Clinton's successful first nominee, Ruth Bader Ginsburg, is being congratulated by Senator Dianne Feinstein (D., Cal.) and Carol Moseley-Braun (D., Ill.).

gressional responsibilities set the stage for a greatly expanded role for the national government relative to the states. It also constitutes, at least in theory, a check on the expansion of presidential powers.

THE FUNCTIONS OF CONGRESS

The Constitution provides the foundation for congressional powers. Yet a complete understanding of the role that Congress plays requires a broader study of the functions that the national legislature performs for the American political system.

Congress, as an institution of government, is expected by its members, by the public, and by other centers of political power to perform a number of functions. Our perceptions of how good a job Congress is doing overall are tied closely to evaluations of whether and how it fulfills certain specific tasks. These tasks include the following:

1. Lawmaking.
2. Service to constituents.
3. Representation.
4. Oversight.
5. Public education.
6. Conflict resolution.

The Lawmaking Function

LAWMAKING

The process of deciding the legal rules that govern our society. Such laws may regulate minor affairs or establish broad national policies.

The principal and most obvious function of any legislature is **lawmaking.** Congress is the highest elected body in the country charged with making binding rules for all Americans. Lawmaking requires decisions about the size of the federal budget, about health-care reform and gun control, and about the long-term prospects for war or peace. This does not mean, however, that Congress initiates most of the ideas for legislation that it eventually considers. Most of the bills that Congress acts on originate in the executive branch, and many other bills are traceable to interest groups and political party organizations. Through the processes of compromise and **logrolling** (offering to support a fellow member's bill in exchange for that member's promise to support your bill in the future), backers of legislation attempt to fashion a winning majority coalition.

LOGROLLING

An arrangement by which two or more members of Congress agree in advance to support each other's bills.

Service to Constituents

Individual members of Congress are expected by their constituents to act as brokers between private citizens and the imposing, often faceless, federal government. **Casework** is the usual form taken by this function of providing service to constituents. The legislator and his or her staff spend a considerable portion of their time in casework activity, such as tracking down a missing Social Security check, explaining the meaning of particular bills to people who may be affected by them, promoting a local business interest, or interceding with a regulatory agency on behalf of constituents who disagree with proposed agency regulations.

CASEWORK

Personal work for constituents by members of Congress.

Legislators and many analysts of congressional behavior regard this **ombudsperson** role as an activity that strongly benefits the members of Congress. A government characterized by a large, confusing bureaucracy and complex public programs offers innumerable opportunities for legislators to come to the assistance of (usually) grateful constituents. Morris P. Fiorina suggests somewhat mischievously that senators and representatives prefer to maintain bureaucratic confusion in order to maximize their opportunities for performing good deeds on behalf of their constituents:

OMBUDSPERSON

An individual in the role of hearing and investigating complaints by private individuals against public officials or agencies.

Some poor, aggrieved constituent becomes enmeshed in the tentacles of an evil bureaucracy and calls upon Congressman St. George to do battle with the dragon. . . . In dealing with the bureaucracy, the congressman is not merely one vote of 435. Rather, he is a nonpartisan power, someone whose phone call snaps an office to attention. He is not kept on hold. The constituent who receives aid believes that his congressman and his congressman alone got results.[1]

The Representation Function

If constituency service carries with it nothing but benefits for most members of Congress, the function of **representation** is less certain and even carries with it some danger that the legislator will lose his or her bid for reelection. Generally, representation means that the many competing interests in society should be represented in Congress. It follows that Congress should be a body acting slowly and deliberately and that its foremost concern should be to maintain a carefully crafted balance of power among competing interests.

How is representation to be achieved? There are basically two points of view on this issue.

The Trustee View of Representation.   The first approach to the question of how representation should be achieved is that legislators should act as **trustees** of the broad interests of the entire society and that they should vote against the narrow interests of their constituents as their conscience and their perception of national needs dictate. For example, some Democratic legislators voted for the North American Free Trade Agreement (NAFTA) in late 1993 in spite of strong opposition from unions in their districts.

The Instructed-Delegate View of Representation.   Directly opposed to the trustee view of representation is the notion that the members of Congress should behave as **instructed delegates.** That is, they should mirror the views of the majority of the constituents who elected them to power in the first place. On the surface, this approach is plausible and rewarding. For it to work, however, we must assume that constituents actually have well-formed views on the issues that are decided in Congress and, further, that they have clear-cut preferences about these issues. Neither condition is likely to be satisfied very often. Most people generally do not have well-articulated views on major issues. Among those who do, there frequently is no clear majority position but rather a range of often conflicting minority perspectives.

In a major study of the attitudes held by members of Congress about their proper role as representatives, Roger Davidson found that neither a pure trustee view nor a pure instructed-delegate view was held by most legislators. Davidson's sampling of members of Congress showed that about the same proportion endorsed the trustee approach (28 percent) and delegate approach (23 percent) to representation. The clear preference, however, was for the **politico** position—which combines both perspectives in a pragmatic mix.[2]

The Oversight Function

Oversight of the bureaucracy is essential if the decisions made by Congress are to have any force. **Oversight** is the process by which Congress follows up

REPRESENTATION

The function of members of Congress as elected officials to represent the views of their constituents.

TRUSTEE

In regard to a legislator, one who acts according to his or her conscience and the broad interests of the entire society.

INSTRUCTED DELEGATE

A legislator who is an agent of the voters who elected him or her and who votes according to the views of constituents regardless of personal assessments.

POLITICO

The legislative role that combines the instructed-delegate and trustee concepts. The legislator varies the role according to the issue under consideration.

OVERSIGHT

The responsibility Congress has for following up on laws it has enacted to ensure that they are being enforced and administered in the way in which they were intended.

---

[1]Morris P. Fiorina, *Congress: Keystone of the Washington Establishment,* 2d ed. (New Haven, Conn.: Yale University Press, 1989), pp. 44, 47.
[2]Roger Davidson, *The Role of the Congressman* (New York: Pegasus, 1969), p. 117.

LEGISLATIVE VETO

A provision in a bill reserving to Congress or to a congressional committee the power to reject an action or regulation of a national agency by majority vote; declared unconstitutional by the Supreme Court in 1983.

on the laws it has enacted to ensure that they are being enforced and administered in the way Congress intended. This is done by holding committee hearings and investigations, changing the size of an agency's budget, and cross-examining high-level presidential nominees to head major agencies. Also, until 1983, Congress could refuse to accede to proposed rules and regulations by resorting to the **legislative veto.** This allowed one, or sometimes both, chambers of Congress to disapprove of an executive rule within a specified period of time by a simple majority vote and thereby prevent its enforcement. In 1983, however, the Supreme Court ruled that such a veto violated the separation of powers mandated by the Constitution, because the president had no power to veto the legislative action. Thus, the legislative veto was declared unconstitutional.[3]

Senators and representatives increasingly see their oversight function as a critically important part of their legislative activities. In part, oversight is related to the concept of constituency service, particularly when Congress investigates alleged arbitrariness or wrongdoing by bureaucratic agencies.

The Public-Education Function

Educating the public is a function that is exercised whenever Congress holds public hearings, exercises oversight over the bureaucracy, or engages in committee and floor debate on such major issues and topics as political assassinations, aging, illegal drugs, or the concerns of small businesses. In so doing, Congress presents a range of viewpoints on pressing national questions. Congress also decides what issues will come up for discussion and decision; **agenda setting** is a major facet of its public-education function. Congress is currently implementing a plan to make all congressional documents available online.

AGENDA SETTING

Determining which public policy questions will be debated or considered by Congress.

The Conflict-Resolution Function

Congress is commonly seen as an institution for resolving conflicts within American society. Organized interest groups and representatives of different racial, religious, economic, and ideological interests look on Congress as an access point for airing their grievances and possibly for stimulating government action on their behalf. A logical extension of the representation function, this focus on conflict resolution puts Congress in the role of trying to resolve the differences among competing points of view by passing laws to accommodate as many interested parties as possible. Clearly, this is not always achieved. Every legislative decision results in some winners and some losers. Congress commonly is regarded as the place to go in Washington to get a friendly hearing or a desired policy result. To the extent that Congress meets pluralist expectations in accommodating competing interests, it tends to build support for the entire political process by all branches of government.

HOUSE-SENATE DIFFERENCES

Congress is composed of two markedly different—although coequal—chambers. Although the Senate and the House of Representatives exist within the same legislative institution, each has developed certain distinctive features that clearly distinguish life on one end of Capitol Hill from conditions on the

---

[3]*Immigration and Naturalization Service v. Chadha,* 454 U.S. 812 (1983).

other (the Senate wing is on the north side of the Capitol building, and the House wing is on the south side). A summary of these differences is given in Table 12–1.

Size and Rules

The central difference between the House and the Senate is simply that the House is much larger than the Senate. The House has 435 representatives, plus delegates from the District of Columbia, Puerto Rico, Guam, American Samoa, and the Virgin Islands, compared with just 100 senators. This size difference means that a greater number of formal rules are needed to govern activity in the House, whereas correspondingly looser procedures can be followed in the less crowded Senate. This difference is most obvious in the rules governing debate on the floors of the two chambers.

The Senate normally permits extended debate on all issues that arise before it. In contrast, the House operates with an elaborate system in which its **Rules Committee** normally proposes time limitations on debate for any bill, and a majority of the entire body accepts or modifies those suggested time limits. As a consequence of its stricter time limits on debate, and despite its greater size, the House often is able to act on legislation more quickly than the Senate.

Debate and Filibustering

According to historians, the Senate tradition of unlimited debate, which is known as **filibustering,** dates back to 1790, when a proposal to move the U.S. capital from New York to Philadelphia was stalled by such time-wasting tactics. This unlimited-debate tradition—which also existed in the House until 1811—is not absolute, however.

Under Senate Rule 22, debate may be ended by invoking **cloture,** or shutting off discussion on a bill. Amended in 1975 and 1979, Rule 22 states that debate may be closed off on a bill if sixteen senators sign a petition requesting it and if, after two days have elapsed, three-fifths of the entire member-

DID YOU KNOW . . .
That before the Republicans reorganized House services in 1995, all members had buckets of ice delivered to their offices each day, at an annual cost of $500,000?

RULES COMMITTEE

A standing committee of the House of Representatives that provides special rules under which specific bills can be debated, amended, and considered by the House.

FILIBUSTERING

In the Senate, unlimited debate to halt action on a particular bill.

CLOTURE

A method to close off debate and to bring the matter under consideration to a vote in the Senate.

Table 12–1

Differences between the House and the Senate

HOUSE*	SENATE*
Members chosen from local districts	Members chosen from an entire state
Two-year term	Six-year term
Originally elected by voters	Originally (until 1913) elected by state legislatures
May impeach (indict) federal officials	May convict federal officials of impeachable offenses
Larger (435 voting members)	Smaller (100 members)
More formal rules	Fewer rules and restrictions
Debate limited	Debate extended
Less prestige and less individual notice	More prestige and more media attention
Originates bills for raising revenues	Has power to advise the president on, and to consent to, presidential appointments and treaties
Local or narrow leadership	National leadership

*Some of these differences, such as the term of office, are provided for in the Constitution. Others, such as debate rules, are not.

Senator Strom Thurmond leaves the chamber after completing a record-setting filibuster that lasted for twenty-four hours and eighteen minutes. The purpose of the filibuster was to thwart the passage of the 1957 Civil Rights Act. The senator from South Carolina was reelected in 1996 at the age of ninety-three.

ship (sixty votes, assuming no vacancies) vote for cloture.[4] After cloture is invoked, each senator may speak on a bill for a maximum of one hour before a vote is taken.

In 1979, the Senate extended Rule 22 to provide that a final vote must take place within one hundred hours of debate after cloture has been imposed. It further limited the use of multiple amendments to stall postcloture final action on a bill.

Prestige

As a consequence of the greater size of the House, representatives generally cannot achieve as much individual recognition and public prestige as can members of the Senate. Senators, especially those who openly express presidential ambitions, are better able to gain media exposure and to establish careers as spokespersons for large national constituencies. To obtain recognition for his or her activities, a member of the House generally must do one of two things. He or she might survive in office long enough to join the ranks of the leadership on committees or within the party. Alternatively, the representative could become an expert on some specialized aspect of legislative policy—such as tax laws, the environment, or education.

Other Differences

Other major differences between the House and the Senate are unrelated to the size of each chamber. The Constitution, in Article I, provides that members of the House serve shorter terms (two years) than senators (six years). All 435 voting members of the House must run for reelection in November of even-numbered years, but only about one-third of the Senate seats are contested in the same biennial election. Their longer term in office generally gives senators more time to act as national leaders before facing the electorate again.

---

[4]Edward V. Schneier and Bertram Gross, *Congress Today* (New York: St. Martin's Press, 1993), p. 221.

CONGRESSPERSONS AND THE CITIZENRY: A COMPARISON

Government institutions are given life by the people who work in them and shape them as political structures. Who, then, are the members of Congress, and how are they elected?

Members of the U.S. Senate and the U.S. House of Representatives are not typical American citizens, as can be seen in Table 12–2. Members of Congress are, of course, older than most Americans, partly because of constitutional age requirements and partly because a good deal of political experience normally is an advantage in running for national office. Members of Congress are also disproportionately white, male, Protestant, and trained in higher-status occupations.

Some recent trends in the social characteristics of Congress should be noted, however. The average age of members of the 105th Congress is 52.2 years—a slight decrease from an average age of 53 three decades ago. The Protestant domination of Congress has been loosened, with substantial increases being made in the representation of Jews and Roman Catholics. Some Protestant denominations, notably Episcopalians and Presbyterians, are overrepresented in Congress. Baptists and Lutherans are underrepresented, relative to their numbers among U.S. Protestants.

Lawyers are by far the largest occupational group among congresspersons: 54 senators and 170 representatives in the 105th Congress reported that they were trained in the legal profession. The proportion of lawyers in the House is lower now than at nearly any time in the last thirty years, however.

CONGRESSIONAL ELECTIONS

The process of electing members of Congress is decentralized. Congressional elections are operated by the individual state governments, which must conform to the rules established by the U.S. Constitution and by national

Table 12–2

Characteristics of the 105th Congress (1997 to 1999)

CHARACTERISTIC	U.S. POPULATION (1990)	HOUSE	SENATE
Age (median)	33.0	50.9	58.4
Percentage minority	28.0	13.5	4
Religion			
Percentage church members	61.0	98	99
Percentage Roman Catholic	39.0	30	24
Percentage Protestant	56.0	63	61
Percentage Jewish	4.0	5.5	9
Percentage female	51.9	11	9
Percentage with college degrees	21.4	93	94
Occupation			
Percentage lawyers	2.8	39	54
Percentage blue-collar workers	20.1	0	0
Family income			
Percentage of families earning over $50,000 annually	22.0	100	100
Personal wealth			
Percentage of population with assets over $1 million	0.7	16	33

After African Americans gained the right to vote in 1870, several southern states elected African American senators and representatives to Congress.

statutes. The Constitution states that representatives are to be elected every second year by popular ballot, and the number of seats awarded to each state is to be determined by the results of the decennial census. Each state has at least one representative, with most congressional districts having about half a million residents. Senators are elected by popular vote (since the passage of the Seventeenth Amendment) every six years; approximately one-third of the seats are chosen every two years. Each state has two senators. Under Article I, Section 4, of the Constitution, state legislatures are given control over "[T]he Times, Places and Manner of holding Elections for Senators and Representatives"; however, "the Congress may at any time by Law make or alter such Regulations."

Candidates for Congressional Elections

Candidates for seats in Congress generally are recruited by local political party activists, or they are self-starters. Potential candidates who are selected or self-selected usually share many of the social characteristics of their prospective constituents. Religion, race, and ethnic background are especially important considerations. Prior political experience may be an important asset, especially in states with strong political parties or restrictive nominating systems.

Reasons for Making the Race.   At least three major factors are important in determining who will run for congressional office and whether party leaders are willing to recruit someone for the race. As discussed by James David Barber, these are *motivation, resources,* and *opportunity.*[5] Motivation means that a candidate must be able to achieve a sense of self-satisfaction from participating in the contest. It also implies that a candidate must project a positive attitude toward electoral politics. Important resources for the campaign include money, the political skills of the candidate and of his or her supporters, the ability of the candidate and staff to take time off from their regular jobs and other commitments, and the candidate's access to the mass media. Opportunity relates to such questions as whether an incumbent is running for office, whether many candidates are contending for the same nomination, how strong the opposition party may be in November, and whether the local party activists form a positive image of the candidate.[6]

The Nomination Process.   Since the early part of the century, control over the process of nominating congressional candidates has been shifting from party conventions—which reformers charged with being corrupt and boss controlled—to **direct primaries,** in which **party identifiers** in the electorate select the candidate who will carry that party's endorsement into the actual election. All fifty states currently use the direct primary to select party nominees for senator or representative. In general, there are more candidates running and the competition is more intense when a party is strong and a November victory is likely.

The Congressional Campaign.   Most candidates win through the effectiveness of their personal organizations, although sometimes with assistance from the state party organization. It is important to realize that congressional

DIRECT PRIMARY

An intraparty election in which the voters select the candidates who will run on a party's ticket in the subsequent general election.

PARTY IDENTIFIER

A person who identifies with a political party.

[5]James David Barber, *The Lawmakers: Recruitment and Adaptation to Legislative Life* (New Haven, Conn.: Yale University Press, 1965), pp. 10–15.
[6]See the work of Gary Jacobson, *The Politics of Congressional Elections,* 4th ed. (New York: Longman Publishers, 1997).

candidates have only a loose affiliation to the party at the national and state level. Even the effect of presidential "coattails," in which a victorious president helps bring into office legislators who would not have won otherwise, is minimal. For example, Richard Nixon's landslide victory over George McGovern in 1972, with 61 percent of the popular vote and 520 out of 538 electoral votes, resulted in a gain of only twelve Republican seats in the House.

In midterm congressional elections—those held between presidential contests—voter turnout falls sharply. In these elections, party affiliation of the voters who turn out is a stronger force in deciding election outcomes, and the party controlling the White House normally loses seats in Congress. Additionally, voters in midterm elections often are responding to incumbency issues, because there is no presidential campaign. The result is a fragmentation of party authority and a loosening of ties between Congress and the president. Table 12–3 shows the pattern for midterm elections since 1942.

The Power of Incumbency

The power of incumbency in the outcome of congressional elections cannot be overemphasized. Table 12–4 shows that the overwhelming majority of representatives and a smaller proportion of senators who decide to run for reelection are successful. This conclusion holds for both presidential-year and midterm elections.

David R. Mayhew argues that the pursuit of reelection is the strongest motivation behind the activities of members of Congress. The reelection goal

Table 12–3

Midterm Losses by the Party of the President, 1942 to 1994

SEATS LOST BY THE PARTY OF THE PRESIDENT IN THE HOUSE OF REPRESENTATIVES	
1942	−45 (D.)
1946	−55 (D.)
1950	−29 (D.)
1954	−18 (R.)
1958	−47 (R.)
1962	−4 (D.)
1966	−47 (D.)
1970	−12 (R.)
1974	−48 (R.)
1978	−15 (D.)
1982	−26 (R.)
1986	−5 (R.)
1990	−8 (R.)
1994	−52 (D.)

Table 12–4

The Power of Incumbency

	PRESIDENTIAL-YEAR ELECTIONS						MIDTERM ELECTIONS						
	1976	1980	1984	1988	1992	1996	1970	1974	1978	1982	1986	1990	1994
House													
Number of incumbent candidates	384	398	409	409	368	382	401	391	382	393	393	407	382
Reelected	368	361	390	402	325	359	379	343	358	352	385	391	347
Percentage of Total	95.8	90.7	95.4	98.3	88.9	93.4	94.5	87.7	93.7	90.1	98.0	96.1	90.8
Defeated	16	37	19	7	43	23	22	48	24	39	8	16	35
In primary	3	6	3	1	19	2	10	8	5	10	2	1	1
In general election	13	31	16	6	24	21	12	40	19	29	6	15	34
Senate													
Number of incumbent candidates	25	29	29	27	28	21	31	27	25	30	28	32	26
Reelected	16	16	26	23	23	19	24	23	15	28	21	31	24
Percentage of total	64.0	55.2	89.6	85	82.1	90	77.4	85.2	60.0	93.3	75.0	96.9	92.3
Defeated	9	13	3	4	5	2	7	4	10	2	7	1	2
In primary	0	4	0	0	1	1	1	2	3	0	0	0	0
In general election	9	9	3	4	4	1	6	2	7	2	7	1	2

SOURCE: Norman Ornstein, Thomas E. Mann, and Michael J. Malbin, *Vital Statistics on Congress, 1993–1994* (Washington, D.C.: Congressional Quarterly Press, 1994), pp. 56–57; *Congressional Quarterly Weekly Report*, November 7, 1992, pp. 3551, 3576; and authors' update.

CRITICAL PERSPECTIVE
Gridlock or Constitutional Balance?

By the end of George Bush's presidency, the relationship between Congress and the president was frequently described as one of gridlock. The term described the political stand-off between Bush and the Democratic majority in Congress. Few of the bills that the president introduced could be passed, and he successfully vetoed a number of bills that the Democrats in Congress passed. In fact, the Democratic party used Bush's presidential term to try to convince the electorate that it was time, after twelve years, to put a Democrat in the White House, because the Democratic-controlled Congress would work more effectively with a Democratic administration.

The relationship between the president and Congress is structured constitutionally to prevent either branch from being totally dominant. Because of checks and balances, including the veto, the veto override, the nomination and treaty processes, and the different constituencies and terms in office of members of the House and the Senate, presidential success with the Congress is difficult to achieve. Some presidents of the same party as the majority in Congress have had great success after landslide elections, such as Franklin Roosevelt in 1933 and Lyndon Johnson in 1965. This happened, in part, because many new Democrats were elected with the president. Sometimes, as in Ronald Reagan's case, a president who does not control the chambers of Congress still can have great legislative success. Reagan's personal electoral victory and great popularity with the public seemed to generate congressional cooperation.

Remember that checks and balances were put into the Constitution to assure exactly what has happened—to make sure that it would not be too easy for an electoral majority, either for the president or in Congress, to make changes too quickly. In fact, most opinion polls in the 1990s found that the public approved of a divided government, believing that it kept the political parties and the government under better control. Polling data on elections and partisanship, as noted in Chapters 8 and 9, also show that Americans are more likely than ever before to split their tickets between congressional candidates and the president and that partisan identity provides less and less of a cue for voting.

In 1992, the voters were presented with a choice between a continuation of divided government, a Democratic-controlled government, or (in the case of H. Ross Perot) a nonpartisan presidency. Historically, there have been cycles of divided government, as shown in the accompanying table, with higher proportions before 1894 and since 1968. The question for consideration is whether a "unified" government is more likely than a "divided government" to pass legislation.

At the end of his first year in office, President Bill Clinton declared that "gridlock was over." He saluted the effectiveness of the Democratic leadership in Congress in passing his tax increase/deficit reduction plan; the family leave plan; the national service plan; and the North American Free Trade Agreement (NAFTA). The president vetoed no bills in 1993.

---

is pursued in three major ways: by *advertising*, by *credit claiming*, and by *position taking*.[7] Advertising includes using the mass media, making personal appearances with constituents, and sending newsletters—all to produce a favorable image and to make the incumbent's name a household word. Members of Congress try to present themselves as informed, experienced, and responsive to people's needs. Credit claiming focuses on the things a legislator claims to have done to benefit his or her constituents—by fulfilling the congressional casework function or by supplying material goods in the form of, say, a new post office or a construction project, such as a dam or highway. Position taking occurs when an incumbent explains his or her voting record on key issues; makes public statements of general support for presidential decisions; or indicates that he or she specifically supports positions on key

---

[7]David R. Mayhew, Congress: The Electoral Connection (New Haven, Conn.: Yale University Press, 1974).

CRITICAL PERSPECTIVE
Gridlock or Constitutional Balance? Continued

Scholars, however, suggest that the election of a Democrat to the White House, along with the Democratic majority in Congress, does not guarantee smooth sailing or the end of legislative deadlock. Both David Mayhew and Roger Davidson argue that historically divided government is not related to deadlock in legislation.* Dwight Eisenhower, Richard Nixon, Ronald Reagan, and George Bush all were able to pass important legislation with Democratic control of one or both chambers of Congress. Democratic Presi-

dent Jimmy Carter, with a Democratic majority, had as much difficulty as any other president.

President Bill Clinton's chance to work with a Democratic Congress ended abruptly with the 1994 election. For the first year after the election of the Republican-controlled House and Senate, the president and Congress seemed to be truly ineffective. The fight over the passage of the federal budget brought some areas of the government to a halt before the president and the congressional leadership were able to forge a deal. Actually, Clinton gained in popularity when he vetoed Republican bills that he felt he could not approve, and the Republicans in Congress gained in respect when they were able to pass major bills after compromising with their Democratic colleagues. The combination of a Democratic president and a Republican Congress succeeded in writing a budget, cutting spending by 9 percent, and approving major overhauls of agricultural, telecommunications, and welfare policies. Polls showed that the public continued to approve of a divided government and voted to continue divided government in the 1996 elections.

The Occurrence of Divided Government Following Presidential and Midterm Elections, 1864–1996

ELECTION YEARS	ELECTIONS RESULTING IN DIVIDED GOVERNMENT		
	% PRESIDENTIAL ELECTIONS	% MIDTERM ELECTIONS	% ALL ELECTIONS
1864–1894	25 (2/8)	75 (6/8)	50 (8/16)
1896–1966	6 (1/18)	28 (5/18)	17 (6/36)
1968–1996	71 (6/8)	86 (6/7)	79 (12/15)

NOTE: The numbers in parentheses are the actual number of elections in the category that resulted in divided government and the total number of presidential or midterm elections held in that period.
SOURCE: James E. Campbell, *The Presidential Pulse of Congressional Elections* (Lexington, Ky.: University Press of Kentucky, 1993), p. 212, and authors' update.

For Critical Analysis

1. Who would be in favor of gridlock?
2. How did the Constitution provide for the possibility of gridlock?

*David Mayhew, *Divided We Govern* (New Haven: Yale University Press, 1991); and Roger Davidson, "The Presidency and Three Eras of the Modern Congress," in *Divided Democracy*, ed. by James A. Thurber (Washington, D.C.: Congressional Quarterly Press, 1991).

issues, such as gun control or anti-inflation policies. Position taking carries with it certain risks, as the incumbent may lose support by disagreeing with the attitudes of a large number of constituents.

Because of the many scandals and the stalemate between President George Bush and Congress over many issues (see this chapter's *Critical Perspective*), 1992 was a year of change. Public disgust was reflected in the approval of term-limitation legislation in fourteen states by that time. A record number of the legislators who were up for reelection in 1992 decided to retire rather than face bitter campaigns. For a few representatives, there was a financial incentive to retire as well: they belonged to the group that would be allowed to convert campaign funds to personal use if they left office before 1994. When the polls closed, forty-eight incumbents had been defeated.

The movement to limit congressional terms of office continued after the 1992 election. Many states provide for term limits for their state legislatures,

and such limits were also approved for members of Congress by the voters of more than twenty states In 1995, however, the United States Supreme Court, in *Term Limits v. Arkansas*,[8] held that an Arkansas state constitutional amendment limiting the terms of congresspersons was unconstitutional. The Court stated that the states could not change the terms of office that are specified in the Constitution. Of course, the constitutional provision could be changed by a constitutional amendment, but even the Republican conservatives who held power after the 1994 elections could not find enough votes to pass such an amendment.

The Shakeup in the 1994 Elections

The 1994 midterm elections swept the Democratic majority in both houses of Congress out of power and brought in a Republican majority in a nationwide change of government that surprised and shocked the members of Congress and the parties themselves. According to exit polls taken on election day, Republican candidates for the Congress won the votes of their own party identifiers, of the majority of independents, and of those who had voted for Perot in 1992, but from very few of the Democratic voters. Republicans captured the votes of white males, with a gender gap of about 8 percent. Republicans won 19 more seats in the South, giving them a 73–64 seat majority in that region. In Washington, the speaker of the House, Tom Foley, was defeated, the first Speaker to be denied reelection since 1862. In total, the Democrats lost 53 seats, with 190 incumbents reelected and 35 defeated. All Republican incumbents in the house were reelected. (See the feature entitled *Thinking Politically about the Contract with America* for a discussion of the Republicans' platform in 1994.)

ELECTIONS '96

Congress After the 1996 Elections

As Congress and the president began to cooperate in passing legislation in 1996, public approval ratings for Congress rose. The elections of 1996 appeared to confirm the voters' approval of the Republican controlled Congress working with the Democratic president.

The House of Representatives was widely thought to be the best chance for Democrats to make major gains. With the president's lead in the polls, some "coattail" effects were expected to congressional seats. In addition, the funds raised by labor unions in 1996 were intended to target the conservative freshmen Republicans who had been elected in 1994. The National Rifle Association and the Christian Coalition entered the campaign on behalf of many of these conservative members. As the results of the congressional races became known, the Democrats did pick up some seats but not enough to gain control of the House of Representatives. In all, Democrats gained nine seats to make the Republican margin of control 236 to 198. Of the 73 freshmen Republicans, however, only 16 lost their seats in the 1996 elections.

The Supreme Court's decision requiring the redrawing of the "minority-majority" districts in four states put the House elections in several states into a state of chaos. In Texas, thirteen districts were redrawn too close to the election to have a primary. The rules required that candidates receive an absolute majority in the election to win a seat. Three districts required "run-off" elections in December 1996 to determine the winners. In the other states, minority incumbents were reelected even though their districts were redrawn.

---

[8]115 S.Ct. 1842 (1995).

Thinking Politically about the Contract with America

The centerpiece of the Republican congressional campaign of 1994 was the Contract with America, a pledge signed by most of the candidates for the House to accomplish certain kinds of legislative action in the first one hundred days of the 104th Congress. The accompanying table shows what happened to those promises. As you can see, some legislation was passed, particularly in regard to congressional reform. The budget legislation became a nightmare struggle between the president and Congress and resulted in two limited "shutdowns" of the government. Other items, such as

Speaker of the House, Newt Gingrich, and other Republicans celebrate the completion of the Contract With America at a flag waving rally on Capitol Hill.

The Contract with America

THE REPUBLICANS PROMISED TO BRING THESE ITEMS TO THE FLOOR OF THE HOUSE OF REPRESENTATIVES IN THE FIRST ONE HUNDRED DAYS OF THE 104TH CONGRESS.

Preface: Put Congress under workplace laws	Law
Revise House rules	Passed House
1) Budget reform:	
Balanced Budget Amendment	Passed House
Line-item veto	Law
2) Toughen crime bill	Passed House
3) Reform welfare programs	Law
4) Strengthen families:	
Tax credits for adoptions	Passed House
Penalties for sex crimes with children	Passed House
Enforce child support	Passed House
5) Middle class tax cut	Passed House
6) National security: keep U.S. troops from U.N. command	Passed House
7) Social Security: decrease taxes on retirees' income and benefits	Passed House
8) Capital gains and regulations:	
Curb new unfunded mandates on states	Law
Reduce federal paperwork	Law
Cut capital gains tax rate	Passed House
Require risk assessment on regulations	Passed House
9) Civil law and liability:	
Change product liability law	Passed House
Change lawsuit rules	Passed House
10) Term-limits constitutional amendment	Failed in House

campaign finance reform and term limits for Congress, lost favor with the new Republican majority. By the time the Republicans selected their presidential nominee in 1996, the Contract with America seemed to have disappeared. Conservative voters may have wondered why it was never mentioned at the national convention. The explanation is that it never had gained support among the public, even though individual items were popular, and its originator, Speaker Newt Gingrich, had very poor approval ratings among the public. As an election device, the contract was viewed as a detriment to further Republican victories.

For Critical Analysis

What impact has the Contract with America had on the average citizen?

The 1996 elections saw the Republican margin in the Senate increase from 53–47 to 55–45. Although the one incumbent Republican senator was defeated (Larry Pressler of South Dakota), Republicans picked up formerly Democratic seats in Alabama, Arkansas, and Nebraska.

In the 104th Congress, Newt Gingrich's House was considered to be far more conservative than was Bob Dole's Senate. The 1996 election produced a Congress in which the Senate with its new members is likely to become more divided between liberal Democrats and conservative Republicans while the House may become more moderate.

CONGRESSIONAL REAPPORTIONMENT

By far the most complicated aspects of the mechanics of congressional elections are the issues of **reapportionment** (the allocation of seats in the House to each state after each census) and **redistricting** (the redrawing of the boundaries of the districts within each state).[9] In a landmark six-to-two vote in 1962, the Supreme Court made reapportionment a **justiciable** (that is, a reviewable) **question** in the Tennessee case of *Baker v. Carr*[10] by invoking the Fourteenth Amendment principle that no state can deny to any person "the equal protection of the laws." This principle was applied directly in the 1964 ruling, *Reynolds v. Sims*,[11] when the Court held that *both* chambers of a state legislature must be apportioned with equal populations in each district. This "one person, one vote" principle was applied to congressional districts in the 1964 case of *Wesberry v. Sanders*,[12] based on Article I, Section 2, of the Constitution, which requires that congresspersons be chosen "by the People of the several States."

Severe malapportionment of congressional districts prior to *Wesberry* had resulted in some districts containing two or three times the populations of other districts in the same state, thereby diluting the effect of a vote cast in the larger districts. This system generally had benefited the conservative populations of rural areas and small towns and harmed the interests of the more heavily populated and liberal urban areas. In fact, suburban areas have benefited the most from the *Wesberry* ruling, as suburbs account for an increasingly larger proportion of the nation's population, and cities include a correspondingly smaller segment of the population.

Gerrymandering

Although the general issue of reapportionment has been dealt with fairly successfully by the one person, one vote principle, the **gerrymandering** issue has not yet been resolved. This term refers to the legislative boundary-drawing tactics that were used by Elbridge Gerry, the governor of Massachusetts, in the 1812 elections (see Figure 12–1). A district is said to have been gerrymandered when its shape is altered substantially by the dominant party in a state legislature to maximize its electoral strength at the expense of the minority party. This can be achieved by either concentrating the opposition's voter support in as few districts as possible or by diffusing the minority party's strength by spreading it thinly across many districts.

In 1986, the Supreme Court heard a case that challenged gerrymandered congressional districts in Indiana. The Court ruled for the first time that redistricting for the political benefit of one group could be challenged on constitutional grounds. In this specific case, *Davis v. Bandemer*,[13] the Court, however, did not agree that the districts were drawn unfairly, because it could not be proved that a group of voters would consistently be deprived of its influence at the polls as a result of the new districts.

"Minority-Majority Districts"

Although the Supreme Court had declared as unconstitutional districts that are uneven in population or that violate norms of size and shape to maximize the advantage of one party in the early 1990s, the federal government encour-

---

[9]For an excellent discussion of these issues, see *Congressional Districts in the 1990s* (Washington, D.C.: Congressional Quarterly Press, 1993).
[10]369 U.S. 186 (1962).
[11]377 U.S. 533 (1964).
[12]376 U.S. 1 (1964).
[13]478 U.S. 109 (1986).

REAPPORTIONMENT

The allocation of seats in the House to each state after each census.

REDISTRICTING

The redrawing of the boundaries of the districts within each state.

JUSTICIABLE QUESTION

A question that may be raised and reviewed in court.

GERRYMANDERING

The drawing of legislative district boundary lines for the purpose of obtaining partisan or factional advantage. A district is said to be gerrymandered when its shape is manipulated by the dominant party in the state legislature to maximize electoral strength at the expense of the minority party.

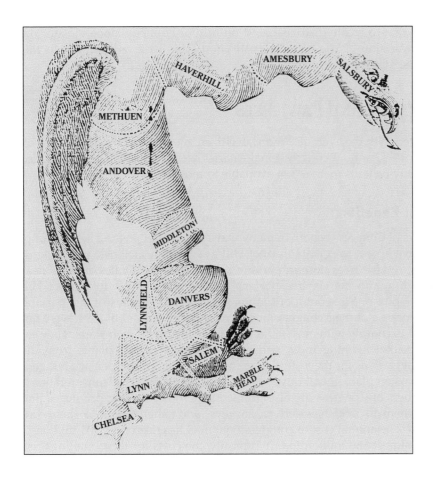

Figure 12–1
• • • • • • • • • • • • • • • •
The Original Gerrymander

The practice of "gerrymandering"—
the excessive manipulation of the
shape of a legislative district to benefit a certain incumbent or party—is
probably as old as the republic, but
the name originated in 1812. In that
year, the Massachusetts legislature
carved out of Essex County a district
that historian John Fiske said had a
"dragonlike contour." When the
painter Gilbert Stuart saw the mis-
shapen district, he penciled in a
head, wings, and claws and
exclaimed, "That will do for a sala-
mander!" Editor Benjamin Russell
replied, "Better say a Gerrymander"
(after Elbridge Gerry, then governor
of Massachusetts).

SOURCE: *Congressional Quarterly's Guide to
Congress,* 3d ed. (Washington, D.C.:
Congressional Quarterly Press, 1982), p. 695.

aged another type of gerrymandering that made possible the election of a
minority representative from a "minority-majority" area. Under the mandate
of the Voting Rights Act of 1965, the Justice Department issued directives to
states after the 1990 census instructing them to create congressional districts
that would maximize the voting power of minority groups—that is, create
districts in which minority voters were the majority. One such district—the
Twelfth District of North Carolina—was 165 miles long, following Interstate
85 for the most part (see Figure 12–2). According to a local joke, the district
was so narrow that a car traveling down the interstate highway with both
doors open would kill most of the voters in the district. Many of these
"minority majority" districts were challenged in court by citizens who

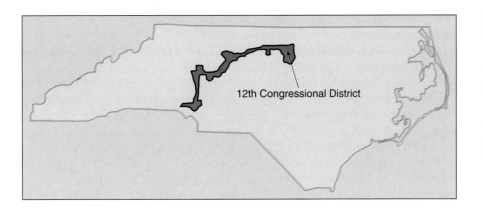

12th Congressional District

Figure 12–2
• •
**The Twelfth District of
North Carolina**

The Twelfth District, which was
declared unconstitutional by the
United States Supreme Court in
1996, was created to make possible
the election of a minority representative. It snaked through North
Carolina along Interstate 85.

DID YOU KNOW...

That Samuel Morse demonstrated his telegraph to Congress in 1843 by stretching wire between two committee rooms?

FRANKING

A policy that enables members of Congress to send material through the mail by substituting their facsimile signature (frank) for postage.

claimed that to create districts based on race or ethnicity alone violates the equal protection clause of the Constitution. This issue is explored in this chapter's *Politics and the Constitution.*

PAY, PERKS, AND PRIVILEGES

Compared with the average American citizen, members of Congress are well paid. In 1997, annual congressional salaries were $133,600. Legislators also have many benefits that are not available to most workers.

Special Benefits

Members of Congress benefit in many ways from belonging to a select group. They have access to private Capitol Hill gymnasium facilities; get low-cost haircuts; receive free, close-in parking at National and Dulles airports near Washington; and get six free parking spaces per member in Capitol Hill garages—plus one free outdoor Capitol parking slot. They also avoid parking tickets because of their congressional license plates and, until 1994, were not required to comply with most labor laws in dealing with their staffs. They eat in a subsidized dining room and take advantage of free plants from the Botanical gardens for their offices, free medical care, an inexpensive but generous pension plan, liberal travel allowances, and special tax considerations.

Members of Congress are also granted generous **franking** privileges that permit them to mail newsletters, surveys, and other letters to their constituents. The annual cost of congressional mail has risen from $11 million in 1971 to almost $60 million today. Typically, the costs for these mailings rise enormously during election years.

Permanent Professional Staffs

More than 38,660 people are employed in the Capitol Hill bureaucracy. About half of this total consists of personal and committee staff members. The personal staff includes office clerks and secretaries; professionals who deal with media relations, draft legislation, and satisfy constituency requests for service; and staffers who maintain local offices in the member's home district or state.

The average Senate office on Capitol Hill employs about thirty staff members, and twice that number work on the personal staff of senators from the most populous states. House office staffs typically are about half as large as those of the Senate. As Figure 12–3 on page 410 shows, the number of staff members has increased dramatically since 1960. With the bulk of those increases coming in assistance to individual members, some scholars question whether staff members are really advising on legislation or are primarily aiding constituents and gaining votes.

Congress also benefits from the expertise of the professional staffs of agencies that were created to produce information for members of the House and Senate. The Congressional Research Service (CRS), a section of the Library of Congress, furnishes a computer-based record of the contents and current legislative status of major bills that are under consideration. This record can be reviewed by staff members using computer terminals available in most offices. The General Accounting Office (GAO) audits the spending of money by federal agencies, investigates agency practices, and makes policy recommendations to Congress, especially concerning financial activities of the government. The Office of Technology Assessment (OTA) was designed to eval-

POLITICS AND THE CONSTITUTION
Racial Gerrymandering

The concept of equality is a basic American value. The meaning of equality, though, depends to a great extent on how the United States Supreme Court interprets such laws as the equal protection clause of the Constitution. In the 1990s, the Supreme Court's views on equal protection clearly came into conflict with those of the Justice Department with respect to racial gerrymandering—the creation of "minority-majority" congressional districts to enhance the representation of minority groups. After the 1990 census, the Justice Department issued a directive to the states requiring them to create such districts. The motivation for this directive was a desire to ensure more equal treatment for minorities by allowing them a stronger voice in Congress.

As a result of the directive, in the early 1990s a number of states created "minority-majority" districts, some of which had extraordinarily odd shapes (see Figure 12–2, for example) so that they could include more minority residents. Ironically, state compliance with the Justice Department's requirements resulted in several of these new districts being challenged in the courts.

White plaintiffs contended that race-based districting was unconstitutional because it violated the equal protection clause. In 1993, the United States Supreme Court declared that racially gerrymandered districts were subject to strict scrutiny under the equal protection clause—which means that they can only be justified by a "compelling state interest" and must be "narrowly tailored" by the state to serve that interest.*

In 1995, the Supreme Court attacked race-based redistricting even more aggressively when it declared that Georgia's new Eleventh District was unconstitutional. The district stretched from Atlanta to the Atlantic, splitting eight counties and five municipalities along the way. The Court referred to the district as a "monstrosity" linking "widely spaced urban centers that have absolutely nothing to do with each other." The Court went on to say that when a state assigns voters on the basis of race, "it engages in the offensive and demeaning assumption that voters of a particular race, because of their race, think alike, share the same political interests, and will prefer the same candidates at

the polls." The Court also chastised the Justice Department for concluding that race-based districting was mandated under the Voting Rights Act of 1965: "When the Justice Department's interpretation of the Act compels race-based districting, it by definition raises a serious constitutional question."†

In two cases decided in 1996, the Court affirmed its position that when race is the dominant factor in the drawing of congressional district lines, the districts are unconstitutional. In these two cases, the Court ruled that the Twelfth District in North Carolina (see Figure 12–2) and three Texas districts were unconstitutional for this reason.‡

For Critical Analysis

Is the Supreme Court's position on racial gerrymandering consistent with its position on affirmative action programs? Why or why not?

*Shaw v. Reno, 509 U.S. 630 (1993).

†Miller v. Johnson, 115 S.Ct. 2475 (1995).

‡Shaw v. Reno, 116 S.Ct. 1894 (1996); Bush v. Vera, 116 S.Ct. 1941 (1996).

uate national technology policy in such areas as energy and the environment (it was abolished by the 104th Congress). The Congressional Budget Office (CBO) advises Congress on the anticipated effect on the economy of government expenditures and estimates the cost of proposed policies.

Privileges and Immunities under the Law

Members of Congress also benefit from a number of special constitutional protections. Under Article I, Section 6, of the Constitution, they "shall in all Cases, except Treason, Felony and Breach of the Peace, be privileged from Arrest during their Attendance at the Session of their respective Houses, and in going to and returning from the same; and for any Speech or Debate in either House, they shall not be questioned in any other Place." The arrest immunity clause is not really an important provision today. The "speech or debate" clause, however, means that a member may make any allegations or other statements he or she wishes in connection with official duties and normally not be sued for libel or slander or otherwise be subject to legal action.

Figure 12–3
● ● ● ● ● ● ● ● ● ● ● ● ● ● ● ● ● ●

Congressional Staff, 1891 to 1995

As the graph indicates, staff increased dramatically from 1960 to 1980, most notably staff who serve in the members' offices.

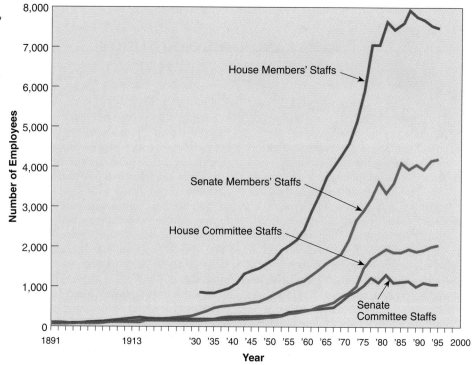

SOURCE: Norman J. Ornstein, Thomas E. Mann, and Michael J. Malbin, *Vital Statistics on Congress, 1993–1994* (Washington, D.C.: Congressional Quarterly Press, 1994), p. 129, and authors' update.

THE COMMITTEE STRUCTURE

Most of the actual work of legislating is performed by the committees and subcommittees within Congress. Thousands of bills are introduced in every session of Congress, and no single member can possibly be adequately informed on all the issues that arise. The committee system is a way to provide for specialization, or a division of the legislative labor. Members of a committee can concentrate on just one area or topic—such as taxation or energy—and develop sufficient expertise to draft appropriate legislation

A committee hearing on a constitutional amendment to balance the budget. Starting from the chair of the committee in the center, Democratic senators sit on the left in order of seniority on the committee, while Republicans take the seats on the right in order of seniority.

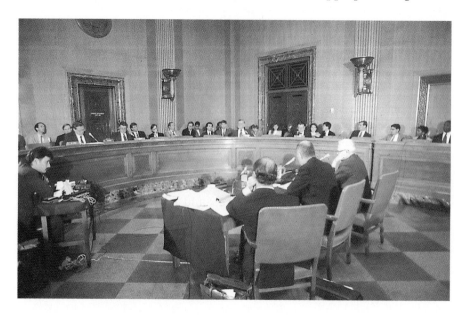

when needed. The flow of legislation through both the House and the Senate is determined largely by the speed with which the members of these committees act on bills and resolutions.

The Power of Committees

Commonly known as "little legislatures," committees usually have the final say on pieces of legislation.[14] Committee actions may be overturned on the floor by the House or Senate, but this rarely happens. Legislators normally defer to the expertise of the chairperson and other members of the committee who speak on the floor in defense of a committee decision. Chairpersons of committees exercise control over the scheduling of hearings and formal action on a bill. They also decide which subcommittee will act on legislation falling within their committee's jurisdiction.

Committees only very rarely are deprived of control over a bill—although this kind of action is provided for in the rules of each chamber. In the House, if a bill has been considered by a standing committee for thirty days, the signatures of a majority (218) of the House membership on a **discharge petition** can pry a bill out of an uncooperative committee's hands. From 1909 to 1996, however, although over nine hundred such petitions were made, only slightly more than two dozen resulted in successful discharge efforts. Of those, twenty passed the House.[15]

Types of Congressional Committees

Over the past two centuries, Congress has created several different types of committees, each of which serves particular needs of the institution.

Standing Committees.   By far the most important committees in Congress are the **standing committees**—permanent bodies established by the rules of each chamber of Congress and that continue from session to session. A list of the standing committees of the 105th Congress is presented in Table 12–5. In addition, most of the standing committees have created several subcommittees to carry out their work. In the 105th Congress, there were 103 subcommittees in the Senate and 139 in the House.[16]

Each standing committee is given a specific area of legislative policy jurisdiction, and almost all legislative measures are considered by the appropriate standing committees. Because of the importance of their work and the traditional influence of their members in Congress, certain committees are considered to be more prestigious than others. If a congressperson seeks to be influential, he or she will usually aspire to a seat on the Appropriations Committee in either chamber, on the Ways and Means Committee in the House, the House Education and Labor Committee, or the Senate Foreign Relations Committee.

Each member of the House serves generally on two standing committees, except when the member sits on the Appropriations, Rules, or Ways and Means Committee—in which case he or she serves on only that one standing committee. Each senator may serve on two major committees and one minor

DID YOU KNOW . . .
That the House members' gym has no locker room for female members, and women must call ahead to warn the men that they are coming to use the gym?

DISCHARGE PETITION

A procedure by which a bill in the House of Representatives may be forced out of a committee (discharged) that has refused to report it for consideration by the House. The discharge petition must be signed by an absolute majority (218) of representatives and is used only on rare occasions.

STANDING COMMITTEE

A permanent committee within the House or Senate that considers bills within a certain subject area.

---

[14]The term *little legislatures* is from Woodrow Wilson, *Congressional Government* (New York: Meridian Books, 1956 [first published in 1885]).

[15]*Congressional Quarterly's Guide to Congress*, 3d ed. (Washington, D.C.: Congressional Quarterly Press, 1982), p. 426; and authors' research.

[16]*Congressional Directory* (Washington, D.C.: U.S. Government Printing Office, various editions).

Table 12–5

Standing Committees of the 105th Congress, 1997 to 1999

House Committee	Chair	Senate Committee	Chair
Agriculture	Bob Smith (R., Ore.)	Agriculture, Nutrition, and Forestry	Richard G. Lugar (R., Ind.)
Appropriations	Bob Livingston (R., La.)	Appropriations	Ted Stevens (R., Alaska)
Banking, Finance, and Urban Affairs	Jim Leach (R., Iowa)	Armed Services	Strom Thurmond (R., S.C.)
		Banking, Housing, and Urban Affairs	Alfonse M. D'Amato (R., N.Y.)
Budget	John Kasich (R., Ohio)	Budget	Pete V. Domenici (R., N.M.)
Commerce	Thomas Bliley, Jr. (R., Fla.)	Commerce, Science, and Transportation	John McCain (R., Ariz.)
Education and Labor	Bill Goodling (R., Pa.)	Energy and Natural Resources	Frank H. Murkowski (R., Alaska)
International Relations	Benjamin A. Gilman (R., N.Y.)	Environment and Public Works	John H. Chafee (R., R.I.)
Judiciary	Henry Hyde (R., Ill.)	Foreign Relations	Jesse Helms (R., N.C.)
National Security	Floyd Spence (R., S.C.)	Finance	William V. Roth, Jr. (R., Del.)
Resources	Don Young (R., Alaska)	Governmental Affairs	Fred Thompson (R., Tenn.).
Rules	Gerald B. H. Solomon (R., N.Y.)	Indian Affairs	John McCain (R., Ariz.)
Science and Technology	Robert S. Walker (R., Pa.)	Judiciary	Orrin Hatch (R., Utah)
Small Business	Jan Meyers (R., Kans.)	Labor and Human Resources	James M. Jeffords (R., Vt.)
Standards of Official Conduct	Nancy L. Johnson (R., Conn.)	Rules and Administration	John W. Warner (R., Va.)
Transportation and Infrastructure	Bud Shuster (R., Pa.)	Small Business	Christopher Bond (R., Mo.)
Veterans' Affairs	Bob Stump (R., Ariz.)	Veterans' Affairs	Arlen Specter (R., Pa.)

committee (only the Rules and Administration Committee and the Veterans' Affairs Committee are considered minor).

SELECT COMMITTEE

A temporary legislative committee established for a limited time period and for a special purpose.

Select Committees. A **select committee** normally is created for a limited period of time and for a specific legislative purpose. For example, a select committee may be formed to investigate a public problem, such as nutrition or aging. Select committees are disbanded when they have reported to the chamber that created them. They rarely create original legislation.

JOINT COMMITTEE

A legislative committee composed of members from both chambers of Congress.

Joint Committees. A **joint committee** is formed by the concurrent action of both chambers of Congress and consists of members from each chamber. Joint committees, which may be permanent or temporary, have dealt with the economy, taxation, and the Library of Congress.

CONFERENCE COMMITTEE

A special joint committee appointed to reconcile differences when bills pass the two chambers of Congress in different forms.

Conference Committees. Special types of joint committees—**conference committees**—are formed for the purpose of achieving agreement between the House and the Senate on the exact wording of legislative acts when the two chambers pass legislative proposals in different forms. No bill can be sent to the White House to be signed into law unless it first passes both chambers in identical form. Sometimes called the "third house" of Congress, conference committees are in a position to make significant alterations in legislation and frequently become the focal point of policy debates.

The House Rules Committee. Because of its special "gatekeeping" power over the terms on which legislation will reach the floor of the House of Representatives, the House Rules Committee holds a uniquely powerful position. A special committee rule sets the time limit on debate and determines whether and how a bill may be amended. This practice dates back to 1883. The Rules Committee has the unusual power to meet while the House is in session, to have its resolutions considered immediately on the floor, and to initiate legislation on its own.

The Selection of Committee Members

In the House, representatives are appointed to standing committees by the Steering and Policy Committee (for Democrats) and by the Committee on Committees (for Republicans). Committee chairpersons normally are appointed according to seniority.

The rule regarding seniority specifies that majority party members with longer terms of continuous service on the committee will be given preference when committee chairpersons—as well as holders of other significant posts in Congress—are selected. This is not a law but an informal, traditional process. The **seniority system,** although deliberately unequal, provides a predictable means of assigning positions of power within Congress.

The general pattern until the 1970s was that members of the House or Senate who represented **safe seats** would be reelected continually and eventually would accumulate enough years of continuous committee service to enable them to become the chairpersons of their committees—if their party gained control of the appropriate chamber of Congress. Traditionally, this avenue of access to power benefited southern Democrats and midwesterners within the Republican party, who seldom faced serious, organized opposition either in their own party's primaries or during the general election. This resulted in a predominance of committee chairpersons from the more conservative ranks of both political parties.

In the 1970s, a number of reforms in the chairperson selection process somewhat modified the seniority system. The reforms introduced the use of a secret ballot in electing House committee chairpersons and established rules for the selection of subcommittee chairpersons that resulted in a greater dispersal of authority within the committees themselves.

SENIORITY SYSTEM

A custom followed in both chambers of Congress specifying that members with longer terms of continuous service will be given preference when committee chairpersons and holders of other significant posts are selected.

SAFE SEAT

A district that returns the legislator with 55 percent of the vote or more.

THE FORMAL LEADERSHIP

The limited amount of centralized power that exists in Congress is exercised through party-based mechanisms. Congress is organized by party. When the Democratic party, for example, wins a majority of seats in either the House or the Senate, Democrats control the official positions of power in that chamber, and every important committee has a Democratic chairperson and a majority of Democratic members. The same process holds when Republicans are in the majority.

We consider the formal leadership positions in the House and Senate separately, but you will note some broad similarities in the way leaders are selected and in the ways they exercise power in the two chambers.

Leadership in the House

The House leadership is made up of the speaker, the majority and minority leaders, and the party whips.

The Speaker. The foremost power holder in the House of Representatives is the **speaker of the House.** The speaker's position is technically a nonparti-

SPEAKER OF THE HOUSE

The presiding officer in the House of Representatives. The speaker is always a member of the majority party and is the most powerful and influential member of the House.

Representative Newt Gingrich
(R., Ga.), speaker of the House. Although
polls showed low approval for him
nationally, Representative Gingrich won
reelection from his Georgia district easily
in 1996.

san one, but in fact, for the better part of two centuries, the speaker has been the official leader of the majority party in the House. When a new Congress convenes in January of odd-numbered years, each party nominates a candidate for speaker. In one of the very rare instances of perfect party cohesion, all Democratic members of the House ordinarily vote for their party's nominee, and all Republicans support their alternative candidate.

The influence of modern-day speakers is based primarily on their personal prestige, persuasive ability, and knowledge of the legislative process—plus the acquiescence or active support of other representatives. The major formal powers of the speaker include the following:

1. Presiding over meetings of the House.
2. Appointing members of joint committees and conference committees.
3. Scheduling legislation for floor action.
4. Deciding points of order and interpreting the rules with the advice of the House parliamentarian.
5. Referring bills and resolutions to the appropriate standing committees of the House.

A speaker may take part in floor debate and vote, as can any other member of Congress, but recent speakers usually have voted only to break a tie.

In general, the powers of the speaker are related to his or her control over information and communications channels in the House. This is a significant power in a large, decentralized institution in which information is a very important resource. With this control, the speaker attempts to ensure the smooth operation of the chamber and to integrate presidential and congressional policies.

In 1975, the powers of the speaker were expanded when the House Democratic caucus gave its party's speaker the power to appoint the Democratic Steering Committee, which determines new committee assignments for House party members.

The election of Newt Gingrich, Republican of Georgia, as speaker in 1994 put a forceful man into an office that had not exercised much direct power, especially for Republicans. Gingrich began his term by handpicking some of the committee chairs so they would work with him. On occasion, he overruled committee chairs, appointed task forces to take issues away from certain members, forced members to debate issues in the Republican caucus, and, by exercising his formal powers, kept extremely tight control of the agenda.

The Majority Leader.   The **majority leader of the House** has been a separate position since 1899, when a power that had usually been exercised by the chairperson of the Ways and Means Committee was transferred to a new office. The majority leader is elected by a caucus of party members to foster cohesion among party members and to act as a spokesperson for the party. The majority leader influences the scheduling of debate and generally acts as the chief supporter of the speaker. The majority leader cooperates with the speaker and other party leaders, both inside and outside Congress, to formulate the party's legislative program and to guide that program through the legislative process in the House. The majority leader's post is a very prestigious one because of the power and responsibility inherent in the office and also because, at least among Democrats, future speakers are recruited from that position.

The Minority Leader.   The **minority leader of the House** is the candidate nominated for speaker by a caucus of the minority party. Like the majority leader, the leader of the minority party has as his or her primary responsibility the maintaining of cohesion within the party's ranks. As the official spokesperson for the minority party, he or she consults with the ranking minority members of the House committees and encourages them to adhere to the party position. The minority leader also acts as a morale booster for the usually less successful minority and speaks on behalf of the president if the minority party controls the White House. In relations with the majority party, the minority leader consults with both the speaker and the majority leader on recognizing members who wish to speak on the floor, on House rules and procedures, and on the scheduling of legislation. Minority leaders have no actual power in these areas, however.

Whips.   The formal leadership of each party includes assistants to the majority and minority leaders, who are known as **whips.** These positions have existed throughout this century. Over the past fifty years, they have developed into a complex network of deputy and regional whips supervised by the chief party whip. The whips assist the party leader by passing information down from the leadership to party members and by ensuring that members show up for floor debate and cast their votes on important issues. Whips conduct polls among party members about the members' views on major pieces of legislation, inform the leaders about whose vote is doubtful and whose is certain, and may exert pressure on members to support the leader's position.

Leadership in the Senate

The Senate is less than one-fourth the size of the House. This fact alone probably explains why a formal, complex, and centralized leadership structure is less necessary in the Senate than it is in the House.

The two highest-ranking formal leadership positions in the Senate are essentially ceremonial in nature. Under the Constitution, the vice president of the United States is the president (that is, the presiding officer) of the Senate and may vote to break a tie. The vice president, however, only rarely is pre-

DID YOU KNOW...
That the Constitution does not require that the speaker of the House of Representatives be an elected member of the House?

MAJORITY LEADER OF THE HOUSE

A legislative position held by an important party member in the House of Representatives. The majority leader is selected by the majority party in caucus or conference to foster cohesion among party members and to act as spokesperson for the majority party in the House.

MINORITY LEADER OF THE HOUSE

The party leader elected by the minority party in the House.

WHIP

An assistant who aids the majority or minority leader of the House and the Senate majority or minority floor leader.

PRESIDENT PRO TEMPORE

The temporary presiding officer of the Senate in the absence of the vice president.

MAJORITY FLOOR LEADER

The chief spokesperson of the major party in the Senate, who directs the legislative program and party strategy.

MINORITY FLOOR LEADER

The party officer in the Senate who commands the minority party's opposition to the policies of the majority party and directs the legislative program and strategy of his or her party.

sent for a meeting of the Senate. The Senate elects instead a **president pro tempore** ("pro tem") to preside over the Senate in the vice president's absence. Ordinarily, the president pro tem is the member of the majority party with the longest continuous term of service in the Senate. The president pro tem is mostly a ceremonial position. Junior senators take turns actually presiding over the sessions of the Senate.

The real leadership power in the Senate rests in the hands of the **majority floor leader,** the **minority floor leader,** and their respective whips. The Senate majority and minority leaders have the right to be recognized first in debate on the floor and generally exercise the same powers available to the House majority and minority leaders. They control the scheduling of debate on the floor in conjunction with the majority party's Policy Committee, influence the allocation of committee assignments for new members or for senators attempting to transfer to a new committee, influence the selection of other party officials, and participate in selecting members of conference committees. The leaders are expected to mobilize support for partisan legislative initiatives or for the proposals of a president who belongs to the same party. The leaders act as liaisons with the White House when the president is of their party, try to get the cooperation of committee chairpersons, and seek to facilitate the smooth functioning of the Senate through the senators' unanimous consent. Floor leaders are elected by their respective party caucuses.

Democratic leaders of the Senate potentially have more power than Republican leaders. The Democratic floor leader is also simultaneously the chairperson of the Democratic Conference (Caucus); the Steering Committee, which makes committee assignments; and the Policy Committee, which schedules legislation for floor action. In contrast, four different Republican senators hold these comparable positions, in a much more decentralized pattern of leadership.

Senate party whips, like their House counterparts, maintain communication within the party on platform positions and try to ensure that party colleagues are present for floor debate and important votes. The Senate whip system is far less elaborate than its counterpart in the House, simply because there are fewer members to track.

A list of the formal party leaders of the 105th Congress is presented in Table 12–6. Party leaders are a major source of influence over the decisions about public issues that senators and representatives must make every day. We consider the nature of partisan and other pressures on congressional decision making in the next section.

HOW MEMBERS OF CONGRESS DECIDE

Why congresspersons vote as they do is difficult to know with any certainty. One popular perception of the legislative decision-making process is that legislators take cues from other trusted or more senior colleagues.[17] This model holds that because most members of Congress have neither the time nor the incentive to study the details of most pieces of legislation, they frequently arrive on the floor with no clear idea about what they are voting on or how they should vote. Their decision is simplified, according to the cue-taking model, by quickly checking how key colleagues have voted or intend to vote. More broadly, verbal and nonverbal cues can be taken from fellow committee

---

[17]Donald Matthews and James Stimson, *Yeas and Nays: Normal Decision Making in the U.S. House of Representatives* (New York: Wiley, 1975).

Table 12–6

Party Leaders in the 105th Congress, 1997 to 1999

POSITION	INCUMBENT	PARTY/ STATE	LEADER SINCE
House			
Speaker	Newt Gingrich	R., Ga.	Jan. 1995
Majority leader	Dick Armey	R., Tx.	Jan. 1995
Majority whip	Tom DeLay	R., Tx.	Jan. 1995
Chairperson of the Republican Conference	John Boehner	R., Ohio	Jan. 1995
Minority leader	Richard Gephardt	D., Mo.	Jan. 1995
Minority whip	David Bonior	D., Mich.	Jan. 1995
Chairperson of the Democratic Caucus	Vic Fazio	D., Calif.	Jan. 1995
Senate			
President pro tempore	Strom Thurmond	R., S.C.	Jan. 1995
Majority floor leader	Trent Lott	R., Miss.	June 1996
Assistant majority leader	Don Nickles	R., Okla.	June 1996
Secretary of the Republican Conference	Connie Mack	R., Fla.	Jan. 1995
Minority floor leader	Tom Daschle	D., S.D.	Jan. 1995
Assistant floor leader	Wendell Ford	R., Okla.	Jan. 1995
Chairperson of the Democratic Caucus	Barbara Mikulski	D., Md.	Jan. 1995

members and chairpersons, party leaders, state delegation members, or the president.

A different theory of congressional decision making places the emphasis on the policy content of the issues being decided, on the desires of a congressperson's constituents, and on the pressures brought to bear by his or her supporters.[18] The degree of constituency influence on congressional voting patterns depends on the extent to which a state or district is urbanized, the region and state that a member represents, and the blue-collar proportion of the labor force.

Most people who study the decision-making process in Congress agree that the single best predictor for how a member will vote is the member's party membership.[19] Republicans tend to vote similarly on issues, as do Democrats. Of course, even though liberals predominate among the Democrats in Congress and conservatives predominate among the Republicans, the parties still may have internal disagreements about the proper direction that national policy should take. This was generally true for the civil rights legislation of the 1950s and 1960s, for example, when the greatest disagreement was between the conservative southern wing and the liberal northern wing of the Democratic party.

One way to measure the degree of party unity in Congress is to look at how often a majority of one party votes against the majority of members from

---

[18]Aage R. Clausen, *How Congressmen Decide* (New York: St. Martin's Press, 1973).
[19]David Mayhew, *Party Loyalty among Congressmen* (Cambridge, Mass.: Harvard University Press, 1966).

Roll-call votes posted in the House. Since electronic voting was instituted, attendance at roll calls has increased. Legislators were quite aware that their absences would also be recorded.

CONSERVATIVE COALITION

An alliance of Republicans and southern Democrats that can form in the House or the Senate to oppose liberal legislation and support conservative legislation.

the other party. Table 12–7 displays the percentage of all votes in the House and the Senate when this type of party voting has occurred.

Regional differences, especially between northern and southern Democrats, may overlap and reinforce basic ideological differences among members of the same party. One consequence of the North-South split among Democrats has been the **conservative coalition** policy alliance between southern Democrats and Republicans. This conservative, cross-party grouping formed regularly on votes that split liberals and conservatives. The coalition was active during the Reagan years, declined under Bush, and further weakened under Clinton.

HOW A BILL BECOMES LAW

Each year, Congress and the president propose and approve many laws. Some are budget and appropriation laws that require extensive bargaining but must be passed for the government to continue to function. Other laws are relatively free of controversy and are passed with little dissension between the branches of government. Still other proposed legislation is extremely controversial and reaches to the roots of differences between Democrats and Republicans and between the executive and legislative branches. Such a piece of legislation was the Brady Bill, or the Handgun Violence Prevention Act of 1993, a bill that had been debated by Congress for seven years. The Brady Bill illustrates the path a bill may take that, although involving relatively few committees, still generates an extraordinary amount of legislative action.

The Brady Bill

At the end of his first year in the presidency, in 1981, Ronald Reagan was the target of an assassination attempt as he left a Washington hotel. Although the president was wounded, his injuries were not nearly as serious as those sustained by his press secretary, James Brady. Brady, hit by shots fired from a handgun that had been purchased by a former mental patient, had extremely serious head injuries that damaged his ability to speak and partially paralyzed him. From the time of his recovery until 1993, Brady and his wife, Sarah, headed a national campaign to institute a waiting period for purchasers of handguns. The waiting period would allow gun sellers to check the backgrounds of prospective purchasers.

The first version of the now-named Brady Bill was debated in 1987. The bill was opposed by Ronald Reagan, many western and southern members of Congress, and the National Rifle Association. In September 1988, the waiting-period proposal was defeated in the House by a vote of 228 to 182. After the election of George Bush, the bill was reintroduced even though Bush, a gun owner, was ambivalent about it. In 1991, the House of Representatives passed the bill, in a stunning victory for the Bradys. Although it was clear that the Senate would not pass the bill in 1991, it seemed likely that the Senate might be ready to approve some version of it in the future.

The Bradys and the House sponsors of gun control legislation reintroduced the bill in February 1993 after the election of Bill Clinton. The bill was referred to the House Judiciary Committee for hearings. The bill was then referred to a subcommittee for hearings—in this case, it was the House Subcommittee on Crime and Criminal Justice. After hearings in September, the bill was reported back to the full committee and then approved. The bill was sent to the House Rules Committee before it was sent to the House floor. (Figure 12–4 shows the typical path of proposed legislation.)

The bill came to the House floor on November 10, 1993, where it was debated and amended. Most of the amendments dealt with the date on which the law would expire, subject to the institution of a national "instant check" system to be in place at that time. Finally, the bill passed with a six-year limit to substitute the instant check system for the waiting period. The House then requested the "concurrence" of the Senate.

On November 13, 1993, the bill was read for the first time (that is, introduced) in the Senate. Because the bill was well known and had been debated several times before, the Senate went right to conference to request amendment of the bill. The chair of the Judiciary Committee and several of its members formed a conference committee with the House members. The Senate

Table 12–7

Party Voting in Congress

This table lists the percentage of all roll calls in which a majority of Democratic legislators voted against a majority of Republican legislators.

YEAR	HOUSE	SENATE
1996	N/A	N/A
1995	73.0	69.0
1994	61.8	51.7
1993	65.0	67.0
1992	64.0	53.0
1991	55.0	49.0
1990	49.0	54.0
1989	55.0	35.0
1988	47.0	42.0
1987	64.0	41.0
1986	57.0	52.0
1985	61.0	50.0
1984	47.1	40.0
1983	55.6	43.6
1982	36.4	43.4
1981	37.4	47.8
1980	37.6	45.8
1979	47.3	46.7
1978	33.2	45.2
1977	42.2	42.4
1976	35.9	37.2
1975	48.4	47.8
1974	29.4	44.3
1973	41.8	39.9

SOURCE: *Congressional Weekly Report,* January 27, 1996, p. 245.

President Clinton signs into law August 22, 1996, a bill reforming welfare that ends the 61-year-old federal guarantee of aid to the poor. With the president, left to right, are Delaware Governor Thomas Carper, former welfare mothers Lillie Harden and Janet Ferrel, Vice President Al Gore, West Virginia Governor Gaston Caperton, Senator John Breaux (D., La.), and former welfare mother Penelope Howard.

Figure 12–4

• •

How a Bill Becomes Law

This illustration shows the most typical way in which proposed legislation is enacted into law. The process is illustrated with two hypothetical bills. House bill No. 100 (HR 100) and Senate bill No. 200 (S 200). Bills must be passed by both chambers in identical form before they can be sent to the president. The path of HR 100 is traced by a blue line, and that of S 200 by a red line. In practice, most bills begin as similar proposals in both chambers.

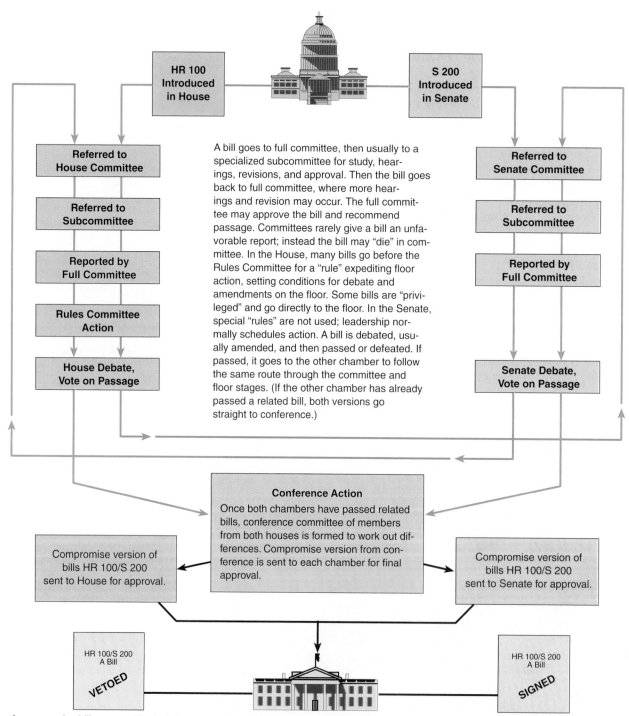

A compromise bill approved by both houses is sent to the president, who can sign it into law or veto it and return it to Congress. Congress may override veto by a two-thirds majority vote in both houses; the bill then becomes law without the president's signature.

passed its own version of the bill and sent it to the House, which rejected it. Then the two chambers went to conference. The House passed the conference report, which was the result of intensive negotiations between House and Senate representatives, on November 22.

As the Thanksgiving recess loomed, the Senate needed to take up the bill and make a decision. Republicans, claiming that the Senate Democrats had bargained away their own agreement to have a five-year period for the bill, began a filibuster. The first two cloture votes failed. Finally, Senators Robert Dole, Joseph Biden, and George Mitchell ironed out a compromise that the Republicans would support. They agreed to the five-year sunset period and to reconsider the legislation with some changes in the next session. The Senate then ended the filibuster and passed the Brady Bill by voice vote on November 24, 1993. It was signed into law by the president on November 30. As Jim Brady put it, "It's an awfully nice Thanksgiving present for the American people."[20]

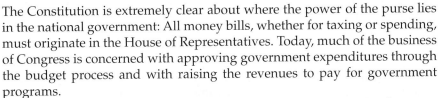

HOW MUCH WILL THE GOVERNMENT SPEND?

The Constitution is extremely clear about where the power of the purse lies in the national government: All money bills, whether for taxing or spending, must originate in the House of Representatives. Today, much of the business of Congress is concerned with approving government expenditures through the budget process and with raising the revenues to pay for government programs.

From 1922, when Congress required the president to prepare and present to the legislature an **executive budget,** until 1974, the congressional budget process was so disjointed that it was difficult to visualize the total picture of government finances. The president presented the executive budget to Congress in January. It was broken down into thirteen or more appropriations bills. Some time later, after all of the bills were debated, amended, and passed, it was more or less possible to estimate total government spending for the next year.

Frustrated by the president's ability to impound funds and dissatisfied with the entire budget process, Congress passed the Budget and Impoundment Control Act of 1974 to regain some control over the nation's spending. The act required the president to spend the funds that Congress had appropriated, frustrating the president's ability to kill programs of which the president disapproved by withholding funds. The other major accomplishment of the act was to force Congress to examine total national taxing and spending at least twice in each budget cycle.

The budget cycle of the federal government is described in the following sections. (See Figure 12–5 for a graphic illustration of the budget cycle.)

Preparing the Budget

The federal government operates on a **fiscal year (FY).** The fiscal year runs from October through September, so that fiscal 1998, or FY98, runs from October 1, 1997, through September 30, 1998. Eighteen months before a fiscal year starts, the executive branch begins preparing the budget. The Office of Management and Budget (OMB) receives advice from the Council of Economic

DID YOU KNOW . . .
That retiring members of Congress can start collecting a pension at age fifty after twenty years of work or at age sixty after ten years of service?

EXECUTIVE BUDGET

The budget prepared and submitted by the president to Congress.

FISCAL YEAR (FY)

The twelve-month period that is used for bookkeeping, or accounting, purposes. Usually, the fiscal year does not coincide with the calendar year. For example, the federal government's fiscal year runs from October 1 through September 30.

[20]"Brady Bill Goes to the Brink, but the Senate Finally Clears It," *Congressional Quarterly Weekly Report,* November 27, 1993, p. 3271.

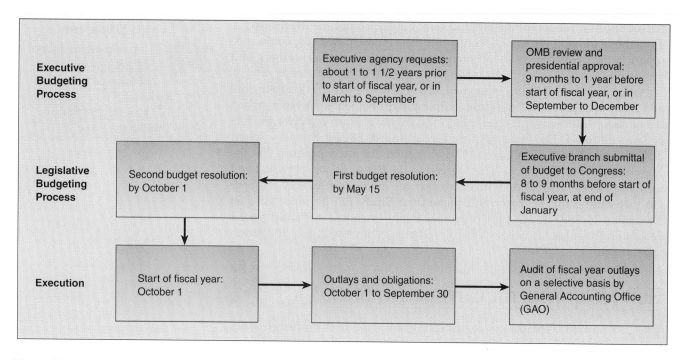

Figure 12–5
• •
The Budget Cycle

Advisers (CEA) and the Treasury Department. The OMB outlines the budget and then sends it to the various departments and agencies. Bargaining follows, in which—to use only two of many examples—the Department of Health and Human Services argues for more welfare spending, and the armed forces argue for fewer defense spending cuts.

Even though the OMB has only six hundred employees, it is known as one of the most powerful agencies in Washington. It assembles the budget documents and monitors the agencies throughout each year. Every year, it begins the budget process with a **spring review,** in which it requires all of the agencies to review their programs, activities, and goals. At the beginning of each summer, the director of the OMB sends out a letter instructing agencies to submit their requests for funding for the next fiscal year. By the end of the summer, each agency must submit a formal request to the OMB.

In actuality, the "budget season" begins with the **fall review.** At this time, the OMB looks at budget requests and, in almost all cases, routinely cuts them back. Although the OMB works within guidelines established by the president, specific decisions often are left to the director and the director's associates. By the beginning of November, the director's review begins. The director meets with cabinet secretaries and budget officers. Time becomes crucial. The budget must be completed by January so that it can go to the printer to be included in the *Economic Report of the President.*

Congress Faces the Budget

In January, nine months before the fiscal year starts, the president takes the OMB's proposed budget, approves it, and submits it to Congress. Then the congressional budgeting process takes over. Congressional committees and subcommittees look at the proposals from the executive branch. The Congressional Budget Office (CBO) advises the different committees on economic matters, just as the OMB and the CEA advise the president. The **first budget resolution** by Congress is supposed to be passed in May. It sets overall rev-

SPRING REVIEW

The time every year when the Office of Management and Budget requires federal agencies to review their programs, activities, and goals and submit their requests for funding for the next fiscal year.

FALL REVIEW

The time every year when, after receiving formal federal agency requests for funding for the next fiscal year, the Office of Management and Budget reviews the requests, makes changes, and submits its recommen-

FIRST BUDGET RESOLUTION

A resolution passed by Congress in May that sets overall revenue and spending goals and hence, by definition, the size of the deficit for the following fiscal year.

enue goals and spending targets and, by definition, the size of the deficit (or surplus, if that were ever to occur again).

During the summer, bargaining among all the concerned parties takes place. Spending and tax laws that are drawn up during this period are supposed to be guided by the May congressional budget resolution. By September, Congress is supposed to pass its **second budget resolution,** one that will set "binding" limits on taxes and spending for the fiscal year beginning October 1. Bills passed before that date that do not fit within the limits of the budget resolution are supposed to be changed.

In actuality, between 1978 and 1996, Congress did not pass a complete budget by October 1. In other words, generally, Congress does not follow its own rules. Budget resolutions are passed late, and when they are passed, they are not treated as binding. In each fiscal year that starts without a budget, every agency operates on the basis of **continuing resolutions,** which enable the agencies to keep on doing whatever they were doing the previous year with the same amount of funding. Even continuing resolutions have not always been passed on time.

Dealing with the budget is a recurring nightmare for Congress and the president. George Bush's 1990 budget battle, which forced him to raise taxes, may have cost him the presidency in 1992. President Bill Clinton won his first big budget fight in 1993 by a margin of one vote in the Senate, cast by Vice President Al Gore to break the tie, and by a single vote in the House. Clinton's deficit reduction package included large new taxes on the rich, on gasoline, and on tobacco.

The Republican sweep of 1994 changed the budget dynamics completely in the 104th Congress. The Republicans in the House, who had pledged to balance the budget as part of the Contract with America, tried to force the presi-

SECOND BUDGET RESOLUTION

A resolution passed by Congress in September that sets "binding" limits on taxes and spending for the next fiscal year beginning October 1.

CONTINUING RESOLUTION

A temporary law that Congress passes when an appropriations bill has not been decided by the beginning of the new fiscal year on October 1.

POLITICS AND ETHICS
Congress Examines Its Own for Improprieties

Public approval of Congress as a body has continued to be very low, in part because of the succession of ethical problems and improprieties that have become public. Both the House and the Senate have attempted to deal with the ethical lapses of their respective members through internal processes, but the public perception continues to be that many members are involved in shady dealings that the ordinary citizen finds hard to justify.

Ethical problems for elected representatives fall into several categories. The most flamboyant involve sexual misconduct involving staff members or constituents. In recent years, Representative Gus Savage of Illinois was accused of making sexual advances to a Peace Corps volunteer while on an official trip, and Representative Donald "Buz" Lukens of Ohio was convicted of having sex with a sixteen-year-old girl. Both representatives were defeated in subsequent elections. Representative Barney Frank of Massachusetts, who has acknowledged his own homosexuality, was reprimanded by the House Ethics Committee for hiring a former lover as a staff assistant and allowing that person the use of his office for personal business.

The Senate's most famous case recently has been that of Senator Robert Packwood of Oregon, who was accused of sexually harassing a number of women. Packwood admitted some of his guilt, citing abuse of alcohol as the reason for his misbehavior. Packwood's case put the Senate in the limelight, because some of its female members petitioned for the Senate to deny him his seat on the basis that he was elected fraudulently (that is, Packwood denied allegations of wrongdoing before the election and pressured the media to suppress them). Packwood resigned in September 1995, after the Senate Ethics Committee voted to expel him from the Senate.

Both the House and the Senate have also dealt with the ethical problems that arise when a member takes advantage of his or her office for personal benefit. Several House members—including Jim Wright, a former speaker, and Tony Coelho, a former Democratic whip—resigned from Congress after investigations of their personal finances. Five Senators, known as the Keating Five for their association with the convicted Arizona financier Charles Keating, were reprimanded for their attempts to limit the investigation of Keating's failed savings and loans. None of the five was censured (which is a stronger action). One did not seek reelection.

In a 1994 ethics incident, Representative Dan Rostenkowski, the one-time powerful chair of the House Ways and Means Committee, was indicted for violating House rules in the purchase of stamps and personal gifts from House stores and for misusing funds for staff and office expenses. The indictment of this powerful congressperson forced him, under House rules, to resign his chairmanship. (He lost his congressional seat in 1994, when the voters did not reelect him, and was convicted in a federal court in 1995.) In 1995, Illinois Representative Melvin Reynolds resigned following his conviction for having had sexual relations with a sixteen-year-old girl.

For Critical Analysis
Do you think that the public's perception of congressional behavior is influenced by media coverage?

---

dent to accept a budget with big cuts in domestic spending. President Clinton resisted the pressure. By October 1, 1995, only two of the thirteen bills needed to finance government for fiscal year 1996 had been passed. When the president and Congress could not agree on the spending bills, the government partially "shut down" twice over the next three months. Finally, after painstakingly working out the budget for each of the remaining bills, the FY96 budget was completed in April 1996, seven months after it was due.

THE QUESTION OF CONGRESSIONAL ETHICS

Ethics is the most serious public relations problem confronting Congress today. Perhaps nothing has so tarnished the public's perception of Congress as the revelations concerning the abuse of staff members, the misuse of public funds, and the personal indiscretions and corruption of members of that institution.

Congress's response to revelations of member misconduct has been mixed. The House Democratic caucus in June 1980 voted 160 to 0 to require that chairpersons of committees or subcommittees be stripped of their posts automatically if they have been censured or indicted on a felony charge carrying a prison sentence of at least two years. This rule can be waived, however, by the same caucus.

Public financing of congressional campaigns may offer a partial solution to recurring problems of financial misconduct. Nonetheless, Congress has refused to use tax money for, or to impose spending limits on, its members' campaigns, even though it adopted such provisions for presidential campaigns in 1974. Part of the campaign-funding problem is illustrated by the former member of Congress who used leftover campaign funds to make a down payment on a fifty-five-foot houseboat in Florida and to finance a limousine carrying the congressional seal. The practice of diverting unused campaign funds to personal use was outlawed in January 1980, but members of Congress were exempted from coverage by the law until 1992. By the 1990s, the public's regard for Congress had reached an all-time low (see this chapter's *Politics and Ethics* on the previous page).

THE CONGRESS: UNFINISHED WORK

The U.S. Congress, although respected by the public for its history and for its authority, continues to slide downward with respect to public approval of its activities. To many voters, the House and the Senate seem like arcane institu-

CONCEPT OVERVIEW
The Changing Congress

In some ways, the Congress of the United States remains a very traditional institution in which manners and rituals are important. It has changed significantly over the last four decades, however, both because of the changing politics of the nation and because of reforms enacted by Democrats in 1972 and, most recently, by Republicans in 1995.

THEN	NOW
• Speaker's power decreasing.	• Speaker's power increasing.
• Parties controlled members.	• Senators and representatives frequently act independently.
• Junior members rarely spoke or took action on the floor.	• Junior members are full participants, even pushing action.
• Committee chairs had significant power.	• Committee chairs have limited power.
• House Rules Committee held independent power.	• House Rules Committee is under the control of the speaker.
• Almost all members were white and male.	• Many minority and female members.
• Budget compiled from many bills; president's responsibility.	• Congress takes more responsibility in the budget process.

tions that spend too much time in political battles with each other and with the president. Too little legislation that matters to the people seems to be produced by Congress, and too many members of Congress seem to hold office just to satisfy their own ambitions.

One of the results of the public's cynical attitude toward Congress is the popularity of term limits for elected officials. Although the Supreme Court struck down state laws limiting the terms of congresspersons, a constitutional amendment providing for term limits remains a viable alternative. The question today is whether enough support can be garnered to pass the amendment.

Other unfinished work of Congress relates to the problem that minority groups in the United States are underrepresented in that institution. The Supreme Court has made it clear that racial gerrymandering to increase minority representation in Congress is not an acceptable solution to this problem. Finding alternate solutions may be one of the most difficult challenges facing Congress—and American society—today.

Given the complexity of national problems and the attempts by hundreds of interest groups to influence congressional action, both the House and the Senate continue to try to meet the expectations of the people in the media age. The president continues to garner far more credit for whatever legislation is enacted, while Congress tries to find a way to balance interests and produce policies that meet modern needs. The members of Congress, however, continue to go home to their districts and, in most cases, build trusting relationships with their constituents—which helps build support for the institution as a whole.

GETTING INVOLVED
How to Be an Intern in Washington, D.C.

John Stuart Mill, the British political philosopher and economist, wrote in the last century, "There are many truths of which the full meaning cannot be realized until personal experience has brought it home." Hundreds of students each year flock to Washington, D.C., for a summer, a semester, or a full year to gain personal experience in one of the myriad institutions of the nation's capital. For those with "Potomac fever," an internship in Washington earning college credit while working is an extraordinary opportunity. If you are interested in a Washington experience, here are some things to keep in mind.

First, make sure that you discuss your internship plan with your faculty adviser. He or she will have useful tips. Some colleges have strict rules on who may obtain credit for internships, what preparation is necessary, in what year students are allowed to participate in internships, and other such matters. Internships are most useful if you are in your junior or senior year.

There are several ways to plan an internship. First, contact an existing program, such as the following:

THE WASHINGTON CENTER
1101 14th St. N.W.
Suite 500
Washington, D.C. 20005
202-336-7600
http://www.twc.edu/

Such an organization will assist you in finding a suitable internship in government, the private sector, foundations, and nonprofit or volunteer organizations, as well as in considering other opportunities. "Organized" internship programs will also find you housing and usually provide field trips, special seminars, internship advisers, and other support. Ask if your college or university is affiliated with a Washington program or has an internship program of its own.

Second, find your own internship. There are several avenues for identifying and pursuing opportunities. Contact the local office of your representative or senator, which is usually listed in the telephone directory under "United States Government." Many members of Congress have internship coordinators andlarge, well-supervised programs. Some even may be able to pay part of your expenses.

Always make sure that you explore in detail what a specific job offers. Think carefully about internships that are glorified secretarial jobs in which all you do is typing and filing. Good internships should give you an insider's view on how a profession works. It should furnish some real "hands-on" opportunities to do research, deal with the public, learn about legislation, and watch government officials in action.

Remember that most internships are nonpaying. Make sure that you understand all the costs involved. Arrange for financing through your college, a guaranteed student loan, personal savings, or family support.

Finally, keep in mind that there are also internships in most members' district offices close to home. Such jobs may not have the glamor of Washington, but they may offer excellent opportunities for political experience.

A very useful booklet with which you should start is *Storming Washington: An Intern's Guide to National Government*, by Stephen E. Frantzich. It is available from the following source:

AMERICAN POLITICAL SCIENCE ASSOCIATION
1527 New Hampshire Ave. N.W.
Washington, DC 20036
202-483-2512
http://www2.dgsys.com/~APSA/

KEY TERMS

CHAPTER SUMMARY

❶ The authors of the Constitution, believing that the bulk of national power should be in the legislature, set forth the structure, power, and operation of Congress. The Constitution states that Congress will consist of two chambers. Partly an outgrowth of the Connecticut Compromise, this bicameral structure established a balanced legislature, with the membership in the House of Representatives based on population and the membership in the Senate based on the equality of states.

❷ The first seventeen clauses of Article I, Section 8, of the Constitution specify most of the enumerated, or expressed, powers of Congress, including the right to impose taxes, to borrow money, to regulate commerce, and to declare war. Besides its enumerated powers, Congress enjoys the right to "make all Laws which shall be necessary and proper for carrying into Execution the foregoing Powers, and all other Powers vested by this Constitution in the Government of the United States, or in any Department or Officer thereof." This is called the elastic, or necessary and proper, clause.

❸ The functions of Congress include (a) lawmaking, (b) service to constituents, (c) representation, (d) oversight, (e) public education, and (f) conflict resolution.

❹ There are 435 members in the House of Representatives and 100 members in the Senate. Owing to its larger size, the House has a greater number of formal rules. The Senate tradition of unlimited debate, or filibustering, dates back to 1790 and has been used over the years to frustrate the passage of bills. Under Senate Rule 22, cloture can be used to shut off debate on a bill.

❺ Members of Congress are not typical American citizens. They are older than most Americans; disproportionately white, male, and Protestant; and trained in professional occupations.

❻ Congressional elections are operated by the individual state governments, which must abide by rules established by the Constitution and national statutes. The process of nominating congressional candidates has shifted from party conventions to the direct primaries currently used in all states. The overwhelming majority of incumbent representatives and a smaller proportion of senators who run for reelection are successful. The most complicated aspect of the mechanics of congressional elections is reapportionment—the allocation of legislative seats to constituencies. The Supreme Court's one person, one vote rule has been applied to equalize the populations of state legislative and congressional districts.

❼ Members of Congress are well paid and enjoy other benefits, including franking privileges. Members of Congress have personal and committee staff members available to them and also benefit from a number of legal privileges and immunities.

❽ Most of the actual work of legislating is performed by committees and subcommittees within Congress. Legislation introduced into the House or Senate is assigned to the appropriate standing committees for review. Select committees are created for a limited period of time for a specific legislative purpose. Joint committees are formed by the concurrent action of both chambers and consist of members from each chamber. Conference committees are special joint committees set up to achieve agreement between the House and the Senate on the exact wording of legislative acts passed by both chambers in different forms. The seniority rule specifies that longer-serving members will be given preference when committee chairpersons and holders of other important posts are selected.

❾ The foremost power holder in the House of Representatives is the speaker of the House. Other leaders are the House majority leader, the House minority leader, and the majority and minority whips. Formally, the vice president is the presiding officer of the Senate, with the majority party choosing a senior member as the president pro tempore to preside when the vice president is absent. Actual leadership in the Senate rests with the majority floor leader, the minority floor leader, and their respective whips.

❿ A bill becomes law by progressing through both chambers of Congress and their appropriate standing and joint committees to the president.

⓫ The budget process for a fiscal year begins with the preparation of an executive budget by the president. This is reviewed by the Office of Management and Budget and then sent to Congress, which is supposed to pass a final budget by the end of September. Since 1978, Congress has not followed its own time rules.

⓬ Ethics is the most serious public relations problem facing Congress. Financial misconduct, sexual improprieties, and other unethical behavior on the part of several House and Senate members have resulted in a significant lowering of the public's regard for the institution of Congress. Despite congressional investigations of ethical misconduct and, in some cases, reprimands of members of Congress, the overall view of the public is that Congress has little control over the actions of its members in respect to ethics.

QUESTIONS FOR REVIEW AND DISCUSSION

❶ What should be the balance of power between the president and Congress? Should Congress be a reactive body, waiting for presidential proposals and then debating them, or should Congress take the initiative? How does the Constitution constrain this relationship? Under what conditions would the Constitution favor congressional leadership in policymaking?

❷ Think about your senator or representative. As a constituent, what are your expectations of him or her? To what extent do you expect your member of Congress to try to represent the constituents' views or to take a national perspective? What are the political risks to a member of being oriented more to national problems than to local ones?

❸ Given the emphasis on media campaigning and the growth in campaign expenditures, how should congressional campaigning be reformed to reduce the amount of time and energy that candidates must spend on fund raising? Should the public fund campaigns? Should campaign spending for the House and Senate be limited? How would limits change the process of campaigning?

❹ Is it possible for an assembly of elected officials to make complex public policies, or is the task too difficult? What sources of information do members of Congress need in order to write and understand public policies? Which political actors and forces focus their concerns on certain interests or regional problems? Is that focus on constituent concerns important in drafting important legislation, such as health-care reform?

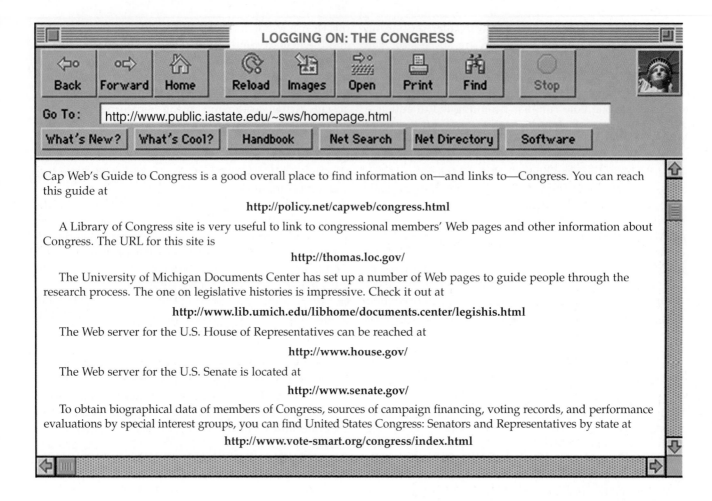

LOGGING ON: THE CONGRESS

Go To: http://www.public.iastate.edu/~sws/homepage.html

What's New?   What's Cool?   Handbook   Net Search   Net Directory   Software

Cap Web's Guide to Congress is a good overall place to find information on—and links to—Congress. You can reach this guide at

http://policy.net/capweb/congress.html

A Library of Congress site is very useful to link to congressional members' Web pages and other information about Congress. The URL for this site is

http://thomas.loc.gov/

The University of Michigan Documents Center has set up a number of Web pages to guide people through the research process. The one on legislative histories is impressive. Check it out at

http://www.lib.umich.edu/libhome/documents.center/legishis.html

The Web server for the U.S. House of Representatives can be reached at

http://www.house.gov/

The Web server for the U.S. Senate is located at

http://www.senate.gov/

To obtain biographical data of members of Congress, sources of campaign financing, voting records, and performance evaluations by special interest groups, you can find United States Congress: Senators and Representatives by state at

http://www.vote-smart.org/congress/index.html

SELECTED REFERENCES

Barone, Michael, and Grant Ujifusa. *The Almanac of American Politics, 1997.* Washington, D.C.: National Journal, 1996. This is a comprehensive summary of current political information on each member of Congress, his or her state or congressional district, recent congressional election results, key votes and ratings of roll-call votes by various organizations, sources of campaign contributions, and records of campaign expenditures.

Benjamin, Gerald, and Michael J. Malbin, eds. *Limiting Legislative Terms,* Washington, D.C.: Congressional Quarterly Press, 1992. This collection of essays looks at the history of term-limit proposals and the campaigns for their passage, and suggests possible effects on the legislature if term limits are imposed.

Campbell, James E. *The Presidential Pulse of Congressional Elections.* Lexington, Ky.: University Press of Kentucky, 1993. The author examines and compares various theories of the surge and decline in party strength in Congress relative to presidential elections.

Casey, Chris. *The Hill on the Net: Congress Enters the Information Age.* Boston, Mass.: Academic Press, 1996. A staff member of Senator Edward Kennedy provides a brief history of how Congress came to embrace the Internet and gives advice on how to access information sources on Capitol Hill.

Congress A to Z: A Ready Reference Encyclopedia. 2d ed. Washington, D.C.: Congressional Quarterly Press, 1993. The most recent edition of this reference work includes essays on aspects of Congress, historical treatment of many topics, and a wealth of tables and statistics about Congress.

Curtis, Thomas B., and Donald L. Westerfield. *Congressional Intent.* Westport, Conn.: Praeger, 1992. Curtis and Westerfield examine the current state of Congress and its inability to engage in national debate, contrary to the intentions of the founders of the nation. They suggest reforms to make

Congress a coequal partner with the president in regard to policymaking.

Deering, Christopher J., and Steven S. Smith. *Committees in Congress*. 3d Ed. Washington, D.C.: Congressional Quarterly Press, 1997. This new edition of a classic work on committees expands its coverage of reforms in Congress and now includes those that have been initiated by the Republican majority since 1995.

Fenno, Richard F., Jr. *Senators on the Campaign Trail: The Politics of Representation*. Norman, Okla.: University of Oklahoma Press, 1996. One of the outstanding scholars of congressional elections details the relationship between senators and their constituents on the campaign trail.

Fiorina, Morris P. *Congress: Keystone of the Washington Establishment*. 2d ed. New Haven, Conn.: Yale University Press, 1989. An extensive update to the 1977 original, this book examines the sources of the criticism that the unconstrained pursuit of personal goals by members of Congress has resulted in their failure to meet the responsibilities imposed by the nation.

Harris, Fred R. *Deadlock or Decision: The U.S. Senate and the Rise of National Politics*. New York: Oxford University Press, 1993. Harris, a former senator, presents an excellent overview of the forces that have affected the Senate over the years. He believes that those forces have weakened the Senate's ability to debate and write policy for the nation.

Kingdon, John W. *Congressmen's Voting Decisions*. 3d ed. Ann Arbor: University of Michigan Press, 1990. This is considered to be one of the best studies of the ways in which members of Congress vote. It includes the roles played in this process by constituents, colleagues, interest groups, the executive branch, and staff members.

Ornstein, Norman J., Thomas E. Mann, and Michael J. Malbin. *Vital Statistics on Congress, 1995–1996*. Washington, D.C.: Congressional Quarterly Press, 1995. The authors bring together from various sources information on eight areas related to Congress, including data on the members themselves, elections, campaign finances, budgeting, committees, and so on.

Peterson, Paul E., ed. *The President, the Congress and the Making of Foreign Policy*. Norman, Okla.: University of Oklahoma Press, 1996. This collection of essays reexamines the relationship between the president and the members of both houses of Congress in regard to foreign policy issues. The editor concludes that today's chaotic world enhances the president's leadership on these issues.

Reeves, Andree E. *Congressional Committee Chairmen: Three Who Made an Evolution*. Lexington, Ky.: University Press of Kentucky, 1993. Reeves examines the careers of three very strong House committee chairpersons of the House Education and Labor Committee. Her work shows how committees develop and change under the direction of different chairpersons.

Schneier, Edward V., and Bertram Gross. *Congress Today*. New York: St. Martin's Press, 1993. Two individuals with extensive experience on Capitol Hill provide an excellent overview of Congress and the changing context in which it works.

Sinclair, Barbara. *Legislators, Leaders and Lawmaking: The U.S. House of Representatives in the Postreform Era*. Baltimore, Md.: Johns Hopkins University Press, 1995. The author provides an excellent analysis of the changes that have taken place in the House of Representatives since the reform era of the 1970s.

13
The Presidency

CHAPTER OUTLINE

- ☆ Who Can Become President?
- ☆ The Process of Becoming President
- ☆ The Many Roles of the President
- ☆ The President as Party Chief and Superpolitician
- ☆ The Special Uses of Presidential Power
- ☆ Abuses of Executive Power and Impeachment
- ☆ The Executive Organization
- ☆ The Vice Presidency

The First Lady Were a Paid Government Employee?

WHAT IF THE FIRST LADY WERE A PAID GOVERNMENT EMPLOYEE?

Given the expectation that the First Lady will, indeed, work at her job and spend her time to benefit the president and his programs or the nation in her ceremonial duties, why shouldn't the First Lady be an official, paid government employee?

In fact, given the dependence of the executive branch on the office of the First Lady for certain kinds of planning and entertaining, there probably would be little opposition to making the First Lady a paid, professional employee. Today, with the increasing likelihood that a president's spouse has a career that must be put aside for the term of office, most individuals would say that the person should be paid for the duties performed. The real controversy would swirl around the definition of the First Lady's duties.

DEFINING THE POSITION

In the history of the presidency, First Ladies have performed a number of functions for the office. These functions include ceremonial and social duties (all First Ladies), speaking for certain constituencies (Hillary Rodham Clinton for children), doing on-site investigations for the president (Eleanor Roosevelt for her physically impaired spouse),

working for policy changes (Lady Bird Johnson for highway beautification), and playing a policy advisory role to the president (Hillary Rodham Clinton in the health policy proposals of the Clinton administration). Which of these duties should be specified as part of a job description?

Then there is the matter of performance. What if the First Lady were widely perceived to be doing less than an exemplary job in some of her duties? As a government employee, she could be subject to congressional investigation, which, currently, she is not because of her informal (unpaid) position. The problem could be resolved by creating the position of the First Lady as a political appointment within the White House Office staff. Then, Congress's power to investigate her position would be limited by the president's claim of executive privilege if the position involved discussions of delicate policy issues.

As more and more political candidates are members of two-career families, the idea of making the First Lady's position official is likely to take hold. What this might mean is that if a First Lady preferred to hold a position outside government, the president could name someone else to take on part of the First Lady's duties and compensate that person as a staff member. The First Lady's duties then would be simply to act as a social companion and hostess at White House events. The conflict of interest that might arise if a First Lady held an outside paid employment position raises yet another set of issues that would need to be discussed in the future.

FOR CRITICAL ANALYSIS

1. *Which duties of the First Lady are actually necessary to the presidency, and which are necessary primarily to her husband's political interests?*
2. *Would making the First Lady an official staff member lessen the influence of other staff members or of the vice president or the president?*

The writers of the Constitution created the presidency of the United States without any models on which to draw. Nowhere else in the world was there a democratically selected chief executive. What the founders did not want was a king. In fact, given their previous experience with royal governors in the colonies, many of the delegates to the Constitutional Convention wanted to create a very weak executive who could not veto legislation. Other delegates, especially those who had witnessed the need for a strong leader in the revolutionary army, believed a strong executive to be necessary for the republic. The delegates, after much debate, created a chief executive who had enough powers granted in the Constitution to balance those of the Congress.[1]

The power exercised by each president who has held the office has been scrutinized and judged by historians, political scientists, the media, and the public. Indeed, it would seem that Americans are fascinated by presidential power and by the persons who hold the office. (As the *What If . . .* that opens this chapter notes, the American fascination with the president extends to the president's spouse.) In this chapter, after looking at who can become president and at the process involved, we examine closely the nature and extent of the constitutional powers held by the president.

WHO CAN BECOME PRESIDENT?

The requirements for becoming president, as outlined in Article II, Section 1, of the Constitution, are not overwhelmingly stringent:

> No person except a natural born Citizen, or a Citizen of the United States, at the time of the Adoption of this Constitution, shall be eligible to the Office of President; neither shall any Person be eligible to that Office who shall not have attained to the Age of thirty-five Years, and been fourteen Years a Resident within the United States.

The only question that arises about these qualifications relates to the term "natural born Citizen." Does that mean only citizens born in the United States and its territories? What about a child born to a U.S. citizen (or to a couple who are U.S. citizens) while visiting or living in another country? Although the question has not been dealt with directly by the Supreme Court, it is reasonable to expect that someone would be eligible if his or her parents were Americans. The first presidents, after all, were not even American citizens at birth, and others were born in areas that did not become part of the United States until later. These questions were debated when George Romney, who was born in Chihuahua, Mexico, made a serious bid for the Republican presidential nomination in the 1960s.[2]

The great American dream is symbolized by the statement that "anybody can become president of this country." It is true that in modern times, presidents have included a haberdasher (Harry Truman—for a short period of time), a peanut farmer (Jimmy Carter), and an actor (Ronald Reagan). But if you examine Appendix C, you will see that the most common previous occupation of presidents in this country has been the legal profession. Out of forty-two presidents, twenty-six have been lawyers, and many have been wealthy.

Although the Constitution states that the minimum-age requirement for the presidency is thirty-five years, most presidents have been much older

Abraham Lincoln is usually classified as one of the greatest presidents because of his dedication to preserving the Union.

---

[1]Forrest McDonald, *The American Presidency: An Intellectual History* (Lawrence, Kans.: University Press of Kansas, 1994), p. 179.
[2]George Romney was governor of Michigan from 1963 to 1969. Romney was not nominated, and the issue remains unresolved.

From left to right, the first cabinet—Henry Knox, Thomas Jefferson, Edmund Randolph, Alexander Hamilton, and the first president—George Washington.

than that when they assumed office. John F. Kennedy, at the age of forty-three, was the youngest elected president, and the oldest was Ronald Reagan, at age sixty-nine. The average age at inauguration has been fifty-four. There has clearly been a demographic bias in the selection of presidents. All have been male, white, and Protestant, except for John F. Kennedy, a Roman Catholic. Presidents have been men of great stature—such as George Washington—and men in whom leadership qualities were not so pronounced—such as Warren Harding.

THE PROCESS OF BECOMING PRESIDENT

Major and minor political parties nominate candidates for president and vice president at national conventions every four years. As discussed in Chapter 10, the nation's voters do not elect a president and vice president directly but rather cast ballots for presidential electors, who then vote for president and vice president in the electoral college. (See this chapter's *Politics and the Fifty States* for a discussion of how electoral votes affect campaign strategy.)

Because the election is governed by a majority in the electoral college, it is conceivable that someone could be elected to the office of the presidency without having a plurality of the popular vote cast. Indeed, in three cases, candidates won elections even though their major opponents received more popular votes. In cases in which there were more than two candidates running for office, many presidential candidates have won the election with less than 50 percent of the total popular votes cast for all candidates—including Abraham Lincoln, Woodrow Wilson, Harry S Truman, John F. Kennedy, and Richard Nixon. In the 1992 election, Bill Clinton, with only 43 percent of the vote, defeated incumbent George Bush. Independent candidate H. Ross Perot garnered a surprising 19 percent of the vote. (See the feature entitled *Politics and Presidential Elections* in this chapter.)

On occasion, the electoral college has failed to give any candidate a majority. At this point, the election is thrown into the House of Representatives. The president is then chosen from among the three candidates having the most electoral college votes. Only two times in our past has the House had to decide on a president. Thomas Jefferson and Aaron Burr tied in the electoral college in 1800. This happened because the Constitution had not been explicit in indicating which of the two electoral votes was for president and which was for vice president. In 1804, the **Twelfth Amendment** clarified the matter. In 1824 the House again had to make a choice, this time among William H. Crawford, Andrew Jackson, and John Quincy Adams. It chose Adams, even though Jackson had more electoral and popular votes.

TWELFTH AMENDMENT

An amendment to the Constitution, adopted in 1804, that specifies the separate election of the president and vice president by the electoral college.

THE MANY ROLES OF THE PRESIDENT

The Constitution speaks briefly about the duties and obligations of the president. Based on a brief list of powers and the precedents of history, the presidency has grown into a very complicated job that requires balancing at least five constitutional roles. These are (1) *chief of state,* (2) *chief executive,* (3) *commander in chief* of the armed forces, (4) *chief diplomat,* and (5) *chief legislator* of the United States. Here we examine each of these significant presidential functions, or roles. It is worth noting that one person plays all these roles simultaneously and that the needs of these roles may at times be contradictory.

POLITICS AND THE FIFTY STATES
Campaigning for Electoral Votes

The map of the United States shown here is distorted to show the relative weight of the states in terms of electoral votes. Considering that a candidate must win 270 electoral votes to be elected, the president's staff plots his visits around the nation to maximize exposure in the most important states. In the first three years of his administration, Bill Clinton, for example, visited California twenty-five times.

For Critical Analysis
What other factors, besides the number of electoral votes, might be taken into account when presidents plan their visits to states for campaign effects?

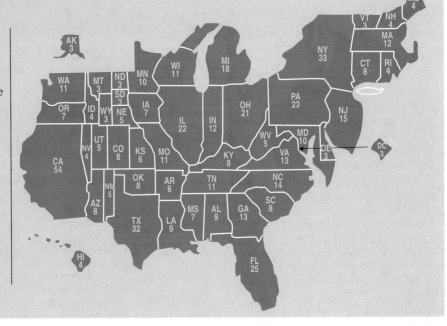

Chief of State

Every nation has at least one person who is the ceremonial head of state. In most democratic governments, the role of **chief of state** is given to someone other than the chief executive, who is the head of the executive branch of government (see this chapter's *Politics and Comparative Systems*). In Britain, for example, the chief of state is the queen. In France, where the prime minister

CHIEF OF STATE

The role of the president as ceremonial head of the government.

President Clinton, along with International Olympic Committee President Juan Antonio Samaranch (left) and Atlanta Olympic Games President William Porter Payne, stand at attention for the U.S. national anthem during the opening ceremonies for the XXVI Olympic games. President Clinton's participation in events like the Olympics or throwing out the first pitch at a season opening game of a baseball season are traditional activities within the role of chief of state.

POLITICS AND PRESIDENTIAL ELECTIONS
How Popular Is the "Popular Vote"?

No president of the United States has ever been elected by a majority of all adults of voting age, even though many presidents have been elected by very large majorities of votes from citizens who actually cast ballots. As you can see from the accompanying table, Martin Van Buren was elected president by a record low of just 11.4 percent of voting-age Americans in 1836.

The proportion of voting-age citizens who have elected presidents has generally increased over time. This has happened largely because of several important extensions of voting rights—the Fifteenth Amendment in 1870, which removed race as a barrier to voting for African American males; the Nineteenth Amendment in 1920, which enfranchised women; the Twenty-fourth Amendment in 1964, which abolished the poll tax in federal elections; and the Twenty-sixth Amendment in 1971, which lowered the minimum voting age to eighteen. Lyndon Johnson, in 1964, came the closest of any president in history to being elected by a majority of the voting-age public, and even he gained the votes of less than 40 percent of those who were old enough to cast a ballot.

These results are especially useful to keep in mind whenever a president claims to have received a "mandate" from the people to govern the nation. In reality, no president has ever been elected with sufficient popular backing to make this a serious claim.

For Critical Analysis
Considering the data presented in this table, is it legitimate for any winning presidential nominee to declare that the nominee received a mandate? Why or why not?

Year	Winning Candidate	Percentage of Total Vote	Percentage of Voting-Age Population
1828	Andrew Jackson	56.0	12.4
1832	Andrew Jackson	56.5	11.6
1836	Martin Van Buren	50.8	11.4
1840	William Harrison	52.9	16.9
1844	James Polk	49.5	15.1
1848	Zachary Taylor	47.3	13.5
1852	Franklin Pierce	50.6	13.8
1856	James Buchanan	45.3	13.8
1860	Abraham Lincoln	39.8	12.5
1864	Abraham Lincoln	55.0	13.4
1868	Ulysses Grant	52.8	16.7
1872	Ulysses Grant	55.7	17.8
1876	Rutherford Hayes	47.9	17.8
1880	James Garfield	48.3	17.5
1884	Grover Cleveland	48.5	17.3
1888	Benjamin Harrison	47.9	17.4
1892	Grover Cleveland	46.1	16.1
1896	William McKinley	51.1	18.8
1900	William McKinley	51.7	17.6
1904	Theodore Roosevelt	56.4	16.8
1908	William Taft	51.6	15.4
1912	Woodrow Wilson	41.9	11.7
1916	Woodrow Wilson	49.3	15.8
1920	Warren Harding	60.4	25.6
1924	Calvin Coolidge	54.0	23.7
1928	Herbert Hoover	58.1	30.1
1932	Franklin Roosevelt	57.4	30.1
1936	Franklin Roosevelt	60.8	34.6
1940	Franklin Roosevelt	54.7	32.2
1944	Franklin Roosevelt	53.4	29.9
1948	Harry Truman	49.6	25.3
1952	Dwight Eisenhower	55.1	34.0
1956	Dwight Eisenhower	57.4	34.1
1960	John Kennedy	49.7	31.2
1964	Lyndon Johnson	61.1	37.8
1968	Richard Nixon	43.4	26.4
1972	Richard Nixon	60.7	33.7
1976	Jimmy Carter	50.1	27.2
1980	Ronald Reagan	51.0	26.7
1984	Ronald Reagan	58.7	32.0
1988	George Bush	53.4	26.7
1992	Bill Clinton	43.0	23.1
1996	Bill Clinton	49.2	23.3

POLITICS AND COMPARATIVE SYSTEMS
Filling the Ceremonial Role

For decades, scholars have felt that the president of the United States spends far too much time on the duties of chief of state—largely ceremonial tasks, such as greeting the Super Bowl champions or receiving foreign dignitaries. In virtually every other Western nation, the chief of state is a separate position from that of the chief executive.

In the seven Western European countries headed by royalty, the monarch is considered the chief of state and plays a ceremonial role. In the United Kingdom, for example, Queen Elizabeth represents the state at ceremonial occasions, such as the opening sessions of Parliament, the christening of ships, and receptions for foreign ambassadors.

In the monarchies of the Netherlands and Norway, the king or queen initiates the process of forming a government after national elections by determining which parties can combine to rule in coalition. This process really depends on the results of the election and the desires of the political parties—but the monarch must certify it.

The majority of European states are not monarchies, but they split the duties of government between a prime minister and a president. In Switzerland, for example, the president is

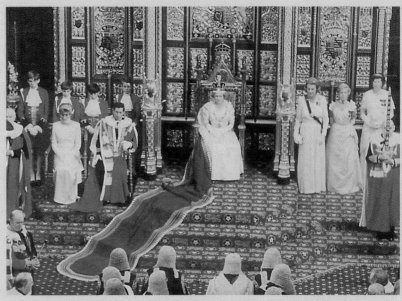

Queen Elizabeth of the United Kingdom is the chief of state of that nation, but she has no political power.

elected indirectly by the legislature. The president is selected from among members of a governing council, but, once chosen, assumes purely ceremonial duties.

Throughout Western Europe, the pattern in the same: Presidents have ceremonial powers only. The single exception to this rule is France, which has a presidential system in which the head of state has real political power, particularly in foreign affairs.

In the new governments of Eastern Europe, presidents or other executive officials were established more on the American model.

For Critical Analysis
If the United States were to create a ceremonial head of state, what duties would be given to that position? How would that help or hinder the president in performing presidential roles?

is the chief executive, the chief of state is the president. But in the United States, the president is both chief executive and chief of state. According to William Howard Taft, as chief of state, the president symbolizes the "dignity and majesty" of the American people. In his capacity as chief of state, the president engages in a number of activities that are largely symbolic or ceremonial, such as the following:

- Decorating war heroes.
- Throwing out the first ball to open the baseball season.
- Dedicating parks and post offices.
- Receiving visiting chiefs of state at the White House.
- Going on official state visits to other countries.
- Making personal telephone calls to congratulate the country's heroes.

• Representing the nation at times of national mourning, such as after the 1995 bombing of the Alfred P. Murrah Federal Building in Oklahoma City.

Many students of the American political system believe that having the president serve as both the chief executive and the chief of state drastically limits the time available to do "real" work. Not all presidents have agreed with this conclusion, however—particularly those presidents who have been able to blend skillfully these two roles with their role as politician. Being chief of state gives the president tremendous public exposure, which can be an important asset in the campaign for reelection. When that exposure is positive, it helps the president deal with Congress over proposed legislation and increases the chances of being reelected—or getting the candidates of the president's party elected. (See the feature entitled *Thinking Politically about the First Lady* for a discussion of whether the First Lady's behavior influences approval ratings of presidential actions.)

Chief Executive

According to the Constitution, "The executive Power shall be vested in a President of the United States of America.... [H]e may require the Opinion, in writing, of the principal Officer in each of the executive Departments, upon any Subject relating to the Duties of their respective Offices . . . and he shall nominate, and by and with the Advice and Consent of the Senate, shall appoint . . . Officers of the United States.... [H]e shall take Care that the Laws be faithfully executed."

As **chief executive** the president is constitutionally bound to enforce the acts of Congress, the judgments of federal courts, and treaties signed by the United States. To assist in the various tasks of the chief executive, the president has a federal bureaucracy (see Chapter 14), which currently consists of 2.9 million federal civilian employees and which spends over 1.5 trillion dollars per year.

The Powers of Appointment and Removal. You might think that the president, as head of the largest bureaucracy in the United States, wields enor-

CHIEF EXECUTIVE

The role of the president as head of the executive branch of the government.

One of the president's jobs is to act as chief of state, thereby representing the United States throughout the world. Here President Clinton gives a speech commemorating the fiftieth anniversary of D-Day, which began about 12:15 A.M. on June 6, 1944. This campaign, which started on the beaches of Normandy, France, was credited with causing the German war effort on the Western front to collapse. Germany signed an unconditional surrender on May 7, 1945.

Thinking Politically about the First Lady

Hillary Rodham Clinton is the best-educated First Lady in American history as well as the first to have had a professional career in addition to being a political spouse. Her dual role as wife to the president and as a professional woman with strong opinions on public policy issues has put her into the political spotlight since the early days of Bill Clinton's primary campaign. Her involvement in the Whitewater investigation further complicated her image and standing in the public's view. Polling data suggest that she might be the most controversial First Lady since Eleanor Roosevelt, who also challenged the public's understanding of the First Lady's role.

What political advantages and disadvantages can the president expect from the public's perception of the First Lady? Even if she is controversial, is she, like the vice presidential candidate, likely to have little real impact on voters' decisions?

The advantages to the president or presidential candidate of having a popular spouse are many. When she represents him on the campaign trail or at public appearances, she is well received. Barbara Bush came, in time, to be more popular than her husband and has continued a career of speaking on behalf of her favorite cause—literacy—after the end of the Bush presidency. First Ladies can greatly influence the climate of public opinion with regard to the image of the White House both at home and abroad. No First Lady is likely to replicate Jacqueline Kennedy's flair for entertaining, fashion, and social grace. A popular First Lady can "soften" the less flattering characteristics of the president.

The disadvantages to the president of having a controversial or unpopular spouse are also many. If she is outspoken on controversial policy issues, she may cause voters to reject the president as well. Her image may lessen public support for the office, although there really are no examples of this happening in the United States. Perhaps, most importantly, a First Lady who is unpopular or controversial has limited political usefulness. Staff time must be spent to remake her public image, and she is unable to represent the president and the administration on issues for which she will generate negative feelings.

An assessment of the impact of Hillary Rodham Clinton on American politics is not easy. While most Americans (62 percent) believe that she has more influence on the president than other First Ladies have had, just under half (40 to 49 percent) continue to believe that she has "about the right amount of power." When asked about her influence on the administration, voters have moved from thinking that she has the right amount of influence to perhaps having too much influence. There is no doubt that more survey questions have been asked about Hillary Rodham Clinton than about any other First Lady and that her popularity is a matter of media attention. There is no evidence, however, that the public perceptions of a First Lady—Barbara Bush, Nancy Reagan, or Hillary Clinton—have had any impact on public approval of her husband's actions.

For Critical Analysis

When the United States elects its first female president, what kind of attention will be paid to her spouse? What will be expected of him?

mous power. The president, however, only nominally runs the executive bureaucracy, for most of its jobs are protected by **civil service.**[3] Therefore, even though the president has **appointment power,** it is not very extensive, being limited to cabinet and subcabinet jobs, federal judgeships, agency heads, and about two thousand lesser jobs. This means that most of the three million federal employees owe no political allegiance to the president. They are more likely to owe loyalty to congressional committees or to interest groups representing the sector of the society that they serve. Table 13–1 shows what percentage of the total employment in each executive department is available for political appointment by the president.

The president's power to remove from office officials who are not doing a good job or who do not agree with the president is not explicitly granted by the Constitution and has been limited. In 1926, however, a Supreme Court

CIVIL SERVICE

A collective term for the body of employees working for the government. Generally, civil service is understood to apply to all those who gain government employment through a merit system.

APPOINTMENT POWER

The authority vested in the president to fill a government office or position. Positions filled by presidential appointment include those in the executive branch, the federal judiciary, commissioned officers in the armed forces, and members of the independent regulatory commissions.

[3]See Chapter 14 for a discussion of the Civil Service Reform Act.

Table 13–1

Total Civilian Employment in Cabinet Departments Available for Political Appointment by the President

EXECUTIVE DEPARTMENT	TOTAL NUMBER OF EMPLOYEES	POLITICAL APPOINTMENTS AVAILABLE	PERCENTAGE
Agriculture	119,558	501	0.42
Commerce	37,642	399	1.06
Defense	879,651	853	0.10
Education	4,813	252	5.24
Energy	19,899	503	2.53
Health and Human Services	128,244	541	0.42
Housing and Urban Development	13,218	188	1.42
Interior	80,704	311	0.39
Justice	97,910	543	0.55
Labor	16,732	214	1.28
State	25,596	454	1.77
Transportation	64,896	429	0.66
Treasury	156,373	283	0.18
Veterans' Affairs	262,432	364	0.14
TOTAL	1,907,668	5,835	0.31

SOURCE: U.S. Department of Commerce; *The American Almanac: Statistical Abstract of the United States, 1995–1996* (Washington, D.C.: U.S. Government Printing Office, 1996).

decision prevented Congress from interfering with the president's ability to fire those executive-branch officials whom the president had appointed with Senate approval.[4]

The ten agencies whose directors the president can remove at any time are as follows:

1. ACTION (coordinates volunteer programs).
2. Arms Control and Disarmament Agency.
3. Commission on Civil Rights.
4. Energy Research and Development Agency.
5. Environmental Protection Agency.
6. Federal Mediation and Conciliation Service.
7. General Services Administration.
8. National Aeronautics and Space Administration.
9. Postal Service.
10. Small Business Administration.

In addition, the president can remove all heads of cabinet departments, all individuals in the Executive Office of the President, and all political appointees listed in Table 13–1.

Harry Truman spoke candidly of the difficulties a president faces in trying to control the executive bureaucracy. Upon leaving office, he referred to the problems that Dwight Eisenhower, as a former general of the army, was going to have: "He'll sit here and he'll say do this! do that! and nothing will happen. Poor Ike—it won't be a bit like the Army. He'll find it very frustrating."[5]

The Power to Grant Reprieves and Pardons.   Section 2 of Article II of the Constitution gives the president the power to grant **reprieves** and **pardons**

REPRIEVE

The presidential power to postpone the execution of a sentence imposed by a court of law; usually done for humanitarian reasons or to await new evidence.

PARDON

The granting of a release from the punishment or legal consequences of crime; a pardon can be granted by the president before or after a conviction.

---

[4]*Meyers v. United States*, 272 U.S. 52 (1926).

[5]Quoted in Richard E. Neustadt, *Presidential Power: The Politics of Leadership* (New York: Wiley, 1960), p. 9.

for offenses against the United States except in cases of impeachment. All pardons are administered by the Office of the Pardon Attorney in the Department of Justice. In principle, pardons are granted to remedy a mistake made in a conviction.

The Supreme Court upheld the president's right to reprieve in a 1925 case concerning the pardon granted by the president to an individual convicted of contempt of court. The judiciary had contended that only judges had the authority to convict individuals for contempt of court when court orders were violated and that the courts should be free from interference by the executive branch. The Supreme Court simply stated that the president could reprieve or pardon all offenses "either before trial, during trial, or after trial, by individuals, or by classes, conditionally or absolutely, and this without modification or regulation by Congress."[6] In a controversial decision, President Gerald Ford pardoned former president Richard Nixon for his role in the Watergate affair before any charges were brought in court. After his defeat in the 1992 presidential election, George Bush also exercised the right of executive pardon for six former members of the Reagan administration who had been charged with various offenses in regard to the Iran-*contra* investigation.

Commander in Chief

The president, according to the Constitution, "shall be Commander in Chief of the Army and Navy of the United States, and of the Militia of the several States, when called into the actual Service of the United States." In other words, the armed forces are under civilian, rather than military, control.

Certainly those who wrote the Constitution had George Washington in mind when they made the president the **commander in chief.** Although we no longer expect our president to lead the troops to battle, presidents as commanders in chief have wielded dramatic power. Harry Truman made the awesome decision to drop atomic bombs on Hiroshima and Nagasaki in 1945 to force Japan to surrender and thus bring to an end World War II. Lyndon Johnson ordered bombing missions against North Vietnam in the 1960s, and

---

[6]*Ex parte Grossman,* 267 U.S. 87 (1925).

DID YOU KNOW...
That Thomas Jefferson was the first president to be inaugurated in Washington, D.C., where he walked to the Capitol from a boarding house, took the oath, made a brief speech in the Senate chamber, and then walked back home?

COMMANDER IN CHIEF

The role of the president as supreme commander of the military forces of the United States and of the state national guard units when they are called into federal service.

President Clinton talks to soldiers during a visit to Bosnia.

DID YOU KNOW...
That John F. Kennedy was the youngest elected president, taking office at the age of forty-three, but that Theodore Roosevelt assumed office at the age of forty-two after the assassination of President William McKinley?

WAR POWERS ACT

A law passed in 1973 spelling out the conditions under which the president can commit troops without congressional approval.

he personally selected some of the targets. Richard Nixon decided to invade Cambodia in 1970. Ronald Reagan sent troops to Lebanon and Grenada in 1983 and ordered U.S. fighter planes to attack Libya in 1986. George Bush sent troops to Panama in 1989 and to the Middle East in 1990. Bill Clinton sent troops to Haiti in 1994 and to Bosnia in 1995.

The president is the ultimate decision maker in military matters. Everywhere he goes, so too goes the "football"—a briefcase filled with all the codes necessary to order a nuclear attack. Only the president has the power to order the use of nuclear force.

As commander in chief, the president has probably exercised more authority than in any other role. Constitutionally, Congress has the sole power to declare war, but the president can send the armed forces into a country in situations that are certainly the equivalent of war. When William McKinley ordered troops into Peking to help suppress the Boxer Rebellion in 1900, he was sending them into a combat situation. Harry Truman dispatched troops to Korea as part of a "police action" in 1950. Kennedy, Johnson, and Nixon waged an undeclared war in Southeast Asia, where over 58,000 Americans were killed and 300,000 were wounded. In none of these situations did Congress declare war.

In an attempt to gain more control over such military activities, in 1973 Congress passed a **War Powers Act**—over President Nixon's veto—requiring that the president consult with Congress before sending American forces into action. Once they are sent, the president must report to Congress within forty-eight hours. Unless Congress has passed a declaration of war within sixty days or has extended the sixty-day time limit, the forces must be withdrawn. The War Powers Act was tested in the fall of 1983, when Reagan requested that troops be left in Lebanon. The resulting compromise was a congressional resolution allowing troops to remain there for eighteen months. Shortly after the resolution was passed, however, more than 240 sailors and marines were killed in the suicide bombing of a U.S. military housing compound in Beirut. That event provoked a furious congressional debate over the role American troops were playing in the Middle East, and all troops were withdrawn shortly afterward.

President Clinton is shown here working in the Oval Office. This oval-shaped office in the White House, with its immense seal of the United States in the carpet, is often used to represent the power of the presidency and of the United States. Indeed, common references to "the Oval Office" mean specifically the president who is in power at that time.

In spite of the War Powers Act, the powers of the president as commander in chief are more extensive today than they were in the past. These powers are linked closely to the president's powers as chief diplomat, or chief crafter of foreign policy.

Chief Diplomat

The Constitution gives the president the power to recognize foreign governments; to make treaties, with the **advice and consent** of the Senate; and to make special agreements with other heads of state that do not require congressional approval. In addition, the president nominates ambassadors. As **chief diplomat,** the president dominates American foreign policy.

Recognition Power.   An important power of the president as chief diplomat is **recognition power,** or the power to recognize—or refuse to recognize—foreign governments. In the role of ceremonial head of state, the president has always received foreign diplomats. In modern times, the simple act of receiving a foreign diplomat has been equivalent to accrediting the diplomat and officially recognizing his or her government. Such recognition of the legitimacy of another country's government is a prerequisite to diplomatic relations or negotiations between that country and the United States.

Deciding when to recognize a foreign power is not always simple. The United States, for example, did not recognize the Soviet Union until 1933—sixteen years after the Russian Revolution of 1917. It was only after all attempts to reverse the effects of that revolution—including military invasion of Russia and diplomatic isolation—had proved futile that Franklin Roosevelt extended recognition to the Soviet government. U.S. presidents faced a similar problem with the Chinese communist revolution. In December 1978, long after the communist victory in China, Jimmy Carter granted official recognition to the People's Republic of China.[7]

The diplomatic recognition issue that faced the Clinton administration was different from the previous ones because it involved recognizing a former enemy—the Republic of Vietnam. An odd coalition of liberals who believed we needed to heal the wounds of the war and perhaps more conservative business leaders who saw tremendous economic opportunities supported the reestablishment of diplomatic relations with the communist nation. Many Americans, particularly those who believed that Vietnam had not been forthcoming in the efforts to find the remains of missing American soldiers or to find out about former prisoners of war, opposed any formal relationship with that nation. After the U.S. government had negotiated with the Vietnamese government for many years over the missing-in-action issue and engaged in limited diplomatic contacts for several years, President Clinton announced on July 11, 1995, that the United States would recognize the government of Vietnam and move to establish normal diplomatic relations. Support for the decision came from several Vietnam veterans in Congress, including Senator John McCain, a former prisoner of war. Although the decision was not opposed in legislation, members of Congress who disagreed with Clinton planned to continue to hamper future moves by the administration by attacking the funding to build an embassy in Vietnam and in other ways.

Proposal and Ratification of Treaties.   The president has the sole power to negotiate treaties with other nations. These treaties must be presented to the

ADVICE AND CONSENT

The power vested in the U.S. Senate by the Constitution (Article II, Section 2) to give its advice and consent to the president on treaties and presidential appointments.

CHIEF DIPLOMAT

The role of the president in recognizing foreign governments, making treaties, and making executive agreements.

RECOGNITION POWER

The president's power, as chief diplomat, to extend diplomatic recognition to foreign governments.

---

[7]The Nixon administration first encouraged new relations with the People's Republic of China by allowing a cultural exchange of ping-pong teams.

DID YOU KNOW...
That President William Henry Harrison gave the longest inaugural address (8,445 words) of any American president, lasting two hours? (The weather was chilly and stormy, and Harrison caught a cold, got pneumonia and pleurisy, and died a month later.)

EXECUTIVE AGREEMENT

An international agreement made by the president, without senatorial ratification, with the head of a foreign state.

Senate, where they may be modified and must be approved by a two-thirds vote. After ratification, the president can approve the senatorial version of the treaty. Approval poses a problem when the Senate has tacked on substantive amendments or reservations to a treaty, particularly when such changes may require reopening negotiations with the other signatory governments. Sometimes a president may decide to withdraw a treaty if the senatorial changes are too extensive—as Woodrow Wilson did with the Versailles Treaty in 1919. Wilson felt that the senatorial reservations would weaken the treaty so much that it would be ineffective. His refusal to accept the senatorial version of the treaty led to the eventual refusal of the United States to join the League of Nations.

President Jimmy Carter was successful in lobbying for the treaties that provided for the return of the Panama Canal to Panama by the year 2000 and neutralizing the canal. He was unsuccessful, however, in his attempts to gain ratification of the Strategic Arms Limitation Treaty, known as SALT II. That treaty, which provided for limits on nuclear-armed long-range bombers and intercontinental ballistic missiles, encountered fierce opposition from Senate conservatives and from the subsequent Reagan administration.

President Bill Clinton won a major political and legislative victory in 1993 by persuading Congress to ratify the North American Free Trade Agreement (NAFTA). In so doing, he had to overcome opposition from Democrats and most of organized labor.

Executive Agreements. Presidential power in foreign affairs is enhanced greatly by the use of **executive agreements** made between the president and other heads of state. Such agreements do not require Senate approval, although the House and Senate may refuse to appropriate the funds necessary to implement them. Whereas treaties are binding on all succeeding administrations, executive agreements are not binding without each new president's consent.

Among the advantages of executive agreements are speed and secrecy. The former is essential during a crisis; the latter is important when the administration fears that open senatorial debate may be detrimental to the best interests of the United States or to the interests of the president. There have been

U.S. President Jimmy Carter, Egyptian President Anwar el-Sadat, and Israeli Prime Minister Menachem Begin sign the Camp David accords, bringing peace between Egypt and Israel.

POLITICS AND ECONOMICS
Traveling with the President

Whenever the president travels in the United States or overseas, reporters for national newspapers and for television networks travel with him. Sometimes these correspondents are invited to travel on *Air Force One,* the president's plane. More often, a press plane is chartered. Early in the Clinton presidency, the staff members of the White House Travel Office were fired from their jobs, and the task of arranging presidential and press travel was turned over to a private travel agency. After some criticism, most of those workers were reinstated on a temporary basis. Republican members of Congress pursued an investigation of the firing in an attempt to embarrass the president and Mrs. Clinton politically.

One of the duties of the White House Travel Office is to arrange travel for the press and then to bill the press for those trips. The cost for a reporter to travel with the president is approximately three times the cost of a first-class ticket, with no discounts for Saturday night stayovers.

The president's airplane, the Boeing 747 *Air Force One*, was inaugurated in 1990. It costs $30,000 per hour to operate *Air Force One.*

The bill for one Associated Press reporter traveling with Bill Clinton to Brussels, Prague, Kiev, Moscow, Minsk, and Geneva totaled $6,658.18, exclusive of ground transportation and other expenses. The charges for travel within Russia were modest, but the return trip from Geneva to Washington, D.C., cost $2,904.93.

---

far more executive agreements (about 9,000) than treaties (about 1,300). Many executive agreements contain secret provisions calling for American military assistance or other support. For example, Franklin Roosevelt used executive agreements to bypass congressional isolationists in trading American destroyers for British Caribbean naval bases and in arranging diplomatic and military affairs with Canada and Latin American nations.

Negotiating treaties and executive agreements often requires the president to travel abroad. For a discussion of the cost of traveling with the president, see this chapter's *Politics and Economics.*

Chief Legislator

Constitutionally, presidents must recommend to Congress legislation that they judge necessary and expedient. Not all presidents have wielded their powers as **chief legislator** in the same manner. President John Tyler was almost completely unsuccessful in getting his legislative programs implemented by Congress. Presidents Theodore Roosevelt, Franklin Roosevelt, and Lyndon Johnson, however, saw much of their proposed legislation put into effect.

CHIEF LEGISLATOR

The role of the president in influencing the making of laws.

STATE OF THE UNION MESSAGE

An annual message to Congress in which the president proposes a legislative program. The message is addressed not only to Congress but also to the American people and to the world. It offers the opportunity to dramatize policies and objectives and to gain public support.

VETO MESSAGE

The president's formal explanation of a veto when legislation is returned to the Congress.

POCKET VETO

A special veto power exercised by the chief executive after a legislative body has adjourned. Bills not signed by the chief executive die after a specified period of time. If Congress wishes to reconsider such a bill, it must be reintroduced in the following session of Congress.

Each year the president presents his State of the Union message, which is required by Article II, Section 3, of the Constitution and is usually given in late January, shortly after Congress reconvenes. Because the floor of the House of Representatives is so much larger than that of the Senate, the State of the Union speech is given there. Attendees are, of course, all members of Congress, plus usually the justices of the U.S. Supreme Court, the heads of the executive departments, and certain others, such as the chairman of the Federal Reserve Board of Governors. The press, of course, is in attendance, too.

In modern times, the president has played a dominant role in creating the congressional agenda. In the president's annual **State of the Union message,** which is required by the Constitution (Article II, Section 3) and is usually given in late January shortly after Congress reconvenes, the president as chief legislator presents his program. The message gives a broad, comprehensive view of what the president wishes the legislature to accomplish during its session. It is as much a message to the American people and to the world as it is to Congress. Its impact on public opinion can determine the way in which Congress responds to the president's agenda.

Getting Legislation Passed. The president can propose legislation, but Congress is not required to pass any of the administration's bills. How, then, does the president get those proposals made into law? One way is the power of persuasion. The president writes to, telephones, and meets with various congressional leaders; makes public announcements to force the weight of public opinion onto Congress in favor of a legislative program; and, as head of the party, exercises legislative leadership through the congresspersons of the president's party.

To be sure, a president whose party represents a majority in both houses of Congress may have an easier time getting legislation passed than does a president who faces a hostile Congress. But one of the ways in which a president who faces a hostile Congress still can wield power is through the ability to veto legislation. After the 1994 congressional elections, Bill Clinton faced a Republican-controlled Congress. He used the veto liberally (see Table 13–2) to force Republicans to rewrite their legislative proposals to gain his approval. The Republicans, not having enough votes to overturn Clinton's veto, modified some of their legislation in 1995 and 1996 to make it into law.

Saying No to Legislation. The president has the power to say no to legislation through use of the veto, by which the White House returns a bill unsigned to the legislative body with a **veto message** attached.[8] Because the Constitution requires that every bill passed by the House and the Senate must be sent to the president before it becomes law, the president must act on each bill:

1. If the bill is signed, it becomes law.
2. If the bill is not sent back to Congress after ten congressional working days, it becomes law without the president's signature.
3. The president can reject the bill and send it back to Congress with a veto message setting forth objections. Congress then can change the bill, hoping to secure presidential approval and repass it. Or it can simply reject the president's objections by overriding the veto with a two-thirds roll-call vote of the members present in each house.
4. If the president refuses to sign the bill and Congress adjourns within ten working days after the bill has been submitted to the president, the bill is killed for that session of Congress. If Congress wishes the bill to be reconsidered, the bill must be reintroduced during the following session. This is called a **pocket veto.**

Presidents employed the veto power infrequently until the administration of Andrew Johnson, but it has been used with increasing vigor since then (see Table 13–2). The total number of vetoes from George Washington through Bill Clinton's fourth year in office was 2,510, with about two-thirds of those

---

[8]*Veto* in Latin means "I forbid."

Table 13–2

Presidential Vetoes, 1789 to 1996

Years	President	Regular Vetoes	Vetoes Overridden	Pocket Vetoes	Total Vetoes
1789–1797	Washington	2	0	0	2
1797–1801	J. Adams	0	0	0	0
1801–1809	Jefferson	0	0	0	0
1809–1817	Madison	5	0	2	7
1817–1825	Monroe	1	0	0	1
1825–1829	J. Q. Adams	0	0	0	0
1829–1837	Jackson	5	0	7	12
1837–1841	Van Buren	0	0	1	1
1841–1841	Harrison	0	0	0	0
1841–1845	Tyler	6	1	4	10
1845–1849	Polk	2	0	1	3
1849–1850	Taylor	0	0	0	0
1850–1853	Fillmore	0	0	0	0
1853–1857	Pierce	9	5	0	9
1857–1861	Buchanan	4	0	3	7
1861–1865	Lincoln	2	0	5	7
1865–1869	A. Johnson	21	15	8	29
1869–1877	Grant	45	4	48	93
1877–1881	Hayes	12	1	1	13
1881–1881	Garfield	0	0	0	0
1881–1885	Arthur	4	1	8	12
1885–1889	Cleveland	304	2	110	414
1889–1893	Harrison	19	1	25	44
1893–1897	Cleveland	42	5	128	170
1897–1901	McKinley	6	0	36	42
1901–1909	T. Roosevelt	42	1	40	82
1909–1913	Taft	30	1	9	39
1913–1921	Wilson	33	6	11	44
1921–1923	Harding	5	0	1	6
1923–1929	Coolidge	20	4	30	50
1929–1933	Hoover	21	3	16	37
1933–1945	F. Roosevelt	372	9	263	635
1945–1953	Truman	180	12	70	250
1953–1961	Eisenhower	73	2	108	181
1961–1963	Kennedy	12	0	9	21
1963–1969	L. Johnson	16	0	14	30
1969–1974	Nixon	26*	7	17	43
1974–1977	Ford	48	12	18	66
1977–1981	Carter	13	2	18	31
1981–1989	Reagan	39	9	28	67
1989–1993	Bush	37	1	0	38
1993–1996	Clinton	14	0	0	14
TOTAL		1,470	104	1039	2,510

*Two pocket vetoes, overruled in the courts, are counted here as regular vetoes.

Source: Louis Fisher, *The Politics of Shared Power: Congress and the Executive*, 2d ed. (Washington, D.C.: Congressional Quarterly Press, 1987), p. 30: *Congressional Quarter Weekly Report*, October 17, 1992, p. 3249; and authors' update.

vetoes being exercised by Grover Cleveland, Franklin Roosevelt, Harry Truman, and Dwight Eisenhower.

Ronald Reagan lobbied strenuously for Congress to give another tool to the president—the **line-item veto.** Reagan saw the ability to veto *specific* spending provisions of legislation that he was sent by Congress as the only way that the president could control overall congressional spending. In 1996, Congress passed a law providing for the line-item veto. Signed by President Clinton, the law grants the president the power to rescind any item in an

LINE-ITEM VETO

The power of an executive to veto individual lines or items within a piece of legislation without vetoing the entire bill.

State *of the* **UNION:**
President Clinton presents his **VISION** *of the* **FUTURE.**

"... IT'S KINDA GRAY AND VERY WRINKLY ..."

Distributed by King Features Syndicate

Reprinted with special permission of King Features Syndicate

President Clinton fulfills his campaign promise to enlarge what he considered to be a successful government program—Head Start. This program targets "at risk" children before and after they enter kindergarten. Its goal has been to form strong educational and other positive values so that such children will continue to do well in school.

appropriations bill unless Congress passes a "disapproval" bill, which could be vetoed. The law did not take effect until after the 1996 election.

A veto is a clear-cut indication of the president's dissatisfaction with congressional legislation. Nonetheless, Congress rarely overrides a presidential veto. Consider that two-thirds of the members of each chamber who are present must vote to override the president's veto in a roll-call vote. This means that if only one-third plus one of the members voting in one of the chambers of Congress do not agree to override the veto, the veto holds. Table 13–2 tells us that it was not until the administration of John Tyler that Congress overrode a presidential veto. In the first sixty-five years of American federal government history, out of thirty-three regular vetoes, Congress overrode only one, or less than 3 percent. Overall, only about 4 percent of all vetoes have been overridden.

Measuring the Success or Failure of a President's Legislative Program.
One way of determining a president's strength is to evaluate that president's success as chief legislator. A strong president is one who has achieved much of the administration's legislative program; a weak president is one who has achieved little. Using these definitions of strong and weak, it is possible to rank presidents according to their legislative success.

Figure 13–1 shows the percentages of presidential victories measured by congressional votes in situations in which the president took a clear-cut position. Based on this information, John Kennedy appears to have been the most successful president in recent years until Clinton, whose high success rate (86.4 percent) in the first two years of his presidency tumbled to 36 percent after the Republican victory in the 1994 elections. Such data provide a statistical measure but do not indicate the importance of the legislation, the bills not introduced, or whether the president was perceived as a successful national leader regardless of this measure.

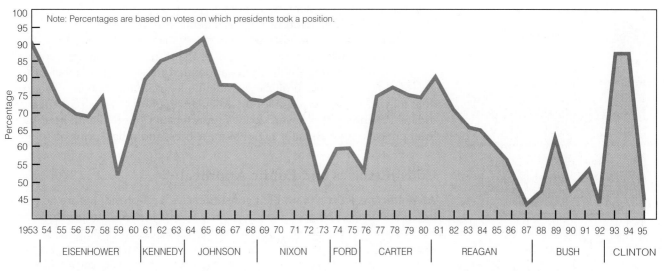

Note: Percentages are based on votes on which presidents took a position.

EISENHOWER | KENNEDY | JOHNSON | NIXON | FORD | CARTER | REAGAN | BUSH | CLINTON

SOURCE: *Congressional Quarterly Weekly Report*, various issues.

Figure 13–1
● ● ● ● ● ● ● ● ● ● ● ● ● ● ● ● ● ●
Presidential Support on Congressional Votes, 1953 to 1996
Most presidents have their greatest successes in the first years of their terms in office.

Other Presidential Powers

The powers of the president discussed in the preceding sections are called **constitutional powers,** because their basis lies in the Constitution. In addition, Congress has established by law, or statute, numerous other presidential powers—such as the ability to declare national emergencies. These are called **statutory powers.** Both constitutional and statutory powers have been labeled the **expressed powers** of the president, because they are expressly written into the Constitution or into law.

Presidents also have what have come to be known as **inherent powers.** These depend on the loosely worded statement in the Constitution that "the executive Power shall be vested in a President" and that the president should "take Care that the Laws be faithfully executed." The most common example of inherent powers are those emergency powers invoked by the president during wartime. Franklin Roosevelt used his inherent powers to relocate the Japanese living in the United States during World War II.

THE PRESIDENT AS PARTY CHIEF AND SUPERPOLITICIAN

Presidents are by no means above political partisanship, and one of their many roles is that of chief of party. Although the Constitution says nothing about the function of the president within a political party (the mere concept of political parties was abhorrent to most of the authors of the Constitution), today presidents are the actual leaders of their parties.

The President as Chief of Party

As party leader, the president chooses the national committee chairperson and can try to discipline party members who fail to support presidential policies. One way of exerting political power within the party is by **patronage**— appointing individuals to government or public jobs. This power was more extensive in the past, before the establishment of the civil service in 1882 (see Chapter 14), but the president still retains impressive patronage power. As we

CONSTITUTIONAL POWER

A power vested in the president by Article II of the Constitution.

STATUTORY POWER

A power created for the president through laws established by Congress.

EXPRESSED POWER

A constitutional or statutory power of the president, which is expressly written into the Constitution or into congressional law.

INHERENT POWER

A power of the president derived from the loosely worded statement in the Constitution that "the executive power shall be vested in a president" and that the president should "take care that the laws be faithfully executed"; defined through practice rather than through constitutional or statutory law.

PATRONAGE

Rewarding faithful party workers and followers with government employment and contracts.

WASHINGTON COMMUNITY

Individuals regularly involved with politics in Washington, D.C.

noted earlier, the president can appoint several thousand individuals to jobs in the cabinet, the White House, and the federal regulatory agencies.

Presidents have a number of other ways of exerting influence as party chief. The president may make it known that a particular congressperson's choice for federal judge will not be appointed unless that member of Congress is more supportive of the president's legislative program.[9] The president may agree to campaign for a particular program or for a particular candidate. Presidents also reward loyal supporters in Congress with funding for local projects, tax breaks for regional industries, and other forms of "pork."

Constituencies and Public Approval

All politicians worry about their constituencies, and presidents are no exception. Presidents, however, have numerous constituencies. In principle, they are beholden to the entire electorate—the public of the United States—even to those who did not vote. They are certainly beholden to their party constituency, because its members put them in office. The president's constituencies also include members of the opposing party whose cooperation the president needs. Finally, the president has to take into consideration a constituency that has come to be called the **Washington community.** This community consists of individuals who—whether in or out of political office—are intimately familiar with the workings of government, thrive on gossip, and daily measure the political power of the president.

All of these constituencies are impressed by presidents who maintain a high level of public approval, partly because this is very difficult to accomplish. Presidential popularity, as measured by national polls, gives the president an extra political resource to use in persuading legislators or bureaucrats to pass legislation. After all, refusing to do so might be going against public sentiment. President Reagan showed amazing strength in the public opinion polls for a second-term chief executive, as Figure 13–2 indicates, although there was a one-month drop of 20 points during the Iran-*contra* hearings.

Figure 13–2
● ● ● ● ● ● ● ● ● ● ● ● ● ● ●
Public Popularity of Bill Clinton and His Predecessors

[9]"Senatorial courtesy" (see Chapter 15) often puts the judicial appointment in the hands of the Senate, however.

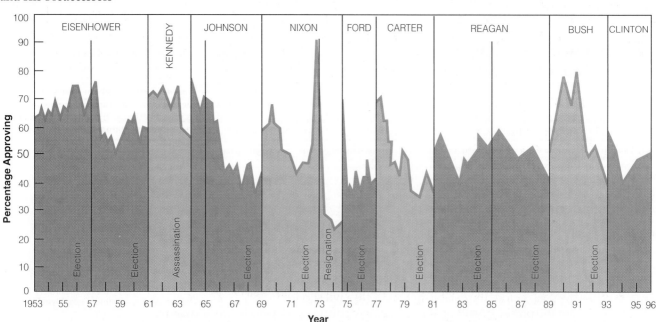

SOURCE: *Public Opinion*, February/March 1988, pp. 36–39; and Gallup Polls, March 1992, June 1994, September 1995, and August, 1996.

President Clinton began his term in office with a 58 percent approval rating and then saw it plummet to 38 percent six months later. By the end of his first year, his rating returned to 48 percent approving his performance, although in the following year, it dropped to 38 percent again. Before the 1996 elections, it had climbed to 51 percent, however.

The presidential preoccupation with public opinion has been criticized by at least one scholar as changing the balance of national politics. Samuel Kernell proposed that the style of presidential leadership since World War II has changed, owing partly to the influence of television.[10] Presidents frequently go over the heads of Congress and the political elites, taking their case directly to the people. This strategy, which Kernell dubbed "going public," gives the president additional power through the ability to persuade and manipulate public opinion. By identifying their own positions so clearly, presidents make compromises with Congress much more difficult and weaken the legislators' positions. Given the increasing importance of the media as the major source of political information for citizens and elites, presidents will continue to use public opinion as part of their arsenal of weapons to get support from Congress and to achieve their policy goals.

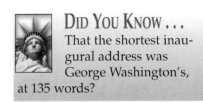

THE SPECIAL USES OF PRESIDENTIAL POWER

Presidents have at their disposal a variety of special powers and privileges not available in other branches of the U.S. government. These include (1) emergency powers, (2) executive orders, (3) executive privilege, and (4) impoundment of funds.

Emergency Powers

If you were to read the Constitution, you would find no mention of the additional powers that the executive office may exercise during national emergencies. Indeed, the Supreme Court has indicated that an "emergency does not create power."[11] But it is clear that presidents have used their inherent powers during times of emergency, particularly in the realm of foreign affairs. The **emergency powers** of the president were first enunciated in the Supreme Court's decision in *United States v. Curtiss-Wright Export Corp.*[12] In that case, President Franklin Roosevelt, without authorization by Congress, ordered an embargo on the shipment of weapons to two warring South American countries. The Court recognized that the president may exercise inherent powers in foreign affairs and that the national government has primacy in foreign affairs.

Examples of emergency powers are abundant, coinciding with real or contrived crises in domestic and foreign affairs. Abraham Lincoln's suspension of civil liberties at the beginning of the Civil War, his calling of the state militias into national service, and his subsequent governance of conquered areas and even of areas of northern states were justified by claims that such actions were essential to preserve the Union. Franklin Roosevelt declared an "unlimited national emergency" following the fall of France in World War II and mobilized the federal budget and the economy for war.

President Harry Truman authorized the federal seizure of steel plants and their operation by the national government in 1952 during the Korean War. Truman claimed that he was using his inherent emergency power as chief

EMERGENCY POWER

An inherent power exercised by the president during a period of national crisis, particularly in foreign affairs.

---

[10]Samuel Kernell, *Going Public: New Strategies of Presidential Leadership*, 2d ed. (Washington, D.C.: Congressional Quarterly Press, 1992).
[11]*Home Building and Loan Association v. Blaisdell*, 290 U.S. 398 (1934).
[12]229 U.S. 304 (1936).

CRITICAL PERSPECTIVE
Which Presidential Leadership Style Is Best?

All candidates for the presidency share some characteristics—extensive political experience, strong attachment to a political party or set of beliefs, a competitive spirit, a belief that he or she can be a leader of the nation, and an enjoyment of the political process. Richard Nixon, who many believed did not much enjoy the presidency, acknowledged that he really enjoyed the competition of politics. Dwight Eisenhower is often remembered as a reluctant leader. He had earned an international reputation, however, as leader of the combined armies of the Western Allies against Adolf Hitler and, it turns out, had an understated but shrewd leadership style in the White House.

What are the qualities of leadership that would best serve the presidency of the United States and the country itself? Many scholars have examined the question of presidential leadership and offered schemes for evaluating and predicting the capacity of candidates for leadership.

Presidents must not only make decisions in crises, be able to articulate their views to the public, persuade legislators and others in private, and maintain a favorable public image but also must be good managers. The president of the United States is the chief executive officer of the largest business in the country, with about 2.8 million civilian employees, nearly two million military employees, and a budget of over 1.5 trillion dollars. As the chief executive

officer, the president must gather a staff that will serve him or her well, choose managers to run the cabinet departments, gather and process information well, sift through competing points of view, and make decisions about which course of action to take.

In his 1960 classic book *Presidential Power: The Politics of Leadership,* political scientist Richard Neustadt suggested some principles for leadership.* He noted that it was very important to follow through and do what you say you are going to do, or else no one will believe your threats or promises. In his book entitled *Presidential Character,* James David Barber took a psychological approach to the topic, developing a scheme for analyzing all presidents and then classifying them according to their personality traits, especially whether they took a positive or negative view of the world and whether they were active or passive in their approach to problems.† Barber believed that an active/positive president had the best chance of succeeding, because that type of person could learn on the job, be resilient, tackle many tasks, and take criticism with confidence.

Other analysts are not so sure that personality type is that important. They point to the management style of successful presidents as the key factor to watch. Franklin Roosevelt managed the presidency by seeking different points of view before making a decision. Establishing what might be called a *competitive* system,

executive and commander in chief to safeguard the nation's security, as the ongoing steel mill strike threatened the supply of weapons to the armed forces. The Supreme Court did not agree, holding that the president had no authority under the Constitution to seize private property or to legislate such action.[13] According to legal scholars, this was the first time a limit was placed on the exercise of the president's emergency powers.

Executive Orders

Congress allows the president (as well as administrative agencies) to issue **executive orders** that have the force of law. These executive orders can do the following: (1) enforce legislative statutes, (2) enforce the Constitution or treaties with foreign nations, and (3) establish or modify practices of executive administrative agencies.

An executive order, then, represents the president's legislative power. The only apparent requirement is that under the Administrative Procedure Act of

EXECUTIVE ORDER

A rule or regulation issued by the president that has the effect of law. Executive orders can implement and give administrative effect to provisions in the Constitution, to treaties, and to statutes.

---

[13]*Youngstown Sheet and Tube Co. v. Sawyer,* 343 U.S. 579 (1952).

CRITICAL PERSPECTIVE
Which Presidential Leadership Style Is Best? Continued

he provoked his staff members into disagreeing with one another, rearranged their duties, and kept them off guard so that he could learn more from their discussions. John Kennedy used some elements of the competitive system but also implemented a *collegial* style, relying on teamwork and the wisdom of a small group of advisers. He was helped in this approach by the presence of his own brother (the U.S. attorney-general) in that group to report on disagreements between participants. Other presidents use a more *formalistic* style, with a hierarchy of staff whose access to the president is controlled by a strong chief of staff. Generally, Republican presidents have been more likely to have a formalistic structure, whereas Democratic presidents have preferred either the collegial or competitive style.

Fundamentally, a president must find a way to deal with a tremendous flow of information, decide how much of a decision or action to delegate to others, and determine the degree to which dissent or conflict within the staff is helpful. Many scholars believe that the competitive style gives a president more alternatives to consider before making a choice. Presidents who are protected from alternative points of view may make serious errors.

Ronald Reagan clearly preferred the formalistic structure so that he could avoid dealing with many details. George Bush tended to prefer a more collegial style, relying on his advisers for

decision-making consultation. Bill Clinton seems to be operating by mixing competition among staff members with a need to have collegial advice in making decisions. The situation is further complicated by the fact that First Lady Hillary Rodham Clinton also has her own circle of advisers and that the president and the First Lady both try to seek advice from old friends from Arkansas. Most observers of the Clinton White House have noted that the president tends to first gain a great deal of information, listen to myriad voices, and delegate few decisions. Then he tries to get collegial support for a decision.

For Critical Analysis

1. Why is it necessary for a president to make a careful choice about how the White House staff is organized and how information is gathered for the chief executive?

2. To what extent does an individual's personality influence the way he or she will interact with subordinates and deal with conflict? Is it more important for a president to avoid conflict or to be comfortable with it?

*Richard E. Neustadt, *Presidential Power: The Politics of Leadership* (New York: Wiley, 1960).

†James D. Barber, *Presidential Character: Predicting Performance in the White House,* 5th ed. (Englewood Cliffs, N.J.: Prentice-Hall, 1982).

1946, all executive orders must be published in the *Federal Register,* a daily publication of the U.S. government. Executive orders have been used to establish some procedures for appointing noncareer administrators, to implement national affirmative action regulations, to restructure the White House bureaucracy, to ration consumer goods and to administer wage and price controls under emergency conditions, to classify government information as secret, and to regulate the export of restricted items.

FEDERAL REGISTER

A publication of the executive branch of the U.S. government that prints executive orders, rules, and regulations.

Executive Privilege

Another inherent executive power that has been claimed by presidents concerns the ability of the president and the president's executive officials to refuse to appear before, or to withhold information from, Congress or the courts. This is called **executive privilege,** and it relies on the constitutional separation of powers for its basis. Critics of executive privilege believe that it can be used to shield from public scrutiny actions of the executive branch that should be open to Congress and to the American public. (The power of the executive branch and the White House staff is discussed more fully in this chapter's *Critical Perspective* on presidential leadership styles.)

EXECUTIVE PRIVILEGE

The right of executive officials to refuse to appear before, or to withhold information from, a legislative committee. Executive privilege is enjoyed by the president and by those executive officials accorded that right by the president.

DID YOU KNOW ...
That President Jimmy Carter was the first president to hold a phone-in television broadcast, with Walter Cronkite as the moderator?

Limits to executive privilege went untested until the Watergate affair in the early 1970s. The Supreme Court subpoenaed secret tapes containing Richard Nixon's Oval Office conversations during his tenure at the White House. Nixon refused to turn them over, claiming executive privilege. He argued that "no president could function if the private papers of his office, prepared by his personal staff, were open to public scrutiny." In 1974, in one of the Court's most famous cases, *United States v. Nixon*,[14] the justices unanimously ruled that Nixon had to hand over the tapes to the Court. The court held that executive privilege could not be used to prevent evidence from being heard in criminal proceedings.

Impoundment of Funds

By law, the president proposes a budget, and Congress approves it. But there is no clear-cut constitutional indication that the president, as chief executive, is required by law to *spend* all of the funds appropriated by Congress, and many presidents have not done so. In 1803, Thomas Jefferson deferred a $50,000 appropriation for gunboats. Ulysses Grant returned to the Treasury unspent money for public works. In 1932, Herbert Hoover canceled projects funded by Congress. Franklin Roosevelt deferred spending on a number of appropriations to later fiscal years. Harry Truman did not spend all of the money that Congress had allocated for the military, nor did Lyndon Johnson the money allocated for highway construction. John Kennedy did not spend all of the money allocated for weapons systems.

The question of whether the president is required to spend all appropriated funds came to a head during the Nixon administration after a number of confrontations over this issue between the Republican president and an antagonistic, Democratic-controlled Congress. When Nixon vetoed appropriation bills, Congress often overrode his veto. In retaliation, Nixon refused to spend the appropriated funds, claiming that he wanted to reduce overall federal spending.

As part of its Budget and Impoundment Control Act of 1974, Congress required that the president spend all appropriated funds, although Congress gave the president some leeway. A president who is not going to spend all appropriated funds must tell Congress, and only if Congress agrees within forty-five days can the president withhold spending. If the president simply wishes to delay spending, this must be indicated to Congress. If Congress does not agree, it can pass a resolution requiring the immediate spending of the appropriated funds. While Congress was deliberating on the budget bill, cities, states, and certain members of Congress sued President Nixon over his refusal to spend appropriated funds. The Supreme Court in 1975 unanimously ruled that the president had to spend money appropriated by Congress because of his constitutional obligation to "take care that the laws be faithfully executed."[15]

ABUSES OF EXECUTIVE POWER AND IMPEACHMENT

Presidents normally leave office either because their first term has expired and they do not seek (or win) reelection or because, having served two full terms, they are not allowed to seek reelection (owing to the Twenty-second

---

[14]318 U.S. 683 (1974).
[15]*Train v. City of New York,* 420 U.S. 35 (1975).

Amendment, passed in 1951). Eight presidents have died in office. But there is still another way for a president to leave office—by **impeachment.** Articles I and II of the Constitution authorize the House and Senate to remove the president, the vice president, or other civil officers of the United States for crimes of "Treason, Bribery, or other high Crimes and Misdemeanors." No one has really defined "high Crimes and Misdemeanors," but at least twice Congress and the American public were pretty sure that a president had engaged in them.

The authority to impeach (that is, to accuse) is vested in the House of Representatives, and formal impeachment proceedings are initiated there. In the House, a representative must list the charges against the president, vice president, or other civil officer. The impeachment charges are referred either to the Judiciary Committee or to a special investigating committee. If a majority in the House votes for impeachment, then articles of impeachment are drawn up, which set forth the basis for the removal of the executive-branch officer. The actual trial of impeachment is conducted in the Senate, with all members sitting in judgment. The chief justice of the United States Supreme Court presides over the Senate. A two-thirds vote of the senators present is required for conviction. The only punishment that Congress can mete out is removal from office and disqualification from holding any other federal office. The convicted official, however, is subject to further punishment according to law.

In the history of the United States, no president has ever been impeached and also convicted. The only president who was actually impeached by the House was Andrew Johnson, but he was acquitted by the Senate by the margin of a single vote in 1868. Some argue that Johnson's impeachment was simply a case of partisan politics. Impeachment attempts also were made against John Tyler, Herbert Hoover, and Vice President Schuyler Colfax.

The case of Richard Nixon and the Watergate affair, however, was more serious and certainly less questionable in terms of its political motivation. In 1974, the House was ready to vote on Nixon's impeachment and to send the articles of impeachment to the Senate when Nixon resigned from office, making his vice president, Gerald Ford, president of the United States. The House committee recommended impeachment of the president for his role in the cover-up of the Watergate break-in in 1972. Five men had broken into the headquarters of the Democratic National Committee and were caught searching for documents that would damage the candidacy of the Democratic nominee, George McGovern. Later investigation showed that the break-in was planned by members of Nixon's campaign committee and that Nixon and his closest advisers had devised a strategy for impeding the investigation of the crime, using the Central Intelligence Agency for illegal activities. Additionally, when it became known that all of the conversations held in the Oval Office had been tape-recorded on a secret system, Nixon refused to give the tapes to the investigators in Congress. Three days after the Supreme Court ordered the release of the tapes, which showed the president's involvement in the cover-up, the House committee passed the first article of impeachment. Nixon then resigned the presidency.

THE EXECUTIVE ORGANIZATION

Gone are the days when presidents answered their own mail, as George Washington did. It was not until 1857 that Congress authorized a private secretary for the president, to be paid by the federal government. Woodrow Wilson typed most of his correspondence, even though he did have several

IMPEACHMENT

As authorized by Article I of the Constitution, an action by the House of Representatives and the Senate to remove the president, vice president, or civil officers of the United States from office for crimes of "Treason, Bribery, or other high Crimes and Misdemeanors."

Richard Nixon (right) leaves the White House after his resignation on August 9, 1974. Next to him are his wife, Pat, Betty Ford, and Gerald Ford, the new president.

Reprinted with permission of the News-Press of Fort Myers

secretaries. At the beginning of Franklin Roosevelt's long tenure in the White House, the entire staff consisted of thirty-seven employees. It was not until the New Deal and World War II that the presidential staff became a sizable organization.

Today, the executive organization includes a White House Office staff of about 600, including some workers who are part-time employees and others who are detailed from their departments to the White House. Not all of these employees have equal access to the president, nor are all of them likely to be equally concerned about the administration's political success. The more than 350 employees who work in the White House Office itself are closest to the president. They often include many individuals who worked in the president's campaign. These assistants are most concerned with preserving the president's reputation (see this chapter's feature entitled *Politics and Ethics: The Whitewater Affair*). Also included in the president's staff are a number of councils and advisory organizations, such as the National Security Council (NSC). Although the individuals who hold staff positions in these offices are appointed by the president, they are really more concerned with their own area than with the president's overall success. The group of appointees who perhaps are least helpful to the president is the cabinet, each member of which is the principal officer of a government department.

The Cabinet

Although the Constitution does not include the word *cabinet*, it does state that the president "may require the Opinion, in writing, of the principal Officer in each of the executive Departments." Since the time of our first president, there has always been an advisory group, or **cabinet,** to which the president turns for counsel. Originally, the cabinet consisted of only four officials—the secretaries of state, treasury, and war, and the attorney general. Today, the cabinet numbers thirteen secretaries and the attorney general. (See Table 13–1 on page 442 for the names of the cabinet departments.)

The cabinet may consist of more than the secretaries of the various departments. The president at his or her discretion can, for example, ascribe cabinet

CABINET

An advisory group selected by the president to aid in making decisions. The cabinet presently numbers thirteen department secretaries and the attorney general. Depending on the president, the cabinet may be highly influential or relatively insignificant in its advisory role.

POLITICS AND ETHICS:
The Whitewater Affair

During the 1980s, Bill Clinton, then governor of Arkansas, and his wife, Hillary Rodham Clinton, a lawyer with a prominent Little Rock, Arkansas, law firm, invested in a real estate development called the Whitewater Development Company. Although the total amount of money that the Clintons invested and lost was only about $68,000, the irregularities surrounding that investment triggered a sequence of events starting in 1994 that has raised a number of issues about the ethical decisions of White House staff and other political appointees.

The Whitewater investment had raised interest among Republicans and other opponents of the Clinton administration soon after the Clinton victory. Although the Clintons dismissed the investment as a bad family financial decision, their partner in the scheme, James McDougal, was also the owner of a failed savings and loan that was under investigation by the federal regulators in 1984.

The thrift's failure cost the American taxpayers about $68 million to repay depositors. Furthermore, McDougal was a close political friend of the Clintons and had arranged political fund raisers for the gover-

nor's campaigns as well as lending money to Clinton's presidential campaign in its early months. After much delay, in January 1994, Attorney General Janet Reno named a special prosecutor, Robert Fiske, who later was replaced by Kenneth Starr, to investigate the matter. As a result of Starr's investigation, James and Susan McDougal and Arkansas governor Jim Guy Tucker were tried for federal crimes and found guilty in 1996. In several cases, including that of the McDougals, President Clinton was called as a witness for the defense and testified via videotape in their behalf. Other outcomes of the investigations by Starr and by congressional committees chaired by Republicans included the following:

• The embarrassment of a number of Treasury officials for alerting the Clintons in advance of the pending investigation of Madison Guaranty Savings. Several of those officials resigned from the department after the investigation.
• The questionable handling of presidential adviser Vincent Foster's papers after his suicide, with evidence that advisers to the Clintons had removed some items from Foster's office after

his death.
• The disappearance and reappearance of Mrs. Clinton's billing records from the Rose law firm in Arkansas that had handled some of the savings and loan business.
• Continued investigations by Special Prosecutor Starr and congressional committees into every aspect of the savings and loan business, the Whitewater development, and Mrs. Clinton's ties to these political and business transactions throughout 1996.

Although polls showed that the public had little continuing interest in the details of the Whitewater affair, the continued investigation into the business and political associates of the Clintons, with some of them actually going to trial in Arkansas, certainly cast a shadow over the presidential campaign of 1996 and provided ample material for media discussions.

For Critical Analysis
What impact might such investigations and unresolved scandals have on a president's ability to persuade Congress to pass his initiatives? Should they have any effect?

rank to the National Security Council adviser, to the ambassador to the United Nations, or to others. Because neither the Constitution nor statutory law requires the president to consult with the cabinet, its use is purely discretionary. Some presidents have relied on the counsel of their cabinets more than others. Dwight Eisenhower frequently turned to his cabinet for advice on a wide range of governmental policies—perhaps because he was used to the team approach, from his experience in the U.S. Army, to solving problems. Other presidents solicited the opinions of their cabinets and then did what they wanted to do anyway. Lincoln supposedly said—after a cabinet meeting in which a vote was seven nays against his one aye—"Seven nays and one aye, the ayes have it."[16]

In general, few presidents have relied heavily on the advice of their cabinet members. Jimmy Carter thought he could put his cabinet to good use and

---

[16]Quoted in Thomas E. Cronin, *The State of the Presidency*, 2d ed. (Boston: Little, Brown, 1980), p. 11.

KITCHEN CABINET

The informal advisers to the president.

held regular cabinet meetings for the first two years of his tenure. Then he fired three cabinet members and forced two others to resign, while reorganizing his "inner government." He rarely met with the members of his cabinet thereafter. In recent years, the growth of other parts of the executive branch has rendered the cabinet less significant as an advisory board to the president.

Often, a president will use a **kitchen cabinet** to replace the formal cabinet as a major source of advice. The term *kitchen cabinet* originated during the presidency of Andrew Jackson, who relied on the counsel of close friends who often met with him in the kitchen of the White House. A kitchen cabinet is a very informal group of advisers, such as Bill Clinton's Arkansas friends, who may or may not otherwise be connected with the government.

It is not surprising that presidents meet with their cabinet heads only reluctantly. Often the departmental heads are more responsive to the wishes of their own staffs or to their own political ambitions than they are to the president. They may be more concerned with obtaining resources for their departments than with helping presidents achieve their goals. So there is often a strong conflict of interest between presidents and their cabinet members. It is likely that formal cabinet meetings are held more out of respect for the cabinet tradition than for their problem-solving value.

The Executive Office of the President

When President Franklin Roosevelt appointed a special committee on administrative management, he knew that the committee would conclude that the president needed help. Indeed, the committee proposed a major reorganization of the executive branch. Congress did not approve the entire reorganization, but it did create the **Executive Office of the President (EOP)** to provide staff assistance for the chief executive and to help coordinate the executive bureaucracy. Since that time, a number of agencies within the EOP have been created to supply the president with advice and staff help. These agencies are as follows:

EXECUTIVE OFFICE OF THE PRESIDENT (EOP)

Established by President Franklin D. Roosevelt by executive order under the Reorganization Act of 1939, the EOP currently consists of nine staff agencies that assist the president in carrying out major duties.

- White House Office (1939).
- Council of Economic Advisers (1946).
- National Security Council (1947).
- Office of the United States Trade Representative (1963).
- Council on Environmental Quality (1969).
- Office of Management and Budget (1970).
- Office of Science and Technology Policy (1976).
- Office of Administration (1977).
- Office of National Drug Control Policy (1988).

Several of the offices within the EOP are especially important, including the White House Office, the Council of Economic Advisers, the Office of Management and Budget, and the National Security Council.

The White House Office.   One of the most important of the agencies within the EOP is the **White House Office,** which includes most of the key personal and political advisers to the president. Among the jobs held by these aides are those of legal counsel to the president, secretary, press secretary, and appointments secretary. Often, the individuals who hold these positions are recruited from the president's campaign staff. Their duties—mainly protecting the president's political interests—are similar to campaign functions. In all recent administrations, one member of the White House Office is named **chief of**

WHITE HOUSE OFFICE

The personal office of the president, which tends to presidential political needs and manages the media.

staff. This person, who is responsible for coordinating the office, is one of the president's chief advisers.

Employees of the White House Office have been both envied and criticized. The White House Office, according to most former staffers, grants its employees access and power. They are able to use the resources of the White House to contact virtually anyone in the world by telephone, cable, fax, or electronic mail as well as to use the influence of the White House to persuade legislators and citizens. Because of this influence, staffers are often criticized for overstepping the bounds of the office (see this chapter's feature entitled *Politics and Ethics: The Whitewater Affair*). It is the appointments secretary who is able to grant or deny senators, representatives, and cabinet secretaries access to the president. It is the press secretary who grants to the press and television journalists access to any information about the president. White House staff members are closest to the president and may have considerable influence over the administration's decisions. Often, when presidents are under fire for their decisions, the staff is accused of keeping the chief executive too isolated from criticism or help. Presidents insist that they will not allow the staff to become too powerful, but given the difficulty of the office, each president eventually turns to staff members for loyal assistance and protection.

The Council of Economic Advisers.   The Employment Act of 1946 created a three-member **Council of Economic Advisers (CEA)** to advise the president on economic matters. Their advice serves as the basis for the president's annual economic report to Congress. Each of the three members is appointed by the president and can be removed at will. In principle, the CEA was also created to advise the president on economic policy, but for the most part the function of the CEA has been to prepare the annual report.

The Office of Management and Budget.   The **Office of Management and Budget (OMB)** was originally the Bureau of the Budget, which was created in 1921 within the Department of the Treasury. Recognizing the importance of this agency, Franklin Roosevelt moved it into the White House Office in 1939. Richard Nixon reorganized the Bureau of the Budget in 1970 and changed its name to reflect its new managerial function. It is headed by a director, who must make up the annual federal budget that the president presents to Congress each January for approval. In principle, the director of the OMB has broad fiscal powers in planning and estimating various parts of the federal budget, because all agencies must submit their proposed budget to the OMB for approval. In reality, it is not so clear that the OMB truly can affect the greater scope of the federal budget. The OMB may be more important as a clearinghouse for legislative proposals initiated in the executive agencies.

The National Security Council.   The **National Security Council (NSC)** is a link between the president's key foreign and military advisers and the president. Its members consist of the president, the vice president, and the secretaries of state and defense, plus other informal members. The NSC has the resources of the National Security Agency (NSA) at its disposal in giving counsel to the president. (The NSA protects U.S. government communications and produces foreign intelligence information.) Included in the NSC is the president's special assistant for national security affairs. Richard Nixon had Henry Kissinger in this post; Jimmy Carter had the equally visible Zbigniew Brzezinksi. In the Reagan years, staff members of the NSC, including Lieutenant Colonel Oliver North and Admiral John Poindexter, became involved in an illegal plan to aid the *contras* in Nicaragua.

CHIEF OF STAFF

The person who is named to direct the White House Office and advise the president.

COUNCIL OF ECONOMIC ADVISERS (CEA)

A staff agency in the Executive Office that advises the president on measures to maintain stability in the nation's economy; established in 1946.

OFFICE OF MANAGEMENT AND BUDGET (OMB)

A division of the Executive Office created by executive order in 1970 to replace the Bureau of the Budget. The OMB's main functions are to assist the president in preparing the annual budget, to clear and coordinate all departmental agency budgets, to help set fiscal policy, and to supervise the administration of the federal budget.

NATIONAL SECURITY COUNCIL (NSC)

A staff agency in the Executive Office established by the National Security Act of 1947. The NSC advises the president on domestic and foreign matters involving national security.

DID YOU KNOW...
That only two U.S. presidents and their wives are buried together at Arlington National Cemetery—John Kennedy and his wife, Jacqueline Kennedy Onassis; and William Taft and his wife, Helen Herron Taft?

THE VICE PRESIDENCY

The Constitution does not give much power to the vice president. The only formal duty is to preside over the Senate—which is rarely necessary. This obligation is fulfilled when the Senate organizes and adopts its rules and when the vice president is needed to decide a tie vote. In all other cases, the president pro tempore manages parliamentary procedures in the Senate. The vice president is expected to participate only informally in senatorial deliberations, if at all.

The Vice President's Job

Vice presidents have traditionally been chosen by presidential nominees to balance the ticket or to reward or appease party factions. If a presidential nominee is from the North, it is not a bad idea to have a vice presidential nominee who is from the South or the West. If the presidential nominee is from a rural state, perhaps someone with an urban background would be most suitable as a running mate. Presidential nominees who are strongly conservative or strongly liberal would do well to have vice presidential nominees who are more in the middle of the political road.

Presidential nominee Bill Clinton ignored almost all of the conventional wisdom when he selected Senator Al Gore of Tennessee as his running mate in 1992. Not only was Gore close in age and ideology to Clinton, but he also came from the mid-South. The advantage gained from choosing Gore was his experience in the Senate, his strong position on issues such as the environment, and his compatibility with Clinton. Clinton and Gore and their families became a very successful campaign team whose friendship continued after the inauguration. Although Clinton's position as president has not been challenged by Gore's activity, the vice president continues to lead the administration on most environmental issues. He maintains a close relationship with the president, meeting with him as regularly as he does with members of the White House staff.

Vice presidents infrequently have become elected presidents in their own right. John Adams and Thomas Jefferson were the first to do so. Then Martin Van Buren was elected president in 1836 after he had served as Andrew Jackson's vice president for the previous eight years. In 1988, George Bush was elected to the presidency after eight years as Ronald Reagan's vice president.

The job of vice president is not extremely demanding, even when the president gives some specific task to the vice president. Typically vice presidents spend their time supporting the president's activities. All of this changes, of course, if the president becomes disabled or dies in office.

Presidential Succession

Eight vice presidents have become president because of the death of the president. John Tyler, the first to do so, took over William Henry Harrison's position after only one month. No one knew whether Tyler should simply be a caretaker until a new president could be elected three and a half years later or whether he actually should be president. Tyler assumed that he was supposed to be the chief executive and he acted as such—although he was commonly referred to as "His Accidency." On all occasions since then, vice presidents taking over the position of the presidency because of the incumbent's death have assumed all of the presidential powers.

Vice President Al Gore

But what should a vice president do if a president becomes incapable of carrying out necessary duties while in office? When James Garfield was shot in 1881, he stayed alive for two and a half months. What was Vice President Chester Arthur's role?

This question was not addressed in the original Constitution. Article II, Section 1, says only that "in Case of the Removal of the President from Office, or of his Death, Resignation, or Inability to discharge the Powers and Duties of the said Office, the same shall devolve on the Vice President." There have been many instances of presidential disability. When Dwight Eisenhower became ill a second time in 1958, he entered into a pact with Richard Nixon that provided that the vice president could determine whether the president was incapable of carrying out his duties if the president could not communicate. John Kennedy and Lyndon Johnson entered into similar agreements with their vice presidents. Finally, in 1967, the **Twenty-fifth Amendment** was passed, establishing procedures in case of presidential incapacity.

The Twenty-fifth Amendment

According to the Twenty-fifth Amendment, when the president believes that he is incapable of performing the duties of office, he must inform the Congress in writing. Then the vice president serves as acting president until the president can resume his normal duties. When the president is unable to communicate, a majority of the cabinet, including the vice president, can declare that fact to Congress. Then the vice president serves as acting president until the president resumes his normal duties. If a dispute arises over the return of the president's ability to discharge his normal functions, a two-thirds vote of Congress is required to decide whether the vice president shall remain acting president or whether the president shall resume his duties.

Although President Reagan did not formally invoke the Twenty-fifth Amendment during his surgery for the removal of a cancerous growth in his

DID YOU KNOW...
That President Richard Nixon served 56 days without a vice president, and that President Gerald Ford served 132 days without a vice president?

TWENTY-FIFTH AMENDMENT

An amendment to the Constitution adopted in 1967 that establishes procedures for filling vacancies in the two top executive offices and that makes provisions for situations involving presidential disability.

An attempted assassination of Ronald Reagan occurred on March 31, 1981. In the foreground, press secretary James Brady lies seriously wounded. In the background, two men bend over President Reagan.

Spiro Agnew was Richard Nixon's vice president from 1969 to 1973. Agnew resigned amid allegations of income tax evasion in connection with money he received when he was govenor of Maryland.

Table 13–3

Line of Succession to the Presidency of the United States

1. Vice president.
2. Speaker of the House of Representatives.
3. Senate president pro tempore.
4. Secretary of State.
5. Secretary of the Treasury.
6. Secretary of Defense.
7. Attorney General.
8. Secretary of the Interior.
9. Secretary of Agriculture.
10. Secretary of Commerce.
11. Secretary of Labor.
12. Secretary of Health and Human Services.
13. Secretary of Housing and Urban Development.
14. Secretary of Transportation.
15. Secretary of Energy.
16. Secretary of Education.
17. Secretary of Veterans Affairs.

colon on July 13, 1985, he followed its provisions in temporarily transferring power to the vice president, George Bush. At 10:32 A.M., before the operation began, Reagan signed letters to the speaker of the House and the president pro tempore of the Senate directing that the vice president "shall discharge those powers and duties in my stead commencing with the administration of anesthesia to me." In the early evening of that same day, Reagan transmitted another letter to both officials announcing that he was again in charge. During this period, Vice President Bush signed no bills and took no actions as acting president. Although the Reagan administration claimed that the president's action set no precedents, most legal experts saw Reagan's acts as the first official use of the Twenty-fifth Amendment.

When the Vice Presidency Becomes Vacant

The Twenty-fifth Amendment also addresses the issue of how the president should fill a vacant vice presidency. Section 2 of the amendment simply states, "Whenever there is a vacancy in the office of the Vice President, the President shall nominate a Vice President who shall take office upon confirmation by a majority vote of both Houses of Congress." This is exactly what occurred when Richard Nixon's vice president, Spiro Agnew, resigned in 1973 because of his alleged receipt of construction contract kickbacks during his tenure as governor of Maryland. Nixon turned to Gerald Ford as his choice for vice president. After extensive hearings, both houses confirmed the appointment. Then, when Nixon resigned on August 9, 1974, Ford automatically became president and nominated as his vice president Nelson Rockefeller. Congress confirmed Ford's choice. For the first time in the history of the country, both the president and the vice president were individuals who were not elected to their positions.

The question of who shall be president if both the president and vice president die is answered by the Succession Act of 1947. If the president and vice president die, resign, or are disabled, the speaker of the House will act as president, after resigning from Congress. Next in line is the president pro tempore of the Senate, followed by the cabinet officers in the order of the creation of their department (see Table 13–3).

THE PRESIDENCY: UNFINISHED WORK

In the twentieth century, the responsibilities of world leadership and the growth of government have led to enormous changes in the American presidency. The office has changed from being that of "chief clerk" to being leader of the most powerful military in the Western world and the chief operating officer of a huge organization that affects the lives of everyone in the nation. At the same time, the relationship between the president and the electorate has changed, most notably through the growth of television as the most often used source of news. Most Americans find out what the president is doing through television news. Presidential staffs work continuously to gain favorable images and reports in the media. It may be that our nation's fixation on image and popularity keeps us from considering the substance of public policy and tackling the work of making real policy choices. Perhaps the media stardom of presidents eventually undermines the public's trust of the president, because so much attention is paid to image rather than to accomplishments. This issue will continue to attract discussion in the years to come.

The Modern President

The office of the presidency has changed drastically since the early years of the nineteenth century when presidents "walked" to work and had small clerical staffs. Today's president is a world leader as well as the head of a huge bureaucracy. The nature of the office has changed as well.

THEN	NOW
• Limited presidential responsibilities in domestic and foreign affairs.	• The president is the chief executive of the government and is seen as responsible for peace and the economic health of the nation.
• Presided over a small, mostly clerical staff.	• Presides over a huge bureaucracy.
• Elected after a relatively low-level campaign.	• Campaign continues throughout the presidential term; national campaign costs tens of millions of dollars.
• Conveyed messages to the public via newspapers.	• Conveys messages to the public via radio, TV, print, and electronic media.
• Never traveled outside the United States.	• Travels throughout the world.
• Reacted to congressional initiatives.	• Sets initiatives for Congress; proposes legislation.
• No budgetary power except the veto.	• The Office of Management and Budget (OMB) prepares the budget.

Additionally, Congress, faced with impossible tasks in regulating the huge economy and overseeing the government, has delegated much of its lawmaking power to the president. When President Clinton faced a Republican Congress in 1995, a new set of tensions arose. An activist congressional party tried to initiate legislation to scale back government. The president, using the veto power, then acted as a braking mechanism on the conservative agenda. The resulting "gridlock" reminds us that congressional-presidential relationships can change over time, and certainly they will continue to do so.

Another unresolved issue in American politics is the role of the president in engaging the nation in military action. To what extent does the War Powers Act limit presidential action? How can Congress play a role in critical war-related decisions? Combined with that concern is the uncertainty about what role the United States should play in a world without any superpower competition.

GETTING INVOLVED
Communicating with the White House

Writing to the president of the United States long has been a way for citizens to express their political opinions. The most traditional form of communication is, of course, by letter. Letters to the president should be addressed to:

THE PRESIDENT OF THE UNITED STATES
The White House
1600 Pennsylvania Avenue N.W.
Washington, D.C. 20500

If you wish to write to Hillary Rodham Clinton, letters may be sent to the First Lady at the same address. Will you get an answer? Almost certainly. The White House mail room is staffed by volunteers and paid employees who sort the mail for the president and tally the public's concerns. You may receive a standard response to your comments or a more personal, detailed response.

You can also call the White House on the telephone and leave a message for the president or First Lady. To call the switchboard, call 202-456-1414, a number publicized by former Secretary of State James Baker when he told the Israelis publicly, "When you're serious about peace, call us at . . . ." The switchboard received more than eight thousand calls in the next twenty-four hours.

The White House also has a round-the-clock comment line, which you can reach at 202-456-1111. When you call that number, an operator will take down your comments and forward them to the president's office. Again, the operators tally the calls to give the president a measurement of opinion on specific topics.

In this electronic age, the Clinton White House has been aggressive in its use of the Internet and the World Wide Web. The home page for the White House is listed in the *Logging On* feature at the end of this chapter. It is always designed to be entertaining and to convey information about the president. You can, however, easily send your comments and ideas to the White House via the Internet. Send comments to the president to

President@whitehouse.gov

Address electronic mail (e-mail) to the First Lady at

First.Lady@whitehouse.gov

You will receive an electronic response to your mail from the White House staff. Due to the extremely heavy e-mail load, you will only receive one response per day regardless of how many messages you send. Since the opening of the president's electronic mailbox in June 1993, more than a million messages have been sent to him and the First Lady.

KEY TERMS

advice and consent 445

appointment power 441

cabinet 458

chief diplomat 445

chief executive 440

chief legislator 447

chief of staff 461

chief of state 437

civil service 441

commander in chief 443

constitutional power 451

Council of Economic Advisers
  (CEA) 461

emergency power 453

executive agreement 446

Executive Office of the President
  (EOP) 460

executive order 454

executive privilege 455

expressed power 451

Federal Register 455

impeachment 457

inherent power 451

kitchen cabinet 460

line-item veto 449

National Security Council (NSC)
  461

Office of Management and
  Budget (OMB) 461

pardon 442

patronage 451

pocket veto 448

recognition power 445

reprieve 442

State of the Union message 448

statutory power 451

Twelfth Amendment 436

Twenty-fifth Amendment 463

veto message 448

War Powers Act 444

Washington community 452

White House Office 460

CHAPTER SUMMARY

❶ The office of the presidency in the United States, combining as it does the functions of chief of state and chief executive, is unique. The framers of the Constitution were divided over whether the president should be a weak executive controlled by the legislature or a strong executive.

❷ The requirements for the office of the presidency are outlined in Article II, Section 1, of the Constitution. The president's roles include both formal and informal duties. The president is chief of state, chief executive, commander in chief, chief diplomat, chief legislator, and party chief.

❸ As chief of state, the president is ceremonial head of the government. As chief executive, the president is bound to enforce the acts of Congress, the judgments of the federal courts, and treaties. The chief executive has the power of appointment and the power to grant reprieves and pardons.

❹ As commander in chief, the president is the ultimate decision maker in military matters. As chief diplomat, the president recognizes foreign governments, negotiates treaties, signs agreements, and nominates and receives ambassadors.

❺ The role of chief legislator includes recommending legislation to Congress, lobbying for the legislation, approving laws, and exercising the veto power. The president also has statutory powers written into law by Congress. The president is also leader of his or her political party. Presidents use their power to persuade and their access to the media to fulfill this function.

❻ Presidents have a variety of special powers not available to other branches of the government. These include emergency power, executive power, executive privilege, and impoundment of funds.

❼ Abuses of executive power are dealt with by Articles I and II of the Constitution, which authorizes the House and Senate to impeach and remove the president, vice president, or other officers of the federal government for crimes of "Treason, Bribery or other high Crimes and Misdemeanors."

❽ The president gets assistance from the cabinet and from the Executive Office of the President (including the White House Office).

❾ The vice president is the constitutional officer assigned to preside over the Senate and to assume the presidency in case of the death, resignation, removal, or disability of the president. The Twenty-fifth Amendment, passed in 1967, established procedures to be followed in case of presidential incapacity and when filling a vacant vice presidency.

QUESTIONS FOR REVIEW AND DISCUSSION

❶ What talents and skills must an individual have to be successful in the job of the president? To what extent should a candidate's experience, personality, and organizational skills be relevant to voting for a president?

❷ How do the president and Congress share power in policymaking and legislation? What resources does each bring to this joint lawmaking process? Should the president play a leading role in most major legislation?

❸ What factors make the presidency seem to be powerful? To what extent does the president's command of the media and access to the news enhance the public's expectations of the president and contribute to a powerful image? How does that presidential image of power contribute to the president's ability to persuade members of Congress or other national leaders to take a particular position?

LOGGING ON: THE PRESIDENCY

Back | Forward | Home | Reload | Images | Open | Print | Find | Stop

Go To: `http://www.public.iastate.edu/~sws/homepage.html`

What's New? | What's Cool? | Handbook | Net Search | Net Directory | Software

This is a site from which you can obtain all kinds of information on the White House and the presidency:

http://www.whitehouse.gov/WH/Welcome.html

The Library of Congress White House page is a great source of information and has numerous presidency-related links. The URL is

http://lcweb.loc.gov/global/executive/white_house.html

The White House archives at Texas A&M is a different type of resource. It is good for researching documents and other academic resources. You can reach it at

http://www.tamu.edu/whitehouse/

Inaugural addresses of American presidents from Washington to Clinton can be found at

http://www.columbia.edu/acis/bartleby/inaugural/index.html

The site offers biographical information, the full text of speeches, and a picture of each president. You can compare what presidents said in different periods.

A new location is

http://www.itd.umd.edu/UMS/UMCP/MCK/GUIDES/presidency/html

This guide is an annotated bibliography of the most useful general sources of information on the U.S. presidency and the federal executive branch available in the University of Maryland Libraries. Here are the current contents of this URL:

Bibliographies and Guides
Biographical Sources
Dictionaries and Encyclopedias
Directories
Indexes and Abstracts
Internet Resources
Miscellaneous
Speeches and Documents

SELECTED REFERENCES

Brace, Paul, and Barbara Hinckley. *Follow the Leader: Opinion Polls and the Modern Presidents.* New York: Basic Books, 1992. This study examines the nature, conduct, and interpretation of public opinion polls that generate presidential approval ratings. The authors identify factors, including events, that influence these ratings and question the use of such data.

Burke, John P. *The Institutional Presidency.* Baltimore: Johns Hopkins University Press, 1992. Burke gives a detailed examination of the interplay between the White House staff system and the style and management abilities of particular presidents, from Franklin Roosevelt to George Bush.

Ellis, Richard J. *Presidential Lightning Rods: The Politics of Blame Avoidance.* Lawrence, Kans.: University Press of Kansas, 1995. The author examines the tactics that presidents and their advisers use to enhance their reputations and the techniques that can be used to avoid blame for mistakes or crises.

Hinck, Edward A. *Enacting the Presidency: Political Argument, Presidential Debates, and Presidential Character.* Westport, Conn.: Praeger, 1993. The author examines the candidates in presidential debates from the Kennedy-Nixon debates through 1988. He shows how candidates used the debates in shaping their public images and how the debates demonstrate the leadership style each would bring to the office.

Jones, Charles O. *The Presidency in a Separated System.* Washington, D.C.: The Brookings Institution, 1994. Rather than decrying the gridlock of Congress and the president or looking for an imperial president, Jones discusses the constitutionally required tension between the two branches of government. By looking at twenty-eight different pieces of legislation, he is able to demonstrate the many patterns of interaction and partisanship that occur in the process of lawmaking.

Kernell, Samuel. *Going Public: New Strategies of Presidential Leadership.* 2d ed. Washington, D.C.: Congressional Quarterly Press, 1992. This fascinating book explores how presidents increasingly have bypassed the traditional process of bargaining with Congress and have "gone public" with presidential priorities in an effort to bring direct public pressure on Congress.

McDonald, Forrest. *The American Presidency: An Intellectual History.* Lawrence, Kans.: University Press of Kansas, 1994. This intellectual history traces the development of the presidency and its powers from the early colonial governors through the American Revolution, the Constitutional Convention, and the early presidents.

Mezey, Michael L. *Congress, the President, and Public Policy.* 2d ed. Boulder, Colo.: Westview Press, 1993. This book studies the relationship between the executive branch and Congress that makes it possible to pass legislation, particularly on major public policy issues. The tendency to stalemate, according to this author, is rooted in our institutions and Constitution rather than in a particular president.

Milkis, Sydney M., and Michael Nelson. *The American Presidency: Origins and Development, 1776–1990.* Washington, D.C.: Congressional Quarterly Press, 1990. This is a comprehensive overview of the American presidential office, how it has changed over time, and the factors influencing that change.

Pious, Richard M. *The Presidency.* Boston: Allyn and Bacon, 1996. In this comprehensive look at the presidency, the author uses examples from many presidencies, including the Clinton administration, to illustrate his discussions of presidential influence.

Rourke, John T. *Presidential Wars and American Democracy: Rally 'Round the Chief.* New York: Paragon House, 1993. The author traces the recent history of presidents who have chosen military action, including the Persian Gulf War, and raises a number of constitutional and theoretical issues about how a democracy should decide to use military force.

Thomas, Norman C., Joseph A. Pika, and Richard A. Watson. *The Politics of the Presidency.* 4th ed. Washington, D.C.: Congressional Quarterly Press, 1996. This excellent, up-to-date book covers the changing presidency as well as the relationship between the president and the other two branches of government.

Watson, Richard A. *Presidential Vetoes and Public Policy.* Lawrence, Kans.: University Press of Kansas, 1995. Watson discusses the use of the veto by presidents and its influence on lawmaking.

14
The Bureaucracy

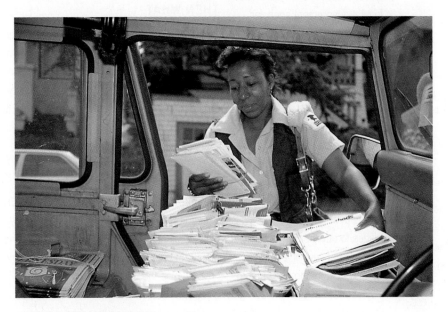

CHAPTER OUTLINE

☆ The Nature of Bureaucracy

☆ Theories of Bureaucracy

☆ The Size of the Bureaucracy

☆ The Organization of the Federal Bureaucracy

☆ Staffing the Bureaucracy

☆ Modern Attempts at Bureaucratic Reform

☆ Bureaucrats as Politicians and Policymakers

☆ Congressional Control of the Bureaucracy

Some Agencies Were Privatized?

BACKGROUND

THE FEDERAL BUREAUCRACY CURRENTLY INCLUDES NUMEROUS INDEPENDENT EXECUTIVE AGENCIES, INDEPENDENT REGULATORY AGENCIES, AND SO-CALLED GOVERNMENT CORPORATIONS. MANY OF THESE FEDERAL GOVERNMENT AGENCIES, SUCH AS THE CENTRAL INTELLIGENCE AGENCY, PROVIDE SERVICES THAT ARE HIGHLY SENSITIVE. OTHERS, SUCH AS THE NATIONAL SCIENCE FOUNDATION, EXIST SIMPLY TO GIVE AWAY MONEY FOR SPECIFIC PURPOSES. STILL OTHERS, SUCH AS THE U.S. POSTAL SERVICE, PROVIDE FOR-FEE SERVICES THAT IN EFFECT COMPETE WITH PRIVATE-SECTOR SERVICES.

WHAT IF SOME AGENCIES WERE PRIVATIZED?

Throughout the world, governments are selling all or part of government-owned agencies and companies to private investors, including both individuals and existing corporations. Certainly, in the United States, we cannot imagine auctioning off, say, the Central Intelligence Agency to the highest private bidder. Nonetheless, numerous federal government agencies conceivably could be privatized. In particular, it has been proposed that the Federal Aviation Administration (FAA), the U.S. Postal Service, and the National Mediation Board could be privatized.

There are many methods by which government-owned operations can be privatized. One option would be to issue and sell shares directly to anybody who wishes to buy them. Eventually, a group would control a large enough percentage of shares to elect a board of directors so that the group could steer the newly privatized agency in a particular direction.

Another option would be to offer to sell a government agency to existing corporations that already might be engaged in similar lines of business. The U.S. Postal Service, for example, could be offered for sale to existing delivery companies, such as United Parcel Service (UPS), Federal Express, DHL, and Airborne. Finally, some of the larger agencies that are spread throughout the United States, such as the FAA, could be offered for sale in small chunks. For example, each airport control system could be offered for sale to investors in that particular city.

AFTER PRIVATIZATION, THEN WHAT?

It is certain that any federal government agency that became privatized would be subject to a much greater extent to the not-so-tender mercies of the marketplace. If the Tennessee Valley Authority (a government agency that provides electricity to a wide region at relatively low rates) were privatized, it would be forced to take account of the true costs of all of its operations. Ultimately, to meet its costs, it would have to raise the price of electricity to its customers.

Consider other examples. The U.S. Postal Service probably would be run more like Federal Express and UPS. If it were, U.S. postal workers, who are now part of a very strong union, would find privatized postal management much less willing to accept union demands for higher wages. The National Mediation Board would have to bill unions and businesses for its mediation services in labor-management disputes.

THE DOWN SIDE TO PRIVATIZATION

Critics of the concept of privatizing certain federal agencies point out that not everything should be run for a profit. They argue, for example, that if the U.S. Postal Service were privatized, mail delivery to rural Americans might become too expensive. This might cause more people to move to the cities, which already are overcrowded. If the National Mediation Board had to charge the full cost for all of its services, perhaps some labor-management disputes would take longer to resolve because of the reluctance of the parties to pay more for mediation services.

FOR CRITICAL ANALYSIS

1. *Which additional agencies and government operations are likely candidates for privatization? Why?*
2. *Which government agencies and operations clearly are not candidates for privatization? Why?*

Virtually every modern president, at one time or another, has proclaimed that his administration was going to "fix government." Virtually every modern president has claimed that government is too big and unwieldy. As you can see in Table 14–1, all modern presidents also have put forth plans to end government inefficiency. While none has come out in favor of privatizing selected federal government agencies, as this chapter's opening *What If . . .* suggested, they all have declared war on government waste and inefficiency. Their success has been, in a word, underwhelming.

Presidents have been virtually powerless to affect significantly the structure and operation of the federal bureaucracy. It has been called the "fourth branch of government," even though you will find no reference to the bureaucracy in the original Constitution or in the twenty-seven amendments that have been passed since 1787. But Article II, Section 2, of the Constitution gives the president the power to appoint "all other Officers of the United States, whose Appointments are not herein otherwise provided for." Article II, Section 3, states that the president "shall take Care that the Laws be faithfully executed, and shall Commission all the Officers of the United States." Constitutional scholars believe that the legal basis for the bureaucracy rests on these two sections in Article II.

THE NATURE OF BUREAUCRACY

A **bureaucracy** is the name given to a large organization that is structured hierarchically to carry out specific functions. Generally, most bureaucracies are characterized by an organization chart. The units of the organization are divided according to the specialization and expertise of the employees.

Public and Private Bureaucracies

We should not think of bureaucracy as unique to government. Any large corporation or university can be considered a bureaucratic organization. The fact is that the handling of complex problems requires a division of labor. Individuals must concentrate their skills on specific, well-defined aspects of a problem and depend on others to solve the rest of it.

Public or government bureaucracies differ from private organizations in some important ways, however. A private corporation, such as Microsoft, has a single set of leaders, its board of directors. Public bureaucracies, in contrast,

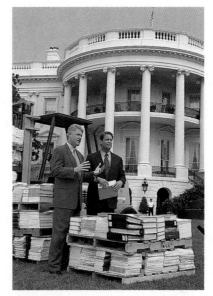

One of Vice President Gore's first tasks was to help President Clinton "change government as we know it." Gore was responsible for managing a project that became known as "reinventing government." Here Clinton and Gore announce the publication of their program on how to reinvent government. The book and manuals surrounding them represent existing government regulations, many of which they suggested should be eliminated.

BUREAUCRACY

A large organization that is structured hierarchically to carry out specific functions.

Table 14–1

Selected Presidential Plans to End Government Inefficiency

PRESIDENT	NAME OF PLAN
Lyndon Johnson (1963–1969)	Programming, Planning, and Budgeting Systems
Richard Nixon (1969–1974)	Management by Objectives
Jimmy Carter (1977–1981)	Zero-Based Budgeting
Ronald Reagan (1981–1989)	President's Private Sector Survey on Cost Control (the Grace Commission)
George Bush (1989–1993)	Right-Sizing Government
Bill Clinton (1993–)	"From Red Tape to Results: Creating a Government That Works Better and Costs Less"

DID YOU KNOW...
That in Great Britain, bureaucrats have only one boss—the head of the particular ministry in which they are employed—but in the United States, authority over the bureaucracy is divided between the legislative and the executive branches of government?

do not have a single set of leaders. Although the president is the chief administrator of the federal system, all bureaucratic agencies are subject to the desires of Congress for their funding, staffing, and indeed, for their continued existence. Furthermore, public bureaucracies supposedly serve the citizen rather than the stockholder.

One other important difference between private corporations and government bureaucracies is that government bureaucracies are not organized to make a profit. Rather, they are supposed to perform their functions as efficiently as possible to conserve the taxpayers' dollars. Perhaps it is this aspect of government organization that makes citizens hostile toward government employees when citizens experience inefficiency and red tape.

These characteristics, together with the prevalence and size of the government bureaucracies, make them an important factor in American life.

Bureaucracies Compared Across Countries

The federal bureaucracy in the United States enjoys a greater degree of autonomy than do federal or national bureaucracies in most other countries. Much of the insularity that is commonly supposed to characterize the bureaucracy in this country may stem from the sheer size of the government organizations needed to implement a budget that exceeds $1.7 trillion. Because the lines of authority often are not well defined, some bureaucracies may be able to operate with a significant degree of autonomy.

The federal nature of the American government also means that national bureaucracies regularly provide financial assistance to their state counterparts. Both the Department of Education and the Department of Housing and Urban Development, for example, distribute funds to their counterparts at the state level. In contrast, most bureaucracies in European countries have a top-down command structure so that national programs may be implemented directly at the lower level. This is due not only to the small size of most European countries but also to the fact that public ownership of such things as telephone companies, airlines, railroads, and utilities is far more common in Europe than in the United States.

The fact that the U.S. government owns relatively few enterprises does not mean, however, that its bureaucracies are comparatively powerless. Indeed, there are numerous **administrative agencies** in the federal bureaucracy—such as the Environmental Protection Agency, the Nuclear Regulatory Commission, and the Securities and Exchange Commission—that extensively regulate private companies even though they virtually never have an ownership interest in those companies.

ADMINISTRATIVE AGENCY

An agency that forms part of the executive branch, an independent agency, or an independent regulatory agency (for example, the Federal Trade Commission, the Securities and Exchange Commission, and the Federal Communications Commission). State and local governments also have administrative agencies.

THEORIES OF BUREAUCRACY

Several theories have been offered to help us understand better the ways in which bureaucracies function. Each of these theories focuses on specific features of bureaucracies.

The Weberian Model

WEBERIAN MODEL

A model of bureaucracy developed by the German sociologist Max Weber, who viewed bureaucracies as rational, hierarchical organizations in which power flows from the top downward and decisions are based on logical reasoning and data analysis.

The classic model, or **Weberian model,** of the modern bureaucracy was proposed by the German sociologist Max Weber.[1] He argued that the increas-

---

[1]Max Weber, *Theory of Social and Economic Organization,* ed. by Talcott Parsons (New York: Oxford University Press, 1974).

The Department of Agriculture inspects meat-packing facilities throughout the United States, certifying the quality and condition of the meat to be sold.

ingly complex nature of modern life, coupled with the steadily growing demands placed on governments by their citizens, made the formation of bureaucracies inevitable. According to Weber, most bureaucracies—whether in the public or private sector—are hierarchically organized and governed by formal procedures. The power in a bureaucracy flows from the top downward. Decision-making processes in bureaucracies are shaped by detailed technical rules that promote similar decisions in similar situations. Bureaucrats are specialists who attempt to resolve problems through logical reasoning and data analysis instead of "gut feelings" and guesswork. Individual advancement in bureaucracies is supposed to be based on merit rather than political connections. Indeed, the modern bureaucracy, according to Weber, should be an apolitical organization.

The Acquisitive Model

Other theorists do not view bureaucracies in terms as benign as Weber's. Some believe that bureaucracies are acquisitive in nature. Proponents of the **acquisitive model** argue that top-level bureaucrats will always try to expand, or at least to avoid any reductions in, the size of their budgets. Although government bureaucracies are not-for-profit enterprises, bureaucrats want to maximize the size of their budgets and staffs, because these things are the most visible trappings of power in the public sector. These efforts are also prompted by the desire of bureaucrats to "sell" their product—national defense, public housing, agricultural subsidies, and so on—to both Congress and the public.

ACQUISITIVE MODEL

A model of bureaucracy that views top-level bureaucrats as seeking constantly to expand the size of their budgets and the staffs of their departments or agencies so as to gain greater power and influence in the public sector.

The Monopolistic Model

Because government bureaucracies seldom have competitors, some theorists have suggested that bureaucratic organizations may be explained best by using a **monopolistic model.** The analysis is similar to that used by economists to examine the behavior of monopolistic firms. Monopolistic bureaucracies—like monopolistic firms—are less efficient and more costly to operate because they have no competitors. Because monopolistic bureaucracies are

MONOPOLISTIC MODEL

A model of bureaucracy that compares bureaucracies to monopolistic business firms. Lack of competition within a bureaucracy leads to inefficient and costly operations, just as it does within monopolistic firms. Because bureaucracies are not penalized for inefficiency, there is no incentive to save costs or use resources more productively.

Figure 14–1

● ● ● ● ● ● ● ● ● ● ● ● ● ● ● ● ● ● ●

Federal Agencies and Their Respective Numbers of Civilian Employees

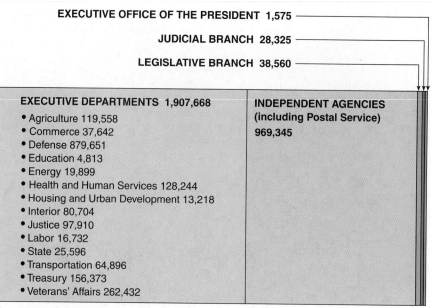

EXECUTIVE OFFICE OF THE PRESIDENT **1,575**

JUDICIAL BRANCH **28,325**

LEGISLATIVE BRANCH **38,560**

EXECUTIVE DEPARTMENTS **1,907,668**	INDEPENDENT AGENCIES (including Postal Service) **969,345**
• Agriculture 119,558 • Commerce 37,642 • Defense 879,651 • Education 4,813 • Energy 19,899 • Health and Human Services 128,244 • Housing and Urban Development 13,218 • Interior 80,704 • Justice 97,910 • Labor 16,732 • State 25,596 • Transportation 64,896 • Treasury 156,373 • Veterans' Affairs 262,432	

SOURCE: U.S. Department of Commerce, *Statistical Abstract of the United States* (Washinton, D.C.: U.S. Government Printing Office, 1996).

GARBAGE CAN MODEL

A model of bureaucracy that characterizes bureaucracies as rudderless entities with little formal organization in which solutions to problems are based on trial and error rather than rational policy planning.

Figure 14–2

● ● ● ● ● ● ● ● ● ● ● ● ● ● ● ● ● ● ●

Government Employment at Federal, State, and Local Levels

There are more local government employees than federal and state employees combined.

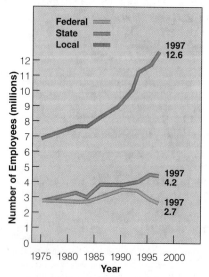

SOURCE: U.S. Department of Labor, Bureau of Labor Statistics, *Monthly Labor Review*, October 1994. 1997 data are estimates.

not usually penalized for chronic inefficiency, they have little reason to adopt cost-saving measures or to make more productive uses of their resources. Some economists have argued that such problems can be cured only by privatizing certain bureaucratic functions.

The Garbage Can Model

The image of a bumbling, rudderless organization is offered by proponents of the **garbage can model** of bureaucracy. This theory presupposes that bureaucracies rarely act in any purposeful or coherent manner but instead bumble along aimlessly in search of solutions to particular problems. This model views bureaucracies as having relatively little formal organization. The solutions to problems are obtained not by the smooth implementation of well-planned policies but instead by trial and error. Choosing the right policy is tricky, because usually it is not possible to determine in advance which solution is best. Thus, bureaucrats may have to try one, two, three, or even more policies before they obtain a satisfactory result.

THE SIZE OF THE BUREAUCRACY

In 1789, the new government's bureaucracy was minuscule. There were three departments—State (with nine employees), War (with two employees), and Treasury (with thirty-nine employees). This bureaucracy was still small in 1798. At that time, the secretary of state had seven clerks and spent a total of $500 (about $5,500 in 1997 dollars) on stationery and printing. In that same year, the Appropriations Act allocated $1.4 million to the War Department (or $15 million in 1997 dollars).[2]

Times have changed, as we can see in Figure 14–1, which lists the various federal agencies and the number of civilian employees in each. Excluding the military, approximately 2.9 million government employees constitute the fed-

[2]Leonard D. White *The Federalists: A Study in Administrative History, 1789–1801* (New York: Free Press, 1948).

eral bureaucracy. That number has remained relatively stable for the last several decades. It is somewhat deceiving, however, because there are many others working directly or indirectly for the federal government as subcontractors or consultants and in other capacities.

The figures for federal government employment are only part of the story. Figure 14–2 shows the growth in government employment at the federal, state, and local levels. Since 1970, this growth has been mainly at the state and local levels. If all government employees are counted, then, over 15 percent of all civilian employment is accounted for by the government.

The costs of the bureaucracy are commensurately high and growing. The share of the gross national product taken up by government spending was only 8.5 percent in 1929, but today it exceeds 40 percent.

THE ORGANIZATION OF THE FEDERAL BUREAUCRACY

Within the federal bureaucracy are a number of different types of government agencies and organizations. Figure 14–3 outlines the several bureaucracies

DID YOU KNOW...
That the federal government spends over $1 billion every 6 hours, 365 days a year?

Figure 14–3
● ●
Organization Chart of the Federal Government

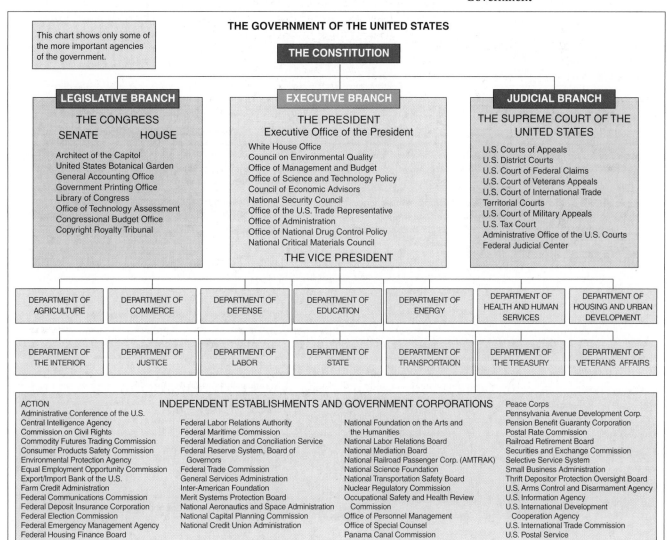

SOURCE: *U.S. Government Manual, 1995–1996.*

DID YOU KNOW ...
That the Commerce Department's U.S. Travel and Tourism Administration recently gave away $440,000 in so-called disaster relief to western ski resort operators because there hadn't been enough snow?

within the executive branch, as well as the separate organizations that provide services to Congress, to the courts, and directly to the president. In Chapter 13, we discussed those agencies that are considered to be part of the Executive Office of the President.

The executive branch, which employs most of the bureaucrats, has four major types of bureaucratic structures. They are (1) cabinet departments, (2) independent executive agencies, (3) independent regulatory agencies, and (4) government corporations. Each has a distinctive relationship to the president, and some have unusual internal structures, overall goals, and grants of power.

Cabinet Departments

CABINET DEPARTMENT

One of the fourteen departments of the executive branch (State, Treasury, Defense, Justice, Interior, Agriculture, Commerce, Labor, Health and Human Services, Housing and Urban Development, Education, Energy, Transportation, and Veterans Affairs).

LINE ORGANIZATION

Government or corporate units that provide direct services or products for the public.

The fourteen **cabinet departments** are the major service organizations of the federal government. They can also be described in management terms as **line organizations.** This means that they are directly accountable to the president and are responsible for performing government functions, such as printing money or training troops. These departments were created by Congress when the need for each department arose. The first department to be created was State, and the most recent one was Veterans Affairs, established in 1988. A president might ask that a new department be created or an old one abolished, but the president has no power to do so without legislative approval from Congress.

Table 14–2

Executive Departments

DEPARTMENT AND YEAR ESTABLISHED	PRINCIPAL DUTIES	MOST IMPORTANT SUBAGENCIES
State (1789) (25,596 employees)	Negotiates treaties; develops foreign policy; protects citizens abroad.	Passport Agency; Bureau of Diplomatic Security; Foreign Service; Bureau of Human Rights and Humanitarian Affairs; Bureau of Consular Affairs.
Treasury (1789) (156,373 employees)	Pays all federal bills; borrows money; collects federal taxes; mints coins and prints paper currency; operates the Secret Service; supervises national banks.	Internal Revenue Service (IRS); Bureau of Alcohol, Tobacco, and Firearms; U.S. Secret Service; U.S. Mint; Customs Service.
Interior (1849) (80,704 employees)	Supervises federally owned lands and parks; operates federal hydroelectric power facilities; supervises Native American affairs.	U.S. Fish and Wildlife Service; National Park Service; Bureau of Indian Affairs; Bureau of Land Management.
Justice (1870)* (97,910 employees)	Furnishes legal advice to the president; enforces federal criminal laws; supervises the federal corrections system (prisons).	Federal Bureau of Investigation (FBI); Drug Enforcement Administration (DEA); Bureau of Prisons (BOP); Immigration and Naturalization Service (INS).
Agriculture (1889) (119,558 employees)	Provides assistance to farmers and ranchers; conducts research to improve agricultural activity and to prevent plant disease; works to protect forests from fires and disease.	Soil Conservation Service; Agricultural Research Service; Food and Safety Inspection Service; Federal Crop Insurance Corporation; Farmers Home Administration.
Commerce (1913)† (37,642 employees)	Grants patents and trademarks; conducts a national census; monitors the weather; protects the interests of businesses.	Bureau of the Census; Bureau of Economic Analysis; Minority Business Development Agency; Patent and Trademark Office; National Oceanic and Atmospheric Administration; U.S. Travel and Tourism Administration.
Labor (1913) (16,732 employees)	Administers federal labor laws; promotes the interests of workers.	Occupational Safety and Health Administration (OSHA); Bureau of Labor Statistics; Employment Standards Administration; Office of Labor-Management Standards.

*Formed from the Office of the Attorney General (created in 1789).
†Formed from the Department of Commerce and Labor (created in 1903).

Each department is headed by a secretary (except for the Justice Department, which is headed by the attorney general) and has several levels of undersecretaries, assistant secretaries, and so on.

Presidents theoretically have considerable control over the cabinet departments, because presidents are able to appoint or fire all of the top officials. Even cabinet departments do not always respond to the president's wishes, though. One reason for the frequent unhappiness of presidents with their departments is that the entire bureaucratic structure below the top political levels is staffed by permanent employees, many of whom are committed to established programs or procedures and who resist change. As we can see from Table 14–2, each cabinet department employs thousands of individuals, only a handful of whom are under the control of the president. The table also describes the functions of each of the cabinet departments.

Independent Executive Agencies

Independent executive agencies are bureaucratic organizations that are not located within a department and report directly to the president, who appoints their chief officials. When a new federal agency is created—the Environmental Protection Agency, for example—a decision is made by Congress about where it will be located in the bureaucracy. In this century, presidents often have asked that a new organization be kept separate or independent rather than added to an existing department, particularly if a

DID YOU KNOW...
That the Pentagon and the Central Intelligence Agency spent over $11 million on psychics who were supposed to provide special insights regarding various foreign threats?

INDEPENDENT EXECUTIVE AGENCY

A federal agency that is not part of a cabinet department but reports directly to the president.

Table 14–2, Continued

Executive Departments

DEPARTMENT AND YEAR ESTABLISHED	PRINCIPAL DUTIES	MOST IMPORTANT SUBAGENCIES
Defense (1947)‡ (879,651 employees)	Manages the armed forces (army, navy, air force, and marines); operates military bases; is responsible for civil defense.	National Guard; National Security Agency; Joint Chiefs of Staff; Departments of the Air Force, Navy, Army.
Housing and Urban Development (1965) (13,218 employees)	Deals with the nation's housing needs; develops and rehabilitates urban communities; promotes improvement in city streets and parks.	Assistant Secretary for Community Planning and Development; Government National Mortgage Association; Assistant Secretary for Housing—Federal Housing Commissioner; Assistant Secretary for Fair Housing and Equal Opportunity.
Transportation (1967) (64,896 employees)	Finances improvements in mass transit; develops and administers programs for highways, railroads, and aviation; is involved with offshore maritime safety.	Federal Aviation Administration (FAA); Federal Highway Administration; National Highway Traffic Safety Administration; U.S. Coast Guard; Federal Transit Administration.
Energy (1977) (19,899 employees)	Is involved in the conservation of energy and resources; analyzes energy data; conducts research and development.	Office of Civilian Radioactive Waste Management; Bonneville Power Administration; Office of Nuclear Energy; Energy Information Administration; Office of Conservation and Renewable Energy.
Health and Human Services (1979)§ (128,244 employees)	Promotes public health; enforces pure food and drug laws; is involved in health-related research.	Food and Drug Administration; Administration for Children and Families; Health Care Financing Administration; Public Health Service.
Education (1979)§§ (4,813 employees)	Coordinates federal programs and policies for education; administers aid to education; promotes educational research.	Office of Special Education and Rehabilitation Services; Office of Elementary and Secondary Education; Office of Postsecondary Education; Office of Vocational and Adult Education.
Veterans Affairs (1988) (262,432 employees)	Promotes the welfare of veterans of the U.S. armed forces.	Veterans Health Administration; Veterans Benefits Administration; National Cemetery System.

‡Formed from the Department of War (created in 1789) and the Department of Navy (created in 1798).
§Formed from the Department of Health, Education, and Welfare (created in 1953).
§§Formed from the Department of Health, Education, and Welfare (created in 1953).

department may in fact be hostile to the agency's creation. Table 14–3 describes the functions of several selected independent executive agencies.

Independent Regulatory Agencies

INDEPENDENT REGULATORY AGENCY

An agency outside the major executive departments charged with making and implementing rules and regulations to protect the public interest.

The **independent regulatory agencies** are typically responsible for a specific type of public policy. Their function is to make and implement rules and regulations in a particular sector of the economy to protect the public interest. The earliest such agency was the Interstate Commerce Commission (ICC), which was established in 1887 when Americans began to seek some form of government control over the rapidly growing business and industrial sector. This new form of organization, the independent regulatory agency, was supposed to make technical, nonpolitical decisions about rates, profits, and rules that would be for the benefit of all and that did not require congressional legislation. In the years that followed the creation of the ICC, other agencies were formed to regulate communication (the Federal Communications Commission), nuclear power (the Nuclear Regulatory Commission), and so on. (The ICC was abolished on December 30, 1995.)

The Purpose and Nature of Regulatory Agencies. The regulatory agencies are administered independently of all three branches of government. They were set up because Congress felt it was unable to handle the complexities and technicalities required to carry out specific laws in the public interest. The regulatory commissions in fact combine some functions of all three branches of government—executive, legislative, and judicial. They are legislative in that they make rules that have the force of law. They are executive in that they provide for the enforcement of those rules. They are judicial in that they decide disputes involving the rules they have made.

Table 14–3

Selected Independent Executive Agencies

NAME	DATE FORMED	PRINCIPAL DUTIES
Central Intelligence Agency (CIA)*	1947	Gathers and analyzes political and military information about foreign countries so that the United States can improve its own political and military status; conducts activities outside the United States, with the goal of countering the work of intelligence services operated by other nations whose political philosophies are inconsistent with our own.
General Services Administration (GSA) (16,698 employees)	1949	Purchases and manages all property of the federal government; acts as the business arm of the federal government in overseeing federal government spending projects; discovers overcharges in government programs.
National Science Foundation (NSF) (1,250 employees)	1950	Promotes scientific research; provides grants to all levels of schools for instructional programs in the sciences.
Small Business Administration (SBA) (5,524 employees)	1953	Protects the interests of small businesses; provides low-cost loans and management information to small businesses.
National Aeronautics and Space Administration (NASA) (21,996 employees)	1958	Is responsible for the U.S. space program, including the building, testing, and operating of space vehicles.
Environmental Protection Agency (EPA) (18,297 employees)	1970	Undertakes programs aimed at reducing air and water pollution; works with state and local agencies to help fight environmental hazards. (It has been suggested recently that its status be elevated to that of a cabinet department.)

*The CIA will not release information on the number of employees who work for this agency (because it is "classified information").

Regulatory agency members are appointed by the president with the consent of the Senate, although they do not report to the president. By law, the members of regulatory agencies cannot all be from the same political party. Presidents can influence regulatory agency behavior by appointing people of their own parties or people who share their political views when vacancies occur, in particular when the chair is vacant. Members may be removed by the president only for causes specified in the law creating the agency. Table 14–4 describes the functions of several selected independent agencies.

Over the last several decades, some observers have concluded that these agencies, although nominally independent may in fact not always be so. They also contend that many independent regulatory agencies have been **captured** by the very industries and firms that they were supposed to regulate. The results have been less competition rather than more competition, higher prices rather than lower prices, and less choice rather than more choice for consumers.

Deregulation and Reregulation.   During the presidency of Ronald Reagan in the 1980s, some significant deregulation (the removal of regulatory restraints—the opposite of regulation) occurred, much of which started under President Jimmy Carter. For example, Carter appointed a chairperson of the Civil Aeronautics Board (CAB) who gradually eliminated regulation of airline fares and routes. Then, under Reagan, the CAB was eliminated on January 1, 1985. During the Bush administration, calls for *re*regulation of many businesses increased. Indeed, under President Bush, the Americans with Disabilities Act of 1990, the Civil Rights Act of 1991, and the Clean Air Act Amendments of 1991, all of which increased or changed the regulation of many businesses, were passed. Additionally, there was the passage of the

DID YOU KNOW...
That there are nineteen military golf courses around Washington, D.C., yet the Pentagon announced that it would spend over $5 million to build a new one at Andrews Air Force Base in suburban Maryland?

CAPTURE

The act of gaining direct or indirect control over agency personnel and decision makers by the industry that is being regulated.

Table 14–4

Selected Independent Regulatory Agencies

NAME	DATE FORMED	PRINCIPAL DUTIES
Federal Reserve System Board of Governors (Fed) (1,760 employees)	1913	Determines policy with respect to interest rates, credit availability, and the money supply.
Federal Trade Commission (FTC) (1,000 employees)	1914	Prevents businesses from engaging in unfair trade practices; stops the formation of monopolies in the business sector; protects consumer rights.
Securities and Exchange Commission (SEC) (2,803 employees)	1934	Regulates the nation's stock exchanges, in which shares of stocks are bought and sold; requires full disclosure of the financial profiles of companies that wish to sell stocks and bonds to the public.
Federal Communications Commission (FCC) (2,055 employees)	1934	Regulates all communications by telegraph, cable, telephone, radio, and television.
National Labor Relations Board (NLRB) (1,945 employees)	1935	Protects employees' rights to join unions and bargain collectively with employers; attempts to prevent unfair labor practices by both employers and unions.
Equal Employment Opportunity Commission (EEOC) (2,838 employees)	1964	Works to eliminate discrimination based on religion, sex, race, color, national origin, age, or disability; examines claims of discrimination.
Federal Election Commission (FEC) (390 employees)	1974	Ensures that candidates and states follow the rules established by the Federal Election Campaign Act.
Nuclear Regulatory Commission (NRC) (3,264 employees)	1974	Ensures that electricity-generating nuclear reactors in the United States are built and operated safely; regularly inspects the operations of such reactors.

GOVERNMENT CORPORATION

An agency of government that administers a quasi-business enterprise. These corporations are used when activities are primarily commercial. They produce revenue for their continued existence, and they require greater flexibility than is permitted for departments and agencies.

Cable Reregulation Act of 1992. Under President Clinton, the Interstate Commerce Commission was eliminated, but there has been increased environmental regulation and regulation of the banking industry. Additionally, major attempts to institute general regulatory reform were made in Congress. So far, no significant legislation of that nature has been passed.

Government Corporations

The newest form of bureaucratic organization to be adopted in the United States is the **government corporation.** Although the concept is borrowed from the world of business, distinct differences exist between public and private corporations.

A private corporation has shareholders (stockholders) who elect a board of directors, who in turn choose the corporate officers, such as president and vice president. When a private corporation makes a profit, it must pay taxes (unless it avoids them through various legal loopholes). It either distributes part or all of the after-tax profits to shareholders as dividends or plows the profits back into the corporation to make new investments.

A government corporation has a board of directors and managers, but it does not have any stockholders. We cannot buy shares of stock in a government corporation. If the government corporation makes a profit, it does not distribute the profit as dividends. Also, if it makes a profit, it does not have to pay taxes; the profits remain in the corporation. Table 14–5 describes the functions of selected government corporations.

STAFFING THE BUREAUCRACY

There are two categories of bureaucrats: political appointees and civil servants. As noted earlier, the president is able to make political appointments to most of the top jobs in the federal bureaucracy. The president also can appoint ambassadors to the most important foreign posts. All of the jobs that are considered "political plums" and that usually go to the politically well connected are listed in *Policy and Supporting Positions*, published by the Government Printing Office after each presidential election. This has been infor-

U.S. Postal Service employees sort the mail during the night shift at a New York post office.

mally (and correctly) called "The Plum Book." The rest of the individuals who work for the national government belong to the civil service and obtain their jobs through a much more formal process.

Political Appointees

To fill the positions listed in "The Plum Book," the president and the president's advisers solicit suggestions from politicians, businesspersons, and other prominent individuals. Appointments to these positions offer the president a way to pay off outstanding political debts. But the president must also take into consideration such things as the candidate's work experience, intelligence, political affiliations, and personal characteristics. Presidents have differed over the importance they attach to appointing women and minorities to plum positions. Presidents often use ambassadorships, however, to reward selected individuals for their campaign contributions.

Political appointees are in some sense the aristocracy of the federal government. But their powers, although appearing formidable on paper, are often exaggerated. Like the president, a political appointee will occupy his or her position for a comparatively brief time. Political appointees often leave office before the president's term actually ends. The average term of service for political appointees is less than two years. As a result, the professional civil servants who make up the permanent civil service but serve under a normally temporary political appointee may not feel compelled to carry out their current boss's directives quickly, because they know that he or she will not be around for very long.

This inertia is compounded by the fact that it is extremely difficult to discharge civil servants. In recent years, less than one-tenth of 1 percent of federal employees have been fired for incompetence. Because discharged employees may appeal their dismissals, many months or even years may pass before the issue is resolved conclusively. This occupational rigidity helps to ensure that most political appointees, no matter how competent or driven, will not be able to exert much meaningful influence over their subordinates, let alone implement dramatic changes in the bureaucracy itself. Of course, there are excep-

> **DID YOU KNOW...**
> That the federal Helium Program was started in 1925 to keep our blimps afloat, and that thirty-two billion cubic feet of helium are still stored today in Amarillo, Texas?

Table 14–5

Selected Government Corporations

NAME	DATE FORMED	PRINCIPAL DUTIES
Tennessee Valley Authority (TVA) (16,587 employees)	1933	Operates a Tennessee River control system and generates power for a seven-state region and for the U.S. aeronautics and space programs; promotes the economic development of the Tennessee Valley region; controls floods and promotes the navigability of the Tennessee River.
Federal Deposit Insurance Corporation (FDIC) (15,712 employees)	1933	Insures individuals' bank deposits up to $100,000; oversees the business activities of banks.
Export/Import Bank of the United States (Ex/Im Bank) (438 employees)	1933	Promotes American-made goods abroad; grants loans to foreign purchasers of American products.
National Railroad Passenger Corporation (AMTRAK) (23,000 employees)	1970	Provides a balanced national and inter-city rail passenger service network; controls 23,000 miles of track with 505 stations.
U.S. Postal Service* (839,381 employees)	1970	Delivers mail throughout the United States and its territories; is the largest government corporation.

*Formed from the Office of the Postmaster General in the Department of the Treasury (created in 1789).

DID YOU KNOW...
That the U.S. Postal Service, with almost 840,000 employees, is the largest civilian employer in the United States?

NATURAL ARISTOCRACY

A small ruling clique of the state's "best" citizens, whose membership is based on birth, wealth, and ability. The Jeffersonian era emphasized government rule by such a group.

SPOILS SYSTEM

The awarding of government jobs to political supporters and friends; generally associated with President Andrew Jackson.

MERIT SYSTEM

The selection, retention, and promotion of government employees on the basis of competitive examinations.

PENDLETON ACT (CIVIL SERVICE REFORM ACT)

The law, as amended over the years, that remains the basic statute regulating federal employment personnel policies. It established the principle of employment on the basis of merit and created the Civil Service Commission to administer the personnel service.

CIVIL SERVICE COMMISSION

The initial central personnel agency of the national government; created in 1883.

tions. Under the Civil Service Reform Act of 1978, for example, senior employees can be transferred within their departments and receive salary bonuses and other benefits as incentives for being productive and responsive to the goals and policy preferences of their politically appointed superiors.

History of the Federal Civil Service

When the federal government was formed in 1789, it had no career public servants but rather consisted of amateurs who were almost all Federalists. When Thomas Jefferson took over as president, he found that few in his party were holding federal administrative jobs, so he fired more than one hundred officials and replaced them with members of the so-called **natural aristocracy**—that is, with his own Jeffersonian (Democratic) Republicans. For the next twenty-five years, a growing body of federal administrators gained experience and expertise, becoming in the process professional public servants. These administrators stayed in office regardless of who was elected president. The bureaucracy had become a self-maintaining, long-term element within government.

To the Victor Belong the Spoils. When Andrew Jackson took over the White House in 1828, he could not believe how many appointed officials (appointed before he became president, that is) were overtly hostile toward him and his Democratic party. The bureaucracy—indeed an aristocracy—considered itself the only group fit to rule. But Jackson was a man of the people, and his policies were populist in nature. As the bureaucracy was reluctant to carry out his programs, Jackson did the obvious: he fired federal officials—more than had all his predecessors combined. The **spoils system**—an application of the principle that to the victor belong the spoils—reigned. The aristocrats were out, and the common folk were in. The spoils system was not, of course, a Jacksonian invention. Thomas Jefferson, too, had used this system of patronage in which the boss, or patron, rewards those who worked to get him or her elected.

The Civil Service Reform Act of 1883. Jackson's spoils system survived for a number of years, but it became increasingly corrupt. Also, the size of the bureaucracy increased by 300 percent between 1851 and 1881. Reformers began to examine the professional civil service that was established in several European countries, which operated under a **merit system** in which job appointments were based on competitive examinations. The cry for civil service reform began to be heard more loudly.

In 1883, the **Pendleton Act**—or **Civil Service Reform Act**—was passed, bringing to a close the period of Jacksonian spoils. The act established the principle of employment on the basis of open, competitive examinations and created the **Civil Service Commission** to administer the personnel service. Only 10 percent of federal employees were covered initially by the merit system. Later laws, amendments, and executive orders, however, increased the coverage to more than 90 percent of the federal civil service.

The Supreme Court put an even heavier lid on the spoils system in *Elrod v. Burns*[3] in 1976 and *Branti v. Finkel*[4] in 1980. In those two cases, the Court used the First Amendment to forbid government officials from discharging or threatening to discharge public employees solely for not being supporters of

[3] 427 U.S. 347 (1976).
[4] 445 U.S. 507 (1980).

The assassination of President James A. Garfield on September 19, 1881, was by a disappointed office seeker, Charles J. Guiteau. The long-term effect of this event was to replace the spoils system with a permanent career civil service, with the passage of the Pendleton Act in 1883, which established the Civil Service Commission.

the political party in power unless party affiliation is an appropriate requirement for the position. Additional curbs on political patronage were added in *Rutan v. Republican Party of Illinois*[5] in 1990. The Court's ruling effectively prevented the use of partisan political considerations as the basis for hiring, promoting, or transferring most public employees. An exception was permitted, however, for senior policymaking positions, which usually go to officials who will support the programs of the elected leaders. (See the *Politics and the Constitution* in Chapter 9 for a more detailed discussion of political patronage and the First Amendment.)

The Hatch Act of 1939.   The growing size of the federal bureaucracy created the potential for political manipulation. In principle, a civil servant is politically neutral. But civil servants certainly know that it is politicians who pay the bills through their appropriations and that it is politicians who decide about the growth of agencies. In 1933, when President Franklin D. Roosevelt set up his New Deal, a virtual army of civil servants was hired to staff the numerous new agencies that were created. Because the individuals who worked in these agencies owed their jobs to the Democratic party, it seemed natural for them to campaign for Democratic candidates. The Democrats controlling Congress in the mid-1930s did not object. But in 1938, a coalition of conservative Democrats and Republicans took control of Congress and forced through the **Hatch Act**—or the **Political Activities Act**—of 1939.

The main provision of this act is that civil service employees cannot take an active part in the political management of campaigns. It also prohibits the use of federal authority to influence nominations and elections and outlaws the use of bureaucratic rank to pressure federal employees to make political contributions.

In 1972, a federal district court declared the Hatch Act prohibition against political activity to be unconstitutional. The United States Supreme Court, however, reaffirmed the challenged portion of the act in 1973, stating that the government's interest in preserving a nonpartisan civil service was so great that the prohibitions should remain.[6]

HATCH ACT
(POLITICAL ACTIVITIES ACT)

The act that prohibits the use of federal authority to influence nominations and elections or the use of rank to pressure federal employees to make political contributions. It also prohibits civil service employees from active involvement in political campaigns.

---

[5]497 U.S. 62 (1990).
[6]*United States Civil Service Commission v. National Association of Letter Carriers*, 413 U.S. 548 (1973).

MODERN ATTEMPTS AT BUREAUCRATIC REFORM

As long as the federal bureaucracy exists, there will continue to be attempts to make it more open, efficient, and responsive to the needs of U.S. citizens. The most important actual and proposed reforms in the last few years include sunshine and sunset laws, contracting out, and more protection for so-called whistleblowers.

Sunshine Laws

GOVERNMENT IN THE SUNSHINE ACT

A law that requires all multiheaded federal agencies to conduct their business regularly in public session.

In 1976, Congress enacted the **Government in the Sunshine Act.** It required for the first time that all multiheaded federal agencies—about fifty of them—hold their meetings regularly in public session. The bill defined *meetings* as almost any gathering, formal or informal, of agency members, including conference telephone calls. The only exceptions to this rule of openness are discussions of matters such as court proceedings or personnel problems, and these exceptions are specifically listed in the bill.

Sunset Laws

SUNSET LEGISLATION

A law requiring that an existing program be reviewed regularly for its effectiveness and be terminated unless specifically extended as a result of this review.

A potential type of control on the size and scope of the federal bureaucracy is **sunset legislation,** which would place government programs on a definite schedule for congressional consideration. Unless Congress specifically reauthorized a particular federally operated program at the end of a designated period, it would be terminated automatically; that is, its sun would set.

The idea of sunset legislation—the first hint at the role of the bureaucracy in the legislative process—was initially suggested by Franklin D. Roosevelt when he created the plethora of New Deal agencies. His assistant, William O. Douglas, recommended that each agency's charter should include a provision allowing for its termination in ten years. Only an act of Congress could revitalize it. Obviously, the proposal was never adopted. It was not until 1976 that a state legislature—Colorado's—adopted sunset legislation for state regulatory commissions, giving them a life of six years before their suns set. Today most states have some type of sunset law.

Civil Service Reform Act of 1978

In 1978, the Civil Service Reform Act abolished the Civil Service Commission and created two new federal agencies to perform its duties. To administer the civil service laws, rules, and regulations, the act created the Office of Personnel Management (OPM). The OPM is empowered to recruit, interview, and test potential government workers and determine who should be hired. The OPM makes recommendations to the individual agencies as to which persons meet the standards (typically, the top three applicants for a position), and the agencies generally decide whom to hire. To oversee promotions, employees' rights, and other employment matters, the act created the Merit Systems Protection Board (MSPB). The MSPB evaluates charges of wrongdoing, hears employee appeals from agency decisions, and can order corrective action against agencies and employees. (Some critics point out that civil service has not actually been reformed at all. See this chapter's *Politics and the Bureaucracy*.)

Contracting Out

CONTRACTING OUT

The replacement of government services with services provided by private firms.

One approach to bureaucratic reform is **contracting out.** Contracting out occurs when government services are replaced by services from the private

POLITICS AND THE BUREAUCRACY
Firings from the Federal Government Are Few and Far Between

When a long-time employee of the Labor Department told a young part-timer that too much work was piling up, the subordinate broke her superior's jaw. Was the subordinate fired? No; the American Federation of Government Employees intervened. Rather than fight an uphill battle, the Labor Department decided not to fire the worker but to transfer her. The lucky transferred worker got a permanent job and a raise of almost $4,000 a year.

The fact is, according to James King, director of the Office of Personnel Management, "Only somebody who aggressively seeks to be terminated" is likely ever to be fired from the federal government. In a typical year, out of the nearly 3 million federal civil service workers, only about 200 will be fired for incompetence and another 2,000, for misconduct. Increasingly, fired federal civil service workers are filing claims with the Equal Employment Opportunity Commission.

The way to envision how much firing occurs in the federal bureaucracy is to imagine that all of the nearly 3 million employees are reduced to a single office of 100 federal workers. One would be fired for serious misconduct about every ten years. Another would resign under pressure from upper management about every fifteen years. Finally, one such federal employee would be fired for incompetence about every seventy years.

Of those who are fired or pressured to resign, they file complaints with the Equal Employment Opportunity Commission twelve times more frequently than do private-sector workers. And they go to court three times more often than do private-sector workers.

The United States would have a very different work force (not to mention an entirely different basis for its economy) if private-sector workers were permitted to have comparable levels of job security and associated rights. That would have to be an attractive prospect for many workers, especially with the layoffs, downsizing, mergers, and restructuring that have characterized American economic developments in recent years.

For Critical Analysis
Fifty years ago, it was much easier to discharge a government employee than it is today. Why?

sector. For example, the government might contract with private firms to operate prisons. Supporters of contracting out argue that some services could be provided more efficiently by the private sector. Another scheme is to furnish vouchers to "clients" in lieu of services. For example, it has been proposed that instead of federally supported housing assistance, the government should offer vouchers that recipients could use to "pay" for housing in privately owned buildings.

The contracting-out strategy has been most successful on the local level. Municipalities, for example, can form contracts with private companies for such things as trash collection. Such an approach is not a cure-all, however, as there are many functions, particularly on the national level, that cannot be contracted out in any meaningful way. For example, the federal government could not contract out national defense to a private firm.

Incentives for Efficiency and Productivity

An increasing number of state governments are beginning to experiment with a variety of schemes to run their operations more efficiently and capably. They focus on maximizing the efficiency and productivity of government workers by providing incentives for improved performance.[7] (See this chapter's *Critical Perspective.*)

---

[7]See, for example, David Osborne and Ted Gaebler, *Reinventing Government: How the Entrepreneurial Spirit Is Transforming the Public Sector* (Reading, Mass.: Addison-Wesley, 1992).

DID YOU KNOW...
That even though the Clinton administration reduced the federal work force by over 200,000 people between 1994 and 1997, virtually all of the work formerly done by federal employees is now being contracted out (that is, the number of people working on federal programs has not decreased)?

WHISTLEBLOWER
Someone who brings to public attention gross governmental inefficiency or an illegal action.

Tough economic times have forced many governors, mayors, and city administrators to consider ways in which government can be made more entrepreneurial. Some of the more promising measures have included such tactics as permitting agencies that do not spend their entire budgets to keep some of the difference and rewarding employees with performance-based bonuses.

These measures are supported by the assertion that although society and industry have changed enormously in the past century, the form of government used in Washington, D.C., and in most states has remained the same. Some observers believe that the nation's diverse economic base cannot be administered competently by traditional bureaucratic organizations. Consequently, government must become more responsive to cope with the increasing number of demands placed on it.

Helping Out the Whistleblowers

The term **whistleblower** as applied to the federal bureaucracy has a special meaning: it is someone who blows the whistle on a gross governmental inefficiency or illegal action. Whistleblowers may be clerical workers, managers, or even specialists, such as scientists. Dr. Aldric Saucier is an army research scientist who had claimed since 1987 that the Strategic Defense Initiative, known as "Star Wars," was plagued by mismanagement. Saucier asserted that the army tried to dismiss him for reporting his criticisms about the program to his superiors. In particular, Saucier charged that the program had been beset by wasteful and flawed research and that his dismissal was ordered after he submitted detailed reports documenting those criticisms to the military. Representative John Conyers (D., Mich.) intervened on Saucier's behalf and obtained the assistance of the federal Office of Special Counsel. The office conducted a preliminary examination and concluded in March 1992 that some of Saucier's claims might have merit. Shortly thereafter, the army agreed to suspend Saucier's dismissal until his claims could be investigated fully.

The 1978 Civil Service Reform Act prohibits reprisals against whistleblowers by their superiors, and it set up the Merit Systems Protection Board as part of this protection. There is little evidence, though, that potential whistle-

Members of a Federal Aviation Administration investigation team try to find the cause of a crash at the Los Angeles airport. The federal government essentially controls all air traffic in the United States and sets the regulations for commercial and private aircraft.

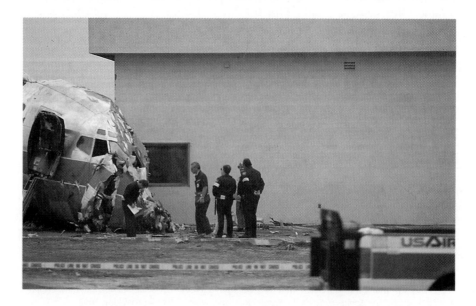

blowers truly have received more protection as a result. An attempt by Congress to increase protection for whistleblowers was vetoed by President Ronald Reagan in 1988.

Many federal agencies also have toll-free hotlines that employees can use anonymously to report bureaucratic waste and inappropriate behavior. About 35 percent of all calls result in agency action or follow-up. Some calls lead to dramatic savings for the government. The General Accounting Office (GAO) hotline was reported to have generated $25 million in savings in 1996 alone. Excluding crank calls, the GAO hotline received more than eleven thousand calls during that period, which resulted in the conviction or reprimand of 250 federal employees.

BUREAUCRATS AS POLITICIANS AND POLICYMAKERS

Agencies in the federal bureaucracy are created by Congress to implement legislation. Because Congress is unable to oversee the day-to-day administration of its programs, it must delegate certain powers to administrative agencies. In theory, the agencies should put into effect laws passed by Congress. Laws are often drafted in such vague and general terms, however, that they provide little guidance to administrators as to how they should be put into effect. This means that the agencies themselves must decide how best to carry out the wishes of Congress.

The discretion given to administrative agencies is not accidental. Congress has long realized that it lacks the technical expertise and the resources to monitor the implementation of its laws. Hence, the administrative agency is created to fill the gaps. This gap-filling role requires the agency to formulate administrative rules (regulations) to put flesh on the bones of the law. But it also forces the agency itself to assume the role of an unelected policymaker.

The Rulemaking Environment

Rulemaking does not occur in a vacuum. Suppose that Congress passes a new air-pollution law. The Environmental Protection Agency (EPA) might decide to implement the new law by a technical regulation relating to factory emissions. This proposed regulation would be published in the *Federal Register* so that interested parties would have an opportunity to comment on it. Individuals and companies that opposed parts or all of the rule might then try to convince the EPA to revise or redraft the regulation. Some parties might try to persuade the agency to withdraw the proposed regulation altogether. In any event, the EPA would consider these comments in drafting the final version of the regulation following the expiration of the comment period.

Once the final regulation has been published in the *Federal Register*, the regulation might be challenged in court by a party having a direct interest in the rule, such as a company that could expect to incur significant costs in complying with it. The company could argue that the rule misinterprets the applicable law or goes beyond the agency's statutory purview. An allegation by the company that the EPA made a mistake in judgment probably would not be enough to convince the court to throw out the rule. The company instead would have to demonstrate that the rule itself was "arbitrary and capricious." To meet this standard, the company would have to show that the rule reflected a serious flaw in the EPA's judgment—such as a steadfast refusal by the agency to consider reasonable alternatives to its rule.

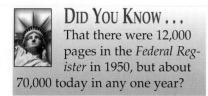

In a budget package signed by the president in 1996, some regulatory relief was obtained. When an agency now issues a new rule, it has to wait sixty days (instead of only thirty days, as was previously required) before enforcing the rule. During that waiting period, businesses, individuals, and state and local governments can ask Congress to overturn the regulation rather than having to sue the agency after the rule takes effect.

Negotiated Rulemaking

Since the end of World War II, companies have filed lawsuits regularly to block the implementation of agency regulations. Environmentalists and other special interest groups have also challenged government regulations. In the 1980s and 1990s, however, the sheer wastefulness of attempting to regulate through litigation has become more and more apparent. A growing number of federal agencies have been encouraging businesses and public interest groups to become involved directly in the drafting of regulations. Agencies hope that such participation might help to prevent later courtroom battles over the meaning, applicability, and legal effect of the regulations.

Congress formally approved such a process, which is called *negotiated rulemaking*, in the Negotiated Rulemaking Act of 1990. The act authorizes agencies to allow those who will be affected by a new rule to participate in the rule-drafting process. If an agency chooses to engage in negotiated rulemaking, it must publish in the *Federal Register* the subject and scope of the rule to be developed, the parties that will be affected significantly by the rule, and other information. Representatives of the affected groups and other interested parties then may apply to be members of the negotiating committee. The agency is represented on the committee, but a neutral third party (not the agency) presides over the proceedings. Once the committee members have reached agreement on the terms of the proposed rule, notice of the proposed rule is published in the *Federal Register,* followed by a period for comments by any person or organization interested in the proposed rule.

One example of negotiated rulemaking was the EPA's decision to seek an agreement with business interests and environmental groups about implementing certain provisions of the Clean Air Act of 1990. The only condition was that the participants—which included such perennial targets of environmentalists as the National Petroleum Refiners Association (NPRA)—promise not to challenge in court the outcome of any agreement to which they were a party and to support the agreement if one of the other participating companies filed suit to have the agreement overturned. Representatives of the NPRA and other business organizations have hailed this process as being more productive than the past practice of simply challenging agency regulations in court. This new approach has also been supported by environmental groups, such as the Environmental Defense Fund, which view such agreements as a way to conserve their own limited resources and to deal with potential pollution problems before they arise.

Bureaucrats Are Policymakers

Theories of public administration once assumed that bureaucrats do not make policy decisions but only implement the laws and policies promulgated by the president and legislative bodies. Many people continue to make this assumption (see the feature entitled *Thinking Politically about the Bureaucracy*). A more realistic view of the role of the bureaucracy in policymaking, which is now held by most bureaucrats and elected officials, is that the agencies and

Thinking Politically about the Bureaucracy

To some extent, just using the word *bureaucracy* is loading the dice against the entire concept. Most people think of bureaucracy only in negative terms. Often, the term conjures up a vision of an impersonal, machine-like organization consisting of people who do not think or act for themselves, but who merely carry out the wishes of others, such as Congress, the president, and the courts. The fact is that all administrative agencies exercise a considerable amount of discretion as they carry out policies dictated by others. That's why there are politics within administrative agencies and why there is a give and take among the people who are required to implement such policies.

Clearly, the administrative agencies that constitute the bureaucracy are much more than mere extensions of presidential power. Agency directors and managers actually are decision makers in their own right, apart from the president, or Congress, or a governor (at the state level). Agency actions are influenced by numerous pressures in their political environment. This political environment consists of, at a minimum, Congress, interest groups, the courts, the Constitution, the president, the media, the Office of Management and Budget, public opinion, and even other agencies. These pressures influence the decisions made by agency personnel. These pressures also constitute checks on the behavior of those who run each agency, thus helping to ensure that these non-elected decision makers are accountable for their decisions.

The fact is that the government always has and always will consist of people. It is people who make the decisions in all branches of government, including the "fourth" branch. The people who staff administrative agencies, like the people in the other government branches, ultimately are influenced by politics—the give and take within our democratic system.

For Critical Analysis

What would your response be to an agency head who told you that politics did not enter into his or her actions because he or she is "just following the rules"?

---

departments of government play important roles in policymaking. As we have seen, many government rules, regulations, and programs are in fact initiated by the bureaucracy, based on its expertise and scientific studies. How a law passed by Congress eventually is translated into concrete action—from the forms to be filled out to decisions about who gets the benefits—usually is determined within each agency or department. Even the evaluation of whether a policy has achieved its purpose usually is based on studies that are commissioned and interpreted by the agency administering the program.

Policy is made by several groups. The bureaucracy's policymaking role can be better understood by examining what has been called the **iron triangle.**

The Iron Triangle

Consider the bureaucracy within the Department of Agriculture. It consists of 119,558 employees working directly for the federal government and thousands of others who, directly or indirectly, work as contractors, subcontractors, or consultants to the department. Now consider that there are various interest, or client, groups that are concerned with what the federal government does for farmers. These include the American Farm Bureau Federation, the National Cattleman's Association, the National Milk Producers Association, the Corn Growers Association, and the Citrus Growers Association. Finally, go directly to Congress, and you will see that there are two major congressional committees concerned with agriculture—the House Committee on Agriculture and the Senate Committee on Agriculture, Nutrition, and Forestry—each of which has seven subcommittees.

IRON TRIANGLE

The three-way alliance among legislators, bureaucrats, and interest groups to make or preserve policies that benefit their respective interests.

CRITICAL PERSPECTIVE
Can Common Sense Be Put Back into Government?

Early in the Clinton administration, with great fanfare, Vice President Al Gore put out a report called "From Red Tape to Results: Creating a Government That Works Better and Costs Less." This report was produced by the National Performance Review, a task force created by the Clinton administration to "reinvent" the federal government by focusing on federal agencies. One of the authors of the report was David Osborne, who also was a coauthor, with Ted Gaebler, of *Reinventing Government: How the Entrepreneurial Spirit is Transforming the Public Sector.** This book contains ideas about reforming the bureaucracy that were noted elsewhere in this chapter. Among the premises of both the National Performance Review report and Osborne's book is that agency employees need to be freer to make decisions without being tied down by countless rules.

Less than two years later, another book, *The Death of Common Sense: How Law Is Suffocating America,*† written by Philip K. Howard, became a best seller. Much of the book was filled with horror stories about how inefficient government has become. Politicians quickly jumped onto the bandwagon. The governor of Florida bought two hundred copies and sent them to all of his agency directors. During the early days of the Clinton/Dole presidential campaign, both candidates were vying for Howard's blessing. At one point, Dole had Howard invited to testify before the Senate Judiciary Committee. Clinton's team arranged a private meeting between Howard and Al Gore. Clinton personally endorsed Howard and his book at a "reinventing regulatory reform" event.

The Goals of Reinventing Government

The goals of reinventing government are straightfoward:

- Reduce the size of government.
- Decentralize hiring.
- Improve incentives for efficiency.
- Improve incentives for performance.
- Implement speedier firing procedures.
- Eliminate government monopolies.
- Most of all, eliminate the literally hundreds of thousands, if not millions, of seemingly stupid petty regulations and the accompanying paperwork that plague American businesses.

How to Get Results

Philip Howard stated, "I wanted to figure out why everyone who deals with the government has the same basic reaction—anger, frustration. I decided that it's because we ban *judgment*." Howard believes that government regulation is based on a false premise: if government can stipulate every regulatory circumstance, government inspectors can simply go out and enforce the rules. Of course, each set of circumstances is different, so no one rule can fit all circumstances.

Figure 14–4
• •
The Iron Triangle

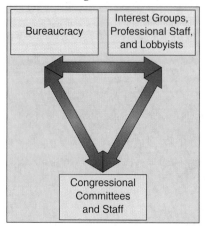

Figure 14–4 is a schematic view of the iron triangle. This triangle, or subgovernment, is an alliance of mutual benefit among some unit within the bureaucracy, its interest or client group, and committees or subcommittees of Congress and their staff members. The workings of iron triangles are complicated, but they are well established in almost every subgovernment.

Consider again the Department of Agriculture. The secretary of agriculture is nominated by the president (and confirmed by the Senate) and is nominally the head of the Department of Agriculture. But that secretary cannot even buy a desk lamp if Congress does not approve the appropriations for the Department of Agriculture's budget. Within Congress, the responsibility for considering the Department of Agriculture's request for funding belongs first to the House and Senate appropriations committees and to the Agriculture subcommittees under them. The members of those committees, most of whom represent agricultural states, have been around a long time. They have their own ideas about what amount of funds is appropriate for the Agriculture Department's budget. They have their own program concepts. They carefully scrutinize the ideas of the president and the secretary of agriculture.

CRITICAL PERSPECTIVE
Can Common Sense Be Put Back into Government? Continued

So, Howard wants us to have continuing standards—for example, for food and drugs, clean air, and water—but with one change: the government should not specify precisely how standards should be met. In other words, bureaucrats should have more power; they should be able to use their discretion.

Consistent with Howard's policy prescription, President Clinton set up a pilot program a few years ago in the Environmental Protection Agency. This program allows companies to "toss out the rule book" and negotiate how they will come into compliance with clean air and water standards.

Ignoring the Iron Triangle

The problem with all attempts at "reinventing government" is never the recommendations—many of which, if given effect, could be a step toward the elimination of government waste and efficiency. The problem with all such attempts is that they ignore the most formidable obstacle in the path of implementation: the iron triangle.

The three components of the iron triangle are Congress, special interest groups, and the bureaucracy itself. The report asks Congress to stop micromanaging agency budgets. Experimental projects have shown that allowing agency personnel to manage their own funds can increase productivity. But micromanagement is how Congress satisfies special interest groups, generates campaign contributions, and exercises its own power. There is no indication that special interest groups intend to relinquish their control or that Congress intends to change its role.

Cutting spending under the weight of the iron triangle is extraordinarily difficult. As proof, this is not the first time that the iron triangle has crushed an administration's attempt to make government leaner, more responsive, and less confusing. At the beginning of this chapter, we noted the different "reinventing government" plans that had been proffered by previous administrations. As long as there are new presidents, there probably will be other plans. With each new administration, there will be attempts at reinventing government. But unless the iron triangle disappears, none of these reform blueprints will have much support.

For Critical Analysis

1. Can you think of situations in which Congress, government agencies, or special interest groups have acted in ways that adversely affect their own interests (relinquishing control of spending, reducing staffs, and so on) to benefit the general public?
2. Is there any practical way to reduce the influence of the iron triangle without radically restructuring the federal government?

*Reading, Mass.: Addison-Wesley, 1992.
†New York: Random House, 1994.

Finally, the various interest groups—including producers of farm chemicals and farm machinery, agricultural cooperatives, grain dealers, and exporters—have vested interests in whatever the Department of Agriculture does and in whatever Congress lets the Department of Agriculture do. Those interests are well represented by the lobbyists who crowd the halls of Congress. Many lobbyists have been working for agricultural pressure groups for decades. They know the congressional committee members and Agriculture Department staff members extremely well and meet with them routinely. Industry representatives may be named to administrative positions in the Department of Agriculture, or they may be former bureaucrats. When the president proposes policies that benefit or harm the interests or constituents of groups of the triangle, they present a united front either to pass or to oppose such legislation.

Such iron triangles—of which there are many, not only on Capitol Hill but also in state capitals—at times have completely thwarted efforts by the president to get the administration's programs enacted. (See this chapter's *Critical Perspective: Can Common Sense Be Put Back into Government?* for a discussion of the role played by iron triangles in almost guaranteeing that no matter what the administration proposes in terms of "reinventing government," very little change actually will occur.)

CONGRESSIONAL CONTROL OF THE BUREAUCRACY

Although Congress is the ultimate repository of political power under the Constitution, many political pundits doubt whether Congress can meaningfully control the burgeoning federal bureaucracy. These commentators forget that Congress has the power of the purse and could, theoretically, refuse to authorize or appropriate money for a particular agency. Whether Congress would actually take such a drastic measure in exercising its responsibility of legislative oversight would depend on the circumstances. It is clear, however, that Congress does have the legal authority to decide whether to fund or not to fund administrative agencies.

Creating Administrative Agencies

Nearly every administrative agency is created by "enabling legislation" passed by Congress (for an example of enabling legislation, see the feature entitled *Politics and Agency Creation*). The legislation that results in the creation of an agency is usually proposed to address a pressing national problem. The Occupational Safety and Health Act of 1970, for example, was created to address the problem of workplace hazards. But the act itself would have been rendered nearly useless had it not included provisions for the creation of a regulatory agency, the Occupational Safety and Health Administration (OSHA), to create and enforce safety standards. Although Congress delegated significant powers to OSHA in the enabling legislation, Congress did define the parameters within which the agency could operate.

Authorizing Funds

Once an agency is created by enabling legislation, Congress must authorize funds for it. The **authorization** is a formal declaration by the appropriate leg-

AUTHORIZATION

A formal declaration by a legislative committee that a certain amount of funding may be available to an agency. Some authorizations terminate in a year; others are renewable automatically without further congressional authorization.

The space shuttle Discovery landing in the California desert. While the National Aeronautics and Space Administration works to build support for its programs in the future, many members of the public question the need for this expensive public program.

POLITICS AND AGENCY CREATION
The Popcorn Board

It doesn't take much to start a new agency within the federal government. All that is needed is enabling legislation, which can be tacked onto a bill that is signed by the president. To give you some idea of what enabling legislation looks like, we present here excerpts from part of the farm bill passed by the Senate in 1996, which were aimed at establishing a federal Popcorn Board. The Popcorn Board received strong support from the chairman of the Senate Agricultural Committee, Richard G. Lugar of Indiana, as well as from the Popcorn Institute.

Subtitle A—Popcorn
SEC. 901. SHORT TITLE
This subtitle may be cited as the "Popcorn Promotion, Research, and Consumer Information Act."
SEC. 902. FINDINGS AND DECLARATIONS OF POLICY.
(a) FINDINGS—Congress finds that—
(1) popcorn is an important food that is a

valuable part of the human diet;
(2) the production and processing of popcorn plays a significant role in the economy of the United States in that popcorn is processed by several popcorn processors, distributed through wholesale and retail outlets and consumed by millions of people throughout the United States and foreign countries;
(3) popcorn must be of high quality, readily available, handled properly, and marketed efficiently to ensure that the benefits of popcorn are available to the people of the United States;
. . . .

(b) POLICY—It is the policy of Congress that it is in the public interest to authorize the establishment, through the exercise of the powers provided in this subtitle, of an orderly procedure for developing, financing (through adequate assessments on unpopped popcorn processed domestically), and carrying out an effective, continuous, and coordinated program of promotion, research, consumer information, and industry information designed to—

(1) strengthen the position of the popcorn industry in the marketplace; and
(2) maintain and expand the markets for all popcorn products . . .
. . . .

SEC. 905. REQUIRED TERMS IN ORDERS
(a) IN GENERAL—An order shall contain the terms and conditions specified in this section.
(b) ESTABLISHMENT AND MEMBERSHIP OF POPCORN BOARD—
(1) IN GENERAL—The order shall provide for the establishment of, and appointments of members to, a Popcorn Board that shall consist of not fewer than 4 members and not more than 9 members . . . .

For Critical Analysis
Why do you think so few Americans ever hear about such legislation?

---

islative committee that a certain amount of funding may be available to the agency. The authorization itself may terminate in a year, or it may be renewed automatically without further action by Congress. The National Aeronautics and Space Administration (NASA) is one agency in which authorizations must be periodically renewed; Social Security, in contrast, is funded through a permanent authorization. Periodic authorizations enable Congress to exercise greater control over the spending programs of an agency, whereas permanent authorizations free Congress from the task of having to review the authorization each year. The drawback of permanent authorizations is that they can become almost impossible to control politically.

Appropriating Funds

After the funds are authorized, they must be appropriated by Congress. The appropriations committees of both the House and the Senate forward spending bills to their respective bodies. The **appropriation** of funds occurs when the final bill is passed. Congress is not required to appropriate the entire authorized amount. It may appropriate less if it so chooses. If the appropriated funds are substantially less than the authorized amount, however, it may signal that the agency's agenda soon may be revamped by Congress.

Investigations and Hearings

Congressional committees conduct investigations and hold hearings to oversee an agency's actions, reviewing them to ensure compliance with congres-

APPROPRIATION

The passage, by Congress, of a spending bill, specifying the amount of authorized funds that actually will be allocated for an agency's use.

DID YOU KNOW...
That the federal government owns one-third of the land in the United States (744 million acres), an area the size of all the states east of the Mississippi River plus Texas?

sional intentions. The agency's officers and employees can be ordered to testify before a committee about the details of an action. Through these oversight activities, especially in the questioning and commenting by members of the House or Senate during the hearings, Congress indicates its positions on specific programs and issues. Congress can also ask the General Accounting Office (GAO) to investigate particular agency actions. The Congressional Budget Office (CBO) also conducts oversight studies. The results of a GAO or CBO study may encourage Congress to hold further hearings or make changes in the law. Even if a law is not changed explicitly by Congress, however, the views expressed in any investigations and hearings are taken seriously by agency officials, who often act on those views.

THE BUREAUCRACY: UNFINISHED WORK

As this chapter's *Critical Perspective* indicated, there probably will be serious unfinished business with respect to reforming the bureaucracy as long as we have a representative democratic form of government. The way members of the House and Senate get reelected and the way in which lobbyists fit into that process practically guarantee that the bureaucracy will never be reformed completely.

This does not mean that we will not see improvements. Indeed, competition in the private marketplace is forcing changes on some federal government institutions. For example, the efficiency of private overnight delivery services, such as Federal Express, Airborne, and United Parcel Service (UPS), has forced many changes on the U.S. Postal Service. Increasingly, the use of fax machines, high-speed modems, and e-mail also has put added pressure on the U.S. Postal Service to become more efficient. Such changes are bound to continue as communications technology improves.

The actual job of the federal bureaucracy, of course, will never disappear. Federal agencies are the primary means by which the laws of Congress are put into practice. This "gap-filling" power gives federal agencies significant discretion to make policy. Such policymaking has certain advantages: bureaucrats are often specialists in their fields and are more knowledgeable than members of Congress about specific issues relating to the legislation passed by Congress.

GETTING INVOLVED
What the Government Knows about You

The federal government collects billions of pieces of information on tens of millions of Americans each year. These are stored in files and gigantic computers and often are exchanged among agencies. You probably have at least several federal records (for example, those in the Social Security Administration; the Internal Revenue Service; and, if you are a male, the Selective Service).

The 1966 Freedom of Information Act requires that the federal government release, at your request, any identifiable information it has in the administrative agencies of the executive branch. This information can be about you or about any other subject. Ten categories of material are exempted, however (classified material, confidential material dealing with trade secrets, internal personnel rules, personal medical files, and the like). To request material, you must write the Freedom of Information Act officer directly at the agency in question (say, the Department of Education). You must also have a relatively specific idea about the document or information you wish to obtain.

A second law, the Privacy Act of 1974, gives you access specifically to information the government may have collected about you. This is a very important law, because it allows you to review your records on file with federal agencies (for example, with the Federal Bureau of Investigation) and to check those records for possible inaccuracies. Cases do exist in which two people with similar or the same names have had their records confused. In some cases, innocent persons have had the criminal records of another person erroneously inserted into their files.

If you wish to look at any records or find out if an agency has a record on you, write to the agency head or Privacy Act officer, and address your letter to the specific agency. State that "under the provisions of the Privacy Act of 1974, 5 U.S.C. 522a, I hereby request a copy of (or access to) _____." Then describe the record that you wish to investigate.

If you have trouble finding out about your records or wish to locate an attorney in Washington, D.C., to help you with this matter, you can contact the following organization:

LAWYER REFERRAL SERVICE
Washington Bar Association
1819 H St. N.W., Suite 300
Washington, DC 20036
202-289-4247

KEY TERMS

acquisitive model 475

administrative agency 474

appropriation 495

authorization 494

bureaucracy 473

cabinet department 478

capture 481

Civil Service Commission 484

contracting out 486

garbage can model 476

government corporation 482

Government in the Sunshine Act 486

Hatch Act (Political Activities Act) 485

independent executive agency 479

independent regulatory agency 480

iron triangle 491

line organization 478

merit system 484

monopolistic model 475

natural aristocracy 484

Pendleton Act (Civil Service Reform Act) 484

spoils system 484

sunset legislation 486

Weberian model 474

whistleblower 488

CHAPTER SUMMARY

1 Presidents have long complained about their inability to control the federal bureaucracy. There is no reference to the bureaucracy itself in the Constitution, but Article II gives the president the power to appoint officials to execute the laws of the United States. Most scholars cite Article II as the constitutional basis for the federal bureaucracy.

2 Bureaucracies are rigid hierarchical organizations in which the tasks and powers of lower-level employees are defined clearly. Job specialties and extensive procedural rules set the standards for behavior. Bureaucracies are the primary form of organization of most major corporations and universities.

3 Several theories have been offered to explain bureaucracies. The Weberian model posits that bureaucracies have developed into centralized hierarchical structures in response to the increasing demands placed on governments by their citizens. The acquisitive model views top-level bureaucrats as pressing for ever greater funding, staffs, and privileges to augment their own sense of power and security. The monopolistic model focuses on the environment in which most government bureaucracies operate, stating that bureaucracies are inefficient and excessively costly to operate because they often have no competitors. Finally, the garbage can model posits that bureaucracies are rudderless organizations that flounder about in search of solutions to problems.

4 Since the founding of the United States, the federal bureaucracy has grown from 50 to nearly 3 million employees (excluding the military). Federal, state, and local employees together make up some 15 percent of the nation's civilian labor force. The federal bureaucracy consists of fourteen cabinet departments, as well as numerous independent executive agencies, independent regulatory agencies, and government corporations. These entities enjoy varying degrees of autonomy, visibility, and political support.

5 A self-sustaining federal bureaucracy of career civil servants was formed during Thomas Jefferson's presidency. Andrew Jackson implemented a spoils system through which he appointed his own political supporters. A civil service based on professionalism and merit was the goal of the Civil Service Reform Act of 1883. Concerns that the civil service be freed from the pressures of politics prompted the passage of the Hatch Act in 1939.

6 There have been many attempts to make the federal bureaucracy more open, efficient, and responsive to the needs of U.S. citizens. The most important reforms have included sunshine and sunset laws, the Civil Service Reform Act of 1978, contracting out, schemes to provide incentives for increased productivity and efficiency, and protection for whistleblowers.

7 Congress delegates much of its authority to federal agencies when it creates new laws. The bureaucrats who run these agencies may become important policymakers, because Congress has neither the time nor the technical expertise to oversee the administration of its laws. In the agency rulemaking process, a proposed regulation is published. A comment period follows, during which interested parties may offer suggestions for changes. Because companies have challenged many regulations in court, federal agencies now are allowed to involve parties that will be affected by new regulations in the rule-drafting process.

8 Congress exerts ultimate control over all federal agencies, because it controls the federal government's purse strings. It also establishes the general guidelines by which regulatory agencies must abide. The appropriations process may also provide a way to send messages of approval or disapproval to particular agencies, as do congressional hearings and investigations relating to agency actions.

QUESTIONS FOR REVIEW AND DISCUSSION

1 The size of the federal bureaucracy has been declining in recent years. Yet the total size of the government at all levels has risen. Does it matter to individuals which part of the government bureaucracy is growing and which part is not? If so, why? If not, why not?

2 How do the interests of private businesses and individuals help create inefficiency in government?

3 What might some of the conflicts be between different bureaucracies within the federal government? [Hint: Do the Central Intelligence Agency (CIA) and the Federal Bureau of Investigation (FBI) cooperate smoothly?]

4 "Congress purposely creates vague laws that the federal bureaucracy must interpret. In this way, members of Congress make sure that they always have areas in the economy in which they can intervene to help voters in their jurisdictions." Do you agree or disagree with this quote? Why would Congress purposely make vague laws?

5 The U.S. Postal Service is a government corporation. How does this corporation differ from a private, non-government corporation?

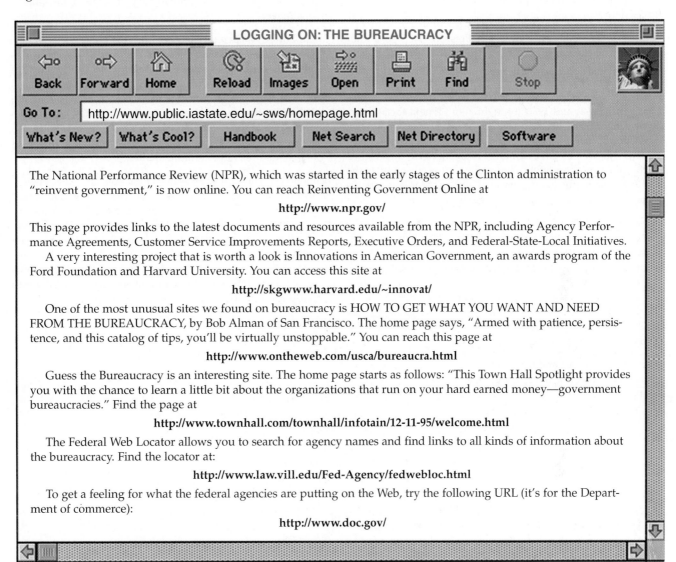

LOGGING ON: THE BUREAUCRACY

Back | Forward | Home | Reload | Images | Open | Print | Find | Stop

Go To: http://www.public.iastate.edu/~sws/homepage.html

What's New? | What's Cool? | Handbook | Net Search | Net Directory | Software

The National Performance Review (NPR), which was started in the early stages of the Clinton administration to "reinvent government," is now online. You can reach Reinventing Government Online at

http://www.npr.gov/

This page provides links to the latest documents and resources available from the NPR, including Agency Performance Agreements, Customer Service Improvements Reports, Executive Orders, and Federal-State-Local Initiatives.

A very interesting project that is worth a look is Innovations in American Government, an awards program of the Ford Foundation and Harvard University. You can access this site at

http://skgwww.harvard.edu/~innovat/

One of the most unusual sites we found on bureaucracy is HOW TO GET WHAT YOU WANT AND NEED FROM THE BUREAUCRACY, by Bob Alman of San Francisco. The home page says, "Armed with patience, persistence, and this catalog of tips, you'll be virtually unstoppable." You can reach this page at

http://www.ontheweb.com/usca/bureaucra.html

Guess the Bureaucracy is an interesting site. The home page starts as follows: "This Town Hall Spotlight provides you with the chance to learn a little bit about the organizations that run on your hard earned money—government bureaucracies." Find the page at

http://www.townhall.com/townhall/infotain/12-11-95/welcome.html

The Federal Web Locator allows you to search for agency names and find links to all kinds of information about the bureaucracy. Find the locator at:

http://www.law.vill.edu/Fed-Agency/fedwebloc.html

To get a feeling for what the federal agencies are putting on the Web, try the following URL (it's for the Department of commerce):

http://www.doc.gov/

SELECTED REFERENCES

Burnham, David. *A Law unto Itself: The IRS and the Abuse of Power.* New York: Random House, 1990. This is a very critical study of the role of the Internal Revenue Service, one of the largest, most powerful, and least accountable enforcement agencies in the federal government.

Cook, Brian J. *Bureaucracy and Self-Government: Reconsidering the Role of Public Administration in American Politics.* Baltimore, Md.: Johns Hopkins University Press, 1996. The author examines the tension between two traditional perceptions of the bureaucracy in American political life. One perception views bureaucrats as implementers of the orders given by elected officials. The other perception views bureaucrats as policymakers.

Downs, Anthony. *Inside Bureaucracy.* Boston: Little, Brown, 1967. In this classic work, Downs provides an economist's explanation of why the bureaucracy is what it is and why bureaucrats and their agencies conduct themselves as they do.

Dunleavy, Patrick. *Democracy, Bureaucracy, and Public Choice: Economic Approaches in Political Science.* Englewood Cliffs, N.J.: Prentice-Hall, 1994. The author examines the public choice theory of bureaucracy and shows how the public choice model can help predict governmental actions.

Eisner, Marc Allen. *Regulatory Politics in Transition.* Baltimore, Md.: Johns Hopkins University Press, 1993. The author argues that the only way to understand the importance of regulatory policy fully is to understand the policy shifts that have occurred during the Progressive period (1890–1920), during the New Deal (1932–1945), and today. He argues that the 1960s and 1970s brought about a new social structure in which policies addressed the social consequences of economic activities in the areas of occupational health and safety, as well as environmental protection. He then claims that there was an efficiency regime that occurred after the 1970s, when the competence of the government and its processes to perform its tasks were under scrutiny.

Ingraham, Patricia W. *The Foundation of Merit: Public Service in American Democracy.* Baltimore, Md.: Johns Hopkins University Press, 1995. Ingraham discusses the evolution of the merit system and concludes that federal personnel policy is not based on any coherent scheme but rather consists of a collection of various rules and regulations created at different times for different political ends. She examines six "harsh realities" that face those who would like to reform the federal bureaucracy.

Johnson, Ronald N., and Gary D. Libecap. *The Federal Civil Service System and the Problem of Bureaucracy: The Economics and Politics of Institutional Change.* Chicago: University of Chicago Press, 1994. The authors examine the evolution of the civil service system from the Pendleton Act of 1883 to the 1990s and explain why, in spite of numerous attempts, reforming the federal bureaucracy remains a formidable challenge.

Light, Paul C. *Thickening Government: Federal Hierarchy and the Diffusion of Accountability.* Washington, D.C.: Brookings Institution, 1995. The author describes the "thickening" of government, both horizontally (by the creation of agencies) and vertically (by creating new layers of management). Whether the bureaucracy can be "thinned" depends, according to the author, on whether the president and Congress are "willing to abandon their prevailing image of what organizations should look like."

Schoenbrod, David. *Power without Responsibility.* New Haven, Conn.: Yale University Press, 1993. The author claims that the president and Congress do not make laws that govern us but rather give bureaucrats the power to make laws through agency regulations. He argues that delegation then allows the president and Congress to wield power by pressuring agency lawmakers in private and at the same time, to shed responsibility by avoiding the need personally to support or oppose these "laws."

15
The Judiciary

CHAPTER OUTLINE

Supreme Court Justices Were Elected?

BACKGROUND

THE FOUNDERS OF THIS COUNTRY ESTABLISHED A REPRESENTATIVE DEMOCRACY, IN WHICH THOSE WHO PASS LAWS AND MAKE POLICY ARE ELECTED. THEORETICALLY, AT LEAST, THEIR JOB IS TO REPRESENT THE INTERESTS OF THE PEOPLE. THE NINE JUSTICES WHO SIT ON THE BENCH OF THE SUPREME COURT ARE AMONG THE MOST IMPORTANT POLICYMAKERS OF THIS NATION. THIS IS BECAUSE THEY HAVE THE FINAL SAY ON HOW THE U.S. CONSTITUTION—THE "SUPREME LAW OF THE LAND"—SHOULD BE INTERPRETED, WHICH CAN HAVE SIGNIFICANT CONSEQUENCES FOR THE NATION. SUPREME COURT JUSTICES, HOWEVER, ARE NOT ELECTED BUT RATHER ARE APPOINTED BY THE PRESIDENT AND CONFIRMED BY THE SENATE—AS ARE ALL FEDERAL JUDGES. THE JUSTICES ALSO HOLD OFFICE FOR LIFE, BARRING GROSS MISCONDUCT.

WHAT IF SUPREME COURT JUSTICES WERE ELECTED?

Many contend that if Supreme Court justices were elected, they would be less able to resist the fierce winds of politics. Under the existing system, however, once approved by the Senate and seated on the high court's bench, a justice is free to decide cases as he or she wishes. Supreme Court justices, because they hold office for life, do not have to worry about job security.

If Supreme Court justices were elected, they might give greater consideration to public opinion than they currently do when deciding cases. For example, assume that public opinion polls show that most Americans are against laws protecting gay and lesbian rights. An elected justice about to run for reelection might be more inclined than an appointed justice to deem such laws unconstitutional.

Of course, some argue that Supreme Court justices *should* be concerned about public opinion and what the public wants.

After all, implementing the wishes of the electorate is the appropriate function of government institutions in a representative democracy. Certainly, the justices on the Supreme Court bench today take public opinion into consideration when deciding cases—albeit not to the extent they might if they were elected.

INTEREST GROUPS AND CAMPAIGN COSTS

Supreme Court justices, by virtue of their lifetime appointments, are immunized from the pressures brought to bear on the legislative and executive branches by various interest groups. If Supreme Court justices were elected, they certainly would lose this immunity. A person seeking election (or reelection) to the Court might be tempted to give in to pressure to vote in accordance with a particular interest group's wishes in return for the group's political support.

POLITICAL IDEOLOGY

Humorist Finley Peter Dunne once said that "th' Supreme Court follows th' iliction returns." In other words, Democratic presidents tend to appoint liberal justices, and Republican presidents tend to appoint conservative justices. Ultimately, then, the Supreme Court does change in response to election returns, but this process takes time because justices might end up sitting on

the Court for decades. If Supreme Court justices were elected, the ideological complexion of the Court probably would change much more quickly. A voting bloc of liberal or conservative justices might be short lived, with new alliances being formed after the next election. As a result, the decisions made by the Court, as the final interpreter of the Constitution, might not be very "final." If the next election brought in justices with different ideological views, the Court could overturn the precedents set by the Court during the previous term. Of course, staggered terms could be used, as in the Senate, to ensure more continuity in judicial decision making.

FOR CRITICAL ANALYSIS

1. *Should Supreme Court justices be influenced by public opinion when making their decisions? Why or why not?*
2. *If Supreme Court justices were elected, would their decisions be less authoritative? Explain.*

As indicated in this chapter's opening *What If . . .* , the judges and justices[1] of the federal court system are not elected but rather are appointed by the president and confirmed by the Senate. This fact does not mean that the federal judiciary is apolitical, however. Indeed, our courts play a larger role in making public policy than courts in any other country in the world today. To understand the extensive policymaking powers of the Supreme Court, for example, consider how the history of the United States might read if Chief Justice John Marshall, in the early 1800s, had not interpreted the commerce clause to mean that the national government had the exclusive authority to regulate interstate commerce (see Chapter 3). Similarly, what might have happened if Chief Justice Earl Warren, during the 1950s, had not decided that racial segregation and the "separate-but-equal" doctrine were unconstitutional (see Chapter 5)? This quasi-legislative role played by the courts was not envisioned by the framers of the Constitution, who were concerned primarily with abuses of power by the national government. Rather, the role evolved over time.

As Alexis de Tocqueville, a nineteenth-century French commentator on American society, noted, "scarcely any political question arises in the United States that is not resolved, sooner or later, into a judicial question."[2] Our judiciary forms part of our political process. The instant that judges interpret the law, they become actors in the political arena—policymakers working within a political institution. As such, the most important political force within our judiciary is the United States Supreme Court. Because of its preeminence, we devote the major portion of this chapter to it. The remainder of the chapter deals with the lower federal courts and the state court systems.

FUNDAMENTAL SOURCES OF AMERICAN LAW

Because of our colonial heritage, most of American law is based on the English legal system, in which the decisions made by court judges constitute an important source of law. We look here at this legal system and how it functions, as well as at the other major sources of law in the United States.

The Courts and *Stare Decisis*

In 1066, the Normans conquered England, and William the Conqueror and his successors began the process of unifying the country under their rule. One of the ways they did this was to establish the king's courts, or *curia regis*. Before the conquest, disputes had been settled according to local custom. The king's courts sought to establish a common or uniform set of rules for the whole country. As the number of courts and cases increased, portions of the more important decisions of each year were gathered together and recorded in *Year Books*. Judges settling disputes similar to ones that had been decided before used the *Year Books* as the basis for their decisions. If a case was unique, judges had to create new laws, but they based their decisions on the general principles suggested by earlier cases. The body of judge-made law that developed under this system is still used today and is known as the **common law.**

COMMON LAW

Judge-made law that originated in England from decisions shaped according to prevailing custom. Decisions were applied to similar situations and gradually became common to the nation. Common law forms the basis of legal procedures in the fifty states.

---

[1]The terms *justice* and *judge* are two designations given to judges in various courts. All members of the United States Supreme Court are referred to as *justices.* In most states' highest appellate courts, the formal title given to the judge is *justice* also, although the converse is true in the state of New York.
[2]Alexis de Tocqueville, *Democracy in America* (New York: Harper & Row, 1966), p. 248.

PRECEDENT

A court rule bearing on subsequent legal decisions in similar cases. Judges rely on precedents in deciding cases.

STARE DECISIS

To stand on decided cases; the policy of courts to follow precedents established by past decisions.

The practice of deciding new cases with reference to former decisions—that is, according to **precedent**—became a cornerstone of the English and American judicial systems and is embodied in the doctrine of *stare decisis* (pronounced *ster*-ay dih-*si*-ses), a Latin phrase that means "to stand on decided cases". The rule of *stare decisis* performs many useful functions. First, it helps the courts to be more efficient. It would be time consuming if each judge had to establish reasons for deciding what the law should be for each case brought before the court. If other courts have confronted the same issue and reasoned through the case carefully, their opinions can serve as guides. Second, *stare decisis* creates a more uniform system. All courts try to follow precedent, and thus different courts often use the same rule of law. (Some variations occur, however, because different states and regions follow different precedents, as will be discussed shortly.) Also, the rule of precedent tends to neutralize the personal prejudices of individual judges to the degree that they feel obliged to use precedent as the basis for their decision. Finally, the rule makes the law more stable and predictable than it otherwise would be. If the law on a subject is relatively well settled, someone bringing a case to court usually can rely on the court to make a decision based on what the law has been.

Note that the doctrine of *stare decisis* obligates judges to follow the precedents set previously only by their own court or by higher courts that have authority over them. For example, a lower state court in California would be obligated to follow a precedent set by the California Supreme Court. That lower court, however, would not be obligated to follow a precedent set by the supreme court of another state, because each state court system is independent. Of course, when the United States Supreme Court decides an issue, all of the nation's other courts are obligated to abide by the Court's decision—because the Supreme Court is the highest court in the land. The decisions of the Supreme Court (and of the lower courts, unless their decisions are overturned by the Supreme Court) constitute an important source of American law.

The doctrine of *stare decisis* provides a basis for judicial decision making in all countries that have common law systems. (For a discussion of an alternative legal system used in many nations of the world, see this chapter's *Politics and Comparative Systems*.)

Constitutions

The constitutions of the federal government and the states set forth the general organization, powers, and limits of government. The U.S. Constitution is the supreme law of the land. A law in violation of the Constitution, no matter what its source, may be declared unconstitutional and thereafter cannot be enforced. Similarly, the state constitutions are supreme within their respective borders (unless they conflict with the U.S. Constitution or laws and treaties made in accordance with it). The Constitution thus defines the political playing field on which state and federal powers are reconciled. The idea that the Constitution should be supreme in certain matters stemmed from widespread dissatisfaction with the weak federal government that had existed previously under the Articles of Confederation adopted in 1781.

Statutes and Administrative Regulations

Although the English common law provides the basis for both our civil and criminal legal systems, statutes (laws enacted by legislatures) increasingly have become important in defining the rights and obligations of individuals.

POLITICS AND COMPARATIVE SYSTEMS
Legal Systems of the World

Basically, there are two legal systems in today's world. One of these systems is the common law system of England and the United States, as described in this chapter. The other system is based on Roman civil law, or "code law." The term *civil law*, as used here, refers not to civil as opposed to criminal law but to *codified* law—an ordered grouping of legal principles enacted into law by a legislature or governing body. In a *civil law system*, the primary course of law is a statutory code, and case precedents are not judicially binding, as they normally are in a common law system. Although judges in a civil law system commonly refer to previous decisions as sources of legal guidance, they are not bound by precedent; in other words, the doctrine of *stare decisis* does not apply.

The accompanying table lists the countries that today follow either the common law system or the civil law system. Generally, those countries that were once colonies of Great Britain

The Legal Systems of Nations

CIVIL LAW		COMMON LAW	
Argentina	Indonesia	Australia	Nigeria
Austria	Iran	Bangladesh	Singapore
Brazil	Italy	Canada	United Kingdom
Chile	Japan	Ghana	United States
China	Mexico	India	Zambia
Egypt	Poland	Israel	
Finland	South Korea	Jamaica	
France	Sweden	Kenya	
Germany	Tunisia	Malaysia	
Greece	Venezuela	New Zealand	

retained their English common law heritage after they achieved their independence. Similarly, the civil law system, which is followed in most of the continental European countries, was retained in the Latin American, African, and Asian countries that were once colonies of those nations. Japan and South Africa also have civil law systems, and ingredients of the civil law system are found in the Islamic courts of predominantly Muslim countries. In the United States, the state of Louisiana, because of its historical ties to France, has in part a civil law system. The legal systems of Puerto Rico, Québec, and Scotland are similarly characterized as having elements of the civil law system.

For Critical Analysis

How does the doctrine of **stare decisis** *affect the legal systems of common law countries?*

Federal statutes may relate to any subject that is a concern of the federal government and may cover areas ranging from hazardous waste to federal taxation. Statutes are often extremely detailed and complex on both the federal and state levels. State statutes include criminal codes, commercial laws, and laws relating to a variety of other matters. Cities, counties, and other local political bodies also pass statutes, which are called ordinances. These ordinances may deal with such things as zoning schemes and public safety. Rules and regulations issued by administrative agencies are another source of law.

Legislative bodies and administrative agencies have assumed an ever-increasing share of lawmaking. Today, much of the work of courts consists of interpreting these laws and regulations and applying them to circumstances in cases before the courts.

THE JUDICIARY'S ROLE IN AMERICAN GOVERNMENT

The body of American law is vast and complex. It includes the federal and state constitutions, statutes passed by legislative bodies, administrative law, and the legal principles that form the body of common law. These laws would be meaningless, however, without the courts to interpret and apply them.

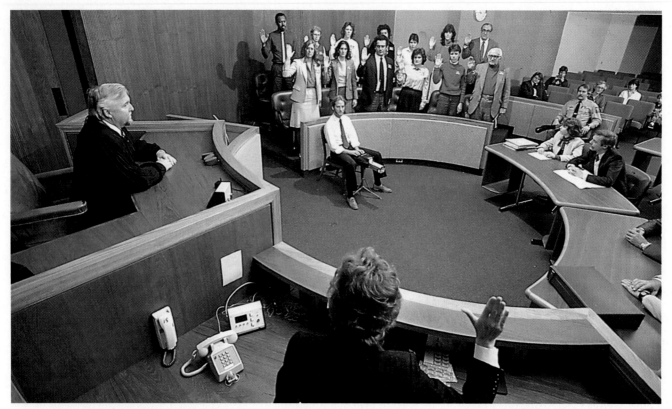

A jury is being sworn in. Most jury trials have between six and twelve jurors. Some trials are held without juries.

This is the essential role of the judiciary—the courts—in the American governmental system: to interpret and apply the laws to specific situations. Additionally, as the branch of government entrusted with interpreting the laws, the judiciary can decide whether the laws or actions of the other two branches are constitutional.

Judicial Review

Remember from Chapter 2 that the power of the courts to determine whether a law or action by the other branches of government is constitutional is known as the power of *judicial review.* This power of the judiciary enables the judicial branch to act as a check on the other two branches of government, in line with the checks and balances system established by the U.S. Constitution.

The power of judicial review is not mentioned in the Constitution, however. Rather, it was established by the United States Supreme Court's decision in *Marbury v. Madison.*[3] In that case (see this chapter's *Politics and the Law*), in which the Court declared that a law passed by Congress violated the Constitution, the Court claimed such a power for the courts:

> It is emphatically the province and duty of the Judicial Department to say what the law is. Those who apply the rule to a particular case, must of necessity expound and interpret that rule. If two laws conflict with each other, the courts must decide on the operation of each.

The Supreme Court has ruled parts or all of acts of Congress to be unconstitutional only about 150 times in its history. State laws, however, have been

---

[3]5 U.S. 137 (1803).

POLITICS AND THE LAW
Judicial Review—*Marbury v. Madison* (1803)

In the edifice of American public law, the *Marbury v. Madison* decision in 1803 can be viewed as the keystone of the constitutional arch. The story is often told, and for a reason—it shows how seemingly insignificant cases can have important and enduring results.

Consider the facts behind *Marbury v. Madison*. John Adams had lost his bid for reelection to Thomas Jefferson in 1800. Adams, a Federalist, thought the Jeffersonian (Democratic) Republicans (Anti-Federalists) would weaken the power of the national government by asserting states' rights. He also feared the Anti-Federalists' antipathy toward business. During the final hours of Adams's presidency, he worked feverishly to "pack" the judiciary with loyal Federalists just before Jefferson took office.

All of the judicial appointments had to be certified and delivered. The task of delivery fell on Adams's secretary of state, John Marshall. Out of the fifty-nine midnight appointments, Marshall delivered only forty-two. Of course, Jefferson refused to have his new secretary of state, James Madison, deliver the remaining commissions. William Marbury, along with three other Federalists to whom the commissions had not been delivered, decided to sue. The suit was brought directly to the Supreme Court, seeking a writ of *mandamus* (an order issued by a court to compel the performance of an act), authorized by the Judiciary Act of 1789.

As fate would have it, the man responsible for the lawsuit, John Marshall, had stepped down as Adams's secretary of state only to become chief

John Marshall

James Madison

justice. He was now in a position to decide the case for which he was responsible.* Marshall was faced with a dilemma: If he ordered the commissions delivered, the new secretary of state could simply refuse. The Court had no way to compel action, because it has no police force. Also, Congress was controlled by the Democratic Republicans. It might impeach Marshall for such an action.† But if Marshall simply allowed Secretary of State Madison to do as he wished, the Court's power would be eroded severely.

Marshall masterfully fashioned a decision that did not require anyone to do anything but at the same time enlarged the power of the Supreme Court. He stated that the highest court did not have the power to issue a writ of *mandamus* in this particular case. Marshall pointed out that Article III of the Constitution, which spelled out the Court's original jurisdiction (its

authority to decide cases brought directly to the Court instead of on appeal), did not mention writs of *mandamus*. Because Congress did not have the right to expand the Supreme Court's jurisdiction, this section of the Judiciary Act of 1789 was unconstitutional—and thus void. The decision still stands today as a judicial and political masterpiece.

For Critical Analysis
What might result if the courts could not exercise the power of judicial review?

*Today, any justice who has been involved in an issue before the Court would probably disqualify himself or herself because of a conflict of interest.
†In fact, in 1805, Congress did impeach Supreme Court Justice Samuel Chase, a Federalist, although he was not convicted. The charge was abusive behavior under the Sedition Act.

declared unconstitutional by the Court much more often—about 1,000 times. Most of these rulings date from the period after the Civil War, before which time only two acts of Congress were declared unconstitutional. There have been two periods of relatively extensive use of the process of judicial negation—in the 1920s and 1930s, when a conservative Court upheld private interests over public statutes, and in the 1960s and 1970s, when more liberal justices upheld individual and group rights to racial and political equality.

A significant modern example of judicial review was the Supreme Court's ruling in *Term Limits v. Arkansas,*[4] a case decided in 1995. The Court held that an Arkansas state constitutional amendment limiting the terms of congresspersons was unconstitutional. As a consequence of this decision, laws establishing term limits in twenty-three other states were also invalidated. Other examples include the Supreme Court's 1996 ruling that certain state attempts to redraw congressional districts to increase minority representation violated the equal protection clause (see Chapter 12); and the decisions of two lower courts holding that the Communications Decency Act of 1996, enacted by Congress to regulate indecent speech on the Internet, was unconstitutional (see Chapter 4).

Whether a court will declare an action of the legislative or executive branch unconstitutional, depends, of course, on how the court interprets the Constitution. We now turn to a discussion of what many have termed the "policymaking" function of the judiciary—interpreting the laws.

Interpreting the Laws

How the courts interpret and apply the laws necessarily has a broad impact on our society. As the final interpreter of the Constitution, the Supreme Court plays a leading role in giving shape to the rights and liberties of Americans set forth in that document. Similarly, when applying statutory law to specific situations, the Court must determine the meaning of statutory provisions. Deciding what the framers of the Constitution or a legislative body meant by a certain phrase or provision is never easy, and inevitably, at least to some extent, the personal attributes and ideological persuasions of the justices come into play during the process.

Generally, conservative justices tend to interpret the law based on the ordinary meaning given to the words being examined. Liberal justices tend to assume that the broader social and political context should be considered when determining the meaning of particular words. The Supreme Court justices' different interpretations of Title VI of the Civil Rights Act of 1964 in *Regents of the University of California v. Bakke*[5] illustrate these two approaches. Recall from Chapter 5 that this was one of the first cases challenging the constitutionality of affirmative action programs. The case was brought by Allan Bakke, who was denied admission to a University of California medical school even though his academic record was better than those of some of the minority applicants who had been admitted to the program under an affirmative action program.

Four of the Court's justices took a conservative approach, concluding that the university's affirmative action program violated the plain language of Title VI, which reads, "No person in the United States shall, on the ground of race, color, or national origin, be excluded from participation in, be denied the benefits of, or be subjected to discrimination under any program or activity receiving federal financial assistance." Four other justices, of a more liberal persuasion, concluded that the words of the statute did not necessarily mean what they said. It was "inconceivable" in their minds that Congress would attempt to eliminate racial discrimination without permitting the use of "race-conscious remedies." The Court's decision in the matter marked a com-

---

[4]115 S.Ct. 1842 (1995).
[5]438 U.S. 265 (1978).

POLITICS AND THE CONSTITUTION
The Changing Meaning of Equal Protection

As you no doubt have learned by this time, the Constitution essentially means what the Supreme Court says it does. The Court's varying interpretations of the equal protection clause of the Fourteenth Amendment provide a good illustration of how the meaning of a constitutional provision or amendment can change over time.

After the passage of the Fourteenth Amendment following the Civil War, for example, the Court faced the question of how continued discrimination against African Americans could be justified in view of the equal protection clause. The Court's answer to this question was the "separate but equal" doctrine enunciated in 1896 in *Plessy v. Ferguson.** The Court held that racial segregation—separate facilities for African Americans and whites—did not violate the Fourteenth Amendment. The Court stated that the amendment "could not have been intended to abolish distinctions based upon color, or to enforce social . . . equality." The "separate but equal" doctrine was upheld by the Court for nearly sixty years thereafter.

By the 1950s, the mood of the nation had changed considerably, as had the ideological make-up of the high court. Under Chief Justice Earl Warren, the Court actively sought not

only to end racial discrimination but also to undo the effects of past discrimination by integrating the public schools. As discussed in Chapter 5, in the 1960s Congress passed a series of acts protecting the rights of all Americans to be free from discriminatory practices. The Civil Rights Act of 1964, for example, prohibited discrimination on the basis of race, color, national origin, gender, or religion. Affirmative action programs were established to make up for the effects of past discrimination—against African Americans and other minorities, as well as women. The Warren Court upheld these and other laws protecting Americans' civil rights. To a significant extent, so did the Court under the more conservative leadership of Warren Burger from 1969 to 1986.

In the 1990s, the meaning of the equal protection clause again is undergoing a metamorphosis. The Rehnquist Court of today seems to have concluded, with some historical irony, that affirmative action programs, because they treat people unequally, are constitutionally suspect. Although the Court has not ruled that all affirmative action programs are unconstitutional, it has subjected them to strict scrutiny. Under this standard of judicial review, unless such programs are

tailored narrowly to remedy specific past discriminatory practices, they will violate the equal protection mandate. The Court also has let stand the decisions of several lower courts that have held affirmative action programs to be unconstitutional.

Many have been puzzled by the Court's "conservative" approach to affirmative action on the one hand, and its "liberal" approach to gay and lesbian rights and male-only school policies on the other hand.[†] The connecting link here is the Court's view of the equal protection clause. The Court apparently has decided that equal protection means just what it says—no more and no less.

For Critical Analysis
Do all federal laws or policies that require unequal treatment violate the equal protection clause? [Hint: What about the Americans with Disabilities Act of 1990?]

*163 U.S. 537 (1896). This case and the civil rights legislation referred to in this feature are discussed in greater detail in Chapter 5.

[†]See the discussion in Chapter 6 of *Romer v. Evans,* 116 S.Ct. 1620 (1996); and *United States v. Virginia,* 116 S.Ct. 2263 (1996).

promise: race could be one of a number of factors governing admission to the medical school but not the only factor. (See this chapter's *Politics and the Constitution* for another example of how these two approaches to judicial decision making have been applied to the equal protection clause of the Constitution over time.)

OUR COURT SYSTEM TODAY

The United States has a dual court system. There are state courts and federal courts. Each of the fifty states, as well as the District of Columbia, has its own fully developed, independent system of courts. The federal court system derives its power from the U.S. Constitution, Article III, Section 1.

JURISDICTION

The authority of a court to decide certain cases. Not all courts have the authority to decide all cases. Where a case arises and what its subject matter is are two jurisdictional factors.

FEDERAL QUESTION

A question that pertains to the U.S. Constitution, acts of Congress, or treaties. A federal question provides a basis for federal jurisdiction.

DIVERSITY OF CITIZENSHIP

A basis for federal court jurisdiction over a lawsuit between (1) citizens of different states, (2) a foreign country and citizens of a state or of different states, or (3) citizens of a state and citizens or subjects of a foreign country. The amount in controversy must be more than $75,000 before a federal court can take jurisdiction in such cases.

TRIAL COURT

The court in which most cases usually begin and in which questions of fact are examined.

State courts can exercise **jurisdiction** (the power to hear and decide cases) over most cases touching on persons or property within their borders. Federal court jurisdiction is more limited—because the federal government is a limited government.[6] One basis for federal jurisdiction arises when a lawsuit involves a **federal question** (a question concerning, at least in part, the U.S. Constitution, a treaty, or a federal law). Another basis for federal jurisdiction is **diversity of citizenship,** which exists when a lawsuit is between (1) citizens of different states, (2) a foreign country and citizens of a state or of different states, or (3) citizens of a state and citizens or subjects of a foreign country. The amount in controversy must be more than $75,000 before a federal court can take jurisdiction in diversity cases. (See this chapter's *Thinking Politically about Diversity Jurisdiction* for more details on diversity jurisdiction.)

The Federal Court System

Both the federal and state court systems have several tiers of authority. Figure 15–1 shows the components of the federal judiciary. There are ninety-four federal district courts, which are the basic **trial courts** in the federal system. The majority of cases that are appropriately within the jurisdiction of the federal courts start here.

When cases that have been decided in a federal trial court are appealed, they usually go to one of the federal circuit courts of appeals, the boundaries of which are outlined in Figure 15–2 on page 512. Under normal circumstances, the decisions of the courts of appeals are final, but appeal to the United States Supreme Court is possible. At the top of the federal judiciary is the Supreme Court of the United States. According to the language of Article III of the U.S. Constitution, there can only be one Supreme Court, with all other courts in the federal system "inferior" to it.

Figure 15–1
• •
The Federal Court System

[6]The jurisdiction of the federal courts is limited by Article III, Section 2, of the U.S. Constitution.

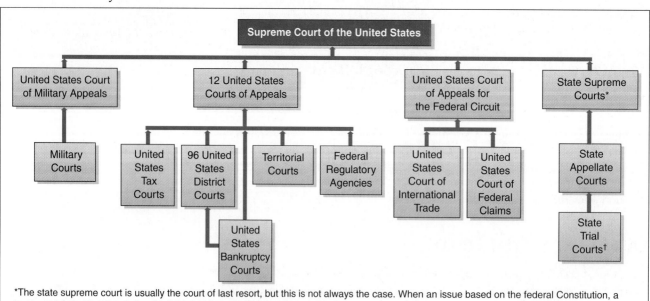

*The state supreme court is usually the court of last resort, but this is not always the case. When an issue based on the federal Constitution, a treaty, or a federal statute is involved, it might be possible to appeal a state supreme court decision to the United States Supreme Court.

† It is also possible to transfer a case from a state court to a U.S. district court on a writ of *habeas corpus.*

Thinking Politically about Diversity Jurisdiction

Diversity jurisdiction arose out of what were basically considerations of fairness. Apparently, the authors of the Constitution felt that a state might be biased in favor of its own citizens and, therefore, when a dispute involved citizens from different states, a federal forum should be available to protect the out-of-state party. Today, the possibility of moving a case to federal court when diversity jurisdiction exists is often an attractive option. For example, a California plaintiff who wants to sue a New York business firm for damages that exceed $75,000 can file the suit in a federal court located in California—the plaintiff does not have to initiate the suit in a New York court.

Diversity jurisdiction offers many advantages, but there is also a major disadvantage—the federal courts end up spending a good deal of their time deciding issues that arise under state law. Like the state courts, the federal courts are facing a growing backlog of cases, and there is little hope that the federal judiciary's budget will be expanded greatly. Rather, ways are being explored to trim that budget.

Some people see limiting or abolishing diversity jurisdiction as a solution to this problem. For example, the Long Range Planning Committee of the Judicial Conference of the United States (the official organization of the federal judiciary) recently recom-

mended that diversity jurisdiction be eliminated entirely except in cases involving foreigners or in cases in which local prejudice in a state court clearly can be demonstrated. This is not the first such proposal. In fact, since the 1920s bills to curtail or abolish diversity jurisdiction have been introduced periodically in Congress. So far, none of the proposals has been adopted into law.

For Critical Analysis

Are the benefits of diversity jurisdiction worth its costs to the federal court system?

State Court Systems

State court systems are similar to the federal court system, except that only twenty-three states have intermediate courts of appeals, or **appellate courts,** between the trial courts (in which the majority of cases originate) and the highest reviewing courts of the states. Many cases that appear before trial courts require juries. A trial jury normally consists of six or twelve jurors, who determine the innocence or guilt of the defendant in criminal and civil trials. A **grand jury,** in contrast, is called for a *pretrial* proceeding. The grand jury consists of from six to twenty-three persons who are called to hear evidence and determine whether indictments should be issued against persons suspected of having committed a crime. Grand juries decide whether there is enough evidence to warrant a formal accusation by the state of wrongdoing; they do not determine guilt.

The decisions of each state's highest court on questions of state law are final. Only when issues relating to the U.S. Constitution or other federal laws are involved can the United States Supreme Court overrule a state court's decision. Recall that the Constitution reserves all powers to the states that are not expressly granted to the federal government. The federal courts, which derive their power from the Constitution, thus have no authority to rule on issues relating solely to state law.

APPELLATE COURT

A court having jurisdiction to review cases and issues that were originally tried in lower courts.

GRAND JURY

A jury called to hear evidence and determine whether indictments should be issued against persons suspected of having committed crimes.

Parties and Procedures

In most lawsuits, the parties are the plaintiff (the person or organization that initiates the lawsuit) and the defendant (the person or organization against whom the lawsuit is brought). There may be numerous plaintiffs and defendants in a single lawsuit. In the last several decades, many lawsuits have been

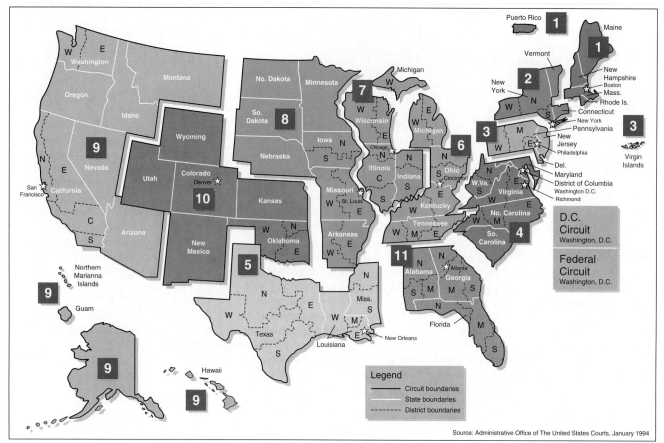

Figure 15–2
● ● ● ● ● ● ● ● ● ● ● ● ● ● ● ● ● ● ●
Geographic Boundaries of Federal Circuit Courts of Appeals

LITIGATE

To engage in a legal proceeding or seek relief in a court of law; to carry on a lawsuit.

AMICUS CURIAE BRIEF

A brief (a document containing a legal argument supporting a desired outcome in a particular case) filed by a third party, or *amicus curiae* (Latin for "friend of the court"), who is not directly involved in the litigation but who has an interest in the outcome of the case.

CLASS-ACTION SUIT

A lawsuit filed by an individual seeking damages for "all persons similarly situated."

brought by interest groups (see Chapter 8). Interest groups play an important role in our judicial system, because they **litigate**—bring to trial—or assist in litigating most cases of racial or gender-based discrimination, virtually all civil liberties cases, and more than one-third of the cases involving business matters. Interest groups also file *amicus curiae* **briefs** in more than 50 percent of these kinds of cases.

Sometimes, interest groups or other plaintiffs will bring a **class-action suit,** in which whatever the court decides will affect all members of a class similarly situated (such as users of a particular product manufactured by the defendant in the lawsuit). The strategy of class-action lawsuits was pioneered by such groups as the National Association for the Advancement of Colored People (NAACP), the Legal Defense Fund, and the Sierra Club, whose members believed that the courts—rather than Congress—would offer the most sympathetic forum for their views.

Both the federal and the state courts have established procedural rules that shape the litigation process. These rules are designed to protect the rights and interests of the parties, to ensure that the litigation proceeds in a fair and orderly manner, and to identify the issues that must be decided by the court—thus saving court time and costs. (See this chapter's *Politics and the Judiciary* for a discussion of the budget problems facing the federal courts.) The parties must comply with procedural rules and with any orders given by the judge during the course of the litigation. When a party does not follow a court's order, the court can cite him or her for contempt. A party who commits *civil* contempt (failing to comply with a court's order for the benefit of another party to the proceeding) can be taken into custody, fined, or both,

POLITICS AND THE JUDICIARY
Budget-Crunching and Judicial Accommodations

Judges traditionally have been the masters of their courtrooms. In addition to determining how the opposing parties will or will not behave while in court, judges also have some say in designing new courthouses. For example, for the new federal courthouse being constructed in Boston, the judges requested that the courtrooms be paneled with a rare and expensive type of English oak. They also wanted the vanities in the judges' private bathrooms to have marble tops. For the new federal courthouse in New York City, the judges insisted on having showers and private kitchens in their chambers, as well as mahogany wood paneling in the courtrooms.

Many judges seem unconcerned about courtroom costs. Others, including Judge Martin Feldman, a U.S. district court judge in New Orleans, think that they are entitled to comfortable accommodations. "Would anyone criticize the opulence of the speaker's office or the extent to which senators enjoy comfort in Washington?" asks Judge Feldman.*

Other government officials, though, are concerned about the judiciary's total expenses, and judicial lifestyles increasingly are coming under scrutiny. According to a report released by the Senate Environment and Public Works Committee, the "unrestrained demands" of federal judges have caused courthouse construction costs to escalate. For example, the new New York courthouse, which originally was supposed to cost $354 million to construct, ended up costing $500 million after the judges' various requests were met.

Compared to the other two branches of government, the judiciary's annual budget is relatively meager—around $2.7 billion. What has the government worried is the fact that the judiciary's budget has grown over 1,000 percent during the past twenty years, compared to a 330 percent increase in the legislative budget and a 435 percent increase in the executive branch's budget. Even so, some judicial officials maintain that the budget increases have not kept pace with the increasing demands placed on the judiciary. In the past decade, the federal courts have faced an expanding caseload, particularly with respect to environmental and criminal law cases. The question is, how can the judiciary handle its backlog of some 20,000 cases and still trim its budget?

For Critical Analysis

If the decision were up to you, would you trim the judiciary's budget, or would you reduce funding for some other government agency or program? If the latter, which agency or program would be your target? Why?

*As quoted in Constance Johnson, "Federal Judiciary's Budget Is Scrutinized," *The Wall Street Journal,* June 30, 1995, p. B4.

until the party complies with the court's order. A party who commits *criminal* contempt (obstructing the administration of justice or bringing the court into disrepute) also can be taken into custody and fined but cannot avoid punishment by complying with a previous order.

THE SUPREME COURT—CHOOSING, HEARING, AND DECIDING CASES

Alexander Hamilton, writing in *Federalist Paper* No. 78, believed that the Supreme Court would be the "least dangerous branch" of the federal government, because it had no enforcement powers, nor could it raise money. The other two branches had to cooperate with it, and the public had to accept its decisions, or the Supreme Court would be superfluous.

In the Court's earliest years, it appeared that Hamilton's prediction would come true. The first Supreme Court chief justice, John Jay, resigned to become governor of New York because he thought the Court would never play an important role in American society. The next chief justice, Oliver Ellsworth, quit to become an envoy to France. In 1801, when the federal capital was moved to Washington, somebody forgot to include the Supreme Court in the plans. It met in the office of the clerk of the Senate until 1935.

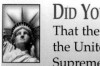

Of the total number of cases that are decided each year, those reviewed by the Supreme Court represent less than one-half of 1 percent. Included in these, however, are decisions that profoundly affect our lives—even issues of life and death. In recent years, the United States Supreme Court has decided numerous issues, including issues involving capital punishment, affirmative action programs, abortion, busing, term limits for congresspersons, sexual harassment, and pornography. Because the Supreme Court exercises a great deal of discretion over the types of cases it hears, it can influence the nation's policies by issuing decisions in some types of cases and refusing to hear appeals in others, thereby allowing lower court decisions to stand.

Which Cases Reach the Supreme Court?

Many people are surprised to learn that in a typical case, there is no absolute right of appeal to the United States Supreme Court. The Supreme Court is given original, or trial court, jurisdiction in a small number of situations. Under Article III, Section 2, Paragraph 2, the Supreme Court has original jurisdiction in all cases affecting foreign diplomats and in all cases in which a state is a party. The Eleventh Amendment, passed in 1798, removed from the judicial power of the United States suits commenced by, or prosecuted against, citizens of another state or by citizens or subjects of any foreign nation. Therefore, the Supreme Court today rarely acts as a court of original jurisdiction except in cases involving suits by one state against another, such as suits relating to territorial disputes or cross-border pollution. In all other cases, its jurisdiction is appellate "with such Exceptions, and under such Regulations as the Congress shall make." Appellate jurisdiction means the authority of the Court to review decisions of a lower court. With the Judicial Improvements and Access to Justice Act of 1988, Congress made the Court's appellate jurisdiction almost entirely discretionary—the court can choose which cases it will decide.

WRIT OF *CERTIORARI*

An order issued by a higher court to a lower court to send up the record of a case for review. It is the principal vehicle for United States Supreme Court review.

With a **writ of *certiorari*** (pronounced sur-shee-uh-*rah*-ree), the Supreme Court orders a lower court to send it the record of a case for review. A party can petition the Supreme Court to issue a writ of *certiorari*. Typically, however, only petitions that raise the possibility of important constitutional questions or problems of statutory interpretation are granted. Within these limits, the granting of *certiorari* (or "cert," as it is popularly called) is done entirely at the discretion of the Court and seems to depend on such factors as who the petitioners are, the kinds of issues involved, and the ideologies of the individual justices of the Court.

The following situations indicate when the Court will issue a writ, although they are not a limit on the Court's discretion:

1. When a state court has decided a substantial federal question that has not been determined by the Supreme Court before, or the state court has decided it in a way that is probably in disagreement with the trend of the Supreme Court's decisions.
2. When two federal courts of appeals are in disagreement with each other.
3. When a federal court of appeals has decided an important state question in conflict with state law, has decided an important federal question not yet addressed by the Supreme Court but that should be decided by the Court, has decided a federal question in conflict with applicable decisions of the Court, or has departed from the accepted and usual course of judicial proceedings.
4. When a federal court of appeals holds a state statute to be invalid because it violates federal law.

5. When the state's highest court holds a federal law invalid or upholds a state law that has been challenged as violating a federal law.

6. When a federal court holds an act of Congress unconstitutional and the federal government or one of its employees is a party.

More than 90 percent of the petitions for writs of *certiorari* are denied. A denial is not a decision on the merits of a case, nor does it indicate agreement with the lower court's opinion. (The judgment of the lower court remains in force, however.) Therefore, denial of the writ has no value as a precedent.[7] The Court will not issue a writ unless at least four justices approve of it. This is called the **rule of four.**[8]

The Supreme Court at Work

The Supreme Court, by law, begins its regular annual term on the first Monday in October and usually adjourns in late June or early July of the next year. Special sessions may be held after the regular term is over, but only a few cases are decided in this way. More commonly, cases are carried over until the next regular session.

The United States Supreme Court normally does not hear any evidence, as is true with all appeals courts. The Court's consideration of a case is based on the abstracts, the record, and the briefs. The attorneys are permitted to present **oral arguments.** The Court hears oral arguments on Monday, Tuesday, Wednesday, and sometimes Thursday, usually for seven two-week sessions scattered from the first week in October to the end of April or the first week in May. Recesses are held between periods of oral argument to allow the justices to consider the cases and handle other Court business. Oral arguments run from 10 A.M. to noon and again from 1 to 3 P.M., with thirty minutes for each side unless a special exception is granted. All statements and the justices' questions are tape-recorded during these sessions. Unlike the practice in most courts, lawyers addressing the Supreme Court can be (and often are) questioned by the justices at any time during oral argument.

Deciding a Case: Private Research. All of the crucial work on accepted cases is done through private research and reflection. Each justice is entitled to four law clerks (recent graduates of law schools), who undertake much of the research and preliminary drafting necessary for the justice to form an opinion. It is sometimes suspected that because of their extensive assistance, the law clerks form a kind of junior court in themselves, deciding the fate of appeals and petitions to the Court. Some disgruntled lawyers have even suggested that the Senate should no longer confirm the appointment of justices but rather the appointment of law clerks. Such criticism is probably too harsh. Clerks do help in screening the large volume of petitions and in the preliminary research work for cases under review, but the justices make the decisions.

Deciding a Case: The Wednesday and Friday Conferences. Each Wednesday and Friday during the annual Court term, the justices meet in conference to discuss cases then under consideration and to decide which new appeals and petitions the Court will accept. These conferences take place in the oak-paneled chamber and are strictly private—no stenographers, tape recorders,

RULE OF FOUR

A United States Supreme Court procedure requiring four affirmative votes to hear the case before the full Court.

ORAL ARGUMENTS

The verbal arguments presented in person by attorneys to an appellate court. Each attorney presents reasons to the court why the court should rule in his or her client's favor.

---

[7]*Singleton v. Commissioner of Internal Revenue,* 439 U.S. 940 (1978).
[8]The "rule of four" is modified when seven or fewer justices participate, which occurs from time to time. When that happens, as few as three justices can grant *certiorari.*

DID YOU KNOW . . .
That only four American presidents—William Henry Harrison, Zachary Taylor, Andrew Johnson, and Jimmy Carter—appointed no Supreme Court justices?

or video cameras are allowed. Two pages used to be in attendance to wait on the justices while they were in conference, but fear of information leaks caused the Court to stop this practice.[9]

In the justices' conference, certain procedures traditionally are observed. On entering the room, each justice shakes hands with all present. The justices then sit by order of seniority around a large, rectangular table. Each case is discussed by each justice in that order, with the chief justice starting the discussion. The chief justice determines the order in which the cases are called, guides the discussion generally, and in most cases, sets the tone for the proceedings.

Starting with the Court of John Marshall, after each discussion, a vote was taken in reverse order of seniority. Today, the justices seldom vote formally. Since 1965, decisions have been announced on any day that they are ready to be released. They are usually presented orally, in summary form, in open session by the author of the decision. Other views may be stated by members who have written concurring or dissenting opinions. After the necessary editing and the publication of preliminary prints, the official Court decision is placed in the *United States Reports,* the official record of the Court's decisions, which is available in most college libraries. (See this chapter's *Logging On* to learn how you can access Supreme Court opinions via the Internet almost immediately after the decisions are announced.)

Cases that are brought on petition (or appeal) to the Court are scheduled for an oral argument or denied a hearing in a written "orders list" released on Mondays.

Decisions and Opinions. When the Court has reached a decision, its opinion is written. The **opinion** contains the Court's reasons for its decision, the rules of law that apply, and the judgment. In general, the Court will not **reverse** findings of fact unless the findings are unsupported or contradicted by the evidence. Rather, it will review the record for errors of law. If the Supreme Court feels that a reversible error was committed during the trial or that the jury was instructed improperly, the judgment will be reversed. Sometimes the case will be **remanded** (sent back to the court that originally heard the case) for a new trial or other proceeding. In many cases, the decision of the lower court is **affirmed,** resulting in the enforcement of that court's judgment or decree.

The Court's written opinion sometimes is brief and unsigned; this is called a *per curiam* opinion. Often, it is long and is signed by all the justices who agree with it. Usually, when in the majority, the chief justice will write the opinion. Whenever the chief justice is in the minority, the senior justice on the majority side decides who writes the opinion.

There are four types of written opinions for any particular case decided by the Supreme Court. When all justices unanimously agree on an opinion, the opinion is written for the entire Court (all the justices) and can be deemed a **unanimous opinion.** When there is not a unanimous opinion, a **majority opinion** is written, outlining the views of the majority of the justices involved in the particular case. Often, one or more justices who feel strongly about making or emphasizing a particular point that is not made or emphasized in the unanimous or majority written opinion will write a **concurring opinion.** That means the justice writing the concurring opinion agrees (concurs) with the conclusion given in the unanimous or majority written opinion, but for different reasons. Finally, in other than unanimous opinions, one or more dis-

OPINION

The statement by a judge or a court of the decision reached in a case tried or argued before it. The opinion sets forth the law that applies to the case and details the legal reasoning on which the judgment was based.

REVERSE

To annul or make void a judgment on account of some error or irregularity.

REMAND

To send a case back to the court that originally heard it.

AFFIRM

To declare that a judgment is valid and must stand.

UNANIMOUS OPINION

An opinion or determination on which all judges agree.

MAJORITY OPINION

The views of the majority of the judges.

CONCURRING OPINION

A separate opinion, prepared by a judge who supports the decision of the majority of the court but who wants to make or clarify a particular point or to voice disapproval of the grounds on which the decision was made.

---

[9]Even though it turned out that one supposed information leak came from lawyers making educated guesses.

senting opinions are usually written by those justices who do not agree with the majority. The **dissenting opinion** is important because it often forms the basis of the arguments used years later that cause the Court to reverse the previous decision and establish a new precedent.

DISSENTING OPINION
A separate opinion in which a judge dissents from (disagrees with) the conclusion reached by the majority of the court and expounds his or her own views about the case.

After a Decision Is Reached

President Andrew Jackson was once supposed to have said, after Chief Justice John Marshall made an unpopular decision, that "John Marshall has made his decision; now let him enforce it."[10] This purported quote goes to the heart of **judicial implementation,** or the way in which court decisions are actually translated into policy and thereby affect the behavior of individuals, businesspersons, police personnel, and the like. The Court does not have the executive power to implement its decisions, nor does it have control of the budget to pay for such implementation when government funds are required. Other units of government have to carry out the Court's decisions.

JUDICIAL IMPLEMENTATION
The way in which court decisions are translated into action.

That means that the process of judicial implementation may take time, or it may never occur at all. Prayers were banned in public schools in 1962, yet it was widely known that the ban was (and still is) ignored in many southern districts. After the Court ordered schools to desegregate "with all deliberate speed" in 1955,[11] the inflammatory rhetoric against desegregation expounded by the governor and state legislators in Little Rock, Arkansas, encouraged citizens to take the law into their own hands. A riot broke out in 1957, and the president finally decided to act. President Dwight Eisenhower federalized (subjected to federal authority) the state's national guard, which quelled the riot.

Initially, the media reporting on Supreme Court decisions provide the most widespread information about what the Court has decided. (Often, though, such paraphrased information may be inaccurate.) Those persons affected by Supreme Court decisions somehow have to become aware of their new-found rights (or of the stripping of their existing rights). For example, the Supreme Court, in *Miranda v. Arizona* in 1966, set guidelines for police questioning of suspects (see Chapter 4).[12] It has been estimated that it took seventeen months before all of the police departments around the country were aware of the decision, and it certainly took even longer for suspected criminals to be aware that they should be "read their *Miranda* rights."

THE SELECTION OF FEDERAL JUDGES

All federal judges are appointed. The Constitution, in Article II, Section 2, states that the president appoints the justices of the Supreme Court with the advice and consent of the Senate. Congress has provided the same procedure for staffing other federal courts. This means that the Senate and the president jointly decide who shall be a federal judge, no matter what the level.

There are over eight hundred federal judgeships in the United States. Once appointed to such a judgeship, a person holds that job for life. Judges serve until they resign, retire voluntarily, or die.

Federal judges may be removed through impeachment, although such action is extremely rare. Moreover, the conduct must be blatantly illegal, as

---

[10]The decision referred to was *Cherokee Nation v. Georgia,* 5 Pet. 1 (1831). *Pet.* in an abbreviation of *Petrarch,* a nineteenth-century reporter of Supreme Court cases.
[11]*Brown v. Board of Education,* 349 U.S. 294 (1955), the second *Brown* decision.
[12]384 U.S. 436 (1966).

was illustrated by the impeachment proceedings against federal judges Alcee Hastings and Walter Nixon. Hastings was impeached by the U.S. House of Representatives on a charge of conspiracy to obtain a $150,000 bribe and lying about his actions to a jury. Nixon was impeached for lying to a grand jury about a discussion he had had with a district county attorney in Mississippi. The discussion concerned charges brought against the son of a wealthy friend. Both Hastings and Nixon were removed from office.

Nominating Judicial Candidates

Judicial candidates for federal judgeships are suggested to the president by the Department of Justice, senators, other judges, the candidates themselves, and bar associations and other interest groups.

Since the Truman administration, the American Bar Association, through its Committee on the Federal Judiciary, furnishes the president with evaluations of those individuals being considered. No president is required to refer any nominees to the committee, but most presidents have done so.

The nomination process—no matter how the nominees are obtained—always works the same way. The president does the actual nomination, transmitting the name to the Senate. The Senate then either confirms or rejects the nomination. To reach a conclusion, the Senate Judiciary Committee (operating through subcommittees) invites testimony, both written and oral, at its various hearings. In the case of federal district court judgeship nominations, a practice used in the Senate, called **senatorial courtesy,** is a constraint on the president's freedom to appoint whomever the administration chooses. Senatorial courtesy allows a senator of the president's political party to veto a judicial appointment in his or her state.

Federal District Court Judgeship Nominations. Although the president nominates federal judges, the nomination of federal district court judges typically originates with a senator or senators of the president's party from the state in which there is a vacancy. If the Committee on the Federal Judiciary of the American Bar Association deems the nominee unqualified, as a matter of political courtesy the president will discuss with the senator or senators who originated the nomination whether the nomination should be withdrawn. Also, when a nomination is unacceptable politically to the president, the president will consult with the appropriate senator or senators, indicate that the nomination is unacceptable, and work with the senator or senators to seek an alternative candidate.

Federal Courts of Appeals Appointments. There are many fewer federal courts of appeals appointments than federal district court appointments, but they are more important. This is because federal appellate judges handle more important matters, at least from the point of view of the president, and therefore presidents take a keener interest in the nomination process for such judgeships. Also, appointments to the U.S. courts of appeals have become "stepping stones" to the Supreme Court. Typically, the president culls the Circuit Judge Nominating Commission's list of nominees for potential candidates. The president may also use this list to oppose senators' recommendations that may be unacceptable politically to the president.

SUPREME COURT APPOINTMENTS AND IDEOLOGY

The nomination of Supreme Court justices belongs solely to the president, as we have described. That is not to say that the president's nominations are

SENATORIAL COURTESY

In regard to federal district court judgeship nominations, a Senate tradition allowing a senator of the president's political party to veto a judgeship appointment in his or her state simply by indicating that the appointment is personally not acceptable. At that point, the Senate may reject the nomination, or the president may withdraw consideration of the nominee.

always confirmed, however. In fact, almost 20 percent of presidential nominations for the Supreme Court have been either rejected or not acted on by the Senate. Numerous acrimonious battles over Supreme Court appointments have ensued when the Senate and the president have not seen eye to eye about political matters.

The Senate's Role

The U.S. Senate had a long record of refusing to confirm the president's judicial nominations from the beginning of Andrew Jackson's presidency in 1829 to the end of Ulysses Grant's presidency in 1877. During a fairly long period of relative acquiescence on the part of the Senate to presidential nominations, from 1894 until 1968, only three nominees were not confirmed. From 1968 through 1986, however, there were two rejections of presidential nominees to the highest court. Both were Nixon appointees, rejected because of questions about their racial attitudes. In 1987, two of President Ronald Reagan's nominees failed to be confirmed—Robert Bork was rejected for his views on the Constitution, and Douglas Ginsburg withdrew his nomination when it was reported that he had used marijuana in the 1970s.

President George Bush decided to use a different strategy when Justice William J. Brennan announced his retirement from the bench in 1989. Bush chose David H. Souter, a recent appointee to a federal court of appeals with extensive experience as a justice on the New Hampshire Supreme Court. Souter was dubbed a "stealth" candidate, because he had not written extensively on controversial social issues, such as abortion or racial equality. During the Senate Judiciary Committee hearings, various members attempted to elicit Souter's views on these subjects, but he refused to speculate as to how he would rule in any particular hypothetical case.

The same tactic was followed by Bush's second nominee, Clarence Thomas, who underwent an extremely volatile confirmation hearing replete with charges of sexual harassment. Were it not for the dramatic and televised allegations by his former aide, Anita Hill, Thomas's confirmation hearings might have been more similar in tone to those of Souter. Both men were confirmed, however, although members of the Senate Judiciary Committee complained about the lack of information concerning the nominees' views.

Demonstrators protest the possible confirmation of Judge Clarence Thomas in 1991, after Professor Anita Hill charged him with sexually harassing her while she was his employee. After long and difficult hearings on the subject, the Senate voted to confirm Judge Thomas.

In 1993, President Clinton had little trouble gaining approval for his nominee to take the seat left vacant by Justice Byron White. Ruth Bader Ginsburg became the second female Supreme Court Justice. In 1994, Clinton nominated Stephen Breyer, a federal court of appeals judge, to fill the seat of retiring Supreme Court Justice Harry Blackmun. Seen by many as a consensus builder who might effectively pull together justices with divergent views, Breyer was confirmed without significant opposition.

Partisanship and Supreme Court Appointments

Ideology plays an important role in the president's choices for the Supreme Court (and for nominations to the lower federal courts, too). Ideology also plays a large role in the Senate's confirmation hearings. There has been an extremely partisan distribution of presidential appointments to the federal judiciary. In the over two hundred years of the Supreme Court's history, fewer than 13 percent of the justices nominated by a president have been from an opposing political party. Presidents see their federal judiciary appointments as the one sure way to institutionalize their political views long after they have left office. By 1993, for example, Presidents Reagan and Bush together had appointed nearly three-quarters of all federal court judges. This preponderance of Republican-appointed federal judges strengthened the legal moorings of the conservative social agenda on a variety of issues, ranging from abortion to civil rights.

Nevertheless, President Bill Clinton has had the opportunity to appoint about two hundred federal judges, marking a different shift in the ideological makeup of the federal judiciary. Also, Clinton's appointees matched more closely the actual U.S. demographics—nearly 38 percent of Clinton's nominees are women, for example, compared to Bush's 17 percent and Reagan's 8 percent. By 1997, Clinton had appointed more women and members of minority groups to federal judgeships than any other president.

The fact that all presidents attempt to strengthen their legacy through the appointment of federal judges with similar political and ideological philosophies has been noted already. But the fact that a president appoints a justice who has supported the president's policies in the past is no guarantee that the newly appointed justice will continue to do so in the future. President Dwight Eisenhower, a conservative Republican, appointed Earl Warren, the former governor of California, to be chief justice of the Supreme Court in 1953. Warren's past moderate-to-conservative policies gave no indication that he would lead the Court in an unprecedented revision of the nation's existing laws, greatly expanding the protections afforded to minorities and criminal defendants. Indeed, Eisenhower later characterized his appointment of Warren as the biggest single mistake of his presidency.

Similarly, Richard Nixon appointed Warren Burger as chief justice in 1969 to replace Earl Warren. Nixon believed that Burger's conservative views would ensure that the court would minimize its involvement in controversial issues, such as school desegregation. But within two years, Burger authored the opinion of the Court in *Swann v. Charlotte-Mecklenburg Board of Education*,[13] in which school authorities were directed to desegregate dual school systems. Perhaps the ultimate irony of Nixon's appointment was that Burger wrote the Court's opinion in *United States v. Nixon*,[14] in which the Court unanimously rejected the president's claim of executive privilege.

[13]402 U.S. 1 (1971).
[14]418 U.S. 683 (1974).

WHO BECOMES A SUPREME COURT JUSTICE?

The make-up of the federal judiciary is far from typical of the American public. Table 15–1 summarizes the background of all of the 108 Supreme Court justices to 1997. The justices' partisan attachments have been mostly the same as those of the president who appointed them. There have been some exceptions, however. Nine nominal Democrats have been appointed by Republican presidents, three Republicans by Democratic presidents, and one Democrat by Whig president John Tyler.[15]

[15]Actually, Tyler was a member of the Democratic party who ran with William H. Harrison on the Whig ticket. When Harrison died, much to the surprise of the Whigs, Tyler—a Democrat— became president, although they tried to call him "acting president." Thus, there are historians who quibble over the statement that Tyler was a Whig.

Table 15–1

Background of Supreme Court Justices to 1997

	NUMBER OF JUSTICES (108 = TOTAL)
Occupational Position before Appointment	
Private legal practice	25
State judgeship	21
Federal judgeship	28
U.S. attorney general	7
Deputy or assistant U.S. attorney general	2
U.S. solicitor general	2
U.S. senator	6
U.S. representative	2
State governor	3
Federal executive post	9
Other	3
Religious Background	
Protestant	83
Roman Catholic	11
Jewish	6
Unitarian	7
No religious affiliation	1
Age on Appointment	
Under 40	5
41–50	31
51–60	58
61–70	14
Political Party Affiliation	
Federalist (to 1835)	13
Democratic Republican (to 1828)	7
Whig (to 1861)	1
Democrat	44
Republican	42
Independent	1
Educational Background	
College graduate	92
Not a college graduate	16
Sex	
Male	106
Female	2
Race	
Caucasian	106
Other	2

SOURCE: Congressional Quarterly, *Congressional Quarterly's Guide to the U.S. Supreme Court* (Washington, D.C.: Congressional Quarterly Press, 1996), and author's update.

As you will note, the most common occupational background of the justices at the time of their appointments has been private legal practice or state or federal judgeships. Those nine justices who were in federal executive posts at the time of their appointments held the high offices of secretary of state, comptroller of the treasury, secretary of the navy, postmaster general, secretary of the interior, chairman of the Securities and Exchange Commission, and secretary of labor. In the "Other" category under "Occupational Position before Appointment" in Table 15–1 are two justices who were professors of law (including William H. Taft, a former president) and one justice who was a North Carolina state employee with responsibility for organizing and revising the state's statutes.

Most justices were in their fifties when they assumed office, although two were as young as thirty-two and one as old as sixty-six. The average age of newly sworn justices is about fifty-three.

The great majority of justices have had a college education. By and large, those who did not attend college or receive a degree lived in the late eighteenth and early nineteenth centuries, when a college education was much less common than it is today. In recent years, degrees from such schools as Yale, Harvard, Columbia, and other prestigious institutions have been typical. Note that many of the earlier college-educated justices did not hold their degrees in law. In fact, it was not until 1957 that all of the sitting members of the Supreme Court were graduates of law schools.

The religious background of Supreme Court justices is clearly not typical of that of the American population as a whole, even making allowances for changes over time in the religious composition of the nation. Catholics (and certain Protestant denominations, notably Baptists and Lutherans) have been underrepresented, whereas Protestants in general (Episcopalians, Presbyterians, Methodists, and others), as well as Unitarians, have been overrepresented among the justices. Typically, there has been a "Catholic seat" on the Court, with interruptions, and a "Jewish seat" existed without a break from 1916 until 1969, when Abe Fortas resigned.

THE REHNQUIST COURT

William H. Rehnquist became the sixteenth chief justice of the Supreme Court in 1986 after fifteen years as an associate justice. He was known as a strong anchor of the Court's conservative wing. With Rehnquist's appointment as chief justice, it seemed to observers that the Court necessarily would become more conservative. Proponents of civil liberties feared that the Rehnquist Court would eventually erode many of those liberties that the previous Courts under Earl Warren (1953 to 1969) and Warren Burger (1969 to 1986) had established or maintained.

In the late 1980s, the Rehnquist Court ruled on several extremely important matters that raised the question of the direction in which the Court was moving ideologically. These rulings also caused renewed speculation about the impact on the Court if one or more of the aging "liberal" justices should die or resign and be replaced with appointees of President George Bush. That is precisely what did happen following the resignations of William Brennan and Thurgood Marshall in 1990 and 1991, respectively, and the subsequent appointments by President Bush of conservative justices David Souter and Clarence Thomas.

The perception that the Rehnquist Court would take a rightward shift in the late 1980s and first half of the 1990s appeared to be borne out by its con-

The Rehnquist Court

· ·

LIBERAL/MODERATE

John Paul Stevens

David Souter

Ruth Bader Ginsburg

Stephen Breyer

SWING VOTES

Sandra Day O'Connor

Anthony Kennedy

CONSERVATIVE

William Rehnquist

Antonin Scalia

Clarence Thomas

servative rulings in cases involving criminal confessions, racial disparities in death-penalty sentencing, the burden of proof placed on litigants in civil rights cases, and the availability of abortion. Indeed, a primary impetus behind Congress's passage of the 1991 Civil Rights Act, which amended several civil rights laws to clarify their meaning and add more protective features, was its desire to overturn a group of Supreme Court cases. These cases, which had been decided by the Court in 1989 and 1990, had greatly restricted the ease with which discrimination suits could be brought by increasing the burden of proof on plaintiffs.

The conservative shift of the Rehnquist Court also forced many special interest groups, including the American Civil Liberties Union and the National Association for the Advancement of Colored People, to view the

Court as a brake on, rather than an accelerator of, the engine of social progress. Consequently, these groups began petitioning Congress to enact laws to overturn Court rulings they considered to be undesirable. Congress was now viewed as the primary guarantor of civil liberties by these groups. This marked a stunning reversal of the situation that had existed in the late 1950s and early 1960s, at which time the Court was vehemently attacked by many members of Congress and by other prominent politicians for its expansive civil rights rulings. A series of rulings in the mid-1990s again has raised concerns that a conservative Supreme Court may be placing in jeopardy many of the gains in civil rights made during the last three decades.

JUDICIAL ACTIVISM AND JUDICIAL RESTRAINT

JUDICIAL ACTIVISM

A doctrine holding that the Supreme Court should take an active role in using its powers to check the activities of Congress, state legislatures, and administrative agencies when those government bodies exceed their authority.

JUDICIAL RESTRAINT

A doctrine holding that the Supreme Court should defer to the decisions made by the elected representatives of the people in the legislative and executive branches.

Judicial scholars like to characterize different Supreme Courts and different Supreme Court justices as being either activist or restraintist. The doctrine of **judicial activism** rests on the conviction that the Supreme Court should take an active role in using its powers to check the activities of Congress, state legislatures, and administrative agencies when those government bodies exceed their authority. One of the Court's most activist eras was the period from 1953 to 1969 when the Court was headed by Chief Justice Earl Warren. The Warren Court propelled the civil rights movement forward by holding, among other things, that laws permitting racial segregation violated the equal protection clause.

In contrast, the doctrine of **judicial restraint** rests on the assumption that the Court should defer to the decisions made by the legislative and executive branches, because members of Congress and the president are elected by the people whereas justices of the Supreme Court are not. Because administrative agency personnel normally have more expertise than the Court does in the areas regulated by the agencies, the Court likewise should defer to agency rules and decisions. In other words, under the doctrine of judicial restraint, the Court should not thwart the implementation of legislative acts and agency rules unless they are clearly unconstitutional.

Judicial activism sometimes is linked with liberalism, and judicial restraint with conservatism. In fact, a conservative Court can be activist, just as a liberal Court can be restraintist—and vice versa. In the 1950s and 1960s, the Court was activist and liberal. An activist decision in the 1970s was *Roe v. Wade*,[16] in which the Supreme Court held that women have the right to an abortion during the first and second trimesters of pregnancy. The Court's decision in this case rendered unconstitutional all state statutes that provided otherwise. Some critics fear that the current Court, with its conservative majority, is becoming increasingly activist, especially with respect to states' rights. (See this chapter's *Critical Perspective* for a further discussion of judicial activism and restraint, and the role of political ideology in framing Supreme Court decisions in general.)

WHAT CHECKS OUR COURTS?

Our judicial system is probably the most independent in the world. But the courts do not have absolute independence, for they are part of the political process. Political checks limit the extent to which courts can exercise judicial

---

[16]410 U.S. 113 (1973).

review and engage in an activist policy. These checks are exercised by the legislature, the executive, the public, and, finally, the judiciary itself.

Legislative Checks

Courts may make rulings, but often the legislatures at local, state, and federal levels are required to appropriate funds to carry out the courts' rulings. When such funds are not appropriated, the court that made the ruling, in effect, has been checked. A court, for example, may decide that prison conditions must be improved. Then a legislature has to find the funds to carry out such a ruling.

Courts' rulings can be overturned by constitutional amendments at both the federal and state levels. Many of the amendments to the U.S. Constitution (such as the Eleventh, Fourteenth, Sixteenth, and Twenty-sixth Amendments) check the state courts' ability to allow discrimination, for example. Proposed constitutional amendments that were created by a desire to reverse courts' decisions on school prayer and abortion have failed.

Finally, legislatures can rewrite (amend) old laws or pass new laws to overturn courts' rulings. This may happen particularly when a court interprets a statute in a way that Congress had not intended or when a court finds no relevant statute to apply in certain cases. The legislature can then pass a new statute to negate the court's ruling, as was the case with the Civil Rights Act of 1991 discussed earlier.

Executive Checks

Presidents have the power to change the direction of the Supreme Court and the federal judiciary. The president can appoint new judges who, in principle, have philosophies more in line with that of the administration. Also, a president, governor, or mayor can refuse to enforce courts' rulings. The possibility that a president might refuse to enforce an order is not merely theoretical. Several presidents, including Abraham Lincoln and Andrew Jackson, have refused to obey orders issued by the Supreme Court.[17] Such conduct does not appear to constitute an explicit violation of the Constitution, because there is no language in that document expressly authorizing the federal courts to review the actions of the executive and legislative branches.

Public Opinion and Response

Despite its lack of tangible enforcement mechanisms, the Supreme Court is widely perceived by the general public to be the final arbiter of national laws. Moreover, its decisions are regarded as the least partisan of all of the three branches of government. Had Richard Nixon refused to hand over the materials for which he claimed executive privilege after the Court's unanimous ruling in *United States v. Nixon*, for example, the Nixon presidency would have seen what little public support it still had further eroded and the chances of a conviction from an impeachment trial increased to a near certainty. In the absence of any threat of impeachment by Congress, however, the main

DID YOU KNOW...
That among the 108 persons who have served on the Supreme Court from 1789 to 1997, only two (Thurgood Marshall and Clarence Thomas) have been African American and only two (Sandra Day O'Connor and Ruth Bader Ginsburg) have been women?

---

[17]Lincoln refused to obey a direct order by the Court in *Ex parte Merryman*, 17 F.Cas. 144 (C.C.D.Md. 1861), whereas Jackson challenged the Court to enforce its order in *Cherokee Nation v. Georgia*, 5 Pet. 1 (1831), as mentioned in footnote 10. *F.Cas.* stands for *Federal Cases*—an eighteenth- and nineteenth-century reporter of cases decided in the federal courts of appeals that was abolished in 1912.

CRITICAL PERSPECTIVE
Do Personal Policy Preferences Shape Supreme Court Decisions?

The question of the extent to which personal policy preferences affect the Supreme Court's decisions has been asked—and answered—time and again. The question is not an idle one, because how the Court decides issues that affect national policy sometimes can have consequences as serious as any of the laws passed by Congress.

Among those who have scrutinized the Court's decisions closely in an effort to explain the Court's voting behavior are Supreme Court scholars Jeffrey Segal and Harold Spaeth. In *The Supreme Court and the Attitudinal Model,** Segal and Spaeth posit two models of judicial decision making: the legal model and the attitudinal model. The legal model postulates that "the decisions of the Court are based on the facts of the case in light of the plain meaning of statutes and the Constitution, the intent of the framers, precedent, and a balancing of societal interests." The attitudinal model, in contrast, "holds that the Supreme Court decides disputes in light of the facts of the case vis-à-vis the ideological attitudes and values of justices. Simply put, Rehnquist votes the way he does because he is extremely conservative."

The Legal Model Explains "Nothing and Everything"

According to Segal and Spaeth, the legal model of judicial decision making does not explain Supreme Court decision making at all. The authors point out, as many others have before them, that the "plain meaning" of statutes never really is plain; nor is the "intent of the framers" ever all that clear. Hence, there is much room for different judicial interpretations of statutory or constitutional provisions. There also is a vast array of case precedents from which the Justices can pick and choose to support their positions. Certainly, a dissenting opinion often contains as many, if not more, references to case precedents than the Court's majority opinion. In short, conclude Segal and Spaeth, the legal model doesn't apply because it "explains nothing and everything." They claim that only the attitudinal model can explain Supreme Court decision making.

The Attitudinal Model

The attitudinal model suggests that Supreme Court justices base their decisions on policy preferences simply because they are free to do so—they face no external constraints. First, they are virtually immune from political accountability—they do not have to answer to the electorate. Second, "legislative inertia and the majorities needed to pass legislation" make it difficult for Congress to overturn, by statutory or constitutional amendment, the Court's interpretation of a particular statute or constitutional provision. Third, unlike lower court judges, the desire for higher office or not to be overruled by a higher court is not a factor in the Court's decision

weapon at the Court's disposal would appear to be public pressure. Whether a politician would be able to withstand the public firestorm that would likely result from a deliberate refusal to obey an order from the Supreme Court would depend, in large part, on the factual circumstances of the case and whether the Court's decision otherwise appeared to be legally justified.

Additionally, if a Supreme Court decision is noticeably at odds with public opinion, persons affected by the decision might simply ignore it. Suppose, for example, that a teacher continues to lead his or her students in prayer every day despite a Supreme Court ruling that such a practice violates the establishment clause. What can the courts do in this situation? Unless someone complains about the teacher's actions and initiates a lawsuit, the courts can do nothing.

Judicial Traditions and Doctrines

Supreme Court justices (and other federal judges) typically exercise self-restraint in fashioning their decisions. In part, this restraint stems from their

CRITICAL PERSPECTIVE
Do Personal Policy Preferences Shape Supreme Court Decisions? Continued

making. This is because the Supreme Court is the highest position on the judicial career ladder.

The attitudinal model, according to Segal and Spaeth, also suggests that judicial activism and judicial restraint are merely tools used by the justices to cloak their personal ideological preferences. If a justice disagrees with a particular law or agency rule, he or she will assert that the Court should use its power to check the other two branches of government, thus taking an activist stance. If a justice agrees with a particular law or agency rule, he or she will argue the need for judicial restraint and deference to the elected legislative body or the expertise of the administrative agency.

The Critics Respond

Critics of the attitudinal model point out that the legal model is and always has been a fiction, and thus it is not a very worthy target. As Segal and Spaeth themselves state, even the justices do not claim that the legal model explains their decisions. Furthermore, no one ever has doubted that Supreme Court decisions are shaped by the attitudes of the decision makers. Critics say that there is no real evidence indicating that personal preferences affect decisions to the extent suggested by Segal and Spaeth, however. Justices sometimes admit to making decisions that fly in

the face of their personal values and preferences, simply because they feel obligated to do so in view of existing law. Additionally, Supreme Court justices traditionally have exercised a great degree of self-restraint. More often than not, the justices narrow their rulings to focus on just one aspect of an issue, even though there may be nothing to stop them from broadening their focus and thus widening the impact of their policy preferences.

For Critical Analysis

1. Is it possible for Supreme Court justices to put aside their personal biases and policy preferences when rendering a decision? Should they?

2. How does the political process of appointing Supreme Court justices promote judicial restraint?

3. Unlike members of Congress, Supreme Court justices explain the reasons for their decisions in written opinions. Does this mean that the Supreme Court, in fact, may be more accountable to the public than congresspersons?

*New York: Cambridge University Press, 1993.

knowledge that the other two branches of government can exercise checks on the judiciary, as previously discussed. To a large extent, however, this restraint is mandated by various judicially established traditions and doctrines. For example, in exercising its discretion to hear appeals, the Supreme Court will not hear a meritless appeal just so it can rule on the issue. Additionally, the doctrine of *stare decisis* acts as a restraint because it obligates the courts, including the Supreme Court, to follow established precedents when deciding cases. Only rarely will courts overrule a precedent.

Other judicial doctrines and practices also act as restraints. The courts will hear only what are called **justiciable disputes,** which are disputes that arise out of actual cases and that can be settled by legal methods. In other words, a court will not hear a case that involves merely a hypothetical issue. A party must have some stake in a real controversy before that party can bring a case before a court. Furthermore, under the doctrine of exhaustion of remedies, a court will not hear an appeal from an administrative agency's ruling unless the party bringing the appeal has exhausted the remedies available through the agency itself. If the party could have appealed to the head of the agency

JUSTICIABLE DISPUTE

A dispute that raises questions about the law and that is appropriate for resolution before a court of law.

and failed to do so, the court will not review the case. Finally, when reviewing a case, the Supreme Court typically narrows its focus to just one issue or one aspect of an issue involved in the case. The Court rarely makes broad, sweeping decisions on issues.

Often, if a political question is involved, the Supreme Court will exercise judicial restraint and refuse to rule on the matter. A **political question** is one that the Supreme Court declares should be decided by the elected branches of government—the executive branch, the legislative branch, or those two branches acting together. For example, for many years the Supreme Court refused to rule on the constitutionality of laws concerning legislative apportionment (the shaping of electoral districts), even when those laws resulted in grossly obvious gerrymandering (reshaping a district to enhance the political support of one political party—see Chapter 12). It was not until 1962, in *Baker v. Carr*,[18] that the Court changed its attitude and decided to rule on the issue. More recently, the Supreme Court has refused to rule on the controversy

POLITICAL QUESTION

An issue that a court believes should be decided by the executive or legislative branch.

---

[18]369 U.S. 186 (1962).

CONCEPT OVERVIEW
Changes in Judicial Interpretation

The lower federal courts are obligated to abide by the principles of law enunciated in Supreme Court decisions. How the Supreme Court interprets a particular law or constitutional provision therefore has a significant impact on the federal courts—and thus throughout society. Here we list some of the ways in which the Rehnquist Court of today has changed directions from those taken by the Warren Court during the 1950s and 1960s.

THEN	NOW
• Affirmative action programs were constitutional.	• Affirmative action programs are subject to strict scrutiny; they may violate the equal protection clause.
• The constitutional authority of the national government's regulatory powers was being expanded.	• The constitutional authority of the national government's regulatory powers is being limited.
• Equal protection meant unequal treatment (affirmative action).	• Equal protection means equal treatment, regardless of race, color, national origin, gender, or religion.
• More cases classified as involving political questions.	• Fewer cases classified as involving political questions.
• Judicial activism to promote civil rights.	• Judicial restraint with respect to civil rights, criminal procedures, and states' rights.
• Predominantly liberal justices on the Supreme Court.	• Relatively conservative justices on the Supreme Court.
• The Supreme Court decided up to 150 cases per year.	• The Supreme Court decides about half that number of cases.

regarding the rights of gays and lesbians in the military, preferring instead to defer to the executive branch's decisions on the matter. Generally, fewer questions are deemed political questions by the Supreme Court today than in the past.

Higher courts can reverse the decisions of lower courts. Lower courts can act as a check on higher courts, too. Lower courts can ignore—and have ignored—Supreme Court decisions. Usually, this is done indirectly. A lower court might conclude, for example, that the precedent set by the Supreme Court does not apply to the exact circumstances in the case at bar (before the court); or the lower court may decide that the Supreme Court's decision was ambiguous with respect to the issue before the lower court. The fact that the Supreme Court rarely makes broad and clear-cut statements on any issue facilitates different interpretations of the Court's decisions by the lower courts.

THE JUDICIARY: UNFINISHED WORK

The judiciary remains one of the most active and important institutions in American political life. Particularly at the federal level, judicial decision making through the years has affected the way all of us live and work.

During the Reagan-Bush years (1981 to 1993), there appeared to be a trend toward a noticeably more conservative federal judiciary. Some argued that this "conservative" legacy would remain effective for years to come. The election of Bill Clinton, however, may have changed that. When he took office, over one hundred judicial openings in the lower federal courts existed. By 1997, he had already been able to appoint about two hundred federal court judges, including two Supreme Court justices. Consequently, some argue that the direction of the federal judiciary will not necessarily continue to be in a conservative direction.

A number of key constitutional issues will continue to be brought before the federal judiciary. These issues include affirmative action programs, congressional redistricting to maximize minority representation, indecent speech on the Internet, privacy rights, and a variety of other civil rights issues. The work of the judiciary in this sense will always remain unfinished. Even when an issue seems to be "resolved," it may come up again many years later. After all, the Supreme Court decision in *Roe v. Wade* appeared to have put an end to discussion about restrictions on abortion. Yet in the 1990s, the issue continues to come back to the courts and is currently being settled there, as well as through decisions and movements in public opinion. In a dynamic nation with a changing population, we can never expect issues to be resolved once and for all.

GETTING INVOLVED
Changing the Legal System

Although impressed by the power of judges in American government, Alexis de Tocqueville stated:

The power is enormous, but it is clothed in the authority of public opinion. They are the all-powered guardians of a people which respects law; but they would be impotent against public neglect or popular contempt.*

The U.S. court system may seem all powerful and too complex to be influenced by one individual, but its power nonetheless depends on our support. A hostile public has many ways of resisting, modifying, or overturning rulings of the courts. Sooner or later a determined majority will prevail. Even a determined minority can make a difference. As Alexander Hamilton suggested in *The Federalist Papers*, the people will always hold the scales of justice in their hands, and ultimately all constitutional government depends on their firmness and wisdom.

One example of the kind of pressure that can be exerted on the court system began with a tragedy. On a spring afternoon in 1980, thirteen-year-old Cari Lightner was hit from behind and killed by a drunk driver while walking in a bicycle lane. The driver turned out to be a forty-seven-year-old man with two prior drunk-driving convictions. He was at that time out on bail for a third arrest. Cari's mother, Candy, quit her job as a real estate agent to form Mothers Against Drunk Driving (MADD) and launched a personal campaign to stiffen penalties for drunk-driving convictions.

The organization grew to 20,000 members, with 91 regional offices and a staff of 160. Outraged by the estimated 23,000 lives lost every year because of drunk driving, the group not only seeks stiff penalties against drunk drivers but also urges police, prosecutors, and judges to crack down on such violators. MADD, by becoming involved, has gotten results. Owing to its efforts and the efforts of other citizen-activist groups, many states have responded with

stronger penalties and deterrents. If you feel strongly about this issue and want to get involved, contact the following:

MADD
511 E. John Carpenter Freeway
Suite 700
Irving, TX 75062
214-744-6233
http://www.gran-net.com/madd/madd.html

Several other organizations have been formed by people who want to change or influence the judicial system. A few of them follow:

HALT—AN ORGANIZATION OF AMERICANS FOR LEGAL REFORM
1319 F. St. N.W. #300
Washington, DC 20004
202-347-9600
http://www.halt.org

NATIONAL LEGAL CENTER FOR THE PUBLIC INTEREST
1000 16th St. N.W.
Washington DC 20036
202-296-1683

If you want information about the Supreme Court, contact the following by telephone or letter:

CLERK OF THE COURT
The Supreme Court of the United States
1 First St. N.E.
Washington, DC 20543
202-479-3000
http://www.law.cornell.edu/supct/justices/fullcourt.html

*Alexis de Tocqueville, *Democracy in America*, Vol. 1 (New York: Schocken Books, 1961), p. 166.

KEY TERMS

affirm 516	justiciable dispute 527	precedent 504
amicus curiae brief 512	judicial activism 524	remand 516
appellate court 511	judicial implementation 517	reverse 516
class-action suit 512	judicial restraint 524	rule of four 515
common law 503	jurisdiction 510	senatorial courtesy 518
concurring opinion 516	litigate 512	*stare decisis* 504
dissenting opinion 517	majority opinion 516	trial court 510
diversity of citizenship 510	opinion 516	unanimous opinion 516
federal question 510	oral arguments 515	writ of *certiorari* 514
grand jury 511	political question 528	

CHAPTER SUMMARY

❶ One of the fundamental sources of American law is the common law tradition, which was part of our legal heritage from England. The common law doctrine of *stare decisis* (which means "to stand on decided cases") obligates judges to follow precedents established previously by their own courts or by higher courts in their jurisdiction. Precedents established by the United States Supreme Court, the highest court in the land, are binding on all lower courts. Other fundamental sources of American law include the U.S. Constitution and state constitutions, statutes enacted by legislative bodies, and regulations issued by administrative agencies.

❷ The judiciary's role in American government basically is to interpret and apply the laws. The United States Supreme Court has a significant influence on the rights and liberties of Americans. As the final interpreter of the Constitution, the Supreme Court (and other courts) can determine the constitutionality of actions taken by the other branches of government. This power of judicial review was claimed by the Supreme Court in *Marbury v. Madison* in 1803. The ideological attitudes of the judges or justices deciding a case necessarily come into play to a certain extent when they interpret the law. Thus, constitutional provisions may be interpreted differently at different times by the courts, including the Supreme Court.

❸ The federal court system and most state court systems have several tiers. All trials are conducted in the trial, or district, courts. The outcome of a trial may then be appealed to an intermediate court, or court of appeals. Whether a litigant can further appeal a claim to the state or federal supreme court will depend on the nature of the claim and the access afforded to litigants by the particular court. The United States Supreme Court, for example, exercises almost total discretion over the types of cases it chooses to hear. State courts can exercise jurisdiction over most cases concerning persons or property within the state's borders. Federal courts have limited jurisdiction and can hear cases only if they involve federal questions or diversity of citizenship. Both the federal courts and the state courts have established procedural rules that frame the litigation process.

❹ There is no absolute right of appeal to the United States Supreme Court. Parties can petition the Court for a writ of *certiorari*, but the Court has almost complete discretion as to whether or not to take any particular case. Typically, the Court will issue writs for selected types of cases, such as when the lower courts have issued conflicting opinions on a federal law.

❺ The confirmation process for federal judges, particularly those who will sit on the Supreme Court, is often extremely politicized. Democrats and Republicans alike realize that justices may occupy a seat on the Court for decades and naturally want to have persons appointed who share their basic views. Nearly one-fifth of all United States Supreme Court appointments have been either rejected or not acted on by the Senate—often for ideological reasons. The overwhelming majority of persons appointed to the Supreme Court have been white male Protestants. Of the 108 persons who have sat on the

Court so far, only two have been African American, and only two have been women. The Court is perhaps the least representative government institution in the United States.

6 The Rehnquist Court is noticeably conservative in its rulings, so much so that at one point in the early 1990s liberals looked to Congress to overturn Court decisions that they disliked. There is no longer a large enough liberal voting bloc to prevent more conservative rulings in certain areas, such as affirmative action.

7 Proponents of judicial activism argue that the Supreme Court should take an active role in using its powers to check the activities of the other branches of government. Proponents of judicial restraint contend that the Court should defer to the decisions made by elected representatives of the people—in Congress and in the executive branch—or to the expertise of adminis-

trative agencies. Judicial activism and restraint are not linked necessarily to liberal or conservative ideologies. Both liberal and conservative justices may take an activist (or restraintist) position on issues.

8 The power of the judiciary is checked by the other branches of government. Presidents may influence the federal courts through the use of their appointment power. Legislatures can check court rulings by not appropriating the funds necessary to implement those rulings. Legislatures can also amend old laws (or pass new ones) to clarify the law on certain issues and effectively overturn contrary decisions on those issues by the Supreme Court. Public opinion and judicial traditions and doctrines, such as the doctrine of *stare decisis,* also act as restraints on the courts. Finally, lower courts may find ways to avoid applying a widely unpopular Supreme Court decision.

QUESTIONS FOR REVIEW AND DISCUSSION

1 The United States Supreme Court has no police force and a relatively small budget. How, then, can it be sure that its decisions are enforced?

2 What are some of the reasons why cases are not heard by the Supreme Court?

3 Why has the nomination of Supreme Court justices become so politicized?

4 "Judges are just making too much legislation." What

does this quotation mean? How is it possible for a judge to "make legislation"?

5 The Supreme Court has never allowed television cameras in its chambers, but other courts have. What would be some of the arguments against videotaping the Supreme Court at work? What are some of the arguments in favor of doing so?

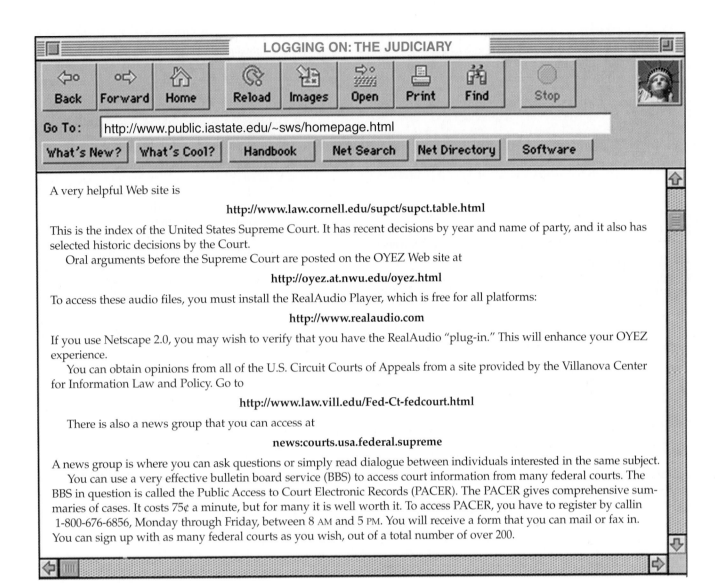

LOGGING ON: THE JUDICIARY

Go To: http://www.public.iastate.edu/~sws/homepage.html

A very helpful Web site is

http://www.law.cornell.edu/supct/supct.table.html

This is the index of the United States Supreme Court. It has recent decisions by year and name of party, and it also has selected historic decisions by the Court.

Oral arguments before the Supreme Court are posted on the OYEZ Web site at

http://oyez.at.nwu.edu/oyez.html

To access these audio files, you must install the RealAudio Player, which is free for all platforms:

http://www.realaudio.com

If you use Netscape 2.0, you may wish to verify that you have the RealAudio "plug-in." This will enhance your OYEZ experience.

You can obtain opinions from all of the U.S. Circuit Courts of Appeals from a site provided by the Villanova Center for Information Law and Policy. Go to

http://www.law.vill.edu/Fed-Ct-fedcourt.html

There is also a news group that you can access at

news:courts.usa.federal.supreme

A news group is where you can ask questions or simply read dialogue between individuals interested in the same subject.

You can use a very effective bulletin board service (BBS) to access court information from many federal courts. The BBS in question is called the Public Access to Court Electronic Records (PACER). The PACER gives comprehensive summaries of cases. It costs 75¢ a minute, but for many it is well worth it. To access PACER, you have to register by callin 1-800-676-6856, Monday through Friday, between 8 AM and 5 PM. You will receive a form that you can mail or fax in. You can sign up with as many federal courts as you wish, out of a total number of over 200.

SELECTED REFERENCES

Abraham, Henry J. *The Judiciary: The Supreme Court in the Governmental Process.* 9th ed. Madison, Wis.: Brown & Benchmark, 1994. This classic textbook treats in much more detail virtually every topic in the chapter you have just read.

Barnum, David G. *The Supreme Court and American Democracy.* New York: St. Martin's Press, 1993. The author attempts to describe the unique status of the Supreme Court as a special type of democratic institution. He points out that the justices theoretically are accountable only to their own consciences for their decisions, even when such decisions may affect the most sensitive of personal affairs for the rest of the nation.

Cardozo, Benjamin N. *The Nature of the Judicial Process.* New Haven, Conn.: Yale University Press, 1985 (originally published in 1921). In this classic work on legal philosophy and judicial decision making, Cardozo, an associate justice on the Supreme Court from 1932 to 1938, wrote of the "uncertainty" that the flexibility of the Constitution ultimately must lend to the law, and of the creative nature of the judicial process that naturally follows this uncertainty.

Carp, Robert A., and Ronald Stidham. *Judicial Process in America.* 3d ed. Washington, D.C.: Congressional Quarterly Books, 1995. The authors look at variables affecting the judicial process and conclude that all judges engage in policymaking.

Cushman, Clare, ed. *The Supreme Court Justices: Illustrated Biographies, 1789–1995.* 2d ed. Washington, D.C.: Congressional Quarterly Books, 1995. These biographies of the Supreme Court justices are interspersed with lively anecdotes and reveal the human side of the Supreme Court. Each biography summarizes the justice's background, interests, and legal philosophy, and discusses the issues in major cases on which the justice ruled.

Gangi, William. *Saving the Constitution from the Courts.* Norman, Okla.: University of Oklahoma Press, 1995. The author, after several introductory chapters on American constitutionalism and nineteenth-century court decisions, argues in defense of judicial restraint and against judicial activism, which he suggests is threatening the survival of self-government in America.

Goldstein, Joseph. *The Intelligible Constitution: The Supreme Court's Obligation to Maintain the Constitution as Something We the People Can Understand.* New York: Oxford University Press, 1992. Goldstein criticizes the Supreme Court for its failure to present its opinions concerning constitutional matters in a clear and comprehensible manner. The author argues that the Supreme Court has an obligation not only to decide cases but also to explicate, with candor and integrity, the principles embedded in the Constitution and to make the Constitution understandable for today's citizens.

Hall, Kermit L., ed., with James W. Ely, Jr., Joel B. Grossman, and William M. Wiecek. *The Oxford Companion to the Supreme Court of the United States.* New York: Oxford University Press, 1992. This volume contains more than a thousand entries on every aspect of the United States Supreme Court, biographies of all the justices who ever sat on the Court through 1992, the details concerning more than four hundred major decisions of the Court, and articles on important legal and constitutional debates.

Hazard, Geoffrey C., Jr., and Michele Taruffo. *American Civil Procedure: An Introduction.* New Haven, Conn.: Yale University Press, 1993. The authors describe and analyze civil litigation in the United States. They discuss specific details and broad themes, explaining the jury trial, the adversary system, the power of the courts to make law as well as declare it, and the role of civil justice in the government and in the resolution of controversial social issues.

Nagel, Robert F. *Judicial Power and American Character: Censoring Ourselves in an Anxious Age.* New York: Oxford University Press, 1994. In his introduction, the author states that his book contains statements that will "irritate the reader"—and his attacks on Supreme Court justices' decision making may irritate many. He concludes generally that the exercise of judicial review (by intolerant and "morally imperious judges") should give way to politics and policy-making exercised by elected officials and democratic institutions.

Rakove, Jack N. *Original Meanings: Politics and Ideas in the Making of the Constitution.* New York: Knopf, 1996. The author both describes the political and ideological issues that framed the writing of the Constitution and the difficulty faced by today's courts when trying to interpret that document.

Schwartz, Bernard. *Decision: How the Supreme Court Decides Cases.* Cary, N.C.: Oxford University Press, 1996. This noted author provides a unique, behind-the-scenes look at the Supreme Court and how the justices go about their work. He includes discussions of cases, as well as the positions taken by the justices on various issues.

PART FIVE

Public Policy

16
Domestic Policy

CHAPTER OUTLINE

Welfare Programs Were *Completely* Controlled by the States?

BACKGROUND

TRADITIONALLY, WELFARE PROGRAMS HAVE BEEN ADMINISTERED BY THE FEDERAL GOVERNMENT AS WELL AS BY STATE AND LOCAL GOVERNMENTS. MOST WELFARE PROGRAMS ADMINISTERED AT THE STATE AND LOCAL LEVELS HAVE BEEN REGULATED EXTENSIVELY BY FEDERAL GOVERNMENT MANDATES, AND FEDERAL EXPENDITURES ON HEALTH, MEDICARE, AND INCOME SECURITY ROUTINELY HAVE ADDED UP TO OVER ONE-THIRD OF THE FEDERAL BUDGET.

THERE HAVE BEEN OVER ONE HUNDRED FEDERAL ANTIPOVERTY PROGRAMS, INCLUDING TWELVE DIFFERENT PROGRAMS TO PROVIDE FOOD TO THE NEEDY AND SEVEN HOUSING PROGRAMS. IN 1996, CONGRESS ENACTED A WELFARE REFORM BILL THAT GAVE THE STATES MORE CONTROL OVER CERTAIN WELFARE PROGRAMS. IN ESSENCE, HOWEVER, THE FEDERAL GOVERNMENT RETAINED A SIGNIFICANT DEGREE OF CONTROL OVER THE WELFARE SYSTEM.

WHAT IF WELFARE PROGRAMS WERE *COMPLETELY* CONTROLLED BY THE STATES?

Assume for the moment that the federal government simply sent back to the states—*with no strings attached*—all of the hundreds of billions of dollars that it currently spends on federal welfare programs. In this situation, we probably would see a massive realignment of how welfare dollars are allocated and spent. Much of the current thinking on welfare is that it should be transformed into "workfare," which, loosely speaking, would require that welfare recipients perform some type of work or services in return for welfare assistance. (Indeed, the 1996 welfare reform law conditioned the receipt of welfare assistance, after an initial two-year period, on the recipients working at either a public service job or for a private employer.)

To be sure, some states would become aggressive in the use of job retraining programs for the poor. Welfare-to-work programs are costly, though, because they require additional state employees to implement and oversee the programs. Furthermore, job-training efforts to help welfare recipients work their way off the welfare rolls have not been very successful in the past.

Some states might not want to provide job-training programs or create public-service jobs to put welfare recipients to work. (In fact, immediately after the 1996 reform law was passed, some states requested—and received—permission from the federal government to waive the reform law's requirement that welfare recipients must be employed within two years.)

INNOVATIVE PROGRAMS

If the states *completely* controlled welfare, they probably would experiment with new programs to use welfare funds more effectively and to reduce poverty generally. Studies could be done to identify those policies that do the best or worst job of making people self-sufficient.

No one can say for sure whether *complete* state control over welfare programs would ultimately lead to a better welfare system, however, or to a better life for the nation's poor. Generally, the poor have never been a popular political group. They do not have the resources to organize and lobby state legislatures for beneficial programs and policies. We simply cannot predict whether the states, in the face of budget problems, would increase or decrease welfare spending or invest in new, innovative programs to reduce long-term welfare costs.

FOR CRITICAL ANALYSIS

1. *Which group or groups would be most likely to oppose turning over* all *federal welfare dollars to the states?*

2. *Which group or groups would be most likely to support this policy action?*

Literally thousands of policy proposals are debated in the halls of Congress, in state capitols, and in municipal government halls every year. Just about any policy proposal can be subjected to a rigorous analysis. As an example, consider the question discussed in this chapter's opening *What If . . . .* This policy issue has numerous pros and cons, and the costs and benefits of such a proposal must be analyzed carefully. Some groups are in favor of such a policy change. Others, including federal government employees who administer welfare programs from Washington, D.C., oppose such a policy change.

Part of the public policy debate in our nation involves domestic problems. **Domestic policy** can be defined as all of the laws, government planning, and government actions that affect each individual's daily life in the United States. Consequently, the span of such policies is enormous. Domestic policies range from relatively simple issues, such as what the speed limit should be on interstate highways, to more complex issues, such as how best to protect our environment. Many of our domestic policies are formulated and implemented by the federal government, but many others are the result of the combined efforts of federal, state, and local governments.

In this chapter we look at domestic policy issues concerned with poverty and welfare, immigration, violence and crime, and the environment. In the next chapter, we examine national economic policies undertaken solely by the federal government. Before we start our analysis, we must look at how public policies are made.

DOMESTIC POLICY

Those public plans or courses of action that concern issues of national importance, such as poverty, crime, and the environment, in contrast to economic policies that normally relate only to issues of inflation, interest rates, unemployment, and international trade deficits.

THE POLICYMAKING PROCESS

How does any issue, such as the possibility of completely reforming how the federal government regulates agriculture, food stamps, and rural development, first become a problem and then get solved? First, of course, the issue has to become identified as a problem. Policymakers can obtain information on the costs of the federal farm policy, the complexity of the many programs, the use of food stamps, and the plight of rural areas from numerous nationally published statistics.

Often, policymakers simply have to open their local newspapers—or letters from their constituents—to discover that a problem is brewing. Like most Americans, however, policymakers receive much of their information from the media. Finally, different lobbying groups will provide information to members of Congress. In the area of agricultural policy, these groups include farmers themselves, as well as users of farm products, such as corporations that make breakfast foods and the like.

During the 1990s, because the federal budget deficit continued to be a problem, many traditionally sacrosanct federal programs were put under the microscope. One of these programs was the federal farm program. Congress and the White House gradually accepted that a new farm policy was desirable.

Protesters demonstrate outside the White House in August 1996 to show their opposition to the Welfare Reform Bill of 1996. Grass-roots expressions of public opinion like this demonstration plays a significant role in the policymaking process.

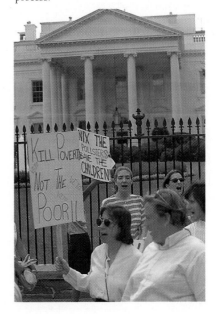

The Role of Debate in the Policymaking Process

As mentioned above, the first step in the policymaking process is the acknowledgment that a problem exists and needs a solution. Problems and possible solutions often emerge through public debate. For example, there has been debate about America's federal farm program since its beginnings in the 1930s. To raise the incomes of American farmers, the federal government has offered them an array of payment systems. In effect, for decades the

American taxpayer has subsidized American farmers to the tune of tens of billions of dollars every year. Another consequence of U.S. farm policy is that American consumers have had to pay higher food prices than they otherwise would have had to pay. Part of the U.S. farm policy has also been the maintenance of a massive Department of Agriculture that has been staffed by over one hundred thousand federal employees for many years.

PRICE SUPPORTS

Minimum prices set by the government for particular products.

While farmers and their supporters have argued that **price supports** and the like have been necessary to keep many farmers "afloat," some policy research groups have continually called for either the abolition of such price supports or at least a reduction in the amount of taxpayer dollars that has been going to U.S. farmers.

Part of the debate, to be sure, has been guided not so much by partisan politics as by "home-based" politics. Specifically, members of Congress from the principal farming states generally have supported the continuation of generous payments to farmers. Members of Congress from nonfarming states often have been vocal about reducing such generous payments. As discussed in Chapter 8, such diverse groups reached a compromise in 1996 and passed the Freedom to Farm Act (formally titled the Federal Agriculture Improvement and Reform Act). How this farm bill was passed is a good example of the policymaking process.

Steps in the Policymaking Process

The problem, the reaction to the problem, and the solution to the problem all form part of the public policymaking process in the United States. No matter how simple or how complex the problem, those who make policy follow a number of steps. Based on observation, we can divide the process of policymaking into at least five steps.

1. Agenda Building: *The issue must get on the agenda.* This occurs through crisis, technological change, or mass media campaigns, as well as through the efforts of strong political personalities and effective lobbying groups. In the case of a new farm bill, members of Congress, in response to the public's concern over budget deficits and perceived over-regulation by government, included farm policy reform as part of their proposed legislative agenda in late 1995 and early 1996.

2. Agenda formulation: *The proposals are discussed among government officials and the public.* Such discussions may take place in the printed media, on television, and in the halls of Congress. Congress holds hearings, the president voices the administration's views, and the topic may even become a campaign issue. For example, President Clinton held an agriculture "summit" meeting at Iowa State University at which leaders of farm, consumer, and rural development groups were invited to speak out on the proposed farm bill. This summit was given extensive national news coverage. Some groups, such as peanut and sugar producers, fiercely opposed proposed cuts in government subsidies for those products. Other groups voiced strong support for generous food-stamp allotments.

3. Agenda adoption: *A specific strategy is chosen from among the proposals discussed.* That is, Congress must enact legislation, executive departments must write new regulations, or the courts must interpret past policies differently. Much of the congressional year prior to the passage of the new farming legislation, for example, was taken up by work on that legislation. After extensive debate, a bill was passed, and the president signed it in 1996. The new legislation was, of course, a compromise: it attempted to meet the objectives of cost cutting and deregulation while at the same time trying to satisfy the interests of some of the more powerful lobbying groups.

4. Agenda implementation: *Government action must be implemented by bureaucrats, the courts, police, and individual citizens.* The benefits outlined by the new legislation have to be implemented, over a seven-year period, by the same federal and state organizations that coordinated all previous farm programs.

5. Agenda evaluation: *Increasingly, after a policy is implemented, groups undertake policy evaluation.* Groups both inside and outside government conduct studies to show what actually happens after a policy has been implemented for a given period of time. Based on this "feedback" and the perceived success or failure of the program, a new round of policymaking initiatives will be undertaken to correct and hopefully improve on the effort. Research groups, for example, will determine how much the average cost of food per family dropped as a result of the 1996 farm bill.

It is worth noting that although the flow of the policy process is well understood, there are competing models of how and for whose benefit that process works. Table 16–1 lists a number of competing models for the policymaking process and gives a brief summary of each model.

Analyzing the Freedom to Farm Act

Like all legislation, the farm bill reflected a compromise. To satisfy critics of the government's regulation of farm prices, the Freedom to Farm Act eliminated price supports for most farm products. In the future, market forces of supply and demand will determine the price people pay for wheat, corn, and the like. For the most part, in the future, farmers can grow crops on any land that they own, although some land is still not allowed to be used because it

DID YOU KNOW...
That from 1986 to 1996, the federal government mailed to urban zip codes a total of 1.6 million farm subsidy checks valued at $1.3 billion, including checks to 47 "farmers" in Beverly Hills, California?

Table 16–1

Selected Models of the Policymaking Process

1. The Bureaucratic Politics Model. In the bureaucratic politics model, the relative power of the large bureaucracies in Washington determines which policy becomes part of the national agenda and which is implemented. This theory of American politics is based on the struggle among competing interest groups.

2. The Power Elite, or Elitism, Model. Powerful economic interests determine the outcome of policy struggles, according to the power elite, or elitism, model. The rich and those who know the rich determine what gets done. More important, the power elite decides what items do *not* get on the public agenda and which items get removed if they are already on it.

3. The Marxist Model. Closely aligned with the power elite model is the Marxist model of public policymaking, in which the ruling class institutes public policy, often at the expense of the working class. The Marxist solution is revolution and the seizure of government by the working class.

4. The Incremental Model. Public policy evolves through small changes or adjustments, according to the incrementalist model. Consequently, policymakers examine only a few alternatives in trying to solve national problems. A good public policy decision is made when there is agreement among contesting interests, and agreement is obtained most easily when changes are minimal.

5. The Rationalist Model. The rationalist model, sometimes thought of as a pure textbook abstraction, hypothesizes a rational policymaker who sets out to maximize his or her own self-interest, rather than determining what the public, or collective, interest might be. Rational policymakers will rank goals and objectives according to their benefit to the policymakers. Such a model is often viewed as an alternative to the incrementalist model. This model is sometimes known as the theory of public choice.

6. The Systems Model. The most general, and perhaps the most ambitious, approach to modeling public policymaking is a systems approach, in which policy is a product of the relationships between the institutions of government and the socioeconomic-political environment. Such a model has (a) inputs from public opinion and crises; (b) a political process including legislative hearings, debates, court deliberations, party conventions, and so on; (c) a set of policy outputs consisting of legislation, appropriations, and regulations; and (d) policy outcomes, which may provide, for example, more job security, less unemployment, more research on AIDS, and so on.

has been deemed environmentally sensitive. To satisfy groups of farmers whose lobbyists fought hard during the policy negotiations, the total price tag for the bill—about $50 billion—is only $2 billion less than the government was projected to spend on the old farm programs anyway.

What Supporters of the Bill Say.   Supporters of the Freedom to Farm Act say that farmers now will know exactly how much they will receive from the federal government. They will be able to plan ahead and hence save money for hard times. Supporters of the legislation argue that government policies distorted the market by creating incentives for farmers to grow too much of a subsidized crop, thereby making it necessary for the government to guarantee prices in order to save farmers from bankruptcy. In general, most supporters of the law believe that the deregulation of farming is its main benefit.

What the Critics Say.   Critics of the new bill first point out that the federal government still is paying lavishly to allow tens of millions of acres of America's best farmland to lie fallow. Both Democrats and Republicans supported and obtained a continuation of the Conservation Reserve Program, which currently is paying farmers to leave idle about thirty-six million acres—about 10 percent of America's cropland. This program, which began in 1985, has been used as a way to increase direct federal subsidies to farmers. Any farmer who enrolls in the program has to sign a contract in which the farmer agrees to leave land idle for ten years in return for receiving annual payments—payments that are routinely the equivalent of double or even triple the local rental rate for such land.

Critics of the new system maintain that without price supports, farmers might be vulnerable to low world prices for food. Critics also argue that taxpayers will be offended that payments to farmers, which are paid directly from the U.S. Treasury, bear no relation to production or prices—it looks like a straight welfare bill for farmers. Additionally, the bill's critics contend that the legislation will benefit agribusinesses (corporate farms) much more than family-run farms. Indeed, as he signed the bill, President Clinton had some reservations because the bill "fails to provide an adequate safety net for family farmers."

POVERTY AND WELFARE

Throughout the world, historically poverty has been accepted as inevitable. Even today, little has been done on an international level to eliminate worldwide poverty (see this chapter's *Politics and Global Coordination*). The United States and other industrialized nations, however, have sustained enough economic growth in the past several hundred years to eliminate *mass* poverty. In fact, considering the wealth and high standard of living in the United States, the persistence of poverty here appears bizarre and anomalous. How can there still be so much poverty in a nation of so much abundance? And what can be done about it?

A traditional solution has been **income transfers.** There are methods of transferring income from relatively well-to-do to relatively poor groups in society, and as a nation, we have been using such methods for a long time. Today, we have a vast array of welfare programs set up for the sole purpose of redistributing income. We know, however, that these programs have not been entirely successful. Before we examine the problems posed by the welfare system, let's look at the concept of poverty in more detail and at the characteristics of the poor.

INCOME TRANSFER

A transfer of income from some individuals in the economy to other individuals. This is generally done by way of the government. It is a transfer in the sense that no current services are rendered by the recipients.

POLITICS AND GLOBAL COORDINATION
Poverty Worldwide and How to Cure It:
Suggestions from the Latest UN Summit

According to the United Nations (UN), almost 1.5 billion people of the world's total population of 5.6 billion live in poverty. For a week in 1995, delegations from over 140 countries from around the world gathered in Copenhagen, Denmark, for the United Nations World Summit for Social Development. Those attending this conference agreed to a document that commits them to the goal of "eradicating poverty in the world." Nobel Prize–winning economist James Tobin offered one solution: tax speculative international currency transactions

(the buying or selling of foreign currencies in the hope of making a profit) to raise $50 billion a year for the United Nations to support development programs. The delegates also argued for a "20-20 compact." Donor nations should agree to direct 20 percent of their foreign aid to alleviate poverty in developing countries, and recipient developing countries should direct 20 percent of their national budgets to the same programs.

From a political point of view, the UN summit accomplished very little. The United Nations has no power to

enforce any of the declarations signed by delegates attending any of its summits. Nonetheless, the world problem of poverty was brought into focus, at least for a short period of time.

For Critical Analysis
How could the solution of taxing speculative international currency transactions be put into practice? In other words, who would collect the tax, given that the United Nations does not have taxing power?

The Low-Income Population

We can see in Figure 16–1 that the number of individuals classified as poor fell rather steadily from 1959 through 1996. For about a decade, the number of poor leveled off, until the recession of 1981 to 1982. The number then fell somewhat until the early 1990s when it began to increase—until 1995, when it again fell slightly.

Defining Poverty. The threshold income level, which is used to determine who falls into the poverty category, was originally based on the cost of a nutritionally adequate food plan designed by the U.S. Department of Agriculture for emergency or temporary use. The threshold was determined by multiplying the food-plan cost times three, on the assumption that food expenses constitute approximately one-third of a poor family's expenditures. In 1969, a federal interagency committee examined the calculations of the threshold and decided to set new standards. Until then, annual revisions of

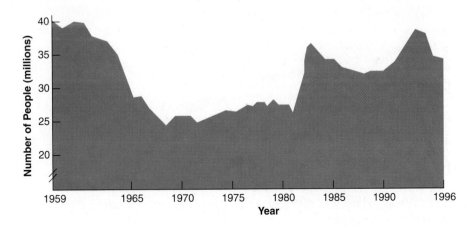

Figure 16–1

The Official Number of Poor in the United States

The number of individuals classified as poor fell steadily from 1959 through 1996. From 1970 to 1981, the number stayed about the same. It then increased during the 1981–1982 recession. The number of poor then fell somewhat, until the early 1990s. After rising a few years, the number started to fall in 1995.

the threshold level had been based only on price changes in the food budget. After 1969, the adjustments were made on the basis of changes in the consumer price index (CPI). The CPI is based on the average prices of a specified set of goods and services bought by wage earners in urban areas.

The low-income poverty threshold thus represents an absolute measure of income needed to maintain a specified standard of living as of 1963, with the constant-dollar value, or purchasing-power value, increased year by year in relation to the general increase in prices. For 1996, for example, the official poverty level for a family of four was about $16,000. It has gone up since then by the amount of the change in the CPI during the intervening period. (The poverty level varies with family size and location.)

Transfer Payments as Income.   The official poverty level is based on pre-tax income, including cash but not **in-kind subsidies**—food stamps, housing vouchers, and the like. If we correct poverty levels for such benefits, the percentage of the population that is below the poverty line drops dramatically, as can be seen in Figure 16–2. Some economists argue that the way in which the official poverty level is calculated makes no sense in a nation that redistributed about $900 billion in cash and noncash transfers in 1996.

Major Welfare Programs

Welfare assistance to the poor traditionally has taken a variety of forms. One of the key welfare programs has been **Aid to Families with Dependent Children (AFDC),** which was designed to furnish aid to families in which dependent children do not have the financial support of the father because of desertion, disability, or death. The **Supplemental Security Income (SSI)** program was established in 1974 to establish a nationwide minimum income for elderly persons and persons with disabilities who do not qualify for Social Security benefits.

The government also issues **food stamps,** coupons that can be used to purchase food. Food stamps are available for low-income individuals and families. Recipients must prove that they qualify by showing that they do not make very much money (or no money at all). In 1964, about 367,000 Ameri-

---

IN-KIND SUBSIDY

A good or service—such as food stamps, housing, or medical care—provided by the government to lower-income groups.

AID TO FAMILIES WITH DEPENDENT CHILDREN (AFDC)

A state-administered program that furnished assistance for families in which dependent children do not have the financial support of the father, owing to the father's desertion, disability, or death. The program has been financed partially by federal grants.

SUPPLEMENTAL SECURITY INCOME (SSI)

A federal program established to provide assistance to elderly persons and disabled persons.

FOOD STAMPS

Coupons issued by the federal government to low-income individuals to be used for the purchase of food.

Figure 16–2
●●●●●●●●●●●●●●●●●●●
Three Measures of Poverty

The percentage of the U.S. population living in poverty depends on what one includes in the definition of income. If one looks at private money income only, the percentage of the population in poverty during the 1980s and 1990s was well above 20 percent. If one adds cash benefits paid to individuals by the government during most of the 1980s and 1990s, less than 14 percent of the U.S. population was living in poverty. Finally, if one takes account of cash benefits, in-kind benefits, and the underreporting of income, the share of the U.S. population in poverty was estimated to be about 7.9 percent in 1996.

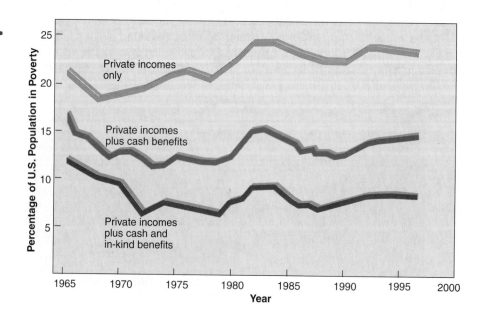

cans were receiving food stamps. In 1997, the estimated number of those receiving food stamps is over 26,000,000. The annual cost of funding food stamps jumped from $860,000 in 1964 to an estimated $22 billion in 1997. Workers who find themselves on strike, and even some college students, are eligible to receive food stamps.

The food-stamp program has become a major part of the welfare system in the United States. Although it was started in 1964 mainly to shore up the nation's agricultural sector by distributing surplus food through retail channels.

Total social welfare spending by governments at all levels on these and other welfare programs exceeds $25,000 per year for every family of four below the poverty level. Nonetheless, as can be seen in Figure 16–3, even though welfare spending started to rise dramatically at the end of the 1960s, there seems to be no improvement in the number of people who are defined as poor in this country. The poverty rate, if anything, is stable or only slightly falling. It is not surprising that at least one presidential candidate in every election over the past twenty-five years, including Bill Clinton in his 1992 campaign for the presidency, has said that he will change "welfare as we know it." On August 22, 1996, welfare reform became a reality when Clinton signed into law a welfare reform bill passed by Congress.

The Welfare Reform Bill of 1996

Traditionally, the federal government and the states have shared the cost of welfare, but the federal government determined how the programs would be implemented and increased the funds allocated for welfare programs as the number of welfare recipients rose. The welfare reform bill of 1996, however, gave more control over welfare to state governments.

Under the new system, federal and state governments continue to share the costs of welfare assistance, but the states play a greater role in establishing welfare rules (such as who will receive what type of benefits) and in managing the welfare programs. With respect to AFDC, for example, the reform

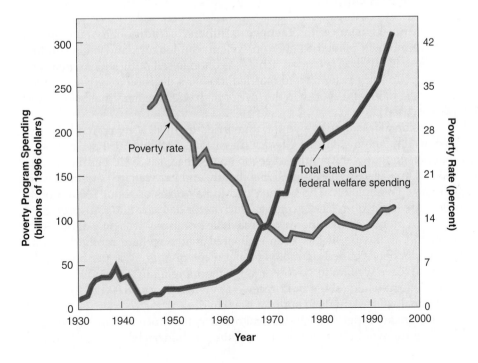

Figure 16–3
● ● ● ● ● ● ● ● ● ● ● ● ● ● ● ● ● ● ●
Welfare Spending and the Poverty Rate

Welfare spending has increased dramatically since the late 1960s. Nonetheless, the measured poverty rate has remained relatively stable.

bill abolished the current program and provided that the federal government will turn over to the states, in lump-sum ("block") grants, the funds that would otherwise go to the AFDC program. The states, not the federal government, have to meet the costs of any increased welfare spending. Although the federal government retained control over the food stamp program, benefits under this program were reduced. For example, with the exception of those in certain states, legal immigrants who are not citizens will no longer be eligible to receive food stamps.

In part, the welfare reform bill of 1996 shifted to state governments some of the financial burden of the welfare system. One of the basic aims of the bill, however, was to reduce welfare spending by all governments in the long run. To do this, the bill made two significant changes in the welfare system. These changes relate to work requirements and benefits for unmarried teenage mothers.

Work Requirements.   One of the problems with the traditional welfare system was that most programs were "means-tested." When a person's or family's income (means) increased by a certain amount, welfare benefits were reduced or eliminated. In other words, the more a welfare recipient earned, the fewer benefits he or she received. In the AFDC program, for example, a $1 increase in income earned by the recipient family reduced the benefits by $1—which amounts to a 100 percent effective marginal tax rate. In effect, the welfare system created disincentives for welfare recipients to find work. (See this chapter's feature entitled *Politics and Economics: The Earned Income Tax Credit Program* for another example of a federal program that creates such disincentives.)

The 1996 reform bill addressed this problem by limiting most welfare recipients to only two years of welfare assistance. After two years, welfare payments are to be discontinued unless the recipient is working, either at a public-service job or in the private sector. The bill also limited lifetime welfare assistance to five years. (The federally established five-year limit can be avoided by the states, however, if they use their own funds to pay for continued welfare benefits.)

Denial of Assistance to Teenage Mothers.   Traditionally, unmarried teenage mothers tended to stay on welfare the longest, and their children were less likely than others to achieve economic self-sufficiency when they grew up. To some extent, an unmarried mother's decision to remain on welfare was a rational response in the face of high effective marginal tax rates, as just discussed.

Consider, for example, a young unmarried mother receiving food stamps, cash welfare payments, and Medicaid assistance totaling $950 per month. If that person took a minimum-wage job and earned, say, $820 per month, her food stamps were reduced by $125 a month, and her welfare payments were eliminated completely. The woman had to pay taxes of about $60 a month, and if she faced job-related expenses (such as for day care and transportation) of $100 a month, the net increase in real take-home pay was only about $60 a month. Nationwide, it has been estimated that a welfare mother without work experience ended up making a net wage of only $1.50 per hour if she chose to leave welfare to go to work. Furthermore, if an unwed mother had an additional child, she would receive anywhere from $8,000 to $15,000 in additional welfare funds to support that child.

Thus, many experts concluded that one way to reduce welfare spending in the long run would be to reduce the number of children born out of wedlock.

POLITICS AND ECONOMICS
The Earned Income Tax Credit Program

In 1975, when the Earned Income Tax Credit (EITC) program was created, it provided only for rebates of Social Security taxes to low-income workers. It was increased sharply in 1990 and again in 1993. In fiscal year 1995–1996, the EITC program is estimated to have cost about $21 billion, more than the federal cost of Aid to Families with Dependent Children. An estimated one-fifth of all tax returns for 1996 claimed an EITC. The Internal Revenue Service mails out more than ten million letters a year encouraging more people to sign up for the program. The estimate for 1996 is that 45.1 percent of families in Mississippi became eligible for the EITC, and 42.3 percent in the District of Columbia qualified. The EITC program has become the fastest-growing welfare program in the nation. It also appears to be a program that discourages work more than it rewards work.

Consider how the EITC operates. Families earning up to $8,425 receive a payment representing 30 percent of their earnings from the EITC program. Those earning between $8,426 and $11,000 receive a flat $2,528. A family that earns between $11,000 and $25,300 receives that amount *minus* 17.68 cents for every dollar they earn above $11,000. This is a type of punitive tax on earnings over $11,000. Consequently, it is not surprising that almost three times as many EITC recipients are in the lower range of income than in the higher ranges. The former chair of the President's Council of Economic Advisors, Laura Tyson, declared that the EITC was "a way to reward hard-working Americans who work full time." Yet the General Accounting Office reported that the average EITC recipient works only 1,300 hours, compared with the normal work year of in excess of 2,000 hours.

Has the EITC program been successful in raising people out of poverty? Not according to the General Accounting Office, which claims that the EITC decreased the poverty rate by less than 1 percentage point.

For Critical Analysis
Why do you think the EITC program has not affected the poverty rate to any significant degree?

The 1996 reform bill attempts to discourage illegitimate births in two ways: by offering "bonus payments" to states that reduce their rates of illegitimate births among welfare mothers and by allowing states to deny benefits to unmarried teenage mothers.

Welfare Reform, or Welfare Repeal?

Supporters of the 1996 reform bill claim that it will reduce federal government spending on welfare by $55 billion over a six-year period. They also believe that the bill will go a long way toward achieving the goal of getting people off the welfare rolls and into productive jobs. Many, though, contend that the bill as passed is far from an optimal solution to the welfare problem. Senator Daniel Patrick Moynihan of New York, one of several Senate Democrats who bitterly opposed the reform bill, went so far as to say that the legislation is less "welfare reform" than "welfare repeal."

Perhaps the most controversial provisions of the bill are those allowing the states to deny welfare assistance to unwed teenage mothers. Supporters of the bill maintain that these provisions are necessary to remove the purported financial incentives to have children that traditionally have been provided by the welfare system. Critics contend that the only real effect of these provisions will be to reduce aid to poor children. They see the provisions as a simplistic attempt to remedy a problem that is rooted deeply in social and economic factors, such as urban decay and unemployment, as well as in the disincentives to work mentioned earlier. If a state chooses to deny benefits to unmarried teenage mothers, who will provide for the needs of illegitimate children?

Problems Facing the States

The 1996 welfare reform bill gave the states more control over welfare, but it also created many problems for which the states must find solutions. For example, consider the state of New York. Its constitution requires the state to provide for the "aid, care and support of the needy," as determined by the state legislature. The welfare bill, by denying some benefits to legal immigrants and imposing five-year lifetime limits on welfare assistance to adults, in effect passes on the costs of providing aid to the "needy" to New York state and local governments.

Furthermore, implementing the "workfare" requirements of the bill may be costly and difficult. The concept of workfare—performing public service jobs in return for welfare benefits—is not new, and welfare reform proposals often have been couched in such terms. Many point out, though, that the work requirements of the 1996 reform bill, although they play into the public's feeling that no one should "get something for nothing," are not free. For one thing, making the state the employer of last resort adds yet another layer to the bureaucracy—those state officials who will manage the state-provided jobs. This will only add to the costs of welfare that the states must pay. According to the Congressional Budget Office, each public service job costs $3,500 a year to monitor. If it involves mothers, an additional $3,000 a year has to be paid for child-care costs. Clearly, the success of the work requirements will depend on whether the states and industry can create and monitor the millions of jobs needed to put welfare recipients to work.

Finally, it may take many months, and even years, for states to develop the computer capability to enforce the restrictions that the bill imposes on welfare benefits. For example, suppose that a person receives welfare assistance in Tennessee for a year, then moves to New York and receives welfare benefits in that state for a year. The following year, the person moves to California and applies for welfare benefits there. To determine how long the person has received welfare payments, the state of California would have to have access to data stored in other states' computer files. At present, there is no national computer system that allows states to exchange such data on welfare recipients, and it may take some time for such a system to be developed.

IMMIGRATION

Immigration, like welfare, has become a political lightning rod in recent years. Although much of the debate has focused on illegal immigration and the share of welfare payments going to immigrants, the scope of the debate over immigration raises the following general question: Should *any* immigration into the United States be permitted, and if so, just who and how many individuals should be permitted to immigrate to this country?

Is Recent Immigration Greater Than in the Past?

The immigration issue has become more important in recent years because of the upsurge in immigration rates in the last several decades, as shown in panel (a) of Figure 16–4. Currently, about twenty-five million foreign-born persons are living in the United States, or 9 percent of the total U.S. population (which is about 268 million), as shown in panel (b) of Figure 16–4. Although these numbers may seem impressive, when measured as a proportion of the population, immigrants are far less significant than they were in

Panel (a)

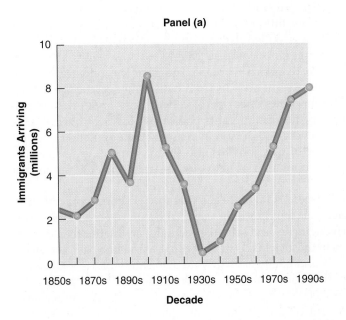

Panel (b)

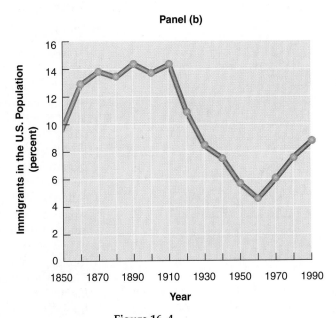

years past. For example, between 1880 and 1920, foreign-born persons constituted over 14 percent of the U.S. population, as shown in panel (b) of Figure 16–4. Subsequent legal restrictions reduced immigration sharply, leading to a forty-year decline in the proportion of the U.S. population that was foreign born. Indeed, only in the last thirty or so years has the foreign-born population begun to rebound.

Changing Federal Immigration Policy

Prior to 1965, federal immigration policy favored white Europeans. Starting in 1965, that policy changed as the federal government began to make family unification the centerpiece of its immigration policy. As a result, children, spouses, and siblings poured in from around the world to join immigrants who originally had entered alone. Additionally, the flood of immigrants was stimulated by the growing sentiment that individuals fleeing persecution in then-communist countries should receive special status as political refugees. Additional entry visas were set aside for such persons, thereby pushing legal immigration totals above what they would have been otherwise.

Do Immigrants Push Down Wage Rates for All Americans?

One of the major complaints by those who wish to limit or halt immigration is that legal immigrants have a dampening effect on everyone else's wage rates. After all, they argue, a larger supply of labor due to increased immigration allows employers to offer lower wage rates than they otherwise would have to offer. This argument has been used particularly with respect to the markets for low-skilled jobs, because of the lower average skills possessed by many new immigrants. If immigration indeed represses wage rates in these markets, some native-born workers may become unemployed or drop out of the labor force all together.

Although this argument superficially appears accurate, a closer analysis of immigration data suggests a different conclusion. A number of studies have examined whether the influx of immigrant workers has affected native-born

Figure 16–4
● ● ● ● ● ● ● ● ● ● ● ● ● ● ●
Immigrants in America

Since the 1850s, immigrant arrivals peaked in the 1900–1910 period but have almost returned to that high level today, as is seen in panel (a). Nonetheless, the percentage of the U.S. population that is foreign born is still lower than it was from the 1850s to the 1920s, as is seen in panel (b).

SOURCES: U.S. Census Bureau; U.S. Immigration and Naturalization Service.

workers adversely, and these studies all have come essentially to the same conclusion: there has been little or no negative impact on employment or unemployment rates of less-skilled native-born Americans.[1]

Apparently, new immigrants compete chiefly for low-skilled jobs with other immigrants, not native-born workers. The garment industry of New York is a prime example. Recent arrivals from Latin America, the Caribbean, and the Far East sit at machines once operated by Italians and Jews. On balance, then, the arrival of new immigrants boosts employment overall. One study showed that for every 100-person increase in the population of adult immigrants, the number of new jobs rose by 46. In contrast, for every 100-person increase in the population of native-born Americans, the number of new jobs rose by only 25.

In the skilled areas, there is no evidence that foreign-born workers cause wages to fall. In fact, just the opposite seems to occur: average wage rates among foreign-born engineers and scientists actually are higher than among native-born workers in those fields. Data show that within the past five years, foreign-born scientists and engineers had a median salary of $44,400, versus $40,000 for their native-born counterparts. Foreign-born Ph.D.'s earned a median income of $70,000 versus $60,000 for their native-born counterparts. Indeed, the Department of Labor's own data show that out of more than 230,000 outstanding "critical-need" visas granted to the foreign born to work in the United States, only 418 were found to be for jobs that paid less than the prevailing wage.

Do Immigrants, on Balance, Contribute to the Economy?

Critics of immigration contend that new immigrants are likely to be heavy users of publicly provided or subsidized services, such as education and some forms of health care. Indeed, the adverse impact that new immigrants sometimes have on state and local budgets often is the most visible and easily quantifiable measure and thus also is an important source of opposition to immigration. At times, this political opposition has reached extraordinary intensity. Thus, in California, voters passed Proposition 187, a 1994 ballot initiative that stripped illegal immigrants of rights to many government services, including education and nonemergency health care. Proposition 187 was challenged immediately in the courts, however, and therefore has had little impact.

Some statistics do bear out this criticism of immigration. Immigrants constitute around 8.5 percent of households in America, yet they receive 13.1 percent of public assistance. In California, foreign households receive 32 percent of all public cash assistance. These overall numbers, though, mask the fact that the behavior of immigrants is not uniform. Two-thirds of all immigrants arrive legally under the regular immigration system. Normally, they are well educated and highly motivated and receive proportionately about the same amount of welfare payments as native-born people. Furthermore, a significant percentage of the research and development personnel in American corporations is foreign born (see the feature entitled *Politics and Diversity: Immigrants and High Technology*).

Illegal immigrants as well as legal immigrants arriving as refugees from former communist countries are another story. Overall, 16 percent of political refugees receive welfare assistance from the government, in contrast to 8 percent of other legal immigrants. Thirty-one percent of such recent refugee arrivals are on welfare. Additionally, although illegal immigrants typically

These individuals are illegally crossing the Mexico-U.S. border. Images such as this contribute to the perception that immigrants coming to the U.S. are overwhelmingly poor and illegal. In actuality more than two-thirds of the immigrants arrive legally.

---

[1]See, for example, George Borjas, *Friends or Strangers: The Impact of Immigrants on the U.S. Economy* (New York: Basic Books, 1990).

POLITICS AND DIVERSITY
Immigrants and High Technology

Lost in much of the discussion of immigration reform is a serious analysis of the positive effects that the foreign born have had on America's way of life, standard of living, and industrial might. Consider, for example, the career of just one immigrant, Andrew S. Grove. In 1957, Grove arrived at the Brooklyn Naval Yard after escaping from communist Hungary. He had $20 in his pocket. He enrolled as an engineering student at the City College of New York and went on to earn his Ph.D. in chemical engineering at the University of California. Just eleven years after arriving as a poor immigrant, Grove joined forces with two other scientists to start the Intel Corporation. Today, Intel's microprocessor architecture is used by 80 percent of the world's computers, and Grove is the president and chief executive offi-

cer of one of the most important companies in the world.

Grove is not alone. As of the beginning of 1997, immigrants started or currently preside over such high-tech companies as AST, Borland, Compaq, LSI Logic, Sun Microsystems, and others. Consider also that about one-third of the engineers in California's Silicon Valley are foreign born, as are the engineers at the main labs of IBM and AT&T.

Other industries have benefited from immigrants, too. Italian A. P. Giannini started BankAmerica, and Scotsman Andrew Carnegie was responsible for technologies that significantly reduced the cost of steel production. The American chemical industry was developed by a Frenchman named E. I. du Pont. The co-inventor of the modern digital com-

puter, John Vincent Attanasoff, was of Bulgarian extraction. Germans were responsible for the birth of many large companies, including Weyerhaeuser, Bausch & Lomb, Chrysler, Hershey, and Anheuser-Busch. Hispanic immigrants have started tens of thousands of small businesses. Finally, immigrants helped develop America's nuclear and missile technologies, as well as the ability to land on the moon.

For Critical Analysis

Consider the policy proposal that only educated and skilled individuals should be allowed to immigrate to this country. How might the United States suffer from such a policy, given the above information?

may not receive any cash assistance, many are regular consumers of other forms of taxpayer-funded public assistance. For example, one study estimated that during the early 1990s, many of the births in the Los Angeles area were to illegal immigrant mothers and were paid for chiefly with public funds.

With respect to refugees, our government policy has been to encourage the use of welfare. In contrast to other legal immigrants, who have to wait at least three years to receive welfare assistance, political refugees are eligible for welfare immediately. In other words, refugees from countries such as Cambodia, Vietnam, the former Soviet Union, and Cuba can obtain welfare assistance immediately, as well as a wide variety of benefits that exceed what native-born Americans can receive legally.

Although public assistance to refugees is costly, studies suggest that, overall, immigration offers a net gain to the economy. Even illegal aliens, such as those in California, eventually may contribute to this gain. According to the Tomás Rivera Center, a nonprofit public policy research institute affiliated with the Claremont Graduate School, immigrants—legal and illegal—contribute more to California in taxes than they cost in government services. The most recent research takes the position that most of California's immigrants will spend the rest of their lives there and that ultimately they will pay their fair share of state taxes.

The Immigration Reform Act of 1996

In response to public pressure to curb immigration, particularly illegal immigration, and the amount of public benefits going to noncitizen residents in the

A proud new U.S. citizen displays her cetificate of citizenship at a ceremony on Ellis Island in New York.

United States, Congress passed the Immigration Reform Act of 1996. To conform with the welfare reform act that had been passed earlier in the year, the act prohibited immigrants, including legal immigrants who are not yet citizens, from receiving most forms of public assistance. (*Not* included in the act as passed, however, was a controversial provision that would have prevented children of immigrants from attending public schools.) To stem the influx of illegal immigrants, the act also did as follows:

• Doubled the number of border patrol agents.
• Increased penalties for immigrant smuggling and document fraud.
• Authorized an expedited deportation process for illegal aliens (including undocumented political refugees).
• Provided for the establishment, in five states, of pilot programs to assist employers in verifying workers' status.
• Provided that any person who "sponsors" an immigrant, such as a family member, must have an income of at least 125 percent of the poverty level (which in 1996 was about $16,000 for a family of four).

CRIME: THE COLD WAR OF THE 1990S AND BEYOND

The issue of crime has been on the national agenda for years now. Virtually all polls taken in the United States in the last few years show that crime is one of the major concerns of the public. Recall from Chapter 7 that Americans regularly rank violence and crime as the nation's number one problem (see Table 7–4). Although there is some evidence that certain crime rates have fallen, on average, the public's concern has not been misplaced. (See the feature entitled

Thinking Politically about Crime

For years the American public has been concerned over crime and violence. Consequently, "getting tough on crime" has been a standard campaign strategy for many politicians. During the 1996 election, for example, President Clinton used every available opportunity to preempt Bob Dole on the crime issue. Historically, Republicans have been viewed as "harder" on crime than Democrats. It is perhaps not surprising that even before the 1996 Republican nominating convention

Bob Dole endorsed a constitutional amendment to protect crime victims' rights.

Soon thereafter, the Clinton administration announced that it would present its own version of such an amendment. Almost immediately, the administration asked the Justice Department to "sign off" on what would become Clinton's first proposed constitutional amendment. Some Justice Department officials were not pleased, arguing that the Constitution should not be used to score political

points. The criminal division of the Justice Department argued that the amendment might allow victims to disrupt routine plea bargains. The White House pushed ahead nonetheless, because it was determined to portray the president as "tough on crime."

For Critical Analysis
Are there any circumstances in which a major social issue will not become a political football, to be used between candidates?

Thinking Politically about Crime for a discussion of political campaign strategies and the crime issue.)

Crime in American History

In every period in the history of this nation, people have voiced their apprehension about crime. Some criminologists argue that crime was probably as frequent around the time of the American Revolution as it is currently. During the Civil War, mob violence and riots erupted in numerous cities. After the Civil War, people in San Francisco were told that "no decent man is in safety to walk the streets after dark; while at all hours, both night and day, his property is jeopardized by incendiarism and burglary."[2] In 1910, one author stated that "crime, especially in its more violent forms and among the young, is increasing steadily and is threatening to bankrupt the Nation."[3]

From 1900 to the 1930s, social violence and crime increased dramatically. Labor union battles and racial violence were common. Only during the three-decade period from the mid-1930s to the early 1960s did the United States experience, for the first time in its history, stable or slightly declining overall crime rates.

Violent Crime. What most Americans are worried about is violent crime. From the mid-1980s to 1994, its rate rose relentlessly, until 1995, when it declined by 9 percent. Look at Figure 16–5, where you see the changes in violent crime rates from 1970 to 1995. Going back even further, the murder rate per 100,000 people in 1964 was 4.9, whereas in 1994 it was estimated at 9.3, an almost 100 percent increase. These nationwide numbers, however, do not tell the full story. Murder rates in some major U.S. cities are between 50 and 100

[2]President's Commission on Law Enforcement and Administration of Justice, *Challenge of Crime in a Free Society* (Washington, D.C.: Government Printing Office, 1967), p. 19.
[3]President's Commission, *Challenge of Crime*, p. 19.

Figure 16–5
● ● ● ● ● ● ● ● ● ● ● ● ● ● ● ● ● ●
Changes in Violent Crime Rates from 1970 to 1995

Violent crime in the United States rose from 1970 to the beginning of the 1980s. Then crime rates dropped relatively dramatically until about 1986, when they again started to climb. By 1994, they were at their highest recorded levels. In 1995, violent crime dropped 9 percent.

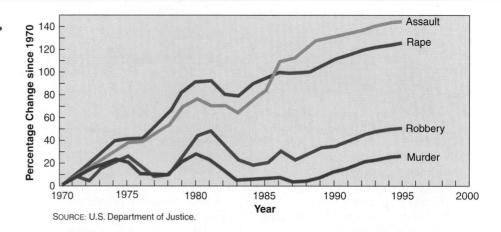

SOURCE: U.S. Department of Justice.

per 100,000 people. These cities include Washington, D.C.; Detroit; New Orleans; St. Louis; and Birmingham.

A disturbing element with respect to crime is the number of serious crimes committed by juveniles. As you can see in Figure 16–6, the number of violent crimes committed by juveniles increased dramatically from the mid-1980s to 1994. Since 1995, however, that number has declined somewhat. (See this chapter's *Politics and Crime* for a further examination of the problem of juvenile crime.)

Crime Rates Soaring in Mid-sized Cities. Violent crime actually has started to peak in major cities like New York City and Los Angeles. In contrast, violent crimes have had their most significant increases in cities with populations between 100,000 and 500,000. For example, violent crimes, including murders, rapes, robberies, and assaults, declined in cities of over one million people during the 1990s but increased in virtually all other cities. (See this chapter's *Politics and the Fifty States* for crime rates in selected U.S. cities.)

The Total Cost of Crime to American Society

Figure 16–6
● ● ● ● ● ● ● ● ● ● ● ● ● ● ● ● ● ●
Arrest Rates For Violent Crime

Rates per 100,000 for youths aged 10 through 17 and for adults

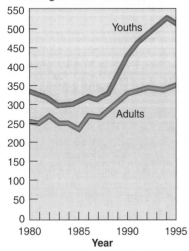

SOURCE: Federal Bureau of Investigation.

For the perpetrator, crime may pay in certain circumstances—a successful robbery or embezzlement, for example—but crime certainly costs the American public. Consider one typical new home in Pico Rivera, a small city southeast of Los Angeles. The new two-story frame house has motion-sensitive floodlights, infrared alarms, video monitors, and a spiked fence topped with razor wire. The patio is surrounded by a metal cage, and bars are over every window. In the yard are two Doberman pinschers. Private security guards patrol the community. The additional costs of building that new house in terms of crime protection are part of the nationwide cost of crime. Table 16–2 summarizes what crime is costing us every year.

The Prison Population Bomb

Virtually the instant a new prison is built, it is filled, and complaints arise about overcrowding. In 1994, for example, the state prison population was about 900,000, yet state prisons only had the capacity to hold about 500,000 inmates. The federal prison population, which is currently over 95,000, also far exceeds prison capacity. In 1996, the Department of Justice announced that the total U.S. prison population had climbed even further—to about 1.6 million in all—and is now nearly twice what it was a decade ago. (For a com-

POLITICS AND CRIME
Attacking the Problem of Juvenile Crime

Although serious adult crimes have declined overall since 1980, those by persons aged ten through seventeen rose dramatically until 1994. As you can see in the accompanying figure, the number of arrest rates for murders committed by youths surpassed that for adults in the late 1980s—and continues to be higher. Furthermore, teenage killings with firearms quadrupled in the ten years after 1984. Currently, handguns are used in two-thirds of juvenile homicides.

The political response to this rise in serious juvenile crimes has been varied. Some cities have established juvenile curfews. Several states have begun to try more and more juveniles as adults, particularly juveniles charged with homicides. Still other states are operating juvenile "boot camps" to try to "shape up" the less violent juvenile criminals. Additionally, victims of juvenile crime and vic-

tims' relatives are attempting to pry open the traditionally secret juvenile-court system. Even the White House in 1996 sent to Congress a plan for federal prosecutors to try some juveniles as adults without seeking judicial permission.*

The number of youths between the ages of fifteen and seventeen will rise from about nine million today to almost thirteen million in the year 2010. It is thus understandable that there is grave concern about preventing an even worse juvenile crime problem in the years to come.

For Critical Analysis
What are the pros and cons of trying more juvenile criminals as adults?

*For more details on the rights of juveniles in our legal system, see Chapter 6.

Youths and Murder

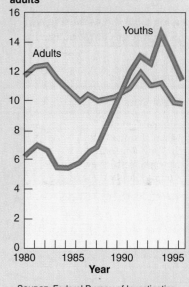

Murder arrest rates per 100,000 for youths aged 10 through 17 and for adults

SOURCE: Federal Bureau of Investigation.

parison of U.S. incarceration rates with those of other countries, see this chapter's feature entitled *Politics and Comparative Systems: Incarceration Worldwide.*)

As the number of arrests and incarcerations in the United States increases, so does the cost of building and operating prisons. An additional 1,500 new

Table 16–2

The Total Yearly Cost of Crime in America

EXPENDITURE	EXPLANATION	TOTAL COST (PER YEAR)
Criminal justice	All the spending on police, courts, and prisons at the federal, state, and local levels	$ 95 billion
Private protection	Spending on private guards, security systems, alarms, etc.	$ 70 billion
Urban decay	The cost of lost jobs and fleeing residents because of excessive crime in inner cities	$ 50 billion
Property loss	The value of stolen goods and vandalized buildings	$ 50 billion
Destroyed lives	The economic value of lost lives (death) and broken lives as a result of robberies, rapes, loss of loved ones, etc.	$175 billion
Medical care	The cost of treating victims	$ 10 billion
TOTAL		**$450 billion**

SOURCE: Federal Bureau of Investigation; and *Business Week*, various issues.

POLITICS AND THE FIFTY STATES
Crime Rates in Selected U.S. Cities

Serious crime continues to drop in the United States, according to reports issued by the Federal Bureau of Investigation. There is a dramatic difference in crime rates, however, across the states. More specifically, there is a difference in crime rates across cities in the United States. The accompanying table shows the five best cities and the five worst cities with respect to serious crime.

For Critical Analysis
What are some of the factors that determine crime rates across cities?

Serious Crimes

WORST CITIES	PER 100,000	BEST CITIES	PER 100,000
Atlanta, Georgia	16,783	San Jose, California	4,428
Miami, Florida	15,607	Virginia Beach, Virginia	4,744
St. Louis, Missouri	15,300	Santa Ana, California	5,184
Newark, New Jersey	14,894	San Diego, California	5,496
Tampa, Florida	13,943	Pittsburgh, Pennsylvania	5,900

prison beds are needed each week. When operational costs are included and construction costs are amortized over the life of a facility, the cost of sentencing one person to one year in jail averages between $25,000 and $40,000. Thus, the annual nationwide cost of building, maintaining, and operating prisons is about $35 billion today.

When imprisonment keeps truly violent felons behind bars longer, it prevents them from committing more crimes. The average predatory street criminal commits fifteen or more crimes each year when not behind bars. But most prisoners are in for a relatively short time and released on parole early, often

To help ease the overcrowding, inmates at the New York State Prison at Watertown are incarcerated in barrack-style prison blocks.

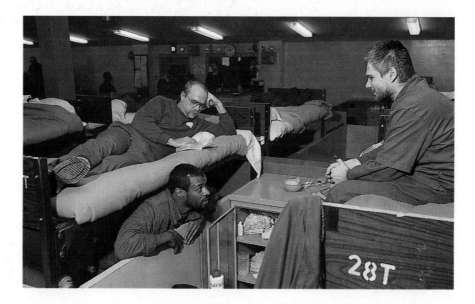

POLITICS AND COMPARATIVE SYSTEMS
Incarceration Worldwide

The United States is known as "the home of the free and the land of the brave." It therefore may surprise many Americans to discover that the United States has the highest incarceration rate of any country in the world today. Just look at the figure in this feature. These data, relatively speaking, would have looked about the same ten years ago, when the Gulag prison camps still existed in the former Soviet Union and when repression in South Africa was at its peak.

For Critical Analysis
Why does the U.S. prison population continue to rise while at the same time the number of violent crimes is not significantly reduced?

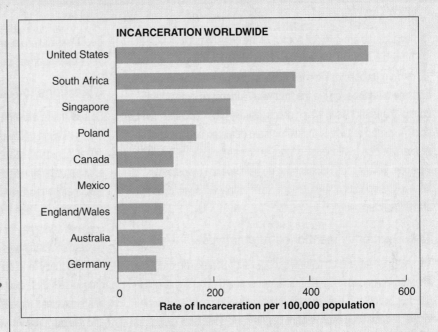

INCARCERATION WORLDWIDE

United States
South Africa
Singapore
Poland
Canada
Mexico
England/Wales
Australia
Germany

0   200   400   600
Rate of Incarceration per 100,000 population

SOURCE: FBI, Bureau of Justice Statistics; The Sentencing Project.

because of prison overcrowding. Then many find themselves back in prison because they have violated parole, typically by using illegal drugs. Indeed, of the over one million people who are arrested each year, the majority are arrested for drug offenses. Given that from twenty to forty million Americans violate one or more drug laws each year, the potential "supply" of prisoners seems virtually without limit. Consequently, it may not matter how many prisons are built; there will still be overcrowding as long as we maintain the same legislation with respect to psychoactive drugs. (See this chapter's *Critical Perspective* for another view of this situation.)

Three Strikes and You're Out

Many states have passed "three-strikes-and-you're-out" legislation. Typically, this legislation states that any "career" criminal who already has two violent felony convictions on his or her record will go to jail for life (without parole) if convicted of a third similar felony. Washington state adopted such a law by public referendum in 1990, and California has a similar law, as do a growing number of other states.[4] The federal crime bill enacted in 1994 adopted this provision, too.

A narcotics officer arrests a cocaine dealer in New York. The war against drugs seemed to make little headway during the 1980s and 1990s, although government expenditures on the effort continued to rise.

---

[4]In June 1996, the California Supreme Court ruled that judges do have some discretion in applying the three-strikes-and-you're-out law, however. The court stated that a trial court judge's refusal to consider two prior felony allegations of a criminal defendant did not violate the three-strikes law. See *People v. Superior Court*, 13 Cal. 4th 497 (1996).

CRITICAL PERSPECTIVE
Drugs and a Constitutional Alternative

Illegal drugs are a major source of the crisis in public safety in America. A rising percentage of arrests are for illegal drug use or drug trafficking. Violence accompanies the illegal drug trade, and one of the reasons is the "turf wars" among drug dealers to control the territories in which drugs, usually crack cocaine, can be sold. A related reason is that when drug deals go bad, drug dealers cannot turn to the legal system to help them out. They turn to violence. Finally drug addicts who do not have the income to finance their habits often turn to a life of crime—assault, robbery, and sometimes murder.

Two Frequently Mentioned Alternatives

Two alternatives are commonly proposed for solving the drug problem in America. The first is to "get serious" about fighting illegal drug sales and use. Proponents of get-tough policies include former federal drug czar William Bennett and 1992 and 1996 presidential candidate H. Ross Perot. A get-tough policy would involve major shifts in the use of government resources to fight drug trafficking and drug use. Advocates of such a policy believe that a true "war"—including use of the military—is what is needed.

At the other extreme are those who want to legalize all drugs. They argue that the prohibition against alcohol was a complete failure during this nation's "dry" period from 1920 to 1933. Under Prohibition, murder and assault rates increased, and so did the growth of organized crime. They argue that the legalization (or decriminalization) of most or all drugs would eliminate the main impetus that drives people to deal in drugs—huge profits.

Objections to These Two Alternatives

Both of these extreme views have met with numerous objections. The get-tough policy did not work during Prohibition. Moreover, all of the increased spending on drug interdiction has had virtually no effect on overall illegal drug consumption in the United States. In fact, there is more and higher-quality cocaine available today than at any other time in the history of this country. The price of cocaine, corrected for inflation and quality increases, is about 10 percent of what it was in the early 1960s.

An equally long list of objections to the laissez-faire view of drug legalization exists. What if nationwide legalization leads to an unprecedented increase in the use of cocaine, marijuana, heroin, and the like? Are we willing to pay the social costs of larger-scale use? If we are not, it might then be impossible for this country to revert to criminalization of drug trading and use. Also, what about those individuals who do not want to live in a nation that allows all drugs to be freely produced, distributed, and consumed?

A Middle Ground—
The Constitutional Alternative

A middle ground has been offered by Daniel K. Benjamin and Roger LeRoy Miller in their book *Undoing Drugs: Beyond Legaliza-*

There are several problems with the three-strikes-and-you're-out plan. One of the most important relates to what we have already talked about: overcrowded prisons. A nationwide adoption of the plan definitely would increase the number of prisoners. Those convicted under such a law would be in prison for life. Thus, we would have a large population of aging prisoners who would require more health-care expenditures—all paid for by the state (or federal) government.

Additionally, in states that do not have capital punishment, the three-strikes-and-you're-out legislation actually reduces the potential cost of crime to those already convicted of two felonies. Consider an individual who already has spent time in prison for two felonies. While he is robbing a store, the police pull up. The robber knows that if he gets caught and convicted, he will stay in prison forever with no chance of parole. He therefore has an increased incentive to kill the police and all witnesses: it will make no differ-

CRITICAL PERSPECTIVE
Drugs and a Constitutional Alternative, Continued

tion.*They point out that there is a precedent for a new way of solving the drug problem. It is contained in Section 2 of the Twenty-first Amendment, which repealed Prohibition. That section states that "the transportation or importation into any State, Territory, or possession of the United States for delivery or use therein of intoxicating liquors, in violation of the laws thereof, is hereby prohibited." In other words, the repeal of Prohibition did not make alcoholic beverages legal everywhere in the United States. Rather, they remain illegal in any jurisdiction that continues to have laws against them.

Why not do the same thing with today's illegal drugs? Currently, every state has its own drug laws, which, of course, are influenced by federal legislation. All the Congress would have to do, according to Benjamin and Miller, is amend the Comprehensive Drug Abuse Prevention and Control Act of 1970. This amendment would simply take the federal government out of the business of controlling drugs and leave it to the states and their subjurisdictions. The federal government still would be available to help states when requested to do so. It would still make sure that federal laws with respect to taxation were followed, much as it does today with federal excise taxes on beer, wine, and liquor.

Benjamin and Miller predict that under their constitutional alternative, different states would undertake different ways of solving their drug problems, depending on the wishes of their electorates. Some jurisdictions might make methadone freely available for heroin addicts so they would not need to engage in crime to support their habits. This would also reduce the transmission of AIDS through dirty needles. Some states might decriminalize marijuana but get much tougher on crack cocaine. No one really knows what would happen. At a minimum, though, the states would be able to innovate and experiment with alternative systems. Some states might devote resources to education and rehabilitation, whereas others might stress incarceration. Individuals would have the option of "voting with their feet"; they could move to those jurisdictions that have the right combination.

In essence, the Benjamin and Miller proposal is an argument in favor of federalism. They want the states to assume police power over all psychoactive substances just as they now have over all alcoholic beverages.

For Critical Analysis

1. What political forces would be in favor of eliminating the federal monopoly in the drug policy and enforcement area? What political forces would be against this proposal?

2. Nicotine causes more deaths than all other psychoactive drugs combined. Alcohol causes greater losses in productivity, more broken homes, and more violence than any other psychoactive drug. Why do you think these two drugs currently are not illegal?

*New York: Basic Books, 1993.

ence to his fate. If he ends up being caught anyway, the most he can get is life imprisonment, which he was going to receive anyway.

Although such reasoning may not affect all criminals who find themselves in similar situations, it may affect enough of them to actually increase the murder rate. If it did, this would be the result of the law of unintended consequences—legislation sometimes leads to what is not desired, because it changes the incentives facing individuals.

Politics and Crime: The New Iron Triangle

In Chapter 14, you discovered the iron triangle at work within the federal government. The example used was the U.S. Department of Agriculture. The three points of the iron triangle were (1) the members of Congress who deal with agriculture; (2) the bureaucrats in Congress who administer the pro-

DID YOU KNOW...
That the average cost of construction per prison bed ranges from $50,000 at a minimum-security site to $100,000 or more at a maximum-security facility?

grams; and (3) interest groups, their professional staffs, and lobbyists paid for by agribusiness.

A similar type of iron triangle is now developing in the area of crime. A new version of the old military-industrial complex has been born. It is an infrastructure dependent on political rhetoric and federal, state, and local dollars. The politicians are trying to outdo each other as they stand up to the common enemy—crime. During the Eisenhower era in the 1950s, politicians did the same thing when the common enemy was communism. Instead of looking to military bases, communities today look to new prison sites to create jobs and improve their economies. Large and small businesses scramble to get contracts for developing prisons, new anticrime weapons, and so on.

As illustrated in Figure 16–7, the iron triangle in today's cold war against crime involves, on the legislative side, the appropriate congressional committees, such as the Senate Judiciary Committee and the House Judiciary Committee, as well as related subcommittees. Additionally, there are the lobbyists for prison contractors and those making sophisticated anticrime weapons. Finally, the bureaucracy in the Department of Justice—particularly in the Federal Bureau of Investigation, the Drug Enforcement Administration, and the Office of National Drug Control Policy—completes the triangle.

Even prison guards are forming lobbies to keep the prison population growing. The prison guards' union has become a powerful voice in the iron triangle. For example, in a recent California election, the California Correctional Peace Officer's Association was the second-largest donor in the state in terms of campaign contributions. The association spends over a million dollars on political contributions for the governorship as well as for the legislature during each electoral cycle.

Communities seeking job growth via crime-related activities are numerous. According to Keith Cunningham of Business Executives for National Security, "There's a food fight among communities that want these prisons." When Senator Edward Kennedy (D., Mass.) announced that Fort Devons, which was supposed to be closed, would be converted to a federal prison, businesspersons in the audience stood up and cheered.

Figure 16–7
• • • • • • • • • • • • • • • • • • • •
Comparing the Iron Triangle for the Old Cold War with the Iron Triangle for the New Cold War against Crime

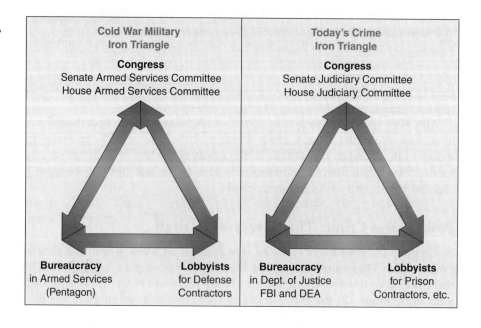

ENVIRONMENTAL POLICY

Human actions may create unwanted side effects—including the destruction of the environment and the ecology (the total pattern of environmental relationships). Every day, humans, through their actions, emit pollutants into the air and the water. Each year, the world atmosphere receives twenty million metric tons of sulfur dioxide, eighteen million metric tons of ozone pollutants, and sixty million metric tons of carbon monoxide.

The Government's Response to Air and Water Pollution

The government has been responding to pollution problems since before the American Revolution, when the Massachusetts Bay Colony issued regulations to try to stop the pollution of Boston Harbor. In the nineteenth century, states passed laws controlling water pollution after scientists and medical researchers convinced most policymakers that dumping sewage into drinking and bathing water caused disease. At the national level, the Federal Water Pollution Control Act of 1948 provided research and assistance to the states for pollution control efforts, but little was done. In 1952, the first state air-pollution law was passed in Oregon. The federal Air Pollution Control Act of 1955 gave some assistance to states and cities. Table 16–3 describes the major environmental legislation in the United States.

The National Environmental Policy Act. The year 1969 marked the start of the most concerted national government involvement in solving pollution problems. In that year, the conflict between oil exploration interests and environmental interests literally erupted when a Union Oil Company's oil well six

A number of urban areas have a landfill problem. The price of landfill has been going up in many of the major cities for many years. Nationwide, in contrast, the average per-ton price of landfill has gone down. In other words, cities in many regions of the United States pay less today to dump their garbage into landfills than they did ten years ago.

Table 16–3

Major Federal Environmental Legislation

1899 Refuse Act. Made it unlawful to dump refuse into navigable waters without a permit. A 1966 court decision made all industrial wastes subject to this act.

1948 Federal Water Pollution Control Act. Set standards for the treatment of municipal water waste before discharge. Revisions to this act were passed in 1965 and 1967.

1955 Air Pollution Control Act. Authorized federal research programs for air-pollution control.

1963 Clean Air Act. Assisted local and state governments in establishing control programs and coordinated research.

1965 Clean Air Act Amendments. Authorized the establishment of federal standards for automobile exhaust emissions, beginning with 1968 models.

1965 Solid Waste Disposal Act. Provided assistance to local and state governments for control programs and authorized research in this area.

1965 Water Quality Act. Authorized the setting of standards for discharges into waters.

1967 Air Quality Act. Established air quality regions, with acceptable regional pollution levels. Required local and state governments to implement approved control programs or be subject to federal controls.

1969 National Environmental Policy Act. Established the Council for Environmental Quality (CEQ) for the purpose of coordinating all federal pollution control programs. Authorized the establishment of the Environmental Protection Agency (EPA) to implement CEQ policies on a case-by-case basis.

1970 Clean Air Act Amendments. Authorized the Environmental Protection Agency to set national air-pollution standards and restricted the discharge of six major pollutants into the lower atmosphere. Automobile manufacturers were required to reduce nitrogen oxide, hydrocarbon, and carbon monoxide emissions by 90 percent (in addition to the 1965 requirements) during the 1970s.

1972 Federal Water Pollution Control Act Amendments. Set national water quality goal of restoring polluted waters to swimmable, fishable waters by 1983.

1972 Federal Environmental Pesticide Control Act. Required that all pesticides used in interstate commerce be approved and certified as effective for their stated purpose. Required certification that they were harmless to humans, animal life, animal feed, and crops.

1974 Clean Water Act. Originally called the Safe Water Drinking Act, this law set (for the first time) federal standards for water suppliers serving more than twenty-five people, having more than fifteen service connections, or operating more than sixty days a year.

1976 Resource Conservation and Recovery Act. Encouraged the conservation and recovery of resources. Put hazardous waste under government control. Prohibited the opening of new dumping sites. Required that all existing open dumps be closed or upgraded to sanitary landfills by 1983. Set standards for providing technical, financial, and marketing assistance to encourage solid waste management.

1977 Clean Air Act Amendments. Postponed the deadline for automobile emission requirements.

1980 Comprehensive Environmental Response, Compensation, and Liability Act. Established a "Superfund" to clean up toxic waste dumps.

1990 Clean Air Act Amendments. Provided for precise formulas for new gasoline to be burned in the smoggiest cities, further reduction in carbon monoxide and other exhaust emissions in certain areas that still have dangerous ozone levels in the year 2003, and a cap on total emissions of sulfur dioxide from electricity plants. Placed new restrictions on toxic pollutants.

1990 Oil Pollution Act. Established liability for the clean-up of navigable waters after oil-spill disasters.

---

miles off the coast of Santa Barbara, California, exploded, releasing 235,000 gallons of crude oil. The result was an oil slick, covering an area of eight hundred square miles, that washed up on the city's beaches and killed plant life, birds, and fish. Hearings in Congress revealed that the Interior Department did not know which way to go in the energy-environment trade-off. Congress did know, however, and passed the National Environmental Policy Act in 1969. This landmark legislation established, among other things, the Council for Environmental Quality. Also, it mandated that an **environmental impact statement (EIS)** be prepared for every recommendation or report on legislation or major federal actions that significantly affected the quality of the environment. The act gave citizens and public interest groups concerned with the environment a weapon against the unnecessary and inappropriate use of natural resources by the government.

ENVIRONMENTAL IMPACT STATEMENT (EIS)

As a requirement mandated by the National Environmental Policy Act, a report that must show the costs and benefits of major federal actions that could significantly affect the quality of the environment.

The Clean Air Act of 1990.　The most comprehensive government attempt at cleaning up our environment occurred in 1990. After years of lobbying by environmentalists and counterlobbying by industry, the Clean Air Act of 1990 was passed. This act amended the 1970 Clean Air Act, which, among other things, had required a reduction of 90 percent of the amount of carbon monoxide and other pollutants emitted by automobiles. In spite of the fact that an automobile purchased today emits only 4 percent of the pollutants that a 1970 model did, there is more overall air pollution. This is because so many more automobiles are being driven today. Currently, the urban ground-level ozone is as great as it was before any clean-air legislation. The 1990 Clean Air Act requires automobile manufacturers to cut new automobiles' exhaust emissions of nitrogen oxide by 60 percent and the emission of other pollutants by 35 percent. These requirements must be met by 1998.

Stationary sources of air pollution are also subject to more regulation. To reduce **acid rain,** 110 of the oldest coal-burning power plants in the United States must cut their emissions by 40 percent by the year 2001. Controls on other factories and businesses are intended to reduce ground-level ozone pollution in ninety-six cities to healthful levels by 2005 (except in Los Angeles, which has until 2010 to meet the standards). The act also requires that the production of chlorofluorocarbons (CFCs) be stopped completely by the year 2002. CFCs are thought to deplete the ozone layer and increase global warming. CFCs are used in air conditioning and other refrigeration units.

The Costs of Clean Air. Before the mid-1980s, environmental politics seemed to be couched in terms of "them against us." "Them" was everyone involved in businesses that cut down rain forests, poisoned rivers, and created oil spills. "Us" was the government, and it was the government's job to stop "them." Today, particularly in the United States, more people are aware that the battle lines are blurred. According to the Environmental Protection Agency (EPA), we are already spending well over $100 billion annually to comply with federal environmental rules. When the 1990 Clean Air Act is fully implemented, that amount may be as much as 50 percent higher. The government, particularly in Washington, D.C., has become interested in how to solve the nation's environmental problems at the lowest cost. Moreover, U.S. corporations are becoming increasingly engaged in producing recyclable and biodegradable products, as well as pitching in to solve some environmental problems.

Cost concerns clearly were in the minds of the drafters of the Clean Air Act of 1990 when they tackled, for example, the problem of sulfur emissions from electric power plants. Rather than tightening the existing standards, the new law simply limits total sulfur emissions. Companies have a choice of either rebuilding old plants or buying rights to pollute. The result is that polluters have an incentive to not even attempt to deal with exceptionally dirty plants. When closing down such plants, they can sell their pollution rights to those who value them more. The law is straightforward: An electric utility power plant is allowed to emit up to one ton of sulfur dioxide into the air in a given year. If the plant emits one ton of sulfur dioxide, the allowance disappears. If a plant switches to a low-sulfur-dioxide fuel, for example, or installs scrubbing equipment that reduces sulfur dioxide, it may end up emitting less than one ton. In this case, it can sell or otherwise trade its unused pollution allowance, or it can bank it for later use.

These rights to pollution allowances are being traded in the marketplace. Indeed, there is a well-established market in "smog futures" offered on the Chicago Board of Trade and the New York Mercantile Exchange.

There Have Been Improvements. The United States is making fairly substantial strides in the war on toxic emissions. From 1988 to 1994, the latest years for which we have data, the Environmental Protection Agency showed

DID YOU KNOW...
That Greenpeace USA sends out thirty-five million pieces of mail a year and that the National Wildlife Federation annually mails sixty million pieces?

ACID RAIN

Rain that has picked up pollutants, usually sulfur dioxides, from industrial areas of the earth that are often hundreds of miles distant from where the rain falls.

that the volume of chemicals released into the environment declined 37 percent. In 1988, annual toxic emissions totaled 4.848 billion pounds, and in 1994, they totaled only 3.047 billion pounds. One reason for these successes is the increased awareness of the American public of the need for environmental protection—and consequent pressure on Congress to take action. (For a discussion of the role played by the school system in educating Americans on environmental issues—and the reasons why environmental education has become a sensitive political issue—see this chapter's *Politics and the Environment.*)

Regulating Hazardous Waste: Superfund

In 1980, Congress passed the Comprehensive Environmental Response, Compensation, and Liability Act (CERCLA), commonly known as Superfund. The basic purpose of Superfund, which was amended in 1986 by the Superfund Amendments and Reauthorization Act, is to regulate the clean-up of leaking hazardous waste disposal sites. A special federal fund was created for that purpose. Superfund provides that when a release or a threatened release from a site occurs, the EPA can clean up the site and recover the cost of the clean-up from (1) the person who generated the wastes disposed of at the site, (2) the person who transported the wastes to the site, (3) the person who owned or operated the site at the time of the disposal, or (4) the current owner or operator. Liability is usually assessed on anyone who might have been responsible—for example, a person who generated only a fraction of the hazardous waste disposed of at the site may nevertheless be liable for all of the clean-up costs.

By the early 1990s, only 84 of the 1,245 designated sites on Superfund's high-priority list had been cleaned up. The cost has been $11.1 billion. Critics of the Superfund program point out that only 10 percent of the money spent by insurance companies to settle Superfund claims is used to clean up hazardous materials. According to the Rand Corporation, in Santa Monica, California, the remaining 90 percent goes to legal fees and related costs. Other critics point out that the potential benefits of such expensive toxic waste clean-ups are not worth the cost.

The EPA believes that one thousand cancer cases result each year from exposure to hazardous waste sites (although some sources estimate the number of cancer cases to be much higher). Through Superfund, the EPA is allocating $1.75 billion for clean-up. That comes out to $1.75 million per predicted cancer case—under the assumption, of course, that a significant number of the hazardous waste sites actually are cleaned up. In contrast, the National Cancer Institute's 1995 budget for breast cancer research was about $150 million, when there are an estimated 175,000 breast cancer cases diagnosed each year (that is, a cost of $857 per diagnosed case). Furthermore, new EPA studies suggest that other environmental problems pose a greater cancer risk than do hazardous wastes, in terms of the number of people who get cancer. For example, indoor air pollution may cause more cancer deaths per year than do uncleaned Superfund sites.

Recycling and Precycling

The current ecology movement includes intensive efforts to save scarce resources via recycling. **Recycling** involves reusing paper products, plastics, glass, and metals rather than putting them into solid waste dumps. Many cities have instituted mandatory recycling programs.

RECYCLING

The reuse of raw materials derived from already manufactured products

POLITICS AND THE ENVIRONMENT
Environmental Education and Ideology

In the last several decades, the American public has become much more aware of environmental problems and of possible solutions to these problems. Much of this public awareness is due to an increasing amount of environmental education, particularly in grades kindergarten through junior high school. What could be more appropriate, claim environmentalists, than teaching young children about global warming, recycling, and the like? Nonetheless, the issue has become highly political. In Arizona, the legislature overturned a 1990 law requiring environmental education in public schools. The state withdrew its curriculum guide and reduced dramatically the funds for classroom environmental projects, starting in 1996. The legislature specifically warned school districts that if they do continue to teach environmental issues, they cannot encourage advo-

cacy or activism. That means that teachers cannot collect money to save whales or trees, and they cannot encourage students and their parents to send letters of protest to business firms that reportedly pollute the environment. Similar legislation is pending in Wisconsin, North Carolina, Florida, and Texas.

Environmental education has become a politically sensitive issue because some critics maintain that it is less education than indoctrination. Critics contend further that those who teach the subject often have little training in environmental issues. Consequently, children may learn that acid rain creates an environmental crisis, whereas a recent congressionally funded study concluded that acid rain is much less harmful than had been feared. In some schools, young students were told not to use aerosol spray cans even though ozone-

destroying chlorofluorocarbons have been eliminated from most aerosols since 1978.

Environmental teachers have formed their own political organization to fight back against their critics. The North American Association of Environmental Educators (NAAEE) started developing standards in the early 1990s. It soon will conduct program evaluations. NAAEE's executive director, Ed McRea, claims that the attacks on the environmental programs are "motivated by ideology rather than reason."

For Critical Analysis
McRea also made the following comment: "Kids should be encouraged to think, to become activists. Isn't that what teaching is about?" Do you agree with McRea? Explain.

The benefits of recycling are straightforward: fewer *natural* resources are used. But some commentators argue that recycling does not necessarily save *total* resources. For example, recycling paper products may not necessarily save trees in the long run, according to A. Clark Wiseman, an economist for Resources for the Future, in Washington, D.C. He argues that an increase in paper recycling eventually will lead to a reduction in the demand for virgin paper and, thus, in the demand for trees. Because most trees are planted specifically to produce paper, a reduction in the demand for trees will mean that certain land now used to grow trees will be put to other uses. The end result may be smaller, rather than larger, forests. Nonetheless, every ton of recycled paper does save seventeen trees and three cubic yards of landfill space in the short run.

Recycling's Invisible Costs.   The recycling of paper can also pollute. Used paper has ink on it that has to be removed during the recycling process. According to the National Wildlife Federation, one hundred tons of de-inked fiber generates forty tons of sludge. This sludge has to be disposed of, usually in a landfill. Many paper companies, however, are beginning to produce nondyed, nonbleached paper, but its recycling still creates waste that has to be disposed of somehow.

Additionally, recycling requires human effort. The labor resources involved in recycling are often many times more costly than the potential sav-

Typical recycling laws in different cities and counties require that recyclable materials be separated by each household. In this photo, the household has carefully separated newspapers from glass and plastic bottles.

ings in scarce natural resources. This means that net resource use—counting all sources—may sometimes be greater with recycling than without it.

Is Precycling the Answer? One way to reduce the amount of our waste is to precycle. Although this term does not have a strict definition, it usually is used to mean making products in such a way that they are not overpackaged, can be refilled, or both. Detergent companies, for example, have found it beneficial for themselves, consumers, and the environment to package and sell concentrated forms of detergent. The packages are smaller, the resources used in packaging are fewer, and there is less waste to get rid of than is the case with the nonconcentrated forms of detergent. In principle, concentrated juices also represent a form of precycling. In short, the packaging of products in a more concentrated form may help the environment.

Environmental versus Economic Issues

An ongoing debate with respect to environmental policy involves the extent to which economic interests should be sacrificed to preserve the environment. The economic well-being of the timber industry in the northwestern United States, for example, has suffered significantly from environmental regulations intended to preserve the natural habitat for the spotted owl and other endangered species. As you read in the opening *What If . . .* in Chapter 3, environmental policies with respect to federally owned lands can involve significant constitutional issues. Environmental laws and regulations that place restrictions on how these lands can be used have fueled the rebellion against federal land ownership, particularly in the western states.

DOMESTIC POLICY: UNFINISHED WORK

It seems strange that programs to reduce poverty are still on the domestic policy agenda. After all, the federal government started its "war on poverty" back in the early 1960s. By some estimates, we have transferred well over a trillion dollars to eliminate poverty since then. Yet poverty remains a blight on the record of one of the world's richest countries—the United States. Presidential candidate Bill Clinton claimed he would eliminate welfare "as we know it." Although the welfare reform bill of 1996 represented a step toward that goal, the outcome of the bill remains uncertain. Certainly, finding ways to meet the needs of the poor without creating disincentives to work will continue to challenge the government at all levels.

The fact that a significant amount of public benefits go to immigrants, particularly illegal immigrants and political refugees, has linked the domestic policy debate on welfare with the debate on immigration. Although the 1996 Immigration Reform Act authorized actions that will help to curb illegal immigration and reduce welfare spending on immigrants, certain issues—such as emergency medical services and public schooling for the children of immigrants—will continue to spark debate.

Additional unfinished work with respect to domestic policy involves crime and violence in the United States. There is little indication that this problem will be solved in the foreseeable future. The attempt to "get tough on crime" in the form of "three-strikes-and-you're-out" legislation creates the further problem of how to pay for the building and maintenance of additional prisons. Furthermore, the effectiveness of the legislation may be curbed through court interpretation of particular "three-strikes" laws—as has already occurred in California. We probably will see continuing violence among those engaged in the illegal drug trade. No doubt, we also will hear political candidates stress that our high crime rates are a reflection of the breakdown of American values and family structure.

Finally, Congress probably will never remove environmental policy from its domestic policy agenda. Even if the United States miraculously solved many of its environmental problems, there still would be the rest of the world to worry about. Although steps have been taken toward the global coordination of environmental-protection efforts, the practical implementation of global policies remains to be achieved.

GETTING INVOLVED
Working for a Cleaner Environment

Energy undoubtedly will be among the more important domestic issues in the coming decades. Ultimately, every energy policy involves environmental questions. Not only is this issue central to our everyday lives, but also, it is argued, the fate of the planet may hang in the balance of today's decisions made about energy production and environmental protection. To make things more complicated, these parallel struggles of coping with energy problems and preserving our environment tend to work at cross-purposes. In the pursuit of secure and abundant energy, the interests of clean air, water, and land—as well as people—sometimes are sacrificed.

When objectives clash, difficult political trade-offs must be made. To a large group of environmentalists in this country, the choice is clear. Through citizen action groups, environmentalists have challenged the government on these and other issues. They argue that if we want to improve or even preserve our quality of life, we must stop environmental degradation.

Although these diverse groups work on a host of issues from solar power to mass transit and from wildlife preservation to population control, they are bound by certain commonly held beliefs.

If you feel strongly about these issues and want to get involved, contact the following groups:

ENVIRONMENTAL DEFENSE FUND
1875 Connecticut Ave. N.W., Suite 1016
Washington, DC 20036

ENVIRONMENTAL POLICY INSTITUTE
1100 17thSt. N.W., Suite 330
Washington, DC 20036

FRIENDS OF THE EARTH
1025 Vermont Ave. N.W., Suite 300
Washington, DC 20005

GREENPEACE USA
1436 U St. N.W.
Washington, DC 20009

IZAAK WALTON LEAGUE OF AMERICA
707 Conservation Lane
Gaithersburg, MD 20878

LEAGUE OF CONSERVATION VOTERS
1707 L St. N.W., Suite 750
Washington, DC 20036

NATIONAL AUDUBON SOCIETY
700 Broadway
New York, NY 10003

NATIONAL PARKS CONSERVATION ASSOCIATION
1776 Massachusetts Ave. N.W., Suite 200
Washington, DC 20036

NATIONAL WILDLIFE FEDERATION
1400 16th St.
Washington, DC 20036

NATURAL RESOURCES DEFENSE COUNCIL
1200 New York Ave. N.W., Suite 400
Washington, DC 20005

SIERRA CLUB
85 2d St.
San Francisco, CA 94105

WILDERNESS SOCIETY
900 7th St. N.W.
Washington, DC 20006

KEY TERMS

acid rain 563

Aid to Families with Dependent Children (AFDC) 544

domestic policy 539

environmental impact statement (EIS) 562

food stamps 544

income transfer 542

in-kind subsidy 544

price supports 540

recycling 564

Supplemental Security Income (SSI) 544

CHAPTER SUMMARY

1 Domestic policy consists of all of the laws, government planning, and government actions that affect the lives of American citizens. Policies are created in response to public problems or public demand for government action. Four major policy problems now facing this nation are poverty and welfare, immigration, crime, and the environment.

2 The policymaking process is initiated when policymakers become aware—through the media or from their constituents—of a problem that needs to be addressed by the legislature and the president. The process of policymaking includes five steps: agenda building, agenda formulation, agenda adoption, agenda implementation, and agenda evaluation. All policy actions necessarily result in both costs and benefits for society.

3 In spite of the wealth of the United States, a significant number of Americans live in poverty or are homeless. The low-income poverty threshold represents an absolute measure of income needed to maintain a specified standard of living as of 1963, with the constant-dollar, or purchasing-power, value increased year by year in relation to the general increase in prices. The official poverty level is based on pretax income, including cash, and does not take into consideration in-kind subsidies (food stamps, housing vouchers, and so on).

4 The United States spends about $900 billion annually on various welfare programs. The welfare system has been criticized because it creates a disincentive for recipients to increase their work effort, because the more a recipient earns, the fewer benefits he or she will receive. The 1996 welfare reform bill transferred more control over welfare programs to the states, imposed work requirements on welfare recipients, and allowed states to deny welfare benefits to unwed teenage mothers. The reform bill has generated a significant amount of controversy, and its critics maintain that it is far from an optimal solution to the welfare problem.

5 Like welfare, immigration has become a controversial issue in recent years. The number of immigrants entering the United States has been rising at a rapid rate during the last several decades, and many maintain that immigration should be limited. Although many complain that immigrants push down wage rates for Americans, analysis of immigration data reveals that legal immigrants have no negative impact on employment rates for native-born Americans. In response to the public backlash against immigrants, particularly illegal immigrants, Congress passed the Immigration Reform Act in 1996. The act increased the number of border patrol agents, imposed sterner penalties for document fraud and immigrant smuggling, authorized an expedited deportation process for illegal aliens, and provided for the establishment of pilot programs to help employers verify the status of job applicants. The act also prohibited immigrants from receiving most forms of public benefits.

6 There is widespread concern in this country over the high rates of violent crime, and particularly, the large number of crimes that are committed by juveniles. While the overall rate of violent crime declined 9 percent in 1995, crime rates continue to soar in certain areas and are rising in mid-sized cities. Drug dealing and drug abusers have contributed significantly not only to escalating crime rates but also to overcrowded prisons. The prison "population bomb" presents a major challenge to today's policymakers.

7 Pollution problems continue to plague the United States and the world. Since the nineteenth century, a number of significant federal acts have been passed in an attempt to curb the pollution of our environment. The National Environmental Policy Act of 1969 established the Council for Environmental Quality. That act also mandated that environmental impact statements be prepared for all legislation or major federal actions that might significantly affect the quality of the environment. Substantial strides have been made in the war on toxic emissions, but the war has not been won. In 1980, Congress passed the Comprehensive Environmental Response, Compensation and Liability Act, commonly known as Superfund, to regulate the clean-up of leaking hazardous waste disposal sites. By the mid-1990s, however, only a small percentage of the sites had been cleaned up.

8 Intensive efforts to save resources include recycling. The benefits of recycling are straightforward—fewer natural resources are consumed—but the costs, in terms of *all* resources used, may be greater with recycling than without it. Other efforts to reduce waste include precy-cling (packaging products in more concentrated forms, for example).

QUESTIONS FOR REVIEW AND DISCUSSION

1 In some major cities, crime rates have either stayed constant or fallen slightly over the last three or four years. Nonetheless, opinion polls still show that crime is considered to be one of the most serious problems by citizens in those same cities. How can you explain this anomaly?

2 If you had to come up with an agenda for solving the crime problem in the United States, what would be the four most important policy decisions you would implement?

3 Does the United States have a moral obligation to keep its doors open to political refugees? Explain.

4 "You can never eliminate poverty if you define it in relative terms." Is this statement correct or incorrect? Why?

5 How have certain welfare programs discouraged work?

6 Why do we have literally hundreds of different welfare programs rather than simply giving money directly to the poor?

7 Is it possible to have perfectly clean air and water in our nation? Why or why not?

8 Develop a theory of the iron triangle with respect to environmental policy.

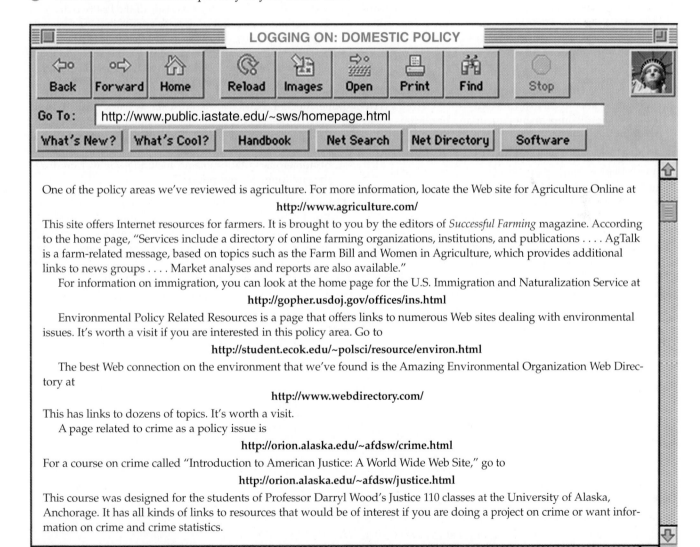

LOGGING ON: DOMESTIC POLICY

Go To: http://www.public.iastate.edu/~sws/homepage.html

One of the policy areas we've reviewed is agriculture. For more information, locate the Web site for Agriculture Online at

http://www.agriculture.com/

This site offers Internet resources for farmers. It is brought to you by the editors of *Successful Farming* magazine. According to the home page, "Services include a directory of online farming organizations, institutions, and publications . . . . AgTalk is a farm-related message, based on topics such as the Farm Bill and Women in Agriculture, which provides additional links to news groups . . . . Market analyses and reports are also available."

For information on immigration, you can look at the home page for the U.S. Immigration and Naturalization Service at

http://gopher.usdoj.gov/offices/ins.html

Environmental Policy Related Resources is a page that offers links to numerous Web sites dealing with environmental issues. It's worth a visit if you are interested in this policy area. Go to

http://student.ecok.edu/~polsci/resource/environ.html

The best Web connection on the environment that we've found is the Amazing Environmental Organization Web Directory at

http://www.webdirectory.com/

This has links to dozens of topics. It's worth a visit.

A page related to crime as a policy issue is

http://orion.alaska.edu/~afdsw/crime.html

For a course on crime called "Introduction to American Justice: A World Wide Web Site," go to

http://orion.alaska.edu/~afdsw/justice.html

This course was designed for the students of Professor Darryl Wood's Justice 110 classes at the University of Alaska, Anchorage. It has all kinds of links to resources that would be of interest if you are doing a project on crime or want information on crime and crime statistics.

SELECTED REFERENCES

Bane, Mary Jo, and David T. Ellwood. *Welfare Realities: From Rhetoric to Reform.* Cambridge, Mass.: Harvard University Press, 1994. Based on extensive data collection and analysis, the authors conclude, among other things, that the data tend to support the "rational choice" model of welfare dynamics. In other words, being on welfare represents a rational choice on the part of many welfare recipients, including single mothers with limited work skills.

Benjamin, Daniel K., and Roger LeRoy Miller. *Undoing Drugs: Beyond Legalization.* New York: Basic Books, 1993. This is a complete analysis of past and present U.S. drug policies, plus a new solution—the "constitutional alternative"—to the drug problem.

J. Clarence Davies, ed. *Comparing Environmental Risks: Tools for Setting Government Priorities.* Baltimore, Md.: Johns Hopkins University Press, 1996. For some time, the U.S. government has been criticized for its allegedly haphazard way of establishing environmental priorities. This collection of essays explores the concept of determining environmental priorities based on risk factors.

Davis, Charles E. *The Politics of Hazardous Waste.* Englewood Cliffs, N.J.: Prentice-Hall, 1993. The author argues that state and local political institutions must be viewed as critical actors in the implementation of any hazardous waste program.

Harris, Nigel. *The New Untouchables: Immigration and the New World Worker.* New York: St. Martin's Press, 1996. The author looks at the migration of workers from one country to another in the context of a changing world economy. Harris argues that fears of immigration are largely unjustified and that more immigration usually means more jobs and more income for native populations.

Katz, Michael B. *Improving Poor People: The Welfare State, the "Underclass," and Urban Schools as History.* Princeton, N.J.: Princeton University Press, 1995. An evaluation of today's welfare and educational systems by a leading historian of social welfare. Katz contends that public policy with respect to welfare relies on the erroneous assumption that poverty results from the character of poor people rather than on an examination of the structural causes of poverty.

Kopel, David B., ed. *Guns: Who Should Have Them?* Amherst, N.Y.: Prometheus, 1995. An examination of the gun-control issue and gun-control policies. Among other contentions, the authors of the contributed chapters to this book argue that gun-control policies are an ineffective solution to the problems of crime and violence in American society.

Landy, Marc K., ed. *The New Politics of Public Policy.* Baltimore, Md.: The Johns Hopkins University Press, 1995. Most of the authors of this collection of essays share the view that traditional models of policymaking do not explain the policymaking that has been characteristic of the last two decades. The authors argue that a "dramatic shift" in the policymaking process has occurred and that, to understand how public policy is made, analysts must give more attention to the role played by other factors, such as changes in values and an increased emphasis on rights.

Miller, Roger LeRoy, *et al. The Economics of Public Issues.* 10th ed. New York: HarperCollins, 1999. Chapters 3, 4, 8, 14–18, and 24–27 are especially useful. The authors use short essays of three to seven pages to explain the purely economic aspects of numerous social problems, including the war on drugs, the environment, and poverty.

Oates, Wallace E. *The Economics of Environmental Regulation.* Brookfield, Vt.: Edward Elgar Publishing Co., 1996. The author contends that environmental policies increasingly are being influenced by economic considerations.

17
Economic Policy

CHAPTER OUTLINE

We Switched to a Flat Tax?

BACKGROUND

Currently, the federal personal income tax system is progressive. Individuals pay a higher tax rate on additional income as they earn more income. Except for a brief period during the Civil War, there was no federal personal income tax until passage of the Sixteenth Amendment in 1913, which authorized Congress "to lay and collect taxes on incomes." For many years, most people paid little or no federal income taxes. Today, in contrast, virtually everyone who works pays some income taxes. The top marginal tax rate was 94 percent in 1944, 92 percent in 1952, 50 percent in 1982, and currently it is almost 40 percent.

WHAT IF WE SWITCHED TO A FLAT TAX?

For decades, some have argued in favor of scrapping our progressive income tax system and replacing it with a so-called *flat tax.* Members of Congress at various times have praised this approach as well. The idea behind a flat tax is simple: to calculate what you owe, simply subtract the appropriate exemption from your income and multiply the rest by the flat tax rate, which would be a certain percentage of your taxable income, such as 20 percent. Only incomes exceeding a certain threshold would be subject to the flat tax. For example, a family of four might be able to earn as much as $25,000 or $35,000 a year before it paid any income tax.

THE BENEFITS OF A FLAT TAX

According to its proponents, a flat tax would, at a minimum, reduce all of the resources devoted to figuring out one's taxes. It has been estimated that people spend, at a minimum, the equivalent of $50 billion a year computing their federal income taxes. Additionally, a large number of attorneys and accountants who specialize in tax law and accounting would no longer be needed. They could then engage in more productive activities.

On a national basis, no matter what the highest marginal tax rate has been, the federal government has never collected more than about 20 percent of the nation's annual income as tax revenues. What has happened and continues to occur is that those with relatively high incomes do the following:

1. They hire more tax lawyers and accountants to help them find loopholes in the tax system so that they can avoid high marginal tax rates.
2. They change their investment strategies to take advantage of loopholes that allow them to pay lower marginal tax rates.
3. They engage in off-the-books ("underground") activities for which they are paid in cash and do not pay taxes on the undocumented income.

WHAT WOULD HAPPEN TO FEDERAL TAX REVENUES?

Any proposal to switch to a flat tax must deal with an important question: What would happen to federal tax revenues? Proponents of the flat tax system claim that a flat tax would have no serious effect on total federal tax revenues. Because fewer resources would be devoted to avoiding taxes, more income would be reported overall. Additionally, these proponents argue that a low flat tax rate would encourage economic growth.

Why? Because people would want to save more and businesses would want to invest more.

Opponents of a flat tax are worried that the rich would "get away with something." From a practical point of view, however, the rich always have shown superb ingenuity in avoiding high taxes—even when the highest rate was 94 percent. Thus, it is not clear that a flat tax would actually reduce the total amount of taxes accounted for by the rich.

FOR CRITICAL ANALYSIS

1. *What group or groups within the federal bureaucracy would be against a switch to a flat tax?*
2. *Even though in reality the "rich" as a group are able to avoid the effects of high tax rates, many politicians still talk about taxing the rich more. Why is this?*

As you saw in Chapter 16, public policymaking is complicated, and clear-cut answers to public policy issues seldom are obvious. Nowhere are the principles of public policymaking more obvious than in the area of economic decisions undertaken by the federal government. The president and Congress (and to a growing extent, the judiciary) are faced constantly with questions concerning economic policy. Consider some of them:

1. Should federal income taxes be raised on high-income-earning individuals in order to reduce the federal budget deficit?

2. Should Congress pass laws that restrict the ability of foreigners to buy U.S. companies and real estate?

3. Should interest rates be raised by the Federal Reserve System in order to quell potential overheating of the economy?

4. Should the United States restrict imports from Japan in an attempt to force that country to open up its domestic markets to U.S. exporters?

There are no clear-cut answers to such questions. Each policy action carries with it costs and benefits, known as **policy trade-offs.** The costs are typically borne by one group and the benefits enjoyed by another group.

This chapter's opening *What If . . .* described some policy trade-offs in switching from our current progressive federal income tax system to a flat tax. In the process of making this switch, some groups would be helped in the economy, and some groups would be hurt. This is the reality of all economic policymaking. We start our analysis of economic policymaking with something that affects everybody directly—taxes and subsidies.

THE POLITICS OF TAXES AND SUBSIDIES

Taxes are not just given to us from above. Rather, they are voted on by members of Congress. Members of Congress also vote on *subsidies,* which are a type of negative taxes or gifts to certain businesses and individuals.

We begin our analysis with the premise that in the world of taxes and subsidies, the following is always true: *For every action on the part of the government, there will be a reaction on the part of the public.* Eventually, the government will react with another action, followed by the public's further reaction. The **action-reaction syndrome** is a reality that has plagued government policymakers since the beginning of this nation.

The Tax Code, Tax Rates, and Tax Loopholes

An examination of the Internal Revenue Code, encompassing thousands of pages, thousands of sections, and thousands of subsections, gives some indication that our tax system is not very simple. The 1986 Tax Reform Act was supposed to simplify it somewhat, but once you understand the action-reaction principle of taxation, you can predict that whatever simplification occurred in 1986 will be undone over time.

People are not assessed a lump-sum tax each year; each family does not just pay $1,000 or $10,000 or $20,000. Rather, individuals and businesses pay taxes based on tax rates. (Table 17–1 shows the 1996 tax rates for individuals and married couples.) The higher the tax rate—the action on the part of the government—the greater the public's reaction to that tax rate. Again, it is all a matter of costs and benefits. If the tax rate on all the income you make is 15 percent, that means that any method you can use to reduce your taxable income by one dollar saves you fifteen cents in tax liabilities that you owe the

POLICY TRADE-OFFS

The cost to the nation of undertaking any one policy in terms of all of the other policies that could have been undertaken. For example, an increase in the expenditures on one federal program means either a reduction in expenditures on another program or an increase in federal taxes (or the deficit).

ACTION-REACTION SYNDROME

For every action on the part of government, there is a reaction on the part of the affected public. Then the government attempts to counter the reaction with another action, which starts the cycle all over again.

Table 17–1

1996 Tax Rates for Individuals and Married Couples

| SINGLE PERSONS | | MARRIED COUPLES | |
MARGINAL TAX BRACKET	MARGINAL TAX RATE	MARGINAL TAX BRACKET	MARGINAL TAX RATE
$0–$23,999	15 %	$0–$40,099	15 %
$24,000–$58,149	28	$40,100–$96,899	28
$58,150–$121,299	31	$96,900–$147,699	31
$121,300–$263,749	36	$147,700–$263,749	36
$263,750 and up	39.6	$263,750 and up	39.6

federal government. Therefore, those individuals paying a 15 percent rate have a relatively small incentive to avoid paying taxes. But consider individuals who were faced with a tax rate of 94 percent in the 1940s They had a tremendous incentive to find legal ways to reduce their taxable incomes. For every dollar of income that was somehow deemed nontaxable, these taxpayers would reduce tax liabilities by 94 cents.

So, individuals and corporations facing high tax rates will always react by making concerted attempts to get Congress to add **loopholes** in the tax law that allow them to reduce their taxable incomes. When the Internal Revenue Code imposed very high tax rates on high incomes, it also provided for more loopholes. There were special provisions that enabled investors in oil and gas wells to reduce their taxable income. There were loopholes that allowed people to shift income from one year to the next. There were loopholes that allowed individuals to form corporations outside the United States in order to avoid some taxes completely. The same principles apply to other interest groups. As long as one group of taxpayers sees a specific benefit from getting the law changed and that benefit means a lot of money per individual, the interest group will aggressively support lobbying activities and the election and reelection of members of Congress who will push for special tax loopholes. In other words, if there are enough benefits to be derived from influencing tax legislation, such influence will be exerted by the affected parties.

LOOPHOLE

A legal method by which individuals and businesses are allowed to reduce the tax liabilities owed to the government.

President Clinton signs the budget package into law in 1993. He had campaigned on a platform that included tax cuts for the middle class and significant "jobs programs." The compromise budget package that he was forced to accept included neither, but it did include significant increases in the marginal tax rate for America's high-earning citizens.

Why We Probably Will Never Have a Truly Simple Tax System

After 1986, the federal tax code was simplified for most people. But astute policymakers then predicted that it would not stay simple for long. The federal government was running large deficits in the late 1980s, and these have continued into the 1990s. When faced with the proposition of having to cut the growth of federal government spending, Congress has balked. Instead, it has raised tax rates. This occurred under the Bush administration in 1990 and under the Clinton administration in 1993. Indeed, at the upper end of income earners, the tax rate paid on each extra dollar earned went up from 28 percent, based on the 1986 tax reform act, to 39.6 percent after the 1993 tax bill passed. That is an increase in the effective tax rate of 41.4 percent.

In response, the action-reaction syndrome is certainly going into effect as you read this text. As tax rates go up, those who are affected spend more time and effort to get Congress to legislate special exceptions, exemptions, loopholes, and the like, so that the *full* impact of such tax-rate increases will not be felt by richer Americans. The U.S. tax code has become as complex as, or more complicated than, it was before the Tax Reform Act of 1986. The average U.S. tax burden still may be lower than that in other countries, however. (See this chapter's feature entitled *Politics and Comparative Systems: Is the Average Tax Burden Relatively Low in the United States?*)

The Underground Economy

The other reaction by those who face a higher federal income tax rate is to seek relief in the underground economy. The **underground economy** consists of individuals who work for cash payments without paying any taxes. (It also consists of individuals who engage in illegal activities, such as prostitution, gambling, and drug trafficking.) As tax rates increase, individuals find a greater incentive to work "off the books."

The question, of course, is how big the underground economy is. If it is small, it is not a serious problem. Various researchers have come up with different estimates as to the size of the U.S. underground economy. These estimates range from 5 to 15 percent of total national income each year. This means that the underground economy in the United States represents anywhere from $400 billion to $1.2 trillion a year. See Table 17–2 for estimates of the percentage of services supplied by the underground economy. The extent of the underground economy is estimated to be even greater in some other countries. (See this chapter's feature entitled *Politics and Comparative Systems: The Worldwide Underground Economy.*)

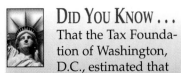

DID YOU KNOW...
That the Tax Foundation of Washington, D.C., estimated that Americans worked for the federal, state, and local governments a total of 128 days, until May 7, during 1996?

UNDERGROUND ECONOMY

The part of the economy that does not pay taxes and so is not directly measured by government statisticians; also called the *subterranean economy or* unreported economy.

Table 17–2

Estimated Percentage of Services Supplied by the Underground Economy in the United States

Lawn Maintenance	90%
Domestic Help	83%
Child Care	49%
Home Improvements/Repairs	34%
Sewing and Laundry Services	25%
Appliance Repairs	17%
Car Repairs	13%

SOURCE: U.S. Department of Labor and the University of Michigan Institute for Social Research.

POLITICS AND COMPARATIVE SYSTEMS
Is the Average Tax Burden Relatively Low in the United States?

Numerous studies have shown that the average person in the United States today has a tax burden that is less than in other industrialized countries in the world. Look at the accompanying graph. It would appear that the United States is at the bottom of the ladder in the tax burden faced by the average citizen.

But these data are somewhat flawed. In the countries with relatively high taxes—Denmark, France, Germany, Italy, the United Kingdom, and Canada—90 percent or more of medical costs are paid for by the government out of tax revenues. As of 1996, in the United States, about 44 percent of medical costs were covered by the government through Medicaid and Medicare. The remainder were paid for by private-sector employers and individuals. That means that the U.S. private sector's medical bill equals about 7.5 percent of total U.S. national income each year. If you add this amount to total federal, state, and local tax receipts, the United States

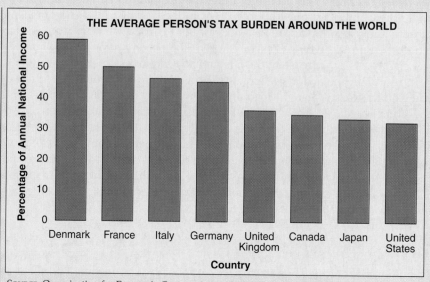

THE AVERAGE PERSON'S TAX BURDEN AROUND THE WORLD

(Bar graph. Y-axis: Percentage of Annual National Income, from 0 to 60. X-axis: Country. Bars from highest to lowest: Denmark ~59, France ~50, Italy ~46, Germany ~45, United Kingdom ~35, Canada ~34, Japan ~32, United States ~31.)

SOURCE: Organization for Economic Cooperation and Development, 1996.

would place right after France in total tax revenues as a percentage of annual national income, and ahead of Japan, Canada, the United Kingdom, Italy, and Germany.

For Critical Analysis
Why is a nation's tax burden an important issue?

A particularly thorny aspect of the underground economy came under intense public scrutiny during the first year of President Bill Clinton's administration. Several of his appointees were discovered to have avoided paying the "nanny tax" for household help. In effect, the Clinton nominees in question had paid their nannies and housekeepers in cash, thus avoiding any payment of federal taxes owed. Those nannies and other household helpers were, in effect, part of the underground economy. (In 1994, Congress took action to reduce the "nanny tax" problem.)

SOCIAL SECURITY IN TROUBLE

Closely related to the question of taxes in the United States is the viability of the Social Security system. Social Security taxes came into existence when the Federal Insurance Contribution Act (FICA) was passed in 1935. When the FICA tax was first levied, it was 1 percent of earnings up to $3,000. By 1963, the percentage rate had increased to 3.625 percent. As of 1996, a 6.2 percent rate was placed on each employee's wages up to a maximum of $62,700 to pay for Social Security. In addition, employers must pay in ("contribute") an

POLITICS AND COMPARATIVE SYSTEMS
The Worldwide Underground Economy

As a rule, the higher the taxation rate, the bigger the underground economy (the part of the economy that does not pay taxes) will be. A country like the United States has a smaller underground economy than Greece and Italy, where taxes are higher and hiring-and-firing laws are stricter. Both workers and employers alike have a greater incentive to go "underground."

For Critical Analysis

Does it appear from the accompanying graph that the United States has a problem with the underground economy?

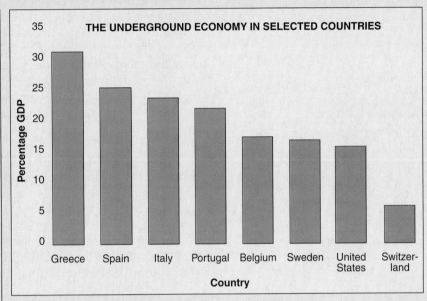

Source: Organization for Economic Cooperation and Development, 1996.

---

equal percentage. Also, there is a combined employer/employee 2.9 percent tax rate assessed for Medicare on all wage income, with no upper limit.

Social Security Is a Regressive Tax

When people with higher incomes pay lower tax rates than people with lower incomes, we call it **regressive tax.** Social Security taxes are regressive, because once individuals' incomes exceed the maximum taxable amount, they pay no more FICA taxes. The Medicare portion of this tax is no longer regressive, because it applies to all wage income, but the Social Security portion remains regressive. A person earning a million dollars in a year pays the same total Social Security taxes as a person earning $62,700.

The Grim Future of the Social Security System

In 1996, Senator Bob Kerrey (D., Neb.) stated that "we are damning our children to a very grim future if we continue to hide our heads in the sand." He was referring to the projected bankruptcy of the Social Security system sometime around the year 2010. After that date, Social Security taxes will have to be raised, Social Security benefits will have to be dramatically curtailed, or spending on other federal programs will have to be reduced. Medicare appears to be in even worse shape. As the number of Americans aged sixty-five and older increases from about thirty-three million today to forty million in the year 2010, and to seventy million in the year 2030, Medicare expenditures as a percentage of total national income are expected to grow dramatically, as can be seen in Figure 17–1.

REGRESSIVE TAX

A tax system in which tax rates go down as income goes up.

Figure 17–1

Medicare Expenditures as a Percentage of Total National Income

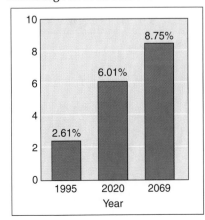

The Real Problem

The real problem with the Social Security system is that people who pay into Social Security think that they are actually paying into a fund, perhaps with their name on it. This is what you do when you pay into a private pension plan. It is not the case, however, with the federal Social Security system. That system is basically a pay-as-you-go transfer system in which those who are working are paying benefits to those who are retired.

Currently, the number of people who are working relative to the number of people who are retiring is declining. Therefore, those who work will continue to have to pay more of their income in Social Security taxes in order to pay for the benefits of those who retire. In the year 2025, when the retirement of the baby boom generation is complete, benefits are projected to cost almost 23 percent of taxable payroll income in the economy. Today this figure is only 14 percent. In today's dollars, that amounts to more than a trillion dollars of additional taxes annually.

As long as Congress continues to increase Social Security benefits while at the same time the labor force grows less rapidly than the number of retirees, financial strain will plague the Social Security system. Social Security also will continue to be a political issue, as well as a focal point of lobby efforts, particularly by groups that represent older Americans. One alternative to the current system that is being debated today is the full or partial privatization of Social Security (see the feature entitled *Thinking Politically about Social Security* for a further discussion of this alternative).

THE POLITICS OF FISCAL AND MONETARY POLICY

FISCAL POLICY

The use of changes in government spending or taxes to alter national economic variables, such as the rate of unemployment.

MONETARY POLICY

The use of changes in the amount of money in circulation to alter credit markets, employment, and the rate of inflation.

Changes in the tax code sometimes form part of an overall fiscal policy change. **Fiscal policy** is defined as the use of changes in government expenditures and taxes to alter national economic variables, such as the rate of inflation, the rate of unemployment, the level of interest rates, and the rate of economic growth. The federal government also controls **monetary policy,** defined as the use of changes in the amount of money in circulation so as to affect interest rates, credit markets, the rate of inflation, and employment. Fiscal policy is the domain of Congress and the president. Monetary policy, as we shall see, is much less under the control of Congress and the president, because the monetary authority in the United States, the Federal Reserve System, or the Fed, is an independent agency not directly controlled by either Congress or the president.

Fiscal Policy: Theory and Reality

The theory behind fiscal policy changes is relatively straightforward: When the economy is going into a recession (a period of rising unemployment), the federal government should stimulate economic activity by increasing government expenditures, by decreasing taxes, or both. When the economy is becoming overheated with rapid increases in employment and rising prices (a condition of inflation), fiscal policy should become contractionary, reducing government expenditures and increasing taxes. That particular view of fiscal policy was first implemented in the 1930s and again became popular during the 1960s. It was an outgrowth of the economic theories of the English economist John Maynard Keynes. Keynes's ideas, published during the Great Depression of the 1930s, influenced the economic policymakers guiding President Franklin D. Roosevelt's New Deal.

Thinking Politically about Social Security

The unthinkable is being discussed in the halls of Congress today—the partial or full privatization of the Social Security system. Such a change would allow individuals to opt for either staying with the current government-financed Social Security system or taking the same amount of money that they now pay in Social Security taxes and placing it in private pension plans. This kind of system actually was instituted in Chile in 1981. Within a couple of years, more than 90 percent of the workers there chose the private option. Under the private option, workers pay 10 percent of their wages to the investment firm of their choice.

According to recent surveys conducted in the United States, the majority of adults queried liked the idea of directing part of their Social Security taxes to a personal retirement account in the private sector. Even some of the members of the Advisory Commission on Social Security have advocated the option of allowing workers to shift all of their shares of Social Security payroll taxes to private alternatives. Those who disagree with proposals to privatize the Social Security system typically argue that even partial privatization is just a scheme to destroy the benefits that currently are available to recipients.

For Critical Analysis
Why might current retirees be against the privatization of Social Security?

Keynes believed that the forces of supply and demand operated too slowly in a serious recession and that government should step in to stimulate the economy. Such actions thus are guided by **Keynesian economics.** Keynesian economists believe, for example, that the Great Depression resulted from a serious imbalance in the economy. The public was saving more than usual, and businesses were investing less than usual. According to Keynesian theory, at the beginning of the depression, the government should have filled the gap that was created when businesses began limiting their investments. The government could have done so by increasing government spending or cutting taxes.

KEYNESIAN ECONOMICS

An economic theory, named after English economist John Maynard Keynes, that gained prominence during the Great Depression of the 1930s. It is typically associated with the use of fiscal policy to alter national economic variables—for example, increased government spending during times of economic downturns.

Wall Street during the stock market crash of 1929.

FEDERAL OPEN MARKET COMMITTEE (FOMC)

The most important body within the Federal Reserve System. The FOMC decides how monetary policy should be carried out by the Federal Reserve.

Monetary Policy: Politics and Reality

The theory behind monetary policy, like that behind fiscal policy, is relatively straightforward. In periods of recession and high unemployment, we should stimulate the economy by expanding the rate of growth of the money supply. (The money supply is defined loosely as currency—see this chapter's *Politics and Economics* on eliminating the dollar bill—and checking account balances, plus other types of account balances that generally serve as money.) An easy-money policy is supposed to lower interest rates and induce consumers to spend more and producers to invest more. With rising inflation, we should do the reverse: reduce the rate of growth of the amount of money in circulation. Interest rates should rise, choking off some consumer spending and some business investment. But the world is never so simple as the theory we use to explain it. If the nation experiences stagflation—rising inflation *and* rising unemployment—expansionary monetary policy (expanding the rate of growth of the money supply) will lead to even more inflation. Ultimately, the more money there is in circulation, the higher prices will be—there will be inflation.

The Monetary Authority—The Federal Reserve System. Congress established our modern central bank, the Federal Reserve System, in 1913. It is governed by a board of governors consisting of seven individuals, including the very powerful chairperson. All of the governors, including the chairperson, are nominated by the president and approved by the Senate. Their appointments are for fourteen years.

Through the Federal Reserve System, called the Fed, and its **Federal Open Market Committee (FOMC),** decisions about monetary policy are made eight times a year. The Board of Governors of the Federal Reserve System is independent. The president can attempt to convince the board, and Congress can threaten to merge the Fed with the Treasury, but as long as the Fed retains its independence, its chairperson and governors can do what they please. Hence, talking about "the president's monetary policy" or "Congress's monetary policy" is inaccurate. To be sure, the Fed has, on occasion, yielded to presidential pressure, and for a while the Fed's chairperson felt constrained to follow a congressional resolution requiring him to report monetary targets

The Board of Governors of the Federal Reserve System meets in Washington, D.C.

POLITICS AND ECONOMICS
How to Save Billions a Year—Eliminate the Dollar Bill

Because inflation has depreciated the purchasing power of our money, it takes ever larger denominations of money to make the same purchases that we did years ago with simple coins. Nonetheless, the cost of keeping the dollar bill instead of replacing it with an equivalent-valued coin is high. Half of the 8.4 billion bills printed annually by the Bureau of Engraving and Printing are one-dollar bills. Each costs about four cents to make. In contrast, a one-dollar coin would cost more—eight cents. But such coins last thirty years compared with the seventeen months for a dollar bill. On a yearly basis, dollar bills cost ten times more to keep in circulation than does a dollar coin.

The handling of dollar bills is difficult and costly to automate. It costs about $22 per thousand to count dollar bills, whereas coins cost less than $2 per thousand to count. Counting such bills is so difficult that the Los Angeles County Metropolitan Transportation Authority does not bother to sort them. Rather, it sells them by weight to private-sector contractors for ninety-eight cents on the dollar.

Other countries already have switched to high-denomination coins. Canada introduced the dollar coin in 1987 (and vending machine use has boomed since then). France has even introduced a coin with the face value of one hundred francs, the equivalent of about twenty dollars at current exchange rates.

There have been efforts in the United States to introduce dollar coins: the Eisenhower silver dollar in 1971 and the Susan B. Anthony dollar in 1979. Both were failures, however. The Susan B. Anthony dollar looked at a distance just like a quarter. Moreover, in both cases, the U.S. government continued to print one-dollar bills, contrary to what other countries have done when they introduced coins of higher denominations to replace bills.

So far, The Coin Coalition, a lobbying group representing thirty industry organizations, has been unable to get the Clinton administration to support legislation replacing the dollar bill with a dollar coin.

For Critical Analysis
Who will benefit if the dollar bill is eliminated?

over each six-month period. But now, more than ever before, the Fed remains one of the truly independent sources of economic power in the government.

Monetary Policy and Lags.   Monetary policy does not suffer from the same lengthy time lags as fiscal policy does, because the Fed can, within a very short period, put its policy into effect. Nonetheless, researchers have estimated that it takes almost fourteen months for a change in monetary policy to become effective, measured from the time the economy either slows down or speeds up too much to the time the economy feels the policy change.[1] This means that by the time monetary policy goes into effect, a different policy might be appropriate.

The Fed's Record.   Federal Reserve monetary policy, in principle, is supposed to be countercyclical. The economy goes through so-called business cycles, made up of recessions (and sometimes depressions) when unemployment is high, and boom times when unemployment is low and businesses are straining capacity. For the Fed to "ride against the wind," it must create policies that go counter to business activity. Researchers examining the evidence since 1914 have uniformly concluded that, on average, the Fed's policy has turned out to be pro-cyclical. That is, by the time the Fed started pumping money into the economy, it was time to do the opposite; by the time the Fed started reducing the rate of growth of the money supply, it was time for it to start increasing it. Perhaps the Fed's biggest pro-cyclical blunder occurred

---

[1]Robert Gordon, *Macroeconomics*, 7th ed. (New York: HarperCollins, 1996), p. 431.

Alan Greenspan, the chairman of the Federal Reserve. The Federal Reserve is responsible for our nation's monetary policy. Greenspan is often called to testify before various congressional committees. He finds himself frequently in the "hot seat" if interest rates are rising.

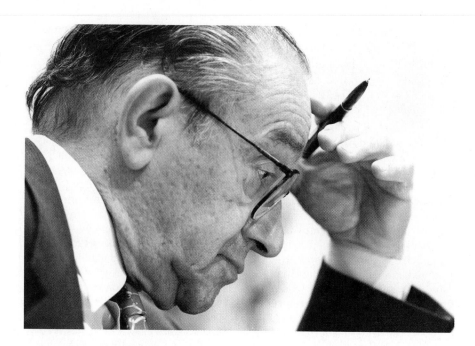

U.S. TREASURY BOND

Evidence of debt issued by the federal government; similar to corporate bonds but issued by the U.S. Treasury.

PUBLIC DEBT, OR NATIONAL DEBT

The total amount of debt carried by the federal government.

Table 17–3

Net Public Debt of the Federal Government

YEAR	TOTAL (BILLIONS OF CURRENT DOLLARS)
1940	$ 42.7
1945	235.2
1950	219.0
1960	237.2
1970	284.9
1980	709.3
1990	2,410.1
1992	2,998.6
1993	3,247.5
1994	3,432.1
1995	3,603.4
1996	3,747.1
1997	3,900.0*

*Estimate.
SOURCE: U.S. Office of Management and Budget.

during the Great Depression. Many economists believe that what would have been a severe recession turned into the Great Depression in the 1930s because the Fed's action resulted in almost a one-third decrease in the amount of money in circulation. It has also been argued that the rapid inflation experienced in the 1970s was in part the result of the Fed's increasing the rate of growth of the money supply too much.

In addition, some observers of Federal Reserve policy claim that former head of the Fed Paul Volcker created one of the worst recessions since the Great Depression in 1981–1982, when he caused the Fed to engage in an extremely restrictive monetary policy. Others argue that he needed to do so to "break inflation's back." In fact, inflation did slow down to almost zero during the middle of the 1980s. It averaged about 4 percent in the early 1990s.

While inflation actually fell somewhat below 4 percent in certain years, Alan Greenspan, chairman of the Fed, seemed to be worried about a resurgence of inflation in 1994. He came under criticism from Treasury Secretary Lloyd M. Bentsen, Henry B. Gonzalez (head of the House Banking Committee), and others when he caused the Fed to increase interest rates several times. Each small increase in the interest rate that the Fed charges depository institutions when they borrow money from the Fed has far-reaching effects. On at least some of the occasions when Greenspan raised such interest rates, the stock market responded negatively.

REFLECTIONS ON THE PUBLIC DEBT AND BIG DEFICITS

The federal government has run a deficit—spent more than it received—in every year except two since 1960. Every time a budget deficit occurs, the federal government issues debt instruments in the form of **U.S. Treasury bonds.** The sale of these bonds to corporations, private individuals, pension plans, foreign governments, foreign businesses, and foreign individuals adds to the **public debt,** or **national debt,** defined as the total amount owed by the federal government. Thus, the relationship between the annual federal government budget deficit and the public debt is clear: If the public debt is, say,

$4 trillion this year and the federal budget deficit is $150 billion during the year, then at the end of the year the public debt will be $4.15 trillion. Table 17–3 shows what has happened to the net public debt over time.

It would seem that the nation increasingly is mortgaging its future. But this table does not take into account two important variables: inflation and increases in population. In Figure 17–2, we correct the net public debt for inflation and increases in population. The per capita net public debt in so-called **constant dollars** (dollars corrected for inflation) reached its peak, as you might expect, during World War II and fell steadily thereafter until the mid-1970s. Since then, except for a slight reduction in 1980, it has continued to rise. If we are not careful, it will exceed (in per capita constant-dollar terms) what it was during World War II.

Is the Public Debt a Burden?

We often hear about the burden of the public debt. Some argue that the government eventually is going to go bankrupt, but that, of course, cannot happen. As long as the government has the ability to pay for interest payments on the public debt through taxation, it will never go bankrupt. What happens is that when Treasury bonds come due, they are simply "rolled over." That is, if a $1 million Treasury bond comes due today, the U.S. Treasury pays it off and sells another $1 million bond.

What about the interest payments? Interest payments are paid by taxes, so what we are really talking about is taxing some people to pay interest to others who loaned money to the government. This cannot really be called a burden to all of society. There is one hitch, however. Not all of the interest payments are paid to Americans. A significant amount is paid to foreigners, because foreigners own almost 15 percent of the public debt. This raises the fear of too much foreign control of U.S. assets. So it is no longer the case that we "owe it all to ourselves."

Another factor is also important. Even though we are paying interest to ourselves for the most part, the more the federal government borrows, the greater the percentage of the federal budget that is committed to interest payments. The ever-increasing portion of the budget committed to interest payments reduces the federal government's ability to purchase public goods, such as more national parks, in the future. In 1976, interest costs to the government were less than 9 percent of total federal outlays. The estimate for 1997 is about 17 percent. Indeed, if you wish to do a simple projection of current trends, some time in the next century the federal government will be spending almost 100 percent of its budget on interest payments! This, of course, will not occur, but it highlights the problem of running larger and larger deficits and borrowing more and more money to cover them.

The Problem of "Crowding Out"

Although it may be true that we owe the public debt to ourselves (except for what is owed to foreigners), another issue is involved. A large public debt is made up of a series of annual federal government budget deficits. Each time the federal government runs a deficit, we know that it must go into the financial marketplace to borrow the money. This process, in which the U.S. Treasury sells U.S. Treasury bonds, is called **public debt financing.** Public debt financing, in effect, "crowds out" private borrowing. Consider that to borrow, say, $100 billion, the federal government must bid for loanable funds in the marketplace, just as any business does. It bids for those loanable funds by offering to pay higher interest rates. Consequently, interest rates are increased when

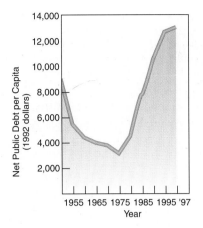

Figure 17–2
● ● ● ● ● ● ● ● ● ● ● ● ● ● ● ● ● ● ● ●
Per Capita Public Debt of the United States in Constant 1992 Dollars

If we correct the public debt for intergovernmental borrowing, the growth in the population, and changes in the price level (inflation), we obtain a graph that shows the per capita net public debt in the United States expressed in constant 1992 dollars. The public debt reached its peak during World War II and then dropped consistently until about 1975. In the last twenty years, it has risen steadily and is starting to approach World War II levels.

CONSTANT DOLLARS

Dollars corrected for inflation; dollars expressed in terms of purchasing power for a given year.

PUBLIC DEBT FINANCING

The government's spending more than it receives in taxes and paying for the difference by issuing U.S. Treasury bonds, thereby adding to the public debt.

the federal government runs large deficits and borrows money to cover them. Higher interest rates can stifle or slow business investment, which reduces the rate of economic growth. (To see how the U.S. public debt compares with that of other nations, see this chapter's feature entitled *Politics and Comparative Systems: How the U.S. Public Debt Compares with That of Other Nations.*)

BALANCING THE BUDGET: A CONSTITUTIONAL AMENDMENT?

Some argue that the way not to have deficits is to have a constitutional convention to draft a balanced-budget amendment to the U.S. Constitution. Two-thirds of the state legislatures need to petition the Congress for a convention to be called. To date, the required number of legislative petitions has not been filed.

A Congress-Generated Amendment

Congress also has the option of passing a constitutional amendment, which it could then submit to the states for ratification. In 1986, the Senate voted on such an amendment. In 1992, Texas Democrat Charles Stenholm put forth an amendment bill in the House with 268 co-sponsors. Simultaneously in the Senate, Democrat Paul Simon of Illinois introduced his own amendment. Both amendments would have required that whenever the federal government ran a deficit, Congress and the president would have to eliminate it. This could be done either by lowering spending or raising taxes. Some argue that such an amendment would automatically create tax increases, because members of Congress, pressured by powerful lobby groups, have always found it difficult to cut spending. In any event, neither bill passed.

Alternatives to a Balanced-Budget Amendment

Critics of the balanced-budget amendment concept argue that even if such an amendment were passed, Congress simply would figure out ways to put

Every president is responsible for formulating the president's budget message to Congress. Here President Clinton is shown with his budget advisors, including former Secretary of Labor Robert Reich. Note that the president can only suggest a budget. It is Congress that passes the budget. Every single budget submitted by the last five presidents has been exceeded by what Congress has actually budgeted.

POLITICS AND COMPARATIVE SYSTEMS
How the U.S. Public Debt
Compares with That of Other Nations

The U.S. national debt held by the public is estimated to be a little over $3.7 trillion in 1997, but that number alone does not tell us much. We need to compare the federal debt with a year's annual output in this country (gross domestic product, or GDP). The estimated U.S. GDP for 1997 is about $7.8 trillion. Therefore, the public debt expressed as a percentage of annual U.S. output is about 50 percent.

To know whether that is comparatively a low or high percentage, we need to compare the U.S. debt as a percentage of annual GDP with that of other industrialized countries. Look at the accompanying table. You will see that relative to the public debt of most countries in the European Union (EU), the U.S. public debt is comparatively low.

The United States may, however, catch up with Ireland, Belgium, Italy, and Greece fairly soon. After all, at the beginning of the 1980s, the debt held by the public amounted to only 25 percent of annual U.S. output. By 1986, the percentage had risen to 40 percent, and it is now 50 percent.

For Critical Analysis
Why does the size of the national debt matter?

COUNTRY	FEDERAL DEBT AS A PERCENTAGE OF ANNUAL GDP
Belgium	143
Ireland	109
Italy	109
Greece	101
The Netherlands	85
Portugal	74
Denmark	72
Spain	53
United States	50
France	49
Great Britain	49
Germany	44

SOURCE: European Union, extrapolated from 1995 data.

excessive spending "off budget." In 1985, Congress passed the Gramm-Rudman-Hollings Deficit Reduction Act in an effort to require that Congress reduce the size of its budget deficits. The deficit was required to drop from $171.9 billion in 1986 to zero in 1991. After the first two years of failure to comply with the target deficit reductions, Congress passed a revised act requiring that the 1988 deficit be $144 billion and that it drop to zero by 1993. The first three years of the Revised Deficit Reduction Act saw Congress again fail to meet deficit reductions. In 1990, another revised set of Gramm-Rudman targets was proposed, allowing for a 1991 deficit of over $200 billion, excluding the cost of the savings and loan bailout. In fact, the true deficit in 1991 turned out to be closer to $270 billion and was almost $300 billion in 1992.

Some observers believe that Congress's inability to comply with its own law indicates that our governing body can no longer be fiscally responsible. In reality, the prospect of ever balancing the budget is dim. Apparently giving up, Congress in 1990 passed a deficit reduction act that rendered the Gramm-Rudman Act and its revisions ineffective.

HOW LARGE DEFICITS AND AN INCREASING PUBLIC DEBT AFFECT THE AVERAGE AMERICAN

Large federal deficits make headlines, and so does the increasing public debt. But the average American has seen such headlines for at least a decade now. How has the average American been affected? How will that average American be affected in the future if, as predicted, federal budget deficits continue at record rates?

DID YOU KNOW ...

That one thing that Presidents Carter, Reagan, Bush, and Clinton have in common is that the proposed federal government budgets that they offered Congress were all exceeded by actual federal government outlays?

As with all issues in politics and economics, the answer is not simple. We already have discussed the crowding-out effect of government spending financed by deficits. The more that federal budget deficits crowd out investment, the poorer our children and our grandchildren will be. Why? Because we will have invested less today in machines, equipment, research and development, and the like.

Another way in which the average American has been affected by such large deficits is that the deficits have caused lawmakers in Washington to mandate many rules and regulations that the states and municipalities must now carry out on their own. We discussed this important issue in Chapter 3 when we talked about federal mandates. Congress, presumably embarrassed by the continuing large federal budget deficits, would rather see its programs carried out by the states with state money so that federal deficits will not be any larger.

Some observers argue, however, that the size of the deficit is irrelevant. Currently, federal, state, and local governments spend anywhere from 33 to 42 percent of annual national economic output.[2] The figures are high because governments are large. The public policy question, according to these observers, is "What is the optimal size of government?" rather than "How should we finance government spending?"

GLOBAL COMPETITIVENESS AND THE WORLD TRADE ORGANIZATION

At the close of World War II, the United States was clearly the most powerful and influential nation on earth. Japan, Europe, and the Soviet Union were all in shambles. From the end of the war through most of the 1960s, America retained its economic hegemony. In the last twenty-five years, however, U.S. dominance in the global marketplace has been challenged. Japan has risen from its wartime defeat to become one of the top world economic powers.

---

[2]The estimates vary widely, depending on who is doing the measuring.

Periodically, the Group of Seven, or G-7, nations meet to discuss economic policy. This photo shows the participants in the Naples meeting on August 7, 1994. At that meeting, President Boris Yeltsin of Russia asked to join the G-7.

Some of its Pacific Rim neighbors—Taiwan, Hong Kong, Singapore, Malaysia, and Thailand—are starting to catch up.

On the other side of the world, the fifteen countries of the former European Community (EC) became one consumer market—the European Union, or EU—on December 31, 1992. For the first time in more than a hundred years, the U.S. economy slipped to second place, behind the 360-million-consumer economy of the EU. Adding to the EU's formidable economic power is the untapped low-cost labor that is available from the former republics of the Soviet Union and from Eastern Europe, plus, of course, Latin America.

America's Current Competitive Position

"The United States is falling behind." "We need to stay competitive internationally." These and similar statements have been heard in government circles during virtually all of the 1990s. Discussions of this issue encounter several problems, however. A major problem has to do with the definition of *global competitiveness.* What does this phrase really mean? For a controversial view on this issue, see this chapter's *Critical Perspective,* which explores the question of whether the American economy has been globalized.

However competitiveness is defined, one organization, the Institute for Management Development in Lausanne, Switzerland, has declared that the United States continues to lead the pack in world competitiveness; the United States is ahead of Japan, Hong Kong, Germany, and the rest of the European Union. According to the report, America's top-class ranking is due to, at a minimum, America's widespread entrepreneurship and the absence of extensive government regulation. Other factors include America's sophisticated financial system and large investments in scientific research.

Opening Up World Trade—GATT and the WTO

In general, over the last decade the United States has been in the forefront of those trying to ease restrictions on international trade. In particular, the United States had been an active participant in the negotiations for reducing

Part of the negotiations during the Uruguay Round of the General Agreement on Tariffs and Trade (GATT) involved severely reducing government subsidies to farmers throughout the world. During the GATT deliberations, farmers from all over Europe demonstrated against it in Strasbourg, France. Nonetheless, the Uruguay Round that began in 1986 was successful. GATT has been replaced by the World Trade Organization.

CRITICAL PERSPECTIVE
Has the American Economy Been Globalized?

The term *globalization* has been used so much that almost every-one accepts globalization as a fact. After all, superfast worldwide telecommunications, the Internet, the opening of the closed economies of the former Soviet Union and its satellites, and other events all have meant that the United States no longer stands alone. The United States is no longer the most powerful economic nation on earth, but instead has to compete in an increasingly competitive global environment in which the rapidly growing coun-tries of Southeast Asia—particularly Japan, Malaysia, Singapore, Thailand, and the Philippines—are becoming more efficient and more aggressive. Additionally, American companies presumably must compete more aggressively than they have in the past against a unified Europe (the European Union) and the developing nations of Central Europe and Latin America. Politicians increas-ingly have used the threat of increased foreign competition because of globalization as a reason to undertake all sorts of new policies.

A Voice From the Wilderness

Not all observers of the domestic and global economic scene agree that the American economy has become more globalized. According to Stanford University Professor Paul R. Krugman, "It is a late twentieth-century conceit that we invented the global econ-omy just yesterday."* He discovered, for example, that one hun-dred years ago Chicago meat packers were more acutely aware of their competition with New Zealand than they are today. At the time, railroads converged on Chicago, bringing beef and wheat that were destined for European markets. Those railroads were built with European capital. Additionally, on the eve of World War I (1914–1918), Great Britain's overseas investments were larger than its domestic investments. Krugman points out that since then, this record has never been matched by a major country.

Krugman further discovered that one hundred years ago, the chemical companies that provided Chicago residents with dyes for their fabrics and aspirin for their headaches were primarily multina-tional corporations headquartered in Germany. Although at that time international money transfers took a few hours instead of a split second to complete, the more serious substance of economic affairs was just as global as it is today, if not more so.

The grand opening of Kentucky Fried Chicken in Tiananmen Square in Beijing, China.

World Trade, Past and Present

World trade as a share of total world production was greater in 1913 than it was in any year until 1970. The flow of money capital around the world constituted a larger share of world savings prior to World War I than it does today. Additionally, people migrated internationally to a far greater extent prior to World War I than they have ever since.

Let's just consider the actual percentage of their income that Americans spend on imports. Today, that percentage is about 11 percent. In 1890, the corresponding figure was about 8 percent.

CRITICAL PERSPECTIVE
Has the American Economy Been Globalized? Continued

How can this be, given that trade is so much more open today, we have cheaper modern transportation, and the communications revolution has made it possible for any one good to be manufactured in a series of steps throughout many countries? Taiwanese workers take an American microprocessor, wire it up to a disc drive made in Singapore, put the whole thing in a case made in China, and then ship it back to America. It is true that we ship manufactured goods back and forth around the world as never before—*but manufactured goods constitute a shrinking share of the things that we buy.* Since 1970, U.S. residents have decreased their spending on manufactured goods from 46 percent to around 40 percent. As a nation, we are buying more health care, entertainment, legal services, travel, restaurant meals, and so on than we did in the past. These are the kinds of services that foreigners cannot sell us very easily.

What about International Competitiveness?

Both within and outside politics, the concern about *international competitiveness* has taken on increasing proportions. There is a common view that we live in a world in which nations, like large corporations, are engaged in fierce competition for global markets. So, according to this logic, the United States competes with Japan in the same way that Pepsi competes with Coca-Cola. The United States is, in effect, in a race for the twenty-first century.

There is a basic problem, though, with the concept of international competitiveness. One can compare two corporations' profitability rates to determine which one is "winning" a competitive race. The less competitive corporation may eventually go out of business. Countries, however, do not "go out of business." They have no well-defined "bottom line." Additionally, Coke and Pepsi are true rivals. Very few of Coca-Cola's sales go to employees of Pepsi and vice versa. Thus, if Coke is successful, Pepsi is less successful.

Such is not the case with major countries, according to those who applaud the trend toward globalization. They argue that each country may sell products that compete with each other, but each country also constitutes an export market for other countries and is a supplier of useful imports to other countries. Indeed, this per-

spective holds that if one part of the world starts doing better than another world sector economically, the U.S. economy benefits—because that other part of the world simply becomes a larger market for U.S. exports. The argument is that the United States is not worse off because Europe or Asia is getting richer; in fact, the United States is better off.

Others who have examined the pattern of globalization argue that, in reality, corporations simply are trying to reduce their wage costs, reduce employee benefits, and take advantage of cheaper labor and raw materials wherever they can. Critics argue that globalization, far from providing better lives for all of those concerned, seems more likely to disrupt societies and impoverish many people. The ones who are enriched are the few who have the skills and resources to exploit such opportunities for their own advantage.

For Critical Analysis

1. Assume that there actually is increased competition from abroad. How could the U.S. economy benefit from this situation?

2. When competition from, say, Alabama causes a job loss in a competing company in Texas, the U.S. Congress normally does not react. If the same job loss occurs from increased competition in, say, Asia, however, the U.S. Congress may react. From a political perspective, what is the difference in these two situations?

*Pop Internationalism (Cambridge, Mass.: MIT Press, 1996).

POLITICS AND THE ENVIRONMENT
The WTO Overrules U.S. Gasoline Standards

As nations become more aware of environmental problems, more legislation is being passed in an attempt to improve the quality of our environment. One such regulation was issued by the U.S. Environmental Protection Agency (EPA) in 1993. It required that the cleanliness of gasoline sold in America's most polluted cities be improved by 15 percent over 1990 levels. Because the agency realized that such an improvement could not be achieved rapidly without dramatically increasing the cost of gasoline at the pump, it allowed most refiners a five-year grace period to meet the single, absolute cleanliness target. It did not give the same grace period to foreign refiners.

First, Venezuela and Brazil, and then the European Union and Norway, claimed "foul." Those countries petitioned the World Trade Organization (WTO) to declare that the U.S. rules were discriminatory and thus in violation of the WTO's nondiscrimination clauses. According to the complaint, forcing all foreign refiners to comply immediately with the new cleanliness requirements, while at the same time giving American refiners five years to comply, constituted a gross and obvious way to reduce competition from abroad.

The first WTO panel ruled against the United States. The U.S. government decided to appeal. In the first appellate ruling it has ever made, the WTO upheld the initial ruling. The United States can appeal to no higher authority and must do one of the following things:

1. Obey the WTO immediately and change the EPA regulation with respect to foreign refiners.
2. Do nothing—and face annual trade sanctions of $150 million, which the United States would have to pay to Venezuela and the other countries involved.
3. Negotiate the terms of the sanctions, offering compensation in the form of new trade benefits with Venezuela and the other nations.

Critics of the WTO argue that this latest ruling is strong evidence that the WTO is simply a political body whose members are determined to keep the American economy more open to their exports than their economies are to U.S. exports.

For Critical Analysis
What is the importance of the fact that under the new WTO system, the United States has surrendered its veto power?

TARIFF

A tax on imported goods.

tariffs (taxes on imports) as part of the General Agreement on Tariffs and Trade, or GATT.

The origins of a worldwide trade liberalization policy date to 1947, when the initial GATT was signed. Under GATT, countries met periodically to negotiate tariff reductions that are mutually advantageous to all members. The 117 member nations of GATT account for between 85 and 90 percent of all world trade. The latest round of negotiations was called the Uruguay Round, because the meetings were held in Uruguay. The final act of the Uruguay Round was signed in Marrakesh, Morocco, by over one hundred representatives in 1994. Starting in 1995, GATT ceased to exist. It was replaced by the World Trade Organization (WTO).

The ratification of the last round of GATT by the United States and the establishment of the WTO will result in a roughly 40 percent cut in tariffs worldwide. Agricultural subsidies will be reduced and eventually eliminated. Protection of patents will be extended worldwide.

The WTO raises serious political issues. Although the WTO has arbitration boards to settle international disputes over trade issues, no country has a veto. Opponents argue that a "vetoless" America will repeatedly be outvoted by the mercantile countries of Western Europe and East Asia. Some citizens' groups have warned that the unelected WTO international trade bureaucrats based in Geneva, Switzerland, might be able to weaken environmental health and consumer safety laws if such laws affect international trade flows.

Indeed, some of the critics' worst fears came true in the first ruling ever by the WTO's appellate body in 1996. (See the feature entitled *Politics and the Environment: The WTO Overrules U.S. Gasoline Standards.*)

ECONOMIC POLICY: UNFINISHED WORK

Economic policymaking will always consist of unfinished work. The very nature of the federal government seems to be to engage in economic policymaking. Certainly, the federal government will never really get its house in order until it grapples successfully with continuing federal budget deficits and the consequent growing national debt. Thus, we expect to see a balanced-budget proposal to pop up regularly in Congress.

Political issues will continue to swirl around Social Security. Older Americans will continue to make Social Security a focal point of their lobbying efforts, as they have in the past, and policymakers will continue to consider alternatives to the current system.

The independence of the Federal Reserve System probably will be an issue, also. Many in Congress resent the Fed's ability to alter economic policy without consulting legislators. Debates over the effectiveness of the Fed's policies will never end, because even economists disagree.

If federal income tax rates continue to rise, another debate will become more strident. It will involve questioning whether high federal income tax rates reduce the incentives of individuals and businesses to work, save, and invest.

Certainly, the U.S. economic role in a global economy will continue to be an issue for economic policy. While the United States has become strong in the global marketplace, international trade issues continue to come to the fore. Congress and the president will always take these issues seriously.

GETTING INVOLVED
The Importance of Government in Your Life

The federal budgetary process is a complex system that has many players. The ultimate test of the effectiveness of the federal budgetary process is how it affects each individual American. One way for you to take stock of how the federal government affects your life is as follows: (1) List what you have as assets (everything that you own). (2) List what you do during the day as activities. Then note the extent to which government is involved in your life—and at what cost. The emphasis should always be on the services that must be paid for, either directly or indirectly.

Consider the following example:

1. Rode bicycle to class—highway usage. How are the highways paid for? Who pays for them?

2. Checked out book from public library. Who paid for that library? Who owns it?

3. Received student loan—a subsidy from the government. Who ultimately paid for it?

4. Went to class. On average, in the United States, taxpayers pay approximately 70 percent of the cost of higher education, and students and their families directly pay only 30 percent.

5. Got groceries. How much of the meat was government inspected?

Where else did government intervene?

KEY TERMS

action-reaction syndrome 573

constant dollars 583

Federal Open Market Committee
(FOMC) 580

fiscal policy 578

Keynesian economics 579

loophole 574

monetary policy 578

policy trade-offs 573

public debt, or national debt 582

public debt financing 583

regressive tax 577

tariff 590

underground economy 575

U.S. Treasury bond 582

CHAPTER SUMMARY

① In the area of taxes and subsidies (negative taxes), policymakers have long had to contend with what is known as the action-reaction syndrome. For every action on the part of the government, there will be a reaction on the part of the public, to which the government will react with another action, to which the public will again react, and so on. In regard to taxes, as a general rule, individuals and corporations that pay the highest tax rates will react to those rates by pressuring Congress into creating exceptions and tax loopholes (loopholes allow high-income earners to reduce their taxable incomes). This action on the part of Congress results in a reaction from another interest group—consisting of those who want the rich to pay more taxes. In response, higher tax rates will be imposed on the rich, and so the cycle continues.

② Closely related to the question of taxes is the viability of the Social Security system. As the number of people who are working relative to the number of people who are retiring declines, those who work will have to pay more Social Security taxes to pay for the benefits of those who retire.

③ Fiscal policy is the use of changes in government expenditures and taxes to alter national economic variables, such as the rate of inflation or unemployment. Monetary policy is defined as the use of changes in the amount of money in circulation so as to affect interest rates, credit markets, the rate of inflation, and employment. Fiscal policy was made popular by the English economist John Maynard Keynes, whose ideas influenced Franklin D. Roosevelt's New Deal legislation, as well as the fiscal policies of the government during the 1960s. Keynesian fiscal policy economics usually means increasing government spending during recessionary periods and increasing taxes during inflationary boom periods. The problem with fiscal policy and monetary policy is the lag between the time a problem occurs in the economy and the time when policy changes are actu-

ally felt in the economy.

④ Whenever the federal government spends more than it receives, it runs a deficit. The deficit is met by U.S. Treasury borrowing. This adds to the public debt of the federal government. Although the public debt has grown dramatically, when corrected for increases in population and inflation, it fell from the end of World War II to the middle of the 1970s. Since then, it has increased almost to its previous level at the height of the World War II. Those who oppose large increases in government spending argue that one effect of the federal deficit is the crowding out of private investment.

⑤ One congressional option for balancing the federal budget is passing a constitutional amendment. Such an amendment would require that whenever the federal government ran a deficit, Congress and the president would have to eliminate it by either lowering spending or raising taxes. Perhaps as an alternative to a constitutional amendment, Congress passed the Gramm-Rudman-Hollings Deficit Reduction Act in 1985. Its goal was to force the federal government to balance its budget. Unable to meet this goal, Congress passed an act in 1990 that rendered the Gramm-Rudman Act's provisions ineffective.

⑥ From the end of World War II through the 1960s, the United States dominated the global marketplace. In the past twenty-five years, however, economic developments in Europe, Japan, and the Pacific Rim countries have challenged the economic hegemony of the United States. The Uruguay Round of the General Agreement on Tariffs and Trade (GATT) reduced tariffs worldwide on manufactured goods and made other areas of world trade more competitive. As of January 1995, GATT ceased to exist and has been replaced by the World Trade Organization (WTO). The WTO raises serious political issues, particularly in relation to its dispute-settling authority.

QUESTIONS FOR REVIEW AND DISCUSSION

1 Does the existence of the action-reaction syndrome imply that it is impossible to "soak the rich" through higher tax rates? Explain your answer.

2 What accounts for differences in the relative size of the underground economy across nations?

3 A growing percentage of the U.S. population consists of senior citizens. What would you predict, therefore, about the future of legislation that reduces Social Security benefits?

4 Is there truly such a thing as fiscal policy in the United States? Why or why not? Explain your answer.

5 If the national debt is owned primarily by Americans, how can it ever be a burden on Americans?

6 The Uruguay Round of the General Agreement on Tariffs and Trade (GATT) was signed by the member nations in the spring of 1994. It remained to be ratified by the U.S. Congress. The president was required to indicate where taxes could be raised in order to make up for revenues that would be lost due to the elimination of many tariffs over the following five years. What assumption was being used in requiring the president to "make up" the predicted lost tax revenues?

LOGGING ON: ECONOMIC POLICY

| Back | Forward | Home | Reload | Images | Open | Print | Find | Stop |

Go To: http://www.public.iastate.edu/~sws/homepage.html

| What's New? | What's Cool? | Handbook | Net Search | Net Directory | Software |

The federal budget-making process often involves substantial controversy and discussion. Information on past federal budgets and proposed budgets for the upcoming fiscal year can be obtained through the University of North Carolina at

http://sunsite.oit.unc.edu/nc/nchome.html

Choose **Sunsite Archives/US and World Politics/Sunsite Political Archives/US-Budget** . . . This service allows you to gather information on the federal budget in its final form. It also gives you information on the president's budget, as well as various other alternative budgets.

A Web site with numerous links to sources on economic policy, prosperity, economics and politics, taxes, jobs, and other topics is Idea Central—Economics and Politics. You can find its home page at

http://epn.org/idea/economy.html

If you want to look at the Federal Reserve Bank home page, it is located at

http://woodrow.mpls.frb.fed.us/info/policy/

This site offers extensive information on the Fed and monetary policy.

The Urban Institute, a nonprofit policy research organization located in Washington, D.C., has a Web page at

http://www.urban.org/

The institute's staff "investigates the social and economic problems confronting the nation and government policies and public and private programs designed to alleviate them." The institute tends to be on the "liberal" side. Its topics include Assessing the New Federalism Project; Medicare; Medicaid; Welfare Reform; The Future of the Public Sector; and Tax Reform.

SELECTED REFERENCES

Axford, Barrie. *The Global System: Politics, Economics, and Culture.* New York: St. Martin's Press, 1996. This book on the nature and economic effects of globalization also includes a discussion of political and cultural globalization.

Creedy, John. *Fiscal Policy and Social Welfare: An Analysis of Alternative Tax and Transfer Systems.* Brookfield, Vt.: Edward Edgar Publishing Co., 1996. This is an examination of alternative tax and transfer systems and their implications for social welfare and income distribution.

Feldstein, Martin. "The Effect of Marginal Tax Rates on Taxable Income." Working Paper 4496. Cambridge, Mass.: National Bureau of Economic Research, 1994. The author examines how individuals respond to changing tax rates. He examines data that show that the taxed income of those in the highest tax brackets increased somewhat dramatically when their tax rates were reduced. Feldstein also predicts that because of the action-reaction syndrome, the 1993 tax rate increase actually will yield very little additional government revenue due to the way people will react to increased tax rates.

Friedman, Milton, and Walter Heller. *Monetary versus Fiscal Policy.* New York: Norton, 1969. This is a classic presentation of the pros and cons of monetary and fiscal policy given by a noninterventionist (Friedman) and an advocate of federal government intervention in the economy (Heller).

Hinshaw, Randall, ed. *The World Economy in Transition: What Leading Economists Think.* Brookfield, Vt.: Edward Elgar Publishing Co., 1996. In this collection of essays, leading economists discuss different aspects of current domestic and international monetary issues.

Johnson, Haynes. *Divided We Fall: Gambling with History in the 90s.* New York: Norton, 1994. Haynes Johnson is a Washington reporter who put together this "report card" on President Bill Clinton's first year in office. He examines what the president did to put the economy back on the right track. He points out that the U.S. economy is dividing itself increasingly into hostile camps based on gender, race, and ethnicity. But he sees hope in the future, because people are changing and are thinking beyond just today.

Miller, Roger LeRoy, and Daniel K. Benjamin. *The Economics of Macro Issues.* 10th ed. St. Paul, Minn.: West, 1996. This short paperback consists of twenty-nine topical chapters examining the major issues facing economic policymakers today. It is lively, up to date, and easily understood.

Phelps, Edmond. *Structural Slumps: The Modern Equilibrium Theory of Unemployment, Interest, and Assets.* Cambridge, Mass.: Harvard University Press, 1994. This highly respected economist presents his ideas on the causes of modern recessions. Phelps examines the costs of hiring and training new workers. This book requires a knowledge of basic economics to understand everything the author presents.

The President's Council of Economic Advisers. *Economic Report of the President.* Washington, D.C.: U.S. Government Printing Office, published annually. This volume contains a wealth of details concerning current monetary and fiscal policy and what is happening to the economy.

Schaling, Eric. *Institutions and Monetary Policy: Credibility, Flexibility, and Central Bank Independence.* Brookfield, Vt.: Edward Edgar Publishing Co., 1995. The author examines rule-based versus discretionary monetary policy and looks at the relationship between domestic monetary institutions and economic performance in selected countries.

18
Foreign and Defense Policy

CHAPTER OUTLINE

The UN
Enforced
Human Rights
Worldwide?

BACKGROUND

EARLY IN THE HISTORY OF THE UNITED NATIONS (UN), THE GENERAL ASSEMBLY PASSED THE UNIVERSAL DECLARATION OF HUMAN RIGHTS, OUTLINING THE FUNDAMENTAL RIGHTS OF *ALL* PEOPLE ON EARTH. A NUMBER OF NATIONS, INCLUDING THE UNITED STATES, HAVE NOT SIGNED THE DECLARATION. MEMBERS OF THE U.S. CONGRESS HAVE LONG FELT THAT THE DECLARATION COULD BE INTERPRETED AS A TREATY, THUS OVERRIDING AMERICAN LAW. THE DECLARATION MIGHT BE IN CONFLICT WITH THE U.S. CONSTITUTION OR ADD RIGHTS THAT ARE NOT INCLUDED IN OUR CONSTITUTION OR OTHER LAWS. THEN, THE QUESTION WOULD ARISE AS TO HOW SUCH CONFLICTS WOULD BE RESOLVED AND WHO WOULD ENFORCE THESE ADDITIONAL RIGHTS.

WHAT IF . . . THE UN ENFORCED HUMAN RIGHTS WORLDWIDE?

If the UN enforced human rights throughout the world, some agency or commission of the UN would have to be empowered either to survey the worldwide situation or, more likely, to receive complaints from aggrieved individuals or groups. Of course, there would be other organizational problems: How could the impartiality of UN commissioners be assured? How could UN officials gain access to witnesses and victims in nations that do not cooperate? Furthermore, how could the UN commission enforce its judgment on an uncooperative nation or group of people?

WHAT RIGHTS TO PROTECT?

Considering the scope of the assignment, the new human rights body would need to decide its priorities. The Universal Declaration of Human Rights begins with the basic rights of survival— the right to food, shelter, and physical safety. Would these basic rights be the first priority for the UN? If so, then the starvation of millions of individuals in various countries around the world would be the first problem to be confronted. But starvation is not always the result of scarcity. Many times, starvation occurs because of civil wars or other political conflicts.

Another set of rights includes the freedom of speech, political freedoms, and the right of assembly. Would the UN be willing to use force to ensure free elections in nations such as China? Would the UN take on the task of assuring political freedom for gypsies in Eastern Europe or Palestinians in Israel?

Each of these situations involves not only the basic human rights of people but also internal political problems. Although the UN advocates democracy and individual freedom, rarely has it been willing even to discuss the internal political issues of its members. These topics have been off limits so that its members will continue to support the organization.

SOME PRACTICAL PROBLEMS

Finally, who would pay for investigations concerning human rights? Which nations would be willing to send investigators or armed police into other nations to enforce human rights in those countries? By 1997, the annual cost of peacekeeping operations was estimated to top $3 billion. Not only are many nations spending money, but others contribute troops, transportation, and equipment to support these efforts. Would any nation be willing to commit such resources to preserve human rights in a faraway land? It seems more likely that the UN's authority on these matters will continue to be mainly moral.

FOR CRITICAL ANALYSIS

1. *Would Americans be willing to send troops to enforce human rights in another country?*
2. *What proportion of nations would allow the UN to investigate human rights within their own borders?*
3. *Which human rights should take precedence over political considerations? Why?*

Americans view a world that is changing so rapidly that their first response can be to turn inward and focus on domestic problems. Presidents and members of Congress also are tempted to pay less attention to foreign affairs in the post–Cold War world. The instability of world politics, however, which has been fueled by the disintegration of the Soviet Union, the rise of ethnic nationalism, the continuing threat of terrorism, and the existence of multiple regional "hot spots," presents serious threats to American security.

Without a guiding theme to foreign policy—confrontation with the communist states—the creation and implementation of foreign policy and a national security strategy have become much more complex. The United States, faced with pressing domestic needs, could lower defense spending. Without the need to compete with the Soviet Union in different regions of the world, the United States could decide not to become engaged in regional conflicts. It could allow the United Nations to monitor human rights, as suggested in this chapter's *What If . . .* feature.

The Clinton administration, which has focused on domestic policies, including welfare reform, has been criticized for not developing an equally clearly focused foreign policy. Yet it was certainly not clear what the right policy should be toward Bosnia, Rwanda, Haiti, Cuba, or North Korea, to name just a few trouble spots. It was clear, however, that in times of crisis, the nation still needed guiding principles for action.

WHAT IS FOREIGN POLICY?

As the cultural, military, and economic interdependence of the nations of the world has increased, it has become even more important for the United States to establish and carry out foreign policies to deal with external situations and to carry out its own national goals. By **foreign policy,** we mean both the goals the government wants to achieve in the world and the techniques and strategies to achieve them. For example, if one national goal is to achieve stability in Eastern Europe and to encourage the formation of pro-American governments there, U.S. foreign policy in that area may be carried out with the techniques of **diplomacy, economic aid, technical assistance,** or military intervention. Sometimes foreign policies are restricted to statements of goals or ideas, such as helping to end world poverty, whereas at other times foreign policies are comprehensive efforts to achieve particular objectives.

In the United States, the **foreign policy process** usually originates with the president and those agencies that provide advice on foreign policy matters. Foreign policy formulation often is affected by congressional action and national public debate.

National Security Policy

As one aspect of overall foreign policy, **national security policy** is designed primarily to protect the independence and the political integrity of the United States. It concerns itself with the defense of the United States against actual or potential (real or imagined) enemies, domestic or foreign.

U.S. national security policy is based on determinations made by the Department of Defense, the Department of State, and a number of other federal agencies, including the **National Security Council (NSC).** The NSC acts as an advisory body to the president, but it has increasingly become a rival to the State Department in influencing the foreign policy process. This was particularly evident when it was revealed, in November 1986, that the Reagan

FOREIGN POLICY

A nation's external goals and the techniques and strategies used to achieve them.

DIPLOMACY

The total process by which states carry on political relations with each other; settling conflicts among nations by peaceful means.

ECONOMIC AID

Assistance to other nations in the form of grants, loans, or credits to buy the assisting nation's products.

TECHNICAL ASSISTANCE

The sending of experts with technical skills in agriculture, engineering, or business to aid other nations.

FOREIGN POLICY PROCESS

The steps by which external goals are decided and acted on.

NATIONAL SECURITY POLICY

Foreign and domestic policy designed to protect the independence and political and economic integrity of the United States; policy that is concerned with the safety and defense of the nation.

NATIONAL SECURITY COUNCIL (NSC)

A board created by the 1947 National Security Act to advise the president on matters of national security.

administration had largely bypassed the Department of State (and Congress) in using the NSC to direct sales of U.S. military equipment to Iran.

Diplomacy

Diplomacy is another aspect of foreign policy. Diplomacy includes all of a nation's external relationships, from routine diplomatic communications to summit meetings among heads of state. More specifically, diplomacy refers to the settling of disputes and conflicts among nations by peaceful methods. Diplomacy is the set of negotiating techniques by which a nation attempts to carry out its foreign policy.

Diplomacy may or may not be successful, depending on the willingness of the parties to negotiate. For example, after years of refusing to negotiate or even recognize the other's existence, Israel and representatives of the Palestine Liberation Organization (the PLO) in 1993 agreed to return control of Jericho and part of the West Bank to Palestinian control. The 1993 agreement left open the possibility of a Palestinian state.

MORALITY VERSUS REALITY IN FOREIGN POLICY

From the earliest years of the republic, Americans have felt that their nation had a special destiny. The American experiment in democratic government and capitalism, it was thought, would provide the best possible life for men and women and be a model for other nations. As the United States assumed greater status as a power in world politics, Americans came to believe that the nation's actions on the world stage should be guided by American political and moral principles. As Harry Truman stated, "The United States should take the lead in running the world in the way that it ought to be run."

This view of America's mission has led to the adoption of many foreign policy initiatives that are rooted in **moral idealism,** a philosophy that sees the world as fundamentally benign and other nations as willing to cooperate for the good of all.[1] In this perspective, nations should come together and agree to keep the peace, as President Woodrow Wilson (1913–1921) proposed for the League of Nations. Nations should see the wrong in violating the human rights of ethnic or religious minorities and should work to end such injustice. Many of the foreign policy initiatives taken by the United States have been based on this idealistic view of the world, but few of these actions have been very successful.

The Peace Corps, however, which was created by John Kennedy in 1961, is one example of an effort to spread American goodwill and technology that has achieved some of its goals. The Clinton administration's actions in 1994 to return the democratically elected president of Haiti to power were rooted partly in moral conviction, although elements within the U.S. government regarded President Jean-Bertrand Aristide as unstable or left-leaning. Foreign policy based on moral imperatives often is unsuccessful because it assumes that other nations agree with American views of morality and politics.

In opposition to the moral perspective is **political realism.** Realists see the world as a dangerous place in which each nation strives for its own survival and interests. Foreign policy decisions must be based on a cold calculation of what is best for the United States without regard for morality. Realists believe

MORAL IDEALISM

A philosophy that sees all nations as willing to cooperate and agree on moral standards for conduct.

POLITICAL REALISM

A philosophy that sees each nation acting principally in its own interest.

---

[1]Charles W. Kegley, Jr., and Eugene Wittkopf, *American Foreign Policy, Pattern and Process,* 3d ed. (New York: St. Martin's Press, 1987), p. 73.

that the United States must be prepared militarily to defend itself, because all other nations are, by definition, out to improve their own situations. A strong defense will show the world that the United States is willing to protect its interests. The practice of political realism in foreign policy allows the United States to sell weapons to military dictators who will support its policies, to support American business around the globe, and to repel terrorism through the use of force. Political realism leads, for example, to a policy of not negotiating with terrorists who take hostages, because such negotiations simply will lead to the taking of more hostages.

It is important to note that the United States never has been guided by only one of these principles. Instead, both moral idealism and political realism affect foreign policymaking. President Clinton wrestled with the situation in Bosnia to try to find a way for the United States to practice a pragmatic policy based on moral principles. Strongly opposed to using U.S. troops to establish peace in Bosnia, the president tried to convince the warring parties—the Bosnian Serbs and the Bosnian Muslims—to negotiate and accept a cease-fire. Finally, under pressure from the United States, the warring parties hammered out an agreement to divide the territory into ethnic nations. The United States and other NATO nations guaranteed military forces to patrol the new boundaries for a period of time.

WHO MAKES FOREIGN POLICY?

Is foreign policy made by the president, by the Congress, or by joint executive and congressional action? There is no easy answer to this question, because, as constitutional authority Edwin S. Corwin once observed, the U.S. Constitution created an "invitation to struggle" between the president and Congress for control over the foreign policy process. Let us look first at powers given to the president by the Constitution.

President Franklin D. Roosevelt signs the declaration of war against Japan on December 8, 1941.

Constitutional Powers of the President

The Constitution confers on the president broad powers that are either explicit or implied in key constitutional provisions. Article II vests the executive power of the government in the president. The presidential oath of office given in Article II, Section 1, requires that the president "solemnly swear" to "preserve, protect and defend the Constitution of the United States."

In addition, and perhaps more important, Article II, Section 2, designates the president as "Commander in Chief of the Army and Navy of the United States." Starting with Abraham Lincoln, all presidents have interpreted this authority dynamically and broadly. Indeed, since the Washington administration, the United States has been involved in at least 125 undeclared wars that were conducted under presidential authority. For example, Harry Truman ordered U.S. armed forces in the Pacific to enter into North Korea's conflict with South Korea. Dwight Eisenhower threatened China and North Korea with nuclear weapons if the Korean peace talks were not successfully concluded. Bill Clinton sent troops to Haiti and Bosnia.

Article II, Section 2, of the Constitution also gives the president the power to make treaties, provided that two-thirds of the senators present concur. Presidents usually have been successful in getting treaties through the Senate. In addition to this formal treaty-making power, the president makes use of **executive agreements** (discussed in Chapter 13). Since World War II, executive agreements have accounted for almost 95 percent of the understandings reached between the United States and other nations.

EXECUTIVE AGREEMENT

A binding international obligation made between chiefs of state without legislative sanction.

Executive agreements have a long and important history. Significant in their long-term effects were the several agreements Franklin Roosevelt reached with the Soviet Union and other countries, especially at Yalta, during World War II. The government of South Vietnam and the government of the United States, particularly under Dwight Eisenhower, John Kennedy, and Lyndon Johnson, made a series of executive agreements in which the United States promised support. All in all, between 1946 and 1997, over eight thousand executive agreements with foreign countries were made. There is no way to get an accurate count, because perhaps several hundred of these agreements have been secret.

An additional power conferred on the president in Article II, Section 2, is the right to appoint ambassadors, other public ministers, and consuls. In Section 3 of that article, the president is given the power to recognize foreign governments through receiving their ambassadors.

Informal Techniques of Presidential Leadership

Other broad sources of presidential power in the U.S. foreign policy process are tradition, precedent, and the president's personality. The president can employ a host of informal techniques that give the White House overwhelming superiority within the government in foreign policy leadership.

First, the president has access to information. More information is available to the president from the Central Intelligence Agency (CIA), the State Department, and the Defense Department than to any other governmental official. This information carries with it the ability to make quick decisions—and that ability is used often.

Second, the president is a legislative leader who can influence the amount of funds that are allocated for different programs. For example, with a large budget deficit and the end of the Cold War, President Clinton proposed large cuts in defense spending.

Third, the president can influence public opinion. President Theodore Roosevelt once made the following statement:

> People used to say to me that I was an astonishingly good politician and divined what the people are going to think. . . . I did not "divine" how the people were going to think; I simply made up my mind what they ought to think and then did my best to get them to think it.[2]

Presidents are without equal in this regard, partly because of their ability to command the media. Depending on their skill in appealing to patriotic sentiment (and sometimes fear), they can make people think that their course in foreign affairs is right and necessary. Public opinion often seems to be impressed by the president's decision to make a national commitment abroad. Presidents normally, although certainly not always, receive the immediate support of the American people when reacting to (or creating) a foreign policy crisis (see Chapter 7).

Finally, the president can commit the nation morally to a course of action in foreign affairs. Because the president is the head of state and the leader of one of the most powerful nations on earth, once the president has made a commitment for the United States, it is difficult for Congress or anyone else to back down on that commitment.

Other Sources of Foreign Policymaking

There are at least four foreign policymaking sources within the executive branch, in addition to the president. These are (1) the Department of State,

[2]Sidney Warren, *The President as World Leader* (New York: McGraw-Hill, 1964), p. 23.

(2) the National Security Council, (3) the intelligence community and informational programs, and (4) the Department of Defense.

The Department of State.   In principle, the State Department is the executive agency that is most directly concerned with foreign affairs. It supervises U.S. relations with the nearly two hundred independent nations around the world and with the United Nations and other multinational groups, such as the Organization of American States. It staffs embassies and consulates throughout the world. It has about 25,600 employees. This may sound impressive, but it is small compared with, say, the Department of Health and Human Services with its more than 128,000 employees. Also, the State Department had an annual operating budget of only $5.5 billion in fiscal year 1997—one of the smallest budgets of the cabinet departments.

Newly elected presidents usually tell the American public that the new secretary of state is the nation's chief foreign policy adviser. Nonetheless, the State Department's preeminence in foreign policy has declined dramatically since World War II. The State Department's image within the White House Executive Office and Congress (and even foreign governments) is quite poor—a slow, plodding, bureaucratic maze of inefficient, indecisive individuals. There is even a story about how Premier Nikita Khrushchev of the Soviet Union urged President John Kennedy to formulate his own views rather than to rely on State Department officials who, according to Khrushchev, "specialized in why something had not worked forty years ago."[3] In any event, since the days of Franklin Roosevelt, the State Department sometimes has been bypassed and often has been ignored when crucial decisions are made.

It is not surprising that the State Department has been overshadowed in foreign policy. It has no natural domestic constituency as does, for example, the Department of Defense, which can call on defense contractors for support. Instead, the State Department has what might be called **negative constituents**—U.S. citizens who openly oppose American foreign policy. One of the State Department's major functions, administering foreign aid, often elicits criticisms (see the discussion in this chapter's feature entitled *Thinking Politically about Foreign Aid*). Also, within Congress, the State Department is often looked on as an advocate of unpopular and costly foreign involvement. It is often called "the Department of Bad News."

The National Security Council.   The job of the National Security Council (NSC), created by the National Security Act of 1947, is to advise the president on the integration of "domestic, foreign, and military policies relating to the national security." Its larger purpose is to provide policy continuity from one administration to the next. As it has turned out, the NSC—consisting of the president, the vice president, the secretaries of state and defense, the director of emergency planning, and often the chairperson of the joint chiefs of staff and the director of the CIA—is used in just about any way the president wants to use it.

The role of national security adviser to the president seems to fit the player. Some advisers have come into conflict with heads of the State Department. Henry A. Kissinger, Nixon's flamboyant and aggressive national security adviser, rapidly gained ascendancy over William Rogers, the secretary of state, in foreign policy. When Jimmy Carter became president he appointed Zbigniew Brzezinski as national security adviser. Brzezinski competed openly with Secretary of State Cyrus Vance (who apparently had little

NEGATIVE CONSTITUENTS
Citizens who openly oppose government foreign policies.

---

[3]Theodore C. Sorensen, *Kennedy* (New York: Harper & Row, 1965), pp. 554–555.

Thinking Politically about Foreign Aid

When asked which government program should be cut first, the number one response of American voters is always "foreign aid." Surveys have shown that Americans vastly overestimate the amount of foreign aid that is sent abroad each year and its impact on the budget. A recent report by the United Nations characterized the United States as one of the least generous of nations, with foreign assistance accounting for only 0.18 percent of our gross domestic product (GDP). Norway, Sweden, and Denmark top the list of assisting nations, each donating 1 percent of their GDP to aid. Japan and Australia earmark 0.32 percent of their GDP for foreign aid, and Ger-many donates 0.38 percent of its GDP. Japan even outspends the United States in actual dollars.

Senator Jesse Helms of North Carolina has been attacking foreign assistance for many years on the basis of waste and corruption. Much of foreign aid, however, is in the form of grants and loans to buy American goods—so-called tied aid. A considerable portion of foreign economic assistance is given to regions of the world that pose a security threat to the United States—Israel, Egypt, Turkey, Korea, and Eastern Europe. The goal of such aid is to assist those nations in reaching political stability and to preserve the peace in the region, thus keeping American troops out of any conflict there.

Foreign aid always will be subject to attack because it is a trade-off of risks: Do we spend the money to keep peace and help other nations, or do we save the relatively low amounts of money and risk military conflicts? Because the money goes to foreign nations and sometimes gets diverted through corruption and bribery, it always is a good political target for politicians and citizens alike.

For Critical Analysis
What message would the United States give to other nations of the world if it discontinued foreign economic assistance?

power). In the Clinton administration, neither National Security Adviser Anthony Lake nor Secretary of State Warren Christopher dominated the policy process.

The Intelligence Community.   No discussion of foreign policy would be complete without some mention of the **intelligence community.** This consists of the forty or more government agencies or bureaus that are involved in intelligence activities, informational and otherwise. On January 24, 1978, President Carter issued Executive Order 12036, in which he formally defined the official major members of the intelligence community. They are as follows:

INTELLIGENCE COMMUNITY

The government agencies involved in gathering information about the capabilities and intentions of foreign governments and that engages in activities to further U.S. foreign policy aims.

1. Central Intelligence Agency (CIA).
2. National Security Agency (NSA).
3. Defense Intelligence Agency (DIA).
4. Offices within the Department of Defense.
5. Bureau of Intelligence and Research in the Department of State.
6. Federal Bureau of Investigation (FBI).
7. Army intelligence.
8. Air Force intelligence.
9. Department of the Treasury.
10. Drug Enforcement Administration (DEA).
11. Department of Energy.

The CIA was created as part of the National Security Act of 1947. The National Security Agency and the Defense Intelligence Agency were created by executive order. Until recently, Congress voted billions of dollars for intelligence activities with little knowledge of how the funds were being used. Intelligence activities consist mostly of overt information gathering, but covert actions also are undertaken. Covert actions, as the name implies, are done secretly, and rarely does the American public find out about them. In the late 1940s and early 1950s, the CIA covertly subsidized anticommunist labor unions in Western Europe. The CIA covertly aided in the overthrow of the Mossadegh regime in Iran, which allowed the restoration of the shah in 1953. The CIA helped to overthrow the Arbenz government of Guatemala in 1954 and apparently was instrumental in destabilizing the Allende government in Chile from 1970 to 1973.

During the mid-1970s, the "dark side" of the CIA was at least partly uncovered when the Senate undertook an investigation of its activities. One of the major findings of the Senate Select Committee on Intelligence was that the CIA had routinely spied on American citizens domestically—a supposedly strictly prohibited activity. Consequently, the CIA came under the scrutiny of six, and later eight, oversight committees within Congress, which restricted the scope of its activity. By 1980, however, the CIA had regained much of its lost power to engage in covert activities. In the early 1990s, as the relationships with the states of the former Soviet Union eased, the attention of the CIA and other agencies began to turn from military to economic intelligence. During the first Clinton administration, the CIA suffered damage to its reputation when a high-ranking agent, Aldrich Ames, was convicted of spying against the United States.

In addition to intelligence activities, U.S. foreign policy also makes use of propaganda and information programs. The United States Information Agency (which for a while was called the United States International Communication Agency) is part of an attempt to spread information and propaganda throughout the world on behalf of the American government.

The Department of Defense. The Department of Defense (DOD) was created in 1947 to bring all of the various activities of the American military establishment under the jurisdiction of a single department headed by a civilian secretary of defense. At the same time, the joint chiefs of staff, consisting of the commanders of each of the military branches and a chairperson, was created to formulate a unified military strategy.

Although the Department of Defense is larger than any other federal department, it has declined in size since the fall of the Soviet Union in 1991.

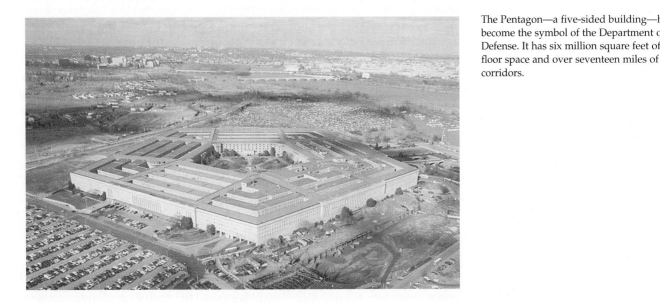

The Pentagon—a five-sided building—has become the symbol of the Department of Defense. It has six million square feet of floor space and over seventeen miles of corridors.

In the last ten years, the total number of civilian employees has been reduced by about 200,000, to the current number of 880,000. Military personnel have also been reduced from 2.1 million in 1985 to about 1.7 million today. While the defense budget has decreased by about $35 billion since 1990, to $255 billion in 1997, the Republican majority in Congress forced the president to accept a $7 billion increase in the defense budget for fiscal year 1996. Many Republicans believed that the nation's security was in jeopardy from previous cuts.

Congress often does not agree with the plans of the DOD, particularly if the plans call for closing a military base or ending a contract in a powerful legislator's state or district. Also, the branches of the military often differ in their points of view, thus weakening the department's political influence.

LIMITING THE PRESIDENT'S POWER

A new interest in the balance of power between Congress and the president on foreign policy questions developed during the Vietnam War (1964–1975). Sensitive to public frustration over the long and costly war and angry at Richard Nixon for some of his other actions as president, Congress attempted to establish some limits on the power of the president in setting foreign and defense policy. In 1973, Congress passed the War Powers Act over President Nixon's veto. The act limited the president's use of troops in military action without congressional approval (see Chapter 13). Most presidents, however, have not interpreted the "consultation" provisions of the act as meaning that Congress should be consulted before military action is taken. Instead, Presidents Ford, Carter, Reagan, and Bush ordered troop movements and then informed congressional leaders. Critics note that it is quite possible for a president to commit troops to a situation from which the nation could not withdraw without incurring heavy losses, whether or not Congress is consulted.

Congress also has exerted its authority to limit or deny the president's requests for military assistance to Angolan rebels and to the government of El Salvador, and requests for new weapons, such as the B-1 bomber. In general, Congress has been far more cautious in supporting the president in situations where military involvement of American troops is possible.

At times, Congress can take the initiative in foreign policy. In 1986, Congress initiated and passed a bill instituting economic sanctions against South Africa to pressure that nation into ending apartheid. President Reagan vetoed the bill, but the veto was overridden by large majorities in both the House and the Senate.

DOMESTIC SOURCES OF FOREIGN POLICY

The making of foreign policy is often viewed as a presidential prerogative because of the president's constitutional power in that area and the resources of the executive branch that the president controls. Foreign policymaking is also influenced by a number of other sources, however, including elite and mass opinion and the military-industrial complex.

Elite and Mass Opinion

Public opinion influences the making of U.S. foreign policy through a number of channels. Elites in American business, education, communications, labor, and religion try to influence presidential decision making through several strategies. Some individuals, such as former secretary of state Henry Kissinger and the late president Richard Nixon, had a long-standing interest in foreign policy and were asked to advise the president privately. Several elite organizations, such as the Council on Foreign Relations and the Trilateral Commission, work to increase international cooperation and to influence foreign policy through conferences, publications, and research.

The members of the American elite establishment also exert influence on foreign policy through the general public by encouraging debate over foreign policy positions, by publicizing the issues, and by use of the media. Generally, the efforts of the president and the elites are most successful with the segment of the population called the **attentive public.** This sector of the mass public, which probably constitutes 10 to 20 percent of all citizens, is more interested in foreign affairs than most Americans. These Americans are also likely to transmit their opinions to the less interested members of the public through conversation and local leadership.

ATTENTIVE PUBLIC
That portion of the general public that pays attention to policy issues.

The Military-Industrial Complex

A fear is often expressed that the military influences the making of U.S. foreign policy. Civilian fear of the relationship between the defense establishment and arms manufacturers (the **military-industrial complex**) dates back many years. In the 1930s, Franklin Roosevelt raised the specter of mammoth improper military influence in the domestic economy. On the eve of a Senate investigation of the munitions industry, he said that the arms race was a "grave menace . . . due in no small measure to the uncontrolled activities of the manufacturers and the merchants of the engines of destruction and it must be met by the concerted actions of the people of all nations."

MILITARY-INDUSTRIAL COMPLEX
The mutually beneficial relationship between the armed forces and defense contractors.

During President Eisenhower's eight years in office, the former five-star general of the army experienced firsthand the kind of pressure that could be brought against him and other policymakers by arms manufacturers. Eisenhower decided to give the country a solemn and, as he saw it, necessary warning of the consequences of this influence. On January 17, 1961, in his last official speech, he said,

> In the councils of government, we must guard against the acquisition of unwarranted influence, whether sought or unsought, by the military-industrial complex. The potential for the disastrous rise of misplaced power exists and will persist. . . . Only an alert and knowledgeable citizenry can compel the proper meshing of the huge industrial and military machinery of defense with our peaceful methods and goals, so that security and liberty may prosper together.[4]

The Pentagon has supported a large sector of our economy through defense contracts. It also has supplied retired army officers as key executives to large defense-contracting firms. Perhaps the Pentagon's strongest allies have been members of Congress whose districts or states benefited from the economic power of military bases or contracts. As Russia and the United States worked to conclude treaties reducing their armaments, however, the Pentagon and defense contractors began to reassess their roles. They looked for new directions and programs to avoid anticipated cutbacks in military spending.

THE MAJOR FOREIGN POLICY THEMES

Although some observers might suggest that U.S. foreign policy is inconsistent and changes with the current occupant of the White House, the long

[4]*Congressional Almanac* (Washington, D.C.: Congressional Quarterly Press, 1961), pp. 938–939.

view of American diplomatic ventures reveals some major themes underlying foreign policy. In the early years of the nation, presidents and the people generally agreed that the United States should avoid foreign entanglements and concentrate instead on its own development. From the beginning of the twentieth century until today, one major theme has been increasing global involvement, with the United States taking an active role in assisting the development of other nations, dominating the world economy, and in some cases acting as a peacemaker. The major theme of the post–World War II years was the containment of communism. In the following brief review of American diplomatic history, these three themes predominate. The theme for the next century has not yet emerged.

The Formative Years: Avoiding Entanglements

U.S. foreign policy dates back to the colonial uprising against the British Crown. The Declaration of Independence formalized the colonists' desired break from Britain. Then, on September 3, 1783, the signing of the Treaty of Paris not only ended the War of Independence but also recognized the United States as an independent nation. In addition, the Treaty of Paris probably helped to reshape the world, for the American colonies were the first to secure independence against a "superpower."

Foreign policy was largely negative during the formative years. Remember that the new nation was operating under the Articles of Confederation. The national government had no right to levy and collect taxes, no control over commerce, no right to make commercial treaties, and no power to raise an army (the army was disbanded in 1783). The government's lack of international power was made clear when the United States was unable to recover American hostages who had been seized in the Mediterranean by Barbary pirates but ignominiously had to purchase the hostages in a treaty with Morocco.

The founders of this nation had a basic mistrust of corrupt European governments. George Washington said it was the U.S. policy "to steer clear of permanent alliances," and Thomas Jefferson echoed this sentiment when he said America wanted peace with all nations but "entangling alliances with none." This was also a logical position at a time when the United States was so weak militarily that it could not influence European development directly. Moreover, being protected by oceans that took weeks to traverse certainly allowed the nation to avoid entangling alliances. During the 1700s and 1800s, the United States generally stayed out of European conflicts and politics.

The Monroe Doctrine and the Americas

President James Monroe, in his message to Congress on December 2, 1823, stated that this country would not accept foreign intervention in the Western Hemisphere. In return, the United States would not meddle in European affairs. The **Monroe Doctrine** was the underpinning of the U.S. **isolationist foreign policy** toward Europe, which continued throughout the nineteenth century.

In contrast to its isolationist policy toward Europe, the United States pursued an actively expansionist policy in the Americas and the Pacific area during the nineteenth century. The nation purchased Louisiana in 1803, annexed Texas in 1845, gained half of Mexico's territory in the 1840s, purchased Alaska in 1867, and annexed Hawaii in 1898. By first becoming a power in the Western Hemisphere, the United States laid the groundwork for becoming a world power in the twentieth century.

MONROE DOCTRINE

The policy statement included in President James Monroe's 1823 annual message to Congress, which set out three principles: (1) European nations should not establish new colonies in the Western Hemisphere, (2) European nations should not intervene in the affairs of independent nations of the Western Hemisphere, and (3) the United States would not interfere in the affairs of European nations.

ISOLATIONIST FOREIGN POLICY

Abstaining from an active role in international affairs or alliances, which characterized U.S. foreign policy toward Europe during most of the nineteenth century.

A 1912 painting shows President James Monroe explaining the Monroe Doctrine to a group of government officials. Essentially, the Monroe Doctrine made the Western Hemisphere the concern of the United States.

The Spanish-American War and World War I

The end of the isolationist policy started with the Spanish-American War in 1898. Winning that war gave the United States possession of Guam, Puerto Rico, and the Philippines (which gained independence in 1946). On the heels of that war came World War I (1914 to 1918). In his reelection campaign of 1916, President Woodrow Wilson ran on the slogan "He kept us out of war." Nonetheless, on April 6, 1917, the United States declared war on Germany. It was evident to Wilson that without help, the Allies would be defeated, and American property and lives, already under attack, increasingly would be endangered. Wilson also sought to promote American democratic ideals in Europe and to end international aggression by having the United States enter into the war.

In the 1920s, the United States did indeed go "back to normalcy," as President Warren G. Harding urged it to do. U.S. military forces were largely disbanded, defense spending dropped to about 1 percent of total national income, and the nation entered a period of isolationism.

The Era of Internationalism

Isolationism was permanently shattered and relegated to its place in history by the bombing of the U.S. naval base at Pearl Harbor, Hawaii, on December 7, 1941. The surprise attack by the Japanese resulted in the deaths of 2,403 American servicemen and the wounding of 1,143 others. Eighteen warships were sunk or seriously damaged, and 188 planes were destroyed at the airfields. Tales of the horrors experienced by the wounded survivors quickly reached the mainland. The American public was outraged. President Franklin Roosevelt asked Congress to declare war on Japan immediately, and the United States entered World War II.

This unequivocal response was certainly due to the nature of the provocation. American soil had not been attacked by a foreign power since the burning of Washington, D.C., by the British in 1814. World War II marked a lasting change in American foreign policy. It also produced a permanent change in defense spending. Except for brief periods during the Civil War and World War I, defense spending had been a fairly trivial part of total national income. By the end of World War II, in 1945, however, defense spending had increased to almost 40 percent of total national income. The number of U.S. military bases overseas increased from three at the beginning of 1940 to almost 450 by the end of World War II. National security had become a priority item on the federal government's agenda.

The United States was the only major participating country to emerge from World War II with its economy intact, and even strengthened. The Soviet Union, Japan, Italy, France, Germany, Britain, and a number of minor participants in the war were all economically devastated. The United States was also the only country to have control over operational nuclear weapons. President Harry S Truman had personally made the decision to use two atomic bombs, on August 6 and August 9, 1945, to end the war with Japan. (Historians still dispute the necessity of this action, which ultimately killed more than 100,000 Japanese civilians and left an equal number permanently injured.) The United States truly had become the world's superpower.

The Cold War

The United States had become an uncomfortable ally of the Soviet Union after Adolf Hitler's invasion. Soon after the war ended, relations between the Soviet Union and the West deteriorated. The Soviet Union wanted a weakened Germany, and to achieve this it insisted that the country be divided in two, with East Germany becoming a buffer. Little by little, the Soviet Union helped to install communist governments in Eastern European countries, which collectively became known as the **Soviet bloc**. In response, the United

The atomic bomb explodes over Nagasaki, Japan, on August 9, 1945.

SOVIET BLOC

The Eastern European countries that installed communist regimes after World War II.

Joseph Stalin, Franklin Roosevelt, and Winston Churchill met at Yalta from February 4 to 11, 1945, to resolve their differences over the shape that the international community would take after World War II.

States encouraged the rearming of Western Europe. The **Cold War** had begun.[5]

In Fulton, Missouri, on March 5, 1946, Winston Churchill, in a striking metaphor, declared that from the Baltic to the Adriatic seas "an iron curtain has descended across the [European] continent." The term **iron curtain** became even more appropriate when the Soviet Union built a wall separating East Berlin from West Berlin on August 17 and 18, 1961.

Tests of Strength

In 1947, a remarkable article was published in *Foreign Affairs.* The article was signed by "X." The actual author was George F. Kennan, chief of the policy-planning staff for the Department of State. The doctrine of **containment** set forth in the article became—according to many—the Bible of Western foreign policy. "X" argued that whenever and wherever the Soviet Union could successfully challenge Western institutions, it would do so. He recommended that our policy toward the Soviet Union be "firm and vigilant containment of Russian expansive tendencies."[6]

The containment theory was expressed clearly in the **Truman Doctrine,** which was enunciated by President Harry S Truman in his historic address to Congress on March 12, 1947. In that address, he announced that the United States must help countries in which a communist takeover seemed likely, and he proposed the Greek-Turkish aid program specifically to counter Soviet influence in the eastern Mediterranean area. Greece was involved in a civil war that included communist forces, and Turkey was being pressured by the Soviet Union for political concessions. Truman proposed $400 million in aid to those two countries. He put the choice squarely before Congress—it either must support those measures required to preserve peace and security abroad or risk widespread global instability and perhaps World War III.[7]

During the Cold War, there was never any direct military confrontation between the United States and the Soviet Union. Rather, confrontations among "client" nations were used to carry out the policies of the superpowers. Only on occasion did the United States directly enter into a conflict in a significant way. Two such occasions were in Korea and Vietnam.

In 1950, North Korean troops were embroiled in a war with South Korea. President Truman asked for and received a Security Council order from the United Nations for the North Koreans to withdraw their troops. The Soviet Union was absent from the council on that day, protesting the exclusion of the People's Republic of China from the UN, and did not participate in the discussion. Truman then authorized the use of American forces in support of the South Koreans. For the next three years, American troops were engaged in a land war in Asia, a war that became a stalemate and a political liability to President Truman. One of Dwight Eisenhower's major 1952 campaign promises was to end the Korean war—which he did. An armistice was signed on July 27, 1953. (American troops have been stationed in South Korea ever since, however.)

U.S. involvement in Vietnam began shortly after the end of the Korean conflict. When the French army in Indochina was defeated by the communist

COLD WAR

The ideological, political, and economic impasse that existed between the United States and the Soviet Union following World War II.

IRON CURTAIN

The term used to describe the division of Europe between the Soviet Union and the West; popularized by Winston Churchill in a speech portraying Europe as being divided by an iron curtain, with the nations of Eastern Europe behind the curtain and increasingly under Soviet control.

CONTAINMENT

A U.S. diplomatic policy adopted by the Truman administration to "build situations of strength" around the globe to contain communist power within its existing boundaries.

TRUMAN DOCTRINE

The policy adopted by President Harry Truman in 1947 to halt communist expansion in southeastern Europe.

---

[5]See John Lewis Gaddis, *The United Nations and the Origins of the Cold War* (New York: Columbia University Press, 1972).

[6]X, "The Sources of Soviet Conduct," *Foreign Affairs*, July 1947, p. 575.

[7]*Public Papers of the Presidents of the United States: Harry S Truman, 1947* (Washington, D.C.: U.S. Government Printing Office, 1963), pp. 176–180.

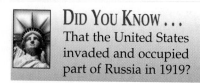

forces of Ho Chi Minh and the two Vietnams were created in 1954, the United States assumed the role of supporting the South Vietnamese government against North Vietnam. President John Kennedy sent 16,000 "advisers" to help South Vietnam, and after Kennedy's death, President Lyndon Johnson greatly increased the scope of that support. American forces in Vietnam at the height of the U.S. involvement totaled more than 500,000 troops. In excess of 58,000 Americans were killed and 300,000 wounded in the conflict. The debate over U.S. involvement in Vietnam divided the American electorate and, as mentioned previously, spurred congressional efforts to limit the ability of the president to commit forces to armed combat.

The Cuban Missile Crisis

Nuclear power spread throughout the world. The two superpowers had enough nuclear bombs to destroy everyone at least twice and maybe three times. Obviously, confrontation between the United States and the Soviet Union could have taken on world-destroying proportions. Perhaps the closest we came to such a confrontation was the Cuban missile crisis in 1962. The Soviets had decided to place offensive missiles ninety miles off the U.S. coast, in Cuba, to help prevent an American-sponsored invasion like the Bay of Pigs. (In 1961, Cuban exiles who were trained, armed, and directed by U.S. government agents invaded Cuba's "Bay of Pigs" to overthrow Fidel Castro's communist regime.)

President Kennedy and his advisers rejected the possibility of armed intervention, setting up a naval blockade around the island instead. When Soviet vessels, apparently carrying nuclear warheads, appeared near Cuban waters, the tension reached its height. After intense negotiations between Washington and Moscow, the Soviet ships turned around on October 25, and on October 28 the Soviet Union announced the withdrawal of its missile operations from Cuba. In exchange, the United States agreed not to invade Cuba and to remove some of its own missiles that were located near the Soviet border.

A Period of Détente

DÉTENTE

A French word meaning the relaxation of tension. The term characterizes U.S.–Soviet policy as it developed under President Richard Nixon and Secretary of State Henry Kissinger. Détente stresses direct cooperative dealings with Cold War rivals but avoids ideological accommodation.

STRATEGIC ARMS LIMITATION TREATY (SALT I)

A treaty between the United States and the Soviet Union to stabilize the nuclear arms competition between the two countries. SALT I talks began in 1969, and agreements were signed on May 26, 1972.

The French word **détente** means a relaxation of tensions between nations. By the end of the 1960s, it was clear that some efforts had to be made to reduce the threat of nuclear war between the United States and the Soviet Union. The Soviet Union gradually had begun to catch up in the building of strategic nuclear delivery vehicles in the form of bombers and missiles, thus balancing the nuclear scales. Each nation acquired the military capacity to destroy the other with nuclear weapons.

As the result of protracted negotiations, in May 1972, the United States and the Soviet Union signed the **Strategic Arms Limitation Treaty (SALT I).** That treaty "permanently" limited the development and deployment of antiballistic missiles (ABMs), and it limited for five years the number of offensive missiles each country could deploy. To further reduce tensions, under the policy of Secretary of State Henry Kissinger and President Nixon, new scientific and cultural exchanges were arranged with the Soviets, as well as new opportunities for Jewish emigration out of the Soviet Union.

The policy of détente was not limited to U.S. relationships with the Soviet Union. Seeing an opportunity to capitalize on increasing friction between the Soviet Union and the People's Republic of China, Kissinger secretly began negotiations to establish a new relationship with that nation. President Nixon eventually visited the People's Republic of China and set the stage for the for-

President Richard Nixon signs SALT I, a Cold War agreement with the Soviet Union, in 1972.

mal diplomatic recognition of that country during the Carter administration (1977–1981).

The late 1970s saw increased tension between the United States and the Soviet Union. The Soviet Union intervened militarily in Afghanistan and suppressed the Polish Solidarity movement, which it saw as a threat to its political control throughout Eastern Europe.

The Reagan-Bush Years

President Ronald Reagan took a hard line against the Soviet Union during his first term, proposing the strategic defense initiative (SDI), or "Star Wars," in 1983. SDI was designed to serve as a space-stationed defense against enemy missiles. Reagan and others in his administration argued that the program would deter nuclear war by shifting the emphasis of defense strategy from offensive to defensive weapons systems.

In November 1985, President Reagan and Mikhail Gorbachev, the Soviet leader, held summit talks in Geneva. The two men agreed to reestablish cultural and scientific exchanges and to continue the arms control negotiations. Progress toward an agreement was slow, however.

In 1987, representatives of the United States and the Soviet Union continued work on an arms reduction agreement. Although there were setbacks throughout the year, the negotiations resulted in a historic agreement signed by Reagan and Gorbachev in Washington, D.C., on December 8, 1987. The terms of the Intermediate-Range Nuclear Force (INF) Treaty required the superpowers to dismantle a total of four thousand intermediate-range mis-

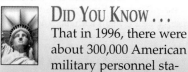

siles within the first three years of the agreement. The verification procedures allowed each nation to keep a team of inspectors on the other nation's soil and to conduct up to twenty short-notice inspections of the disassembly sites each year. The Senate ratified the treaty in a vote of ninety-three to five on May 27, 1988, and the agreement was formally signed by Reagan and Gorbachev at the Moscow summit in 1988.

George Bush continued the negotiations with the Soviet Union after he became president. The goal of both nations was to reduce the number of nuclear weapons and the number of armed troops in Europe. The developments in Eastern Europe, the drive by the Baltic republics for independence, the unification of Germany, and the dissolution of the Soviet Union (December 1991) made the process much more complex, however. American strategists worried as much about who now controlled the Soviet nuclear arsenal as about completing the treaty process. In 1992, the United States signed the Strategic Arms Reduction Treaty (START) with four former Soviet republics—Russia, Ukraine, Belarus, and Kazakhstan—to reduce the number of long-range nuclear weapons.

CHALLENGES IN WORLD POLITICS

The end of the Cold War, the dissolution of the Soviet Union, the economic unification of Europe, and the political changes in Eastern Europe have challenged U.S. foreign policy in ways that were unimaginable a few years ago. The United States had no contingency plans for these events. Also, predicting the consequences of any of these changes for world politics is all but impossible. Furthermore, such sweeping changes mean not only that the United States must adjust its foreign policy to deal with new realities but also that it must consider adjustments in the American military and intelligence establishments.

The Dissolution of the Soviet Union

After the fall of the Berlin Wall in 1989, it was clear that the Soviet Union had relinquished much of its political and military control over the states of Eastern Europe that formerly had been part of the Soviet bloc. Sweeping changes within the Soviet Union had been proposed by Gorbachev, and talks to reduce nuclear armaments were proceeding. No one expected the Soviet Union to dissolve into separate states as quickly as it did, however. While Gorbachev tried to adjust the Soviet constitution and political system to allow greater autonomy for the republics within the union, demands for political, ethnic, and religious autonomy grew. In August 1991, the Soviet military tried to slow the process by arresting Gorbachev. Led by Boris Yeltsin, then president of Russia, the coup attempt was successfully resisted.

The result of the failed attempt to gain control by military leaders was to hasten the process of creating an independent Russian state led by Yeltsin. On the day after Christmas in 1991, the Soviet Union was officially dissolved. A few months later, the majority of the former republics had joined a loose federation called the Commonwealth of Independent States, although a few of the larger republics, including Georgia and Ukraine, refused to join.

Another uprising in Russia, this time led by anti-Yeltsin members of the new parliament who wanted to restore the Soviet Union immediately, failed in 1993. The first free elections of the new nation produced a divided parliament, with a majority of delegates who opposed Yeltsin and his programs. Yeltsin, however, won the election for president in 1996, although he appeared

Russian President Boris Yeltsin celebrated his August 1991 success against forces fighting to preserve the Soviet Union by waving the Russian flag.

to be in ill health during the campaign and soon after his inauguration had heart surgery. Yeltsin's presidency continued to be plagued by domestic economic problems and the uprising in Chechnya, a breakaway ethnic region.

Nuclear Proliferation

The dissolution of the Soviet Union brought a true lowering of tensions between the major powers in the world. The United States and Russia agreed to continue negotiating the dismantling of nuclear warheads and delivery systems. The problems of nuclear proliferation were far from solved, how-

The threat of nuclear destruction was perhaps reduced when President Clinton signed a nuclear accord with Russia, represented by President Boris Yeltsin, and Ukraine, then represented by Leonid Kravchuk. Russia currently owns the majority of nuclear warheads from the former Soviet Union. One continuing problem today is that weapons-grade enriched uranium is being sold on the black market to certain countries that are working secretly on the development of their own nuclear bombs.

One of the continuing "hot spots" in the world has been Korea. This country was divided into South and North Korea after World War II. After the Korean War (1950–1953), a demilitarized zone (DMZ) was established between the North and the South. Here President Clinton is shown with American soldiers at the DMZ. Such soldiers have been there since the end of the Korean War. Tension mounted between North and South Korea when North Korea prohibited international inspectors from attempting to ascertain whether North Korea was developing nuclear bombs. Tension also increased when Kim Il Sung died in 1994. The octogenarian had stayed in power since the official formation of his country on May 1, 1948.

ever. As shown in Table 18–1, the number of warheads known to be in stock worldwide is nearly twenty thousand; other nations do not report the extent of their nuclear stockpiles. In 1994, North Korea defied the efforts of the International Atomic Energy Commission to inspect parts of its nuclear power plant, particularly at a time when fuel rods were to be changed. The international inspectors suspected that spent fuel would be reprocessed to make a nuclear bomb or warhead. When North Korea continued to defy international pressure to comply with inspection, the United States sought approval

Table 18–1

The Nuclear Club

LOCATION	KNOWN AND SUSPECTED NUMBER OF WARHEADS	
Official estimates:		
United States	8,500 (to be reduced to 3,500 by 2003)	
Former Soviet Union	9,853 (to be reduced to 3,500 by 2003)	
	In possession of:	
	Russia	8,362
	Kazakhstan	1,410
	Belarus	81
France	482	
China	284	
Britain	234	
Unofficial estimates:		
Israel	50 to 200	
India	Capability for 80	
Pakistan	Capability for 15 to 25	
Nations that are capable of building weapons and/or suspected of having a nuclear program:		
Algeria, Argentina, Brazil, Iran, Iraq, Libya, North Korea, South Africa, and Syria.		

SOURCE: *Newsweek,* July 24, 1995, p. 36–37, and authors' update.

for sanctions on the nation from the United Nations. Former U.S. president Jimmy Carter went to North Korea in mid-1994 and negotiated a deal by which the North Koreans would give up their nuclear power plant in exchange for a new one. The new one would not have the capability to produce similar fuel rods and would be built with money loaned to North Korea by the United States.

Terrorism

Dissident groups, rebels, and other revolutionaries always have engaged in some sort of terrorism to gain attention and to force their enemy to the bargaining table. Over the last two decades, terrorism has continued to threaten world peace and the lives of ordinary citizens.

Terrorism can be a weapon of choice in domestic or civil strife. The conflict in the Middle East between Israel and the Arab states has been lessened by a series of painfully negotiated agreements between Israel and some of the other states. In recent years, Israel and the Palestinians have tried to reach agreement on some of their differences. Those opposed to the peace process, however, have continued to disrupt the negotiations through assassinations, mass murders, and bomb blasts in the streets of major cities within Israel. At this point, most of the terrorist attacks are carried out by groups (either Israeli or Arab) that reject the peace process. Similar "domestic" terrorist acts continue to disrupt talks between Britain and Ireland over the fate of Northern Ireland. Terrorist acts by rebels or separatist groups occurred in Sri Lanka (the Tamils), Paris (Algerian extremists), Russia (Chechen rebels), and Japan (secret cults).

In other cases, terrorist acts are planned against the civilians of foreign nations to make an international statement and to frighten the citizens of a faraway land. Perhaps one of the most striking of these attacks was that launched against Israeli athletes at the Munich Olympics in 1972. Others have included ship hijackings, airplane hijackings, and the bombing of the World Trade Center in New York. In 1996, two incidents brought the fear of terrorism home to Americans; first, radical elements in Saudi Arabia bombed an American military compound there, killing a number of American military personnel; then, TWA flight 800 exploded soon after take-off on a flight to Paris from New York City. It is not yet clear, however, that terrorists were responsible for the latter.

What can nations do to prevent terrorism? Besides taking a clear stand about the consequences of such acts and punishing the perpetrators, as the Israelis do, the best defense of nations is to be vigilant. This includes stronger security measures and a commitment to intelligence gathering. The Clinton administration requested a strengthening of U.S. intelligence capabilities in 1996, but that proposal met with opposition from civil liberties groups as well as conservative Republicans. The problem that faces a democracy that upholds liberty for its citizens is how to balance the needs of increased surveillance for criminals against the rights of citizens to be free of police spying and record keeping.

The Global Economy

Although the United States derives only about 10 percent of its total national income from world trade, it is deeply dependent on the world economy. A serious stock market crash of 1987 showed how closely other markets watch the economic situation of the United States and, conversely, how U.S. markets follow those of London and Japan. Furthermore, since the 1980s, the United

DID YOU KNOW...
That foreigners owned only about 6 percent of U.S. stocks and 14 percent of U.S. corporate bonds in 1996?

States has become a debtor nation, meaning that we owe more to foreigners than foreigners owe to us. The reason for this is a huge trade deficit and the willingness of foreign individuals and nations to finance part of the U.S. national debt by purchasing U.S. government securities.

Because the United States imports more goods and services than it exports, it has a net trade deficit. These imports include BMWs, Sonys, Toshibas, and Guccis, as well as cheaper products such as shoes manufactured in Brazil and clothes from Taiwan. As Figure 18–1 shows, the biggest trade deficit is with Asian countries.

No one can predict how a unified Europe will affect world trade. With the European Union having become one economic "nation" on December 31, 1992, some expect Europe to close gradually some markets to outside economic powers. Others see a united Europe as a market opportunity for American and multinational corporations.

Regional Conflicts

The United States has played a role—sometimes alone, sometimes in conjunction with other powers—in many regional conflicts. During the 1990s, the United States has been involved in conflicts in countries and regions around the globe.

Haiti and Cuba. The Caribbean nation of Haiti became a focal point of U.S. policy in the 1990s. The repressive military regime there ousted the democratically elected president Jean-Bertrand Aristide in 1992. The Clinton administration announced that it would support sanctions and other measures to reinstate Aristide in office. At the same time, the administration tried to stem the tide of refugees who tried to reach Florida by sea from the island nation.

Figure 18–1

● ●

U.S. Exports and Imports, 1994

In 1994, the U.S. trade deficit continued to grow, reaching $151 billion. It is important to note, however, that Canada is the most important market for U.S. products and that Canada and Mexico together account for about 30 percent of all U.S. exports and imports. China is rapidly increasing its exports to the United States.

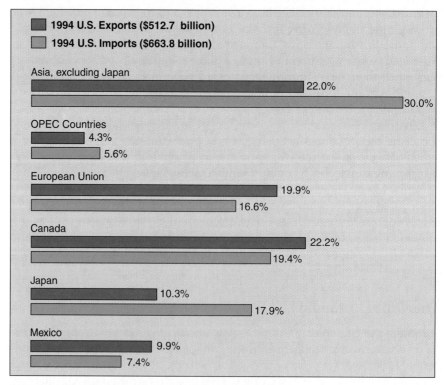

SOURCE: *Survey of Current Business*, March 1994, updated by authors.

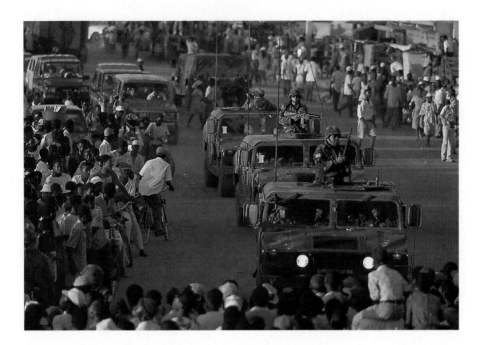

U.S. troops arrive in Port-au-Prince, Haiti, in September of 1994.

Although Clinton had promised in his campaign to admit the Haitian "boat people," he maintained the Bush policy of returning them to their native land. By 1994, he announced that the United States would at least listen to pleas for political asylum if refugees could reach Jamaica or other Caribbean islands. The Clinton administration also increased the sanctions on Haiti in 1994, and then sent troops to Haiti to assist in the reinstatement of President Aristide.

The United States continued to face problems with Cuba. In the last days of the summer of 1994, Castro threatened to "swamp" the United States with Cuban refugees. True to his word, he allowed thousands to leave the island on anything that would float. President Clinton was forced to rescind the U.S. open-door policy for Cuban refugees. He ordered the Coast Guard to return all refugees picked up at sea to the U.S. naval base at Guantanamo in Cuba. Then U.S. and Cuban authorities reached an agreement under which the United States would accept 20,000 legal Cuban immigrants a year. In exchange, Castro agreed to police Cuba's shores to prevent an exodus of Cuban refugees.

In 1996, another incident occurred. Cuban military aircraft shot down two planes flown by anti-Castro American residents who were searching for Cubans escaping by sea. The pilots were conducting the search for an anti-communist organization that had violated Cuban air space repeatedly on previous occasions. The United States, refusing to accept Cuba's explanation that the two planes were in Cuban territorial waters, retaliated by passing the Helms-Burton Act. The act, which punished owners of foreign firms (and their family members) for investing in formerly American-owned business firms that had been nationalized by Cuba, sparked international opposition.

The Middle East.   The United States has also played a role in the Middle East. As a long-time supporter of Israel, the United States has undertaken to persuade the Israelis to agree to negotiations with the Palestinians who live as refugees within the occupied territories of the state of Israel. The conflict, which began in 1948, has been extremely hard to resolve. One reason is that

Part of America's foreign policy involves deciding how to deal with political and economic refugees. As the situation under military rule in Haiti worsened in 1994, the Coast Guard picked up an increasing number of fleeing Haitians who wished to reestablish themselves in the United States. They were virtually all sent to the Guantanamo naval base in Cuba. By the middle of the summer of 1994 there were 15,000 Haitians living there under U.S. protection. They were then joined by tens of thousands of Cuban refugees.

Israeli Prime Minister Benjamin Netanyahu and PLO Chairman Yasir Arafat shake hands at their first meeting. Before becoming prime minister, Netanyahu had opposed the peace accords negotiated by his predecessor, Yitzhak Rubin. This handshake was interpreted as a symbol of his willingness to continue the implementation of the accords.

it requires all the Arab states in the region to recognize Israel's right to exist. Another reason is that resolution of the conflict would require Israel to make some settlement with the Palestine Liberation Organization (PLO), which has launched attacks on Israel from within and outside its borders and which Israel has regarded as a terrorist organization. In December 1988, the U.S. began talking directly to the PLO, and in 1991, under great pressure from the United States, the Israelis opened talks with representatives of the Palestinians and other Arab states.

In 1993, the Israeli-Palestinian peace talks reached a breakthrough, with both parties agreeing to set up Palestinian territories in the West Bank and Gaza. The historic agreement, signed in Cairo on May 4, 1994, put in place a process by which the Palestinians would assume self-rule in the Gaza Strip and in the town of Jericho. In the months that followed, Israeli troops withdrew from much of the territory, Palestinians assumed police duties, and many Palestinian prisoners were freed by the Israelis. During an election campaign speech, however, Israeli prime minister Yitzhak Rabin was assassinated by a right-wing Israeli student who opposed the peace process. In the election, the voters elected a new prime minister, Benjamin Netanyahu, who represented more conservative ideas. Since that time, conditions in the Palestinian areas have worsened, and it is unclear to what degree Israel will go forward with the peace process.

U.S. Response to Iraq's Invasion of Kuwait.   On August 2, 1990, the Middle East became the setting for a major challenge to the authority of the United States and its ability to buy oil from its allies there. President Saddam Hussein of Iraq initially sent more than 100,000 troops into the neighboring oil sheikdom of Kuwait, occupying the entire nation. Within less than two days, President George Bush took the position that the annexation of Kuwait must not be tolerated by the Western world and that the oil fields of Saudi Arabia must be protected. At the formal request of the king of Saudi Arabia, American troops were dispatched to set up a defensive line at the Kuwaiti border. In addition, the president announced an economic boycott of Iraq (supported by the United Nations) and sent American carrier groups to seal off the Iraqi ports, cutting off shipments of oil.

American tanks carry out maneuvers in Saudi Arabia during Operation Desert Shield. Subsequently, the United States, together with a coalition of other nations, instituted Operation Desert Storm—the Persian Gulf "hot war" that lasted for only one hundred hours on the ground, following prolonged air attacks. Such maneuvers again were undertaken in Kuwait in the fall of 1994, when Saddam Hussein moved troops close to the Kuwaiti border.

Bush continued to send troops—including reserve units called up from the United States—to Saudi Arabia. By the end of 1990, more than half a million troops were in place. After the United Nations approved a resolution authorizing the use of force if Saddam Hussein did not respond to sanctions, the U.S. Congress reluctantly also approved such an authorization. On January 17, 1991, two days after the deadline for President Hussein to withdraw, the coalition forces launched a massive air attack on Iraq. After several weeks of almost unopposed aerial bombardment, the ground offensive began. Iraqi troops retreated from Kuwait a few days later, and the Persian Gulf War ended within another week. This war was a testing ground for a new technological "weapon"—see this chapter's *Politics and Technology*.

After the end of the armed conflict, many Americans criticized the Bush administration for not sending troops to Baghdad, where they might have deposed Saddam Hussein. Others faulted the effort for raising the expectations of the Kurdish people that the United States would eliminate President Hussein if they revolted. When no one helped their uprising, the entire community risked retaliation by the Iraqi dictator. Belatedly, American troops were sent to preserve peace. The war also created an enormous environmental disaster owing to the destruction of the oil fields by the Iraqis when they retreated from Kuwait. In 1996, Saddam Hussein sent troops to recapture some of the Kurdish region when fighting broke out between competing Kurdish factions. The United States responded by firing cruise missiles at Iraqi bases as a warning. Hussein continues to hold great power in the region.

President Clinton ordered two cruise missile attacks against Iraq to deter that regime from attacking Kurdish villages in the north of Iraq. The attacks ceased, but several cities remained under Iraq's control at the end of the attacks.

Eastern Europe. Eastern Europe, a region that had been extremely stable while under Soviet domination, suddenly became an unknown quantity in U.S. policy. With the decision of the Soviet Union to allow free elections and non-Marxist governments in Eastern Europe, these nations took separate paths to becoming democratic states with mixed or market-oriented economies. Some nations moved immediately to democratic elections; some struggled first to repair damaged economies; and still others attempted to deal with ethnic tensions within their populations.

POLITICS AND TECHNOLOGY
Developing an Infowar Strategy

One of the problems facing Pentagon officials in the 1990s is how to prepare for *infowar*—defined by the Pentagon as the effort to seize control of electronic information systems during a conflict. One infowar weapon has already been developed: the Army's Sandscrab jammer that was used to disrupt long-range radio links in Iraq during the Persian Gulf War in 1991. Since that time, Pentagon officials have become concerned not only with finding out how secure its own computer systems are against potential enemy hackers but also in developing "weapons" to attack other nations' information systems.

How secure are Pentagon computers? In 1994, the Defense Information Systems Agency (DISA) learned the answer to this question after it arranged to have several in-house hackers try to break into Pentagon computers to see how vulnerable they were to external attack. The hackers apparently succeeded in penetrating 88 percent of the 8,900 computers they attacked. Furthermore, the Defense Department was aware of only 4 percent of the break-ins.*

A major problem for the U.S. military in preparing for infowar is the fact that over 95 percent of military communications take place over civilian electronic communications networks, like the Internet. If enemy hackers succeeded in jamming or disabling these networks, military operations, and the nation's business generally, would come to a standstill. Unlike in years past, when the outcome of war depended to a great extent on the economic ability to produce weaponry, the outcome of wars in cyberspace will depend on the ability to develop sophisticated, high-tech techniques to attack (and defend) electronic information systems. The United States isn't alone in its concerns about cyberspace wars. At least thirty other countries around the globe are developing infowar techniques and strategies.

Developing an infowar strategy is not easy, as Pentagon officials are learning. For one thing, to develop the necessary high-tech products costs more than the Pentagon currently has to spend. Additionally, the Pentagon would find it difficult to compete with high-tech products created by commercial developers, which are not directly controlled by the government. Finally, because the military is so dependent on civilian communications systems, securing those systems against external attacks would require extensive control over them—which the government does not have. This is probably the most significant obstacle in developing an infowar strategy. Americans are unlikely to accept the degree of government intrusion into their personal and business lives that would be necessary to protect civilian information and communications systems.

For Critical Analysis

What might result if an enemy hacker succeeded in jamming New York's telephone exchange?

*Neil Munroe, "Our Electronic Achilles' Heel," *The Washington Post*, August 14–20, 1995, p. 24.

It is difficult to overestimate the potential for civil disorder in these nations, particularly with regard to ethnic differences. (See this chapter's feature entitled *Politics and Ethics.*) The world watched in 1991 as Yugoslavia split into a number of independent states. As former provinces of Yugoslavia—Slovenia, Croatia, and Bosnia and Herzegovina—tried to declare independence, Serbian military and government leaders launched attacks on their neighbors. The fighting was caused by historic conflicts and by strong ethnic and religious differences.

The fighting was fiercest in the former province of Bosnia, where Serbs and Muslims launched attacks on each other's villages and cities. News reports suggested that many women were raped, and that the men were sent to camps to force their families to leave their homes. The United States and European nations forced the Serbs to withdraw their weapons from the city and to begin a process for permanent disengagement. With guarantees from the United States and other NATO allies, the warring parties began the process of establishing separate ethnic provinces and returning to their home villages. Troops from the United States and other European nations patrolled

POLITICS AND ETHICS
The Demands of Ethnic Nationalism

The slaughter of civilians in Rwanda in 1994 and the fighting between Serbian and Moslem Bosnians is but a prelude to things to come. As new states are created from the wreckage of the Soviet Union and as postcolonial states mature, more and more people identifying with ethnic subnationalities will be claiming the right to sovereignty as new states or, at a minimum, the right to international protection for their culture and identity. According to one commentator, the first wave of twentieth-century nationalism followed World War II, when colonial powers like Great Britain and France allowed their former colonies to become independent states. At that time, the new states, including India, Pakistan, Vietnam, and others, fought to establish national unity against the colonial powers.*

Since that time, several more waves of ethnic nationalism have followed, as people of ethnic nationalities within these new nations (and within old nations) claim independence or the need for greater rights within the nation. The response of the world's international organizations has also changed in this century; they now support human rights in every case.

The result has been an explosion of ethnic conflicts in developing nations, in the states of the former Soviet Union, and even in the industrialized nations. A few years ago the *Los Angeles Times* listed fifty-three separate ethnic conflicts in the world. Although Rwanda was mentioned, at that time, the mass killings of more than 500,000 people had not yet occurred. In India, at least twenty thousand people have been killed in violence between the Sikhs and the Hindu government. In Azerbaijan, three thousand deaths have occurred since 1988. In Sri Lanka, twenty thousand Tamils have died in their revolt against the Buddhist Sinhalese. In Iraq, persecution of the Kurds and the "marsh Arabs" continues. Within Russia, Chechen rebels successfully fended off Russian troops sent to subdue their uprising. In late 1996, ethnic strife in Rwanda again erupted into violence.

The international community faces an ethical dilemma in these situations. Should all peoples who claim an ethnic identity be protected, either by outside forces or through the creation of a separate political entity? If that is the case, what is the right of a nation as a whole to protect its sovereignty and its borders for the good of all the citizens? It cannot be correct morally to allow the oppression of one group by another, but can outsiders intervene in the domestic affairs of a nation? Finally, the solution cannot be separate states for each people. Such a solution would produce a world of nations too small to survive and would require large-scale migrations of peoples back to their homelands.

For Critical Analysis
What can the United States and other members of the world community do to curb increasing ethnic violence?

*Joane Nagel, "Ethnic Nationalism: Politics, Ideology, and the World Order," *International Journal of Comparative Sociology,* Vol. 34 (1993), p. 107.

the new borders and assisted in the process. Prospects for a lasting peace after the troops leave are not great due to the degree of ethnic hatred in this region.

Africa.   The continent of Africa witnessed both great strides for freedom and savage civil strife during the mid-1990s. In South Africa, the first all-race elections were held—mostly in an orderly and peaceful manner—and Nelson Mandela was elected as the first president under a new constitution. Most South African constituencies took part in the election and seemed ready to support the new black-majority regime. The economic sanctions applied by the United States had helped bring the white South African government to a position of economic hardship and led, in part, to its negotiations with Mandela and his African National Congress party.

In central Africa, another situation arose that seemed to be totally beyond the influence of the United States, France, or the United Nations. After a plane crash that killed the presidents of Rwanda and of neighboring Burundi, civil war erupted in Rwanda. The political war between the government and the rebel forces was complicated by a terrible ethnic struggle between the Hutu

CRITICAL PERSPECTIVE
Can the United Nations Keep the Peace?

The fundamental purpose of the United Nations (UN) at its inception was to prevent the outbreak of another global conflict. The UN Security Council—with its permanent seats (and votes) for the strongest international powers, namely, the United States, the Soviet Union, Great Britain, France, and China—was intended to be a forum that could negotiate disputes among the greater powers and decide how to stop all other disputes. The Cold War, however, made agreement by the United States and the Soviet Union impossible for more than forty years. Additionally, the Chinese seat was given to Taiwan until the 1980s, when the People's Republic of China took its place at the UN. During those four decades, most regional conflicts became tests of strength between the two superpowers, with the threat of nuclear war ever present. The United States and the Soviet Union "faced off" in Europe, Vietnam, Cuba, Yemen, and other "hot spots."

End of the Cold War

With the breaking up of the Soviet Union and the end of the Cold War in the 1990s, the UN has been asked to increase its peacekeeping role tremendously. The questions to be answered in the future are whether the UN really is able to mount and sustain peacekeeping operations around the world and whether those operations can solve ethnic and regional conflicts. As the secretary-general of the UN, Boutros Boutros-Ghali, put it, "We are in a period of transition, and the world hasn't decided yet what will be the new rules of the game. The member states haven't decided whether they really want a strong United Nations."*

*Julia Preston, "Vision of a More Aggressive U.N. Is Dimming," *The Washington Post,* January 5, 1994, p. A24.

Most scholars trace the origins of UN peacekeeping operations to the United Nations Truce Supervision Organization (UNTSO), a group of unarmed observers who monitored the truce between Israel and the Arab states after the first Israeli-Arab war in 1948. Since that time, the UN has participated in thirteen operations, including those in Korea (a major war), Egypt, the Congo, the Middle East (after the 1973 war), and Lebanon. Most of the UN operations in the Middle East have used unarmed troops to monitor borders and truce conditions, and most have been very successful. As the Cold War came to an end, both the United States and the Soviet Union agreed to let the UN try to establish peace in a number of other trouble spots, stretching the institution's capabilities to the limit.

Increase in Peacekeeping Operations

By the beginning of 1997, the UN was carrying out fourteen operations concurrently, at an estimated expense of $2.8 billion. It had more than sixty thousand peacekeepers in the field. The UN took over peacekeeping operations in Somalia, relieving the American troops who had been delivering food and maintaining peace between warring factions. It also was being asked to play a more substantial role in the Bosnian conflict and, in 1994, to stop the slaughter of civilians in Rwanda. The rapid increase in operations put a strain on the organization and raised questions about the support it would get from the member nations. For example, with perhaps more than half a million people murdered in Rwanda, the UN asked for troops from African and Asian nations to join a force to protect civilians and to deliver food and medical supplies to the refugees in Rwanda. The operation was crippled at the onset,

and Tutsi tribes. Observers estimated that more than half a million people were killed within a few weeks, with many bodies dumped in the rivers. About 250,000 refugees arrived in Uganda, setting up a small city in less than a week. Over a million others fled into neighboring Zaire. The United Nations called for troops to assist in relief efforts, but only France responded (and pulled out shortly thereafter). The United States played virtually no part in this situation until small military and civilian contingents were sent to assist with the refugee crisis. In 1996, ethnic hostilities flared up again, resulting in more killings. (See this chapter's *Critical Perspective,* which examines the UN's role as a peacekeeper).

CRITICAL PERSPECTIVE
Can the United Nations Keep the Peace? Continued

because only France would commit large numbers of troops to this effort.

According to Marrack Goulding, the former UN undersecretary-general for peacekeeping operations, the UN forces operate under a set of informal principles:

• Peacekeeping operations are UN operations, not those of member states. Thus, they need UN command and control.
• Peacekeeping operations can be set up only if the parties to the conflict consent.
• Peacekeepers must be neutral in the conflict.
• Peacekeeping forces use borrowed troops, because the UN does not maintain a standing army. If no troops can be made available, there will be no operation.
• Force will be used at a minimum level. Most operations use force only in self-defense.†

These principles make it possible for the UN to be effective, but they also raise problems. The Somalia operation, utilizing troops from many nations, was less than effective, and some members of the peacekeeping forces seemed to be out of control. If there is no consent by the warring parties, then there will be no operation. Finally, if force is necessary to keep the terms of a truce or cease-fire, the UN peacekeepers generally will not use it. They will rely, as in the past, on major powers to exert armed force.

As noted above, the Rwanda situation provided a frightening example of the inability of the UN to deal with a terrible case of genocide. Hundreds of thousands of civilians were massacred by

warring factions in Rwanda while the world stood by helplessly. In this case, it was not possible to find enough troops to support a peacekeeping operation.

Bosnia was a complex situation. The "blue helmets," or UN forces, could protect convoys of relief supplies and, at one point, try to guard weapons turned in by the Bosnians and the Serbs. Whenever one of the combatants want to use force to attack a town or to take back the weapons, however, they succeeded. The United States and the European nations forced the combatants to the bargaining table and committed military personnel to keep the peace, something the UN could not do.

The American Position

Further complicating the issue was a reconsideration of putting American forces under UN command. In 1994, the Clinton administration announced a new policy that limits the service of U.S. troops under a UN command to highly specific situations decided on a case-by-case basis. Thus, the United States, still the strongest military power in the world, essentially has withdrawn its forces from the expanded role of the UN. This leaves the burden to other nations and weakens the ability of the UN to sustain its expanded operations.

For Critical Analysis

1. Should the UN have its own military force, with a single command and troops that are loyal to the international organization?
2. Why should the United States ever put its troops under UN command? What is the risk to American troops if they stay?

†Marrack Goulding, "The Evolution of United Nations Peacekeeping," *International Affairs*, Vol. 69 (1993), pp. 453–455.

FOREIGN AND DEFENSE POLICY: UNFINISHED WORK

No president or secretary of state can predict the future of world politics. There is simply no way of knowing whether the states of the former Soviet Union will be a source of future conflicts, whether ethnic tensions will erupt in more nations, or whether the United Nations will be able to assemble an effective peacekeeping force. Nonetheless, it is necessary for U.S. leaders to try to plan for the future. The United States needs to plan a strategy for self-defense rather than a strategy for confronting Russia. Among the foreign pol-

CONCEPT OVERVIEW

The Changing Role of the United States in the World

American foreign and national security policy certainly has been challenged in the years since World War II, which ended in 1945. Then, the United States faced the challenge of the Soviet Union and its allies during the Cold War. Now, within the same lifetime of most Americans, the United States must craft policies to face a world with new issues and no real fixed structures of power or influence. Listed below are some of the ways in which the U.S. role in world politics has changed since the Cold War.

THEN	NOW
• The Soviet Union and China were major threats to American dominance.	• No specific nations pose such a threat; regions are unstable; China is increasing in power.
• Nuclear weapons development and defense were paramount.	• Treaties have been signed to destroy nuclear warheads; small nations pose a threat of nuclear terror.
• The United Nations was in stalemate.	• Peacekeeping efforts by the United Nations are increasing.
• The United States and its NATO allies were the most powerful nations militarily.	• The United States is the only great military power.
• Congress was bipartisan on issues of defense.	• Congress is more partisan; it may try to restrict presidential action.
• The defense budget was increasing.	• The defense budget has been cut.
• The United States held primary economic power.	• Japan, China, the European Union, and other nations and regions are also very strong.

icy issues to be confronted, it is vitally important for the United States to plan an economic strategy that will increase U.S. exports and hold imports steady—in order to reduce the trade deficit.

Other issues that need to be resolved include the role that the United States sees for the United Nations, the degree to which the United States must keep a vital intelligence service, the strategies for supporting American interests in the Western Hemisphere and throughout the world, and the degree to which the United States will play an active role in the world. Without the structure of the Cold War, it is likely that foreign policy for the United States, as well as for other leading nations, will need to be much more flexible than it has been in the past to deal with changing conditions and complex situations.

As the world approaches the twenty-first century, the international experiences of the 1990s—and of the whole twentieth century—may be seen as a time of transition. The events of this century created the economic and social basis for the United States to change from a nation interested primarily in domestic policy to a major player on the world stage. The next century is likely to see that role grow, perhaps making possible a new variety of world politics.

GETTING INVOLVED
Working for Human Rights

In many countries throughout the world, human rights are not protected to the extent that they are in the United States. In some nations, people are imprisoned, tortured, or killed because they oppose the current regime. In other nations, certain ethnic or racial groups are oppressed by the majority population. In nations such as Somalia, in which civil war has caused starvation among millions of people, international efforts to send food relief to the refugee camps were hampered by the fighting among rival factions that raged within that country.

What can you do to work for the improvement of human rights in other nations? One way is to join one of the national and international organizations listed to the right that attempt to keep watch over human rights violations. By publicizing human rights violations, these organizations try to pressure nations into changing their tactics. Sometimes, such organizations are able to apply enough pressure and cause enough embarrassment that selected individuals may be freed from prison or allowed to emigrate.

Another way to work for human rights is to keep informed about the state of affairs in other nations and to write personally to those governments or to their embassies, asking them to cease these violations. Again, the organizations listed in the next column have newsletters or other publications to keep you aware of developments in other nations.

If you want to receive general information about the position of the United States on human rights vio-

lations, you could begin by contacting the State Department:

U.S. DEPARTMENT OF STATE
Bureau of Democracy, Human Rights, and Labor
2201 C St. N.W.
Washington, DC 20520
202-647-4000

You can also contact the United Nations:

UNITED NATIONS
777 United Nations Plaza
New York, NY 10017
212-867-8878

The following organizations are best known for their watchdog efforts in countries that violate human rights for political reasons.

AMNESTY INTERNATIONAL U.S.A.
322 8th Ave., Fl. 10
New York, NY 10001
212-807-8400

AMERICAN FRIENDS SERVICE COMMITTEE
1501 Cherry St.
Philadelphia, PA 19102
215-241-7000

KEY TERMS

CHAPTER SUMMARY

1 Foreign policy includes national goals and the techniques used to achieve them. National security policy, which is one aspect of foreign policy, is designed to protect the independence and the political and economic integrity of the United States. Diplomacy involves the nation's external relationships and is an attempt to resolve conflict without resort to arms. Sometimes U.S. foreign policy is based on moral idealism. At other times, U.S. policies stem from political realism.

2 The formal power of the president to make foreign policy derives from the U.S. Constitution, which makes the president responsible for the preservation of national security and designates the president as commander in chief of the army and navy. Presidents have interpreted this authority broadly. They also have the power to make treaties and executive agreements. In principle, the State Department is the executive agency most directly involved with foreign affairs. The National Security Council (NSC) advises the president on the integration of "domestic, foreign, and military policies relating to the national security." The intelligence community consists of forty or more government agencies engaged in intelligence activities varying from information gathering to covert actions. In response to presidential actions in the Vietnam War, Congress attempted to establish some limits on the power of the president in foreign policy by passing the War Powers Act in 1973.

3 Three major themes have guided U.S. foreign policy. In the early years of the nation, isolationism was the primary focus. With the start of the twentieth century, this view gave way to global involvement. From the end of World War II through the 1980s, the major goal was to contain communism and the influence of the Soviet Union.

4 During the 1700s and 1800s, the United States had little international power and generally stayed out of European conflicts and politics. The nineteenth century has been called the period of isolationism. The Monroe Doctrine of 1823 stated that the United States would not accept foreign intervention in the Western Hemisphere and would not meddle in European affairs. The United States pursued an actively expansionist policy in the Americas and the Pacific area during the nineteenth century, however.

5 The end of the policy of isolationism toward Europe started with the Spanish-American War of 1898. U.S. entanglement in European politics became more extensive when the United States entered World War I on April 6, 1917. World War II marked a lasting change in American foreign policy. The United States was the only major country to emerge from the war with its economy intact and the only country with operating nuclear weapons.

6 Soon after the close of World War II, the uncomfortable alliance between the United States and the Soviet Union ended, and the Cold War began. A policy of containment, which assumed an expansionist Soviet Union, was enunciated in the Truman Doctrine. Following the frustrations of the Vietnam War and the apparent arms equality of the United States and the Soviet Union, the United States was ready for détente. As the arms race escalated, arms control became a major foreign policy issue. Although President Ronald Reagan established a tough stance toward the Soviet Union in the first term of his administration, the second term saw serious negotiations toward arms reduction, culminating with the signing of the Intermediate-Range Nuclear Force Treaty at the Moscow summit in 1988. Negotiations toward further arms reduction continued in the Bush administration. The Strategic Arms Reduction Treaty, which limited long-range nuclear missiles, was signed in 1992 with Russia and several other states of the former Soviet Union.

7 Nuclear proliferation continues to be an issue due to the breakup of the Soviet Union and the loss of control over its nuclear arsenal, along with the continued efforts of other nations to gain nuclear warheads. The number of warheads is known to be nearly twenty thousand.

8 Ethnic tensions and political instability in many regions of the world provide challenges to the United States. The nations of Central America and the Caribbean, including Haiti, require American attention because of their proximity. Negotiations have brought agreement in the Middle East and South Africa, whereas civil wars have torn apart Rwanda and Yugoslavia.

9 The United States is dependent on the world economy, as shown by the vulnerability of its stock market to world forces, its status as a debtor nation, and its significant trade deficit. The effects of a united Europe on world trade are yet to be fully realized.

QUESTIONS FOR REVIEW AND DISCUSSION

❶ Without a clear enemy to confront, should the United States play an active role in the world? What advantages and disadvantages might accompany a return to isolationism?

❷ Traditionally, the State Department has focused on diplomacy and on representing U.S. interests abroad, whereas the Defense Department has planned strategy for war. Should the State Department play a larger role in a post–Cold War world? Should the Treasury and Commerce Departments be more important in foreign policy decisions than they have been in recent decades?

❸ As one of the founders of the United Nations and a permanent member of the Security Council, should the United States welcome the United Nation's expanded efforts in peacekeeping? Can you think of instances in which UN efforts might contradict the interests of the United States? To what extent should the United States support UN peacekeepers?

❹ What are the interests of the United States today in world affairs? Identify three or four goals that you believe should be pursued by American diplomats and leaders. Why are those goals important to ordinary citizens? Which institutions of government must work to achieve those goals?

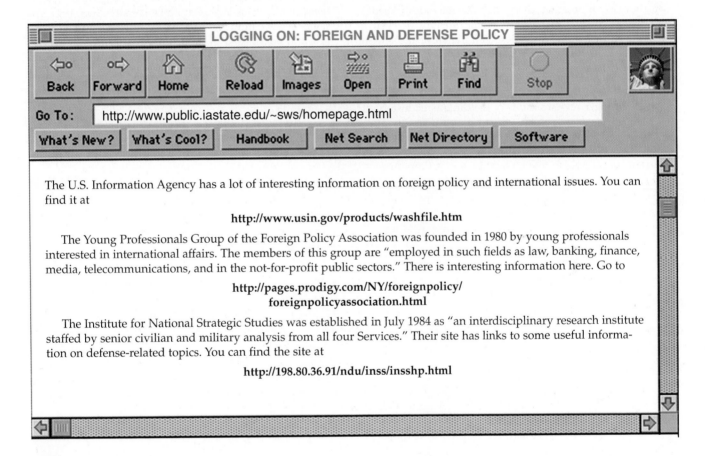

LOGGING ON: FOREIGN AND DEFENSE POLICY

Go To: http://www.public.iastate.edu/~sws/homepage.html

The U.S. Information Agency has a lot of interesting information on foreign policy and international issues. You can find it at

http://www.usin.gov/products/washfile.htm

The Young Professionals Group of the Foreign Policy Association was founded in 1980 by young professionals interested in international affairs. The members of this group are "employed in such fields as law, banking, finance, media, telecommunications, and in the not-for-profit public sectors." There is interesting information here. Go to

**http://pages.prodigy.com/NY/foreignpolicy/
foreignpolicyassociation.html**

The Institute for National Strategic Studies was established in July 1984 as "an interdisciplinary research institute staffed by senior civilian and military analysis from all four Services." Their site has links to some useful information on defense-related topics. You can find the site at

http://198.80.36.91/ndu/inss/insshp.html

SELECTED REFERENCES

Allison, Graham, and Gregory F. Treverton, eds. *Rethinking America's Security: Beyond the Cold War to New World Order.* New York: Norton, 1992. This book, which was sponsored by the American Assembly and the Council on Foreign Relations, brings together the insights of leading experts on foreign policy and provides in-depth scrutiny of national security in the post–Cold War period.

Clarke, Jonathan, and James Clad. *After the Crusade: American Foreign Policy for the Post–Superpower Age.* Lanham, Md.: University Press of America, 1995. In this volume, the authors examine the future of U.S. foreign relations and suggest that American elites should rethink their vision of the world.

Clinton, W. David. *The Two Faces of National Interest.* Baton Rouge: Louisiana State University Press, 1994. The concept of national interest is examined in this volume in the context of four major crisis points in the twentieth century. The author finds that this concept can be helpful in choosing foreign policy directions.

Diehl, Paul F. *International Peacekeeping.* Baltimore, MD.: Johns Hopkins University Press, 1996. The author investigates the successes and failures of peacekeeping expeditions.

Durch, William J., ed. *The Evolution of UN Peacekeeping.* New York: St. Martin's Press, 1993. A collection of essays that discuss UN peacekeeping operations on different continents.

Gottlieb, Gideon. *Nation against State: A New Approach to Ethnic Conflicts and the Decline of Sovereignty.* New York: Council on Foreign Relations, 1993. Gottlieb explores the conflicts that arise when ethnic groups or nationalities demand physical territory to support their community. He reminds the reader that it is possible to have an ethnic identity or even a nation—for example, the Palestinian nation or the Jewish nation—without having the boundaries of a legally sovereign state.

Kissinger, Henry. *Diplomacy.* New York: Simon & Schuster, 1994. Kissinger reviews much of the diplomatic history of the nineteenth century to provide a foundation for understanding America's twentieth-century foreign policy dilemmas. He remains committed to the national interest and to using national power in politics to create a more stable world.

Klare, Michael. *Rogue State and Nuclear Outlaws: America's Search for a Foreign Policy.* New York: Hill and Wang, 1995. The author concludes that the American military may have exaggerated the threat of nuclear terrorism and lost nuclear materials to inflate the defense budget.

Miller, Judith. *God Has Ninety-Nine Names: Reporting from a Militant Middle East.* New York: Simon & Schuster, 1996. A journalist provides a lucid account of the forces at work in the Arab world of the Middle East and offers special insights into the possibilities there for terrorism and for accord.

Moynihan, Daniel Patrick. *Pandaemonium: Ethnicity in International Politics.* New York: Oxford University Press, 1993. The senior senator from New York discusses the rise of ethnicity in world politics and the difficulty of both encouraging ethnic groups to retain their separate identities and cultures and discouraging ethnic violence.

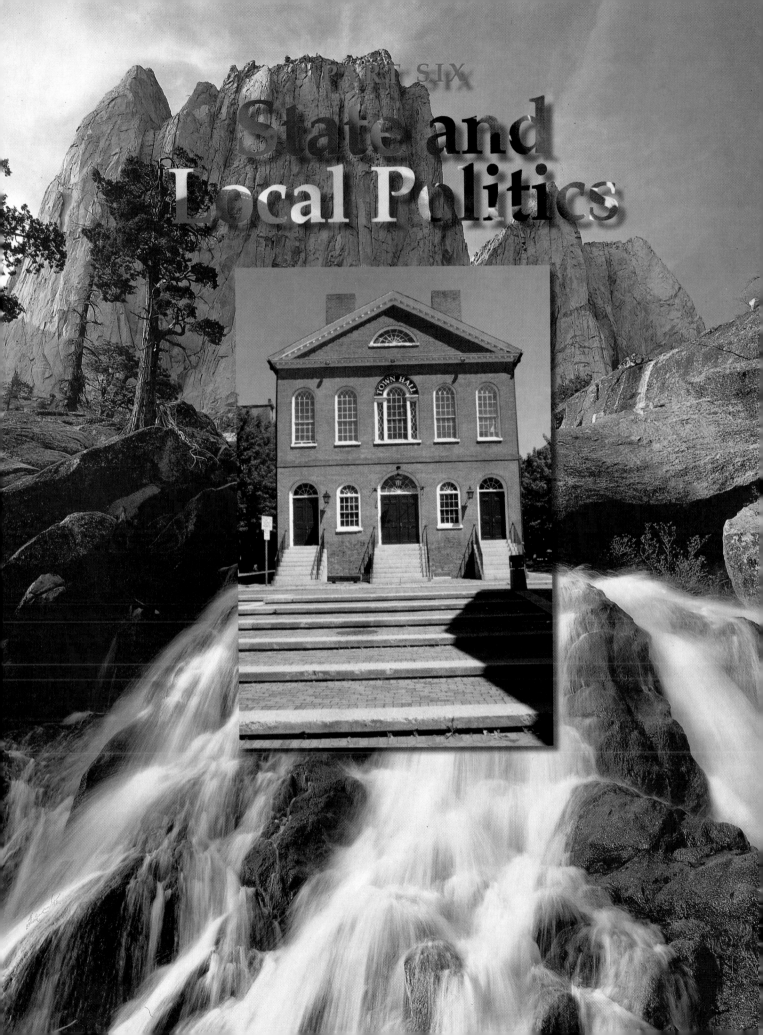

TOWN HALL

19
State and Local Government

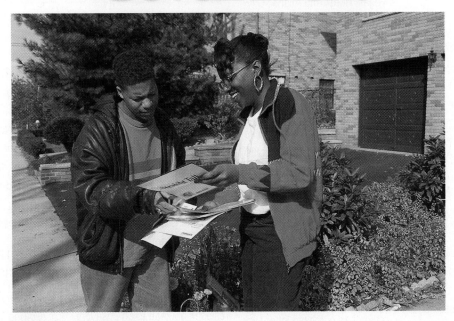

CHAPTER OUTLINE

⭐ State and Local Government Spending

⭐ Paying for State and Local Government

⭐ The U.S. Constitution and the States

⭐ State Constitutions

⭐ The State Executive Branch

⭐ The State Legislature

⭐ The State Judiciary

⭐ How Local Government Operates

All States Allowed Gambling?

BACKGROUND

IN THE UNITED STATES TODAY, ALL BUT A FEW STATES HAVE SOME FORM OF LEGALIZED GAMBLING. IN 1931, LAS VEGAS AND RENO LEGALIZED FULL CASINO GAMBLING—ROULETTE, DICE, CARD GAMES, AND SO ON. ATLANTIC CITY, NEW JERSEY, LEGALIZED CASINO GAMBLING IN 1978. BY 1997, CASINO GAMBLING HAD BEEN LEGALIZED IN MISSISSIPPI, SOUTH DAKOTA, AND SEVERAL OTHER STATES, AS WELL AS ON NUMEROUS NATIVE AMERICAN RESERVATIONS. IOWA HAD ALSO LEGALIZED GAMBLING ON MISSISSIPPI RIVER BOATS. ADDITIONALLY, TODAY THIRTY-SIX STATES HAVE SOME FORM OF STATE LOTTERY, OFTEN WITH A PART OF THE PROCEEDS GOING TO FUND EDUCATION. BY 1997, THESE PROCEEDS TOTALED ABOUT $32 BILLION.

WHAT IF GAMBLING WERE LEGALIZED IN ALL OF THE STATES?

Assume for a moment that every state legislature passed a law allowing legalized gambling. No longer would the cities of Las Vegas, Reno, and Atlantic City be "the only game in town." Casinos undoubtedly would crop up just about everywhere, including Miami Beach, downtown Chicago, New York City, Los Angeles, and Dallas.

To the extent that the states and municipalities taxed profits made from legalized gambling, by institutions as well as individuals, state and local tax revenues certainly would increase. The "take" from state lotteries, though, might decline. Those with an urge to gamble might decide to gamble at casinos rather than purchase lottery tickets. States that currently obtain revenues from race tracks, dog tracks, and the like also might find their revenues falling. Betting on horses certainly would not disappear if gambling were legalized everywhere, but the amount of such betting probably would fall.

A REDUCTION IN ORGANIZED CRIME?

In major cities, organized crime purportedly runs the illegal "numbers" games, as well as illegal "bookie" operations that allow for betting on sporting events and horse races. If all of the states legalized gambling, the public's desire to engage in illegal gambling might diminish considerably. Only to the extent that illegal gambling operations offered a higher probability of winning would such operations continue to exist. In any event, we can be fairly certain that organized crime would lose a valuable income source if gambling were legalized everywhere.

QUALITY OF LIFE ISSUES

One of the reasons that voters, when asked, have often turned down initiatives to legalize casino gambling is that they worry about changes in the quality of life. In particular, they fear that the concentration of gambling establishments in particular areas of their cities might lead to an unsavory environment that would encourage an increase in Mafia-type involvement in those areas. Additionally, people who have voted against casino gambling typically fear that legalized gambling would lead breadwinners to renege on their family financial responsibilities because of the lure of "striking it rich" in the casinos.

There is no way to predict with certainty what the societal outcomes of legalized gambling would be. The outcomes perhaps would depend on the extent to which each state would regulate gambling operations within its borders. If limits were placed on the location, number, and size of casinos, perhaps there would be little change in the social fabric of each state. No matter how legalized gambling would be regulated, though, one thing is certain—the Native American tribes that currently are earning tens of millions of dollars a year would be affected seriously. Their current riches probably would dwindle significantly.

FOR CRITICAL ANALYSIS

1. *What is the argument in favor of allowing legalized state lotteries but no other forms of legalized gambling?*
2. *If all states except one were to legalize gambling, how would that single state be affected by being the only one without legalized gambling?*

As you read in this chapter's *What If . . .* , it is up to the individual states to determine whether to legalize gambling. There is no federal law that determines the issue, at least not yet. Within each state, even if a law allowing gambling was passed, local restrictions could prevent legalized gambling. The reason is that the states and cities are separate political units within the United States.

Indeed, the United States has more than eighty thousand separate governmental units—more than do most other countries in the world. As discussed in Chapter 1, under the political doctrine of pluralism, different groups that are autonomous actively compete in the decision-making processes for the use of resources in the country. But having more than eighty thousand separate governmental units goes beyond any concept of pluralism and enters into the realm of **hyperpluralism,** in which authority is so fragmented that nothing gets done. The reality is that when people think of government, they are usually thinking of an agency or a set of individuals who work for one of those eighty thousand separate government units; they are not thinking about the federal government or the state governments. Most individuals come in contact with government workers only at the local levels.

By the time you read this text, more than twenty million U.S. civilians will be working directly for state and local governmental units. Millions of others work indirectly for such governments. Therefore, just from a practical point of view, knowing how these governments operate is relevant for every citizen.

STATE AND LOCAL GOVERNMENT SPENDING

Examining the spending habits of a household often gives relevant information about the personalities and priorities of the household members. Examination of the expenditure patterns of state and local governments likewise can be illuminating. Table 19–1 shows state expenditures for the latest fiscal year for which data are available. Table 19–2 on the following page shows the same data for local governments. There is a clear-cut pattern. State and city expenditures are concentrated in the areas of education, public welfare, highways, health, and police protection. Education is the biggest category of expenditure, particularly at the local level. Contrast this expenditure pattern with that of the federal government, which allocates only about 4 percent of its budget to education. (For a discussion of how some local governments are reducing their costs, see the feature entitled *Politics and Economics: Competition for Municipal Services.*)

PAYING FOR STATE AND LOCAL GOVERNMENT

In 1996, state and local expenditures totaled about $1 trillion. These expenditures had to be paid for somehow. Until the twentieth century, almost all state and local expenditures were paid for by state and local revenues raised within state borders. Starting in the twentieth century, however, federal grants to state and local governmental units began to pay some of these costs. In 1902, federal grants to state and local governments accounted for 0.7 percent of state and local revenues. By 1996, they accounted for 24 percent.

State and local governments generally are very willing to accept federal money. Indeed, they have entire staffs that devote all of their time to obtaining federal grants. For obvious reasons, politicians usually prefer to obtain money through federal, rather than direct state or local, taxation.

HYPERPLURALISM

An extreme form of pluralism in which government is so decentralized and authority so fragmented that it does not get much accomplished.

Table 19–1

State Expenditures (in percentages)

EXPENDITURE	PERCENTAGE
Education	26.66
Public welfare	21.04
Highways	15.51
Health and hospitals	10.28
Interest on general debt	4.32
Natural resources	3.80
Corrections	2.46
Financial administration	2.03
General control	1.67
Social insurance administration	1.63
Police	1.48
General public building	.59
Air transportation	.30
Housing and urban renewal	.28
Water transport and terminals	.24
Libraries	.10
Other	7.61

SOURCE: Tax Foundation, *Facts and Figures on Government Finance, 1996.*

POLITICS AND ECONOMICS
Competition for Municipal Services

As municipalities search for ways to reduce expenses without reducing services, many have experimented with "contracting out." Contracting out involves asking for bids from the private sector to perform municipal services. Municipalities have contracted out for garbage collection, fire protection, street cleaning, and the like. In some instances, simply asking for bids from private firms for a particular municipally provided service can save a city money.

Consider the example of Flint, Michigan. When the mayor of that city, Woodrow Stanley, decided to contract out for garbage collection, the

city received five private company bids. By contracting out, the city could have saved $2 million out of a $6.2 million annual budget, or almost one-third. Rather than lose city garbage-collection jobs, the municipality's public sector unions offered to reduce the city's expenditures on garbage collection by $1.5 million a year. The unions agreed to increase the number of stops on each garbage-collection route, reduce the number of shifts, and reduce the number of staff.

The experience of Flint, Michigan, is mirrored in Indianapolis, where the Transportation Department has to compete with private companies for

its services. Indianapolis claims to be saving $28 million a year. Philadelphia has done the same thing for its waste water treatment. Phoenix has done so for a whole range of city-provided activities. Clearly, the concept of competition for municipal services is growing in popularity.

For Critical Analysis

Do you think that city residents are concerned about whether services for residents are performed by the public sector or the private sector? What, if anything, would residents stand to lose from the contracting out of services?

GENERAL SALES TAX

A tax levied as a proportion of the retail price of a commodity at the point of sale.

PROPERTY TAX

A tax on the value of real estate. This tax is limited to state and local governments and is a particularly important source of revenue for local governments.

Table 19–2

Local Expenditures (in percentages)

EXPENDITURE	PERCENTAGE
Education	44.88
Public welfare	7.06
Health and hospitals	6.78
Highways	5.66
Police	5.08
Interest on general debt	3.84
Sewerage	3.72
General control	2.58
Fire protection	2.44
Parks and recreation	2.42
Housing and urban renewal	1.80
Sanitation (other than sewerage)	1.44
Financial administration	1.26
General public building	1.25
Corrections	.89
Air transportation	.76
Libraries	.72
Natural resources	.64
Water transport and terminals	.30
Parking facilities	.21
Other	6.27

SOURCE: Tax Foundation, *Facts and Figures on Government Finance*, 1996.

Tax Revenue

Figure 19–1(a) shows the percentages of taxes in various categories raised by state governments, and Figure 19–1(b) gives the same information for local governments. By far the most important tax at the state level is the **general sales tax** and at the local level, the **property tax.** Whereas the federal government obtains 42 percent of its total revenues from the personal income tax, states obtain only about 17 percent in this way. In 1996, there were still six states that did not have a personal income tax. Other taxes assessed by states include corporate income taxes and fees, permits, and licenses at both the state and local governmental level, as well as inheritance and gift taxes at the state level. Generally, the types of taxes that states levy vary widely from state to state.

A tremendous amount of variation also exists in the total amounts of state and local taxes collected. Look at the table in this chapter's *Politics and the Fifty States.* This table shows that among the states receiving the highest amounts in tax revenues are Alaska, New York, and the District of Columbia. Those levying the lowest taxes are Arkansas, Mississippi, and Alabama.

Nontax Revenue

Nontax revenue includes funds granted to state and local governments and transfer payments by the federal government. These funds provide nearly 15 percent of state and local government income. The grants are not always without "strings," however. Federal programs in such areas as education, highway construction, health care, and law enforcement may dispense cash subject to certain conditions. For example, the funds may be used only for a specific purpose or only if matching funds are contributed.

Profits generated by publicly operated businesses are another source of revenue for state and local governments. Publicly operated businesses

POLITICS AND THE FIFTY STATES
Total State and Local Tax Collections, Per Capita

As you can see from the table, state and local taxation varies significantly from one state to another. Note that Alaska's tax collections per capita are more than three times those of Mississippi.

For Critical Analysis
What factors might explain the variations in state and local tax levies?

Alaska	$3,604.68	Pennsylvania	1,627.48
District of Columbia	3,339.28	Oregon	1,602.24
New York	2,934.04	Ohio	1,568.54
Connecticut	2,280.78	Nebraska	1,557.47
Hawaii	2,258.58	Montana	1,538.27
New Jersey	2,216.86	Florida	1,521.96
Massachusetts	2,160.26	Texas	1,495.50
Maryland	2,092.82	North Carolina	1,494.72
Minnesota	2,076.44	Georgia	1,491.00
Wyoming	2,045.97	New Mexico	1,472.07
California	1,948.47	New Hampshire	1,471.99
Wisconsin	1,888.76	Utah	1,459.64
Michigan	1,883.92	Indiana	1,440.97
Vermont	1,863.31	Oklahoma	1,402.07
Delaware	1,853.54	North Dakota	1,389.22
Rhode Island	1,837.34	Missouri	1,371.54
Maine	1,831.72	South Carolina	1,337.37
Washington	1,782.68	Louisiana	1,328.70
Illinois	1,781.69	South Dakota	1,321.09
U.S. average	**1,772.43**	Kentucky	1,271.00
Arizona	1,690.47	Idaho	1,259.92
Virginia	1,686.85	Tennessee	1,242.08
Colorado	1,685.61	West Virginia	1,211.75
Kansas	1,676.27	Alabama	1,141.58
Iowa	1,656.85	Arkansas	1,112.56
Nevada	1,655.37	Mississippi	1,087.73

SOURCE: Taxpayers' Federation of Illinois.

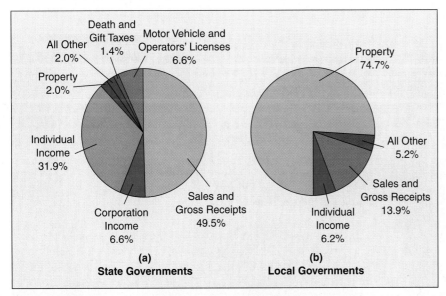

(a) **State Governments**

Death and Gift Taxes 1.4%
All Other 2.0%
Property 2.0%
Motor Vehicle and Operators' Licenses 6.6%
Individual Income 31.9%
Corporation Income 6.6%
Sales and Gross Receipts 49.5%

(b) **Local Governments**

Property 74.7%
All Other 5.2%
Sales and Gross Receipts 13.9%
Individual Income 6.2%

SOURCE: Council of State Governments, *Book of the States, 1996–1997*.

Figure 19–1
• • • • • • • • • • • • • • •
Taxes Raised by State and Local Governments

States generally are dependent on sales taxes, whereas towns and cities depend on property taxes.

include toll roads and bridges, as well as water, electric power, and mass transportation systems. More than a third of the states sell liquor through state-operated stores that earn profits. Other state-operated businesses include Washington's ferries and North Dakota's commercial banks. Some states receive lease payments for public lands, and some cities rent space in publicly owned buildings.

Other nontax revenue sources include court fines and interest on loans and investments. In the 1980s, state-run lotteries became an increasingly popular way to raise money. By 1997, nearly two-thirds of the states and the District of Columbia sponsored lotteries. It is expected that the rest of the states will follow.

Fiscal Policy Lessons

In the 1980s, when state budgets more than doubled, most states tried to close the gap between state income and spending by raising taxes. Many of these states continued this policy into the early 1990s. The states that approved the largest tax increases in the early 1990s, however, also approved the greatest increases in spending.

By 1994, it became clear that states attempting to reduce their budget deficits by increasing taxes were not especially successful at lowering those deficits. In fact, many states actually harmed, rather than helped, their states' economies. This was the lesson learned by such states as California, Connecticut, New Jersey, Pennsylvania, and Rhode Island.

At the same time, states such as Massachusetts, Michigan, Mississippi, and Virginia attempted to balance their budgets by cutting spending instead of raising taxes. This policy proved more successful, resulting in balanced budgets and improved state economies. By the mid-1990s, many of these states were proposing state tax cuts to encourage the development of business and further improve their local economies.

As states entered the second half of the 1990s, the following states had budget surpluses of half a billion dollars or more: Arizona, California, Indiana, Minnesota, North Carolina, South Carolina, Texas, and Washington. Not surprisingly, cries for state tax cuts were heard throughout the nation. Look at Table 19–3. There you see the significant state tax cuts that were enacted for fiscal year 1996. In all, twenty-one states cut taxes. While the tax cuts gener-

Public education is one of the primary functions of state and local government. In recent years, a number of states have begun school-reform efforts, often delegating more control over local schools to parents and to the community.

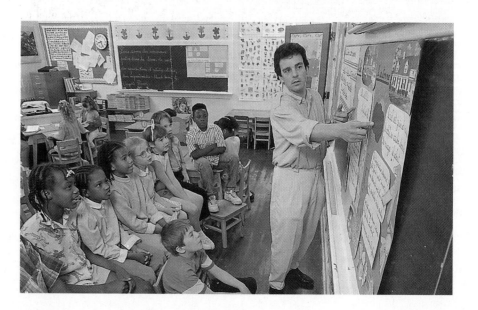

ally did not represent major reductions in general state revenues, they did indicate a change in the trend toward ever-increasing taxes.

THE U.S. CONSTITUTION AND THE STATES

We live in a federal system in which there are fifty separate state governments and one national government. The U.S. Constitution reserves a broad range of powers for state governments. It also prohibits state governments from engaging in certain activities. The U.S. Constitution does not say explicitly what the states actually may do. Rather, state powers are simply reserved, or residual: States may do anything that is not prohibited by the Constitution or anything that is not expressly within the realm of the national government.

The major reserved powers of the states are the powers to tax, spend, and regulate intrastate commerce, or commerce within a given state. The states also have general **police power,** meaning they can impose their will on their citizens in the areas of safety (through, say, traffic laws), health (immunizations), welfare (child-abuse laws), and morals (regulation of pornographic materials).

Restrictions on state and local governmental activity are implied by the Constitution in Article VI, Paragraph 2:

> This Constitution, and the Laws of the United States which shall be made in Pursuance thereof; and all Treaties made, or which shall be made, under the Authority of the United States, shall be the supreme Law of the Land; and the Judges in every State shall be bound thereby, any Thing in the Constitution or Laws of any State to the Contrary notwithstanding.

In other words, it is the U.S. Constitution that is the supreme law of the land. No state or local law can be in conflict with the Constitution, with laws made by the national Congress, or with treaties entered into by the national government. Judicially, the United States Supreme Court has been the final arbiter of conflicts arising between the national government and state governments.

STATE CONSTITUTIONS

The U.S. Constitution is a model of brevity, although at the cost of specificity. State constitutions, however, typically are excessively long and detailed. The U.S. Constitution has endured for two hundred years and has been amended only twenty-seven times. State constitutions are another matter. Louisiana has had eleven constitutions; Georgia, nine; South Carolina, seven; and Alabama, Florida, and Virginia, six. The number of amendments that have been submitted to voters borders on the absurd. For example, by 1997, the citizens of Alabama had been asked to approve over 650 amendments—of which they adopted over 450.

Why Are State Constitutions So Long?

According to historians, the length and mass of detail of many state constitutions reflect the loss of popular confidence in state legislatures between the end of the Civil War and the early 1900s. During that period, forty-two states adopted or revised their constitutions. Those constitutions adopted before or after that period are shorter and contain fewer restrictions on the powers of state legislatures. Another equally important reason for the length and detail of state constitutions is that state constitution makers apparently have had a difficult time distinguishing between constitutional and statutory law. Does

POLICE POWER

Authority to promote and safeguard the health, morals, safety, and welfare of the people.

Table 19–3

Selected State Tax Cuts for Fiscal Year 1996

STATE	AS % OF GENERAL REVENUE	IN MILLIONS
Kansas	3.3%	$191.7
North Carolina	2.5	410.1
Arizona	2.3	200.0
Utah	2.0	90.0
Indiana*	2.0	266.5
Connecticut†	1.8	200.0
Wisconsin	1.7	230.0
Washington†	1.6	236.1
Idaho	1.5	42.2
Iowa	1.3	92.9
New Jersey	1.2	284.0
Michigan	1.2	283.6
New York	0.9	575.0
Delaware	0.7	18.9
Pennsylvania	0.7	215.9
New Mexico	0.5	27.3
Montana	0.5	12.1
Kentucky	0.4	34.0
Illinois	0.4	103.0
Maryland	0.1	13.0
Nebraska	0.1	1.9

*Enacted tax cut figure is for FY 1997.
†Multi-year figure was divided by number of years.

SOURCE: *In the States: Everything's Comin Up Supply Side,* A. B. Laffer, V. A. Canto & Associates.

The Massachusetts gun law is an example of the police power of the states. Other powers reserved to the states under the U.S. Constitution include taxing, spending, and regulatory powers.

the Louisiana constitution need an amendment to declare Huey Long's birthday a legal holiday? Is it necessary for the constitution of South Dakota to authorize a cordage and twine plant at the state penitentiary? Does Article XX of the California constitution need to discuss the tax-exempt status of the Huntington Library and Art gallery? The U.S. Constitution contains no such details. It leaves to the legislature the nuts-and-bolts activity of making specific statutory laws.

In all fairness to the states, their courts do not interpret their constitutions as freely as the United States Supreme Court interprets the U.S. Constitution. Therefore, the states feel compelled to be more specific in their own constitutions. Additionally, the framers of state constitutions may feel compelled to fill in the gaps left by the very brief federal constitution.

The Constitutional Convention and the Constitutional Initiative

Two of the several ways to effect constitutional changes are the state constitutional convention and the constitutional initiative. As of 1997, over 230 state constitutional conventions had been used to write an entirely new constitution or to attempt to amend an existing one. A major feature of the constitutions of seventeen states is the **constitutional initiative**.[1] An initiative allows citizens to place a proposed amendment on the ballot without calling a constitutional convention. The number of signatures required to get a constitutional initiative on the ballot varies from state to state; it is usually between 5 and 10 percent of the total number of votes cast for governor in the last elec-

CONSTITUTIONAL INITIATIVE

An electoral device whereby citizens can propose a constitutional amendment through petitions signed by the required number of registered voters.

---

[1]These states are Arizona, Arkansas, California, Colorado, Florida, Illinois, Massachusetts, Michigan, Missouri, Montana, Nebraska, Nevada, North Dakota, Ohio, Oklahoma, Oregon, and South Dakota.

tion. The initiative process has been used most frequently in California and Oregon. Relatively few initiative amendments are approved by the electorate.

THE STATE EXECUTIVE BRANCH

All state governments in the United States have executive, legislative, and judicial branches. Here the similarity ends. State governments do not always have strong executive branches. Additionally, in some states citizens can initiate legislation.

A Weak Executive

During the colonial period, governors were appointed by the Crown and had the power to call the colonial assembly (the colonial legislative body) into session, recommend legislation, exercise veto power, and dissolve the assembly. The colonial governor acted as commander in chief of each colony's military forces, and the governor was head of the judiciary.

Not surprisingly, the colonies' revolt against English rule centered on the all-powerful colonial governors. When the first states were formed after the Declaration of Independence, hostility toward the governor's office ensured a weak executive branch and an extremely strong legislative branch. By the 1830s, however, the state executive office had become more important. Since Andrew Jackson's presidency, all governors (except in South Carolina) have been elected directly by the people. Simultaneously, there was an effort to democratize state government by popularly electing other state government officials as well.

Under the tenets of Jacksonian democracy, the more public officials who are elected (and not appointed), the more democratic (and better) the system will be. The adoption of the long ballot (see Chapter 10) was a result of applying these tenets. Even today, some states have numerous state offices with independently elected officials. Michigan, for example, has thirty-six. There is a problem with the long ballot, however. The direct election of so many executive officials means it is likely that no one will have much power, because each official is working to secure his or her own political support. Only if the elected officials happen to be able to work together cohesively can they get much done.

A slight majority of the states require that the candidates for governor and lieutenant governor run for election as a team. In some states where this is not required, however, the voters have at times chosen a governor from one political party and a lieutenant governor from another. One result may be to make the governor unwilling to leave the state in order to keep the lieutenant governor from exerting power during his or her travels.

Reforming the System

Most states follow the practice of electing numerous executive officials. Nonetheless, governors have exercised the authority of their office with increasing frequency in recent years. Governors have become a significant force in legislative policymaking. The governor, in theory, enjoys the same advantage that the president has over Congress in his or her ability to make policy decisions and to embody these in a program on which the state legislative body can act. How the governor exercises this ability often depends on his or her powers of persuasion. A strong personality can make for a strong executive office. Personal skill, the strength of political parties and special interest groups, and the governor's use of the media can affect how much actual power he or she has.

Reorganization of the state executive branch to achieve greater efficiency has been attempted numerous times and in many states. There are many obstacles to reorganizing state executive branches. Voters do not want to lose their ability to influence politics directly. Both the voters and the legislators fear that reorganization will concentrate too much authority in the hands of the governor. Finally, many believe that numerous governmental functions, such as control of the highway program, should remain administrative rather than political.

Despite the fragmentation of executive power and doubts about the concentration of power in an executive's hands, the trend toward modernization has increased the powers of many of the states' highest executives. Based on a governor's ability to make major appointments, formulate a state budget, veto legislation, and exercise other powers, the National Governors Association ranks the governors of twenty-five states as powerful or very powerful executives. Only eleven states are assessed as giving their executives little or very little power.

The Governor's Veto Power

The veto power gives the president of the United States immense leverage. Simply the threat of a presidential veto often means that legislation will not be passed by Congress. In some states, governors have strong veto power, but in other states, governors have no veto power at all. Some states give the governor veto power but allow only five days in which to exercise it. Thirteen states give the governor a pocket veto power (see Chapter 13).

ITEM VETO

The power exercised by the governors of most states to veto particular sections or items of an appropriations bill, while signing the remainder of the bill into law.

In forty-three states, the governor has some form of **item veto** power on appropriations. If the governor in such a state does not particularly like one item, or line, in an appropriations bill, he or she can veto that item. In twelve states, the governor can reduce the amount of the appropriation but cannot reduce it to zero. Nineteen states give governors the ability to use the item veto on more than just appropriations.

THE STATE LEGISLATURE

Although there has been a move in recent years to increase the power of governors, state legislatures are still an important force in state politics and state governmental decision making. The task of these assemblies is to legislate on such matters as taxes and the regulation of business and commerce, highways, school systems and the funding of education, and welfare payments. Allocation of funds and program priorities are vital issues to local residents and communities, and conflicts between regions within the state or between the cities and the rural areas are common.

State legislatures have been criticized for being unprofessional and less than effective. It is true that state legislatures sometimes spend their time considering trivial legislation (such as the official state pie in Florida), and lobbyists often have too much influence in state capitals. At the same time, state legislators are often given few resources with which to work. In many states, legislatures are limited to meeting only part of the year, and in some the pay is a disincentive to real service. In at least eight states, state legislators are paid less than $10,000 per year. A complete list of state legislators' salaries, as well as other characteristics of state legislatures, is given in Table 19–4.

Table 19–4

Characteristics of State Legislatures

	SEATS IN SENATE	LENGTH OF TERM	SEATS IN HOUSE	LENGTH OF TERM	YEARS SESSIONS ARE HELD	SALARY*
Alabama	35	4	105	4	Annual	$10(d)†
Alaska	20	4	40	2	Annual	24,012†
Arizona	30	2	60	2	Annual	15,000
Arkansas	35	4	100	2	Odd	12,500†
California	40	4	80	2	Even	72,000†
Colorado	35	4	65	2	Annual	17,500
Connecticut	36	2	151	2	Annual	16,760†
Delaware	21	4	41	2	Annual	26,000†
Florida	40	4	120	2	Annual	23,244†
Georgia	56	2	180	2	Annual	10,854†
Hawaii	25	4	51	2	Annual	32,000†
Idaho	35	2	70	2	Annual	12,360†
Illinois	59	—†	118	2	Annual	42,265†
Indiana	50	4	100	2	Annual	11,600†
Iowa	50	4	100	2	Annual	18,800
Kansas	40	4	125	2	Annual	63(d)†
Kentucky	38	4	100	2	Even	100(d)†
Louisiana	39	4	105	4	Annual	16,800†
Maine	35	2	151	2	Even	9,975§
Maryland	47	4	141	4	Annual	28,840†
Massachusetts	40	2	160	2	Annual	46,410†
Michigan	38	4	110	2	Annual	49,155†
Minnesota	67	4	134	2	Odd	29,675†
Mississippi	52	4	122	4	Annual	10,000†
Missouri	34	4	163	2	Annual	24,313
Montana	50	—‡	100	2	Odd	57.06(d)†
Nebraska"	49	4	—	—	Annual	12,000†
Nevada	21	4	42	2	Odd	130(d)†
New Hampshire	24	2	400	2	Annual	200(b)
New Jersey	40	—‡	80	2	Annual	35,000
New Mexico	42	4	70	2	Annual	—†
New York	61	2	150	2	Annual	57,500†
North Carolina	50	2	120	2	Odd	13,951†
North Dakota	49	4	98	2	Odd	90(d)†
Ohio	33	4	99	2	Annual	42,427
Oklahoma	48	4	101	2	Annual	32,000†
Oregon	30	4	60	2	Odd	—†
Pennsylvania	50	4	203	2	Annual	47,000†
Rhode Island	50	2	100	2	Annual	5(d)
South Carolina	46	4	124	2	Annual	10,400†
South Dakota	35	2	70	2	Annual	4,267#
Tennessee	33	4	99	2	Odd	16,500†
Texas	31	4	150	2	Odd	7,200†
Utah	29	4	75	2	Annual	85(d)†
Vermont	30	2	150	2	Odd	480†
Virginia	40	4	100	2	Annual	18,000†
Washington	49	4	98	2	Annual	25,900†
West Virginia	34	4	100	2	Annual	15,000
Wisconsin	33	4	99	2	Annual	38,056†
Wyoming	30	4	60	2	Annual	125(d)†

*Salaries annual unless otherwise noted as (d)—per day, (b)—biennium, or (w)—per week.
†Plus per diem living expenses.
‡Terms vary from two to four years.
§For odd year; $7,500 for even year.
"Unicameral legislature.
#For odd year; $3,733 for even year.

SOURCE: Adapted from Council of State Governments, *Book of the States, 1996–1997.*

We have seen earlier how a bill becomes a law in the U.S. Congress. A similar process occurs at the state level. Figure 19–2 traces how a bill becomes a law in the Florida legislature. Similar steps are followed in other states (note that Nebraska has a unicameral legislature, however, so there is no second chamber process).

Legislative Apportionment

Drawing up legislative districts—state as well as federal—has long been subject to gerrymandering—creative cartography designed to guarantee that one political party maintains control of a particular voting district. Malapportionment is the skewed distribution of voters in a state's legislative districts. The United States Supreme Court indicated in 1962 that malapportioned state legislatures violate the equal protection clause of the Fourteenth Amendment.[2] In a series of cases that followed, the Court held that legislative districts must be as nearly equal as possible in terms of population, and the grossest examples of state legislative malapportionment were eliminated.[3] The Burger Court, however, allowed "benevolent, bipartisan gerrymandering" in certain states. Indeed, in 1977, the Supreme Court held that the state had an obligation imposed under the 1965 Voting Rights Act to draw district boundaries to maximize minority legislative representation.[4] Thus, each decade, state and

[2]*Baker v. Carr*, 369 U.S. 186 (1962).
[3]*Reynolds v. Sims*, 377 U.S. 533 (1964), and other cases.
[4]*United Jewish Organizations of Williamsburg v. Cary*, 430 U.S. 144 (1977).

Figure 19–2
● ●
How an Idea Becomes a Law

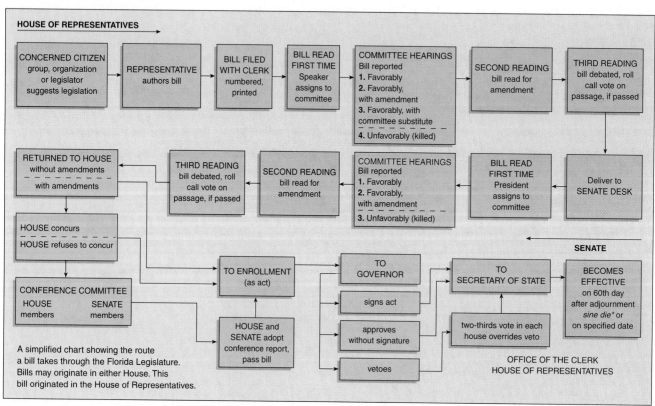

A simplified chart showing the route a bill takes through the Florida Legislature. Bills may originate in either House. This bill originated in the House of Representatives.

SOURCE: Allen Morris, *The Florida Handbook 1983–1984*, 19th ed. (Tallahassee, Fla.: Peninsular Publishing Co., 1983), pp. 84–85.
Sine die means "without assigning a day for a further meeting."

federal legislative districts must be redrawn to ensure that every person's vote is roughly equal and that minorities are represented adequately.

By the mid-1990s, however, the Supreme Court had reversed its position on what has been called "racial gerrymandering." In 1996, the Court held that voting districts that are redrawn with the goal of maximizing the electoral strength and representation of minority groups violate the equal protection clause. (See Chapter 12 for a more detailed discussion of this issue.)

Direct Democracy: The Initiative, Referendum, and Recall

There is a major difference between the legislative process as outlined in the U.S. Constitution and the legislative process as outlined in the various state constitutions. Many states exercise a type of direct democracy through the initiative, the referendum, and the recall—procedures that allow voters directly to control the government.

The Initiative.   One technique lets citizens bypass legislatures by proposing new statutes or changes in government for citizen approval. Most states that permit the citizen **legislative initiative** require that the initiative's backers circulate a petition to place the issue on the ballot and that a certain percentage of the registered voters in the last gubernatorial election sign the petition. Twenty-two states use the legislative initiative, typically those states in which political parties are relatively weak and nonpartisan groups are strong. Legislative initiatives have involved protecting crime victims' rights, authorizing tougher penalties for certain crimes, allowing certain types of legalized gambling, limiting campaign contributions, limiting corporate spending on ballot questions, changing a state capital from one city to another, denying state services to illegal immigrants, establishing uniform state regulation of smoking, restricting the rights of homosexuals, and allowing terminally ill patients to obtain a doctor's prescription for drugs to end a life. (For a further discussion of legislative initiatives, see the feature entitled *Thinking Politically about the Voter Initiative.*)

DID YOU KNOW . . .
That in 1996, twenty-three state legislatures had enacted some form of law making English the official language of those states?

LEGISLATIVE INITIATIVE

A procedure by which voters can propose a change in state or local laws by gathering signatures on a petition and submitting it to the legislature for approval.

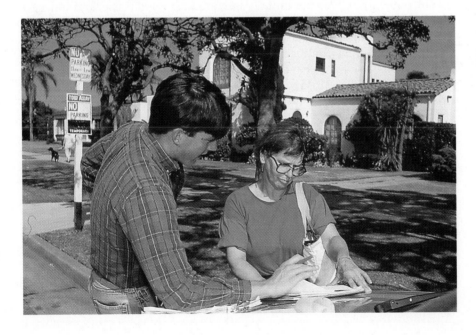

This volunteer is working to make sure that a local referendum is passed in California. A referendum is an issue or constitutional change that is proposed first by the legislature and then directed to the voters for their approval. An initiative, in contrast, lets citizens bypass legislatures completely by proposing new statutes or changes in government for citizen approval.

Thinking Politically about the Voter Initiative

The voter initiative has been around since the nineteenth century. The idea seems laudable—at the grassroots, the people can make a difference by proposing and voting for the passage of an initiative. California is a good example. The initiative started there in 1911. By 1996, in two separate elections, voters were faced with a total of over twenty initiatives. These initiatives deal with issues ranging from reforming the legal liability system to reforming campaign funding. There are also local initiatives. In one recent year, residents of Los Angeles had, on average, fifteen to eighteen minutes to vote on a total of forty-five state and local initiatives, plus a full assortment of candidates.

When one examines the initiative process, though, it is not simply grass-roots politicking. Rather, it has become big business. For example, in 1996 Californians who were for and against legal liability reforms spent almost $18 million to promote their views. Some initiatives in California will see $40 million spent by opponents and proponents alike. For the proponents, at least a million dollars goes into gathering the hundreds of thousands of signatures needed for an initiative to be put on the ballot. About half of each initiative's budget goes to television advertising. A large part of the budget goes to fund raising itself. Indeed, what has happened in California and other states that use the initiative regularly is that it has become a straight business. Certainly, special interest groups continue to push initiatives or to fight them, but at a minimum they are helped by those who profit most from the process—consultants, fund raisers, and signature gatherers.

For Critical Analysis
Why would special interest groups propose an initiative rather than working directly with the legislature?

REFERENDUM

An electoral device whereby legislative or constitutional measures are referred by the legislature to the voters for approval or disapproval.

The Referendum. The **referendum** is similar to the initiative, except that the issue (or constitutional change) is proposed first by the legislature and then directed to the voters for their approval. The referendum is most often used for approval of local school bond issues and for amendments to state constitutions. In a number of states that provide for the referendum, a bill passed by the legislature may be suspended by obtaining the required number of voters' signatures on petitions. A statewide referendum election is then held. If a majority of the voters disapprove of the bill, it is no longer valid.

The referendum was not initially intended for regular use, and indeed it has been used infrequently in the past. Its opponents argue that it is an unnecessary check on representative government and that it weakens legislative responsibility. In recent years, the referendum has become increasingly popular as citizens have attempted to control their state and local governments. Interest groups have been active in sponsoring the petition drives necessary to force a referendum. Thirty-six states provided for the referendum as of 1997.

RECALL

A procedure enabling voters to remove an elected official from office before his or her term has expired.

The Recall. The right of citizens to recall, or remove, elected officials is not exercised frequently. **Recall** is a provision written into the constitutions of fifteen states. It allows voters to remove elected state officials, including the governor, before the expiration of their terms of office. In the case of judges, the recall can terminate a lifetime appointment.

Citizens begin the recall process by circulating petitions demanding a statewide vote to remove the offending officeholder. The number of signatures required to bring about the election ranges from 10 to 40 percent of the last vote for the office in question. If the required number of signatures is obtained, the question of whether to remove the incumbent is decided in a general election.

The fifteen states that sanction the recall are Alaska, Arizona, California, Colorado, Georgia, Idaho, Kansas, Louisiana, Michigan, Montana, Nevada, North Dakota, Oregon, Washington, and Wisconsin. All but three of these states lie west of the Mississippi; one of them is in the Southeast. Their distribution supports the idea that different regions of the country have distinctive political cultures, or commonly held beliefs about how politics should be conducted. It is probably not a coincidence that most of the states that permit the removal of state officials also permit the passage of laws by initiative—that is, the ability of citizens to place proposed laws on a ballot and submit them to a popular vote without the intervention of the state legislature.

The recall and the initiative are examples of "pure democracy," in which the people as a whole vote directly on important issues. Such measures are distinct in theory and in practice from the norms of "representative democracy," in which the people govern only indirectly, through their elected representatives.

THE STATE JUDICIARY

Each of the fifty states, as well as the District of Columbia, has its own separate court system (which is in addition to the federal courts—see Chapter 15). Figure 19–3 shows a sample state court system. It appears quite similar to the model of the federal court system, with its various levels of courts—including trial courts, intermediate courts of appeal, and a supreme court. Again, the trial courts are of two types: those having limited jurisdiction and those having general jurisdiction.[5] Cases heard before these courts can be appealed to the state appellate court and ultimately to the state supreme court.

State courts confront severe problems of underfunding and overwork. Lack of funds—due to an increased case load and inflation—has slowed down, and occasionally even threatened to shut down, operations. State courts annually process the equivalent of one court case for every adult in the United States, or more than 100 million per year. Almost 70 percent of those cases are traffic or other minor cases. But criminal cases account for over 13 million of the total, up by 45 percent at the beginning of 1997 compared with 1985. Short on judicial personnel and frequently delayed by complex cases with lengthy appeals, the state courts are not always able to function efficiently or fairly. The consequence is all too often a resort to plea-bargained convictions or a denial of justice to plaintiffs in civil and criminal cases.

The state courts of last resort are usually called simply supreme courts, although they are also labeled the supreme judicial court (Maine and Massachusetts), the court of appeals (Maryland and New York), the court of criminal appeals (Oklahoma and Texas, which also have separate supreme courts for appeals in noncriminal cases), or the supreme court of appeals (West Virginia). Judges for these highest courts may be chosen either at large from the state as a whole or by judicial district. Chief justices may be chosen by the public in an election, by fellow justices, by gubernatorial appointment with or without legislative approval, by a judicial nominating commission, by seniority, by rotation, or by the legislature. Terms of the chief justice and associate justices range from six years to life, though typically a limit of a certain number of years is set.

All states have major trial courts, commonly called circuit courts, district courts, or superior courts. The number of judges and their terms in office vary

[5]See Chapter 15 for a definition of these terms.

widely. Many, though not all, states have intermediate appellate courts between the trial courts of original jurisdiction and the court of last resort. These are usually called courts of appeal. Salaries of state judges also vary widely, but higher pay is given to appellate and supreme court members.

HOW LOCAL GOVERNMENT OPERATES

Local governments are difficult to describe because of their great dissimilarities and because, if we include municipalities, counties, towns, townships, and special districts, there are so many of them. We limit the discussion here to the most important types and features of local governments.

Figure 19–3
• •
A Sample State Court System

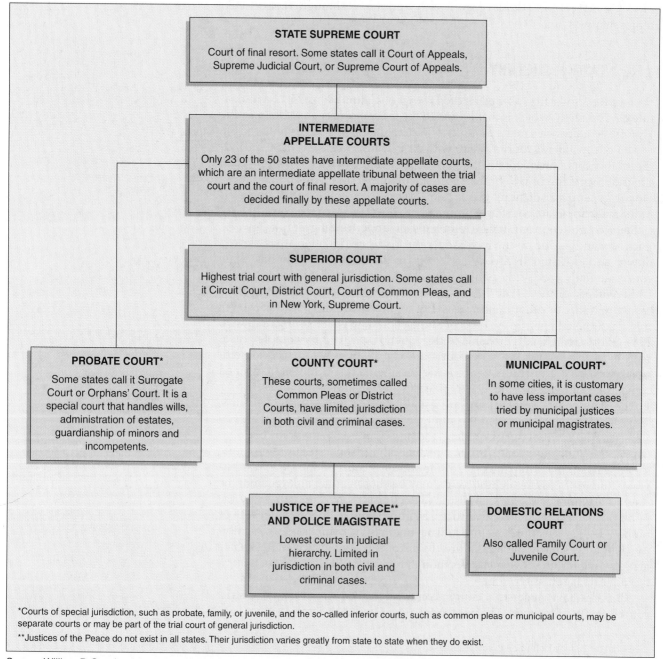

STATE SUPREME COURT

Court of final resort. Some states call it Court of Appeals, Supreme Judicial Court, or Supreme Court of Appeals.

INTERMEDIATE APPELLATE COURTS

Only 23 of the 50 states have intermediate appellate courts, which are an intermediate appellate tribunal between the trial court and the court of final resort. A majority of cases are decided finally by these appellate courts.

SUPERIOR COURT

Highest trial court with general jurisdiction. Some states call it Circuit Court, District Court, Court of Common Pleas, and in New York, Supreme Court.

PROBATE COURT*

Some states call it Surrogate Court or Orphans' Court. It is a special court that handles wills, administration of estates, guardianship of minors and incompetents.

COUNTY COURT*

These courts, sometimes called Common Pleas or District Courts, have limited jurisdiction in both civil and criminal cases.

MUNICIPAL COURT*

In some cities, it is customary to have less important cases tried by municipal justices or municipal magistrates.

JUSTICE OF THE PEACE AND POLICE MAGISTRATE**

Lowest courts in judicial hierarchy. Limited in jurisdiction in both civil and criminal cases.

DOMESTIC RELATIONS COURT

Also called Family Court or Juvenile Court.

*Courts of special jurisdiction, such as probate, family, or juvenile, and the so-called inferior courts, such as common pleas or municipal courts, may be separate courts or may be part of the trial court of general jurisdiction.

**Justices of the Peace do not exist in all states. Their jurisdiction varies greatly from state to state when they do exist.

SOURCE: William P. Statsky, *Introduction to Paralegalism*, 4th ed. (St. Paul: West, 1992), p. 333.

The Legal Existence of Local Government

The U.S. Constitution makes no mention of local governments. Article IV, Section 4, states that "[t]he United States shall guarantee to every State in this Union a Republican Form of Government." Actually, then, the states do not even have to have local governments. Consequently, every local government is a creature of the state. The state can create a local government, and the state can terminate the right of a local government to exist. Indeed, states often have abolished entire counties, school districts, cities, and special districts. Since World War II, almost twenty thousand school districts have gone out of existence as they were consolidated with other school districts.

Because the local government is the legal creation of the state, does that mean the state can dictate everything the local government does? For many years that seemed to be the case. The narrowest possible view of the legal status of local governments follows **Dillon's rule,** outlined by Judge John F. Dillon in his *Commentaries on the Law of Municipal Corporations* in 1811. He stated that municipal corporations may possess only powers "granted in express words . . . [that are] necessarily or fairly implied in or incident to the powers expressly granted."[6] Cities governed under Dillon's rule have been dominated by the state legislature. Those communities wishing to obtain the status of a municipal corporation have simply petitioned the state legislature for a **charter.** The charter has typically been extremely narrow.

In a revolt against state legislative power over municipalities, the home rule movement began. It was based on **Cooley's rule,** derived from an 1871 decision by Michigan judge Thomas Cooley stating that cities should be able to govern themselves.[7] Since 1900, about four-fifths of the states have allowed **municipal home rule,** but only with respect to local concerns for which no statewide interests are involved. A municipality must choose to become a **home rule city;** otherwise, it operates as a **general law city.** In the latter case, the state makes certain general laws relating to cities of different sizes, which are designated as first-class cities, second-class cities, or towns. Once a city, by virtue of its population, receives such a ranking, it follows the general law put down by the state. Only if it chooses to be a home rule city can it avoid such state government restrictions. In most states, only cities with populations of 2,500 or more can choose home rule.

Local Governmental Units

There are four major types of local governmental units: municipalities, counties, towns and townships, and special districts.

Municipalities. A municipality is a political entity created by the people of a city or town to govern themselves locally. As of 1997, there were about nineteen thousand municipalities within the fifty states. Almost all municipalities are fairly small cities. Only about five hundred cities have populations over fifty thousand, and only six municipalities (Chicago, Detroit, Houston, Los Angeles, New York, and Philadelphia) have populations over a million. In 1996, all the municipalities combined spent about $681 billion—primarily for water supply and other utilities, police and fire protection, and education. About three-fourths of municipal tax revenues come from property taxes. Municipalities rely very heavily on financial assistance from both the federal and state governments. (For an issue that involves the use of municipal tax dollars, see this chapter's *Critical Perspective.*)

DID YOU KNOW...
That nine states have no minimum age and fourteen states have no U.S. citizenship requirements for a person to run for governor?

DILLON'S RULE

The narrowest possible interpretation of the legal status of local governments, outlined by Judge John F. Dillon, who in 1811 stated that a municipal corporation can exercise only those powers expressly granted by state law.

CHARTER

A document issued by a government that grants rights to a person, a group of persons, or a corporation to carry on one or more specific activities. A state government can grant a charter to a municipality allowing that group of persons to carry on specific activities.

COOLEY'S RULE

The view that cities should be able to govern themselves, presented in an 1871 Michigan decision by Judge Thomas Cooley.

MUNICIPAL HOME RULE

The power vested in a local unit of government to draft or change its own charter and to manage its own affairs.

HOME RULE CITY

A city with a charter allowing local voters to frame, adopt, and amend their own charter.

GENERAL LAW CITY

A city operating under general state laws that apply to all local governmental units of a similar type.

---

[6]John F. Dillon, *Commentaries on the Law of Municipal Corporations,* 5th ed. (Boston: Little, Brown, 1911), Vol. 1, Sec. 237.
[7]*People v. Hurlbut,* 24 Mich. 44 (1871).

CRITICAL PERSPECTIVE
Should Cities Be Able to Stop Sports Franchises from Moving Away?

Professional sports represent a major business activity in the United States. The National Football League alone generates almost $700 million a year. Many sports fans are extremely loyal to their city's teams. The Cubs have been in Chicago since 1876, the Yankees have been in New York since 1902, the Celtics have been in Boston since 1946, and the Forty-Niners have been in San Francisco since 1946. To some extent, the fans consider their city's teams as "their own." Not surprisingly, then, when the owners of a particular professional sports team decide to move that team to another city, the fans feel cheated and become outraged.

The Dance of the Dollar

When the Brooklyn Dodgers moved to Los Angeles in 1957, the residents of Brooklyn said they would never recover. In more recent times, in the National Football League, the Los Angeles Rams moved to St. Louis, and the Cleveland Browns became the Baltimore Ravens.

The Issue of Investing Tax Dollars

When a city takes a sports franchise owner to court to prevent the owner from moving a franchise, the city typically argues that the franchise cannot be moved because the city has made huge investments of taxpayers' dollars in the team. In fact, many cities have spent millions of dollars of taxpayers' money either to keep or to lure a sports team. Taxpayers do not give money directly to baseball, football, and basketball players—or to team owners. Rather, taxpayers give these groups money indirectly by subsidizing new stadiums. Consider that in 1950, not a single stadium for baseball's National League was owned by the public; today, more than 80 percent of that league's stadiums are publicly owned. For the American League, the comparable numbers are 12 percent in 1950 and almost 90 percent today. For the National Football League, 36 percent of stadiums were publicly owned in 1950; today that number is 96 percent. For basketball, the number went from 46 to 76 percent and for hockey from 0 to 52 percent.

Listed below are some of the sums of money that taxpayers transferred:

- Camden Yards, Baltimore: $200 million
- Comiskey Park, Chicago: $135 million
- Jacobs Field, Cleveland: $236 million
- Arlington Hall, Arlington, TX: $135 million

COUNTY

The chief governmental unit set up by the state to administer state law and business at the local level. Counties are drawn up by area, rather than by rural or urban criteria.

Counties. The difference between a **county** and a municipality is that a county may not be created at the behest of its inhabitants. The state sets up counties on its own initiative to serve as political extensions of the state government. Counties apply state law and administer state business at the local level. Counties are not municipal corporations, even though in some states the law treats counties as involuntary, quasi-municipal corporations.

County governments, of which there are over three thousand within the United States, vary from Los Angeles County, California, with more than eight million people, to Loving County, Texas, with less than one hundred people. San Bernardino County, California, has more than twenty thousand square miles—half the size of Pennsylvania—but Bristol County, Rhode Island, has only twenty-five square miles.

County governments' responsibilities include zoning, building regulations, health, hospitals, parks, recreation, highways, public safety, justice, and record keeping. Typically, when a municipality is established within a county, the county withdraws most of its services from the municipality; for example, the municipal police force takes over from the county police force. County governments are extremely complex entities, a product of the era of Jacksonian democracy and its effort to bring government closer to the people.

CRITICAL PERSPECTIVE
Should Cities Be Able to Stop Sports Franchises from Moving Away? Continued

All in all, just since 1992 over $1.5 billion of taxpayers' money has been spent on professional sports stadiums, with another $2 billion under construction today and plans for yet another $5 billion by the year 2000.

So the argument that sports teams should not be allowed to move away from a particular city is based more on the fact that taxpayers have subsidized such teams than on any sense of the "fans owning the team."

The Pros and Cons

Clearly, if there were a ban on the movement of sports teams, cities would not feel compelled to subsidize stadium construction or renovation to the extent they do now. Sports teams that wanted better facilities might have to raise the money privately, as they did in the past and as was done for Miami's Joe Robbie Stadium. On the negative side of the ledger, teams that are not doing well financially might not be able to raise the funds to improve their stadiums. A vicious circle might occur. Team owners might then find themselves declaring bankruptcy.

Many commentators are in favor of allowing the owners of sports franchises to move at will. They argue that, after all, any other business can move when it wants to, so why can't a sports team? They point out that city governments are at fault in subsidizing stadiums so heavily today. Perhaps if more teams move, thereby "burning" the taxpayers in the process, fewer cities will want to spend such large amounts of money on new stadium facilities.

Studies of the fiscal impact of bringing a sports team to a city via a heavily subsidized public stadium are conclusive. The city's taxpayers almost never recover—in additional visitors, business, and profits—the $100 million plus that they put into a new stadium.

For Critical Analysis

1. What constitutional issues would be raised in trying to pass a law to prevent sports franchises from moving away?
2. Who are the beneficiaries of the subsidization by taxpayers of new professional sports stadiums?

There is no easy way to describe their operation in summary form. Indeed, the county has been called by one scholar "the dark continent of American politics."[8]

Towns and Townships. A unique governmental creation in the New England states is the **New England town**—not to be confused with the word *town* when used as just another name for a city. In Maine, Massachusetts, New Hampshire, Vermont, and Connecticut, the unit called the town combines the roles of city and county into one governing unit. A New England town typically consists of one or more urban settlements and the surrounding rural areas. Consequently, counties have little importance in New England. In Connecticut, for example, they are simply geographic units.

From the New England town is derived the tradition of the annual **town meeting,** at which direct democracy was—and continues to be—practiced. Each resident of a town is summoned to the annual meeting at the town hall. Those who attend levy taxes, pass laws, elect town officers, and appropriate money for different activities.

NEW ENGLAND TOWN

A governmental unit that combines the roles of city and county into one unit in the New England states.

TOWN MEETING

The governing authority of a New England town. Qualified voters may participate in the election of officers and in the passage of legislation.

[8]Henry S. Gilbertson, *The County, the "Dark Continent of American Politics"* (New York: National Short Ballot Association, 1917).

A recycling program in Portland, Oregon, is an example of a local government's successful tackling of a policy problem.

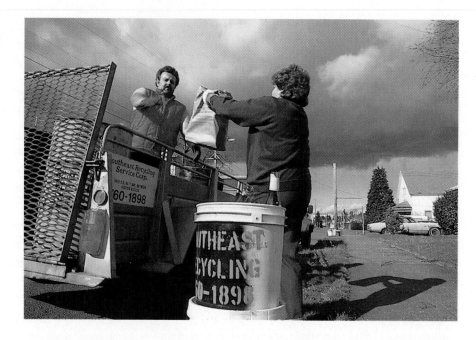

TOWN MANAGER SYSTEM

A form of city government in which voters elect three selectpersons, who then appoint a professional town manager, who in turn appoints other officials.

SELECTPERSON

A member of the governing group of a town.

TOWNSHIP

A rural unit of government based on federal land surveys of the American frontier in the 1780s. They have declined significantly in importance.

UNINCORPORATED AREA

An area not located within the boundary of a municipality.

Normally, few residents show up for town meetings today unless a high-interest item is on the agenda or unless family members want to be elected to office. The town meeting takes a day or more, and few citizens are able to set aside such a large amount of time. Because of the declining interest in town meetings, many New England towns have adopted a **town manager system:** The voters simply elect three **selectpersons,** who then appoint a professional town manager. The town manager in turn appoints other officials.

Townships operate somewhat like counties. Where they exist, there may be several dozen within a county. They perform the same functions that the county would do otherwise. Indiana, Iowa, Kansas, Michigan, Minnesota, New Jersey, New York, Ohio, Pennsylvania, and Wisconsin all have numerous townships. A township is not the same thing as a New England town, because it is meant to be a rural government rather than a city government. Moreover, it is never the principal unit of local government, as are New England towns. The boundaries of most townships are based on federal land surveys that began in the 1780s, mapping the land into six-mile squares called townships. They were then subdivided into thirty-six blocks of one square mile each, called sections. Along the boundaries of each section, a road was built.

Although townships have few functions left to perform in many parts of the nation, they are still politically important in others. In some metropolitan areas, townships are the political unit that provides most public services to residents who live in suburban **unincorporated areas.**

Special Districts. The most numerous form of local government is the special district, which includes school districts. As of 1997, there were more than forty-four thousand special districts, of which slightly less than fifteen thousand were school districts (see Figure 19–4). Special districts are one-function governments that usually are created by the state legislature and governed by a board of directors. After school districts, districts for fire protection are the most numerous. There are also districts for mosquito control, cemeteries, and numerous other concerns. Special districts may be called authorities, boards, corporations—or simply districts.

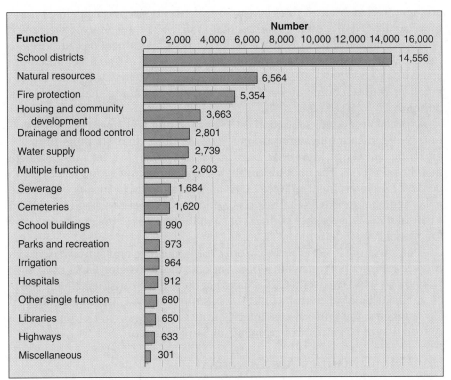

Function	Number
School districts	14,556
Natural resources	6,564
Fire protection	5,354
Housing and community development	3,663
Drainage and flood control	2,801
Water supply	2,739
Multiple function	2,603
Sewerage	1,684
Cemeteries	1,620
School buildings	990
Parks and recreation	973
Irrigation	964
Hospitals	912
Other single function	680
Libraries	650
Highways	633
Miscellaneous	301

SOURCE: U.S. Department of Commerce, *Statistical Abstract of the United States,* (Washington, D.C.: U.S. Government Printing Office, 1995).

Figure 19–4
●●●●●●●●●●●●●●●●●●●●
Special Districts According to Their Functions

One important feature of special districts is that they cut across geographic and governmental boundaries. Sometimes special districts even cut across state lines. For example, the Port of New York Authority was established by an **interstate compact** between New Jersey and New York in 1921 to develop and operate the harbor facilities in the area. A mosquito control district may cut across both municipal and county lines. A metropolitan transit district may provide bus service to dozens of municipalities and to several counties.

Except for school districts, the typical citizen is not very aware of most special districts. Indeed, most citizens do not know who furnishes their weed control, mosquito control, water, or sewage control. Part of the reason for the low profile of special districts is that most special district administrators are appointed, not elected, and therefore receive little public attention.

Consolidation of Governments

With approximately eighty thousand separate and often overlapping governmental units within the United States, the trend in recent years toward consolidation is understandable. **Consolidation** is defined as the union of two or more governmental units to form a single unit. Typically, a state constitution or a state statute will designate consolidation procedures.

Consolidation is often recommended for metropolitan-area problems, but to date there have been few consolidations within metropolitan areas. The most successful consolidations have been **functional consolidations**—particularly of city and county police, health, and welfare departments. In some cases, functional consolidation is a satisfactory alternative to the complete consolidation of governmental units. The most successful form of functional consolidation was started in 1957 in Dade County, Florida. The county gov-

INTERSTATE COMPACT

An agreement between two or more states to cooperate on a policy or problem, such as sharing water resources. It must first be approved by Congress.

CONSOLIDATION

The union of two or more governmental units to form a single unit.

FUNCTIONAL CONSOLIDATION

The cooperation of two or more units of local government in providing services to their inhabitants.

ernment, called Metro-Dade, is a union of twenty-six municipalities. Each municipality has its own governmental entity, but the county government operates under a home rule charter. The county government has authority to furnish water, planning, mass transit, and police services and to set minimum standards of performance. The governing body of Metro-Dade is an elected board of county commissioners, which appoints a county manager and an attorney.

A special type of consolidation is the **council of government (COG),** a voluntary organization of counties and municipalities that attempts to tackle areawide problems. More than two hundred COGs have been established, mainly since 1966. The impetus for their establishment was, and continues to be, federal government grants. COGs are an alternative means of treating major regional problems that various communities are unwilling to tackle on a consolidated basis either by true consolidation of governmental units or by functional consolidation.

The power of COGs is advisory only. Each member unit simply selects its council representatives, who report back to the unit after COG meetings. Nonetheless, today several COGs have begun to have considerable influence on regional policy. These include the Metropolitan Washington Council of Governments, the Supervisors' Inter-County Commission in Detroit, and the Association of Bay Area Governments in San Francisco.

How Municipalities Are Governed

We can divide municipal representative governments into four general types: (1) the commission plan, (2) the council-manager plan, (3) the mayor-administrator plan, and (4) the mayor-council plan.

The Commission Plan.   The commission form of municipal government consists of a commission of three to nine members who have both legislative and executive powers. The salient aspects of the commission plan are as follows:

1. Executive and legislative powers are concentrated in a small group of individuals, who are elected at large on a (normally) nonpartisan ballot.
2. Each commissioner is individually responsible for heading a particular municipal department, such as the department of public safety.

COUNCIL OF GOVERNMENT (COG)

A voluntary organization of counties and municipalities concerned with areawide problems.

A billboard in Blue Earth, Minnesota, supports a referendum to construct a new school. School districts represent by far the largest share of special districts.

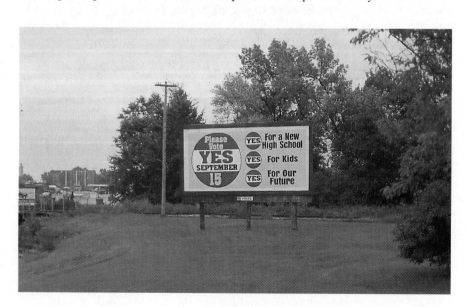

3. The commission is collectively responsible for passing ordinances and controlling spending.

4. The mayor (an office that is only ceremonial) is selected from the members of the commission.

The commission plan, originating in Galveston, Texas, in 1901, had its greatest popularity during the first twenty years of this century. It appealed to municipal government reformers. They looked on it as a type of business organization that would eliminate the problems they believed to be inherent in the long ballot and in partisan municipal politics. Unfortunately, vesting both legislative and executive power in the hands of a small group of individuals means that there are no checks and balances on administration and spending. Also, because the mayoral office is ceremonial, there is no provision for strong leadership. Not surprisingly, only about one hundred cities today use the commission plan—Tulsa, Salt Lake City, Mobile, Topeka, and Atlantic City are a few of them.

The Council-Manager Plan. In the council-manager form of municipal government, a city council appoints a professional manager, who acts as the chief executive. He or she typically is called the city manager. In principle, the manager is there simply to see that the general directions of the city council are carried out. The important features of the council-manager plan are as follows:

1. A professional, trained manager can hire and fire subordinates and is responsible to the council.

2. The council or commission consists of five to seven members, elected at large on a nonpartisan ballot.

3. The mayor may be chosen from within the council or from outside, but he or she has no executive function. As with the commission plan, the mayor's job is largely ceremonial. The city manager works for the council, not the mayor (unless, of course, the mayor is part of the council).

Today, about two thousand cities use the council-manager plan. About one-third of the cities with populations of more than 5,000 and about one-half of the cities with populations of more than 25,000 operate with this type of plan. Only four large cities with populations of more than 500,000—Cincinnati, Dallas, San Antonio, and San Diego—have adopted this plan.

The major defect of the council-manager scheme, as with the commission plan, is that there is no single, strong political executive leader. It is therefore not surprising that large cities rarely use such a plan.

The Mayor-Administrator Plan. The mayor-administrator plan is often used in large cities where there is a strong mayor. It is similar to the council-manager plan except that the political leadership is vested in the mayor. The mayor is an elective chief executive. He or she appoints an administrative officer, whose function is to free the mayor from routine administrative tasks, such as personnel direction and budget supervision.

The Mayor-Council Plan. The mayor-council form of municipal government is the oldest and most widely used. The mayor is an elected chief executive, and the council is the legislative body. Virtually all councils are unicameral except in Everett, Massachusetts. There are typically five to nine members of the council except in very large cities, such as Chicago, which has fifty members. Council members are popularly elected for terms as long as six, but normally four, years.

DID YOU KNOW...
That because Texas was the only state to enter the Union after having sovereign status, it is the only state that can fly its state flag at the same height as the U.S. flag?

The mayor-council plan can either be a strong-mayor type or a weak-mayor type. In the *strong mayor–council plan*, the mayor is the chief executive and has virtually complete control over hiring and firing employees, as well as preparing the budget. The mayor exercises strong and positive leadership in the formation of city policies. The *weak mayor–council plan* separates executive and legislative functions completely. The mayor is elected as chief executive officer; the council is elected as the legislative body. This traditional separation of powers allows for checks and balances on spending and administration.

About 50 percent of American cities use some form of the mayor-council plan. Most recently, the mayor-council plan has lost ground to the council-manager plan in small and middle-sized cities.

Machine versus Reform in City Politics

For much of the late nineteenth and early twentieth centuries, many major cities were run by "the machine." The machine was an integrated political organization. Each city block within the municipality had an organizer, each neighborhood had a political club, each district had a leader, and all of these parts of the machine had a boss—such as Richard Daley in Chicago, Edward Crump in Memphis, or Tom Pendergast in Kansas City. The machine became a popular form of city political organization in the 1840s, when the first waves of European immigrants came to the United States to work in urban factories. Those individuals, often lacking the ability to communicate in English, needed help; and the machine was created to help them.[9] The urban machine drew on the support of the dominant ethnic groups to forge a strong political institution that was able to keep the boss (usually the mayor) in office year after year. The machine was oiled by **patronage**—rewarding faithful party workers and followers with government employment and contracts. The party in power was often referred to as the patronage party.[10]

According to sociologist Robert Merton, the machine offered personalized assistance to the needy, helped to establish local businesses, opened avenues of upward social mobility for the underprivileged, and afforded a locus of strong political authority and responsibility.[11] More critical of the political machine are Edward Banfield and James Wilson, who argue that

> machine government is, essentially, a system of organized bribery. The destruction of machines . . . permit[s] government on the basis of appropriate motives, that is, public-regarding ones. In fact it has other highly desirable consequences—especially greater honesty, impartiality, and (in routine matters) efficiency.[12]

When the last of the big-city bosses, Mayor Richard Daley of Chicago, died in December 1976, with him died an era. The big-city machine began to be in serious trouble in the 1960s, when community activists organized to work for a more professional and efficient municipal government. Soon a government of administrators rather than politicians began to appear. Fewer offices were elective; more were appointive.

Switching from a political to an administrative form of urban government was a way to break up the centralized urban political machine. In some cities, the results have been beneficial to most citizens. In others, decentralization has gone so far that there is no strong leader who can pull together discordant

PATRONAGE

Rewarding faithful party workers and followers with government employment and contracts.

---

[9]See Harvey W. Zorbaugh, *The Gold Coast and the Slum: A Sociological Study of Chicago's Near North Side* (Chicago: University of Chicago Press, 1929).

[10]See, for example, Harold F. Gosnell, *Machine Politics: Chicago Model* (Chicago: University of Chicago Press, 1937).

[11]Robert Merton, *Social Theory and Social Structure* (Glencoe, Ill.: Free Press, 1957), pp. 71–81.

[12]Edward C. Banfield and James Q. Wilson, *City Politics* (New York: Vintage Books, 1963), p. 12.

factions to create and follow a coherent policy. Consequently, in cities with a greatly decentralized government typified by numerous independent commissions and boards, a lot that should be done does not get done, particularly when an area-wide problem is involved. This is an especially severe problem for less economically privileged people, who used to be able to rely on machine-sponsored activities and on the machine's political clout to help them compete against wealthier citizens for a share of the city's services. Reform is in some ways a middle-class preoccupation, whereas the less advantaged may find themselves better served by machine politics.

DID YOU KNOW . . .
That the first African American mayors of big cities were Richard G. Hatcher of Gary, Indiana, and Carl B. Stokes of Cleveland, both elected in 1967?

Governing Metropolitan Areas

Large cities are often faced with problems that develop in part from a shrinking employment base. When employers move out of a city, there is a smaller tax base, and more people are out of work. Less tax revenue means less money to pay for schools and to meet other municipal obligations, including fighting crime and assisting those who are out of work. These developments feed on themselves, leading to more crime, more poverty, an even smaller job base, and other problems.

But crime, as well as such problems as traffic congestion and pollution, are not contained within municipal political boundaries. For this reason, solutions are sometimes sought to govern a metropolitan area as a whole. Annexation by a city of the surrounding suburbs is one solution; consolidation of city and county governments into one government is another. People who live in the suburbs often oppose such measures, however, particularly when they and the residents of a city are of different races or social classes, or have different political agendas.

A third attempt to deal with problems that spread beyond limited political boundaries is represented by a system of metropolitan government. With this method, a single entity, such as a county, concerns itself with the problems of an entire metropolitan area, and smaller entities, such as individual city governments, concern themselves with local matters. People who live in the suburbs often oppose this solution, however, for the same reasons that they oppose other measures: they want to preserve their communities and lifestyles as they are.

A fourth solution is the creation of special districts, each of which is concerned with a specific service—an area's water supply or public transportation system, for example. Special districts are more popular than the other solutions, in part because they can deal with a single matter relatively more efficiently without concern for social issues or class conflict.

STATE AND LOCAL GOVERNMENT: UNFINISHED WORK

The states face a broad array of problems, the solutions to which no longer can be found in Washington, D.C. Specifically, as the federal government continues to give the states more responsibilities, the states are expected to solve more problems—such as crime, education, and welfare—than they had in previous years. At the same time, some states are attempting to lure population and businesses by reducing taxes. The friction between the need to solve problems and the need to expand the business base will remain part of the unfinished work of states for years to come.

Local governments will continue to be expected to solve the local problems of crime, pollution, congestion, and the like. Many municipalities have seen their tax bases decline as residents move to the suburbs. Nonetheless, fiscal help from the state and federal governments is less available today than ever before. Consequently, local governments must continue to seek ways to streamline the provision of public services, perhaps by more contracting out or by better management.

State and local governments also will continue to search for new ways to meet the pressing challenge of how to improve the quality of education and at the same time keep educational expenditures in check. States across the nation are experimenting with various systems, including school vouchers (discussed in Chapter 4), in their attempt to meet this challenge. How the states resolve the educational issues confronting them certainly will have a significant effect on America's future electorate.

GETTING INVOLVED
Learning about Local Politics and Government in Your Community

What government does or fails to do in the areas of education, health, employment, and crime affects you, your family, and your friends. Your sense of adventure, concern, curiosity, or injustice may urge you to take an active part in the government of a society with which you might not be particularly content. Yet getting involved on the national level may seem complicated, and national issues may not be of immediate concern. You may not even know exactly where you stand on many of those issues.

Every week, however, decisions are being made in your community that affect directly your local environment, transportation, education, health, employment, rents, schools, utility rates, freedom from crime, and overall quality of life. The local level is a good place to begin discovering who you are politically.

Many neighborhoods have formed neighborhood associations for the purposes of protecting their interests. One way to learn about issues that directly affect you (such as whether a street in your neighborhood should be widened or a park created) is to attend a local neighborhood association meeting. Another way to familiarize yourself with local political issues is to attend a city council meeting. Think about the issues being discussed. How do these issues and their outcomes concern you as an individual? What is your position on each issue?

If you are interested in education and educational reform, you can attend a school board meeting. Typically, the board will devote a substantial amount of time to budgetary decisions. Pay close attention to how the board feels school funds should be allocated. What are the board's primary concerns and priorities? Do you agree with the board's views? Find out if the school district is considering proposals to implement innovational educational programs.

Virtually all communities have groups that are working to improve the environment at the state or local level. At the local level, environmental issues may concern efforts to beautify the city (by restricting billboards or yard signs, for example) or implementing recycling programs to control waste. State environmental organizations may need volunteers to go door-to-door in your community to distribute information on their lobbying efforts before the state legislature, to gather signatures for petitions, and the like. If you look in the Yellow Pages under "Environment" or "Environmental," you probably will find a listing of several local and state organizations to contact.

Getting involved in a campaign for a local or state office is another way to learn about political issues that affect your community or your state. You also can participate at the local level in campaigns by candidates seeking national office, such as candidates running for Congress. Working at the "grassroots" level for a political candidate gives you first-hand knowledge of how the politics of democracy actually work.

Finally, to observe the judicial branch of government at work, you can observe proceedings in your local courts. An important court at the local level is the small claims court. Small claims courts hear disputes involving claims under a certain amount, such as $1,000 or $2,500 (the amount varies from state to state). Lawyers are not required, and many small claims courts do not permit lawyers. Other local courts are described in Figure 19–3. For information on your local courts and on when you can attend court proceedings, call the courthouse clerk.

KEY TERMS

charter 647	home rule city 647	recall 644
consolidation 651	hyperpluralism 633	referendum 644
constitutional initiative 638	interstate compact 651	selectperson 650
Cooley's rule 647	item veto 640	town manager system 650
council of government (COG) 652	legislative initiative 643	town meeting 649
county 648	municipal home rule 647	township 650
Dillon's rule 647	New England town 649	unincorporated area 650
functional consolidation 651	patronage 654	
general law city 647	police power 637	
general sales tax 634	property tax 634	

CHAPTER SUMMARY

❶ The United States has more than eighty thousand separate governmental units. Some believe that such decentralized authority makes it impossible to get anything done. Despite this perception, however, state and local government workers perform a wide variety of highly visible functions, such as education, police and fire protection, and so on. State and local government spending is concentrated in the areas of education, public welfare, highways, health, and police protection. State services are funded primarily by sales taxes, whereas local services are financed by property taxes.

❷ Under the U.S. Constitution, powers not delegated expressly to the federal government are reserved to the states. The states may exercise taxing, spending, and general police powers. State constitutions are often very long, owing to the desire of their framers to include much of what we would consider statutory law because of a loss of popular confidence in state legislatures at the end of the nineteenth century. Other reasons include state courts' reluctance to interpret state constitutions as freely as the United States Supreme Court interprets the U.S. Constitution.

❸ In colonial America, the governors of the colonies were vested with extensive powers. Following the Revolutionary War, most states established forms of government in which the governor was given extremely limited powers. After Andrew Jackson's presidency, however, all governors (except in South Carolina) were elected directly by the people. Most governors have the right to exercise some sort of veto power; some enjoy item veto power.

❹ State legislatures deal with matters such as taxes, schools, highways, and welfare. They also must redraw state and federal legislative districts each decade to ensure that every person's vote is roughly equal to that of others and that minorities are adequately represented in both the state legislature and Congress. Voters may exercise some direct control over state government through the use of the initiative, referendum, and recall. Every state has its own court system. Most such systems have several levels of courts—including trial courts, intermediate courts of appeal, and a supreme court. State courts are overburdened with over 100 million cases each year, the majority of which are traffic offenses.

❺ Municipal revenues are obtained primarily from property taxes; these funds are spent on utilities, police and fire protection, and education. Counties are merely extensions of state authority and apply state laws at the local level. Many of the functions of municipalities and counties are combined in towns or townships, particularly in the New England area. Municipalities may be governed by a commission consisting of members with executive and legislative powers, or they may be administered according to a council-manager, mayor-administrator, or mayor-council plan. Most major cities used to be run by political machines, which freely dispensed favors to supporters. In recent decades, however, machine politics has fallen into disfavor, particularly among the middle class.

QUESTIONS FOR REVIEW AND DISCUSSION

❶ One of the main thrusts of the new federalism was to cut back *federal* spending on social programs. The philosophy underlying this effort is that the people and the states can decide for themselves whether they want these programs to continue. What factors are likely to influence *state* decisions about financing social programs?

❷ What are some of the features of state governments that give greater control to the voters? To what extent do these features limit the flexibility and effectiveness of state government?

❸ The structures and practices of state governments vary widely, revealing many adaptations of national institutions. What reasons can you give for the unique features of state governments?

❹ Some people suggest that the reason we have more than eighty thousand separate governmental units is that Americans fear placing too much power in any centralized structure. What are some of the advantages and disadvantages of having multiple governments, particularly within one urban area? What functions of government would be easiest to consolidate? Which functions do you think the voters are least likely to grant to any form of metro government or centralized authority?

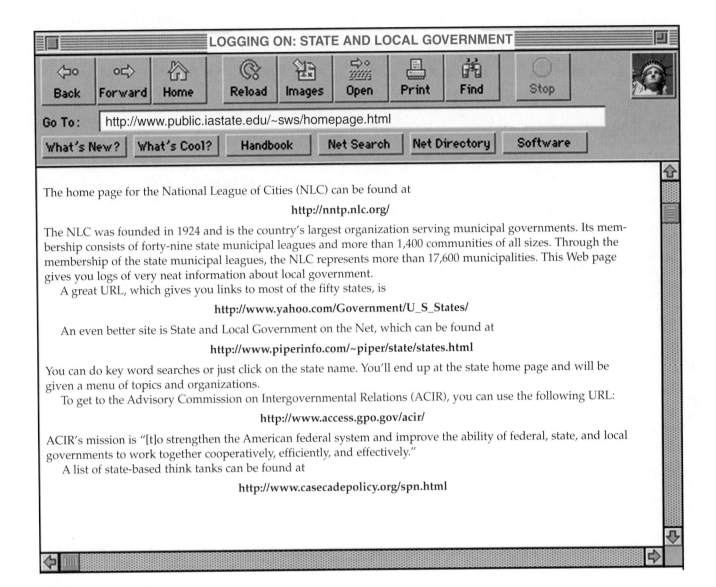

LOGGING ON: STATE AND LOCAL GOVERNMENT

Go To: http://www.public.iastate.edu/~sws/homepage.html

The home page for the National League of Cities (NLC) can be found at

http://nntp.nlc.org/

The NLC was founded in 1924 and is the country's largest organization serving municipal governments. Its membership consists of forty-nine state municipal leagues and more than 1,400 communities of all sizes. Through the membership of the state municipal leagues, the NLC represents more than 17,600 municipalities. This Web page gives you logs of very neat information about local government.

A great URL, which gives you links to most of the fifty states, is

http://www.yahoo.com/Government/U_S_States/

An even better site is State and Local Government on the Net, which can be found at

http://www.piperinfo.com/~piper/state/states.html

You can do key word searches or just click on the state name. You'll end up at the state home page and will be given a menu of topics and organizations.

To get to the Advisory Commission on Intergovernmental Relations (ACIR), you can use the following URL:

http://www.access.gpo.gov/acir/

ACIR's mission is "[t]o strengthen the American federal system and improve the ability of federal, state, and local governments to work together cooperatively, efficiently, and effectively."

A list of state-based think tanks can be found at

http://www.casecadepolicy.org/spn.html

SELECTED REFERENCES

Banfield, Edward C., and James Q. Wilson. *City Politics.* New York: Vintage Books, 1963. A classic work describing competing interests and ideas in city life.

Berman, David R. *State and Local Politics.* 7th ed. Madison, Wis.: WCB Brown and Benchmark, 1993. This standard text examines all aspects of state and local politics, including the intergovernmental environment.

Council of State Governments. *Book of the States.* Lexington, Ky.: Council of State Governments, 1996–1997. This annual publication, the bible of state government, contains a variety of statistics and other facts on state governments. It examines problems and major issues in state finances, as well as the relationship between the judicial system and the executive and legislative branches in the various states.

It contains detailed information on state elections and constitutions.

Dye, Thomas R. *Politics in States and Communities.* 8th ed. Englewood Cliffs, N.J.: Prentice-Hall, 1994. This text explores the inner workings of political systems by comparing and analyzing state and local perspectives on public policy. The author focuses on conflicts in states and communities and the structures and processes designed to manage conflict.

Gold, Steven D., ed. *The Fiscal Crisis of the States: Lessons for the Future.* Washington, D.C.: Georgetown University Press, 1995. This volume offers an informative look, as well as detailed case studies, at how state governments responded to their latest fiscal crises. In an era of growing support for turning over various federal programs to the states, the book offers some insights into how states might respond to future fiscal crises. The book shows that in times of fiscal crises, the state governments are likely to transfer obligations to others or to reduce or cut funding for crucial programs in order to balance their budgets.

Lilley, William, III, Laurence J. DeFranco, and William M. Diefenderfer III. *The State Atlas of Political and Cultural Diversity*. Washington, D.C.: Congressional Quarterly Books, 1996. The authors have collected and analyzed data on the ethnic and ancestral makeup of the over six thousand state legislative districts in the United States. The book, the first of its kind, is a comprehensive resource on racial and ethnic populations in state legislatures.

Peterson, Paul E. *The Price of Federalism*. Washington, D.C.: Brookings Institution, 1995. The author looks at theories of federalism, arguing that how we divide power among governments is a central question in self-government. He states that the United States seems to have arrived at a rational division of labor among the various levels of government. He suggests that certain functions (such as building roadways) are performed best at the state and local level, whereas other functions (such as Social Security) are handled best at the national level.

Royko, Mike. *Boss: Richard J. Daley of Chicago*. New York: Signet Books, 1971. Royko delves into the personal and social forces of the Chicago Democratic party machine and the leadership of its famous mayor.

Van Horn, Carl E., ed. *The State of the States*. 3d ed. Washington, D.C.: Congressional Quarterly Books, 1996. This collection of essays describes state government institutions and political processes, and looks at some of the challenges, such as welfare and educational reform, facing state governments today.

Zimmerman, Joseph F. *State-Local Relations: A Partnership Approach*. 2d ed. Westport, Conn.: Praeger, 1995. The author has revised and updated his classic study of state-local relations. Zimmerman examines numerous aspects of the relations between state and local governments, including the legal and constitutional basis for state government authority, the control by state governments over local governing units and how that control has changed over time, and the state-local partnership in terms of fiscal relations.

A

The Declaration of Independence

In Congress, July 4, 1776

A Declaration by the Representatives of the United States of America, in General Congress assembled. When in the Course of human Events, it becomes necessary for one People to dissolve the Political Bands which have connected them with another, and to assume among the Powers of the Earth, the separate and equal Station to which the Laws of Nature and of Nature's God entitle them, a decent Respect to the Opinions of Mankind requires that they should declare the causes which impel them to the Separation.

We hold these Truths to be self-evident, that all Men are created equal, that they are endowed by their Creator with certain unalienable Rights, that among these are Life, Liberty, and the Pursuit of Happiness—That to secure these Rights, Governments are instituted among Men, deriving their just Powers from the Consent of the Governed, that whenever any Form of Government becomes destructive of these Ends, it is the Right of the People to alter or to abolish it, and to institute new Government, laying its Foundation on such Principles, and organizing its Powers in such Forms, as to them shall seem most likely to effect their Safety and Happiness. Prudence, indeed, will dictate that Governments long established should not be changed for light and transient Causes; and accordingly all Experience hath shewn, that Mankind are more disposed to suffer, while Evils are sufferable, than to right themselves by abolishing the Forms to which they are accustomed. But when a long Train of Abuses and Usurpations, pursuing invariably the same Object, evinces a Design to reduce them under absolute Despotism, it is their Right, it is their Duty, to throw off such Government, and to provide new Guards for their future Security. Such has been the patient Sufferance of these Colonies; and such is now the Necessity which constrains them to alter their former Systems of Government. The History of the present King of Great-Britain is a History of repeated Injuries and Usurpations, all having in direct Object the Establishment of an absolute Tyranny over these States. To prove this, let Facts be submitted to a candid World.

He has refused his Assent to Laws, the most wholesome and necessary for the public Good.

He has forbidden his Governors to pass Laws of immediate and pressing Importance, unless suspended in their Operation till his Assent should be obtained; and when so suspended, he has utterly neglected to attend to them.

He has refused to pass other Laws for the Accommodation of large Districts of People, unless those People would relinquish the Right of Representation in the Legislature, a Right inestimable to them, and formidable to Tyrants only.

He has called together Legislative Bodies at Places unusual, uncomfortable, and distant from the Depository of their Public Records, for the sole Purpose of fatiguing them into Compliance with his Measures.

He has dissolved Representative Houses repeatedly, for opposing with manly Firmness his Invasions on the Rights of the People.

He has refused for a long Time, after such Dissolutions, to cause others to be elected; whereby the Legislative Powers, incapable of Annihilation, have returned to the People at large for their exercise; the State remaining in the mean time exposed to all the Dangers of Invasion from without, and Convulsions within.

He has endeavoured to prevent the Population of these States; for that Purpose obstructing the Laws for Naturalization of Foreigners; refusing to pass others to encourage their Migrations hither, and raising the Conditions of new Appropriations of Lands.

He has obstructed the Administration of Justice, by refusing his Assent to Laws for establishing Judiciary Powers.

He has made Judges dependent on his Will alone, for the Tenure of their offices, and the Amount and payment of their Salaries.

He has erected a Multitude of new Offices, and sent hither Swarms of Officers to harrass our People, and eat out their Substance.

He has kept among us, in Times of Peace, Standing Armies, without the consent of our Legislatures.

He has affected to render the Military independent of, and superior to the Civil Power.

He has combined with others to subject us to a Jurisdiction foreign to our Constitution, and unacknowledged by our Laws; giving his Assent to their Acts of pretended Legislation:

For quartering large Bodies of Armed Troops among us:

For protecting them, by a mock Trial, from Punishment for any Murders which they should commit on the Inhabitants of these States:

For cutting off our Trade with all Parts of the World:

For imposing Taxes on us without our Consent:

For depriving us, in many cases, of the Benefits of Trial by Jury:

For transporting us beyond Seas to be tried for pretended Offences:

For abolishing the free System of English Laws in a neighbouring Province, establishing therein an arbitrary Government, and enlarging its Boundaries, so as to render it at once an Example and fit Instrument for introducing the same absolute Rule into these Colonies:

For taking away our Charters, abolishing our most valuable Laws, and altering fundamentally the Forms of our Governments:

For suspending our own Legislatures, and declaring themselves invested with Power to legislate for us in all Cases whatsoever.

He has abdicated Government here, by declaring us out of his Protection and waging War against us.

He has plundered our Seas, ravaged our Coasts, burnt our towns, and destroyed the Lives of our People.

He is, at this Time, transporting large Armies of foreign Mercenaries to compleat the works of Death, Desolation, and Tyranny, already begun with circumstances of Cruelty and Perfidy, scarcely paralleled in the most barbarous Ages, and totally unworthy the Head of a civilized Nation.

He has constrained our fellow Citizens taken Captive on the high Seas to bear Arms against their Country, to become the Executioners of their Friends and Brethren, or to fall themselves by their Hands.

He has excited domestic Insurrections amongst us, and has endeavoured to bring on the Inhabitants of our Frontiers, the merciless Indian Savages, whose known Rule of Warfare, is an undistinguished Destruction, of all Ages, Sexes and Conditions.

In every state of these Oppressions we have Petitioned for Redress in the most humble Terms: Our repeated Petitions have been answered only by repeated Injury. A Prince, whose Character is thus marked by every act which may define a Tyrant, is unfit to be the Ruler of a free People.

Nor have we been wanting in Attentions to our British Brethren. We have warned them from Time to Time of Attempts by their Legislature to extend an unwarrantable Jurisdiction over us. We have reminded them of the Circumstances of our Emigration and Settlement here. We have appealed to their native Justice and Magnanimity, and we have conjured them by the Ties of our common Kindred to disavow these Usurpations, which, would inevitably interrupt our Connections and Correspondence. They too have been deaf to the Voice of Justice and of Consanguinity. We must, therefore, acquiesce in the Necessity, which denounces our Separation, and hold them, as we hold the rest of Mankind, Enemies in War, in Peace, Friends.

We, therefore, the Representatives of the UNITED STATES OF AMERICA, in General Congress Assembled, appealing to the Supreme Judge of the World for the Rectitude of our Intentions, do, in the Name, and by the Authority of the good People of these Colonies, solemnly Publish and Declare, That these United Colonies are, and of Right ought to be, Free and Independent States; that they are absolved from all Allegiance to the British Crown, and that all political Connection between them and the State of Great-Britain, is and ought to be totally dissolved; and that as Free and Independent States, they have full Power to levy War, conclude Peace, contract Alliances, establish Commerce, and to do all other Acts and Things which Independent States may of right do. And for the support of this declaration, with a firm Reliance on the Protection of divine Providence, we mutually pledge to each other our lives, our Fortunes, and our sacred Honor.

B

The Constitution of the United States of America*

The Preamble

We the People of the United States, in Order to form a more perfect Union, establish Justice, insure domestic Tranquility, provide for the common defence, promote the general Welfare, and secure the Blessings of Liberty to ourselves and our Posterity, do ordain and establish this Constitution for the United States of America.

The Preamble declares that "We the People" are the authority for the Constitution (unlike the Articles of Confederation, which derived their authority from the states). The Preamble also sets out the purposes of the Constitution.

Article I. (Legislative Branch)

The first part of the Constitution is called Article 1; it deals with the organization and powers of the lawmaking branch of the national government, the Congress.

Section 1. Legislative Powers

All legislative Powers herein granted shall be vested in a Congress of the United States, which shall consist of a Senate and House of Representatives.

Section 2. House of Representatives

Clause 1: Composition and Election of Members. The House of Representatives shall be composed of Members chosen every second Year by the People of the several States, and the Electors in each State shall have the Qualifications requisite for Electors of the most numerous Branch of the State Legislature.

Each state has the power to decide who may vote for members of Congress. Within each state, those who may vote for state legislators may also vote for members of the House of Representatives (and, under the Seventeenth Amendment, for U.S. senators). When the Constitution was written, nearly all states limited voting rights to white male property owners or taxpayers at least twenty-one years old. Subsequent amendments granted voting power to African-American men, all women, and eighteen-year-olds.

Clause 2: Qualifications. No Person shall be a Representative who shall not have attained to the Age of twenty five Years, and been seven Years a Citizen of the United States, and who shall not, when elected, be an Inhabitant of that State in which he shall be chosen.

Each member of the House must (1) be at least twenty-five years old, (2) have been a U.S. citizen for at least seven years, and (3) be a resident of the state in which she or he is elected.

Clause 3: Apportionment of Representatives and Direct Taxes. Representatives [and direct Taxes][1] shall be apportioned among the several States which may be included within this Union, according to their respective Numbers [which shall be determined by adding to the whole Number of free Persons, including those bound to Service for a Term of Years, and excluding Indians not taxed, three fifths of all other Persons].[2] The actual Enumeration shall be made within three Years after the first Meeting of the Congress of the United States, and within every subsequent Term of ten Years, in such Manner as they shall by Law direct. The Number of Representatives

---

*The spelling, capitalization, and punctuation of the original have been retained here. Brackets indicate passages that have been altered by amendments to the Constitution.

---

[1] Modified by the Sixteenth Amendment.
[2] Modified by the Fourteenth Amendment.

shall not exceed one for every thirty Thousand, but each State shall have at Least one Representative; and until such enumeration shall be made, the State of New Hampshire shall be entitled to chuse three, Massachusetts eight, Rhode Island and Providence Plantations one, Connecticut five, New York six, New Jersey four, Pennsylvania eight, Delaware one, Maryland six, Virginia ten, North Carolina five, South Carolina five, and Georgia three.

A state's representation in the House is based on the size of its population. Population is counted in each decade's census, after which Congress reapportions House seats. Since early in this century, the number of seats has been limited to 435.

Clause 4: Vacancies. When vacancies happen in the Representation from any State, the Executive Authority thereof shall issue Writs of Election to fill such Vacancies.

The "Executive Authority" is the state's governor. When a vacancy occurs in the House, the governor calls a special election to fill it.

Clause 5: Officers and Impeachment. The House of Representatives shall chuse their Speaker and other Officers; and shall have the sole Power of Impeachment.

The power to impeach is the power to accuse. In this case, it is the power to accuse members of the executive or judicial branch of wrongdoing or abuse of power. Once a bill of impeachment is issued, the Senate holds the trial.

Section 3. The Senate
Clause 1: Term and Number of Members. The Senate of the United States shall be composed of two Senators from each State [chosen by the Legislature thereof],[3] for six Years; and each Senator shall have one Vote.

Every state has two senators, each of whom serves for six years and has one vote in the upper chamber. Since the Seventeenth Amendment in 1913, all senators are elected directly by voters of the state during the regular election.

Clause 2: Classification of Senators. Immediately after they shall be assembled in Consequence of the first Election, they shall be divided as equally as may be into three Classes. The Seats of the Senators of the first Class shall be vacated at the Expiration of the second Year, of the second Class at the Expiration of the fourth Year, and of the third Class at the Expiration of the sixth Year, so that one third may be chosen every second Year; [and if Vacancies happen by Resignation, or otherwise, during the Recess of the Legislature of any State, the Executive thereof may make temporary Appointments until the next Meeting of the Legislature, which shall then fill such Vacancies].[4]

One-third of the Senate's seats are open to election every two years (unlike the House, all of whose members are elected simultaneously).

Clause 3: Qualifications. No Person shall be a Senator who shall not have attained to the Age of thirty Years, and been nine Years a Citizen of the United States, and who shall not, when elected, be an Inhabitant of that State for which he shall be chosen.

Every senator must be at least thirty years old, a citizen of the United States for a minimum of nine years, and a resident of the state in which he or she is elected.

Clause 4: The Role of the Vice President. The Vice President of the United States shall be President of the Senate, but shall have no Vote, unless they be equally divided.

The vice president presides over meetings of the Senate but cannot vote unless there is a tie. The Constitution gives no other official duties to the vice president.

Clause 5: Other Officers. The Senate shall chuse their other Officers, and also a President pro tempore, in the Absence of the Vice President, or when he shall exercise the Office of President of the United States.

The Senate votes for one of its members to preside when the vice president is absent. This person is usually called the president pro tempore because of the temporary situation of the position.

Clause 6: Impeachment Trials. The Senate shall have the sole Power to try all Impeachments. When sitting for that Purpose, they shall be on Oath or Affirmation. When the President of the United States is tried, the Chief Justice shall preside: And no Person shall be convicted without the Concurrence of two thirds of the Members present.

The Senate conducts trials of officials that the House impeaches. The Senate sits as a jury, with the vice president presiding if the president is not on trial.

Clause 7: Penalties for Conviction. Judgment in Cases of Impeachment shall not extend further than to removal from Office, and disqualification to hold and enjoy any

---

[3]Repealed by the Seventeenth Amendment.

[4]Modified by the Seventeenth Amendment.

Office of honor, Trust, or Profit under the United States: but the Party convicted shall nevertheless be liable and subject to Indictment, Trial, Judgment, and Punishment, according to Law.

On conviction on impeachment charges, the Senate can only force an official to leave office and prevent him or her from holding another office in the federal government. The individual, however, can still be tried in a regular court.

Section 4. Congressional Elections: Times, Manner, and Places

Clause 1: Elections.   The Times, Places and Manner of holding Elections for Senators and Representatives, shall be prescribed in each State by the Legislature thereof; but the Congress may at any time by Law make or alter such Regulations, except as to the Places of chusing Senators.

Congress set the Tuesday after the first Monday in November in even-numbered years as the date for congressional elections. In states with more than one seat in the House, Congress requires that representatives be elected from districts within each state. Under the Seventeenth Amendment, senators are elected at the same places as other officials.

Clause 2: Sessions of Congress.   [The Congress shall assemble at least once in every Year, and such Meeting shall be on the first Monday in December, unless they shall by Law appoint a different Day.][5]

Congress has to meet every year at least once. The regular session now begins at noon on January 3 of each year, subsequent to the Twentieth Amendment, unless Congress passes a law to fix a different date. Congress stays in session until its members vote to adjourn. Additionally, the president may call a special session.

Section 5. Powers and Duties of the Houses

Clause 1: Admitting Members and Quorum.   Each House shall be the Judge of the Elections, Returns, and Qualifications of its own Members, and a Majority of each shall constitute a Quorum to do Business; but a smaller Number may adjourn from day to day, and may be authorized to compel the Attendance of absent Members, in such Manner, and under such Penalties as each House may provide.

Each chamber may exclude or refuse to seat a member-elect.

The quorum rule requires that 218 members of the House and 51 members of the Senate be present in order to conduct business. This rule is normally not enforced in the handling of routine matters.

Clause 2: Rules and Discipline of Members.   Each House may determine the Rules of its Proceedings, punish its Members for disorderly Behaviour, and, with the Concurrence of two thirds, expel a Member.

The House and the Senate may adopt their own rules to guide their proceedings. Each may also discipline its members for conduct that is deemed unacceptable. No member may be expelled without a two-thirds majority vote in favor of expulsion.

Clause 3: Keeping a Record.   Each House shall keep a Journal of its Proceedings, and from time to time publish the same, excepting such Parts as may in their Judgment require Secrecy; and the Yeas and Nays of the Members of either House on any question shall, at the Desire of one fifth of those Present, be entered on the Journal.

The journals of the two houses are published at the end of each session of Congress.

Clause 4: Adjournment.   Neither House, during the Session of Congress, shall, without the Consent of the other, adjourn for more than three days, nor to any other Place than that in which the two Houses shall be sitting.

Congress has the power to determine when and where to meet, provided, however, that both houses meet in the same city. Neither house may recess in excess of three days without the consent of the other.

Section 6. Rights of Members

Clause 1: Compensation and Privileges.   The Senators and Representatives shall receive a Compensation for their services, to be ascertained by Law, and paid out of the Treasury of the United States. They shall in all Cases, except Treason, Felony and Breach of the Peace, be privileged from Arrest during their Attendance at the Session of their respective Houses, and in going to and returning from the same; and for any Speech or Debate in either House, they shall not be questioned in any other Place.

Congressional salaries are to be paid by the U.S. Treasury rather than by the members' respective states. The original salaries were $6 per day; in 1857 they were $3,000 per year. Both representatives and senators currently are paid $133,600 each year.

Members cannot be arrested for things they say during speeches and debates in Congress. This immunity applies to the Capitol Building itself and not to their private lives.

Treason is defined in Article III, Section 3. A felony is any serious crime. A breach of the peace is any indictable offense

---

[5]Changed by the Twentieth Amendment.

less than treason or a felony. Members cannot be arrested for anything they say in speeches or debates in Congress.

Clause 2: Restrictions. No Senator or Representative shall, during the Time for which he was elected, be appointed to any civil Office under the Authority of the United States, which shall have been created, or the Emoluments whereof shall have been encreased during such time; and no Person holding any Office under the United States, shall be a Member of either House during his Continuance in Office.

During the term for which a member was elected, he or she cannot concurrently accept another federal government position.

Section 7. Legislative Powers: Bills and Resolutions

Clause 1: Revenue Bills. All Bills for raising Revenue shall originate in the House of Representatives; but the Senate may propose or concur with Amendments as on other Bills.

All tax and appropriation bills for raising money have to originate in the House of Representatives. The Senate, though, often amends such bills and may even substitute an entirely different bill.

Clause 2: The Presidential Veto. Every Bill which shall have passed the House of Representatives and the Senate, shall, before it becomes a Law, be presented to the President of the United States; If he approve he shall sign it, but if not he shall return it, with his Objections to the House in which it shall have originated, who shall enter the Objections at large on their Journal, and proceed to reconsider it. If after such Reconsideration two thirds of that House shall agree to pass the Bill, it shall be sent together with the Objections, to the other House, by which it shall likewise be reconsidered, and if approved by two thirds of that House, it shall become a Law. But in all such Cases the Votes of both Houses shall be determined by Yeas and Nays, and the Names of the Persons voting for and against the Bill shall be entered on the Journal of each House respectively. If any Bill shall not be returned by the President within ten Days (Sundays excepted) after it shall have been presented to him, the Same shall be a Law, in like Manner as if he had signed it, unless the Congress by their Adjournment prevent its Return in which Case it shall not be a Law.

When Congress sends the president a bill, he or she can sign it (in which case it becomes law) or send it back to the house in which it originated. If it is sent back, a two-thirds majority of each house must pass it again for it to become law. If the president neither signs it nor sends it back within ten days, it becomes law anyway, unless Congress adjourns in the meantime.

Clause 3: Actions on Other Matters. Every Order, Resolution, or Vote to which the Concurrence of the Senate and House of Representatives may be necessary (except on a question of Adjournment) shall be presented to the President of the United States; and before the Same shall take Effect, shall be approved by him, or being disapproved by him, shall be repassed by two thirds of the Senate and House of Representatives, according to the Rules and Limitations prescribed in the Case of a Bill.

The president must either sign or veto everything that Congress passes, except votes to adjourn and resolutions not having the force of law.

Section 8. The Powers of Congress

Clause 1: Taxing. The Congress shall have Power To lay and collect Taxes, Duties, Imposts and Excises, to pay the Debts and provide for the common Defence and general Welfare of the United States; but all Duties, Imposts and Excises shall be uniform throughout the United States;

Duties are taxes on imports and exports. Impost is a generic term for tax. Excises are taxes on the manufacture, sale, or use of goods.

Clause 2: Borrowing. To borrow Money on the credit of the United States;

Congress has the power to borrow money, which is normally carried out through the sale of U.S. treasury bonds on which interest is paid. Note that the Constitution places no limit on the amount of government borrowing.

Clause 3: Regulation of Commerce. To regulate Commerce with foreign Nations, and among the several States, and with the Indian Tribes;

This is the commerce clause, which gives to the Congress the power to regulate interstate and foreign trade. Much of the activity of Congress is based on this clause.

Clause 4: Naturalization and Bankruptcy. To establish a uniform Rule of Naturalization, and uniform Laws on the subject of Bankruptcies throughout the United States;

Only Congress may determine how aliens can become citizens of the United States. Congress may make laws with respect to bankruptcy.

Clause 5: Money and Standards. To coin Money, regulate the Value thereof, and of foreign Coin, and fix the Standard of Weights and Measures;

Congress mints coins and prints and circulates paper money. Congress can establish uniform measures of time, distance, weight, etc. In 1838, Congress adopted the English system of weights and measurements as our national standard.

Clause 6: Punishing Counterfeiters.   To provide for the Punishment of counterfeiting the Securities and current Coin of the United States;

Congress has the power to punish those who copy American money and pass it off as real. Currently, the fine is up to $5,000 and/or imprisonment for up to fifteen years.

Clause 7: Roads and Post Offices.   To establish Post Offices and post Roads;

Post roads include all routes over which mail is carried—highways, railways, waterways, and airways.

Clause 8: Patents and Copyrights.   To promote the Progress of Science and useful Arts, by securing for limited Times to Authors and Inventors the exclusive Right to their respective Writings and Discoveries;

Authors' and composers' works are protected by copyrights established by copyright law, which currently is the 1978 Copyright Act. Copyrights are valid for the life of the author or composer plus fifty years. Inventors' works are protected by patents, which vary in length of protection from three and a half to seventeen years. A patent gives a person the exclusive right to control the manufacture or sale of her or his invention.

Clause 9: Lower Courts.   To constitute Tribunals inferior to the supreme Court;

Congress has the authority to set up all federal courts, except the Supreme Court, and to decide what cases those courts will hear.

Clause 10: Punishment for Piracy.   To define and punish Piracies and Felonies committed on the high Seas, and Offences against the Law of Nations;

Congress has the authority to prohibit the commission of certain acts outside U.S. territory and to punish certain violations of international law.

Clause 11: Declaration of War.   To declare War, grant Letters of Marque and Reprisal, and make Rules concerning Captures on Land and Water;

Only Congress can declare war, although the president, as commander in chief, can make war without Congress's formal declaration. Letters of marque and reprisal authorized private

parties to capture and destroy enemy ships in wartime. Since the middle of the nineteenth century, international law has prohibited letters of marque and reprisal, and the United States has honored the ban.

Clause 12: The Army.   To raise and support Armies, but no Appropriation of Money to that Use shall be for a longer Term than two Years;

Congress has the power to create an army; the money used to pay for it must be appropriated for no more than two-year intervals. This latter restriction gives ultimate control of the army to civilians.

Clause 13: Creation of a Navy.   To provide and maintain a Navy;

This clause allows for the maintenance of a navy. In 1947, Congress created the air force.

Clause 14: Regulation of the Armed Forces.   To make Rules for the Government and Regulation of the land and naval Forces;

Congress sets the rules for the military mainly by way of the Uniform Code of Military Justice, which was enacted in 1950 by Congress.

Clause 15: The Militia.   To provide for calling forth the Militia to execute the Laws of the Union, suppress Insurrections and repel Invasions;

The militia is known today as the National Guard. Both Congress and the president have the authority to call the National Guard into federal service.

Clause 16: How the Militia Is Organized.   To provide for organizing, arming, and disciplining the Militia, and for governing such Part of them as may be employed in the Service of the United States, reserving to the States respectively, the Appointment of the Officers, and the Authority of training the Militia according to the discipline prescribed by Congress;

This clause gives Congress the power to "federalize" state militia (National Guard). When called into such service, the National Guard is subject to the same rules that Congress has set forth for the regular armed services.

Clause 17: Creation of the District of Columbia.   To exercise exclusive Legislation in all Cases whatsoever, over such District (not exceeding ten Miles square) as may, by Cession of particular States, and the Acceptance of Congress, become the Seat of the Government of the

United States, and to exercise like Authority over all Places purchased by the Consent of the Legislature of the State in which the Same shall be, for the Erection of Forts, Magazines, Arsenals, dock-Yards, and other needful Buildings;—And

Congress established the District of Columbia as the national capital in 1791. Virginia and Maryland had granted land for the District, but Virginia's grant was returned because it was believed it would not be needed. Today, the District covers sixty-nine square miles.

Clause 18: The Elastic Clause.   To make all Laws which shall be necessary and proper for carrying into Execution the foregoing Powers, and all other Powers vested by this Constitution in the Government of the United States, or in any Department or Officer thereof.

This clause—the necessary and proper clause, or the elastic clause—grants no specific powers, and thus it can be stretched to fit different circumstances. It has allowed Congress to adapt the government to changing needs and times.

Section 9. The Powers Denied to Congress
Clause 1: Question of Slavery.   The Migration or Importation of such Persons as any of the States now existing shall think proper to admit, shall not be prohibited by the Congress prior to the Year one thousand eight hundred and eight, but a Tax or duty may be imposed on such Importation, not exceeding ten dollars for each Person.

"Persons" referred to slaves. Congress outlawed the slave trade in 1808.

Clause 2: Habeas Corpus.   The privilege of the Writ of Habeas Corpus shall not be suspended, unless when in Cases of Rebellion or Invasion the public Safety may require it.

A writ of habeas corpus is a court order directing a sheriff or other public officer who is detaining another person to "produce the body" of the detainee so the court can assess the legality of the detention.

Clause 3: Special Bills.   No Bill of Attainder or ex post facto Law shall be passed.

A bill of attainder is a law that inflicts punishment without a trial. An ex post facto law is a law that inflicts punishment for an act that was not illegal when it was committed.

Clause 4: Direct Taxes.   [No Capitation, or other direct, Tax shall be laid, unless in Proportion to the Census or Enumeration herein before directed to be taken.][6]

---
[6]Modified by the Sixteenth Amendment.

A capitation is a tax on a person. A direct tax is a tax paid directly to the government, such as a property tax. This clause was intended to prevent Congress from levying a tax on slaves per person and thereby taxing slavery out of existence.

Clause 5: Export Taxes.   No Tax or Duty shall be laid on Articles exported from any State.

Congress may not tax any goods sold from one state to another or from one state to a foreign country. (Congress does have the power to tax goods that are bought from other countries, however.)

Clause 6: Interstate Commerce.   No Preference shall be given by any Regulation of Commerce or Revenue to the Ports of one State over those of another: nor shall Vessels bound to, or from, one State, be obliged to enter, clear, or pay Duties in another.

Congress may not treat different ports within the United States differently in terms of taxing and commerce powers. Congress may not tax goods sent from one state to another. Finally, Congress may not give one state's port a legal advantage over those of another state.

Clause 7: Treasury Withdrawals.   No Money shall be drawn from the Treasury, but in Consequence of Appropriations made by Law; and a regular Statement and Account of the Receipts and Expenditures of all public Money shall be published from time to time.

Federal funds can be spent only as Congress authorizes. This is a significant check on the president's power.

Clause 8: Titles of Nobility.   No Title of Nobility shall be granted by the United States: And no Person holding any Office of Profit or Trust under them, shall, without the Consent of the Congress, accept of any present, Emolument, Office, or Title, of any kind whatever, from any King, Prince, or foreign State.

On no person in the United States may be bestowed a title of nobility, such as a duke or duchess. This clause also discourages bribery of American officials by foreign governments.

Section 10. Those Powers Denied to the States
Clause 1: Treaties and Coinage.   No State shall enter into any Treaty, Alliance, or Confederation; grant Letters of Marque and Reprisal; coin Money; emit Bills of Credit; make any Thing but gold and silver Coin a Tender in Payment of Debts; pass any Bill of Attainder, ex post facto Law, or Law impairing the Obligation of Contracts, or grant any Title of Nobility.

Prohibiting state laws "impairing the Obligation of Contracts" was intended to protect creditors. (Shays' Rebellion—an attempt to prevent courts from giving effect to creditors'

legal actions against debtors—occurred only one year before the Constitution was written.)

Clause 2: Duties and Imposts. No State shall, without the Consent of the Congress, lay any Imports or Duties on Imports or Exports, except what may be absolutely necessary for executing its inspection Laws; and the net Produce of all Duties and Imposts, laid by any State on Imports or Exports, shall be for the Use of the Treasury of the United States; and all such Laws shall be subject to the Revision and Controul of the Congress.

Only Congress can tax imports. Further, the states cannot tax exports.

Clause 3: War. No State shall, without the Consent of Congress, lay any Duty of Tonnage, keep Troops, or Ships of War in time of Peace, enter into any Agreement or Compact with another State, or with a foreign Power or engage in War, unless actually invaded, or in such imminent Danger as will not admit of delay.

A duty of tonnage is a tax on ships according to their cargo capacity. No states may effectively tax ships according to their cargo unless Congress agrees. Additionally, this clause forbids any state to keep troops or warships during peacetime or to make a compact with another state or foreign nation unless Congress so agrees. States can, in contrast, maintain a militia, but its use has to be limited to internal disorders that occur within a state—unless, of course, the militia is called into federal service.

Article II. (Executive Branch)

Section 1. The Nature and Scope of Presidential Power

Clause 1: Four-Year Term. The executive Power shall be vested in a President of the United States of America. He shall hold his Office during the Term of four Years, and, together with the Vice President, chosen for the same Term, be elected, as follows.

The president has the power to carry out laws made by Congress, called the executive power. He or she serves in office for a four-year term after election. The Twenty-second Amendment limits the number of times a person may be elected president.

Clause 2: Choosing Electors from Each State. Each State shall appoint, in such Manner as the Legislature thereof may direct, a Number of Electors, equal to the whole Number of Senators and Representatives to which the State may be entitled in the Congress; but no Senator or Representative, or Person holding an Office of Trust or Profit under the United States, shall be appointed an Elector.

The "Electors" are more commonly known as the "electoral college." The president is elected by electors—that is, representatives chosen by the people—rather than by the people directly.

Clause 3: The Former System of Elections. [The Electors shall meet in their respective States, and vote by Ballot for two Persons, of whom one at least shall not be an Inhabitant of the same State with themselves. And they shall make a List of all the Persons voted for, and of the Number of Votes for each; which List they shall sign and certify, and transmit sealed to the Seat of the Government of the United States, directed to the President of the Senate. The President of the Senate shall, in the Presence of the Senate and House of Representatives, open all the Certificates, and the Votes shall then be counted. The Person having the greatest Number of Votes shall be the President, if such Number be a Majority of the whole Number of Electors appointed; and if there be more than one who have such Majority, and have an equal Number of Votes, then the House of Representatives shall immediately chuse by Ballot one of them for President; and if no Person have a Majority, then from the five highest on the List the said House shall in like Manner chuse the President. But in chusing the President, the Votes shall be taken by States, the Representation from each State having one Vote; A quorum for this Purpose shall consist of a Member or Members from two thirds of the States, and a Majority of all the States shall be necessary to a Choice. In every Case, after the Choice of the President, the Person having the greater Number of Votes of the Electors shall be the Vice President. But if there should remain two or more who have equal Votes, the Senate shall chuse from them by Ballot the Vice President.][7]

The original method of selecting the president and vice-president was replaced by the Twelfth Amendment. Apparently, the framers did not anticipate the rise of political parties and the development of primaries and conventions.

Clause 4: The Time of Elections. The Congress may determine the Time of chusing the Electors, and the Day on which they shall give their Votes; which Day shall be the same throughout the United States.

Congress set the Tuesday after the first Monday in November every fourth year as the date for choosing electors. The electors cast their votes on the Monday after the second Wednesday in December of that year.

Clause 5: Qualifications for President. No person except a natural born Citizen, or a Citizen of the United States, at the time of the Adoption of this Constitution,

---

[7]Changed by the Twelfth Amendment.

shall be eligible to the Office of President; neither shall any Person be eligible to that Office who shall not have attained to the Age of thirty five Years, and been four-teen Years a Resident within the United States.

The president must be a natural-born citizen, be at least thirty-five years of age when taking office, and have been a resident within the United States for at least fourteen years.

Clause 6: *Succession of the Vice President.* [In Case of the Removal of the President from Office, or of his Death, Resignation or Inability to discharge the Powers and Duties of the said Office, the same shall devolve on the Vice President, and the Congress may by Law pro-vide for the Case of Removal, Death, Resignation or Inability, both of the President and Vice President, declaring what Officer shall then act as President, and such Officer shall act accordingly, until the Disability be removed, or a President shall be elected.][8]

This former section provided for the method by which the vice president was to succeed to the presidency, but its wording is ambiguous. It was replaced by the Twenty-fifth Amendment.

Clause 7: *The President's Salary.* The President shall, at stated Times, receive for his Services, a Compensa-tion, which shall neither be encreased nor diminished during the Period for which he shall have been elected, and he shall not receive within that Period any other Emolument from the United States, or any of them.

The president maintains the same salary during each four-year term. Moreover, she or he may not receive additional cash payments from the government. Originally set at $25,000 per year, it is currently $200,000 a year plus a $50,000 taxable expense account.

Clause 8: *The Oath of Office.* Before he enter on the Execution of his Office, he shall take the following Oath or Affirmation: "I do solemnly swear (or affirm) that I will faithfully execute the Office of President of the United States, and will to the best of my Ability, pre-serve, protect and defend the Constitution of the United States."

The president is "sworn in" prior to beginning the duties of the office. Currently, the taking of the oath of office occurs on January 20, following the November election. The ceremony is called the inauguration. The oath of office is administered by the chief justice of the United States Supreme Court.

Section 2. Powers of the President
Clause 1: *Commander in Chief.* The President shall be Commander in Chief of the Army and Navy of the

United States, and of the Militia of the several States, when called into the actual Service of the United States; he may require the Opinion, in writing, of the principal Officer in each of the executive Departments, upon any Subject relating to the Duties of their respective Offices, and he shall have Power to grant Reprieves and Par-dons for Offences against the United States, except in Cases of Impeachment.

The armed forces are placed under civilian control because the president is a civilian, but still commander in chief of the mil-itary. The president may ask for the help of the heads of each of the executive departments (thereby creating the cabinet). The cabinet members are chosen by the president with the consent of the Senate, but they can be removed without Sen-ate approval.

The president's clemency powers extend only to federal cases. In those cases, he or she may grant a full or conditional pardon, or reduce a prison term or fine.

Clause 2: *Treaties and Appointment.* He shall have Power, by and with the Advice and Consent of the Sen-ate, to make Treaties, provided two thirds of the Sena-tors present concur; and he shall nominate, and by and with the Advice and Consent of the Senate, shall appoint Ambassadors, other public Ministers and Con-suls, Judges of the supreme Court, and all other Officers of the United States, whose Appointments are not herein otherwise provided for, and which shall be estab-lished by Law; but the Congress may by Law vest the Appointment of such inferior Officers, as they think proper, in the President alone, in the Courts of Law, or in the Heads of Departments.

Many of the major powers of the president are identified in this clause, including the power to make treaties with foreign governments (with the approval of the Senate by a two-thirds vote) and the power to appoint ambassadors, Supreme Court justices, and other government officials. Most such appoint-ments require Senate approval.

Clause 3: *Vacancies.* The President shall have Power to fill up all Vacancies that may happen during the Recess of the Senate, by granting Commissions which shall expire at the end of their next Session.

The president has the power to appoint temporary officials to fill vacant federal offices without Senate approval if the Con-gress is not in session. Such appointments expire automati-cally at the end of Congress's next term.

Section 3. Duties of the President
He shall from time to time give to the Congress Infor-mation of the State of the Union, and recommend to

---

[8]Modified by the Twenty-fifth Amendment.

their Consideration such Measures as he shall judge necessary and expedient; he may, on extraordinary Occasions, convene both Houses, or either of them, and in Case of Disagreement between them, with Respect to the Time of Adjournment, he may adjourn them to such Time as he shall think proper; he shall receive Ambassadors and other public Ministers; he shall take Care that the Laws be faithfully executed, and shall Commission all the Officers of the United States.

Annually, the president reports on the state of the union to Congress, recommends legislative measures, and proposes a federal budget. The State of the Union speech is a statement not only to Congress but also to the American people. After it is given, the president proposes a federal budget and presents an economic report. At any time he or she so chooses, the president may send special messages to Congress while it is in session. The president has the power to call special sessions, to adjourn Congress when its two houses do not agree for that purpose, to receive diplomatic representatives of other governments, and to ensure the proper execution of all federal laws. The president further has the ability to empower federal officers to hold their positions and to perform their duties.

Section 4. Impeachment

The President, Vice President and all civil Officers of the United States, shall be removed from Office on Impeachment for, and Conviction of, Treason, Bribery, or other high Crimes and Misdemeanors.

Treason denotes giving aid to the nation's enemies. The definition of high crimes and misdemeanors is usually given as serious abuses of political power. In either case, the president or vice president may be accused by the House (called an impeachment) and then removed from office if convicted by the Senate. (Note that impeachment *does not mean removal, but rather the state of being accused of treason or high crimes and misdemeanors.)*

Article III. (Judicial Branch)

Section 1. Judicial Powers, Courts, and Judges

The judicial Power of the United States, shall be vested in one supreme Court, and in such inferior Courts as the Congress may from time to time ordain and establish. The Judges, both of the supreme and inferior Courts, shall hold their Offices during good Behaviour, and shall, at stated Times, receive for their Services a Compensation, which shall not be diminished during their Continuance in Office.

The Supreme Court is vested with judicial power, as are the lower federal courts that Congress creates. Federal judges serve in their offices for life unless they are impeached and convicted by Congress. The payment of federal judges may not be reduced during their time in office.

Section 2. Jurisdiction

Clause 1: Cases Under Federal Jurisdiction. The judicial Power shall extend to all Cases, in Law and Equity, arising under this Constitution, the Laws of the United States, and Treaties made, or which shall be made, under their Authority;—to all Cases affecting Ambassadors, other public Ministers and Consuls;—to all Cases of admiralty and maritime Jurisdiction;—to Controversies to which the United States shall be a Party;—to Controversies between two or more States; [—between a State and Citizens of another State;—][9] between Citizens of different States;—between Citizens of the same State claiming Lands under Grants of different States, [and between a State, or the Citizens thereof, and foreign States, Citizens or Subjects.][10]

The federal courts take on cases that concern the meaning of the U.S. Constitution, all federal laws, and treaties. They also can take on cases involving citizens of different states and citizens of foreign nations.

Clause 2: Cases for the Supreme Court. In all Cases affecting Ambassadors, other public Ministers and Consuls, and those in which a State shall be a Party, the supreme Court shall have original Jurisdiction. In all the other Cases before mentioned, the supreme Court shall have appellate Jurisdiction, both as to Law and Fact, with such Exceptions, and under such Regulations as the Congress shall make.

In a limited number of situations, the Supreme Court acts as a trial court and has original jurisdiction. These cases involve a representative from another country or involve a state. In all other situations, the cases must first be tried in the lower courts and then can be appealed to the Supreme Court. Congress may, however, make exceptions. Today the Supreme Court acts as a trial court of first instance on rare occasions.

Clause 3: The Conduct of Trials. The Trial of all Crimes, except in Cases of Impeachment, shall be by Jury; and such Trial shall be held in the State where the said Crimes shall have been committed; but when not committed within any State, the Trial shall be at such Place or Places as the Congress may by Law have directed.

Any person accused of a federal crime is granted the right to a trial by jury in a federal court in that state in which the crime was committed. Trials of impeachment are an exception.

Section 3. Treason

Clause 1: The Definition of Treason. Treason against the United States, shall consist only in levying War

---

[9]Modified by the Eleventh Amendment.
[10]Modified by the Eleventh Amendment.

against them, or, in adhering to their Enemies, giving them Aid and Comfort. No Person shall be convicted of Treason unless on the Testimony of two Witnesses to the same overt Act, or on Confession in open Court.

Treason is the making of war against the United States or giving aid to its enemies.

Clause 2: Punishment. The Congress shall have Power to declare the Punishment of Treason, but no Attainder of Treason shall work Corruption of Blood, or Forfeiture except during the Life of the Person attainted.

Congress has provided that the punishment for treason ranges from a minimum of five years in prison and/or a $10,000 fine to a maximum of death. "No Attainder of Treason shall work Corruption of Blood" prohibits punishment of the traitor's heirs.

Article IV. (Relations Among the States)

Section 1. Full Faith and Credit
Full Faith and Credit shall be given in each State to the public Acts, Records, and judicial Proceedings of every other State. And the Congress may by general Laws prescribe the Manner in which such Acts, Records and Proceedings shall be proved, and the Effect thereof.

All states are required to respect one another's laws, records, and lawful decisions. There are exceptions, however. A state does not have to enforce another state's criminal code. Nor does it have to recognize another state's grant of a divorce if the person obtaining the divorce did not establish legal residence in the state in which it was given.

Section 2. Treatment of Citizens
Clause 1: Privileges and Immunities. The Citizens of each State shall be entitled to all Privileges and Immunities of Citizens in the several States.

A citizen of a state has the same rights and privileges as the citizens of another state in which he or she happens to be.

Clause 2: Extradition. A Person charged in any State with Treason, Felony, or other Crime, who shall flee from Justice, and be found in another State, shall on Demand of the executive Authority of the State from which he fled, be delivered up, to be removed to the State having Jurisdiction of the Crime.

Any person accused of a crime who flees to another state must be returned to the state in which the crime occurred.

Clause 3: Fugitive Slaves. [No Person held to Service or Labour in one State, under the Laws thereof, escap-

ing into another, shall, in Consequence of any Law or Regulation therein, be discharged from such Service or Labour, but shall be delivered up on Claim of the Party to whom such Service or Labour may be due.][11]

This clause was struck down by the Thirteenth Amendment, which abolished slavery in 1865.

Section 3. Admission of States
Clause 1: The Process. New States may be admitted by the Congress into this Union; but no new State shall be formed or erected within the Jurisdiction of any other State; nor any State be formed by the Junction of two or more States, or Parts of States, without the Consent of the Legislatures of the States concerned as well as of the Congress.

Only Congress has the power to admit new states to the union. No state may be created by taking territory from an existing state unless the state's legislature so consents.

Clause 2: Public Land. The Congress shall have Power to dispose of and make all needful Rules and Regulations respecting the Territory or other Property belonging to the United States; and nothing in this Constitution shall be so construed as to Prejudice any Claims of the United States, or of any particular State.

The federal government has the exclusive right to administer federal government public lands.

Section 4. Republican Form of Government
The United States shall guarantee to every State in this Union a Republican Form of Government, and shall protect each of them against Invasion; and on Application of the Legislature, or of the Executive (when the Legislature cannot be convened) against domestic Violence.

Each state is promised a form of government in which the people elect their representatives, called a republican form. The federal government is bound to protect states against any attack by foreigners or during times of trouble within a state.

Article V. (Methods of Amendment)
The Congress, whenever two thirds of both Houses shall deem it necessary, shall propose Amendments to this Constitution, or on the Application of the Legislatures of two thirds of the several States, shall call a Convention for proposing Amendments, which, in either Case, shall be valid to all Intents and Purposes, as Part of this Constitution, when ratified by the Legislatures of three fourths of the several States, or by Conventions in three fourths thereof, as the one or the other Mode of

---

[11]Repealed by the Thirteenth Amendment.

Ratification may be proposed by the Congress; Provided that no Amendment which may be made prior to the Year One thousand eight hundred and eight shall in any Manner affect the first and fourth Clauses in the Ninth Section of the First Article; and that no State, without its Consent, shall be deprived of its equal Suffrage in the Senate.

Amendments may be proposed in either of two ways: a two-thirds vote of each house (Congress) or at the request of two-thirds of the states. Ratification of amendments may be carried out in two ways: by the legislatures of three-fourths of the states or by the voters in three-fourths of the states. No state may be denied equal representation in the Senate.

Article VI. (National Supremacy)

Clause 1: Existing Obligations. All Debts contracted and Engagements entered into, before the Adoption of this Constitution shall be as valid against the United States under this Constitution, as under the Confederation.

During the Revolutionary War and the years of the Confederation, Congress borrowed large sums. This clause pledged that the new federal government would assume those financial obligations.

Clause 2: Supreme Law of the Land. This Constitution, and the Laws of the United States which shall be made in Pursuance thereof; and all Treaties made, or which shall be made, under the Authority of the United States, shall be the supreme Law of the Land; and the Judges in every State shall be bound thereby, any Thing in the Constitution or Laws of any State to the Contrary notwithstanding.

This is typically called the supremacy clause; it declares that federal law takes precedence over all forms of state law. No government, at the local or state level, may make or enforce any law that conflicts with any provision of the Constitution, acts of Congress, treaties, or other rules and regulations issued by the president and his or her subordinates in the executive branch of the federal government.

Clause 3: Oath of Office. The Senators and Representatives before mentioned, and the Members of the several State Legislatures, and all executive and judicial Officers, both of the United States and of the several States, shall be bound by Oath or Affirmation, to support this Constitution; but no religious Test shall ever be required as a Qualification to any Office or public Trust under the United States.

Every federal and state official must take an oath of office promising to support the U.S. Constitution. Religion may not be used as a qualification to serve in any federal office.

Article VII. (Ratification)

The Ratification of the Conventions of nine States shall, be sufficient for the Establishment of this Constitution between the States so ratifying the Same.

Nine states were required to ratify the Constitution. Delaware was the first and New Hampshire the ninth.

Done in Convention by the Unanimous Consent of the States present the Seventeenth Day of September in the Year of our Lord one thousand seven hundred and Eighty seven and of the Independence of the United States of America the Twelfth. In witness whereof we have hereunto subscribed our Names,

Go. WASHINGTON
Presid't. and deputy from Virginia

Attest
WILLIAM JACKSON
Secretary

DELAWARE
Geo. Read
Gunning Bedfordjun
John Dickinson
Richard Basset
Jaco. Broom

MASSACHUSETTS
Nathaniel Gorham
Rufus King

CONNECTICUT
Wm. Saml. Johnson
Roger Sherman

NEW YORK
Alexander Hamilton

NEW JERSEY
Wh. Livingston
David Brearley.
Wm. Paterson.
Jona. Dayton

PENNSYLVANIA
B. Franklin
Thomas Mifflin
Robt. Morris
Geo. Clymer
Thos. FitzSimons
Jared Ingersoll
James Wilson.
Gouv. Morris

NEW HAMPSHIRE
John Langdon
Nicholas Gilman

MARYLAND
James McHenry
Dan of St. Thos. Jenifer
Danl. Carroll.

VIRGINIA
John Blair
James Madison Jr.

NORTH CAROLINA
Wm. Blount
Richd. Dobbs Spaight.
Hu. Williamson

SOUTH CAROLINA
J. Rutledge
Charles Cotesworth Pinckney
Charles Pinckney
Pierce Butler.

GEORGIA
William Few
Abr. Baldwin

Articles in addition to, and amendment of the Constitution of the United States of America, proposed by Congress and ratified by the Legislatures of the several states, pursuant to the Fifth Article of the original Constitution.

Amendments to the Constitution of the United States

The Bill of Rights[12]

Amendment I.
Religion, Speech, Assembly, and Politics

Congress shall make no law respecting an establishment of religion, or prohibiting the free exercise thereof; or abridging the freedom of speech, or of the press; or the right of the people peaceably to assembly, and to petition the Government for a redress of grievances.

Congress may not create an official church or enact laws limiting the freedom of religion, speech, the press, assembly, and petition. These guarantees, like the others in the Bill of Rights (the first ten amendments), are not absolute—each may be exercised only with regard to the rights of other persons.

Amendment II.
Militia and the Right to Bear Arms

A well regulated Militia, being necessary to the security of a free State, the right of the people to keep and bear Arms, shall not be infringed.

To protect itself, each state has the right to maintain a volunteer armed force. States and the federal government regulate the possession and use of firearms by individuals.

Amendment III.
The Quartering of Soldiers

No Soldier shall, in time of peace be quartered in any house, without the consent of the Owner, nor in time of war, but in a manner to be prescribed by law.

Before the Revolutionary War, it had been common British practice to quarter soldiers in colonists' homes. Military troops do not have the power to take over private houses during peacetime.

---

[12]On September 25, 1789, Congress transmitted to the state legislatures twelve proposed amendments, two of which, having to do with congressional representation and congressional pay, were not adopted. The remaining ten amendments became the Bill of Rights. In 1992, the amendment concerning congressional pay was adopted as the Twenty-seventh Amendment.

Amendment IV.
Searches and Seizures

The right of the people to be secure in their persons, houses, papers, and effects, against unreasonable searches and seizures, shall not be violated, and no Warrants shall issue, but upon probable cause, supported by Oath or affirmation, and particularly describing the place to be searched, and the persons or things to be seized.

Here the word warrant means "justification" and refers to a document issued by a magistrate or judge indicating the name, address, and possible offense committed. Anyone asking for the warrant, such as a police officer, must be able to convince the magistrate or judge that an offense probably has been committed.

Amendment V.
Grand Juries, Self-incrimination, Double Jeopardy, Due Process, and Eminent Domain

No person shall be held to answer for a capital, or otherwise infamous crime, unless on a presentment or indictment of a Grand Jury, except in cases arising in the land or naval forces, or in the Militia, when in actual service in time of War or public danger; nor shall any person be sub- ject for the same offence to be twice put in jeopardy of life or limb; nor shall be compelled in any criminal case to be a witness against himself, nor be deprived of life, liberty, or property, without due process of law; nor shall private property be taken for public use, without just compensation.

There are two types of juries. A grand jury considers physical evidence and the testimony of witnesses, and decides whether there is sufficient reason to bring a case to trial. A petit jury hears the case at trial and decides it. "For the same offence to be twice put in jeopardy of life or limb" means to be tried twice for the same crime. A person may not be tried for the same crime twice or forced to give evidence against herself or himself. No person's right to life, liberty, or property may be taken away except by lawful means, called the due process of law. Private property taken for use in public purposes must be paid for by the government.

Amendment VI.
Criminal Court Procedures

In all criminal prosecutions, the accused shall enjoy the right to a speedy and public trial, by an impartial jury of the State and district wherein the crime shall have been committed, which district shall have been previously ascertained by law, and to be informed of the nature and cause of the accusation; to be confronted with the witnesses against him; to have compulsory process for obtaining witnesses in his favor, and to have the assistance of counsel for his defence.

Any person accused of a crime has the right to a fair and public trial by a jury in the state in which the crime took place. The charges against that person must be so indicated. Any accused person has the right to a lawyer to defend him or her and to question those who testify against him or her, as well as the right to call people to speak in his or her favor at trial.

Amendment VII.
Trial by Jury in Civil Cases
In Suits at common law, where the value in controversy shall exceed twenty dollars, the right of trial by jury shall be preserved, and no fact tried by jury, shall be otherwise re-examined in any Court of the United States, than according to the rules of the common law.

A jury trial may be requested by either party in a dispute in any case involving more than $20. If both parties agree to a trial by a judge without a jury, the right to a jury trial may be put aside.

Amendment VIII.
Bail, Cruel and Unusual Punishment
Excessive bail shall not be required, nor excessive fines imposed, nor cruel and unusual punishments inflicted.

Bail is that amount of money that a person accused of a crime may be required to deposit with the court as a guarantee that she or he will appear in court when requested. The amount of bail required or the fine imposed as punishment for a crime must be reasonable compared with the seriousness of the crime involved. Any punishment judged to be too harsh or too severe for a crime shall be prohibited.

Amendment IX.
The Rights Retained by the People
The enumeration in the Constitution, of certain rights, shall not be construed to deny or disparage others retained by the people.

Many civil rights that are not explicitly enumerated in the Constitution are still held by the people.

Amendment X.
Reserved Powers of the States
The powers not delegated to the United States by the Constitution, nor prohibited by it to the States, are reserved to the States respectively, or to the people.

Those powers not delegated by the Constitution to the federal government or expressly denied to the states belong to the

states and to the people. This clause in essence allows the states to pass laws under its "police powers."

Amendment XI
(Ratified on February 7, 1795).
Suits Against States
The Judicial power of the United States shall not be construed to extend to any suit in law or equity, commenced or prosecuted against one of the United States by Citizens of another State, or by Citizens or Subjects of any Foreign State.

This amendment has been interpreted to mean that a state cannot be sued in federal court by one of its citizens, by a citizen of another state, or by a foreign country.

Amendment XII
(Ratified on June 15, 1804).
Election of the President
The Electors shall meet in their respective states, and vote by ballot for President and Vice-President, one of whom, at least, shall not be an inhabitant of the same State with themselves; they shall name in their ballots the person voted for as President, and in distinct ballots the person voted for as Vice-President, and they shall make distinct lists of all persons voted for as President, and of all persons voted for as Vice-President, and of the number of votes for each, which lists they shall sign and certify, and transmit sealed to the seat of the government of the United States, directed to the President of the Senate;—The President of the Senate shall, in the presence of the Senate and House of Representatives, open all the certificates and the votes shall then be counted;—The person having the greatest number of votes for President, shall be the President, if such number be a majority of the whole number of Electors appointed; and if no person have such majority, then from the persons having the highest numbers not exceeding three on the list of those voted for as President, the House of Representatives shall choose immediately, by ballot, the President. But in choosing the President, the votes shall be taken by States, the representation from each State having one vote; a quorum for this purpose shall consist of a member or members from two-thirds of the States, and a majority of all States shall be necessary to a choice. [And if the House of Representatives shall not choose a President whenever the right of choice shall devolve upon them, before the fourth day of March next following, then the Vice-President shall act as President, as in the case of the death or other constitutional disability of the President.][13]—The person having the greatest number of votes as Vice-President, shall be the Vice-President, if

---

[13]Changed by the Twentieth Amendment.

such number be a majority of the whole number of Electors appointed, and if no person have a majority, then from the two highest numbers on the list, the Senate shall choose the Vice President; a quorum for the purpose shall consist of two-thirds of the whole number of Senators, and a majority of the whole number shall be necessary to a choice. But no person constitutionally ineligible to the office of President shall be eligible to that of Vice-President of the United States.

The original procedure set out for the election of president and vice-president in Article II, Section 1, resulted in a tie in 1800 between Thomas Jefferson and Aaron Burr. It was not until the next year that the House of Representatives chose Jefferson to be president. This amendment changed the procedure by providing for separate ballots for president and vice president.

Amendment XIII
(Ratified on December 6, 1865).
Prohibition of Slavery

Section 1.
Neither slavery nor involuntary servitude, except as a punishment for crime whereof the party shall have been duly convicted, shall exist within the United States, or any place subject to their jurisdiction.

Some slaves had been freed during the Civil War. This amendment freed the others and abolished slavery.

Section 2.
Congress shall have power to enforce this article by appropriate legislation.

Amendment XIV
(Ratified on July 9, 1868).
Citizenship, Due Process, and [lbEqual Protection of the Laws

Section 1.
All persons born or naturalized in the United States, and subject to the jurisdiction thereof, are citizens of the United States and of the State wherein they reside. No State shall make or enforce any law which shall abridge the privileges or immunities of citizens of the United States; nor shall any State deprive any person of life, liberty, or property, without due process of law; nor deny to any person within its jurisdiction the equal protection of the laws.

Under this provision, states cannot make or enforce laws that take away rights given to all citizens by the federal government. States cannot act unfairly or arbitrarily toward, or discriminate against, any person.

Section 2.
Representatives shall be apportioned among the several States according to their respective numbers, counting the whole number of persons in each State, excluding Indians not taxed. But when the right to vote at any election for the choice of electors for President and Vice President of the United States, Representatives in Congress, the Executive and Judicial officers of a State, or the members of the Legislature thereof, is denied to any of the male inhabitants of such State, being [twenty-one][14] years of age, and citizens of the United States, or in any way abridged, except for participation in rebellion, or other crime, the basis of representation therein shall be reduced in the proportion which the number of such male citizens shall bear to the whole number of male citizens twenty-one years of age in such State.

Section 3.
No person shall be a Senator or Representative in Congress, or elector of President and Vice President, or hold any office, civil or military, under the United States, or under any State, who having previously taken an oath, as a member of Congress, or as an officer of the United States, or as a member of any State legislature, or as an executive or judicial officer of any State, to support the Constitution of the United States, shall have engaged in insurrection or rebellion against the same, or given aid or comfort to the enemies thereof. But Congress may by a vote of two-thirds of each House, remove such disability.

This provision forbade former state or federal government officials who had acted in support of the Confederacy during the Civil War to hold office again. It limited the president's power to pardon those persons. Congress removed this "disability" in 1898.

Section 4.
The validity of the public debt of the United States, authorized by law, including debts incurred for payment of pensions and bounties for services in suppressing insurrection or rebellion, shall not be questioned. But neither the United States nor any State shall assume or pay any debt or obligation incurred in aid of insurrection or rebellion against the United States, or any claim for the loss or emancipation of any slave, but all such debts, obligations and claims shall be held illegal and void.

Section 5.
The Congress shall have power to enforce, by appropriate legislation, the provisions of this article.

---

[14]Changed by the Twenty-sixth Amendment.

Amendment XV
(Ratified on February 3, 1870).
The Right to Vote

Section 1.

The right of citizens of the United States to vote shall not be denied or abridged by the United States or by any State on account of race, color, or previous condition of servitude.

No citizen can be refused the right to vote simply because of race or color or because that person was once a slave.

Section 2.

The Congress shall have power to enforce this article by appropriate legislation.

Amendment XVI
(Ratified on February 3, 1913).
Income Taxes

The Congress shall have power to lay and collect taxes on incomes, from whatever source derived, without apportionment among the several States, and without regard to any census or enumeration.

This amendment allows Congress to tax income without sharing the revenue so obtained with the states according to their population.

Amendment XVII
(Ratified on April 8, 1913).
The Popular Election of Senators

The Senate of the United States shall be composed of two Senators from each State, elected by the people thereof, for six years; and each Senator shall have one vote. The electors in each State shall have the qualifications requisite for electors of the most numerous branch of the State legislatures.

When vacancies happen in the representation of any State in the Senate, the executive authority of such State shall issue writs of election to fill such vacancies: *Provided,* That the legislature of any State may empower the executive thereof to make temporary appointments until the people fill the vacancies by election as the legislature may direct.

This amendment shall not be so construed as to affect the election or term of any Senator chosen before it becomes valid as part of the Constitution.

This amendment modified portions of Article I, Section 3, that related to election of senators. Senators are now elected by the voters in each state directly. When a vacancy occurs, either

the state may fill the vacancy by a special election, or the governor of the state involved may appoint someone to fill the seat until the next election.

Amendment XVIII
(Ratified on January 16, 1919).
Prohibition.

Section 1.

After one year from the ratification of this article the manufacture, sale, or transportation of intoxicating liquors within, the importation thereof into, or the exportation thereof from the United States and all territory subject to the jurisdiction thereof for beverage purposes is hereby prohibited.

Section 2.

The Congress and the several States shall have concurrent power to enforce this article by appropriate legislation.

Section 3.

This article shall be inoperative unless it shall have been ratified as an amendment to the Constitution by the legislatures of the several States, as provided in the Constitution, within seven years from the date of the submission hereof to the States by the Congress.[15]

This amendment made it illegal to manufacture, sell, and transport alcoholic beverages in the United States. It was repealed by the Twenty-first Amendment.

Amendment XIX
(Ratified on August 18, 1920).
Women's Right to Vote.

The right of citizens of the United States to vote shall not be denied or abridged by the United States or by any State on account of sex.

Congress shall have power to enforce this article by appropriate legislation.

Women were given the right to vote by this amendment, and Congress was given the power to enforce this right.

Amendment XX
(Ratified on January 23, 1933).
The Lame Duck Amendment

Section 1.

The terms of the President and Vice President shall end at noon on the 20th day of January, and the terms of Senators and Representatives at noon on the 3d day of

---

[15]The Eighteenth Amendment was repealed by the Twenty-first Amendment.

January, of the years in which such terms would have ended if this article had not been ratified; and the terms of their successors shall then begin.

This amendment modified Article I, Section 4, Clause 2, and other provisions relating to the president in the Twelfth Amendment. The taking of the Oath of Office was moved from March 4 to January 20.

Section 2.

The Congress shall assemble at least once in every year, and such meeting shall begin at noon on the 3d day of January, unless they shall by law appoint a different day.

Congress changed the beginning of its term to January 3. The reason the Twentieth Amendment is called the Lame Duck Amendment is because it shortens the time between when a member of Congress is defeated for reelection and when he or she leaves office.

Section 3.

If, at the time fixed for the beginning of the term of the President, the President elect shall have died, the Vice President elect shall become President. If a President shall not have been chosen before the time fixed for the beginning of his term, or if the President elect shall have failed to qualify, then the Vice President elect shall act as President until a President shall have qualified; and the Congress may by law provide for the case wherein neither a President elect nor a Vice President elect shall have qualified, declaring who shall then act as President, or the manner in which one who is to act shall be selected, and such person shall act accordingly until a President or Vice President shall have qualified.

This part of the amendment deals with problem areas left ambiguous by Article II and the Twelfth Amendment. If the president dies before January 20 or fails to qualify for office, the presidency is to be filled in the order given in this section.

Section 4.

The Congress may by law provide for the case of the death of any of the persons from whom the House of Representatives may choose a President whenever the rights of choice shall have devolved upon them, and for the case of the death of any of the persons from whom the Senate may choose a Vice President whenever the right of choice shall have devolved upon them.

Congress has never created legislation subsequent to this section.

Section 5.

Sections 1 and 2 shall take effect on the 15th day of October following the ratification of this article.

Section 6.

This article shall be inoperative unless it shall have been ratified as an amendment to the Constitution by the legislatures of three-fourths of the several States within seven years from the date of its submission.

Amendment XXI
(Ratified on December 5, 1933).
The Repeal of Prohibition.

Section 1.

The eighteenth article of amendment to the Constitution of the United States is hereby repealed.

Section 2.

The transportation or importation into any State, Territory, or possession of the United States for delivery or use therein of intoxicating liquors, in violation of the laws thereof, is hereby prohibited.

Section 3.

This article shall be inoperative unless it shall have been ratified as an amendment to the Constitution by conventions in the several States, as provided in the Constitution, within seven years from the date of the submission hereof to the States by the Congress.

The amendment repealed the Eighteenth Amendment but did not make alcoholic beverages legal everywhere. Rather, they remained illegal in any state that so designated them. Many such "dry" states existed for a number of years after 1933. Today, there are still "dry" counties within the United States, in which alcoholic beverages are illegal.

Amendment XXII
(Ratified on February 27, 1951).
Limitation of Presidential Terms.

Section 1.

No person shall be elected to the office of the President more than twice, and no person who has held the office of President, or acted as President, for more than two years of a term to which some other person was elected President shall be elected to the office of President more than once. But this Article shall not apply to any person holding the office of President when this Article was proposed by the Congress, and shall not prevent any person who may be holding the office of President, or acting as President, during the term within which this Article becomes operative from holding the office of President or acting as President during the remainder of such term.

Section 2.

This article shall be inoperative unless it shall have been ratified as an amendment to the Constitution by the legislatures of three-fourths of the several States within seven years from the date of its submission to the States by the Congress.

No president may serve more than two elected terms. If, however, a president has succeeded to the office after the halfway point of a term in which another president was originally elected, then that president may serve for more than eight years, but not to exceed ten years.

Amendment XXIII
(Ratified on March 29, 1961).
Presidential Electors for the District of Columbia.

Section 1.
The District constituting the seat of Government of the United States shall appoint in such manner as the Congress may direct:

A number of electors of President and Vice President equal to the whole number of Senators and Representatives in Congress to which the District would be entitled if it were a State, but in no event more than the least populous State; they shall be in addition to those appointed by the States, but they shall be considered, for the purposes of the election of President and Vice President, to be electors appointed by a State; and they shall meet in the District and perform such duties as provided by the twelfth article of amendment.

Section 2.
The Congress shall have power to enforce this article by appropriate legislation.

Citizens living in the District of Columbia have the right to vote in elections for president and vice president. The District of Columbia has three presidential electors, whereas before this amendment it had none.

Amendment XXIV
(Ratified on January 23, 1964).
The Anti-Poll Tax Amendment.

Section 1.
The right of citizens of the United States to vote in any primary or other election for President or Vice President, for electors for President or Vice President, or for Senator or Representative in Congress, shall not be denied or abridged by the United States, or any State by reason of failure to pay any poll tax or other tax.

Section 2.
The Congress shall have power to enforce this article by appropriate legislation.

No government shall require a person to pay a poll tax in order to vote in any federal election.

Amendment XXV
(Ratified on February 10, 1967).
Presidential Disability and Vice Presidential Vacancies.

Section 1.
In case of the removal of the President from office or of his death or resignation, the Vice President shall become President.

Whenever a president dies or resigns from office, the vice president becomes president.

Section 2.
Whenever there is a vacancy in the office of the Vice President, the President shall nominate a Vice President who shall take office upon confirmation by a majority vote of both Houses of Congress.

Whenever the office of the vice presidency becomes vacant, the president may appoint someone to fill this office, provided Congress consents.

Section 3.
Whenever the President transmits to the President pro tempore of the Senate and the Speaker of the House of Representatives his written declaration that he is unable to discharge the powers and duties of his office, and until he transmits to them a written declaration to the contrary, such powers and duties shall be discharged by the Vice President as Acting President.

Whenever the president believes she or he is unable to carry out the duties of the office, she or he shall so indicate to Congress in writing. The vice president then acts as president until the president declares that she or he is again able to properly carry out the duties of the office.

Section 4.
Whenever the Vice President and a majority of either the principal officers of the executive departments or of such other body as Congress may by law provide, transmit to the President pro tempore of the Senate and the Speaker of the House of Representatives their written declaration that the President is unable to discharge the powers and duties of his office, the Vice President shall immediately assume the powers and duties of the office as Acting President.

Thereafter, when the President transmits to the President pro tempore of the Senate and the Speaker of the

House of Representatives his written declaration that no inability exists, he shall resume the powers and duties of his office unless the Vice President and a majority of either the principal officers of the executive department or of such other body as Congress may by law provide, transmit within four days to the President pro tempore of the Senate and the Speaker of the House of Representatives their written declaration that the President is unable to discharge the powers and duties of his office. Thereupon Congress shall decide the issue, assembling within forty-eight hours for that purpose if not in session. If the Congress, within twenty-one days after receipt of the latter written declaration, or, if Congress is not in session, within twenty-one days after Congress is required to assemble, determines by two-thirds vote of both Houses that the President is unable to discharge the powers and duties of his office, the Vice President shall continue to discharge the same as Acting President; otherwise, the President shall resume the powers and duties of his office.

Whenever the vice president and a majority of the members of the cabinet believe that the president cannot carry out his or her duties, they shall so indicate in writing to Congress. The vice president shall then act as president. When the president believes that she or he is able to carry out her or his duties again, she or he shall so indicate to the Congress. If, though, the vice president and a majority of the Cabinet do not agree, Congress must decide by a two-thirds vote within three weeks who shall act as president.

Amendment XXVI
(Ratified on July 1, 1971).
The Eighteen-Year-Old Vote.

Section 1.
The right of citizens of the United States, who are eighteen years of age or older, to vote shall not be denied or abridged by the United States or by any State on account of age.

No one over eighteen years of age can be denied the right to vote in federal or state elections by virtue of age.

Section 2.
The Congress shall have power to enforce this article by appropriate legislation.

Amendment XXVII
(Ratified on May 7, 1992).
Congressional Pay.
No law varying the compensation for the services of the Senators and Representatives shall take effect, until an election of representatives shall have intervened.

This amendment allows the voters to have some control over increases in salaries for congressional members. Originally submitted to the states for ratification in 1789, it was not ratified until 203 years later, in 1992.

C
The Presidents of the United States

	Term of Service	Age at Inauguration	Political Party	College or University	Occupation or Profession
1. George Washington	1789–1797	57	None		Planter
2. John Adams	1797–1801	61	Federalist	Harvard	Lawyer
3. Thomas Jefferson	1801–1809	57	Democratic-Republican	William and Mary	Planter, Lawyer
4. James Madison	1809–1817	57	Democratic-Republican	Princeton	Lawyer
5. James Monroe	1817–1825	58	Democratic-Republican	William and Mary	Lawyer
6. John Quincy Adams	1825–1829	57	Democratic-Republican	Harvard	Lawyer
7. Andrew Jackson	1829–1837	61	Democrat		Lawyer
8. Martin Van Buren	1837–1841	54	Democrat		Lawyer
9. William H. Harrison	1841	68	Whig	Hampden-Sydney	Soldier
10. John Tyler	1841–1845	51	Whig	William and Mary	Lawyer
11. James K. Polk	1845–1849	49	Democrat	U. of N. Carolina	Lawyer
12. Zachary Taylor	1849–1850	64	Whig		Soldier
13. Millard Fillmore	1850–1853	50	Whig		Lawyer
14. Franklin Pierce	1853–1857	48	Democrat	Bowdoin	Lawyer
15. James Buchanan	1857–1861	65	Democrat	Dickinson	Lawyer
16. Abraham Lincoln	1861–1865	52	Republican		Lawyer
17. Andrew Johnson	1865–1869	56	Nat/I. Union†		Tailor
18. Ulysses S. Grant	1869–1877	46	Republican	U.S. Mil. Academy	Soldier
19. Rutherford B. Hayes	1877–1881	54	Republican	Kenyon	Lawyer
20. James A. Garfield	1881	49	Republican	Williams	Lawyer
21. Chester A. Arthur	1881–1885	51	Republican	Union	Lawyer
22. Grover Cleveland	1885–1889	47	Democrat		Lawyer
23. Benjamin Harrison	1889–1893	55	Republican	Miami	Lawyer
24. Grover Cleveland	1893–1897	55	Democrat		Lawyer
25. William McKinley	1897–1901	54	Republican	Allegheny College	Lawyer
26. Theodore Roosevelt	1901–1909	42	Republican	Harvard	Author
27. William H. Taft	1909–1913	51	Republican	Yale	Lawyer
28. Woodrow Wilson	1913–1921	56	Democrat	Princeton	Educator
29. Warren G. Harding	1921–1923	55	Republican		Editor
30. Calvin Coolidge	1923–1929	51	Republican	Amherst	Lawyer
31. Herbert C. Hoover	1929–1933	54	Republican	Stanford	Engineer
32. Franklin D. Roosevelt	1933–1945	51	Democrat	Harvard	Lawyer
33. Harry S. Truman	1945–1953	60	Democrat		Businessman
34. Dwight D. Eisenhower	1953–1961	62	Republican	U.S. Mil. Academy	Soldier
35. John F. Kennedy	1961–1963	43	Democrat	Harvard	Author
36. Lyndon B. Johnson	1963–1969	55	Democrat	Southwest Texas State	Teacher
37. Richard M. Nixon	1969–1974	56	Republican	Whittier	Lawyer
38. Gerald R. Ford‡	1974–1977	61	Republican	Michigan	Lawyer
39. James E. Carter, Jr.	1977–1981	52	Democrat	U.S. Naval Academy	Businessman
40. Ronald W. Reagan	1981–1989	69	Republican	Eureka College	Actor
41. George H. W. Bush	1989–1993	64	Republican	Yale	Businessman
42. Bill Clinton	1993–	46	Democrat	Georgetown	Lawyer

*Church preference; never joined any church.
†The National Union Party consisted of Republicans and War Democrats. Johnson was a Democrat.
**Inaugurated Dec. 6, 1973, to replace Agnew, who resigned Oct. 10, 1973.
‡Inaugurated Aug. 9, 1974, to replace Nixon, who resigned that same day.
§Inaugurated Dec. 19, 1974, to replace Ford, who became president Aug. 9, 1974.

C
The Presidents of the United States

	Religion	Born	Died	Age at Death	Vice President	
1.	Episcopalian	Feb. 22, 1732	Dec. 14, 1799	67	John Adams	(1789–1797)
2.	Unitarian	Oct. 30, 1735	July 4, 1826	90	Thomas Jefferson	(1797–1801)
3.	Unitarian*	Apr. 13, 1743	July 4, 1826	83	Aaron Burr	(1801–1805)
					George Clinton	(1805–1809)
4.	Episcopalian	Mar. 16, 1751	June 28, 1836	85	George Clinton	(1809–1812)
					Elbridge Gerry	(1813–1814)
5.	Episcopalian	Apr. 28, 1758	July 4, 1831	73	Daniel D. Tompkins	(1817–1825)
6.	Unitarian	July 11, 1767	Feb. 23, 1848	80	John C. Calhoun	(1825–1829)
7.	Presbyterian	Mar. 15, 1767	June 8, 1845	78	John C. Calhoun	(1829–1832)
					Martin Van Buren	(1833–1837)
8.	Dutch Reformed	Dec. 5, 1782	July 24, 1862	79	Richard M. Johnson	(1837–1841)
9.	Episcopalian	Feb. 9, 1773	Apr. 4, 1841	68	John Tyler	(1841)
10.	Episcopalian	Mar. 29, 1790	Jan. 18, 1862	71		
11.	Methodist	Nov. 2, 1795	June 15, 1849	53	George M. Dallas	(1845–1849)
12.	Episcopalian	Nov. 24, 1784	July 9, 1850	65	Millard Fillmore	(1849–1850)
13.	Unitarian	Jan. 7, 1800	Mar. 8, 1874	74		
14.	Episcopalian	Nov. 23, 1804	Oct. 8, 1869	64	William R. King	(1853)
15.	Presbyterian	Apr. 23, 1791	June 1, 1868	77	John C. Breckinridge	(1857–1861)
16.	Presbyterian*	Feb. 12, 1809	Apr. 15, 1865	56	Hannibal Hamlin	(1861–1865)
					Andrew Johnson	(1865)
17.	Methodist*	Dec. 29, 1808	July 31, 1875	66		
18.	Methodist	Apr. 27, 1822	July 23, 1885	63	Schuyler Colfax	(1869–1873)
					Henry Wilson	(1873–1875)
19.	Methodist*	Oct. 4, 1822	Jan. 17, 1893	70	William A. Wheeler	(1877–1881)
20.	Disciples of Christ	Nov. 19, 1831	Sept. 19, 1881	49	Chester A. Arthur	(1881)
21.	Episcopalian	Oct. 5, 1829	Nov. 18, 1886	57		
22.	Presbyterian	Mar. 18, 1837	June 24, 1908	71	Thomas A. Hendricks	(1885)
23.	Presbyterian	Aug. 20, 1833	Mar. 13, 1901	67	Levi P. Morton	(1889–1893)
24.	Presbyterian	Mar. 18, 1837	June 24, 1908	71	Adlai E. Stevenson	(1893–1897)
25.	Methodist	Jan. 29, 1843	Sept. 14, 1901	58	Garret A. Hobart	(1897–1899)
					Theodore Roosevelt	(1901)
26.	Dutch Reformed	Oct. 27, 1858	Jan. 6, 1919	60	Charles W. Fairbanks	(1905–1909)
27.	Unitarian	Sept. 15, 1857	Mar. 8, 1930	72	James S. Sherman	(1909–1912)
28.	Presbyterian	Dec. 29, 1856	Feb. 3, 1924	67	Thomas R. Marshall	(1913–1921)
29.	Baptist	Nov. 2, 1865	Aug. 2, 1923	57	Calvin Coolidge	(1921–1923)
30.	Congregationalist	July 4, 1872	Jan. 5, 1933	60	Charles G. Dawes	(1925–1929)
31.	Friend (Quaker)	Aug. 10, 1874	Oct. 20, 1964	90	Charles Curtis	(1929–1933)
32.	Episcopalian	Jan. 30, 1882	Apr. 12, 1945	63	John N. Garner	(1933–1941)
					Henry A. Wallace	(1941–1945)
					Harry S. Truman	(1945)
33.	Baptist	May 8, 1884	Dec. 26, 1972	88	Alben W. Barkley	(1949–1953)
34.	Presbyterian	Oct. 14, 1890	Mar. 28, 1969	78	Richard M. Nixon	(1953–1961)
35.	Roman Catholic	May 29, 1917	Nov. 22, 1963	46	Lyndon B. Johnson	(1961–1963)
36.	Disciples of Christ	Aug. 27, 1908	Jan. 22, 1973	64	Hubert H. Humphrey	(1965–1969)
37.	Friend (Quaker)	Jan. 9, 1913	Apr. 22, 1994	81	Spiro T. Agnew	(1969–1973)
					Gerald R. Ford**	(1973–1974)
38.	Episcopalian	July 14, 1913			Nelson A. Rockefeller§	(1974–1977)
39.	Baptist	Oct. 1, 1924			Walter F. Mondale	(1977–1981)
40.	Disciples of Christ	Feb. 6, 1911			George H. W. Bush	(1981–1989)
41.	Episcopalian	June 12, 1924			J. Danforth Quayle	(1989–1993)
42.	Baptist	Aug. 19, 1946			Albert A. Gore	(1993–)

D

Federalist Papers
No. 10, No. 51, and No. 78

#10

Among the numerous advantages promised by a well-constructed Union, none deserves to be more accurately developed than its tendency to break and control the violence of faction. The friend of popular governments never finds himself so much alarmed for their character and fate as when he contemplates their propensity to this dangerous vice. He will not fail, therefore, to set a due value on any plan which, without violating the principles to which he is attached, provides a proper cure for it. The instability, injustice, and confusion introduced into the public councils have, in truth, been the mortal diseases under which popular governments have everywhere perished, as they continue to be the favorite and fruitful topics from which the adversaries to liberty derive their most specious declamations. The valuable improvements made by the American constitutions on the popular models, both ancient and modern, cannot certainly be too much admired; but it would be an unwarrantable partiality to contend that they have as effectually obviated the danger on this side, as was wished and expected. Complaints are everywhere heard from our most considerate and virtuous citizens, equally the friends of public and private faith and of public and personal liberty, that our governments are too unstable, that the public good is disregarded in the conflicts of rival parties, and that measures are too often decided, not according to the rules of justice and the rights of the minor party, but by the superior force of an interested and overbearing majority. However anxiously we may wish that these complaints had no foundation, the evidence of known facts will not permit us to deny that they are in some degree true. It will be found, indeed, on a candid review of our situation, that some of the distresses under which we labor have been erroneously charged on the operation of our governments; but it will be found, at the same time, that other causes will not alone account for many of our heaviest misfortunes; and, particularly, for that prevailing and increasing distrust of public engagements and alarm for private rights which are echoed from one end of the continent to the other. These must be chiefly, if not wholly, effects of the unsteadiness and injustice with which a factious spirit has tainted our public administration.

By a faction I understand a number of citizens, whether amounting to a majority or minority of the whole, who are united and actuated by some common impulse of passion, or of interest, adverse to the rights of other citizens, or the permanent and aggregate interests of the community.

There are two methods of curing the mischiefs of faction: the one, by removing its causes; the other, by controlling its effects.

There are again two methods of removing the causes of faction: the one, by destroying the liberty which is essential to its existence; the other, by giving to every citizen the same opinions, the same passions, and the same interests.

It could never be more truly said than of the first remedy that it was worse than the disease. Liberty is to faction what air is to fire, an aliment without which it instantly expires. But it could not be a less folly to abolish liberty, which is essential to political life, because it nourishes faction than it would be to wish the annihilation of air, which is essential to animal life, because it imparts to fire its destructive agency.

The second expedient is as impracticable as the first would be unwise. As long as the reason of man continues fallible, and his is at liberty to exercise it, different opinions will be formed. As long as the connection subsists between his reason and his self-love, his opinions and his passions will have a reciprocal influence on each other; and the former will be objects to which the latter will attach themselves. The diversity in the faculties of men, from which the rights of property originate, is not less an insuperable obstacle to a uniformity of interests.

The protection of these faculties is the first object of government. From the protection of different and unequal faculties of acquiring property, the possession of different degrees and kinds of property immediately results; and from the influence of these on the sentiments and views of the respective proprietors ensues a division of the society into different interests and parties.

The latent causes of faction are thus sown in the nature of man; and we see them everywhere brought into different degrees of activity, according to the different circumstances of civil society. A zeal for different opinions concerning religion, concerning government, and many other points, as well of speculation as of practice; an attachment to different leaders ambitiously contending for pre-eminence and power; or to persons of other descriptions whose fortunes have been interesting to the human passions, have, in turn, divided mankind into parties, inflamed them with mutual animosity, and rendered them much more disposed to vex and oppress each other than to co-operate for their common good. So strong is this propensity of mankind to fall into mutual animosities that where no substantial occasion presents itself the most frivolous and fanciful distinctions have been sufficient to kindle their unfriendly passions and excite their most violent conflicts. But the most common and durable source of factions has been the various and unequal distribution of property. Those who hold and those who are without property have ever formed distinct interests in society. Those who are creditors, and those who are debtors, fall under a like discrimination. A landed interest, a manufacturing interest, a mercantile interest, a moneyed interest, with many lesser interests, grow up of necessity in civilized nations, and divide them into different classes, actuated by different sentiments and views. The regulation of these various and interfering interests forms the principal task of modern legislation and involves the spirit of party and faction in the necessary and ordinary operations of government.

No man is allowed to be a judge in his own cause, because his interest would certainly bias his judgment, and, not improbably, corrupt his integrity. With equal, nay with greater reason, a body of men are unfit to be both judges and parties at the same time; yet what are many of the most important acts of legislation but so many judicial determinations, not indeed concerning the rights of single persons, but concerning the rights of large bodies of citizens? And what are the different classes of legislators but advocates and parties to the causes which they determine? Is a law proposed concerning private debts? It is a question to which the creditors are parties on one side and the debtors on the other. Justice ought to hold the balance between them. Yet the parties are, and must be, themselves the judges; and the most numerous party, or in other words, the most powerful faction must be expected to prevail. Shall domestic manufacturers be encouraged, and in what degree, by restrictions on foreign manufacturers? Are questions which would be differently decided by the landed and the manufacturing classes, and probably by neither with a sole regard to justice and the public good. The apportionment of taxes on the various descriptions of property is an act which seems to require the most exact impartiality; yet there is, perhaps, no legislative act in which greater opportunity and temptation are given to a predominant party to trample on the rules of justice. Every shilling with which they overburden the inferior number is a shilling saved to their own pockets.

It is in vain to say that enlightened statesmen will be able to adjust these clashing interests and render them all subservient to the public good. Enlightened statesmen will not always be at the helm. Nor, in many cases, can such an adjustment be made at all without taking into view indirect and remote considerations, which will rarely prevail over the immediate interest which one party may find in disregarding the rights of another or the good of the whole.

The inference to which we are brought is that the *causes* of faction cannot be removed and that relief is only to be sought in the means of controlling its *effects*.

If a faction consists of less than a majority, relief is supplied by the republican principle, which enables the majority to defeat its sinister views by regular vote. It may clog the administration, it may convulse the society; but it will be unable to execute and mask its violence under the forms of the Constitution. When a majority is included in a faction, the form of popular government, on the other hand, enables it to sacrifice to its ruling passion or interest both the public good and the rights of other citizens. To secure the public good and private rights against the danger of such a faction, and at the same time to preserve the spirit and the form of popular government, is then the great object to which our inquiries are directed. Let me add that it is the great desideratum by which alone this form of government can be rescued from the opprobrium under which it has so long labored and be recommended to the esteem and adoption of mankind.

By what means is this object attainable? Evidently by one of two only. Either the existence of the same passion or interest in a majority at the same time must be prevented, or the majority, having such coexistent passion or interest, must be rendered, by their number and local situation, unable to concert and carry into effect schemes of oppression. If the impulse and the opportunity be suffered to coincide, we well know that neither moral nor religious motives can be relied on as an adequate control. They are not found to be such on the injustice and violence of individuals, and lose their efficacy in proportion to the number combined together, that is, in proportion as their efficacy becomes needful.

From this view of the subject it may be concluded that a pure democracy, by which I mean a society consisting of a small number of citizens, who assemble and administer the government in person, can admit of no cure for the mischiefs of faction. A common passion or interest will, in almost every case, be felt by a majority of the whole; a communication and concert results from the form of government itself; and there is nothing to check the inducements to sacrifice the weaker party or an obnoxious individual. Hence it is that such democracies have ever been spectacles of turbulence and contention; have ever been found incompatible with personal security or the rights of property; and have in general been as short in their lives as they have been violent in their deaths. Theoretic politicians, who have patronized this species of government, have erroneously supposed that by reducing mankind to a perfect equality in their political rights, they would at the same time be perfectly equalized and assimilated in their possessions, their opinions, and their passions.

A republic, by which I mean a government in which the scheme of representation takes place, opens a different prospect and promises the cure for which we are seeking. Let us examine the points in which it varies from pure democracy, and we shall comprehend both the nature of the cure and the efficacy which it must derive from the Union.

The two great points of difference between a democracy and a republic are: first, the delegation of the government, in the latter, to a small number of citizens elected by the rest; secondly, the greater number of citizens and greater sphere of country over which the latter may be extended.

The effect of the first difference is, on the one hand, to refine and enlarge the public views by passing them through the medium of a chosen body of citizens, whose wisdom may best discern the true interest of their country and whose patriotism and love of justice will be least likely to sacrifice it to temporary or partial considerations. Under such a regulation it may well happen that the public voice, pronounced by the representatives of the people, will be more consonant to the public good than if pronounced by the people themselves, convened for the purpose. On the other hand, the effect may be inverted. Men of factious tempers, of local prejudices, or of sinister designs, may, by intrigue, by corruption, or by other means, first obtain the suffrages, and then betray the interests of the people. The question resulting is, whether small or extensive republics are most favorable to the election of proper guardians of the public weal; and it is clearly decided in favor of the latter by two obvious considerations.

In the first place it is to be remarked that however small the republic may be the representatives must be raised to a certain number in order to guard against the cabals of a few; and that however large it may be they must be limited to a certain number in order to guard against the confusion of a multitude. Hence, the number of representatives in the two cases not being in proportion to that of the constituents, and being proportionally greatest in the small republic, it follows that if the proportion of fit characters be not less in the large than in the small republic, the former will present a greater option, and consequently a greater probability of a fit choice.

In the next place, as each representative will be chosen by a greater number of citizens in the large than in the small republic, it will be more difficult for unworthy candidates to practice with success the vicious arts by which elections are too often carried; and the suffrages of the people being more free, will be more likely to center on men who possess the most attractive merit and the most diffusive and established characters.

It must be confessed that in this, as in most other cases, there is a mean, on both sides of which inconveniencies will be found to lie. By enlarging too much the number of electors, you render the representative too little acquainted with all their local circumstances and lesser interests; as by reducing it too much, you render him unduly attached to these, and too little fit to comprehend and pursue great and national objects. The federal Constitution forms a happy combination in this respect; the great and aggregate interests being referred to the national, the local and particular to the State legislatures.

The other point of difference is the greater number of citizens and extent of territory which may be brought within the compass of republican than of democratic government; and it is this circumstance principally which renders factious combinations less to be dreaded in the former than in the latter. The smaller the society, the fewer probably will be the distinct parties and interests composing it; the fewer the distinct parties and interests, the more frequently will a majority be found of the same party; and the smaller the number of individuals composing a majority, and the smaller the compass within which they are placed, the more easily will they concert and execute their plans of oppression. Extend the sphere and you take in a greater variety of parties and interests; you make it less probable that a majority of the whole will have a common motive to invade the rights of other citizens; or if such a common motive exists, it will be more difficult for all who feel it to discover their own strength and to act in unison with each other. Besides other impediments, it may be remarked that, where there is a consciousness of unjust or dishonorable purposes, communication is always checked by distrust in proportion to the number whose concurrence is necessary.

Hence, it clearly appears that the same advantage which a republic has over a democracy in controlling the effects of faction is enjoyed by a large over a small republic—is enjoyed by the Union over the States composing it. Does this advantage consist in the substitution of representatives whose enlightened views and virtuous sentiments render them superior to local prejudices and to schemes of injustice? It will not be denied that the representation of the Union will be most likely to possess these requisite endowments. Does it consist in the greater security afforded by a greater variety of parties, against the event of any one party being able to outnumber and oppress the rest? In an equal degree does the increased variety of parties comprised within the Union increase this security. Does it, in fine, consist in the greater obstacles opposed to the concert and accomplishment of the secret wishes of an unjust and interested majority? Here again the extent of the Union gives it the most palpable advantage.

The influence of factious leaders may kindle a flame within their particular States but will be unable to spread a general conflagration through the other States.

A religious sect may degenerate into a political faction in a part of the Confederacy; but the variety of sects dispersed over the entire face of it must secure the national councils against any danger from that source. A rage for paper money, for an abolition of debts, for an equal division of property, or for any other improper or wicked project, will be less apt to pervade the whole body of the Union than a particular member of it, in the same proportion as such a malady is more likely to taint a particular county or district than an entire State.

In the extent and proper structure of the Union, therefore, we behold a republican remedy for the diseases most incident to republican government. And according to the degree of pleasure and pride we feel in being republicans ought to be our zeal in cherishing the spirit and supporting the character of federalists.

Publius
(James Madison)

#51

To what expedient, then, shall we finally resort, for maintaining in practice the necessary partition of power among the several departments as laid down in the Constitution? The only answer that can be given is that as all these exterior provisions are found to be inadequate the defect must be supplied, by so contriving the interior structure of the government as that its several constituent parts may, by their mutual relations, be the means of keeping each other in their proper places. Without presuming to undertake a full development of this important idea I will hazard a few general observations which may perhaps place it in a clearer light, and enable us to form a more correct judgment of the principles and structure of the government planned by the convention.

In order to lay a due foundation for that separate and distinct exercise of the different powers of government, which to a certain extent is admitted on all hands to be essential to the preservation of liberty, it is evident that each department should have a will of its own; and consequently should be so constituted that the members of each should have as little agency as possible in the appointment of the members of the others. Were this principle rigorously adhered to, it would require that all the appointments for the supreme executive, legislative, and judiciary magistracies should be drawn from the same fountain of authority, the people, through channels having no communication whatever with one another. Perhaps such a plan of constructing the several departments would be less difficult in practice than it may in

contemplation appear. Some difficulties, however, and some additional expense would attend the execution of it. Some deviations, therefore, from the principle must be admitted. In the constitution of the judiciary department in particular, it might be inexpedient to insist rigorously on the principle: first, because peculiar qualifications being essential in the members, the primary consideration ought to be to select that mode of choice which best secures these qualifications; second, because the permanent tenure by which the appointments are held in that department must soon destroy all sense of dependence on the authority conferring them.

It is equally evident that the members of each department should be as little dependent as possible on those of the others for the emoluments annexed to their offices. Were the executive magistrate, or the judges, not independent of the legislature in this particular, their independence in every other would be merely nominal.

But the great security against a gradual concentration of the several powers in the same department consists in giving to those who administer each department the necessary constitutional means and personal motives to resist encroachments of the others. The provision for defense must in this, as in all other cases, be made commensurate to the danger of attack. Ambition must be made to counteract ambition. The interest of the man must be connected with the constitutional rights of the place. It may be a reflection on human nature that such devices should be necessary to control the abuses of government. But what is government itself but the greatest of all reflections on human nature? If men were angels, no government would be necessary. If angels were to govern men, neither external nor internal controls on government would be necessary. In framing a government which is to be administered by men over men, the great difficulty lies in this: you must first enable the government to control the governed; and in the next place oblige it to control itself. A dependence on the people is, no doubt, the primary control on the government; but experience has taught mankind the necessity of auxiliary precautions.

This policy of supplying, by opposite and rival interests, the defect of better motives, might be traced through the whole system of human affairs, private as well as public. We see it particularly displayed in all the subordinate distributions of power, where the constant aim is to divide and arrange the several offices in such a manner as that each may be a check on the other—that the private interest of every individual may be a sentinel over the public rights. These inventions of prudence cannot be less requisite in the distribution of the supreme powers of the State.

But it is not possible to give to each department an equal power of self-defense. In republican government, the legislative authority necessarily predominates. The remedy for this inconveniency is to divide the legislature into different branches; and to render them, by different modes of election and different principles of action, as little connected with each other as the nature of their common functions and their common dependence on the society will admit. It may even be necessary to guard against dangerous encroachments by still further precautions. As the weight of the legislative authority requires that it should be thus divided, the weakness of the executive may require, on the other hand, that it should be fortified. An absolute negative on the legislature appears, at first view, to be the natural defense with which the executive magistrate should be armed. But perhaps it would be neither altogether safe nor alone sufficient. On ordinary occasions it might not be exerted with the requisite firmness, and on extraordinary occasions it might be perfidiously abused. May not this defect of an absolute negative be supplied by some qualified connection between this weaker department and the weaker branch of the stronger department, by which the latter may be led to support the constitutional rights of the former, without being too much detached from the rights of its own department?

If the principles on which these observations are founded be just, as I persuade myself they are, and they be applied as a criterion to the several State constitutions, and to the federal Constitution, it will be found that if the latter does not perfectly correspond with them, the former are infinitely less able to bear such a test.

There are, moreover, two considerations particularly applicable to the federal system of America, which place that system in a very interesting point of view.

First. In a single republic, all the power surrendered by the people is submitted to the administration of a single government; and the usurpations are guarded against by a division of the government into distinct and separate departments. In the compound republic of America, the power surrendered by the people is first divided between two distinct governments, and then the portion allotted to each subdivided among distinct and separate departments. Hence a double security arises to the rights of the people. The different governments will control each other, at the same time that each will be controlled by itself.

Second. It is of great importance in a republic not only to guard the society against the oppression of its rulers, but to guard one part of the society against the injustice of the other part. Different interests necessarily exist in different classes of citizens. If a majority be united by a common interest, the rights of the minority will be insecure. There are but two methods of providing against this evil: the one by creating a will in the community independent of the majority—that is, of the society itself; the other, by comprehending in the society so many separate descriptions of citizens as will render an unjust combination of a majority of the whole very improbable, if not impracticable. The first method prevails in all governments possessing an hereditary or self-appointed authority. This, at best, is but a precarious security; because a power independent of the society may as well espouse the unjust views of the major as the rightful interests of the minor party, and may possibly be turned against both parties. The second method will be exemplified in the federal republic of the United States. Whilst all authority in it will be derived from and dependent on the society, the society itself will be broken into so many parts, interests and classes of citizens, that the rights of individuals, or of the minority, will be in little danger from interested combinations of the majority. In a free government the security for civil rights must be the same as that for religious rights. It consists in the one case in the multiplicity of interests, and in the other in the multiplicity of sects. The degree of security in both cases will depend on the number of interests and sects; and this may be presumed to depend on the extent of country and number of people comprehended under the same government. This view of the subject must particularly recommend a proper federal system to all the sincere and considerate friends of republican government, since it shows that in exact proportion as the territory of the Union may be formed into more circumscribed Confederacies, or States, oppressive combinations of a majority will be facilitated; the best security, under the republican forms, for the rights of every class of citizen, will be diminished; and consequently the stability and independence of some member of the government, the only other security, must be proportionally increased. Justice is the end of government. It is the end of civil society. It ever has been and ever will be pursued until it be obtained, or until liberty be lost in the pursuit. In a society under the forms of which the stronger faction can readily unite and oppress the weaker, anarchy may as truly be said to reign as in a state of nature, where the weaker individual is not secured against the violence of the stronger; and as, in the latter state, even the stronger individuals are prompted, by the uncertainty of their condition, to submit to a government which may protect the weak as well as themselves; so, in the former state, will the more powerful factions or parties be gradually induced, by a like motive, to wish for a government which will protect all parties, the weaker as well as the more powerful. It can be little doubted that if the State of Rhode Island was separated from the Confederacy and left to itself, the insecurity of rights under the popular form of government within such narrow limits would be displayed by such reiterated oppressions of factious majorities that some power altogether independent of

the people would soon be called for by the voice of the very factions whose misrule had proved the necessity of it. In the extended republic of the United States, and among the great variety of interests, parties, and sects which it embraces, a coalition of a majority of the whole society could seldom take place on any other principles than those of justice and the general good; whilst there being thus less danger to a minor from the will of a major party, there must be less pretext, also, to provide for the security of the former, by introducing into the government a will not dependent on the latter, or, in other words, a will independent of the society itself. It is no less certain than it is important, notwithstanding the contrary opinions which have been entertained, that the larger the society, provided it lie within a practicable sphere, the more duly capable it will be of self-government. And happily for the *republican cause*, the practicable sphere may be carried to a very great extent by a judicious modification and mixture of the *federal principle*.

Publius
(James Madison)

#78

WE PROCEED now to an examination of the judiciary department of the proposed government.

In unfolding the defects of the existing Confederation, the utility and necessity of a federal judicature have been clearly pointed out. It is the less necessary to recapitulate the considerations there urged, as the propriety of the institution in the abstract is not disputed; the only questions which have been raised being relative to the manner of constituting it, and to its extent. To these points, therefore, our observations shall be confined.

The manner of constituting it seems to embrace these several objects: 1st. The mode of appointing the judges. 2d. The tenure by which they are to hold their places. 3d. The partition of the judiciary authority between different courts, and their relations to each other.

First. As to the mode of appointing the judges; this is the same with that of appointing the officers of the Union in general, and has been so fully discussed in the last two numbers, that nothing can be said here which would not be useless repetition.

Second. As to the tenure by which the judges are to hold their places; this chiefly concerns their duration in office; the provisions for their support; the precautions for their responsibility.

According to the plan of the convention, all judges who may be appointed by the United States are to hold their offices during good behavior; which is conformable to the most approved of the State constitutions and

among the rest, to that of this State. Its propriety having been drawn into question by the adversaries of that plan, is no light symptom of the rage for objection, which disorders their imaginations and judgments. The standard of good behavior for the continuance in office of the judicial magistracy, is certainly one of the most valuable of the modern improvements in the practice of government. In a monarchy it is an excellent barrier to the despotism of the prince; in a republic it is a no less excellent barrier to the encroachments and oppressions of the representative body. And it is the best expedient which can be devised in any government, to secure a steady, upright, and impartial administration of the laws.

Whoever attentively considers the different departments of power must perceive, that, in a government in which they are separated from each other, the judiciary, from the nature of its functions, will always be the least dangerous to the political rights of the Constitution; because it will be least in a capacity to annoy or injure them. The Executive not only dispenses the honors, but holds the sword of the community. The legislature not only commands the purse, but prescribes the rules by which the duties and rights of every citizen are to be regulated. The judiciary, on the contrary, has no influence over either the sword or the purse; no direction either of the strength or of the wealth of the society; and can take no active resolution whatever. It may truly be said to have neither force nor will, but merely judgment; and must ultimately depend upon the aid of the executive arm even for the efficacy of its judgments.

This simple view of the matter suggests several important consequences. It proves incontestably, that the judiciary is beyond comparison the weakest of the three departments of power; that it can never attack with success either of the other two; and that all possible care is requisite to enable it to defend itself against their attacks. It equally proves, that though individual oppression may now and then proceed from the courts of justice, the general liberty of the people can never be endangered from that quarter; I mean so long as the judiciary remains truly distinct from both the legislature and the Executive. For I agree, that "there is no liberty, if the power of judging is not separated from the legislative and executive powers." And it proves, in the last place, that as liberty can have nothing to fear from the judiciary alone, but would have everything to fear from its union with either of the other departments; that as all the effects of such a union must ensue from a dependence of the former on the latter, notwithstanding a nominal and apparent separation; that as, from the natural feebleness of the judiciary, it is in continual jeopardy of being overpowered, awed, or influenced by its co-ordinate branches; and that as nothing can contribute so much to its firmness and independence as permanency in office, this quality may therefore be justly regarded as an indispensable ingredient in its constitution, and, in a great measure, as the citadel of the public justice and the public security.

The complete independence of the courts of justice is peculiarly essential in a limited Constitution. By a limited Constitution, I understand one which contains certain specified exceptions to the legislative authority; such, for instance, as that it shall pass no bills of attainder, no ex-post-facto laws, and the like. Limitations of this kind can be preserved in practice no other way than through the medium of courts of justice, whose duty it must be to declare all acts contrary to the manifest tenor of the Constitution void. Without this, all the reservations of particular rights or privileges would amount to nothing. Some perplexity respecting the rights of the courts to pronounce legislative acts void, because contrary to the Constitution, has arisen from an imagination that the doctrine would imply a superiority of the judiciary to the legislative power. It is urged that the authority which can declare the acts of another void, must necessarily be superior to the one whose acts may be declared void. As this doctrine is of great importance in all the American constitutions, a brief discussion of the ground on which it rests cannot be unacceptable.

There is no position which depends on clearer principles, than that every act of a delegated authority, contrary to the tenor of the commission under which it is exercised, is void. No legislative act, therefore, contrary to the Constitution, can be valid. To deny this, would be to affirm, that the deputy is greater than his principal; that the servant is above his master; that the representatives of the people are superior to the people themselves; that men acting by virtue of powers, may do not only what their powers do not authorize, but what they forbid.

If it be said that the legislative body are themselves the constitutional judges of their own powers, and that the construction they put upon them is conclusive upon the other departments, it may be answered, that this cannot be the natural presumption, where it is not to be collected from any particular provisions in the Constitution. It is not otherwise to be supposed, that the Constitution could intend to enable the representatives of the people to substitute their will to that of their constituents. It is far more rational to suppose, that the courts were designed to be an intermediate body between the people and the legislature, in order, among other things, to keep the latter within the limits assigned to their authority. The interpretation of the laws is the proper and peculiar province of the courts. A constitution is, in fact, and must be regarded by the judges, as a fundamental law. It therefore belongs to them to ascertain its meaning, as well as the meaning of any particular act proceeding from the legislative body. If there should happen to be an irreconcilable variance between the two, that which has the superior obligation and validity ought, of course, to be preferred; or, in other words, the Constitution ought to be preferred to the statute, the intention of the people to the intention of their agents.

Nor does this conclusion by any means suppose a superiority of the judicial to the legislative power. It only supposes that the power of the people is superior to both; and that where the will of the legislature, declared in its statutes, stands in opposition to that of the people, declared in the Constitution, the judges ought to be governed by the latter rather than the former. They ought to regulate their decisions by the fundamental laws, rather than by those which are not fundamental.

This exercise of judicial discretion, in determining between two contradictory laws, is exemplified in a familiar instance. It not uncommonly happens, that there are two statutes existing at one time, clashing in whole or in part with each other, and neither of them containing any repealing clause or expression. In such a case, it is the province of the courts to liquidate and fix their meaning and operation. So far as they can, by any fair construction, be reconciled to each other, reason and law conspire to dictate that this should be done; where this is impractable, it becomes a matter of necessity to give effect to one, in exclusion of the other. The rule which has obtained in the courts for determining their relative validity is, that the last in order of time shall be preferred to the first. But this is a mere rule of construction, not derived from any positive law, but from the nature and reason of the thing. It is a rule not enjoined upon the courts by legislative provision, but adopted by themselves, as consonant to truth the propriety, for the direction of their conduct as interpreters of the law. They thought it reasonable, that between the interfering acts of an equal authority, that which was the last indication of its will should have the preference.

But in regard to the interfering acts of a superior and subordinate authority, of an original and derivative power, the nature and reason of the thing indicate the converse of that rule as proper to be followed. They teach us that the prior act of a superior ought to be preferred to the subsequent act of an inferior and subordinate authority; and that accordingly, whenever a particular statute contravenes the Constitution, it will be the duty of the judicial tribunals to adhere to the latter and disregard the former.

It can be of no weight to say that the courts, on the pretense of a repugnancy, may substitute their own pleasure to the constitutional intentions of the legislature. This might as well happen in the case of two contradictory statutes; or it might as well happen in every adjudication upon any single statute. The courts must declare the sense of the law; and if they should be disposed to exercise will instead of judgment, the consequence would equally be the substitution of their pleasure to that of the legislative body. The observation, if it prove anything, would prove that there ought to be no judges distinct from that body.

If, then, the courts of justice are to be considered as the bulwarks of a limited Constitution against legislative encroachments, this consideration will afford a strong argument for the permanent tenure of judicial offices, since nothing will contribute so much as this to that independent spirit in the judges which must be essential to the faithful performance of so arduous a duty.

The independence of the judges is equally requisite to guard the Constitution and the rights of individuals from the effects of those ill humors, which the arts of designing men, or the influence of particular conjunctures, sometimes disseminate among the people themselves, and which, though they speedily give place to better information, and more deliberate reflection, have a tendency, in the meantime, to occasion dangerous innovations in the government, and serious oppressions of the minor party in the community. Though I trust the friends of the proposed Constitution will never concur with its enemies, in questioning that fundamental principle of republican government, which admits the right of the people to alter or abolish the established Constitution, whenever they find it inconsistent with their happiness, yet it is not to be inferred from this principle, that

the representatives of the people, whenever a momentary inclination happens to lay hold of a majority of their constituents, incompatible with the provisions of the existing Constitution, would, on that account, be justifiable in a violation of those provisions; or that the courts would be under a greater obligation to connive at infractions in this shape, than when they had proceeded wholly from the cabals of the representative body. Until the people have, by some solemn and authoritative act, annulled or changed the established form, it is binding upon themselves collectively, as well as individually; and no presumption, or even knowledge, of their sentiments, can warrant their representatives in a departure from it, prior to such an act. But it is easy to see, that it would require an uncommon portion of fortitude in the judges to do their duty as faithful guardians of the Constitution, where legislative invasions of it had been instigated by the major voice of the community.

But it is not with a view to infractions of the Constitution only, that the independence of the judges may be an essential safeguard against the effects of occasional ill humors in the society. These sometimes extend no farther than to the injury of the private rights of particular classes of citizens, by unjust and partial laws. Here also the firmness of the judicial magistracy is of vast importance in mitigating the severity and confining the operation of such laws. It not only serves to moderate the immediate mischiefs of those which may have been passed, but it operates as a check upon the legislative body in passing them; who, perceiving that obstacles to the success of iniquitous intention are to be expected from the scruples of the courts, are in a manner compelled, by the very motives of the injustice they meditate, to qualify their attempts. This is a circumstance calculated to have more influence upon the character of our governments, than but few may be aware of. The benefits of the integrity and moderation of the judiciary have already been felt in more States than one; and though they may have displeased those whose sinister expectations they may have disappointed, they must have commanded the esteem and applause of all the virtuous and disinterested. Considerate men, of every description, ought to prize whatever will tend to beget or fortify that temper in the courts; as no man can be sure that he may not be to-morrow the victim of a spirit of injustice, by which he may be a gainer to-day. Any every man must now feel, that the inevitable tendency of such a spirit is to sap the foundations of public and private confidence, and to introduce in its stead universal distrust and distress.

That inflexible and uniform adherence to the rights of the Constitution, and of individuals, which we perceive to be indispensable in the courts of justice, can certainly not be expected from judges who hold their offices by a temporary commission. Periodical appointments, however regulated, or by whomsoever made, would, in some way or other, be fatal to their necessary independence. If the power of making them was committed either to the Executive or legislature, there would be danger of an improper complaisance to the branch which possessed it; if to both, there would be an unwillingness to hazard the displeasure of either; if to the people, or to persons chosen by them for the special purpose, there would be too great a disposition to consult popularity, to justify a reliance that nothing would be consulted but the Constitution and the laws.

There is yet a further and a weightier reason for the permanency of the judicial offices, which is deducible from the nature of the qualifications they require. It has been frequently remarked, with great propriety, that a voluminous code of laws is one of the inconveniences necessarily connected with the advantages of a free government. To avoid an arbitrary discretion in the courts, it is indispensable that they should be bound down by strict rules and precedents, which serve to define and point out their duty in every particular case that comes before them; and it will readily be conceived from the variety of controversies which grow out of the folly and wickedness of mankind, that the records of those precedents must unavoidably swell to a very considerable bulk, and must demand long and laborious study to acquire a competent knowledge of them. Hence it is, that there can be but few men in the society who will have sufficient skill in the laws to qualify them for the stations of judges. And making the proper deductions for the ordinary depravity of human nature, the number must be still smaller of those who unite the requisite integrity with the requisite knowledge. These considerations apprise us, that the government can have no great option between fit character; and that a temporary duration in office, which would naturally discourage such characters from quitting a lucrative line of practice to accept a seat on the bench, would have a tendency to throw the administration of justice into hands less able, and less well qualified, to conduct it with utility and dignity. In the present circumstances of this country, and in those in which it is likely to be for a long time to come, the disadvantages on this score would be greater than they may at first sight appear; but it must be confessed, that they are far inferior to those which present themselves under other aspects of the subject.

Upon the whole, there can be no room to doubt that the convention acted wisely in copying from the models of those constitutions which have established good behavior as the tenure of their judicial offices, in point of duration; and that so far from being blamable on this account, their plan would have been inexcusably defective, if it had wanted this important feature of good government. The experience of Great Britain affords an illustrious comment on the excellence of the institution.

Publius
(Alexander Hamilton)

E

How to Do Research in Political Science

You are expected to complete a political science research project for your class and present the results in a paper. Research, you have learned, is a tool of science. At first you may ask, what is there about politics that is "scientific"? You can't study people the way you do rats in a maze, nor can you conduct experiments in the same manner as in the biology lab. Yet much of what we know today about how political processes work, and especially about how people act in political situations, is the result of scientific research. For the modern political scientist, the acts of voters, the decisions of presidents and Supreme Court justices, and the policy decisions of state and municipal governments are data to be analyzed according to the methods of science.

I. The Scientific Approach to Politics

When you conduct a research project, it is essential to adhere to certain rules of *epistemology*. Epistemology has to do with *how* we know what we think is true, and the answer to this question lies in whether our work is valid and reliable. A research result is *valid* if it tells you something that actually is true, and it is *reliable* if you or other researchers could reproduce the same results (or at least get approximately the same findings). Validity and reliability are the two hallmarks of the scientific method, which is applied to political science research as much as it is to other scientific research.

How do you know when your results are valid and reliable? The validity of your findings is difficult to establish, but your results are more likely to be valid if you follow these steps in the research process:

1. Formulate a fairly narrow problem to research in such a way that you can make a conclusion based on empirical evidence, that is, evidence based on observation or experience.
2. Set up one or more concrete research hypotheses, which are statements about what you expect to find from your observations.
3. Put together a research design, or a strategy for getting your observations (which might involve doing a sample survey, observing a city council meeting, or gathering information from an almanac or a computer file.)
4. Find an appropriate way to measure the key pieces of information, or data, that you need in order to determine whether your research hypotheses are supported by the factual evidence of your observations.
5. Go out and collect the data.
6. Conduct a careful analysis of the data that you have gathered (usually with appropriate statistical procedures).
7. Make some general conclusions about whether the data tend to support your research hypotheses.

This list of procedures makes empirical research in political science look very mechanical. In part, it is. However it takes intuition and clear thinking to decide how to study political phenomena. There are certain pitfalls to be avoided in analyzing data.

Pitfalls to Avoid. For one thing, you must show that there is some meaningful relationship, or covariation, between or among the variables on which you have collected information. For example, before you claim that Republicans tend to be in higher-income brackets, you must be able to show that the percentage of people who are Republicans is greater among those who have incomes over, say, $50,000 a year than the percentage of Republicans you find among those with incomes under $50,000 a year. The simple fact that you find this pattern of covariation, by itself, though, doesn't necessarily mean that income is what really causes people to choose political sides. It turns out that people's income level is closely related to how much education they have, what kind of job they hold (medical doctors make more money than secretaries), and even how old they are and whether they are married. In other words, you must attempt to eliminate possibly spurious relationships, that is, explanations that don't take into account the complex relationships among variables.

Sometimes empirical covariation can be completely misleading. You probably remember the old story about how storks bring babies. Well, it really is true that birthrates in Europe are higher when storks are busy with their own nesting activities. This empirical fact, however, doesn't mean that the storks bring human babies with them; it just means that there is a similar pattern of human and stork behavior. As another example, you can easily find that the more fire trucks that go to fight a fire, the greater is the amount of damage from the fire. Does sending more fire trucks actually cause the fire to be worse? Of course not. Rather, the correct conclusion would be that a bigger fire requires that more trucks be called in to help fight it, and the bigger fire also produces more property damage. The covariation between the number of fire trucks and the amount of damage is spurious, because both of those variables are affected by the severity of the fire.

The fire truck example also brings us to another point of caution—deciding what "causes" what. You might be led astray in your conclusions if you aren't careful about the order of causal patterns. The fact that you took an examination in your American government course before you went to the polls and voted a straight Democratic ticket doesn't mean that your course (or the exam) caused you to vote that way. Such an incorrect conclusion would be an example of the *post hoc ergo propter hoc* (after, and therefore because of) fallacy. As another example, consider the relationship between your decision to protest ROTC on your campus and your parents' views on whether it is legitimate for people to engage in protest behavior. What "causes" what here? Assume your parents in general support public protests. Does your parents' general approval of protesting tend to determine whether you participate in the protest, or does your protesting gradually intensify your parents' view? Or could your behavior and their attitudes be mutually "causal"? Probably, the fact that you grew up under your parents' influence (not that you listened to or did everything they said) meant that you absorbed their tolerance for protest behavior. They had a much better chance to influence your behavior than you had a chance to influence their attitudes. In other words, it is important to take into consideration the *time ordering* of the variables that you might measure. In general, a later event logically is not able to "cause" an earlier event. Still, there likely is some tendency for parents to modify their previous views if they can be persuaded that your way of doing things politically is legitimate.

How to Increase Reliability. For your results to be valid, they must first be reliable. Whether your conclusions are reliable depends on how carefully you designed the study to take into account random variation from what otherwise might be observed. There are four different ways to test for reliability in your work.

1. Measure everything a second time. This is called the **test–retest method.**

2. Measure the same phenomenon in more than one way. This is the **parallel forms method** for assessing reliability.
3. Split your sample of observations into two groups and see if the results correspond closely. This is the **split-half method.**
4. Conduct an **item analysis,** which entails looking at the degree to which any one item that you have measured relates to the entire set of results. Any variable that doesn't fit closely with the overall pattern may need to be thrown out, or at least be remeasured. (Incidentally, this is precisely what many university instructors do when they prepare computer analyses for the results of a multiple-answer examination).

II. Choosing a Topic

Choosing a topic is the most important decision you'll make. Avoid being too broad ("Civil Rights in the U.S."). Avoid being too current (you will find almost nothing published and little analysis on the subject). Your freedom to choose will depend on the instructions you have received. In any case, make sure the topic fits the course. Be specific and focused. Consider the data or variables you will need to complete your project, keeping in mind the need to present valid and reliable facts. Also pick a subject that interests and even excites you. Your research will be more fun and your written report more lively if your heart is really in the project.

III. Writing the Paper

After you have read the pamphlet that accompanies your text entitled, *Handbook on Critical Thinking and Writing in American Politics,* you are ready to start.

Begin with an outline. It is your road map, so, for most research papers, make sure you cover at least the following:

Title page (title, your name, class, date.)

1. Introduction (what you plan to do).
2. Problem statement or thesis (what you plan to prove; why this is an important topic).
3. Body of project (logically arranged discussion of facts; interpretation/analysis of the information).
4. Conclusion (what generalizations or overall insights you have gained from the study. Make sure these relate back to 2).
5. Endnotes or footnotes.
6. Appendix (put tables, charts, and other material here that are important to the paper but are not directly relevant in the body of the study).
7. Sources (bibliography).

Other Tips.   Take notes on index cards or a yellow pad. Write down the complete citation, including page numbers of material. You may think it will be easy to do that later but it won't! The book or magazine may be gone, checked out, or missing. You may forget where it was. Label cards or pages so you can sort and organize them to fit the structure of your project.

Try to Be Objective.   Let the facts lead you to conclusions. DON'T start with a conclusion (or bias) and then look for facts to prove you are right!

Type Your Paper.   Make sure you number all pages. Cite sources, especially quotations or close paraphrasing. DON'T PLAGIARIZE (in other words, don't use ideas, analyses, or conclusions from other sources and pretend they are your own).

IV. Where to Find Information

Knowing where to find information quickly and efficiently is every researcher's goal. The following are excellent places to start:

We assume that you are familiar with the card catalog in your library and know how to search for books and other items indexed there. However, you will want to go beyond books (perhaps the subject is too recent for books or no one has quite focused on the subject the way you plan to approach it). You should also be familiar with the *Reader's Guide to Periodical Literature*, which cites material in popular periodicals such as *Time* and *People* magazines.

The Public Affairs Information Service (PAIS) publishes the *PAIS Bulletin*, which is an index (cumulated each year) with diverse citations on public affairs including books, journals, government documents, periodicals, fliers, and pamphlets.

Facts on File may be helpful in pinpointing and succinctly informing you about an event or person in the news. Its index is very complete and cross referenced. The *New York Times Index* is an annotated reference to the articles and stories that have appeared in the nation's complete newspaper, the *New York Times*.

The periodicals section of your library should have what we call *scholarly journals*. These are research-oriented publications in which political scientists report the results of their studies. Look for articles on your topic in *ABC POL SCI A Bibliography of Contents; Political Science and Government, Santa Barbara, CA: American Bibliographical Center, Clio Press*. This index is published five times a year and leads you to nearly 300 periodicals.

Familiarize yourself with some of the following scholarly journals: *The American Political Science Review, The Journal of Politics, Comparative Politics, Political Science Quarterly, The Western Political Quarterly, The American*
Journal of Political Science, Polity, Foreign Affairs, Presidential Studies Quarterly, Public Administration Review.

For public opinion one of the most widely used sources is the *Gallup Opinion Index.*

The *Congressional Quarterly Weekly Report (CQWR)* is absolutely essential for every researcher. It comes to your library every week, is indexed, and is bound by volume every year. This source contains useful information on members of Congress, issues, scandals, political action committees, legislation, international affairs, and other material related to Congress. Tables and charts are excellent sources of information.

The *National Journal* covers material similar to the *CQWR.*

The *Supreme Court Reporter* (West Publishing) is one of the best-annotated sources of Supreme Court cases. It provides detailed information about the case and background as well as reference to other relevant cases.

The *Book of the States* is the authoritative source on the structure of state government, statistics, finances, and other information about the fifty states. This is published every two years.

The *Encyclopedia of Associations* is a multivolume source of information on organizations. You will be amazed at the number and diversity of organized groups, associations, and other organizations that exist. The *Encyclopedia* tells you the objectives, organizations, budget, membership, names of officers, address, and telephone numbers.

V. Using Government Publications

One of the best sources of information for research is the U.S. government, the largest publisher in the world. There are federal government publications for virtually every research topic. Because of the sheer volume, only specially designated *depository libraries* receive most of these publications. Ask your librarian where the nearest one is located. Remember that you can obtain this material through interlibrary loan.

Federal publications include statistics; congressional material including hearings, pamphlets, and bulletins; technical reports; presidential statements and documents; court rulings; and agency-specific publications. To find this material, you may want to use the following:

The *CIS* (Congressional Information Service) *Index*. This is published monthly and bound into a volume each year. It covers congressional hearings, reports, and special publications. Each item listed includes an abstract.

The *Congressional Monitor* is the best source of information on congressional hearings, which are listed by subject area for each House and Senate committee.

The *American Statistics Index* covers over five hundred federal government sources of information including numerical data.

The *Guide to U.S. Government Publications,* by John L. Andriot, is an annual guide to the reports and regular publications (magazines, for example) that are produced by more than 2,000 government agencies.

The following are selected United States government publications by topic:

Foreign Policy: *United States Foreign Policy: A Report of the Secretary of State.* This annual report reviews U.S. foreign policy, military and technical assistance, and other international activities country by country.

Federalism: *Catalog of Federal Domestic Assistance.* This publication is compiled by the Office of Management and Budget and lists virtually all federal grant programs to state and local governments. *Intergovernmental Perspective* is published by the Advisory Commission on Intergovernmental Relations four times a year and contains statistical information, analysis, and listings on all aspects of intergovernmental relations.

Voting/Elections: The *Journal of Election Administration* is published by the Federal Election Commission (FEC), which also publishes an array of statistical information on campaigns, voting, and related matters (call toll free, 800-424-9530).

Congress: The *Congressional Record* is published every day Congress is in session and contains the proceedings as well as supplemental documents inserted by members of Congress.

Presidency: The *Weekly Compilation of Presidential Documents* is issued every week and compiled annually as *Public Powers of the President of the United States.* It contains the speeches, messages, statements, and press conferences of the president.

The Supreme Court: The *United States Reports,* published since 1790, is the official publication of Supreme Court decisions. Citation of a case is usually to the *Reports.* For example Miranda v. Arizona, 348 U.S. 436 (1966) means volume 348 of the U.S. Reports, page 436 in the year 1966.

Domestic Policy: One of the best sources of information is the *Budget of the United States* and its appendices or the *United States Budget in Brief,* which contain the specific spending plans and revenue sources of the federal government.

Public Welfare Policy: The book *Characteristics of General Assistance in the United States* provides state-by-state data on federal and state assistance programs for the needy.

Education: data are found in the *Digest of Educational Statistics* published by the Department of Education each year.

The Economy and the Society: Statistics on general aspects of the society and the economy can be found in *Social Indicators: Selected Statistics on Social Conditions and Trends in the U.S.,* published by the Office of Management and Budget.

The U.S. Federal Government: The *United States Government Manual,* describes the agencies of the executive branch, their activities and the names and addresses of key officials. This book can be considered the "official" directory of U.S. government agencies. Government publication can also be obtained from your representative and senators. Find their nearest office in the government section of your local phone book. Ask for the publication by title, date, publication number, and issuing agency. (Have as much of this information as possible.) You can also write or call their office and tell them what general topic you are researching; they will send you material. However, be aware that this will be a random selection from publications they have in their office. You will still need to do further research to make certain you've covered the subject fully.

VI. Computerized Research Sources

Computerized searching capabilities are rather recent. The *Logging On* features at the end of the chapters in this text can serve as a guide to the types of sources that can be accessed through the Internet. The following sources are also useful for students doing research in American government:

The *Social Science Index* is available on CD-ROM floppy disks and also on-line through various library services.

DIALOG Information Service Inc. contains over 350 databases with more than 200 million individual records (units of information generally citations to sources). A typical ten-minute search costs from $5 to $15. It is available twenty-four-hours a day except from 3 A.M. to 1 P.M. EST on Sundays.

One of the most useful files is *U.S. Political Science Documents #93.* This contains 48,970 records starting in 1975 and consisting of detailed abstracts and indexes from roughly 150 of the major American scholarly journals in political science.

Social Science #7 contains over 2.5 million records indexed from the 1,500 most important social science journals throughout the world. It covers every area of the social and behavioral sciences.

PAIS International #49 has 338,817 records with bibliographic information on the public policy literature in a range of disciplines.

Another separate computerized source is the *Monthly Catalog of Government Publications,* which is available on CD-ROM disks under the name MARCIVE, GPO CAT/PAC.

The research librarian at your library is an excellent source for other and computerized sources of information for research projects and papers.

VII. More on Research

For a more detailed discussion of how to do research in political science, the following are excellent: Carl Kalvelage, Albert P. Melone, and Morley Segal, *Bridges to Knowledge in Political Science: A Handbook for Research,* (Pacific Palisades, CA: Palisades Publishers, 1984), or Robert Weissberg, *Politics: A Handbook for Students* (New York: Harcourt Brace Jovanovich, Publishers, 1985).

Jay M. Shafritz, *The Dorsey Dictionary of American Government and Politics* (Chicago: The Dorsey Press, 1988) is a 661-page treasure of detailed information and reference that you should consider owning. It is richly illustrated and very easy to use.

F

Justices of the U.S. Supreme Court in the Twentieth Century

Chief Justices

NAME	YEARS OF SERVICE	STATE APP'T FROM	APPOINTING PRESIDENT	AGE APP'T	POLITICAL AFFILIATION	EDUCATIONAL* BACKGROUND
Fuller, Melville Weston	1888–1910	Illinois	Cleveland	55	Democrat	Bowdoin College; studied at Harvard Law School
White, Edward Douglass	1910–1921	Louisiana	Taft	65	Democrat	Mount St. Mary's College; Georgetown College (now University)
Taft, William Howard	1921–1930	Connecticut	Harding	64	Republican	Yale; Cincinnati Law School
Hughes, Charles Evans	1930–1941	New York	Hoover	68	Republican	Colgate University; Brown; Columbia Law School
Stone, Harlan Fiske	1941–1946	New York	Roosevelt, F.	69	Republican	Amherst College; Columbia
Vinson, Frederick Moore	1946–1953	Kentucky	Truman	56	Democrat	Centre College
Warren, Earl	1953–1969	California	Eisenhower	62	Republican	University of California, Berkeley
Burger, Warren Earl	1969–1986	Virginia	Nixon	62	Republican	University of Minnesota; St. Paul College of Law (Mitchell College)
Rehnquist, William Hubbs	1986–	Virginia	Reagan	62	Republican	Stanford; Harvard; Stanford University Law School

*SOURCE: Educational background information derived from Elder Witt, *Guide to the U.S. Supreme Court*, 2d ed. (Washington, D.C.: Congressional Quarterly Press, Inc., 1990) Reprinted with the permission of the publisher.

Associate Justices

NAME	YEARS OF SERVICE	STATE APP'T FROM	APPOINTING PRESIDENT	AGE APP'T	POLITICAL AFFILIATION	EDUCATIONAL BACKGROUND
Harlan, John Marshall	1877–1911	Kentucky	Hayes	61	Republican	Centre College; studied law at Transylvania University
Gray, Horace	1882–1902	Massachusetts	Arthur	54	Republican	Harvard College; Harvard Law School
Brewer, David Josiah	1890–1910	Kansas	Harrison	53	Republican	Wesleyan University; Yale; Albany Law School
Brown, Henry Billings	1891–1906	Michigan	Harrison	55	Republican	Yale; studied at Yale Law School and Harvard Law School
Shiras, George, Jr.	1892–1903	Pennsylvania	Harrison	61	Republican	Ohio University; Yale; studied law at Yale and privately
White, Edward Douglass	1894–1910	Louisiana	Cleveland	49	Democrat	Mount St. Mary's College; Georgetown College (now University)

Associate Justices (continued)

Name	Years of Service	State App't from	Appointing President	Age App't	Political Affiliation	Educational Background
Peckham, Rufus Wheeler	1896–1909	New York	Cleveland	58	Democrat	Read law in father's firm
McKenna, Joseph	1898–1925	California	McKinley	55	Republican	Benicia Collegiate Institute, Law Dept.
Holmes, Oliver Wendell, Jr.	1902–1932	Massachusetts	Roosevelt, T.	61	Republican	Harvard College; studied law at Harvard Law School
Day, William Rufus	1903–1922	Ohio	Roosevelt, T.	54	Republican	University of Michigan; University of Michigan Law School
Moody, William Henry	1906–1910	Massachusetts	Roosevelt, T.	53	Republican	Harvard; Harvard Law School
Lurton, Horace Harmon	1910–1914	Tennessee	Taft	66	Democrat	University of Chicago; Cumberland Law School
Hughes, Charles Evans	1910–1916	New York	Taft	48	Republican	Colgate University; Brown University; Columbia Law School
Van Devanter, Willis	1911–1937	Wyoming	Taft	52	Republican	Indiana Asbury University; University of Cincinnati Law School
Lamar, Joseph Rucker	1911–1916	Georgia	Taft	54	Democrat	University of Georgia; Bethany College; Washington and Lee University
Pitney, Mahlon	1912–1922	New Jersey	Taft	54	Republican	College of New Jersey (Princeton); read law under father
McReynolds, James Clark	1914–1941	Tennessee	Wilson	52	Democrat	Vanderbilt University; University of Virginia
Brandeis, Louis Dembitz	1916–1939	Massachusetts	Wilson	60	Democrat	Harvard Law School
Clarke, John Hessin	1916–1922	Ohio	Wilson	59	Democrat	Western Reserve University; read law under father
Sutherland, George	1922–1938	Utah	Harding	60	Republican	Brigham Young Academy; one year at University of Michigan Law School
Butler, Pierce	1923–1939	Minnesota	Harding	57	Democrat	Carleton College
Sanford, Edward Terry	1923–1930	Tennessee	Harding	58	Republican	University of Tennessee; Harvard; Harvard Law School
Stone, Harlan Fiske	1925–1941	New York	Coolidge	53	Republican	Amherst College; Columbia University Law School
Roberts, Owen Josephus	1930–1945	Pennsylvania	Hoover	55	Republican	University of Pennsylvania; University of Pennsylvania Law School
Cardozo, Benjamin Nathan	1932–1938	New York	Hoover	62	Democrat	Columbia University; two years at Columbia Law School
Black, Hugo Lafayette	1937–1971	Alabama	Roosevelt, F.	51	Democrat	Birmingham Medical College; University of Alabama Law School
Reed, Stanley Forman	1938–1957	Kentucky	Roosevelt, F.	54	Democrat	Kentucky Wesleyan University; Foreman Yale; studied law at University of Virginia and Columbia University; University of Paris
Frankfurter, Felix	1939–1962	Massachusetts	Roosevelt, F.	57	Independent	College of the City of New York; Harvard Law School
Douglas, William Orville	1939–1975	Connecticut	Roosevelt, F.	41	Democrat	Whitman College; Columbia University Law School

Associate Justices (continued)

Name	Years of Service	State App't From	Appointing President	Age App't	Political Affiliation	Educational Background
Murphy, Frank	1940–1949	Michigan	Roosevelt, F.	50	Democrat	University of Michigan; Lincoln's Inn, London; Trinity College
Byrnes, James Francis	1941–1942	South Carolina	Roosevelt, F.	62	Democrat	Read law privately
Jackson, Robert Houghwout	1941–1954	New York	Roosevelt, F.	49	Democrat	Albany Law School
Rutledge, Wiley Blount	1943–1949	Iowa	Roosevelt, F.	49	Democrat	University of Wisconsin; University of Colorado
Burton, Harold Hitz	1945–1958	Ohio	Truman	57	Republican	Bowdoin College; Harvard University Law School
Clark, Thomas Campbell	1949–1967	Texas	Truman	50	Democrat	University of Texas
Minton, Sherman	1949–1956	Indiana	Truman	59	Democrat	Indiana University College of Law; Yale Law School
Harlan, John Marshall	1955–1971	New York	Eisenhower	56	Republican	Princeton; Oxford University; New York Law School
Brennan, William J., Jr.	1956–1990	New Jersey	Eisenhower	50	Democrat	University of Pennsylvania; Harvard Law School
Whittaker, Charles Evans	1957–1962	Missouri	Eisenhower	56	Republican	University of Kansas City Law School
Stewart, Potter	1958–1981	Ohio	Eisenhower	43	Republican	Yale; Yale Law School
White, Byron Raymond	1962–1993	Colorado	Kennedy	45	Democrat	University of Colorado; Oxford University; Yale Law School
Goldberg, Arthur Joseph	1962–1965	Illinois	Kennedy	54	Democrat	Northwestern University
Fortas, Abe	1965–1969	Tennessee	Johnson, L.	55	Democrat	Southwestern College; Yale Law School
Marshall, Thurgood	1967–1991	New York	Johnson, L.	59	Democrat	Lincoln University; Howard University Law School
Blackmun, Harry A.	1970–1994	Minnesota	Nixon	62	Republican	Harvard; Harvard Law School
Powell, Lewis F., Jr.	1972–1987	Virginia	Nixon	65	Democrat	Washington and Lee University; Washington and Lee University Law School; Harvard Law School
Rehnquist, William H.	1972–1986	Arizona	Nixon	48	Republican	Stanford; Harvard; Stanford University Law School
Stevens, John Paul	1975–	Illinois	Ford	55	Republican	University of Colorado; Northwestern University Law School
O'Connor, Sandra Day	1981–	Arizona	Reagan	51	Republican	Stanford; Stanford University Law School
Scalia, Antonin	1986–	Virginia	Reagan	50	Republican	Georgetown University; Harvard Law School
Kennedy, Anthony M.	1988–	California	Reagan	52	Republican	Stanford; London School of Economics; Harvard Law School
Souter, David Hackett	1990–	New Hampshire	Bush	51	Republican	Harvard; Oxford University
Thomas, Clarence	1991–	District of Columbia	Bush	43	Republican	Holy Cross College; Yale Law School
Ginsburg, Ruth Bader	1993–	District of Columbia	Clinton	60	Democrat	Cornell University; Columbia Law School
Breyer, Stephen, G.	1994–	Massachusetts	Clinton	55	Democrat	Stanford University; Oxford University; Harvard Law School

G

Party Control of Congress in the Twentieth Century

CONGRESS	YEARS	PRESIDENT	MAJORITY PARTY IN HOUSE	MAJORITY PARTY IN SENATE
57th	1901–1903	T. Roosevelt	Republican	Republican
58th	1903–1905	T. Roosevelt	Republican	Republican
59th	1905–1907	T. Roosevelt	Republican	Republican
60th	1907–1909	T. Roosevelt	Republican	Republican
61st	1909–1911	Taft	Republican	Republican
62d	1911–1913	Taft	Democratic	Republican
63d	1913–1915	Wilson	Democratic	Democratic
64th	1915–1917	Wilson	Democratic	Democratic
65th	1917–1919	Wilson	Democratic	Democratic
66th	1919–1921	Wilson	Republican	Republican
67th	1921–1923	Harding	Republican	Republican
68th	1923–1925	Coolidge	Republican	Republican
69th	1925–1927	Coolidge	Republican	Republican
70th	1927–1929	Coolidge	Republican	Republican
71st	1929–1931	Hoover	Republican	Republican
72d	1931–1933	Hoover	Democratic	Republican
73d	1933–1935	F. Roosevelt	Democratic	Democratic
74th	1935–1937	F. Roosevelt	Democratic	Democratic
75th	1937–1939	F. Roosevelt	Democratic	Democratic
76th	1939–1941	F. Roosevelt	Democratic	Democratic
77th	1941–1943	F. Roosevelt	Democratic	Democratic
78th	1943–1945	F. Roosevelt	Democratic	Democratic
79th	1945–1947	Truman	Democratic	Democratic
80th	1947–1949	Truman	Republican	Democratic
81st	1949–1951	Truman	Democratic	Democratic
82d	1951–1953	Truman	Democratic	Democratic
83d	1953–1955	Eisenhower	Republican	Republican
84th	1955–1957	Eisenhower	Democratic	Democratic
85th	1957–1959	Eisenhower	Democratic	Democratic
86th	1959–1961	Eisenhower	Democratic	Democratic
87th	1961–1963	Kennedy	Democratic	Democratic
88th	1963–1965	Kennedy/Johnson	Democratic	Democratic
89th	1965–1967	Johnson	Democratic	Democratic
90th	1967–1969	Johnson	Democratic	Democratic
91st	1969–1971	Nixon	Democratic	Democratic
92d	1971–1973	Nixon	Democratic	Democratic
93d	1973–1975	Nixon/Ford	Democratic	Democratic
94th	1975–1977	Ford	Democratic	Democratic
95th	1977–1979	Carter	Democratic	Democratic
96th	1979–1981	Carter	Democratic	Democratic
97th	1981–1983	Reagan	Democratic	Republican
98th	1983–1985	Reagan	Democratic	Republican
99th	1985–1987	Reagan	Democratic	Republican
100th	1987–1989	Reagan	Democratic	Democratic
101st	1989–1991	Bush	Democratic	Democratic
102d	1991–1993	Bush	Democratic	Democratic
103d	1993–1995	Clinton	Democratic	Democratic
104th	1995–1997	Clinton	Republican	Republican

H

Spanish Equivalents for Important Terms in American Government

Acid Rain: Lluvia Acida
Acquisitive Model: Modelo Adquisitivo
Actionable: Procesable, Enjuiciable
Action-reaction Syndrome: Sídrome de Acción y Reacción
Actual Malice: Malicia Expresa
Administrative Agency: Agencia Administrativa
Advice and Consent: Consejo y Consentimiento
Affirmative Action: Acción Afirmativa
Affirm: Afirmar
Agenda Setting: Agenda Establecida
Aid to Families with Dependent Children (AFDC): Ayuda para Familias con Niños Dependientes
Amicus Curiae **Brief:** Tercer persona o grupo no involucrado en el caso, admitido en un juicio para hacer valer el intéres público o el de un grupo social importante.
Anarchy: Anarquía
Anti-Federalists: Anti-Federalistas
Appellate Court: Corte de Apelación
Appointment Power: Poder de Apuntamiento
Appropriation: Apropiación
Aristocracy: Aristocracia
Attentive Public: Público Atento
Australian Ballot: Voto Australiano
Authority: Autoridad
Authorization: Autorización

Bad-Tendency Rule: Regla de Tendencia-mala
"Beauty Contest": Concurso de Belleza
Bicameralism: Bicameralismo
Bicameral Legislature: Legislatura Bicameral
Bill of Rights: Declaración de Derechos
Blanket Primary: Primaria Comprensiva
Block Grants: Concesiones de Bloque
Bureaucracy: Burocracia
Busing: Transporte público

Cabinet: Gabinete, Consejo de Ministros
Cabinet Department: Departamento del Gabinete
Cadre: El núcleo de activistas de partidos políticos encargados de cumplir las funciones importantes de los partidos políticos americanos.
Canvassing Board: Consejo encargado con la encuesta de una violación.
Capture: Captura, toma
Casework: Trabajo de Caso
Categorical Grants-in-Aid: Concesiones Categóricas de Ayuda
Caucus: Reunión de Dirigentes

Challenge: Reto
Checks and Balances: Chequeos y Equilibrio
Chief Diplomat: Jefe Diplomático
Chief Executive: Jefe Ejecutivo
Chief Legislator: Jefe Legislador
Chief of Staff: Jefe de Personal
Chief of State: Jefe de Estado
Civil Law: Derecho Civil
Civil Liberties: Libertades Civiles
Civil Rights: Derechos Civiles
Civil Service: Servicio Civil
Civil Service Commission: Comisión de Servicio Civil
Class-action Suit: Demanda en representación de un grupo o clase.
Class Politics: Política de Clase
Clear and Present Danger Test: Prueba de Peligro Claro y Presente
Climate Control: Control de Clima
Closed Primary: Primaria Cerrada
Cloture: Cierre al voto
Coattail Effect: Effecto de Cola de Chaqueta
Cold War: Guerra Fría
Commander in Chief: Comandante en Jefe
Commerce Clause: Clausula de Comercio
Commercial Speech: Discurso Comercial
Common Law: Ley Común, Derecho Consuetudinario

Comparable Worth: Valor Comparable
Compliance: De acuerdo
Concurrent Majority: Mayoría Concurrente
Concurring Opinion: Opinión Concurrente
Confederal System: Sistema Confederal
Confederation: Confederación
Conference Committee: Comité de Conferencia
Consensus: Concenso
Consent of the People: Consentimiento de la Gente
Conservatism: Calidad de Conservador
Conservative Coalition: Coalición Conservadora
Consolidation: Consolidación
Constant Dollars: Dólares Constantes
Constitutional Initiative: Iniciativa Constitucional
Constitutional Power: Poder Constitucional
Containment: Contenimiento
Continuing Resolution: Resolució Contínua
Cooley's Rule: Régla de Cooley
Cooperative Federalism: Federalismo Cooperativo
Corrupt Practices Acts: Leyes Contra Acciones Corruptas
Council of Economic Advisers (CEA): Consejo de Asesores Económicos
Council of Government (COG): Consejo de Gobierno
County: Condado
Credentials Committee: Comité de Credenciales
Criminal Law: Ley Criminal

De Facto **Segregation:** Segregación de Hecho
De Jure **Segregation:** Segregación Cotidiana
Defamation of Character: Defamación de Carácter
Democracy: Democracia
Democratic Party: Partido Democratico
Dillon's Rule: Régla de Dillon
Diplomacy: Diplomácia
Direct Democracy: Democracia Directa
Direct Primary: Primaria Directa
Direct Technique: Técnica Directa
Discharge Petition: Petición de Descargo
Dissenting Opinion: Opinión Disidente
Divisive Opinion: Opinión Divisiva
Domestic Policy: Principio Político Doméstico
Dual Citizenship: Ciudadanía Dual
Dual Federalism: Federalismo Dual
Détente: No Spanish equivalent.

Economic Aid: Ayuda Económica
Economic Regulation: Regulación Económica
Elastic Clause, or Necessary and Proper Clause: Cláusula Flexible o Cláusula Propia Necesaria
Elector: Elector
Electoral College: Colegio Electoral
Electronic Media: Media Electronica
Elite: Elite (el selecto)
Elite Theory: Teoría Elitista (de lo selecto)
Emergency Power: Poder de Emergencia
Enumerated Power: Poder Enumerado
Environmental Impact Statement (EIS): Afirmación de Impacto Ambiental
Equality: Igualdad
Equalization: Igualación
Equal Employment Opportunity Commission (EEOC): Comisión de Igualdad de Oportunidad en el Empleo
Era of Good Feeling: Era de Buen Sentimiento
Era of Personal Politics: Era de Política Personal
Establishment Clause: Cláusula de Establecimiento
Euthanasia: Eutanasia
Exclusionary Rule: Regla de Exclusión
Executive Agreement: Acuerdo Ejecutivo

Executive Budget: Presupuesto Ejecutivo
Executive Office of the President (EOP): Oficina Ejecutiva del Presidente
Executive Order: Orden Ejecutivo
Executive Privilege: Privilegio Ejecutivo
Expressed Power: Poder Expresado
Extradite: Entregar por Extradición

Faction: Facción
Fairness Doctrine: Doctrina de Justicia
Fall Review: Revision de Otoño
Federalist: Federalista
Federal Mandate: Mandato Federal
Federal Open Market Committee (FOMC): Comité Federal de Libre Mercado
Federal Register: Registro Federal
Federal System: Sistema Federal
Federalists: Federalistas
Fighting Words: Palabras de Provocación
Filibuster: Obstrucción de iniciativas de ley
Fireside Chat: Charla de Hogar
First Budget Resolution: Resolució Primera Presupuesta
First Continental Congress: Primér Congreso Continental
Fiscal Policy: Politico Fiscal
Fiscal Year (FY): Año Fiscal
Fluidity: Fluidez
Food Stamps: Estampillas para Comida
Foreign Policy: Politica Extranjera
Foreign Policy Process: Proceso de Politica Extranjera
Franking: Franqueando
Fraternity: Fraternidad
Free Exercise Clause: Cláusula de Ejercicio Libre
Full Faith and Credit Clause: Cláusula de Completa Fé y Crédito
Functional Consolidation: Consolidación Funcional
Gag Order: Orden de Silencio
Garbage Can Model: Modelo Bote de Basura

Gender Gap: Brecha de Género
General Law City: Regla General Urbana
General Sales Tax: Impuesto General de Ventas
Generational Effect: Efecto Generacional
Gerrymandering: División arbitraria de los distritos electorales con fines políticos.
Government: Gobierno
Government Corporation: Corporación Gubernamental
Government in the Sunshine Act: Gobierno en la acta: Luz del Sol
Grandfather Clause: Clausula del Abuelo
Grand Jury: Gran Jurado
Great Compromise: Grán Acuerdo de Negociación

Hatch Act (Political Activities Act): Acta Hatch (acta de actividades politicas)
Hecklers' Veto: Veto de Abuchamiento
Home Rule City: Regla Urbana
Horizontal Federalism: Federalismo Horizontal
Hyperpluralism: Hiperpluralismo

Ideologue: Ideólogo
Ideology: Ideología
Image Building: Construcción de Imágen
Impeachment: Acción Penal Contra un Funcionario Público
Inalienable Rights: Derechos Inalienables
Income Transfer: Transferencia de Ingresos
Incorporation Theory: Teoría de Incorporación
Independent: Independiente
Independent Candidate: Candidato Independiente
Independent Executive Agency: Agencia Ejecutiva Independiente
Independent Regulatory Agency: Agencia Regulatoria Independiente
Indirect Technique: Técnica Indirecta
Inherent Power: Poder Inherente

Initiative: Iniciativa
Injunction: Injunción, Prohibición Judicial
Institution: Institución
Instructed Delegate: Delegado con Instrucciones
Intelligence Community: Comunidad de Inteligencia
Intensity: Intensidad
Interest Group: Grupo de Interés
Interposition: Interposición
Interstate Compact: Compacto Interestatal
In-kind Subsidy: Subsidio de Clase
Iron Curtain: Cortina de Acero
Iron Triangle: Triágulo de Acero
Isolationist Foreign Policy: Politica Extranjera de Aislamiento
Issue Voting: Voto Temático
Item Veto: Artículo de Veto

Jim Crow Laws: No Spanish equivalent.
Joint Committee: Comité Mancomunado
Judicial Activism: Activismo Judicial
Judicial Implementation: Implementacion Judicial
Judicial Restraint: Restricción Judicial
Judicial Review: Revisión Judicial
Jurisdiction: Jurisdicción
Justiciable Dispute: Disputa Judiciaria
Justiciable Question: Pregunta Justiciable

Keynesian Economics: Economía Keynesiana
Kitchen Cabinet: Gabinete de Cocina

Labor Movement: Movimiento Laboral
Latent Public Opinion: Opinión Pública Latente
Lawmaking: Hacedores de Ley
Legislative History: Historia Legislativa
Legislative Initiative: Iniciativa de legislación
Legislative Veto: Veto Legislativo

Legislature: Legislatura
Legitimacy: Legitimidad
Libel: Libelo, Difamación Escrita
Liberalism: Liberalismo
Liberty: Libertad
Limited Government: Gobierno Limitado
Line Organization: Organización de Linea
Literacy Test: Exámen de alfabetización
Litigate: Litigar
Lobbying: Cabildeo
Logrolling: Práctica legislativa que consiste en incluir en un mismo proyecto de ley temas de diversa ídole.
Loophole: Hueco Legal, escapatoria

Madisonian Model: Modelo Madisónico
Majority: Mayoría
Majority Floor Leader: Líder Mayoritario de Piso
Majority Leader of the House: Líder Mayoritario de la Casa
Majority Opinion: Opinión Mayoritaria
Majority Rule: Regla de Mayoría
Managed News: Noticias Manipuladas
Mandatory Retirement: Retiro Mandatorio
Matching Funds: Fondos Combinados
Material Incentive: Incentivo Material
Media: Media
Media Access: Acceso de Media
Merit System: Sistema de Mérito
Military-Industrial Complex: Complejo Industriomilitar
Minority Floor Leader: Líder Minoritario de Piso
Minority Leader of the House: Líder Minorial del Cuerpo Legislativo
Monetary Policy: Politica Monetaria
Monopolistic Model: Modelo Monopólico
Monroe Doctrine: Doctrina Monroe
Moral Idealism: Idealismo Moral

Municipal Home Rule: Regla Municipal

Narrow Casting: Mensaje Dirigído

National Committee: Comité Nacional

National Convention: Convención Nacional

National Politics: Politica Nacional

National Security Council (NSC): Concilio de Seguridad Nacional

National Security Policy: Politica de Seguridad Nacional

Natural Aristocracy: Aristocracia Natural

Natural Rights: Derechos Naturales

Necessaries: Necesidades

Negative Constituents: Constituyentes Negativos

New England Town: Pueblo de Nueva Inglaterra

New Federalism: Federalismo Nuevo

Nullification: Nulidad, Anulación

Office-Block, or Massachusetts, Ballot: Cuadro-Oficina, o Massachusetts, Voto

Office of Management and Budget (OMB): Oficina de Administració y Presupuesto

Oligarchy: Oligarquía

Ombudsman: Funcionario que representa al ciudadano ante el gobierno.

Open Primary: Primaria Abierta

Opinion: Opinión

Opinion Leader: Líder de Opinión

Opinion Poll: Encuesta, Conjunto de Opinión

Oral Arguments: Argumentos Orales

Oversight: Inadvertencia, Omisión

Paid-for-Political Announcement: Anuncios Politicos Pagados

Pardon: Perdón

Party-Column, or Indiana, Ballot: Partido-Columna, o Indiana, Voto

Party Identification: Identificación de Partido

Party Identifier: Identificador de Partido

Party-in-Electorate: Partido Electoral

Party-in-Government: Partido en Gobierno

Party Organization: Organización de Partido

Party Platform: Plataforma de Partido

Patronage: Patrocinio

Peer Group: Grupo de Contemporáneos

Pendleton Act (Civil Service Reform Act): Acta Pendleton (Acta de Reforma al Servicio Civil)

Personal Attack Rule: Regla de Ataque Personal

Petit Jury: Jurado Ordinario

Pluralism: Pluralismo

Plurality: Pluralidad

Pocket Veto: Veto de Bolsillo

Police Power: Poder Policiaco

Policy Trade-offs: Intercambio de Politicas

Political Action Committee (PAC): Comité de Acción Política

Political Consultant: Consultante Político

Political Culture: Cultura Politica

Political Party: Partido Político

Political Question: Pregunta Politica

Political Realism: Realismo Político

Political Socialization: Socialización Politica

Political Tolerance: Tolerancia Política

Political Trust: Confianza Política

Politico: Político

Politics: Politica

Poll Tax: Impuesto sobre el sufragio

Poll Watcher: Observador de Encuesta

Popular Sovereignty: Soberanía Popular

Power: Poder

Precedent: Precedente

Preferred-Position Test: Prueba de Posición Preferida

Presidential Primary: Primaria Presidencial

President Pro Tempore: Presidente Provisoriamente

Press Secretary: Secretaría de Prensa

Prior Restraint: Restricción Anterior

Privileges and Immunities: Privilégios e Imunidades

Privitization, or Contracting Out: Privatización

Property: Propiedad

Property Tax: Impuesto de Propiedad

Public Agenda: Agenda Pública

Public Debt Financing: Financiamiento de Deuda Pública

Public Debt, or National Debt: Deuda Pública o Nacional

Public Interest: Interes Público

Public Opinion: Opinión Pública

Purposive Incentive: Incentivo de Propósito

Ratification: Ratificación

Rational Ignorance Effect: Effecto de Ignorancia Racional

Reapportionment: Redistribución

Recall: Suspender

Recognition Power: Poder de Reconocimiento

Recycling: Reciclaje

Redistricting: Redistrictificación

Referendum: Referédum

Registration: Registración

Regressive Tax: Impuestos Regresivos

Relevance: Pertinencia

Remand: Reenviar

Representation: Representación

Representative Assembly: Asamblea Representativa

Representative Democracy: Democracia Representativa

Reprieve: Trequa, Suspensión

Republic: República

Republican Party: Partido Republicano

Resulting Powers: Poderes Resultados

Reverse: Cambiarse a lo contrario

Reverse Discrimination: Discriminación Reversiva

Rules Committee: Comité Regulador

Rule of Four: Regla de Cuatro

Run-off Primary: Primaria Residual

Safe Seat: Asiento Seguro
Sampling Error: Error de Encuesta
Secession: Secesión
Second Budget Resolution: Resolución Segunda Presupuestal
Second Continental Congress: Segundo Congreso Continental
Sectional Politics: Política Seccional
Segregation: Segregación
Selectperson: Persona Selecta
Select Committee: Comité Selecto
Senatorial Courtesy: Cortesia Senatorial
Seniority System: Sistema Señiorial
Separate-but-Equal Doctrine: Separados pero iguales
Separation of Powers: Separación de Poderes
Service Sector: Sector de Servicio
Sexual Harassment: Acosamiento Sexual
Sex Discrimination: Discriminacion Sexual
Slander: Difamación Oral, Calumnia
Sliding-Scale Test: Prueba Escalonada
Social Movement: Movimiento Social
Social Security: Seguridad Social
Socioeconomic Status: Estado Socioeconómico
Solidary Incentive: Incentivo de Solideridad
Solid South: Súr Sólido
Sound Bite: Mordida de Sonido
Soviet Bloc: Bloque Soviético
Speaker of the House: Vocero de la Casa
Spin: Girar/Giro
Spin Doctor: Doctor en Giro
Spin-off Party: Partido Estático
Spoils System: Sistema de Despojos
Spring Review: Revisión de Primavera
Stare Decisis: El principio característico del ley comú por el cual los precedentes

jurisprudenciales tienen fuerza obligatoria, no sólo entre las partes, sino tambien para casos sucesivos análogos.
Stability: Estabilidad
Standing Committee: Comité de Sostenimiento
State Central Committee: Comité Central del Estado
State: Estado
State of the Union Message: Mensaje Sobre el Estado de la Unión
Statutory Power: Poder Estatorial
Strategic Arms Limitation Treaty (SALT I): Tratado de Limitación de Armas Estratégicas
Subpoena: Orden de Testificación
Subsidy: Subsidio
Suffrage: Sufrágio
Sunset Legislation: Legislación Sunset
Superdelegate: Líder de partido o oficial elegido quien tiene el derecho de votar.
Supplemental Security Income (SSI): Ingresos de Seguridad Suplementaria
Supremacy Clause: Cláusula de Supremacia
Supremacy Doctrine: Doctrina de Supremacia
Symbolic Speech: Discurso Simbólico

Technical Assistance: Asistencia Técnica
Third Party: Tercer Partido
Third-party Candidate: Candidato de Tercer Partido
Ticket Splitting: División de Boletos
Totalitarian Regime: Régimen Totalitario
Town Manager System: Sistema de Administrador Municipal
Town Meeting: Junta Municipal
Township: Municipio
Tracking Poll: Seguimiento de Encuesta
Trial Court: Tribunal de Primera
Truman Doctrine: Doctrina Truman
Trustee: Depositario
Twelfth Amendment: Doceava Enmienda

Twenty-fifth Amendment: Veinticincoava Enmienda
Two-Party System: Sistema de Dos Partidos

Unanimous Opinion: Opinión Unánime
Underground Economy: Economía Subterráea
Unicameral Legislature: Legislatura Unicameral
Unincorporated Area: Area no Incorporada
Unit Rule: Regla de Unidad
Unitary System: Sistema Unitario
Universal Suffrage: Sufragio Universal
U.S. Treasury Bond: Bono de la Tesoreria de E.U.A.

Veto Message: Comunicado de Veto
Voter Turnout: Renaimiento de Votantes

War Powers Act: Acta de Poderes de Guerra
Washington Community: Comunidad de Washington
Weberian Model: Modelo Weberiano
Whip: Látigo
Whistleblower: Privatización o Contratista
White House Office: Oficina de la Casa Blanca
White House Press Corps: Cuerpo de Prensa de la Casa Blanca
White Primary: Sufragio en Elección Primaria/Blancos Solamente
Writ of *Certiorari:* Prueba de certeza; orden emitida por el tribunal de apelaciones para que el tribunal inferior dé lugar a la apelación.
Writ of *Habeas Corpus:* Prueba de Evidencia Concreta
Writ of *Mandamus:* Un mandato por la corte para que un acto se lleve a cabo.

Yellow Journalism: Amarillismo Periodístico

I

A Citizen's Survival Guide

We cannot foresee every situation that you are likely to confront during your career as a college student. This guide, however, will provide you with information about several topics that may interest you or problems that you may face as a college or university student.

YOU AND THE POLITICAL SYSTEM

Any person, providing that he or she fulfills certain minimal requirements, can participate in the American political system. Here we provide information on how you can register to vote; how to obtain information about political candidates, as well as events occurring in state legislatures and the U.S. Congress; and what to do if you wish to become a political candidate.

How Do I Register to Vote?

In most states, you must register before you go to the polls on election day.

Who May Register?   In general, you are eligible to vote if you are a citizen of the United States, will be eighteen years old on election day, and are a resident of the state in which you wish to register.

How Do I Register?   You may register to vote at the appropriate county office in your state, or you may complete a postcard registration form and return it to the correct official. To find out which county official or office you need to contact (whether the appropriate official or office is the county clerk, county auditor, or county board of elections, for example), check the information pages of your local telephone directory.

Registration forms are available throughout your county in places such as banks, union halls, city halls, savings and loans, utility offices, libraries, and political party headquarters. If you cannot register by one of the above methods, call your county clerk, political party headquarters, or the League of Women Voters.

For How Long Is My Registration Valid?   In general, your registration will be valid indefinitely if you vote at least once every four calendar years and if you remain in the county in which you are registered. These rules vary somewhat from state to state, because some states have regular "purges" of their voter registration lists and others do this less routinely.

When May I Register?   In states that require pre-voting registration, you must register no later than 5:00 P.M. on the tenth calendar day prior to the primary and general elections, or the eleventh calendar day prior to any other election in which you wish to vote. Postcard registration forms must be postmarked no later than fifteen days prior to the election in which you wish to vote.

If I Move, How Do I Record My Change of Address?   If you move within a county, write a letter to the appropriate county official. State the full name under which you are registered, your old address, your new address, and any other information to assist the county official in identifying you. The letter must include a signature from each affected voter. You may also record the change at the county offices in person, at the polls on election day, or by completing a postcard registration form. If you move to a different county, you must register as a new voter.

May I Vote Using an Absentee Ballot?   Yes. If you are properly registered and you expect to be out of your precinct on election day, or if you are ill or physically disabled, you may vote by sending in an absentee ballot. Incidentally, if you are voting via an absentee ballot from another state, check with a local notary public; a notary public's signature may be required for the out-of-state absentee ballot to be acceptable back home. If you are using an absentee ballot within your state, you can have it notorized at the county auditor's office during regular office hours.

You may request a ballot by mail not more than seventy days prior to an election. If the request is for a primary election ballot and you are in a state that requires party registration, you must include your party preference. Persons who are residents of health-care facilities or patients in hospitals may have a ballot delivered to them upon request to the registration official. Your completed absentee ballot must be postmarked no later than one day before the election. An absentee ballot must be returned, regardless of whether it is completed.

Where Do I Get Information about the Candidates?

Apart from paying attention to political and election news on television and radio, take the time to read a national newspaper (such as the *New York Times*) or a news magazine (such as *Time* or *Newsweek*). Also, watch C-Span or CNN on cable television, or contact interested groups. Local election headquarters for a candidate are probably the most direct source of information, but you should also contact the county or state party headquarters, look in your local public library for campaign material, or rely on nonpartisan activist groups, such the League of Women Voters, for unbiased information.

How Can I Find Out What's Going on in Congress or in My State Legislature?

To find out what is happening in Congress, you can call the offices of a U.S. senator or congressional representative from your state. To obtain information about events in your state legislature, you can call the legislature and leave a message for an individual state senator or representative, or you can ask for information about upcoming votes or events in the legislature. Most legislatures have a number with a recorded message describing the day's events in the legislature and a separate number with information on the status of bills, public hearings, and legislative agendas.

How Can I Become a Candidate?

If you want to be a candidate, contact one of the following offices:

- For county positions, contact the county clerk's office.
- For state and federal positions, contact the secretary of state's office.
- For municipal positions, contact the city clerk's office in your city.
- For school district positions, contact the secretary of the school district in your district.

Note that candidates must also file campaign finance disclosure reports. Federal candidates should write or call the Federal Election Commission, 999 E Street N.W., Washington, DC 20463 (800–424–9530). All other candidates should write or call the Campaign Finance Disclosure Commission for their state.

YOU AND THE JUSTICE SYSTEM

One of the essential "survival skills" in today's world is knowing what to do if you are a victim of a crime or have an encounter with the police. The following sections provide information on how to deal with such situations. Additionally, any American citizen has a chance of being called up for jury duty. If you should be called, you should know what jury duty entails.

What If I Am the Victim of a Crime?

If you are the victim of a crime, you should, of course, report the crime to the proper authorities. At a college or university, this may involve contacting the campus security office, the local municipal police, or both. Many campus security personnel have powers of arrest, as well as training comparable to local police, and they probably can respond more quickly than the local police if the crime occurred on campus. Help with legal services is available through many student governments or university administrations.

Beyond that, many states have crime-victim compensation programs that help victims with costs related to injuries resulting from criminal acts. In general, you may be eligible for this form of assistance if you have been physically or emotionally injured in a violent crime; if you are the victim of drunk driving, hit-and-run driving, reckless driving, or driving in which a car is used as a weapon; or if you are the survivor of a homicide victim. To qualify for such financial compensation, generally you must report the crime to local law-enforcement officers within a specified amount of time (for example, seventy-two hours), unless there is an explanation of why you could not do so; file an application with the program within a time limit (for example, two years) from the date of the crime; cooperate with the reasonable requests of law-enforcement officers in their investigation or prosecution of the crime; not have consented to, provoked, or incited the crime; and not have been assisting in, or committing, the criminal act causing your injuries. Payments generally will be made when all required information is received.

Within established limits, you may be compensated for medical or nursing care needed for crime injuries, crime-related counseling, wages lost due to crime injuries, loss of support (for dependents of deceased victims or victims who cannot work), funeral and burial costs for homicide victims, grief counseling for survivors of homicide victims, cleaning the homicide location in a home, or replacing clothing and bedding held as evidence by law-enforcement officials. Depending on particular state legislation, you may not be eligible under these programs to be compensated for property loss or repair, legal fees, travel, telephone bills, meals, or pain and suffering.

What Happens If I Have an Encounter with the Police?

Let's say that you are involved in a traffic accident, and the police start asking questions. Then again, you might be stopped as you leave a store at the mall and be charged with shoplifting. What kinds of things do you need to know to help you get through experiences such as these?

We will assume in what follows that you will be dealing with state law-enforcement and court authorities rather than federal officials, because by far the greatest number of violations of the law involve transgressions against state laws or local ordinances.

Criminal laws are passed to protect the public from conduct that is dangerous or offensive. When a criminal law is broken, the city, county, or state brings criminal charges against an individual. Criminal law is divided into two classifications: felonies and misdemeanors. A *felony* is a major crime (such as murder, robbery, or sexual assault) and may be punishable by an imprisonment for anywhere from one year to life (or death, for that matter, in states that provide for capital punishment), depending on the severity and classification of the felony. In contrast, a *misdemeanor* is a comparatively minor offense that is punishable by a fine, imprisonment for up to one year, or both.

Criminal Procedures. Most arrests are for misdemeanors, and in such situations, the arresting officers often release the suspect with a citation rather than taking him or her to the police station. The *citation* instructs the person to appear in court at some later date to respond to the charges. If, after arrest, the suspect is not released with a citation, he or she will be taken into custody. Within twenty-four hours, the suspect will be brought before a magistrate or a judge. At this time, the suspect is informed of the charges against him or her, and bail or conditions of release are set. In some serious cases, state law may prohibit a release on bail. Within a relatively short time (twenty days, for example), the accused person may receive a preliminary hearing before a district judge or a district associate judge. The purpose of this hearing is to determine if there is enough evidence ("probable cause") to continue to prosecute the case. If a preliminary hearing is held and the court finds probable cause, the defendant will be held for further proceedings.

Depending on state law or other factors, the case may be presented to a grand jury. A *grand jury* is a panel consisting of six to twenty-three citizens who decide whether to return an indictment against the defendant. If a specified number of the grand jurors feel that there is enough evidence to bring the accused person to trial, they *indict* the defendant, which means that the case is presented to the court for filing. Few criminal cases are heard by grand juries. Usually, the county attorney will file an *information*, which is a statement of the charges and the evidence in the case. After the indictment or the filing of an information, the defendant appears before a judge or magistrate for arraignment, generally within forty-five days of the preliminary hearing. At the arraignment, the defendant hears the charges and enters a plea, which is usually either "guilty" or "not guilty." The judge will either dismiss the case, accept the not guilty plea, or accept the guilty plea. If the guilty plea is accepted, the judge will announce the sentence, which may be a fine, confinement in a jail or prison, probation, and/or other treatment. Sometimes, if a judge is not convinced that a defendant is guilty, he or she may require that a trial be held.

If the defendant pleads not guilty, a trial date is set. The defendant has the right to a trial by jury. If a jury is not requested, a *bench trial* is scheduled. In a bench trial, the judge will hear the evidence and render a verdict. If a jury is requested, the jury will hear and weigh the evidence and render a verdict. If the jury is not convinced beyond a reasonable doubt of the defendant's guilt, a not guilty verdict must be returned. In a criminal trial, the jurors' decision as to whether the defendant is guilty or not guilty must be unanimous. If the jury cannot reach a unanimous verdict, the judge will declare a *mistrial*. The state then will decide whether to retry the case before another jury or to dismiss the charges. If the jury returns a guilty verdict, a sentencing date will be set. The judge will also order a complete investigation of the defendant's background and the circumstances of the case.

After weighing the information from the investigation, the judge at a sentencing hearing may sentence the defendant to a fine, confinement in a jail or prison, probation, other form of special correctional treatment, or a combination of these punishments. If the sentence is a fine or confinement, the judge may suspend the sentence. If the sentence is suspended, the fine or confinement does not have to be paid or served, and the defendant is placed on probation. If the defendant fails to follow the rules and conditions of the probation, it may be revoked and the original sentence reinstated.

Traffic Violations.   For traffic-related matters, a somewhat different pattern is followed. Fines and costs are listed on tickets when they are issued for minor violations, such as parking and most moving violations (speeding violations, for example). These costs are usually paid by mail but can be paid at the traffic clerk's or district clerk's office. Usually, a court appearance is not required for a minor violation. Some jurisdictions, though, may require you to go through a "shock" session before a judge. If damages from an accident exceed a specified amount, a court appearance may be required. More serious traffic violations—such as reckless driving, operating a motor vehicle while intoxicated, or driving when your license is suspended—require a court appearance before a judge or magistrate.

What If I Am Called for Jury Duty?

Eligibility to serve on a jury is a basic obligation of citizenship. In general, any registered voter (and, in many locations, people who are registered as owning motor vehicles or whose names appear on other publicly available lists) may be called up periodically (the frequency varies) to show up at the county courthouse for possible selection to serve on a jury. Jurors may be excused from service for reasons of serious hardship, inconvenience, or public necessity. The United States Supreme Court has stated that, during the jury-selection process, potential jurors may not be excluded because of their race or gender. In general, to "qualify" for jury duty, you must be at least eighteen years old, be a citizen of the United States, and be able to understand spoken and written English (those with hearing disabilities will be accommodated).

In many states, there are few, if any, blanket exemptions from jury duty for students or others whose lives or jobs might be disrupted by having to take the time to sit on a jury. It may be possible, however, to ask that your period of eligibility for jury duty be delayed to a later date. Whether you will be allowed to delay jury duty often depends on the cooperation of the local judge and, possibly, of the court clerks. One situation that normally would excuse you from jury duty is if you were solely responsible for the daily care of a permanently disabled person living in your own household.

Although many trials may last no more than one or two days and many potential juries are dissolved before they actually meet (because defendants plea-bargain for a lesser sentence from the judge), you will have no control over the length of time you must serve on the jury. It is quite possible that you might be required to participate for a week or longer, during which time you may not be permitted to watch or listen to certain broadcasted news reports or to read certain printed news articles. There is no guarantee that you will not be chosen on more than one occasion to serve on a jury.

If you or any member of your immediate family has been a party to a lawsuit involving the principal persons involved in the trial or has had any other significant interaction with those principals or the law-enforcement officers participating in the case, or if you feel that physical or mental circumstances would make it difficult for you to make an informed and impartial decision, then you may be excused by the judge.

YOU AND YOUR PERSONAL PROTECTION

Being a victim of crimes against persons is not inevitable, but these crimes are certainly commonplace. An important survival skill today is knowing what you can do to avoid becoming a victim of crime. You should also be aware of what steps you can take if you are the victim of a sexual assault or battering.

Suggestions for Guaranteeing Your Personal Safety

Anticrime experts have a number of tips that can help you avoid being a victim. Here are some of them:

1. Always park your car near a light and as close to a gate or to a security booth as you can. When possible, use valet parking. Only give the valet your ignition key. Otherwise, a simple wax impression of your home keys can easily be made by an enterprising valet.

2. Never stop on the street to look at your watch if someone asks the time. While you are looking at your watch, you are extremely vulnerable. Simply approximate the time, and give the person the approximate time while you continue walking.

3. If you are traveling or simply worried about a robbery at your house or hotel room, do the following: Leave a $20 bill about four feet inside the entry door. Few criminals will walk past that money without pocketing it. Thus, when you return and open the door, if you notice that the $20 bill has disappeared, you should immediately close the door and not return until you are with a police officer or a security guard.

4. According to many self-defense experts and police personnel, meekness often invites aggression. An alternative to meekness is "cerebral self-defense." This is the state of being mentally prepared for trouble. One of the first things to do when accosted by a criminal is to use "choice speech." Most attackers, if made to speak, will become somewhat distracted. The attacker's talking buys you time either to make an escape or to signal for help. In some situations, it even changes the attacker's mind. Some examples of choice speech are "You don't want to hurt me. After all, I hate the same people you do," or "I'll bet you were probably abused as a child."*

---

*These suggestions come from Tony Blauer, a self-defense instructor in Montreal, as reported in *Forbes*, March 14, 1994, p. 122.

What Can I Do If I Am the Victim of a Sexual Assault or Battering?

Many cities, counties, and towns have assault care shelters and telephone hotlines for reporting serious crises that happen to you in your relationships. Local facilities often provide some or all of the following services: a twenty-four-hour crisis telephone line for listening, support, information, and advocacy; a shelter to provide safe, temporary housing for women and their children; children's programs for counseling, advocacy, outings, and therapeutic play groups; free, short-term individual counseling provided to adult survivors of child sexual abuse, rape, and battering; support groups for battered women or victims of sexual assault, with child care; and education programs for community groups and public agencies.

You may be a victim of battering if your partner hits, kicks, or shoves you; uses his or her temper, jealous rages, or anger to frighten you; isolates you from your social support system; calls you names, puts you down, or plays mind games; threatens to commit suicide; threatens to report you to the authorities; controls access to money, food, and necessities; or forces sex on you against your will.

Many colleges and universities have affirmative action offices, sexual-harassment offices, or both that you may contact if these or related events occur to you while you are a student. Particular rules and guidelines may apply in your institution. To find out about those rules, contact your student government, the campus affirmative action office, or the campus women's center. Some universities and colleges have a sexual-harassment hotline.

Protecting Yourself on the Electronic Superhighway

To protect yourself against huge phone bills and the ability of others to get into your electronic mail, (*e-mail*), it is important that you choose a password that cannot be easily discovered by others. Here are some rules for choosing a password and keeping your password secret:

- Do not use any words that are in any dictionary.
- Use at least eight characters.
- Do not use obvious passwords, such as sports teams or your birthday.
- Mix up numbers, special characters, and letters. Mix upper and lower case.
- Never write your password anyplace where people can find it.
- Change passwords frequently.
- Do not "lend" your password to anyone else.
- Do not tell your password to someone over the phone.

YOU AND YOUR EMPLOYER

Finding and keeping a job is clearly important to your future well-being. In the past, an employer could hire and fire workers with virtually no legal restrictions. Today, many laws restrict the employer's discretion in hiring and firing employees and ensure that employees are treated more fairly. These laws do not guarantee fairness in the workplace, but they do prevent certain specific forms of unfairness.

Legislation Prohibiting Employment Discrimination

Until the early 1960s, private employers were free to discriminate openly against minorities, women, or any other group. Title VII of the Civil Rights Act of 1964 prohibited employment discrimination based on race, color, national origin, religion, or gender. The Equal Employment Opportunity Commission (EEOC) was created to help resolve or prosecute discrimination cases for employees. Two other federal acts—the Age Discrimination in Employment Act of 1967 and the Americans with Disabilities Act of 1990—prohibited employment discrimination on the basis of age and disability, respectively.

These laws prohibit employment discrimination at any stage of employment. A business may not discriminate on the basis of race, color, national origin, religion, gender, age, or disability in hiring new employees, in setting pay scales, in granting promotions, or in firing employees. The law also prohibits discrimination regarding the "terms and conditions of employment." This means that an employer cannot expect a person who falls into one of the categories, or groups, protected by the laws mentioned above to work longer hours or suffer less desirable working conditions than other employees. Indeed, employers must be very careful about giving preferential treatment to the members of any protected class. Sexual or racial harassment is a prohibited act, as is discrimination on the basis of pregnancy. An employer cannot refuse to hire a pregnant woman, fire her because of her pregnancy, or force her to take maternity leave. Pregnancy must be treated the same as any other temporary disability. For example, pregnancy must be covered under health insurance if other temporary disabilities are covered.

Under the Family and Medical Leave Act of 1993, employers with fifty or more workers must provide up to twelve weeks of leave during any twelve-month period to employees for family or medical reasons, which include caring for a newborn baby. During the leave, the employer must continue the worker's health-care coverage and guarantee employment in the same position or a comparable position when the employee returns to work.

Intentional and Unintentional Discrimination

The initial focus of Title VII of the Civil Rights Act of 1964 was on intentional discrimination against the classes of employees designated by the act. As the law evolved, courts began to recognize the presence of discriminatory practices (such as certain educational requirements) that had a discriminatory effect, or *disparate impact*. For example, suppose that a fire department had a rule requiring all job applicants to be at least 6 feet tall and weigh at least 175 pounds. Although this rule is applied equally to everyone, the requirements exclude a disproportionate number of women who might want to become firefighters. This rule has a disparate impact.

An employer may justify a rule or policy having a discriminatory impact by claiming that the rule or policy is a *business necessity*. If the fire department were sued for discriminating against women, for example, the fire department might respond that firefighters need to be strong, and therefore the rule is necessary to perform the job. The plaintiff could rebut (counter) this claim by showing that an alternative test of strength or other measure—one that does not have a discriminatory impact—could serve the fire department's needs. An employer may also justify a rule by claiming that the rule is a *bona fide occupational qualification* (BFOQ). The BFOQ exception is very limited, however, and it generally applies only in obvious situations, such as those involving fashion models or actors.

Affirmative Action Programs

To make up for past discriminatory practices against certain groups, many employers have instituted *affirmative action programs*. For such a program to be lawful, the employer must show a reason, or need, for affirmative action. Such a reason might be that the company has an extremely low number of minority employees relative to the number of qualified workers in the community. Any affirmative action program must be temporary and limited to correcting the need to create a balanced workforce. Affirmative action programs cannot unduly restrict the opportunities of groups, such as white males, that are not protected under employment-discrimination laws. Courts in the mid-1990s are increasingly reluctant to uphold affirmative action programs on the ground that they violate the equal protection clause of the Constitution.

What Can I Do If I Am a Victim of Employment Discrimination?

If you believe that you have suffered unlawful discrimination, you should first file a claim with your state government human rights agency, which will investigate and pursue your case if it is deemed meritorious. If you receive no relief at the state level, you can file a claim with the EEOC. You must file a claim with the EEOC within 180 days of suffering the discrimination. The EEOC, if it decides to investigate your claim, will try to reach a voluntary settlement with your employer that protects your interests. If no settlement can be reached, the EEOC will determine whether there is reasonable cause to suspect unlawful discrimination. If it finds reasonable cause, the EEOC may take the case to court for you. If it does not find reasonable cause, the EEOC will give you a "right-to-sue" letter, and you can initiate a lawsuit against your employer for illegal employment discrimination. You must file your lawsuit within 90 days of obtaining a right-to-sue letter. If your claim is successful, you may be awarded back pay (wages for up to two years), compensatory damages, attorneys' fees, and job reinstatement.

Other Laws Protecting Employees

In addition to the discrimination laws discussed above, a number of statutes provide a variety of protections to workers. Many of these laws protect the economic and safety interests of workers and are summarized below.

Fair Labor Standards Act.   The Fair Labor Standards Act (FLSA) of 1938 governs the hours and wages of work. The coverage of the FLSA is very broad and reaches virtually every employer in the country. This law establishes a minimum wage, which is now set at $4.70 per hour and will be raised to $5.15 per hour as of September 1997. Some states have a higher minimum wage. Employers must pay the applicable minimum-wage rate for the first forty hours worked in a week. If you work more than forty hours a week, you are entitled to one-and-one-half times your regular wage rate (usually called "overtime" wages) for the hours worked beyond the first forty.

Not every worker is protected by the FLSA. For example, agricultural workers, many salespeople, and professional, managerial, and supervisory employees are exempted from the law. The FLSA also has child-labor provisions that generally prevent the employment of persons younger than fourteen years of age and that restrict the terms of employment of persons between the ages of fourteen and seventeen.

Worker Safety.   The Occupational Safety and Health Act of 1970 was enacted to help ensure safe and healthful working conditions on the job. Numerous standards have been set under this law, including limits on exposures to harmful chemicals and various workplace standards to avert accidents. In addition, the law obligates employers to keep the workplace free of recognized hazards to health, even in the absence of a standard. Employees can file complaints about unsafe conditions and cannot be required to work when they have reason to fear that their safety is in jeopardy.

When an on-the-job accident does occur, the employee may apply for *workers' compensation*. Each state has a workers' compensation system that pays benefits for accidents or diseases that arise out of or during the course of normal employment. A worker may recover even if his or her own negligence contributed to the injury, but there is no recovery for intentionally self-inflicted harms. The injured worker may not file suit against the employer but may be able to bring a case against a manufacturer of the product that caused the injury. Some workers have been afraid to file for compensation, lest they be fired. In most states, a person cannot be discharged in retaliation for filing a legitimate workers' compensation claim.

Unemployment Compensation. The United States has an unemployment compensation system, in which employers pay taxes into a fund, and the proceeds are paid out to workers who qualify for such compensation. Each state has authority to set rules determining which workers are entitled to unemployment benefits. Some typical state requirements are as follows:

- The employee must have been fired without good cause or have quit the job with good cause.
- The employee must be unemployed for some minimum amount of time, such as a week.
- The employee must have worked on a reasonably regular basis prior to unemployment.
- The employee must register with a state-operated employment agency, seek a new job, and accept any reasonably suitable new job offer.
- The employee must be able to work and not be a striker.

If the worker qualifies for unemployment compensation, he or she will receive regular, but temporary, benefits based on a formula. The formula is generally based on a fraction of the worker's average wages during a recent period up to a certain maximum. Benefits are available for up to twenty-six weeks, and this time period has been extended during times of serious unemployment. This income may be taxable.

Employee Privacy

Employee privacy rights are a major new concern of the law. In general, employees have little on-the-job privacy protection under the common law. Some statutes have been passed to provide a measure of privacy protection to workers, but this protection is still quite limited.

Lie Detector Tests. In most occupations, you cannot be forced to take a lie detector test and therefore cannot be fired for refusing to take the test. There are some exceptions when such testing is allowed. Workers holding certain sensitive jobs, such as security personnel, may be subjected to lie detector testing. An employer may also force an employee to take such a test if the company is conducting an ongoing investigation of losses and has a reasonable suspicion that the employee was involved in the losses.

Even if you are lawfully subject to testing, federal law contains further protections. You cannot be asked needlessly intrusive or degrading questions.

You must be informed of the purpose of the testing, and disclosure of the test results is limited to those who have a need to know them. The testing must follow accepted standards for accuracy.

Drug Testing.   Recent years have seen a significant increase in the use of employer drug testing, as the costs to employers of drug abuse are increasingly recognized. With the exception of a few states, such drug tests are legal. Although drug tests plainly intrude upon your privacy, the tests are generally held to be a reasonable exercise of the employer's rights. Courts may require that steps be taken to ensure the tests' accuracy and that the privacy invasion resulting from drug testing be no greater than necessary.

Employee Monitoring.   With the advance of new technologies, employers are increasingly able to monitor the work of their employees. Companies may monitor your telephone calls or your computer work. Closed-circuit monitors may be installed in the workplace to observe your work habits. Like drug testing, such monitoring is considered to be a private matter between employer and employee and is generally legal. A few states have laws restricting such monitoring in certain areas, such as nonwork areas.

Personnel Records.   Federal law provides no right for workers to see their personnel records, though a number of states grant such a right, as do many employers' voluntary policies. Moreover, an employer may lawfully disclose the contents of your personnel file to individuals either inside or outside the company. If the revealed information is false, you may sue for *defamation*.

Glossary

ACID RAIN   Rain that has picked up pollutants, usually sulfur dioxides, from industrial areas of the earth that are often hundreds of miles distant from where the rain falls.

ACQUISITIVE MODEL   A model of bureaucracy that views top-level bureaucrats as seeking constantly to expand the size of their budgets and the staffs of their departments or agencies so as to gain greater power and influence in the public sector.

ACTION-REACTION SYNDROME   For every action on the part of government, there is a reaction on the part of the affected public. Then the government attempts to counter the reaction with another action, which starts the cycle all over again.

ACTIONABLE   Furnishing grounds for a lawsuit. Actionable words, for example, in the law of libel are such words that naturally imply damage to the individual in question.

ACTUAL MALICE   Actual desire and intent to see another suffer by one's actions. Actual malice in libel cases generally consists of intentionally publishing any written or printed statement that is injurious to the character of another with either knowledge of the statement's falsity or a reckless disregard of the truth.

ADMINISTRATIVE AGENCY   An agency that forms part of the executive branch, an independent agency, or an independent regulatory agency (for example, the Federal Trade Commission, the Securities and Exchange Commission, and the Federal Communications Commission). State and local governments also have administrative agencies.

ADVICE AND CONSENT   The power vested in the U.S. Senate by the Constitution (Article II, Section 2) to give its advice and consent to the president on treaties and presidential appointments.

AFFIRM   To declare that a judgment is valid and must stand.

AFFIRMATIVE ACTION   A policy in job hiring that gives special consideration or compensatory treatment to traditionally disadvantaged groups in an effort to overcome present effects of past discrimination.

AGENDA SETTING   Determining which public policy questions will be debated or considered by Congress.

AID TO FAMILIES WITH DEPENDENT CHILDREN (AFDC)   A state-administered program that furnishes assistance for families in which dependent children do not have the financial support of the father, owing to the father's desertion, disability, or death. The program is financed partially by federal grants.

AMICUS CURIAE BRIEF   A brief (a document containing a legal argument supporting a desired outcome in a particular case) filed by a third party, or *amicus curiae* (Latin for "friend of the court"), a party not directly involved in the litigation but who has an interest in the outcome of the case.

ANARCHY   The condition of having no government and no laws. Each member of the society governs himself or herself.

ANTI-FEDERALISTS   Those who opposed the adoption of the Constitution because of its centralist tendencies and attacked the failure of the Constitution's framers to include a bill of rights.

APPELLATE COURT   A court having jurisdiction to review cases and issues that were originally tried in lower courts.

APPOINTMENT POWER   The authority vested in the president to fill a government office or position. Positions filled by presidential appointment include those in the executive branch, the federal judiciary, commissioned officers in the armed forces, and members of the independent regulatory commissions.

APPROPRIATION   The passage, by Congress, of a spending bill, specifying the amount of authorized funds that actually will be allocated for an agency's use.

ARISTOCRACY   Rule by the best suited, through virtue, talent, or education; in later usage, rule by the upper class.

ATTENTIVE PUBLIC   That portion of the general public that pays attention to policy issues.

AUSTRALIAN BALLOT   A secret ballot prepared, distributed, and tabulated by government officials at public expense. Since 1888, all states have used the Australian ballot rather than an open, public ballot.

AUTHORITY   The features of a leader or an institution that compel obedience, usually because of ascribed legitimacy. For most societies, government is the ultimate authority in the allocation of values.

AUTHORIZATION   A formal declaration by a legislative committee that a certain amount of funding may be available to an agency. Some authorizations terminate in a year; others are renewable automatically without further congressional authorization.

BAD-TENDENCY RULE   A rule stating that speech or other First Amendment freedoms may be curtailed if there is a possibility that such expression might lead to some "evil."

"BEAUTY CONTEST"   A presidential primary in which contending candidates compete for popular votes but the results have little or no impact on the selection of delegates to the national convention, which is made by the party elite.

BICAMERAL LEGISLATURE   A legislature made up of two chambers, or parts. The U.S. Congress, composed of the House of Representatives and the Senate, is a bicameral legislature.

BICAMERALISM   The division of a legislature into two separate assemblies.

BILL OF RIGHTS   The first ten amendments to the U.S. Constitution. They contain a listing of the freedoms that a person enjoys and that cannot be infringed upon by the government, such as the freedoms of speech, press, and religion.

BLOCK GRANTS   Federal programs that provide funding to the state and local governments for general functional areas, such as criminal justice or mental-health programs.

BUNDLING   The practice of adding together maximum individual campaign contributions to increase their impact on the candidate.

BUREAUCRACY   A large organization that is structured hierarchically to carry out specific functions.

BUSING The transportation of public school students from areas where they live to schools in other areas to eliminate school segregation based on residential patterns.

CABINET An advisory group selected by the president to aid in making decisions. The cabinet presently numbers thirteen department secretaries and the attorney general. Depending on the president, the cabinet may be highly influential or relatively insignificant in its advisory role.

CABINET DEPARTMENT One of the fourteen departments of the executive branch (State, Treasury, Defense, Justice, Interior, Agriculture, Commerce, Labor, Health and Human Services, Housing and Urban Development, Education, Energy, Transportation, and Veterans Affairs).

CADRE The nucleus of political party activists carrying out the major functions of American political parties.

CANVASSING BOARD An official group at the county, city, or state level that receives vote counts from every precinct in the area, tabulates the figures, and sends them to the state canvassing authority, which certifies the winners.

CAPTURE The act of gaining direct or indirect control over agency personnel and decision makers by the industry that is being regulated.

CASEWORK Personal work for constituents by members of Congress.

CATEGORICAL GRANTS-IN-AID Federal grants-in-aid to states or local governments that are for very specific programs or projects.

CAUCUS A closed meeting of party leaders to select party candidates or to decide on policy; also, a meeting of party members designed to select candidates and propose policies.

CHALLENGE An allegation by a poll watcher that a potential voter is unqualified to vote or that a vote is invalid; designed to prevent fraud in elections.

CHARTER A document issued by a government that grants rights to a person, a group of persons, or a corporation to carry on one or more specific activities. A state government can grant a charter to a municipality allowing that group of persons to carry on specific activities.

CHECKS AND BALANCES A major principle of the American governmental system whereby each branch of the government exercises a check on the actions of the others.

CHIEF DIPLOMAT The role of the president in recognizing foreign governments, making treaties, and making executive agreements.

CHIEF EXECUTIVE The role of the president as head of the executive branch of the government.

CHIEF LEGISLATOR The role of the president in influencing the making of laws.

CHIEF OF STAFF The person who is named to direct the White House Office and advise the president.

CHIEF OF STATE The role of the president as ceremonial head of the government.

CIVIL LAW The law regulating conduct between private persons over noncriminal matters. Under civil law, the government provides the forum for the settlement of disputes between private parties in such matters as contracts, domestic relations, and business relations.

CIVIL LIBERTIES Those personal freedoms that are protected for all individuals and generally that deal with individual freedom. Civil liberties typically involve restraining the government's actions against individuals.

CIVIL RIGHTS Those powers or privileges that are guaranteed to individuals or protected groups and that are protected from arbitrary removal by government or by individuals.

CIVIL SERVICE A collective term for the body of employees working for the government. Generally, civil service is understood to apply to all those who gain government employment through a merit system.

CIVIL SERVICE COMMISSION The initial central personnel agency of the national government; created in 1883.

CLASS POLITICS Political preferences based on income level, social status, or both.

CLASS-ACTION SUIT A lawsuit filed by an individual seeking damages for "all persons similarly situated."

CLEAR AND PRESENT DANGER TEST The test proposed by Justice Holmes for determining when government may restrict free speech. Restrictions are permissible, he argued, only when speech provokes a "clear and present danger" to the public order.

CLIMATE CONTROL The use of public relations techniques to create favorable public opinion toward an interest group, industry, or corporation.

CLOTURE A method to close off debate and to bring the matter under consideration to a vote in the Senate.

COATTAIL EFFECT The influence of a popular or unpopular candidate on the electoral success or failure of other candidates on the same party ticket. The effect is increased by the party-column ballot, which encourages straight-ticket voting.

COLD WAR The ideological, political, and economic impasse that existed between the United States and the Soviet Union following World War II.

COMMANDER IN CHIEF The role of the president as supreme commander of the military forces of the United States and of the state national guard units when they are called into federal service.

COMMERCE CLAUSE The section of the Constitution in which Congress is given the power to regulate trade among the states and with foreign countries.

COMMERCIAL SPEECH Advertising statements, which have increasingly been given First Amendment protection.

COMMON LAW Judge-made law that originated in England from decisions shaped according to prevailing customs. Decisions were applied to similar situations and thus gradually became common to the nation. Common law forms the basis of legal procedures in the United States.

COMPARABLE WORTH The idea that compensation should be based on the worth of the job to an employer and that factors unrelated to the worth of a job, such as the sex of the employee, should not affect compensation.

COMPLIANCE Accepting and carrying out authorities' decisions.

CONCURRENT POWERS Powers held jointly by the national and state governments.

CONCURRING OPINION A separate opinion, prepared by a judge who supports the decision of the majority of the court but who wants to make or clarify a particular point or to voice disapproval of the grounds on which the decision was made.

CONFEDERAL SYSTEM A system of government consisting of a league of independent states, each having essentially sovereign powers. The central government created by such a league has only limited powers over the states.

CONFEDERATION A political system in which states or regional governments retain ultimate authority except for those powers they expressly delegate to a central government. A voluntary association of independent states, in which the member states agree to limited restraints on their freedom of action.

CONFERENCE COMMITTEE A special joint committee appointed to reconcile differences when bills pass the two chambers of Congress in different forms.

CONSENSUS General agreement among the citizenry on an issue.

CONSENT OF THE PEOPLE The idea that governments and laws derive their legitimacy from the consent of the governed.

CONSERVATISM A set of beliefs that includes a limited role for the national government in helping individuals, support for traditional values and lifestyles, and a cautious response to change.

CONSERVATIVE COALITION An alliance of Republicans and southern Democrats that can form in the House or the Senate to oppose liberal legislation and support conservative legislation.

CONSOLIDATION The union of two or more governmental units to form a single unit.

CONSTANT DOLLARS Dollars corrected for inflation; dollars expressed in terms of purchasing power for a given year.

CONSTITUTIONAL INITIATIVE An electoral device whereby citizens can propose a constitutional amendment through petitions signed by the required number of registered voters.

CONSTITUTIONAL POWER A power vested in the president by Article II of the Constitution.

CONTAINMENT A U.S. diplomatic policy adopted by the Truman administration to "build situations of strength" around the globe to contain communist power within its existing boundaries.

CONTINUING RESOLUTION A temporary law that Congress passes when an appropriations bill has not been decided by the beginning of the new fiscal year on October 1.

CONTRACTING OUT The replacement of government services with services provided by private firms.

COOLEY'S RULE The view that cities should be able to govern themselves, presented in an 1871 Michigan decision by Judge Thomas Cooley.

COOPERATIVE FEDERALISM The theory that the states and the national government should cooperate in solving problems.

CORRUPT PRACTICES ACTS A series of acts passed by Congress in an attempt to limit and regulate the size and sources of contributions and expenditures in political campaigns.

COUNCIL OF ECONOMIC ADVISERS (CEA) A staff agency in the Executive Office that advises the president on measures to maintain stability in the nation's economy; established in 1946.

COUNCIL OF GOVERNMENT (COG) A voluntary organization of counties and municipalities concerned with areawide problems.

COUNTY The chief governmental unit set up by the state to administer state law and business at the local level. Counties are drawn up by area, rather than by rural or urban criteria.

CREDENTIALS COMMITTEE A committee used by political parties at their national conventions to determine which delegates may participate. The committee inspects the claim of each prospective delegate to be seated as a legitimate representative of his or her state.

CRIMINAL LAW The law that defines crimes and provides punishment for violations. In criminal cases, the government is the prosecutor, because crimes are against the public order.

DE FACTO SEGREGATION Racial segregation that occurs not as a result of deliberate intentions but because of past social and economic conditions and residential patterns.

DE JURE SEGREGATION Racial segregation that occurs because of laws or administrative decisions by public agencies.

DEFAMATION OF CHARACTER Wrongfully hurting a person's good reputation. The law has imposed a general duty on all persons to refrain from making false, defamatory statements about others.

DEMOCRACY A system of government in which ultimate political authority is vested in the people. Derived from the Greek words demos ("the people") and kratos ("authority").

DEMOCRATIC PARTY One of the two major American political parties evolving out of the Democratic (Jeffersonian) Republican group supporting Thomas Jefferson.

DÉTENTE A French word meaning the relaxation of tension. The term characterizes U.S.–Soviet policy as it developed under President Richard Nixon and Secretary of State Henry Kissinger. Détente stresses direct cooperative dealings with Cold War rivals but avoids ideological accommodation.

DILLON'S RULE The narrowest possible interpretation of the legal status of local governments, outlined by Judge John F. Dillon, who in 1811 stated that a municipal corporation can exercise only those powers expressly granted by state law.

DIPLOMACY The total process by which states carry on political relations with each other; settling conflicts among nations by peaceful means.

DIRECT DEMOCRACY A system of government in which political decisions are made by the people directly, rather than by their elected representatives; probably possible only in small political communities.

DIRECT PRIMARY An intraparty election in which the voters select the candidates who will run on a party's ticket in the subsequent general election.

DIRECT TECHNIQUE An interest group activity that involves interaction with government officials to further the group's goals.

DISCHARGE PETITION A procedure by which a bill in the House of Representatives may be forced out of a committee (discharged) that has refused to report it for consideration by the House. The discharge petition must be signed by an absolute majority (218) of representatives and is used only on rare occasions.

DISSENTING OPINION A separate opinion in which a judge dissents from (disagrees with) the conclusion reached by the majority of the court and expounds his or her own views about the case.

DIVERSITY OF CITIZENSHIP A basis for federal court jurisdiction over a lawsuit between (1) citizens of different states, (2) a foreign country and citizens of a state or of different states, or (3) citizens of a state and citizens or subjects of a foreign country. The amount in controversy must be more than $75,000 before a federal court can take jurisdiction in such cases.

DIVISIVE OPINION Public opinion that is polarized between two quite different positions.

DOMESTIC POLICY Those public plans or courses of action that concern issues of national importance, such as poverty, crime, and the environment, in contrast to economic policies that normally relate only to issues of inflation, interest rates, unemployment, and international trade deficits.

DUAL FEDERALISM A system of government in which the states and the national government each remain supreme within their own spheres. The doctrine looks on nation and state as coequal sovereign powers. It holds that acts of states within their reserved powers could be legitimate limitations on the powers of the national government.

ECONOMIC AID Assistance to other nations in the form of grants, loans, or credits to buy the assisting nation's products.

ELASTIC CLAUSE, OR NECESSARY AND PROPER CLAUSE The clause in Article I, Section 8, that grants Congress the power to do whatever is necessary to execute its specifically delegated powers.

ELECTOR A person on the partisan slate that is selected early in the presidential election year according to state laws and the applicable political party apparatus. Electors cast ballots for president and vice president. The number of electors in each state is equal to that state's number of representatives in both houses of Congress.

ELECTORAL COLLEGE A group of persons called electors selected by the voters in each state and Washington, D.C.; this group officially elects the president and vice president of the United States. The number of electors in each state is equal to the number of each state's representatives in both houses of Congress. The Twenty-third Amendment to the Constitution permits Washington, D.C., to have as many electors as a state of comparable population.

ELECTRONIC MEDIA Broadcasting media (radio and television). The term derives from their method of transmission, in contrast to printed media.

ELITE An upper socioeconomic class that controls political and economic affairs.

ELITE THEORY A perspective holding that society is ruled by a small number of people who exercise power in their self-interest.

EMERGENCY POWER An inherent power exercised by the president during a period of national crisis, particularly in foreign affairs.

ENUMERATED POWERS Powers specifically granted to the national government by the Constitution. The first seventeen clauses of Article I, Section 8, specify most of the enumerated powers of Congress.

ENVIRONMENTAL IMPACT STATEMENT (EIS) As a requirement mandated by the National Environmental Policy Act, a report that must show the costs and benefits of major federal actions that could significantly affect the quality of the environment.

EQUAL EMPLOYMENT OPPORTUNITY COMMISSION (EEOC) A commission established by the 1964 Civil Rights Act to (1) end discrimination based on race, color, religion, gender, or national origin in conditions of employment and (2) promote voluntary action programs by employers, unions, and community organizations to foster equal job opportunities.

EQUALITY A concept that all people are of equal worth.

EQUALIZATION A method for adjusting the amount of money that a state must put up to receive federal funds. The formula used takes into account the wealth of the state or its ability to tax its citizens.

ERA OF GOOD FEELING The years from 1817 to 1825, when James Monroe was president and there was, in effect, no political opposition.

ERA OF PERSONAL POLITICS An era when attention centers on the character of individual candidates rather than on party identification.

ESTABLISHMENT CLAUSE The part of the First Amendment prohibiting the establishment of a church officially supported by the national government. It is applied to questions of state and local government aid to religious organizations and schools, questions of the legality of allowing or requiring school prayers, and questions of the teaching of evolution versus fundamentalist theories of creation.

EUTHANASIA Killing incurably ill people for reasons of mercy.

EXCLUSIONARY RULE A policy forbidding the admission at trial of illegally seized evidence.

EXECUTIVE AGREEMENT A binding international agreement made between chiefs of state that does not require legislative sanction.

EXECUTIVE BUDGET The budget prepared and submitted by the president to Congress.

EXECUTIVE OFFICE OF THE PRESIDENT (EOP) Established by President Franklin D. Roosevelt by executive order under the Reorganization Act of 1939, the EOP currently consists of nine staff agencies that assist the president in carrying out major duties.

EXECUTIVE ORDER A rule or regulation issued by the president that has the effect of law. Executive orders can implement and give administrative effect to provisions in the Constitution, to treaties, and to statutes.

EXECUTIVE PRIVILEGE The right of executive officials to refuse to appear before, or to withhold information from, a legislative committee. Executive privilege is enjoyed by the president and by those executive officials accorded that right by the president.

EXPRESSED POWER A constitutional or statutory power of the president, which is expressly written into the Constitution or into congressional law.

EXTRADITE To surrender an accused or convicted criminal to the authorities of the state from which he or she has fled; to return a fugitive criminal to the jurisdiction of the accusing state.

FACTION A group or bloc in a legislature or political party acting together in pursuit of some special interest or position.

FAIRNESS DOCTRINE An FCC regulation affecting broadcasting media, which required that fair or equal opportunity be given to legitimate opposing political groups or individuals to broadcast their views.

FALL REVIEW The time every year when, after receiving formal federal agency requests for funding for the next fiscal year, the Office of Management and Budget reviews the requests, makes changes, and submits its recommendations to the president.

FEDERAL MANDATE A requirement in federal legislation that forces states and municipalities to comply with certain rules.

FEDERAL OPEN MARKET COMMITTEE (FOMC) The most important body within the Federal Reserve System. The FOMC decides how monetary policy should be carried out by the Federal Reserve.

FEDERAL QUESTION A question that pertains to the U.S. Constitution, acts of Congress, or treaties. A federal question provides a basis for federal jurisdiction.

FEDERAL REGISTER A publication of the executive branch of the U.S. government that prints executive orders, rules, and regulations.

FEDERAL SYSTEM A system of government in which power is divided by a written constitution between a central government and regional, or subdivisional, governments. Each level must have some domain in which its policies are dominant and some genuine political or constitutional guarantee of its authority.

FEDERALISTS The first American political party, led by Alexander Hamilton and John Adams. Many of its members had strongly supported the adoption of the new Constitution and the creation of the federal union.

FIGHTING WORDS Words that, when uttered by a public speaker, are so inflammatory that they could provoke the average listener to violence; the words are usually of a racial, religious, or ethnic type.

FILIBUSTER In the Senate, unlimited debate to halt action on a particular bill.

FIRESIDE CHAT One of the warm, informal talks by Franklin D. Roosevelt to a few million of his intimate friends—via the radio. Roosevelt's fireside chats were so effective that succeeding presidents have been urged by their advisers to emulate him by giving more radio and television reports to the nation.

FIRST BUDGET RESOLUTION A resolution passed by Congress in May that sets overall revenue and spending goals and hence, by definition, the size of the deficit for the following fiscal year.

FIRST CONTINENTAL CONGRESS The first gathering of delegates from twelve of the thirteen colonies, held in 1774.

FISCAL POLICY The use of changes in government spending or taxes to alter national economic variables, such as the rate of unemployment.

FISCAL YEAR (FY) The twelve-month period that is used for bookkeeping, or accounting, purposes. Usually, the fiscal year does not coincide with the calendar year. For example, the federal government's fiscal year runs from October 1 through September 30.

FLUIDITY The extent to which public opinion changes over time.

FOCUS GROUP A small group of individuals who are led in discussion by a professional consultant to gather opinions and responses to candidates and issues.

FOOD STAMPS Coupons issued by the federal government to low-income individuals to be used for the purchase of food.

FOREIGN POLICY A nation's external goals and the techniques and strategies used to achieve them.

FOREIGN POLICY PROCESS The steps by which external goals are decided and acted on.

FRANKING A policy that enables members of Congress to send material through the mail by substituting their facsimile signature (frank) for postage.

FRATERNITY From the Latin *fraternus* (brother), a term that came to mean, in the political philosophy of the eighteenth century, the condition in which each individual considers the needs of all others; a brotherhood. In the French Revolution of 1789, the popular cry was "liberty, equality, and fraternity."

FREE EXERCISE CLAUSE The provision of the First Amendment guaranteeing the free exercise of religion.

FRONT-LOADING The practice of moving presidential primary elections to the early part of the campaign, to maximize the impact of certain states or regions on the nomination.

FRONT-RUNNER The presidential candidate who appears to have the most momentum at a given time in the primary season.

FULL FAITH AND CREDIT CLAUSE A section of the Constitution that requires states to recognize one another's laws and court decisions. It ensures that rights established under deeds, wills, contracts, and other civil matters in one state will be honored by other states.

FUNCTIONAL CONSOLIDATION The cooperation of two or more units of local government in providing services to their inhabitants.

GAG ORDER An order issued by a judge restricting the publication of news about a trial in progress or a pretrial hearing in order to protect the accused's right to a fair trial.

GARBAGE CAN MODEL A model of bureaucracy that characterizes bureaucracies as rudderless entities with little formal organization in which solutions to problems are based on trial and error rather than rational policy planning.

GENDER DISCRIMINATION Any practice, policy, or procedure that denies equality of treatment to an individual or to a group because of gender.

GENDER GAP A term most often used to describe the difference between the percentage of votes a candidate receives from women and the percentage the candidate receives from men. The term was widely used after the 1980 presidential election.

GENERAL LAW CITY A city operating under general state laws that apply to all local governmental units of a similar type.

GENERAL SALES TAX A tax levied as a proportion of the retail price of a commodity at the point of sale.

GENERATIONAL EFFECT A long-lasting effect of events of a particular time period on the political opinions or preferences of those who came of political age at that time.

GERRYMANDERING The drawing of legislative district boundary lines for the purpose of obtaining partisan or factional advantage. A district is said to be gerrymandered when its shape is manipulated by the dominant party in the state legislature to maximize electoral strength at the expense of the minority party.

GOVERNMENT A permanent structure (institution) composed of decision makers who make society's rules about conflict resolution and the allocation of resources and who possess the power to enforce them.

GOVERNMENT CORPORATION An agency of government that administers a quasi-business enterprise. These corporations are used when activities are primarily commercial. They produce revenue for their continued existence, and they require greater flexibility than is permitted for departments and agencies.

GOVERNMENT IN THE SUNSHINE ACT A law that requires all multiheaded federal agencies to conduct their business regularly in public session.

GRAND JURY A jury called to hear evidence and determine whether indictments should be issued against persons suspected of having committed crimes.

GRANDFATHER CLAUSE A device used by southern states to exempt whites from state taxes and literacy laws originally intended to disenfranchise African American voters. It restricted the voting franchise to those who could prove that their grandfathers had voted before 1867.

GREAT COMPROMISE The compromise between the New Jersey and the Virginia plans that created one chamber of the Congress based on population and one chamber that represented each state equally; also called the Connecticut Compromise.

HATCH ACT (POLITICAL ACTIVITIES ACT) An act passed in 1939 that prohibited a political committee from spending more than $3 million in any campaign and limited individual contributions to a committee to $5,000. The act was designed to control political influence buying.

HECKLERS' VETO Boisterous and generally disruptive behavior by listeners of public speakers that, in effect, vetoes the public speakers' right to speak.

HOME RULE CITY A city with a charter allowing local voters to frame, adopt, and amend their own charter.

HORIZONTAL FEDERALISM Activities, problems, and policies that require state governments to interact with one another.

HYPERPLURALISM An extreme form of pluralism in which government is so decentralized and authority so fragmented that it does not get much accomplished.

IDEOLOGUE An individual whose political opinions are carefully thought out and relatively consistent with one another. Ideologues are often described as having a comprehensive world view.

IDEOLOGY A comprehensive and logically ordered set of beliefs about the nature of people and about the institutions and role of government.

IMPEACHMENT As authorized by Article I of the Constitution, an action by the House of Representatives and the Senate to remove the president, vice president, or civil officers of the United States from office for crimes of "Treason, Bribery, or other high Crimes and Misdemeanors."

IN-KIND SUBSIDY A good or service—such as food stamps, housing, or medical care—provided by the government to lower-income groups.

INALIENABLE RIGHTS Rights held to be inherent in natural law and not dependent on government; as asserted in the Declaration of Independence, the rights to "life, liberty, and the pursuit of happiness."

INCOME TRANSFER A transfer of income from some individuals in the economy to other individuals. This is generally done by way of the government. It is a transfer in the sense that no current services are rendered by the recipients.

INCORPORATION THEORY The view that most of the protections of the Bill of Rights are incorporated into the Fourteenth Amendment's protection against state governments.

INDEPENDENT A voter or candidate who does not identify with a political party.

INDEPENDENT CANDIDATE A political candidate who is not affiliated with a political party.

INDEPENDENT EXECUTIVE AGENCY A federal agency that is not part of a cabinet department but reports directly to the president.

INDEPENDENT REGULATORY AGENCY An agency outside the major executive departments charged with making and implementing rules and regulations to protect the public interest.

INDIRECT TECHNIQUE A strategy employed by interest groups that uses third parties to influence government officials.

INHERENT POWER A power of the president derived from the loosely worded statement in the Constitution that "the executive power shall be vested in a president" and that the president should "take care that the laws be faithfully executed"; defined through practice rather than through constitutional or statutory law.

INITIATIVE A procedure by which voters can propose a law or a constitutional amendment.

INJUNCTION An order issued by a court to compel or restrain the performance of an act by an individual or government official.

INSTITUTION A long-standing, identifiable structure or association that performs functions for society.

INSTRUCTED DELEGATE A legislator who is an agent of the voters who elected him or her and who votes according to the views of constituents regardless of personal assessments.

INTELLIGENCE COMMUNITY The government agencies involved in gathering information about the capabilities and intentions of foreign governments and that engages in activities to further U.S. foreign policy aims.

INTENSITY The strength of a position for or against a public policy or an issue. Intensity is often critical in generating public action; an intense minority can often win on an issue of public policy over a less intense majority.

INTEREST GROUP An organized group of individuals sharing common objectives who actively attempt to influence policymakers in all three branches of the government and at all levels. Also called pressure group or lobby.

INTERSTATE COMPACT An agreement between two or more states. Agreements on minor matters are made without congressional consent, but any compact that tends to increase the power of the contracting states relative to other states or relative to the national government generally requires the consent of Congress. Such compacts serve as a means by which states can solve regional problems.

IRON CURTAIN The term used to describe the division of Europe between the Soviet Union and the West; popularized by Winston Churchill in a speech portraying Europe as being divided by an iron curtain, with the nations of Eastern Europe behind the curtain and increasingly under Soviet control.

IRON TRIANGLE The three-way alliance among legislators, bureaucrats, and interest groups to make or preserve policies that benefit their respective interests.

ISOLATIONIST FOREIGN POLICY Abstaining from an active role in international affairs or alliances, which characterized U.S. foreign policy toward Europe during most of the nineteenth century.

ISSUE VOTING Voting for a candidate based on how he or she stands on a particular issue.

ITEM VETO The power exercised by the governors of most states to veto particular sections or items of an appropriations bill, while signing the remainder of the bill into law.

JOINT COMMITTEE A legislative committee composed of members from both chambers of Congress.

JUDICIAL ACTIVISM A doctrine holding that the Supreme Court should take an active role in using its powers to check the activities of Congress, state legislatures, and administrative agencies when those government bodies exceed their authority.

JUDICIAL IMPLEMENTATION The way in which court decisions are translated into action.

JUDICIAL RESTRAINT A doctrine holding that the Supreme Court should defer to the decisions made by the elected representatives of the people in the legislative and executive branches.

JUDICIAL REVIEW The power of the Supreme Court or any court to declare unconstitutional federal or state laws and other acts of government.

JURISDICTION The authority of a court to decide certain cases. Not all courts have the authority to decide all cases. Where a case arises and what its subject matter is are two jurisdictional factors.

JUSTICIABLE DISPUTE A dispute that raises questions about the law and that is appropriate for resolution before a court of law.

JUSTICIABLE QUESTION A question that may be raised and reviewed in court.

KEYNESIAN ECONOMICS An economic theory, named after English economist John Maynard Keynes, that gained prominence during the Great Depression of the 1930s. It is typically associated with the use of fiscal policy to alter national economic variables—for example, increased government spending during times of economic downturns.

KITCHEN CABINET The informal advisers to the president.

LABOR MOVEMENT Generally, the full range of economic and political expression of working-class interests; politically, the organization of working-class interests.

LATENT PUBLIC OPINION Unexpressed political opinions that have the potential to become manifest attitudes or beliefs.

LAWMAKING The process of deciding the legal rules that govern our society. Such laws may regulate minor affairs or establish broad national policies.

LEGISLATIVE INITIATIVE A procedure by which voters can propose a change in state or local laws by gathering signatures on a petition and submitting it to the legislature for approval.

LEGISLATIVE VETO A provision in a bill reserving to Congress or to a congressional committee the power to reject an action or regulation of a national agency by majority vote; declared unconstitutional by the Supreme Court in 1983.

LEGISLATURE A government body primarily responsible for the making of laws.

LEGITIMACY A status conferred by the people on the government's officials, acts, and institutions through their belief that the government's actions are an appropriate use of power by a legally constituted governmental authority following correct decision-making policies. These actions are regarded as rightful and entitled to compliance and obedience on the part of citizens.

LIBEL A written defamation of a person's character, reputation, business, or property rights. To a limited degree, the First Amendment protects the press from libel actions.

LIBERALISM A set of beliefs that includes the advocacy of positive government action to improve the welfare of individuals, support for civil rights, and tolerance for political and social change.

LIBERTY The greatest freedom of individuals that is consistent with the freedom of other individuals in the society.

LIMITED GOVERNMENT A form of government based on the principle that the powers of government should be clearly limited either through a written document or through wide public understanding; characterized by institutional checks to ensure that government serves the public rather than private interests.

LINE ORGANIZATION Government or corporate units that provide direct services or products for the public.

LINE-ITEM VETO The power of an executive to veto individual lines or items within a piece of legislation without vetoing the entire bill.

LITERACY TEST A test administered as a precondition for voting, often used to prevent African Americans from exercising their right to vote.

LITIGATE To engage in a legal proceeding or seek relief in a court of law; to carry on a lawsuit.

LOBBYING The attempt by organizations or by individuals to influence the passage, defeat, or contents of legislation and the administrative decisions of government.

LOGROLLING An arrangement by which two or more members of Congress agree in advance to support each other's bills.

LOOPHOLE A legal method by which individuals and businesses are allowed to reduce the tax liabilities owed to the government.

MADISONIAN MODEL The model of government devised by James Madison in which the powers of the government are separated into three branches: executive, legislative, and judicial.

MAJORITY More than 50 percent. Full age; the age at which a person is entitled by law to the right to manage his or her own affairs and to the full enjoyment of civil rights.

MAJORITY FLOOR LEADER The chief spokesperson of the major party in the Senate, who directs the legislative program and party strategy.

MAJORITY LEADER OF THE HOUSE A legislative position held by an important party member in the House of Representatives. The majority leader is selected by the majority party in caucus or conference to foster cohesion among party members and to act as spokesperson for the majority party in the House.

MAJORITY OPINION The views of the majority of the judges.

MAJORITY RULE A basic principle of democracy asserting that the greatest number of citizens in any political unit should select officials and determine policies.

MANAGED NEWS Information generated and distributed by the government in such a way as to give government interests priority over candor.

MANDATORY RETIREMENT Forced retirement when a person reaches a certain age.

MATCHING FUNDS For many categorical grant programs, money with which the state must "match" the federal funds. Some programs only require the state to raise 10 percent of the funds, whereas others approach an even share.

MATERIAL INCENTIVE   A reason or motive having to do with economic benefits or opportunities.

MEDIA ACCESS   The public's right of access to the media. The Federal Communications Commission and the courts gradually have taken the stance that citizens do have a right to media access.

MEDIA   The technical means of communication with mass audiences.

MERIT SYSTEM   The selection, retention, and promotion of government employees on the basis of competitive examinations.

MILITARY-INDUSTRIAL COMPLEX   The mutually beneficial relationship between the armed forces and defense contractors.

MINORITY FLOOR LEADER   The party officer in the Senate who commands the minority party's opposition to the policies of the majority party and directs the legislative program and strategy of his or her party.

MINORITY LEADER OF THE HOUSE   The party leader elected by the minority party in the House.

MONETARY POLICY   The use of changes in the amount of money in circulation to alter credit markets, employment, and the rate of inflation.

MONOPOLISTIC MODEL   A model of bureaucracy that compares bureaucracies to monopolistic business firms. Lack of competition within a bureaucracy leads to inefficient and costly operations, just as it does within monopolistic firms. Because bureaucracies are not penalized for inefficiency, there is no incentive to save costs or use resources more productively.

MONROE DOCTRINE   The policy statement included in President James Monroe's 1823 annual message to Congress, which set out three principles: (1) European nations should not establish new colonies in the Western Hemisphere, (2) European nations should not intervene in the affairs of independent nations of the Western Hemisphere, and (3) the United States would not interfere in the affairs of European nations.

MORAL IDEALISM   A philosophy that sees all nations as willing to cooperate and agree on moral standards for conduct.

MUNICIPAL HOME RULE   The power vested in a local unit of government to draft or change its own charter and to manage its own affairs.

NARROWCASTING   Broadcasting that is targeted to one small sector of the population.

NATIONAL COMMITTEE   A standing committee of a national political party established to direct and coordinate party activities during the four-year period between national party conventions.

NATIONAL CONVENTION   The meeting held every four years by each major party to select presidential and vice presidential candidates, to write a platform, to choose a national committee, and to conduct party business. In theory, the national convention is at the top of a hierarchy of party conventions (the local and state conventions are below it) that consider candidates and issues.

NATIONAL POLITICS   The pursuit of interests that are of concern to the nation as a whole.

NATIONAL SECURITY COUNCIL (NSC)   A staff agency in the Executive Office established by the National Security Act of 1947. The NSC advises the president on domestic and foreign matters involving national security.

NATIONAL SECURITY POLICY   Foreign and domestic policy designed to protect the independence and political and economic integrity of the United States; policy that is concerned with the safety and defense of the nation.

NATURAL ARISTOCRACY   A small ruling clique of the state's "best" citizens, whose membership is based on birth, wealth, and ability. The Jeffersonian era emphasized government rule by such a group.

NATURAL RIGHTS   Rights held to be inherent in natural law, not dependent on governments. John Locke stated that natural law, being superior to human law, specifies certain rights of "life, liberty, and property." These rights, altered to become "life, liberty, and the pursuit of happiness," are asserted in the Declaration of Independence.

NECESSARIES   In contract law, necessaries include whatever is reasonably necessary for suitable subsistence as measured by age, state, condition in life, and so on.

NEGATIVE CONSTITUENTS   Citizens who openly oppose government foreign policies.

NEW ENGLAND TOWN   A governmental unit that combines the roles of city and county into one unit in the New England states.

NEW FEDERALISM   A plan to limit the national government's power to regulate, as well as to restore power to state governments. Essentially, the new federalism is designed to give the states greater ability to decide for themselves how government revenues should be spent.

NULLIFICATION   The act of nullifying, or rendering void. Prior to the Civil War, southern supporters of states' rights claimed that a state had the right to declare a national law to be null and void and therefore not binding on its citizens, on the assumption that ultimate sovereign authority rested with the several states.

OFFICE OF MANAGEMENT AND BUDGET (OMB)   A division of the Executive Office created by executive order in 1970 to replace the Bureau of the Budget. The OMB's main functions are to assist the president in preparing the annual budget, to clear and coordinate all departmental agency budgets, to help set fiscal policy, and to supervise the administration of the federal budget.

OFFICE-BLOCK, OR MASSACHUSETTS, BALLOT   A form of general election ballot in which candidates for elective office are grouped together under the title of each office. It emphasizes voting for the office and the individual, rather than for the party.

OLIGARCHY   Rule by a few members of the elite, who generally make decisions to benefit their own group.

OMBUDSPERSON   An individual in the role of hearing and investigating complaints by private individuals against public officials or agencies.

OPINION   The statement by a judge or a court of the decision reached in a case tried or argued before it. The opinion sets forth the law that applies to the case and details the legal reasoning on which the judgment was based.

OPINION LEADER   One who is able to influence the opinions of others because of position, expertise, or personality. Such leaders help to shape public opinion.

OPINION POLL   A method of systematically questioning a

small, selected sample of respondents who are deemed representative of the total population. These polls are widely used by government, business, university scholars, political candidates, and voluntary groups to provide reasonably accurate data on public attitudes, beliefs, expectations, and behavior.

ORAL ARGUMENTS The verbal arguments presented in person by attorneys to an appellate court. Each attorney presents reasons to the court why the court should rule in his or her client's favor.

OVERSIGHT The responsibility Congress has for following up on laws it has enacted to ensure that they are being enforced and administered in the way in which they were intended.

PARDON The granting of a release from the punishment or legal consequences of crime; a pardon can be granted by the president before or after a conviction.

PARTY IDENTIFICATION Linking oneself to a particular political party.

PARTY IDENTIFIER A person who identifies with a political party.

PARTY ORGANIZATION The formal structure and leadership of a political party, including election committees; local, state, and national executives; and paid professional staff.

PARTY PLATFORM A document drawn up by the platform committee at each national convention, outlining the policies, positions, and principles of the party; it is then submitted to the entire convention for approval.

PARTY-COLUMN, OR INDIANA, BALLOT A form of general election ballot in which candidates for elective office are arranged in one column under their respective party labels and symbols. It emphasizes voting for the party, rather than for the office or individual.

PARTY-IN-ELECTORATE Those members of the general public who identify with a political party or who express a preference for one party over the other.

PARTY-IN-GOVERNMENT All of the elected and appointed officials who identify with a political party.

PATRONAGE Rewarding faithful party workers and followers with government employment and contracts.

PEER GROUP A group consisting of members sharing common relevant social characteristics. These groups play an important part in the socialization process, helping to shape attitudes and beliefs.

PENDLETON ACT (CIVIL SERVICE REFORM ACT) The law, as amended over the years, that remains the basic statute regulating federal employment personnel policies. It established the principle of employment on the basis of merit and created the Civil Service Commission to administer the personnel service.

PERSONAL ATTACK RULE The rule promulgated by the Federal Communications Commission that allows individuals or groups airtime to reply to attacks that have been aired previously.

PLURALISM A theory that views politics as a conflict among interest groups. Political decision making is characterized by bargaining and compromise.

PLURALITY The total votes cast for a candidate who receives more votes than any other candidate but not necessarily a majority. Most national, state, and local electoral laws provide for winning elections by a plurality vote.

POCKET VETO A special veto power exercised by the chief executive after a legislative body has adjourned. Bills not signed by the chief executive die after a specified period of time. If Congress wishes to reconsider such a bill, it must be reintroduced in the following session of Congress.

POLICE POWER The authority to legislate for the protection of the health, morals, safety, and welfare of the people. In the United States, most police power is a reserved power of the states.

POLICY TRADE-OFFS The cost to the nation of undertaking any one policy in terms of all of the other policies that could have been undertaken. For example, an increase in the expenditures on one federal program means either a reduction in expenditures on another program or an increase in federal taxes (or the deficit).

POLITICAL ACTION COMMITTEE (PAC) A committee set up by and representing a corporation, labor union, or special interest group. PACs raise and give campaign donations on behalf of the organizations or groups they represent.

POLITICAL CONSULTANT A paid professional hired to devise a campaign strategy and manage a campaign. Image building is the crucial task of the political consultant.

POLITICAL CULTURE The collection of beliefs and attitudes toward government and the political process held by a community or nation.

POLITICAL PARTY A group of political activists who organize to win elections, to operate the government, and to determine public policy.

POLITICAL QUESTION An issue that a court believes should be decided by the executive or legislative branch.

POLITICAL REALISM A philosophy that sees each nation acting principally in its own interest.

POLITICAL SOCIALIZATION The process through which individuals learn a set of political attitudes and form opinions about social issues. The family and the educational system are two of the most important forces in the political socialization process.

POLITICAL TRUST The degree to which individuals express trust in the government and political institutions, usually measured through a specific series of survey questions.

POLITICO The legislative role that combines the instructed-delegate and trustee concepts. The legislator varies the role according to the issue under consideration.

POLITICS According to David Easton, the "authoritative allocation of values" for a society; according to Harold Lasswell, "who gets what, when, and how" in a society.

POLL TAX A special tax that must be paid as a qualification for voting. The Twenty-fourth Amendment to the Constitution outlawed the poll tax in national elections, and in 1966 the Supreme Court declared it unconstitutional in all elections.

POLL WATCHER An individual appointed by a political party to scrutinize the voting process on election day. Usually, there are two poll watchers at every voting place, representing the Democratic and the Republican parties, both attempting to ensure the honesty of the election.

POPULAR SOVEREIGNTY The concept that ultimate political authority rests with the people.

POWER The ability to cause others to modify their behavior and to conform to what the power holder wants.

PRECEDENT A court rule bearing on subsequent legal decisions in similar cases. Judges rely on precedents in deciding cases.

PREFERRED-POSITION DOCTRINE A judicial doctrine under which limitations on speech are permissible only if they are necessary to avoid imminent, serious, and important evils.

PRESIDENT PRO TEMPORE The temporary presiding officer of the Senate in the absence of the vice president.

PRESIDENTIAL PRIMARY A statewide primary election of delegates to a political party's national convention to help a party determine its presidential nominee. Such delegates are either pledged to a particular candidate or unpledged.

PRESS SECRETARY The individual responsible for representing the White House before the media. The press secretary writes news releases, provides background information, sets up press conferences, and so on.

PRICE SUPPORTS Minimum prices set by the government for particular products.

PRIOR RESTRAINT Restraining an action before the activity has actually occurred. It involves censorship, as opposed to subsequent punishment.

PRIVILEGES AND IMMUNITIES Special rights and exceptions provided by law. Article IV, Section 2, of the Constitution requires states not to discriminate against one another's citizens. A resident of one state cannot be treated as an alien when in another state; he or she may not be denied such privileges and immunities as legal protection, access to courts, travel rights, or property rights.

PROPERTY Anything that is or may be subject to ownership. As conceived by the political philosopher John Locke, the right to property is a natural right superior to human law (laws made by government).

PROPERTY TAX A tax on the value of real estate. This tax is limited to state and local governments and is a particularly important source of revenue for local governments.

PUBLIC AGENDA Issues that commonly are perceived by members of the political community as meriting public attention and governmental action. The media play an important role in setting the public agenda by focusing attention on certain topics.

PUBLIC DEBT, OR NATIONAL DEBT The total amount of debt carried by the federal government.

PUBLIC DEBT FINANCING The government's spending more than it receives in taxes and paying for the difference by issuing U.S. Treasury bonds, thereby adding to the public debt.

PUBLIC FIGURES Public officials, movie stars, and generally all persons who become known to the public because of their positions or activities.

PUBLIC INTEREST The best interests of the collective, overall community; the national good, rather than the narrow interests of a self-serving group.

PUBLIC OPINION The aggregate of individual attitudes or beliefs shared by some portion of adults. There is no one public opinion, because there are many different "publics."

PURPOSIVE INCENTIVE A reason or motive having to do with ethical beliefs or ideological principles.

RATIFICATION Formal approval.

RATIONAL IGNORANCE EFFECT When people purposely and rationally decide not to become informed on an issue because they believe that their vote on the issue is not likely to be a deciding one; a lack of incentive to seek the necessary information to cast an intelligent vote.

REAPPORTIONMENT The allocation of seats in the House to each state after each census.

RECALL A procedure enabling voters to remove an elected official from office before his or her term has expired.

RECOGNITION POWER The president's power, as chief diplomat, to extend diplomatic recognition to foreign governments.

RECYCLING The reuse of raw materials derived from already manufactured products.

REDISTRICTING The redrawing of the boundaries of the districts within each state.

REFERENDUM An electoral device whereby legislative or constitutional measures are referred by the legislature to the voters for approval or disapproval.

REGISTRATION The entry of a person's name onto the list of eligible voters for elections. Registration requires meeting certain legal requirements relating to age, citizenship, and residency.

REGRESSIVE TAX A tax system in which tax rates go down as income goes up.

RELEVANCE The extent to which an issue is of concern at a particular time. Issues become relevant when the public views them as pressing or of direct concern to daily life.

REMAND To send a case back to the court that originally heard it.

REPRESENTATION The function of members of Congress as elected officials to represent the views of their constituents.

REPRESENTATIVE ASSEMBLY A legislature composed of individuals who represent the population.

REPRESENTATIVE DEMOCRACY A form of government in which representatives elected by the people make and enforce laws and policies.

REPRIEVE The presidential power to postpone the execution of a sentence imposed by a court of law; usually done for humanitarian reasons or to await new evidence.

REPUBLIC The form of government in which sovereignty rests with the people, who elect agents to represent them in lawmaking and other decisions.

REPUBLICAN PARTY One of the two major American political parties, which emerged in the 1850s as an antislavery party. It was created to fill the vacuum caused by the disintegration of the Whig party.

REVERSE To annul or make void a judgment on account of some error or irregularity.

REVERSE DISCRIMINATION The charge that affirmative action programs requiring preferential treatment or quotas discriminate against those who do not have minority status.

RULE OF FOUR A United States Supreme Court procedure requiring four affirmative votes to hear the case before the full Court.

RULES COMMITTEE A standing committee of the House of Representatives that provides special rules under which specific bills can be debated, amended, and considered by the House.

SAFE SEAT A district that returns the legislator with 55 percent of the vote or more.

SAMPLING ERROR The difference between a sample's

results and the true result if the entire population had been interviewed.

SECESSION The act of formally withdrawing from membership in an alliance; the withdrawal of a state from the federal union.

SECOND BUDGET RESOLUTION A resolution passed by Congress in September that sets "binding" limits on taxes and spending for the next fiscal year beginning October 1.

SECOND CONTINENTAL CONGRESS The 1775 congress of the colonies that established an army.

SECTIONAL POLITICS The pursuit of interests that are of special concern to a region or section of the country.

SELECT COMMITTEE A temporary legislative committee established for a limited time period and for a special purpose.

SELECTPERSON A member of the governing group of a town.

SENATORIAL COURTESY In regard to federal district court judgeship nominations, a Senate tradition allowing a senator of the president's political party to veto a judgeship appointment in his or her state simply by indicating that the appointment is personally not acceptable. At that point, the Senate may reject the nomination, or the president may withdraw consideration of the nominee.

SENIORITY SYSTEM A custom followed in both chambers of Congress specifying that members with longer terms of continuous service will be given preference when committee chairpersons and holders of other significant posts are selected.

SEPARATE-BUT-EQUAL DOCTRINE The doctrine holding that segregation in schools and public accommodations does not imply that one race is superior to another; rather, it implies that each race is entitled to separate but equal facilities.

SEPARATION OF POWERS The principle of dividing governmental powers among the executive, the legislative, and the judicial branches of government.

SERVICE SECTOR The sector of the economy that provides services—such as food services, insurance, and education—in contrast to the sector of the economy that produces goods.

SEXUAL HARASSMENT Unwanted physical or verbal conduct or abuse of a sexual nature that interferes with a recipient's job performance, creates a hostile environment, or carries with it an implicit or explicit threat of adverse employment consequences.

SLANDER The public uttering of a false statement that harms the good reputation of another. The statement must be made to, or within the hearing of, persons other than the defamed party.

SOCIAL MOVEMENT A movement that represents the demands of a large segment of the public for political, economic, or social change.

SOCIOECONOMIC STATUS A category of people within a society who have similar levels of income and similar types of occupations.

SOFT MONEY Campaign contributions that evade contribution limits by being given to parties and party committees to help fund general party activities.

SOLID SOUTH A term describing the tendency of the post–Civil War southern states to vote for the Democratic party. (Voting patterns in the South have changed, though.)

SOLIDARY INCENTIVE A reason or motive having to do with the desire to associate with others and to share with others a particular interest or hobby.

SOUND BITE A brief, memorable comment that easily can be fit into news broadcasts.

SOVIET BLOC The Eastern European countries that installed communist regimes after World War II.

SPEAKER OF THE HOUSE The presiding officer in the House of Representatives. The speaker is always a member of the majority party and is the most powerful and influential member of the House.

SPIN An interpretation of campaign events or election results that is most favorable to the candidate's campaign strategy.

SPIN DOCTOR A political campaign adviser who tries to convince journalists of the truth of a particular interpretation of events.

SPIN-OFF PARTY A new party formed by a dissident faction within a major political party. Usually, spin-off parties have emerged when a particular personality was at odds with the major party.

SPOILS SYSTEM The awarding of government jobs to political supporters and friends; generally associated with President Andrew Jackson.

SPRING REVIEW The time every year when the Office of Management and Budget requires federal agencies to review their programs, activities, and goals and submit their requests for funding for the next fiscal year.

STABILITY The extent to which public opinion remains constant over a period of time.

STANDING COMMITTEE A permanent committee within the House or Senate that considers bills within a certain subject area.

STARE DECISIS To stand on decided cases; the policy of courts to follow precedents established by past decisions.

STATE A group of people occupying a specific area and organized under one government; may be either a nation or a subunit of a nation.

STATE CENTRAL COMMITTEE The principal organized structure of each political party within each state. This committee is responsible for carrying out policy decisions of the party's state convention.

STATE OF THE UNION MESSAGE An annual message to Congress in which the president proposes a legislative program. The message is addressed not only to Congress but also to the American people and to the world. It offers the opportunity to dramatize policies and objectives and to gain public support.

STATUTORY POWER A power created for the president through laws established by Congress.

STRATEGIC ARMS LIMITATION TREATY (SALT I) A treaty between the United States and the Soviet Union to stabilize the nuclear arms competition between the two countries. SALT I talks began in 1969, and agreements were signed on May 26, 1972.

SUBPOENA To serve with a legal writ requiring a person's appearance in court to give testimony.

SUBSIDY Financial assistance given by the government to business firms or individuals.

SUFFRAGE The right to vote; the franchise.

SUNSET LEGISLATION A law requiring that an existing program be reviewed regularly for its effectiveness and be terminated unless specifically extended as a result of this review.

SUPER TUESDAY The date on which a number of presidential primaries are held, including those of most of the southern states.

SUPERDELEGATE A party leader or elected official who is given the right to vote at the party's national convention. Superdelegates are not elected at the state level.

SUPPLEMENTAL SECURITY INCOME (SSI) A federal program established to provide assistance to elderly persons and disabled persons.

SUPREMACY CLAUSE The constitutional provision that makes the Constitution and federal laws superior to all conflicting state and local laws.

SUPREMACY DOCTRINE A doctrine that asserts the superiority of national law over state or regional laws. This principle is rooted in Article VI of the Constitution, which provides that the Constitution, the laws passed by the national government under its constitutional powers, and all treaties constitute the supreme law of the land.

SYMBOLIC SPEECH Nonverbal expression of beliefs, which is given substantial protection by the courts.

TARIFF A tax on imported goods.

TECHNICAL ASSISTANCE The sending of experts with technical skills in agriculture, engineering, or business to aid other nations.

THIRD PARTY A political party other than the two major political parties (Republican and Democratic). Usually, third parties are composed of dissatisfied groups that have split from the major parties. They act as indicators of political trends and as safety valves for dissident groups.

THIRD-PARTY CANDIDATE A political candidate running under the banner of a party other than the two major political parties.

TICKET SPLITTING Voting for candidates of two or more parties for different offices. For example, a voter splits her ticket if she votes for a Republican presidential candidate and for a Democratic congressional candidate.

TOTALITARIAN REGIME A form of government that controls all aspects of the political and social life of a nation. All power resides with the government. The citizens have no power to choose the leadership or policies of the country.

TOWN MANAGER SYSTEM A form of city government in which voters elect three selectpersons, who then appoint a professional town manager, who in turn appoints other officials.

TOWN MEETING The governing authority of a New England town. Qualified voters may participate in the election of officers and in the passage of legislation.

TOWNSHIP A rural unit of government based on federal land surveys of the American frontier in the 1780s. They have declined significantly in importance.

TRACKING POLL A poll taken for the candidate on a nearly daily basis as election day approaches.

TRIAL COURT The court in which most cases usually begin and in which questions of fact are examined.

TRUMAN DOCTRINE The policy adopted by President Harry Truman in 1947 to halt communist expansion in southeastern Europe.

TRUSTEE In regard to a legislator, one who acts according to his or her conscience and the broad interests of the entire society.

TWELFTH AMENDMENT An amendment to the Constitution, adopted in 1804, that specifies the separate election of the president and vice president by the electoral college.

TWENTY-FIFTH AMENDMENT An amendment to the Constitution adopted in 1967 that establishes procedures for filling vacancies in the two top executive offices and that makes provisions for situations involving presidential disability.

TWO-PARTY SYSTEM A political system in which only two parties have a reasonable chance of winning.

U.S. TREASURY BOND Evidence of debt issued by the federal government; similar to corporate bonds but issued by the U.S. Treasury.

UNANIMOUS OPINION An opinion or determination on which all judges agree.

UNDERGROUND ECONOMY The part of the economy that does not pay taxes and so is not directly measured by government statisticians; also called the subterranean economy or unreported economy.

UNICAMERAL LEGISLATURE A legislature with only one legislative body, as compared with a bicameral (two-house) legislature, such as the U.S. Congress. Nebraska is the only state in the union with a unicameral legislature.

UNINCORPORATED AREA An area not located within the boundary of a municipality.

UNIT RULE All of a state's electoral votes are cast for the presidential candidate receiving a plurality of the popular vote.

UNITARY SYSTEM A centralized governmental system in which local or subdivisional governments exercise only those powers given to them by the central government.

UNIVERSAL SUFFRAGE The right of all adults to vote for their representatives.

VETO MESSAGE The president's formal explanation of a veto when legislation is returned to the Congress.

VOTER TURNOUT The percentage of citizens taking part in the election process; the number of eligible voters that actually "turn out" on election day to cast their ballots.

WAR POWERS ACT A law passed in 1973 spelling out the conditions under which the president can commit troops without congressional approval.

WASHINGTON COMMUNITY Individuals regularly involved with politics in Washington, D.C.

WATERGATE BREAK-IN The 1972 illegal entry into the Democratic campaign offices by participants in Richard Nixon's reelection campaign.

WEBERIAN MODEL A model of bureaucracy developed by the German sociologist Max Weber, who viewed bureaucracies as rational, hierarchical organizations in which power flows from the top downward and decisions are based on logical reasoning and data analysis.

WHIG PARTY One of the foremost political organizations in the United States during the first half of the nineteenth century, formally established in 1836. The Whig party was dominated by the same anti-Jackson elements that organized the National Republican faction within the Democratic (Jeffersonian) Republicans and represented a variety of regional interests. It fell apart as a national party in the early 1850s.

WHIP   An assistant who aids the majority or minority leader of the House and the Senate majority or minority floor leader.

WHISTLEBLOWER   Someone who brings to public attention gross governmental inefficiency or an illegal action.

WHITE HOUSE OFFICE   The personal office of the president, which tends to presidential political needs and manages the media.

WHITE HOUSE PRESS CORPS   A group of reporters assigned full time to cover the presidency.

WHITE PRIMARY   A state primary election that restricts voting to whites only; outlawed by the Supreme Court in 1944.

WRIT OF *CERTIORARI*   An order issued by a higher court to a lower court to send up the record of a case for review. It is the principal vehicle for United States Supreme Court review.

WRIT OF *HABEAS CORPUS*   *Habeas corpus* means, literally, "you have the body." A writ of *habeas corpus* is an order that requires jailers to bring a person before a court or judge and explain why the person is being held in prison.

YELLOW JOURNALISM   A term for sensationalistic, irresponsible journalism. Reputedly, the term is short for "Yellow Kid Journalism," an allusion to the cartoon "The Yellow Kid" in the old *New York World*, a newspaper especially noted for its sensationalism.

Index

Photo Credits